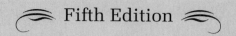 Fifth Edition

Instruction of Students with Severe Disabilities

Martha E. Snell
University of Virginia

Fredda Brown
Queens College,
City University of New York

Merrill,
an imprint of Prentice Hall
Upper Saddle River, New Jersey • Columbus, Ohio

Library of Congress Cataloging-in-Publication Data

Instruction of students with severe disabilities / [edited by]
  Martha E. Snell, Fredda Brown. — 5th ed.
      p.   cm.
    Includes bibliographical references and indexes.
    ISBN 0–13–014247–6
      1. Handicapped children—Education—United States.
    2. Special education—United States.   I. Snell, Martha E.
    II. Brown, Fredda.
    LC4031.I572 2000
    371.91'0973—dc21   99-42790
                                                           CIP

Editor: Ann Castel Davis
Production Editor: Sheryl Glicker Langner
Production Coordination: Holly Henjum, Clarinda
    Publication Services
Design Coordinator: Karrie Converse-Jones
Cover Designer: Dan Eckel
Cover Art: Stephen Schildbach
Production Manager: Laura Messerly
Electronic Text Management: Karen Bretz
Editorial Assistant: Pat Grogg
Director of Marketing: Kevin Flanagan
Marketing Manager: Meghan Shepherd
Marketing Coordinator: Krista Groshong

This book was set in Novarese by The Clarinda Company
and was printed and bound by Courier Corp. The cover was
printed by Phoenix Color Corp.

©2000 by Prentice-Hall, Inc.
Pearson Education
Upper Saddle River, New Jersey 07458

Earlier editions © 1993 by Macmillan Publishing Company,
a division of Macmillan, Inc.; previous editions, entitled
Systematic Instruction of Persons with Severe Handicaps, copyright
© 1987 by Macmillan Publishing Company; copyright ©
1983, 1978 by Merrill Publishing Company.

Photo Credits: All photos copyrighted by individuals or
companies listed. Philippa Campbell and the Children's
Hospital Audiovisual Department, pp. 307, 311, 314, 319,
321; Douglas Siegel-Causey, pp. 427, 442, 444; Philip and
Dianne Ferguson, pp. 636, 647, 650, 651; Wally Kempe &
Associates, p. 632; Courtesy of Lehigh University Supported
Employment, used with permission, pp. 557, 568;
Marquette Elementary, p. 25; Warren C. Rommacher,
p. 352; Karen Schooley, p. 337; Martha Snell, pp. 348, 368,
375, 504, 562, 576; Martha Snell and Karen Schooley, p. 351;
Tom Watson/Merrill, p. 382; Amy Weatherby, pp. 410, 414,
416, 421; Larry Wilson, Kennedy Center, Peabody
College/Vanderbilt University, pp. 462, 463, 468.

Printed in the United States of America

10 9 8 7 6 5 4 3

ISBN 0-13-014247-6

Prentice-Hall International (UK) Limited, *London*
Prentice-Hall of Australia Pty. Limited, *Sydney*
Prentice-Hall of Canada, Inc., *Toronto*
Prentice-Hall Hispanoamericana, S. A., *Mexico*
Prentice-Hall of India Private Limited, *New Delhi*
Prentice-Hall of Japan, Inc., *Tokyo*
Prentice-Hall (Singapore) Pte. Ltd., *Singapore*
Editora Prentice-Hall do Brasil, Ltda., *Rio de Janeiro*

*For David and Matthew who are gone
and the many children and adults still
here who have taught us without
knowing so. For our students who
teach us as we teach them, and for
the many others whose integrity and
work have inspired us.*

*For our children—Emilie and Claire and
Grayson and Lea, for our partners,
and for our friends who have provided
us support without reservation.*

Preface

In this fifth edition, we describe many of the same principles about teaching students with severe disabilities that were present in earlier editions because these principles have continued relevance. For example,

- Inclusive schools create new opportunities for *all* students to learn and to form supportive social relationships.
- Teams of people, not isolated individuals, are responsible for designing, implementing, and evaluating educational programs.
- The skills identified for each student to learn should be functional (matching the student's current and future needs), suited to the student's chronological age, and respectful of the student's preferences.
- To be appropriate, instruction must be planned to suit an individual student.

In addition, some principles we present are new to this fifth edition. For example:

- School efforts should be organized toward the achievement of three outcomes in our students: membership, belonging, and skills.
- There is great value in building self-determination in our students as there is for all students; the challenge is to understand the many individualized ways this characteristic can be developed (e.g., matching job training opportunities to preferences, teaching the skill of making choices and initiating preferred activities, examining students' problem behaviors as a form of communication).
- To improve education for all students, special education needs to be merged with general education rather than always being viewed separately, while the diverse talents of both special and general educators are retained.
- The teaching methods we use need to be research-based and effective and appropriate for a variety of students in inclusive settings.

In addition to these principles, we have incorporated several features into the text in the hope of making the text more useful to its readers. One of the most effective ways we learn is through examples. Thus, we begin each chapter with case studies of students and then apply chapter concepts to these individuals. Because heterogeneity is characteristic of severe disabilities, our examples are also diverse and include individuals ranging in age from preschool to young adult with a variety of disabilities—cognitive, movement, sensory, behavioral, and emotional. The applications are highlighted from the rest of the text so readers can predict concrete illustrations easily as they progress through each chapter.

Over the years this text has gained a reputation for being both comprehensive and current. The aim of earlier editions was to present issues and strategies documented as effective and not to "jump on treatment bandwagons." The fifth edition maintains this reputation. Because our students often challenge the available supply of teaching methods, we have described guidelines for designing instruction and procedures for evaluating the effects of instruction on students. We have added a new chapter on social relationships, expanded several chapters to include new authors, and extensively rewritten or revised all 16 chapters in the book. The contributors provide activities at the end of each chapter that will help readers apply concepts to individuals and teaching situations. Also, we have written as we aim to speak—using respectful, people-first language. Finally, there are two editors for this edition—Fredda Brown is the welcomed addition!

Organization of the Text

We begin this 5th edition with five chapters that lay the foundation for the rest of the book. The first two chapters focus on basic concepts central to the education of students with severe disabilities: inclusion and families. The discussion by Wayne Sailor, Kathy Gee, and Tricia Karasoff sets the stage for viewing inclusion as central to the educational reform movement that is occurring now in all schools and for all children. These authors provide not just a focus on current public policy in education as it affects children and youth with severe disabilities, but also demonstrate practical models and examples of how inclusion can be effective and beneficial for all children.

Students grow up as members of families, and families are most often the primary advocates for their children throughout life. Ann and Rud Turnbull explore the factors that make successful partnerships between home and school. Two such factors are ongoing, reciprocal communication between home and school and interactions that reflect and respect families of diverse cultural backgrounds.

Chapters 3, 4, and 5, written by the editors, set forth the basic strategies and tools educators use in concert with other team members to equip students for functioning at home, in schools, in communities, and on the job. Three key words sum up the content of this section: assessment, teaching, and evaluation. We have written this section to acquaint the reader with the resources educators rely upon; because there are many resources, these chapters are comprehensive and lengthy.

In chapter 6, Rob Horner and his three co-authors (Rick Albin, Jeff Sprague, and Anne Todd) set forth the principles of positive behavior support. Using a comprehensive case example, these authors describe how the process of functional assessment is conducted and used to design an effective behavioral support plan that is based in the values of self-determination, respect, and inclusion.

Marilyn Ault and her three co-authors (Jane Rues, Carolyn Graff, and Jennifer Holvoet) undertake the task of describing health care procedures required by some students during the school day. Chapter 7 tells how to incorporate special health care procedures into the educational day and how educators can contribute to the prevention of related health problems and conditions.

In Chapter 8, Pip Campbell addresses the related topic of movement disabilities that often are present in our students. Because all team members interact with a student over a range of daily activities, practical knowledge about motor disabilities must be shared.

Students deserve to have consistency and competence in the ways they are positioned, moved, fed, and guided through daily routines that involve movement.

One of the most important elements schools can offer students is social relationships with peers. In chapter 10, Debbie Staub, along with Cap Peck, Chrysan Gallucci, and Ilene Schwartz, describe and illustrate techniques that teams can use to promote membership or a sense of belonging and to build a variety of personal relationships between students in classrooms and schools.

The skills of caring for oneself, toileting, eating, dressing, and grooming, are important goals for all individuals, regardless of severity of disability. In chapter 9, Leslie Farlow and Marti Snell provide a comprehensive review of effective methods for teaching self-care skills while also showing how these methods apply to specific students.

Chapters 11 and 12 address communication. First, in chapter 11, Ellin Siegel and Amy Wetherby describe nonsymbolic communication and the use of movement, gestures, facial expression, and other behaviors to express messages to others. Many of our students reach this level of communication but their teams may not recognize their skills or use their abilities to express themselves without symbols. These two authors provide a clear framework for understanding nonsymbolic communication and relating effectively to students who communicate in these ways.

In chapter 12, Ann Kaiser follows with teaching guidelines for students learning to use symbols to express themselves: words, signs, and picture symbols. She explains a set of naturalistic or Milieu Teaching methods that have been found to be effective in expanding students' beginning communication abilities, whether spoken or augmented, with manual or two-dimensional, pictured symbols.

The basic academic skills of reading, writing, and arithmetic can be useful and important to many of our students when these skills are taught within daily routines. In Chapter 13, Diane Browder and Marti Snell address an array of functional academic skills and instructional strategies that have been proven effective. Additionally, this chapter provides guidelines for selecting academic goals as well as for substituting less difficult alternatives to academic goals.

Learning skills that increase active participation in home and community life is the topic for Chapter 14.

Diane Browder and Linda Bambara begin with a series of guiding values and principles that characterize the outcomes of skill instruction referenced to students' homes and communities. These themes are coupled with instructional methods found effective with students.

Our special education laws have broadened the focus of transition and lowered the age at which transition activities are to begin. Preparing students for real work in the community is a longitudinal process requiring extensive team effort over the teen-age years. In Chapter 15, Sherril Moon and Katty Inge describe the essential elements of secondary vocational programs that will allow students to plan the transition from school to adulthood with their teams and then make the transition.

The book closes with Chapter 16 in which Phil and Dianne Ferguson discuss, both as parents and as scholars, the promises that adulthood can offer. The Fergusons take us on a remarkable journey across the years with their son Ian. This family's story gives us a glimpse of a path that has been ". . . often confusing and frustrating, but also filled with many exciting achievements." The concept of supported adulthood is discussed within the context of current policy, social services, educational practices and societal expectations.

Acknowledgments

Many people have assisted in the task of developing the 5th edition. We are grateful for the helpful comments of these reviewers: Edwin Helmstetter, Washington State University; Merri Jamieson, Ashland University (OH); Ann Riall, University of Wisconsin—Whitewater; and Tony Russo, Marywood College (PA). Their thoughtful comments on different portions of the manuscript and at various stages in the revision process were of immeasurable help in shaping this 5th edition. We want to give special thanks to Felix Billingsley of the University of Washington who once again has provided us with support and advice for the revision of this text. His ongoing influence over successive editions of this text is both valuable and evident.

Next, the contributions of several valued professionals merit recognition. We would like to identify the copy editor, Cynthia Hake, the production editors, Sheryl Langner and Holly Henjum, the editorial assistant, Pat Grogg, and the administrative editor, Ann Davis. Their combined efforts have been central to the final quality of this text.

Finally, we are indebted to a small group of students—the children, adolescents, and young adults who add reality to each chapter and whose abilities and disabilities have challenged and shaped our own skills and those of our contributors. Their families and their educators deserve equal votes of gratitude for providing a vast array of teaching ideas, for granting permission to use photographs, and for giving us extensive examples and information.

Martha E. Snell
Fredda Brown

～ Contents ～

5

Measurement, Analysis, and Evaluation   173

Fredda Brown and Martha E. Snell

6

Positive Behavior Support   207

Robert H. Horner, Richard W. Albin, Jeffrey R. Sprague, and Anne W. Todd

7

Special Health Care Procedures   245

Marilyn M. Ault, Jane P. Rues, J. Carolyn Graff, and Jennifer F. Holvoet

15

16

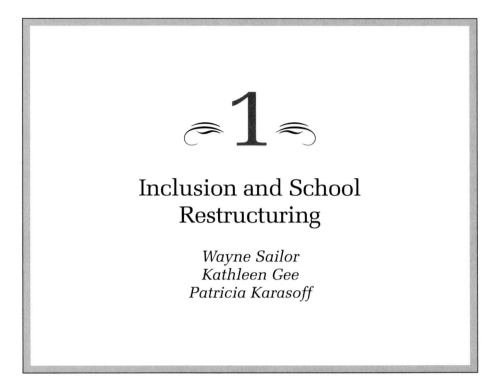

1

Inclusion and School Restructuring

Wayne Sailor
Kathleen Gee
Patricia Karasoff

A generation ago, Bob Dylan wrote, "The times, they are a-changing," and the schools provide an excellent place to witness the effects of that process in action. Millions of newcomers have arrived in our country since those words were sung, bringing with them diverse cultures, rich languages, and children with a rich variety of learning styles. Technology, scientific investigations, and information access have made it possible for teachers and their students to be connected all over the world. Children are involved in highly developed programs for the fine arts and sports at younger ages than ever before. Over the same period of time, however, misguided and almost unbelievably shortsighted economic policies have created an underclass of chronically unemployed and homeless people whose children reflect the ravages of poverty. Youth gangs, drugs, vandalism, teen pregnancy, and high school dropouts have become common in a significant number of our nation's secondary schools (Tyack & Cuban, 1995).

The well-being of children and families in America is deteriorating, with the income of increasing numbers of people being below the poverty line, despite a near full-employment economy (Cibulka & Kritec, 1996). Factors such as increasing rates of births to teenaged parents (Bruner, 1996), drug and alcohol abuse among teens (National Center for Children's Disease Prevention and Health Promotion, 1997), and rates of high school dropout for reasons of poverty (The Urban Institute, 1996) create a significant negative impact on the ability of schools to fulfill their primary function of enabling children to learn to become productive citizens.

Many of these problems are likely to be exacerbated with the recent passage of the Personal Responsibility and Work Opportunity Reconciliation Act of 1996. This landmark welfare reform legislation will directly and adversely affect millions of American children over the near term by greatly reducing their access to needed services and supports. Over the next

1

5 years, according to Gerry (in press), more than 2 million children, about a quarter of the current welfare caseload, will lose Aid to Families with Dependent Children (AFDC) support; about 16% of the current caseload will lose food stamp eligibility; and approximately 32% of the current caseload of children with disabilities (about 300,000) will be dropped from Social Security Insurance (SSI) eligibility. The net affect, according to Gerry's analysis, will be to force about 1.1 million more children into poverty status, an increase of about 12%.

According to the Children's Defense Fund (1998), about one-fifth of American children (70 million) are poor by federal poverty standards. Of these, 62.5% are white, including Latino children, and 31% are African American. At least 4 million children go hungry in the U.S., at least for part of each month. One-half of all present food stamp recipients in the U.S. are children, and that program is being phased out (The Urban Institute, 1996). As if these statistics were not frightening enough, the new welfare reform legislation also cuts close to $3 billion from child nutrition programs over the next 6 years (Gerry, in press).

All of these serious social challenges, in juxtaposition to the "state of the art" opportunities available to some but not all, have continued to place an enormous burden on the public educational system. Educators, researchers, administrators, and parents are seeking workable answers to difficult questions related to excellence and equity, accountability, diversity, choice, and safety. Two major pedagogical, social, and political issues for current educational and instructional reform are the extent to which all children and youth will be included in the transformation of our school systems and the extent to which the learning of every child is valued. One underlying premise for this chapter is that the very basis for the transformation, and thus the reality of the transformation, cannot occur without the inclusion of all students.

Special education across the U.S. serves over 5 million students, with costs exceeding $20 billion per year, considering all levels of government (Lipsky & Gartner, 1997). Approximately one-third of all students in special education programs are served in general education classes, one-third in special classes for students with disabilities only, and one-third in partial placement situations between, for example, general education classes and resource rooms. Two-thirds of all students labeled as mentally retarded (including severe disability) are served in special classes. The pattern of placement distribution by states is extremely variable: some states serve almost all students with severe disabilities in separate settings; other states, such as Vermont, serve the same population almost exclusively in general education classes. When the data reported by the states to the federal government in compliance with the Individuals with Disabilities Education Act (IDEA) are broken down by ethnic group, it is clear that African Americans and Latinos are disproportionately represented. In Connecticut, for example, based on 1993 data as reported in Lipsky and Gartner (1997, p. 20), 14% of the total school population is African American, but 22% of students in special education are of that ethnic group. Similarly, the federal data from the same year revealed that the category "mental retardation" contained 26% African American students, 11% white, and 8% Latino students, based on the total count by Lipsky and Gartner (1997, p. 20).

In the past two decades an extensive amount of research and demonstration of effort has taken place in the fields of education, employment, and supported living for individuals with severe disabilities by many creative and innovative professionals, consumers, and family members. The best practices generated by these efforts make it possible to more effectively support individuals with serious behavioral challenges; multiple cognitive, sensory, and physical disabilities; and those who have significant differences from typical people in the way they communicate. Special education reformers have taken on many issues in this period of time, with an increasing focus on the positive effects of instruction and participation in general education classrooms, meaningful employment in real work environments, and supported lifestyles that reflect informed choices that are determined by the consumer. As a result, some children and youth with severe disabilities are educated in inclusive schools alongside their nondisabled peers, where they make meaningful friendships and gain valuable academic, functional, and living skills. Some adults with severe disabilities live in the community in homes of their choice, with individuals supporting them in a quality of life that is respected, self-determined, and valued by members of their social circle. Despite these advances our ever-growing database of strategies, technologies, and processes for making these practices a reality for all individuals with severe disabilities, the majority of children and youth in this population do not yet go to inclusive schools, do not yet have meaningful employment, and do not yet live a lifestyle valued by their closest friends and relatives.

As we approach the year 2000, special education is still in need of reform—not only in new and innovative practices—but also in how to best organize to implement the federal legislation, that is, IDEA of 1997, which has been reauthorized and guarantees a free and appropriate public education to all students in the least restrictive environment. Together, educational leaders in both general and special education have been increasingly discussing the fact that classrooms in the United States are vital environments to children and youth who bring with them a rich variety of intelligences, abilities, learning styles, cultures, languages, and families. Through collaboration and transdisciplinary research efforts, there has been a growing acceptance of the fact that improving the education of students with disabilities cannot occur without improving the education of all the students in the school. Taking a close look at state-of-the-art practices in educating students with severe disabilities must be done, therefore, in the context of understanding the larger educational picture and how developments in the field of severe disabilities have both influenced, and are influenced by, the broader system.

In this chapter, we focus on current public policy in education, particularly as it affects children and youth with severe disabilities. We address three important policy developments: (a) new efforts to bring the educational system into a coordinated, working relationship with social and health systems of the greater community; (b) inclusive schooling; and (c) the unification of school resources and reforms. Children and youth with severe disabilities, their families, and the professionals who serve them have contributed to and benefited from these new efforts. The remaining chapters of this book focus on the best practices for educating individuals with severe disabilities. Threaded throughout this wide range of practical, research-based efforts is information that has guided policy efforts toward the inclusion of individuals with disabilities in all aspects of school life, community life, and work life, with the realization that self-determination and quality of life cannot be achieved without drastic reforms in the way special education services have been provided in the past.

In order to illustrate the complex interactions of policy and practice and the implications for students, families, and teachers directly, we provide some of the practical details of the reform efforts and practices through the real-life experiences of several students with severe disabilities and their educational teams. Four of these students are introduced to you in Tables 1–1 through 1–4.

The Community Schools Movement

The decade of the 90s represents a significant shift in the way that schools engaged in reform have involved communities and families. These new approaches to educational reform acknowledge that the challenges confronting students with and without disabilities in schools are multifaceted and closely linked to the complex community conditions in which they live (Sailor, 1996). Therefore, to improve educational and social outcomes for all students, schools are increasingly working in partnerships with their communities to jointly design solutions to persistent problems, particularly those arising from circumstances of poverty.

Although community schools are just beginning to appear in reasonable numbers across the country, they can best be viewed as "setting the standard" for how comprehensive supports and services can be organized to enhance the quality of life and outcomes from public education for all students, including those with severe disabilities. For these reasons, we begin this chapter with a close look at community schools. A community school can be defined as a school with strong ties to families, local community businesses, and service-provider systems through carefully designed "partnership" arrangements (Sailor, in press; Lawson & Briar-Lawson, 1997; Adelman & Taylor, 1997; Benson & Harkavy, 1997).

Community schools represent an approach to educational reform that focuses on improving outcomes through community building and economic revitalization (Benson & Harkavy, 1997). This approach acknowledges that for schools and the teachers within them to be successful in educating their students, they must work in concert with communities, families, and the agencies that serve them. Moreover, this approach not only strives to link schools with their communities to make the job of

TABLE 1–1

Description of Shalila

Shalila Is a Second Grader

Shalila is a delightful girl with an outgoing personality. She is anxious to communicate and socialize and uses many gestures and vocalizations to get her messages across. She likes being pushed fast in her wheelchair, driving in circles in her power wheelchair, and being pulled in a wagon over bumpy sidewalks. Shalila is happiest in school during math workshop, science, and recess. Some of the things she is working on in school include: communicating with a picture/talk communication device; developing sequences of communication with pictures; using a walker to get around; using her power wheelchair; making friends; using her cognitive and motor skills to participate in science and social studies; manipulating objects and developing some mathematics concepts; answering yes and no questions about stories that have been read to her; completing classroom jobs and following classroom rules; completing homework; using the bathroom as independently as she can; and using adaptations at lunch to assist her in eating and drinking.

Shalila has never been in a segregated educational program. She received infant development services at home at an early age, when it was determined that she had cerebral palsy, and attended the same preschool that her older brother attended, with special education support and services provided by her school district. When Shalila reached kindergarten age, some of her team members thought this would be the time to separate her from her nondisabled peers, but her parents and other team members did not feel this way. The principal at Shalila's urban elementary school and the educational community for the school fully anticipated having the third child of this family in their school, and when the time came, Shalila was enrolled. Shalila is now in second grade. Her Individualized Educational Plan (IEP) team for the 1997/98 year met to determine her goals and objectives and the educational services that she would need. The first and second grade teachers and the principal attended the IEP meeting and were integral parts of the process. Some of the support Shalila needs is: a special education teacher trained to collaborate with the general education teacher and to design specialized adaptations and instructional strategies; a physical therapist to work collaboratively with the school; an instructional assistant to assist her during certain periods of the day and in the bathroom and at lunch.

Shalila follows the same schedule as her nondisabled peers, completing objectives that are of priority for her and participating in all aspects of the curriculum, with only a few exceptions. After lunch and recess, when the other students are doing silent reading, Shalila takes a little longer in the bathroom, fulfilling some of her self-care objectives. During the independent math work time, twice a week, Shalila and two other second grade students from her class do a community mathematics problem, which is different each time. Shalila works on using her electric wheelchair and social and communication skills and the other students solve the problem of the day.

TABLE 1–2

Description of Daren

Daren Is a Seventh Grader

Daren is a middle-school student in an urban community. He enjoys going to football games at the high school with friends and assisting in running the lights and sound for drama productions at school. Daren is fascinated with the computer, and although he can use words to make understandable phrases, he prefers to type messages on the computer. When he is at the computer, he does not like to be interrupted or share the computer. Daren has been included since he was in elementary school. His teachers and his mother have grown in their understanding of the most effective ways to support Daren to enjoy friendships and the activities of school. Daren has continuously improved his ability to handle his emotions and his impulses. The community school model adopted by Daren's schools has facilitated the ability of his team to provide "seamless" services for Daren.

Daren has a syndrome that makes it very difficult for him to tolerate other people being too close to him physically. In addition to developmental delays, he also has obsessive-compulsive disorder and other emotional disabilities. Daren has a few very close friends who understand his emotional disabilities and ways to support him. He has many other acquaintances who enjoy being with him at school. His team has worked hard to find the best ways for Daren to both learn new skills and increase his comfort level with school and community environments.

While Daren has some academic skills, his combination of significant challenges require a high level of adult and peer support. In his seventh grade Individualized Educational Plan (IEP), Daren's academic objectives included English: expressive writing of sentences and discussing the literature of focus (after listening on tape); history: adapting basic facts, project completion, responding to modified questions; computer: word processing; mathematics: using the calculator to do functional math problems (adding and subtracting); social skills: using a social story book to assist in preparation for activities, using a conversation book, using strategies to tolerate crowded social situations, relationships with friends; communication skills: increasing verbal skills and increasing use of computer with more fluid sentences; participation in drama class as light and sound assistant.

TABLE 1–3
Description of Jeremy

Jeremy Is a Seventh Grader

Jeremy is a middle-school student who likes loud music, going to concerts, and being in the middle of lots of action. His friends at school tape recorded cheering and "boo-ing" so that he could be assisted to activate the appropriate noise while they played basket-ball. He likes being outside, and his favorite teacher is Ms. S. because she has a very dynamic style, and sometimes she gets "goofy"—but most of all, she interacts with Jeremy a lot. Jeremy's sources of voluntary movement are his small eye movements, his ability to use a deep breath to make his head turn about 1/4 in. to the left, and his eyebrow movements. He communicates nonsymbolically by using his eyebrows, his ability to be very still, his ability to blow air and make noise out of the tracheotomy tube in his throat, and the changes in color in his face. Due to a severe trauma in his infancy, Jeremy lost the physical functioning in most of his body. His blink reflex is gone, and he wears special goggles to moisturize his eyes.

Jeremy's family went through many challenges after his trauma. He was in the hospital for nearly two years, and the recommenda-tion of many medical personnel was to institutionalize Jeremy. Jeremy's mother persevered, and succeeded in bringing him home; but this was not easy, because Jeremy required 24-hour assistance due to the many special health care procedures required to keep Jeremy alive and comfortable. At age 5, he was offered only a couple of hours of home instruction by the school system, which stated that Jeremy "could not benefit" from attending school. After this went on for a few years, Jeremy's mother was ready for another chal-lenge. After a fair hearing, the school system was required to admit Jeremy to school with the supports and services he required; how-ever, he was in a segregated class. Jeremy then moved to a segregated special education class on a general education campus with opportunities to integrate only at lunch and recess and some opportunities to interact with peers who came into the special education classroom.

Jeremy was not included as a full member of his same-age peer group or in regular classes until the sixth grade, when his family moved because of his mother's job. The school system receiving Jeremy called the local university for assistance in developing an ap-propriate program. When the suggestion was made by the consultant and the school team that the majority of Jeremy's Individualized Educational Plan (IEP) goals (except those requiring community or nonclassroom settings) could best be met in general education classrooms, his mother was skeptical and decided to wait for the IEP process and a clear delineation of Jeremy's needs, thinking that after hearing about the serious nature of his disabilities, the team may change their minds. However, at Jeremy's initial IEP meeting, the team said that Jeremy's cognitive, physical, sensory, and health impairments required the least restrictive environment in which the maximum amount of interactions could occur, where he would have capable peer partners who could learn to communicate with him, and where he would be motivated by the engagement of others—the general education classrooms. His previous instructional environ-ments had caused extreme loneliness and isolation and had often put Jeremy to sleep for lack of activity.

The team identified the following priorities: (a) developing friendships and social relationships; (b) learning to use his breath to cre-ate a slight head movement to activate a microswitch, which could control a variety of technological devices; (c) using nonsymbolic communication signals (through slight changes in facial expression and breathing) to express needs and choices; (d) learning an orga-nized and clearly presented, auditory object-receptive communication system; (e) increasing methods of control and choice; (f) utilizing his right eye to fixate on objects and people; (g) participating in general education school activities: academic, nonacademic, and recre-ational; (h) participating in the community; and (i) maintaining health and current physical status.

Because of Jeremy's many specialized health care needs at the start of the day, his team determined a class schedule that would allow him to arrive at the start of the second period; participate in the literacy and social studies core periods; break for a variety of specialized health care needs (e.g., catheterization, respiratory therapy); return for three more periods: computer, science, and perform-ing arts. Community-based instruction would occur twice per week. Because he had not been through elementary school with the stu-dents in this school, Jeremy's team planned ways in which they would actively support the development of friendships and social rela-tionships for Jeremy. A "circle of friends" (Forest & Lusthaus, 1989) was recruited from his core classes and the special education teacher met with them weekly at first to facilitate ways to communicate and spend time together. In addition, Jeremy required several types of ongoing support: an available adult to provide suctioning at least two to three times per hour and assist with all necessary movements in and out of his chair; his equipment; health maintenance issues, such as eye moisture and heat regulation; an augmenta-tive communication system; a computer and various microswitch technologies with an environmental switch; and consultation from a registered nurse, occupational therapist, and an education specialist from a nearby university to assist the team in the first semester.

Jeremy's mother was initially concerned about whether Jeremy's team would be able to provide instruction for Jeremy's objectives within the general education curriculum. The special education teacher and the consultant met regularly with her to share how Jeremy's instructional priorities were being met within the general education class, his participation plans, instructional plans, and ongoing data that were collected for evaluation purposes (see Tables 6 and 7). She benefited from meeting Jeremy's peers and friends, who were very supportive of Jeremy and became interested in getting together outside of school. Jeremy's peers began to take over many of his support needs during class and eventually became strong advocates for Jeremy's inclusion in all aspects of school life. Together the team began to work hand-in-hand to improve Jeremy's quality of life. Jeremy's mother has since become a strong advocate of inclusion for all students.

TABLE 1–4
Description of Alissa

Alissa Is a Junior in High School

Alissa is a junior in a rural high school to which she has a 30-minute bus ride. She now has a circle of good friends who have learned how to communicate with her and support her in social situations in the community. Alissa likes going to certain places on a regular basis at regular times. On Wednesday afternoons, two of her friends go with her to the local pizza place. On Saturday mornings, Alissa and her mother have a special time just for them to eat breakfast together, and on Sundays, Alissa and her father always leave early for church and have breakfast by themselves. Alissa likes to go out, but she is uncomfortable if things change too much. She enjoys Mr. T.'s biology class the most because she can count on certain things happening on a regular basis.

Alissa's family immigrated to this country when she was 8 years old. At that time her family had no idea that the public schools in this country would serve their oldest daughter. Her disabilities had excluded her from school in their home country, and Alissa's mother had spent most of her time trying to care for and teach her at home. After arriving in the U.S., Alissa was first served in a segregated school and then a segregated classroom on a general education campus. It was determined that Alissa had autism, some cognitive disabilities, and some vision disabilities. When Alissa was 14, her family moved to a different state, where Alissa's father could find better work. Her father was becoming increasingly worried about Alissa's future and her lack of functional skills. Her mother was increasingly worried about Alissa's social skills and her lack of a successful communication system. Alissa's behavioral challenges had increased, and her previous school had increasingly segregated her from others.

Through the family resource center connected with their high school, they met other families whose children were receiving special education services within general education classrooms and in the community. They decided to find a place to rent in the same community in which these other families lived to have support. One of the other parents accompanied them to Alissa's Individualized Educational Plan (IEP). It was determined that a functional assessment should be done to determine a positive behavioral support plan for Alissa (see chapter 6). The team also discussed communication, general classes, vocational opportunities, social and friendship development, and other transition issues. The special education teacher facilitated the functional behavioral assessment and worked with the team to identify a positive behavioral support plan. Alissa's program included general education placement, communication skills instruction, work placements in the community, and friendship development.

This is Alissa's third year in high school. She spends part of her day at school, where she is enrolled in a computer class, Spanish, biology, and drama. Similar to Jeremy, her instructional objectives are embedded throughout the courses she takes with individualized outcomes and strategies planned by her support teacher in conjunction with the regular education teachers. She spends the other part of her day in the community at a supported work placement (one of two she will have this year) and doing other community activities. Alissa now has a successful communication system, which can be increasingly built up. Her positive behavioral support plan is continuously revised, and her transition plan includes methods for increasing friendships as well as specific skills and activities related to semi-independent living and supported work. Alissa has several friends without disabilities who have become a part of her planning team. These students are preparing for their own futures and provide a same-age reference for Alissa's parents in both social and school issues. Alissa's parents continue to get support through a strong family network in their community, which is, in turn, supported by the community school. As her parents increase their knowledge of the types of strategies and supports that can be developed for Alissa, their expectations increase and their advocacy for Alissa sharpens. They know that they will need to work hard with other families to improve opportunities for adults like their daughter in their local communities. Alissa's goals for the future include supported living and supported work. She definitely wants to have her own home and lifestyle.

education more successful, it is also based on a fundamental belief that schools have a responsibility in a democratic society to serve their communities. This approach to education, espoused early in this century by John Dewey (1985), views schools as social centers for the community and dictates a much more reciprocal relationship between families, community members, and schools than is traditional in contemporary society. Simply stated, "Schools of the community should serve the community" (Lawson & Briar-Lawson, 1997, p. 18).

One of the paramount features of the new community schools movement is the welcoming and full-participation agenda established for parents and guardians (Turnbull & Turnbull, 1997). Traditional schools for many families often become messengers of bad news for parents, especially in communities affected by poverty and especially for those families of individuals with learning challenges. Families respond to blame from schools by forming negative attitudes toward schools and withdrawing from participation in school functions (Schorr, 1989). Negative family attitudes toward public education are reflected in children's attitudes in the classroom and the results are poor academic performance, disciplinary problems, and all too frequently, school dropout before graduation (Lawson & Briar-Lawson, 1997).

The community schools approach to reform, such as the Beacon Centers in San Francisco and New York and Caring Communities of Kansas City, create opportunities for communities to capitalize on their assets. In these models, the design and provision of comprehensive neighborhood services are not viewed as the responsibility of the school. Rather, the school works in conjunction with its families, with neighborhood groups and community-based organizations to provide services to support the community. The school facility itself is viewed as an asset and can serve as a hub for needed community services. Community schools typically have extended weekday hours and may stay open on weekends to make the facilities available to the community. The services are designed to address the specific needs of the families of the neighborhood and may include the following types of activities:

Adult education

Employment assistance

Health clinics

Youth or parent workshops

Family night activities

Teen lounge

Conflict resolution classes

Computer literacy classes

Crime and substance prevention programs

One model, known as family-supportive community schools, has been described in detail by Lawson and Briar-Lawson (1997) in *Connecting the Dots: Progress Toward the Integration of School Reform, School-Linked Services, Parent Involvement and Community Schools*. These schools are "based on an understanding of what families want and need; and what makes democracy and civil society work" (p. 42). Schools of this type employ multiple strategies to address both generations within families: parents and students. The following strategies are outlined as characteristic of community schools reform:

Parent empowerment and family support

Paraprofessional jobs and career ladders for parents

School readiness, parent education, and family support

Caring classrooms

Improved classroom support and resources for teachers and children

Collaborative leadership

Community center functions during nonschool hours

Neighborhood development and community organizing

Simultaneous renewal of higher education

Technology enhancement and use (Lawson & Briar-Lawson, 1997 pp. 5–6)

Several different models of school-community reform exist (Schorr, 1997). The two predominant types of community school models are described below: school-linked service integration and school-based community schools—or "full service" schools. Both types of community school reform are grounded in the growing consensus that schools, social service agencies, health care providers, neighborhood groups, and many others must act together in a coordinated and fully integrated fashion to improve outcomes for children and their families. Although this community-family-school partnership reform effort is being impelled largely by the need to respond to issues of poverty and welfare reform and, for schools, is mainly driven by the general education system, the implications for special education and for students with severe disabilities, in particular, are enormous. Systems developed to meet the needs of these students often serve as the "gateway" to the broader assessments described below.

School-Linked Service Integration

School-linked service models of community schools have developed primarily as a response to the complex needs of children and families living in poverty. Urban teachers encounter students daily with significant needs that cannot be adequately addressed by schools. Their efforts to link their students with needed services are often frustrating and unsuccessful and a task for which they are ill-prepared or have little time. Many children and families in need of human services must wait until their needs have reached crisis proportions before becoming eligible for services. Then they may have difficulty navigating the very systems intended to serve them. Both teachers and families become frustrated when, for example, one agency has to be approached for the student's wheelchair and walker, another agency for his mental health needs, and still another agency for his communication system. This makes coordination of services very difficult no matter how capable the teacher or parents are, but especially when family members do not have the time or capability to navigate the maze of individuals and paperwork that must be completed.

> *Daren's former elementary school developed a neighborhood school model of service integration. His current middle school is in the first year of a similar project. In elementary school, the family advocate at the school helped link Daren's mother to counseling services that she could receive and a local agency that helps find quality childcare. This assisted Daren's mother to get a better job and to feel that Daren was supported in the early morning when she had to leave for work. The family advocate worked with parents in the school and two local agencies, which provided the after-school care to establish a collaborative after-school program, which included students with all types of disabilities so that children with and without disabilities were not separated. This allowed Daren to stay with his friends for his after-school care. The same collaborative group worked to integrate the after-school programs in another way: across diverse economic levels. Before this arrangement children who received subsidized after-school care were in a different group than children who paid for their after-school care. The advocate helped the group to create a cohesive program, which brought together parents from a wide range of economic and social backgrounds.*

School-linked models are designed to change the status quo and acknowledge the shortcomings of traditionally fragmented approaches to service delivery. Therefore, they require a paradigm shift, from a crisis orientation to a prevention one; from a specialist to a team approach and from a deficit orientation to a strength-based approach (Adelman & Taylor, 1997; Karasoff, Blonsky, Perry, & Schear, 1996). These models strive to provide services that are child and family centered, prevention-oriented, flexible, comprehensive, holistic, and delivered in an interprofessional team approach (Adelman & Taylor, 1997; Melaville & Blank, 1991; Schorr, 1989, 1997).

School-linked models are based on partnerships with human service agencies in the community. Collaboration is at the very core of planning and implementing these services, and therefore, interagency collaborations are established to provide additional

services in an accessible and comprehensive manner. Often these services are provided by local service agencies near a school site through interagency agreement. Referred to as family resource centers, or FRCs (Langford-Carter, 1993), they may serve one particular school site, as in neighborhood community school models, or may serve several schools in their immediate proximity. Services are linked to the school site by a "facilitator" or "family advocate" who provides the single point of contact for families. A multitude of services and supports may be provided, including the following: (a) health clinic services, such as physical examinations and dental screenings; (b) family advocacy; (c) mental health counseling services; (d) tutoring and family support for education; and (e) public assistance services. In Table 1–4 you are introduced to Alissa:

> *The family resource center associated with Alissa's high school is a place where many services are provided, including a health clinic, job referral, and a tutoring center. When Alissa's school team began planning for work experiences within her high school program, the family advocate from the resource center assigned to Alissa's family assisted in getting the health forms completed, the identification cards, and in other ways. This individual also served as a liaison for Alissa's family with the many different agencies connected with planning for Alissa's transition to adult life. She connected Alissa's parents with other parents in the community who had more experience with the notions of "supported work" and "supported living" (see chapters 16 and 17), and Alissa's parents gained support for themselves through these connections.*

The best "cookbooks" on school-linked service integration are still Melaville and Blank (1991) and Melaville, Blank, and Asayesh (1993). The scholarship and theory underlying the premise is thoroughly analyzed and described in Crowson and Boyd (1993), Gerry (in press), and Kagan and Neville (1993); and a family perspective on school-linked service integration is presented in Turnbull and Turnbull (1997, p. 17, pp. 252–257), in Sailor (1994a, 1994b), and in Sailor, Kleinhammer-Tramill, Skrtic, and Oas (1996). Rigsby, Reynolds, and Wang (1995) discuss school-linked service integration in a review of research on urban school reform movements.

Some communities and states have begun broader innovations in school reform and service integration. One school system recently reported on a pilot project that is a coordinated effort between the state departments of mental health, the department of developmental disabilities, and the school system (Salisbury, Marlowe, & Crawford 1998). The agencies have reached an agreement by which a student's Individualized Educational Plan (IEP) is the central document through which all services are delivered, and other agencies, such as mental health agencies, are coordinated through it. All agency workers tap into the same database and communicate online with each other so that all team members are updated on a regular basis. If this pilot is successful (i.e., the data and outcomes for families are positive), the process will be implemented across the state. Broad-scale state initiatives to undertake school-linked service integration efforts have been undertaken in Colorado, Florida, and Indiana. The reader is referred to Kagan, Goffin, Golub, and Pritchard (1995) for an in-depth, comparative analysis of these state initiatives. The Harvard Family Research Project (1996) examined evaluative approaches from 16 states that report results-based accountability data on their respective efforts.

To sum up, school-linked service integration, as one manifestation of the community schools movement, brings all school resources and processes into a contiguous planning relationship with community resources to accomplish risk prevention for young children and their families and problem abatement strategies for families and youth whose problems are well established (Sailor, in press).

School-Based Community Schools

As mentioned at the outset of this section, community school service integration models come in two forms: those that are linked to schools and those that are a part of the school and physically located on the school site. The school-based model is perhaps best represented in the form of community schools, referred to as "full-service schools" (Dryfoos, 1994, 1996; Dryfoos, Brindis, & Kaplan, 1996). According to Gerry (in press), the full service school model is a comprehensive children's center, providing (in addition to education) a wide range of psychological, physical, social, recreation and other services and supports. It is thus, a kind of "one-stop shop" that seeks to meet the needs of all children and their families through a single point of contact and one easily accessible location. Under this model of a community school, a full-

time coordinator or program director is required in addition to the principal. Typically, a full-service school has teams of culturally sensitive, perhaps bilingual staff. Family and community members are included on the teams, and space is provided at the school for meetings and clinic functions. Most importantly this model provides a coordinated means of linking families and all services and supports for children with the educational program at the school (Sailor, in press).

Research on outcomes associated with both the full-service school version of the community schools movement and the school-linked services version are very encouraging. In the former case, Dryfoos, Brindis, and Kaplan (1996) report higher graduation rates, higher attendance rates, higher scores on math and reading skills assessments and performance, positive family attitudes and response to the schools, and diminished rates of property destruction and violence. In the case of school-linked service integration research, data from implementation of the Kentucky School Reform Act of 1990 afford a similarly encouraging picture (Knitzer & Page, 1996; Kleinert, Kearns, & Kennedy, in press; Doktor & Poertner, 1996).

On the downside, the community schools movement is not without detractors. These reform initiatives engender resistance from many school administrators and even from some teacher organizations who feel that schools should be left to do what they do best—and that is to teach. Health and social science issues, by this argument, are best provided separately by other agencies. These arguments are characteristic of traditional, categorical thinking, but the fact remains that hungry, abused, unhealthy, or homeless children cannot and will not respond to the best efforts of teachers and school administrators without comprehensive assistance in some form (Gerry, 1998).

In her recent book *Common Purpose: Strengthening Families and Neighborhoods to Rebuild America*, Lisbeth Schorr (1997) describes four main lessons worth noting from the community schools movement to date: (a) schools can become hubs for community services and islands of hope in communities; (b) schools cannot be asked to take the full responsibility for service reform and community building, i.e., they must be part of the solution, but not viewed as the solution; (c) intermediaries can be helpful; and (d) services are not enough (p. 289). Schorr cautions that while these services are intended to improve outcomes, sometimes these models do not assist with much-needed systems reform efforts. Schorr notes the potential drawbacks that linking or co-locating existing services may have, by pointing out that simply shifting the location of inadequate services from an inaccessible location to a more convenient one is not likely to improve outcomes. Therefore, it is imperative that whatever educational reform strategy is employed to address the needs of vulnerable children, youth, and families, schools must join together with their communities to design truly responsible and accountable approaches to reform and perhaps to ultimately have the capacity to re-direct funds from services and programs that fail to those that can show demonstrated success through results-based accountability.

In summary, both school-linked and school-based models strive to reduce the fragmentation and complexity of services experienced by so many children with disabilities as well as other vulnerable children and their families. Advocates of school-linked and school-based models view the school as the natural place to provide many needed services. School is the place that children and youth go each day, and therefore, the school itself or a nearby community center is considered an ideal location for the delivery of many services. The strength of this approach, when implemented well, is that it brings all of the providers together to view the child and family as a whole, by addressing the interrelatedness of their problems. Viewed from the special education perspective, these reforms begin to look like the starting point for making education "special" for all children, not just those served under the IDEA.

Inclusion

The second, and perhaps the most significant, policy implication for students with severe disabilities is the concept of inclusive education (Lipsky & Gartner, 1997; McLaughlin Leone, Warren, & Schofield, 1992; Sage & Burrello, 1994; Sailor et al., 1996). Inclusion has been a cornerstone of special education efforts at policy reform for almost a decade, and so we examine it here in some depth.

The term *inclusion* first appeared in the special education literature around 1990 and was picked up in a broader sense to become a central theme in the elec-

tion campaign of President Clinton in 1994. It referred specifically in education to the placement of students with disabilities of all ranges and types in general education classrooms with appropriate supports, adaptations, and services provided primarily in that environment as needed, with additional instruction in other community environments based on specific objectives spelled out in the IEP (Filler, 1996). The term *inclusion* grew out of the earlier rubric *integration*, which characterized 1980s efforts to have students with disabilities, particularly severe disabilities, educated in regular schools (Halvorsen & Sailor, 1990; Sailor, Anderson, Halvorsen, Doering, Filler, & Goetz, 1989). With many students identified for special education being referred out to special schools, "developmental centers," institutions, and even special school districts, the aim of integration as education policy was, for the most part, placement of such students in special classes located in regular schools, with at least some opportunities to interact with and be educated alongside nondisabled peers. Research conducted in the 1980s on the effects of integration across numerous educational and social indicators was overwhelmingly positive and set the stage for the move to inclusive schooling (see Halvorsen & Sailor, 1990 for review).

Where integration had to do with proximity and opportunities for social interaction, inclusion is concerned with full membership and participation in general education classroom activities, where appropriate. Inclusive schools, as originally conceived, are those designed to meet the educational needs of all their community members within common, yet fluid, environments and activities (Sapon-Shevin, 1994). For professionals and families who have been involved in this movement over many years, inclusion signifies something quite different from the earlier "mainstreaming" approaches in which students with disabilities were "allowed access" into general education classrooms at specified times or periods. In the integration model, the students' home base was, and is, the special education classroom. Access to the general education class is arranged for particular periods of the day by agreement with individual teachers (Biklen, 1988). These models rely on the ability of each special education teacher to set up collaborative partnerships with general educators and to design the supports and adaptations. Students often have to "prove" their ability to belong through prerequisite skills or behavior that is deemed acceptable and are just as likely to lose their time in general education classes if they are deemed a distraction to others.

Inclusive schooling is the term used to describe the next step. As educators, researchers, and parents became increasingly skilled at school-site level collaborative efforts in the 1980s and the early 1990s, general educators and special educators alike began to conclude that there were structural and system-wide barriers to effectively including students (Rainforth, York, & Macdonald, 1992; Sailor et al. 1989; Villa & Thousand, 1992; Thousand, Villa, & Nevin, 1994; Rainforth et al., 1996; Schorr, 1989). The 1990s followed, with numerous demonstration and research efforts in many school districts across the country as well as statewide systems change projects, validating the effectiveness of "inclusive schooling" (Gee, 1993; Gee, Graham, & Alwell, 1994; Hunt, Farron-Davis, Beckstead, Curtis, & Goetz, 1994b; Peck, Donaldson, & Pezzoli, 1990; Peck, Carleson, & Helmsstetter, 1992; Schnorr, 1989; Villa & Thousand, 1992; see Lipsky & Gartner, 1997, and Sailor, in press, for review). Inclusive schooling means much more than "where" instruction should occur. By the very nature of its design, an inclusive school reforms the way in which special education services are defined and implemented on site. Operating under the principal of least restrictive environment and individualized instruction, inclusive schools give all students the right to belong to their general education class. This redirects the educational teams to focus on how to teach each child, the specialized supports and instructional strategies required for each child, and how best to facilitate learning of social, academic, functional, and basic skills. The child's team is charged with designing specialized instruction within the general classroom, except when goals and objectives require a different environment to use natural cues and experiences (e.g., street crossing, toothbrushing, grocery shopping).

Sailor (1991) attempted a six-point definition of inclusion that was extended and further elaborated upon by Turnbull, Turnbull, Shank, and Leal (1995). The six points are:

1. All students receive education in the schools they would attend if they had no disability.
2. A natural proportion (that is, representative of the school district at large) of students with disabilities occurs at each school site.
3. A zero-reject philosophy exists, so that typically no student is excluded on the basis of type or extent of disability.
4. School and general education placements are appropriate for age and grade, so that no self-contained special education classes exist.
5. Cooperative learning, peer instruction, and other smaller grouping arrangements are employed as instructional methods.
6. Special education supports exist within the general education class and other integrated environments (p. 116).

On a practical level, inclusive schooling means that all children belong. Their home base is the general education classroom. Through problem solving, collaboration, and creative curricular and instructional design, students of all levels are included in the typical general education schedule, the instructional units, and activities in all core subject areas (Downing, 1996; Gee, in press; Udvari-Solner, 1997). The outcomes and instructional expectations for students with severe disabilities may be very similar to, or very different from, the students without disabilities, depending on the content, the grade level, and the goals. Sometimes alternative instructional activities are designed for small heterogeneous groups of students within the classroom to include

FIGURE 1–1
A 3rd grader and her classmates.

the students with severe disabilities in a more meaningful activity or to assure that instruction on important skills can take place. Over time, collaboration between the general education and special education teachers constantly changes the way in which instruction is designed, making it less and less necessary to create alternatives (Gee, Graham, Sailor, & Goetz, 1995b; Udvari-Solner, 1996). Table 1–5 depicts a sample participation plan for Daren in his social studies class. The teachers at both Daren's and Jeremy's middle schools used the following problem-solving process to plan for their instruction and participation (Gee et al. 1994; Gee et al., 1995; Gee, in press).

TABLE 1–5
Participation and Support Plan for Daren in Social Studies Class

Participation and Support Plan		
Student: Daren (D)		
Subject Area: Social Studies		
Primary Teaching Activities and Expectations for Class	**Adapted Expectations or Modified Outcomes**	**Instructional Support Strategies**
Reading chapters in book • Get more information • Read, answer questions at end of chapter • Test and class discussion preparation	• Provide book chapters on tape • Expectations: listen to chapters, answer the modified questions that the teacher designates by short phrases on the computer.	• Provide D with a plan to listen to the chapters and follow key headlines in book; strategies for answering the modified questions. Practice this in library during study period, and three or four questions can be done for homework periodically.
Class lectures and discussion • Listen, follow outline • Take notes on key concepts • Understand key concepts • Test preparation	• Get a class note buddy. Support teacher or aid highlights key words from the notes for D. • Mr. H. gives disk to D with bullets from overhead projector for D to follow on laptop.	• Assist D with planning time to listen to the chapters before class in order to benefit from the discussion. • Print questions for D and enter questions into the computer and for the notebook. • Remind D to actively listen to the teacher and to the peer responses to questions. • Have D sit facing the teacher.
Class notebook • Include notes, answers to questions, and in-class assignments, and turn in for grade at end of unit.	• Verbally dictated or computer-generated answers to modified questions and chapter summaries • Teacher determines modified questions, summaries, and number.	• If D is absent, assist him to connect with buddy from class. • D has difficulty listening and being ready for questions. Use his social story guide to remind him of the routines. Make sure questions are ready ahead of time for D to plan • Practice listening to chapter a few pages at a time and following key phrases, bold phrases, and photos.
Pop quizzes • Purpose is to make sure students are reading the chapters.	• These move too quickly to complete in class; instead, get a copy and use for study purposes.	

1. Clearly delineate the instructional activities and the expected outcomes or products in the curricular unit.
2. Discuss the purpose behind the activities, the groupings and formats, and the rationale for instructing in particular ways.

3. Share ideas about how to plan for students with a wide range of learning styles and intelligences.
4. Brainstorm the ways in which the content can be provided to the student with disabilities and in what ways the student can be expected to develop new skills and contribute to the class.

Participation and Support Plan

Student: Daren (D)

Subject Area: Social Studies

Primary Teaching Activities and Expectations for Class	Adapted Expectations or Modified Outcomes	Instructional Support Strategies
Class projects • Purpose is to further understanding through applications. • Usually in groups. • Also includes group process objectives.	• Same expectations for social participation. • Additional objectives related to peer interaction and organization and taking initiative. • Determine modified outcome goals for D for each project.	• D needs assistance to select a group and some facilitation in the group. • D needs to do these projects even if it requires time outside of school. Call D's parents to facilitate the process, so that D gets together with students.
In-class assignments, such as reading articles, responding and discussing. • Use real sources; discuss; further understanding.	• Materials should be in large print and done ahead of time. • Support teacher or aid provides modified questions ahead of time.	• Since D's reading ability is at about second grade level, a peer or adult support person reads aloud. • D will verbally indicate answers or write on laptop.
Unit tests • Evaluates what students know.	• Large print test. • Longer period of time to complete it. • Modified questions regarding content.	• Modify for testing materials to match content outcomes for D. • Provide D with assistance to study for the upcoming test (see strategies folder). • Assist D to arrange to meet with teacher in tutorials or study period. • Use study strategies in instructional plan. • Help D connect with peers who might be studying together.

General Support Strategies for Daren

- See D's "social story" planner and file for social studies class
- D's study plan file
- See D's strategies folder
- Books on tape
- Large print materials
- Lecture notes with highlights from buddy
- Homework log and homework communication with home

Reminders to Teachers

- Handouts should be blown up to large print size.
- Support persons check in ahead of class for handouts, so that if there is any that haven't been done, D will do quickly before class starts. Alert Daren to ask buddy to take notes.
- Large projects are given ahead of time to support teacher so that D can plan ahead for materials.

5. Determine what the expected outcomes for the student will be in relationship to IEP goals.
6. Determine the adaptations, accommodations, and supports that are needed.
7. If an alternative activity is necessary, ensure that it includes other students without disabilities and connects or relates to the curricular content of the class.

Table 1–5 depicts some of the greater detail related to how Daren's instructional objectives are actually met within the seventh grade social studies class. Jeremy's instructional objectives and the ways in which they are carried out within his seventh grade English class are very different from Daren's. Jeremy's general education teachers met regularly with the support teacher to plan his participation for the upcoming instructional units (Table 1–6). They met at the beginning of each unit and the support teacher then delineated the ideas in written participation plans for support staff and the general education teacher. Table 1–7 depicts a participation plan for how Jeremy's objectives were reached within a unit on *The Wizard of Earthsea* by Ursula LeGuin. Systematic instructional plans for how each objective was taught were a very important part of his success (see chapter 4 for details on systematic instructional plans). Without systematic instructional methods that use the natural opportunities available in the general education class, Jeremy would not have made progress on his goals as effectively as possible. Similar collaborative planning processes have been described in Falvey (1996); Gee et al. (1994); Gee et al. (1995); Gee (in press); Rainforth, York, and MacDonald (1992), and Udvari-Solner (1996).

There may be some instructional goals on a student's IEP that require instruction in other environments in the community (such as functional shopping skills, for example, or real work experiences) or in other home and school settings (self-care activities, such as showering or toothbrushing, outdoor recreation skills). To make sure these types of goals are addressed, the student's team arranges for time within the school day to use alternate settings or simply extends the use of environments used by all students for similar purposes.

Table 1–8 depicts a matrix of Shalila's second grade school day, demonstrating when and where her instruction on priority goals and objectives takes place. The reader can see that Shalila takes a little longer after lunch to work on some self-care skills in the bathroom, while the other students are doing some silent reading. She also leaves class a little early to go to music, physical education, art, or the library to have time to work on using her walker through the hallways and outside.

Alissa spends half her day in classes at the high school and half her day in the community getting meaningful job experiences to build her resume for job searches when she graduates and important community skills. Table 1–9 depicts her schedule and how it fits in within the high school block schedule.

Providing instruction that is connected to the ongoing curricular and recreational activities of the other students in Daren's, Jeremy's, Shalila's, and Alissa's classes requires an understanding of the whole activity, the skills that can be practiced within it, and the ability to use these natural opportunities as they arrive. This requires that teachers in special education think differently about how instruction on very specific skills is facilitated. Embedded instruction of basic skills within the context of age-appropriate activities has been shown to be a highly effective strategy (Gee et al. 1995; Goetz & Gee, 1987a, 1987b; Hunt, Alwell, & Goetz, 1988; Hunt, Staub, Alwell, & Goetz, 1994a; Palincsar & Brown, 1984; Palincsar, 1986; Palincsar, David, Winn, & Stevens, 1990). Instruction is not "delivered" in the sense of presenting an individual "trial" in isolation from others, but "provided" to Shalila to learn the skill as it relates to the tasks and activities in which she is involved (see chapters 3–5 for more details). Shalila's special education support teacher looks closely at the most common types of activities that the second grade teacher uses. She analyzes the curriculum and the instructional activities and delineates the opportunities that are available for Shalila to practice her instructional objectives.

During daily language or writing time (from 8:30 AM to 9:15 AM), students are reading each other's stories and giving feedback; they are also writing in a journal. Shalila is working on similar objectives by using her augmentative communication device to put together picture sequences for her journal. She shares this with a peer who gives her feedback, and conversation skills can be practiced. Shalila also listens to a story by one of her peers, then makes a comment using her communication device. Shalila can do this with as many peers as possible during

(text continues on p. 20)

TABLE 1–6

Team Planning Tool for Systematic Instruction and Embedded Objectives for Jeremy (J) in the Unit on *The Wizard of Earthsea*

Typical Class Activities	Typical Teaching Strategies	Expectations for General Students	Expectations for Jeremy	How Jeremy Receives Information	How Jeremy Provides Information	Further Integration Ideas
• Reading aloud	• Large group, vary readers, discuss in between passages	• Follow reading, reading aloud, participate in discussion	• Response to name and tactile signal; use of microswitch to activate tape	• Object board • Peers sitting next to him prompt, general teacher provides cues	• Object board • Microswitch attached to tape recorder with prerecorded passages	• Circle of friends • Set aside 5 minutes on a regular basis to train the peers in his support circle how to support him during particular activities and tasks. Make sure they know how to read his eyegaze shifts and can provide consistent ways of interacting. Provide the peers with feedback so that they know when J is looking at them and what he likes and dislikes. At support circle meetings, discuss upcoming projects and look at possibilities for J. Arrange for homework discussions and projects.
• Journal and homework written assignments in Thoughtful Ed. model with four styles	• Independent work or with partner	• Complete assignments after every two chapters • Grammar, spelling, reading for comprehension and understanding, critical thinking	• Computer use with microswitch; with partners, select fantasy pictures for coloring album for class	• Peer partners set context by their assignment; support person provides instructional assistance	• Print out pages for class coloring book	
• Debate	• Room divides in half on a position; students who change their mind physically move	• State arguments clearly, determine agree or disagree, share thoughts, articulate positions	• Contingency awareness: when J moves his eyebrows or eyes, partners move him quickly to the other side	• Peers move him in his chair and make it known when he has made a movement that is relevant	• Changing expression and moving eyebrows or large "sigh"	
• Mandalas	• Students design mandalas based on the themes from the book	• Critical thinking, creative approaches to themes, understanding story themes	• Computer selection of colors and background designs using new program; social interactions	• Support staff and peers provide choices on computer program, Kid Pix	• Shift of gaze; microswitch for output of choice	
• Sociograms	• Students work on sociograms of the characters over the course of the book in groups	• Understanding the relationships between the characters in the book	• Peer interactions; use computer program set up to make sociogram; choice making	• Support staff and peers provide cues and assistance	• Shift gaze, use of microswitch, sigh, facial expression	
• Fantasy play	• Four groups of students: Students design a play which is a fantasy in one act and perform it for the class	• Writing, articulating story plots and themes, understanding fantasy as a literary form, work skills	• Use microswitch to activate lines in play; social interactions; name recognition; object calendar	• Peers	• Tape recorded lines by peers	

TABLE 1–7
Participation Plan for Jeremy in Literature Unit

Student: Jeremy (J)   **Subject: Language Arts—Literature**

Activities: See activities below for unit on The Wizard of Earthsea.
Student Considerations:

- J needs to be suctioned on a regular basis. Try to make sure it is done before the reading aloud times, because it's a little loud.
- The list of partners and his support circle is in his folder.
- Make sure his peers have pre-recorded passages for reading aloud and that they are marked in Ms. S.'s book.
- Make sure the tactile object calendar and communication board are attached to his wheelchair.

Goals and Objectives:

- Primary objectives for J in this period are: recognition of name and shifting of gaze for social response; use of microswitch to operate tape recorder, communication device, and the computer programs; contingency awareness; making choices; building friendships through joint activities; and at every activity, his object communication board should be used.

	Support Needed:	
What the Class Does	**How to Provide Information and Support**	**How J Participates**
Large Group		
• Read aloud and discuss	• Arrange for passages to be pre-recorded for reading, make sure microswitch is ready; peer partner provides extra prompts and assistance with staff input	• Object communication board (see program) • Recognizing name; gaze shift and use of microswitch (see systematic instructional programs for each)
• Debates	• Rotate partners from support circle—this is made for fun!	• Simple contingencies—when he changes expressions, the kids zip him over to the other side—cause and effect
Small Groups		
• Sociograms • Fantasy plays	• Students are in small groups designing this. J's group uses the program on the computer (see the Intellipics program in his file). As students determine choices for this, they need assistance to prompt J to click the mouse with his switch. The peers should do the typing of names. J just activates the circles and the designs.	• Object communication board (see program) • J is working on recognizing the visual cues on the computer and the tactile ones provided by his peers to operate the sociogram program designed (see systematic program and data sheet). He is also expected to use his non-symbolic means to interact—eye gaze, slight eyebrow movement.
	• Provide assistance at the start of each group meeting to assign J a role and help brainstorm ideas. Make sure a group member knows how to operate J's tape recorder system and switch. Assist peers to pre-record lines and determine how to cue J within the play.	• J records the brainstorm session and sample lines; plays back what was said in the first planning sessions. Later he works on recognizing his cues for lines he plays on the tape recorder.
Independent		
• Journal and written homework • Mandalas	• J is designing a fantasy coloring album using the computer program on file. Students are using the stained glass paper and the pens to decorate the windows. Students who finish early come and partner with Jeremy on this.	• Making choices, operating printer, interacting with partners
	• Assist J to find computer file and program. Peers can set up several choices for each part, then watch for his eye gaze choices and prompt him to use his switch	• Making choices, operating microswitch to operate mouse on computer, peer interactions
Unexpected Events		

TABLE 1–8
Shalila's Matrix of Embedded Skill Instruction for the First Quarter

Daily Schedule	Current Objectives										
	Communication with Picture/Voice Output Device and Responding to Yes/No Questions	Sequencing Pictures	Using a Walker to Go Short Distances	Using a Power Wheelchair	Making Friends	Listening and Responding to her Name and Requests for Participation	Fine Motor: Grasping and Releasing and Placing and Directing Others to Use Objects	More and Less Concepts	Completing Classroom Jobs	Completing Homework	Using the Bathroom with Increasing Independence
Daily Opportunities for Instruction of Specific Objectives											
8:30–9:15 Daily Language and Writing	Journals; peer reading	Use pictures to tell story to peers	Entry to room and to desk		Engage peers in the activity	Respond to peer requests	All of the above				
9:15–10:00 Literature Circles	Respond to modified questions	Same as above	From desk to circle area		Respond to peers and choose interactions with peers	Same as above			Complete modified job in literature circle	Complete homework for the circle, modified for her and parents	
10:00–10:20 Recess and Snack	Same as above		From circles to wheelchair	Travel on playground and in halls	Select peers, choose games	Same as above					Same
10:20–11:00 Math Workshop	Same as above	Same as above	From power chair to walker and then to desks		Interact with partners	Same as above	Same as above	Same as above	When clean-up turn is due, assist		
Rotation: 11:00–11:45 Mon, Wed- Phys Ed	Same as above		From desks to power chair	Use power chair to play games	Same as above	Same as above	Same as above	Same as above	Same as above		Same

TABLE 1–8
continued

Daily Schedule	Daily Opportunities for Instruction of Specific Objectives							
11:00–11:45 Tu, Th Music	Same as above	Same as above	Use power chair to music room	Same as above	Same as above	Same as above	Same as above	Same as above
11:00–11:45 Fri, Mon-Art (Rotation then Starts Over)	Same as above	Same as above	Use power chair to art room	Same as above	Same as above	Same as above	Same as above	Same as above
11:45–12:30 Lunch and Recess	Same as above	Same as above	Use power chair to cafeteria	Same as above				
12:30–1:00 Silent Reading or Reading Buddies								Same
1:00–1:45 Mon, Wed Science	Same	Same		Same	Same	Same	Same	Same
1:00–1:45 Tu, Th Social Studies	Same	Same		Same	Same	Same	Same	Same
1:00–1:45 Fri Library	Same	Same	Use power chair to library	Same	Same	Same	Same	Same
1:45–1:55 Short Recess	Same		Use power chair on playground	Same				
2:00–2:20 Math Problems	Same	Same	Use power chair into community on TU and TH	Same	Same	Same	Same	Same

TABLE 1–9
Alissa's Schedule on the High School Campus and in the Community

Monday	Tuesday	Wednesday	Thursday	Friday
Class 1: 8:00–9:30 Computers or keyboard	**Class 5: 8:00–10:15** Off campus work site in the community	**Class 1: 8:00–9:30** Computers	**Class 5: 8:00–10:15** Off campus work site in the community	**Class 1: 8:00–9:30** Computers
Brunch: 9:30–9:45	Return to campus	**Brunch: 9:30–9:45**	Return to campus	**Brunch: 9:30–9:45**
Class 2: 9:45–11:15 Biology	**Class 6: 10:35–12:55** Drama	**Class 2: 9:45–11:15** Science	**Class 6: 10:35–12:55** Drama	**Class 2: 9:45–11:15** Science
Class 3: 11:20–12:50 Spanish		**Class 3: 11:20–12:50**	**Lunch: 12:55–1:25** Alissa has lunch with friends	**Class 3: 11:20–12:50**
Lunch 12:55–1:25 Alissa has lunch with friends	**Lunch: 12:55–1:25** Alissa has lunch with friends	**Lunch 12:55–1:25** Alissa has lunch with friends	**Class 7: 1:30–3:00** Tutorial: same as other students (Alissa does any group project activities or gets materials, does homework)	**Lunch 12:55–1:25** Alissa has lunch with friends
Class 4: 1:30–3:00 Alissa leaves campus to use various services in the community, practice mobility and communication	**Class 7: 1:30–3:00** Tutorial: same as other students (Alissa does any group project activities or gets materials, does homework)	**Class 4: 1:30–3:00** Alissa leaves campus to use various services in the community, practice mobility and communication		**Class 4: 1:30–3:00** Alissa leaves campus to use various services in the community, practice mobility and communication

the time period, giving her many opportunities to practice her communication skills.

The special education teacher makes sure that everyone involved with Shalila knows how to provide the right kind of support and how to fade out that support. She makes sure that the teaching staff is able to evaluate Shalila's performance and facilitate learning using strategies on which the team agrees. Thus, Shalila's teachers, instructional support staff, and peers find multiple opportunities to instruct her throughout the day on all aspects of her IEP (see chapters 3, 4, and 5 for more detail).

When a school commits to an inclusive model, the staff is freed from the responsibility for and the expense of energy and resources that have typically been spent on determining "who should get in." Instead, the staff is given the mission to spend their energies and resources on how to teach every student. While this change may not seem monumental at first, it is actually the most important aspect of inclusive schooling. Since the original Education of the Handicapped Act (P.L. 94–142) in 1974, special education has been intended to focus on individualized and specialized methods of instruction that are added and connected to the regular school curriculum (Turnbull & Turnbull, 1997). In most districts and states in the United States, this quickly translated into a separate system, and student placement became the focus. Services became associated with a special setting, instead of services following the child. Inclusive education and the new IDEA 1997 focuses on a return to instruction and support which is centered on the child and the family, rather than on simple placement of the student.

IDEA, as espoused in 1997, makes it clear that the general education curriculum is to be considered the norm for all students and that performance goals for students with disabilities are to be implemented in the general education classroom (the least restrictive environment) unless particular goals and objectives require different settings, as described above. If IEP teams choose alternative settings, they must show adequate rationale for why a particular goal or objective must be taught outside of the general education classroom.

While some school districts and authors have taken a divergent foray into time as the crucial issue in defining inclusion (i.e., the amount of minutes in regular education as a way of defining inclusion), those involved with inclusive schools as described

above focus on instructional strategies, quality of life, student outcomes, person-centered planning, and successful futures. Students with severe disabilities may need highly intensive instruction to learn new communication, social skills, motor skills, and daily life tasks. This requires creative strategies for embedding instruction of these skills within the general class curriculum, where the natural cues and opportunities exist, as well as finding opportunities for instruction within the community and other parts of the school (Downing, 1996; Falvey, 1996; Hunt et al., 1994a; Ford, Davern, & Schnorr, 1992).

Other students require flexible schedules, or adaptations, in their curriculum and technology to have a successful day at school. Some students need a positive behavioral support plan (see chapter 6) and still others may need specialized health care services (Graff, Ault, Guess, Taylor, & Thompson 1990 (see chapter 7)) or counseling. The excerpt below refers to Table 1–2.

> *Daren has a mental health support group twice a week run by counselors associated with his school's full-service model. Both his special education support teacher and a general education "mentor" (a teacher on site) are trained to provide daily support and guidance to Daren, with support from the psychologist, by regularly "checking in" with Daren during homeroom and his support session in the library with other peers. Daren knows that his mentor and homeroom teacher, Mr. M., and his special education support teacher are there whenever he needs support.*

Students with specific learning disabilities may require intensive instruction in organizational strategies, study strategies, or writing and reading strategies. Each of these students requires an effective team within the inclusive school (including the student, the parents or guardians, a qualified special education support teacher, related support professionals, general educators who consider themselves the student's primary teachers, and peers selected by the student and teacher).

As with all policy reform agendas, not everyone agrees with the goals of inclusive schooling. Arguments surface in the literature of both general and special education professions concerning the difficulty of adapting the general education curriculum to meet the needs of students with disabilities, particularly those with severe disabilities (e.g., Fuchs & Fuchs, 1994). Opponents of inclusive schooling make the mistake of thinking that all children will be asked

FIGURE 1–2
Two friends going for a home run in kickball.

to do the same work or that children with some needs that are very different from others will not receive appropriate instruction. However, the research on inclusive schooling demonstrates that students with severe disabilities can and do learn important functional, academic, and life skills when the instruction of these skills is embedded within the general education activities of their nondisabled peers in general education classrooms (Lipsky & Gartner, 1997; Gee, 1995; Gee et al., 1995; Gee, in press; Hunt et al. 1994b; Skrtic, Sailor, & Gee, 1996; Sailor, Goetz, Anderson, Hunt, & Gee, 1988; Turnbull & Turnbull, 1997). Inclusive schooling provides policy makers with the clearest effort to achieve instruction in the least restrictive environment, while contributing to the overall, positive reform of the entire school.

In fact, a high-quality inclusive school addresses and supports the individual nature of each child and, from an instructional standpoint, is characterized by opportunities to individualize instruction for a wide range of learners (Rainforth et al., 1992; Sapon-Shevin, 1992; Thousand, Villa, & Nevin, 1994). With each new iteration of this well-established trend in education reform policy, beginning with the concept of "mainstreaming" in the 1970s, moving to "integra-

tion" in the 1980s, and focused on inclusion in the present era, the status of the person with disabilities is raised to a point that more closely approximates the status of all the other learners at the school. Students with disabilities are increasingly regarded as less in need of shelter and protection and more in need of support and adaptation.

At the student level, a successful inclusive, learning community fosters collaboration, problem solving, self-directed learning, and critical discourse along with mastery of academic subject areas and functional skills. Fluid instructional groupings within heterogeneous classrooms allow the teachers to work with both heterogeneous and homogeneous partners and groups of students at various times of the day. Intensive instructional support is provided through the combined resources of the general education staff and now-present special education staff, who used to be down the hall. Sometimes teachers may use other space in the school for small reading groups, use other parts of the school building, or do instruction in the community to meet the IEP objectives of students with disabilities. Other students without disabilities may also have instruction in other parts of the school and in the community. The "classroom" is not the only place where instruction occurs. The inclusive school movement represents school improvement on many levels for all students, not just the physical placement of individuals with various abilities and disabilities in general classrooms (Downing, 1996; Falvey, 1992; 1996; Neary, Halvorsen, Kronberg, & Kelly, 1993; Putnam, 1994; Rainforth et al., 1992; Sailor, 1991; Sailor, Gee, & Karasoff, 1993; Sapon-Shevin, 1992; Strully & Strully, 1989; Thousand, Villa, & Nevin, 1994; Villa & Thousand, 1992).

With the growing recognition that diversity is an asset, not a liability, schools are creating learning communities that serve all students more effectively through collaboration of well-trained staff and combined resources. Lipsky and Gartner (1997) reported a review of some 21 state policies that address inclusion and concluded that they share a number of common features in the movement toward inclusion: "the importance of leadership, collaboration across the lines of general and special education, the need for changes in pedagogy and school staffing, and financial issues" (p. 113). As Lipsky and Gartner (1997) point out, inclusion is no longer a matter of "should," but, in terms of education policy, it is now strictly in the realm of "how." The issue for the next decade is not whether to teach students with severe disabilities in inclusive classrooms and the community, but how to make sure that teachers and administrators have the training to implement supports and services in the least restrictive environment (general education classes, schools, and the community) appropriately in accordance with the best practices available. A second issue for the next decade is how to develop schools to be places that facilitate growth for all children, that are flexible for the needs of students who challenge the system, and that collaborate with other disciplines, such as mental health, to design services for the many needs of all children.

In relationship to community schools, inclusion as policy helps to deliver the coordinated resources needed to enhance educational opportunities for all of the students at the school. It also restructures the emphasis of the organization, turning the focus on individual instructional planning versus placement (Gee, in press). For an extended discussion of the position of inclusion in school restructuring and other general education reform movements, see also Sailor, Gee & Karasoff (1993).

Many districts are leaping ahead in providing effective special education services in inclusive schools. However, there are still giant steps that need to be taken to bring our schools closer to the goals of IDEA 1997. Ongoing training and effective leadership, as well as creative organizational strategies, are needed to deliver high-quality services. These needs are consistent across both general and special education systems. Shalila, Jeremy, Daren, and Alissa are all educated in inclusive schools, elementary, middle, and high school respectively. Although their needs vary, each one has severe disabilities. Their schools are in very different communities—urban, suburban, and rural—but each school has made a commitment to provide an excellent education to all students as full members of the general education classroom community. This means that there is a commitment on the part of the principal, faculty, and parent community to improve, on an ongoing basis, the education of all students in their school's zone. Each school has ongoing issues that need to be addressed with staff development and problem solving, some related to individuals with disabilities and some related to school improvement in general. This brings us to our third policy development: the unification of school resources and services.

As we mentioned earlier, the community school movement is related to two other significant school reform policy issues of great importance to the education of students with severe disabilities and, ultimately, to educational outcomes for all children. The first was inclusive education; the second is school unification.

School Unification

School unification policy (Miles & Darling-Hammond, 1998; Sailor, in press) seeks to do two primary things: 1) merge the research-based reform efforts in both general and special education to allow *all* students to benefit from innovative practices developed across fields, and 2) unify school resources and administration so that *all* students benefit from a less fragmented structure.

> At Shalila's school, a site resource team works regularly to review the available staff, their expertise, students with special needs, and students in need of extra assistance. Resources are shared across "categories" so that all students benefit. Shalila's special education support teacher works closely with her second grade teacher and also the other first and second grade teachers. She functions as a regular primary grade team member, contributing ideas and strategies to the overall program. Shalila's computer is shared by other students in the classroom.

Over the past decade there have been numerous hopeful strategies for the redesign of our nation's schools. Bacharach (1990) notes that the first wave of reform efforts in the 1980s resulted in important changes but argues that most of these were made within the general operational patterns of public schools versus the structures themselves. Skrtic (1991, 1995a, 1995b) points out that the process of re-inventing schools requires a deeper analysis of cultural, ethical, and epistemological issues. Other authors suggest that the real heart of restructuring public education lies in each school's belief system regarding the nature and purpose of education and each school's ability to create a shared vision among its staff that incorporates both excellence and equity for all students (Joyce, Wolfe, & Calhoun, 1993; Stainback, Stainback, & Forest 1989; Villa & Thousand, 1992).

The current reform efforts are perceived as different—sensitive to the complexity and systemic nature of the issues (Paul & Rosselli, 1995). In this second wave of reform, educators, researchers, administrators, and parents, in both general and special education, are seeking workable answers to difficult questions related to excellence, equity, choice, accountability, and school climate. One observation (Paul & Rosselli, 1995) is that while general educators were worrying about reforming instruction, special educators were worrying about integration and inclusion. Another view is that educators from both general education and special education have been working on parallel planes on many of the same issues but, until recently, without access to the positive effects of collaboration across disciplines (Gee, in press).

There were many years in which clinical researchers examined the questions of teaching from highly specialized perspectives, reporting results only to highly specific readers, and targeting studies on narrowly defined populations (Skrtic, 1991). While this perspective benefited the field in some ways, it also promoted a lack of common language across disciplines and a general feeling that ideas and strategies from one area could not be applied to another. For many years, this contributed to a lack of dialogue between general and special education professionals and the development of very different language bases for similar and different learning concepts and teaching strategies. Researchers and teachers immersed in the practice of inclusion have noted both the merger and the "mismatch" of professional practices, which often occur when general and special education teachers and related service providers come together on inclusive educational teams (Billingsley, Gallucci, Peck, Schwartz, & Staub, 1996; Dunn, 1991; Gee et al., 1994; Gee, 1993; Rainforth et al. 1992; Thousand et al., 1994; Udvari-Solner, 1994).

There has, however, been a continuous thread of research on effective practices conducted in general education and in special education on a parallel plane (Brown & Campione, 1990; Dunn, 1991; Englert, Tarrant, & Mariage, 1992; Grennon-Brooks & Brooks, 1993; Johnson & Johnson, 1989; Palincsar et al., 1990; Sailor, Goetz, Anderson, Hunt & Gee, 1988; Snell, 1993). Particular developments have brought these lines of teaching and service delivery practices closer together, and the point at which they converge is centered on the inclusive schools movement and the emerging literature on teaching diverse communities of learners (Brown, Palincsar, & Purcell, 1985; Brown

& Campione, 1990; Downing, 1996; Dunn, 1991; Gee, 1995a; Englert et al., 1992; Haring & Ryndak, 1994; Palincsar et al., 1990; Putnam, 1994; Rainforth, York, & MacDonald, 1992; Sapon-Shevin, 1992; Thousand et al., 1994; Udvari-Solner, 1994).

The research on school renewal tells us which reorganization efforts have been successful (Huberman, 1992; Goodlad & Klein, 1970; Cuban, 1989). Major school improvement efforts can be sustained only when the focus is on student learning (Huberman, 1992; Joyce, Showers, & Weil, 1992). Many researchers believe that school improvement efforts that see student learning as central and keep that mission up front at all times will make dramatic positive learning gains for students, as evidenced by the *Success for All* program (Madden, Slavin, Karweil, Dolan, & Wasik, 1991, 1993). In addition, some researchers have noted that it is the abundance of "half-way" and "tip-toe" approaches to change that wear educators out and that strong, well-supported initiatives are easier to make than weak ones (Huberman, 1992).

Joyce, Wolf, and Calhoun (1993) write: "Educators are perfectly capable of rapidly learning the skills and knowledge to sustain the most complex initiatives thus far put forward, provided that adequate support is given. . . . As we struggle to initiate school renewal that sustains healthy learning communities, educators should take comfort from the fact that we can change the whole organization and how it does business—and we can do so quite rapidly. . . . As we change the organization, the creativity and vitality of both educators and students will be enhanced immeasurably" (pp. 20, 21).

What is not clear in many organizations is the extent to which there is agreement on the nature and depth of the changes being sought (Huberman, 1992; Joyce et al., 1993; Madden et al., 1993). A second underlying premise of this argument is that pedagogy and student outcomes must be regarded as the central focus of educational reform for all students (with and without disabilities) with systems and structures designed to support that focus. By unifying the reform efforts from both general education and special education and combining resources, many schools across the nation have been able to achieve significantly positive results for all students (Miles & Darling-Hammond, 1998).

To understand the impulse driving school unification policy, one needs only to examine the organizational structure of a large traditional school in an urban or suburban area. There, one will encounter a maze of federally mandated categorical and highly specialized programs addressed to the needs of discrete groups of students who are in relative isolation at the school. Programs such as special education (which, in fact, often has a myriad complex of further subdivided categorical programs contained within it addressed, e.g., to children labeled autistic, learning disabled, or deaf-blind), Title I, gifted, English as a second language, vocational education, and others often operate in different physical locations within the school and with support from specially trained and licensed personnel who only feel competent to assist students identified for their particular services.

In some urban school settings, after all of the children who have been deemed eligible for one or more of the special programs have been removed from the general education classroom, there may be relatively little support remaining in the school with which to address the needs of those remaining. Yet, these students may face and represent learning challenges that are at least as great as those found eligible for categorical assistance (Lipsky & Gartner, 1997). The fact is that specialized supports for some children have at least some utility for all children. The application, for example, of positive behavioral support programming (Horner, Dunlap, Koegel, Carr, Sailor, Anderson, Albin, & O'Neil, 1990) to help a special education student might be exactly the appropriate intervention for a student with behavioral challenges who is not eligible for special education services.

Resources at the school geared to support special populations are delineated in a manner that benefits the intended recipients in a fully integrated context that allows all children at the school to realize some benefit from their application.

> *Very often an extra staff person is made available in Jeremy's classrooms. While working with Jeremy to provide specialized instruction and support, this faculty or staff person also works with other middle school students on their projects and essays or by answering questions about content.*

In a unified approach, special education is intended to provide specialized services and supports as needed to educate students with disabilities in the least restrictive environment (Turnbull & Turnbull, 1997) but it is also used to benefit all students.

A second aspect of school unification is the increased opportunity, through collaborative instructional planning and unified organization, to address some flawed assumptions in the historically separate systems that still exist in many states and school districts. Referral to the special education process implies an assumption, which is as follows: educators assume that by referring a child to a special education program (really placement, in many instances), they will "get what they need" in the "one hour a day" of resource placement or the "two hours twice a week" or full-day placement in a separate class. In fact, students may get further behind, lose the curriculum content from missed class time, and have less positive communication and fewer social partners. Since there are often no transition criteria or true accountability for progress in systems that operate this way, many students get increasingly segregated with little hope for return.

In addition, the current system in many districts is one of placement versus instructional plans. In other words, "services and supports" often translates to "number of hours of resource support" or placement in a self-contained classroom, rather than a clear plan of instructional strategies that are implemented and regularly evaluated on an individual basis. This flawed system is not in accordance with what federal law (i.e., IDEA) requires in an individualized educational program in the least restrictive environment.

School unification policy seeks to remedy these flaws by bringing faculty, resources, families, and students together in coordinated planning arrangements to address school changes, school activities, school curricula, and school accountability. Schools undergoing unified reform efforts find that teachers from bilingual education, special education, Title 1, Reading Recovery, and general education can effectively team together to make use of their rich pool of skills and experiences, resulting in highly effective programs and instruction that are far better than before (Miles & Darling-Hammond, 1998).

The purpose of these unified efforts is not to water down or lose the expertise of important disciplines but rather to provide the framework in which these highly specialized individuals can work and collaborate together, ultimately benefiting more students. Not everyone on the team has to know everything; however, all team members are empowered to not only care about all the students in the school but to contribute to their education.

At Alissa's high school, the special education teachers are assigned to departmental teams to more carefully collaborate in subject areas of their interest and expertise. Resources from school-to-work programs, special education, and transition planning are combined to provide more students with work experience prior to graduation. As a result, Alissa goes to her work internship with another student without disabilities who works for the same company.

One small school district participating in a federally funded outreach project for inclusive schooling generated its own need to redesign and unify their school resources (Gee et al., 1995). It became clear to the school site principals and many teachers that an effective inclusive program for children with disabilities cannot be developed in a vacuum, separate from all the other important curricular and instructional needs at the school. They have unified their reform efforts with a cohesive focus on improving instruction, curriculum, and school community for all students. Their inservices, faculty meetings, and all other functions reflect this approach, and they are finding it much easier to provide the extra support and instruction that many students with disabilities need. School administrators and teachers participating in small focus groups have a chance to have important discourse about instructional content and strategies. These groups continue to guide the research-based inservices at the school, schoolwide organizational decisions, and instructional improvement.

FIGURE 1–3
General and special education middle school teachers planning for unified school reforms.

School unification policy makes inclusive education and community schools possible. Without a policy of resource sharing to bolster and provide the base for innovation that requires collaboration across disciplines, it is difficult for schools to sustain change in the way individuals with severe disabilities are educated and the way the school system addresses the needs which exist among all students, with and without disabilities.

Summary

In this chapter, we have examined some of the key policy issues that are affecting the education of students with severe disabilities following the reauthorization of IDEA in 1997. From the myriad package of school reforms under way at the close of the millennium, we chose to examine three primary developments that have great influence on the education of students with severe disabilities: the community schools movement, inclusive education, and school unification. The community school, as both a developing concept and a reality in many communities, brings together a number of rapidly emerging new policy developments at the federal and state levels affecting schools, students, families, and community services and businesses. We examined two versions of these partnerships that characterize a number of community schools around the country. First, we examined school-linked service integration models and how these are coming to exemplify school-community linkage arrangements as the basis for a partnership. Second, we examined the concept of full-service schools, as an example of school-based partnership arrangements.

Inclusive schooling, still a focal point of much research, demonstration, and controversy, was described with examples and a glimpse of how it works in practice for students with severe disabilities. Effective inclusive schooling, not to be confused with simply placing students with disabilities in general education classrooms, requires innovation, collaboration, and research-based instruction. Actually, it is important to note that any "effective schooling" requires these same qualities. We noted that when inclusion is not working, most likely these qualities are not in place.

Our discussion of school unification policy examined how various categorical programs at schools are now being harnessed together and integrated for application in the interests of all students at the school, not just those who are eligible for each categorical support. Throughout the chapter, we have sought to highlight the general theme that students with severe disabilities are students first and foremost. They require special support and assistance to learn at their potential, just as do many students, including some who are not in special education. We believe that a preponderance of evidence, much of which will be discussed in the remaining chapters of this text, shows the importance of keeping students of all types and abilities together, as much as possible, for their education experiences. When done properly, all students benefit, not only from having access to all categorical sources of support, new technologies and additional personnel, but also from being able to learn from each other the importance of individual differences and diversity.

Suggested Activities

1. Get a small group together to discuss community schools. As you discuss this topic:
   a. Make a list of the positive results associated with community schools.
   b. Develop an outline for a proposal to create a community school.
2. You are at a party and someone asks you about this "inclusion" thing. Describe what inclusion is and what it isn't, using everyday, non-technical terminology.
3. Develop a visual display useful for organizing information regarding how the needs of children with disabilities are met alongside their nondisabled peers in a general education setting.
4. Imagine that the words "continuum of placements" do not exist. Instead, develop a model for providing supports and services within the school without the need for segregated classrooms.

References

Adelman, H. & Taylor, L. (1997). Addressing barriers to learning: Beyond school-linked services and full service schools. *American Journal of Orthopsychiatry*, 67(3).

Bacharach, S. B. (1990). *Education reform: Making sense of it all*. Boston, MA: Allyn & Bacon.

Benson, L. & Harkavy, I. (1997). School and community in the global society: A Neo-Deweyian theory of community problem-solving schools and cosmopolitan neighborly communities and a Neo-Deweyian "manifesto" to dynamically connect school and community. *Universities and Community Schools*. 5, 11–69.

Biklen, D. (1988). Caught in the continuum: A *critical analysis of the principle of the least restrictive environment*. Journal of the Association for Persons with Severe Handicaps, 13, 41–53.

Billingsley, F., Gallucci, C., Peck, C., Schwartz, I., & Staub, D. (1996). "But those kids can't even do math": An alternative conceptualization of outcomes for inclusive education. *Special Education Leadership Review*, 43–55.

Brown, A., Palincsar, A. S., & Purcell, L. (1985). Poor readers: Teach don't label. In U. Neiser (Ed.), *The Academic Performance of Minority Children: New Perspectives* (pp. 105–143). Hillsdale, NJ: Lawrence Earlbaum.

Brown, A. & Campione, J. (1990). Communities of learning and thinking or a context by any other name. *Developmental Perspectives on Teaching and Learning Thinking Skills*, 21, 108–126.

Bruner, C. (1996). *Realizing a vision for children, families and neighborhoods: An alternative to other modest proposals*. Falls Church, VA: National Center for Service Integration.

Children's Defense Fund. (1992). *The State of America's Children*. Washington DC: Author.

Cibulka, J. G. & Kritec, W. J. (1996). *Coordination among schools, families and communities: Prospects for educational reform*. Albany, NY: State University of New York Press.

Crowson, R. L. & Boyd, W. L. (1993). Coordinated services for children: Designing arks for storms and seas unknown. *American Journal of Education*, 101(140–179).

Cuban, L. (1989). The "at-risk" label and the problem of urban school reform. *Phi Delta Kappan*, 70(10), 780–784, 799–801.

Dewey, J. (1985). *The school and society and the child and the curriculum*. Chicago: University of Chicago Press.

Doktor, J. & Poertner, J. (1996). Kentucky's family resource centers: A community based school-linked services model. *Remedial and Special Education*, 17(5), 293–302.

Downing, J. (1996). *Including students with severe and multiple disabilities in typical classrooms: Practical strategies for teachers*. Baltimore: Paul H. Brookes.

Dryfoos, J. (1994). *Full service schools: A revolution in health and social services for children*. San Francisco: Jossey-Bass.

Dryfoos, J. (1996). Full-service schools. *Educational Leadership*. April, 12–23.

Dryfoos, J., Brindis, C., & Kaplan, D. W. (1996). Research and evaluation in school based health care. *Adolescent Medicine: State of the Art Reviews*, 7(2), 207–220.

Dunn, W. (1991). The sensorimotor systems: A framework for assessment and intervention. In F. O. D. Sobsey (Ed.), *Educating children with multiple disabilities: A transdisciplinary approach*, 2nd. ed. Baltimore: Paul H. Brookes.

Englert, C. S., Tarrant, K. L., & Mariage, T. V. (1992). *Defining and redefining disabilities: A transdisciplinary approach*, 2nd. ed. Baltimore: Paul H. Brookes.

Falvey, M. (1992). *Community based instruction*, 2nd. ed. Baltimore: Paul H. Brookes.

Falvey, M. (1996). *Inclusive education*. Baltimore: Paul H. Brookes.

Filler, J. (1996). A comment on social inclusion: Research and social policy. *Social Policy Report*, X(2/3), 31–32.

Fuchs, D. & Fuchs, L. S. (1994). Inclusive schools movement and the radicalization of special education reform. *Exceptional Children*, 60(4), 294–309.

Gee, K. (1993). An experimental and qualitative investigation into the motivation and competence of peer interactions involving students with severe, multiple disabilities in middle school classrooms. Unpublished doctoral dissertation. University of California, Berkeley.

Gee, K., Graham, N., & Alwell, M. (1994). Team planning for the individual: Setting goals, determining outcomes, and designing supports. In K. Gee et al. (Eds.), Inclusive instructional design: Facilitating informed and active learning for individuals with deaf-blindness. Active Interactions Project, OSERS Validated Practices: Children and Youth with Deaf-Blindness, #HO.

Gee, K. (1995). Facilitating active and informed learning in inclusive settings. In N. H. L. Romer (Ed.), Welcoming students who are deaf-blind into typical classrooms: Facilitating school participation, learning, and friendships. Baltimore: Paul H. Brookes.

Gee, K., Graham, N., Sailor, W., & Goetz, L. (1995). Use of integrated, general education and community settings as primary contexts for skill instruction of students with severe, multiple disabilities. Behavior Modification, 19(1), 33–58.

Gee, K. (in press). New constructions: Linking instructional approaches and successful inclusive education. In W. Sailor (Ed.), Inclusive education and school/community partnerships. New York: Teachers College Press.

Gerry, M. (1998). Service integration and beyond: Implications for lawyers and their training. In J. Heubert (Ed.), Law and school reform: Six strategies for providing educational equity, pp. 244–305. New Haven, CT: Yale University Press.

Gerry, M. (in press). Integration and beyond. In W. Sailor (Ed.), Inclusive education and school/community partnerships. New York: Teachers College Press.

Goetz, L. & Gee, K. (1987a). Teaching visual attention in functional contexts: Acquisition and generalization of complex visual motor skills. Journal of Vision Impairment and Blindness, 81, 115–118.

Goetz, L. & Gee, K. (1987b). Functional vision programming: A model for teaching visual behaviors in natural contexts. In L. Goetz, Guess, D. & Stremell-Campbell, C. (Ed.), Innovative program design for individuals with dual sensory impairments. Baltimore: Paul H. Brookes.

Goodlad, & Klein. (1970). Looking behind the classroom door. Worthington, OH: Charles E. Jones.

Graff, J. C., Ault, M., Guess, D., Taylor, M., & Thompson, B. (1990). Health care for students with disabilities: An illustrated medical guide for the classroom. Baltimore: Paul H. Brookes.

Grennon-Brooks, J. & Brooks, M. G. (1993). The case for constructivist classrooms. Alexandria, VA: Association for Supervision and Curriculum Development.

Halvorsen, A. & Sailor, W. (1990). Integration of students with severe and profound disabilities. In R. Gaylord-Ross (Ed.), Issues and research in special education (Vol. 1). New York: Teachers College Press.

Haring, T. & Ryndak, D. (1994). Strategies and instructional procedures to promote social interactions and relationships. In E. Cipani & F. Spooner (Eds.), Curriculum and instructional approaches for persons with severe disabilities (pp. 289–321). Boston, MA: Allyn & Bacon.

Harvard Family Research Project. (1996). The evaluation exchange: emerging strategies in evaluating child and family services. Cambridge: Harvard Graduate School of Education.

Horner, R. H., Dunlap, G., Koegel, R. L., Carr, E. G., Sailor, W., Anderson, J., Albin, R. W., & O'Neil, R. E. (1990). Toward a technology of "nonadversive" behavioral support. Journal of the Association for Persons with Severe Handicaps, 15(3), 125–132.

Huberman, A. M. (1992). Successful school improvement: Reflections and observations. In M. G. Fullan (Ed.), Successful school improvement. London: Open University Press.

Hunt, P., Allwell, M., & Goetz, L. (1988). Acquisition of conversation skills and the reduction of inappropriate social interaction behaviors. Journal of the Association for Persons with Severe Handicaps, 13, 20–27.

Hunt, P., Staub, D., Allwell, M., & Goetz, L. (1994a). Achievement by all students within the context of cooperative learning groups. Journal of the Association for Persons with Severe Handicaps, 13, 290–301.

Hunt, P., Farron-Davis, F., Beckstead, S., Curtis, D., & Goetz, L. (1994b). Evaluating the effects of placements of students with severe disabilities in general education versus special classes. Journal of the Association for Persons with Severe Handicaps, 19, 200–214.

Johnson, D. W. & Johnson, R. T. (1989). Cooperative learning and mainstreaming. In R. Gaylord-Ross (Ed.), Integration strategies for students with handicaps. Baltimore: Paul H. Brookes.

Joyce, B., Showers, B., & Weil, M. (1992). Models of teaching. (4th ed.). Boston: Allyn and Bacon.

Joyce, B., Wolfe, J., & Calhoun, E. (1993). The self-renewing school. Alexandria, VA: The Association of Supervision and Curriculum Development.

Kagan, S. L. & Neville, P. (1993). Integrating services for children and families. New Haven, CT: Yale University Press.

Kagan, S. L., Goffin, S., Golub, S. A., & Pritchard, E. (1995). Toward systematic reform: Service integration for young children and their families. Falls Church, VA: National Center for Service Integration.

Karasoff, P., Blonsky, H., Perry, K., & Schear, T. (1996). Integrated and collaborative services: A technical assistance planning guide. (Vol. 30). San Francisco: San Francisco State University, California Research Institute.

Kleinert, H. L., Kearns, J. F., & Kennedy S., (in press). Including all students in educational assessment and accountability. In W. Sailor (Ed.), Inclusive education and school/community partnerships. New York: Teachers College Press.

Knitzer, J. & Page, S. (1996). Map and track: State initiatives for young children and families. New York: National Center for Children in Poverty.

Langford-Carter, J. (1993). Moving from principals to practice: Implementing a family-focused approach in schools and community services. Family Resource Center Report, 12, 7–10.

Lawson, H. A. & Briar-Lawson, K. (1997). Connecting the dots: Progress toward the integration of school reform, school-linked services, parent involvement and community schools. Oxford, OH: Institute for Educational Renewal.

Lipsky, D. K. & Gartner, A. (1997). Inclusion and school reform: Transforming America's classrooms. Baltimore: Paul H. Brookes.

Madden, N. A., Slavin, R. E., Karweil, N. L., Donlan, L., & Wasik, B. A. (1991). Success for all. Phi Delta Kappan, 72, 593–599.

Madden, N. A., Slavin, R. E., Karweil, N. L., Donlan, L., & Wasik, B. A. (1993). Success for all: Longitudinal effects of a restructuring program for inner-city elementary schools. American Educational Research Journal, 30(1), 123–148.

McLaughlin, M. J., Leone, P., Warren, S. H., & Schofield, P. F. (1992). Resource implications of inclusion: Impressions of special education administrators at selected sites. Palo Alto, CA: Center for Special Education Finance.

Melaville, A. & Blank, M. (1991). *What it takes: Structuring interagency partnerships to connect children and families with comprehensive services.* Washington, DC: Education and Human Services Consortium.

Melaville, A. I., Blank, M. J., & Asayesh, G. (1993). *Together we can: A guide for crafting a pro-family system of education and human services.* Washington, DC: U. S. Government Printing Office.

Miles, K. H. & Darling-Hammond, L. (1998). Rethinking the allocation of teaching resources: Some lessons from high-performing schools. *Educational Evaluation and Policy Analysis, 21*(1), 9–29.

National Center for Children's Disease Prevention and Health Promotion (1997). *Youth and family violence prevention information update.* Washington, DC: Center for Children's Disease Prevention and Health Promotion.

Neary, T., Halvorsen, A., Kronberg, & Kelly, D. (1993). *Curriculum adaptations for inclusive classrooms.* California Research Institute, San Francisco State University, and California PEERS Project.

Palincsar, A. S. & Brown, A. L. (1984). Reciprocal teaching of comprehension-fostering and comprehension-monitoring activities. *Cognition and Instruction, 1,* 117–175.

Palincsar, A. S. (1986). The role of dialogue in promoting scaffolded instruction. *Educational Psychologist, 21,* 73–98.

Palincsar, A. S., David, Y. M., Winn, J. A., & Stevens, D. (1990). *Examining the differential effects of teacher-versus student-controlled activity in comprehension instruction.* Paper presented at the Annual Meeting of the American Educational Research Association, Boston, MA.

Paul, J. L., Rosselli, H., & Evans, D. (1995). *Integrating school restructuring and special education reform.* Ft. Worth, TX: Harcourt Brace College Publisher.

Peck, C. A., Carleson, P., & Helmstetter, E. (1992). Parent and teacher perceptions of outcomes for typically developing children enrolled in integrated early childhood programs: A statewide survey. *Journal of Early Intervention, 16*(1), 53–63.

Peck, C. A., Donaldson, J., & Pezzoli, M. (1990). Some benefits non-handicapped adolescents perceive for themselves from their social relationships with peers who have severe handicaps. *Journal of the Association for Persons with Severe Handicaps, 15,* 241–249.

Putnam, J. (1994). *Cooperative learning and strategies for inclusion: Celebrating diversity in the classroom.* Baltimore: Paul H. Brookes.

Rainforth, B., York, J., & McDonald, C. (1992). *Collaborative teams for students with severe disabilities: Integrating therapy and educational services.* Baltimore: Paul H. Brookes.

Rigsby, L. C., Reynolds, M. C., & Wang, M. C. (Eds.) (1995). *School-community connections: Exploring issues for research and practice.* San Francisco: Jossey-Bass.

Sage, D. D. & Burrello, L. C. (1994). *Leadership in educational reform: An administrator's guide to changes in special education.* Baltimore: Paul H. Brookes.

Sailor, W., Goetz, L., Anderson, J., Hunt, P., & Gee, K. (1988). Research on community intensive instruction as a model for building functional generalized skills. In R. Horner, G. Dunlap, & R. Kogel (Eds.), *Generalization and maintenance in applied settings* (pp. 67–98). Baltimore: Paul H. Brookes.

Sailor, W., Anderson, J., Halvorsen, A., Doering, K., Filler, J., & Goetz, L. (1989). *The comprehensive local school: Regular education for all students with disabilities.* Baltimore: Paul H. Brookes.

Sailor, W. (1991). Special education in the restructured school. *Remedial and Special Education, 12*(6), 8–22.

Sailor, W., Gee, K., & Karasoff, P. (1993). School restructuring and full inclusion. In M. Snell (Ed.), *Systematic instruction of persons with severe handicaps.* 4th ed. New York: Merrill/Macmillan.

Sailor, W. (1994a). New community schools: Issues for families in three streams of reform. *Coalition Quarterly, 11*(3), 4–7.

Sailor, W. (1994b). Services integration: Parent empowerment through school/community partnerships. *Coalition Quarterly, 11*(3), 11–13.

Sailor, W. (1996). New structures and systems change for comprehensive positive behavioral support. In L. K. Koegel, R. L. Koegel, & G. Dunlap (Eds.), *Positive behavioral support: Including people with difficult behavior in the community* (pp. 163–206). Baltimore: Paul H. Brookes.

Sailor, W., Kleinhammer-Tramill, J., Skrtic, T., & Oas, B. K. (1996). Family participation in new community schools. In G. H. S. Singer, L. E. Powers, & A. L. Olson (Eds.), *Redefining family support: Innovations in public-private partnerships* (pp. 313–332). Baltimore: Paul H. Brookes.

Sailor, W. (in press). Devolution, school/community/family partnerships, and inclusive education. In W. Sailor (Ed.), *Inclusive education and school/community partnerships.* New York: Teachers College Press.

Salisbury, C. L., Marlowe, D., & Crawford, E. W. (1998, December). *Interagency planning and support project: Multiple agencies but only ONE plan!* Paper presented at the International Division for Early Childhood Conference, Chicago, IL.

Sapon-Shevin, M. (1992). Celebrating diversity. In S. Stainback & W. Stainback (Eds.), *Curriculum considerations in inclusive classrooms: Facilitating learning for all children.* Baltimore: Paul H. Brookes.

Schorr, L. B. (1989). *Within our reach: Breaking the cycle of disadvantage.* New York: Doubleday.

Schorr, L. B. (1997). *Common purpose: Strengthening families and neighborhoods to rebuild America.* New York: Anchor Books.

Skrtic, T. M. (1991). *Behind special education: A critical analysis of professional culture and school organization.* Denver, CO: Love Publishing Company.

Skrtic, T. M. (1995a). The organizational context of special education and school reform. In E. Meyen & T. Skrtic (Eds.), *Special education and student disability: Traditional, emerging alternative perspectives.* Denver: Love Publishing.

Skrtic, T. M. (1995b). The special education knowledge tradition: Crisis and opportunity. In E. Meyen & T. Skrtic (Eds.), *Special education and student disability: Traditional, emerging, and alternative perspectives.* Denver: Love Publishing.

Skrtic, T. M., Sailor, W., & Gee, K. (1996). Voice, collaboration, and inclusion: Democratic themes in educational and social reform initiatives. *Remedial and Special Education, 17,* 142–157.

Snell, M. (Ed.) (1993). *Systematic instruction of persons with severe handicaps.* (4th ed.) New York: Merrill/Macmillan.

Stainback, W., Stainback, S., & Forest, M. (1989). *Educating all students in the mainstream or regular education.* Baltimore: Paul H. Brookes.

Strully, J. & Strully, C. (1989). Friendships as an educational goal. In W. Stainback, S. Stainback, & M. Forest (Eds.), *Educating all students in the mainstream of regular education.* Baltimore: Paul H. Brookes.

The Urban Institute (1996). *Potential effects of Congressional welfare reform legislation in family incomes.* Washington, DC: Author.

Thousand, J., Villa, R., & Nevin, A. (1994). *Creativity and collaborative learning: A practical guide to empowering students and teachers*. Baltimore: Paul H. Brookes.

Turnbull, A. P., Turnbull, H. R., Shank, M., & Leal, D. (1998). *Exceptional lives: Special education in today's schools*. 2nd ed. Upper Saddle River, NJ: Merrill/Prentice Hall.

Turnbull, A. P. & Turnbull, H. R. (1997). *Families, professionals, and exceptionality: A special partnership*. (3rd ed.). Upper Saddle River, NJ: Merrill/Prentice Hall.

Tyack, D. & Cuban, L. (1995). *Tinkering toward Utopia: A century of public school reform*. Cambridge, MA: Harvard University Press.

Udvari-Solner, A. (1994). A decision-making model for curricular adaptations in cooperative groups. In R. Villa, J. Thousand, & A. Nevin (Ed.), *Creativity and collaborative learning: A practical guide to empowering students and teachers*. Baltimore: Paul H. Brookes.

Udvari-Solner, A. (1996). Examining teacher thinking: Constructing a process to design curricular adaptations. *Remedial and Special Education*, 17(4), 245–254.

Villa, R. & Thousand, J. S. (1992). Student collaboration: An essential for curriculum delivery in the 21st Century. In S. Stainback, & W. Stainback (Eds.), *Curriculum considerations in inclusive classrooms: Facilitating learning for all students*. Baltimore: Paul H. Brookes.

2

Fostering Family-Professional Partnerships

Ann P. Turnbull
H. R. Turnbull

Mr. and Mrs. Bridge feel that they have been very lucky. Their daughter Libby has been "in the right place at the right time" all of her life. Libby has always been in an inclusive setting of one kind or another, and the Bridge family has enjoyed positive relationships with the educators in Libby's life.

Libby is 11 years old and is in a fifth-grade general education classroom. The fact that Libby has cerebral palsy, mental retardation, epilepsy, and a visual impairment does not stop her from enjoying friendships and camaraderie with her peers and teachers. She loves school and is happy each day to see the school bus slow to a stop outside her Kansas City, Kansas, home.

Libby's first school experience was in an early intervention program affiliated with a local university. From there, she went to a school that employed the practice of "reverse integration"—she was in a special setting, but kids from general education spent time in her class for parts of the day.

Most recently, Mr. and Mrs. Bridge were asked if they would like Libby to participate in their district's full-inclusion program. They were reluctant at first. They had fears that Libby would not receive the attention she needs—that she would get lost in the shuffle. After considering their options and discussing it at length together, they decided to try full inclusion.

Libby has since exceeded their expectations of her. When Libby started the new school, she was unable to walk without assistance. Naturally, one thing that worried her parents was the stairs in the building of the new school. How would Libby ever get around? A few months later, they were thrilled as they watched Libby making her way down the hall and successfully negotiating the steps. Libby's teachers, paraprofessionals, and related service providers had great expectations for her, and they paid off.

Libby also benefits from the support of her family. She lives with her parents and her two sisters, Hilary and Hayley, ages 9 and 4. Her grandparents live nearby and enjoy spending time with Libby and enabling her parents to have time for themselves. They also help with problem solving and brainstorming to help meet Libby's needs.

The family members are also a good source of emotional support. They have always been very accepting of Libby.

A source of concern for the family is Libby's upcoming move to middle school. Libby will go from an inclusive program in an elementary school to a middle school that does not support full inclusion. Instead of going to her home school, she will ride a bus across the city. In addition to the school concerns, Mrs. Bridge is concerned about Libby's developmental changes and what that will mean for the family. Libby is unable to provide any self-care; all of her needs are taken care of by family members when at home and by educators while at school. It will be a continual adjustment as Libby moves from being a child to a teenage girl to a grown woman.

Mr. and Mrs. Bridge have never liked being asked what they see for Libby in the future. Her teachers have asked that question since Libby was a baby and continue to ask it as they work together on Libby's transition needs. Mrs. Bridge explained, "It's hard enough to figure out what she's going to be doing next year, much less where she'll be after high school. I don't think we like to think that far into the future—especially now, because everything is so good. We'd rather she just stay in elementary school the rest of her life and never grow up, and we'll live forever." When they do look into the future, however, they hope to see Libby working in a supported employment setting someday, while remaining at home. "Nobody will love her like her mom, so if you ask me that question now, that's what I'll say—that she'll stay with me forever."

 Introducing the Hanaoka Family

The Hanaoka family is a recently immigrated family. Ms. Hanaoka and her 12-year-old daughter, Emily, have lived in the U.S. for 4 years. They relocated from their native Japan so that Ms. Hanaoka could pursue music therapy studies at the University of Kansas. This was a big move for this small family in more ways than distance.

Emily, a bright-eyed and energetic young lady who shares her mother's love for music, is a person with autism and mental retardation. Ms. Hanaoka has been a single parent since the accidental death of her husband 8 years ago. Needing to re-enter the work force, Ms. Hanaoka, a musicologist, began to investigate further training to advance her career. When she learned of a unique music therapy graduate program in the U.S., she explored the idea of moving to Kansas with her daughter.

Ms. Hanaoka had become discouraged at the educational opportunities available in Japan for children with her daughter's level of disability. She was also very eager for Emily to be in a school where she could interact with her peers who did not have a disability. While some regular schools in Japan are beginning to accommodate children with disabilities, Emily was rejected for admission as having a disability that was too significant. More discouraging was the fact that the special schools to which Emily was referred did not provide individualized teaching; it occurred only if a teacher happened to be trained and motivated to do so. Ms. Hanaoka, however, knew about the comparatively well-developed system of special education for American children and realized that Emily might be able to experience good schooling if they could move to the U.S. After Ms. Hanaoka was accepted into the music therapy graduate program, she began planning the daunting task of helping Emily, who tends to rely on structure and predictability, to adjust to moving far from home.

Once in Kansas, Ms. Hanaoka did discover educational opportunities for Emily. She has been enthusiastic and tireless in both advocating and caring for her daughter as a single parent—not an easy task, given her own workload as a full-time graduate student.

Emily is currently in a specially designed educational program for elementary-aged students with autism in a local public school. She was initially placed in a less specialized program for children with disabilities in a different school, which her mother found very satisfactory. While Ms. Hanaoka has some concerns about the program to which her daughter has now been transferred, she is very pleased with Emily's progress. She has found her own interactions with the school personnel to be fruitful, although she characterizes the processes and legal terms as confusing. She also is delighted with the teachers' enthusiasm and professionalism. This stands in stark contrast, she says, to the preparation and effectiveness of many teachers of special classes in Japan, where there is a severe shortage of specially trained teachers of students with special needs.

Ms. Hanaoka stresses that even well-trained and dedicated teachers in the segregated special schools have fewer supports and more difficult teaching environments than are typical in general education.

She is hopeful that Japanese law will be amended to ensure services that are as appropriate and individualized as those she has experienced in the U.S. In the meantime, she is trying to learn as much as possible about the types of services available in the U.S. to persons with disabilities and their families, so that she can provide information to her Japanese friends who have children with disabilities.

These two families—the Bridges and Hanaokas—offer us a window through which we can gain a clearer understanding of family life. You will continue to learn about these families as we address two major trends that have significantly affected the nature of family-professional partnerships. The first is the Individuals with Disabilities Education Act, which governs how educators interact with families. The second is the family systems perspective, which provides a framework through which professionals can understand families' preferences, strengths, and needs.

Individuals with Disabilities Education Act: Parental Rights and Responsibilities

The Individuals with Disabilities Education Act (IDEA) first became law in 1975 and was initially implemented in 1977. One of its original purposes was to provide a *free, appropriate public education* to all students with disabilities. IDEA also has affected all aspects of educating students with disabilities, including family-professional partnerships related to the delivery of educational services and supports (H.R. Turnbull & Turnbull, 1998).

When Congress reauthorized the IDEA in 1997 (P.L. 105–17), it strengthened parents' roles in their children's education. One of the purposes of the reauthorized laws was to ensure that families will have more "meaningful opportunities" to participate in their children's education "at school and at home." How does IDEA express this intent?

First, IDEA enhances parents' and families' roles by providing the framework of opportunities within which parents, families, and students, on one hand, and educators, on the other hand, can participate together in shared decision making. Second, IDEA increases the procedural safeguards that parents, families, and students may invoke to assure that they have those opportunities. To clarify how IDEA carries out Congressional intent, it will be helpful to examine IDEA's six principles (Turnbull & Turnbull, 1998). For the sake of brevity, we use the word "parent" to refer to parents and other family members covered by IDEA, unless we indicate otherwise. We also use the acronym "LEA" to refer to local educational agencies and "SEA" to refer to state educational agencies.

IDEA's Six Principles

Figure 2–1 highlights the educational process for implementing IDEA's six principles—zero reject, nondiscriminatory evaluation, appropriate education, least restrictive environment, parent and student participation in shared decision making, and procedural due process. In this section, we will briefly highlight key requirements associated with each of these principles—especially ones that are strongly emphasized in the 1997 IDEA reauthorization.

Zero Reject

IDEA's first principle is that of zero reject. This is a rule against the exclusion from school of any age-eligible student who has a disability. The type or severity of the student's disability is irrelevant; zero reject means precisely what it says: All students will be included in a free, appropriate public education. All means all. "All" includes Libby, whose many different disabilities do not exclude her but make it all the more important for her to be educated. "All" includes Emily, who is a legal immigrant and has the right to a free, appropriate public education that is responsive to her disability and that recognizes her cultural and linguistic diversity.

IDEA connects the zero reject principle to parental rights and responsibilities in a myriad of ways. Under IDEA's early intervention provisions, families and their infant or toddler children may receive a large number of services (set out in an individualized family support plan, or IFSP) designed to develop the children's capacities, minimize their potential for developmental delays, and enhance families' capacities to work with their children. If families consent to early intervention, they can benefit from and influence the nature and extent of early intervention services that they are offered. Libby benefited from the early intervention services she received; she was off to a good start with physical therapy and speech therapy at an infant development center.

In light of IDEA's cardinal rule that public education should be "free" to parents, IDEA provides that parents may not be required to use their private insurance benefits to pay for education, but they may offer to have an insurer pay for services that an LEA otherwise must provide without cost. For example, Mr. and Mrs. Bridge do not need to use their health insurance to pay for Libby's educational needs; Libby's education is "free" to her and her parents. But

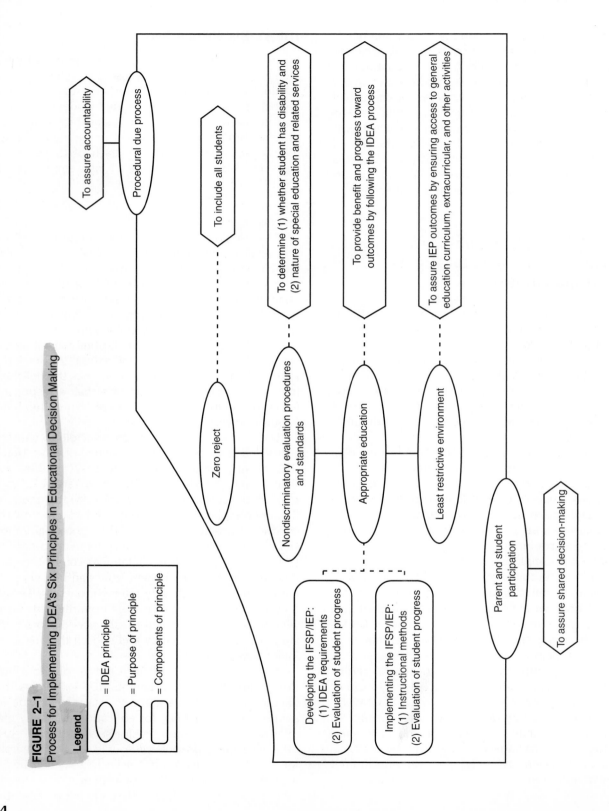

FIGURE 2–1
Process for Implementing IDEA's Six Principles in Educational Decision Making

Legend

⬭ = IDEA principle

⬡ = Purpose of principle

▭ = Components of principle

To assure accountability

Procedural due process

To include all students

To determine (1) whether student has disability and (2) nature of special education and related services

To provide benefit and progress toward outcomes by following the IDEA process

To assure IEP outcomes by ensuring access to general education curriculum, extracurricular, and other activities

Zero reject

Nondiscriminatory evaluation procedures and standards

Appropriate education

Least restrictive environment

Developing the IFSP/IEP:
(1) IDEA requirements
(2) Evaluation of student progress

Implementing the IFSP/IEP:
(1) Instructional methods
(2) Evaluation of student progress

Parent and student participation

To assure shared decision-making

if they want to have their health insurance pay for something that contributes to her education (even though the school is required to pay for it if Libby's IEP so provides), such as physical therapy, then they may—that's the key word, "may"—ask their insurer to pay for it. If their insurance policy obligates the insurer to pay, the insurer must. Only rarely, however, do parents ask their insurance carrier to pay for something that the schools must provide; they try to preserve their insurance for risks that are not covered by IDEA and to stay inside the "cap" that insurance contracts place (a "cap" is the maximum amount of funds that the carrier must pay for the insured).

Finally, ever since the United States Supreme Court decided in *Honig v. Doe* (1988) that IDEA limits the power of LEAs to discipline students with disabilities, the issue of school discipline has been a controversial topic. Concerns about "school safety" and "law and order" brought the matter of school violence and discipline to a head when IDEA's reauthorization was before Congress in 1995 to 1997.

The ultimate resolution of the conflict between those who wanted "no cessation" of IDEA rights and those who wanted safer schools (some people thought schools would be safer if students with disabilities could be expelled or suspended) was manifested in a rule of "no cessation" of services. Whenever a student with a disability is disciplined (under IDEA, discipline is a sanction for violating a school code and consists of in-school or out-of-school suspension or change of placement for more than 10 days in any school year), the LEA must continue to provide free, appropriate public education to the student, regardless of whether or not the behavior for which the discipline is imposed is a "manifestation" of the student's disability. Thus, parents may assume (as a general rule) that, once their children are classified into special education, they will continue to receive special education benefits. An example of this situation is Eddie, who has a long-standing pattern of challenging behavior, especially aggression toward others, property destruction, and self-injury. In the past, students such as Eddie were frequently suspended from school or were allowed only to come to school for a small portion of the school day. When they engaged in challenging behavior, the common response was to call their parents to pick them up from school. Given the new "zero reject" requirements, parents have stronger rights for their children

to remain in special education and to benefit from a functional assessment and the implementation of a comprehensive positive behavioral support plan (Horner & Carr, 1997; Weigle, 1997).

Nondiscriminatory Evaluation

IDEA's second principle is one of nondiscriminatory evaluation, namely, an evaluation that is not biased as a result of the student's language, cultural, or other characteristics. The evaluation has two purposes: (a) to determine whether the student has a disability and (b) if so, to specify what kind of special education and related services the student should receive. The reauthorized IDEA expands parental rights and responsibilities significantly. Parents (a) are members of the evaluation team (indeed, the evaluation team also is the team that develops the student's individualized program); (b) must be given a copy of the evaluation report and documentation concerning their child's eligibility (or lack of eligibility) for special education; (c) may submit to the team and require it to consider evaluations and information that they (the parents) initiate or provide; (d) have a right to be notified that the team has determined that it does not need any additional data for the purposes of deciding whether their child remains eligible for special education (i.e., still has a disability); and (e) have a right to request an assessment to determine whether their child continues to be eligible for special education (i.e., the team does not have to conduct the assessment unless the parents request one).

Ms. Hanaoka brought Emily's Japanese school evaluations with her and gave them to the school district, but Emily herself was evaluated by English-speaking professionals. These professionals used English-language assessment instruments and also relied on their and Emily's teacher's observations of her. In reflecting on the evaluation, Ms. Hanaoka indicated that it never occurred to her that the evaluation could have been in Japanese. She said she thinks Emily could have performed better on the evaluation if it had been administered in Japanese. She feels that Emily was unable to understand the requests made of her—all in English—while she was being observed. Ms. Hanaoka provided written feedback on her daughter's abilities and feels that she was able to give accurate information. However, she feels fortunate to have received help in understanding the assessment instrument's questions from a paraprofessional who, coincidentally, she had hired to tutor Emily at home. Emily was evaluated in the United States before the passage of IDEA's new 1997 regulations. Ms. Hanaoka was not a member of the evaluation team, and she was only the recipient of the evaluation report that the professional team had developed. Had Ms. Hanaoka been a member of the team and had she known her legal rights, she would have been on solid ground to suggest, even require, that the team evaluate Emily in Japanese. If Emily had been evaluated in Japanese, her teachers may have learned something significant about her communication and social skills—two facets of human development that typically are affected by autism. In turn, they would have known how to build on her language skills and precisely what language problems to address.

Because parents are presumed to act in the best interests of their children, they also may give or withhold consent to the initial evaluation, all reevaluations, and any exit evaluation. If they do give their consent, their consent is good for that evaluation only and not for any other evaluations or for the student's placement into or out of special education.

If the school has taken reasonable measures to secure the parents' consent (e.g., certified mail, registered mail, telephone, or fax or home visits) and if the parents have failed to respond to the school's request for consent, the school then may evaluate the student (initial evaluation or reevaluation). If the parents refuse to give consent, the LEA may go to mediation or a due process hearing to try to get permission to evaluate the student. (Mediation and due process hearings are discussed later in the chapter.)

Parents may also secure (at their own expense) an independent evaluation and require the team to consider it. Parents also may charge the cost of an independent evaluation to the LEA if the LEA's evaluation is not appropriate or if the reevaluation was ordered by a due process hearing officer or court. This means that team evaluations may not be completely influenced by only the LEA members. Thus, Ms. Hanaoka may secure a Japanese-language evaluation of Emily's language and communication abilities reported in Japanese and perhaps in English. A multilingual evaluator could use appropriate multilingual evaluation instruments in administering the independent evaluation. Indeed, Ms. Hanaoka could have the school pay for them if a hearing officer or court were to find (as it should) that the English-only evaluation of Emily's communication is linguistically biased.

Appropriate Education

IDEA's third principle is one of appropriate education, namely, one that substantially complies with all of IDEA's processes and that benefits the student (*Board v. Rowley*, 1982). The linchpin for an appropriate education is the student's IFSP (for infants and toddlers, birth through age 2) or Individualized Educational Plan (IEP) (for students ages 3 through 21). The 1997 required IEP content requirements are highlighted in Figure 2–2, which shows that the IEP must provide related services for students. In addition to services for the student, IDEA also provides that parents may benefit from related services for their child. Among these services are (a) family training, counseling, and home visits; (b) parent counseling and training; (c) psychological services; (d) coordination of services for infants and toddlers and their families; (e) social work services; (f) speech-language pathology services; and (g) assistive technology and services. It is clear that the more the parents can take advantage of related services by getting them written into the IEP, the more parents, students, and educators are likely to benefit.

Requirements associated with the IFSP and IEP enable families and professionals to work together as partners in planning and implementing the student's appropriate education. To begin with, in developing an IEP, the team must consider both the parents' concerns and the student's strengths. This requirement rebalances the "power" within the IEP team by requiring parental concerns to be addressed; it also refocuses special education from a purely "pathological," or "fix it," perspective of intervention to one that builds on strengths while it also meets needs, thus blunting the occasional overemphasis on student deficits in special education.

Because parent participation in the student's education, and particularly in developing the IFSP or IEP, is a high priority under IDEA, the LEA must take specified steps to ensure that one or both of the student's parents are members of any group (including the IEP team) that makes decisions on the child's educational placement. These steps include advance notice of the meeting, mutually convenient scheduling of the meeting, and arranging for interpreters for parents who are deaf or non-English-speaking (as the school would have had to do if Ms. Hanaoka had not spoken

FIGURE 2–2

Required Contents of Individualized Educational Plan (IEP)

The IEP is a written statement for each student, ages 3 to 21. Whenever it is developed or revised, it must contain the following:

- The student's present levels of educational performance, including
  - How the disability of a student (age 6 through 21) affects his or her involvement and progress in the general curriculum, or
  - How the disability of a preschooler (age 3 through 5) affects his or her participation in appropriate activities
- Measurable annual goals, including "benchmarks" or short-term objectives, related to
  - Meeting needs resulting from the disability to enable the student to be involved in and progress in the general curriculum
  - Meeting each of the student's other disability-related needs
- The special education and related services and supplementary aids and services that will be provided to the student or on the student's behalf, and the program modifications or supports for school personnel that will be provided so that the student
  - Can advance appropriately toward attaining the annual goals
  - Be involved and progress in the general curriculum and participate in extracurricular and other nonacademic activities
  - Be educated and participate with other students with disabilities and with students who do not have disabilities in general education
- The extent, if any, to which the student will not participate with students who do not have disabilities in general education classes and in extracurricular and other nonacademic activities of the general curriculum
- Any individual modifications in the administration of statewide or districtwide assessments of student achievement, so that the student can participate in those assessments; moreover, if the IEP determines that the student will not participate in a particular statewide or districtwide assessment or any part of an assessment, why that assessment is not appropriate for the student and how the student will be assessed
- The projected date for beginning the services and program modifications and the anticipated frequency, location, and duration of each
- Transition plans, including
  - Beginning at age 14, and each year thereafter, a statement of the student's needs that are related to transition services, including those that focus on the student's courses of study (e.g., the student's participation in advanced-placement courses or in a vocational education program)
  - Beginning at age 16 (or sooner, if the IEP team decides it is appropriate), a statement of needed transition services, including, when appropriate, a statement of the interagency responsibilities or any other needed linkages
  - Beginning at least 1 year before the student reaches the age of majority under state law (usually, at age 18), a statement that the student has been informed of those rights under IDEA that will transfer to the student from the parents when the student becomes of age
- How the student's progress toward annual goals will be measured and how the student's parents will be informed, at least as often as parents of students who do not have disabilities are informed, of the student's progress toward annual goals and the extent to which the progress is sufficient to enable the student to achieve the goals by the end of the school year

---

Note: From *Exceptional Lives: Special Education in Today's Schools* (p. 64), (2nd ed.) by Ann P. Turnbull, H. Rutherford Turnbull, Marilyn Shank, and Dorothy Lean, copyright 1998. Reprinted by permission of Prentice-Hall, Inc., Upper Saddle River, NJ.

English). If the parent(s) cannot attend the meeting, they still may participate through individual or conference telephone calls.

The agency may have an IEP meeting without parent participation only when it can document that it attempted unsuccessfully to have the parents participate. The documentation should include detailed records of telephone calls, copies of letters to and from the parents, and the results of visits to the parents' homes or places of work. Also, the agency must give the parents a copy of the IEP if they ask for it.

Parents are "voting" members of IFSP and IEP teams. Mr. and Mrs. Bridge have attended every IEP

meeting that has been held. Some parents, however, do not exercise this right. Ms. Hanaoka believes that it is important to develop a good relationship with Emily's teachers. This desire for harmony is a belief that governs many Japanese parents in their approaches to teachers, and she feels she has not hesitated to express her questions and concerns about changes proposed in Emily's program. In Japan, she explains, school personnel have as their top priority keeping a harmonious relationship with families. If Emily was injured at school, as she had been once in her American school, the principal would have made a point of coming to the family home to assure Ms.

Hanaoka of the school's concern. In contrast, here she was provided little information about the source of Emily's injury, and her inquiries were met with defensiveness. She now realizes the school was concerned about being sued, but she is perplexed by the tendency of American parents to seek legal solutions to differences with their child's teachers.

Parents may invite other family members or other individuals who are knowledgeable about their child to attend the IFSP and IEP team meetings. This provides parents with supportive allies and the entire team with additional information. Libby's teachers have encouraged Mr. and Mrs. Bridge to invite other family members to meetings concerning Libby. Mrs. Bridge's mother has attended in the past, as has Libby's 9-year old sister, Hilary. Mrs. Bridge said that having other children at a meeting can "be very enlightening. Plus, I think it's helpful just to have their opinions, because I think they, a lot of times, come up with better ideas on how to solve a problem with Libby than the adults do."

At all ages, the IEP must contain a statement of (a) how the student's progress toward the IEP annual goals will be measured and (b) how the child's parents will be informed regularly (at least as often as parents are informed of their nondisabled children's progress) of their child's progress toward the annual goals and the extent to which that progress is sufficient to enable the student to achieve the goals by the end of the year.

Nearly all infants and toddlers (birth to age 3) leave early intervention programs and enter early childhood education programs. That is why their IFSPs must describe the steps that will be taken to assure a smooth transition and to involve the parents in transition planning. Moreover, infants and toddlers who do transition to early childhood programs may now "carry" their IFSPs with them; they do not have to get a new "I-plan" (at age 3, that is the IEP) because their IFSP is "portable." (This is so only if the state chooses to have a policy allowing portability and the parents and the early childhood "receiving" program agree to the IFSP being carried forward.)

The portability provision is important to both the infant and the parents. The infant is assured that there will be no disruption in services and thus no loss of beneficial programming, and the parents continue to have an I-plan that includes services for them. Basically, the portability provisions recognize

that the IFSP approach is solid and that the benefits of early intervention should be sustained over time.

Beginning at age 14 and annually thereafter, the student's IEP must contain a statement of the student's transition service needs and focus on the student's course of study (such as participation in a vocational education program). At age 16, the IEP must contain a statement of transition services for the student (see chapter 15 for a discussion of transition). And when a student attains the age of majority (usually age 18), the student is entitled to exercise his or her IDEA rights independently of his or her parents. Indeed, a year before becoming "of age," a student is entitled to a notice concerning what rights will transfer to him or her upon attaining the age of majority. This provision means that parents need to begin to consider, at least a year before the student's age of majority, how to assure that the student knows about the IDEA rights and is capable of exercising them. A curriculum in self-determination or self-advocacy (including knowledge of rights, responsibilities, and decision-making processes) is especially important. There is a critical need for curriculum development in self-determination to address the preferences, strengths, and needs of students with *severe* disabilities as contrasted to students with *mild* disabilities (Martin & Marshall, 1996; Powers, Singer, & Sowers, 1996; Sands & Wehmeyer, 1996; Van Reusen, Deshler, & Schumaker, 1989).

If the student has been adjudicated by a court to be legally incompetent as an adult, the court-appointed guardian (who may be the parent) is entitled to exercise the student's rights. If, however, a student has not been adjudicated incompetent but is regarded (by whom, it is not clear, but probably by the evaluation or IEP team) to be incapable of providing informed consent regarding his or her educational program, the SEA may appoint the student's parents or another appropriate individual to represent the student's educational interests (the so-called "education surrogate"). These provisions help parents avoid legal guardianships (which involve open court hearings and records, an adversarial process, emotional and financial costs, and the deprivation of rights from the student who is found incompetent). They also require the evaluation or IEP team to make a different kind of judgment (about capacity to consent) than they may have been making in the past; in turn, they may need different kinds of evaluations. This is another area where major work is needed in preparing educators and families to be knowledgeable about the benefits and drawbacks of guardianship (H.R. Turnbull, Turnbull, Bronicki, Summers, & Roeder-Gordon, 1989).

One other matter should be clear, too: When a parent, such as Ms. Hanaoka, is from another culture and especially when the parent (unlike Ms. Hanaoka) does not speak English and the child does not either, the parent's participation in education decision making is especially challenging. Indeed, had it not been for the fact that Ms. Hanaoka enrolled in a graduate course in family-school partnerships, she would not have learned so soon, if at all, exactly what her and Emily's IDEA rights were.

Since IDEA's initial implementation in the mid-1970s, research has consistently reported that parents have limited participation and influence in IEP conferences (Goldstein, Strickland, Turnbull, & Curry, 1980; Harry, Allen, & McLaughlin, 1995; Vaughn, Bos, Harrell, & Lasky, 1988). There is little evidence in the professional literature that a genuine collaborative partnership among families and professionals has characterized many IEP conferences. Research on the participation of families from culturally and linguistically diverse backgrounds especially highlights the "uneven table" (Kritek, 1994) at which many families are expected to negotiate (Harry & Kalyanpur, 1994; Harry, 1992; Harry, Grenot-Scheyer et al., 1995). A Puerto Rican mother in one of Harry's studies commented:

> It is only their opinions that matter. If I do not want the child in a special class or if I want her in a different school, they will still do what they want. Because that is what I try to do, and Vera [the social worker] talked with them, too, and tried to help me, but—no! Our opinions are not valued. Many parents do not want their child in a special class or in a school so far away, but they keep quiet. It is very hard to struggle with these Americans. In America, the schools are for Americans (Harry, 1992, p. 486).

We believe that educators have an affirmative duty to ensure that all parents, especially ones from culturally and linguistically diverse backgrounds, have opportunities for genuine and trusting partnerships with educators throughout the IFSP and IEP process (Harry, Allen et al., 1995). Figure 2–3 highlights state components of the IFSP and IEP conference with sug-

gestions for creating successful family-professional partnerships consistent with the IDEA requirements.

Least Restrictive Environment

IDEA provides that students with disabilities, ages 3 through 21, are to be educated, to the maximum extent appropriate for each, with students who do not have disabilities; the student may be removed from the general education curriculum only when the nature or extent of the student's disability is so great that the student cannot benefit from being educated in the general curriculum even with the use of supplementary aids and services. These provisions create a rebuttable presumption in favor of placement in the general education program.

What is a presumption? A presumption is a rule of law that drives individuals into a predetermined result. For example, there is a presumption of innocence when an individual is charged by the state with a crime. Also, there has been (but is no longer, in most states) a presumption that the mother is the more fit parent to have custody of a child when mother and father divorce. In these cases, the presumption (of innocence or maternal custody) drives the judge or jury to favor the accused or the mother. Both presumptions, however, are rebuttable. That is, they may be set aside if the facts so warrant it. Thus, the state may have sufficient evidence to convict an accused; the presumption of innocence is then rebutted by the facts. Similarly, a father may be able to prove that he, not the child's mother, is a more suitable custodial parent; there, too, the facts will compel a judge or jury to award custody to him, not to the mother.

Under IDEA, the presumption is that the student will be educated with students who do not have disabilities. That presumption, however, may be set aside when the student's needs are so great that, even with related services and with supplementary aids and services, the child cannot benefit from being educated with nondisabled students.

To be educated with students who do not have disabilities, that is, to be placed in the least restrictive environment (LRE), means that the student must have access to the general curriculum. IDEA defines general curriculum as consisting of the academic program, extracurricular activities, or other school-sponsored activities (e.g., field trips or dances). When Emily was in her first American school placement, she was in a setting with students who had a variety of disabilities. At her second placement, all of her classmates are children with autism. Ms. Hanaoka is pleased that, at both sites, she has some opportunities to interact with peers without disabilities outside of the classroom structure. Libby has spent most of her years in inclusive settings of varying degrees. Libby has blossomed in her full inclusion setting and seems to be very happy. Mr. and Mrs. Bridge are concerned about the program Libby will go into in middle school because it will be a step back from inclusion. Hopefully, with IDEA's presumption for inclusion on their side, Libby will continue to receive the kind of inclusive education she and her parents desire.

IDEA also provides that infants and toddlers in early intervention will receive early intervention services in "natural environments," namely, those in which peers without disabilities participate, to the extent appropriate for the child with the disability. Separate settings, such as hospitals, are permissible only when the child requires extensive medical treatment.

The placement decision may not be made until after the child has been given a nondiscriminatory evaluation; and it is made on the basis of that evaluation and by the members of the child's IFSP team when they prepare the IEP or IFSP. They may not decide, without an evaluation and without conforming to the IFSP process, that the child will have a certain placement; placement must always follow evaluation and be decided within the context of the IFSP development. Parents are members of that team and thus have a role in deciding how the LRE rule applies to their child.

Parent and Student Participation in Shared Decision Making

Parents may participate in general ways in making decisions about their child's education. They have the right to have access to their children's school records and to limit the distribution of those records to people who do not "need to know" what they contain. They also have the right of access to the school district's general records about special education, such as the records showing how many students receive special education services and the amount of money the district receives and spends for special education. Obviously, they do not have the right to see the other students' records. In addition to these specific rights,

parents generally have the right to see the state's special education plan, to receive public notice of hearings on the plan, and to comment on the plan. They are entitled to serve on the state advisory council on special education; they must constitute the majority of the council's membership. Finally, parents of infants and toddlers are entitled to serve on the state's interagency coordinating council on early intervention and must constitute a majority of the membership of the council.

Procedural Due Process

Procedural due process is a technique for accountability and refers to IDEA's safeguards for assuring that the student receives a free, appropriate public education. Parents have the right to be informed in writing about an LEA's proposed evaluation of their child for placement into special education, to receive the information in their native language or other mode of communication, and to consent in writing or to withhold their consent. Ms. Hanaoka does not recall ever being asked whether she wished to have any translation assistance. In hindsight, she feels it would have at times been helpful in understanding the educational process in which Emily was becoming newly involved. By law, Ms. Hanaoka is entitled to a notice written in Japanese; and had she also had a visual impairment, she would have been entitled to have the notice read to her by a Japanese-speaking interpreter.

Parents have the right to receive written notice before an LEA proposes to change or refuse to change a student's identification, evaluation, or placement or to change the provisions of a free, appropriate public education to their child. They have the right to receive a written notice (similarly written or translated) of their due process rights on three occasions: at the initial referral of the student for evaluation, upon each notification to them of an evaluation or IEP meeting, and upon their filing of a complaint about the LEA's violation of their child's IDEA rights. These notices must be in the parents' native language or other mode of communication or must be translated orally to the parents if they are unable to read.

Parents are entitled to use mediation to resolve their disputes with an LEA; or, if they do not want to use mediation, to have a due process hearing before an impartial person. The hearing is like a civil trial, with the parents and LEA both having the right to be

FIGURE 2–3
Tips for Collaborating with Parents in IFSP/IEP Conferences

Preparing in Advance
- Appoint a service coordinator to organize the conference.
- Make sure the evaluation has included all relevant areas, is complete, and has clearly synthesized results.
- Ask the family about their preferences regarding the conference.
- Discuss the conference with the student and consider his or her preferences for participation. Assist the student with preparation as appropriate.
- Decide who should attend the conference and include the student, if appropriate.
- Arrange a convenient time and location for the conference.
- Assist families with logistic needs, such as transportation and child care.
- Inform the family (in straightforward, jargon-free language) verbally or in writing of the following:
  - Purpose of the conference
  - Time and location of conference
  - Names and roles of participants
- Give the family the information they want before the conference, including information on their legal rights.
- Encourage and arrange for the student, family members, and their advocates to visit the possible educational placement sites for the student before the conference.
- Encourage the student and family members to talk with each other about the conference.
- Encourage the family to share information and discuss concerns with all participants.
- Review the student's previous IFSP/IEP and ensure that school records document the extent to which each of the goals and objectives (or outcomes) have been accomplished.
- Identify the factors that have most contributed to the attainment of those results and the factors that have been the most significant barriers.
- Request an informal meeting with any teachers or related service providers who will not attend the conference. Document and report their perspectives at the conference.
- Consider whether providing snacks would be appropriate and possible. If so, make necessary arrangements.
- Prepare an agenda to cover the remaining components of the conference.

Connecting and Getting Started
- Greet the students, family, and their advocates.
- Share informal conversation in a comfortable and relaxed way.
- Serve snacks, if available.
- Share an experience about the student that was particularly positive or one that reflects the student's best work.
- Provide a list of all participants or use name tags if there are several people who have not met before.
- Introduce each participant, briefly describing his or her role in the conference.
- State the purpose of the conference. Review the agenda and ask if additional issues should be covered.
- Ask the participants how long they can stay and offer to schedule a follow-up conference if necessary to complete the agenda.
- Ask if family members want you to clarify their legal rights. If so, do so.

Sharing Visions and Great Expectations
- If a Making Action Plans (MAPS) process has been completed, share the results with everyone.
- If a Making Action Plans (MAPS) process has not been completed, consider incorporating it into the conference.
- Encourage the student and family to share their great expectations for the future. Then encourage all committee members to share their visions of the most desirable future for the student, based on the student's preferences, strengths, and needs.
- Affirm the excitement about the great expectations and the connection between the goals and objectives (or outcomes) that are planned at the conference and the achievement of those great expectations.

Review of Formal Evaluation and Current Levels of Performance
- Ensure that the evaluation report includes the statement of how the student's disability affects involvement and progress in the general curriculum (for preschoolers, the statement should address how the disability affects participation in appropriate activities).
- Give family members a written copy of all evaluation results.
- Avoid educational jargon as much as possible and clarify any terms that seem to puzzle the family, students, or others who are attending.

FIGURE 2–3
continued

Review of Formal Evaluation and Current Levels of Performance (continued)

- If a separate evaluation conference has not been scheduled, discuss the evaluation procedures and tests and the results of each.
- Invite families and other conference participants to agree or disagree with the evaluation results and to state their reasons.
- Discuss the meaning and implications of the results in terms of the student's appropriate education, preferences, strengths, great expectations, and needs.
- Review the student's developmental progress and current levels of performance in each subject area or domain.
- Ask families if they agree or disagree with the stated progress and performance levels.
- Strive to resolve any disagreement among participants.
- Proceed with the IFSP/IEP only after all participants agree about the student's current levels of performance.

Sharing Resources, Priorities, and Concerns

- Taking into account the student's and family's strengths, preferences, great expectations, needs, and concerns, encourage each participant to identify the particular resources, expertise, and strengths that they (and absent professionals) can bring to bear.
- Ask participants to share their priorities and reach consensus on the most important issues.
- Encourage all participants to express their concerns about their own roles in supporting the student, especially in areas where they feel they will need support or assistance.
- Plan how all participants can share expertise and resources to create the most comprehensive support system possible in addressing priorities and responding to concerns.

Development of Goals and Objectives (or Outcomes)

- Generate appropriate, measurable goals and objectives for all subject areas that require specially designed instruction consistent with the student's disability-related needs to enable the student to be involved in and progress in a general curriculum.
- Generate appropriate, measurable goals and objectives to enable the student to participate in extracurricular and other nonacademic activities.
- Discuss goals and objectives for the student's future educational and career options based on great expectations.
- Identify goals and objectives to expand the positive contributions the student can make to family, friends, and community.
- Prioritize all goals and objectives by student and family preferences, great expectations, strengths, needs, and concerns.
- Clarify who—the student, family, or professionals—is responsible for reaching the objectives and ensuring their generalization or mastery.
- Determine evaluation criteria, procedures, and schedules for goals and objectives.
- Explain that the IFSP/IEP is not a guarantee that the student will attain the goals and objectives but that it represents a good-faith effort among all participants to work toward the goals and objectives.
- Specify goals and objectives, including individual modifications, to enable the student to participate in the statewide and districtwide assessments. If the committee determines that participation and assessment are not appropriate, include a rationale and a statement of how the student will be assessed.

Determining Placement and Related Services

- Discuss the benefits and drawbacks of less restrictive, more inclusive placement options. Consider the resources that all committee members can bring to bear, especially supplementary aids and related services, in inclusive settings.
- Select a placement option that enables the student to receive appropriate individualized instruction and to develop a sense of belonging with peers without exceptionalities in attaining annual goals.
- Agree on a tentative placement until the student and family can visit and confirm its appropriateness.
- Specify the supplementary aids and related services that the student will receive to ensure the appropriateness of the educational placement and participation in extracurricular and other nonacademic activities.
- If the student is to be placed in a special education program, state why supplementary aids and related services are not capable of assisting the student within a general education setting.
- Document and record the timeline for providing the supplementary aids and related services that will enable the student to make the transition to the general education setting.
- Discuss the benefits and drawbacks of types, schedules, and modes of providing related services that the student needs.
- Provide an explanation of the extent to which the student will not participate in the general education classroom, general curriculum, and in extracurricular and other nonacademic activities.

- Beginning when the student reaches age 14, provide a statement of the student's transition service needs, focusing on the student's course of study (e.g., placement in vocational educational programs).
- Beginning when the student reaches age 16 (or younger if appropriate), include a statement of needed transition services, including interagency responsibilities and linkages.
- Beginning at least 1 year before the student reaches the age of majority, include a statement that the student has been informed of the rights that will transfer from the parents to the student on reaching the age of majority.
- Specify the dates for initiating related services and anticipated duration.
- Share the names and qualifications of all personnel who will provide instruction and related services.

Concluding the Conference

- Assign follow-up responsibility for any task requiring attention.
- Summarize orally and on paper the major decisions and follow-up responsibilities of all participants.
- Set a tentative date for reviewing the IFSP/IEP implementation.
- Review how the student's progress toward annual goals will be measured, and specify how parents will be regularly informed at least as often as parents of students without disability are informed of their children's progress.
- Identify preferred options for ongoing communication among all participants.
- Express appreciation to all team members for their collaborative decision making.
- Affirm the value of a reliable alliance and cite specific examples of how having an alliance enhanced the quality of decision making.

Note: From *Families, Professionals, and Exceptionalities: A Special Partnership* (pp. 234–235), (3rd ed.) by A.P. Turnbull and H.R. Turnbull. Copyright 1997 by Merrill/Prentice Hall. Reprinted with permission.

represented by lawyers and to produce evidence; the losing party may appeal to a state-level hearing officer and then to courts and, if the parents prevail (win), they may recover the fees they paid to their lawyers.

Parents must give the LEA a notice that they are planning to file a complaint against the LEA and set out in the notice the student's name, a description of the problem related to the student, and a proposed resolution of the problem. If they are represented by a lawyer, the lawyer must give this notice or face the possibility that his or her fees will be reduced (if he or she is entitled to recover the fees from the LEA).

Summary of Six Principles

Through each of its six principles, IDEA strengthens parents' rights. Five principles (zero reject, nondiscriminatory evaluation, appropriate education, least restrictive environment, and parent and student participation in shared decision making) establish a framework within which parents acquire rights to affect their children's education; the due process principle establishes a mechanism for the parents to hold the LEA accountable for complying with IDEA.

Supporting Families to Be Educational Advocates

Learning the broad IDEA principles and the specific requirements is a daunting task for professionals who have formal courses in preservice and in-service training. It can be overwhelming, however, for many families. That is why an extensive national resource network exists for parents—Parent Training and Information Centers (PTIs). Currently there are 70 PTIs funded by the U.S. Department of Special Education, Office of Special Education and Rehabilitative Services. Each state has at least one PTI, and some states have two or more. Each PTI must have a private, nonprofit status. Furthermore, typically PTIs are directed by parents of children with disabilities, and under IDEA the majority of staff members must be parents. The resource list at the end of the chapter contains the names and addresses of the currently funded PTIs. Teachers would do well to refer the families of students in their classrooms to their respective state PTIs.

PTIs vary in their specific activities, although they all share the same primary purpose of preparing parents to be effective advocates in educational decision making processes. They provide a broad range of workshops, conferences, other training opportunities, and even one-to-one assistance to families. Furthermore, many of the PTIs have IDEA information in languages other than English and have staff who are from diverse cultural and linguistic groups.

There is a national technical assistance program for the PTIs that is a part of the Minnesota PTI—the PACER Center. This national network—Technical Assistance Alliance for Parent Centers—provides ongoing staff development, technology access, and a range of other informational resources for the national PTI network. Parents should be encouraged to contact their state PTI as well as the Alliance to obtain training opportunities and printed information specifically developed for families.

Another valuable national network aimed at preparing parents to act on their educational rights is a multicultural consortium—Grassroots: A National Multicultural Consortium of Community Parent Resource Centers. The Grassroots Consortium consists of 14 programs in culturally and linguistically diverse communities—African-American, Korean, Vietnamese, Latino, Caucasian, and Native American families are Grassroots constituents. Although none of the Grassroots units specifically focus on Japanese families, some may nevertheless be helpful to Ms. Hanaoka, especially the ones that consist of Korean or Vietnamese families. Members of the Grassroots Consortium strongly believe that social problems are best solved from the perspective of community citizens who create their own solutions and advance their own leadership potential. As stated by Ursula Markey, the Grassroots Consortium convener and editor of their newsletter, *Tapestry*:

As some American families joyfully prepare to cross the famed "bridge to the 21st Century," others must brace themselves for a title wave of cutbacks and changes in welfare, SSI, Medicaid, immigration, and special education legislation that threatens to sweep them away from that promising future.

Most families of children with disabilities will suffer in some way from these cutbacks and changes, however, traditionally underserved groups of families will be especially hard hit. We need all the help we can get to keep our family members with disabilities out of institutions and to access the services and support we need to provide for them at home. Our families are held together by love, determination, and a delicate balance of personal responsibility, disability benefits, and rights guaranteed by special education and disability laws. Without any

one of these supports everything could come tumbling down. . . .

Yet again, we must become as strong as we are tired . . . we must recognize and reject damaging comparisons of our families with the typical majority culture—male head of household, housewife-mother, two-child family structure—revered above all others in the past and value our families in the context of our current reality (Markey, 1997, p. 1).

Many parents participate in educational partnerships to implement all six IDEA principles as illustrated in Figure 2–1. Even with resources and training available, some parents may opt for a less active role. Parents of students with disabilities are a heterogeneous group with different preferences, strengths, and needs.

Indeed, legislative assumptions regarding parents' participation were not based on research data (H.R. Turnbull & Turnbull, 1982); these assumptions were based more on ways that advocates, policy makers, and legislators *think* parents *should* participate. Indeed, the assumption that *many* parents want to be involved has led some professionals to assume that *all* parents want to be involved. Indeed, parent participation in the decision making process may be detrimental to some parents and extremely helpful to others (A.P. Turnbull & Turnbull, 1997). Similar to parents of children without disabilities, some parents of children with disabilities have too many other critical day-to-day concerns; other parents do not value or feel confident about schools; and still other parents believe that all educational decision making is the teacher's job. Research over the last 25 years highlights a consistent pattern that many parents participate passively in educational decision making (A.P. Turnbull & Turnbull, 1997). The evidence clearly contradicts the assumptions and reveals an interesting perspective about families and educators:

The term "parent involvement" sums up the current perspective. It means we want parents involved with us. It means the service delivery system we helped create is at the center of the universe, and families are revolving around it. It brings to mind an analogy about the old Ptolemaic view of the universe with the Earth at the center. . . .

Copernicus came along and made a startling reversal—he put the sun in the center of the universe rather than the Earth. His declaration caused profound shock. The Earth was not the epitome of creation; it was a planet like all other planets. The successful challenge to the entire system of ancient authority required a complete change in philosophical conception of the universe. This is rightly termed the "Copernican revolution."

Let's pause to consider what would happen if we would have a Copernican revolution in the field of disability. Visualize the concept: The family is the center of the universe and the service delivery system is one of the many planets revolving around it. Now visualize the service delivery system at the center and the family in orbit around it. Do you see the difference? Do you recognize the revolutionary change in perspective? We would move from an emphasis on parent involvement (i.e., parents participating in the program) to family support (i.e., programs providing a range of support services to families). This is not a semantic exercise—such a revolution leads us to a new set of assumptions and a new vista of options for service. (A.P. Turnbull & Summers, 1987, pp. 295–296)

The revolution in parent involvement has led researchers and practitioners to recognize families' preferences, strengths, and needs. The next section reviews the progress that has been made in working within this family systems perspective.

A Family Systems Perspective

A system is defined as a "set(s) of elements standing in inter-relation among themselves and with the environment" (Bertalanffy, 1975, p. 159). Systems theory assumes that a system can only be understood as a whole. A familiar saying is that "the whole is greater than the sum of the parts." Professionals can enhance their understanding of the Bridge and Hanaoka families by understanding and applying a family systems perspective.

Systems theory has been applied to family sociology and family therapy in terms of how families interact as a whole system. Before the family systems approach within the field of special education, educators were primarily concerned about how much progress the child with a severe disability was making in acquiring developmental skills. Sometimes their intense concern for development resulted in parents being highly involved in carrying out instructional programs at home (Baker, 1984; Stayton & Karnes, 1994). An unintentional consequence of this emphasis sometimes was that the mother spent her time with the child who had the disability at the expense of

her other children, her spouse, and herself. Another unintentional consequence was to shift the role of parents from being nurturers to teachers and to shift their home from having family activities to having school activities. The family systems view is interested in the well-being of all family members, including recognizing the support needs of parents (including fathers), brothers and sisters, and other family members. Clearly, the "mom at home" approach does not apply to Ms. Hanaoka; but it is exactly the approach that the Bridges have adopted.

The application of family systems theory to special education requires fundamental changes in answer to the following question: Who is the consumer of the services delivered by special education professionals? In the past, the student has been viewed as the sole consumer. The family systems approach identifies the whole family as the consumer of services. Figure 2–4 depicts the family systems framework that we will discuss in the remainder of this chapter. The components of the framework and their interrelationships within the family system follow:

1. *Family characteristics* describe the whole family as a unit (e.g., size and form, cultural background, socioeconomic status, geographic location); the family's personal characteristics (e.g., health, coping styles); and the family's special challenges (e.g., poverty, abuse). From a systems perspective, these characteristics are the underlying *input* to the system that shapes the way in which the family interacts.

2. *Family interaction* is the hub of the system, the *process* of interaction among individual family members and subsystems. Subsystem interactions are influenced by and in turn influence what family members do to respond to individual and collective family needs.

3. *Family functions* are the *output* of the interactional system. Based on its characteristics (input), the family interacts (a process) to produce responses that fulfill family affection, self-esteem, economic, daily care, socialization, recreation, and education needs.

4. *Family life cycle* introduces the element of *change* into the family system. As the family moves through time, developmental and nondevelopmental changes alter the family's characteristics and needs; these, in turn, produce change in the way the family interacts.

FIGURE 2–4
Family Systems Framework:
Emphasis on Family
Characteristics

Note: From *Working with Families
with Disabled Members: A Family
Systems Approach* (p. 60) by A.P.
Turnbull, J.A. Summers, and M.J.
Brotherson, 1984, Lawrence, KS:
The University of Kansas, Kansas
University Affiliated Facility. Copyright
1984 by The University of Kansas.
Adapted by permission.

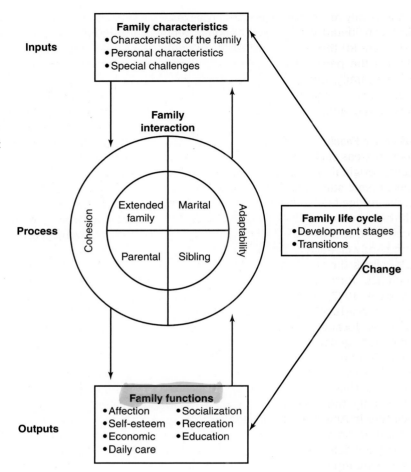

The family systems model enables educators to recognize each family's complexity and uniqueness. Each family is composed of so many attributes that it can interact in an almost endless variety of ways. Furthermore, a family is not a static entity. It is constantly changing, as well as resisting change. The unique characteristics of each family must be considered. To have only one way of interacting with families, one type of policy or program, or one idea of how families "should" be would be a disservice to every family encountered. What may be suitable for the Bridges would not be for the Hanaoka family: For one thing, the Bridges are a two-parent family with grandparents close by, whereas Ms. Hanaoka has only herself to rely on, at least while she is in Kansas.

Each of these four components—characteristics, interaction, functions, and life cycle—provides a different perspective from which the families view their family member's exceptionality, the services that are offered, the professionals they encounter, and their everyday life experiences. The following sections briefly discuss each of the four components outlined in Figure 2–4 and highlight issues relevant for special educators. Given space limitations, we provide illustrative examples of elements within each of the four components, but we are not able to provide a comprehensive description of all elements. For a comprehensive description of these elements, see A.P. Turnbull and Turnbull (1997).

Family Characteristics

When you think of the range of families within your community alone, you will see that family characteristics are infinitely diverse. This diversity greatly influences the impact of a child with a severe disability on the family and family responses to meeting the child's needs. Three considerations in understanding family characteristics are (a) the characteristics of the family as a whole, (b) the personal characteristics of each member of the family, and (c) the characteristics of special challenges. In our discussion, we focus on each of these three family considerations.

Characteristics of the Family

Families vary in areas such as size, form (e.g., dual vs. single parents, original vs. reconstituted family), culture, socioeconomic status, and geographic location. Obviously, the Bridge family differs from the Hanaoka family with respect to number of parents and culture. In this section, we focus on culture as illustrative of variations in family characteristics.

Culture provides the "lens" within which individuals and families form a sense of group identity (Gopaul-McNicol, 1997; Harkness & Super, 1996). It involves many considerations, including race, ethnicity, geographical location, religion, income status, sexual orientation, gender, disability status, and occupation (A.P. Turnbull & Turnbull, 1996). Often people equate culture with race or ethnicity, but culture is a broader concept than that. For example, the Bridges seem to exemplify the apparently dominant Euro-American culture in America: they are white, their ancestors came from an English-speaking country, and they value independence and self-determination for their children. By contrast, Ms. Hanaoka is of a different race and has a different cultural heritage: hers is Asian, specifically, Japanese. These differences can be substantial; but they are by no means bound to be so, especially because Ms. Hanaoka is herself a professional and now is being inculcated with American (Western) influences. Aside from the inculcation, Ms. Hanaoka describes a difference of opinion she had with Emily's teacher concerning the IEP goal that the teacher recommended of teaching Emily proper table place-setting, including the placement of knives. Ms. Hanaoka explained that in her culture knives were rarely used at the table. Chopsticks might be used, and food is prepared in a way so that cutting is not necessary. She felt that this goal, therefore, would be a waste of time for Emily and would not be a functional skill.

A family may not even identify its own behavior patterns as being influenced by cultural roots. Culture influences marriage ceremonies, religious beliefs and practices, rites of passage (e.g., bar or bat mitzvah), celebrations of holidays, observations of holy days, rituals surrounding deaths and burials, a person's perception of his or her relationship to the world, political beliefs, attitudes toward independence and work, and the extent to which it is appropriate for children and youth to be self-determining.

For example, self-determination is a value that suggests that people should be the primary causal agent in their life decisions and that acting autonomously is not only appropriate but preferred (Sands & Wehmeyer, 1996). A study of cultural diversity reveals that some families emphasize values such as family unity and permanence, interdependence, and protectiveness much more than self-determination (A.P. Turnbull & Turnbull, 1996). Quotes from Latin American parents suggest those values:

- "It is against the family for the children to live alone as adults."
- "The family is a service vocation on behalf of the member with the disability."
- "Family interdependence is the soundest possible way of support for each member."
- "Children are always children. They do not go their own way, as a rule." (A.P. Turnbull & Turnbull, 1996, pp. 200–201)

This should not be interpreted to mean that all Latin American parents hold these values; on the contrary, there is tremendous variability *within* cultures as well as *among* cultures. Consider the son or daughter of parents who hold the previous values regarding self-determination and the implications of these values (i.e., family unity and permanence, interdependence, and protectiveness) for what is appropriate to teach in a self-determination curriculum. Furthermore, these values have tremendous implications for the development of transition programs as students move from high school to adulthood. Within a Euro-American perspective, it can be easy to assume that appropriate goals are employment, independent living, and community contribution (Hanson, 1992). Alternatively, some families, given their cultural values, will have very different priorities. Although it is common for traditional Japanese families to take lifelong care of their less abled family members, Ms. Hanaoka is exploring alternative care and housing for her daughter's future. Her preference is partially influenced by her status as a single parent, although she points out that many families in Japan are now fighting for alternative care, but social pressure is still a strong expectation of continuous family caregiving. This is an example of how family characteristics, such as size and form, can influence family values.

While you need to be aware of cultural differences, you also need to be careful not to stereotype families based on this awareness. To say that all people of color, in comparison to the dominant Euro-American culture in the U.S., value family unity and permanence, interdependence, and protectiveness is contrary to the real-life experiences of many individuals in these groups. You should always strive to enhance your cultural self-awareness and cultural competence so that you can, in turn, create partnerships with families that are respectful of their cultural values (Grossman, 1995; Harkness & Super, 1996; Harry, Grenot-Scheyer et al., 1995; Lynch & Hanson, 1992).

Personal Characteristics

Personal characteristics include the characteristics of a member's disability, each family member's mental and physical health status, and individual coping styles. The characteristics of a child's disability contribute to shaping the impact of the child's needs and strengths on the family system and the ability of the family system to be responsive. Libby Bridge's disability—a combination of cerebral palsy, mental retardation, epilepsy, and visual impairment—differ from Emily's, which is autism (including mental retardation). Because the categories of their disabilities are not the same, their families' needs related to the disabilities also may differ. The characteristics of a child's disability include many factors, including the nature of the disability, the extent or degree of the disability, the time of onset, and future prognosis. A child with medically complex needs often requires families to make adaptations in daily routines in providing ongoing assistance, to purchase special equipment, and to interact frequently with medical personnel (Jones, Clatterbuck, Marquis, Turnbull, & Moberly 1996). Children with challenging behavior can place inordinate demands on family members and create stress in activities both within and outside of the home (A.P. Turnbull & Ruef, 1997). A child with a later onset of disability (disability caused from an accident during school years) can cause major family readjustments in dealing with the immediacy of the crisis and in re-

curring long-term rehabilitation (Kreutzer, Serio, & Bergquist, 1994; Singer & Nixon, 1996).

Regardless of the particular nature of the disability, children and youth also provide a broad array of positive contributions to their families, including happiness and fulfillment, strength, personal growth, an expanded social network, career or job growth, and pride in accomplishments (Behr & Murphy, 1993; Glidden, 1989; Summers, Behr, & Turnbull, 1989; H.R. Turnbull, Guess, & Turnbull, 1988). Thus, for professionals to understand the impact of the child with a severe disability, they will need to understand the child's demands on and contributions to the family. Some people assume that a severe disability always produces greater stress on the family than a mild disability. As one parent of a young adolescent commented:

> Don has been labeled profoundly retarded. He is not able to do anything to take care of himself, cannot walk, and has no language. But I remind myself that I never have to chase him around the house, he never talks back or sasses, he doesn't have to enter the rat race of teenage years like my other sons, and he does not try to hurt himself.

According to Mr. and Mrs. Bridge, Libby has contributed to the family by "teaching her sisters how to be helpful and compassionate." Mr. Bridge particularly likes Libby's smile, her eyes, and her laughter; Mrs. Bridge enjoys the times that Libby shows affection and the connection between them is made evident. Thus, while the family experiences challenges related to caring for Libby, they also experience joy from their relationships with her. And just as Libby has affected her family positively, so Emily has affected her mother: Were it not for the fact that Emily has autism, Emma, a musicologist, most likely would not have decided to study music therapy and to have come halfway around the world from Japan to Kansas to do so. Professionals should be encouraged to understand the impact of the disability within the context of each family's individual situation and in light of their values and perceptions.

Special Challenges

The final aspect of family characteristics relates to the underlying special challenges that families face. Families face many challenges over and above a child's exceptionality (Hanson & Carta, 1995). There are a wide range of challenges, from typical ones that many families face at one time or another to challenges that are quite extreme. More typical challenges include unemployment, death of a family member, and crises associated with unpredictable events, such as floods and earthquakes. For example, Mr. Hanaoka was killed in an accident while on a vacation. It was a major shock for the family to experience his death and the end of his roles as a husband, father, and community physician.

Challenges that occur in a smaller subsection of families include substance abuse (Gottwald & Thurman, 1994; Shriver & Piersel, 1994), living with constant exposure to violence (Taylor, Zuckerman, Harik, & Groves; 1994; Vig, 1996), having a family member who is incarcerated, having teenage parents (Muccigrosso, Scavarda, Simpson-Brown, & Thalacker, 1991), having parents with mental retardation (Llewellyn, 1995; Ronai, 1997), and living in poverty (U.S. Department of Education, 1997). We now briefly focus on the challenges of living in poverty.

Poverty challenges many families, especially those whose children have disabilities. Almost 50% of the population that has consistently lived below the poverty line for the past 2 years are children (U.S. Bureau of the Census, 1996). The 1998 National Health Interview Survey reported that the risk of being placed in special education increases 2.4% if a child comes from a low-income family, even after controlling for low birth weight, geographic residence, age, race, family structure, and parent's education (Sherman, 1994). Moreover, household economic status revealed that households with a family member with a developmental disability had significantly lower income and greater reliance on means-tested income support (Fujiura & Yamaki, 1997). Furthermore, cultural and linguistic diversity increased differences in earned income and in access to welfare benefits. Thus, the economic situation of minority households includes less income, larger household size, and greater reliance on welfare benefits.

What are some of the specific effects of poverty on the families of children with severe disabilities? Accessing appropriate medical care, respite care, special equipment, and other supports and resources becomes all the more challenging. Approximately one third of children living in poverty are reported to lack health insurance (O'Hare, 1996).

Poverty can also have an impact on a family's sense of shaping its own destiny. In Jonathan Kozol's (1995) disturbing and compelling analysis of a South Bronx neighborhood, he states:

> So long as there are ghetto neighborhoods and ghetto hospitals and ghetto schools, I am convinced there will be ghetto desperation, ghetto violence, and ghetto fear, because the ghetto is itself an evil and unnatural construction. . . . Perhaps this is one reason why so much of the debate about the "breakdown of the family" has a note of the unreal or incomplete. "Of course the family structure breaks down at a place like the South Bronx!" says a white minister who works in one of New York City's poorest neighborhoods. "Everything breaks down in a place like this. The pipes break down. The phone breaks down. The electricity and heat breaks down. The spirit breaks down. The body breaks down. The immune agents of the heart break down. Why wouldn't a family break down also?"

When the context is so unresponsive to a family, there will, in turn, be an impact on their children's sense of self-determination. Thus, it is imperative to teach students with severe disability skills that will enable them to live the life that they want to live while also addressing systemic barriers that restrict families' abilities to support themselves and their children.

Educational Implications of Understanding Family Characteristics

Families vary widely in their characteristics. These characteristics, in turn, shape the way that families interact, carry-out their functions, and change or stay the same over the life cycle. Rather than adhering to an idealized image of what a family "should be", the most successful way to form partnerships with families is to recognize and honor their diversity across these three elements—characteristics of the family, personal characteristics, and special challenges. By understanding the elements within each of these components, you can identify a family's preferences for involvement in their child's educational program, for ongoing communication with you, and for working together with you to plan for their child's current and future services and supports.

Family Interaction

Parent-professional relationships typically are mother-professional relationships. But do not assume, as many do, that mother and family are synonymous. The members of some families are related by blood or marriage, whereas others are related by preference (a close family friend who is regarded as a family member). The family is a unit of interaction. Each family member is affected by the disability of the child, and the child is affected by each family member.

You should always recognize that any interaction with the child or other member ripples throughout the whole family. A home visit can be a totally positive experience, or it can create family stress because of a perception of having the privacy of one's turf violated or because of the need to alter the schedule of activities or responsibilities (Klass, 1996). Scheduling a parent conference to discuss the child's progress can create an argument between two working parents about which one will take time off from employment. Working on a child's social skills can enhance a sibling relationship that was threatened by embarrassment over inappropriate public behavior. Requesting parents to follow through on instructional programs at home can strengthen their relationship with their child but may also create major tensions. Just how much time does Ms. Hanaoka have to be a "follow-through" educator for Emily? And what support does she have for that role, assuming she wants to perform it? And what does it mean for Libby's sisters, Hilary and Hayley, if Mr. and Mrs. Bridge become Libby's "teachers" at home? The tensions between parent and child can then spill over into the marriage, sibling interactions, and interactions with extended family, neighbors, bosses, and coworkers. Interaction with any member of the system has implications for all members.

> In a mobile, all the pieces, no matter what size or shape, can be grouped together and balanced by shortening or lengthening the strings attached, or rearranging the distance between the pieces. So it is with the family. None of the family members is identical to any others; they are all different and at different levels of growth. As in a mobile, you can't arrange one without thinking of the other (Satir, 1972, pp. 119–120).

From the perspective of family interaction, you would do well to understand two major concepts: (a) family subsystems and (b) ways that families establish balance through their cohesion and adaptability.

Family Subsystems

The family systems framework highlights four major subsystems within traditional nuclear families:

1. Marital subsystem—marital partner interactions
2. Parental subsystem—parent and child interactions
3. Sibling subsystem—child and child interactions
4. Extended family subsystem—whole family or individual member interactions with relatives, friends, neighbors, and professionals

Variations in subsystems exist in many families, such as single parents (like Ms. Hanaoka), stepparents, families with one child (Emily has no siblings), families with extensive extrafamilial subsystems (such as the Bridges), and families where most people are related by preference rather than by blood or marriage. We will highlight information on the marital and sibling subsystems.

Marital Subsystem. There is a common assumption that children with disabilities—particularly severe disabilities—place their parents at great risk for serious marital problems. Some research suggests that there is a higher incidence of marital disharmony and divorce in families who have a child with a disability (Gath, 1977; Murphy, 1982); however, other studies have reported no differences between couples with and without children with disabilities in relation to marital satisfaction (Benson & Gross, 1989; Kazak & Marvin, 1984). Some studies have found that children with disabilities do not affect the marriage in either a positive or a negative way (Abbott & Meredith, 1986; Young & Roopnarine, 1994). Research on effect on marital problems has not specifically addressed the severity of the disability as a factor. Effect on the marriage, like so many other aspects of the family system, is an individual consideration in light of multiple other characteristics operating simultaneously within the family.

Professionals can support families' marital well-being by listening and responding to the parents' preferences for the support that they, themselves, need in caring for their son or daughter. For example, Mr. and Mrs. Bridge make decisions about Libby's education together. The educators working with Libby support this process by scheduling meetings at a time that both parents are able to attend. In many communities, there are a number of resources for marital counseling and support that might be offered to families as a service that they may want to pursue (Lichtenstein, 1993).

Variations in the marital subsystem exist in many families. For example, Ms. Hanaoka describes that her husband tried to hide Emily's disability from his family and to deny that the disability even existed. When it was no longer possible to deny or hide the disability, he avoided sharing the responsibility for the daily care of Emily and often complained about the effects of her behavior on their family life. It was only after his death that Ms. Hanaoka was able to openly and easily solicit assistance and support from sources outside the family.

Nowadays, parents of children with severe disabilities, similar to those of children without disabilities, may be in same-sex marriages, and it is critically important for professionals to support these couples in carrying out their family responsibilities. Increasingly, resources are available for preparing professionals to become comfortable and competent in providing responsive support to lesbian and gay parents (Martin, 1993).

Sibling Subsystem. Just as within the literature on marital subsystems, research on the effects of sibling subsystems are similarly mixed. Some studies have found that brothers and sisters of siblings with disabilities have a higher incidence of emotional problems, lower self-esteem, and greater responsibilities for household chores (McHale & Gamble, 1987; Wilson, Blacher, & Baker, 1989). Other studies have found the opposite to be true (Burton & Parks, 1994; Carr, 1988). Values that Mrs. Bridge wanted to pass on to her children include the acceptance of differences and compassion for others. She is happy that Hilary and Hayley are learning these values through their interactions with Libby. Mrs. Bridge speaks of the unconditional acceptance that the girls show to Libby, saying:

> *It's just normal to them. This is who she is. I have always appreciated that in them. . . . They like to go in her room and watch movies—but they watch them with her, they don't ignore her. They all eat popcorn together. During the movie, they'll reach over and stroke her hair or tickle her or something. I think that's what I like the most.*

For Emily and her mother, however, there is only the two of them: no father and no siblings.

A national resource for siblings is a program called "Sibshops," which has the goal of providing information and emotional support for brothers and sisters (Meyer & Vadasy, 1994) (see box entitled "Sibshops Model").

An especially helpful way to become sensitive to sibling issues is to listen to sibling perspectives.

Siblings can be invited to IEP conferences or to have discussions with teachers or related service providers outside of the IEP conference. Another possibility for gaining information is to read the perspectives of siblings that are often provided in newsletters of family organizations, and now in a new book that provides the perspectives of 45 siblings ranging in age from 4 to 18 (Meyer, 1997). For example, Jessica, 9 years old, has an older brother with autism. She comments:

> In some ways my life is different from kids who have a normal brother, because most of my schedule revolves around Danny. Sometimes I can't go to special activities because my mother has no one to watch Danny and can't take me. I think parents, teachers, and doctors should have more understanding for siblings, because they go through difficult experiences with their brothers or sisters. (Meyer, 1997, p. 27)

Establishing Balance: Cohesion and Adaptability

Family therapists have identified two dimensions in establishing balance in family relationships: cohesion and adaptability. Cohesion is the bridge between close emotional bonding and individual independence. Carnes (1981) uses an example of "the touching of hands" to describe cohesion:

> The dilemma is how to be close yet separate. When the fingers are intertwined, it at first feels secure and warm. Yet when one partner (or family member) tries to move, it is difficult at best. The squeezing pressure may even be painful. . . . The paradox of every relationship is how to touch and yet not hold on. (pp. 70–71)

Professionals must help families learn to touch and yet not hold on by encouraging them to have a balanced view rather than a highly singular focus on the child with the disability, helping them obtain respite care when needed, referring them to community resources on which they can draw, and helping the child with the disability build a social support network. Again, cultural values come into play. As in the example previously given about self-determination, some families set a much stronger cultural value on family interdependence, so they may not encourage individual independence as much as a teacher might think is appropriate for his or her own family. While an educator may think it appropriate to encourage Libby's independence, that same educator will have to consider what "independence" means for Mr. and

Box 2–1

Sibshops Model

Sibshops are opportunities for sisters and brothers of children and teens with disabilities to have shared recreation and opportunities for learning. Sibshops are usually offered on Saturdays and involve games, discussion, eating lunch, and opportunities to gain information about disability issues. They typically are facilitated by professionals and adult siblings of people with disabilities. Participants range in numbers from just a few children to almost 50. A sample schedule includes the following activities (Meyer & Vadasy, 1994):

Trickle-in activity: Group juggling

Warm-up: Human bingo

Discussion #1: Strengths and weaknesses

Game: Sightless sculpture

Lunch: Super nachos

Game: Push-pin soccer

Discussion #2: Dear Aunt Blabby

Guest: Physical therapist

Closing activity: Sound off

For more information on Sibshops:

Project director: Donald Meyer

Project address: Sibling Support Project

    Children's Hospital and Medical Center

    P.O. Box 5371 CL–09

    Seattle, WA 98105-0371

Phone: 206-368-4911

Fax: 206-368-4816

E-mail: Dmeyer@chmc.org

Website: Http:\\www.chmc.org.departmt\sibsupp

Mrs. Bridge. Yes, it includes the prospect that Libby would have supported employment, but it does not yet mean that they see Libby living on her own, away from them. Right now, they see Libby living with them "forever." Some educators might say that the Bridges need more support and encouragement for future planning, but they have a clear preference not to think ahead too far in the future. Ms. Hanaoka sees Emily as needing to be able to function with others without always having her mother close by. As stated earlier, Ms. Hanaoka's values are influenced by the small number of family members available to provide support to Emily.

Adaptability is the ability of a family to change and create new responses when necessary to respond to emerging situations (Olson, Russell, & Sprenkle, 1980). Many families establish patterns of interaction. For example, the mother in a family may assume re-sponsibility for bathing, dressing, feeding, and toileting a child with severe physical disabilities. This pattern may become so ingrained that the mother is unable to leave town for a vacation or a visit with extended family or even to have a break from these duties. If the mother is ill or an emergency arises, a family crisis related to parents' roles is likely to occur. One way to help families achieve successful family interactions is to encourage them to develop an array of alternatives and options, consistent with their cultural values. What, for example, might be culturally appropriate contingency plans for Ms. Hanaoka, given that she is far away from her extended family, at least for now? Because of Emily's difficulty adjusting to new settings, Ms. Hanaoka would most likely prefer that Emily remain in her own home with her familiar routines and to have support people available to come into the home.

Educational Implications of Understanding Family Interaction

Professionals should recognize that supporting families requires developing educational programs that are as responsive to the family system as possible. IEP goals can foster successful family inclusion. For example, students can be taught leisure skills consistent with the recreation interests of the parents and siblings, or priority can be given to self-help, communication, and social skills that lead to increasing contact with grandparents (Seligman, Goodwin, Paschal, Applegate, & Lehman, 1997) and neighbors. You can provide information to extended family or friends and help them gain confidence in handling matters related to the child's seizures, feeding, positioning, and responding to unique language modes.

Families have responsibilities for meeting the needs of all members, not just the child or youth with a disability. Professionals may perceive a parent's absence from a conference or failure to follow through on home teaching as not giving the child adequate attention. An alternative explanation is that the parent is attending to the needs of the marriage, other family members, or himself or herself. Successful families *balance* the needs of *all* members, rather than placing a *single member* in a *focal position* and meeting that person's needs at the expense of the needs of the other members. (It is also critically important for individuals with disabilities to learn to respect the needs and preferences of other family members and to know that they sometimes need to take priority over their own.) Successful families find the level of cohesion and adaptability that works for them. As professionals assist families in planning for experiences with others outside of the family system and for planning for future transitions, respecting the families' definition of cohesion and adaptability are especially important.

Family Functions

Families exist to serve the individual and collective needs of their members. Attending to family functions is one way to characterize how families serve their individual and collective needs. Family functions can be characterized in many ways. A.P. Turnbull and Turnbull (1997) identify seven functions. Figure 2–5 highlights these functions and some tasks performed by family members to meet them.

The family functions are not independent of each other. One function may facilitate another function,

FIGURE 2–5
Family Functions and Tasks

1. *Affection:* developing intimate personal relationships, expressing sexuality, giving and receiving nurturance and love, and expressing emotions

2. *Self-esteem:* establishing self-identity and self-image, identifying personal strengths and weaknesses, and enhancing belonging and acceptance

3. *Economic support:* generating income and handling family finances, paying bills, earning allowances, and handling insurance matters

4. *Daily care:* purchasing food, preparing meals, providing health care, maintaining the home, providing transportation, and taking general safety measures

5. *Socialization:* fostering individual and collective friendships, developing social skills, and engaging in social activities

6. *Recreation:* developing and participating in hobbies or clubs, setting aside everyday demands, and going on vacations

7. *Education:* participating in school-related activities, continuing education for adults, doing homework, providing for career development, and developing a work ethic

as when the socialization function of developing an individual friendship eventually leads to an intimate personal relationship, which meets a teenager's need for affection. On the other hand, one function may impede progress in another functional area. For example, economic hardship often affects a family's other daily care needs (e.g., nutrition, health care), in turn impinging upon a parent or child's self-esteem.

A son or daughter with a disability can impact a family in negative, neutral, and positive ways. In the next section, we highlight effects on the economic function and the socialization function of families. (For a thorough discussion of all family functions, see Turnbull & Turnbull, 1997).

Economic Needs

All families have a need for income and a way to spend the money earned to meet food, clothing, shelter, and other needs. The presence of a son or daughter with a severe disability can create excess expense (Birenbaum & Cohen, 1993; Fujiura, Roccoforte, & Braddock, 1994). Some of the devices and services for a child or teen with a severe disability may include: adaptive feeding utensils; special clothing; lift-equipped vans; bathroom adaptations, such as support and safety bars; ongoing medications required for seizures and other physiologic needs; various body braces; voice synthesizers; hearing aids; adaptive seating equipment; ongoing evaluations by specialists; specially adapted furniture to facilitate lifting; hospital beds; respirators; suctioning equipment; adaptive exercise equipment; remote control devices for televisions, radios, and lights; positioning equipment, such as side lyers and prone standers; adaptive toys; and adaptive mobility devices, such as walkers and crutches. Many devices require ongoing servicing and periodic replacement. Even families fortunate enough to have the best health insurance coverage find that the costs of buying and maintaining many adaptive devices and medical services are not fully covered. Mrs. Bridge comments:

> When we got her first wheelchair we had to pay the majority of that one. I made the comment to one of our friends that we're spending the money that we could have saved over the years for a car . . . probably in the end it all evens out. We probably will end up helping purchase cars for the other girls where she won't need one. Libby is receiving SSI and Medicaid that has been very helpful because that is the reason that I have been able to not work and to take her all the places that she needs to go and attend all the meetings that we need to go to . . . I wouldn't have been able to put the time in if I had to work so I think because of that help, Libby has benefited.

The economic impact on families varies in light of the nature and extent of the child's disability.

Costs associated with providing for the needs of one family member can limit the funds available for the other family members. Parents and other family members may forgo attending to their own needs to afford services for the child with a severe disability. Parents may know that a child could benefit from the purchase of some special piece of equipment and not be able to afford it.

The presence of a family member with a disability may prevent parents from obtaining employment because of the level of care and supervision required. One study found that 32% of the parents of children or adults with a developmental disability reported that they had given up a paying job to provide care, not taken a paying job, or refused a job transfer or a promotion to provide care to the family member with a disability (Agosta, Bass, & Spence, 1986).

This was the case for Mrs. Bridge. She found that she was unable to work outside of the home after Libby joined the family. She explained, "I have found it literally impossible to work. You can't say to [an employer] 'I'd like to work, but I need Tuesday afternoons and Thursday and every other Friday off,' so Libby and I spent all the time going to doctors and therapy and I just have never gone back to work . . . We still haven't found it possible for me to do that."

Many families, however, report that the child with a disability requires less money. Some less active children require less frequent clothing and footwear replacements. The child may not feel compelled to have expensive items associated with growing up, such as a complex stereo system, personal telephone, a car, undergraduate and graduate education, and extensive travel.

Many parents turn to educators for needs beyond the traditional scope of education. Professionals who keep abreast of the range of community services related to economic needs can save families much frustration in accessing needed services. Most states have adopted family support policies and programs that provide some financial subsidies to families who meet certain financial "tests" (Braddock, Hemp, & Parish, 1997; Bradley, Knoll, & Agosta, 1993; Singer, Powers, & Olson, 1996). Unfortunately, the investments in family support are meager in comparison to other types of spending. For example, only five states (Alaska, New Mexico, North Dakota, Oklahoma, and Washington) commit more than one fifth of their total mental retardation and developmental disability resources for individual and family support activities. The national average for states is 7% of the total mental retardation and development disability budget allocated to individual and family support activity (Braddock, Hemp, Parish, & Westrich, 1998).

In terms of how the family support dollars are allocated, some states provide cash to families, and others use vouchers that families can redeem for services. The financial resources can be used for medically related services, assistive technology, case management, respite care, and particular services that the child or teen needs. Because states differ in how this program is administered, we encourage families and professionals to contact state Parent Training and

Information Centers to find out about the state family support resources available, as well as any other programs that provide financial resources to families. The local Social Security Office can provide information about eligibility criteria to receive Supplemental Security Income (SSI) and Social Security Disability Insurance. In many states, people who qualify for SSI are also eligible for Medicaid funds to meet medical expenses. In addition, professionals can provide economic-related information to families in other ways (A.P. Turnbull & Turnbull, 1997):

- Identify appropriate community contacts and provide parents with names and telephone numbers of persons to contact regarding estate planning, disability benefits, or family subsidies.
- Provide information on financial planning and government entitlement funds, such as SSI, as part of a family resource library.
- Encourage parents who have been successful in obtaining financial resources or who have completed financial planning to provide assistance to other parents who have financial questions.
- Provide information to help families investigate scholarships and financial aid.

Socialization Needs
Parents often are disappointed that their sons and daughters with severe disabilities have limited friendships. In a recent study of friendships, over two thirds of 17 families of children, teens, and adults with challenging behavior describe the *absence* of even one friendship for their children with challenging behavior. Parents' comments included:

> Danny has no relationships outside his family.
> Jessie has no friends at school. . . . She has only been there 1 1/2 years (A.P. Turnbull & Ruef, 1997, p. 216)

Interestingly, one of the parents of a young adult in this study warned, "The older you are and the longer you wait, the more difficult it becomes" (A.P. Turnbull & Ruef, 1997, p. 218). Of the 17 families, only one of the parents mentioned even having a vision for future friendship: "My dream is that the phone will ring, and someone will invite her to play" (A.P. Turnbull & Ruef, 1997, p. 218). Brotherson (1985) also found that parents reported that arranging for socialization was their greatest need when they had young adults with

mental retardation. One mother commented, "People with disabilities are lonesome, lonesome people" (Brotherson, 1985, p. 119). Ms. Hanaoka has made it a point to have many respite workers spend time with Emily and to develop a friendship with her. She encourages the respite workers to learn some basic Japanese words and to "connect" with Emily from her own cultural perspective. Ms. Hanaoka has also stocked their home with a variety of typical children's games. She believes that it will be helpful for Emily to learn to play these games so that she might more easily play with other children when opportunities present themselves.

Still other research on parents of students with moderate and severe to profound disabilities indicated that parents believe that approximately one fourth of the school week should be related to friendship and social relationship development (Hamre-Nietupski, 1993). Although parents appear to be very interested in a strong friendship curriculum emphasis (Westling, 1996), the primary focus of school curriculum has been on academics, functional skills, employment, and independent living, so friendship has not gotten adequate attention (Sowers, Glang, Voss, & Cooley, 1996).

Schaffner and Buswell (1992) describe three approaches to friendship facilitation:

1. Finding opportunities—arranging activities and opportunities to bring children and youth with and without disabilities together.
2. Making interpretations—highlighting to others a person's strengths and commonalities.
3. Making accommodations—changing or adapting the environment to increase an individual's participation.

A broad range of people can be friendship facilitators, including general and special education teachers, related service providers, paraprofessionals, family members, community citizens, and classmates (Hamre-Nietupski, Hendrickson, Nietupski, & Sasso, 1993; Hamre-Nietupski, Hendrickson, Nietupski, & Shokoohi-Yekta, 1994; Meyer, Park, Grenot-Scheyer, Schwartz, & Harry, 1998; A.P. Turnbull, Pereira, & Blue-Banning, in press). Many teachers have used the "Circle of Friends" approach with success in students with disabilities (Falvey, Forest, Pearpoint, & Rosenberg, 1994). Chapter 7 provides more information on friendship facilitation.

In addition to what professionals can do directly in friendship facilitation, they also can encourage parents to consider being facilitators of their own children's friendships. The box entitled "Parental Facilitation Strategies" summarizes methods used by parents whose children had at least one successful friendship with a child or teen without a disability (A.P. Turnbull, Pereira, & Blue-Banning, in press). Although all of the parents in the study that focused on parent facilitation reported enjoying their role as a friendship facilitator, other parents may have major problems in addressing this family function. As a parent of a middle school student with mental retardation commented:

> I have found this area [parent facilitation] to be very frustrating. . . . it is a very difficult area . . . how do parents overcome or balance a provider's services and activities and the tendency for a group of kids to take advantage of the parent of the child with a disability. My experience is that we drive to the movies, go to the pool, we are being taken advantage of by kids sometimes. You kiss a lot of frogs before you find the prince. (A.P. Turnbull, Peirera, & Blue-Banning, 1998)

Educational Implications of Family Functions

Educators must recognize all family functions. It can be easy to focus only on the education function and to encourage parents to spend as much time as they possibly can on this one function. The best way to support students with disabilities and their families is to recognize that families are stretched across all of these functions, and for most families there are not enough hours in each day to do each function justice. The feeling of not having enough time to attend to one's family needs is strongly linked to parental stress and even depression (Herman & Marcenko, 1997). Thus, the first point to keep in mind is to ensure that you do "no harm" by putting even more time demands on the family.

IFSPs and IEPs can be developed from the perspective of what the child might learn that would contribute to meeting family functions. For example, children can develop friendships that enable them to have invitations, so that they spend time away from home. This can result in the parents not having to pay for childcare to have time for themselves—a help for the economic family function, as well as for the so-

---

  Parental Facilitation Strategies

Box 2–2

  ### Building a Foundation

Accepting children unconditionally (e.g., loving the "disabled portion" of the child and perceiving the child as "whole" rather than "broken")

Creating Opportunities

Supporting participation in community activities (e.g., enrolling the child for a class at the community arts center and supporting the teacher to interact comfortably with the child)

Advocating for inclusion in the neighborhood school (e.g., working to have the child attend the neighborhood school rather than to be bused to a school across town)

Initiating and facilitating a "Circle of Friends" (e.g., starting a "Circle of Friends" or encouraging someone else to do so to encourage friendships within the school and community settings)

Setting sibling-consistent expectations (e.g., similar to siblings inviting friends over to spend the night, encouraging the child to do the same)

Making Interpretations

Encouraging others to accept the child (e.g., discussing their child's strengths and needs with others and supporting others to know how to communicate comfortably)

Ensuring an attractive appearance (e.g., ensuring that the child is dressed and groomed in a way that is likely to draw positive and appropriate attention)

Making Accommodations

Advocating for partial participation in community activities (e.g., encouraging a scout leader to know how to adapt projects to enable partial participation in completing them)

cialization family function. Additionally, children and youth can learn to attend to their own personal care needs and to complete family chores, such as washing dishes, emptying the trash, and making their bed. All of these tasks can relieve another family member from having to do them, which is a contribution to the daily care family function that might enhance time for family recreation.

Thus, educators need to find the balance with families and their own interests in being friendship facilitators and in encouraging others to take on this role, so that too much responsibility does not fall to the parents alone.

Family Life Cycle

Families differ in *characteristics*, and those differences influence the *interaction* patterns that affect the ability of the family to meet its *functional* needs. Each family is a unique unit. Each unique unit *changes* as it progresses through stages and transitions of the *family life cycle*. Two dimensions of the family life cycle important for educators to understand include: (a) life cycle stages and (b) life cycle transitions.

Life Cycle Stages. In the past, the family life cycle has been described as a series of developmental stages that are periods of time in which family functions are relatively stable (Duvall, 1957). Many tasks facing families of adolescents are different from those facing families of preschoolers. Researchers and theorists disagree concerning the number of life-cycle stages that exist. Some have identified as many as 24 stages, although others have identified as few as six (A.P. Turnbull & Turnbull, 1997). The number is not nearly so important as the tasks that families are responsible for accomplishing at each stage. Six stages are identified here: (a) birth and early childhood, (b) elementary school years, (c) adolescence, (d) early adulthood, (e) middle adulthood, and (f) aging.

Now that Libby Bridge is about to leave elementary school and enter a middle school, she also is about to change physically and perhaps emotionally. The impending changes raise discomfiting issues. Who, for example, will teach or assist her as her menstrual cycles begin? Given that Libby is unable to provide any self-care and that all of her needs have been taken care of by family or teachers, what roles will they have with respect to her adult physical changes?

Table 2–1 identifies possible parental issues encountered at the first four life cycle stages, which are the stages in which families and educators have the most contact.

Although some families' tasks and issues tend to be stage-specific, others tend to permeate all stages. An example of two permeating issues are the families' emphasis on advocating for inclusive experiences and on developing self-determination skills. In regard to advocating for inclusive experiences, many families strongly favor inclusion (Erwin & Soodak, 1995; Guralnick, 1994; Ryndak, Downing, Jacqueline, & Morrison, 1995) and are the major advocates for their children in obtaining inclusive experiences starting during the early childhood stage and continuing throughout the entire life span. As inclusion advocates, families often invest tremendous energy at each life span stage to access experiences that enable their children to be in typical settings:

1. Birth and early childhood: Participating in the nursery within their religious organization, attending neighborhood and community playgroups and childcare, participating in community recreation programs designed for young children
2. Elementary school years: Attending neighborhood schools and being placed in general education programs, taking advantage of typical extracurricular activities such as Scouts and community recreation, developing friendships with classmates with and without disability
3. Adolescence: Attending inclusive secondary schools, participating in extracurricular activities consistent with preferences, enjoying friendships and dating
4. Early adulthood: Participating in supported employment, developing a home of one's own, participating in community activities consistent with preferences.

Families who commit themselves early to inclusion and advocate for inclusive experiences across the lifestyle often spend an incredible amount of time and energy in educating others, making logistic and support arrangements, and trouble-shooting when special issues arise. Many families are unfamiliar with the American school system and the laws that govern it (including especially IDEA). Some parents, like Ms. Hanaoka, come from a cultural tradition of deference to professionals, relatively nondirect advocacy, and

TABLE 2–1
Possible Parental Issues Encountered at Four Life Cycle Stages

Life Cycle Stage	Parents
Early childhood (ages 0–5)	
	Obtaining an accurate diagnosis
	Informing siblings and relatives
	Locating support services
	Clarifying a personal ideology to guide decisions
	Addressing issues of stigma
	Identifying positive contributions of exceptionality
	Participating in IFSP/IEP conferences
	Learning about IDEA rights and responsibilities
Elementary school (ages 6–12)	
	Establishing routines to carry out family functions
	Adjusting emotionally to implications of disability
	Clarifying issues of inclusive practices
	Participating in IEP conferences
	Locating community resources
	Arranging for extracurricular activities
	Establishing positive working relationships with professionals
	Gathering information about educational services available to the family and the child
	Setting great expectations about the future for their child
	Understanding different instructional strategies
Adolescence (ages 12–21)	
	Adjusting emotionally to possible chronicity of disability
	Identifying issues of emerging sexuality
	Addressing possible peer isolation and rejection
	Planning for career and vocational development
	Arranging for leisure-time activities
	Dealing with physical and emotional change of puberty
	Planning for postsecondary education
	Planning for the transition from school to adult life
	Addressing issues of preferred postschool outcomes
Adulthood (from age 21)	
	Addressing the need for preferred living situations
	Adjusting emotionally to adult implications for intensive support
	Addressing the need for socialization opportunities outside the family
	Initiating career choice or vocational program
	Adjusting to the changes that adult life will have on family decision making

close family interdependence. Professionals who tell parents that they "must advocate" for inclusion may be cutting across the grain of family life, even though their efforts are well-intended and may be culturally appropriate for the majority of students in American schools. Professionals can become reliable allies with families in (a) fostering inclusive experiences both within and outside of the school and (b) anticipating future barriers to inclusion and helping to eliminate them. Many families would be relieved to feel that the bulk of advocacy is not on their shoulders (Mlawer, 1993).

A second permeating issue across the life span is the development of self-determination skills. These skills help children and youth with severe disabilities to live their lives according to their own personal values and preferences. Although the major emphasis within the special education field has been on the development of self-determination skills at the adolescent level (Powers et al., 1996; Sands &

Wehmeyer, 1996), it is critically important for families and educators to recognize that the foundation of self-determination starts during the birth and early childhood stage and evolves throughout the entire life span (Brown & Cohen, 1996). Early on, families determine, explicitly or implicitly, the extent to which they value and emphasize opportunities for their son or daughter to express preferences and make choices. Consistent with their cultural values, families carry out tasks at each stage that contribute to either enhancing or impeding the development of self-determination skills.

There are a number of barriers that challenge both families and professionals in the life cycle enhancement of self-determination, including (a) being unclear about the extent of self-determination that is appropriate to expect, (b) being unfamiliar with instructional strategies to teach self-determination skills, (c) having cultural clashes with the expression of self-determination, and (d) giving priority to attending to other needs of the child and placing self-determination at a lower level of priority (Powers et al., 1996). From the earliest years, families and professionals must clarify their values and priorities related to self-determination and recognize that its development is a long-term life cycle issue (Powers et al., 1996). Getting that kind of clarification is important now for the Bridge family and Libby's teachers; her entry into middle school is a good time to discuss these matters, especially since IDEA now requires transition planning to begin when Libby is 14 years old. Likewise, Emily's teachers may want to discuss Ms. Hanaoka's culturally based expectations for Emily's independence.

Life Cycle Transitions. Transitions represent the periods of change as families move from one developmental stage to another. One way to think about life cycle stages and transitions is that stages are similar to plateaus, and transitions resemble peaks and valleys that divide those plateaus. Because transitional times represent changes in expectations and often in service systems, they are typically the times that families identify as the most challenging (Westling, 1996). These transitions involve movement from the intensive care nursery to the home and community, from early intervention to preschool, from preschool to kindergarten, from elementary to middle school (as for Libby Bridge), from middle school to high school, and from high school into adulthood (Able-Boone &

Stevens, 1994; Brown et al., 1988; Halvorsen, Doering, Farron-Davis, Usilton, & Sailor, 1989; Rosenkoetter, Haines, & Fowler, 1994; H.R. Turnbull, Turnbull, Bronicki, Summers, & Roeder-Gordon, 1989).

Cultural values strongly influence life cycle issues—both stages and transitions. For example, Navajo youth typically are regarded as adults just after puberty in contrast to most Euro-American youth, who are generally seen as adults around ages 18 to 21 (Deyhle & LeCompte, 1994). Sexual maturity for females is celebrated in a Navajo puberty ceremony referred to as *Kinaalva*. After this ceremony, pregnancy, even at an early age, has a very different meaning than it does from a Euro-American perspective (Deyhle & LeCompte, 1994). Thus, it is critically important to view appropriate transition timing from a cultural point of view.

Different cultures have various kinds of cultural rituals that they consider appropriate: e.g., baptism, first communion, bar or bat mitzvah, graduation, and voting. Because these rituals serve as symbols of ongoing development for the family, they help to reorient family perspectives toward the changes that are occurring throughout transition. A special challenge for families who have a child with severe disabilities is that the child often does not have access to many of these rituals and therefore does not have the experience of transition. You can support families by encouraging them to participate in rituals and helping them make the inclusion of their child possible. In addition to participation in celebrations and rituals, there are many other ways that professionals can work collaboratively with families in enhancing successful transitions. Figure 2–6 includes tips for doing this.

Educational Implications of Family Life Cycle
We must provide support consistent with life cycle stages and transitions according to each families' preferences, strengths, and needs. A key element is recognizing the individual uniqueness of each family and how that uniqueness influences what they consider to be appropriate at various life cycle stages and during transitional periods. There has been a strong emphasis in the special education literature on the transition of youth with disabilities from school to adulthood; this transitional planning is now mandated to begin at age 14. A key role of educators is to support families throughout the transitional process (Blue-Banning, 1997; Everson & Moon, 1987; McNair

FIGURE 2–6

Tips for Enhancing Successful Transitions

Early Childhood

- Begin preparing for the separation of preschool children from parents by periodically leaving the child with others.
- Gather information and visit preschools in the community.
- Encourage participation in "Parent to Parent" programs, in which veteran parents are matched in one-to-one relationships with parents who are just beginning the transition process.
- Familiarize parents with possible school (elementary and secondary) programs, career options, or adult programs, so they have an idea of future opportunities.

Childhood

- Provide parents with an overview of curricular options.
- Ensure that IEP meetings provide an empowering context for family collaboration.
- Encourage participation in "Parent to Parent" matches, workshops, or family support groups to discuss transitions with others.

Adolescence

- Assist families and adolescents in identifying community leisure-time activities.
- Incorporate into the IEP skills that will be needed in future career and vocational programs.
- Visit or become familiar with a variety of career and living options.
- Develop a mentor relationship with an adult with a similar disability and with an individual who has a career that matches the student's strengths and preferences.

Adulthood

- Provide preferred information to families about guardianship, estate planning, wills, and trusts.
- Assist family members in transferring responsibilities to the individual with an exceptionality, other family members, or service providers, as appropriate.
- Assist the young adult or family members with career or vocational choices.
- Address the issues and responsibilities of marriage and family for the young adult.

  Planning for Angela

  Box 2–3   *Background*

Angela Sloan, who has a moderate-to-severe disability, has just turned age 16 and is in her first year in your high school career education class. You are considering a variety of community jobs for her, but you are faced with a difficult family situation. Angela's parents have gone through an adversarial divorce, and they are not on speaking terms with each other. Ms. Sloan, Angela's mother, regularly attends parent-teacher conferences and IEP meetings and communicates often using a notebook that goes between home and school. Mr. Sloan also has expressed an interest in being kept informed of what is happening with his daughter.

Ms. Sloan is concerned with Angela's functional academic and socialization skills. She has strongly expressed her preference that Angela stay in school and spend her days attending inclusive classes, such as home economics, child development, and computer literacy.

On the other hand, Mr. Sloan has discussed with you his preference that Angela spend as much time working as possible. He has a friend who owns a clothing store. The friend has told Mr. Sloan that Angela will have a job there when she graduates. Mr. Sloan believes that if Angela begins developing job skills for the clothing store now, she can graduate at 18 and go to work.

Angela spent part of last year working in an office through the career education program. She was very proud of her job, and she was sad when school ended and a summer job placement could not be arranged. Angela has expressed her desire to work in an office again. Lately, she has been moody and uncooperative when others in her class leave to go to work, and she attends the computer literacy class. You appreciate all points of view but tend to believe that Angela's preferences should be honored.

Issue: Whose Preferences Are Acted Upon?

Discussing this issue with both parents is going to be difficult. They are at opposite ends of the spectrum, yet both have valid reasons for their positions. Whatever your decision, it will appear that you are siding with one parent over the other or with Angela. Therefore, compromise is needed. In addition, respecting the preference of Angela, who appears to be acting in a self-determining way, is crucial.

You think that a person-centered planning process will prove valuable (see chapter 3). You want to get together with Angela, her parents, friends, advocates, and other professionals to formulate a vision of what Angela's life could look like and to develop an action plan. However, bringing together the parents in a large-group situation may prove either extremely positive or detrimental to the process as a whole. Before jumping into a group situation, you consider the following options:

1. Help Ms. Sloan understand the importance of vocational preparation, and emphasize that such preparation can include more than job skills. Angela can work on social skills and begin to establish a circle of work friends who will still be there when her school friends graduate.
2. Talk with Mr. Sloan about the need to allow maximum growth and opportunities for Angela. Graduation at age 18 may be premature for her. If his friend has promised a job, it may be there in 2 years or in 5 years.
3. Compromise on community vocational experiences for the time being. Set up appropriate in-school job training experiences, such as working in the school office, which would be consistent with Angela's preferences for office work.
4. Start small. Get each stakeholder to compromise on at least one thing. The job in school may appease everyone for the time being, until you can work on the rest.
5. Begin to talk with Mr. and Ms. Sloan about their perceptions of Angela. Look at her desire to establish some independence and to state her preferences. Encourage Angela to make her own decisions at school. It may be difficult for Mr. and Mrs. Sloan to support Angela's self-determination. Keep this in mind. Provide examples of how Angela is expressing her preferences and making decisions at school.
6. Have the parents come to see Angela working in school. Point out her pride and self-esteem when she works.
7. Gradually increase Angela's time in community settings, including vocational sites. It may be for 1 hour this year, 2 hours the next, and so on. As you build trust with Mr. and Ms. Sloan, they will begin to understand your position, and you will begin to understand theirs.

What other options can you suggest?

& Rusch, 1991). Features of person-centered planning, as discussed in chapter 3, can be used (a) to bring together family, professionals, friends, and community citizens; (b) to envision the preferred life from the perspective of the individual and family; and (c) to work together to translate that vision into daily and weekly supports and services (A.P. Turnbull, Blue-Banning, Anderson, Turnbull, Seaton, & Dinas, 1996; A.P. Turnbull & Turnbull, 1996).

Summary

Historically, parent and professional partnerships have not been as positive and productive as they might be. The Individuals with Disabilities Education Act (IDEA) has established ground rules for both educational professionals and parents in their interactions with each other. Associated with each of the six major principles of the law—zero reject,

nondiscriminatory evaluation, appropriate education programs, least restrictive alternative, parent and student participation in shared decision making, and due process—are requirements for family-professional partnerships.

IDEA alone does not ensure collaboration among parents and professionals. All parties must work within the guidelines to develop partnerships to meet families' individual needs and preferences. Preferred educational roles of parents and other family members vary from one family to the next. Likewise, the level of involvement sought by different family members fluctuates.

Professionals must be encouraged to view students within the broader context of family life. A family systems perspective recognizes the true complexity of families and offers a framework to understand the characteristics, interactions, functions, and life cycle issues of families.

The challenge is exciting. Appropriately preparing individuals who have severe disabilities with the academic, social, emotional, and vocational skills to function in society is complex. It requires innovative efforts by families and professionals working toward shared goals. The possibilities are boundless, and the benefits for persons with disabilities are unlimited if all parties apply their energies and imaginations in a partnership of progress.

Suggested Activities

Activity 1: Gaining a Family Systems Perspective

1. Synthesize what you know about the Hanaoka and Bridge families in terms of the four components of the family systems perspective: characteristics, interaction, functions, and life cycle.
2. For each of these components, list two steps that you might take if you were a general or special educator working with these students and families to support them in an individualized way.
3. What steps would you take to establish a partnership with each family regarding nondiscriminatory evaluation and IEP participation, based on the IDEA requirements and what you know about their family system preferences, needs, and strengths?

Activity 2: A Tale of Two Families

The Angelino Family

The Angelino family has five children, and a sixth is on the way. The children are ages 14 (girl), 12 (boy), 10 (girl), 7 (boy), and 6 (girl). They all attend a nearby parochial school. Mr. Angelino owns a butcher shop that had been his father's and that was begun by his grandfather, who immigrated from Italy in 1904. The butcher shop at one time had living quarters upstairs for the family, but about 10 years ago, the family moved into a large, Victorian-style house about a block away.

Mr. Angelino's youngest brother once came back from college with ideas about expanding the business and marketing the family's secret recipe for Italian sausage, but Mr. Angelino (the oldest son) decided against it because it would take too much time away from the family. He is fond of saying, "We ain't rich, but we got a roof over our heads, food in our bellies,

and each other. What more could we want?" This youngest brother is the only one in the family with a college education, and he is also the only one who scandalized the family by marrying a non-Catholic. Mr. Angelino uses his little brother as an example of the detrimental effects of "too much education."

Both Mr. and Ms. Angelino come from large families; most of their brothers and sisters still live in the "Little Italy" section of this large eastern city. All grandparents are dead, with the exception of Ms. Angelino's mother (Mama). Mama lives in the home with them and is very frail. One of Ms. Angelino's brothers or sisters is sure to stop by nearly every day, bringing children, flowers, or food, for a visit with Mama. They often take Mama for drives or to their homes for short visits, depending on her health, and help with her basic care.

Life with the Angelinos can be described as a kind of happy chaos. Kids are always running in and out of the butcher shop, where the older brothers and male cousins are often assigned small tasks in return for a piece of salami or some other treat. The old house is always full of children—siblings and cousins—from teenagers to toddlers. Children are pretty much indulged until they reach age 9 or 10, at which time they are expected to begin taking responsibility, which is divided strictly along traditional gender-role lines. Child care, cooking, and cleaning are accomplished by the women: older sisters or cousins, aunts or mothers. Evening meals are a social event. There is virtually always at least one extended family member or friend at the table, and everyone talks about the events of the day, sometimes all at once, except when Mr. Angelino has something to say, whereupon everyone stops to listen. Mr. Angelino is obviously a very affectionate father, but he expects his word to be obeyed. Bed times, rules about talking at the table, curfews, and other rules are strictly enforced. This situation is beginning to cause conflict with the oldest daughter, who wants to date and spend more time with her friends from school. Ms. Angelino is often sympathetic to her children's requests, but her husband has the final say.

All in all, life in the Angelino home is warm, close, and harmonious. Ms. Angelino, as she approaches her eighth month of pregnancy with this last "surprise" child, shares her contentment with her priest: "I don't know what I have done to deserve so many blessings from the Good Lord."

The McNeil Family

Mr. and Ms. McNeil have been married for 2 years, and she is expecting their first child. Mr. McNeil is the youngest partner in a prestigious law firm in this Midwestern city. Everybody considers him upwardly mobile and thinks it phenomenal that he should achieve a partnership only 3 years out of law school. Ms. McNeil has a degree in interior design. She worked full-time for a while for a decorating firm in another city. After her marriage, Ms. McNeil moved to this city, where she has a part-time, on-call job with an exclusive architectural firm. She has ambitions of starting her own business.

Mr. McNeil is an only child. His parents live on the East Coast. They are both successful in business—his father is a banker, his mother a real estate broker. They have always demanded perfection from their son, and he seems to have lived up to their expectations. Ms. McNeil has one younger sister. Her parents live on the West Coast. They are both professional persons: her father is a college professor and her mother is a social worker. Ms. McNeil's family has always been very close. She calls her parents about once a week, and the family occasionally has conference calls with the parents and the two siblings to decide some important issue or to relay some big news. Ms. McNeil's parents place no demands on her except that she be true to herself. They often tell her how proud they are of her accomplishments.

Both sets of parents are experiencing grandparenthood for the first time with Ms. McNeil's pregnancy. They are thrilled. It sometimes seems to the McNeils that their parents vie with each other in the gifts they give them. The McNeils refuse the more extravagant gifts to make the point that they are indeed making it on their own, and they have discussed some strategies for disentangling themselves from so much contact with their parents.

The McNeils' avant-garde apartment is the scene of much entertaining: his law firm associates and her artistic friends and decorating clients. Although their social spheres overlap somewhat, each has separate groups of friends, and pursues individual interests. They call this "giving each other space," and they consider it an important strength in their marriage. The McNeils believe strongly in supporting each other's careers and in sharing family responsibilities; they divide cooking and cleaning in a flexible way, according to whoever has the time. They are also attending Lamaze classes together and are looking forward to sharing childbirth.

Exercise

The babies Ms. Angelino and Ms. McNeil are expecting will have a severe cognitive and physical disability.

1. Use the family systems framework to predict the preferences, strengths, and needs of both families in terms of characteristics, interaction, function, and life cycle.
2. The Angelinos and McNeils have different cultural values. How would you characterize the cultural values of each family? How do you think these cultural values influence what they consider to be appropriate self-determination for each of the parents (mother and father), as well as for their children with and without a disability (assume that the McNeils have more children who do not have a disability).
3. Given their views on appropriate levels of self-determination, identify two ways that you might work with each family in addressing self-determination within a culturally responsive framework.

References

Abbott, D. A., & Meredeth, W. H. (1986). Strengths of parents with retarded children. *Family Relations, 35,* 371–375.

Able-Boone, H., & Stevens, E. (1994). After the intensive-care nursery experience: Families' perceptions of their well-being. *Children's Health Care, 23*(2), 99–114.

Agosta, J. M., Bass, A., & Spence, R. (1986). *The needs of the family: Results of a statewide survey in Massachusetts.* Cambridge, MA: Human Services Institute.

Baker, B. L. (1984). Interventions with families with young, severely handicapped children. In J. Blacher (Ed.), *Severely handicapped young children and their families: Research in review* (pp. 319–376). Orlando, FL: Academic Press.

Behr, S. K., & Murphy, D. L. (1993). *Kansas inventory of parental perceptions: User's manual.* Lawrence: University of Kansas, Beach Center on Families and Disability.

Benson, B. A., & Gross, A. M. (1989). The effect of a congenitally handicapped child upon the marital dyad: A review of the literature. *Clinical Psychology Review, 9,* 747–758.

Bertalanffy, L. von. (1975). General system theory. In B. D. Ruben & J. Y. Kim (Eds.), *General systems theory and human communication* (pp. 6–20). Rochelle Park, NJ: Hayden.

Birenbaum, A., & Cohen, H. J. (1993). On the importance of helping families: Policy implications from a national study. *Mental Retardation, 31,* 67–74.

Blue-Banning, M. J. (1997). *The transition of Hispanic adolescents with disabilities to adulthood: Parent and professional perspectives.* Unpublished doctoral dissertation, University of Kansas, Lawrence.

Board of Education v. Rowley, 458 U. S. 176, 102 S. Ct. 3034, 73 L. Ed., 2d 690 (1982).

Braddock, D., Hemp, R., & Parish, S. (1997). Emergence of individual and family support in state service-delivery systems. *Mental Retardation, 35*, 497–498.

Braddock, D., Hemp, R., Parish, S., & Westrich, J. (1998). *The state of the states in developmental disabilities* (5th ed.). Washington, DC: American Association on Mental Retardation.

Bradley, V., Knoll, J., & Agosta, J. (1993). *Emerging issues in family support* (Monograph No. 18). Washington, DC: American Association on Mental Retardation.

Brotherson, M. J. (1985). *Planning for adult futures: Parents' self-report of futures planning and its relationship to family functioning and stress with sons and daughters who are disabled.* Unpublished doctoral dissertation, University of Kansas, Lawrence.

Brown & Cohen (1996). Self-determination and young children. *Journal of the Association for Persons with Severe Handicaps, 21*(1), 22–30.

Brown, L., Albright, K. Z., Rogan, P., York, J., Solner, A. U., Johnson, F., VanDeventer, P., & Loomis, R. (1988). An integrated curriculum model for transition. In B. L. Ludlow, A. P. Turnbull, & R. Luckasson (Eds.), *Transitions to adult life for people with mental retardation: Principles and practices* (pp. 45–66). Baltimore: Paul H. Brookes.

Burton, S. L., & Parks, A. L. (1994). College-aged siblings of individuals with disabilities. *Social Work Research, 18*(3), 178–185.

Carnes, P. J. (1981). *Family development 1: Understanding us.* Minneapolis, MN: Interpersonal Communications Programs.

Carr, J. (1988). Six weeks to twenty-one years old: A longitudinal study of children with Down syndrome and their families. *Journal of Child Psychology and Psychiatry, 29*, 407–431.

Deyhle, D., & LeCompte, M. (1994). Cultural differences in child development: Navajo adolescents in middle schools. *Theory into Practice, 33*(3), 156–165.

Duvall, E. (1957). *Family development.* Philadelphia: Lippincott.

Erwin, E. J., & Soodak, L. C. (1995). I never knew I could stand up to the system: Families' perspectives on pursuing inclusive education. *Journal of the Association for Persons with Severe Handicaps, 20*, 136–146.

Everson, J. M., & Moon, M. S. (1987). Transition services for young adults with severe disabilities: Defining professional and parental roles and responsibilities. *Journal of the Association for Persons with Severe Handicaps, 12*(2), 87–95.

Falvey, M. A., Forest, M., Pearpoint, J., & Rosenberg, R. (1994). Building connections. In J. S. Thousand, R. A. Villa, & A. I. Nevin (Eds.), *Creativity and collaborative learning: A practical guide to empowering students and teachers* (pp. 347–368). Baltimore: Paul H. Brookes.

Fujiura, G. T., Roccoforte, J. A., & Braddock, D. (1994). Costs of family care for adults with mental retardation and related developmental disabilities. *American Journal on Mental Retardation, 99*, 250–261.

Fujiura, G. T., & Yamaki, K. (1997). Analysis of ethnic variations in developmental disability prevalence and household economic status. *Mental Retardation, 35*, 286–294.

Gath, A. (1977). The impact of an abnormal child on the parents. *British Journal of Psychiatry, 130*, 405–410.

Glidden, L. M. (1989). *Parents for children, children for parents: The adoption alternative.* Washington, DC: American Association on Mental Retardation.

Goldstein, S., Strickland, B., Turnbull, A. P., Curry, L. (1980). An observational analysis of the IEP conference. *Exceptional Children, 46*, 278–286.

Gopaul-McNicol, S.-A. (1997). *A multicultural/multimodel/multisystems approach to working with culturally different families.* Westport, CT: Praeger.

Gottwald, S. R., & Thurman, S. K. (1994). The effects of prenatal cocaine exposure on mother-infant interaction and infant arousal in the newborn period. *Topics in Early Childhood Special Education, 14*, 217–231.

Grossman, H. (1995). *Special education in a diverse society.* Boston: Allyn & Bacon.

Guralnick, M. J. (1994). Mothers' perceptions of the benefits and drawbacks of early childhood mainstreaming. *Journal of Early Intervention, 18*, 168–183.

Halvorsen, A. T., Doering, K., Farron-Davis, F., Usilton, R., & Sailor, W. (1989). The role of parents and family members in planning severely disabled students' transitions from school. In G. H. S. Singer & L. K. Irvin (Eds.), *Support for caregiving families* (pp. 253–268). Baltimore: Brookes.

Hamre-Nietupski, S. (1993). How much time should be spent on skill instruction and friendship development? Preferences of parents of students with moderate and severe/profound disabilities. *Education and Training in Mental Retardation, 28*, 220–231.

Hamre-Nietupski, S., Hendrickson, J., Nietupski, J., & Sasso, G. (1993, June). Perceptions of teachers of students with moderate, severe, or profound disabilities on facilitating friendships with nondisabled peers. *Education and Training in Mental Retardation*, pp. 111–127.

Hamre-Nietupski, S., Hendrickson, J., Nietupski, J., & Shokoohi-Yekta, M. (1994). Regular educators' perceptions of facilitating friendships of students with moderate, severe, or profound disabilities with nondisabled peers. *Education and Training in Mental Retardation, 29*(2), 102–117.

Hanson, M. J. (1992). Families with Anglo-European roots. In E. W. Lynch & M. J. Hanson (Eds.), *Developing cross-cultural competence: A guide for working with young children and their families* (pp. 63–88). Baltimore: Paul H. Brookes.

Hanson, M. J., & Carta, J. J. (1995). Addressing the challenges of families with multiple risks. *Exceptional Children, 62*, 201–212.

Harkness, S., & Super, C. M. (Eds.). (1996). *Parents' cultural belief systems: Their origins, expressions, and consequences.* New York: Guilford Press.

Harry, B. (1992). An ethnographic study of cross-cultural communication with Puerto Rican-American families in the special education system. *American Educational Research Journal, 29*, 471–494.

Harry, B., Allen, N., & McLaughlin, M. (1995). Communication versus compliance: African-American parents' involvement in special education. *Exceptional Children, 61*, 364–377.

Harry, B., Grenot-Scheyer, M., Smith-Lewis, M., Park, H.S., Xin, F., & Schwartz, I. (1995). Developing culturally inclusive services for individuals with severe disabilities. *Journal of the Association for Persons with Severe Handicaps, 20*(2), 99–109.

Harry, B., Kalyanpur, M. (1994). Cultural underpinnings of special education: Implications for professional interaction with culturally diverse families. *Disability and Society, 9*(2), 145–165.

Herman, S. E., & Marcenko, M. O. (1997). Perceptions of services and resources as mediators of depression among parents of children with developmental disabilities. *Mental Retardation, 35,* 458–467.

Honig v. Doe, 484 U. S. 305, 108 S. Ct. 592, 98 L. Ed. 2d 686 (1988).

Horner, R. H., & Carr, E. G. (1997). Behavioral support for students with severe disabilities: Functional assessment and comprehensive intervention. *Journal of Special Education, 31,* 84–104.

Individuals with Disabilities Education Act, 20 U. S. C. § § 1400 *et seq.* (1997).

Jones, D. E., Clatterbuck, C. C., Marquis, J. G., Turnbull, H. R., & Moberly, R. L. (1996). Educational placements for children who are ventilator assisted. *Exceptional Children, 63,* 47–58.

Kazak, A. E., & Marvin, R. S. (1984). Differences, difficulties, and adaptation: Stress and social networks in families with a handicapped child. *Family Relations, 33,* 67–77.

Klass, C. S. (1996). *Home visiting: Promoting healthy parent and child development.* Baltimore: Paul H. Brookes.

Kozol, J. (1995). *Amazing grace: The lives of children and the conscience of a nation.* New York: Crown.

Kreutzer, J. S., Serio, C. D., & Bergquist, S. (1994). Family needs after brain injury: A quantitative analysis. *Journal of Head Trauma Rehabilitation, 9*(3), 104–115.

Kritek, P. B. (1994). *Negotiating at an uneven table: Developing moral courage in resolving our conflicts.* San Francisco: Jossey-Bass.

Lichtenstein, J. (1993). Help for troubled marriages. In G. H. S. Singer & L. E. Powers (Eds.), *Families, disability, and empowerment* (pp. 259–277). Baltimore: Paul H. Brookes.

Llewellyn, G. (1995). Relationships and social support: Views of parents with mental retardation/intellectual disability. *Mental Retardation, 33,* 349–363.

Lynch, E. W., & Hanson, M. J. (Eds.). (1992). *Developing cross-cultural competence: A guide for working with young children and their families.* Baltimore: Paul H. Brookes.

Markey, U. A. (1997). Valuing all families. *Tapestry: Weaving Sustaining Threads, 1*(3), 1.

Martin, A. (1993). *The lesbian and gay parenting handbook: Creating and raising our families.* New York: HarperCollins.

Martin, J. E., & Marshall, L. H. (1996). ChoiceMaker: Infusing self-determination. In D. J. Sands & M. L. Wehmeyer (Eds.), *Self-determination across the life span: Independence and choice for people with disabilities.* Baltimore: Paul H. Brookes.

McHale, S. M., & Gamble, W. C. (1989). Sibling relationships and the adjustment of children with disabled brothers and sisters. *Journal of Children in Contemporary Science, 19,* 131–138.

McNair, J., & Rusch, F. R. (1991). Parent involvement in transition programs. *Mental Retardation, 29,* 93–101.

Meyer, D. J. (Ed.). (1997). *Views from our shoes: Growing up with a brother or sister with special needs.* Bethesda, MD: Woodbine House.

Meyer, D. J., & Vadasy, P. F. (1994). *Sibshops: Workshops for siblings of children with special needs.* Baltimore: Brookes.

Meyer, H., Park, H. S., Grenot-Scheyer, M., Schwartz, I. S., & Harry, B. (1998). *Making friends: The influences of culture and development.* Baltimore: Brookes.

Muccigrosso, L., Scavarda, M., Simpson-Brown, R., & Thalacker, B. E. (1991). *Double jeopardy: Pregnant and parenting youth in special education.* Reston, VA: Council for Exceptional Children.

Mlawer, M. A. (1993). Who should fight? Parents and the advocacy expectation. *Journal of Disability Policy Studies, 4*(1), 105–115.

Murphy, A. T. (1982). The family with a handicapped child: A review of the literature. *Developmental and Behavioral Pediatrics, 3*(2), 73–82.

O'Hare, W. P. (1996). A new look at poverty in America. *Population Bulletin, 51*(2), 2–48.

Olson, D. H., Russell, C. S., & Sprenkle, D. H. (1980). Marital and family therapy: A decade review. *Journal of Marriage and the Family, 42,* 973–993.

Powers, L. E., Singer, G. H. S., & Sowers, J.-A. (Eds.). (1996). *On the road to autonomy: Promoting self-competence in children and youth with disabilities.* Baltimore: Paul H. Brookes.

Ronai, C. R. (1997). On loving and hating my mentally retarded mother. *Mental Retardation, 35,* 417–432.

Rosenkoetter, S. E., Haines, A. H., & Fowler, S. A. (1994). *Bridging early services for children with special needs and their families: A practical guide for transition planning.* Baltimore: Paul H. Brookes.

Ryndak, D. L., Downing, J. E., Jacqueline, L. R., & Morrison, A. P. (1995). Parents' perceptions after inclusion of their children with mild or severe disabilities. *Journal of the Association for Persons with Severe Handicaps, 20,* 147–157.

Sands, D. J., & Wehmeyer, M. L. (Eds.). (1996). *Self-determination across the life span: Independence and choice for people with disabilities.* Baltimore: Paul H. Brookes.

Satir, V. (1972). *Peoplemaking.* Palo Alto, CA: Science and Behavior Books.

Schaffner, C. B., & Buswell, B. E. (1992). *Connecting students: A guide to thoughtful friendship facilitation for educators and families.* Colorado Springs: PEAK Parent Center.

Seligman, M., Goodwin, G., Paschal, K., Applegate, A., & Lehman, L. (1997, December). Grandparents of children with disabilities: Perceived levels of support. *Education and Training in Mental Retardation and Developmental Disabilities,* 293–303.

Sherman, A. (1994). *Wasting America's future: The Children's Defense Fund report on the costs of child poverty.* Boston: Beacon Press.

Shriver, M. D., & Piersel, W. (1994). The long-term effects of intrauterine drug exposure: Review of recent research and implications for early childhood special education. *Topics in Early Childhood Special Education, 14,* 161–183.

Singer, G. H. S., & Nixon, C. D. (1996). A report on the concerns of parents of children with acquired brain injury. In G. H. S. Singer, A. Glang, & J. Williams (Eds.), *Children with acquired brain injury: Educating and supporting families* (pp. 23–52). Baltimore: Brookes.

Singer, G. H. S., Powers, L. E., & Olson, A. L. (Eds.). (1996). *Redefining family support: Innovations in public/private partnerships.* Baltimore: Paul H. Brookes.

Sowers, J. A., Glang, A. E., Voss, J., & Cooley, E. (1996). Enhancing friendships and leisure involvements of students with traumatic brain injuries and other disabilities. In L. E. Powers, G. H. S. Singer, & J.-A. Sowers (Eds.), *On the road to autonomy: Promoting self-competence in children and youth with disabilities* (pp. 347–372). Baltimore: Paul H. Brookes.

Stayton, V. D., & Karnes, M. B. (1994). Model programs for infants and toddlers with disabilities and their families. In L. J. Johnson, R. J. Gallagher, M. J. LaMontagne, J. B. Jordan, J. J. Gallagher, P. L. Hutinger, M. B. Karnes (Ed.), *Meeting early intervention challenges: Issues from birth to three* (pp. 33–58). Baltimore: Paul H. Brookes.

Summers, J. A., Behr, S. K., & Turnbull, A. P. (1989). Positive adaptation and coping strengths of families who have children with disabilities. In G. H. S. Singer, & Irvin, L. K. (Eds.), *Support for caregiving families: Enabling positive adaptation to disability* (pp. 27–40). Baltimore: Paul H. Brookes.

Taylor, L., Zuckerman, B., Harik, V., & Groves, B. (1994). Witnessing violence by young children and their mothers. *Journal of Developmental and Behavioral Pediatrics*, 15, 120–123.

Turnbull, A. P., Blue-Banning, M. J., Anderson, E. L., Turnbull, H. R., Seaton, K. A., & Dinas, P. A. (1996). Enhancing self-determination through Group Action Planning: A holistic emphasis. In D. J. Sands & M. L. Wehmeyer (Eds.), *Self-determination across the life span: Independence and choice for people with disabilities* (pp. 237–256). Baltimore: Paul H. Brookes.

Turnbull, A. P., Pereira, L., & Blue-Banning, M. J. (in press). Parents' facilitation of friendships between their children with a disability and friends without a disability. *Journal of the Association for Persons with Severe Handicaps*.

Turnbull, A. P., & Ruef, M. (1997). Family perspectives on inclusive lifestyle issues for people with problem behavior. *Exceptional Children*, 63, 211–227.

Turnbull, A. P., & Summers, J. A. (1987). From parent involvement to family support: Evolution to revolution. In S. M. Pueschel, Tingey, C., Rynders, J. W., Crocher, A. C., & Crutcher, D. M. (Eds.), *New perspectives on Down syndrome: Proceedings on the state-of-the-art conference* (pp. 289–306). Baltimore: Paul H. Brookes.

Turnbull, A. P., & Turnbull, H. R. (1996). Self-determination within a culturally responsive family systems perspective: Balancing the family mobile. In L. E. Powers, G. H. S. Singer, & J.-A. Sowers (Eds.), *On the road to autonomy: Promoting self-competence in children and youth with disabilities* (pp. 195–220). Baltimore: Brookes.

Turnbull, A. P., & Turnbull, H. R. (1997). *Families, professionals, and exceptionality: A special partnership.* (3rd ed.). Upper Saddle River, NJ: Merrill/Prentice Hall.

Turnbull, H. R., Guess, D., & Turnbull, A. P. (1988). Vox populi and Baby Doe. *Mental Retardation*, 26, 127–132.

Turnbull, H. R., & Turnbull, A. P. (1982). Parent involvement in the education of handicapped children: A critique. *Mental Retardation*, 20(115–122).

Turnbull, H. R., & Turnbull, A. P., with Buchele-Ash, A., & Rainbolt, K. (1998). *Free appropriate public education: Law and the education of children with disabilities* (5th ed.). Denver, CO: Love.

Turnbull, H. R., Turnbull, A. P., Bronicki, G., Summers, J. A., & Roeder-Gordon, C. (1989). *Disability and the family: A guide to adulthood.* Baltimore: Paul H. Brookes.

U. S. Bureau of the Census. (1996). Almost half of the nation's chronic poor are children. *Census and You*, 31(9), 7.

U. S. Department of Education. (1997). *To assure the free appropriate public education of all children with disabilities: Nineteenth annual report to Congress on the implementation of the Individuals with Disabilities Education Act.* Washington, DC: Author.

Van Reusen, A. K., Deshler, D. D., & Schumaker, J. B. (1989). Effects of a student participation strategy in facilitating the involvement of adolescents with learning disabilities in the individualized education program planning process. *Learning Disabilities*, 1(2), 23–34.

Vaughn, S., Bos, C., Harrell, J., & Lasky, B. (1988). Parent involvement in the initial placement/IEP conference ten years after mandated involvement. *Journal of Learning Disabilities*, 21(2), 82–89.

Vig, S. (1996). Young children's exposure to community violence. *Journal of Early Intervention*, 20, 319–328.

Weigle, K. L. (1997). Positive behavioral support as a model for promoting educational inclusion. *Journal of the Association for Persons with Severe Handicaps*, 22, 36–48.

Westling, D. L. (1996, June). What do parents of children with moderate and severe disabilities want? *Education and Training in Mental Retardation and Developmental Disabilities*, 86–114.

Wilson, J., Blacher, J. & Baker, B. L. (1989). Siblings of children with severe handicaps. *Mental Retardation*, 27, 167–173.

Young, D. M., & Roopnarine, J. L. (1994). Fathers' child care involvement with children with and without disabilities. *Topics in Early Childhood Special Education*, 14, 488–502.

Meaningful Assessment

Fredda Brown
Martha E. Snell

Like their peers, students with more extensive support needs benefit from learning useful skills, from having social connections with others their age, and from belonging to and actively participating in groups (Billingsley, Gallucci, Peck, Schwartz, & Staub, 1996; Staub, Schwartz, Gallucci, & Peck, 1994). These three basic needs—skills, relationships, and membership—should not be a surprise: They are the same for all people. The presence of severe disabilities does not negate such needs, though the challenges for meeting them may be greater.

Timmy does not initiate greetings or play with others, but he knows how to wave when prompted and will play alone with blocks and Legos building blocks for long periods of time. He has just joined a preschool of students his age who do not have autism. His parents and teachers are hoping that this context will enable him to learn how to interact and engage in parallel and cooperative play with others his age. Timothy also participates in one-to-one instruction at home.

Jenny is a member of Ms. Alpern's fifth grade class and just joined Girl Scouts this year. Her classmates know that Jenny has more difficulty remembering things than they do but also that memory strategies, such as her personal daily schedule and calendar, which use picture reminders, a number line, and a calculator, help her to remember.

Christine, like many others with severe disabilities, has spent most of her school years attending self-contained classrooms with little opportunity to interact with nondisabled peers at school. As a result, she is lacking in school friends her age, in taking part in social activities with peers, and in the social skills characteristic of older teens. In the next three chapters, we will use these three student outcomes (i.e., skills, membership, and relationships) as a framework for describing the principles that teams follow as they develop and implement educational programs for students with severe disabilities in inclusive school settings. The outcomes for which team members aim influence the methods they use. Attending

67

school alongside peers without disabilities creates options that do not exist in separate, "handicapped only" settings, but it also changes teachers' roles in many ways. We will describe how these changes can create opportunities and reduce barriers. We recognize that while the number of schools practicing meaningful inclusion has increased in recent years, the majority of students with severe disabilities still experience very isolated lives apart from typical classmates, detached from peers in community activities and at work, and accompanied primarily by their family members or by paid companions. It is true that these patterns of segregated association and education are currently balanced in our country with laws to prevent discrimination against people with disabilities and to create the least restrictive educational environments (Bateman & Linden, 1998). Still, the widespread prevalence of their isolation seems to be maintained both by beliefs that separation is better and by rigid traditions, such as special buildings, programs designed for labeled groups of people, and the methods educators use to place students with disabilities. Another strong force, which blocks movement toward inclusion is the confusion that comes with inexperience and the anticipation of change. As Norm Kunc (1991) has expressed it: "Don't confuse 'I don't know how to do it' with 'it's not a good idea'." These next three chapters, and much of the entire book, are written to address this confusion and to teach readers how to educate students with severe disabilities in inclusive school settings.

In addition to this framework of desirable student outcomes (i.e., relationships, membership, and skills) in the organization of the next three chapters, three students, 4-year-old Timmy, 10-year-old Jenny, and 20-year-old Christine, help us illustrate the concepts we introduce and explain. Their brief case descriptions follow.

Timothy

Timothy is a 4-year-old child who has been diagnosed with autism. He has severe intellectual disabilities and is nonverbal. Timothy lives at home with his parents and his older sister, who is 7 years old. Timothy is a handsome little boy who does not appear to have any disabilities until he engages in any one of a variety of stereotyped behaviors (e.g., hand flapping, jumping up and down) or ritualistic behaviors (e.g., lining up objects, watching videotapes in a ritualistic way). When Timothy was diagnosed with autism at age 2, his mother, Ms. Simms, explored a variety of educational models that were available for young children with autism. Ms. Simms' exploration of autism involved searching the Internet for information on autism. To her delight, there was easy access to chat rooms and list serves on

autism, as well as an abundance of information ranging from basic knowledge about autism to finding family support groups and even how to sue your school district. She also went to a local bookstore and found about a dozen recently published books addressing young children with autism and their families (e.g., Cohen, 1998; Koegel & Koegel, 1995; Maurice, 1996). As she started to sift through all the material, she realized the conflict and controversy that existed in the field. Perhaps the only area in which there was agreement was that education should begin as early as possible, and should be intensive (Cohen, 1998). However, how intensive and what it looked like varied greatly.

Ms. Simms' decision about the best program for Timothy was a difficult one. Each model that she read about seemed to have advantages, focusing on different but important aspects of development. Each boasted successes. What was especially difficult was that most of the special education professionals she approached seemed to promote their own model to the exclusion of the others. No professionals were offering Ms. Simms an integrated, individually determined model for Timothy. Rather, each professional described how Timothy could fit into their model.

After much stress and anxiety about what the best course would be, Timothy's family finally decided to put several pieces together, regardless of the individual messages they received from professionals. The new program that they designed consisted of: 10 hours each week of one-to-one intensive discrete trial instruction at home, delivered by a specially trained graduate student; 3 hours each day in an inclusive preschool program; and two 1-hour sessions each week with a speech and language therapist at a clinic.

Jenny

Jenny is an expressive and energetic fifth grader who experienced trauma during birth, resulting in some degree of neurological impairment. Her seizure disorder causes significant short-term memory difficulties that affect her learning. Her basic academic skills—reading, spelling, and math—are at a mid-first grade level. Jenny's accommodations include use of a calculator and a math facts chart, a written/pictorial schedule, and oral and typed responses in place of written responses. A full-time teaching assistant works with Jenny and others in the classroom. Jenny participates with the fifth grade except for three periods: a daily one-to-one reading tutorial with her special education teacher, alternate activities in place of social studies twice weekly with a small group and the assistant, and speech and phonemic awareness with a speech teacher twice weekly.

Jenny is extremely social and works well with peers during cooperative activities (with little adult involvement). Jenny is very involved in school activities and frequently invites friends to her home to play. Her classmates have been given some very basic information to help explain how Jenny learns and why she engages in certain behaviors.

Her team uses "sensory breaks" across the school day at Jenny's request to give her the opportunity to release energy in appropriate ways. Sensory "overload" results in a high frequency of hand and arm movement, which interferes with peer social interactions.

Across time, Jenny's ability to attend to group direction, take turns as part of a group activity, and participate in a multiple step task has greatly improved.[1]

Christine

Christine, who turned 20 last spring, is actively involved in the transition from school to adulthood. She has a winning personality and often jokes around with others, but she also has clear viewpoints and preferences about her daily and weekly activities, her friends, and her life. Her school day is divided between the community and high school. Because she has cerebral palsy, she uses a wheelchair for much of the day and uses a variety of means to communicate: sounds, facial expressions, gestures, words, yes or no responses, and a computerized, portable communication device. Christine has limited vision, which, along with her cerebral palsy, means she must often depend on others for help. It is her communication skills that enable her to have ongoing active involvement in "running her life" by making choices, stating her preferences, expressing her feelings, and sharing her perspective with her family, friends, and team. Her communication device, a Dynavox, has a low-volume auditory scanning system, which allows Christine to listen and then select her response with a hand-operated switch; she is learning to efficiently select the relevant category of responses from a menu of communication categories, organized with options that fit her daily life. She scans the choices and selects, activating a spoken response. It has taken Christine and her team a long time to identify, refine, and use this complex system; and the system is still growing, as Christine takes on new activities in the community.

This year Christine is involved with Best Buddies High School, a national organization that helps high schools, college groups, and others organize to "match" typical people with people who have mental retardation for the purpose of friendship (Grabowski, 1997). The Best Buddies group at her high school has just started this year, but there are plans to hold group pizza parties monthly in addition to buddies planning their own in and out of school activities. Early in the year, her team and some friends worked with Christine to develop a person-centered plan, which helps guide the direction of instruction and activities this year. Christine has recently started attending a general education drama class; the class was chosen to match her interests and to allow peer interaction with others who do not receive special education services.

Christine's IEP is geared to her transition needs: finding a job she likes and can be actively involved in, learning the job and its related skills (e.g., interacting with others, understanding job responsibility, taking care of her personal needs at the work site), using community services and leisure options, and getting ready to exit school services and enter the adult service system. Christine's teachers are, for her last year of school, planning a post-high school program, which will be located in the community around others in their 20s who are also preparing for their post-school years. Christine already spends a significant amount of time in the community trying out job experiences, performing community activities, and using services that are indicated priorities in her IEP.[2]

References

Bateman, B. D., & Linden, M. A. (1998). Better IEPs (3rd ed.). Longmont, CO: Sopris West.

Billingsley, F. F., Gallucci, C., Peck, C. A., Schwartz, I. S., & Staub, D. (1996). "But those kids can't even do math": An alternative conceptualization of outcomes for inclusive education. The Special Education Leadership Review, 3, 43–56.

Cohen, S. (1998). Targeting autism: What we know, don't know, and can do to help young children with autism and related disorders. Berkeley: University of California Press.

Grabowski, S. (1997). Manual for the faculty advisor, Best Buddies Colleges, Eastern Region. Washington, DC: Best Buddies, Eastern Regional Office.

Koegel, R. L., & Koegel, L. K. (1995). Teaching children with autism: Strategies for initiating positive interactions and improving learning opportunities. Baltimore: Paul H. Brookes.

Kunc, N. (1991, April). Integration: Being realistic isn't realistic. Speech presented at the On Common Ground Conference, Virginia Statewide Systems Change Project, Charlottesville, VA.

Maurice, C. (Ed.)(1996). Behavioral intervention for young children with autism. Austin), TX: Pro-Ed.

Snell, M. E., & Janney, R. E. (in press). Practices for inclusive schools: Sound relationships and peer support. Baltimore: Paul H. Brookes.

Staub, D., Schwartz, I. S., Gallucci, C., & Peck, C. A. (1994). Four portraits of friendship at an inclusive school. Journal of the Association for Persons with Severe Handicaps, 19, 314–325.

---

[1]Jenny's case was contributed by Maria Raynes and adapted from a case used in Snell and Janney (in press).

[2]Christine and her parents provided her case information, with additional input from others who know her well.

Chapters 3, 4, and 5 describe the important process of developing instructional programs for students with severe disabilities. Many phases are involved, from assessing the student through developing an individualized education program (IEP), putting it into place, and evaluating the progress on IEP goals and objectives. Each student is unique, and you must apply the entire process again with each student. To help you understand the material more readily, we apply many of the concepts in the chapter to three students introduced earlier—Timothy, Jenny, and Christine. These students differ in their ages, instructional settings, abilities and disabilities, and behavioral characteristics.

The Importance of Assessment

The first phase of developing instructional programs is the assessment of areas relevant to learning and life quality. Because assessment outcomes influence so many aspects of a student's educational experience, the development of an assessment process that produces meaningful and usable results is critical. There are many reasons that assessments are conducted and still more ways in which the results are used in the development of educational programs. Some assessment strategies contribute to the development of sound educational programs, while others may yield information that is less helpful, or that is perhaps even an obstacle, to the development of high-quality educational programs.

Traditionally, classification and placement decisions in special education have relied on assessments of intellectual functioning (Turnbull & Turnbull, 1998), academic achievement, and perceptual-motor skills (Gresham, 1983). However, the use of these types of assessments for students with more significant levels of disabilities have failed to provide useful information to educators (Downing & Perino, 1992; Silberman & Brown, 1998). As Evans (1991) notes, "Tests and other measures are only as useful as the way in which they are used" (p. 40). Understanding how an assessment can be used inappropriately is as important as understanding its appropriate use. Usually, it is not the instrument itself that is inappropriate but the applications of the assessment information.

Unfortunately, it is not possible to recommend only one or two comprehensive assessment instru-

ments. Students with severe disabilities are likely to have many areas where assessment is of value (e.g., mobility, daily living skills, language, social interactions, quality of life, relationships, and community skills), but no single instrument can measure this wide range of skills. Thus, assessing students with severe disabilities requires an interdisciplinary team effort at all phases of assessment, including selecting the assessments, conducting the assessments, interpreting the results, and determining program priorities. Nor is it possible to rely on just commercial assessments, because assessments should reflect each student's strengths and needs and his or her unique social, emotional, and physical environment. Thus, teachers must design assessments that can be individualized.

The types of assessments that professionals perceive as appropriate and meaningful are strongly influenced by three variables. First, the purpose of the inquiry and the ways in which the data are to be used determine which instruments are appropriate. Second, the team's educational philosophy determines the educational goals seen as appropriate. Consequently, educational philosophy influences the selection of instruments.

A third variable that influences the content and use of assessment is the legal requirements of assessment. The Individuals with Disabilities Education Act (IDEA) requires a multidisciplinary, multifaceted, nonbiased evaluation of a child before classifying and providing special education to that child (Turnbull & Turnbull, 1998). Table 3–1 reflects the assessment and evaluation standards and procedures that are set forth by IDEA.

This chapter reviews assessment issues as they relate to individuals with severe disabilities. Specifically, it discusses the purposes of assessment and the types of assessment used for these purposes, the relationship between assessment and program planning, and most important, meaningful assessment of learning and life quality (see box on page 73).

Definitions of Disability

The issues of testing and assessment are integrally related to the definition of disability. While definitions of disability provide the basis from which identification practices evolve, Ysseldyke and Algozzine (1982) caution that labels or "categories are simply terms used to confirm that individuals in our society differ from each other" (p. 43). It follows then that definitions of disability and evaluation strategies evolve to reflect changing societal values and attitudes (White, 1985; Ysseldyke & Algozzine, 1982). This evolution is illustrated by changes in the definition of mental retardation over the past two decades. In 1983, mental retardation was defined as "significantly subaverage general intellectual functioning existing concurrently with deficits in adaptive behavior and manifested during the developmental period" (Grossman, 1983, p. 1). This definition revised earlier ones that did not include the criteria of adaptive behavior (Heber, 1959, 1961).

The addition of the concept of adaptive behavior reflected a tremendous change in assessment, away from the sole measurement of "intelligence," and toward the gathering of more meaningful and relevant information. The change expanded the types of instruments used to measure the behavior of individuals with disabilities and added a new dimension to assessment, that is, the measure of an individual's adaptation to environmental demands.

More recently, an ecological viewpoint has become the basis for defining individuals with disabilities. For example, The Association for Persons with Severe Handicaps (TASH) (1989) defines individuals with severe disabilities as:

> individuals of all ages who require extensive ongoing support in more than one major life activity in order to participate in integrated community settings and to enjoy a quality of life that is available to citizens with fewer or no disabilities. Support may be required for life activities such as mobility, communication, self-care, and learning as necessary for independent living, employment, and self-sufficiency. (p. 19)

Similarly, the American Association on Mental Retardation (AAMR) has revised its definition to reflect new knowledge about individuals with cognitive disabilities and current views of disability:

> Mental retardation refers to substantial limitations in present functioning. It is characterized by significantly subaverage intellectual functioning, existing concurrently with related limitations in two or more of the following applicable adaptive skill areas: communication, self-care, home living, social skills, community use, self-direction, health and safety, functional academics, leisure, and work. Mental retardation manifests before age 18. (Luckasson et al., 1992.)

In this definition, an individual's disability is related to the degree of functioning in many different areas of adaptive skills; a global measure of adaptive behavior is not used. An emphasis is placed on assessing the level and type of individualized supports needed by the person to function at home, school, and community. Luckasson, et al., (1992) refer to four assumptions essential to the application of this definition:

1. Valid assessment considers cultural and linguistic diversity, and differences in communication and behavioral factors.
2. The existence of limitations in adaptive skills occurs within the context of community environments typical of the individual's age peers and is indexed to the person's individualized needs for support.
3. Specific adaptive limitations often coexist with strengths in other adaptive skills or other personal capabilities.
4. With appropriate supports over a sustained period, the life functioning of the person with mental retardation will generally improve.

Purposes of Assessment

Different types of assessments offer different types of information. Just as teachers should select an educational intervention to match the particular targeted skills, so teachers should select an assessment to match the purpose. Assessments are used to gain information for the purposes of screening, placement, curriculum development, and student evaluation (cf. Browder, 1991; Salvia & Ysseldyke, 1995). The professionals involved in each of these areas, the instruments or strategies used, and the timings of the measurements vary according to the purpose of the assessment. Table 3–2 describes these variations.

Screening

A screening test is a very broad and quickly administered measure. Its intention is not to obtain information precise enough to make instructional decisions or to determine why a problem exists but rather to determine whether a student is significantly different from his peers and requires further testing.

Screening may help ascertain whether referral for evaluation to determine eligibility for special programs or related services (e.g., speech, physical, or

TABLE 3–1
Sample of Nondiscriminatory Evaluation Procedures

Standard	Description	Reference in IDEA
Cultural bias	• Tests and materials are not to be discriminatory on a racial or cultural basis.	20 U.S.C. § 1414(b)(3)(A)(1)
	• Tests and materials are provided and administered in the student's native language or other mode of communication unless it is not feasible to do so.	20 U.S.C. § 1414(b)(3)(A)(ii)
Test validity and administration	• Tests must be validated for the specific purpose for which they are used.	20 U.S.C. § 1414(b)(3)(B)
	• Tests must be administered by trained and knowledgeable personnel.	
	• Test must be administered in accordance with any instructions from the test's producers.	
Evaluation process	• Use a variety of tools and strategies to gather relevant functional and developmental information to determine whether the student has a disability, and the content of the IEP, including information that enables the student to participate in the general curriculum.	20 U.S.C. § 1414(b)(2)(A)
	• Must not use any single procedure as the sole criterion to determine presence of disability, or, if so, student's appropriate education.	20 U.S.C. § 1414(b)(2)(B)
	• Use technically sound instruments to assess across four domains: cognitive, behavioral, physical, and developmental factors.	20 U.S.C. § 1414(b)(2)(C)
	• Use tools and strategies that assist the team directly in determining that the student's educational needs are satisfied.	20 U.S.C. § 1414(b)(3)(D)
	• Review existing evaluation data, classroom-based assessments and observations, and teacher and related services observations.	20 U.S.C. § 1414(C)(1)(A)

occupational therapy) is warranted (Browder, 1991; Lewis & Russo, 1998). Medical personnel and psychologists use screening instruments with young children who are delayed in their development to determine if in-depth assessment is needed. Students with severe or multiple disabilities, however, typically do not go through a formal screening evaluation, as they have obvious disabilities (Gaylord-Ross & Holvoet, 1985). For such students, assessment begins with diagnostic testing.

Screening tests cover a variety of areas, such as vision, hearing, and developmental milestones. Early childhood screening instruments, however, have little value as a child grows older, since such instruments focus on early milestones and do not contribute to curriculum development.

Screening may begin as early as the prenatal period, with the use of amniocentesis to determine the presence of certain genetic disorders. Immediately following birth, screening occurs as physicians check for obvious handicapping conditions or genetic and metabolic disorders (White, 1985). The Apgar scoring system (Apgar, 1953; Apgar & Beck, 1973) and the Brazelton Neonatal Behavioral Assessment Scale (BNBAS) (Brazelton & Nugent, 1995) are screening instruments designed to detect potential problems in newborns. The Apgar scoring system is used to quickly evaluate a newborn's condition after delivery; it assesses the neonate's heart rate, respiration, reflexes, muscle tone, and general appearance at 1 minute, 5 minutes, and 10 minutes after birth. In addition to these developmental and neurologic mea-

TABLE 3–1
continued

Standard	Description	Reference in IDEA
Parent participation	• Parents must be members of the evaluation team.	20 U.S.C. § 1414(d)(1)(B)
	• Parents must be given a copy of the evaluation report and documentation concerning eligibility (or lack of).	
	• Parents may submit to the team and require it to consider evaluations and information that they initiate or provide.	
Parent consent	• Parents may give or withhold consent to initial evaluation, all reevaluations, and any exit evaluation.	20 U.S.C. § 1414(c)(3)
	• If the school has taken reasonable measures to secure parent consent and if parents have failed to respond to the school's request for consent, the school then may evaluate the student.	20 U.S.C. § 1414(a)(1) (C), and (C)(3)
	• If the parents refuse to give consent, the school may go to mediation or a "due process hearing" to evaluate the student.	20 U.S.C. § 1414(a)(1)(C)
Reevaluation	• Must occur at least every 3 years.	20 U.S.C. § 1414(a)(2)(A)
	• Must occur, if "conditions warrant" it, more often than every 3 years (e.g., a dramatic improvement or deterioration in the student).	
	• Must occur if the student's parents or teacher requests it, because they may have or need new information about the student to make the student's special education more effective.	

Note: Adapted, with permission, from Turnbull, H. R.(III), & Turnbull, A. P. (1998). *Free appropriate public education: The law and children with disabilities* (5th edition). Denver: Love.

 Assessment and Evaluation Practices Required by IDEA

Box 3–1

- Team must include parents and student, special educators, specialists, and regular educators who are responsible for evaluation, program delivery, monitoring, and placement decisions.
- Parent participation in assessment must be increased.
- Evaluation must be linked to the IEP and program.
- Evaluation must take into account the student's participation in general curriculum.
- Classroom-based data must be generated and considered.
- Assessment must focus equally on four domains: cognitive, behavioral, physical, and developmental.
- Teams must use "tools and strategies" that indicate whether the school is meeting the student's educational needs.
- Teams must use bias-free assessment instruments and procedures.
- Parent and teacher observation must be reflected in the assessment data that teams gather and use.

Note: Adapted with permission from Turnbull, H. R., III, & Turnbull, A. P. (1998). *Free appropriate public education: The law and children with disabilities* (5th ed.). Denver: Love, p. 115.

TABLE 3–2
Varying Purposes and Characteristics of Assessment in the Education of Students with Severe Disabilities

Assessment Purpose	Types of Assessment	Primary Assessors	Time of Assessment
Screening	• Newborn and infant measures • Motor and sensory functioning measures • Specific domains	• Medical staff • Occupational, physical, and speech therapists • Psychologists	• Early in child's life • After head injury
Diagnosis and placement	• IQ tests • Adaptive behavior tests • Motor and sensory functioning tests	• Psychologist or educational specialist • Occupational, physical, or speech therapists	• Early in the child's life • After head injury
Curriculum and program development	• Ecological analysis • Adaptive behavior tests • Task analytic assessment	• Educational team • Psychologist	• Throughout school years at regular intervals
Evaluation • Student progress	• Direct observation of IEP behaviors and skills under criterion conditions • Training and probe data	• Teacher • Educational team	• Daily, weekly, or bi-weekly
• Program • Quality of Life	• Program evaluations • Quality of life evaluations	• Educational team	• Bi-annually, annually, or as determined by team

sures, the BNBAS includes 27 behavioral measures. These general measures assess alertness, activity level, self-quieting activity, smiles, sleep patterns, and specific behaviors (e.g., the newborn's response to environmental stimuli, such as a light, sounds, and a pinprick on the bottom of the foot). The Apgar test and the BNBAS alert hospital staff to newborns who are in distress or have neurological damage; however, these instruments should not be used to predict long-term outcomes (Fewell & Cone, 1983).

Screening instruments for infants and older children, such as the Denver Developmental Screening Test (DDST) (Frankenburg, Dodds, & Fandal, 1975) and the Developmental Profile II (Alpern, Boll, & Schearer, 1980), cover a variety of domains, such as personal and social, fine and gross motor, language, and self-help development. Again, the purpose of these screening tests for children is to determine if further, more precise assessment is needed, not to determine instructional objectives.

Other screening instruments may focus on only one domain of interest, such as vision or hearing.

Unfortunately, some screening instruments, such as traditional visual acuity tests, cannot be adequately administered to students with severe disabilities because of the complex verbal instructions or the cognitive discriminations required (Cress, Spellman, DeBriere, Sizemore, Northam, & Johnson, 1981). The Parson's Visual Acuity Test (Cress et al., 1981; Spellman, DeBriere, & Cress, 1979) was developed specifically for screening visual problems in individuals with severe disabilities. For individuals who cannot initially perform the response requirements, a training program is included to teach the types of responses needed to participate in the screening test. (For an extensive review of assessments of sensory impairments, see Lewis and Russo, 1998.)

Diagnosis and Placement

The next step in the assessment process is further testing of the child to identify the disorder and possible cause of the delay and to make eligibility, classification, and placement decisions (Salvia & Yesseldyke, 1995). Determination of classification and eligibility is made by the assessment team or the IEP team, which makes its decision based on evidence from several sources, because it is unlawful to determine the presence of a disability on the basis of one test (Lewis & Russo, 1998). Once a delay or a disability is suspected, either through screening or observation, diagnostic testing may be initiated to probe sensory impairments, mental ability, or adaptive functioning. Neurological tests, intelligence tests, and tests of adaptive behavior are used to assess students in each of these areas. Typically, these tests are administered by psychologists, education specialists, or therapists, and the results presented at an IEP meeting. One example of a diagnostic test is the Gilliam Autism Rating Scale (GARS) (Gilliam, 1995), which is designed for use by parents and teachers and other professionals, to help identify and diagnose autism in individuals ages 3 through 22 and to estimate the severity of the problem.

Each type of test yields different information, and teachers must know how, or whether, the information has application in the classroom. For example, performance on a normative developmental test for young children, while providing the education team with information on one level of a student's functioning, is not intended to be translated into instructional objectives for an 8-year-old child. The items may not be age-appropriate or related to functional contexts for the individual.

Curriculum and Program Development

A major purpose of assessment is to gather information useful for the development of an appropriate educational program. Assessment conducted to determine which skills should be taught is considered educational assessment (Gaylord-Ross & Holvoet, 1985). This phase of the assessment process is usually coordinated by the teacher, who directly assesses and observes the student, as well as elicits additional pertinent information from parents, psychologists, and therapists.

Some instruments, such as criterion-referenced tests and certain adaptive behavior scales, are more suited than others for educational assessment. Other instruments, such as intelligence tests, are completely inappropriate for this purpose. In contrast, ecological inventories (which are discussed later) are informal instruments that yield information critical to

the development of age-appropriate and functional curricula for students with severe disabilities. Assessment instruments should be carefully inspected to determine if they were developed for these decision-making capabilities.

Evaluation

Evaluation is another component of the assessment process. It is not enough to develop an educational program for a student; teams must be accountable for the programs they develop and the impact of the educational program on the student and his or her family. Three important areas to evaluate include the progress the student is making, the impact of the educational program on the student's quality of life, and evaluation of the total educational program.

Student Progress

Progress evaluation is a critical, and perhaps the most traditional, form of educational evaluation measure. Teachers must provide ongoing and meaningful evaluations of progress on each objective in each student's IEP. Recently, however, evaluation has expanded from simple measurements of each student's progress on specific IEP objectives to include other broader outcomes.

Quality of Life

Documentation of successful student outcomes has extended beyond the use of quantitative measures of performance and should include qualitative measures as well (Evans & Scotti, 1989; Haring & Breen, 1989; Kazdin, 1977; Meyer & Evans, 1993; Meyer & Janney, 1989; Ulrich, 1991; Voeltz & Evans, 1983; Wolf, 1978). Many efforts are being made to evaluate each individual's quality of life, but because of the subjective nature of this concept, there are wide variations in opinion on exactly what should be measured. There is, however, growing consensus about what the core quality of life dimensions are: emotional well-being, interpersonal relations, material well-being, personal development, physical well-being, self-determination, social inclusion, and human rights (Hatton, 1998; Schalock, 1996). Because an individual's quality of life is determined across settings, environments, and opportunities (Wehmeyer, 1996), assessment strategies must necessarily include this range of personal variables.

Program Evaluation

Program evaluation examines the quality of the program (e.g., educational, residential, vocational) offered to an individual and its impact on the individual and, at times, the individual's family. Many times, an individual's lack of progress can be attributed to inadequacy of services provided. It becomes ludicrous to agonize over instructional modifications when the problem is that the educational program itself does not support the target outcomes (e.g., community integration, interdependence). Some evaluations may focus on specific aspects of a program. For example, the Communication Supports Checklist (McCarthy, et al., 1998) assesses a program's settings and practices in terms of its support and respect for meaningful communication for all individuals in the environment. Bailey, et al. (1998) suggest that focusing solely on the extent to which a program is implementing its practices is not sufficient. They suggest that focus should shift to the actual results, benefits, and impact on the people whom the practices are supposed to serve.

Factors Related to Meaningful Assessment

To understand assessment, familiarity with certain terms and testing issues is necessary. The following sections introduce specific assessment concepts needed to evaluate the potential utility of assessment instruments in educational programs.

Test Reliability

Reliability refers to the extent to which an instrument is consistent in measuring whatever it purports to measure. If an assessment is repeated within a short interval of time, a student should receive the same score or rating. Reliability is usually measured by some form of reliability coefficient, ranging from 0 to 1, or by the standard error of measurement derived from it. Salvia and Ysseldyke (1995) state that tests should have reliability coefficients in excess of .60 if the scores are for administrative purposes or are reported for group scores; however, when tests are used to make decisions regarding individual students, the reliability coefficient should be over .90.

Reliability does not address the content of what is being assessed, only its *consistency*. A teacher may reliably measure a student's ability to "place pegs in a pegboard within 1 minute" as part of an assessment of vocational readiness. The measure may be very reliable (consistent) across time, and two evaluators may agree on the student's test performance (interrater reliability). Yet, although reliability is established, the skill has no relationship to preparing for a vocation. The concept of reliability does not address the purpose or the content (validity) of what is being measured.

Test Validity

Test validity refers to the extent to which a test measures what it is supposed to measure; in other words, validity concerns the *content* of the test. If a test measures irrelevant information, it lacks validity, and the test results cannot be meaningfully interpreted. For example, if Christine's receptive language skills are being assessed by asking her to point to objects and pictures, the test results will not be valid, because Christine has great difficulty using her hands as a result of cerebral palsy and also has limited vision. Instead of measuring receptive language, this test is measuring the motor skill of pointing to visual stimuli. Thus, this test lacks content validity for this student.

Content validity is also lacking if a test does not sample a broad enough range of skills to determine whether competency is sufficient. If the self-help domain of a particular test includes only toileting, dressing, and brushing hair, the test may be deemed insufficient because measuring only three skills will not enable a judgment of a student's general self-help skills. Thus, the test would be judged invalid.

Criterion-related validity refers to the extent to which scores on a test agree with (*concurrent validity*) or predict (*predictive validity*) some given criterion measure. For example, if you are questioning the criterion-related validity of a hypothetical "Smith's Test of Adaptive Behavior," you must determine whether the student's score on this test relates to his or her scores on a test that is presumed to be a valid measure of adaptive behavior or whether the score can accurately predict the student's performance in community settings.

Data Gathering

There are three basic methods of gathering assessment information: direct testing, observation in the natural environment, and interviewing. Each of the methods provides different information and has its own advantages and disadvantages.

Direct Testing

This method of data collection requires the teacher to provide the student with an arranged opportunity to respond to specific stimuli. The teacher presents the student with certain materials or instructions to determine if the student can perform the behavior being assessed. Direct testing may occur in either isolated settings or in more representative settings. Timothy's teacher may take him into the bathroom; provide a toothbrush, toothpaste, cup, and towel; and then ask him to brush his teeth. His teacher then observes what components of the task he performs. Although his teacher, in this testing situation, can observe whether Timothy brushes his teeth in an appropriate setting and with the same materials used at home, Timothy is not being assessed on whether he brushes his teeth at appropriate times.

To the greatest extent possible, direct testing should occur in the criterion environment, at the appropriate times, and using the criterion materials. If his teacher were to assess Timothy by bringing him into the classroom and providing him with an electric toothbrush, the information gathered may not be representative of his performance in the bathroom with the type of toothbrush used at home. Materials used in the assessment process, as well as in instruction, must be selected with several considerations in mind: the availability at home, the student's chronological age, the student's physical abilities, the student's preferences, and school resources.

In the direct testing approach, the student is given the opportunity to demonstrate a behavior. At times, this is a difficult approach to use, because some behaviors do not naturally occur or do not occur frequently enough in a classroom, but they are still important to assess. For example, Jenny's teacher may want to assess her skill in handling money. Although the criterion environment is the school cafeteria, her teacher may want to first use direct testing to gather information in the classroom to get a general idea of Jenny's skill. The teacher must keep in mind, however, that Jenny's performance in the classroom may be different from what it would be in the criterion environment. If Jenny demonstrates the desired skill in the classroom, a second assessment of the skill should take place in the school cafeteria.

The disadvantage of this approach is that very often, the test cues, conditions, and materials are only similar, not the same, as those in the natural environments. The differences may affect a student's test performance negatively, making it unclear whether training is needed to yield competent performance in the criterion setting. In the money handling example, the teacher can arrange to use some of the same materials that are used in the cafeteria when she tests Jenny in the classroom (e.g., one-dollar and five-dollar bills, Jenny's wallet); however, there may not be much that her teacher can do to replicate the great numbers of students on the cafeteria food line or the impatient cashier that awaits her at the end of the line.

Observation in the Natural Environment

In this type of information gathering, the teacher observes the student in the setting in which a behavior naturally occurs. The major advantage is that the teacher may observe typical performance of the target skill and a wider range of related behaviors. In other words, the teacher can see if the student demonstrates associated skills, such as movement to the location of the activity, initiation of the skill, ability to find solutions to problems that arise in the natural environment, and social behaviors. A classroom environment may not offer the natural opportunities to demonstrate the competencies that are needed for skill use in the criterion environment.

Christine and a peer from her drama class, along with her teaching assistant, went to the mall to seek a certain type of makeup that they needed for an upcoming production. Her special education teacher and her teaching assistant planned to assess several of Christine's skills and routines while at the mall (e.g., purchasing from a store, ordering and eating in the food court). Her teacher knew well Christine's skills ordering and eating lunch in the school cafeteria, however, she was interested in determining her skill at the food court where there were many unknown variables. For example, at the food court, Christine would not know the food server, the waiting line would be made up of people whom she did not know, different food choices would be available, and she would have to solve the problem when the food options on her communication device did not match the pictures of the food choices available.

When assessment occurs in the natural environment, a teacher does not have to be concerned about attempting to simulate materials and cues. However, to increase the value of data gathering in the natural environment, observations should sample a range of all the relevant settings (e.g., classroom, home, playground, bathroom) at appropriate times of the day (e.g., before or after lunch, morning, afternoon), using criterion arrangements (e.g., group, one-to-one, free play). Because each of these variables may influence the student's performance, observations over several days are the preferred method to obtain data that accurately represent the student's ability.

One major disadvantage is that the relevant behavior may not naturally occur at the time of the observation. A teacher may decide to take the student into the community to assess the appropriateness of his response to strangers. The ideal way of assessing this would obviously be to take the student to a mall and observe his behavior if a stranger were to approach him; however, there is a good chance that no stranger will approach on that particular day at that particular time. Furthermore, purposely allowing a student to be in a vulnerable situation where a stranger may approach may be dangerous and unethical.

Interviewing

Some assessments require that information be obtained by interviewing others who know the student very well. The Adaptive Behavior Scales (Lambert, Nihira, & Leland, 1993; Nihira, Leland, & Lambert, 1993), and the Vineland Adaptive Behavioral Scales (Sparrow, Balla, & Cicchetti, 1984) are two adaptive behavior assessments that obtain information by interview. O'Neill, et al. (1997) use an interview format for one component of their comprehensive assessment of problem behaviors.

Interviews may include family members, staff from a residential facility (if the student does not live at home), current and past teachers, the student, or any other person who knows the student well. The major advantage is that the information provided by the informants is likely to reflect the student's typical performance in natural settings with naturally occurring cues and consequences. The major disadvantage is that the interview data may be less accurate and more subjective than direct observation.

Interviewing family members is the most direct method of finding out about the activities in which a family engages, parents' preferences for particular activities, and student likes and dislikes. Used in conjunction with the other types of information gathering, teachers and other service providers can become more knowledgeable about the student's home environment. This method is also a constructive way of involving parents in the program and letting them know that their input is critical for the development of a sound educational program. It is important, however, that the interview process and the information gathering be done in a culturally sensitive manner and be respectful of families from diverse cultural backgrounds (Chen & Dote-Kwan, 1998). While adaptive behavior assessments may contain cultural biases, the special education and assessment literature rarely have addressed the need for cultural sensitivity in these contexts (Lim & Browder, 1994).

If family members, for whatever reason, are not available for an interview, an informal written format may help teachers elicit necessary information. Some family members may prefer to complete written questionnaires on their own. A questionnaire should address student likes, dislikes, and preferences, and provide insight into the student's performance in the home environment. Completing such questionnaires before an IEP meeting prepares family members to reflect on functional educational outcomes that are relevant in current and potential environments. Figure 3–1 on pp. 80-81 is an informal questionnaire for families.

Scoring

The scoring systems required in any assessment vary widely. Some tests require a simple *dichotomous response* (e.g., "yes" the student has the skill or "no" the student does not have the skill), while other instruments require more complex or *multiple-level responses* on dimensions such as independence (e.g., can do skill given no assistance, minimal assistance, maximum assistance) or frequency (e.g., can do the skill never, some of the time, frequently, or always).

Each approach has different characteristics and may serve different purposes. The dichotomous scoring method (e.g., + or −) represents broad student outcomes or skill mastery. In terms of assessing a skill in the community, a student either has or has not mastered the skill sufficiently for independent use. If the student can cross a street only "some of the time," certainly the teacher would conclude that this does not represent a sufficient level of mastery! In this case, a dichotomous scoring method is appropriate.

Further, if teachers are interested in what students can do independently in natural settings, then scoring must be related to meaningful units of behavior (Brown, Evans, Weed, & Owen, 1987; Brown & Lehr, 1993). A teacher then knows that an increase in a total score indicates an increase in the functional competence of the person being assessed. Some instruments, however, divide a skill into test items that do not represent meaningful units of the task. Therefore, a student may increase his or her total score, but the increase may represent fairly insignificant improvements across several skills and not an improvement that would help the student function more independently in the community. For example, an assessment might identify six increasingly difficult steps needed to "pull up pants":

1. Child pulls up pants from hip
2. Child pulls up pants from top of thighs
3. Child pulls up pants from knees
4. Child pulls up pants from calves
5. Child pulls up pants from ankles
6. Child pulls up pants independently

The skill of "putting on socks" may include the following six items:

1. Child pulls sock up from ankle
2. Child pulls sock up from heel
3. Child pulls sock up from sole of foot
4. Child pulls sock up over whole foot
5. Child picks up sock and puts on independently
6. Child picks up both socks and puts both on independently

In September, a student may do the first three items of "pulling up pants" and the first two items of "putting on socks" for a total of five items passed. The student cannot, however, do either skill independently. In June, the student's total score on these two skills may increase to nine. An increase of four items offers little information about what the student has mastered. It is possible that the student still cannot perform either skill independently. Or the student may have completed the three remaining items of "pulling up pants" and can now independently put on his pants. In terms of independent functioning, the latter in-

crease of three items is more significant than the former increase of four.

Indeed, a student may have only some part of a skill or may be able to only partially engage in an activity. The Principle of Partial Participation (Baumgart et al., 1982) argues that although some individuals with severe or profound disabilities may not be able to function independently in all environments, they should be taught to perform or to participate at least partially in identified least restrictive environments. If a student's participation in an activity is going to be partial, attention to meaningful components of an activity as an index of progress becomes especially important.

A teacher must work toward participation in activities that a student or others perceive as meaningful and that offers the student control of the activity (Brown, Evans, Weed, & Owen, 1987). For example, Christine, who has severely limited range of arm motion, may partially participate in grocery shopping by pushing a can of food placed 3 inches from her hand into the grocery basket. However, Christine could also participate by activating the switch to her communication device to indicate a particular food item to place in the cart for purchase. Having control over the environment (through choice in this example) and causing desired effects can be more meaningful than performing the actual activity (Brown, Evans, Weed, & Owen, 1987; Brown & Lehr, 1993).

In contrast to the dichotomous scoring method, the *multiple-level scoring* method is most appropriate for monitoring student progress in an instructional program. In terms of instruction, progressing from performing a skill with maximum assistance to performing the same skill with minimum assistance may be significant for a student just learning that skill. Thus, a scoring system sensitive to small student changes in independence or to consistency of performance is most appropriate. Similarly, progress on small components of a task analysis, as in the example of "putting on socks," provides information that a teacher needs to determine the adequacy of the instructional interventions.

The Developmental Approach

The developmental approach looks at the normal sequence of development to determine which skills an individual should be achieving. This approach,

FIGURE 3–1
Family Input Questionnaire

Family member(s) completing form: _____

Child's name: _____

Date: _____

Please answer the following questions so that we may get a better idea of your child's present needs at home and your feelings about his or her needs in the future.

At Home

1. What would you like your child to be doing at home that he or she is not doing at the present time (for example, play by self, stay at table during meals, help clear off table)?
2. Where do you expect your child to live in the future?
3. What types of things may be expected from your child in this setting that your child is not expected to do now (for example, help during eating, get dressed by self, set the table, do the laundry, shower)?
4. Who does your child interact with at home (for example, siblings, neighbors)?
5. What skills would facilitate these interactions?
6. What kinds of activities does your child seem to like most at home?

At School

7. In what curricular areas is your child currently participating (for example, self-help skills, communication training, sight word identification).
8. What curricular areas or skills would you like your child to be studying at school (for example, money skills, street crossing, play independently).
9. With whom does your child have significant relationships at school (for example, teacher, peer with disabilities, peer not labeled with a disability, counselor)?
10. What skills or activities would facilitate these relationships (for example, initiating interactions, participating in school and after-school activities)?

Leisure Activities

11. What places provide leisure opportunities for your child at the present time (for example, school, playroom at home, community center)?

---

prevalent in the early 1970s (Browder, 1991), determined the mental age (MA) of a student with severe disabilities by comparing his or her skills to the age at which a normally developing child acquired those skills. Justification for this approach rests on at least three assumptions: (a) normal development constitutes the most logical ordering of behaviors, (b) many behaviors within normal development are prerequisite behaviors, and (c) behaviors acquired by a nondisabled child are appropriate measures for an individual with a disability who is at the same developmental level (Guess & Noonan, 1982).

Tests sequenced according to normal development are termed norm-referenced tests, which are used to determine the extent of deviation from the norm (Fewell & Cone, 1983) and are standardized around

the average score of the normative group, so that half of the sample scores above the average score and half scores below it (Lewis & Russo, 1998). These measures usually compare the performance of students with disabilities to nondisabled students of the same age. Norm-referenced measures allow the evaluator to determine whether a given student is developing the same skills as the majority of students in the normative sample.

IQ Tests

The IQ test is the most popular developmental test and, along with adaptive behavior scales, it typically makes up the diagnostic component of assessment. IQ tests are designed to measure learning ability, or

FIGURE 3–1
continued

---

12. Who else participates in these activities?

13. What types of leisure activities would you like your child to participate in at these places (for example, watch TV, computer games, board games, playground games)?

14. Are there other places that may have leisure opportunities for your child sometime in the future (for example, break time at work, shopping at the mall, community center)?

15. What are the types of leisure activities that will likely be available to your child in these settings (for example, playing cards, video games, bingo)?

16. What kinds of leisure activities does your child seem to like most?

At Work

17. What type of work setting (or postschool setting) do you expect your child to participate in after completing this present educational program?

18. What types of technical skills do you think will be required there (for example, assembly skills, janitorial skills, bussing tables, computer skills)?

19. What types of work-related skills do you think will be required there that your child will probably need to work on (for example, getting along with co-workers and supervisor, waiting in line for lunch, finding something to do during break time, independent toileting)?

20. What type of work do you think your child would enjoy most?

In the Community

21. What types of community settings would you like your child to participate in now (for example, restaurant, shopping mall, grocery store, doctor's office)?

22. What are the specific activities that you would like your child to do at these settings (for example, walk beside me without hand held, ordering food in a restaurant, purchasing items in a store, walk and not run)?

23. Who would it be appropriate for your child to interact with in these settings (e.g., physician, cashier)?

24. Are there any other community settings or activities that may be available in the future that are not available now? If so, please list.

25. What types of community activities does your child like to participate in most?

"intellectual capacity." "Intelligence," however, is a construct that one infers from a person's performance (Salvia & Ysseldyke, 1995), so the practice of assigning numeric values to a construct (e.g., IQ score) and using these numbers to make important decisions is questionable. Intelligence tests sample behaviors such as discrimination, generalization, motor behavior, vocabulary, inductive reasoning, comprehension, sequencing, detail recognition, understanding of analogies, abstract reasoning, memory, and pattern completion (Salvia & Ysseldyke, 1995).

Some frequently used intelligence tests are the Bayley Scales of Infant Development (Bayley, 1993), Cattell Infant Intelligence Scale (Cattell, 1940), McCarthy Scales of Children's Abilities (McCarthy, 1972), Slosson Intelligence Test (Slosson, 1971), Stanford-Binet Intelligence Scale (Thorndike, Hagen, &

Sattler, 1985), Wechsler Intelligence Scale for Children, Third Edition (Wechsler, 1991), and Wechsler Preschool and Primary Scale of Intelligence, Revised (Wechsler, 1989).

There are many problems in administering IQ tests to students with disabilities and in applying the test results. Certainly, the more severe an individual's disability, the less appropriate is the application of an IQ test. Few, if any, standardized intelligence tests include students with severe disabilities in their normative samples (Sigafoos, Cole, & McQuarter, 1987). Often, and for various reasons, students with severe or profound disabilities are unable to score on these tests; consequently, infant intelligence tests are used (Evans, 1991; Gaylord-Ross & Holvoet, 1985). The inappropriateness of intelligence tests is then further exacerbated by the lack of age-appropriateness. Infant measures focus heavily on perceptual and motor skills, which lack both predictive validity and concurrent validity, or agreement across subtests (Evans, 1991). Evans says:

> Extrapolation of scores or the derivation of IQ scores from scales designed for use with infants or for other special purposes is an especially hazardous practice that provides some continued professional expectation that scores can be meaningfully assigned to people falling within the lower ranges. (p. 40)

Another major disadvantage is the misuse of the information that intelligence tests provide. They are used to make decisions about students and services on the basis of very limited data, and they are inappropriately used to measure student progress (Fewell & Cone, 1983).

Evans (1991) discusses two additional problems in applying IQ tests to students with severe disabilities. First, even though IQ tests are designed to measure fundamental cognitive abilities, they require academic knowledge of variables that many children with severe cognitive disabilities do not have at the time of the testing, such as abstract verbal and pictorial symbols and numbers. Second, individuals with severe disabilities often have multiple disabilities, such as central neural, sensory, and physical impairments, which interfere with test performance.

Much legal controversy exists over the use of intelligence tests in special education. In litigation, such as *Mills v. Board of Education* (1972), *Hobson v. Hansen* (1967), and *Larry P. v. Riles* (1984), courts ruled that exclusion or grouping of students on the basis of standardized tests is unconstitutional.

Developmental Scales

There are several advantages to using developmental scales in the assessment process. Developmental test items are written in observable terms, so presence or absence of a skill can usually be determined reliably. For students with sensory or movement disabilities, however, developmental items must be adapted so that the disability does not prevent assessment of the actual ability being tested. Student progress on the measures can then be noted by periodic administration of the instrument.

Developmental scales give information on functioning in various skill areas, and because skills are listed chronologically, they may provide direction for the next skills to be taught. When used for educational assessment, the items that a student can and cannot do are determined. The first items that a student cannot do are then targeted for intervention. And finally, the familiarity of many disciplines with normal developmental theory may increase communication among disciplines.

There are, however, many problems with applying the developmental approach to students with severe and profound disabilities. First, this approach assumes that the sequences of behavior typical of nondisabled students are relevant for students with severe or profound disabilities. A person who is disabled may develop in a different sequence, and the relationship among skills may be different. Prostheses or environmental adaptations may render typical developmental sequences inappropriate. For example, White (1985) points out that although head control is a prerequisite for normal walking, it is not a prerequisite for a motorized wheelchair. Therefore, although the student failed the head control item, the evaluator should not stop probing higher level gross motor skills. Given individualized adaptations, this student may score on many other higher level functional skills.

Second, because the developmental approach assumes that certain behaviors must be present before other behaviors can be acquired, the results may influence some teachers to instruct students on skills that are neither age-appropriate nor functional for adapting to their daily environments (Guess & Noonan, 1982) and that lead to lower expectations. For example, a 15-year-old student who is severely disabled may fail the item "points to parts of doll" on the Bayley Scales of Infant Development (Bayley, 1993), an item that is usually passed by babies by the time they are 26 months. Instruction on this skill would require materials that are not appropriate for a 15-year-old student, and it is a skill that would have little relevance for that student. Focus on these types of assessment items would naturally have an impact on our expectations of students. Linehan, Brady, and Hwang (1991) found that assessment reports based on developmental measures led respondents to have lower expectations for individuals with severe disabilities than did reports based on functional, ecological approaches.

A third potential danger is that skills within and across curricular or environmental domains may be seen in isolation and, thus, may remain unrelated to each other. For example, the skill of grasping is certainly important and necessary for most physical interactions with the environment. However, unless grasping is related to other skills or examined within functional contexts, it has little meaning. Grasping of a brush during grooming, a spoon while eating, or a toy during play provides more relevant assessment information than does grasping of a 2-inch wooden dowel. Likewise, "scans objects" begins to have meaning if it is in the context of materials used in daily routines (e.g., scan the utensils to find the spoon; scan the toothbrushes to find your own; scan the tapes to find one you like).

Fourth, the purpose for assessing a skill may not be apparent and therefore be left open to inappropriate assessment, administration, and interpretation. Some developmental test items, for example, appear simply because of their high reliability at certain ages, such as the classic item of imitating a bridge built of three 1-inch cubes. However, what ability this item actually is meant to test is not clear (White, 1985). If it is used to assess the fine-motor ability of a student, then a child without limbs and unable to manipulate a prosthetic device would fail the item. However, if the intent is to assess imitation, then some strategy must be developed to allow the child to demonstrate this cognitive ability given his or her physical capabilities.

Fifth, some teachers assume that because an item is on an assessment it must be meaningful for instructional purposes. Many professionals have argued that a normal developmental sequence does not provide information that can be directly used in the educational context (Browder, 1991; Downing & Perino, 1992; Siegel-Causey & Allinder, 1998). For example, the skill "builds tower of three blocks" is an item that is commonly found on developmental scales. Before considering instruction on such an item, the teacher must question the purpose for assessing this particular skill. Is it to determine the motor ability of the student, whether the student can play with blocks, or simply because tower building (like bridge building) is another reliable milestone of development often found in early childhood measures? If a specific rationale for the assessment of that particular item (e.g., motor ability) is determined, then the teacher must decide whether or not this basic function is a relevant instructional objective for the student. If the teacher concludes that the play function of the item is rele-

vant, the teacher should translate the item into a form that is meaningful for the student's age and specific environment (e.g., age-appropriate materials and functional context). Caution must be taken however, not to contrive situations that would not otherwise be considered for instruction.

Some developmental instruments relate more directly to the program development component of the assessment process. These instruments are accompanied by curriculum guides. Some of these assessments include: the Assessment, Evaluation, and Programming System (AEPS) for infants and children (Bricker, 1993); the Carolina Curriculum for Preschoolers with Special Needs (Johnson-Martin, Attermeier, & Hacker, 1990); Learning Accomplishment Profile (LAP) (Sanford, 1974), and Learning Accomplishment Profile for Infants (Early LAP) (Griffin & Sanford, 1981). Although these instruments were developed with instructional implications in mind, a teacher must still carefully evaluate the relevance of particular test items for each student. The student's age, interests, motor or sensory disabilities, and home and community environments must be considered in the decision-making process.

Siegel-Causey and Allinder (1998) suggest that assessment practices based on norm-referenced tests are often "limited in their ability to document and provide instructionally relevant information on those aspects of children's lives most valued by parents and practitioners, specifically children's membership in inclusive settings, their social relationships with nondisabled children, and development of competence in relevant functional skills" (p. 173). Regardless of the well-known problems with using IQ and other norm-referenced tests with individuals having disabilities, the practice continues. Sigafoos, Cole, and McQuarter (1987) examined the cumulative school files of 143 students with severe disabilities, ranging from 6 to 20 years of age. The researchers found that criterion-referenced tests were used infrequently in comparison to norm-referenced tests, including IQ tests. It is our position that IQ tests have no value in planning educational programs for students with disabilities, while norm-referenced developmental measures have general programming value only for younger children with disabilities and when used in combination with consideration of the student's age, interests, motor and sensory abilities, and home and community environments.

Adaptive Behavior

Adaptive behavior is defined as "the effectiveness or degree with which individuals meet the standards of personal independence and social responsibility expected for age and cultural group" (Grossman, 1983, p. 1). The concept of adaptive behavior has encouraged educators to assess behaviors that have relevance to a student's functioning in society. Measures of adaptive behavior are usually checklists of skills required to function in the daily environment. For example the Adaptive Behavior Scale—School (second edition) (Lambert, Nihira, & Leland, 1993) includes the domains of independent functioning, physical development, economic activity, language development, numbers and time, prevocational or vocational activity, self-direction, responsibility, and socialization.

Adaptive behavior measures have been criticized on several counts. First, adaptive behavior is difficult to measure, because the concept is still vague and inadequately defined, making interpretation subjective (Fewell & Cone, 1983). In a survey of state definitions of mental retardation, Frankenberger and Harper (1988) found that 73% of the states surveyed provided criteria for the measurement of IQ, but only 12% of the sample specified criteria for the measurement of adaptive behavior. Second, although these measures focus on skills required in daily living, they often do not assess an individual's ability to adapt to changing circumstances. An item such as "able to catch a bus to work" may assess a skill necessary for functioning in the work world, but it does not address the individual's ability to solve the problem that would arise if the correct bus failed to come on time (Evans & Brown, 1986). Third, the high correlation between adaptive behavior and IQ leads many educators to conclude that adaptive behavior measures and IQ tests may be measuring the same abilities (Adams, 1973; Baumeister & Muma, 1975). Fourth, the information obtained from most current tests of adaptive behavior do not indicate much more about the severity of the problem or its cause than do more simplified screening instruments (Gaylord-Ross & Holvoet, 1985).

Earlier in this chapter, we described recent improvements made in the diagnostic and assessment requirements of disability definitions. Current definitions of mental retardation and severe disabilities emphasize the assessment of specific areas of adaptive behavior (e.g., communication, self-care, home living, social skills, community use, self-direction, health and safety, functional academics, leisure, and work) and the reciprocal measurement of needed supports. As these definitions are applied in the field, there will be a clear demand for improved measures of adaptive behavior.

Criterion-Referenced Tests and Tests of Adaptive Behavior

Unlike norm-referenced tests, which compare a student's performance to other students, *criterion-referenced tests* compare a student's performance to a predetermined level of mastery (criterion), regardless of the performance of other students. The specific adaptive or functional behavior identified in a test provides the measure for the assessment. Depending on how the assessment was developed, adaptive behavior measures may be classified as either norm-referenced or criterion-referenced (Lewis & Russo, 1998).

The advantage of adaptive behavior scales is that, because the items are environmentally determined, they tend to be more relevant to the daily lives of individuals. These scales can provide information that can contribute, at least in part, to the identification of needed functional skills and areas in which to concentrate instruction (Siegel-Causey & Allinder, 1998).

Table 3–3 describes the content areas covered by some frequently used scales that measure adaptive behavior. Some of these scales, such as the Inventory for Client and Agency Planning (ICAP) (Bruininks, Hill, Weatherman, & Woodcock, 1986), Scales of Independent Behavior, Revised (SIB-R) (Bruininks, Woodcock, Weatherman, & Hill, 1996), and Vineland Adaptive Behavior Scales (Sparrow, Balla, & Cicchetti, 1984) include computer components that provide options such as direct scoring, visual profiles of the student's performance across domains, identification of priority areas, items missed, and items successfully passed.

Criterion-Referenced Tests of Specific Domains

The tests just described provide assessments of adaptive behavior across multiple domains. Other instruments assess a single domain. One excellent example is the Assessment of Social Competence (ASC) (Meyer et al., 1985), which was designed as a compre-

TABLE 3–3
Adaptive Behavior Measures Used for Individuals with Severe Disabilities

Instrument, Author, and Publisher	Assessment Methods			Ages Covered			Content Areas									
	Interview	Observation	Direct testing	0–3 yr	3–6 yr	6 yr	Sensory	Gross motor	Fine motor	Language	Cognitive/academic	Social/emotional	Self-help	Independent living	Vocational	Recreation and leisure
Adaptive Behavior Scale—School (1993) Lambert, Nihira, & Leland Austin: Pro Ed	X	X		X	X	X	X	X	X	X		X	X	X	X	X
Checklist of Adaptive Living Skills (CALS) (1991) Morreau & Bruininks Riverside: DLM	X	X		X	X	X						X	X	X	X	
Inventory for Client & Agency Planning (ICAP) (1986) Bruininks, Hill, Weatherman, & Woodcock Riverside: DLM	X			X	X	X	X	X	X	X		X	X	X	X	
Scales of Independent Behavior—Rev. (1996) Bruininks, Woodcock, Weatherman, & Hill Riverside: DLM	X	X		X	X	X		X	X	X		X	X	X	X	X
Vineland Adaptive Behavior Scales (1984) Sparrow, Balla, & Cicchetti Circle Pines, MN: American Guidance Service	X			X	X	X		X	X	X		X	X	X		X

hensive measure of social functions necessary for everyday participation in integrated community environments. In this scale, 11 categories, or functions, are identified to represent the skills involved in social interactions. The concept of function is used to emphasize the idea that the purpose of a skill is more important than the form of the skill.

Many forms can achieve the same purpose for the individual, and the forms of social skills change according to age, setting, and a variety of other factors. Each social function of the ASC is divided into seven or eight levels that represent increasing forms of so-

cial sophistication. The lower levels do not represent younger age equivalents, but instead less complex strategies for accomplishing the same function. For example, function 1 of the ASC is "initiate," which focuses on the individual's joining an ongoing interaction or starting a new one. The following are eight increasingly sophisticated levels of this function, with an example of each level:

1. Initiates behavior inconsistently in the presence of others (e.g., sometimes vocalizes in the presence of other persons).

2. Consistently initiates behavior with other persons (e.g., moves or reaches out to obtain attention).
3. Uses common greetings and initiations (e.g., hovers around a peer activity but joins only when invited).
4. Initiates interactions based on the situation (e.g., shares an object with another person who wants it).
5. Initiates goal-directed social interaction (e.g., after greeting a peer, gets out a favorite game to play).
6. Attends to contextual details when initiating a social interaction (e.g., waits until another person is not busy to initiate interaction).
7. Bases initiations on direct experience with similar activities previously done with a particular person (e.g., initiates activity only with peers who have been friendly in the past).
8. Bases initiations upon indirect knowledge and inference (e.g., invites one friend rather than another, based on the judgment that the selected person likes the chosen activity).

Environmental Assessment Strategies

We have reviewed many issues related to the use of standardized measures for students with developmental disabilities. The most critical point is that these measures provide little useful data for educational programs, while nontraditional, or alternative, assessment procedures provide more relevant and useful data regarding functioning in integrated settings and students' achievement of desired outcomes (Knowlton, 1998; Siegel-Causey & Allinder, 1998). Recently, discussion has focused on the need for alternative strategies of assessment, specifically "authentic" assessment. The term *authentic* refers to assessment that is referenced to independence and lifestyle quality in relevant and actual environments rather than in contrived environments (Knowlton, 1998) and that is based on the evaluation of valued skills (Siegel-Causey & Allinder, 1998).

This section reviews a variety of authentic alternative assessment strategies that focus on the relationship between an individual and specific environmental demands. As is true with all criterion-referenced tests, environmental assessment strategies examine the environment to determine the skills needed by the individual. In this case, however, rather than using commercially prepared instruments, general strate-

gies are applied to assess environments relevant to a particular student. Consequently, the procedure is totally individualized. The purposes of environmental assessments are to identify functional routines and activities required across relevant settings, such as home, school, work, and community, and to measure or estimate a student's performance on specific routines and activities found within those settings.

Before describing specific environmental assessment strategies, it is useful to consider a number of guidelines that increase the validity of the environmentally based assessment process: the who, when, and where of assessment (Silberman & Brown, 1998).

Who Assesses

IDEA formally identifies individuals who must participate on an evaluation team: the student's parents; at least one general education teacher of the student (if the student is or may be participating in the general education setting); at least one special education teacher; a representative of the school district who is qualified to provide or supervise instruction; an individual who can interpret the instructional implications of evaluation results; and, at the parents' or school's discretion, other individuals who have knowledge or special expertise; and the student (when appropriate) (Turnbull & Turnbull, 1998).

Participants in an environmental assessment may include these evaluation team members, but at times may be more inclusive and collaborative. Professionals and others who know the student well are expected to offer information about the student's behavior and performance in a variety of the student's natural environments. Who these people are will vary according to the abilities and disabilities, age, characteristics, and needs of the student (Orelove & Sobsey, 1996; Silberman & Brown, 1998). For example, a bus driver is not likely to be an "informant" on a developmental assessment but may be important in the environmental assessment of the students' traveling routines.

Special education law has long encouraged student participation, *when appropriate*, but student participation in educational planning has been the exception more than the practice (Wehmeyer & Sands, 1998). With increased focus on self-determination, student participation in educational planning is increasing. In fact, IDEA (1990) mandated that students age 16 and older be provided with transition plans based on their needs, interests, and preferences; IDEA amendments of 1997 then mandated that students be invited to participate in the transition planning process (Wehmeyer & Sands, 1998).

Trends in educating students with disabilities emphasize the involvement of each student in critical elements of the education process. Students with severe disabilities represent a challenge to achieving this goal. Participation in programmatic efforts to increase student involvement and self-determination in the education process often requires communication skills that are difficult for individuals with severe, multiple disabilities (Gothelf & Brown, 1998). Increasing participation in the educational process, however, must not be seen as an obstacle, but a challenge. A variety of strategies are available for determining preferences of individuals who have difficulty communicating. For example, effective observational assessments of student preferences may involve: (a) noting the nonverbal forms of communication (e.g., looking towards item, engagement), (b) interviewing people who know the student well, and (c) observing the person's behavior in a variety of environments and contexts (Brown, Gothelf, Guess, & Lehr, 1998; Gothelf, & Brown, 1998; Silberman & Brown, 1998) (see chapter 6 for further discussion on assessing nonverbal behavior).

For example, Timothy's 1:1 home instructor, Juliet, reported that he would intermittently cry and throw his materials on the floor. Mrs. Simms and Juliet decided to more closely observe Timothy's behaviors to try to determine what he might be communicating with his behavior. For 1 week they kept track of variables, such as when the behaviors occurred, in which activities they occurred, and how long he would participate before the behaviors began. They discovered that the disruptive behaviors typically occurred during the same two sessions and would occur after about five trials into the session. The two sessions in which the behavior occurred were the matching colors (using large plastic pegs) and matching shapes (using foam shapes) programs. Mrs. Simms and Juliet made several hypotheses about what Timothy might be expressing about his curriculum. They decided to try several program changes in these two activities to test their hypotheses and note Timothy's response to them: shorten the sessions, take a brief break after three trials, and change the materials to more functional ones. By noting Timothy's response to

these changes they would be testing their hypotheses. Consequent changes in his programs would thus reflect Timothy's contribution to his educational program.

When and Where to Assess

Standardized assessments are conducted in settings that are, to the greatest degree possible, free from distractions (McLoughlin & Lewis, 1994), including, for example, special testing areas or therapy rooms. These practices are used to get as "pure" a reading as possible on the individual's responses to test items. However, environmental assessments have a different mission: to explore the individual's functioning in settings in which he or she routinely participates. Thus, assessment will be conducted, to the greatest degree possible, in those routine settings—including all the distractions that are typically found in those settings (Silberman & Brown, 1998)—and interviews will focus on gaining information concerning the individual's behavior and performance in those settings.

Problems in response generalization and stimulus overselectivity further necessitate assessing performance in everyday settings using materials natural to the context. Some children like Timothy may be able to perform a skill in natural contexts but not in a contrived setting.

Timothy was tested for "verbal imitation" in the speech and language therapy room. Sitting directly across from Timothy, Ms. Rivera, his speech and language therapist, presents a verbal cue (e.g., "say ball"), hoping to elicit an imitation of her verbal stimulus. Timothy makes only a few correct responses to the list of words and frequently leaves his seat during testing. Observations during music group in his preschool, however, indicate that during songs such as "Old MacDonald's Farm," Timothy imitates the teacher or peer's choice of animal sounds. His mother also has reported that, at home, Timothy will imitate his older sister's verbalizations of excitement (e.g., "wow," "cool," "go") when they watch videos together.

Other times, the student may be able to perform a skill in contrived settings, but not in the natural settings. This is particularly likely when skills have been taught only in the isolated setting.

In the speech and language therapy room, Timothy was successfully taught to "sort" objects of like color and shape (e.g., reds go in the red pile and blues go in the blue pile, triangles

*go in the triangle bin and squares in the square bin).
However, when his teacher observed him putting away toys
after free play, Timothy did so randomly, rather than putting
the foam blocks with the other foam blocks and the wood
blocks in the wood block bin.*

Because we are interested in assessing the student's functioning in typical routines, assessment is most valid in those settings, using those materials that are natural to those settings and with all the distractors associated with those settings. Not only is it informative to know what the student *can* or *cannot* do, it is critical to consider the reason for failure. Downing and Demchak (1996) suggested that when a student cannot perform an item on an assessment, we must determine whether the student is actually unable to perform the skill, lacks motivation in that context, or has no reason to perform the skill when requested. This information is critical in designing education programs.

Multidimensional Framework for Conceptualizing Assessment

The assessment process will be only as meaningful as the behavior or skill outcomes that are identified and measured. These outcomes should reflect what current best practice has identified as important. According to Siegel-Causey and Allinder (1998), the best educational practice standards include those that are:

- Grounded both in research and values
- Focused on school and community-based instruction
- Referenced to neighborhood schools
- Facilitative of social and instructional integration of students with and without disabilities
- Coordinated between related services and educational personnel

Meaningful assessment of students with severe disabilities must reflect this range of outcomes. It is clear that assessment of skill acquisition, while important, is not sufficient to demonstrate a meaningful or comprehensive educational experience. Focusing solely on academic development or skill development "fails to acknowledge the breadth of outcomes that may contribute to the ability of students to lead ful-

filling lives" (Billingsley, Gallucci, Peck, Schwartz, & Staub, 1996, p. 44). Billingsley, et al., (1996) conceptualized a three-part outcome framework to represent these broad needs of students with severe disabilities. These domains can be used as a structure to identify assessment needs, plan how assessment information will be collected, and organize assessment information collected (Table 3–4).

One domain of the framework is *skills*. This part of the model focuses on progress in such traditional skill areas as the use of appropriate social or communication skills; the degree of change in using academic skills, such as reading, writing, and math; and progress in using functional skills that increase the student's degree of independence and control of the environment.

A second domain of the conceptual framework refers to the variety of personal *relationships* formed with other children. Billingsley, et al. identified five major patterns of interaction: play or companionship; helpee; helper; peer partner; and adversarial. Third, the model identifies belonging, or *membership*, in formal and informal groups of the classroom and school community. Membership can take at least five forms: role in small group, class membership, friendship cliques, school membership, and activities outside of school.

Taken together, the three components can be used to plan assessment, organize assessment information, and determine if the appropriate range of assessments were conducted. For example, if assessments were conducted for a student that covered the areas of skill acquisition and relationships but did not include any information about "memberships," additional strategies must be initiated to assess needs in this area.

Viewing assessment as being relevant to a broad range of outcomes is responsive to the recent call for greater use of alternative, authentic assessment. Siegel-Causey and Allinder (1998) describe authentic assessment as assessment that is based on the performance of valued skills and focused on what the student actually learns. According to these authors *portfolio assessment* is one type of authentic assessment that meets the standard of a values-based assessment approach. The evaluator is interested in multidimensional assessment data (e.g., functional assessment, curriculum-based assessment, norm-based measures, checklists, permanent products of student work, medical and physical evaluations), and in func-

TABLE 3–4
Definitions of Outcome Categories

Membership	Relationships	Skills
Belonging to a group (treated as a member, accommodations made to include, shared rituals and symbols)	Patterns of interaction that typically develop between peers	Behavioral competencies that develop over time and are the traditional focus of special education
Role in small group Student plays an essential role in multiple groups across the school day. **Class membership** Student involved in class activities, takes turns with class responsibilities, participates in class privileges, and is active in class routines. **Friendship cliques** Student is a stable member of a consistent group of friends. **School membership** Student is involved in schoolwide activities, attends assemblies, and other school functions. **Outside of school activities** Student is a regular participant in extracurricular activities or clubs. Necessary accommodations are present.	**Play/companionship** Student engages in reciprocal social interactions with peers. **Helpee** Student receives and accepts appropriate levels of help from peers. **Helper** Student offers or provides appropriate levels of help to peers. **Peer/reciprocal** Student engages in reciprocal task-related interactions with peers. **Adversarial** Student is involved in negative interactions with one or more peers.	**Social/communication skills** Student learns ways to interact with peers appropriately, to engage cooperatively, to be understood through a system of communication, and to attend to and understand others, even if only in part. **Academic skills** Student learns basic skills or facts in reading, writing, math, science, and social studies. **Functional skills** Student learns practical routines such as dressing, eating, mobility, putting things away, grooming, making purchases, safe street crossing, etc.

Note: Adapted, with permission, from Billingsley, Gallucci, Peck, Schwartz, & Staub, 1997, p. 47.

tional contexts over time and using a variety of means (e.g., videotapes, audiotapes, interviewing, observational data, social validation) (Siegel-Causey & Allinder, 1998; Wesson & King, 1996).

The reauthorized IDEA mandates that states develop and have in place by the year 2000 alternate assessments appropriate for all students with disabilities (Kleinert, Kearns, & Kennedy, 1997; Ysseldyke & Olsen, 1999). As Ysseldyke and Olsen (1999) point out, "States now face a vexing challenge. A small group of students exists (usually students with severe cognitive deficits or multiple disabilities) for whom standard large-scale testing practices and accommodations just do not work" (p. 176). The state of Kentucky has been an innovator in this area. Through the use of the *Alternate Portfolio*, students with moderate and severe cognitive disabilities are included in the statewide educational assessment and accountability system (Kleinert, Kearns, & Kennedy, 1997). In this model, outcomes relevant to students with se-

vere disabilities were generated using the learner outcomes established for all students in the state as a foundation. For each of the identified 75 learner outcomes, or academic expectations, prioritized outcomes were identified for students with severe disabilities, considering how each outcome could apply to or be meaningful to the student with severe disabilities and the outcome's overall educational importance. For example, the statewide outcome of "identifying issues of justice, equality, responsibility, choice, freedom, and applying these democratic principles to real-life situations" was reframed for students with disabilities as "makes choices, and accepts responsibility for own actions." (Kleinert, Kearns, & Kennedy, 1997).

The following sections demonstrate how a wide variety of informal assessment strategies can contribute to the collection of assessment information that focuses on a broad framework of meaningful outcomes.

Ecological Inventories

Ecological inventories are informal assessments that require teachers to consider areas of instruction arranged in "domains of adult functioning," or skill categories (L. Brown, et al., 1979). These domains may include domestic, leisure, community, school, and vocational areas. The *domestic domain* includes skills performed in and around the home—self-care, clothing care, housekeeping, cooking, and yard work. To the extent that an adult might be paid for performing domestic tasks, this domain has some overlap with skills in the vocational domain (e.g., janitorial, factory, fast-food restaurant). In the *leisure domain* are spectator or participant skills that may take place in the community, at school, or at home. The *community domain* includes skills such as street crossing, using public transportation, making purchases in stores, eating in restaurants, and using other public facilities. The *vocational domain* includes skills involved in attaining meaningful employment, some of which occur in the middle school and high school settings, but most of which take place in community locations. Historically, the activities and skills identified under each of the four domains (i.e., domestic, leisure, community, and vocational) were used to develop the school program for a student with severe disabilities. Now, as neighborhood inclusive schools become the standard for best practice, the fifth domain of *school* must be included. Thus, school becomes its own domain, and must be analyzed to determine the school-specific routines (e.g., eating in a cafeteria, using a locker, attending assembly) that should be assessed.

Brown and his colleagues (1979) refer to their functional survey for objectives as a "top-down" approach to skill building. That is, they begin with the requirements of independent adult functioning within each domain. This practice ensures identification of skills that are functional. The ecological approach differs from the developmental approach, in which instructional objectives are chosen from the bottom up, starting with skills normally performed by infants and proceeding to those considered more advanced.

When IEP goals and objectives address skills that are functional for a person, the chances that those skills, once learned, will be used and thus naturally maintained are increased. Since learning is often slow and skill loss through disuse is predictable for stu-

dents with disabilities, target skills that meet the criterion of functionality can facilitate good conditions for skill retention. (At the same time, the criterion of functionality cannot override criteria such as the student's preference and choice and the preferences of the student's family).

Ecological inventories are tailored to encourage skill generalization in several ways. First, *functionality* is defined for each student by a variety of individuals familiar with this student and the student's current and potential home, school, community, and work environments. Second, a skill and activity listing, often rather long, results from interviewing these individuals and studying the environments. Typically, there is some redundancy in skills and activities that are required across environments. Those that are more often required will be deemed "higher priority" and more naturally supported by teachers, peers, and coworkers in those environments.

Another advantage of using ecological inventories over commercially prepared tests is their flexible content (Brown et al., 1979). The content is not predetermined. Rather, it depends on each student's situation. Considering the variability in students and their environments and their subsequent demands, individually determined assessment content is an asset. That is, some students are expected to function in urban settings and others in rural settings. Certainly, recreational options in various communities differ greatly, as do the leisure preferences of students and their families. The age of the student also will be a determining factor in the types of environments and activities in which they engage. If one's goal is to assess a student's ability to adapt within a particular environment, the content of the assessment should reflect the unique requirements of the community and family context.

According to Brown and his colleagues (1979), there are five phases of the ecological inventory process:

1. Identify the curriculum domains.
2. Identify and survey current and future natural environments.
3. Divide the relevant environments into subenvironments.
4. Inventory these subenvironments for the relevant activities performed there.

5. Determine the skills required for performance of the activities.

The teacher proceeds through each phase in order.

Curriculum Domains

For many students, all five domains (i.e., domestic, leisure, school, community, and vocation) are relevant. However, teachers and parents need not concern themselves with the vocational domain until the later elementary years, when classroom jobs may become part of scheduled activities. Rather than the traditional academic or developmental categories, curriculum domains are used because they (a) represent the major life areas, (b) lead to the selection of practical skills, and (c) emphasize the functional goals of self-sufficiency, but use of curriculum domains does not mean that communication, motor, or social skills are forgotten. Rather, the domains may be used as contexts in which to embed and teach those skills.

Most often, the ecological inventory focuses on elementary, middle school, high school, and older students. However, when considering very young children, many professionals do not feel comfortable with trying to predict possible adult environments (Lehr, 1989). Several educators describe application of the *criterion of the next environment* for preschool children. For young children, the skills that are identified should focus on social behavior and survival skills for the next environment, such as an integrated kindergarten (Chandler, 1992; Vincent et al., 1980). Figure 3–2 shows the different domains identified for Timothy and Christine, reflecting the differences in their ages.

Current and Future Natural Environments

The next step requires the teacher to identify and examine the environments in which the student currently lives, learns or studies, works, and plays. Further, to prepare students to function in the settings they will use in the future, these environments must be added to the inspection list.

Although it is difficult to predict future environments, it is necessary to identify them as early as possible. For Timothy, who is only 4 years old, several environments are relevant—his own home (an apartment), the babysitter's home, various shops in his neighborhood, the school yard, and his preschool. A future environment will be the elementary school in his neighborhood. By contrast, Christine's relevant environments at age 20 include her home, various job sites that she is sampling, and the community in which she and her family participate. Figure 3–2 reflects variations in the types of environments identified for assessment for Timothy, who lives in an urban setting, and Christine, who lives in a suburban environment.

Subenvironments

Further division is necessary to isolate the activities most likely to be required in each environment. As with all other steps in this process, the division must be completed with the needs of the individual student in mind. Because Timothy and Christine live in different environments (i.e., apartment and private home), it follows that the subenvironments will also be different (Figure 3–2). One environment has an elevator, while the other has a backyard. The diversity in these two students' ages, living environments, and so on reflect the need for assessments that will be sensitive to individual lifestyles.

Relevant Activities

What are the essential activities that a student is or will be required to perform in these settings, or subenvironments? Because there are potentially an endless number of possible activities that could occur, teachers must consider a variety of factors as they determine which activities are relevant: (a) activities that are considered to be mandatory for successful functioning in the various environments, (b) the number of times an activity (or a variation of it) is needed in other subenvironments in which the student participates, (c) the student's current skills, (d) the student's preferences and interests, (e) the priorities of the parents, (f) the specific physical characteristics of the setting in which the activity will occur, (g) the potential for the student's meaningful partial participation in the activity, and (h) the contribution of this activity to the student's relationships and belonging. Figure 3–3 provides examples of activities found in

FIGURE 3–2
Examples of Domains, Environments, and Subenvironments Individualized for Timothy and Christine

Timothy:

Domain	Domestic	School	Community	Leisure
Environments	Apartment	Preschool	Grocery store	School yard
Subenvironments	Elevator	Classroom	Shopping cart area	Benches
	Kitchen	Bathroom	Food aisles	Playground
	Bathroom	Hallway	Deli counter	Baseball field
	Bedroom	Playground	Cashier	Water fountain
	Fire escape	Main office	Parking lot	Basketball court

Christine:

Domain	Domestic	School	Community	Leisure	Vocational
Environments	Private house	High school	Recycle center	Movie theatre	Library
Subenvironments	Kitchen	Homeroom	Parking lot	Ticket booth	Check out desk
	Bathroom	Cafeteria	Cans area	Concession stand	Hallways
	Bedroom	Classrooms	Newspaper area	Theater	Restroom
	Den	Bus stop	Bottles area	Bathroom	Break area
	Yard	Bathroom	Office	Video games	Stacks

Note: Adapted, with permission, from Silberman, R. K., & Brown, F. (1998). Alternative approaches to assessing students who have visual impairments with other disabilities in classroom and community environments. In S. Z. Sacks & R. K. Silberman (Eds.) *Educating students who have visual impairments with other disabilities* (p. 81). Baltimore: Paul H. Brookes.

one subenvironment of the school domain for Timothy and Christine.

Skills Required

This step requires that activities be broken down into teachable units, or task analyzed. A task analysis (described in more detail in chapter 4) is a detailed description of each behavior needed to accomplish a complex behavior (Alberto & Troutman, 1999; White, 1971). As task analysis relates to assessment, the student is asked to perform a selected task or activity, and the student's performance on each component is recorded (see chapter 5 for examples of evaluating performance on task-analyzed activities). The teacher then knows which components of the chain need to be addressed (e.g., taught, environmental modifications made). Although each skill is separated for measurement and teaching, the teacher must not lose sight of the activity or clusters of related skills that must be performed together in the natural environment. For Christine, the "pledge of allegiance to the flag" includes many related skills: initiating following the cue of the loudspeaker announcement and other students standing up, having her chair turned to face in the direction of the flag, activating the "pledge" on her Dynavox, and turning back to her desk when the pledge is complete.

FIGURE 3–3

Examples of Activities in One Subenvironment in the School Domain for Timothy and Christine

	Timothy	Christine
Environment	**Preschool**	**High School**
Subenvironment	Classroom	Homeroom
Activities	Morning group	Pledge to flag
	Snack	Attendance
	1:1 discrete trial instruction	Hand in notices
	Centers	Pack new notices
	Toileting and handwashing	Review day's schedule
	Recess	
	Music group	

Note: Adapted with permission from Silberman, R. K., & Brown, F. (1998). Alternative approaches to assessing students who have visual impairments with other disabilities in classroom and community environments. In S. Z. Sacks & R. K. Silberman (Eds.) *Educating students who have visual impairments with other disabilities* (p. 82). Baltimore: Paul H. Brookes.

The Component Model of Functional Life Routines: Ensuring Meaningful Task Analysis

Brown, Evans, Weed, and Owen (1987) identify areas of concern in the standard application of task analysis for assessment. First, most task analyses are designed with a very limited scope of skills. Traditionally, tasks are broken down within the context of observable motor skills (e.g., pick up the hairbrush, bring to head, brush down left side of hair). Task analyses may not identify related or critical skills (e.g., social, communication) associated with meaningful performance of an activity in the natural environment. They also may exclude skills such as initiation, problem solving, choice, and monitoring the quality of an activity. Such skills enable a student to have more control over the routine, or self-determination.

Second, the beginning and ending points of behavioral chains are often arbitrary or inconsistent. Often, a task analysis begins with a teacher's verbal cue (e.g., "it's time to go to lunch") rather than an expectation that the student will respond to a natural environmental cue (e.g., the lunch bell sounds; math period is over). In many task-analyzed activities, students are often not expected, as they should be, to end a task. For some students, ending a task may mean putting away the materials that were used (e.g., put the game back in the box and on the shelf); for other students, especially those who do not have the physical ability to put away materials, ending a task may mean indicating when they would like the activity to end.

Third, because the usual division of an activity into smaller steps focuses on the motor aspects of the activity, teachers often promote students' participation on the basis of just those components of the activity. For a student with multiple disabilities, such as Christine, this means that partial participation in activities centers around physical expectations and outcomes. If participation were focused solely on motor components, participation may not be as meaningful or satisfying for the individual, even though the activity itself would be considered functional. Partial participation should allow the student greater control, or self-determination, over the personal routines and events in his or her environment (Brown & Lehr, 1993).

For a student like Timothy who can participate extensively in the routine, teachers should identify an appropriate range of skills to more closely represent mastery. For example, Adaptive Behavior Scales—Public School Version (Lambert, Nihira, & Leland, 1993) breaks down "washing hands and face" into the following components: (a) washes hands and face with soap and water without prompting, (b) washes hands with soap, (c) washes face with soap, (d) washes hands and face with water, and (e) dries hands and face. Would successful performance of these four parts imply that the student has mastered this skill? The core skills do not sample the range of behaviors necessary for functional use of the routine in natural environments. To use this skill in the natural environment, Timothy would also be expected to know, for example, when his hands needed washing, to check to make sure they are clean, and to know where to find more soap when the soap runs out.

The Component Model of Functional Life Routines (Brown, Evans, Weed, & Owen, 1987; Brown & Lehr, 1993) outlines several ways in which an individual can meaningfully participate in activities. Performing motor (or core) skills is only one of three ways that participation can occur in any given routine. *Extension* skills extend the core skills and create a more comprehensive routine and thus provide a more meaningful evaluation of student competence. Extension skills include (a) initiation, (b) preparation, (c) monitoring the quality, (d) monitoring the tempo, (e) problem solving, and (f) terminating.

Extension skills provide options for meaningful participation in the activity without extensive physical requirements. For example, a student may not be able to eat independently, but may *initiate* independently by pointing on her communication board she wants to eat, or *terminate* mealtime by indicating that she is finished eating. The student can also *monitor the quality* of the routine by indicating that her blouse is dirty from lunch and needs to be changed, even though she may not be able to independently change her own blouse.

Enrichment skills are not critical to the independent performance of a routine. They do, however, add to

the quality of the routine and, as such, may be considered to be equally as important as the skills already mentioned. If educators are concerned with the quality of students' lives, then their assessment procedures should reflect this concern. Enrichment skills include expressive communication, social behaviors, and expression of preference. If one were doing the laundry, commenting on the activity may not be crucial to accomplishing the task, but it may make the task a more pleasant experience and also offers functional practice of the communication skill. Choosing between two or more feasible alternatives (e.g., in hairstyle) is also not crucial to the performance of a routine but adds to the quality of a student's experience as well as providing some control over daily life.

Each resulting skill in a component analysis represents a meaningful unit of behavior: all items are relevant to the demands of the natural environment and are particularly important for students with severe physical disabilities. Students like Christine often "bottom out" on many assessments because core motor skills are the usual focus. In interpreting a core skill assessment, a teacher would likely conclude that the student should begin to learn the specific motor movements of the skill as determined by a detailed task analysis. According to the component model, however, the student may be able to engage in other, more meaningful and more satisfying aspects of the routine. With the component model, team members not only assess relevant items and score meaningful dimensions of behavior but also include these items as relevant goals in the student's educational program. The items identified using this approach are closely aligned with the mission of Billingsley's (1996) outcome framework: to identify those skills that would facilitate the individual's membership and belonging in settings that are valued by the individual, family members, and other members of his or her community.

Figure 3–4 is an example of the component model applied to the activity of "plays a game with peer and adult," which was identified as an objective for Timothy. In addition to delineating meaningful units of behavior, the format depicted in Figure 3–4 can be used to provide an informal assessment of baseline and to assess progress during instruction. Note that in this analysis of the activity, "performs basic steps of the game" is only 1 step of 11. This implies that playing the game itself is only one part of the activity and

FIGURE 3–4

Task Analysis of "Plays Game with Peer and Adult" Using The Component Model of Functional Life Routines

Student: _Timothy_

Age: _4_   Date: _____

Domain: _Leisure_

Routine: _Plays game with peer and adult_

Plays Game with Adult	Yes	No	NA	With Adaptations	Comments
1. Lets you or peers know in some way it is time to play game (*initiate*)					
2. Selects game of choice (*preference*)					
3. Selects peer(s) to play with (*preference*)					
4. Arranges play area, gets materials, or arranges with others for things to be done (*prepare*)					
5. Performs basic steps of the game (*core*)					
6. Attempts to improve skills or increase enjoyment for self or others (*monitor quality*)					
7. Spends appropriate amount of time engaged in game (*monitor tempo*)					
8. If a problem arises (e.g., can't find game piece) will take action to remove problem (*problem-solve*)					
9. Puts away materials, arranges for others to put away, or lets other know he is done playing (*terminate*)					
10. Expresses or communicates about any aspect of the activity (e.g., enjoyment, request) (*communication*)					
11. Responds appropriately with peers during game, such as sharing and taking turns (*social*)					

Note: Adapted with permission from Brown, F., Evans, I. M., Weed, K. A., Owen, V. (1987). Delineating functional competencies: A component model. The Journal of the Association for Persons with Severe Disabilities, *12*(2), 122.

that there are many other ways that we are expecting Timothy to participate. If the game playing (e.g., following the rules of the game) was the goal, this step should be further task-analyzed.

Examples of Ecological Inventories

We are not recommending a single format for completing an ecological inventory, because ecological inventories should be individualized to assess the variables deemed critical by the educational team. Figure 3–5 is an example of an environmental inventory format. This inventory does not specify the type of scoring used to measure the core skills (e.g., performance level of the activity or routine) nor does it specify the type of component skills that will be measured. The inventory should be individualized according to variables such as: the context; the student's age, strengths, and needs; and component skills identified by the team as important. For some students, a dichotomous performance score of "yes" or "no" may be appropriate; for others, the team may be interested in the level of prompt needed for the student to complete the activity (e.g., verbal, model, physical assistance). Assessment of component skills will also vary according to the needs of the individual student. Problem solving and initiation may be critical skills of interest for one student; assessing another student's social and communication skills within routines across the school day may be of interest.

Figure 3–6 is a sample portion from an environmental inventory of the school domain for Timothy.

Mr. Grayson and Ms. Johnston (Timothy's special education and preschool teachers) started by generating a list of activities and selecting people to interview. Figure 3–6 shows a section of the ecological inventory they completed to examine the subenvironments and activities involved from the time of Timothy's arrival at school through "centers" time. The activities typically expected of other children in his class in each of the subenvironments (e.g., hallways, bathroom, morning group) were listed down the left side of the form. The team was interested in assessing Timothy's performance in the activities using a three-part scoring system (i.e., assistance needed on most steps, some steps, or independent performance), so these are indicated across the top of the form.

It was also decided by his team that, in addition to assessing his basic performance of the activities, assessment of several component skills would be revealing. Discussion focused on Timothy's inconsistent *initiation* and *termination* of activities. Termination was of particular interest to his teacher, who reported that sometimes Timothy would get upset and cry when he was asked to leave one activity and begin another. On the other hand, Timothy would terminate too quickly when he did not care for the activity or the interaction. Mr. and Mrs. Simms were especially interested in their son exhibiting social and interaction skills with others, so this too was assessed within activities. Finally, everyone agreed that assessing Timothy's choice making and communication skills would address his IEP goals and foster self-determination and cognitive development. The team felt that it would be especially critical to assess these skills within the context of his daily activities, because much instruction in these areas occurred in 1:1 and therapeutic settings.

In addition to the school domain, Mr. Grayson assessed three other domains: leisure, community, and domestic. Peers, family members, and various other teachers and therapists were involved in interviews on one or more of these domain areas.

Applications of the Ecological Model

The ecological assessment strategy can be very time-consuming. Recently, however, professionals have applied the ecological inventory process to specific domains and critical skills. Such applications not only provide teachers with a functional and efficient approach but also offer structure and guidelines for identification of certain types of items within a variety of specific skill areas. This is important because the general process of the ecological inventory does not take into consideration the subjectivity of the assessors. That is, although the process very much ensures identification of skills that are functional for the individual, the skill sequences identified by two raters may be substantially different. One teacher, who has had extensive training in communication, may identify numerous communication opportunities within her ecological inventory. A second teacher, who has had extensive experience teaching students with

FIGURE 3–5

Blank Form for an Environmental Inventory

Student:
Environment:
Date:
Informants:
Methods:

Domain:	Performance Level			Component Skills						Comments
	(Check one)			(Check all that apply)						
Subenvironments/Activity										

FIGURE 3–6

Sample from Environmental Inventory for Timothy

Student:	Timothy
Environment:	Preschool
Date:	October 1999
Informants:	Parents, preschool teacher, teaching assistant, speech therapist, 1:1 instructor
Methods:	Interview and observation

Domain: School	Performance Level (Check one)			Component Skills (Check skills that are displayed)					Comments
Subenvironments/Activity	Assist on most steps	Assist on some steps	Independent	Initiates	Has related social skills	Makes choices	Terminates	Communicates	
Parking lot and building entrance									
• Enters			X	X					
• Greets children	X								
• Greets adults	X								
Hallways									
• Greets others	X								
• Hangs up coat		X		X		X	X		
Bathroom									
• Toilets		X		X			X		Terminates too quickly
• Washes hands		X				X	X		Terminates too quickly
• Checks appearance		X					X		Terminates too quickly
Morning group									
• Sits in place		X				X			
• Interacts with others	X				X		X		Terminates too quickly; only interacts with Melinda

Domain: School	Performance Level (Check one)			Component Skills (Check skills that are displayed)					Comments
Subenvironments/Activity	Assist on most steps	Assist on some steps	Independent	Initiates	Has related social skills	Makes choices	Terminates	Communicates	
Morning group continued									
• Follows instructions	X								
• Uses materials	X								Doesn't want to terminate
• Imitates actions		X							
• Raises hand for attendance		X							
Centers									
• Follows schedule		X				X			Seems to enjoy looking at schedule and choosing
• Shares with others	X					X		X	Shares only with certain peers; terminates quickly
• Uses materials		X							Doesn't want to terminate
• Switches centers following bell cue		X							Hard to switch activities once he is involved in one
• Interacts with others	X				X		X	X	Terminates too quickly; interacts easily with Melinda

multiple disabilities, may focus on the physical demands of an environment.

Teachers need to be sure that ecological inventories identify not only the observable activities and skills that are associated with competent performance in natural environments but also related skills that may not be quite so apparent. In addition to communication and motor skills, subtle social skills, such as smiling at a waitress and giving eye contact to the cashier at a restaurant, may not be consistently identified. Although not always critical to the performance of the routine, these behaviors may nonetheless be crucial to socially appropriate performance of an activity. Similarly, some language competencies may not be observable because they do not occur at that specific place or time of the activity. That is, "going to a movie" may be identified as an activity within the community domain and divided into its component parts, but "communicating about the movie" later in the day or "inviting a friend to the movies" probably would not be identified in an inventory (see earlier section on Component Model of Functional Life Routines).

Several authors have applied the ecological inventory strategy to the assessment of critical, or related, skills, using the life domains as contexts in which critical skills can be identified and functionally assessed. Others have formalized the ecological inventory approach by providing more structure or systematizing the approach. For example, Sigafoos and York (1991) use an ecological inventory approach to determine priority *communication* targets for instruction. In their assessment, the final step of the inventory, or the task analysis, is expanded to include communicative behavior. According to Sigafoos and York, at least six communication variables should be included and explored in an ecological analysis: (a) the *communicative demands* of relevant activities (e.g., ordering food; requesting a movie ticket); (b) the *naturally occurring opportunities* for teaching communication skills (e.g., "more" when you run out of work supplies); (c) the *communicative intents*, or functions, that are required to meet environmental demands and opportunities (e.g., initiate, maintain, reject, comment); (d) the specific *vocabulary needs* of activities, that is, the words frequently used in the activities in which the student will participate; (e) the most effective *communication modes* for specific environments and activities (e.g., a cashier in the fast food restaurant

may understand a picture, but not a sign); and (f) the *natural cues and consequences* that should be used to establish participation in activities (e.g., responding to the school bell to change classes, rather than a teacher prompt).

The Syracuse Community-Referenced Curriculum Guide for Students with Moderate and Severe Disabilities (Ford et al., 1989) is a curriculum guide that uses the ecological approach. This guide focuses on the four domains of (a) self-management and home living, (b) vocational, (c) recreation and leisure, and (d) general community functioning. Also included in this guide are sections on functional academic skills (e.g., reading, writing, money handling, time management) and embedded skills (i.e., social, communication, and motor). Each scope and sequence chart lists the major goal areas of the domain and examples of the sequence of possible activities relevant to students as they progress through the school years. Thus, the goal (or function) remains the same across time, but the form of the activity in which students participate may differ (e.g., a child in kindergarten may learn to prepare a simple snack, a high school student may learn to plan a menu).

Choosing Options and Accommodations for Children (COACH) (Giangreco, Cloninger, & Iverson, 1998) is another assessment and planning tool. It is a comprehensive curriculum guide that helps the team develop annual goals and objectives and determine general supports and accommodations that the student needs to participate in the educational program. There are a wealth of forms to facilitate assessment, implementation, and evaluation of priority goals and objectives. This guide offers a comprehensive system for helping the educational team move from assessment and identification of objectives to implementation and evaluation of the educational plan within the context of the general education program.

Functional Assessment of Problem Behaviors

A comprehensive assessment of problem behaviors is the cornerstone for developing effective and positive behavioral strategies. Recent efforts to reduce severe problem behaviors, such as self-injury, aggression, and property damage, have focused on assessment of the variables that functionally control behavior. In other words, the relationship between the inappropriate behavior and the environment becomes the focus of assessment. The term *functional assessment* refers to the process used to identify the antecedent and consequent events that occasion and maintain problem behavior (Lennox & Miltenberger, 1989). (See chapter 6 for an in-depth review of functional assessment and program development.)

Many problem behaviors are attributed to specific pragmatic intents; that is, the behavior serves a specific function for the individual and is a form of communication for the individual. Durand (1990) classifies controlling variables into four categories, or functions, for the individual: (a) social attention (the behavior elicits attention for the individual), (b) escape (the behavior results in the individual's being removed from an unpleasant situation), (c) access to tangible consequences (the behavior results in access to reinforcing events or materials), and (d) sensory feedback (the behavior provides auditory, visual, or tactile stimulation).

Once the function of the behavior is determined, the student should be provided with, and instructed on, a more appropriate way of communicating the same message. That is, the behavior taught to the individual should be functionally equivalent to the problem behavior (Carr & Durand, 1985; Donnellan, Mirenda, Mesaros, & Fassbender, 1984; Durand & Carr, 1991; Haring & Kennedy, 1990; Koegel, Koegel, & Dunlap, 1996; O'Neill, et al., 1997). This strategy has been termed *functional communication training*.

Functional assessment indicated that some of Timothy's crying, which was typically accompanied by throwing materials and falling to the ground, resulted in his "escape" from nonpreferred activities. His teachers, the speech and language therapist, and his parents scheduled a meeting to design a program to teach him how to indicate "break" to escape from nonpreferred activities, both at school and at home. The goal would be for Timothy to refuse participation or terminate an activity in a socially acceptable way, rather than "tantruming" to escape from or avoid the activity. An important part of the meeting would be to discuss and decide on what communication mode would be used to indicate "break." Timothy's language objectives included both speech and using a communication board (with speech as the goal); however, it would be important to give Timothy a way to indicate "break" that would be quick, easy to exe-

cute, and easily understood by others (e.g., a card with the word "break," a card with the picture of a stop light on it, the sign for "break" or "finished").

Functional communication training is a positive and effective strategy for reducing problem behaviors in individuals with severe disabilities. However, determining the functions of a behavior can be challenging. A comprehensive functional assessment should provide information concerning the function of the behavior as well as other types of environmental variables that maintain the behavior. The range of possible variables that may contribute to the presence of problem behavior is as wide, varied, and unique as are individuals (Brown, 1996). Many of these variables relate to issues concerning the individual's lifestyle, self-determination, and characteristics of the curriculum (Brown, 1996; Dunlap, Kern-Dunlap, Clarke, & Robbins, 1991). Recently, some comprehensive assessments and program development guides utilizing these strategies have become available. The guides include: Behavioral Assessment Guide (Willis, LaVigna, & Donnellan, 1993); Severe Behavior Problems: A Functional Communication Training Approach (Durand, 1990); Functional Assessment and Program Development for Problem Behavior: A Practical Handbook (O'Neill et al., 1997); and Practices for Inclusive Schools: Behavior Support (Janney & Snell, in press).

Four strategies frequently used to conduct functional analysis include (a) informant assessment or interview, (b) rating scales, (c) direct observation, and (d) systematic manipulation of controlling variables. Chapter 6 provides a comprehensive description of each strategy used to conduct functional assessment. As an example, we can apply one component of the process, manipulation of controlling variables, to Timothy, who exhibits tantrum behaviors (e.g., cries, throws materials, falls to the ground). Assessments involving the manipulation of variables that control the behavior are referred to as analog assessments. *Analog assessments* "involve the manipulation of various antecedents and consequences that are presumed to be important and observing their effect on an individual's problem behavior" (Durand, 1990, p. 66).

Through the functional assessment process, Timothy's tantrum behaviors were hypothesized to be motivated by a desire to escape from the activities during which they occur. To test this hypothesis, Mr. Grayson, his special education teacher, planned to set up a period of time (e.g., Monday during music group) in which Timothy would be allowed to "escape" each time that he begins a tantrum (i.e., Mr. Grayson reinforces the tantruming). This would be repeated on Wednesday and Thursday. Data from these days would be compared with the data from Tuesday and Friday, in which escaping by tantruming is not reinforced (i.e., his teachers attempted to redirect him back to his activities). If the data reveal higher levels of tantrums on Monday, Wednesday, and Thursday, then Mr. Grayson can conclude that the tantruming is a function of the escape that it produces; that is, the tantruming increases when it is reinforced by escape from the activity. Mr. Grayson could use this information to design or revise current instructional strategies. As described above, he and others from the team might design a functional communication training program to teach Timothy to escape in a more appropriate way (e.g., sign "break," show break card).

Further, Mr. Grayson might examine Timothy's scheduled activities that are associated with tantruming to see if they are (a) needed, (b) preferred or disliked, and (c) on an appropriate difficulty level. Some activities associated with Timothy's tantrums might not be necessary and could be eliminated from his schedule (e.g., matching colored blocks). However, other activities associated with his problem behavior might not be dispensable, so Mr. Grayson would need to investigate further. Are certain activities too difficult and should they be simplified, or should Timothy be taught to request help? Are the activities simply disliked? If so, Mr. Grayson could make one or several program improvements: (a) teaching Timothy to request periodic breaks, (b) preceding the problematic activities with simpler activities (Horner, Day, Sprague, O'Brien, & Heathfield, 1991), (c) allowing Timothy to schedule when he will complete nonpreferred activities (Brown, 1991), or (d) following participation in nonpreferred activities with a choice of preferred activities (positive reinforcement for participation in nonpreferred activities).

Functional assessment of behavior problems is a new element of assessment that teachers should use when developing appropriate programs for students who exhibit serious behavior problems. The assessment process should involve the entire educational team, because functional assessment requires a study of a student throughout his or her daily activities. The outcome of such an assessment is information concerning why behavior problems exist, which is central to the development of effective programs.

Assessment of Student Preferences and Choices

The opportunity to express one's preferences and to make and enjoy choices is part of typical life. Consistent with this basic life quality tenet, recent law requires that educational and rehabilitation programs for persons with disabilities reflect the use of an individual's preferences and allow choice making (Hughes, Pitkin, & Lorden, 1998). While related, choice and preference do not mean the same thing. *Choice* can be observed when an individual acts to get or engage in something as an opportunity occurs, but a *preference* (similar to a positive reinforcer, as discussed in chapter 4) is something consistently chosen over time and is only observed by its effect on the individual over time. "While choice is an observable behavior, preference, on the other hand, is inferred from the act of choice" (Hughes, Pitkin, & Lorden, 1998, p. 299). We usually assume that choices reflect an individual's preferences, although they may not always do so.

Assessment Procedures

There is an abundance of research on the identification of reinforcers and preferences and the effects of offering opportunities for choice making to individuals with severe disabilities (e.g., Hughes et al., 1998; Ivanic & Bailey, 1995; Kern, et al., 1998). An extensive review of research over the past 20 years indicates that increasing choice-making opportunities is associated with the improvement of appropriate behavior and the decline of undesirable responding (Kern et al., 1998). Knowing what an individual prefers is important for several reasons. First, preferred stimuli may be used to reinforce target behaviors or skills. When preferred stimuli are made available singly or offered as a choice of consequence for improvements in target behaviors and skills, the strength or quality of the behavior is likely to improve.

Second, an individual can choose between preferred items or activities. Offering opportunities to choose between preferred activities or events seems to increase active involvement and promote motivation during instruction (Hughes, et al., 1998). These are good reasons to individually assess the activities, events, and objects each student prefers and to offer many opportunities for choices within the context of daily routines across the day (Brown, Belz, Corsi, & Wenig, 1993). Typically, students' preferences vary from day to day, both across teachers and school activities. Since most students with severe disabilities cannot verbally inform us of these changes, initially, more comprehensive assessments should be followed by intermittent (or even daily) "mini-assessments" to determine what activities or items are currently preferred (Mason, McGee, Farmer-Dougan, & Risley, 1989; Raone, Vollmer, Ringdahl, & Marcus, 1998). As a supplement or an alternative to mini-assessment, others suggest that offering a choice of items and letting the student select, rather than having a teacher select, a single preferred item is a simpler way to be sure activities are reinforcing (Horner & Carr, 1997). In the following section, we review several comprehensive and mini-assessment methods that have been successful in identifying preferences with students who have severe disabilities.

Interview
Interviewing those who know the student well to identify a pool of potentially preferred activities and objects has not been found to be an effective method by itself. The opinions of others assessed through interviews do not usually identify reliable preferences when not used in combination with direct observation methods (Green, Reid, White, Halford, Brittain, & Gardner, 1988); however, interviews can provide some idea of activities to assess further through direct observation.

Comprehensive Assessment
A comprehensive assessment of a person's preferences involves multiple opportunities to interact with or choose from a pool of potentially interesting activities, foods, or objects. The outcome is a rank ordered set of potential reinforcers from highly preferred (e.g., approached 80% of the time) to less preferred, not preferred, or avoided. Researchers using these assessment methods have found that when those items that were consistently approached or chosen were then used as consequences for certain behaviors, the preferred items produced consistently higher rates of responding than did nonpreferred items. Usually one of two methods are used for systematic, comprehensive assessment of preferences: approach-avoidance (e.g.,

Pace, Ivancic, Edwards, Iwata, & Page, 1985) or forced choice (e.g., Fisher, Piazza, Bowman, & Amari, 1992).

Approach-avoidance involves presenting single items to a student and waiting for a short, standard period of time (e.g., about 5 seconds). Approach and avoidance responses must be defined individually for each student. Examples of approach responses are: making eye contact with the item; moving toward the item; and making a positive vocal expression. Avoidance responses may include behavior such as: pushing the item away; making a movement away from the item; and making a negative vocalization. If the student approaches the item, that item is made available for another short interval (e.g., 5 seconds). If the student does not approach the item, it is removed, and shortly after, the student is given an opportunity to sample the activity with prompts (e.g., help Timmy turn on a tape recorder to play music). Following any opportunities to sample an activity, the student is given another approach opportunity with the same activity; if the student approaches it, an additional 5 seconds is given to engage with that item.

Another variation of this approach involves free access to a group of 10 or more potentially reinforcing items that involve various types of stimuli and social attention (e.g., tactile: Koosh ball; play: ball; drink: water, cola; social: praise, hugs) (Dyer, 1987). Any items that are consumed are replenished and social attention is provided intermittently. An observer watches and rates the individual's approach and avoidance responses to each item or event.

In a *forced choice method*, items are presented in pairs and each item in the pool of potential reinforcers is presented randomly with every other item. The same general procedures used by Pace in an approach-avoidance method are used, except that items are presented in sets of two. The findings from this method may be more consistent than when items are presented alone.

Brief Assessment
Several brief assessment methods used to update comprehensive assessments also have been shown to be effective with students who have severe disabilities. One brief assessment method used with young children who had autism required variations during the comprehensive assessment (Mason et al., 1989). This variation involved grouping potentially reinforcing items (e.g., common preschool toys, activities,

and consequences) by sensory category: olfactory, gustatory, visual, tactile, vestibular, auditory, and social. A comprehensive approach-avoidance assessment method was initially used to identify preferred items (approached 80% of the time). The daily "mini-assessment" involved presenting only once (but in pairs) each of the items identified as preferred in the comprehensive assessment. A teacher presented two preferred times in a random order and position, but never offered two from the same sensory category together. The student was asked to "pick one," and given as much time as needed to make a choice. The items were removed only after a selection or an active rejection. The next pair was presented until all pairs were assessed. Each item selected was set aside for use as a reinforcer in the upcoming teaching sessions.

A second approach (Roane, Vollmer, Ringdahl, & Marcus, 1998) allows a student to have 5 minutes of free access to a group of items (previously determined to be preferred). Before free access was given, the student was led around a table and given contact with each item in the preferred group; if the student did not initiate contact with the item, the teacher assisted (by modeling or physically prompting the item's use). Then the teacher began the brief preference assessment by: (a) gathering the items, (b) arranging them in a circle on a table, and (c) letting the student manipulate any of them, several at a time, or none at all. No items are removed from the array. The teacher used a 10-second partial interval recording procedure to record the student's contact with any particular item (this recording procedure is explained in chapter 5). This method was reported as taking less time and resulting in less student misbehavior, but still identifying items students found to be reinforcing.

Considerations for Assessing Preferences

While the assessment methods we describe were used with students who have severe disabilities, these students typically did not have motor or sensory limitations, such as Christine's, and demonstrated intentional behavior (see chapter 11). Because our current methods for assessing preferences with students who have severe disabilities are less inclusive of students with extensive motor and sensory limitations or with chronic training problems, team members must make adjustments to these ap-

proaches when they are used with any particular student (Green & Reid, 1996; Ivancic & Bailey, 1995):

- The student's approach and avoidance response should be identified in observable terms.

  Christine does not visually seek out items associated with preferred activities, but smiles and sometimes laughs when engaged in activities she enjoys. Timothy does not show these emotions, but instead simply wants to persist in the activities he likes and cries when they are removed.

- Potential preferred items and activities need to be presented so the student is aware of them.

  Depending on the activity option, Christine's team members tell her the name of the activity, let her experience any movement involved, hear noise associated with the activity, and feel objects involved in the activity.

- Items or activities should be sampled in ways that are meaningful to the student.

  Simply telling Timothy about a new activity (e.g., "Timothy, you can play with the water table today") will not provide a meaningful sample. Timothy needs to watch others use the water table and be encouraged to try it himself before its preference is assessed.

When designing and conducting preference assessments, there are also many considerations that concern the social validity of the assessment process. The following guidelines can increase the social validity of the assessment and its application to inclusive settings (Brown, Gothelf, Guess & Lehr, 1998; Lohrmann-O'Rourke, Browder, & Brown, in preparation).

- Assessments should be conducted in settings and within contexts that are as natural as possible.
- Assessments should be conducted by individuals who know the student well.

  A behavioral consultant recently hired by Timothy's preschool was interested in determining Timothy's preferences. Using a forced choice format, he systematically presented a variety of stimulus items to Timothy. Timothy avoided contact not only with the behavioral consultant, but with all items presented by the consultant. It was concluded that the results did not measure his preference for the stimuli that were being assessed but his level of comfort with the consultant. Plans were made to have his teacher be trained to conduct the assessment.

- Stimuli presented to the individual should be valued by the individual and represent a range of stimuli that reflects events or activities preferred by individuals who do not have disabilities.

  When his teacher presented the stimulus pairs to Timothy, he was able to judge Timothy's approach-avoidance to each item. Mr. Grayson was concerned, however, that although these items were chosen and thus were assumed to be preferred, they did not represent the events and activities that Timothy seemed most to enjoy (e.g., cartoons, building blocks).

- In addition to identifying potential reinforcers, results of preference assessments should lead to information that will contribute to the improvement of daily life (i.e., noncontingent access to preferred events).

  When it was concluded that music was a potential reinforcer for Timothy, some team members suggested that listening to music be contingent on Timothy's performance during group activities. Other team members thought that, because we now know how much Timothy likes music, he should have more access to music, and music should be a context in which he learns other skills. After much discussion, the team decided that there should be more music in his life!

Program Quality and Quality of Life

When professionals view each student with disabilities as having all of the feelings, hopes, and needs of their more typical peers, focus on the assessment and evaluation of small skill changes seems inadequate. Although teachers must still remain accountable for the assessment, instruction, and evaluation of skill learning (process measures), other critical areas in students' lives require evaluation. Outcome measures (see chapter 5 for a more detailed description) refer to the general effect of a program on a person's quality of life. Assessment should reflect a range of meaningful outcomes for the individual, school, family, and community (Billingsley, 1996; Meyer & Janney, 1989). Among the variables assessed are social life (the activities performed with other people), the social network, and the social supports a person has (Kennedy, Horner, & Newton, 1990); control and choices in daily life (Brown, 1991; Meyer & Evans, 1989); and the extent of social and physical integration, family participation, and physical accessibility. The following sec-

tions review some strategies to assess the quality of an individual's program and factors associated with a good quality of life.

Program Quality Indicators (PQI)

The PQI (Meyer & Eichinger, 1994), in its third revision, was developed for use by school districts and consumer groups to evaluate the quality of inclusive schooling and to guide program development and improvement. The PQI checklist contains 38 items, organized into four sections. Within each of these areas are items that represent the most promising practices in educational and related services for students with disabilities.

1. *Local Education Agency District Indicators* include 10 items, among which are policies on placement in home school and inclusive classes, philosophy of mission statement, staff development and unification, and policy for medical and behavioral emergencies.
2. *Building Indicators* include 9 items examining practices related to areas such as family-school relations, transportation, site-based management, extracurricular opportunities, team planning meetings, services in general education, instructional arrangements, and use of paraprofessionals and volunteers.
3. *Educational Placement and Related Services Indicators* lists 9 items focusing on the design of the instructional setting, including areas such as regular education membership and social relationships, daily schedules, regular education instruction, differentiated instruction, curricular and instructional adaptations, student expectations, support services, and transition planning.
4. *Individual Student and Program Indicators* has 9 items that examine the school's response to educational, linguistic, cultural, age-related, and ability-related diversity, as well as opportunities for self-actualization and enrichment.

The PQI was organized into these sections to enable various school personnel to use the specific section for which they have specific responsibility and in which they are most interested. For example, district office personnel may be the most appropriate to evaluate the first component, while district and building level administrators may be most appropriate to evaluate the third component, since they are responsible for decisions regarding educational placement and assignment of services (Meyer & Eichinger, 1994).

Person-Centered Approaches to Assessment

Person-centered planning was designed primarily for persons with severe disabilities who could not easily communicate what they wanted or needed (Cohen, 1998). This approach is qualitatively different from traditional educational, diagnostic, and standardized assessment approaches, because it shifts focus of control from the interdisciplinary team to the person with disabilities and his or her family, and it is their hopes and dreams that determine and direct the education program and supports (Knowlton, 1998; Sands, Bassett, Lehmann, & Spencer, 1998; Turnbull et al., 1996). Kincaid (1996) suggests that person-centered planning activities share a commitment to seeking five essential goals, outcomes, or valued accomplishments in the individual's life: (a) being present and participating in community life; (b) gaining and maintaining satisfying relationships; (c) expressing preferences and making choices in everyday life; (d) having opportunities to fulfill respected roles and to live with dignity; and (e) continuing to develop personal competencies.

Two widely used person-centered planning tools, McGill Action Plans (MAPS) and Personal Futures Planning, will be discussed here. MAPS (Forest & Lusthaus, 1989; Pearpoint, Forest, & O'Brien, 1996; Vandercook, York, & Forest, 1989) involves having typical students, who know the individual well, participate in several planning sessions. In MAPS, the individual and members of the individual's inner circle discuss several questions:

What is the individual's history?

What are your dreams for her or him?

What is your nightmare about him or her (e.g., fears about the future)?

Who is she or he? What does he or she like?

What are his or her strengths, gifts, and talents?

What are his or her needs?

What would an ideal day for her or him look like?

What do we need to make this ideal real?

MAPS serves as a guide for the individual's circle of friends to identify critical areas of focus. The group meets regularly with the facilitating teacher or school staff and the focus individual, informally evaluating their actions, discussing improvements and new ideas, and continuing to support the focus individual.

In Personal Futures Planning (Mount & Zwernik, 1988), a facilitator trained in the planning process leads a group of key people through planning steps. The key people may be related to the focus individual as close friends, family members, staff, or others with whom the person spends a lot of time. Whenever possible, the focus individual is included in the planning process; advocates or spokespersons may be present to help the focus person communicate. The first task of the group is to write a personal profile for the focus individual. Personal profiles consist of three kinds of information about the individual: (a) history, (b) accomplishments, and (c) preferences and desires. A second meeting addresses the individual's future plan. Third, the same participants proceed through seven steps: review the personal profile, review the trends in the environment that may affect the individual, find desirable images of the future, identify obstacles and opportunities, identify strategies to implement the plan, identify actions to get started, and identify any needs for system changes.

For example, in addition to a few of Christine's friends from a nearby college and two high school students who knew her well, Christine, her parents, and the rest of her educational team met before school started to complete a person-centered plan. They hoped the plan would help them further center all their efforts around Christine's interests and life. The first activities took most of an afternoon and involved describing: (a) who was at the meeting; (b) the people in Christine's life; (c) the places she frequents at home, work, school, and in the community; (d) her history; (e) her health issues; (f) her preferences; (g) things that promote respect and detract from the respect of others; (h) strategies that work and don't work; (i) hopes and fears; (j) barriers and opportunities; and (k) the themes of her life (Kincaid, 1996). The group was pleased with their efforts to gather all this information and planned during their second meeting to design a future plan for Christine.

Prioritizing Skills from Assessment Information

Literally hundreds of skills and activities identified in the assessment process are relevant for a student. Teaching all of these is, of course, not possible or desirable. Following the assessment process, the team must select which skills and activities will become the core of the individualized education program. Prioritizing skills and activities is an important step, because it defines the activities in which the student will participate for the year. A team approach is critical in this step of the educational process. Rainforth, York, and Macdonald (1997) reflect that ". . . it is natural for service providers to see priorities from the vantage [point] of their own discipline. A collaborative and consensual approach to determining priorities may be the most difficult aspect of designing the IEP, since it frequently requires one or more team members to let go of what they view as important from their discipline's perspective" (p. 160).

Many criteria for selecting priorities have been discussed in the literature. Figure 3–7, based on the format used by Dardig and Heward (1981) and Helmstetter (1989), identifies many criteria that should be considered when prioritizing objectives from assessment information. No single objective can meet all of the guidelines, and certainly some objectives may meet only a few but are still critical (e.g., health-related objectives). The relative importance of each criterion varies from student to student, especially given variations in family values, lifestyles, and perspectives (Rainforth, York, & Macdonald, 1997). The following are additional questions that should be considered when selecting IEP objectives that reflect current best practices.

Does the objective reflect the student's chronological age, culture, preferences, and profile of strengths and needs? The student must be recognized as an individual with a chronological age and level of physical maturity, a culture, a family history and context, preferences (including likes and dislikes), and personal strengths and needs. Many students have clear strengths in their adaptive skills and in other personal abilities.

Because Christine's vision and spoken communication are very limited, her family, team members, and friends have learned that several strategies are important. For example, it is best when peers, parents, and teachers tell her what will happen next in simple terms, follow familiar routines while avoiding surprises when possible, dodge strategies that rely only on vision, and read her "body language." She is very social and enjoys being around others when these simple guidelines for interaction are respected. This profile of strengths and needs for Christine has guided the team in selecting work sites for her to sample, and the profile also suggested some preparation steps for each site. For example, the team guessed that Christine would enjoy (a) assisting in checking out books at a nearby elementary school library and (b) being a greeter at Wal-Mart. They hypothesized this because both jobs allowed active engagement and offered many social opportunities.

Three preparation steps were taken by team members: (a) analyzing the job routines and needed adaptations to allow active involvement despite her physical limitations; (b) preparing others to communicate with her (teaching others to "read" her body language) and equipping her to communicate in each work site (adding new vocabulary to her communication device); and (c) teaching her over a 3-week to 5-week period, until she knew the routine and team members could judge her job preference and performance.

Does the objective focus on functional skills and lead to meaningful routines and activities? Another guideline for selecting IEP objectives is functionality, or skill usefulness, a measure of how necessary and important a skill is to a particular person, given his or her current and future environments. Applying the functionality guideline to learning objectives means that no generic bank of IEP objectives can be universally taught. What is functional for one person may not be for another.

Applying the functionality guideline also means looking to the future and planning outcomes for the upcoming stages in the student's life cycle: entering preschool, moving into elementary school, starting middle school and becoming an adolescent, going to high school, taking a job, moving away from home, retiring, and facing death. If parents and preschool teachers plan for Timothy, now 4 years old, to be included at age 5 in his neighborhood school kindergarten and identify the necessary supports, this planning will influence the supports and skills delineated in Timothy's current IEP. By using assessment strategies that involve families, friends, present and upcoming teachers or program staff, and observations of kindergarten classrooms, a team will be able to under-

FIGURE 3–7

Examples of Criteria Used for Setting Priorities

Student: _____

Person(s) completing form: _____

Date: _____

List each activity or objective that is being considered for instruction.
Rate each activity or objective using: 3 = strongly agree with statement; 2 = agree somewhat with statement; 1 = disagree somewhat with statement; 0 = disagree strongly with statement

Criteria	Activity/Objective									
1. Can be used in current environments										
2. Can be used in future environments										
3. Can be used across environments and activities										
4. Facilitates interactions with nondisabled peers										
5. Increases student independence										
6. Is chronologically age-appropriate										
7. Student can meaningfully participate										
8. Student rates as high priority or highly preferred										
9. Family rates as high priority										
10. Improves health or fitness										
11. Meets a medical need										
12. Promotes a positive view of the individual										
13. Student shows positive response to activity										
14. Supported by related service staff										
15. Student can achieve, accomplish, or control a meaningful part of the activity										
Total										

Note: Adapted with permission from Dardig, J. D., & Heward, L. (1981). A Systematic Procedure for Prioritizing IEP Goals. *The Directive Teacher, 3,* 6–7; and Helmstetter, E. (1989). Curriculum for school-age students: The ecological model. In F. Brown & D. H. Lehr (Eds.) *Persons with profound disabilities: Issues and practices,* p. 254 Baltimore: Paul H. Brookes.

stand their students' present lives and formulate ideas about future expectations, possibilities, and hopes.

Planning for the future is difficult because it involves examining expectations, predicting accomplishments, and facing the reality of currently available supports and options. Without planning between teachers, service agencies, and families, teaching can get lost in a day-to-day orientation (Turnbull & Turnbull, 1990). Defining future outcomes and planning in those directions can reduce family stress about the future and improve the likelihood of achieving the outcomes (Fowler, Chandler, Johnson, & Stella, 1988).

Can the student participate in the activity in a meaningful way? A student may be able to learn an activity so that it can be performed in its entirety in the natural environment. Thus, the appropriate range of participation necessary for competent performance of the skill in relevant contexts should be ensured (e.g., by initiation, problem solving, quality monitoring). Many students, however, are not able to attain independence in important, needed, or enjoyed skills or activities. Some of the cognitive and motor requirements of tasks may appear to present insurmountable obstacles for an individual student. However, partial participation (Baumgart et al., 1982) can open the door to many possibilities for including that student, instead of excluding him or her because "she (or he) will never be able to do that!" Adaptive or prosthetic aids, adapted materials, rule or schedule adaptations, and personal assistance strategies are ways in which a student can meaningfully participate in an activity (Baumgart et al., 1982).

Meaningful participation can also be facilitated by focusing on extension and enrichment skills. For example, initiating, monitoring quality, terminating, choosing, social interacting, and communicating are ways to participate in a routine that do not require extensive motor participation (Brown, Evans, Weed, & Owen, 1987; Brown & Lehr, 1993).

Does the objective reflect the student's personal and social needs? Planning an IEP by "functional" guidelines alone may mean that personal and social domains are slighted and that supports are viewed narrowly to include only teachers, therapists, and educational materials. This guideline stresses the importance of the relationships and membership domains. Regardless of the presence or degree of a disability, children, adolescents, and adults need friends to participate in activities in a way that increases self-esteem. In fact, the presence of a disability may increase the need for supportive friends. Objectives that facilitate friendships, supports, and membership in the school and community should be given high priority.

Summary

Assessment is a complex but critical component of program development. If used wisely, information gathered from assessments becomes the cornerstone of program development. Although there are no easy formulas for the selection of an appropriate assessment process for any one student, this chapter reviews the advantages and disadvantages of a variety of assessment strategies and describes how they can best be applied. The assessment process determines whether the outcomes that are identified and measured are meaningful. Focusing solely on academic development or skill development, as was done historically, is not sufficient. In addition to academic or skill development, assessment outcomes should also be referenced to the domains of *relationships* and *membership* (Billingsley et al., 1996). Involvement in person-centered planning strategies is an excellent way to guide teams and insure that they focus on those elements that will contribute to the quality of an individual's life.

The chapter discusses developmental approaches to assessment, assessments of adaptive behavior, environmental assessment approaches, assessments of program quality and quality of life, and variables to consider when prioritizing skills for instruction. Teachers must know the appropriate uses, and be aware of the inappropriate uses, of the wide range of assessments and assessment strategies.

Suggested Activities

1. Select one student in your class and carefully examine the assessments that are in his or her file.
   a. How many norm-referenced tests and criterion-referenced tests do you see?
   b. Are there any environmental assessments?
   c. Are there any questionnaires eliciting input from this student's family?

d. If the student has problem behaviors, are there any functional behavioral assessments?
2. Select a different student and carefully examine the instructional objectives targeted on his or her IEP. How do the objectives compare to the 15 criteria listed in Figure 3–7? How do the objectives compare with the following four criteria:
   a. Does the objective reflect the student's chronological age, culture, preferences, and profile of strengths and needs?
   b. Does the objective focus on functional skills and lead to meaningful routines and activities?
   c. Does the objective reflect the student's personal and social needs?
   d. Can the student participate in the activity in a meaningful way?

References

Adams, J. (1973). Adaptive behavior and measured intelligence in the classification of mental retardation. *American Journal of Mental Deficiency*, 78, 77–81.

Alberto, P. A., & Troutman, A. C. (1999). Applied behavior analysis for teachers (5th ed.). Upper Saddle River, NJ: Prentice Hall.

Alpern, G. D., Boll, T. J., & Shearer, M. S. (1980). *Developmental profile II* (Revised ed.). Aspen, CO: Psychological Development Publications.

Apgar, V. (1953). A proposal for a new method of evaluation of the newborn infant. *Current Researches in Anesthesia and Analgesia*, 32, 260–267.

Apgar, V., & Beck, J. (1973). *Is my baby all right?* New York: Trident Press.

The Association for Persons with Severe Handicaps (TASH). (May, 1989). TASH *resolutions and policy statements.* Seattle, WA: Author.

Bailey, D. B., McWilliam, R. A., Darkes, L. A., Hebbeler, K., Simeonsson, R. J., Spiker, D., Wagner, M. (1998). Family outcomes in early intervention: A framework for program evaluation and efficacy research. *Exceptional Children*, 64, 313–328.

Baumeister, A. A., & Muma, J. R. (1975). On defining mental retardation. *Journal of Special Education*, 9, 293–306.

Baumgart, D., Brown, L., Pumpian, I., Nisbet, J., Ford, A., Sweet, M., Messina, R., & Schroeder, J. (1982). Principle of partial participation and individualized adaptations in educational programs for severely handicapped students. *Journal of the Association for the Severely Handicapped*, 7, 17–27.

Bayley, N. (1993). *Bayley scales of infant development—II.* San Antonio: Psychological Corporation.

Billingsley, F. F., Gallucci, C., Peck, C. A., Schwartz, I. S., & Staub, D. (1996). "But those kids can't even *do* math": An alternative conceptualization of outcomes for inclusive education. *Special Education Leadership Review*, 3, 43–55.

Brazelton, T. B., & Nugent, J. K. (1995). *Neonatal behavioral assessment scale (3rd ed.).* London: MacKeith Press.

Bricker, D. (1993). *Assessment, evaluation and programming system* (AEPS) *for infants and children.* Baltimore: Paul H. Brookes.

Browder, D. M. (1991). *Assessment of individuals with severe disabilities:* An *applied behavior approach to life skills assessment.* (2nd ed.). Baltimore: Paul H. Brookes.

Brown, F. (1991). Creative daily scheduling: A nonintrusive approach to challenging behaviors in community residences. *Journal of the Association for Persons with Severe Handicaps*, 16, 75–84.

Brown, F. (1996). Variables to consider in the assessment of problem behaviors. TASH *Newsletter*, 22, 19–20.

Brown, F., Belz, B., Corsi, L., & Wenig, B. (1993). Choice diversity for people with severe disabilities. *Education and Training in Mental Retardation.* 28, 318–326.

Brown, F., Evans, I. M., Weed, K. A., & Owen, V. (1987). Delineating functional competencies: A component model. *Journal of the Association for Persons with Severe Handicaps*, 12, 117–124.

Brown, F., Gothelf, C. R., Guess, D., & Lehr, D. H. (1998). Self-determination for individuals with the most severe disabilities: Moving beyond chimera. *Journal of the Association for Persons with Severe Handicaps*, 23, 17–26.

Brown, F., & Lehr, D. (1993). Meaningful outcomes for students with severe disabilities. *Teaching Exceptional Children*, 4, 12–16.

Brown, L., Branston, M. B., Hamre-Nietupski, S., Pumpian, I., Certo, N., & Gruenewald, L. (1979). A strategy for developing chronological-age-appropriate and functional curricular content for severely handicapped adolescents and young adults. *Journal of Special Education*, 13, 81–90.

Bruininks, R. H., Hill, B. K., Weatherman, R. F., & Woodcock, R. W. (1986). *Inventory for client and agency planning* (ICAP). Riverside: DLM Teaching Resources.

Bruininks, R. H., Woodcock, R. W., Weatherman, R. F., & Hill, B. K. (1996). Scales of independent behavior—revised (SIB-R). Riverside: DLM Teaching Resources.

Carr, E. G., & Durand, V. M. (1985). Reducing behavior problems through functional communication training. *Journal of Applied Behavior Analysis*, 18, 111–126.

Cattell, P. (1940). *Infant intelligence scale.* New York: Psychological Corporation.

Chandler, L. K. (1992). Promoting children's social/survival skills as a strategy for transition to mainstreamed kindergarten programs. In S. L. Odom, S. R. McConnell, & M. A. McEvoy (Eds.), *Social competence of young children with disabilities* (pp. 245–276). Baltimore: Paul H. Brookes.

Chen, D., & Dote-Kwan, J. (1998). Early intervention services for young children who have visual impairments with other disabilities and their families. In S. Z. Sacks & R. I. Silberman (Eds.), *Educating students who have visual impairments with other disabilities* (pp. 303–334). Baltimore: Paul H. Brookes.

Cohen, S. (1998). *Targeting children with autism.* Berkeley: University of California Press.

Cress, P. J., Spellman, C. R., DeBriere, T. J., Sizemore, A. C., Northam, J. K., & Johnson, J. L. (1981). Vision screening for persons with severe handicaps. *Journal of the Association for the Severely Handicapped*, 6(3), 41–50.

Dardig, J. D., & Heward, W. L. (1981). A systematic procedure for prioritizing IEP goals. *The Directive Teacher*, 3, 6–7.

Donnellan, A. M., Mirenda, P. L., Mesaros, R. A., & Fassbender, L. L. (1984). Analyzing the communicative functions of aberrent behavior. *Journal of the Association for Persons with Severe Handicaps, 9*, 201–212.

Downing, J. E., & Demchak, M. A. (1996). First steps: Determining individual abilities and how best to support students. In J. E. Downing (Ed.), *Including students with severe and multiple disabilities in typical classrooms* (pp. 35–61). Baltimore: Paul H. Brookes.

Downing, J., & Perino, D. (1992). Functional vs. standardized assessment procedures: Implications for educational programming. *Mental Retardation, 30*, 289–295.

Dunlap, G., Kern-Dunlap, L., Clarke, S., & Robbins, F. R. (1991). Functional assessment, curricular revision, and severe problem behaviors. *Journal of Applied Behavior Analysis, 22*, 387–397.

Durand, V. M. (1990). *Severe behavior problems: A functional communication training approach.* New York: Guilford Press.

Durand, V. M., & Carr, E. G. (1991). Functional communication training to reduce challenging behavior: Maintenance and application in new settings. *Journal of Applied Behavior Analysis, 24*, 251–264.

Evans, I. M. (1991). Testing and diagnosis: A review and evaluation. In L. H. Meyer, C. A. Peck, & L. Brown (Eds.), *Critical issues in the lives of people with severe disabilities* (pp. 25–44). Baltimore: Paul H. Brookes.

Evans, I. M., & Brown, F. (1986). Outcome assessment of student competence: Issues and implications. *Special Services in the Schools, 2*(4), 41–62.

Evans, I. M., & Meyer, L. (1985). *An educative approach to problem behaviors: A practical decision model for interventions with severely handicapped learners.* Baltimore: Paul H. Brookes.

Evans, I. M., & Scotti, J. R. (1989). Defining meaningful outcomes for persons with profound disabilities. In F. Brown & D. Lehr (Eds.), *Persons and profound disabilities: Issues and practices* (pp. 83–108). Baltimore: Paul H. Brookes.

Fewell, R., & Cone, J. (1983). Identification and placement of severely handicapped children. In M. E. Snell (Ed.), *Systematic instruction of the moderately and severely handicapped* (pp. 46–73). New York: Merrill/Macmillan.

Fisher, W. W., Piazza, C. C., Bowman, L. G., & Amari, A. (1996). Integrating caregiver report with a systematic choice assessment to Enhance reinforcer identification. *American Journal on Mental Retardation, 101*, 15–25.

Ford, A., Schnorr, R., Meyer, L., Davern, L., Black, J., & Dempsey, P. (1989). *The Syracuse community-referenced curriculum guide for students with moderate and severe disabilities.* Baltimore: Paul H. Brookes.

Forest, M., & Lusthaus, E. (1989). Promoting education equality for all students: circles and maps. In S. Stainback, W. Stainback, & M. Forest (Eds.), *Educating all students in the mainstream of regular education* (pp. 43–57). Baltimore: Paul H. Brookes.

Fowler, S. A., Chandler, L. K., Johnson, T. E., & Stella, M. E. (1988). Individualizing family involvement in school transitions: Gathering information and choosing the next program. *Journal of the Division for Early Childhood, 12*, 208–216.

Frankenberg, W. K., Dodds, J. B., & Fandal, A. W. (1975). *Denver developmental screening test.* Denver: Ladoca Project and Publishing Foundation.

Frankenberger, W., & Harper, J. (1988). States' definitions and procedures for identifying children with mental retardation: Comparison of 1981–1982 and 1985–1986 guidelines. *Mental Retardation, 26*, 133–136.

Gaylord-Ross, R. J., & Holvoet, J. (1985). *Strategies for educating students with severe handicaps.* Boston: Little, Brown.

Giangreco, M. F., Cloninger, C. J., & Iverson, V. S. (1998). *C.O.A.C.H.: Choosing outcomes and accommodations for children* (2nd ed.). Baltimore: Paul H. Brookes.

Gilliam, J. E. (1995). *Gilliam autism rating scale* (GARS). Austin, TX: Pro Ed.

Gothelf, C. R., & Brown, F. (1998). Participation in the education process: Students with severe disabilities. In M. L. Wehmeyer & D. J. Sands (Eds.), *Making it happen: Student involvement in education planning, decision making, and instruction* (pp. 99–121). Baltimore: Paul H. Brookes.

Green, C. W., & Reid, D. H. (1996). Defining, validating, and increasing indices of happiness among people with profound multiple disabilities. *Journal of Applied Behavior Analysis, 29*, 67–78.

Green, C. W., Reid, D. H., Canipe, V. S., & Gardner, S. M. (1991). A comprehensive evaluation of reinforcer identification processes for persons with profound multiple handicaps. *Journal of Applied Behavior Analysis, 24*, 537–552.

Green, C. W., Reid, D. H., White, L. K., Halford, R. C., Brittain, D. P., & Gardner, S. M. (1988). Identifying reinforcers for persons with profound handicaps: staff opinion versus systematic assessment of preferences. *Journal of Applied Behavior Analysis, 21*, 31–43.

Gresham, F. M. (1983). Social skills assessment as a component of mainstreaming placement decisions. *Exceptional Children, 49*, 331–336.

Griffin, P. M., & Sanford, A. R. (1981). *Learning accomplishment profile for infants.* Chapel Hill, NC: Chapel Hill Training Outreach Project.

Grossman, H. J. (Ed.) (1983). *Classification in mental retardation.* Washington, DC: American Association on Mental Deficiency.

Guess, D., & Noonan, M. J. (1982). Curricula and instructional procedures for severely handicapped students. *Focus on Exceptional Children, 4*, 1–12.

Haring, T. G., & Breen, C. (1989). Units of analysis of social interaction outcomes in supported education. *Journal of the Association of Persons with Severe Handicaps, 14*, 255–262.

Haring, T. G., & Kennedy, C. H. (1990). Contextual control of problem behaviors in students with severe disabilities. *Journal of Applied Behavior Analysis, 23*, 235–243.

Hatton, C. (1998). Whose quality of life is it anyway? Some problems with the emerging quality of life consensus. *Mental Retardation, 36*, 104–115.

Heber, R. (1959). A *manual on terminology and classification in mental retardation.* Willimantic, CT: American Association on Mental Deficiency.

Heber, R. (1961). Modifications in the manual on terminology and classification in mental retardation. *American Journal of Mental Deficiency, 65*, 499–500.

Helmstetter, E. (1989). Curriculum for school-age students: The ecological model. In F. Brown & D. Lehr (Eds.), *Persons with profound disabilities: Issues and practices* (pp. 239–264). Baltimore: Paul H. Brookes.

Hobson v. Hansen, 269 F. Supp. 401 (D.D.C. 1967).

Horner, R. H., & Carr, E. G. (1997). Behavioral support for students with severe disabilities: Functional assessment and comprehensive intervention. *The Journal of Special Education, 31*, 84–104.

Horner, R. H., Day, M. H., Sprague, J. R., O'Brien, M., & Heathfield, L. T. (1991). Interspersed requests: A nonaversive procedure for reducing aggression and self-injury during instruction. *Journal of Applied Behavior Analysis, 24*, 265–278.

Hughes, C., Pitkin, S. E., & Lorden S. W. (1998). Assessing preferences and choices of persons with severe and profound mental retardation. *Education and Training in Mental Retardation and Developmental Disabilities, 33,* 299–316.

Ivancic, M. T., & Bailey, J. S. (1995). Current limits to reinforcer identification for some persons with profound disabilities. *Research in Developmental Disabilities, 17,* 77–92.

Janney, R. E., & Snell, M. E. (in press). Practices for inclusive schools: Behavior support. Baltimore: Paul H. Brookes.

Johnson-Martin, N. M., Attermeier, S. M., Hacker, B. (1990). *The Carolina Curriculum for Preschoolers with Special Needs.* Baltimore: Paul H. Brookes.

Kazdin, A. E. (1977). Assessing the clinical or applied importance of behavior change through social validation. *Behavior Modification, 1,* 427–452.

Kennedy, C. H., Horner, R. H., & Newton, J. S. (1990). The social networks and activity patterns of adults with severe disabilities: A correlational analysis. *Journal of the Association for Persons with Severe Handicaps, 15,* 86–90.

Kern, L., Vorndran, C. M., Hilt, A., Ringdahl., J. E., Adelman, B. E., & Dunlap, G. (1998). Choice as an intervention to improve behavior: A review of the literature. *Journal of Behavioral Education, 8,* 151–169.

Kincaid, D. 1996. Person-centered planning. In L. K. Koegel, R. L. Koegel, & G. Dunlap (Eds.), *Positive behavioral support: Including people with difficult behavior in the community* (pp. 439–465). Baltimore: Paul H. Brookes.

Kleinert, H. L., Kearns, J. F., & Kennedy, S. (1997). Accountability for *all* students: Kentucky's alternate portfolio assessment for students with moderate and severe cognitive disabilities. *Journal of the Association for Persons with Severe Handicaps, 22,* 88–101.

Knowlton, E. (1998). Considerations in the design of personalized curricular supports for students with developmental disabilities. *Education and Training in Mental Retardation and Developmental Disabilities, 33,* 95–107.

Koegel, R. L., & Koegel, L. K. (Eds.). (1995). *Teaching children with autism: Strategies for initiating positive interactions and improving learning opportunities.* Baltimore: Paul H. Brookes.

Koegel, R. L., Koegel, L. K., & Dunlap, G. (1996). *Positive behavioral support: Including people with difficult behavior in the community.* Baltimore: Paul H. Brookes.

Lambert, N., Nihira, K., & Leland, H. (1993). *Adaptive Behavior Scale-School.* Austin: Pro-Ed.

Larry P. v. Riles, 793 F2d. 969 (9th Cir. 1984).

Lehr, D. (1989). Educational programming for young children with the most severe disabilities. In F. Brown & D. Lehr (Eds.), *People with profound disabilities: Issues and practices* (pp. 213–238). Baltimore: Paul H. Brookes.

Lennox, D. B., & Miltenberger, R. G. (1989). Conducting a functional assessment of problem behavior in applied settings. *Journal of the Association for Persons with Severe Handicaps, 14,* 304–311.

Lewis, S., & Russo, R. (1998). Educational assessment for students who have visual impairments with other disabilities. In S. Z. Sacks & R. I. Silberman (Eds.) *Educating students who have visual impairments with other disabilities* (pp. 39–71). Baltimore: Paul H. Brookes.

Lim, L. H. F., & Browder, D. M. (1994). Multicultural life skills assessment of individuals with severe disabilities. *The Journal of the Association for Persons with Severe Handicaps, 19,* 130–138.

Linehan, S. A., Brady, M. P., & Hwang, C. (1991). Ecological versus developmental assessment: Influences on instructional expectations. *The Journal of the Association for Persons with Severe Handicaps, 16,* 146–153.

Lohrmann-O'Rourke, S., Browder, D. M., & Brown, F. Increasing the social validity of preference assessment of individuals with severe disabilities. Manuscript in preparation.

Lord, C., & Schopler, E. (1989). TEACCH services for preschool children. In S. L. Harris, & J. S. Handleman (eds.) *Preschool programs for children with autism* (pp. 87–106). Austin, TX: Pro-Ed.

Luckasson, R., Coulter, D. L., Polloway, E. A., Reiss, S., Schalock, R. L., Snell, M. E., Spitalnik, D. M., & Stark, J. A. (1992). *Mental retardation: Definition, classification, and systems of supports* (9th ed.). Washington, DC: American Association on Mental Retardation.

Mason, S. A., McGee, G. G., Farmer-Dougan, V., & Risley, T. R. (1989). A practical strategy for ongoing reinforcer assessment. *Journal of Applied Behavior Analysis, 22,* 171–179.

Maurice, C. (1996). *Behavioral intervention for young children with autism: A manual for parents and professionals.* Austin, TX: Pro-Ed.

McCarthy, C. F., Miller, J. F., Romski, M. A., McLean, L. K., Paul-Brown, D. Rourk, J. D., & Yoder, D. E. (1998). *Communication supports checklist for programs serving individuals with severe disabilities.* Baltimore: Paul H. Brookes.

McCarthy, D. (1972). *Manual for the McCarthy scales of children's abilities.* New York: Psychological Corporation.

McEachin, J. J., Smith, T., & Lovaas, O. I. (1993). Long-term outcome for children with autism who received early intensive behavioral treatment. *American Journal on Mental Retardation, 87,* 359–372.

McGee, G., Daly, T., & Jacobs, H. A. (1992). The Walden Project. In S. L. Harris, & J. S. Handleman (Eds.), *Preschool programs for children with autism.* Austin, TX: Pro-Ed.

McLoughlin, J. A., & Lewis, R. B. (1994). *Assessing special students* (4th ed.). New York: Merrill.

Meyer, L. H., & Eichinger, J. (1994). *Program quality indicators (PQI): A checklist of most promising practices in educational programs for students with severe disabilities* (3rd edition). Seattle, WA: The Association for Persons with Severe Handicaps.

Meyer, L. H., & Evans, I. H. (1993). Meaningful outcomes in behavioral intervention: Evaluating positive approaches to the remediation of challenging behaviors. In J. Reichle & D. P. Wacker (Eds.), *Communication and language intervention series: Vol. 3. Communicative alternatives to challenging behavior: Integrating functional assessment and intervention strategies* (pp. 407–428). Baltimore: Paul H. Brookes.

Meyer, L. H., & Evans, I. H. (1989). *Nonaversive intervention for behavior problems: A manual for home and community.* Baltimore: Paul H. Brookes.

Meyer, L. H., & Janney, R. E. (1989). User-friendly measures of meaningful outcomes: Evaluating behavioral interventions. *Journal of the Association for Persons with Severe handicaps, 14,* 263–270.

Meyer, L. H., Reichle, J., McQuarter, R. J., Cole, D., Vandercook, T., Evans, I. M., Neel, R., & Kishi, G. (1985). *The assessment of social competence (ASC): A scale of social competence functions.* Minneapolis, MN: University of Minnesota Consortium Institute.

Mills v. Board of Education of the District of Columbia. 348F. Supp. 866 (D.D.C. 1972).

Morreau, L. E., & Bruininks, R. H. (1991). *Checklist of adaptive living skills (CALS).* Allen, TX: DLM.

Mount, B., & Zwernik, K. (1988). *It's never too early, it's never too late: A booklet about personal futures planning.* St. Paul: St. Paul Metropolitan Council.

Nihira, K., Leland, H., & Lambert, N. (1993). Adaptive Behavior Scales—Residential & Community (2nd ed). Austin, TX: Pro-Ed.

Odom, S., McConnell, R., & McEvoy, M. A. (Eds.). *Social competence of young children with disabilities* (pp. 245–276). Baltimore: Paul H. Brookes.

O'Neill, R. E., Horner, R. H., Albin, R. W., Sprague, J. R., Story, K., & Newton, J. S. (1997). *Functional assessment and program development for problem behavior: A practical handbook* (2nd ed.). Pacific Grove, CA: Brooks/Cole.

Orelove, F. P., & Sobsey, D. (1996). *Educating children with multiple disabilities* (3rd ed.). Baltimore: Paul H. Brookes.

Pace, G. M., Ivancic, M. R., Edwards, G. L., Iwata, B. A., & Page, T. J. (1985). Assessment of stimulus preference and reinforcer value with profoundly retarded individuals. *Journal of Applied Behavior Analysis, 18,* 249–255.

Parsons, M. B., Reid, D. H., Reynolds, J., & Baumgarner, M. (1990). Effects of chosen versus assigned jobs on the work performance of persons with severe handicaps. *Journal of Applied Behavior Analysis, 23,* 253–258.

Pearpoint, J., Forest, M., & O'Brien, J. (1996). MAPS, circles of friends, and PATH: Powerful tools to help build caring communities. In S. Stainback & W. Stainback (Eds.), *Inclusion: A guide for educators* (pp. 67–86). Baltimore: Paul H. Brookes.

Rainforth, B., York, J., & Macdonald, C. (1997). *Collaborative teams for students with severe disabilities: Integrating therapy and educational services.* (2nd Edition). Baltimore: Paul H. Brookes.

Roane, H. S., Vollmer, T. R., Ringdahl, J. E., & Marcus, B. A. (1998). Evaluation of a brief stimulus preference assessment. *Journal of Applied Behavior Analysis, 31,* 605–620.

Salvia, J., & Ysseldyke, J. E. (1995). *Assessment* (6th ed.). Boston: Houghton Mifflin.

Sands, D. J., Bassett, D. S., Lehmann, J., & Spencer, K. C. (1998). Factors contributing to and implications for student involvement in transition-related planning, decision making, and instruction. In M. L. Wehmeyer & D. J. Sands (Eds.) *Making it happen: Student involvement in education planning, decision making, and instruction* (pp. 25–44). Baltimore: Paul H. Brookes.

Sanford, A. R. (Ed.). (1974). *Learning accomplishment profile.* Chapel Hill, NC: Chapel Hill Training Outreach Project.

Schalock, R. L. (1996). Reconsidering the conceptualization and measurement of quality of life. In R. L. Schalock (Ed.), *Quality of Life: Vol. 1: Conceptualization and measurement* (pp. 123–139). Washington, D.C.: American Association on Mental Retardation.

Siegel-Causey, E., & Allinder, R. M. (1998). Using alternative assessment for students with severe disabilities: Alignment with best practices. *Education and Training in Mental Retardation and Developmental Disabilities, 33,* 168–178.

Sigafoos, J., Cole, D. A., & McQuarter, R. J. (1987). Current practices in the assessment of students with severe handicaps. *Journal of the Association for Persons with Severe Handicaps, 12,* 264–273.

Sigafoos, J., & York, J. (1991). Using ecological inventories to promote functional communication. In J. Reichle, J. York, & J. Sigafoos (Eds.), *Implementing augmentative and alternative communication: Strategies for learners with severe disabilities* (pp. 61–70). Baltimore: Paul H. Brookes.

Silberman, R. K., & Brown F. (1998). Alternative approaches to assessing students who have visual impairments with other disabilities in classroom and community environments. In S. Z. Sacks & R. K. Silberman (Eds.), *Educating students who have visual impairments with other disabilities* (pp. 73–98). Baltimore: Paul H. Brookes.

Slosson, R. L. (1971). *Slosson intelligence test.* East Aurora, NY: Slosson Educational Publications.

Somerton-Fair, M. E., & Turner, K. D. (1975). *Pennsylvania training model: Individual assessment guide.* Harrisburg, PA: Pennsylvania Department of Education.

Sparrow, S. S., Balla, D. A., & Cicchetti, D. V. (1984). *Vineland adaptive behavior scales.* Circle Pines, MN: American Guidance Service Incorporated.

Spellman, C. R., DeBriere, T. J., & Cress, P. J. (1979). *Final report, from the project Research and Development of Subjective Visual Acuity Assessment Procedures for Severely Handicapped Persons,* BEH Grant #G00-76-02592.

Strain, P. S., Kohler, F. W., & Goldstein, H. (1996). Learning experiences . . . an alternative program: Peer mediated interventions for young children with autism. In E. D. Hibbs & P. S. Jensen (Eds.) *Child and adolescent disorders: Empirically based strategies for clinical practice* (pp. 573–587). Washington, D.C.: American Psychological Association.

The Association for Persons with Severe Handicaps. (1991). Definition of the people TASH serves (Document 1.1). In L. H. Meyer, C. A. Peck, & L. Brown (Eds.) *Critical issues in the lives of people with severe disabilities,* (p. 19). Baltimore: Paul H. Brookes.

Thorndike, R. L., Hagen, E., & Sattler, J. (1985). *Stanford-Binet intelligence scale.* Chicago: Riverside Publishing.

Turnbull, A. P., Blue-Banning, M. J., Anderson, E. L., Turnbull, H. R., Seaton, K. A., & Dinas, P. A. (1996). Enhancing self-determination through group action planning. In D. J. Sands & M. L. Wehmeyer (Eds.), *Self-determination across the life span* (pp. 237–256). Baltimore: Paul H. Brookes.

Turnbull, A. P., & Turnbull, H. R. (1990). *Families, professionals, and exceptionality.* Upper Saddle River, NJ: Merrill/Prentice Hall.

Turnbull, H. R., & Turnbull, A. P. (1998). *Free appropriate public education: The law and children with disabilities* (5th Edition). Denver: Love.

Ulrich, M. (1991). Evaluating evaluation: A "fictional" play. In L. H. Meyer, C. A. Peck, & L. Brown (Eds.), *Critical issues in the lives of people with severe disabilities* (pp. 93–100). Baltimore: Paul H. Brookes.

Vandercook, T., York, J., & Forest, M. (1989). The McGill action planning system (MAPS): A strategy for building the vision. *Journal of the Association for Persons with Severe Handicaps, 14,* 205–215.

Vincent, L. J., Salisbury, C., Walter, G., Brown, P., Gruenewald, L., & Powers, M. (1980). Program evaluation and curriculum development in early childhood/special education: Criteria of the next environment. In W. Sailor, B. Wilcox, & L. Brown (Eds.), *Methods of instruction for severely handicapped students* (pp. 303–328). Baltimore: Paul H. Brookes.

Voeltz, L. M., & Evans, I. M. (1983). Educational validity: Procedures to evaluate outcomes in programs for severely handicapped learners. *Journal of the Association for the Severely Handicapped, 8*(1), 3–15.

Wechsler, D. (1989). Wechsler preschool and primary scale of intelligence—revised. San Antonio: Psychological Corporation.

Wechsler, D. (1991). Wechsler intelligence scale for children—third edition. San Antonio: Psychological Corporation.

Wehmeyer, M. L. (1996). Self-determination as an educational outcome: Why is it important to children, youth, and adults with disabilities? In D. J. Sands, & M. L. Wehmeyer (eds.). *Self-determination across the life span: Independence and choice for people with disabilities* (pp. 17–36). Baltimore: Paul H. Brookes.

Wehmeyer, M. L., & Sands, D. (Eds.). (1998). *Making it happen: Student involvement in education planning, decision making, and instruction.* Baltimore: Paul H. Brookes.

Welch, R. J., O'Brian, J. J., & Ayers, F. (1974). *Cambridge assessment development rating and evaluation (CADRE).* Cambridge, MN: CADRE Center, Cambridge Isanti Public Schools.

Wesson, C. L., & King, R. P. (1996). Portfolio assessment and special education students. *Teaching Exceptional Children, 28,* 44–48.

White, O. R. (1971). *A glossary of behavioral terminology.* Eugene, OR: Research Press.

White, O. R. (1985). The evaluation of severely mentally retarded individuals. In B. Bricker & J. Filler (Eds.), *Severe mental retardation: From theory to practice* (pp. 161–184). Reston, VA: Council for Exceptional Children.

Willis, T. J., LaVigna, G. W., & Donnellan, A. M. (1993). *Behavior assessment guide.* Los Angeles: Institute for Applied Behavior Analysis.

Wolf, M. M. (1978). Social validity: The case for subjective measurement, or how applied behavior analysis is finding its heart. *Journal of Applied Behavior Analysis, 11,* 203–214.

Wolfensberger, W. (1972). *Normalization: The principle of normalization in human services.* Toronto: National Institute on Mental Retardation.

Wolfensberger, W. (1983). Social role valorization: A proposed new term for the principle of normalization. *Mental Retardation, 21,* 234–239.

Wolfensberger, W., & Glenn, L. (1975). *Program analysis of service systems (PASS): A method for the quantitative evaluation of human services: Handbook* (Rev. 3rd ed.). Toronto: National Institute on Mental Retardation.

Ysseldyke, J. E., & Algozzine, B. (1982). *Critical issues in special and remedial education.* Boston: Houghton Mifflin.

Ysseldyke, J., & Olsen, K. (1999). Putting alternate assessments into practice: What to measure and possible sources of data. *Exceptional Children, 65,* 175–185.

4

Development and Implementation of Educational Programs

Martha E. Snell
Fredda Brown

Developing Educational Programs

The development of educational programs is influenced by many factors. In this chapter, we describe how teams write students' individualized educational programs (IEPs) and then design and implement instructional programs for each IEP objective. Several important *school practices*, not present in all schools, can create a supportive context for developing appropriate educational programs. Furthermore, when teams that develop students' programs are guided by the set of *principles* we describe, the resulting programs are even more likely to achieve the three desirable student *outcomes* we set forth in chapter 3: memberships, relationships, and skills (Table 3-4). Our initial discussion in this chapter addresses the three elements in this relationship: (1) supportive school practices combined with (2) guiding team principles lead to (3) desirable student outcomes. Then the discussion shifts to the design of supports that foster relationships and promote membership

and, finally, to the design and implementation of skill instruction programs.

Desirable Student Outcomes

Often the best way to develop a process is to begin by identifying the outcomes we want. Even with educators, the targeted destination influences the directions taken with students. As described in chapter 3, Staub et al. and Billingsley et al. (Billingsley, Gallucci, Peck, Schwartz, & Staub, 1996; Staub, Schwartz, Gallucci, & Peck, 1994) identified three desirable outcomes that students with severe disabilities achieved when they attended inclusive school settings (Table 4–1).

- The *skills outcome* encompasses the abilities that an individual needs to acquire, such as functional academics; proficiency in useful social, motor, and communication skills; and other behaviors that schools and special education address. Being educated in general education classrooms and participating in activities with the necessary supports, in

TABLE 4–1
Supportive Practices, Principles, and Outcomes

Supportive School Practices	Guiding Team Principles For Program Development	Desirable Student Outcomes
Inclusion	Student-centered	
Collaborative teams	Team-generated	Skills
Integrated therapy	Practical and valid	
Systematic, activity-based Instruction	Socially valid	Memberships
Data-based decision making	Reflect functional priorities	
Positive behavior support	Promote active participation	Relationships
	Foster self-determination	
	Individualized	

contrast to self-contained classrooms, appears to offer more opportunity to learn useful and age-appropriate skills and to generalize them to a variety of settings (Billingsley et al., 1996).

- The *membership outcome* encompasses belonging to a group and being treated as a group member (i.e., sharing group symbols, participating in activities even when accommodations are needed, and having knowledge about the group). Inclusive schools present more and varied occasions to join peer groups and experience affiliation with classmates during and after school hours than do noninclusive schools.

- The *relationships outcome* includes ongoing, familiar, social interactions with other individuals that may take on various patterns, including play and companionship, helper, helpee, reciprocal peer, and adversarial. Inclusive schools provide the context for one or more of these relationships to develop among students with disabilities and those without, which in turn creates learning opportunities and social benefits.

Students' achievement of membership and relationships in addition to skills occurs not by accident but by the careful planning of many people. Unfortunately, unless a school has "bought into inclusion" and many other supportive practices, a lot of teacher effort goes into creating opportunities for stu-

dents to interact and participate in school activities with a variety of other students their age. This is because scheduling for both groups of students does not coincide, and lunches, assemblies, class changes, and class times are not shared times. Historically, educators have focused mainly on the differences between groups of students with and without disabilities, rather than on their similarities. The result is that schools often base the design of educational programs on the assumption that such groups cannot learn meaningfully together.

When teachers are employed in school systems that do not practice *inclusion*, or even *integration* (terms are defined in Box 4–1), the responsibility is theirs to initiate these practices piecemeal or to influence administrative leaders to assist. If these schools have relied primarily on self-contained classrooms for educating students with severe disabilities, *systemic* changes are required for inclusion (and often, even for integration). The bright side is that we know something about how to accomplish the systemic changes that are needed for these changes (e.g., see chapter 1; Roach, Ashcroft, & Stamp, 1993; Snell & Janney, 2000 a, b; Villa, Thousand, Stainback, & Stainback, 1992; York-Barr, 1997). Fostering positive attitudes toward diversity while creating opportunities for social interaction are two themes evident in schools that have included students with disabilities (Breen, Kennedy, & Haring, 1990).

Supportive School Practices

Not all schools will be characterized by the effective practices of (a) inclusion, (b) collaborative teams, (c) integrated therapy, (d) systematic, activity-based instruction, (e) data-based decision making, and (f) positive behavior support. However, these six practices are often cited as being central to excellent school programs for students with severe disabilities (e.g., Hunt & Goetz, 1997; Orelove & Sobsey, 1997; Rainforth & York-Barr, 1997). When practices are deficient or missing, it becomes important to repair or build the practice while still focusing on the design and implementation of appropriate student programs. This process requires that administrators and school staff critically examine their current methods, engage in creative problem solving, learn more about the effective practices we describe next, and tackle the politics of making changes.

Box 4–1

What Do Inclusive *and* Integrated *Schools Mean?*

Inclusive schools create a mainstream where all students belong and learn. Inclusion affects the location of students, the supports provided, and the roles of school staff. These characteristics require that:

- All students attend their neighborhood school, the one they would otherwise attend if they had no disabilities.
- The number of students with disabilities reflect the natural proportions of students with disabilities.
- Special education supports follow students wherever they are scheduled to be.
- Students with disabilities are members of general education classrooms with their age peers.
- Inclusion is planned on an individual basis: the classroom(s), the amount and kinds of support, and the types of accommodations and adaptations used to enable active and meaningful participation in learning and social activities.
- Inclusion does not preclude the use of "pull-out" with collaboration.

Integrated schools have some of these characteristics, but not all. Students with disabilities are present alongside nondisabled peers, but integrated schools do not serve all students within the nearby area. Therefore, integrated schools do not reflect the natural proportion of students with disabilities (there may be far fewer or far more students with disabilities present). These schools may discourage development of after-school friendships because of the long distances between students with disabilities and their nondisabled classmates.

Inclusion

Inclusion and integration are pivotal school practices that influence students with disabilities and their teams (Box 4–1). Both practices are complex but strongly influence school attitudes and opportunities for learning and interaction between peers (Hunt & Goetz, 1997). Over the past decade, studies of including students with severe disabilities in general education have led to an accumulation of evidence on the potential benefits that may result (e.g., Hunt & Goetz, 1997; Staub & Peck, 1995). We know that inclusion can lead to social benefits and skill improvements for students with severe disabilities (e.g., Dugan, Kamps, Leonard, Watkins, Rheinberger, & Stackhaus, 1995;

Fryxell & Kennedy, 1995; Haring & Breen, 1992; Hunt, Staub, Alwell, & Goetz, 1994; Kennedy, Shukla, & Fryxell, 1997; Shukla, Kennedy, & Cushing, 1998) (Table 4–2). The outcomes of inclusion for students without disabilities have been studied and found beneficial (Cushing & Kennedy, 1997; Dugan et al., 1995; Evans, Salisbury, Palombaro, & Goldberg, 1994; Kishi & Meyer, 1994; Shukla et al., 1998).

Inclusion is encouraged, though not legally mandated by law. As noted by Bateman and Linden (1998, p. 13): "The law continues to express a preference rather than a mandate for placement of children with disabilities in the regular classroom." The Individuals with Disabilities Education Act (IDEA) of 1997 and its

---

TABLE 4–2
Potential Benefits of Inclusion

Benefits for Students with Severe Disabilities	Benefits for Students without Disabilities
• Increased social participation with typical peers and social networks • Age-appropriate models for social interaction, behavior, dress, preferences, etc. • Better acceptance by peers and more interactions and positive social relationships with peers • More participation in general education classes, curriculum, and activities • Improvement in skills (e.g., awareness and alertness, social maturation and interaction, academic outcomes) and independence	• Increased opportunity to socialize with peers who have disabilities and larger social networks • Improvements in attitudes toward people with disabilities and in awareness of, comfort with, and appreciation for these individuals • Replacement of fear and avoidance of peers with disabilities with an increased understanding and acceptance of them • Improvements in other positive character traits: tolerance of differences, increased responsibility, improvements in understanding and appreciation of self-worth, self-esteem, and empathy

earlier versions require that the least restrictive environment for each student be used "to the maximum extent appropriate" and that "supplementary aids and services" be added to the general education classroom and activities when needed to make that setting work satisfactorily for students with disabilities. While the inclusion of students with disabilities has been quietly working in many schools for years, a number of professionals and disability organizations still draw rigid battle lines and debate the meaning and values of inclusion. Educators and parents of students with severe disabilities typically are more vocal in their support of inclusion. Court decisions on inclusion have shifted back and forth between being supportive and nonsupportive in recent years. Because the move from separate programs to inclusive programs is difficult and motivated more through modeling than mandating, schools are often left to choose their own course of action. This means that inclusion is practiced very unevenly; for example, where a student with severe disabilities lives may be the single strongest factor determining whether or not a student attends an inclusive school or receives special education primarily in a self-contained classroom.

Collaborative Teams

One of the simplest ways to define *collaborative teams* is that they are two or more people working together toward a common goal (Snell & Janney, 2000). *Working* can mean goal setting, problem identification, assessment of student's needs and skills, information exchange, resolution of problems, and the design and use of action plans. *Working together* refers to the "positive interdependence" that exists among team members who agree to pool their resources, share their rewards, and operate within a framework of shared values. Team members cooperate rather than compete by helping and lending support to each other (Rainforth & York-Barr, 1997). The *common goals* of a team are its mutually agreed upon aims.

Core teams are the smaller subset of members from the extended team who have regular and frequent contact with a particular student and therefore with each other. Core members on many student's teams include a family member, the student, the special education teacher, and a general education teacher; but others may be part of the core team (e.g., paraprofessionals, speech and language pathologist [SLP], occu-

pational therapist [OT], physical therapist [PT]). Family members and students are typically not present for all core team interactions, although their input is routinely heard through interaction with team members. *Extended teams* are larger and include all members who contribute to a student's educational program in some way.

To accomplish their work, teams must interact frequently; formal meetings occur less often than informal meetings and exchanges "on the fly" during the school day. Regardless of the type of interaction, effective communication and trust are crucial to teamwork. Communication and trust involve two-way talents: communication requires skills in listening and in speaking, while trust involves both trusting and being trustworthy.

There are several important team activities. First, teams must identify their shared values and set ground rules by which to operate. *Shared values* include philosophical guidelines upon which members agree and that influence the actions teams take with students and each other (e.g., "we believe that all students can communicate in some way"; "family members have a primary say in all planning"). *Ground rules* define a team's operating standards and guidelines for working together (e.g., "arrive on time, end on time"; "listen to what all members have to say"). Second, teams should take time each meeting to *examine their teaming process*: the quality of their communication, progress made on their agenda items, and barriers and benefits they are feeling as a team. When such introspection becomes part of a team's routine, it serves as a health check and a means for facing team weaknesses before they become serious. Third, teams must learn how to resolve problems, particularly those concerning their focus student(s). *Problem solving* involves identifying problems, gathering relevant information concerning a problem and the situation, brainstorming potential solutions, evaluating those ideas against team criteria, formulating a solution, designing an action plan, carrying the plan out, and making needed improvements along the way. Figure 4–1 summarizes the typical steps involved in problem solving and the team and procedural considerations for each step (Cook & Friend, 1993; Snell & Janney, in press, a).

Teams require supports. They cannot get started or easily maintain their efforts in schools without ad-

FIGURE 4–1

Elements of Problem Solving: Interpersonal and Procedural Considerations

Interpersonal Considerations		Procedural Considerations
• Establish a climate of trust. • Share relevant information.	1. IDENTIFY THE PROBLEM	• Focus on the problem, not the solution. • Reach agreement on the problem.
• Encourage input from all parties. • Defer judgment about the solutions.	2. BRAINSTORM POSSIBLE SOLUTIONS	• Generate as many alternative solutions as possible.
• Be supportive rather than attacking. • Evaluate the solutions, not people. • Elicit input from all parties. • Be accepting of differences.	3. EVALUATE THE POSSIBLE SOLUTIONS	• Identify criteria by which the solutions are judged. • Modify and combine the solutions as needed.
• Ascertain that all participants feel some ownership of the trial solution. • Reach a decision by consensus.	4. CHOOSE A SOLUTION	• Select a trial solution.
	5. WRITE AN ACTION PLAN	• Determine what materials will be needed (if any). • Assign responsibility for the specific steps. • Set a time line. • Establish measurement procedures. • Schedule a follow-up meeting

Note: Interpersonal and procedural considerations of collaborative teams and problem-solving (p. 44) by L. Cook & M. Friend in R. Beck (Ed.) , *Project RIDE: Responding to individual differences in education* (p. 44). Longmont, CO: Sopris West. Reprinted with permission.

ministrative support for their values, without in-service training or consultation for the skills required, and without time to do their work. Simultaneously, educational programs for students with severe disabilities rely on collaborative teamwork because any one individual rarely has the skills and resources needed to develop, implement, and monitor an appropriate program.

For example, it took the combined efforts of many (Christine's parents, her SLP, OT, and PT, her job coach, and special education teacher) working with staff in each work setting to plan for Christine's communication and job sampling last semester. Christine worked as an elementary school library assistant checking out books, as a greeter at Wal-Mart, and as an activity assistant in a nearby day care center. Her team planned for her physical and communication needs in each work setting. At the day care center and Wal-Mart, Christine could use preprogrammed stories or greetings. However, in the library, when assisting in scanning books, she needed to rely more on saying "yes" or "no" and her gestures and facial expressions to communicate, be-

cause her somewhat bulky communication device got in the way of the books and scanner. For each job, team members needed to actively explore Christine's role to meet their team's guiding principles.

Integrated Therapy

Students are more likely to benefit when their therapy needs (e.g., physical, occupational, speech and communication, mobility) are synthesized into their daily routine (Giangreco, 1986). Integrated therapy ". . . provides the most educationally relevant services in the least restrictive environments" (Rainforth & York-Barr, 1997, p. 203). For example:

1. Therapists address actual, not simulated, skill difficulties in the context of routine school or community activities, which requires that therapy be functionally matched to a student's skill needs.

   By going to the library job with Christine, her OT and SLP could experiment with position, switches, and communication modes until they figured out how she could best perform the job and still communicate effectively.

2. A student's daily routine provides the therapy setting, materials, and performance conditions, thus
making it easier for students to maintain the gains
they achieve in therapy.

*In October after a month of daily focus on greeting his teach-
ers and the SLP when he arrived at school, Timothy began to
do so without any reminders.*

3. Students are more apt to generalize their learning
to other similar activities at school, home, and in
the community when therapy is applied in realistic
and familiar locations.

*Several months after the OT and Jenny's team instituted a
plan for her to take brief "exercise breaks" when she became
fidgety, unable to sit, and inattentive, Jenny now tells her
parents when she needs a break at home.*

Plugging therapy into the routines where the skills
are required is the best way to guarantee that the
therapy relates to reality. When therapy occurs in isolated speech or therapy rooms, it is more likely that
nonuseful skills are addressed and that there will be
little transfer of learning from therapy to daily routines. Instead, therapy should be scheduled as part of
integrated activities like lunch (language and eating),
physical education (transfers, balance, and muscle
tone), and interactions (greetings, requests, using a
pocket communication book).

Systematic, Activity-Based Instruction
Teaching skills in the context of familiar, functional
activities is referred to as *activity-based instruction*. The
logic of activity-based instruction is similar to integrated therapy: teach when targeted skills are needed
so the conditions are realistic and learning is more
likely to be maintained and generalized. Some also
suggest that a student's motivation may be higher
when instruction is activity-based, particularly if the
student chooses the activity or if an instructor follows the student's lead within an activity (Bricker &
Cripe, 1993; Kaiser, Hancock, & Hester, 1998). The
objectives teams target for students involve functional skills that are both frequently required and
embedded within regular routines at school or home,
or in the community. When activity-based instruction
is *systematic*, it takes place reliably and consistently
and is characterized by being team-planned and
purposeful.

*For example, Timothy receives instruction on several related
IEP objectives just before and during lunch time: using his
picture schedule to identify lunch, washing his hands, going
to the cafeteria with his lunch partners, greeting the cafeteria
workers who greet him, and waiting in line and getting lunch
materials without engaging in stereotypic behavior.*

Data-Based Decision Making
Teams use student performance data to decide what to
teach, how to teach, when instruction is working, and
when it misses the mark. As we described in chapter 3,
assessment information is the team's primary guide
for defining a student's current level of performance,
need for special education and related services, and
IEP objectives. Students are observed and tested in
natural as well as new situations; family members and
others who know students well are interviewed to
gather information on student behavior and preferences and on care-provider hopes and concerns. Then
teams pool, discuss, and analyze the assessment information, identify needed skills, write IEPs, and design teaching programs to address IEP objectives.
Only by measuring students' *present levels of performance*
through the observation of their behavior or work samples and then comparing these levels to changes that
result from instruction, can team members determine
if and how much progress has been made. *Data-based
decision making* is an active, ongoing process involving
repeated assessment of relevant student behavior,
careful team examination of those data, and decisions
that logically reflect the changes in student performance over time (Farlow & Snell, 1995).

Positive Behavior Support
The old rules of "behavior mod" advised teachers and
parents that problem behavior should simply be reduced by taking two steps: (a) selecting consequences
from a menu of procedures often involving punishment (such as reprimands, removal of privileges, time
out, overcorrection), and (b) presenting the consequences immediately following each instance of the
behavior (Horner & Carr, 1997). Rarely did team members seek to discover *immediate antecedents* that might
predict the behavior's occurrence. For example, did
the time of day or the type of task (e.g., too difficult or
too boring) make a difference in the occurrence of
problem behavior? Were some settings more likely to
spark problem behavior (e.g., too crowded with people or noisy)? Was problem behavior usually associ-

ated with a desire for attention or a particular tangible? In some cases, might more distant *setting events* cause any of these antecedent conditions to be less tolerable for students? For example, without breakfast, Jenny has little tolerance for copying the day's date from the blackboard and will get fidgety and refuse to work.

Over the past decade, we have come to better understand the relationships between students' serious problem behavior and several important factors: (a) the individualized role antecedent conditions play in triggering problem behavior, (b) the ways people respond to problem behavior that act to maintain or accelerate it, (c) students' ability to communicate and be recognized, and (d) the opportunities available for students to make choices, have active control, and participate in meaningful activities (Horner & Carr, 1997). Three primary strategies are used in a positive behavior support approach: (a) searching for and sometimes testing hypotheses that explain the function of problem behavior (e.g., to get desired items or activities, to escape from activities or situations, to obtain attention, etc.) and variables associated with the behavior (e.g., quality of instruction, noise level, number of choice opportunities, etc.); (b) acting on those hypotheses by teaching skills that replace the problem behavior but serve a similar function; and (c) arranging the environment to address factors associated with the problem behavior (e.g., adapting a task to promote success, reducing noise level, giving many options for students to make choices about their schedule and activities).

> To address the escape function of Timothy's tantrums in the speech therapy room and in other nonpreferred activities (e.g., clearing his dishes, going into the mall), his team teaches him to show a break card (with a red stop sign) when he first exhibits signs of being anxious (e.g., whining, pulling away from adults). They also offer him choices of which activities to complete.

Also in these cases, the existing "rules" for the problem behaviors are changed so that adults and peers do not allow tantrums, self-injury, or aggression for example, to yield the outcome a student seeks (e.g., toys or food, help or escape, and attention of others); while the alternate, appropriate behavior easily and effectively yields the desired outcome. Additionally, programs that rely on positive behavior support often involve multiple, individualized im-

provements in students' routines, instructional programs, and environments. Particular attention is given to students' (a) communication (i.e., expressing themselves understandably and being understood and recognized by others), (b) priority skills, and (c) interests, preferences, and choice making (see chapter 6).

Schools that exhibit these six practices offer a supportive environment to teachers and their teammates as they work to create appropriate educational programs for students with severe disabilities.

Guiding Team Principles

Next, we review eight principles that characterize educational teamwork and influence how teams make decisions about teaching (Table 4–1). While these guiding principles determine the directions teams take, the strength of their influence is affected by the supportive practices previously described that are operating in a school (e.g., inclusion, teaming, positive behavior support).

Educational Programs Are Student-Centered

Teams consider students' well-being as their core purpose. To this end, teams look to the student and to family members for their personal knowledge and long-term commitment, to the student's peers for their awareness of existing relationships and sensitivity to their age group, and to service providers for their knowledge of students and expertise. Being student-centered can mean different things: (a) the student has team input, (b) peers make contributions, (c) the student participates in some team meetings, or (d) team members use a student-centered tool like McGill Action Planning System (MAPS), or person-centered planning to help design programs (Vandercook, York, & Forest, 1989) (see chapter 3).

Because many factors can influence student participation in their own planning, teams need to find appropriate ways to promote student-centeredness (Wehmeyer, 1998). Recently, a group of researchers found that both a student's style of conversation (e.g., gregarious or withdrawn) and the size of the meeting had an impact on the student's participation (Whitney-Thomas, Shaw, Honey, & Butterworth, 1998). Withdrawn students often preferred smaller meetings but still needed to be "drawn out" to participate. Meeting facilitators needed to establish a clear pattern of communication, such as using short, clear questions and then asking: "Anything else?" or stating questions in the form of two choices (while holding out one hand or symbol for each choice) and asking the student to choose a hand or symbol. The level of abstraction in the meetings was another critical factor identified by Whitney-Thomas et al. (1998). For example, it was easier to have students answer questions about what they liked or didn't like at work or school than to plan future events (i.e., "What are your dreams?"). Student participation could be increased by: (a) speaking directly to students rather than generally to the group; (b) confirming the student's responses or answers to questions; (c) speaking in ways that students understand; (d) augmenting spoken words (and displayed meeting notes) with pictures, gestures, and objects to increase understanding; (e) waiting for students to respond; (f) following the student's lead to change the topic, take more time on a topic, or take a break; and (g) keeping a positive meeting tone.

> *For example, Christine joins team members for all IEP and transition meetings and is given time to respond to questions and make choices. Her parents and teachers prepare her for these meetings, and she seems to grasp how they affect her daily school routines. Last summer, her extended team and friends gathered to complete a person-centered future plan with her. Many themes were revealed: she has lots of friends in and out of school; her community support requires enlarging; her health is finally not a dominant priority; her communication is good; and she needs more opportunities to be independent.*

Educational Programs Are Team-Generated

Students' educational programs are designed by cohesive teams of two or more individuals; the decisions that teams make reflect the input and consensus of all members, synthesizing the ideas of many.

> *For example, Christine's team is large; the size reflects her needs and age. Besides Christine and her parents, regular core members include a special education teacher, several general education teachers, her teaching assistant, OT, PT, SLP, and a transition coordinator. The team also draws upon a vision specialist and staff from Christine's current work settings. Because her core team has a common vision of what Christine wants when she completes her schooling, they often find that they achieve consensus with little debate.*

Educational Programs Are Both Practical and Valid

To design educational programs, teams select and combine ideas that are not only usable and efficient but also substantiated, logical, consistent with current knowledge, and likely to realize change in the desired directions (Worrall, 1990). This *principle of parsimony* (Etzel & LeBlanc, 1979) cautions against selecting either overly complex or questionable methods: When several approaches work, select the simplest approach.

Tim's team regularly asks five questions when considering specific treatments for his autism:

- *Will the treatment result in harm?*
- *Is the treatment developmentally appropriate for Timothy?*
- *How will failure of the treatment affect Timothy and his family?*
- *What type of scientific validation exists to support the treatment?*
- *How will the treatment be integrated into Timothy's current program and not result in the elimination or reduction of other valued treatments? (Freeman, 1997, p. 649)*

Educational Programs Are Socially Valid

Teams also need to apply societal standards for judging the quality, value, and acceptability of educational programs. *Social validity* encompasses the significance of resultant learning, the acceptability of teaching methods, and the importance of chosen goals (Wolf, 1978). Just as some goals are not important or useful for all students, neither are some teaching methods socially acceptable to teachers, parents, or peers (Wolfe, 1994). An example of the social validity of methods (through subjective opinion) occurred when Timothy's mom evaluated an approach some team members advocated to increase attention in students with autism, learning disabilities, and attention deficit disorder:

> *After reading materials on auditory integration training (AIT) and watching a child in a session, Timothy's mom, Ms. Simms, decided against using the approach. She judged it to be unacceptable: "The boy looked bored and then very unhappy; and he had to come back for more sessions. We can't waste Timothy's time with something like that. Also, I question the so-called evidence behind it." Timothy's OT, who wants to try AIT, says that she will search for additional literature on it to consider at their next meeting.*

Judging the social validity of changes in student behavior involves looking beyond objective data and graphs and asking, "So what? Is this change important to me?" Typically, social validation of skill gains in a student (or methods used to teach skills) depend on one of two tests. First, a student's performance can be compared to his or her peers' performance (e.g., Christine can use the Dynovox, but do others understand her when she orders a hamburger at McDonald's or tries to purchase a movie ticket?). Second, the subjective, honest opinion about the skill change can be sought from "consumers" who have a vested interest in the student (e.g., asking parents, friends, or potential employers if they think Christine's skill on the job is good enough). In fact, when the opinion of Christine's "boss" was sought after 3 weeks on the job, the librarian socially validated her skills:

> The elementary school librarian in one of Christine's job sites was overheard to say, "I need her here! On days when Christine is around, my day goes so much better and the kids using the library are much happier too!"

Educational Programs Reflect Functional Priorities

Functional skills are those skills that, if not performed in part or full by a student, must be completed for the student by someone else. Students with severe disabilities often must be guided in learning these practical skills that are needed regularly in life and may not be part of their typical peers' school curriculum. What is functional for one student may not be for another, because, as was discussed in chapter 3, functionality depends on individual characteristics and must be determined through ecological or environmental assessment.

Educational Programs Require Active Participation

A student's participation in an activity may be partial or complete, but it is best when performance is meaningful and active rather than nonpurposeful and passive. When students are unable to achieve independence or to participate meaningfully in a valued routine, the routine or the ways it is performed must be adapted to promote their active participation. The *principle of partial participation*, as this viewpoint is called, promotes involvement in one or more ways: by changing the way or order in which a task is per-

formed, modifying the materials used, adding personal assistance on the difficult steps, or making changes in the rules or setting (Baumgart et al., 1982; Ferguson & Baumgart, 1991). The decision to use partial participation needs regular review to prevent holding the student back from learning more.

> For example, until recently, Christine relied on others to turn on her communication device because this step was too difficult, but she could turn the Dynovox off by clicking her hand switch when she heard that option scanned on the main menu (i.e., "school, home, or shut down"). Over the Christmas holiday, her parents experimented with the device and her switches. After some practice, Christine learned to use her head switch to turn on the device, and to wait until she heard the device power up and saw the screen light up.

Educational Programs Foster Self-Determination

All humans seem to benefit from learning to make decisions about themselves, attain independence in useful routines, evaluate their own performance, and make needed adjustments to improve themselves. People with disabilities are no different. These skills, which are components of being self-determined (Wehmeyer, Agran, & Hughes, 1998), are highly interrelated with "the three Cs" (i.e., communicating, choice making, and control) and with improvements in behavior and learning (Williams, 1991):

- Having a recognized means for communicating with others (being understood and understanding others)
- Making choices (i.e., having opportunities to choose, choosing, and experiencing the choice) (Kern, et al., 1998)
- Being taught to exercise responsible control of oneself, routine events, and more significant aspects of life.

Educational Programs Are Individualized

A central tenet of appropriate programs is that they are tailored to the individual student. *Individualized instruction* means that teaching is tailored to the student's strengths, needs, and individual characteristics and must not be confused with individual or one-to-one instruction (Rainforth & England, 1997, p. 95). Individualized instruction reflects the student's stage of learning for a given skill; his or her preferences, priorities, and chronological age; and specific assets or limitations that may require adaptation in materials, environment, or teaching methods.

Designing Supports that Foster Relationships and Promote Membership

In this section, we address some general ways teams can aim for two of the three desired student outcomes: fostering relationships and promoting membership. Some recent research on these outcomes with students who have severe disabilities lends strong support to what may be quite obvious: The best way to enhance social relationships of students with severe disabilities is to enroll them in general education classes and give them the necessary supports. Enrollment in general education classrooms results in more frequent interactions with nondisabled peers, higher proportions of social support, and bigger and more long-lasting social networks of typical peers than occurs for similar students served in special education classrooms (Kennedy, Cushing, & Itkonen, 1997; Kennedy, Shukla, et al., 1997). Several practices have emerged that facilitate membership and relationships with peers. The following section provides an overview of these strategies; chapter 10 provides more depth.

How Can Membership Be Promoted?

Membership can be promoted by planned placement of students with peers in general education classes.

For the first time, Christine is enrolled in a "regular" high school class! She has goals and objectives to guide her instruction and she has the needed support. Her special education teacher knows how to work with the drama teacher and other team members to plan for the needed modifications.

Jenny has been included in general education classrooms since first grade. She has learned the social skills that make her a good companion and attract an active set of friends. Her team is planning for the changes that will come in middle school in order to continue her inclusion with peers.

Timothy spends every weekday morning in a community preschool. There he has numerous natural opportunities to use the communication, pre-academic, and social skills that he has been learning in a one-to-one arrangement for the past 2 years. His team members are alert to the importance of generalizing these skills to this setting and his nondisabled classmates.

A second strategy for promoting membership is to involve students with disabilities in peer networks or cliques. Often, mere proximity in a supportive school setting results in numerous examples of membership for many students with disabilities. Sometimes the addition of adult and peer support or the creation of friendship clubs optimizes the opportunity for membership in classroom groupings, friendship groups, and extracurricular and school clubs and activities (Shukla et al., 1998; Snell & Colley, in press).

For example, Timothy's team noticed that block time was one of his favorite activities. They formed a "Builder's Club" for those who especially enjoyed blocks, about 6 of the 15 kids. With some initially added support, Timothy has learned to work alongside peers as the group grew from two members to the limit of six. The "club" has led to more interactions between Timothy and peers at other times during preschool, now that most of them understand his signs, gestures, and use of pictures to communicate.

Jenny has been in Scouts for 2 years and is a member of the soccer team; both groups include some kids from her fifth grade class.

Christine's recent membership in Best Buddies holds great promise for participating in activities that others her age enjoy. This is the first club she has joined at her high school.

How Can Relationships Be Fostered?

Relationships are central to all human beings; children and adolescents with severe disabilities are no exception. Some have argued that friendships be included as educational goals for students who do not have them (Strully & Strully, 1989). Others who examined the IEPs of a variety of students with disabilities found that while students' current functioning on peer interaction was often described accurately, their actual needs did not get the support necessary to promote improved interaction with peers (Gelzheiser, McLane, Meyers, & Pruzek, 1998). We agree it is crucial to foster relationships both by targeting IEP goals and by providing the variety of supports necessary to achieve them.

As adults we can either help or hinder the formation and growth of relationships our students have with nondisabled peers. Adult support that promotes peer relationships, called *adult facilitation*, is not easily accomplished. Schnorr (1997) found that teachers and teaching assistants could either facilitate or prevent social interactions between middle and high school students with severe disabilities and their peers in general education. The strategies adults used to promote successful interactions between the student they supported and his or her classmates included:

- Being alert to times when student interactions naturally occurred (e.g., before and between classes, while attendance was taken, during seatwork following a group lesson) and encouraging the student's participation.
- Understanding the social role successfully played by the student they supported (e.g., Mark laughed at class jokes even though he could not tell them, and he always greeted others).
- Responding to the student's vocalizations in conversational ways, and, as needed, sensitively interpreting the student's vocalizations aloud by connecting them to the class context, giving them meaning, and encouraging interactions (e.g., "Nicole, Mark wants to show you something," Schnorr, 1997, p. 13).
- Considering the student's physical location among classmates in a classroom, being aware of peer social groups and memberships, and recognizing partners who interacted with the student.
- Understanding that peers needed to know a student's communication system in order to interact with him or her.
- Recognizing that a student's modes of communicating (e.g., vocalizations, gestures, signs, words, pictures, electronic devices) and their vocabulary needed to be flexible, suitable, and supportive of social interactions specific to each class context (Schnorr, 1997).

In addition to adult facilitation, a second general strategy for building relationships among students is to shape and use *peer supports* (Salisbury, Gallucci, Palombaro, & Peck, 1995; Snell & Colley, in press). There are many successful models for peer support, and it is evident that active engagement of students with severe disabilities tends to be as good or better

when peers lend support than when adults do (Shukla et al., 1998). There are three models for peer support.

Peer problem-solving groups are facilitated by an adult to solve difficulties that arise in the class or school. As the students' skills for recognizing and resolving problems improves, the adult reduces assistance. Groups may focus on a single student with disabilities (e.g., peer networks, MAPS, person-centered planning) or may address a wider scope of issues that include peer acceptance (e.g., peer planning, collaborative problem solving) (Forest & Lusthaus, 1989; Haring and Breen, 1992; Salisbury, Evans, & Palombaro, 1997; Salisbury & Palombaro, 1993; Snell & Colley, in press)

Friendship pairs or groups involve careful pairing of individuals or connecting small friendship networks of students without disabilities with single students who have disabilities. Typical peers volunteer to support students with disabilities and participate with them in activities. Peers receive varying amounts of training, guidance, and supervision. Examples of this type of peer support include the PAL Club (Partners at Lunch), student aide program, friendship volunteers, peer connections, and Best Buddies High School (Breen & Lovinger, 1990; Grabowski, 1997; Kamps, Potucek, Lopez, Kravits, & Kemmerer, 1997; Keachie, 1997; Peck, Donaldson, & Pezzoli, 1990; Staub, Spaulding, Peck, Gallucci, & Schwartz, 1996).

Natural activities with support are more loosely organized activities that bring together students with and without disabilities, usually for leisure experiences during and after school. These groups might include a community service club that regularly pairs up with students who have severe disabilities in their school for service activities, as well as adapted sports groups, buddy systems, and advocacy clubs (Perske, 1988).

A final set of strategies that contribute to building social relationships with students who have severe disabilities is broadly identified as "social skill instruction." These strategies may focus on (a) building prosocial behaviors and interaction skills; (b) promoting age-appropriate behavior, dress, and improvements in appearance and social acceptability; and (c) replacing problem behavior with socially acceptable behavior. Usually social skill instruction is most successful if paired with adult facilitation and peer support.

Designing and Putting Skill Programs into Place

Designing programs to teach skills involves the consideration of many factors by team members: students' current level of skill performance, needed goals and objectives, and the design and use of programs to teach specific objectives. In this last but longest section, we tackle these topics. We start by giving some background on stages of learning and then link this to students' present level of performance of skills identified as individually functional and important. Given an awareness of students' present performance of priority skills, teams can discuss and determine IEP goals and objectives. Then teams must turn their attention to basic program questions: Who will teach? Where and when will teaching occur? What teaching arrangement will be used? What adaptations will be applied, if any? And what teaching methods (logistics, arrangements, and procedures) will be used?

Stages of Learning

Think of two skills you have: one that is known and easily performed and one you are just learning. Now describe how you feel when you perform both skills. Have you used phrases like the following?

In the skill I am competent in performing

- I'm confident and at ease. It seems automatic to perform this skill.
- I am pretty fast.
- I make few errors (unless some task feature has changed).

In the skill I am learning to perform

- I'm cautious and hesitant, checking each step before I perform it.
- I am very slow.
- I make a lot of mistakes, but keep trying.

For all individuals, learning appears to move through different stages related to the grasp of the target skill (Browder, 1991; Liberty, 1985). Because some teaching strategies are more influential at certain points in learning than at other points, instructional plans should address the stage of learning or the present level of performance that students demonstrate for each priority skill. As shown in Figure 4–2, there are at least four stages of learning:

- *Acquisition stage* ("learn it"). Typically, skills in this stage are new skills, performed with accuracy varying from 0% to about 60% or 70% of the steps correct (Farlow & Snell, 1995). While the focus of early learning is often accurate performance of the core steps of a skill, instruction need not be limited to these steps. As was explained in chapter 3, teaching can be expanded to include extension and enrichment skills, such as initiating the task, preparing for the task, terminating the task, and making choices in the task (Brown, Evans, Weed, & Owen, 1987). Probably, most research on skill instruction has addressed learning during the acquisition stage. We seem to focus on and understand the three later stages of learning, despite their importance, less well than acquisition.

- *Maintenance stage* ("use it routinely"). Skills in this stage are still imperfect but are good enough to use with some level of independence. The adage "practice makes perfect" applies to this stage and reminds us of two things: (a) forgetting is best remedied through regular use; and (b) functional skills, because they are needed, offer extensive opportunities for practice. Researchers have addressed various aspects of promoting skill maintenance in situations with little or no supervision.

- *Fluency, or proficiency, stage* ("make it faster and better"). Skills in this stage of learning are performed with an accuracy usually above 60%, but the quality of performance at this level still needs improvement (Farlow & Snell, 1995). For example, some students learn to monitor the tempo (rate and duration) of the task performance (e.g., Can I count out the money fast enough not to hold up the line of customers? Am I emptying the dishwasher quickly enough?). Other students focus on improving the quality of task performance (e.g., Is the floor clean enough? Did I staple the top left corner of the pages?). Still other students work on both tempo and quality; however, many continue to emphasize their accuracy.

- *Generalization stage* ("use it anywhere and whenever it is needed"). In this stage, students are exposed to more variations of task materials and environments. They particularly need to learn problem solving as natural stimuli change and adaptations in response are required.

FIGURE 4–2
Stages of Learning

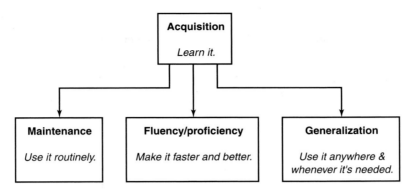

Teaching Structure

Teaching structure refers to the actions teachers take and the control they have over students during instruction. For example, structure includes what the teacher does before and after the student responds:

- Antecedent to a student's response: materials, proximity, requests, opportunities for choice, response latency, prompts.
- Consequent to the response: reinforcement, corrections, task change.

Furthermore, the behavior that is expected from the student is part of teaching structure (e.g., accuracy, complexity, duration, self-correction). Finally, the context and logistics of the activity contribute to structure (arrangement, location, and frequency and duration of instruction).

The teaching structure used should relate to a student's present ability to perform each IEP objective—their stage of learning. Generally, somewhat greater structure is used when teaching a new skill (acquisition stage) to prevent errors or to keep errors at a minimum. For example, students require more assistance to avoid errors but that assistance should be gradually faded out; they benefit from having ongoing feedback on their accuracy (e.g., praise for correct responses as well as for attempts or prompted correct responses, more assistance after errors). To teach skills in the acquisition stage, teachers are closer than usual to the student. Also, students need to have some repetition in the task steps and stimuli so that they can master a chain of responses; only later in learning should they be expected to adjust the skill to suit wide variations in the task materials, method, or setting. This does not mean that teaching in real locations or natural situations should be avoided nor that initial training be limited to one setting. However, teachers should provide enough structure initially to avoid confusing learning conditions.

For example, Timothy's greeting skills are still in the acquisition stage of learning. His teachers talk with his parents to define the target behavior. How Timothy will be taught to greet others depends on what he already can do and what his peers do. Next, the team plans how to prompt his response, emphasizing the natural cues that ultimately signal greeting. Given his beginning social and language skills, Timothy should not yet be taught a different greeting for everyone; instead, he'll learn to use the same raised hand movement for saying "hello" and "good-bye" to everyone.

During later stages of learning, teachers should gradually "pull away" from the learner, give less direct supervision, emphasize natural forms of reinforcement and error correction, and teach the student to self-monitor performance, while external reinforcement, supervision, and assistance are reduced. For example, during the maintenance stage of learning: (a) students should have regular opportunities to use the same skill under familiar conditions, (b) structure should be gradually reduced, and (c) teachers should reduce their assistance and fade their presence and approval so that the skill comes more under the control of natural cues and stimuli.

For example, Jenny automatically gets her daily schedule from her desk each morning and checks with the teacher for any schedule symbols to move or new symbols to add. With minimal reminders, she uses it regularly throughout the day, moving completed symbols to the back of the card and checking what's next.

Maintenance is a stage that many teachers forget or at least find difficult to implement, because it requires shifting from an active teaching role (e.g., prompting, praising) to distancing themselves and giving intermittent attention. Researchers have found that when students cannot predict teachers' supervision of their work on a task they know fairly well, they attend better and complete more of the task (Dunlap & Johnson, 1985).

Multiple-Step Tasks and Stages of Learning

Often, skills are composed of a sequence of behaviors or subskills. The skills involved in performing an activity may be multiple, with some students learning simplified versions and others learning more complex versions. Furthermore, a student's competence on different composite skills may not be equal or at the same stage of learning.

For example, one of Christine's mini-work experiences was being a greeter at Wal-Mart. Some of the skills involved in this job were new (e.g., having people take advertising flyers from a box on her tray, greeting customers she did not know), but other parts of the job involved skills used before in other settings (greeting using her speaking communication device, ordering a drink, taking a work break). She filled this job for 3 weeks and came to know the routine for which she was responsible. Many task steps (Table 4–3) were partially performed with the personal assistance of the teacher.

During acquisition, Christine's special education teacher, Ms. Washington, focused on the core steps of Christine's greeting customers either when signaled by a teacher or in response to a customer's greeting. Christine was good at greeting others with her Dynovox, but not as a greeter at Wal-Mart. Using her signaling watch to start or stop work or break and ordering and purchasing a drink during break were not new skills, though using them at Wal-Mart was (skill generalization stage). Slowly, Christine's performance improved in accuracy on the core steps even as Ms. Washington started to fade out her prompts and reduce her praise. When Christine met the initial acquisition criterion of 70% accuracy, Ms. Washington modified her teaching methods to promote skill maintenance. First, Ms. Washington spent less time directly instructing Christine and required Christine to continue greeting, while she remained quiet alongside. Ms. Washington also modified the reinforcement system used during acquisition, which had initially consisted of continuous praise for each task step completed. Ms.

TABLE 4–3
Task Steps in Christine's Job at Wal-Mart

1. Prepare materials for work (communication device and switch, money for drink, sales bill box that fits on tray). (Assistance placing in backpack)
2. Take school bus to Wal-Mart. (Assistance with wheelchair)
3. Report to work supervisor, sign in using name stamp. (Assistance with wheelchair)
4. Find out which greeting station to fill.
5. Pick up any sales pages to give to customers; place in box on tray. (Assistance putting sales pages in box)
6. Report to greeting station. (Assistance with wheelchair)
7. Position chair so that it maximizes her view of customers who have entered the store and allows them to pass close to her chair. (Assistance with wheelchair)
8. Use Dynovox to greet each customer, using one of several greetings (e.g., "Welcome to Wal-Mart. Help yourself to a sales sheet.").
9. Refer customer's questions to assistant or respond directly, as appropriate.
10. Leave job when watch signals a break; take 20-minute break in cafeteria. (Assistance with wheelchair and getting money from backpack)
11. Return to job when watch signals the end of break. (Assistance with wheelchair)
12. Work until watch signals the time to go. (Assistance with wheelchair)
13. Report to the supervisor, sign out. (Assistance with wheelchair)
14. Take bus back to school. (Assistance with wheelchair)

Washington began giving praise only for completion of the entire task.

When the priority skill involves a chain or sequence of steps or several routines together, as do many functional tasks, students' present level of performance may be uneven. They may perform at several different stages of learning within one routine. The teaching structure (context, logistics, and methods) used must be adjusted to mesh with a student's varying performance, as Ms. Washington did when working with Christine at Wal-Mart. As we discuss in chapter 5, by far the best way to make decisions about changing a teaching program is for team members to observe the student performing and collect and examine performance data as a team; by pooling relevant information and solving problems together, a team can reach agreement on the needed change (if any), implement that change, and then observe the outcome.

Writing IEPs

What Is a High-Quality IEP?

IEPs are complex and crucial documents that special education teachers must fully understand; readers are referred to Bateman and Linden (1998) for more depth (Box 4–2). "The IEP is a firm, legally binding commitment of resources" (Bateman & Linden, 1998, p. 60) by a school system and thus must be written with great care. Resources range widely from basic to specialized services and supports: (a) basic resources include buildings, transportation, professional and paraprofessional staff, instructional materials, and staff development; and (b) more specialized services and supports include related services personnel, educational programs designed to teach specific objectives, curriculum modifications, training on and support for collaborative teams and positive behavior support, augmentative and alternative communication devices, transportation to job settings in the community, and job coaches. The IEP is a document in which a student's many unique needs (e.g., functional academic, social, motor, communication, and, if old enough, vocational skills) are addressed in a highly individualized way.

To develop a student's IEP, teams should conduct a "threefold inquiry":

1. **Characteristics or needs**: Based on assessment information, what are a student's unique educational needs or characteristics that the IEP should address? What is a student's present level of performance?
2. **Services**: What will the educational team and district do, and what services will be furnished in response to each unique need or characteristic? When will these services begin; what will their frequency, location, and duration be?
3. **Annual goals and objectives**: What student accomplishments (written as measurable goals or objectives) will verify that the services provided are effective (Bateman & Linden, 1998, p. 100)?

The IEP constitutes what the educational team and district design in terms of special education, related services, supplementary aides and services, assistance technology, program modifications, and personnel support. IEP objectives are written to be indicators of learning and program evaluation. Objectives enable a school to judge if the services and educational program are successful or not.

Another important element of the IEP concerns transition. At age 14 (or younger, if appropriate), IEPs must include a statement of each student's transition service needs, while by age 16 (or younger,

---

Box 4–2

The Eight Essential Items Each Student's IEP Must Contain

1. A statement of the student's present levels of educational performance.
2. A statement of annual goals in measurable terms, including short-term objectives that meet each of the student's identified needs and enable involvement and learning in the general curriculum.
3. A statement of the needed services (special education, related services, and supplementary aids and services), program modifications, or school personnel supports that will be provided for the student.
4. An explanation of the extent, if any, to which the student will not participate with nondisabled students in general education classrooms and activities.
5. A statement of individual modifications, if any, in state or district assessments that are needed for the student to participate in assessment. If the team determines that the student will not participate, a statement of why participation is not appropriate and how the student will be assessed.
6. The projected date for needed services and modifications to begin and the anticipated frequency, location, and duration of those services and modifications.
7. A statement of how the student's progress toward the annual IEP goals will be measured; and how the student's parents will be regularly informed (at least as often as parents of nondisabled students are informed). Progress statements include the progress a student makes toward annual goals and the extent to which that progress is sufficient to enable the student to reach IEP goals by the end of the year.
8. A statement of transition services for students aged 16 or older; a statement of transition service needs if the student is 14 or older (younger than these ages, if appropriate).

[Adapted from Better IEPs (pp. 38–39) by B. D. Bateman & M. A. Linden, 1998, Longmont, CA: Sopris West. Reprinted with permission.

TABLE 4–4
A Partial Listing of Christine's Goals and Objectives for Building Vocational Skills

What Are This Student's Unique Needs and Characteristics?	What Educational Services Will Address These Needs and Characteristics?	What Goals and Objectives Will Be Indicators that the Services Are Appropriate?
Vocational Skills At age 19, Christine does not yet understand the meaning of paid work. She doesn't have routine responsibilities at home or school, nor has she participated in any volunteer or paid jobs in the community. While she gets an allowance and shops regularly, she does not connect reliable work with earning money. (Limited vision and control of movements.) **Present Level of Performance:** She has trouble paying attention to an independent school task for longer than 10 minutes and completing it without adult assistance. She communicates well with family and some staff, but she often is unable to make herself understood by other people.	The team will identify Christine's preferences for work/activity settings by using a structured interview of team members (including Christine). Team members will develop a set of work criteria that delineates characteristics of a desirable and acceptable work environment. This listing will be regularly revised to reflect Christine's experiences. The team will obtain inservice training in supported employment from a state project. With supported employment coordinator, team will identify 5 to 6 work placements for Christine, visit those sites, and make arrangements for mini-work experiences. These placements will be revised consistent with Christine's experiences. Related service team members will visit sites and assist team in adaptations (positioning, job arrangement) and communication (Dynovox vocabulary needed on job) for each work experience.	*Annual goal.* Christine will participate in work/volunteer activities that will lead to skills needed for meaningful day activities. *Objective 1:* Given 5 to 6 mini-work/volunteer experiences that are consistent with the ecological inventory and the team criteria for work experience, Christine will participate in each experience. Each experience will last 2 to 3 weeks at a community location for 3 or more days a week for 2 or more hours a day. *Objective 2:* For each work/volunteer experience, Christine will demonstrate an increase in time on task from 10 to 30 minutes over the successive work experiences. *Objective 3:* For each work/volunteer experience, Christine will communicate with her work supervisors and co-workers through signs, gestures, words, and the Dynovox by greeting and requesting her needs.

if appropriate), transition services must be addressed in the IEP; this statement may well include interagency linkages between the school and adult services. Transition services are "a coordinated set of activities," not a haphazard plan, aimed at fostering movement from school to postschool life. These services include instruction, related services, community experiences, development of employment and adult living skills, and, as is often needed with most students who have severe disabilities, the acquisition of daily living skills and functional vocational assessment. Thus the focus of the IEP changes during the teen years to include the transition to the postschool years: higher education (for some students), adult life, and work.

Listed among the "worst sins" of an IEP are five failures: failure to individualize; failure to address all a student's educational needs; failure to specify needed services; failure to write clear, meaningful, and measurable goals and objectives; and failure to clearly describe a student's present levels of functioning (Bateman & Linden, 1998, p. 88). When IEP objectives are written following the "threefold inquiry" listed earlier, many of these failures can be prevented. Christine's vocational goals and objectives, as set forth in Table 4–4, illustrate this advantageous practice.

The Logistics and Context of Teaching Programs

Once goals and objectives are written, team members shift their focus to designing specific teaching programs, while being guided by the principles set forth earlier. Teams address a series of questions:

- Who will teach, when, and where?
- What arrangement (e.g., individual, small group, tutoring, large group) will be used?
- What adaptations will be applied, if any?
- What teaching methods will be employed?

Teaching plans are ultimately the responsibility of the special education teacher with input from other team members. When the student is taught in the general education classroom or during integrated activities (such as library, lunch, art), teaching programs must mesh with classroom schedules, planned activities, available staff, and feasible grouping arrangements to take advantage of the opportunities for learning with and around peers. In this section, we describe the options available to address the first two questions, which involve logistics (who will teach and when) and context (where and in what arrangement).

Who Will Teach?

Teams have many options for instructors: the general or special education teacher, a paraprofessional, or a related services staff member. The more cohesive the team, the more likely that teaching plans will fit into ongoing school activities and suit multiple instructors. If cooperative learning groups are used in classrooms, peers will help teach each other. Finally, older students (typical or with disabilities), in a cross-age tutoring program, may be taught to serve as the tutor of younger students (typical or with disabilities). Any adult who teaches also needs to be involved in team conversations about the student so that all instructors are informed of progress and involved with problem solving. When instructors communicate as a team, having multiple instructors can be beneficial because it: (a) encourages students to generalize their learning across people, (b) provides the team with broader experience in teaching the student, and (c) prevents overinvolvement or isolation of instructors with students.

Several researchers have studied students in inclusive elementary classrooms and found that who was teaching made little difference (general or special educator, paraprofessional, or another student) in the student's level of academic responding (Logan, Brakeman, & Keefe, 1997; McDonnell, Thorson, & McQuivey, 1998). What seems to influence a student's academic responding in these classrooms is a combination of factors: (a) the arrangement: the rate of en-

gagement was slightly higher when the number of students were fewer (one-on-one and small group) than in whole class instruction; (b) being the *focus of* instruction seemed to improve a student's rate of responding (i.e., having opportunities to respond directed toward a student, materials provided, and feedback given); and (c) having individualized instruction: academic responding increased when teaching was tailored to the student.

A practice often used by schools and IEP teams is to pair off students having more extensive support needs with paraprofessionals for much of the day. Sometimes, however, when a single teaching assistant spends much of the school day with a single student, problems can result. Giangreco, Edelman, Luiselli, and MacFarland (1997, p. 11) studied this staffing practice and identified eight undesirable patterns that may develop when teaching assistants are in the exclusive role of assisting a single student. Teaching assistants may:

1. Obstruct the general educator's role and responsibility by having complete control in implementing the student's program.
2. Isolate the student from classmates by removing or distancing the student from groups of students and activities.
3. Promote dependency on adults.
4. Affect peer interactions negatively by their constant proximity and their sometimes protective approach to the student.
5. Use less than competent teaching methods with students.
6. Encourage a loss of personal control in the students they were responsible for by failing to promote choice making or peer interaction.
7. Be insensitive to the student's gender by, for example, taking male students into female bathrooms.
8. Distract classmates by, for example, involving the student in activities that differed from classmates.

Schools and educational teams are advised to rethink their practices and policies concerning the use of paraprofessionals so that these problems are eliminated. Individuals who have written about pairing paraprofessionals with students who need support have made some suggestions about addressing these potential difficulties (Giangreco et al., 1997; Hall, McClannahan, & Krantz, 1995; Snell & Colley, in press). First, it is important to broaden the responsibilities of classroom teachers so that they are involved in the supervision of special education teaching assistants. Second, classroom teachers and paraprofessionals should have basic training in systematic instruction, including ways to promote peer interaction. Third, the classroom teacher should feel ownership of the students with disabilities in their classrooms. Fourth, paraprofessionals need to be team members so that they have input and benefit from team thinking. Fifth, students' schedules should be designed so they are truly integrated into class activities and peer interactions, using adaptations as needed to promote meaningful involvement; simply being present with an assistant does not constitute meaningful inclusion. And finally, for students who need more personal assistance and the support of a paraprofessional, several practices may reduce the possibility of overisolation: (a) assign two assistants to a single student for part of the day and let assistants rotate among other students, (b) assign assistants to classrooms rather than to students, (c) vary a student's support so it rotates among team members, and (d) design teaching arrangements so team members avoid one-to-one arrangements but include nondisabled students and teach in pairs, teams, or small groups.

When and Where Will Teaching Occur?

Many students with severe disabilities learn both inside and outside the classroom: in hallways, other classrooms, the cafeteria, and outside the school on playgrounds, at the bus loading areas, and in the community. As students with severe disabilities grow older and their IEP objectives include skills or activities not targeted for most nondisabled peers, their instruction will expand into alternative settings, beyond the general education classroom. As a general rule, some alternate teaching settings away from the general education classroom but in the school (with or apart from peers) are necessary during the later elementary and middle school years.

For example, Jenny is not enrolled in language arts but instead receives one-to-one instruction in following school routines more independently.

During the middle school, high school, and post-high school years, as the instructional focus for students with severe disabilities shifts to include more functional academic, community, and job-related skills, the alternative teaching settings expand to include stores, offices, libraries, streets and sidewalks, restaurants, and work settings in the nearby community. Teams still must plan for general education classes or school activities that maximize students' continued contact with peers.

For example, Christine spends the bulk of her school week learning vocational skills in community settings, but she is taking a general education drama class and is active in an after school club.

In inclusive schools, special education instruction may take place in at least four different ways (Snell & Janney, 2000 a), each of which must involve team planning.

- *General education teacher with team planning and "consultation" from special education:* The student with disabilities is taught with peers using the same or adapted methods, but with no extra staff support.
- *Collaborative teaching* (also called team teaching or co-teaching): Two or more team members plan and teach the entire class (students with and without disabilities) cooperatively, usually for part of the day.
- *Pull-in with collaborative teaming:* Special education teacher or another team member (e.g., related services staff) teaches or provides support to the student(s) with disabilities in the context of a general education classroom or school activity. Classmates typically are involved in the same or similar activities as the students with disabilities and may participate together in small or large groups or alongside.
- *Pull-out with collaborative teaming* (also called alternative activities): Support is provided by special education staff or other team members (e.g., related services staff, vocational teacher) to the student with disabilities in a setting away from the general education classroom for a particular reason identified by the team (e.g., to give privacy, more space, access to materials not in the classroom). The student who is removed from the general education setting may be accompanied by other classmates. Any use of pull-out depends on team collaboration to be effective and needs to be regularly reevaluated.

Often students with severe disabilities receive their special education services in more than one of these ways. Teams determine what approaches to use depending on the student's needs and characteristics, the services offered, and the skills targeted. For example, the schedules for Timothy, Jenny, and Christine reflect use of all four approaches, despite their differences in age and needs (Figure 4–3).

What Teaching Arrangement?

Most students with severe disabilities, much like their nondisabled peers, can acquire the ability to learn in groups and can also benefit from observing others learn. The skill objective, the setting, and the instructor influence whatever teaching arrangement is chosen (one-to-one, student pair, small group, or large group). When students present difficulties attending or staying with a small group, the team must build these skills.

One-to-One Instruction. On a practical level, one-to-one instruction has not proven to be as beneficial to

FIGURE 4–3

Team Support Approaches for Three Students

	Team Support Approaches			
Student	**Pull-Out with Collaborative Planning**	**Pull-In with Collaborative Planning**	**Collaborative Teaching**	**General Educator with Team**
Timothy (age 4) Preschool	Timothy leaves daily with the SLP for intensive communication training. Special educator and paraprofessional teach Timothy self-toileting.	All special staff provide Timothy with support in classroom activities. Special educator facilitates peer support twice a week; the SLP alternates.	Special and general educators regularly "run" a craft group, oversee centers during structured play, and participate in teaching special unit activities. Timothy is part of these activities.	During recess and two free play sessions a week, Ms. Johnson and her assistant carry out Timothy's communication and social objectives using methods designed by the team.
Jenny (age 10) 5th grade	SLP, assistant, and tutor work for 30-minute sessions, 3 times a week, in the library, cafeteria, playground, and around the school on self-management and errands.	M–F: Teaching assistant and special educator are scheduled to provide support to Jenny in the classroom (math, reading, writing). On Fridays, special educator runs "lunch bunch" peer support group for 4th/5th graders.	MWF: Special educator and classroom teacher conduct science classes and related cooperative group activities.	Ms. Alpern follows the team plans for Jenny's arrival and departure; monitors Jenny's work during shared reading; and oversees the "lunch bunch" group twice a week.
Christine (age 20) High school and community	Christine participates in community-based instruction for part of each day accompanied by one of several team members, depending on the teaching plans and schedule. Every 6 weeks, the PT checks her equipment. M–F: Christine is pulled out for bathroom breaks.	Paraprofessional and SLP alternate in accompanying Christine to drama class and to lunch with peers from the Lunch Club; services are focused on communicating with others effectively	Periodically used; Special education teacher spent time initially in drama class teaching students how to communicate with Christine.	This is the first year Christine has attended regular education classes; Ms. Washington (her TA) is always present in drama, but Mr. Fullen now interacts confidently with Christine and directs questions to her.

SLP, Speech-language pathologist; M–F, Monday through Friday; MWF, Monday, Wednesday, Friday; PT, physical therapist; TA, teaching assistant.

students with severe disabilities as many educators have thought. The rationale for this approach is to minimize distractions and thus enable stimulus control (Rotholz, 1987). Some confuse the notion of *individualized* instruction for students with *individual* instruction, but they are not synonymous. Individualized instruction is teaching designed to suit a specific student and can be delivered in a variety of teaching arrangements.

One disadvantage of one-to-one instruction is the failure of generalization. Skills mastered by students with autism and other severe disabilities in individual or one-to-one arrangements do not automatically generalize to larger groups of students (Koegel & Rincover, 1974) or to people other than the original teacher (Rincover & Koegel, 1975). Another disadvantage is the exclusion from other pupils, which means that opportunities are lost for peer-to-peer teaching, peer reinforcement, social interaction, and students' incidental learning of other students' material through observation (Farmer, Gast, Wolery, & Winterling, 1991; Stinson, Gast, Wolery, & Collins, 1991). In contrast, group instruction allows opportunities to acquire taking turns, waiting, and imitation of others—skills that have practical value in everyday life. Finally, one-to-one instruction is not cost-effective in terms of teacher time. It results in increased "down time" (noninstructional time) for students (Rotholz, 1987). Thus, one-to-one instruction should be reserved for teaching tasks in which: (a) privacy is required, (b) other students cannot easily be included (e.g., job training), (c) an older student teaches a younger student in a supervised tutoring program, and (d) short-term intensive instruction is needed.

When a student's IEP objectives include learning to work in groups, teams will want to consider several strategies which build these skills by varying the arrangement: tandem instruction, sequential instruction, concurrent instruction, and combination instruction are explained in Table 4–5. Another method called *enhanced group instruction* (EGI) (Kamps, Dugan, Leonard, & Daoust, 1994; Kamps, Leonard, Dugan, Boland, & Greenwood, 1991) has been found to promote effective responding and learning in small groups for students with intellectual disabilities and autism. Teachers working with groups of three to five students made tasks interesting and promoted learning by: (a) requesting frequent student-to-student responding, (b) using fast-paced and random trials,

(c) rotating materials and concepts taught, (d) using multiple examples of each concept taught (a minimum of three sets per concept), and (e) using individualized sets of materials for each student. While all the students in these studies had disabilities, some of the strategies for making instruction interesting and focused have the same effect with more diverse groups in general education classrooms.

Observation Learning. It is not surprising that students with severe disabilities can learn by watching others. Recent work has shown positive learning effects from having one student observe another student acquire academic skills (e.g., spelling one's name, adding, using a calculator, identifying community signs) and nonacademic skills (e.g., sharpening a pencil) (Doyle, Gast, Wolery, Ault, & Farmer, 1990; Singleton, Schuster, & Ault, 1995; Stinson et al., 1991; Whalen, Schuster, & Hemmeter, 1996). In these studies, which involved only pairs or small groups of students with disabilities, students not only learned the skills they were taught directly but also acquired some of their classmates' skills that they observed or that had been presented to them incidentally. Learning through observation in small groups can be improved:

- If group members have the same type of task (identifying over-the-counter medications) but are taught with different materials (each student learns two different medications), rather than when all have the same materials.
- When nondisabled peers model functional tasks for students with severe disabilities while simply verbalizing each step they perform (e.g., spelling their name with letter tiles, using a calculator) (Werts, Caldwell, & Wolery, 1996).

> *For example, during preschool, Timothy's teacher often pairs Timothy with two peers to help teach routines such as putting things in his cubby, picking a center, and getting ready for a snack. Josh and Meredith are good models; they make sure Timothy is watching and then perform one small step at a time while telling what they are doing in simple words and gestures.*

Students as Tutors. Students without disabilities have been found to be effective instructors of students with severe disabilities in one-to-one arrangements. First, when tutors learned to use enhanced group instruc-

TABLE 4–5
Methods to Build Group Participation Skills

Tandem Instruction

Start with one-to-one instruction and fade in other students one at a time until there is a group. Use with students who appear to have difficulties following requests to "sit quietly," "put your hands down," or "look at this," or participating without continuous reinforcement. Koegel and Rincover (1974) found that while gradually increasing the group size from one to eight students, attending skills were shaped along with students' ability to tolerate less reinforcement. However, the same attending skills can be shaped in the context of the group itself. Thus, tandem instruction can be used part of the day while the same student participates in some groups for short periods during other portions of the day, a strategy that reduces the disadvantages of gradually fading out one-to-one teaching (Rincover & Koegel, 1977).

Sequential Instruction

Teach students in a sequential manner (each student gets one turn, while others wait their turn) (Brown, Holvoet, Guess, & Mulligan, 1980). Reinforcing group members who attend to others as they take a turn increases the possibility for observational learning. Alternately, waiting time can be replaced with another activity for students who are not good at waiting, but students involved in other activities have less opportunity for learning by observing others. When sequential instruction is used, it is better to give turns contingent on being ready or contingent on being prompted to be ready than to give turns to students who are inattentive or misbehaving. Thus, turns may not be given in strict sequential order around a group.

Concurrent Instruction

Direct instruction toward an entire group, with individuals responding or with group responding in unison (Reid & Favell, 1984). When the diversity of a group is increased, teachers must adjust their presentation of content so all students can understand (e.g., use words, signs, and concrete objects to describe the group task or concept being taught) and allow a variety of response levels and modes so that all students can participate.

Combination Groups

In many classrooms, it is not unusual to address a large group or class on a concept, give instructions for an activity applying that concept (concurrent), and then divide into smaller groups, often of mixed ability levels (heterogeneous groups). Groups may have both independent or cooperative activities geared to individual abilities and goals. The teacher may provide directions to one group at a time or teach each group using turn taking (sequential). Students who have difficulty working in a group may be faded gradually into a group (tandem model) from a one-to-one teaching arrangement in the same classroom, as Koegel and Rincover (1974) did with students having autism. Likewise, students first may be taught to work independently for brief periods (e.g., cutting out 10 words and matching them to 10 pictures), after which they join a small group, where individualized instruction is continued during turn taking (Rincover & Koegel, 1977). The latter example is a combination of tandem and sequential models.

tion (Kamps, Walker, Locke, Delquadri, & Hall, 1990) and to teach word reading, their tutees made as much progress as they did when taught one-on-one or in small groups by teachers or paraprofessionals. Shukla et al. (1998) recently demonstrated that adolescents who were underachievers could learn to be as effective as special educators in getting their tutees to engage in class tasks, while also improving their own engagement.

In order to be effective instructors, student instructors must (a) indicate an interest and volunteer, (b) be provided with teaching methods and supervision, and (c) be involved in one-to-one arrangements, not small groups. Good student tutoring programs are often combined with peer support groups and problem solving (Snell & Janney, 2000 b). We think that the best practice is cross-age tutoring, a common practice in many school that involves students teaching younger students rather than students of their age. Except for reciprocal peer tutoring, in which two students teach each other (one student may have a disability), peer tutoring typically involves one-way instruction and makes the relationship a teaching or helping one, not a reciprocal or balanced relationship (Delano & Snell, 2000).

For example, twice a week Jenny looks forward to sessions with her seventh grade tutor Rita. After checking in at the tutoring office and getting the lesson plan, materials, and Jenny's record book, Rita gets Jenny. They start by reviewing what Jenny has done over the past few days with adult staff who have taught the same skill: getting around the school, carrying out tasks without being distracted, and using picture or word guides to help her remember task steps.

After the lesson, Jenny self-evaluates with Rita. Before returning to the middle school next door, Rita shows the tutoring supervisor Jenny's record; once a month, Rita is observed by the tutoring supervisor. Rita takes pride in her work and knows that it will help Jenny next year in middle school.

Cooperative Learning Groups. Strategies to promote cooperation among students working toward a group goal have had widespread application in regular education programs (Johnson & Johnson, 1997). Many of the strategies for successful group instruction are evident in cooperative learning groups, with the added advantage that students learn to cooperate with others while shifting competition with others to competition with oneself (Delano & Snell, in press). Slavin (1991) defines *cooperative learning methods* as "instructional techniques in which students work in heterogeneous learning teams to help one another learn academic material" (p. 177). In contrast to the group arrangements just described, cooperative learning groups work more independently from the teacher (although cooperative learning groups receive instructions on the purpose of the activity, have ongoing supervision, interact with the teacher, and require a great deal of planning.

In preschool, Timothy's teachers make frequent use of cooperative groupings. For example, the 4-year-olds and 5-year-olds form groups of five children for cooperative activities. These activities change daily and involve art (making a mural together), music and dance, building with blocks or other materials, science, cooking, or games. The small groups are balanced so that children who need extra assistance or accommodation are spread across the groups, as are children who are more independent. Group membership changes several times a year. Following simple directions given by Ms. Johnson, the groups move to the activity, get settled, receive instructions, participate together, finish the activity, and clean up, if necessary. After instructions or a demonstration of the activity, Ms. Johnson and Mr. Grayson help group members decide who will do what to contribute to the activity. For example, when cleanup is needed, Timothy, who likes to put things in their places, is often given the responsibility of putting materials away in his group. Marion and Charles, each in different groups, enjoy passing out items to group members and need practice naming group members, so they are often given such tasks.

Two recent examples of cooperative learning groups have involved students with severe disabilities in general education classrooms. First, Dugan et al. (1995) demonstrated that fourth graders with autism could learn skills such as word recognition, peer interaction, and academic engagement alongside their peers in social studies cooperative groups. Second, Hunt, et al., (1994) taught second graders to use positive feedback and prompts to assist classmates with severe movement, cognitive, and communication disabilities to respond in cooperative groups. The students with disabilities rotated to new cooperative groups in the classroom every 8 to 10 weeks. Not only did peers achieve their academic objectives even when serving as mediators, but target students also learned motor and communication objectives that were embedded within the cooperative activity and generalized these skills to new groups, peers, and activities. While the typical students focused on learning geometry from shapes and money skills, their classmates with disabilities worked on communication and motor IEP objectives, since the group activity allowed many opportunities to request turns and to move task materials.

Group Instructional Guidelines. Teachers can facilitate observational learning and maximize motivation in several ways, thereby adding to the benefits that group instruction has over one-to-one instruction. For example, when teaching small groups of students the same general content:

1. Involve all members by using individualized instruction, teaching the same concept at multiple levels of complexity, and allowing for different response modes and modified materials.
2. Keep the group instruction interesting by (a) keeping turns short, (b) giving everyone turns, (c) making turns dependent on attending, (d) giving demonstrations, and (e) using a variety of materials that can be handled.
3. Encourage students to listen and watch other group members as they take their turns. Praise them when they do.
4. Actively involve students in the process of praising and prompting others.
5. Allow students to participate in demonstrations and handle materials related to the skill or concept being taught.

6. Keep waiting time to a minimum by controlling group size, teacher talk, and the number of student responses made in a single turn.
7. Prompt cooperation among group members and discourage competition among them.

Adapting General Education Class Work and Activities

Often students with severe disabilities require planned adaptations to participate meaningfully in classroom activities and school work with their peers in general education. The best rule is that when teams decide adaptations are needed they should be "only as special as necessary" (Janney & Snell, in press). While adaptations need not be intrusive, annoying, distracting, or pushy to students, nor to their peers or to staff, they should enable meaningful involvement and facilitate learning. Teachers often report that adaptations for students with severe disabilities *do not meet* these requirements (Coots, Bishop, & Grenot-Scheyer, 1998; Werts, Wolery, Snyder, & Caldwell, 1996).

Ways to Conceptualize Adaptations

General and special education teachers in inclusive elementary classrooms make modifications in three areas in order to include students with severe disabilities (Janney & Snell, 1997): (a) their roles and responsibilities (changing who does what so that the student with disabilities can learn alongside peers); (b) class routines and physical environment, in order to keep students together; and (c) instructional activities. To include students with disabilities, teachers modified instructional activities by using: academic adaptations, such as simplified tasks (e.g., fewer spelling words); social participation strategies that allow social, though not academic, responding (e.g., holding a book that others are reading); and parallel activities that differ from classmates' and are carried out separately but in the classroom (e.g., doing money problems at a table, while classmates add and subtract in the front of the classroom).

There are other ways to conceptualize modifications that team members make to include students with severe disabilities among nondisabled peers. First, the principle of partial participation suggests that teams work together to plan for each student's active and meaningful involvement in typical school and community activities, even if full participation is not a realistic goal for that student (Baumgart et al. 1982). Second, Giangreco and Putnam's (1991) system for making adaptations views all school and classroom activities as being one of three types:

- Same activity: A student with disabilities participates in the same class activity or school work, with no adaptations required.

   Examples: Jenny uses the restroom just like other fifth grade girls; like his peers, Timothy usually hangs up his coat and backpack; Christine and Jenny answer roll call as do classmates.

- Multilevel activity: One or more students with disabilities (or without) participate in the same activity as the rest of the class, but learn at different levels of difficulty.

   Examples: Timothy uses a picture schedule rather than using words to remember. Jenny has fewer spelling words and uses a calculator in place of adding in her head. Christine and Jenny listen to books on tape instead of reading.

- Curriculum overlapping activity: One or more students with disabilities participate in the same class activity but work on different target skills from classmates.

   Examples: Jenny passes out corrected papers to become fluent with classmates' names, while others complete division and fraction problems. Christine moves through the halls when her peers change classes in order to practice greeting and responding to peers by vocalizing and using her communication device.

Although general, these approaches are helpful ways to organize adaptations. Many authors have contributed to schoolwork adaptation methods for students with severe disabilities (e.g., Giangreco, Cloninger, & Iverson, 1993; Falvey, 1995; Salisbury, Mangino, Rainforth, Syryca, & Palombaro, 1994; Udvari-Solner, 1994).

A Model for Making Adaptations

We now briefly summarize a comprehensive model that builds on other adaptation approaches and suits students with many types of special education or other learning needs who are members of general education classes (Janney & Snell, in press). Our discussion is limited to adaptations for students with more severe disabilities (Box 4–3); we encourage readers to seek more in-depth analysis (Janney & Snell, in

The Differences Between Accommodations and Adaptations

Box 4–3

Accommodations

"Accommodations are modifications that are documented by the eligibility process and specified on the IEP as part of a student's special education program." Accommodations are provided to help students access the general classroom or curriculum.

Examples: Allowing extra time to complete a test; seating a student close to the blackboard; giving a student a quiet study or test location; permitting a student to use a calculator instead of making mental calculations or by hand; having support from a part- or full-time teaching assistant; being permitted to take breaks from class.

Adaptations

"Adaptations are changes to the requirements of the learning task, and may include changes to the instructional content, teaching methods and materials, or the physical environment." Adaptations are often temporary or reduced over time; when students become independent with adaptations that continue to be needed, they may be included as accommodations on the IEP (e.g., a calculator).

Examples: Instructing a student in the use of a calculator to solve math problems or make purchases; listening to a taped book rather than reading it; learning shorter lists of simpler spelling words than peers have; having a student learn and demonstrate an alternate skill (recognizing peers by name and returning papers) that is more functional than what peers are focusing on (writing an essay).

[Adapted from *Practices in inclusive schools: Modifying school work*, by R. E. Janney & M. E. Snell, in press, Baltimore, MD: Paul H. Brookes. Reprinted with permission.]

press). Figure 4–4 portrays the three types of adaptations in this model (curricular, instructional, and ecological adaptations) and their categories:

- Curricular: Adapt *what* is taught (supplementary, simplified, and alternative)
- Instructional: Adapt *how* it is taught and how student learning is demonstrated (instructional stimulus, or *input*, and student response, or *output*)

- Ecological: Adapt the learning situation; *when* (schedule), *where* (place), and with *whom* (staffing and grouping).

Curricular Adaptations. Curricular adaptations, or changing what is taught, will be primarily of the simplified and alternative subtypes for students like Timothy, Jenny, and Christine. Simplified adaptations make the same content less difficult than that taught to others

FIGURE 4–4

Model for Making Adaptations

[Adapted from *Practices in inclusive schools: Modifying school work*, by R. E. Janney & M. E. Snell, in press, Baltimore, MD: Paul H. Brookes. Reprinted with permission.]

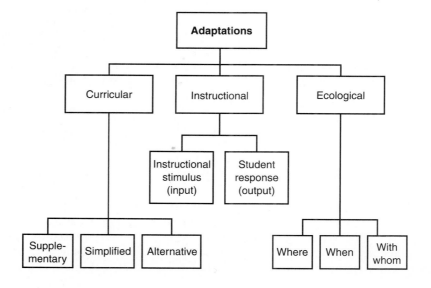

in the class or group, and are similar to multilevel adaptations.

> *For example: Jenny has a shorter weekly spelling word list and reading passages for social studies at a first, not a fifth, grade level and is learning to use a calculator to add and subtract to 25. Timothy is learning to associate pictures with new classroom vocabulary words (his peers learn to say the words) and to select and show pictures to request things (his peers are learning to say "please" to request).*

The second kind of curriculum adaptation common to our students involves changing to an alternative or functional curriculum (Ford, et al., 1989). This adaptation means emphasizing skills needed for participation in priority activities at school, in the home and community, and on the job. Some alternative or functional activities are a natural part of the school routine, though they are not instructional goals for most typical students (e.g., expressing needs clearly; eating in the cafeteria at lunch; using the restroom; changing clothing in some way, such as shoes at gym time, paint smock during art, coats on and off; getting around the school). Functional activities may be informal goals for typical children when they are very young; these same activities may become the functional curriculum for school-aged students with severe disabilities (e.g., self-care routines, using functional academics in the school cafeteria and community, crossing streets safely). What is functional or a priority for a student is determined through individualized assessments (ecological inventories) of the environments a student routinely uses or will use (described in chapter 3).

> *For example, Jenny is learning to identify coins and match coins to values, to tell time to the hour, and to run routine errands around the school without getting lost or distracted. Most of her simplified and alternative curriculum objectives are taught within fifth grade class activities.*
>
> *At age 20, Christine's curriculum involves primarily functional skills: fluent communication with others using her multiple modes, ability to work on tasks at a real job with meaningful involvement, partial participation in all self-care routines, and interaction and participation in social activities with typical peers in and out of school. Christine's team members teach her alternative curriculum within the community and at school (e.g., during Best Buddy activities, at lunch, in drama class, and during pull-out sessions).*

Instructional Adaptations. The two categories of instructional adaptations involve either how an instructor teaches (instructional stimulus, or input) or how the student behaves or performs during instruction (student's response, or output). Both input and output can be adapted in three ways: (a) level of difficulty or amount, (b) modality, and (c) format or materials (Table 4–6). The general rule is that teams should use adaptations only when necessary, keep them simple, and avoid adaptations that stigmatize students. Usually input adaptations fit these three requirements more easily than do output adaptations, which require changing what the student does so it differs from peers.

> *For example, Jenny's classroom teacher gives short and simple instructions for a task accompanied by a demonstration (input adaptations). Jenny, along with some classmates, understands the instructions more naturally and with less teacher effort than if the teacher developed special task worksheets or teaching materials for Jenny (output adaptations).*

Ecological Adaptations. Sometimes teams make adaptations in the learning environment in order to improve a student's success in learning. These adaptations could include changing the location for instruction, the arrangement or number of people, the schedule, and the instructor. Earlier we discussed the many possibilities that exist for location, instructor, time, and arrangement. Ecological adaptations are often selected as part of a behavioral support plan and used as a temporary means to encourage positive behavior, facilitate attending, and promote success. Teams who choose ecological adaptations to support students must regularly review these adaptations to prevent student dependencies and allow the development of student self-management. For example:

- *Consider changing the schedule: Jenny is encouraged to request a limited number of short breaks when she is unable to sit and work. At these times, she goes to one of several locations and jumps rope, runs in place, or uses the exercise bike; then records her time and reports back to class. She shares her exercise times each week with her physical education (PE) and classroom teachers. Jenny now manages her activity level well.*
- *Consider changing the place: To minimize visual distractions, Jenny's desk is always located someplace at the front of the room and positioned by one of several students from her support circle.*

TABLE 4–6
Instructional Adaptations of Input and Output

Adapting the Instructional Stimulus (Input)		
Level of Difficulty/Amount	**Modality**	**Format/Materials**
• Use simpler vocabulary with gestures for explanations. • Record a passage (others read) at simpler level and add pictures. • Reduce the number of problems. • Use more cues, prompts, and feedback during practice activities.	• Read text to students. • Use slides, overhead pictures, and manipulative objectives to accompany oral presentations. • Give demonstrations with simple explanations. • Provide audiotapes or CD-ROM with textbook.	• Use large print books and materials. • Enlarge worksheet to allow more space for larger handwriting style. • Add pictures or symbols to text. • Give demonstrations, simulations, and role plays.
Adapting the Student's Response (Output)		
Level of Difficulty/Amount	**Modality**	**Format/Materials**
• Circles numbers named by teacher rather than completes math problems. • Completes selected steps in an art or science project. • Reads content in same area but at simpler level and with pictures.	• Listens and gives yes or no answers to questions rather than written responses to written questions. • Demonstrates how to do something rather than tells how. • Draws pictures in journal rather than writes.	• Carries out functional task rather than solves nonapplied problems (e.g., count out needed pencils for group, hand them out to check). • Completes a drawing, molds clay, or makes music to describe a book character's feelings rather than writes an essay.

[Adapted from *Practices in inclusive schools: Modifying school work*, by R. E. Janney & M. E. Snell, 2000, Baltimore, MD: Paul H. Brookes. Reprinted with permission.]

• *Consider changing the people or arrangement: Jenny spends time daily receiving direct instruction on reading with one or two other students.*

General and Special Adaptations. Of all the adaptations just described any that are used within predictable school routines like arrival, circle, and lunch and can be used over and over are called *general adaptations*. Once put in place (during the first month of school), general adaptations require little adjustment or planning. By contrast, *specific adaptations* relate to the changes teachers make regularly as their instructional content shifts, as new themes are addressed, and as more advanced skills are taught. Specific adaptations are planned by teachers on a regular basis as classroom content changes.

For example, the predictable morning routines in Jenny's fifth grade include: arrival, journal, reading, language skills, break, spelling, math, shared reading, and lunch. A set of general adaptations was planned by the team for each routine

and used daily. During arrival and journal, Jenny followed the same routine as others, but general adaptations were added to the journal activity to enable her participation (simplified curriculum adaptation with input and output instructional adaptations). For example, Jenny narrates her journal entry to a teaching assistant who helps her write down the content in simple sentences. Then Jenny locates word cards of known words from her word bank; she reads her journal entry, independently rewrites it on the computer, and reads it again. During reading, Jenny and two others (ecological adaptation) receive direct instruction from the special education teacher in the classroom (simplified curriculum adaptation involving input and output instructional adaptations).

Jenny leaves the classroom during language skills (ecological adaptation) to participate with either the speech and language pathologist (SLP) or the teaching assistant in various activities to build her independence and communication (e.g., using the library, running errands without distractions or getting lost) (functional curriculum adaptation). Her seventh grade peer tutor visits twice weekly at this time with oth-

ers on a tutoring team from the middle school next door; the tutor continues work on independence (ecological and functional curriculum adaptations). After a social break with classmates, Jenny participates in spelling by learning her own shortened list of useful words (simplified curriculum adaptation). In math, Jenny works on her math objectives with the teacher or assistant in a small group (functional curriculum and ecological adaptations); her individualized problems involve instruction followed by independent problem solving with coins, calculator, number line, counting out amounts, and solving story problems (output adaptations). During shared reading, Jenny tutors a first grader on word drill games and reads a story with extra monitoring from teachers (simplified curriculum adaptation), while classmates also work with other first graders.

Because preschools and elementary schools have identifiable morning and afternoon routines, they will have a morning and an afternoon set of general adaptations that are used daily. Since secondary classes each have individual routine patterns and repeated activities, a set of general adaptations is needed for each class. After general adaptations are in place, teams shift their focus to specific adaptations, which define the changes teachers make on a daily, weekly, or monthly basis as their instruction shifts to new topics, skills, or activities. Specific adaptations link the student to the topics and themes being studied by classmates; these adaptations depend on regular short-term planning among the core team members, particularly the general and special education teachers.

> For example, the specific content for each reading group in Jenny's classroom changes every 1 to 2 weeks and requires new words (e.g., American Revolution, settling the frontier, women authors). The special and general educators discuss the specific content during their weekly planning sessions and find or create simpler reading materials that are related (simplified curriculum adaptation); they also plan the math activities, relating them to Jenny's IEP objectives and defining practical classroom applications that can be used for practice (counting out necessary science materials for each cooperative group, e.g., table one needs four magnifying glasses, one work sheet, and four specimen trays) (functional curriculum adaptations). To promote her ability to follow directions independently, Jenny is in charge of getting and returning library books for various unit topics in science and social studies, so the SLP checks weekly on the books needed (functional curriculum).

Using the Model. Applying this model to plan for the inclusion of students in general education, team members follow six steps (Janney & Snell, in press).

1. *Gather information about the student, classroom, and routines (before school starts or in first month):* The team gathers information about the student and the classroom during preparation before an IEP meeting, before school starts, or in the first few weeks of school. A "Program at a Glance" form will be completed for each student with an IEP (Figure 4–5), which summarizes IEP objectives, accommodations, academic and management needs, and any special needs. More detailed confidential information forms often are completed which specify for team members the special education and related services, medical or health issues, what promotes learning and what doesn't, likes and dislikes, and other important information.

   Knowing when and what kind of adaptations will be necessary depends a lot on the classroom routines and structure, types of activities and teaching approaches, curriculum, climate, behavior rules and expectation, testing, and homework practices. Information about the classroom is gathered by the special education teacher through class observations and teacher interviews early in the school year. Information is used to identify when and what adaptations will be necessary so that they fit with ongoing routines. In secondary schools, information must be gathered for *each* class, as classes often differ while elementary classrooms are divided into predictable routines. Elementary "specials" like music, PE, and art often have fairly individualized routines and thus should be observed separately.

   When a student's main focus in general education is the embedded social, motor, and communication skills (as is Christine's in drama class), the special educator will provide more detailed assessment of the student's performance in order to explore ways to improve participation. Table 4–7 shows a detailed assessment of Christine during the second week of drama class when typical class routines were already in place (e.g., socialize before bell; when the bell rings, go to seat; roll call; review homework as group; attend to lesson with intermittent student responding; get homework assignment; socialize; when the bell rings, leave).

FIGURE 4–5

Jenny's Program at a Glance

Student: <u>Jenny</u>	**Date:** <u>9/10/99</u> **Grade:** <u>5</u>

IEP Objectives (simplified)

Math:
- "Count on" for addition to 15
- "Count on" for subtraction from 15
- Use calculator to add and subtract from 25
- Identify coins, match to values, and count combinations of pennies, nickels, and dimes
- Count out named amounts of coins (pennies, nickels, dimes)
- Count quarters by 25s; count combinations of all coins and state value
- Compare 2-digit numbers: state bigger or smaller
- Tell time to hour and match time to events
- Identify month, day, year

Reading and Writing:
- Decode consonant-vowel-consonant words
- Decode short vowel words with blends and digraphs
- Write 2 related sentences in journal
- Use of correct beginning, ending, and medial vowels in writings
- Answers comprehension questions about reading

Social:
- Approach peers to initiate task
- Complete cooperative task with peers, without adult prompting
- Socialize in age-appropriate ways during class breaks and at lunch ("Lunch Bunch" group)

Self-Management Needs:
- Self-monitor activity level; ask for breaks to use extra energy or use relaxation exercises
- School independence: complete routine errands around the school without getting lost
- Make snacks, pack lunch independently

Accommodations & Adaptations

Accommodations:
- Calculator
- Number line
- Manipulatives to aid adding/subtracting
- "Money" chart (modification of 100s chart)
- Personal schedule
- Personal calendar
- Full-time teaching assistant in her classroom.

Adaptations:
- Curriculum: use both simplified and functional curriculum adaptations
- Instructional: use input and output (see Classroom Participation Plan)
- Ecological: Special education teaches the 1:1 or 1:2 reading tutorial for 40 minutes every day in classroom. Desk near front of class and next to model peers. Pull-out (functional curriculum) during language arts with speech-language pathologist, teaching assistant, and peer tutor.

Comments/Special Needs

- Use "beat the clock" system to speed task completion
- Peers provide model and help with organizational issues

[Adapted from *Practices in inclusive schools: Collaborative teaming*, by M. E. Snell & R. E. Janney, 2000 a, Baltimore, MD: Paul H. Brookes. Reprinted with permission.]

The observation provided useful ideas to the team on ways to improve Christine's participation through additional skills or adaptations.

2. *Determine when adaptations are needed:* A program *matrix* is especially valuable for students who have an altered (functional) curriculum. The matrix is a form for plotting a student's IEP objectives against class activities and times. Matrices help teams determine when and where all objectives, but especially altered curriculum objectives, will be taught. Figure 4–6 illustrates when and where Jenny's sim-

plified academic objectives and her alternative objectives will be taught and her self-management and social skills will be embedded during the day. With one exception, Jenny's morning schedule is spent with her class; during language activities, she works with her assistant or the SLP on self-management and communication and twice a week with her middle school tutor on the same activities.

3. *Decide how team members will plan:* We have found that planning goes more smoothly when the special ed-

TABLE 4–7
Assessment of Classroom Procedures to Plan Adaptations

Typical Sequence of Steps/Procedures	Target Student Participation
Class: Drama (Grades 11 and 12) **Teacher:** Mr. Fullen **Date:** 9/15 Time: 10 AM	**Student:** Christine **Teaching Assistant:** Ms. Washington
1. Students visit, joke in clusters, then move to their seats as bell rings.	1. Christine is wheeled in to her location away from students; interacts only with Ms. W.
2. Mr. Fullen calls role; students respond.	2. Christine responds when name is called.
3. Mr. Fullen reviews homework assignment, calling on students to give their answers or comment.	3. Christine completes adapted homework, but teacher calls on assistant rather than Christine. Christine tries to answer, but needs new vocabulary or a yes or no question.
4. Mr. Fullen moves to the lesson on doing basic improvisations, using brief explanations and lively demonstrations. Each example is followed by having the group try.	4. Christine attends. She cannot see facial expressions but is close enough to see large movements and feel the vibrations of jumping on the floor. She laughs but does not try when peers do.
Skills Needed to Increase Participation:	**Adaptations Needed to Increase Participation:**
1. Teach peers how to interact with Christine.	1. Position Christine by peers before bell.
2. Raise hand to signal teacher for response or turn.	2. Assistant provides translation of Christine's remarks or intent as needed; direct others to talk to Christine or prompt Christine to respond.
3. Ability to access and use Dynovox categories programmed for class.	3. Program Dynovox with vocabulary suited to class content and homework comments.
4. Practice and adapt improvisations to suit Christine; teacher involve class in obtaining suggestions.	4. Position Christine close to demonstrations, use extra lighting to improve her perception.

[Adapted from *Practices in inclusive schools: Modifying school work*, by R. E. Janney & M. E. Snell, in press, Baltimore, MD: Paul H. Brookes. Reprinted with permission.]

ucator and the classroom teacher(s) determine planning strategies early in the year. Planning strategies include: when and where to meet, how long and how often, how materials that need adapting will be exchanged between general and special education teachers, and what to do if problems arise. Therefore, in late August or early September, the special educator completes a planning form that addresses these questions with each teacher who has students with disabilities. These regular meetings may be sometimes attended by related services staff, usually are of short duration (15 to 20 minutes), and are scheduled for the whole year on a weekly or alternate weekly basis.

For example, Ms. Dailey (Jenny's special educator) meets weekly for 30 minutes during prep time with Ms. Alpern (her fifth grade teacher) to review Jenny's progress, solve any problem issues that have arisen, and to exchange the materials that need adaptations (e.g., journal topics, reading fo-

cus, classroom applications for functional math, spelling words, science unit).

4. *Plan and implement general adaptations:* Once designed, general adaptations do not require weekly planning and can be put into place early on, often during the first few weeks of school. Both general (and specific adaptations) still need to reflect the principles we addressed earlier (e.g., be practical, team-generated, socially valid, and individualized) while also being "only as special as necessary." Since students with severe disabilities have simplified and alternative curriculum objectives, the adaptation plan uses three columns to detail: (a) the class schedule of activities, (b) the student's objectives for each activity, and (c) the general adaptations made in procedures and materials to teach or support the student in that activity. For preschool and elementary students, these plans reflect the morning and afternoon "chunks" of the day (see Figure 4–7 for part of Jenny's morning

FIGURE 4–6

Program Planning Matrix for Jenny's Morning Schedule

Student: Jenny   **Class:** Alpern/5th   **Date:** 9/99

IEP Objectives	Arrival	Journal	Reading	Language Arts	Break	Spelling	Math	Shared Reading	Lunch
Pull-out with Collaborative Planning	No	No	No	Yes	No	No	No	No	No
Math:									
Count on for add/subtract							X		
Calculator for add/subtract							X		
ID coins, match to value							X		X
Tell time to hour, associate	X	X	X	X	X	X	X	X	X
ID month, day, year		X	X			X	X		X
Reading & Writing:									
Decode CVC, short vowel		X	X					X	
Write 2 related sentences		X	X					X	
Write using B,E,M vowels		X	X					X	
Answers comp. questions		X	X	X				X	
Functional Skills:									
Self-monitor activity level	X	X	X	X	X	X	X	X	X
Use personal schedule	X	X	X	X	X	X	X	X	X
Use personal calendar	X						X		
Run routine errands				X					
Social Skills:									
Approach peer, initiate task	X			X	X		X	X	
Complete task with peer	X			X	X		X	X	

ID, Identify ___ ; CVC, Consonant-vowel-consonant ___ ; B,E,M, Beginning, ending, medial placement ___ .

144

FIGURE 4–7

A Sample of Jenny's Classroom Participation Plan with General Adaptations

Time & Activity	IEP Objectives	General Adaptations in Procedures and Materials
8:40–9:00 Arrival	• Use personal calendar and schedule • Put things away, no prompt • Socialize with peers • Approach peer to initiate task • Complete task, no prompt	• With TA, locates and names month and day; adds special events: identifies activities for arrival; completes them. • Monitor checking off "things away" on schedule. • Keep her with class during social opportunities. • Monitor asking peer to help class task. • Monitor task completion with peer; check off "task done."
9:00–9:30 Journal Writing	• Write two related short sentences; type on computer • Decode CVC and short vowel words with blends & digraphs • Use correct vowels (B,E,M) in writings	• Narrates journal entry in topical area to TA. • Writes known words from memory or copies from word bank card. • Writes letters for other words. • Reads aloud. • Copies independently on computer file, prints, adds to journal and rereads to peer at table.
9:30–10:15 Reading Groups	• Prior three objectives • Comprehension questions about reading	• Select 2–3 reading vocabulary words from content being read; J. points to and reads: adds to word bank if correct 3 times. • Teacher reads selection to group (alternate with students reading first) • Ask J. simplified questions about content of reading similar to other students in group. Restate if wrong; prompt as needed. • Students read aloud sentences from their version of story adjusted to reading level. • Students complete worksheet or activity-matched reading content and vocabulary.

[Adapted from *Practices in inclusive schools: Modifying school work*, by R. E. Janney & M. E. Snell, in press, Baltimore, MD: Paul H. Brookes. Reprinted with permission.]

plan), while secondary students have a plan for every general education class they are enrolled in.

5. *Plan and implement specific adaptations*: Once general adaptations are planned and in place, teams meet to determine the specific adaptations for changing class content (e.g., unit topics, topics from classroom curriculum, science focus, spelling words). Teams will find it helpful to record their decisions on weekly forms that address morning and afternoon periods (elementary classrooms) or specific classes in secondary school. Figure 4–8 shows a partially completed afternoon form illustrating a weekly plan for Jenny's science class.

6. *Plan and implement alternative activities, if needed*: Teams may identify a need to supplement classroom activities with alternative or functional instruction.

Alternative instruction may involve pull-out or may take place in the classroom.

For example, while his classmates are involved in free play, Timothy has daily 20-minute intensive training in another room on using his picture and signing communication systems.

As an alternative to fifth grade language skills period, Jenny is taught to carry out errands around the school without prompts or getting lost (second row in Figure 4–6).

Christine receives daily community-based instruction apart from peers.

There are several reasons for teams adding alternative or functional activities to a student's schedule: (a) intensive instruction in basic academic or communication skills, (b) opportunities for instruction or intensive support in self-care skills, and (c) community-based instruction on functional skills. Alternative activities should be designed to give intensive instruction on important IEP objectives that a student would not otherwise receive. When used, alternative

FIGURE 4–8
Partially Completed Weekly Plan for Specific Adaptations for Science

Subject	Class Objectives	Activities	Specific Adaptations
Science: Pollution and Ecology	• Define pollution, give examples from nearby community and distant community • Key concepts: clean water, litter, land fill, sewage, sewage treatment, compost, run-off, fertilizers, and animal waste	• Slide show from forestry agent on farm pollution • Videos and readings on pollution and solutions • Cooperative groups research and present one method to curb pollution	• Picture-word vocabulary cards for class; personal set for Jenny • Homework worksheets on content covered; simplified for Jenny • Group work: locate, cut and mount pictures to illustrate presentation; type captions written by or with others

activities are meant to supplement instruction alongside peers and, when possible, should be designed to meet several guidelines (Janney & Snell, in press):

- The activity is not scheduled during important class routines.
- The student comes and goes from the activity at natural class breaks when others also are in transit.
- Peers are added into the activity as appropriate.
- Classroom themes are coordinated with the alternative activity to prevent isolation from classmates.
- An alternative activity matches the same activity times for other students.

In this section we have described a model for adapting curricular content (simplified and functional or alternative), instructional methods (input and output), and ecological factors (where, when, and with whom).

Initial Steps in Choosing Teaching Procedures

When teams are guided by the eight principles discussed earlier (Table 4–1), the probability that their teaching plans are successful is improved. The teaching procedure teams select must suit the type of skill (discrete or multiple-stepped) and students' abilities, preferences, and stage of learning. Instructional planning begins with an objective taken from the IEP. Next, a teaching skill sequence or a task analysis of the target skill is developed, along with a means to

measure the student's current level of performance. After the student's performance is measured, the instructional objective is adjusted to suit current performance.

Initial Planning Steps: Discrete and Multiple-Stepped Skills Objectives
Target behaviors that involve a single, isolated response are called *discrete responses*; these responses are individually distinctive and can stand alone (e.g., matching prices to coins, identifying pictures of class activities by going to the location or materials, reading words). By contrast, most other target behaviors are viewed as being *multiple-stepped responses* and require task analyses. Discrete behaviors may be taught separately (e.g., reading prices) or taught as a step within a larger chain of behaviors (e.g., the chain of getting a snack from a vending machine). The distinction between discrete and multiple-stepped behaviors is not always clear. Many discrete behaviors can be divided into steps. For example, reading words involves a sequence of behaviors: look at word, make initial letter sound, blend with medial and final sounds to say word. How teams decide to view a target behavior depends on the behavior and the student and also influences instruction and measurement.

Discrete Behavior Objectives. Often discrete behavior objectives (e.g., counting, labeling) are taught through *skill sequences*—a listing of related skills arranged from simple to more difficult, which are taught separately in sequence over a period of time. For example, Timothy first learned to match pictures, then to locate named pictures, and finally to name pictures by signing. The money management skills that Jenny is learning are part of a generalized math skill sequence for using coins and bills (Table 4–8). Many of the skills are discrete, while some may be more logically taught as a chain of responses.

> *After several years of instruction, Jenny has mastered steps 1 through 12; she is now working on counting quarters and soon will learn to count combinations of all coins. Her teachers schedule regular application of these skills in school to make small purchases. For example, skills 7 and 12 require Jenny to count out a given amount of money, which is required when paying library fines (5 cents a day), buying her school lunch (80 cents) or milk (20 cents), and buying pencils (25 to 35 cents) and paper (2 to 5 cents) in the school store.*

Multiple-Step Skill Objectives. Many target skills involve the performance of a sequence of multiple behaviors or steps to complete a task; these skills require a *task analysis* of the responses that are performed in order to complete an activity or routine. For exam-

ple, the following tasks involve multiple steps: sweeping the floor, eating at a fast-food restaurant, brushing one's teeth, and counting out combinations of coins to pay for a product. Typically, the last response is followed by reinforcement, either natural (e.g., completing a task and doing something else, eating lunch, getting help with a jacket zipper) or artificial (e.g., teacher praise, participation in a preferred activity). As Timothy learns each of the 12 behaviors in the arrival routine, the stimulus preceding each response becomes discriminated as a signal for the next response and for eventual reinforcement (Table 4–9).

Task Analysis. Analyzing a task is not trivial. Consider how Timothy's teachers planned for his active participation in the arrival routine.

> *Before teaching Timothy the morning routine, the special education teacher, Ted Grayson, watched others perform the task and analyzed the steps. Ted also asked Timothy's preschool teacher, Carlene Johnson, to use the preliminary task analysis and observe students at arrival to double-check the steps. Carlene piloted the analysis for Timothy to be sure that the steps made sense for him. When she found that some steps were too hard for Timothy (the car door and the*

TABLE 4–8
Jenny's Skill Sequence for Using Coins to Make Purchases

---

1. Identification of pennies and stating their value (discrete responses)
2. Counting pennies by ones (chained response) and identifying the total amount (discrete)
3. Identification of nickels and stating their value (discrete responses)
4. Identification and stating the values of nickels and pennies in a mixed order (discrete responses)
5. Counting nickels by fives (chained response) and identifying the total amount (discrete)
6. Counting combinations of pennies and nickels (counting by fives, then counting on by ones) (chained response) and stating the total amount (discrete response)
7. Counting combinations of pennies and nickels to yield a written or stated price (chained response)*
8. Identification of dimes and stating their value (discrete responses)
9. Identification and stating the values of dimes, nickels, and pennies in a mixed order (discrete responses)
10. Counting dimes by tens (chained response) and identifying the total amount (discrete response)
11. Counting combinations of pennies, nickels, and dimes (counting by tens, then counting on by fives and then ones) (chained response) and stating the total amount (discrete response)
12. Counting combinations of pennies, nickels, and dimes to match a written or stated price (chained response)*
13. Identification of quarters and stating their value (discrete responses)
14. Identification and stating the values of nickels and pennies in a mixed order (discrete responses)
15. Counting quarters by twenty-fives (chained response) and identifying the total amount (discrete response)
16. Counting combinations of pennies, nickels, dimes, and quarters (counting by twenty-fives, then counting by tens, fives, and ones) (chained response) and stating the total amount (discrete response)
17. Counting combinations of pennies, nickels, dimes, and quarters to match a written or stated price (chained response)*

---

*Making purchases.

TABLE 4–9
A Sequence of Stimuli and Responses Involved
in Timothy's Arrival Routine

Stimulus	Response
Car stops	Get out of car
See school, hear mom say and gesture, "Let's go"	Walk into school
See school door	Open and walk through door
See hallway	Walk down hall
See blue classroom door	Open door and go in
See cubbies and others removing jacket	Remove jacket
See hook with his photo and others hanging jackets	Hang jacket
Smiles and praise from teacher	Move away from cubby
Teacher shows activity board, "What do you want to do, Timothy?"	Get his photo card. Look at the activity board and pick activity to do. Attach his photo beneath the activity picture.
Teacher: "You want the sand box! Good choice."	Go to the sand box.

building door were too difficult for him to open alone), she added adult help to those steps or made one step into two steps: (a) getting his photo card and (b) selecting an activity by placing his photo beneath the activity picture. Next, Timothy's mother looked at the task analysis and added her ideas. Because Timothy could perform very little of the task during the initial pilot, Ted and Carlene anticipated that Timothy would be in the acquisition stage of learning and thus left the focus of the task analysis on the core steps of the task. However, the preschool staff suggested adding the enrichment skill of communicating a greeting.

Task analysis typically proceeds through a process:

1. Use ecological inventory results to identify an individually functional and age-appropriate skill that is an important target for a particular student.
2. Define the target skill simply, including a description of the settings and materials most suited to the natural performance of the task.
3. Perform the task and observe peers performing the task, using the chosen materials in the natural settings, while noting the steps involved.

4. Adapt the steps to suit the student's disabilities and skill strengths, employing the principle of partial participation and component analysis as needed to enable participation that is both age-appropriate and functional.
5. Validate the task analysis by having the student perform the task, but provide assistance on steps that are unknown, so that performance of all steps can be viewed.
6. Explore adding simple, nonstigmatizing adaptations to steps that appear to be unreasonable targets in an unadapted form; revise the task analysis.
7. Write the task analysis on a data collection form so that steps (a) are stated in terms of observable behavior, (b) result in a visible change in the product or process, (c) are ordered in a logical sequence, and (d) are written in second-person singular so that they could serve as verbal prompts (if used), using language that is not confusing to the student and enclosing in parentheses details essential to assessing performance.

Figure 4–9 shows the task analysis of Timothy's arrival routine. Note how the steps in Table 4–9 were modified when the team followed this validation process. The form in Figure 4–9 allows team members to easily record teaching and testing data and anecdotal comments to explain a student's performance.

Assessing Current Performance and Revising Instructional Objectives

Sometimes, IEP objectives must be adjusted to match changes in the teaching conditions or a student's performance. Often IEP objectives are written in the spring and taught the following fall. While the general skill priority is not likely to change, some aspects of the conditions, behaviors, or criteria may change, especially if the student has changed schools or classrooms. Often the student's current level of performance has only been estimated, not assessed.

Informal Assessment. The method of informal assessment must suit the target skill. Most often, informal assessment involves direct observation of a student as he or she attempts to perform the task or discrete behavior under criterion conditions. Sometimes informal assessment involves examining the "permanent product" that results from a student's performance of

FIGURE 4-9
A Task Analysis of Timothy's Arrival Routine at Preschool

Teachers: Carlene Johnson (preschool), Ted Grayson (special ed.), Jo Milano (SLP)

Student: Timothy

Target Behavior: Morning arrival

Baseline/Probe: Every 2 weeks, Multiple Opportunity

Instructional Cue: Arrival at preschool in family car; parent/sitter says "Let's go to preschool"

Setting: Bus/car arrival area, sidewalk, hallway, classroom

Location: St. Stephens Preschool   **Day(s):** Daily at arrival

Stage of Learning: Acquisition

		9/23	9/24	9/25	9/26	9/27	9/30
	% Totals	21	21	14			
1	Unbuckle your seat belt (assist buckle and straps)	−	−	−			
2	Open your door (assist from outside car)	−	−	−			
3	Get out of car and close the door (assist one hand)	−	+	−			
4	Walk to preschool (on sidewalk)	−	−	−			
5	Open the door (assist pulling)	−	−	−			
6	Walk to your room	+	+	+			
7	Open the door and go in	−	−	−			
8	Look at teacher or peer, wave	−	−	−			
9	Find your cubby	+	+	+			
10	Take off your coat	−	−	−			
11	Grab it (by the collar)	−	−	−			
12	Hang it up (on hook)	+	−	+			
13	Get your picture (from table)	−	−	−			
14	Put your picture (on board) where you want to play	−	−	−			
15	Go play (goes to selected activity)	−	−	−			

(back page of form)

Task Analysis: Arrival

Student: Timothy

Date	Teacher	Anecdotal Comments
9/23	Carlene	Waited for help on most steps
9/25	Ted	Seemed sleepy; on ear infection meds

Recording Key: **Train:** (time delay): Gestural/Partial Physical (GPP), + (correct). **Test:** + (correct), − (incorrect).

Criterion: 10 of 15 steps correct (67%) for 3 of 5 training days

Materials: Activity picture chart, garment, or backpack

Latency period: 0 sec, 4 sec

*Greeting can occur at any point when peer or staff are seen.

a skill: e.g., examining, then determining the number of correct place settings, the fraction of a lunch packed, or whether a coat and backpack are hung up. (Evaluation methods are described in more detail in chapter 5.) When planning the informal assessment of target behaviors, teachers should remember that the assessment conditions must represent the conditions stated in the behavioral objective. The conditions should be as natural as possible and match the times and places for performance, as well as the materials, adaptations, and individuals present (if any).

For example, on several mornings when Timothy arrives, he is assessed on the morning arrival routine. These are the same conditions under which Timothy will be taught. Since the routine is similar to the one he follows when he leaves before lunch (steps 1 through 12 are reversed in order and the last three are omitted), his team decides to target the departure routine for instruction as well. Teaching will occur naturally on arrival and departure, but testing will take place once a week during arrival. When Timothy's baseline performance of the morning routine was assessed (baseline data measure performance before instruction), he could carry out 3 (20%) of 15 task steps the first day, followed by 3 (20%) and 2 (13%) of 15 on each of the next 2 days. He consistently got several steps correct (Figure 4–9). If the baseline data are accurate, Timothy's performance places him in the acquisition stage of learning, which means that

some teaching is necessary to guarantee his success and learning.

Refine Instructional Objectives. Baseline data and observations should be used to refine an instructional objective, set a performance criterion, and identify an *aim date* (the date a student is predicted to meet the criteria for an objective). Timothy's original instructional objectives were adjusted to reflect his baseline performance and the modified target skill (Table 4–10).

When teachers set *aim dates*, it is easier to judge how a student's current level of skill performance compares with the goal or criterion level (Farlow & Snell, 1995; Liberty & Haring, 1990). An aim date is the date teachers expect a particular student to reach the criterion for an instructional objective. Once training begins, teachers combine this date with the student's performance during the first 3 training days to create an *aim line* by which to judge progress. When progress dips below the aim line, teams determine whether or not to modify the program. (The procedure of setting and using an aim date is discussed in more detail in chapter 5.)

Timothy's team sets their aim date for 8 weeks after the initiation of training, because all preschoolers receive performance evaluations just before the holiday break. Because

TABLE 4–10
A Sample of Timothy's Goals and Objectives for Self-Management and Social Interaction

---

Goal: Timothy will follow preschool routines on his own by the end of the year (self-management).

Objective 1: Upon arrival at and departure from preschool, Timothy will exit the car, walk to enter the preschool class, greet familiar people, remove and hang his outer garments in his cubby, and select and go to a play activity at a criterion level of 10 of 15 steps (67%) during two training sessions (using partial participation on some steps as indicated in the task analysis).
  Aim Date: December 17, 1999

Objective 2: When given an opportunity in preschool to select a play activity using a picture activity chart, Timothy will get his photo card and place it under an activity picture and then go to that activity on three out of four opportunities (embedded across morning).
  Aim Date: December 17, 1999

Goal: Timothy will interact socially with his teachers and some peers at preschool by looking at them, greeting, making requests, and playing with or alongside peers (social interaction).

Objective 1: Timothy will greet the familiar adults and peers at preschool at the time of their and his arrival and departure by looking at them and using a wave on three out of four opportunities (embedded across the day).
  Aim Date: December 17, 1999

Timothy performed accurately on only a few steps, the teachers judged Timothy's learning to be in the acquisition stage. Thus they planned to use structured antecedent and consequence methods, and they established criteria at far less than 100%. The teachers reasoned that once the acquisition criteria were met, they would modify the teaching methods (e.g., provide less structure for partially learned steps), increase the performance criteria, and make the task analysis more complex to suit the later stages of learning. The teachers were pleased, though, that even now, Timothy performed several steps, although not consistently, and attempted performance on six to seven other steps.

Selecting Antecedent Teaching Methods

The initial steps Timothy's team took to plan his morning routine instruction involved: (a) defining the skills or behavior chains and identifying teaching conditions, (b) assessing his current or baseline level of performance for the routine, and (c) refining his instructional objectives. Next, the team planned how he would be given assistance (*prompts*) on the steps that he could not or did not complete, in a manner that drew his attention to the relevant stimuli to be learned (*discriminative stimuli*). They also decided how that assistance would be faded. This phase of writing an instructional plan focuses on the antecedents.

Instructional antecedents are the planned and incidental stimuli in the learning situation: a teacher's instructional cues or task directions, setting, teaching and task materials, opportunities for choice making, and prompts and procedures for fading prompts. Closely related are the instructional *consequences*, which address the ways instructors and others in the environment respond to student behavior. Both the instructional antecedents and consequences selected to teach an objective are related to a student's stage of learning for that skill and other general characteristics, such as age, preferences, communication abilities, and teaching arrangement.

Discriminative Stimuli

Learning is a process of understanding how to respond to specific and changing signals or stimuli in the environment.

For example: Timothy has learned that in the presence of food at the kitchen table when he is hungry, he will get food if he makes the "eat" or the "drink" sign or if he says "Mmm" for

"more." Timothy has also learned to indicate through his own personalized gestures and facial expressions some of the things he wants and does not want at meals.

Timothy's use of certain signs in the presence of food and drinks have been reinforced for so long that he has learned which responses lead to food. Discriminative stimuli (also referred to as S^Ds) are those relevant aspects of a task or situation in the presence of which a particular behavior is frequently reinforced. Discriminative stimuli can include aspects of a task setting, teacher requests, materials, the time of day, the student's physical state (e.g., empty stomach, full bladder), and other contextual stimuli. Initially a teacher's prompts are the stimuli that control a student's responses, but once the task discriminated stimuli are learned, they control the student's response and therefore prompts from others are not needed.

Last month, when Christine started the job at the school library checking out books, she did not understand what to do when someone asked her to scan or check out a book. She did not know what to do when someone placed a book into the book holder on her lap tray. Now, she is alert to critical stimuli that "tell" her it is time to press the book scanning switch: a child asking her to check out a book, followed by the thud of the book against the metal end of the slanted book holder on her tray, which signals that the book is in position to be scanned. She also knows that if she does not hear a beep from the scanner, the book was not put in the holder correctly (with the bar code positioned up and under the scanner). The absence of a beep is a different stimulus, which she responds to by pushing her communication device to say: "Oops! Can you put the book in the right way?"

Teaching involves shifting the control from prompting stimuli to natural task stimuli. For most students, the goal is to respond in the presence of natural cues rather than teacher-applied stimuli: requests and prompts. For example, students should respond to the discriminated stimulus of a dirty mirror or the fact that cleaning it is part of their job *before* a teacher requests its cleaning. Similarly, students should initiate a search for a needed or desired material rather than do so only after the teacher asks, "What do you want?" If natural task stimuli are to control behavior, teachers must incorporate them into the instructional plan. Teaching in natural settings and at natural times lets teachers use environmental cues. Initially, for most tasks in the acquisition phase of learning, an instructional cue or request is necessary to evoke the behavior. Instructional requests need to be carefully planned:

1. State requests in terms easily understood by the student.
2. Phrase them as requests ("Tie your shoes"), not questions ("Can you tie your shoes?").
3. Provide them only when the student is attending.
4. Give them only once at the beginning of the task, rather than repeating requests over and over.
5. Match the request to the conditions stated in the instructional objective (e.g., give the request "Clean the mirror" in the presence of a dirty mirror and a basket of cleaning materials).
6. Pair the request with relevant, natural task stimuli provided by realistic settings (i.e., real bathrooms with mirrors) and materials (i.e., dirty mirrors, containers of glass cleaner, and paper towels).

Choice-Making Opportunities

The use of choice-making as an antecedent strategy is relatively new in the literature. For example, a student might be offered one of a number of choices at the beginning of a task (or during or afterward): (a) Which of several activities or chores will you work on? (b) Where do you want to do this activity? (c) Who would you like as a work partner? (d) When do you want to take a break? and (e) What do you want to do on break or after you are done? (Brown, 1991). Reviews of choice-making research over the past several decades lend strong support to the practice of increasing choice-making opportunities as part of teaching; giving students choices is associated both with the improvement of appropriate behavior and the decline of problem behavior (Horner & Carr, 1997; Kern et al., 1998).

At the same time, there is much we do not know about the best ways to suit choice-making strategies to students or how choice works. For example, is it the opportunity to make a choice and have some control that results in the generally favorable effects on a student's behavior or do the effects of choice-making strategies primarily result from experiencing reinforcing or preferred events (Kern et al., 1998)? Horner and Carr (1997) suggested two reasons why choice may reduce problem behavior: first, when given a choice, a student will choose the most preferred at that time (while the teacher may not); and second, when an ac-

tivity is chosen by a student (rather than the same activity chosen by a teacher and offered to the student), it seems less likely to result in problem behavior because "choosing may reduce the aversive properties of tasks and activities" (p. 97). What we do know is that having opportunities to make choices is both a recommended element of teaching programs and behavioral support interventions and a valued feature in quality of life. Thus, it is important to both teach students to make choices and to include choice making in students' daily schedules.

Student Skills Involved in Choice Making. Independent choice making requires several student skills: (a) being aware of the options (visually, tactilely, or auditorily scan the choices), (b) having some preferred activities or events, (c) having the ability to express intent or choice by making an observable response (gazing at, pointing to, or picking up an item), (d) making a choice when offered options, and (e) engaging in the choice. One of these crucial skills is intent (described in more detail in chapter 11), which can be inferred from a person's behavior but not measured directly. Intentional behaviors are the communicative behaviors by which we judge that a person prefers one thing over another. For example, a student shows intent when one or several behaviors occur (Siegel-Causey & Wetherby, in press), such as:

- Persistent responding until a goal is accomplished.
- Changing one's signal or response until a goal is accomplished (e.g., pointing, whining, then taking a person by the hand and leading him or her to the location of the goal activity).
- Using certain communicative forms or signals in specific contexts because they are recognized.
- Alternating one's gaze between a goal and another individual in the vicinity (looking up at a toy on the shelf, then looking at parent, and back to the toy).
- Waiting for a response from a listener.
- Stopping communication signals when the goal is met.
- Showing satisfaction when the goal is met (smiles, engage with activity) or dissatisfaction if the goal is not met (crying, problem behavior).

Perhaps the best way to teach intent (as well as the other related skills of choice making) is to identify reinforcing or preferred activities and to offer them on a predictable and frequent basis, while varying the choice options and using communication that is consistent with the student's level of understanding. (See chapter 3 for assessment of preferences.)

Teacher Skills. Choice making involves not only several student skills but also certain teacher or adult behaviors. To use choice making as an antecedent strategy, teachers must: (a) be aware of an individual's preferences, (b) know how to offer choice options so the student is aware of them, (c) offer a choice that is compatible with the ongoing activity and student, (d) pause for the student to respond, (e) know what student response indicates a favorable choice and a rejection, and (f) provide the choice and time to engage in that choice activity.

Stimulus and Response Prompting

Prompting is another major category of antecedent strategies. Behavior must occur before it can be shaped, and various types of assistance given before the response increase the likelihood that the learner will perform the desired behavior or a better approximation. Prompts may be associated primarily with the task stimuli (materials) or the response. *Stimulus prompts*, which involve manipulations of the relevant and irrelevant task stimuli, are used by teachers to improve the chance of a correct response. Stimulus fading, a type of stimulus prompt, is exemplified by color coding various parts of bicycle brake pieces to make the assembly task easier (Gold, 1972). Given color-coded parts, the workers simply match the colors of the parts to be joined. Eventually, the color coding is eliminated or faded. Stimulus prompts are more time consuming to prepare and use than response prompts.

Response prompts are actions taken by the teacher before a student responds (or after an error) to increase the probability of a correct response. Typical response prompts include verbal instructions, gestures or pointing movements, models, and physical assists. Regardless of the type of prompt, all prompts should be faded as students learn to respond to natural task, environmental, and internal stimuli (Wolery & Gast, 1984). To do this, teachers should draw students' attention to natural stimuli by:

- Matching verbal prompts with the actual terminology used in the setting where the skill ultimately will be performed.

For example, on her library job, Christine's teachers use the words "scanner" and "beep" because that's what library staff and the students say.

- Emphasizing the type of prompt most prevalent in the natural setting.
For example, Jenny missed the teacher's directions; her assistant tells her to watch what her friends seated nearby are getting from their desks and do the same.

- When a student skips an important task step, calling attention (with gestures, words, and positioning) to the step that occurred just before the omitted step so that the student attends to the relevant natural stimuli.
For example, Timothy pulled up his pants, flushed the toilet, then started to leave the bathroom when the teacher called him back, positioned him facing the sink, and said, "What's next?"

- Using natural prompts and correction procedures whenever possible during the fluency, maintenance, and generalization phases.
For example, Christine has learned to listen for the scanner beep after she activates the switch in order to judge if the library book was placed in the book holder correctly.

- Teaching students performing in the later learning phases to ask for assistance when prompts are faded.
For example, while learning to return the classroom's books to the library, Jenny performs well enough that, if she needs help, she must ask for it; otherwise her instructors only assist if danger is a possibility.

Types of Instructional Prompts. Prompts come in many forms (e.g., words, visual demonstrations, physical movement) and are often combined. Prompts differ in the amount of assistance they provide, the student skills required, and their intrusiveness. Teams should choose single prompts or combinations of prompts that suit the skill and setting and the student's preferences, abilities, and stage of learning. Arranged roughly in an order from requiring more student skill to be effective to requiring less student skill, Table 4–11 provides some information on prompts and considerations in using each type (Wolery, Ault, & Doyle, 1992).

Response Latency. In terms of giving instructional prompts, *response latency* can be defined as the period of time allowed for a student to respond without assistance or to respond following a prompt. Without

TABLE 4–11

Definitions, Examples, and Pros and Cons of Common Prompts

Type of Prompt	Definition and Examples	Pros and Cons
Verbal (Signed) Prompts	Words or signs that tell the student how to respond ("Spray the mirror"); not the same as instructional cues (e.g., "Clean the bathroom") or directions. Match to fit student's comprehension of words/signs and the amount of prompt needed (e.g., nonspecific prompts like "What's next?" may be good later in learning, but provide little information).	Pros: Can be given to a group and used from a distance; do not require visual attention; involve no physical contact. Cons: Must be heard and understood by student and followed. Level of complexity varies highly. May be hard to fade.
Pictorial or Written Prompts	Pictures or line drawings that tell the student how to perform a behavior. Pictures may show the completed task or one or more steps in the task. Words may accompany pictures if student can read. May be used as permanent prompts that are not faded. Level of abstraction needs to fit student (e.g., photos, drawings, line drawings, letters, numbers, words).	Pros: Can be used unobtrusively; does not require reading. Can promote independence even when used as permanent prompts. Standard symbols may help maintain consistency. Cons: Pictures may be poorly drawn or taken; if lost, pictures may not be replaceable. Some actions are difficult to illustrate. Must be seen and understood by student and followed. Level of abstraction varies.
Gestural Prompts	Movements made to direct a person's attention to something relevant to a response. Pointing toward the desired direction; tapping next to the material needed.	Pros: Unobtrusive, more natural cues. Can be given to a group and used from a distance; requires no physical contact. Cons: Must be seen and understood by student and followed.
Model Prompts	Demonstrations of the target behavior that students are expected to imitate. Models often involve movement (showing a step in shoe tying) but may involve no movement, as in showing a finished task (show one place set at a table and match to sample) or be verbal ("sign 'want ball'"). Models may be complete (show entire step) or partial (show part of the step). If the model is done on a second set of materials, it need not be undone. Model prompts usually match task steps.	Pros: No physical contact with person is needed, can be used with a group and given from a distance. Versatile: models suit many target behaviors. Complexity of model can be adjusted to suit student's level of performance. Others can be effective models on a planned or incidental basis. Modeling can be unobtrusive. Cons: Requires students to attend (see, feel, or hear the model) and to imitate. If model is too long or complex, imitation will be difficult.
Partial Physical Prompts	Brief touching, tapping, nudging, or lightly pulling or pushing a student's hand, arm, leg, trunk, jaw, etc. Used to help a student initiate a response or a sequence of responses. Follow the rule: "as little as necessary."	Pro: Gives some control over student responding with little physical contact. Useful when vision is limited. Con: Can be intrusive. Some students do not like to be touched; can't be used at a distance. Care must be taken not to injure or throw student off balance.
Full Physical Prompts	Full guidance through a behavior, often involving hand-over-hand assistance (as in using a spoon or smoothing a bed spread) or movement of the trunk and legs (as in assisting crawling or walking forward). Physical prompts should match task steps. Follow the rule: "as little as necessary," while being sensitive to any student movement and easing physical control. Does not involve force.	Pros: Allows total control over response, thereby reducing errors. Useful when vision is limited. Cons: Highly intrusive, unnatural, and stigmatizing in public. Some students do not like to be touched; can't be used at a distance. Care must be taken not to injure through tight holding, to force compliance with a movement, or to throw student off balance.

(Adapted from *Teaching students with moderate to severe disabilities* (pp. 38–41) by M. Wolery, M.J. Ault, & P.M. Doyle (1992), New York: Longman Press. Adapted with permission.)

the opportunity to initiate, students may become prompt-dependent and fail to learn the target response. The length of the response latency period depends primarily on the student and, in part, on the response, or task step. For many students without significant movement difficulties and for many tasks, a latency of 3 to 5 seconds often suits students during the acquisition stage of learning. The full latency is provided both before any assistance is given (allowing the student time to initiate the response without help) and after assistance is given (allowing the student time to act on the prompt).

For example, when Timothy is standing by his cubby, Carlene waits 5 seconds to see if he will take off his jacket. If he does not or starts to but stops, she uses a combined gestural and physical prompt (points then tugs at his jacket) and then waits 5 more seconds for him to initiate.

If a student makes an error before the latency is over, it is important to gently interrupt the error with a second prompt or with a prompt that provides more assistance. If a student seems to require more time to initiate responding, the teacher must determine the student's *natural response latency* by timing the student as he or she performs a known task involving similar movements. The time that it takes for the student to "get the response going" should be the latency used.

For example, because of her cerebral palsy, Christine is aware of the need to move before she can actually make a required move. Her teachers use response latencies longer than 5 seconds for responses that involve her hands and arms.

Prompt Fading. Fading is the gradual changing of prompts controlling a student's performance to less intrusive and more natural prompts, without noticeably increasing student errors or reducing student performance. Fading of prompts is not an exact science (Riley, 1995). Often teams must observe a student's performance and adjust their methods so that fading is not too fast (thus keeping errors low) and not too slow (thus keeping motivation for the task high).

Prompts are faded in many ways: for example, reducing the number of prompts provided (model and verbal instructions faded to just verbal instructions), decreasing the amount of information provided by a prompt, or reducing the amount of physical control.

Although it is important to transfer behavior control from training prompts to natural cues quickly, removal of prompts too quickly is certain to hamper successful transition. Fading is most successful when it is planned and completed systematically. Making observations of the student without any prompts is the best way to judge if they can perform without assistance. Once all prompts have been faded and the student still makes the correct response, learning or independent performance is demonstrated.

Prompt Systems

Prompts may be used singularly, in combination, or as part of a *prompting system*. Some systems employ a hierarchy; that is, prompts are arranged either in a most-to-least order of intrusiveness, called "most to least prompting" (e.g., physical-model-verbal), or in a least-to-most order of intrusiveness, called "system of least prompts" or "least to most prompting" (e.g., verbal-model-physical). Several other prompt systems (time delay, graduated guidance, and simultaneous prompts) have been used to teach a variety of skills during the acquisition stage of learning to students who have severe disabilities. Table 4–12 sets forth a description of prompt systems ordered roughly from the simplest to use and potentially least intrusive to the most complex and most intrusive. One of the main advantages of these systems, if used correctly, is that students generally learn with few errors. The reader is referred to several other sources for more extensive detail on these methods and their use with students (Billingsley, 1998; Demchak, 1990; Schuster, et al., 1998; Snell, 1997; Wolery et al., 1992).

The prompts, prompt system, and the response latency a team selects to teach a student should be chosen to suit individual students' skills (e.g., their ability to wait, to follow spoken or signed requests, to imitate models, to respond to pointing, to tolerate physical touch) and their preferences (Demchak, 1990). Perhaps the most efficient approaches for learners in the acquisition stage are constant time delay and *prescriptive* increasing of assistance (a least prompts system in which prompts are individually selected). Both these approaches also can be used in later learning stages if the prompts are simplified, reduced in number (using single not combination prompts with time delay, using only two prompts in the least prompts

TABLE 4–12

Commonly Used Response Prompt Systems and Considerations for Use

Description of Prompt System	Supportive Research and Considerations for Use
Constant Time Delay	

Select prompt that controls the response and determine how many trials will be given at 0-sec delay. During initial requests to respond, the prompt is given at the same time as the request (0-sec delay), making early trials look like simultaneous prompting. After a trial, several trials, or session(s), the delay between the task request and the prompt is lengthened to 4 sec. If the student does not respond correctly in 4 sec, the prompt is given. Initially reinforce prompted correct responses, later differentially reinforce. Always reinforce unprompted correct responses. Continue giving delayed prompts until learning occurs. If errors occur, interrupt with the prompt; after several consecutive errors, reintroduce 0-sec delay for 1 trial or more. Response fading is part of the procedure as students learn that anticipating the delayed prompt enables faster reinforcement and/or completion of the task.	*Supportive Research:* Evidence of success for both discrete and chained responses within a range of students with disabilities and tasks. *Considerations:* Initially student does not have to wait for assistance. Easier to use than progressive delay or prompt hierarchy. Only one prompt or two combined (verbal + model) are used; prompt(s) must work for student. Requires practice in using; need to count off the delay silently. Responses made before 4 sec (correct anticipations) should receive more reinforcement than prompted responses. If repeated errors, use progressive delay, change program, or simplify task. Can be used with forward or backward chaining or when a total task format is used. *Recommended Use:* During early to late acquisition, as well as other phases, but with less intrusive prompt. Good with chained or discrete tasks; equally effective but easier to use than progressive delay and more efficient than increasing assistance system.
Simultaneous Prompting	
Request student to perform the target behavior while prompting at the same time. Model prompts are often used. Reinforce both prompted correct and independent correct responses. Before every training session, give an opportunity to perform without prompting (probes) (or following a set number of trials) to determine when to fade prompts. Fading of prompts occurs when probes alert teacher to stop prompting, prompting is stopped, and student continues to respond correctly.	*Supportive Research:* Limited application; successful with discrete behaviors (naming photos and reading) and the chained task of dressing with preschoolers with disabilities. *Considerations:* Student does not have to wait for a prompt. Procedure is relatively easy to use. Must use probes to determine when to fade. *Recommended Use:* During early to late acquisition phase. Seems to work well when student cannot use less intrusive prompts. Perhaps less useful in later stages of learning.
System of Least Prompts (Increasing Assistance)	
Select a response latency and two to four different prompts that suit student and task; arrange prompts in an order from least assistance to most (e.g., verbal, verbal + model, verbal + physical). Student is asked to perform the task and allowed the latency to respond. Whenever a correct response (or a prompted correct) is made, reinforcement is given and the next training step/trial is provided. If student makes an error or no response, the first prompt in the hierarchy is given and the latency is waited. If the student again makes an error or no response, the next prompt is given and the latency provided, and so on through the last level of prompt. Errors are interrupted with the next prompt. The last prompt should be adequate to produce the response. Prompt fading generally occurs as students learn to respond to less intrusive prompts and then become independent.	*Supportive Research:* Extensive with both discrete and chained tasks; less support with students who have multiple, severe disabilities and with basic self-care tasks. In comparisons with delay, outcomes are the same or less efficient (errors, time to criterion, etc.). More efficient to use a *prescriptive* (individually suited) set of prompts than the traditional three (verbal, model, physical), but may be more difficult for staff. *Considerations:* While hierarchies of verbal, model, and physical prompts are most prevalent, many options for simpler hierarchies exist (gestural, gestural + partial physical, gestural + full physical). Requires a lot of practice to use consistently, but versatile across tasks. May be intrusive and stigmatizing. Some question the amount of time between task stimuli and responding, and the change of response modalities across different prompts. Can be used with forward or backward chaining or when a total task format is used. *Recommended Use:* If learning is in fluency stage, this is more efficient than decreasing assistance. Reduce intrusiveness of prompts for use in later learning phases.

Description of Prompt System	Supportive Research and Considerations for Use

Progressive Time Delay

Similar to constant delay, except delay interval is gradually increased from 0 sec to 8 or more seconds.

Determine delay levels and how many trials will be given at each level; plan error approach.

During initial requests to respond, the prompt is given at the same time as the request (0-sec delay), making early trials look like simultaneous prompting.

After a trial, several trials, or session(s), the delay between the task request and the prompt is lengthened by 1 to 2 sec increments up to 8 (or more) sec, where delay remains until student learns.

Errors and corrects are handled as in constant delay, except delay may be reduced partially or completely when errors occur and then increased gradually or quickly when prompted correct responding returns.

Response fading is part of the procedure as students learn that anticipating the delayed prompt enables faster reinforcement and/or completion of the task.

Supportive Research: Extensive support for discrete tasks, good for chained tasks across a range of students with disabilities and tasks.

Considerations: Same as for constant delay. Progressive is more difficult to use, particularly with chained tasks. Reducing and then increasing delay for repeated errors is also complex. Produces fast learning with few errors. Better than constant delay for students who have difficulty waiting because the delay is gradually increased and the ability to wait is shaped. Can be used with forward or backward chaining or when a total task format is used.

Recommended Use: During early to late acquisition; good with chained or discrete tasks; equally effective with constant delay but less easy to use; and more efficient than increasing assistance system.

Most-to-Least Prompt Hierarchy (Decreasing Assistance)

Select a response latency and two to four different prompts that suit student and task; arrange prompts in an order from most assistance to least (e.g., verbal + physical, verbal + model, verbal).

The first prompt should be adequate to produce the response.

Determine the criterion for progressing to a less intrusive prompt (e.g., so many minutes of training at each level; a certain number of corrects in a row).

Student is asked to perform the task and allowed the latency to respond. Whenever a correct response (or a prompted correct) is made, reinforcement is given and the next training step/trial is provided.

Prompt fading generally occurs when teachers substitute less intrusive prompts for more intrusive ones and students learn to respond to less intrusive prompts and then become independent.

Supportive Research: Convincing support for use with students having severe disabilities and a range of skills (self-care, mobility, following directions).

Considerations: Teachers must plan how to fade prompts and implement these plans or students may become prompt dependent. Can be used with forward or backward chaining or when a total task format is used.

Recommended Use: Better for teaching skills in acquisition than a least-to-most system. Works well when student cannot use less intrusive prompts (e.g., cannot follow verbal direction, imitate, or does not wait for prompts) and makes many errors. Good when target task is chained and requires fluent movement. Less useful in later stages of learning.

Graduated Guidance

Select a general procedure to use:
(a) Gradually lighten physical assistance from full to partial to light touch to shadowing;
(b) Hand to shoulder fading, which uses a full physical prompt applied at the hand and then faded to the wrist, the fore-arm, the elbow, the upper arm, the shoulder, and then to shadowing; hand to shoulder fading has been accompanied by ongoing verbal praise and tactile reinforcement, with concrete reinforcers given at the end of a task chain.
(c) Reducing the amount of pressure from initial full hand-over-hand assistance, to two-finger assistance, to one-finger guiding, and then shadowing. Shadowing means that the teacher's hands are close to the student's involved body part (hand, mouth, arm) but not in contact, ready to assist if needed.

Prompts are delivered simultaneously with task request and the student's movements through the task are continuous.

Develop a plan to fade prompts. Begin fading when there is evidence that student can perform with less assistance: (a) sensing the student's assistance with the response through tactile cues, (b) improved performance (less help or no help) during probe or test trials, (c) student initiates the task, or (d) what seems like an adequate amount of training.

Supportive Research: Supported by mostly older, research in institutional groups and self-care tasks with intensive training methods.

Considerations: Typically used with chained tasks, a total task format, no latency, and intensive training, but can be used without intensive training. A latency may be used to help judge when fading is appropriate (Reese & Snell, 1991). While procedure is not complex (physical prompt only and then fading), it requires many teacher judgments about when to fade prompts; not systematic. Prompts may be faded too quickly causing errors. Can be highly intrusive, because only physical prompts are used.

Recommended Use: Use during early to later acquisition only and after other, less intrusive systems have not worked.

Prompts are arranged roughly in an order from requiring more student skill to be effective to requiring less student skill.

system), and reduced in intrusiveness. Thus a teacher might use indirect verbal prompts (such as "What's next?", or confirmation "That's right," or just say "Keep going" if a student pauses too long); or replace more extensive prompts with small cues or gestures that the student understands (teacher looks in direction of next step or nods towards materials used in forgotten step and gives hand motions to speed up).

Researchers have found that time delay is one of the most effective and efficient prompting methods and also is versatile across skills (Wolery et al., 1992). For example, time delay yielded fewer errors and less disruptive behavior than did the system of least prompts when young children with autism were taught academic tasks (matching pictures to objects, receptive identification of objects, numeral identification, word reading) (Heckaman, Alber, Hooper, & Heward, 1998). Clearly, teams must select prompt procedures to suit individual students and then monitor each student's progress as instruction progresses.

Applications of Several Prompt Systems

Constant Time Delay. Jenny's teachers use *constant time delay* to teach the skill sequence for using coins to make purchases (Table 4–8). When teaching Jenny to name quarters and state their value (step 12), Ms. Alpern and Ms. Lee both started with 0-second delay trials, using a model (verbal or visual) prompt:

Teacher: [Shows quarter] "Name this coin . . . quarter." [Verbal model prompt, zero seconds delay]
Jenny: "It's a quarter."
Teacher: "Right, quarter. What's a quarter worth?" [Immediately holds up a card with the 25 cent price on it: a visual model prompt at zero delay].
Jenny: "Twenty-five cents."
Teacher: "Right! A quarter's worth twenty-five cents."

Next the teacher gave a second zero delay trial on the quarter. Then the teacher paused 4 seconds before giving the model, hoping that Jenny would try to answer if she knew or wait if she was uncertain:

Teacher: [Shows a quarter] "Name this coin." [Counts off 4 seconds to herself and then gives a verbal model prompt.] "Quarter."
Jenny: [Waits for the prompt] "It's a quarter."

Teacher: "Right, quarter. What's a quarter worth?" [Counts off 4 seconds to herself and then holds up a card with the 25 cents price on it: a visual model prompt].
Jenny: [Before the card is shown, Jenny responds.] "Twenty-five cents."
Teacher: "That's exactly right! A quarter's worth twenty-five cents."

The teacher continued trials at 4 second delays until Jenny was able to name the coin and the value without the delayed prompt, which happened during one 15-minute session. The next day they reviewed this step (one trial at 0-seconds, one or several trials at 4 seconds until Jenny was able to respond without the prompt) and then worked on step 13: opportunities to name all four coins and their values in a mixed order. Step 13 started again at 0-second delay and moved to 4-second delay after all coins had been reviewed.

System of Least Prompts. Timothy's teachers are using a prescriptive system of least prompts to teach him to use the bathroom. They teach across all steps in the task (total task approach). They start by giving him a 3-second latency to respond. If he does not respond or makes an error, they use a gestural prompt (point to the item associated with the step) and wait 3 more seconds. If this does not work, they give a gestural and physical prompt (point and touch him lightly or nudge him toward the materials). These prompts suit him better than verbal or full physical prompts. Instruction on the first three teaching steps looked like this:

Teacher: "It's time to use the bathroom." [Instructional cue]
Timothy continues sitting during latency as others head to the bathroom. [No response]
Teacher goes close to him, gets in his view, and points toward the bathroom. [Gestural prompt]
Timothy looks in that direction but does not move. [Approximation but incomplete response]
Teacher tugs on his sleeve and points toward the bathroom. [Gestural and physical prompt]
Timothy gets up and moves to the bathroom door. [Prompted correct on first task step]
Teacher: "Good job Timothy!"
Timothy continues into bathroom and stops by toilet. [Unprompted correct on second task step]
Teacher: "Great!"
Timothy stands without taking further action for the latency. [No response on third step]
Teacher points to his pants. [Gestural prompt]

Timothy grabs his pants and pulls them down and sits on the toilet. [Prompted correct on third step]

Teacher: "Good pulling your pants down, Timothy!" [Pats him on the shoulder]

Instruction continues through each remaining step of the chained task.

Prompt systems are effective, systematic ways to teach, but these two examples emphasize the importance of designing the specific method to suit the student and then practicing the methods until team members are consistent in their use.

Alternatives to Response Prompt Systems

There are alternatives to the response prompting systems described in Table 4–12. Naturalistic teaching or prompting procedures (described in chapter 12) include such approaches as model, mand-model, naturalistic time delay, and incidental teaching. These methods use a flexible response latency, planned prompts, a means to handle errors, and reinforcing consequences, but they are always used in the context of ongoing routines. The student's interest is used as a guide for when to teach. Naturalistic teaching procedures have been very successful with communication and social skills and with young students (e.g., Kaiser et al., 1998).

> *Timothy's team was most successful in teaching him to sign "help" when he needed it. For example, they approached and taught him when he was seen struggling with his jacket, trying to reach a toy, fussing because he could not get on the swing, or looking for a paintbrush or crayon. His team used a model approach for signals that were in acquisition and a delay approach for signals he knew fairly well, but failed to use. The "help" sign was not readily used by Timothy, so staff began by getting close to him and establishing "joint attention" on the item of interest (kneel down and look with him at his zipper). If Timmy signed help, immediate help was given to him; but if he didn't or if he used his other signals (whining, moving the teacher's hands to his jacket), the teacher silently modeled the help sign. If Timothy signed correctly, the teacher said, "You need help with your zipper!" and gave help. If his signing was unclear, the teacher repeated the model closer to his view. Help was given when his sign was clear.*

Stimulus modification procedures also can be useful in some teaching situations, particularly when teaching academic skills. *Stimulus modification procedures* involve a gradual change in the teaching stimuli over successive teaching trials, from an easy discrimination to a more difficult discrimination. The change in the stimulus is so gradual that difficulty on any given trial is about the same if the student has learned each previous discrimination. Most examples of these methods require vision, reduce errors to a minimum, and have excellent research support, but often demand extensive preparation of teaching materials (Wolery et al., 1992). Computer-assisted versions of stimulus modification procedures may be an efficient option to teacher-made materials and have been applied to reading instruction for students with severe disabilities.

Two commonly used stimulus modification procedures include stimulus fading and stimulus superimposition. Stimulus fading involves the pairing of an irrelevant stimulus (color or size) with a relevant stimulus (the word on the red card matches the picture shown, the big object matches the picture shown), and gradual fading of the irrelevant stimulus (background color or object size). Stimulus superimposition involves the placement of a known stimulus (a picture) over another that is not known (the word for the picture) and slowly modifying the intensity, clarity, or salience of the known stimulus until it is not visible. Both methods are used to teach an association between the two stimuli (e.g., teaching words by gradually fading superimposed picture cues, as in Figure 4–10).

A simple application of stimulus modification procedures is to teach with a variety of task materials, allowing the student to become used to changes in the irrelevant stimulus dimensions. Researchers like Kamps and her colleagues (Kamps et al., 1991, 1994) not only rotated materials often during small group instruction, but used multiple exemplars—a minimum of three sets of materials per concept taught—to promote learning. For example, Jenny counts many different sets of materials (e.g., moveable objects, coins, art materials; immovable dots, pictures, words) during a given day as she does practical math problems, but the counting response does not change.

Effective use of prompts or prompt systems involves the following:

1. Select the least intrusive prompt that is effective for the student and task.
2. Select a prompt(s) that suits the student; combine them if necessary.

FIGURE 4–10
Fading Levels for a Superimposed Word Task

Note: Reprinted from *Teaching Sight Words to the Moderately and Severely Mentally Retarded* by D. M. Browder, 1981, unpublished doctoral dissertation. University of Virginia. Reprinted by permission.

3. Choose natural prompts that are related to the target behavior (e.g., responses that involve movement may be best prompted with a gesture or partial physical prompt; verbal responses may be prompted with verbal prompts).
4. Highlight natural prompts (e.g., call attention to others at a table clearing their own dishes).
5. Always wait a latency period (e.g., 3 seconds) before and after the prompt, so learners have a chance to respond without assistance. (An exception is time delay, where a 0-second latency is used initially.)
6. Avoid the repetition of a prompt for the same response. Instead, if a prompt does not work, try more assistance.
7. Prompt only when the student is attending.
8. Devise a plan to fade prompts as soon as possible.
9. Do not introduce prompts unnecessarily.

10. Reinforce a student for responding correctly to a prompt during early acquisition; later, encourage learning through differential reinforcement.

Selecting Consequence Teaching Methods

Recall Timothy's objectives and teaching program for arrival at school. After selecting the prompts and response latency and deciding how to offer choices, the team turned its attention to consequence strategies: (a) planning the reinforcement for step and task completion, (b) deciding if they would use a chaining or a whole-task approach, and (c) determining how errors would be handled. Before they began instruction, they also planned how and when to evaluate Timothy's learning progress.

General *consequence strategies* involve the presentation of positive reinforcement, planned ignoring or extinction, and punishment (the presentation of aversives or the removal of positive reinforcers) following a response. Punishment is an unacceptable strategy. The use of punishment is *not* supported by the 1997 amendments to IDEA. Unfortunately, case law (recent court decisions on punishment and students with disabilities) provides few safeguards for students at risk for aversive interventions from schools (Lohrmann-O'Rourke & Zirkel, 1998). Thus, because the courts continue to lend support to aversive methods, schools and educational teams must be vigilant in advocating for and enforcing the supportive school practice of positive behavior support. We limit our discussion to nonpunitive consequences and ways to effectively manage behavior.

Positive Reinforcement
Positive reinforcement occurs when the presentation of preferred consequences (called positive reinforcers) made contingent on a behavior leads to an increase in the performance of that behavior. Thus, to reinforce means to strengthen behavior by increasing its frequency, duration, or intensity. Positive reinforcement is involved not only in all the prompting methods discussed in the previous section, but also in two of the consequence strategies: shaping and chaining. This interdependent or contingent arrangement between behaviors and consequences lets teachers build behaviors purposefully. What is reinforcing for one person will not necessarily be reinforcing for another,

particularly with students who have more extensive disabilities; therefore the activities and objects an individual student finds reinforcing must be determined through informal assessment involving observation (see chapter 3).

Preference is a newer term than reinforcer but often is used as a synonym for reinforcer. The distinction between the two terms seems to relate more to who is in control: the adult (teacher, therapist, parent) or the student. Traditionally, reinforcement is manipulated by adults for the purpose of increasing the frequency or intensity of a target behavior. Preferences can also be determined in the same manner as reinforcers. By contrast, the opportunity to experience a preferred event may be more under the control of the individual student and may be made available in the context of everyday routines through choice making offered by another or self-initiated by the student. Preference, as a concept, is more consistent with the encouragement of self-determination than is reinforcement. We use the terms as loose synonyms but recognize that opportunities to choose and indicate preferences encourage self-determined behavior, while the tight control of reinforcers may not.

Types of Reinforcement. Although reinforcers (preferred activities and objects) have unlimited range and vary from tangible items and activities to abstract thoughts of self-approval, all reinforcers are either primary (unlearned or unconditioned) or secondary (learned or conditioned). The first category includes the universal, or automatic, reinforcers to which everyone responds (although not continuously) without instruction. Primary reinforcers for someone who is feeling hungry, thirsty, or cold include food, drink, and warmth, respectively; primary reinforcers serve to return a person who is physically uncomfortable to a comfortable state. Secondary reinforcers develop reinforcing value through their association with primary reinforcers. Secondary reinforcers begin as neutral stimuli, but with repeated pairings with already existing reinforcers, they take on their own reinforcing value.

Timothy has learned to enjoy playing with blocks with his classmates because it involves putting blocks in order and creating large structures that he already enjoyed.

Christine began to listen to rock music for pleasure because listening to music was something her peers liked.

Christine smiles when she gets her paycheck for work; she knows that money buys CDs and other things she enjoys.

Secondary reinforcers commonly used in educational settings include task completion, attention, approval, favorite activities, and check marks, stickers, and tokens. It is important to couple simple but specific praise with known reinforcers so that praise acquires reinforcing value for students. The goal is for students to not only enlarge their options for reinforcement but also replace artificial, primary, or age-inappropriate reinforcers for those that are naturally occurring and suited to their chronological age.

Reinforcement Schedules. *Schedules of reinforcement* indicate how many and what pattern of student responses is reinforced. Reinforcement may be given according to the number of responses performed (*ratio* schedules) or the passage of time in relation to the performance (*interval* schedules). Reinforcement schedules may be based upon an absolute or fixed number of responses (which are then called *fixed* ratio schedules) or an absolute amount of time (which are then called *fixed* interval schedules). Presentation of one reinforcer for every occurrence of the target response is a fixed ratio schedule of one, or FR:1. This is commonly called *continuous* reinforcement. All other schedules may be generally called *intermittent* reinforcement. An FR:5 schedule is a fixed pattern of reinforcement for every fifth correct response. It is also an intermittent schedule because reinforcement is not given for every response.

In contrast to fixed schedules, *variable* schedules do not have a fixed, or discrete, number of reinforcements but offer reinforcement on a schedule that is an average of the reinforcement pattern. In a variable ratio schedule of VR:5, reinforcement is delivered on an average of every fifth correct response. This VR:5 pattern may consist of three, seven, two, or eight occurrences of a target behavior followed by reinforcement. These numbers average out to reinforcement every fifth correct response.

In interval schedules, the first target response occurring after a regular time period of so many seconds or minutes (fixed interval, or FI) or an average period (variable interval, or VI) is reinforced. In many classrooms, reinforcement schedules are time-based (at the end of a class period) and teacher-dispensed;

feedback and social praise may be as meager as once every 10 minutes. In a classroom of 25 students, this converts to an even thinner reinforcement schedule. Classroom reinforcement schedules are more often variable than fixed. Teachers may provide opportunities for students to choose a preferred activity when they judge the quality or quantity of work done is good enough or sufficient time has passed. Because "sufficient" and "enough" tend to vary from one day to the next, a variable schedule results.

Because of the powerful influence of reinforcement schedules upon behavior, the following related considerations on scheduling reinforcement should be applied when planning instruction:

- During the acquisition stage of learning, more instances of behavior should be encouraged by the continuous provision of small amounts of contingent reinforcement (e.g., a "high five" touch and words of praise, a few seconds of music plus praise, food) rather than larger amounts of reinforcement given less often.

  When Jenny was first successful counting out combinations of pennies and nickels without help, Ms. Dailey made a "big deal" by cheering whenever she was right (see Table 4–8). After these sessions, she made a point of telling Ms. Alpern and having Jenny show them her new skill.

- After a higher rate of more accurate behavior has been established (later in the acquisition stage), reinforcers should be faded slowly from a continuous to an intermittent schedule, which requires more behavior for each reinforcement. This strengthens the behavior as the student learns to tolerate periods of nonreinforcement rather than to abruptly give up and stop responding when reinforcement is not forthcoming.

  Now Jenny is working on counting out combinations of dimes, nickels, and pennies; she still requires prompts to start with the dimes and count by tens. Ms. Dailey gives praise for every prompted correct response; when Jenny performs without any prompts, Ms. Dailey is extra enthusiastic and lets Jenny write those amounts on her "I Did It By Myself" chart. Periodically, for review, Ms. Dailey also gives easy trials counting out nickels or pennies or the combination. Instead of praising her, Ms. Dailey simply confirms Jenny's accuracy ("OK, 15 cents") or asks her, "Is 15 cents right?"

- Fixed schedules of reinforcement produce uneven patterns of behavior, because the individual can roughly predict how far away reinforcement is,

based on the last instance. Behaviors on fixed schedules extinguish quickly because the students recognize the absence of reinforcement. *To increase her students' responsibility for keeping their classroom neat, Ms. Alpern and the class decided to use "Clean Teams" who would have assigned responsibilities for various parts of the class. Initially, Ms. Alpern gave Friday "Clean Team" inspections and awards which meant the room was clean on Friday but not the rest of the week.*

- Variable schedules generally produce more even patterns of behavior than do fixed schedules, because the individual cannot predict the occasions for reinforcement. Behaviors that have been reinforced by variable reinforcement schedules are also more resistant to extinction, and so they are more durable if reinforcement stops for a given period of time.

  Now, Ms. Alpern gives random spot checks and awards, and the room is usually pretty neat.

- Reinforcers must be reassessed periodically (Mason, McGee, Farmer-Dougan, & Risley, 1989; Roane, Vollmer, Ringdahl, & Marcus, 1998) so that they continue to be reinforcing to the student (see chapter 3).

- Reinforcers must be appropriate for the student's chronological age, the activity, and the learning situation. Aim for replacing less suitable reinforcers with ones that have more availability in natural environments used by the student.

  None of the team members wanted to use food to reinforce Timothy, even though his mom reported this had been successful in his tutoring sessions at home. They talked about what activities he liked, what the other 4-year-old boys liked, and what he could easily do in the preschool. They took this list and tried each activity out, giving him a "sample" first and then letting him choose. He showed clear preferences for block building, the water table, putting blocks away, CD-ROM stories, and riding a tricycle.

- The more immediately the reinforcers are presented following performance of the behavior, the greater their effect.

  Timothy's teachers and his peers respond quickly when he uses his picture symbols to initiate a request or interaction. He is using his picture board more and more to communicate requests because it leads to quick fulfillment of his requests.

- *Satiation* results from the overuse of a reinforcer and its reinforcing effect may be lost. To avoid satiation, teams should (a) explore new reinforcers with students and preserve the special quality of objects or activities selected as reinforcers; (b) use intermittent reinforcement because it requires fewer reinforcers for more behavior and reflects more natural schedules; and (c) give students opportunities to select reinforcing or preferred activities, rather than choosing and presenting reinforcers to students.

Other Consequence Strategies for Building Skills

Two frequently used strategies to build or expand new behaviors include shaping and chaining. Addressing errors is also a basic consequence strategy, including ignoring errors, following errors with assistance, or correcting errors.

Shaping and Chaining. *Shaping* involves the reinforcement of successive approximations of a goal response. Instructors provide praise and other reinforcers for better and better performance over time. Shaping is a strategy involved in most teaching methods that use positive reinforcement.

Chaining refers to teaching students to perform a sequence of functionally related responses in an approximate or exact order to complete a routine or task (e.g., clearing a table of dirty dishes, making a sandwich, brushing teeth, printing one's name, or completing an addition problem). Most skills we perform and teach students to perform consist of a chain of small component responses. Learning a chain or sequence of responses involves performing each discrete step of the chain in the correct order and in close temporal succession. Each component of the chain becomes a conditioned reinforcer for the previous response and a discriminative stimulus for the next response in the chain. Chaining often is used in combination with shaping. Shaping and the three basic chaining strategies (i.e., forward, backward, and total task) that teams choose from when planning teaching programs are described in Table 4–13.

To teach behavior chains, the cluster of responses is first divided into an ordered list of separate teachable behaviors, usually through task analysis. The number of steps into which a chain is divided varies with different students and skills. Since chaining may proceed forward or backward across the sequence of behaviors or may involve instruction across all steps concurrently, a team must select the order in which to teach the task components. The chaining approach selected and the teaching procedures used

depend on the student, how fast the student learns under various teaching conditions, the length and complexity of the chain, the opportunity to perform the chain, and the component responses already known.

Error Correction. The final consequence strategy frequently used in teaching involves handling errors in a way that promotes learning. To maintain a reinforcing environment for learning, it is important to minimize the potential for student errors. When errors do occur, however, the teacher can gently interrupt and correct them in several ways. Most prompt systems we discussed earlier in this chapter come with "built-in" methods for handling errors, but teams still need to decide what approach works best with a given student and task.

> For example, when adults use words to correct Timothy's errors, he does not attend or react. He is often resistant when physical corrections are attempted. But gesture cues (pointing to materials involved or moving materials from the missed step into his view) are often effective.

Table 4–14 on p. 166 gives descriptions of basic error correction procedures and lists considerations for their use. When a student has learned all, or most, of a skill and moves into the fluency or maintenance stage, less structured and informative error correction procedures should be used. Because the student is now more proficient at the skill, errors are less frequent and may be caused by distraction or carelessness rather than by not knowing what to do. In such cases, one of the following procedures may be chosen:

1. The student who makes an error or hesitates may be given a few seconds to self-correct. Some errors, if uninterrupted, will provide natural learning opportunities. If a correction is not forthcoming, then one of the other procedures can be tried.
2. The error may be acknowledged ("No" or "That's not right") without providing negative or harsh feedback. Then, the teacher requests another try on the same step ("Try it again"). If a second error results, some assistance is given.
3. A minimal prompt ("What's next?") or verbal rehearsal of the last step correctly performed ("You just finished getting the plates, now what's next?") may be provided as soon as the error is stopped. If

TABLE 4–13
Skill-Building Consequence Strategies and Considerations for Use

Description	Examples	Considerations for Use
Shaping		
Building skills by reinforcing successive approximations or improved attempts at a target behavior. Precision in skill performance is improved over time. Requires instructor to focus carefully on student's response and make quick judgments about each response in comparison to earlier occurrences and the goal criterion. Rather than wait for the final form, reinforcement is given when the student shows improvement. Involves differential reinforcement, or changing the ongoing rules for what is "good enough."	Useful with many skills, discrete or chained responses (e.g., making transfers from wheelchair to toilet, walking, dressing, social skills, speaking, signing, work tasks, academics, etc.).	A time-consuming process that requires careful observation of the student's small changes in performing the target behavior. Depends on good teaming when multiple instructors are involved. Team must define each expected improvement. Shaping can be made more efficient by using a discriminative stimulus (instructional cue) and combining sometimes with prompts.
Response Chaining: Forward Chaining		
Task analyze steps and measure baseline performance. Instruction begins by starting with the student performing any learned steps in order up to the first unmastered response, at which point instruction occurs. Reinforcement is given quickly after the training step, while more extensive reinforcement may be given after the last step in the chain is completed. The remainder of the chain may be either completed by the teacher or by the student with assistance, but the routine should be finished before another training opportunity. Once this segment of the chain is mastered, through additional trials, instruction shifts to the next unmastered step with prior steps being performed without assistance in sequence.	Useful with many self-care routines (grooming tasks, dressing, using the toilet). May suit many home management and vocational tasks. Appropriate for some chained academics tasks (e.g., use of number line, telephone dialing, calculator). (Not as useful in school or community setting when assistance through the unlearned part of the task is more obvious and may be stigmatizing.)	Usually combined with prompting to teach the target step as well as shaping across the entire chain. May work better than total task for some learners who have multiple disabilities or for longer tasks. Initial mastery of single responses in the chain may be faster, but slower overall. Replace with backward chaining when task has an especially reinforcing end. Replace with total task if chain is performed less often; may want to switch to total task after half the steps are learned. May need to create more training opportunities or learning will be slow. Involves a lot of teacher effort to complete unlearned portion of task.

the student stops before a step is complete, the teacher may confirm and urge the student to continue ("That's right, keep going").

There are many other methods for correcting errors; however, to be effective, error correction procedures must reflect the following characteristics:

- Be suited to the learner's age.
- Be applied immediately and consistently but unemotionally.

- Be nonstigmatizing, humane, socially valid, and not endanger the student.
- Provide enough help to correct the error quickly but not so much as to create dependency on the teacher.
- Be suited in the amount of assistance and reinforcement (if any) to the student's stage of learning for that task.
- Be followed by additional opportunities to respond to the task or step.
- Encourage and reinforce independence.

Description	Examples	Considerations for Use
Response Chaining: Backward Chaining		
Task analyze steps and measure baseline performance. Instruction begins by either completing or helping the student perform the entire chain of behavior up until the last step of the chain, at which point instruction occurs. After additional opportunities and when the student has mastered the last step, teaching shifts to the next to the last step of the chain, but the student is expected to perform the last step(s) unassisted. Reinforcement is given quickly after the training step, while more extensive reinforcement occurs only after the last step in the chain is completed. As the remaining steps are taught, learned, and added in a backward order, the entire chain is performed and the learner is reinforced.	*Similar to forward chaining.*	*Similar to forward chaining.* The main advantage over forward chaining and total task is being assisted through and completing the task quickly and getting reinforcement early in learning. Usually combined with prompting to teach the target step as well as shaping across the entire chain. May work better than total task for some learners who have multiple disabilities or for longer tasks. Initial mastery of single responses in chain may be faster, but slower overall. Replace with total task if chain is performed less often; may want to switch to total task after half the steps are learned. May need to create more training opportunities or learning will be slow. Involves a lot of teacher effort to complete unlearned portion of task.
Response Chaining: Total Task		
Task analyze steps and measure baseline performance. Instruction begins by starting instruction with the first step in the chain, and teaching each successive step in order until the chain of responses are completed. All steps needing instruction are taught in order and concurrently during each performance of the chained routine. Reinforcement is given quickly (e.g., praise) after each response for corrects and improved performances and again at the end of the chain (e.g., a short leisure break).	Has been used successfully with all sorts of chained tasks: self-care; mobility; daily living; community, vocational, and social interactions; and some multiple step academic routines.	Works best if the chain is not too long (chained tasks can be subdivided) or a single training trial can be too lengthy. Main advantages are that all teaching opportunities are used (each step is taught each time) and that the task is completed. May produce faster learning than other chaining methods. May be combined with repeated training just on difficult step(s) of a routine, although this is usually rather unnatural. This seems to be a more natural approach than the other options.

Written Teaching Plans

Responsible teaching is not possible without some written documentation, but if paperwork takes too much time, teaching suffers. Also, when paperwork is not relevant to teaching or reflects inaccurate or unused material, more time is wasted. At the very minimum, teachers need simple data collection forms and readily available guidelines to direct their use of instructional programs. Written programs (i.e., lesson plans, program formats, or teaching guides) should specify the essential elements: the student, objective(s), start and aim date, teaching time and setting, instructor(s), arrangement, materials, evaluation procedure and schedule, teaching procedures (e.g., instructional cue, prompt and fading methods, error correction procedure, reinforcers and schedule), and general instructions for changing procedures during later stages of learning. When programs are described with this level of detail, there are several advantages:

TABLE 4–14
Error Correction Procedures and Considerations for Use

Strategy	Considerations for Use

• In early learning it may be best to gently interrupt error with a prompt (as in most prompt systems).
• After an error, provide another immediate opportunity to perform while increasing the assistance (as in a system of least prompts).
• Gently stop an error and wait to see if the student will self-correct. Direct student's attention to relevant task stimuli, add prompts as needed. Reinforce any self-corrections.
• Later in learning, it may be good to follow some errors by waiting for the student to self-correct; if none occurs, give assistance to correct the error.
• Simplify those responses that are frequently missed or performed wrong.
• Gently interrupt errors and provide repeated practice on those responses (or parts of a chain) that are frequently missed.
	Repeated error correction is aversive for most students and inefficient. Analyze performance data to decide how to improve instruction. Consider the student's stage of learning and motivation for the task as well.
	   Sometimes improving the antecedents may be necessary to reduce errors:
	(a) improve the task analysis of these steps
	(b) use backward chaining for these steps
	(c) use simpler prompts (gestural-model instead of verbal)
	(d) replace a prompt hierarchy with a single prompt system (time delay)
	(e) provide a permanent prompt like a picture book
	(f) use stimulus prompts like color coding temporarily
	   During later learning, allowing or prompting students to self-correct lets them experience the natural stimuli resulting from the error and learn ways to improve the situation. Self-correction needs to be used carefully so as not to endanger or embarrass the student.

• Successful program methods can be used again with the same student, while those that yield little or no learning can be modified more precisely.

• Programs are more likely to be implemented consistently, regardless of who teaches.

Timothy's team has completed a task analysis data form for his arrival program (Figure 4–9) which lists the target behaviors in order, along with the instructional cue, teaching method (constant time delay), the prompt (gestural or partial physical), the response latency, and the recording key. Use of this information encourages consistency in the sequence of skill training, making it easier for Timothy to learn when multiple instructors participate. Staff also refer to the brief teaching guide (Figure 4–11), which describes the constant time delay method they use with Timothy.

Teams should devise or adopt easy-to-use program forms to guide teaching and data collection. Team members may want to combine written program materials with demonstrations and practice using the methods. The special educator often assumes the responsibility for completing, organizing and updating these forms, and making them available to other team members.

Summary

Teaching students effectively involves many steps and decisions. This chapter addresses some of the more important elements involved in developing the IEP, planning the curriculum, adapting general education activities for meaningful participation, designing teaching methods, and scheduling instruction. Special education teachers cannot accomplish best practices if they work alone. Collaboration and problem solving among educators, administrators, and parents are the primary means for successfully including students who have disabilities. Nondisabled peers can be participants in this process, since they also benefit from inclusion. Students with significantly differing abilities need instructional experiences that not only focus on appropriate educational goals and objectives and but also reflect effective and efficient teaching techniques. To keep errors to a minimum during early learning and also to facilitate skill generalization, teams must plan instruction so that structure, support, and stage of learning are properly balanced. But to promote skill maintenance, fluent and proficient performance, and generalization of skills, teams must adjust their

FIGURE 4–11
Brief Teaching Guide for Timothy's Arrival Program

Brief Teaching Guide		

Student: Timothy Simms	**School:** St. Stephen's Preschool	**Start Date:** 9/27/99
Teachers: Carlene Johnson, Ted Grayson, & Jo Milano (SLP)		**Aim Date:** 12/17/99

Objective: Upon arrival at and departure from preschool, Timothy will exit the car, walk to enter the preschool class, greet familiar people, remove and hang his outer garments in his cubby, and select and go to a play activity at a criterion of 10 of 15 steps (67%) during two training sessions (using partial participation on some steps as indicated in the task analysis).

Stage of Learning: Acquisition	**Arrangement:** One to one, naturalistic	
Teaching times: At arrival and departure	**Teaching Days:** M–F	**Test Day:** Alternate F

Setting: car, bus/car area, sidewalk, halls, classroom, cubby

Instructional Cue: Arrival or departure cues, "Let's go to preschool," "Let's go home"

Teaching procedure: Constant time delay (0 or 4 sec) across total task

Prompt(s): Gestural (point, tap) with partial physical (gentle pressure or nudge) Do not use verbal prompts, except stating his name if he is not attending.

Materials: Natural materials involved in task; activity board, student photo cards; task analysis

Reinforcers: Praise, smile, deep pressure rub on shoulder, play activity in AM; car ride at noon

Teaching Procedure: For first 2 days use 0-sec delay; then delay prompt 4 sec. Use 0-sec delay for 1 day after long absences, vacations, or errors on 5 or more steps in one session.

Antecedents: Follow task steps. Start by giving cue, wait delay, then give prompt on time if no response. As successful, include gesture prompts that draw his attention to peers nearby who are performing the same task.

Consequences: Follow unprompted corrects with enthusiastic praise or rub; follow prompted corrects with praise; follow a no response with a prompt. Interrupt errors with a prompt. Encourage peers to praise him when his things are in cubby and when he makes an activity choice.

Maintenance: Thin and fade reinforcer to end of task and activity board choice. Require his use of arrival procedure to participate in play activity.

Fluency: If performance is slower than peers, time him and set goals for shortening the duration.

Generalization: Task analyze home routine, try out and adjust procedure.

teaching procedures to reduce structure, fade prompts, and shift the student's attention to the natural cues and stimuli that must come to control their behavior.

Suggested Activities

1. Use Table 4–1 to evaluate a school program you work in or are familiar with. If possible, gather a group of educators and an administrator and involve them as a focus group in this evaluation process. Rate each supportive school practice, guiding team principle, and student outcome on a scale from 0 to 4:

With the focus group, rank order those needing improvement and brainstorm the actions needed to tackle each using an issue-action problem-solving form, as partially shown after the following rating grid.

Supportive Practice	Not Present	Spoken about but Not Practiced	Some Evidence of Its Application	Good Evidence of Its Application	Schoolwide Evidence of Its Application
List below:	0	1	2	3	4

Issue	Action	Taken by Whom	Taken When

2. Examine the IEP of a student with more extensive support needs. If the student is being included with his or her peers in general education activities, observe over one of several days and check on how adequately his or her IEP objectives are being addressed. Complete a matrix for this student by listing IEP objectives down the left side and the class schedule across the top. Indicate with checks the activities during which it would be logical to teach each objective. Note when (or if) "pull-out" is being used. Explore how inappropriate instances of pull-out might be replaced with adaptation of classroom activities. If the student is not included in general education activities, observe a class (or classes) that might be suitable for the student to be included. Complete a matrix as above; then explore the steps needed to implement change.

3. For this same student, apply the model in Figure 4–4 for making adaptations (Janney & Snell, in press). If the student is assigned to your caseload, then implement the six steps for using the process. If the student is one you work with during a practicum experience, then evaluate the adequacy of adaptations currently used in the student's program. Start with the student's matrix, determine what kinds of curricular, instructional, and ecological adaptations are being used, and decide if they are appropriate or not. Explore how improvements can be made.

References

Ager, C. L., & Browder, D. M. (1991). Assessment of integration and generalization. In D. M. Browder (Ed.), *Assessment of individuals with severe disabilities* (2nd ed.). Baltimore: Paul H. Brookes.

Bateman, B. D., & Linden, M. A. (1998). *Better IEPs* (3rd ed.). Longmont, CO: Sopris West.

Baumgart, D., Brown, L., Pumpian, I., Nisbet, J., Ford, A., Sweet, M., Messina, R., & Schroeder, J. (1982). The principle of partial participation and individualized adaptations in educational programs for severely handicapped students. *Journal of the Association for Persons with Severe Handicaps*, 7(2), 17–27.

Billingsley, F. F. (1998). Behaving independently: considerations in fading instructor assistance. In A. Hilton & R. Ringlaben (Eds.), *Best and promising practices in developmental disabilities* (pp. 157–168). Austin, TX: Pro-Ed.

Billingsley, F. F., Gallucci, C., Peck, C. A., Schwartz, I. S., & Staub, D. (1996). "But those kids can't even *do* math": An alternative conceptualization of outcomes for inclusive education. *The Special Education Leadership Review*, 3, 43–56.

Breen, C. G., Kennedy, C. H., & Haring, T. G. (Eds.) (1990). *Methods for facilitating the inclusion of students with disabilities in integrated school and community contexts* (pp. 23–53). Santa Barbara, CA: Graduate School of Education, University of California.

Breen, C. G. & Lovinger, L. (1990). PAL (Partners at Lunch Club): Evaluation of a program to support social relationships in a junior high school. In C. G. Breen, C. H. Kennedy, & T. G. Haring (Eds.), *Social context research project: Methods for facilitating the inclusion of students with disabilities in integrated school and community contexts* (pp. 106–128). Santa Barbara, CA: University of California.

Bricker, D. & Cripe, J. J. (1993). *An activity-based approach to early intervention*. Baltimore: Paul H. Brookes.

Browder, D. M. (1981). *A comparison of a stimulus prompt and a response prompt with four fading procedures to teach sight words to the moderately and severely retarded*. Unpublished doctoral dissertation, University of Virginia.

Browder, D. M. (Ed.). (1991). *Assessment of individuals with severe disabilities* (2nd ed.). Baltimore: Paul H. Brookes.

Brown, F. (1991). Creative daily scheduling: A non-intrusive approach to challenging behaviors in community residences. *Journal of the Association for Persons with Severe Handicaps*, 16, 75–84.

Brown, F., Evans, I. M., Weed, K. A., & Owen, V. (1987). Delineating functional competencies: A component model. *Journal of the Association for Persons with Severe Handicaps*, 12, 117–124.

Cook, L., & Friend, M. (1993). Interpersonal and procedural considerations of collaborative teams and problem-solving. In R. Beck (Ed.), *Project RIDE: Responding to individual differences in education* (p. 44). Longmont, CO: Sopris West.

Coots, J. J., Bishop, K. D., & Grenot-Scheyer, M. (1998). Supporting elementary age students with significant disabilities in general education classrooms: Personal perspectives on inclusion. *Education and Training in Mental Retardation and Developmental Disabilities*, 33, 317–330.

Cushing, L. S., & Kennedy, C. H. (1997). Academic effects of providing peer support in general education classrooms on students without disabilities. *Journal of Applied Behavior Analysis*, 30, 139–152.

Delano, M., & Snell, M. E. (2000). Models of peer support in instruction. In M. E. Snell & J. E. Janney (Eds.), *Practices in inclusive schools: Social relationships and peer support*. Baltimore, MD: Paul H. Brookes.

Demchak, M. (1990). Response prompting and fading methods: A review. *American Journal on Mental Retardation*, 94, 603–615.

Doyle, P. M., Gast, D. L., Wolery, M., Ault, M. J., & Farmer, J. A. (1990). Use of constant time delay in small group instruction: A study of observational and incidental learning. *The Journal of Special Education*, 23, 369–385.

Dugan, E., Kamps, D., Leonard, B., Watkins, N., Rheinberger, A., & Stackhaus, J. (1995). Effects of cooperative learning groups during social studies for students with autism and fourth-grade peers. *Journal of Applied Behavior Analysis*, 28, 175–188.

Dunlap, G., & Johnson, J. (1985). Increasing the independent responding of autistic children with unpredictable supervision. *Journal of Applied Behavior Analysis*, 18, 227–236.

Evans, I. M., Salisbury, C., Palombaro, M., & Goldberg, J. S. (1994). Children's perceptions of fairness in classroom and interpersonal situations involving peers with severe disabilities. *Journal of the Association for Persons with Severe Handicaps*, 19, 326–332.

Etzel, B. C., & LeBlanc, J. M. (1979). The simplest treatment alternative: The law of parsimony applied to choosing appropriate instructional control and errorless-learning procedures for the difficult-to-teach child. *Journal of Autism and Development Disorders*, 9, 361–382.

Falvey, M. A. (1995). *Inclusive and heterogeneous schooling: Assessment, curriculum, & instruction*. Baltimore, MD: Paul H. Brookes

Farlow, L., & Snell, M. E. (1995). *Making the most of student performance data*. (AAMR Research to Practice Series). Washington, DC: American Association on Mental Retardation.

Farmer, J. A., Gast, D. L., Wolery, M., & Winterling, V. (1991). Small group interaction for students with severe handicaps: A study of observational learning. *Education and Training in Mental Retardation*, 26, 190–201.

Ferguson, D. L., & Barmgart, D. (1991). Partial participation revisited. *Journal of the Association for Persons with Severe Handicaps*, 16, 218–227.

Ford, A., Schnorr, R., Meyer, L., Davern, L., Black, J., & Dempsey, P. (1989). *The Syracuse community-referenced curriculum guide*. Baltimore: Paul H. Brookes.

Forest, M., & Lusthaus, E. (1989). Promoting educational equality for all students: Circles and maps. In S. Stainback, W. Stainback, & M. Forest (Eds.), *Educating all students in the mainstream of regular education* (pp. 43–57). Baltimore: Paul H. Brookes.

Freeman, B. J. (1997). Guidelines for evaluating intervention programs for children with autism. *Journal of Autism and Developmental Disabilities*, 27, 641–651.

Fryxell, D., & Kennedy, C. H. (1995). Placement along the continuum of services and its impact on students' social relationships. *Journal of the Association for Persons with Severe Handicaps*, 20, 259–269.

Gelzheiser, L. M., McLane, M., Meyers, J., & Pruzek, R. M. (1998). IEP-specified peer interaction needs: Accurate but ignored. *Exceptional Children*, 65, 51–65.

Giangreco, M. F., (1986). Effects of integrated therapy: A pilot study. *Journal of the Association for Persons with Severe Handicaps*, 11, 205–208.

Giangreco, M. F., Cloninger, C. J., & Iverson, V. S. (1993). *Choosing options and accommodations for children (COACH): A guide to planning inclusive education*. Baltimore: Paul H. Brookes.

Giangreco, M. F., Edelman, S. W., Luiselli, T. E. & MacFarland, S. Z. C. (1997). Helping or hovering? Effects of instructional assistant proximity on students with disabilities. *Exceptional Children*, 64, 7–18

Giangreco, M. F., & Putnam, J. W. (1991). Supporting the education of students with severe disabilities in regular education. In L. H. Meyer, C. A. Peck, & L. Brown (Eds.), *Critical issues in the lives of people with severe disabilities* (pp. 245–270). Baltimore: Paul H. Brookes.

Gold, M. W. (1972). Stimulus factors in skill training of the retarded on a complex assembly task: Acquisition, transfer, and retention. *American Journal of Mental Deficiency, 76*, 517–526.

Gothelf, C. R., & Brown, F. (1998). Participation in the education process: Students with severe disabilities. In M. L. Wehmeyer, & D. J. Sands (Eds.). *Making it happen: Student involvement in education planning, decision making, and instruction* (pp. 99–121). Baltimore: Paul H. Brookes.

Grabowski, S. (1997). *Manual for the faculty advisor, Best Buddies Colleges, Eastern Region.* Washington DC: Best Buddies, Eastern Regional Office.

Hall, L. J., McClannahan, L. E., & Krantz, P. J. (1995). Promoting independence in integrated classrooms by teaching aides to use activity schedules and decreased prompts. *Education and Training in Mental Retardation and Developmental Disabilities, 30*, 208–217.

Haring, T. G., & Breen, C. G. (1992). A peer-mediated social network intervention to enhance the social integration of persons with moderate and severe disabilities. *Journal of Applied Behavior Analysis, 25*, 319–334.

Heckman, K. A., Alber, S., Hooper, S., & Heward, W. L. (1998). A comparison of least-to-most prompts and progressive time delay on the disruptive behavior of students with autism. *Journal of Behavioral Education, 8*, 171–201.

Horner, R. H., & Carr, E. G. (1997). Behavior support for students with severe disabilities: functional assessment and comprehensive intervention. *Journal of Special Education, 31*, 84–104.

Hunt, P., & Goetz, L. (1997). Research on inclusive educational programs, practices, and outcomes for students with severe disabilities. *The Journal of Special Education, 31*, 3–29.

Hunt, P., Staub, D., Alwell, M., & Goetz, L. (1994). Achievement by all students within the context of cooperative learning groups. *Journal of the Association for Persons with Severe Handicaps, 19*, 290–301.

Janney, R. E., & Snell, M. E. (2000). *Practices in inclusive schools: Modifying school work.* Baltimore, MD: Paul H. Brookes.

Janney, R. E. & Snell, M. E. (1997). How teachers include students with moderate and severe disabilities in elementary classes: The means and meaning of inclusion. *Journal of the Association for Persons with Severe Handicaps, 22*, 159–169.

Johnson, D. W., & Johnson, F. W. (1997). *Joining together: Group theory and skills* (6th ed.). Upper Saddle River, NJ: Prentice Hall.

Kaiser, A., Hancock, T. B., & Hester, P. P. (1998). Parents as co-inventionists: Research on applications of naturalistic language teaching procedures. *Infants and Young Children, 10* (4), 1–11.

Kamps, D. M., Dugan, E. P., Leonard, B. R., & Daoust, P. M. (1994). Enhanced small group instruction using choral responding and student interaction for children with autism and developmental disabilities. *American Journal of Mental Retardation, 99*, 60–73.

Kamps, D. M., Leonard, B. R., Dugan, E. P., Boland, B., & Greenwood, C. R. (1991). The use of ecobehavioral assessment to identify naturally occurring effective procedures in classrooms serving students with autism and other developmental disabilities. *Journal of Behavioral Education, 1*, 367–397.

Kamps, D. M., Potucek, J., Lopez, A. G., Kravits, T., & Kemmerer, K. (1997). The use of peer networks across multiple settings to improve social interaction for students with autism. *Journal of Behavioral Education, 7*, 335–357.

Kamps, D. M., Walker, D., Locke, P., Delquadri, J., & Hall, R. V. (1990). A comparison of instructional arrangements for children

with autism served in a public school setting. *Education and Treatment of Children, 13*, 197–215.

Keachie, J. (1997, Fall). Social inclusion in a high school: The Peer Connections Program. *Impact, 10*, 18–19.

Kennedy, C. H., Cushing, L. S., & Itkonen, T. (1997). General education participation improves the social contacts and friendship networks of students with severe disabilities. *Journal of Behavior Education, 7*, 167–189.

Kennedy, C. H., Shukla, S., & Fryxell, D. (1997). Comparing the effects of educational placement on the social relationships of intermediate school students with severe disabilities. *Exceptional Children, 64*, 31–47.

Kern, L., Vorndran, C. M., Hilt, A., Ringdahl, J. E., Adelman, B. E., & Dunlap, G. (1998). Choice as an intervention to improve behavior: A review of the literature. *Journal of Behavioral Education, 8*, 151–169.

Kishi, G. S., & Meyer, L. H. (1994). What children report and remember: A six-year follow-up of the effects of social contact between peers with and without severe disabilities. *Journal of the Association for Persons with Severe Handicaps, 19*, 277–289.

Koegel, R. L., & Rincover, A. (1974). Treatment of psychotic children in a classroom environment: I. Learning in a large group. *Journal of Applied Behavior Analysis, 7*, 45–59.

Lehr, D. (1985). Effects of opportunities to practice on learning among students with severe handicaps. *Education and Training of the Mentally Retarded, 20*, 268–274.

Liberty, K. A. (1985). Enhancing instruction for maintenance, generalization, and adaptation. In K. C. Lakin & R. H. Bruininks (Eds.), *Strategies for achieving community integration of developmentally disabled citizens* (pp. 29–71). Baltimore: Paul H. Brookes.

Liberty, K. A., & Haring, N. G. (1990). Introduction to decision rule systems. *Remedial and Special Education, 11*, 32–41.

Liberty, K. A., Haring, N. G., & Martin, M. M. (1981). Teaching new skills to the severely handicapped. *Journal of the Association for the Severely Handicapped, 6*(1), 5–13.

Logan, K. R., Brakeman, R., & Keefe, E. B., (1997). Effects of instructional variables on engaged behavior of students with disabilities in general education classrooms. *Exceptional Children, 63*, 481–497.

Lohrmann-O'Rourke, S., & Zirkel, P. A. (1998). The case law on aversive interventions for students with disabilities. *Exceptional Children, 65*, 101–123.

Mason, S. A., McGee, G. G., Farmer-Dougan, V., & Risley, T. R. (1989). A practical strategy for ongoing reinforcer assessment. *Journal of Applied Behavior Analysis, 22*, 171–179.

McDonnell, J., Thorson, N., & McQuivey, C. (1998). The instructional characteristics of inclusive classes for elementary students with severe disabilities. *Journal of Behavioral Education, 8*, 415–437.

Meyer, R. F. (1997). *Preparing instructional objectives* (3rd ed.) Atlanta, GA: Center for Effective Performance.

Orelove F. P., & Sobsey, D. (1997). *Educating children with multiple disabilities* (3rd ed.). Baltimore: Paul H. Brookes.

Peck, C. A., Donaldson, J., & Pezzoli, M. (1990). Some benefits nonhandicapped adolescents perceive for themselves from their social relationships with peers who have severe handicaps. *Journal of the Association for Persons with Severe Handicaps, 15*, 241–249.

Perske, R. (1988). *Circle of friends: People with disabilities and their friends enrich the lives of one another.* Nashville: Abingdon Press.

Rainforth, B., & England, J. (1997). Collaborations for inclusion. *Education and Treatment of Children*, 20, 85–104.

Rainforth, B., & York-Barr, J. (1997). *Collaborative teams for students with severe disabilities* (2nd ed.). Baltimore: Paul H. Brookes.

Riley, G. A. (1995). Guidelines for devising a hierarchy when fading response prompts. *Education and Training in Mental Retardation and Developmental Disabilities*, 30, 231–242.

Rincover, A., & Koegel, R. L. (1975). Setting generality and stimulus control in autistic children. *Journal of Applied Behavior Analysis*, 8, 235–246.

Roach, V., Ashcroft, J., & Stamp, A. (1995, May). *Winning ways: Creating inclusive schools, classrooms, and communities.* Alexandria, VA: National Association of State Boards of Education.

Roane, H. S., Vollmer, T. R., Ringdahl, & Marcus, B. A. (1998). Evaluation of a brief stimulus preference assessment. *Journal of Applied Behavior Analysis*, 31, 605–620.

Rotholz, D. A. (1987). Current considerations on the use of one-to-one instruction with autistic students: Review and recommendations. *Education and Treatment of Children*, 10, 271–278.

Salisbury, C. L., Evans, I. M., & Palombaro, M. M. (1997). Collaborative problem-solving to promote the inclusion of young children with significant disabilities in primary grades. *Exceptional Children*, 63, 195–209.

Salisbury, C. L., Gallucci, C., Palombaro, M. M., & Peck, C. A. (1995). Strategies that promote social relations among elementary students with and without severe disabilities in inclusive schools. *Exceptional Children*, 62, 125–137.

Salisbury, C. L., Mangino, M., Rainforth, B., Syryca, S., & Palombaro, M. M. (1994). Promoting inclusion of young children with disabilities in the primary grades: A curriculum adaptation process. *Journal of Early Intervention*, 18, 311–322.

Salisbury, C. L., & Palombaro, M. M. (Eds.) (1993). *No problem: Working things out our way.* Pittsburgh, PA: Allegheny Singer Research Institute, Child and Family Studies Program.

Schnorr, R. F. (1997). From enrollment to membership: "Belonging" in middle and high school classes. *Journal of the Association for Persons with Severe Handicaps*, 22, 1–15.

Schuster, J. W., Morse, T. E., Ault, M. J., Doyle, P. M., Crawford, M. R., & Wolery, M. (1998). Constant time delay with chained tasks: A review of the literature. *Education and Treatment of Children*, 21, 74–106.

Shukla, S., Kennedy, C. H., & Cushing, L. S. (1998). Adult influence on the participation of peers without disabilities in peer support programs. *Journal of Behavioral Education*, 8, 397–413.

Singleton, K. C., Schuster, J. W., & Ault, M. J. (1995). Simultaneous prompting in a small group instructional arrangement. *Education and Training in Mental Retardation and Developmental Disabilities*, 30, 218–230.

Slavin, R. E. (1991). Cooperative learning and group contingencies. *Journal of Behavioral Education*, 1, 105–115.

Snell, M. E., (1997). Teaching children and young adults with mental retardation in school programs: Current research. *Behaviour Change*, 14, 73–105.

Snell, M. E. & Colley, K. (2000). Approaches for facilitating positive social relationships. In M. E. Snell & R. E. Janney (Eds.). *Practices for inclusive schools: Social relationships and peer support.* Baltimore: Paul H. Brookes.

Snell, M. E., & Janney, R. E. (2000 a). *Practices for inclusive schools: Collaborative teaming.* Baltimore, MD: Paul H. Brookes.

Snell, M. E., & Janney, R. E. (2000 b). *Practices for inclusive schools: Social relationships and peer support.* Baltimore, MD: Paul H. Brookes.

Staub, D., & Peck, C. A. (1995). What are the outcomes for nondisabled students? *Educational Leadership*, 52(4), 36–40.

Staub, D., Schwartz, I. S., Gallucci, C., & Peck, C. A. (1994). Four portraits of friendship at an inclusive school. *Journal of the Association for Persons with Severe Handicaps*, 19, 314–325.

Staub, D., Spaulding, M., Peck, C. A., Gallucci, C., & Schwartz, I. S. (1996). Using nondisabled peers to support the inclusion of students with disabilities. *Journal of the Association for Persons with Severe Handicaps*, 21, 194–205.

Stinson, D. M., Gast, D. L., Wolery, M., & Collins, B. C. (1991). Acquisition of nontargeted information during small-group instruction. *Exceptionality* 2(2), 65–80.

Strully, J., & Strully, C. (1989). Friendship as an educational goal. In S. Stainback, W. Stainback, & M. Forest (Eds.), *Educating all students in the mainstream of regular education* (pp. 59–68). Baltimore: Paul H. Brookes.

Udvari-Solner, A. (1994). A decision-making model for curricular adaptations in cooperative groups. In J. S. Thousand, R. Villa, & A. I. Nevins (Eds.), *Creativity and cooperative learning* (pp. 59–77). Baltimore: Paul H. Brookes.

Vandercook, T., York, J., & Forest, M. (1989). The McGill action planning system (MAPS): A strategy for building the vision. *Journal of the Association for Persons with Severe Handicaps*, 14, 205–215.

Villa, R. A., Thousand, J. S., Stainback, W., & Stainback, S. (Eds.) (1992). *Restructuring for caring and effective education.* Baltimore: Paul H. Brookes.

Wehmeyer, M. L. (1998). Student involvement in education planning, decision making, and instruction: An idea whose time has arrived. In M. L. Wehmeyer, & D. J. Sands (Eds.). *Making it happen: Student involvement in education planning, decision making, and instruction.* (pp. 3–23). Baltimore: Paul H. Brookes.

Wehmeyer, M. L., Agran, M., & Hughes, C. (1998). *Teaching self-determination to students with disabilities.* Baltimore: Paul H. Brookes.

Werts, M. G., Caldwell, N. K., & Wolery, M. (1996). Peer modeling of response chains: Observational learning by students with disabilities. *Journal of Applied Behavior Analysis*, 29, 53–66.

Werts, M. G., Wolery, M., Snyder, E. D., & Caldwell, N. K. (1996). Teachers' perceptions of the supports critical to the success of inclusion programs. *Journal of the Association for Persons with Severe Handicaps*, 21, 9–21.

Whalen, C., Schuster, J. W., & Hemmeter, M. L. (1996). The use of unrelated instructive feedback when teaching in a small group instructional arrangement. *Education and Training in Mental Retardation and Developmental Disabilities*, 31, 188–202.

Whitney-Thomas, J., Shaw, D., Honey, K., & Butterworth, J. (1998). Building a future: A study of student participation in person-centered planning. *Journal of the Association for Persons with Severe Handicaps*, 23, 119–133.

Williams, R. (1991). Choices, communication, and control: A call for expanding them in the lives of people with severe disabilities. In L. H. Meyer, C. A. Peck, & L. Brown (Eds.), *Critical issues in the lives of people with severe disabilities* (pp. 543–544). Baltimore: Paul H. Brookes.

Wolf, M. M. (1978). Social validity: The case for subjective measurement, or how applied behavior analysis is finding its heart. *Journal of Applied Behavior Analysis*, 11, 203–214.

Wolfe, P. S. (1994). Judgment of the social validity of instructional strategies used in community-based instructional sites. *Journal of the Association for Persons with Severe Handicaps*, 19, 43–51.

Wolery, M., Ault, M. J., & Doyle, P. M. (1992). *Teaching students with moderate to severe disabilities*. New York: Longman Press.

Wolery, M., Ault, M. J., Doyle, P. M., Gast, D. L., & Griffen, A. K. (1992). Choral and individual responding during small group instruction: Identification of interactional effects. *Education and Treatment of Children*, 15, 289–309.

Wolery, M., & Gast, D. L. (1984). Effective and efficient procedures for the transfer of stimulus control. *Topics in Early Childhood Special Education*, 4, 57–77.

Worrall, R. S. (1990). Detecting health fraud in the field of learning disabilities. *Journal of Learning Disabilities*, 23, 207–212.

York-Barr, J. (Ed.) (1997). *Creating inclusive school communities*. Baltimore: Paul H. Brookes.

Measurement, Analysis, and Evaluation

Fredda Brown
Martha E. Snell

To evaluate the impact of a school program on a student, educators must formulate specific strategies for measurement. Two basic reasons for developing measurement strategies are (a) to document what has occurred and (b) to identify the variables responsible for the occurrence (Wacker, 1989). A third reason for developing measurement strategies is to enable teachers to better predict future performance, because prediction helps teachers decide if program modifications are necessary.

With the increasing focus on educating students with severe disabilities alongside their typically developing peers in regular education settings, data collection strategies become more of a challenge. Each teacher must balance the need for data to make instructional decisions and to evaluate program effectiveness, with the needs of the regular classroom. Continuous evaluation of student progress is an integral part of the teaching-learning process and should result in the identification of concerns and difficulties quickly and provide a basis for immediate action

(Cullen & Pratt, 1992). Although many teachers question the value of data and find data difficult to manage (Farlow & Snell, 1994; Fisher & Lindsey-Walters, 1987), a growing amount of evidence indicates that teachers make better instructional decisions when they base them on student performance data (Farlow & Snell, 1989; Haring, Liberty, & White, 1981; Meyer & Janney, 1989; Utley, Zigmond, & Strain, 1987). Professionals need to choose data collection strategies that are unobtrusive, but still provide sufficient information to determine program effectiveness (Test & Spooner, 1996). There is an obvious need for data collection strategies that are user friendly (Meyer & Janney, 1989). According to Meyer and Janney (1989), user-friendly methods are those that can be managed in real classrooms and that are reflective of meaningful outcomes (not just isolated behaviors).

Teachers should be concerned with two basic levels of measurement, especially in inclusive settings. These are *outcome measures* and *process measures* (Haring & Breen, 1989). Process measures focus on fine-grain, small

173

units of behavior, such as the individual responses within a complex chain or performance of the entire chain (e.g., steps in a hairbrushing task analysis; frequency of correct signs) (Haring & Breen, 1989). Outcome measures do not provide this level of detailed information on behaviors that occur within a situation. Rather, these measures offer information regarding the general effect of a program on a person's quality of life. Focusing on a specific, discrete target behavior lacks the breadth necessary to assess the broader impact of interventions (Storey, 1997). These measures typically represent only a temporary change in a controlled setting; more meaningful measurement would reflect a range of significant outcomes for the individual, school, family, and community (Meyer & Janney, 1989). As described in chapters 3 and 4, a broad outcome framework, such as the one described by Billingsley, Gallucci, Peck, Schwartz, and Staub (1996), which includes the domains of skills, membership and relationships, is necessary to represent a meaningful educational experience for students with severe disabilities.

It is critical to focus on outcome measures of behavior in supported education contexts (Haring & Breen, 1989). According to Haring and Breen, outcome measures that reflect the success of an inclusive education program include acceptance, friendships, and social participation. Social participation includes such things as the role of the student in the social network, the number of after-school outings with nondisabled friends, and the time spent in social interactions with nondisabled peers. Meyer and Evans (1993) included in their criteria for successful outcomes of behavioral interventions those related to self-determination and quality of life, such as less restrictive placements, greater participation in integrated school experiences, subjective quality-of-life improvements (e.g., happiness, satisfaction, choices, and control), improvements perceived by significant others, and expanded social relationships and informal support networks. Gothelf and Brown (1998) describe the case of a young man who lived in a facility where he received contingent electric shock for the self-injurious behavior of scratching. He wore a shock device 24 hours per day at his school program and in his group home. After many thousands of shocks, his self-injury was significantly reduced, although not entirely. Using the process measure of "rate of scratching" as the only measure of success, it could be concluded that the contingent electric shock was effective. However, Gothelf and Brown point out that

the program was far from effective, because there was little impact on the quality of his life (outcome measures). The following list reflects how ineffective the aversive program *was* on the quality of his life:

Wearing a shock device 24 hours each day

Inability to manage his own behavior without the shock device

Living in a group home with other individuals who had severe behavior problems

Having no control over daily activities (e.g., what to eat; when to go to bed or wake up)

Going to school only with individuals who had severe problem behaviors

Limited social interaction with individuals without disabilities

Limited social interaction with unpaid individuals

Self-reports of being unhappy

No control over his own future

Living far from family (p. 114)

Measurement must reach beyond the traditional assessment of skill increase or behavior reduction to assess the outcomes that make a significant difference in the individual's life. In the previous example of the young man receiving an aversive program, significant outcomes would include, for example, self-management of his behavior, living with a roommate of his choice or alone if he chose, designing his own schedule of activities, pursuing and acquiring a job of his preference, and selecting his own personal care assistants. However, process data are still needed to guide the instruction (Haring & Breen, 1989) and are necessary for measurement of the skill domain.

This chapter reviews a variety of outcome and process measures, as well as some basic concepts, such as defining behavior, measuring behavior, determining reliability, designing data sheets, and graphing data. Furthermore, we discuss measurement and its meaningful implementation within the context of current best practices and philosophy.

Measurement

Data, if wisely used, can provide information critical to the development, evaluation, and revision of instructional efforts (Farlow & Snell, 1994). However, measurements of behavior change are useless if they do not reflect meaningful information. Two components must be considered to determine if a measurement system is meaningful.

- Data must be sufficiently accurate, or reliable.
- Data must reflect important behavior.

Making Measurement Meaningful

Data should reflect important and significant behaviors. Accurate and reliable data are not sufficient. For example, a teacher can accurately measure the number of times Jenny was able to complete a preschool puzzle; however, because a preschool puzzle is not age-appropriate for Jenny, who is in fifth grade, it would not be a meaningful measure. Teams should consider a series of questions to determine if their measurement strategies are meaningful:

- Do these data measure behaviors or skills that are valued by the student, his or her parents, and the community or society?
- Do these data reflect the qualitative changes that we hope to see in this student?
- Are the changes in the student significant?

Many efforts have been made to describe the criteria for evaluating the validity and importance of behavior changes. Researchers and clinicians have used the following five criteria to evaluate the success of behavioral change efforts: (a) statistical significance, (b) clinical significance, (c) social validity, (d) educational validity, and (e) quality of life.

Statistical Significance

Experimental or *statistical significance* is the comparison between behavior during an intervention and what the behavior would have been if the intervention had not been implemented (Kazdin, 1976; Risley, 1970). Often, statistical analysis is used to evaluate the success of an intervention in a research investigation, but it is not sufficient as a sole criterion for evaluating change, nor is it practical for teams to apply in school.

Clinical Significance

Therapeutic or *clinical significance* is the importance of the change in behavior achieved (Kazdin, 1976), or the comparison between the change in behavior that has occurred and the level of change required for the individual to more adequately function in society (Risley,

1970). In other words, if the result of an intervention makes no improvement in the student's life, even though there is statistical significance, the change does not meet the criterion of clinical significance.

For example, a teacher may implement an intervention that increases a student's independent eating from participation in no steps of the routine to participation in five steps. At first glance, the change from zero to five steps may appear significant. After all, independent eating is a functional skill. However, if those five steps are components such as look at the teacher, look at the spoon, touch the spoon, and track the spoon, some people may not consider the progress to be clinically significant. That is not to say that the changes should not be encouraged and reinforced, but as they stand, they do not allow the student more *independence* in eating (see discussions on partial participation in chapters 3 and 4 for clinically significant responses).

Social Validity

Social validity also refers to the significance of a change in an individual's life (see chapter 4 for discussion of social validity). In an analysis of the development of applied behavior analysis, Baer, Wolf, and Risley (1987) state: "We may have taught many social skills without examining whether they actually furthered the subject's social life; many courtesy skills without examining whether anyone actually noticed or cared; many safety skills without examining whether the subject was actually safer thereafter; many language skills without measuring whether the subject actually used them to interact differently than before; many on-task skills without measuring the actual value of those tasks; and, in general, many survival skills without examining the subject's actual subsequent survival" (p. 322).

Social validity is a concept that addresses qualitative aspects of the educational program. It focuses on the acceptability of the educational goals, the instructional methods used, and the importance and social acceptability of the behavior change (Kazdin, 1977; Wolf, 1978). Social validation procedures can be used to determine whether or not the learned behavior is functional or meaningful (Kazdin, 1980). There are two methods for determining social validity. *Social comparison* compares the student's performance with the performance of the student's nondisabled peers. This standard checks against imposing unnecessarily rigorous performance criteria or stopping instruction before the student reaches a socially acceptable level of performance.

> At Timothy's team meeting it was suggested that a behavioral objective be developed to teach him to sit in his seat, and keep his hands in his lap and his feet on the floor for 15 minutes. Mrs. Johnson, his general education teacher, questioned the objective, "I'm not sure ANY of the children in the class can sit like that for 15 minutes!" Mr. Grayson, Timothy's special education teacher, suggested that he observe Mrs. Lombardi's class during a variety of activities and record data on a few typically developing children in the class to determine the range of the duration and the "styles of sitting" displayed by the other students.

The second method used to determine social validity is *subjective evaluation*. In this method, the opinions of significant people, because of their expertise or familiarity with the student, are used to judge the significance of the behavior change. For example, Voeltz, Wuerch, and Bockhaut (1982) validated the outcome of training by asking parents, institutional and community program staff, and nondisabled peers to view pairs of videotapes taken 2 months apart that portrayed adolescents with severe handicaps during their free time. The students who received leisure-skill training during the intervening 2 months were viewed as being more interested in their activity, "looking more OK," and having a more worthwhile activity than were students who had not received training. Such procedures provide some assurance that a student's behavior change is meaningful and will, thus, facilitate functioning within natural environments.

Educational Validity

Voeltz and Evans (1983), in response to the narrow ways in which special education outcomes have been evaluated, offered the term *educational validity* to describe a more inclusive set of criteria for program evaluation for individuals with severe disabilities. To demonstrate educational validity, three criteria must be met. First, *internal validity* (or procedural reliability) criteria must be met. That is, teachers should feel confident that the behavior change occurred as a function of the educational intervention. Second, *educational integrity* should be demonstrated. Educational integrity refers to the implementation of the procedures. It answers the question, "Did the educational intervention occur as specified in the treatment plan?" The final criterion is the qualitative significance of the behavior change. Teams must question whether the behavior

change benefited the student and was considered to be valuable by significant others in the student's natural environment (Voeltz & Evans, 1983).

Quality of Life

In addition to the qualitative aspects of social and educational validity, other criteria are increasingly being suggested as critical in the evaluation of program success. Meyer and Evans (1989) delineate eight possible outcomes to evaluate the effectiveness of a program:

- Improvement in target behavior
- Acquisition of alternative skills and positive behaviors
- Positive collateral effects and absence of side effects
- Reduced need for and use of medical and crisis management services for the individual or others
- Less restrictive placements and greater participation in integrated community experiences
- Subjective quality-of-life improvement—happiness, satisfaction, and choices for the individual
- Perceptions of improvement by the family and significant others
- Expanded social relationships and informal support networks

Certain measurement procedures in community settings promote less than normalized lifestyles and interactions, thus detracting from the individual's quality of life. For example, teaching staff may be so interested in recording prompting levels necessary to complete a leisure activity that they forget to notice whether anyone is having fun (Brown, 1991; Brown & Lehr, 1993)! Professionals are recognizing that critical components of program evaluation are choice and control over one's life (e.g., Bannerman, Sheldon, Sherman, & Harchik, 1990; Brown, 1991; Brown & Lehr, 1993; Meyer & Evans, 1989).

In chapter 4 we discussed the importance of having each individual make meaningful choices concerning the organization and content of his or her day (Brown, 1991). Such choices include the decision to escape, refuse to participate in activities, and to "just say no!" It is critical that each individual, especially at home, have control over the activities in which he or she participates, the option to refuse participation, the sequence in which the activities take place, and the times at which activities occur. Meyer, St. Peter, and Park-Lee (1986) delineate many examples of opportunities to make daily choices. These include deciding what to eat for a meal or a snack, deciding what clothes to wear, deciding what to do in free time, choosing television shows, deciding whether to participate in group activities, deciding if and when to make phone calls, and deciding when to go to bed. The occurrences of choice making and other variables must be related to quality of life be measured and monitored.

As discussed in chapter 4, instructional programs should be designed to teach and monitor choice opportunities in natural contexts. Choice can be systematically taught and evaluated in the same ways as other observable behaviors. Choice is especially critical for students who, because of limited motor skills or the presence of serious problem behaviors, have difficulty expressing choice or do so in inappropriate ways (Brown, 1991; Reichle, York, & Eynon, 1989; Gothelf & Brown, 1996). By identifying choice as a behavioral objective for students, teachers have the advantage of assessing and determining the appropriate level or form that choices take (e.g., selecting between two concrete objects using a visual glance, selecting between symbols representing activities, selecting to leave one's job). Teachers should design ways to monitor progress (e.g., frequency of initiated choices across the day, percent correct pointing responses), and plan for advancing students to "higher" levels of choice in a timely fashion (Brown, 1991, Gothelf & Brown, 1996).

Thus, recent trends look beyond simple quantitative reports and see each individual within the context of a meaningful life. Measurement strategies must support the evaluation of these important outcomes. The next sections discuss specific strategies relevant to process measures.

Making Behavior Observable and Measurable

When a team has decided that a change in a student's behavior is a goal (e.g., increase social interactions, decrease inappropriate verbalizations, extend use of sign language to peers), one of the first steps is to *define the behavior*. A precise description of the behavior is necessary to ensure that everyone is observing the same thing. For example, if "improve manners" is a goal, it is unlikely that the student, his or her parents, teachers, teaching assistants, and therapists automatically agree on what "appropriate manners" are. To some, appropriate table manners mean sitting up straight, arms off the table, napkin in lap, and chewing with one's mouth closed. Others, however, may feel that some of these components are unnecessarily

formal. Indeed, for some students, eating with their mouths closed is physically unrealistic.

To prevent ambiguity, an operational definition of the target behavior must be created; that is, the behavior must be described in a way that is *observable and measurable*. Agreement on what constitutes a behavior is critical to the development of reliable and valid measurement and evaluation systems. The description of a behavior must be specific enough to allow two or more observers to read the definition and make the same judgment about the occurrence, or nonoccurrence, of the behavior (Baer, Wolf, & Risley, 1968). Table 5–1 demonstrates the difference between

TABLE 5–1
Vague Versus Observable Descriptions of Behavior

Student	Vague	Observable
Timothy	Interacts appropriately with peers	Takes turns during board games
		Waves "hi" to peers when enters classroom in the morning
		Passes and receives materials to and from peers during group activities
	Improves grooming	Wipes face after meals
		Asks for assistance to tie shoes
	Increases academic skills	Signs or verbally identifies colors
		Signs or verbally identifies shapes
		Signs or verbally identifies pictures in a book
Christine	Increases community participation	Goes to grocery store with peer once each week to purchase snacks for drama class after-school rehearsals
		Uses communication device to greet the cashier in the grocery store
	Understands job responsibilities	Completes sequence of job tasks recorded on communication device
		Requests help when needed during job tasks

vague terms and descriptions that are observable and measurable. These terms represent a sample of the goals determined for Timothy and Christine. The concepts of "functional" and "meaningful" behaviors should not be confused with the standard of describing behaviors in observable and measurable ways. Designing an operational definition to objectively describe a behavior does not ensure that the definition is functional or meaningful to an individual. For example, the statement, "When shown either a red or blue block, Jenny will point to the red or blue block placed in front of her," is observable and measurable. It is not, however, a meaningful activity for Jenny.

Quantitative Measures

Teams must feel confident that each student's instructional program is effective in helping the student accomplish the objectives delineated in his or her Individualized Educational Plan (IEP). Thus, process measures (or formative evaluation) are crucial to the ongoing assessment of intervention strategies. Many teachers resist data collection because they feel they cannot afford the time. However, such teachers may find 4 months into the school year that their intervention is not working! A student with severe disabilities, or any other student, cannot afford to participate in an ineffective intervention for 4 months! Frequent and ongoing data collection provides teachers with ongoing feedback about the student's progress and provides important information to guide program modification.

Rationale

Research has shown that instructional decisions are enhanced with the use of data and that such decisions positively influence student performance (Farlow & Snell, 1989; Farlow & Snell, 1994; Fuchs & Fuchs, 1986; Holvoet, O'Neil, Chazdon, Carr, & Warner, 1983; Utley, Zigmond, & Strain, 1987; White, 1986). Fuchs and Fuchs (1986) found that teachers are more effective and efficient when they use student performance data rather than teacher judgment for making instructional decisions. These researchers also found greater improvements in student performance when the teachers used graphed data rather than ungraphed data to make their decisions. Utley, Zigmond, and Strain (1987) found that teachers, and teachers-in-training, make more accurate judgments about student performance when they use

data (graphed, ungraphed, or both) than when they base their judgments on observation.

When teachers begin to measure individual student performance, some other advantages become obvious. Precise measurement of behavior allows teams to see even small changes in the behavior, giving everyone the message "Keep up the good work!" It also discourages teams from changing a strategy that has some promise. Continuing an instructional strategy is frustrating when one does not feel that any progress is being made.

Student performance data can enhance communication with others in the same ways that precise definitions of behavior do. Saying, based on intuition, that someone is "Doing better in cooking," or "seems to be using signs more frequently," is vague, subjective, and possibly inaccurate. Making a statement, such as "Jenny is now preparing a sandwich with only two verbal prompts" or "Timothy now waves hello correctly four out of five opportunities each day," communicates a clearer and more objective message.

Testing and Training Data

Different levels of evaluation can occur for each objective identified on an IEP. *Test* conditions and *training* conditions provide two conditions for obtaining valuable data (Farlow & Snell, 1994). *Testing* means that a person's performance is checked under criterion conditions (i.e., conditions that as closely as possible use natural contexts, cues, and consequences). Thus, the teacher typically provides no prompting or teaching assistance, no reinforcement for task success or improvement, nor any corrections. The goal of testing is to learn about a student's current performance under criterion conditions (specified in the objective), not to teach the student.

During *training*, or *teaching*, conditions, data are recorded while a student is assisted as needed to "get responding going," is provided instructional feedback, is given corrections for errors, and is provided with appropriate reinforcement. Learning is the goal of training, so conditions are planned to promote improvement in performance and to advance the learner through the various stages of learning.

Typically, a student's performance under testing conditions is less proficient than under training conditions, simply because of the absence of prompts and reinforcement. Test data thus represent conservative measures of learning but may more accurately represent a student's performance in natural, unaided situations. Test data taken on a skill before a teaching program is initiated is called *baseline* data; data taken on a skill under testing conditions once a teaching program has been initiated is called *probe* data. Because probe data are not collected each and every time teaching occurs, instructors avoid the problem of trying to teach and collect data at the same time (Test & Spooner, 1996).

> *When Christine was first learning how to use her communication board to greet the cashier in the grocery store, her teacher initially "tested" her at the grocery store (i.e., she did a baseline test). Test data showed that Christine was unable to activate the correct greeting symbol. Instruction was implemented to teach her this skill during daily sessions at school, in which her teacher recorded training data. When Christine went to the grocery store, her teacher recorded test data (probe data) to determine how she was performing the skill in the natural context.*

Measurement Strategies

In this section, we review several ways to measure student performance. The strategy selected should suit the behavior to be measured and the situation. Some of the strategies are easy to use and require little time away from the usual routine. A few of the strategies, however, take more planning and time. Therefore, they may be used when a challenging situation in the class warrants additional investigation. Table 5–2 summarizes these measurement strategies: (a) permanent products, (b) frequency recording, (c) percentage, (d) rate, (e) duration, (f) task analytic measurement, and (g) interval recording and time sampling.

Permanent Products

Many behaviors have a concrete result, or product, that lasts. Unlike behaviors that must be directly observed as they occur, behaviors that have an outcome can be evaluated after the individual has performed the behavior. For example, parents need not sit by their child's bed all night long to observe toileting accidents. Rather, evidence of accidents can be observed by looking at or touching the child's sheet in the morning. A teacher who is interested in measuring the number of dishes a student can wash in 20 minutes can simply count the dishes washed and in the drainer after 20 minutes. The teacher does not

have to observe the student washing each dish. Because measurement of permanent products does not require continuous observation, it is convenient for classroom use. Permanent product measures provide opportunities to detect error and quality patterns (e.g., the tops of the plates and cups are clean, but the bottoms are still dirty).

Frequency Recording

Some behaviors are transitory and must be measured as they occur. Frequency recording measures the number of times a behavior (appropriate or inappropriate) occurs within a specified period of time (e.g., the number of times that a student throws his or her work materials onto the floor during a 30-minute work session, the number of times that the student greets people appropriately throughout the school day). Frequency has been used to measure many types of behaviors. For example, Kennedy and Itkonen (1994) measured the frequency of contacts that three high school students with severe disabilities had with their nondisabled peers, and Cooper and Browder (1998) counted the frequency of independent choices three adults with severe disabilities made in a variety of fast food restaurants.

In order to have meaningful frequency data, it is necessary to specify the time period and to compare data from the same time period only. For example, a teacher may report that her student bit her hand 15 times on Monday, but only 5 times on Tuesday. This certainly sounds like excellent progress. However, if the teacher observed the student for 3 hours on Monday, but only for 1 hour on Tuesday, it is not possible to conclude whether there was any progress.

Behaviors measured in this way should be readily divided into discrete units, with a clear beginning and end, and be easily visible and countable. For example, stereotyped behavior, such as hand waving, may occur at such a high rate that it is impossible to count accurately. Attempting a frequency count of vocalizations may also be difficult if each vocalization does not have a clear beginning and a clear end.

Finally, behaviors measured in this way should be relatively uniform in length and not occur for long periods of time. For example, a parent may report that the child sucked his or her thumb only two times. This is not helpful information if each occurrence of thumb sucking lasts 45 minutes! The frequency, in this case, does not reflect the amount of behavior.

TABLE 5–2

Measurement Procedures Appropriate for Classroom

Description of Measurement	Advantages	Disadvantages	Examples of Behaviors Measured
Permanent Products Direct measurement of lasting and concrete results of a target behavior	• Does not require continuous observation • Permits analysis of products for error patterns	• Behavior must have a tangible result • No immediate feedback	• Appropriate behaviors: the number of newsletters folded and stapled • Inappropriate behaviors: the number of buttons ripped from clothing
Frequency Recording The number of times a behavior occurs within a specified period of time	• Is useful with a wide variety of discrete behaviors • Can be easily accomplished in the classroom • May be converted to a rate	• Necessitates continuous attention during the observation period • Yields less accurate results with high rate behaviors or behaviors of varying duration • Inappropriate for behaviors of long duration	• Appropriate behaviors: spontaneous requests for materials needed; initiation of greetings • Inappropriate behaviors: talkouts, hits, incorrect color sorting
Percentage The number correct compared with the number of opportunities (or intervals)	• Useful when the number of opportunities varies across sessions • Can be used to report task analytic measurements, duration, interval, and time sampling data	• Cannot distinguish the number of opportunities from the score • Cannot be used if there is no ceiling on the number of opportunities	• Appropriate behavior: independent eating, correct signing • Inappropriate behavior: hits, self-injury, cursing, etc, if measured through interval recording or time sampling
Rate The frequency of a behavior and its relation to time expressed as a ratio	• Useful when the number of opportunities varies across sessions • Reflects proficiency	• Cannot distinguish the total time of the observation period	• Appropriate behavior: vocational tasks completed per minute, social interactions per hour • Inappropriate behavior: call outs per class period
Duration The total amount of time in which a targeted behavior occurs in a specified observation	• Yields a precise record of the length of the occurrence of a behavior • May be used to record the duration of each incident of behavior	• Necessitates continuous attention during the observation period • Requires a stopwatch for best accuracy • Inappropriate for frequent behaviors of short duration	• Appropriate behavior: attending to lesson, completion of hygiene routine • Inappropriate behavior: tantrums, stereotyped behavior

Description of Measurement	Advantages	Disadvantages	Examples of Behaviors Measured
Task Analytic Measurement A record of the performance of each step in a sequence of behaviors comprising a task	• Useful in most skills in domestic, vocational, leisure and community domains • May be used to guide instruction • Enables a measurement of each behavior that comprises a skill • Can be summarized as a meaningful percentage or number of steps	• Requires a good task analysis of the skill being measured • Not suitable for measuring inappropriate behaviors • May focus too much on motor skills, neglecting qualitative aspects of the task	• Appropriate behaviors: bedmaking, playing a CD, assembly tasks, preparing a snack
Interval Recording A record of the occurrence of behavior within each segment of time (intervals) within a single observation	• Requires less effort than continuous frequency or duration methods • Does not require as precise a definition of a unit of behavior • Applicable to a wide range of behaviors	• Provides an estimate only • The size of the interval must be appropriate for the behavior frequency • Accuracy is facilitated by timers or taperecorded countings of intervals	• Appropriate and inappropriate behaviors: any of the behaviors listed for frequency or duration
Whole Interval Records whether behavior occurred continuously throughout the interval	• Useful when it is important to know that the behavior is not interrupted	• Underestimates the magnitude of the target behavior	
Partial Interval Records whether behavior occurred at any time within the interval	• Useful for behaviors that may occur in fleeting moments	• Overestimates the magnitude of the target behavior	
Momentary Time Sampling Records whether behavior occurred at the moment the interval ends	• Useful for behaviors that tend to persist for a while • Does not require continuous observation • Can be used with more than one student at a time	• Must sample at frequent and relatively short intervals	

Other measures would be more appropriate for such behaviors. Frequency recordings would accurately measure Jenny's correct coin and value identification and the number of times Timothy waved to his teacher and peers.

Percentage

A percentage score can be used when a behavior can occur a fixed number of times in an observation session. This type of measure is used frequently in the regular education system to evaluate mastery of academic concepts. Percentage is calculated by dividing the number of behaviors observed by the number of opportunities to perform that behavior. For example, Timothy passed the materials to his neighbor when it was his turn at two of the five opportunities occurring during the morning song, or 40% of the opportunities.

Percentage measures are not appropriate when the number of opportunities to perform a behavior is not fixed or controlled. For example, it is inappropriate to write an objective that states that Timothy will "greet his peers 80% of the time," if there is no ceiling on the number of times Timothy has the opportunity to greet his peers.

Rate

Rate can be used to determine the frequency of a behavior and its relation to time. A rate is expressed by the ratio of the number of behaviors divided by the unit of time (e.g., Jessie threw her materials on the floor 15 times in a 30-minute session, or 0.5 times per minute). In vocational training situations, for example, educators want to see an increase in the number of custodial cleaning tasks completed in a certain amount of time (e.g., from washing 5 windows in 30 minutes, or .17 per minute, to 10 windows in 30 minutes, or .33 per minute).

Rate is also a helpful measure when the observation time of a session varies, for example, to measure the number of spoonfuls of food Christine eats with her self-feeder when the length of lunch time varies. An advantage of using rate to measure performance is that rate reflects both accuracy and speed, or fluency of performance, rather than just accuracy (Billingsley & Liberty, 1982).

Duration

A duration recording is used if the focus of concern is the amount of time an individual is engaged in a spe-

cific behavior or activity. Sometimes, it is desirable for a person to increase the amount of time engaged in an activity (e.g., brushing teeth, exercising), and sometimes, it is desirable for an individual to decrease the amount of time spent in an activity (e.g., watching television, displaying self-injurious behavior). Duration measures the total amount of time in which a targeted behavior occurs.

Duration measures have been used to record the length of time required to complete a buttoning task (Kramer & Whitehurst, 1981), to record the time that students were engaged in social interaction (Gaylord-Ross, Haring, Breen, & Pitts-Conway, 1984), and to identify reinforcer preferences by comparing duration of time spent operating various battery-controlled devices (Wacker, Berg, Wiggins, Muldoon, & Cavanaugh, 1985).

Duration can be recorded in three ways: (a) a total duration, (b) a percentage of time, and (c) by measuring each occurrence. In the total duration method, the teacher records the total amount of time the individual spent engaged in the behavior in the observation period. For example, the teacher may be interested in measuring the amount of time Timothy spends engaged in independent play. Before starting the duration measure, the teacher must operationally define appropriate and independent play for Timothy, making sure that it is possible to clearly determine the onset and termination of the behavior. The teacher can then monitor the behavior using a stopwatch. All the teacher has to do is to start the stopwatch when Timothy starts playing. As soon as he stops playing (e.g., participates instead in self-stimulatory behavior), the teacher stops the stopwatch. The teacher starts and stops the stopwatch accordingly for the course of the playtime. The amount of time accumulated on the stopwatch at the end of the playtime reflects a total duration.

A percentage of time can be derived by simply dividing the total time by the length of the playtime. For example, Timothy may have played for a total of 5 minutes in a 15-minute playtime. The following equation represents the process for determining the percentage of time:

$$\frac{\text{Total duration of behavior}}{\text{Length of observation period}} = \frac{5 \text{ min}}{15 \text{ min}} = 33\%$$

Although the duration measure is simple and accurate (if the behavior is clearly defined), another piece of information makes the duration measure even more informative: the frequency of each occurrence. For example, we know that Timothy participated in playing for 5 minutes (or 33% of play time); however, these figures do not indicate whether he played for 5 minutes in a row or if he played for only 30 seconds at a time but kept returning to the play area. Such information may be critical in determining the type of intervention to use with Timothy to increase his play skills. The method of measuring each occurrence provides this information. This method is, however, more time-consuming than the previous two methods and so should be used only when this level of information is essential. To measure the occurrences, the teacher would start the stopwatch when Timothy started to play, turn the stopwatch off when he stopped playing, and then record the duration on a data sheet. The teacher would then return the stopwatch to 0. When Timothy started to play again, the teacher would start the stopwatch and have it continue until he stopped playing. When Timothy stopped again, the teacher would record this duration, and so on. At the end of the observation period (e.g., 15 minutes) the teacher would have a record of total duration (e.g., 5 minutes), as well as a count of the number of times Timothy started and stopped playing (e.g., 8 times). In this case, the goal would be to increase the duration of time Timothy spent playing and to decrease the number of times that he got distracted from playing.

Task Analytic Measurement

Task analytic measurement focuses on a student's performance on a sequence, or chain, of behaviors during teaching or during testing. This type of measurement is the most frequently used method of instruction and evaluation of student performance of routines or complex activities. To implement task analytic measurement, a teacher conducts a task analysis (see chapter 4), designs a data sheet to record student performance, and then records the student's performance on each of the steps delineated in the task analysis (or some portion of the steps if using backward or forward chaining).

During teaching, the teacher may evaluate the student by recording a plus (+) or minus (−), the prompt level (e.g., verbal or physical prompt required for the student to complete the step), or another type of measure (e.g., the amount of time to complete a step). If the teacher is using a total task chaining strategy (see

chapter 4), then all of the steps in the task analysis are scored. If the teacher is using a partial participation strategy, forward chaining, or backward chaining, then only the steps that the student is working on are scored. Table 5–3 shows a task analysis for the skill of making a peanut butter sandwich. Because Jenny can participate extensively in this type of activity, her teacher chose to teach the task using a total task chaining strategy and a least-to-most prompting procedure. It was decided that the two levels of prompt that require physical assistance (partial and full physical) would not be used, because observation of Jenny's behavior has clearly indicated that she does not need to be guided and touched in this way; rather, she is able to follow verbal and model prompts. It was agreed that if Jenny did not complete a step of the task analysis independently after a verbal prompt or a model, which was typically sufficient, the teacher would simply complete that step for her and allow her the opportunity to perform the next step of the sequence.

Table 5–4 shows another task analysis for the same activity. Christine, however, is expected to participate partially in the activity. Christine is scored on nine steps of the task, and her teacher completes the steps that are marked with an X. Extension and enrichment skills (e.g., initiation, social skills, monitoring skills) form the steps in which Christine can likely achieve independence. These components allow for meaningful participation and control of the activity even though she cannot perform most of the motor components of the task (see chapters 3 and 4). The prompt procedure for Christine includes physical assistance.

During testing, task analytic measurement can be carried out by using the *single* opportunity method or the *multiple* opportunity method. The easiest, although less informative method, is the single opportunity method. This approach is carried out as follows:

1. Conditions (including materials) are arranged as planned in the instructional program.
2. The instructional cue (if any) is given when the student is attending.
3. The student's response to each step in the task analysis is recorded as correct or incorrect (i.e., performed incorrectly or not performed at all). The following rules can be used to handle errors, periods of no response, and inappropriate behavior:

   • Testing is stopped after the first error and all remaining steps are scored as errors.

TABLE 5–3

Jenny's Task Analysis for Making a Peanut Butter Sandwich

Name:	Jenny	Teacher:

Activity:	Making a peanut butter sandwich

Materials:	Peanut butter sandwich supplies

Record number that indicates amount of assistance: 0-teacher completes; 1-full physical; 2-partial physical; 3-model; 4-verbal; 5-independent

Routine Steps	Dates			
	9/6	9/13	9/27	10/4
1. Initiate snack by going into home economics class	4	4	4	4
2. Go to refrigerator	4	4	4	4
3. Get out peanut butter	4	4	4	4
4. Put peanut butter on counter	4	4	5	5
5. Get bread from bread box	3	3	3	3
6. Put bread on counter	4	4	4	5
7. Get butter knife	3	3	3	4
8. Get plate	3	3	3	3
9. Put knife and plate on counter	5	5	4	5
10. Open bread bag	3	3	3	4
11. Remove 2 slices onto plate	5	5	5	5
12. Open peanut butter jar	0	0	0	0
13. Scoop out peanut butter with knife	3	3	4	3
14. Spread peanut butter on 1 slice	5	5	5	5
15. Repeat until preferred thickness	5	5	5	5
16. Put other slice on top	3	4	3	4
17. Put knife in sink	3	3	3	4
18. Put peanut butter away	4	4	4	4
19. Get napkin	3	4	4	4
20. Bring sandwich & napkin to table	5	5	5	5
TOTAL	73/100	75/100	75/100	80/100

TABLE 5–4

Christine's Task Analysis for Making a Peanut Butter Sandwich

Name:	Christine		Teacher:	Mr. Grayson

Activity:	Making a peanut butter sandwich

Materials:	Peanut butter sandwich supplies; meal preparation overlay for communication board

Record number that indicates amount of assistance: X-teacher completes; 1-full physical; 2-partial physical; 3-model; 4-verbal; 5-independent

Routine Steps	Dates				
	10/7	10/8	10/9	10/10	10/11
1. Initiate snack by activating communication device					
2. Go into home economics class					
3. Press switch when "peanut butter" is scanned on comm. device					
4. Press switch when "bread" is scanned on comm. device					
5. Teacher gets items, puts on counter	X	X	X	X	X
6. Press switch when "knife" is scanned on comm. device					
7. Press switch when "plate" is scanned on comm. device					
8. Press switch when "napkin" is scanned on comm. device					
9. Teacher gets items, puts on counter	X	X	X	X	X
10. Teacher makes sandwich	X	X	X	X	X
11. Teacher gives her a sample of sandwich and asks if sandwich is OK	X	X	X	X	X
12. Press switch when "yes/no" is scanned on comm. device					
13. Teacher fixes sandwich as necessary	X	X	X	X	X
14. Press switch when "thank you" is scanned on comm. device					
TOTAL					

- After a specified period of no response (e.g., 3 seconds), testing is stopped and all remaining steps are scored as errors.
- After a specified period of inappropriate behavior (e.g., 10 seconds of stereotypic behavior) or after a single inappropriate response (e.g., throwing the soap or the towel), testing is stopped, and all remaining steps are scored as errors.

4. For many tasks, the steps performed are scored as correct if they correspond to the task description, regardless of the order in which they are carried out, as long as the result is satisfactory. For example, it is not important whether Timothy pulls his right or left arm out of his coat first. However, for many other tasks, such as some leisure and work tasks, performing each step in order is crucial to the successful completion of the activity. In tasks where order is important, the first step out of sequence is scored as an error. In addition, when the rate of performance is important (as specified in the criteria or standards), the maximum length of time allowed is specified.

The single opportunity method generally is completed quickly. It provides a conservative estimate of the student's skills. Less instructional time is wasted because training can begin immediately after the first error. Further, learning is less likely to occur during testing; therefore, the single opportunity method provides a more accurate estimate of the effect of instruction. However, one disadvantage of the method is that performance on steps in a task analysis that occur after the first error are not measured, because testing is terminated at this point. Thus, probes (testing done once intervention has started) do not initially reflect learning on later steps. If a teacher is using a backward chaining progression (i.e., teaching the last step first), the single opportunity probe does not reflect any progress until training advances to the earlier steps in the chain. Therefore, in these cases, the multiple opportunity probe produces more information.

The multiple opportunity method used the following steps:

1. Conditions are arranged as planned in the instructional program.
2. The instructional cue (if any) is given when the student is attending.
3. The student's responses to each step in the task analysis are recorded as correct or incorrect (i.e., performed correctly or not performed at all).

4. Whenever an error occurs after a specified period of no response or inappropriate behavior, the step is completed by the teacher for the student, rather than by prompting the student to perform the step. Basically, the student is *positioned* for each step that follows an error, so performance on every step can be assessed.

In both assessment approaches, feedback is not provided to the student on the performance of the targeted skill. Withholding feedback differentiates between conditions of testing, which represent the most difficult conditions specified in the objective, and the conditions of teaching, when prompts and reinforcement are available. For some students, noncontingent reinforcement may be made available (i.e., reinforcement for something other than performance of the task) to hold their interest during assessment.

Interval Recording

To use interval recording, the observer divides an observation session into short, equal intervals, and the occurrence of behavior within each interval is recorded. Interval recording is useful for those behaviors that do not have discrete start or stop times and that vary in length (Schloss & Smith, 1998). Interval recording is used frequently in educational research to measure both appropriate behaviors (e.g., peer social initiations and interactions in inclusive settings and inappropriate behaviors (e.g., stereotypic, aggressive), in schools and other community settings (Frea, 1997; Hunt, Alwell, Farron-Davis, & Goetz, 1996; Koegel, Stiebel, & Koegel, 1998; Lee & Odom, 1996; Umbreit & Blair, 1996).

There are two types of interval recording strategies: *whole* interval and *partial* interval. In whole interval strategies, the observer notes if behavior occurred continuously throughout the interval.

Christine's drama teacher thought that she was losing interest in the play. Lately, rehearsals were quite tedious, often focusing on just one or two students, with the other students sitting and reading or doing homework from other classes. In order to assess this, her teacher asked Christine's teaching assistant to conduct a whole interval recording for 5 minutes, once at the beginning of the class, once in the middle of the class session, and once toward the end of the class session. Each of the 5-minute periods were divided into thirty brief 10-second intervals. The teaching assistant noted whether Christine was engaged throughout each 10-second interval in either watching the play or interacting with others. Christine's teacher found that Christine was infrequently attentive to the play and had few interactions with her peers during these times. The first observation at the beginning of class revealed that she was engaged for 10 of 30 intervals (or 33%). In the middle of class, she was engaged for 5 of 30 intervals (or about 17%), and at the end of class it was only 2 of 30 intervals (or 6%). A definite trend became apparent: Christine's engagement decreased as the class period progressed. Christine's teacher, teaching assistant, and two of her friends decided that they needed to make sure that Christine had something to do during these down times.

In partial interval recording, the observer notes if the behavior occurs at all during the interval, rather than if it occurs continuously throughout the interval. Once a behavior is observed and noted on the data sheet, further observation is not required for the remainder of that interval. Exactly how many times the behavior occurs during each interval is not recorded.

Thus, interval recording provides an *estimate* of the occurrence of behavior. Because of this, only limited conclusions can be drawn from the data (Alberto & Troutman, 1999), and the data must be interpreted cautiously.

Timothy seems to be by himself more and more during free play, not interacting with other children. Mr. Grayson, his special education teacher, decides that they will use a partial interval recording to get a better idea of how much time Timothy is spending alone. Mr. Grayson selects a 10-minute period of time in the middle of the 9:30 AM free play and a 10-minute period of time during the 11:30 AM free play. Then, he divides each of these observation sessions into ten equal 1-minute intervals. Mr. Grayson records a plus (+) in the box if Timothy has any type of interaction with another student during the interval and a minus (−) if there is no interaction. Figure 5–1 shows that Timothy had interactions with other children in

FIGURE 5–1

Partial Interval Recording Form for Timothy's Peer Interactions

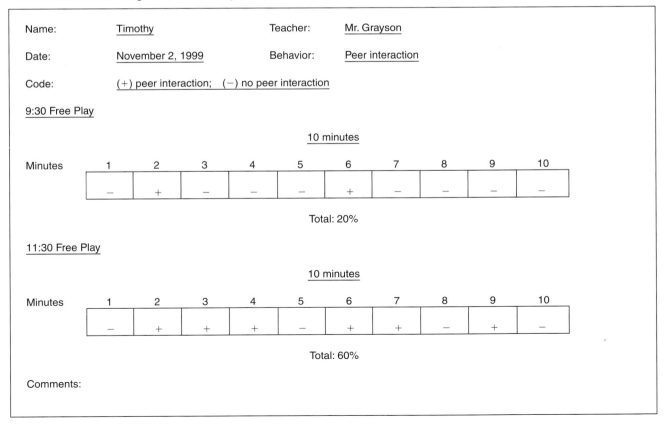

Name:	Timothy		Teacher:	Mr. Grayson
Date:	November 2, 1999		Behavior:	Peer interaction
Code:	(+) peer interaction; (−) no peer interaction			

9:30 Free Play

10 minutes

Minutes	1	2	3	4	5	6	7	8	9	10
	−	+	−	−	−	+	−	−	−	−

Total: 20%

11:30 Free Play

10 minutes

Minutes	1	2	3	4	5	6	7	8	9	10
	−	+	+	+	−	+	+	−	+	−

Total: 60%

Comments:

2 of the 10 intervals during early morning free play (or 20%). The data do not tell us, however, if Timothy had two brief 5-second interactions with other children or spent a full 2 minutes interacting with them.

If Mr. Grayson repeated this observation for a week, following implementation of an instructional strategy to increase interactions, he may still find no change in the data. However, it is possible that Timothy is having a significantly greater number of interactions with his peers, but because the interactions were clustered within two or three of the intervals, the progress cannot be seen. In this case, the results of the interval recording may be misleading.

Data from the 11:30 AM free play interval show a higher percentage of peer interaction (60%). Continued recording will reveal that either this is an unusual day or Timothy typically *does* interact more with his peers in the later free play time. If Timothy interacts more in the later play session, then Mr. Grayson can analyze that play time to determine what variables contribute to the increased level of peer interaction.

Selection of the appropriate interval method should be guided by the characteristics of the behavior and the goals of intervention. If the behavior is brief and the goal is to have the behavior occur on a consistent but not necessarily continuous basis (such as Timothy's interactions), the partial interval method must be used or the behavior will not be detected. Other behaviors, such as attention to a task, appropriately occur in a more continuous fashion (such as Christine's example). Such behaviors are best measured by the whole interval strategy.

When measuring behaviors targeted for reduction, it is best to use the method that provides the most rigorous information. For example, if the whole interval method is used to record the extent of self-injurious behavior, the interval is checked only if the self-injury occurs for the entire length of the interval. It is possible for the data to reflect no occurrences, when in fact the student engaged in extensive self-injury, but not continuous self-injury. Thus, the partial interval method would be more appropriate.

The length of the interval depends on both the behavior being observed (its average length and frequency) and the observer's ability to record the behavior, but interval length usually is measured in seconds (e.g., 5 seconds, 10 seconds, 30 seconds). The more frequent the behavior, the smaller the inter-

val for observation should be, so that the data yield a more accurate representation of behavior.

If large intervals (e.g., 15 minutes) were used with partial interval recording to measure Jenny's frequent behavior of smiling, for example, 100% would be the typical result. In other words, it is almost certain that Jenny would smile at least once within each 15-minute interval. This is not informative, for it does not provide knowledge of the density of the behavior, that is, if Jenny smiled 5 times or 150 times.

For behaviors that occur infrequently, the partial interval method can have longer intervals. For example, because Timothy infrequently initiates interactions with his peers, observing for 30-second intervals makes no sense. It is not likely that Timothy will display the behavior within 30 seconds. However, if the interval is made too large, any instance of the behavior can artificially inflate the percent of intervals. Thus, if Timothy interacts only two times in an hour but the intervals are 30 minutes long, statistically Timothy interacted for 100% of the intervals! This certainly does not reflect the quality of Timothy's behavior. Five minute intervals might be more appropriate.

Interval recording cannot be done casually, as a teacher's total attention must be directed toward the student during the entire observation time. In addition, the teacher must know when to move from one interval to the next. It can be challenging to teach and collect interval data at the same time (Alberto & Troutman, 1999). A watch or clock with a second hand can be used to time the intervals, but checking the time interrupts the observer's concentration; however, a portable tape recorder with a tape of prerecorded intervals and ear plugs may eliminate this problem. Some observers build in a brief time period (e.g., 5 seconds) for recording between observation intervals (Alberto & Troutman, 1999). For longer intervals (e.g., 3–5 minutes), inexpensive egg timers and kitchen timers have been used. Still, teachers must be sensitive to the environment and should be as unobtrusive as possible. For example, it would be distracting to have a beep sound every 10 seconds when observing Christine's attention to the play in her drama class.

Time Sampling

Time sampling is a type of interval measure that can be used more practically in teaching settings. As in the whole or partial interval recording strategy, a specified observation period (e.g., 30 minutes) is divided into small units (e.g., 5-minute intervals). However, unlike interval recording, where a teacher must observe the behavior throughout the entire interval, the teacher observes the student only at the end of the interval. Time sampling usually uses longer intervals (minutes) than does interval recording (seconds). The teacher records on the data sheet whether the student was, or was not, engaging in the target behavior at the end of each interval.

Implementation of time sampling can be done flexibly. Instead of continuously observing and recording at the end of each interval, the teacher can set up random intervals within an observation period. For example, the teacher may decide on an observation period of 1 hour and select six random times to observe (rather than exactly every 10 minutes).

It is also possible to extend time sampling across the day and randomly identify observation times. For example, instead of implementing an interval recording on Timothy's interactions with his peers during free play, Mr. Grayson could choose to use time sampling to record his interactions with peers across the 3-hour day at school (e.g., centers, snack, lunch, circle time). This strategy is relevant if the goal is for Timothy to increase interaction with his peers across many activities, not just during playtime.

Because time sampling does not require continuous observation, teaching and data collection can occur simultaneously (Alberto & Troutman, 1999), and teachers can use the strategy with more than one student at a time. Quilitch and Risley (1973) used this type of strategy to measure the behavior of a group of students. In their Planned Activity Check, the teacher defined the behavior to observe (e.g., on-task behavior) and then counted the students engaged in the target behavior. The teacher also recorded the number of students present in the area, deriving a percentage by dividing the number of students engaged in the target behavior by the total number of students present and then multiplying by 100. Time sampling can also be used to observe a group of students by sequentially rotating observations across the group until all have been observed and repeating the sequence until the observation period is complete (Thomson, Holmberg, & Baer, 1974).

Like interval recording, however, time sampling provides only an estimate of the behavior. In fact, for low-frequency and short-duration behaviors, time sampling is even less accurate than interval recording. The less frequent or briefer a behavior, the shorter the interval must be. As the interval gets longer, the similarity between the data recorded and the actual occurrences is likely to decrease (Alberto & Troutman, 1999). (Because a teacher is checking at the end of the interval only, he may miss the behavior if it does not occur frequently or if it is of short duration). Thus, time sampling is most appropriate for measuring behaviors that are fairly frequent and that occur for long durations.

Data Sheets

Data sheets must allow teachers to systematically record data from their observations (e.g., frequency data, task analytic, interval data). It is important to record in a format that will allow subsequent data analysis. For example, some student performance data can provide the information for error analyses (e.g., which steps of the task analysis are consistently missed), and most data can be converted into graphs for easier visual analysis.

The basic elements of a data sheet are: (a) the student's name; (b) the observer's name; (c) the date, time, and location of the observation; (d) the length of the observation; (e) the behavior(s) observed and, if necessary, a brief observable description of each; (f) adequate space for data recording (e.g., room for a 15-step task analysis, or ten 2-minute intervals); (g) a scoring code; (h) a data summary; and (i) comments (see Figure 5–1, and Tables 5–3 and 5–4). In addition to providing the range of information necessary to make effective instructional decisions, a data sheet can also assist in functional behavioral assessment (Brown, 1991) (see chapter 6 for a discussion of functional behavioral assessment). For example, in the time sampling procedure to measure Timothy's interactions with his peers across the day, his teacher could specify the time of day and the activity in which the data were measured. With this type of information, it is possible to analyze the events or variables (e.g., activities, time of day, different peers, materials) contributing to the presence, or absence, of peer interactions. Adding an extra column on the data sheet for recording the incidence of an inappropriate behavior may enable the teacher to see a trend in the relationship between an inappropriate behavior and the time of day or type of activity.

Measures of Accuracy

Because important decisions are made on the basis of data, team members must have confidence in the data. Consider the following example where the relationship between accurate data collection and effective program evaluation is obvious:

> Data recorded by Jenny's teaching assistant indicate that she can prepare her snack with only two verbal prompts. However, when her teacher assists Jenny in this activity, she finds that Jenny needs not only significant verbal prompts but also gestural cues. The discrepancy in the data may be because Jenny is not accustomed to preparing her snack with her teacher. If this is the case, then certain programmatic changes can help Jenny generalize her snack preparation skills in the presence of others. However, it is also possible that the teaching assistant is not recording Jenny's data accurately. If this is the case, changes focusing on generalization would not be appropriate. Efforts should instead focus on increasing the accuracy, or reliability, of the teaching assistant's data collection.

Interobserver (or Interrater) Reliability

Interobserver reliability is assessed to determine whether the target behavior is being recorded accurately (Miltenberger, 1997). One way to ensure that data are accurate, or reliable, is to have two independent observers record the behavior of a student at the same time, compare the two observations, and mathematically determine the extent of agreement of the data. The percent of interobserver reliability can be calculated by dividing the number of agreements between the two observers by the number of agreements plus disagreements and multiplying by 100. The result of this calculation is a *percent of agreement*.

$$\frac{\text{Agreements}}{\text{Agreements} + \text{Disagreements}} = \text{Percentage of Agreement}$$

For example, two teachers use a partial interval recording to observe the presence of a specified behavior. A 5-minute observation period is divided into ten 30-second intervals. Each time they observe the target behavior they record an X in the correct cell. The results of the observation are:

According to the above formula, the reliability between the two teachers is:

$$\frac{9 \text{ agreements}}{9 \text{ agreements} + 1 \text{ disagreement}} = \frac{9}{10} = 90\% \text{ agreement}$$

Generally, a reliability coefficient of .80, or 80%, is considered acceptable.

Procedural Reliability

Procedural reliability is the degree to which program procedures are implemented accurately. Procedural reliability asks the question: Did the teacher follow the instructional plan? In an extensive discussion of procedural reliability, Billingsley, White, and Munson (1980) point out that all relevant variables of a program must be evaluated. It is not sufficient to explore the reliability of just one or two of the more obvious components of an intervention (e.g., delivery of reinforcers). Procedures related to the areas of program setup, antecedent events, and consequent events should be examined (Billingsley, White, & Munson, 1980). A behavioral checklist of each intervention procedure can be designed and the teacher can "check off" each component addressed (Kerr & Nelson, 1998). Following are some specific questions to consider when assessing procedural reliability:

- Is the instructional plan implemented as frequently as planned?
- Does the instructor use the correct sequence and timing of instructional prompts?
- Does the instructor deliver the appropriate consequences?
- Are instructional cues delivered in the manner designated in the program plan?
- Were all of the necessary instructional materials available?
- Was the program implemented in the correct environment?

Procedural reliability can be calculated in much the same way as interobserver reliability. Billingsley, White, and Munson (1980) offer the following formula:

$$\text{Procedural reliability (\%)} = \frac{(\text{TA} \times 100)}{\text{TT}}$$

30-second intervals	1	2	3	4	5	6	7	8	9	10
Teacher 1	X	X		X		X		X	X	
Teacher 2	X	X	X	X		X		X	X	

In this formula, TA is the number of *teacher* behaviors in *accordance* with the program plan. TT is the *total* number of *teacher* behaviors that could have been performed in accordance with the program plan. As an example, Christine was supposed to participate in the library with her nondisabled peers eight times each month (twice each week) but participated only six times last month. Applying this formula to intervention frequency, the procedural reliability is:

$$\text{Procedural reliability (\%)} = \frac{6 \times 100}{8} = 75\%$$

Graphs

Although analysis of information on a data sheet may provide important details about specific steps performed correctly or missed on a task analysis, there are significant limitations to leaving data in this form. For example, it is difficult to interpret or analyze behavioral data from a data sheet alone, especially when weeks of data are considered. Behavioral data can be most effectively interpreted and analyzed when converted into a graph. Graphs allow teachers to more easily detect trends of progress and thus to make more effective program decisions. When trends are positive, many teachers also find graphs reinforcing, as they are a continual source of feedback.

Although some teachers initially feel apprehensive or intimidated by graphs, most soon discover that graphs are actually simple to design and read. A graph is made up of two axes (Figure 5–2). The abscissa, or the x-axis, is the horizontal line. The abscissa usually represents the time frame of a measurement (e.g., each data point reflects the data from a day, week, or month). The ordinate, or the y-axis, is the vertical line. It is labeled by the target behavior being measured (e.g., peer interaction, eating) and the measurement that was used (e.g., duration, frequency, percent).

Converting Data

Before any points can be plotted on the graph, data must be converted into a single numeric form for each data point. Frequency data can be tallied and presented as the total number in a given time period (e.g., number of times Timothy correctly pointed to or looked at named peers during morning group). Total duration data may be presented as the total number of minutes or seconds during which a behavior occurred within a given time period (e.g., number of minutes spent in leisure activity). Duration data that is collected using the method of measuring each occurrence can be presented in a duration graph (number of minutes spent interacting with peers during morning free play) or as a frequency (number of peer interactions during morning free play). Interval or time sampling data can be converted into the number or percent of intervals in which the behavior occurred. Converting task analytic data, which involves multiple steps and may have a range of scoring codes, is a little more complex. Take the example of Jenny's task analysis of making a peanut butter sandwich, which is 20 steps (see Table 5–3). As described above, Jenny did not need physical prompts within an activity. Because of this, her teacher uses a four-component prompt hierarchy. The steps to convert Jenny's task analytic data into a single numeric form for graph presentation are:

1. Figure out the most points that Jenny can earn in each session. If the teacher multiplies the number of steps in the task analysis (i.e., 20) by the number of points possible in each step (i.e., 5), the most that Jenny can score each session is 100 points.
2. Add the number of points earned in the session. Table 5–3 shows that Jenny scored a total of 73 points on September 6.
3. Divide the number of points earned (i.e., 73) by the total number of points possible (i.e., 100) to calculate the percentage (73%).
4. Plot the percentage of prompt level on the graph.

FIGURE 5–2
Basic Components of a Graph

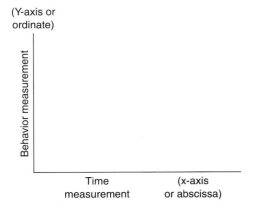

FIGURE 5–3
Four Days of Graphed Data
for Jenny Making a Peanut
Butter Sandwich

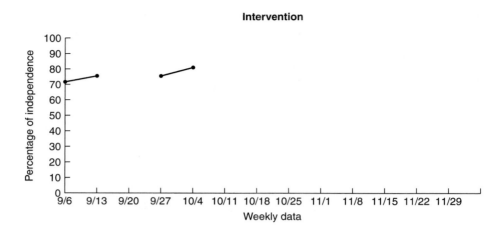

Another option for displaying Jenny's data is to graph the number of steps independently performed (i.e., prompt level 5). Following this approach, on September 6, Jenny scored prompt level 5 on five steps of the task analysis for a total of 25 points out of 100 possible points, or 25%.

Although graphic methods provide a good look at a student's overall progress and trends, a certain level of information is hidden. The raw data should be used for additional analysis concerning where errors are occurring.

Setting Up a Graph
Once raw data have been converted into a single number to graph, it is easy to plot the data point. First, make sure to label the ordinate or vertical line (y-axis) with the behavior being measured and the type of measurement being used (e.g., percent of the vacuuming task analysis steps performed independently, number of verbalizations during lunch). Next, divide the ordinate into equal intervals that cover the possible range of data (e.g., 0–100%, 0–50). If there are no definite upper and lower limits, the range should extend from the baseline level to the target level, with some extra space added at both ends to allow for variability.

Data points within each phase of a program (e.g., baseline, intervention, reinforcer change) are connected by straight lines, but they should not be connected across phase changes. Each program phase is separated by a broken vertical line and should be labeled to indicate the intervention used (e.g., baseline,

prompting, peer model). To enhance the effectiveness of a graph for data analysis, date the graph along the abscissa or horizontal line (x-axis) using the same time intervals as the data (e.g., daily, weekly, monthly). Figure 5–3 lists every week for 3 months because teaching data will be recorded on making a peanut butter sandwich on a weekly basis. It is important to delineate the dates before recording, to allow automatic skipping of spaces for missing sessions. Because missed sessions can have a detrimental effect on a student's performance, it is important to be aware of missed sessions when analyzing a graph. Notice that no data are recorded for September 20 in Figure 5–3. Jenny's teacher should investigate the reason for the absence of data collection and the effect of this absence on her performance.

Plotting Data Points
Figure 5–3 shows 4 days of data taken from Jenny's data sheet. To plot data, place each data point (i.e., the total for the session) at the intersection of the session date (on the abscissa) and the level of performance (on the ordinate). Notice the space between the dates of September 13 and September 27; it is best to skip the space to indicate the missed session. However, all consecutive sessions (according to the scheduled plan of intervention) are connected.

Many teachers find it useful to distinguish between graphs that reflect behavior targeted for acceleration versus graphs that reflect behavior targeted for deceleration. To distinguish, some use a dot to represent acceleration data, and an X for deceleration data (Figure 5–4). This strategy makes successful and unsuccessful

FIGURE 5–4
Use of Graph to Show
Timothy's Progress and
Program Changes During Free
Play

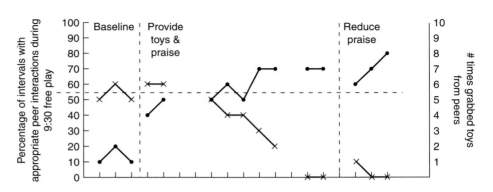

trends even more obvious during data analysis. It also allows two related data paths on the same graph (e.g., the appropriate behavior of asking for materials and the inappropriate behavior of pushing others).

Using Self-Graphing Data Sheets
Some teachers find it efficient to combine the data recording sheet and the graph. This has been done to measure prompting levels (Alberto & Schofield, 1979), task sequences (Holvoet, Guess, Mulligan, & Brown, 1980), and task analysis (Bellamy, Horner, & Inman, 1979). Plotting data from a task analysis in this fashion has been referred to as an upside down or self-graphing format (Test & Spooner, 1996). Figure 5–5 is a self-graphing data sheet to record progress on hairbrushing.

Program: Brush hair

Student: Jenny

Teacher: Ms. Dailey

Task analysis

Task analysis	9/2	9/9	9/16	9/23										
11. Puts brush away	11	11	11	11	11	11	11	11	11	11	11	11	11	11
10. Check hair for neatness	10	10	10	10	10	10	10	10	10	10	10	10	10	10
9. Brush left back of head	9	9	9	9	9	9	9	9	9	9	9	9	9	9
8. Brush left side of head	8	8	8	8	8	8	8	8	8	8	8	8	8	8
7. Brush front	7	7	7	7	7	7	7	7	7	7	7	7	7	7
6. Brush right side of head	6	6	6	6	6	6	6	6	6	6	6	6	6	6
5. Brush right back of head	5	5	5	5	5	5	5	5	5	5	5	5	5	5
4. Pick up brush	4	4	4	4	4	4	4	4	4	4	4	4	4	4
3. Selects desired materials	3	3	3	3	3	3	3	3	3	3	3	3	3	3
2. Locates brushing materials	2	2	2	2	2	2	2	2	2	2	2	2	2	2
1. Initiates brushing	1	1	1	1	1	1	1	1	1	1	1	1	1	1
	9/2	9/9	9/16	9/23										

Key: ╱ = independent
      ╳ = needs assistance

FIGURE 5–5
Self-Graphing Data Sheet For Hairbrushing

A self-graphing data sheet can be used to record probe data by making a slash (/) through the step number if the student responds independently and an X through the step number if the student needs assistance to complete the step. At the end of the session, add the number of slashes and then circle the number correct for the day. A graph is formed by connecting the circles across days.

Frequency of Data Collection

Early in the development of current data-based teaching models, it was fairly common to hear the advice to collect data each time an instructional activity was implemented. In fact, data collection practices recommended for teachers were similar to those used by researchers (Meyer & Janney, 1989). Although this may now sound excessive, it was an important phase, as it afforded educators additional understanding of the learning process of students with severe disabilities and increased knowledge of data analysis and evaluation. However, what were once considered best-practice procedures for data collection (i.e., measuring every response in every instructional activity) are now being questioned (Meyer & Janney, 1989; Test & Spooner, 1996). As educational strategies become more integrated and community-based, data collection procedures must become more appropriate for these settings. At times and in settings where teachers of nondisabled peers are not recording data, conspicuous data collection procedures do not enhance an integrated view of a student with severe disabilities. Smith (1990) points out that data collection procedures should be neither obtrusive nor intrusive; that is, they should not call attention to the individual or the disability and should not interfere with the individual's functioning in the work or home setting. Measures that are most appropriate for inclusive community settings are ones that:

- Do not interrupt instruction
- Take minimal time to complete
- Are unobtrusive and do not stigmatize the individual
- Provide both objective and subjective observations

Just how often a teacher should take data is a subject of great debate. Holvoet et al. (1983) point out that the irony in this debate is that the arguments about data collection do not appear to be data-based. Guidelines for frequency of data collection vary with the literature. Thus, a teacher may read in one book

that data collection should occur at a minimum of once each day during training (Test & Spooner, 1996), once a week for each instructional objective (Gaylord-Ross & Holvoet, 1985), and in another "more often than once a week, but less than every response made during instruction every day" (Browder, 1991, p. 113). Most discussions of frequency of data collection, however, suggest that once a skill is in the maintenance, fluency, or generalization stage of learning, data collection could be reduced (Farlow & Snell, 1994).

Although there are still no definitive answers to the question of exactly how much data are needed to make accurate instructional decisions, the following guidelines can assist teachers in deciding how frequently to collect data:

- High-priority objectives (i.e., those related to the health and safety of the individual or others) warrant daily data collection (Browder, 1991). Not only is daily data collection more sensitive to changes in the trend, but it also contributes to important functional assessment of the behavior (Brown, 1991).
- Lower priority objectives, or objectives that are scheduled to occur on a less than daily basis (e.g., grocery shopping), may be evaluated less frequently, for example, once each week (Browder, 1991).
- Implementation of a new program requires frequent data collection. For the first 2 weeks of the instructional program, data could be collected daily or at every teaching session, if the lessons are not held at least once a day. When the student has shown steady progress (e.g., two weeks of data), data could be reduced to weekly (Farlow & Snell, 1994).
- Data that show progress as planned, with a clear accelerating trend, may be evaluated less frequently (Munger, Snell, & Loyd, 1989; Snell & Loyd, 1991), such as on a weekly basis (Farlow & Snell, 1994).
- Data that do not show progress as planned, or are variable, warrant evaluation on a more continual basis (Munger, Snell, & Loyd, 1989; Snell & Loyd, 1991), minimally twice a week, and ideally on a daily basis (Farlow & Snell, 1994).
- Skills being taught to replace problem behaviors can be measured by using weekly probes. However, these probes should be carried out in the context of relevant situations, persons, and environments (Meyer & Janney, 1989).
- Logs, or anecdotal records, can be used twice weekly to record general information concerning a student's

overall daily performance and to systematically assess responses to program efforts and any conditions that might affect a student's learning (e.g., tasks or activities that the student enjoys; tasks or activities that the student does not enjoy) (Farlow & Snell, 1994; Meyer & Janney, 1989). Such logs may be useful supplements to more precise, quantified data.

Analysis

Teams must feel confident that instruction is having the desired effect on student performance. It is also helpful to know that an intervention is responsible for the change in the student's performance, not just the passage of time or some other event. Some simple *single-subject designs* can help teachers feel more confident about the effect of their instruction. Although an in-depth discussion of single-subject designs is not possible in this text, we recommend further reading in this area. Recent texts that provide excellent reviews of single-subject designs include *Applied Behavior Analysis for Teachers* (Alberto & Troutman, 1999), *Strategies for Managing Behavior Problems in the Classroom* (Kerr & Nelson, 1998), *Applied Behavior Analysis in the Classroom* (Schloss & Smith, 1998), and *Behavior Modification: Principles and Procedures* (Miltenberger, 1997).

Merely collecting data is not sufficient; data must be carefully examined, analyzed, and interpreted to contribute to the instructional process. The remainder of this chapter discusses the analysis of classroom data and ways in which this information can most effectively help teachers make instructional decisions.

To understand the variety of data analysis strategies available for classroom use, teachers must understand three important terms. The behavior to be changed is the *dependent* variable. Examples of dependent variables include: Timothy's peer interactions, Jenny's use of coins to make school purchases, and Christine's performance on the job at Wal-Mart. The instructional strategy that is manipulated by the teacher is the *independent* variable. Examples of independent variables include modeling, prompting procedures, reinforcement, and other procedures that teachers use to try to change a target behavior. The purpose of a single-subject design, or any research design, is to demonstrate a functional relationship between the dependent and the independent vari-

ables, that is, to determine whether application of the independent variable (the teaching procedure) results in changes in the dependent variable (the target behavior). A simple way to remember the distinction between the dependent and the independent variable is to keep in mind that changes in the dependent variable "depend" on changes in the independent variable (Alberto & Troutman, 1999).

Types of Data

To understand whether students are benefiting from instructional programs, teachers should examine students' performance data during teaching as well as data from several other sources. Typically, the data are of several types:

- Anecdotal records (e.g., staff notes on unusual behavior or performance and comments sent by the teacher to the home or from the family to school).
- Ungraphed training data reflecting performance under training conditions on target skills (e.g., individual steps of a task analysis).
- Ungraphed test data reflecting performance on target skills under criterion conditions (e.g., what individual components of the shopping routine the student could perform in the grocery store without instructional prompts).
- Graphed training data on target skills.
- Graphed test data on target skills.

When recording task performance data, we recommend that teachers use data collection sheets similar to those presented in Figure 4–9, Table 5–3, and Table 5–4.

Ungraphed Data

When raw, or ungraphed, data of performance on a multiple-stepped task are summarized and graphed, a certain amount of information is lost (Haring & Kennedy, 1988). For example, teachers looking at a graph on the accuracy of Jenny's sandwich-making know about her overall progress on the task across sessions, but they do not know which steps she missed or did correctly on a given day. Nor do they know if these missed or correct steps were consistent across days.

Teachers should preserve ungraphed data, since response-by-response information may help them make decisions about program implementation when progress is poor (Farlow & Snell, 1994; Snell & Loyd, 1991). For example, if the graphed training data for a new work task (i.e., scanning books at the library) show that Christine has made no progress in a week, her teacher may look at the ungraphed task analytic data collected during training sessions and examine anecdotal notes made during the 5 days of no progress.

Analysis of ungraphed response-by-response data is especially helpful when more than one instructor teaches. Ungraphed data may show that Jenny consistently misses several steps involved in making the peanut butter sandwich (e.g., open peanut butter jar and get bread from the bread box and the plate from the cabinet). Her teacher may then modify these parts of the task into more or different steps or modify the materials or environment. For example, perhaps Jenny can learn to use a rubber jar opener (available in all hardware stores) to open the peanut butter jar. A picture sequence showing the items needed to make the sandwich might serve as a reminder for Jenny, thus decreasing the need for the instructor to model the correct responses.

Ungraphed data may also show inconsistent errors, while anecdotal notes may indicate that Jenny "does not seem to be herself" and that her parents report a cold and possible sore throat. In the latter case, the teacher may not change the task steps but instead may monitor Jenny's health more closely.

Even with non-task analytic, or discrete data (e.g., the number of correct greetings made by Timothy at preschool), graphed summaries lose some of the information that can be preserved on the data collection sheets. For example, Timothy's teacher may be interested in analyzing the ungraphed data to determine if his performance is better in the early part of the morning, or in the later part of his time at school, or if he greeted certain peers or adults more than others. Thus, it is critical to construct data collection sheets that record a range of information useful for future analysis.

Obtaining a Baseline

The first step in implementing systematic classroom instruction is to conduct a baseline measure. *Baseline* is the measure of a behavior (the dependent variable) before intervention (the independent variable). In other words, a baseline describes a student's perfor-

mance under the naturally occurring conditions in his or her environment, without instructional manipulations.

Mr. Grayson uses interval recording to measure Timothy's interactions with his classmates during two free play sessions for 3 days (Figure 5–1 shows recording on 1 day). Because Mr. Grayson observes Timothy in his naturally occurring environment, without intervening in any way, these 3 days are considered baseline. After implementation of an intervention program to increase Timothy's interactions with his classmates, Mr. Grayson compares the baseline data with the intervention data to see whether there was an increase in peer interactions. Mr. Grayson was particularly interested in the effect of the intervention on Timothy's behavior during the 9:30 AM free play time.

A teacher should be cautious about how long a baseline condition is in effect. Generally, the rule is to continue baseline measures until there is a stable trend in the data. It is considered unethical, however, to continue a baseline in certain situations. First, if a behavior is dangerous, it is unacceptable to wait for a stable trend before beginning treatment. Many times, a teacher can find other forms of data to use as a baseline (e.g., incident reports, daily logs).

Second, many students have little or no behavior related to the target objective (e.g., sign language for a student who has never used sign language). Again, it is considered unethical to delay instruction for an extended period of time when a student clearly cannot perform the behavior. Teachers must remember that baseline does not refer to absence of a program or to downtime, but it does refer to the time before a given program is implemented or the time when a particular program is withdrawn or stopped.

Third, if the direction of the baseline trend is opposite to the direction of the desired trend (e.g., the number of peer interactions are decreasing, aggression is increasing), collection of baseline data should be discontinued and intervention should be immediately initiated. When this type of trend occurs, something in the baseline condition is either extinguishing the behavior (e.g., absence of intermittent teacher praise for playing with others was once reinforced and was withdrawn during baseline) or reinforcing the behavior (e.g., lack of teacher consequence for aggressive behavior allows the student to get attention from the other students).

AB, or Baseline-Intervention, Design

Comparing a baseline condition (A) with an intervention condition (B), is called an AB, or baseline-intervention, design. This design is referred to as a quasi-experimental design, because no conclusive demonstration of a cause-effect, or functional, relationship between the intervention and the observed changes in behavior is possible. (See texts mentioned previously for information concerning single-subject experimental designs such as reversal, multiple-baseline, and changing criterion). Since there is no withdrawal of the intervention or replication of treatment effects, rival hypotheses based on factors not controlled by the teacher may have caused the changes in the behavior (e.g., maturation of the student across time, a new student in the class, a parent working on the skill at home).

> Timothy's teacher decides to implement an intervention to increase his interactions during the 11:30 free play. Intervention consists of seating Timothy in proximity to two of his outgoing and friendly classmates, Floyd and Mario, and praising Timothy, Floyd, and Mario for all interactions. Timothy's interactions with his peers increased. Mr. Grayson wondered if it was his new intervention (i.e., praise and environmental manipulation) that increased the peer interaction or if, perhaps, it might be the new Power Ranger figures that Floyd was bringing to school.

Given the lack of experimental control, the AB design rarely is used by researchers, but it is appropriate for monitoring student performance within teaching settings.

When teachers are familiar with a student's typical learning patterns and are aware of various events that affect performance, they can usually judge treatment effects with a considerable degree of certainty. Since student performance is monitored before teaching occurs (in a baseline) and during different phases of teaching (independent variables), the AB design provides an objective (although not scientifically conclusive) description of a student's behavior before and after training, given an adequate record of student progress toward accomplishment of the instructional goal.

If a student's performance during the baseline progresses in the same direction expected during the intervention, teachers have difficulty interpreting the intervention data. That is, unless the intervention has a

FIGURE 5–6
An AB Design for Evaluating the Effects of Intervention on Christine's Engagement During Drama Class

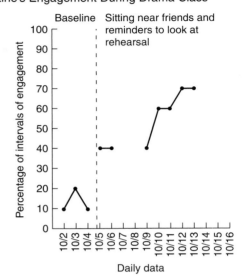

large effect, it is difficult to judge whether the change in the data (from the baseline to the intervention) is the result of the intervention or simply a continuation of the trend seen during the baseline (Parsonson & Baer, 1978). Because of this difficulty, teachers typically wait until baseline performance is relatively stable before starting intervention; however, in some instances (e.g., dangerous behavior), teachers may not wait for a stable baseline or may not take a baseline at all before beginning intervention.

An AB design is shown in Figure 5–6. This example shows an increase in Christine's engagement during drama class (defined as watching the rehearsal or engaging in interactions with her peers) after intervention. Intervention consisted of the simple environmental arrangement of having her sit closer to her friends so she could be part of any conversation that might occur, programming her communication device with vocabulary suited to the class, and having her friends comment intermittently to each other and to Christine about what was happening on the stage.

Graphing Conventions

As described earlier, the main purpose of converting raw data to graphs is to provide a summarizing picture of the student's performance and progress. These interpretations guide program modification. The ability to accurately interpret graphs is enhanced by the use of certain graphing conventions. Three major graphing conventions are recommended (Figure 5–4):

- *Broken vertical lines*, or phase changes, represent changes in the instructional program. These can include planned programmatic changes, such as changing from baseline to intervention (Figure 5–6), modification of the task analysis or materials, change in the time or setting of the instruction, or change in the reinforcement or prompt. Broken vertical lines can also be used to indicate situations or events that might indirectly or incidentally affect the student's performance. These events include, for example, changes in medications, illness, staff changes, or a new student in the class.
- *Broken horizontal lines* (a criterion line) can be used to indicate the criterion for the program. This criterion should match the criterion stated in the behavioral objective of the program. Seeing this line on the graph gives the team a quick visual reminder of what the goal of the program is and where the student is in relation to the goal.
- *Connect data points* only for consecutive days within a phase. Data points should not be connected across phase change lines or across missed data days (e.g., student absent or session missed). This allows a clear picture of the effect of the program change, but also allows the team to note the gaps in instructional opportunities and its effect on performance.
- Teams can quickly note if a graph represents a successful or unsuccessful program effort by using an X to represent behavior that is to be *decelerated*, and dots to represent *skill building*. This graphing convention also allows multiple data paths on one graph (e.g., increasing toy play and decreasing self-stimulatory behavior during free play).

Timothy's teacher graphed his progress on increasing peer interactions in his 9:30 AM free play time. Mr. Grayson decided that it would be helpful not just to note his progress on this social interaction skill, but to analyze the impact of the intervention on Timothy's behavior of grabbing toys from his peers. He drew a criterion line across the graph at 70%, because the objective was to have Timothy engage in appropriate peer interactions in 70% of the intervals of the free play session (a percentage based on his observations of other children in the class

playing together). When Timothy reached criterion on peer interactions, and there was also a significant decrease in grabbing toys, Mr. Grayson decided that he should reduce the amount of praise he was giving to Timothy and his peers so that it was more typical of the frequency of praise he provided other children in the class. He was happy to note that the appropriate peer interactions remained high and the grabbing remained at zero. (See Figure 5–4.)

Visual Analysis

Teachers and researchers often find that their efforts in analyzing the trend in AB graphs are aided by several simple visual aids—the aim line and trend line (Haring, Liberty, & White, 1980, 1981).

Aim Lines

The aim line is a more intensive, sophisticated version of the criterion line (broken horizontal line), calculated from data collected during baseline. The *aim line* begins at the performance level where the student is functioning when you begin instruction and extends over the instructional period to the criterion level and date you have set in the instructional objective (Farlow & Snell, 1994). This visual aid is drawn onto a graph early in a program and allows the team to compare graphed progress to their expectations for progress. Although they might look quite complicated, aim lines are simple to draw and easy to interpret. Aim lines result from connecting two points made by (a) the intersection of the mid-date and the mid-performance of the first 3 training days and (b) the intersection of the criterion performance with the goal date of accomplishment (aim date).

Figure 5–7 reveals that Jenny performs with 30%, 20%, and 20% correct on the first 3 days (September 9, 10, and 11) of her "completing routine errands" instructional program, in which she returns and gets class library books. Jenny's teacher then sets her first endpoint at the intersection of the second, or mid-date, of instruction (September 10) and sets her mid-performance, which is 20% (i.e., the middle number of 30%, 20%, and 20%). An endpoint is set at the intersection of the criterion performance expected of Jenny (i.e., 60%) and the goal date (November 17). (This goal date represents the date when all the teachers in Jenny's school send progress notes home to parents.) Jenny's teacher then draws a straight line between these two endpoints. This line is the aim line.

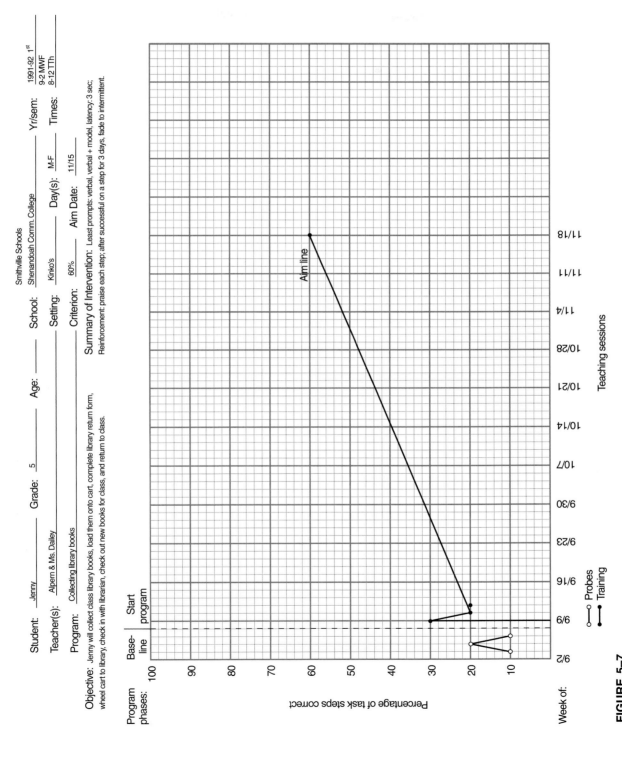

Student: <u>Jenny</u> Grade: <u>5</u> Age: ____ School: <u>Smithville Schools Shenandoah Comm. College</u> Yr/sem: <u>1991-92 1st</u>

Teacher(s): <u>Alpern & Ms. Dailey</u> Setting: <u>Kinko's</u> Day(s): <u>M-F</u> Times: <u>9-2 MWF</u> <u>8-12 TTh</u>

Program: <u>Collecting library books</u> Criterion: <u>60%</u> Aim Date: <u>11/15</u>

Objective: Jenny will collect class library books, load them onto cart, complete library return form, wheel cart to library, check in with librarian, check out new books for class, and return to class.

Summary of Intervention: Least prompts: verbal, verbal + model, latency: 3 sec; Reinforcement: praise each step; after successful on a step for 3 days, fade to intermittent.

Program phases: Base-line | Start program

Percentage of task steps correct

○—○ Probes
●—● Training

Week of: 9/2 9/9 9/16 9/23 9/30 10/7 10/14 10/21 10/28 11/4 11/11 11/18

Teaching sessions

Aim line

FIGURE 5–7
An AB Design, with Aim Line, for Evaluating Jenny's Performance in Collecting Library Books

Selection of an aim date is influenced by several factors, including the school's typical evaluation periods (e.g., every 9 weeks), the urgency (or time line) for learning the skill, the difference between current performance and the criterion, and the speed of learning on similar tasks in the recent past. Aim dates should not be excessively distant from implementation dates and may be set to correspond to more frequent marking periods used in general education (e.g., 9 to 12 weeks).

For students who need extensive progress on a target skill, shorter time lines can be targeted if a lower criterion is set initially or if the task is initially simplified. Once the initial criterion is accomplished, a tougher criterion can be set for the next aim date, allowing teachers to set criteria for fewer gains that are evaluated more often.

Trend Lines

The trend line is a line that roughly averages the direction and slope of a student's performance when the performance is uneven, variable, or difficult to interpret by just looking at the graph. Trend refers to the direction of graphed data as well as the slope, or steepness, of the data path once the data are connected across individual data points. Trend can be of three general types:

1. *Ascending* trends have an upward slope on a graph and are interpreted as indicating improvement or learning when the behavior graphed is a skill or adaptive behavior. (If the goal of the program is to reduce a behavior, the ascending trend would be interpreted as regression, or deterioration.)
2. *Flat* trends have either no slope or a very slight upward or downward slope. Flat trends indicate that no learning or improvement occurs, when the behavior graphed is a skill or an adaptive behavior.
3. *Descending* trends have a downward slope and are interpreted as indicating regression, or deterioration, when the behavior graphed is a skill or adaptive behavior. (If the goal of the program is to reduce a behavior, the downward slope would be interpreted as indicating improvement.)

Because the trend of graphed training data is not always obvious or uniform, trend lines help teachers summarize the fluctuating, or variable, nature of performance and interpret its approximate direction over a period of 6 to 10 teaching sessions (Tawney & Gast, 1984). Some researchers have defined an increasing,

or ascending, slope more precisely, as 30° or more in the positive direction and a decreasing, or descending, slope as 30° or more in the negative direction (DeProspero & Cohen, 1979).

When the trend is obvious, there is no need to draw a trend line over the graphed data, but when a student's progress is below the aim line for 3 of 5 days and the trend is not obvious, a teacher should pencil in a trend line to define the trend. If the line indicates that the trend on a target skill is flat or descending (for skill building programs), then the teacher should further analyze the data and other performance information to decide whether specific program improvements are needed.

There are several ways to draw trend lines, including the "quickie split-middle trend line" (White & Haring, 1980), which can be drawn simply and clarifies the general direction of change in the data as well as the relative rate of change (reflected in the slope). Although teachers may collect test (probe) data intermittently and add them to the same graph using differently coded lines or points, training data constitute the primary information used to make judgments about day-to-day progress (Browder, 1991; Farlow & Snell, 1994; Haring, Liberty, & White, 1980). Teachers should draw a trend line using the following four steps (Figure 5–8):

1. Take the last 6 to 10 days of training data collected.
2. Look at the first half of the data (the first three, four, or five data points) and locate the intersection of the middle date (session) and middle performance level.
   - If an even set of data points is considered (e.g., four), just sketch a pencil line between the dates for the second and third data point; if an odd set is considered (e.g., three or five), draw the line through the middle date.
   - The middle performance level is not the average of the performances for the data points in the set of three to five data points. It is simply the middle performance value. For an odd number of data, select the middle value (e.g., for 10%, 15%, and 12%, the middle performance value is 12%). For an even number of data, select a value halfway between the two middle data points (e.g., for 15%, 10%, 15%, and 11%, the middle value is 13%).
   - Draw the two lines until they intersect.
3. Repeat this process for the other half of the data.

FIGURE 5–8
Drawing a Split-Middle Trend Line

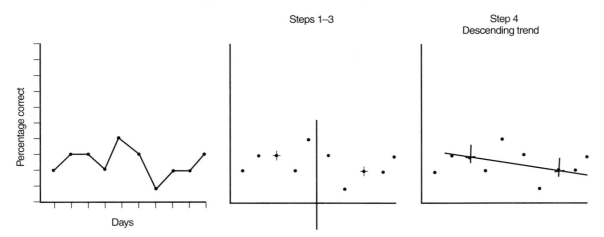

4. Then, draw a line connecting the two points of intersection for both halves of the data.

Once the trend line is drawn, visually judge whether the trend is ascending, flat, or descending. If the trend is flat or descending, teachers should hypothesize or determine why and make program improvements based on the hypotheses or explanations. If the trend is ascending, but not fast enough, teachers may (a) make changes in the program (e.g., modify the materials, change the reinforcer, provide additional instructional prompts) to try to speed progress or (b) adjust the aim line by lowering the criterion or moving the date further into the future. Alternately, teachers may do nothing to the program and look for other explanations for reduced progress.

Evaluation

When a student's progress has been below aim for approximately three out of five sessions or if the trend is flat or descending (or ascending for deceleration programs), teachers should attempt to determine why and to make program improvements based on their analysis of the data (Haring, Liberty, & White, 1980; Farlow & Snell, 1994).

Using a variety of information about the student and the program, along with the data collected on skill performance, team members can systematically develop hypotheses, or possible explanations, for a student's lack of progress. Changes should be implemented that correspond to the probable explanations, or the team may decide not to change the program but to wait and see if there is improvement. It is inappropriate, however, to wait too long before changing an ineffective program; if the team decides to wait beyond 3 weeks, the delay should be justified. The appropriate team members must take steps to modify some element of the curriculum or environment in an effort to improve ineffective programs.

Analyzing the Problem

A number of educators and researchers have developed approaches for analyzing student performance data and making program changes (e.g., Browder, 1991; Browder, Demchak, Heller, & King, 1989; Farlow & Snell, 1994; Ford, Schnorr, Meyer, Davern, Black, & Dempsey, 1989; Haring, Liberty, & White, 1980, 1981; Neel & Billingsley, 1989; Snell, 1988). Some approaches are simple, while others are complex; several approaches rest directly on research, while several do not. Many of the approaches for making data-based decisions build on the work of Norris Haring and his colleagues, Kathleen Liberty and Owen White. This section describes some steps in a procedure that is built on the work of Haring and his colleagues and on that of other researchers and practitioners (Farlow & Snell, 1994; Snell, 1988).

Some of the steps in the process for making data-based program improvements have been described already, but a review of them, plus several more, follows.

1. Determine whether progress is consistently below expected progress (e.g., below the aim for at least 3 of 5 consecutive days, and the trend is flat or descending).
2. If a trend is not clear, use a trend line to define it. If a trend is flat or descending, continue the analysis. If a trend is ascending (but the data are below the aim for 3 of the past 5 days), wait and see, consider adjusting the aim line, or continue searching for reasons.
3. Examine a variety of relevant information and establish hypotheses for poor progress or lack of progress (e.g., training and probe data), including performance data on other objectives, anecdotal records of the student or the teaching session, absentee data, health or medication records, and records of behavior problems.
4. Decide whether you will (a) continue instruction unchanged (wait and see if progress improves), (b) collect more information based on one or more hypotheses before making changes in the program but continue to monitor progress, or (c) make a program change (or several) based on one or more hypotheses while continuing to monitor progress.

A team may use guidelines or checklists to help analyze potential problems with a given instructional program. The Program Analysis Worksheet (Figure 5–9) guides a team to think systematically about why a student is not progressing as planned (Farlow & Snell, 1994).

The process of data analysis is an important one if students are to benefit fully from the systematic data collected by their teachers and from informal observations. Analyzing relevant information about a student's performance during distinct periods of time and drawing evaluative conclusions is an ongoing process, not one that waits until the end of the year. Many factors should be considered before changing a program and deciding what that change or those changes will be. Regardless of what system of data collection and analysis is used, what is important is that teachers use the data they collect on student performance to monitor progress and to improve programs when necessary.

Special Considerations in General Education Settings

This final section of the chapter discusses the importance of being unobtrusive in data collection, storage, and use. First, evaluation information is confidential. It should be available only to the student, family members, and professionals directly involved in the student's program. Just as a typical student's report card is never hung in the hall for public display, neither should a student's progress graphs or data records be displayed in classrooms. All graphs and data collection sheets should be organized and stored in record files accessible to teaching staff.

Unobtrusive collection of data is another challenge for teachers. It is easy to envision a data-collecting teacher or school psychologist armed with a clipboard, stopwatch, and a portable video camera to record students' performance. When teaching staff are so obtrusive in their data collection efforts, they call unnecessary attention to their students and may inadvertently stigmatize them (Test & Spooner, 1996).

Behavior measurement must be relatively accurate and must provide relevant information. However, accuracy and relevance of data need not depend on obvious or bulky recording equipment, excessive adult observers, or measurement procedures that interfere with teaching or learning within the community or school setting. Typically, teaching staff (and sometimes peer tutors) collect data as they teach or record data after an instructional session, basing the data on the permanent products left as a result of a student's performance (e.g., counting the number of clean cafeteria tables). Additional observers usually are not needed or available.

The methods selected for directly measuring behavior in teaching settings should be as simple and time-saving as possible (e.g., frequency or event counts for carefully selected and distinct periods of time or count of permanent products). Typically, teachers avoid methods requiring extensive observation time (e.g., frequency counts taken across an entire day) and avoid measurement equipment that interferes with teaching (e.g., a portable tape recorder and headset for an interval measurement). Teachers must make some compromises to obtain the maximum amount of information with the least effort and time commitment.

FIGURE 5–9
Problem Analysis Worksheet

Problem Analysis Worksheet

Student: _____ Time Period: _____

Program: _____

Team Members present at meeting: _____

Directions: Put a check (√) by the statement that you feel describes the data collected during the latest review period. If you suspect the statement describes the data, but you need more data to address the issue, check the second column. (Check only one column.)

			Seems to be true	Need more data
1. The trend of the data is:	Ascending	1.	_____	NMD
	Flat			
	Descending			
2. The data are:	Not variable	2.	_____	NMD
	Variable			
3. The level of the data is:	Low	3.	_____	NMD
	Moderate			
	High			
4. Student performance is related to medication		4.	_____	NMD
5. Student has experienced a temporary environmental change/problem/stress		5.	_____	NMD
6. The data may not be reliable		6.	_____	NMD
7. The staff are not implementing the program reliably		7.	_____	NMD
8. The trend or level of variability has changed since the last review		8.	_____	NMD
9. The student used to perform the skill at higher levels		9.	_____	NMD
10. The data pattern indicates that variability is random		10.	_____	NMD
11. The data pattern indicates that variability is cyclical		11.	_____	NMD
12. Test data conflict with the instructional data		12.	_____	NMD
13. Test scores tend to be greater than instructional scores		13.	_____	NMD
14. Errors typically occur on the same step(s) of the task analysis		14.	_____	NMD
15. Student is not progressing through prompt levels		15.	_____	NMD
16. Errors typically occur on the first trials of the day/session		16.	_____	NMD
17. Errors typically occur on the latter trials of the day or session		17.	_____	NMD
18. Errors occur more in some settings or with specific staff		18.	_____	NMD
19. Student does not attempt the task		19.	_____	NMD
20. Student is reluctant to participate in the task		20.	_____	NMD
21. Student responds negatively to certain levels of prompts		21.	_____	NMD
22. Student does not attend to the cues		22.	_____	NMD
23. Student is receiving reinforcement for incorrect performance		23.	_____	NMD
24. Student exhibits similar problems in other programs		24.	_____	NMD
25. Interfering behaviors are present		25.	_____	NMD
26. Problem behaviors are staying the same or increasing		26.	_____	NMD
27. The program excludes student interaction with peers		27.	_____	NMD
28. Other:		28.	_____	NMD

State team's hypothesis about the instructional problems based on the above information:

Note: From *Making the Most of Student Performance Data,* by L. J. Farlow and Martha E. Snell, 1994, Innovations: Research to Practice Series, Washington, D.C.: American Association on Mental Retardation. Copyright 1994 by American Association of Mental Retardation. Adapted with permission.

Minimizing the obtrusiveness of data collection typically can be accomplished with a little imagination and brainstorming among educators or between teachers and a student's peers. In some cases, typical measurement methods are used but the equipment is simplified. For example, a teacher who knows a task analysis fairly well can make notes on recipe cards or on small Post-it notes. Some teachers may want to keep 3-inch by 5-inch cards in their pockets for reference, noting the specific step number (correct or prompted) on the card as the student performs the task. Post-it notes can be stuck to purses or watches and hash marks can record the frequency of a target behavior. Wrist-worn or key-chain counters, calculators, or quiet counters also can be used to keep frequency counts unobtrusively and to time the duration of target behaviors. Some teachers have made simple bead counter bracelets using leather shoestrings and 19 plastic beads arranged in two differently colored groups of 9 and 10; the bead arrangement enables counting by ones in the first group and by tens in the second group for a possible total count of 109 before resetting the beads. In those instances when behaviors require the use of interval observations, teachers or psychologists may use headsets and precounted interval tapes on portable cassette recorders fairly unobtrusively; but this works only if the activity does not require the observer to instruct or interact with the student.

In other cases, teachers reduce the obviousness of their evaluation procedures by using less traditional measures. Meyer and Janney (1989) suggest a wide range of measurement tools that they call "user friendly." For example, once Timothy can enter his classroom reliably and safely in his arrival program, the teacher may simply measure two products that result from Timothy's performance of the entire arrival chain: (a) whether his coat or sweater is hung on his hook and (b) whether Timothy is playing at the activity that he placed by his photo on the activity choice chart. This measure would be taken 10 minutes after his arrival. Other examples include using measurement of weight gains and ratings of spillage to evaluate the success of a feeding program, or weight gain to evaluate the effectiveness of a program to reduce rumination and vomiting. Communication logs between home and school may be examined to ascertain a family's perception of student improvement and satisfaction with an instructional program. The list of examples for user-friendly measures depends on the imagination of teachers and

family members about alternate ways to evaluate learning. In all cases, when measurement procedures are simplified to reduce their obviousness, teachers still must transfer the data onto master data sheets and date them in a timely manner, so that the measurements are saved in one place for later use and their accuracy is not threatened.

Summary

Teachers must evaluate each student's progress in his or her school program. Frequent and meaningful data collection that is individualized allows teachers to effectively design, evaluate, and modify their instructional strategies. This chapter discusses quantitative measurement strategies as well as outcome measures that focus on an individual's quality of life. For measurement to be useful and meaningful, it must be reliable (accurate) and it must measure behaviors and skills considered by the individual and significant others as socially valid; that is, the behaviors and skills measured must have a positive impact on the quality of the student's life. Measurement and evaluation strategies must be designed and implemented in ways that respect each student's privacy and participation in integrated and community-based environments.

Suggested Activities

1. Select one student in your class and examine the current measurement strategies used for each of his or her IEP objectives.
   a. For each objective that includes a measurement strategy, consider whether that strategy is the most appropriate one to use. Would a different one be more meaningful?
   b. For each objective that does not include a measurement strategy, describe an appropriate and manageable one that could be used.
2. For this same student, design a graph for each instructional objective not currently displayed in graphic format.

References

Alberto, P. A., & Schofield, P. (1979). An instructional interaction pattern for the severely handicapped. *Teaching Exceptional Children*, 12, 16–19.

Alberto, P. A., & Troutman, A. C. (1999). *Applied behavior analysis for teachers* (5th ed.). Upper Saddle River, NJ: Merrill/Prentice Hall.

Baer, D. M., Wolf, M. M., & Risley, T. R. (1968). Some current dimensions of applied behavior analysis. *Journal of Applied Behavior Analysis, 1,* 91–97.

Baer, D. M., Wolf, M. M., & Risley, T. R. (1987). Some still-current dimensions of applied behavior analysis. *Journal of Applied Behavior Analysis, 20,* 313–327.

Bannerman, D. J., Sheldon, J. B., Sherman, J. A., & Harchik, A. E. (1990). Balancing the right to habilitation with the right to personal liberties: The rights of people with developmental disabilities to eat too many doughnuts and take a nap. *Journal of Applied Behavior Analysis, 23,* 79–89.

Bellamy, G., Horner, R., & Inman, D. (1979). *Vocational habilitation of severely retarded adults: A direct service technology.* Baltimore: University Park Press.

Billingsley, F. F., Gallucci, C., Peck, C. A., Schwartz, I. S., & Staub, D. (1996). "But those kids can't even *do* math": An alternative conceptualization of outcomes for inclusive education. *Special Education Leadership Review,* 43–55.

Billingsley, F. F., & Liberty, K. A. (1982). The use of time-based data in instructional programs for the severely handicapped. *Journal of the Association for the Severely Handicapped, 7,* 47–55.

Billingsley, F. F., White, O. R., & Munson, R. (1980). Procedural reliability: A rationale and an example. *Behavioral Assessment, 2,* 229–241.

Browder, D. M. (1991). *Assessment of individuals with severe disabilities: An applied behavior approach to life skills assessment* (2nd ed). Baltimore: Paul H. Brookes.

Browder, D., Demchak, M., Heller, M., & King, D. (1989). An in vivo evaluation of the use of data-based rules to guide instructional decisions *Journal of the Association for Persons with Severe Handicaps, 14,* 234–240.

Brown, F. (1991). Creative daily scheduling: A nonintrusive approach to challenging behaviors in community residences. *Journal of the Association for Persons with Severe Handicaps, 16,* 75–84.

Brown, F., & Lehr, D. (1993). Meaningful activities meaningful for students with severe multiple disabilities. *Teaching Exceptional Children, 25,* 12–16.

Cooper, K. J., & Browder, D. M. (1998). Enhancing choice and participation for adults with severe disabilities in community-based instruction. *Journal of the Association for Persons with Severe Handicaps, 23,* 252–260.

Cullen, B., & Pratt, T. (1992). Measuring and reporting student progress. In S. Stainback & W. Stainback (Eds.) *Curriculum considerations in inclusive classrooms: Facilitating learning for all students,* (pp. 175–196). Baltimore: Paul H. Brookes.

DeProspero, A., & Cohen, S. (1979). Inconsistent visual analyses of intrasubject data. *Journal of Applied Behavior Analysis, 12,* 574–579.

Farlow, L. J., & Snell, M. E. (1989). Teacher use of student performance data to make instructional decisions: Practices in programs for students with moderate to profound disabilities. *Journal of the Association for Persons with Severe Handicaps, 14,* 13–22.

Farlow, L. J., & Snell, M. E. (1994). Making the most of student performance data. AAMR *Research to Practice Series: Innovations.* Washington, DC: American Association on Mental Retardation.

Fisher, M., & Lindsey-Walters, S. (1987, October). A *survey report of various types of data collection procedures used by teachers and their strengths and weaknesses.* Paper presented at the annual conference of the Association for Persons with Severe Handicaps, Chicago.

Ford, A., Schnorr, R., Meyer, L., Davern, L., Black, J., & Dempsey, P. (1989). *The Syracuse community-referenced curriculum guide.* Baltimore: Paul H. Brookes.

Frea, W. (1997). Reducing stereotypic behavior by teaching orienting responses to environmental stimuli. *Journal of the Association for Persons with Severe Handicaps, 22,* 28–35.

Fuchs, L. S., & Fuchs, D. (1986). Effects of systematic formative evaluation: A meta-analysis. *Exceptional Children, 53,* 199–208.

Gaylord-Ross, R. J., Haring, T. G., Breen, C., & Pitts-Conway, V. (1984). The training and generalization of social interaction skills with autistic youth. *Journal of Applied Behavior Analysis, 17,* 229–247.

Gaylord-Ross, R. J., & Holvoet, J. F. (1985). *Strategies for educating students with severe handicaps.* Boston: Little, Brown.

Gothelf, C. R., & Brown, F. (1996). Instructional support for self-determination in individuals with profound disabilities who are deaf-blind. In D. H. Lehr & F. Brown (Eds.). *People with disabilities who challenge the system* (pp. 355–377). Baltimore: Paul H. Brooks.

Gothelf, C. R., & Brown, F. (1998). Participation in the education process: Students with severe disabilities. In M. L. Wehmeyer & D. J. Sands (Eds.). *Making it happen: Student involvement in education planning, decision making, and instruction* (pp. 99–121). Baltimore: Paul H. Brookes.

Haring, N. G., Liberty, K. A., & White, O. R. (1980). Rules for data-based strategy decisions in instructional programs: Current research and instructional implications. In W. Sailor, B. Wilcox, & L. Brown (Eds.), *Methods of instruction for severely handicapped children* (pp. 159–192). Baltimore: Paul H. Brookes.

Haring, N., Liberty, K., & White, O. R. (1981). An *investigation of phases of learning and facilitating instructional events for the severely/profoundly handicapped learners.* Final project report. Seattle: University of Washington, School of Education.

Haring, T. G., & Breen C. (1989). Units of analysis of social interaction outcomes in supported education. *Journal of the Association for Persons with Severe Handicaps, 14,* 255–262.

Haring, T. G., & Kennedy, C. H. (1988). Units of analysis in task-analytic research. *Journal of Applied Behavior Analysis, 21,* 207–215.

Holvoet, J., Guess, D., Mulligan, M., & Brown, F. (1980). The individualized curriculum sequencing model (II): A teaching strategy for severely handicapped students. *Journal of the Association for the Severely Handicapped, 5,* 337–351.

Holvoet, J., O'Neil, C., Chazdon, L., Carr, D., & Warner, J. (1983). Hey, do we really have to take data? *Journal of the Association for the Severely Handicapped, 8,* 56–70.

Hunt, P., Alwell, M., Farron-Davis, F., & Goetz, L. (1996). Creating socially supportive environments for fully included students who experience multiple disaiblities. *Journal of the Association for Persons with Severe Handicaps, 21,* 53–71.

Kazdin, A. E. (1976). Statistical analysis for single-case experimental designs. In M. Hersen & D. Barlow (Eds.), *Single-case experimental designs: Strategies for studying behavior change* (pp. 265–316). New York: Pergamon Press.

Kazdin, A. E. (1977). Assessing the clinical or applied importance of behavior change through social validation. *Behavior Modification, 1,* 427–452.

Kazdin, A. E. (1980). *Behavior modification in applied settings.* Homewood, IL: Dorsey Press.

Kennedy, C. H., & Itkonen, T. (1994). Some effects of regular class participation on the social contacts and social networks of high school students with severe disabilities.

Kerr, M. M., & Nelson, C. M. (1998). *Strategies for managing behavior problems in the classroom* (3rd ed). Upper Saddle River, NJ: Merrill/ Prentice Hall.

Koegel, L. K., Stiebel, D., & Koegel, R. L. (1998). Reducing aggression in children with autism toward infant or toddler siblings. *Journal of the Association for Persons with Severe Handicaps, 23,* 111–118.

Kramer, L., & Whitehurst, C. (1981). Effects of button features on self-dressing in young retarded children. *Education and Training of the Mentally Retarded, 16,* 277–283.

Lee, S. & Odom, S. L. (1996). The relationship between stereotypic behavior and peer social interaction for children with severe disabilities. *Journal of the Association for Persons with Severe Handicaps, 21,* 88–95.

Meyer, L. H., & Evans, I. M. (1989). *Non-aversive intervention for behavior problems: A manual for home and community.* Baltimore: Paul H. Brookes.

Meyer, L. H., & Evans, I. M. (1993). Meaningful outcomes in behavioral intervention: Evaluating positive approaches to the remediation of challenging behaviors. In J. Reichle & D. P. Wacker (Eds.) *Communicative alternatives to challenging behavior: Integrating functional assessment and intervention strategies* (pps. 407–428). Baltimore: Paul H. Brookes.

Meyer, L. H., & Janney, R. (1989). User-friendly measures of meaningful outcomes: Evaluating behavior interventions. *Journal of the Association for Persons with Severe Handicaps, 14,* 263–270.

Meyer, L. H., St. Peter, S., & Park-Lee, S. H. (1986, November). *The validation of social skills for successful performance in community environments by young adults with moderate to severe/profound disabilities.* Paper presented at the meeting of the Association for Advancement of Behavior Therapy, Chicago.

Miltenberger, R. (1997). *Behavior modification: Principles and procedures.* Pacific Grove, CA: Brooks/Cole.

Munger, G., Snell, M. E., & Loyd, B. H. (1989). A study of the effects of frequency of probe data collection and graph characteristics on teachers' visual analysis. *Research in Developmental Disabilities, 10,* 109–127.

Neel, R. S., & Billingsley, F. F. (1989). IMPACT: *A functional curriculum handbook for students with moderate to severe disabilities.* Baltimore: Paul H. Brookes.

Parsonson, B. S., & Baer, D. M. (1978). The analysis and presentation of graphic data. In T. R. Kratochwill (Ed.). *Single subject research: Strategies for evaluating change* (pp. 101–165). New York: Academic Press.

Quilitch, R. H., & Risley, T. R. (1973). The effects of play materials on social play. *Journal of Applied Behavior Analysis, 6,* 573–578.

Reichle, J., York, J., & Eynon, D. (1989). Influence of indicating preferences for initiating, maintaining, and terminating interactions. In F. Brown & D. Lehr (Eds.). *Persons with profound disabilities: Issues and practices* (pp. 191–211). Baltimore: Paul H. Brookes.

Risley, T. R. (1970). Behavior modification: An experimental-therapeutic endeavor. In L. A. Hamerlynck, P. O. Davidson, & L. E. Acker (Eds.), *Behavior modification and ideal health services* (pp. 103–127). Calgary, Alberta, Canada: University of Calgary Press.

Schloss, P. J., & Smith, M. A. (1998). *Applied behavior analysis in the classroom* (2nd ed.). Boston: Allyn & Bacon.

Smith, M. D. (1990). *Autism and life in the community: Successful interventions for behavioral challenges.* Baltimore: Paul H. Brookes.

Snell, M. E. (1988). *Final report for the effective use of student performance data by teachers of students with severe handicaps* (Final Project Report for Grant #G008530150.) Washington, DC: U.S. Department of Education, Office of Special Education and Rehabilitation Services.

Snell, M. E., & Lloyd, B. H. (1991). A study of the effects of trend variability, frequency, and form of data on teachers' judgments about progress and their decisions about program change. *Research in Developmental Disabilities, 12,* 41–61.

Storey, K. (1997). Quality of life issues in social skills assessment of persons with disabilities. *Education and Training in Mental Retardation and Developmental Disabilities, 32,* 197–200.

Tawney, J., & Gast, D. (1984). *Single subject research in special education.* New York: Merrill/Macmillan.

Test, D. W., & Spooner, F. (1996). Community-based instructional support. AAMR *Research to Practice Series: Innovations.* Washington, DC: American Association on Mental Retardation.

Thomson, C., Holmberg, M., & Baer, D. M. (1974). A brief report on a comparison of time-sampling procedures. *Journal of Applied Behavior Analysis, 7,* 623–626.

Umbreit, J., & Blair, K. W. (1996). The effects of preference, choice, and attention on problem behavior at school. *Education and Training in Mental Retardation and Developmental Disabilities, 31,* 151–162.

Utley, B. L., Zigmond, N., & Strain, P. S. (1987). How various forms of data affect teacher analysis of teacher performance. *Exceptional Children, 53,* 411–422.

Voeltz, L. H., & Evans, I. M. (1983). Educational validity: Procedures to evaluate outcomes in programs for severely handicapped learners. *Journal of the Association for the Severely Handicapped, 8,* 3–15.

Voeltz, L. M., Wuerch, B. B., & Bockhaut, C. H. (1982). Social validation of leisure time activities training with severely handicapped youth. *Journal of the Association for the Severely Handicapped, 7,* 3–13.

Wacker, D. P. (1989). Why measure anything? *Journal of the Association for Persons with Severe Handicaps, 14,* 254.

Wacker, D., Berg, W., Wiggins, B., Muldoon, M., & Cavanaugh, J. (1985). Evaluation of reinforcer preferences for profoundly handicapped students *Journal of Applied Behavior Analysis, 18,* 173–178.

White, O. R. (1986). Precision teaching—precision learning. *Exceptional Children, 53,* 522–534.

White, O. R., & Haring, N. G. (1980). *Exceptional teaching* (2nd ed) New York: Merrill/Macmillan.

Wolf, M. M. (1978). Social validity: The case for subjective measurement or how applied behavior analysis is finding its heart. *Journal of Applied Behavior Analysis, 11,* 203–214.

Wolfe, P. (December, 1991). Social validation of systemic instructional techniques for use with students with severe handicaps. Unpublished doctoral dissertation, University of Virginia, Charlottesville.

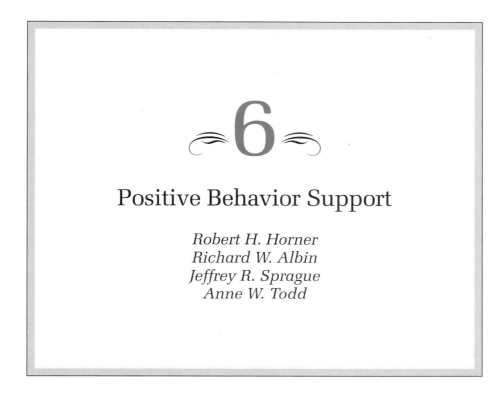

6

Positive Behavior Support

Robert H. Horner
Richard W. Albin
Jeffrey R. Sprague
Anne W. Todd

Positive behavior support is the comprehensive implementation of behavioral interventions that are guided by functional assessment, consistent with basic laws of human behavior and match with the values, skills and resources of those who implement the intervention (Koegel, Koegel, & Dunlap, 1996). Positive behavior support interventions focus on important, durable, generalized outcomes that (a) reduce the full range of problem behaviors that form social or educational barriers for an individual, (b) increase adaptive skills, and (c) improve basic educational, social, employment, and living options. Positive behavior support interventions emphasize the *redesign of environments* (e.g., classrooms, homes, workplaces) to produce broad changes that affect how a person lives in addition to how he/she behaves. Positive behavior support does not include procedures that involve the delivery of pain or result in tissue damage or social humiliation.

Historically, positive behavior support grew from a movement against the use of specific, aversive interventions (e.g., electrical shock, facial screening,

pinching, mechanical restraints, ammonia). More recently, positive behavior support has grown beyond an emphasis on avoiding certain procedures into a clear approach that embraces the technical contributions of applied behavior analysis, demands results that are of lifestyle importance, and requires that procedures be practical for use in homes, schools, communities, and workplaces. In many ways, the emerging technology of positive behavior support reflects the tenets of applied behavior analysis first articulated by Baer, Wolf, and Risley (1968) when they challenged the world to develop procedures that were effective, applied, behavioral, analytic, technological, conceptual and generalized.

Relevance of Positive Behavior Support

In this chapter we offer a vision of the central features defining positive behavior support, the importance of this technology for students with severe disabilities, and implications for the future. Positive behavior support is of particular relevance today for students with severe disabilities, given the impact of (a) inclusion on school reform, (b) the continuing struggle that schools experience educating children with problem behaviors, and (c) the new legal expectation that functional assessment and positive behavior support be incorporated as a regular part of school discipline and behavior support efforts.

Inclusion efforts have transformed many assumptions about special education and special services for children with severe disabilities (Hunt, Farron-Davis, Wrenn, Hirose-Hatae, & Goetz, 1997). The fundamental assumption underlying inclusion efforts is that children with disabilities will be better able to learn essential social skills, academic skills, communication skills, and daily living skills in the context of their peers without disabilities than they can in separate environments. Both our values and our technology argue that personal, social, and academic development will be best achieved when individualized instruction occurs in real contexts rather than in atypical, artificial, and isolated settings (Meyer, Peck, & Brown, 1991; Schmidt & Harriman, 1998). The era of special education as a separate, parallel educational option for children with disabilities is ending. For the foreseeable future, special education will be much more embedded in regular education. Our understanding of effective instructional procedures, our values, and the escalating costs associated with parallel services argue for a closer linkage between special and regular education. Research over the past 30 years documents the ability of children with severe disabilities to learn an impressive range of skills when they receive intensive, well-designed instruction (Meyer, et al, 1991; Snell, 1993). The challenge today is to arrange effective instruction for children with severe disabilities within regular classrooms. We know that inclusion is much more than simply "presence" in regular classrooms, but presence with the support needed to learn, develop, and contribute (Giangreco & Putnam, 1991; Janney & Snell, 1997; Salisbury, Mangino, Rainforth, Syryca, & Palombaro, 1994).

The debate around inclusion has been of special relevance for those interested in behavior support. Just as simple presence is an insufficient outcome for inclusion, so also, simple reduction in problem behaviors is an insufficient outcome for behavior support.

Behavior support is now expected to not only reduce dangerous and disruptive behaviors, but to build new adaptive skills, change activity patterns as well as patterns of problem behavior, and result in durable, generalized, and important changes in how a student lives and learns (Horner et al., 1990). This broadened set of expectations alters the way behavior support is designed, implemented, and evaluated. While there remains a clear expectation that positive behavior support must be effective in reducing problem behavior, the mandate today is that behavior reduction alone will be insufficient if it leaves the student compliant but in a socially, academically, and personally barren situation.

Schools struggle to provide effective education to students with severe problem behavior. Students who engage in self-injury, property destruction, aggression, defiance, and disruption are at major risk for being removed from regular classrooms. Teachers in both regular and special education contexts indicate that they do not feel they have the skills and resources to educate children with severe problem behaviors (Horner, Diemer, & Brazeau, 1992; Sugai & Horner, 1994; Walker, Colvin, & Ramsey, 1995). The impressive gains reported in journal articles and book chapters about our ability to support children with problem behaviors stand in contrast with the struggle that most schools and families face when responding to behavioral challenges (Turnbull & Ruef, 1996, 1997). The technology of positive behavior support must be effective enough to preempt the exclusion of children with problem behaviors, and practical enough that it can be delivered in regular schools and homes by typical school personnel and families.

The Individuals with Disabilities Education Act (IDEA) Amendments of 1997 state (Box 6–1) that functional behavioral assessment and positive behavior support should be considered when behavior support is developed for children with disabilities (Turnbull, Rainbolt, & Buchele-Ash, 1997). These amendments codify positive behavior support as an expected standard within the field of special education and most definitely within the behavior support provided for students with severe disabilities. Teachers, administrators, and families now have an intensified need to be familiar with, and able to deliver, positive behavior support procedures.

To appreciate the recent changes that have occurred in behavior support consider the case of Darin,

Individuals with Disabilities Education Act (IDEA) Amendments of 1997

Box 6–1   **(d) Individualized Education Programs**

(3) Development of IEP.
(B) Consideration of Special Factors—The IEP Team shall (1) In the case of a child whose behavior impedes his or her learning or that of others, consider, when appropriate, strategies, including positive behavioral interventions, strategies, and supports to address that behavior;

(k) Placement in Alternative Educational Setting.

(1) Authority of School Personnel.
(B) Either before or not later than 10 days after taking a disciplinary action described in subparagraph (A)
(1) If the local educational agency did not conduct a functional behavioral assessment and implement a behavioral intervention plan for such child before the behavior that resulted in the suspension described in subparagraph (A), the agency shall convene an IEP meeting to develop an assessment plan to address that behavior;

and compare the options available to him today as opposed to 20 years ago (see next page).

Darin provides an excellent example of the central ways that positive behavior support procedures are used to construct effective environments. Darin's success also highlighted two central processes that characterize positive behavior support: (a) functional assessment and (b) comprehensive support plan design. The next two sections of this chapter provide details about the process of *functional assessment* and the design of *comprehensive plans of support*.

Functional Assessment

Functional assessment is a central feature of positive behavior support. The overall goal of functional assessment is to gather accurate information (Arndorfer, Miltenberger, Woster, Rortvedt, & Gaffaney, 1994) that will improve the effectiveness (Durand, Berotti, & Weiner, 1993; Neef & Iwata, 1994) and efficiency (Horner, 1994; Sturmey, 1994; Wacker et al., 1994) of a behavior support plan. Research conducted over the past 30 years suggests that four types of information are most helpful in the design of support:

1. *Description of problem behaviors*: Behavior support is more effective when everyone involved in providing support agrees on the exact behaviors under consideration. To improve in the consistency and clarity of behavioral intervention implementation, it is useful to develop operational descriptions of *all*

problem behaviors performed by an individual. Describe all of the problem behaviors an individual performs regularly, and describe those behaviors in a manner that is understood by everyone who will implement the intervention. An operational description emphasizes what can be seen and heard rather than what is inferred about behavior. Describing a behavior as "anger" or "frustration" involves significant inference about what is happening within the student. More importantly, such labels carry different images and connotations for the different people who will be providing support. Keep the descriptions simple, clear, and descriptive. Describe "hitting," "spitting," "not doing what is asked by an adult," or "breaking/tearing property." Descriptions such as these will help ensure that different people implementing support will operate with a common understanding of the challenge.

Darin's team agreed that his behaviors of concern were slapping his own face, screaming, and hitting or kicking (attacking) others. For another student, Diane (described in Horner, O'Neill, & Flannery, 1993), problem behaviors described were hitting and biting others and throwing and breaking objects.

2. *Consequences maintaining problem behaviors*: Problem behaviors typically do not continue to occur unless there is some consequence that maintains them. Although some behaviors may be maintained by nonsocial, internal consequences (e.g., body rocking may be maintained by the internal sensations),

Behavior Support Plan for Darin

Darin is 9 years old, lives at home with his family, has autism and severe intellectual disabilities, likes dogs and cats, can communicate with one-word and two-word phrases, will play for long periods of time by himself with a Slinky, but has a history of slapping his face, screaming, and physically attacking adults who work with him. Twenty years ago, Darin most likely would have been placed in a segregated school with a minimalist curriculum, and experienced behavior support that included the delivery of very aversive events (e.g., physical punishment, restraint) when he engaged in problem behaviors.

Today, the assumption is that Darin should receive education in a regular third grade classroom, while also receiving the behavioral support needed to insure that his Individualized Educational Program (IEP) works. The design of behavior support for Darin began with a team of individuals that included his teacher, family, and a behavior specialist. This team completed a personal futures plan (Kincaid, 1996; Mount, 1994), and a functional assessment of Darin's behavior. Darin's preferences and dislikes were identified, and situations were categorized where he was most likely and least likely to engage in slapping, screaming, and aggression. Both through functional assessment interviews with Darin's teacher and family, and through systematic observations of his behavior in the classroom, Darin's team identified three situations where his problem behaviors were most likely to occur: (a) during transitions, when expectations were unclear; (b) during requests to speak in front of the class; and (c) when instructed to do tasks that involved writing. In each case, the team identified that Darin's slapping, screaming, or aggression was rewarded by escaping from something aversive such as: (a) the uncertainty and confusion of transitions, (b) the requirement to speak in front of the class, or (c) the need to write. Based on this assessment, a plan of support was developed that included (1) providing a picture sequence that Darin could use to move predictably through transitions, (2) a shift from speaking in front of the class to working in a small group format with others, and (3) curricular adaptions related to writing tasks, including a sequenced curriculum where he is asked to draw, trace letters and numbers, and then copy words and numbers.

Darin received direct instruction on how to use the picture sequence prompts during transitions, how to follow instructions within small group activities, and how to perform each step of the adapted writing curriculum. He also received direct instruction in how to request a 2-minute "break" from activities by saying, "Break please." Finally, the teacher and a teaching assistant agreed that

if Darin engaged in problem behaviors, he would be told to ask for a break the "right way" (e.g., "Darin say, 'Break please' if you want a break."). However, Darin could not escape the activity through problem behaviors.

In essence, Darin's environment was changed so that his problem behaviors became irrelevant, inefficient, and ineffective. To make his problem behaviors *irrelevant,* the features of Darin's school day (e.g., confusing transitions, speaking in front of the class, difficult writing assignments) were modified to minimize features that were identified as highly aversive. Following the recommendation of Dunlap, Kern-Dunlap, Clarke, and Robbins (1991) the same instructional goals were maintained (e.g., Darin still had a writing objective), but different activities were developed to achieve these goals. Without the aversive events being presented, problem behaviors maintained by escape from these events should be irrelevant (i.e., there is no longer a need to escape).

The problem behaviors became *less efficient* when Darin was taught a simple communication skill (saying "Break please") for obtaining a 2-minute break. He could now escape from those events he perceived as aversive through a socially appropriate request that was physically easier and more likely to be effective than problem behaviors. The new communication skill gave him a more efficient, socially appropriate strategy for escaping.

The problem behaviors became *ineffective* when the teacher and teaching assistant agreed that instead of removing Darin whenever he engaged in problem behaviors, they would redirect him to use his break request and only then allow a break. Although this was difficult during the first few times he became disruptive, Darin quickly learned that problem behaviors were no longer an effective way of escaping unpleasant situations and that asking for a break was effective. Together, the different elements of Darin's behavior support plan transformed the classroom into an environment where Darin's problem behaviors were irrelevant, inefficient, and ineffective. In doing this, however, Darin's behavior was not managed as much as preempted and redirected. He now had activities in which he was successful, plus effective communication skills he could use to let the staff know when he was in distress.

The result of this plan of positive behavior support was that Darin remained an active, and contributing member of his third grade class, his problem behaviors reduced in frequency and intensity, and he made major gains socially and academically. Furthermore, his behavioral competence at school prompted extension of the functional assessment and intervention strategies to his home.

a large proportion of problem behaviors are maintained by external consequences, such as escaping aversive events (e.g., demands, activities, noises), or obtaining social attention, access to activities, or access to objects (e.g., food, toys). It is extremely useful to know the consequence (or consequences) that maintains problem behaviors when designing a plan of support. In fact, if support procedures are designed without attention to maintaining consequences, the support may be as likely to make the problem behavior worse as it is to produce desired changes (e.g., using "time-out" for an escape-maintained behavior will increase the behavior).

Darin's functional assessment indicated that his problem behaviors were maintained by escape from activities and situations that he found aversive. These aversive situations included activities involving writing, speaking in front of the class, and transitions that were confusing and unpredictable.

In the case of Diane, hitting, biting, and throwing or breaking objects all were maintained by escape from hard tasks and from situations where Diane was corrected for errors. However, escape is not the only maintaining consequence for problem behaviors.

A young student named Nina screamed and grabbed for objects (battling to get them) in school and at home; these behaviors were maintained by Nina's success in obtaining objects that she wanted.

3. *Antecedent events that trigger problem behaviors:* Information from a functional assessment identifies conditions when the problem behaviors are most *and least* likely to occur. This is useful for defining exactly what events prompt or occasion problem behaviors. Information about the specific times of day, people, comments, activities, or changes in the day that immediately precede and evoke problem behaviors help in the redesign of environments, and in the identification of alternative behaviors to teach (e.g., alternative communication responses).

For Darin, confusing transitions, requests to speak in front of the class, and tasks involving writing were identified as antecedent events that preceded problem behaviors.

For Nina, objects that she encountered in her environment that she wanted but did not have were antecedents for screaming and grabbing (or attempting to grab).

4. *Setting events that exaggerate the likelihood of problem behaviors:* A recent addition to the list of information needed from a functional assessment is the influence of setting events (Carr, Reeve, & Magito-McLaughlin, 1996; Horner, Day, & Day, 1997; Horner, Vaughn, Day, & Ard, 1996). Setting events (and the more descriptive term: establishing operations) are events that temporarily alter the value of reinforcers that maintain problem behaviors (Michael, 1993). Setting events differ from antecedent events in that setting events, by themselves, do not trigger problem behaviors. However, the presence of a setting event may increase the probability of an antecedent event triggering a problem behavior. For example, hunger is a setting event that increases the value of food, and the likelihood of problem behaviors that produce food (e.g., stealing food). Sleep deprivation is a setting event that may make boring tasks even more aversive than usual and decrease the value of the social praise obtained by doing these tasks. Further, sleep deprivation may increase the value of escaping from boring tasks (e.g., via tantrums) (Durand, 1998). Time spent alone (i.e., a long period of no attention) may be a setting event that increases the value of social attention and, thereby, increases the likelihood of problem behaviors that result in social attention. Setting events help explain why on some days (when no setting event is present) an instructional session goes well, and on other days (when a setting event is present) the exact same instruction is met with dramatic resistance. The design of behavior support is improved when information about powerful setting events is available.

Being tired, defined as less than 6 hours of sleep, was identified as a powerful setting event for Darin. When he was tired, escape from aversive tasks was an even stronger reinforcer, so problem behaviors that produced "escape" were more likely to occur.

Functional assessment is a series of activities used to gather these four types of information (i.e., description of problem behavior, maintaining consequences, immediate antecedents [triggers], setting events). Functional assessment is *not* a process for diagnosis, *nor* a process for determining if a behavior problem is a manifestation of a disability (Sugai, Horner, & Sprague, in press). Functional assessment is a process for defining the events that reliably predict and maintain problem behaviors. The information generated from a functional assessment is useful if it improves the effectiveness and efficiency of a behavior support plan.

The process of functional assessment carries important assumptions about the nature of positive behavior support. The focus of the assessment is on understanding the relationship between environmental events and problem behavior. The goal is to understand how best to change the environment, not the child. Unlike a medical approach, in which the goal is to identify problems in the child to cure (or fix), the focus of functional assessment is to understand existing contingencies in the environment that are maintaining undesirable patterns of behavior. The information is used to modify the environment and to promote and teach more adaptive and desirable patterns of behavior. In this way, functional assessment and positive behavior support emphasize the engineering of effective environments as the key to producing durable, generalized behavior change.

Functional assessment also differs from other forms of diagnosis by focusing less on the fundamental etiology of problem behaviors (i.e., how they began) than on what currently is maintaining them. Problem behaviors may develop initially for very different causes than those that maintain them. Guess and Carr (1991), for example, suggest that some forms of severe self-injury may begin as simple forms of self-stimulation (or responses to short-term illness) and then, through shaping, develop into complex and destructive behaviors that are maintained by social consequences. The point is that a functional assessment focuses attention on the *current* contingencies associated with a problem behavior, not on the long history that may have led to the situation. Functional assessment is not an approach to diagnosis. It shifts the focus of behavior support: (a) from a medical to a behavioral model, (b) from fixing children to fixing environments, and (c) from emphasis on diagnostic labels to emphasis on the specific environmental events that set up, trigger, and maintain problem behaviors.

Outcomes of Functional Assessment

Although there are several strategies for collecting functional assessment information, the overall process typically follows a sequence in which, first, basic infor-mation is gathered, then behavioral hypotheses are developed based on the information, and finally these hypotheses are tested through direct observation (O'Neill, et al., 1997). Confirmed functional assessment information is summarized into hypothesis statements that indicate: (a) setting events, (b) specific antecedent events that predict (occurrence and nonoccurrence of) problem behaviors, (c) problem behaviors (by response class), and (d) maintaining consequences. Given this process, a professionally completed functional assessment will produce the following five outcomes (O'Neill et al., 1997).

1. Operational definitions of the problem behavior(s).
2. Description of setting events and antecedent events that reliably predict when problem behaviors are most likely and situations in which problem behaviors are least likely.
3. Description of the consequences that maintain the problem behaviors.
4. Direct observation data supporting the link between problems and the controlling antecedents and consequences.
5. Summary hypothesis statements that can be used for designing behavioral interventions.

Why Conduct a Functional Assessment?

Conducting a functional assessment has multiple values. The *primary* value of functional assessment is that the information improves the effectiveness and efficiency of the behavior support plan. A plan guided by a functional assessment is more likely to result in desired behavior change. A *second* value, however, is that without a functional assessment, behavior support may be harmful. The most common example is the youngster who engages in tantrums and is removed from the classroom when he tantrums. If tantrums are maintained by avoiding aversive classroom demands, then removal from the classroom not only will be ineffective at reducing tantrums, it will *increase* the likelihood of tantrums. An important value of functional assessment is the use of the information to avoid otherwise harmful interventions.

A *third* value of functional assessment is the improved coherence of multi-element interventions. There is a significant danger when multiple procedures are used in a single intervention (e.g., schedule redesign, teaching new skills, extinction, reinforcement) that, although each procedure may seem logical, the group of procedures collectively may contradict each other. It would not be useful, for example, to teach a student a communication response for taking a break and simultaneously ignore all escape behaviors (including his requests for breaks) so that he learns to "finish his work." If all elements of the intervention are consistent with a single functional assessment, the set of procedures is more likely to be conceptually consistent. Functional assessment information helps ensure that the multiple elements of an intervention work together rather than conflict.

A *fourth* value of functional assessment is that if all the people who will implement a plan of support agree on (a) the exact behaviors of concern, (b) the antecedents that trigger the problem behavior, and (c) the consequences maintaining the problem behavior, they are more likely to implement the intervention with greater consistency. It is impressive how different two people can be in their implementation of a plan of support. The more different the implementers are, the more difficult it is for the student to learn new ways of behaving. While research is just beginning to examine this issue (Albin & Sandler, 1998), an important value of conducting a functional assessment may be improved consistency across all people implementing a behavior support plan.

Functional Assessment as a Three-Step Process

Functional assessment is the gathering of information that defines patterns of problem behavior, the antecedents and setting events that predict occurrence and nonconcurrence of the problem behavior, and the consequences that maintain it. This information is used to shape the content of behavior support plans.

Functional assessment methods vary in terms of the reliability, usefulness, and efficiency (i.e., cost, time to collect) of the information they provide. While we can expect that the sophistication of these methods will continue to improve, most procedures for conducting functional assessment use the following steps:

1. *Define the Challenge.* The first step in conducting a functional assessment is to define the problem behaviors, and the daily (or regular) pattern of problem behavior occurrence. A functional assessment

typically is not limited to a single problem behavior, or a single situation. As such, the assessment typically begins by determining all the problem behaviors a student performs, where they occur, how often they occur, and the topography (form) and intensity with which they occur. One strategy for doing this is to identify basic daily routines that are unlikely to include problem behaviors and daily routines and activities that are likely to include problem behaviors.

2. *Build a Hypothesis (or Multiple Hypotheses).* The main data-gathering tasks in a functional assessment are aimed at building hypothesis statements that indicate *what* problem behaviors occur, *when, where,* and *with whom* they are most and least likely to occur, and *why* they keep occurring. The information for building and refining hypotheses typically is gathered through indirect methods, such as structured interviews and written checklists, and through direct observations (informal or systematic) of student behavior. When indirect methods produce information that is unclear or conflicting, more reliance must be placed on direct observations.

3. *Validate the Hypothesis (or Hypotheses).* Because the hypothesis statements will guide behavior support, and because hypothesis statements are often difficult to define with high confidence, it is necessary to test or validate that a hypothesis is accurate. The two main strategies for testing and confirming hypothesis statements are: (a) systematic direct observation in natural contexts, and (b) formal functional analysis manipulations, where mini-experiments are conducted to prove that the problem behaviors occur under some conditions and under other conditions, they do not.

As a result of this three-step process, a functional assessment results in one or more validated hypothesis statements that can be used to design behavior support. The following subsections review different strategies that have been developed to accomplish each of the three main steps of functional assessment. Table 6–1 provides an overview of strategies and tools used in each step of the functional assessment process. Note that direct observation methods can be used both to build (step 2) and to validate (step 3) hypothesis statements. More detail on each of the three steps for functional assessment is provided in the following sections.

TABLE 6–1

Review of Major Functional Assessment Methods

	Step	Activity	Sample Tools	Strengths	Weaknesses
1.	Define the challenge	Assessment of daily routines and Problem behaviors	• Matrix of daily schedule (Figure 6-1) • Brown, Daily schedule analysis (1991)	• Helps to focus functional assessment efforts	• Information not specific enough for support plan development
2.	Build hypotheses	Structured interviews	• Functional Assessment Interview (O'Neill et al., 1997) • Student-Directed Functional Assessment Interview (O'Neill et al., 1997) • Motivation Assessment Scale (Durand & Crimmins, 1988) • Functional Assessment Checklist for Teachers and Staff (FACTS)(March & Horner, 1998)	• Low cost • Often includes information about setting events, antecedent stimuli, and consequences of behavior	• Summary can be complex • Match between assessment and intervention can be low compared to direct observation or experimental manipulations
3.	Build hypothesis and test hypothesis	Direct observation methods	• ABC Chart (Bijou, Peterson, & Ault, 1968) • Scatterplot (Touchette, MacDonald, & Langer, 1985) • Functional Analysis Observation Form (O'Neill et al., 1997)	• Lower cost than functional analysis • Can pinpoint time of day or other specific variables • More objective and reliable than interviews	• Data are correlational, should be interpreted with caution • Less consistent match between assessment and intervention compared to functional analysis • Difficult to identify setting events
4.	Test hypothesis	Functional analysis manipulations	• Analogue functional analysis (Iwata et al., 1982) • Brief functional analysis (Northup et al., 1991)	• Provides confident link between controlling variables and problem behavior	• Highest cost • Requires more skill to implement • Results may not always generalize • Difficult to identify setting events

Define the Challenge

A central feature of positive behavior support is emphasis on behavior change that covers all relevant parts of the student's day. When defining a student's behavioral challenge, it is important to define not only all the problem behaviors a student performs, but the broad pattern of problem behaviors across typical daily routines.

Assess Daily Routines

Behavioral routines are sequences that are a common part of daily life and result in socially important outcomes. Meals, bathing, travel in the car, eating out, visits to a friend, morning circle at school, recess, transitions from one school activity to another, and reading lessons are all examples of routines. Shoe tying, asking for help, doing a math problem, and sliding down a slide are not routines. They are behaviors that are part of routines. A routine involves a fairly predictable sequence of events that results in fairly predictable outcomes.

We strongly recommend that a functional assessment begin by establishing the student's full daily schedule and identifying where problems are most and least likely to occur in that schedule. Recent research supports both the importance of identifying daily schedules (Turnbull, 1997) and manipulating schedules as an effective strategy for reducing problem behaviors (Brown, 1991). One simple process for achieving the goal of defining the daily schedule involves combining information from the family, teacher, therapists, and others to complete the Assessment of Daily Routines form (Figure 6–1). To complete the form, first fill out the time of day and list the person's typical routines and activities in the first two columns. We often do one routine assessment for school days and a second for weekends. For each routine consider if problem behaviors are likely to be observed at that time. List any problem behavior(s) in the fourth column if it has occurred at least weekly over the past 2 months. In the third column, identify which antecedents are most likely to predict (trigger) the problem behavior in those routines in which problem behaviors are listed. In the last column, indicate what consequence appears most likely to maintain that behavior across time.

The Assessment of Daily Routines form for Darin (Figure 6–1) shows that problem behaviors are occur-

ring in the context of seven routines and activities: traveling to school, the morning greeting routine, the language arts lesson period (activities involving writing), reading period, group project activities involving presentations to the class, the dismissal routine, and the bedtime routine.

The assessment of daily routines serves as a strategy for placing a student's behavior in a broad, daily context. By drawing information from multiple sources (e.g., family, teachers, therapists, bus drivers) the analysis of routines also serves to build a single structure for including the perspectives of the different people who may deliver support.

Build a Hypothesis

Once the broad challenge is defined in terms of daily routines, interviews (or other indirect methods) and direct observations are used to gather information to build hypotheses about the variables affecting problem behavior. This step may involve stages of hypothesis development as information is collected, ranging from preliminary hypotheses that help guide the collection of functional assessment information to fully developed hypothesis statements that summarize functional assessment information about the relationships among these four elements: *setting events, triggering antecedents,* the *behaviors of concern,* and *maintaining consequences.* Table 6–2 presents examples of hypothesis statements. Examine each statement to identify (a) the antecedent events that trigger problem behavior(s), (b) the problem behavior(s), (c) the consequences that appear to maintain the problem behavior(s), and (d) the setting events that make the whole sequence more likely. The outcome of this step is testable hypothesis statements that support team members agree are accurate and that can be validated through systematic observation.

The hypothesis statement for Darin that summarizes information collected through the Assessment of Daily Routines, Functional Assessment Interview (O'Neill et al., 1997), and informal observations in school and at home is: When Darin experiences a transition during which expectations for his behavior are unclear or when he is asked to speak in front of the whole class or perform activities involving writing, he is likely to slap his face, scream, or attack (hit or kick) others. These behaviors all appear to be maintained by Darin's escaping from the situation or activity and are even more likely to occur if Darin has had little sleep and is tired.

FIGURE 6–1
Assessment of Daily Routines

Name: DARIN   **Date: 10/10**

Time	Routine or Activity	Predictors	Problem Behavior(s)	Maintaining Consequence
7:15–7:45 AM	Wake up and morning routine		No problems	
7:45–8:15	Travel to school	Change in route to school	Scream, self-slap	Don't know
8:20–8:30	Morning greeting	Asked to speak to group	Scream, self-hit, hit others	Avoid speaking to class
8:30–9:05	Language arts	Asked to write	Scream, hit others	Avoid writing
9:05–9:40	Math		No problems	
9:40–10:15	Health/PE		No problems	
10:15–10:30	Recess		No problems	
10:30–11:15	Reading	Asked to read out loud	Scream, self-hit, hit teachers	Avoid reading out loud
11:15–12:00	Science/ social studies		No problems	
12:00–12:45 PM	Lunch and recess		No problems	
12:45–1:05	Silent reading		No problems	
1:05–2:20	Group projects	Asked to present project to class	Occasional scream	Avoid presentation
2:20–2:30	Dismissal	Unclear	Screaming	Unclear
2:30–3:10	Travel home		No problem	
3:10–6:00	Afternoon routine		No problem	
6:00–7:00	Dinner and chores		No problem	
7:00–8:00	Evening routine		No problem	
8:30–9:00	Bedtime routine	Told to get in bed	Scream, self-hit	Avoid going to bed?

TABLE 6–2
Examples of Hypothesis Statements
Based on Interview Information

1. When Sarah is getting little attention in morning circle, she is likely to shout profanities and throw things to get attention from her peers. The longer she has gone without direct attention, the more likely she is to engage in shouting profanities.

2. When Monica is asked to do independent seatwork, she is likely to tear up materials and hit her teacher to escape from the task demands. This process is even more likely if she has had a negative interaction with the teacher earlier in the day.

3. When Jolene is prompted to stop using the computer, she is likely to fall on the floor and scream. The problem behaviors are maintained by access to the computer, and the likelihood is greatest when Jolene has had limited time on the computer earlier in the day.

4. In situations with low levels of activity or attention at home, Dan will rock and begin to chew his fingers. These behaviors appear to be maintained by self-stimulation.

5. When Bishara is asked to dress himself or do other nonpreferred self-care routines, he will begin to slap his head. Head slaps appear to be maintained by escape from the self-care routines and are even more likely if he has been asked to stop a preferred activity to engage in the self-care routine.

6. When Anya begins to have difficulty with a reading or math assignment, she will put her head down, refuse to respond, and/or close her books. Anya's refusal is maintained by avoiding the assignment and is far more likely to occur if she has had less than 5 hours sleep the previous night.

Indirect Methods: Interviews and Checklists

Structured interviews (e.g., LaVigna & Donnellan, 1986; O'Neill et al., 1997; Willis, LaVigna & Donnellan, 1987) and checklists such as the Motivation Assessment Scale (MAS) (Durand & Crimmins, 1988) or the Functional Analysis Checklist (Van Houten & Rolider, 1991) organize information about problem behaviors, antecedent stimuli (including setting events), and consequences to help determine behavioral function. In addition, the O'Neill et al. (1997) and Willis et al. (1987) interviews seek information on possible replacement behaviors, communication skills, the quality of the support environment, and the success (or failure) of previous support plans. Most structured interviews and checklists are designed to be conducted with "knowledgeable informants," people who know the student with problem behaviors well (e.g., parents, current or previous teachers). There are also interviews designed to be conducted with the "focus"

student, in cases where the student can provide meaningful information (e.g., Kern, Dunlap, Clarke, & Childs, 1994; O'Neill, et al., 1997). The interview information is used to develop preliminary hypothesis statements regarding the causes and functions of behavior.

Interviews and checklists have the advantages of (a) being relatively low cost to administer, (b) including multiple people who have important information about a student in the assessment process, and (c) providing a rich array of information that can be used to structure more detailed analyses of problem behavior. Although much more research is necessary for strong conclusions about the utility of interviews, it appears that using interviews alone may require considerable caution (Sturmey, 1994). Research on the interrater reliability of the MAS (Arndorfer et al., 1994; Crawford, Brockel, Schauss, & Miltenberger, 1992; Sturmey, 1994; Zarcone, Rodgers, Iwata, Rourke, & Dorsey, 1991) has produced mixed results. Only one study (Arndorfer et al., 1994) has assessed the reliability of the O'Neill et al. (1997) interview and it was found to be reliable. Three additional analyses have been reported that support the reliability of brief interviews, including interviews with higher functioning students (Lewis-Palmer, 1998; Nippe, Lewis-Palmer, & Sprague, 1998; Reed, Thomas, Sprague, & Horner, 1997), but other brief interviews have reported poor reliability (Iwata & Fisher, 1997). Reports of inconsistent reliability from functional assessment interviews may be the result of instrument design, reporting error, or selective reporting. Despite their limitations, the relative ease of use and richness of information make interviews and checklists a good choice for identifying initial functional assessment hypothesis statements. Because of the conflicting research on their reliability, information generated from interviews should be validated before it is used in the design of behavior support plans. We provide an overview of selected interview methods here with a discussion of recommended uses and limitations.

Using Functional Assessment Interviews

Behavior can be very complex. Researchers, direct support personnel, and families are identifying many variables in a person's learning history and physical makeup that can affect behavior. A major purpose of functional assessment interviews is to collect information about a large number of potentially influential variables. Your task is to narrow the focus to those that are important for the specific individual being considered.

Who Should Be Interviewed?

Anyone who knows the student well and has experience with her problem behaviors may be interviewed. This includes teachers, support staff, parents and family members, and other relevant persons who work with or know the individual well. In addition, the student who is exhibiting behaviors of concern also may be able to participate in an interview. For some individuals, talking only with teachers, parents, and support staff makes the most sense. However, when it seems appropriate and productive, the individual of concern should be included in the process (see later section on the Student-Directed Functional Assessment Interview for an example). When interviewing teachers, parents, and other informants, it is most useful to talk with at least two people who have daily contact with the individual.

How Long Should an Interview Take?

A functional assessment interview concerning a complex challenging behavior pattern may take 45 to 90 minutes. In our experience, the time required to complete the interview may vary considerably. Interview length is influenced by factors such as the number and complexity of problem behaviors, the number of people being interviewed, the amount of information that interviewees possess, the degree of agreement among interviewees, and interviewees' interest and willingness to talk. Use of a structured interview or checklist should help to keep the process focused and efficient. Some cases, however, may require more lengthy discussion or multiple interviews.

What Information Is Important to Gather in the Interview?

Although the contents of different interview formats vary, the following list outlines important information to gather from interviewees.

1. *Describe the behaviors.* Have interviewees identify all behaviors that are a problem and not just the most undesirable or intense behaviors. Problem behaviors can be extremely dangerous (e.g., severe self-biting), mildly undesirable (e.g., pushing materials away), or functionally irrelevant (e.g., repetitive movements that do not interfere with ongoing activities). Our experience, however, is that a person with severe problem behaviors seldom performs only one or two behaviors that cause concern. Only one or two behaviors may be dangerous (and thus receive major attention), but obtaining a list of the full range of behaviors that a person performs regularly is important. We have learned that behavior support should not focus only on one or two severe problem behaviors, but rather on the full set of problem behaviors that are maintained by a common consequence (i.e., the response class). For this reason, it is very helpful to begin with a description of the full set of problem behaviors a student performs.

2. *Define setting events.* Information about general medical and physical status; sleep, diet, eating, and social interaction patterns; daily activities; and other potential setting events should be considered and evaluated to determine if any setting events are associated with increased levels of problem behavior. It is useful to review and solicit comments regarding a broad range of potential setting events within an interview to identify any setting events that are relevant to the behavior of the student.

3. *Define specific and immediate antecedent events and situations that predict occurrences and nonoccurrences of the behavior(s).* Ask questions about, and assist interviewees to identify, specific situations in which the problem behaviors happen, including *when* and *where* they occur, *whom* the person is with, and *specific activities* that are problematic. Difficult behaviors are often related to such aspects of a setting. Learning about such relationships can be helpful in determining the pattern of a person's problem behaviors. It is useful to identify specific times of day, settings, people, or other features of the routines or activities identified as problematic (e.g., particular demands or lack of attention or interaction). One or more of these aspects may be more powerful than the others (e.g., the behaviors may occur whenever a certain activity is presented, no matter who does it or where it occurs). However, although you ask about time, place, persons, and activities separately, keep in mind that combinations of these often may be important.

Also ask about situations in which problem behaviors do *not* occur. Much can be learned from identifying antecedent events and situations associated with the nonoccurrence of problem behaviors.

4. *Identify the consequences or outcomes of the undesirable behavior(s) that may be maintaining them.* Another important aspect of behavior-environment relationships has to do with the types of consequences that behaviors produce for a person (i.e., the functions that behaviors appear to serve). Although a function may not be obvious, it is useful to assume that any behavior that occurs repeatedly is serving some useful function or producing some type of outcome that is reinforcing. The question to ask is, "Why is this student doing this?" Behaviors may serve two major types of functions (i.e., produce two kinds of outcomes) for an individual: to *obtain* something desirable and to *avoid* or *escape* something undesirable. In more technical terms, obtaining desirable things is referred to as *positive reinforcement*, while escaping or avoiding undesirable things is referred to as *negative reinforcement* (if such consequences result in continued occurrences of the behaviors). Figure 6–2 provides a framework for organizing the possible functions of problem behaviors into six categories (three under "obtain" and three under "escape/avoid").

A single problem behavior (e.g., screaming) may have multiple functions (e.g., obtain attention, avoid aversive tasks). In general, however, it is useful to (a) organize hypothesis statements around the most powerful function in a specific situation, and (b) define different hypothesis statements for different situations when a behavior serves

FIGURE 6–2
Functions of Behaviors

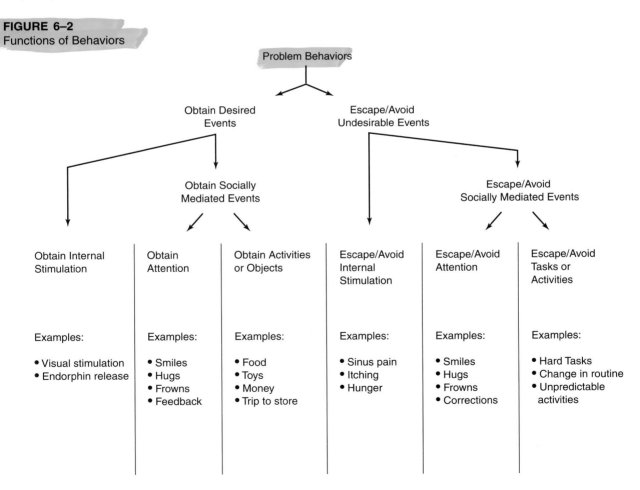

different functions in the different situations (e.g., one hypothesis statement for screaming to get attention at recess, and a separate hypothesis statement for screaming maintained by escape during math).

5. *What functional alternative behaviors has the person already learned*? Teaching and reinforcing persons for engaging in appropriate alternative behaviors are useful strategies in positive behavior support. For example, a student may have demonstrated that she can sometimes ask for help, or ask for a break from an activity, in an appropriate manner by talking, signing, or signaling. In other words, students with problem behaviors already may possess appropriate and desired skills, but may not use them in ways or at times that support providers would desire. Knowing this is helpful in determining whether instruction should focus on teaching new skills versus trying to prompt and reinforce the skills a person already has. Interviews should identify the existing skills on which a support plan can build.

6. *How does the person communicate*? In thinking about appropriate alternative behaviors, communication is the single most important skill to consider for people with severe problem behaviors. Different explanations have been proposed for why this is so, but the consistent conclusion is that effective support requires understanding the ways in which a person communicates information to others in the environment. Positive behavior support plans often include teaching or enhancing communication skills. Therefore, it is essential to know what communication skills a person already uses (Donnellan, Mirenda, Mesaros, & Fassbender, 1984).

7. *What things does the person like that are reinforcing*? Not enough can be said about the importance of identifying preferences and effective reinforcers (e.g., objects, events, activities) in developing effective support strategies. In asking questions about preferred things, you should learn which events or activities the person seeks spontaneously as well as the things that are typically provided by others. Staff or parent reports can be good indicators of preferences and functional reinforcers, but the things that a person seeks on his or her own may be an even better indicator. Although interviews can produce useful information, a comprehensive support plan often requires that you directly test a person's preferences with regard to reinforcing objects, activities, and events. Such assessments typically involve exposing persons to a variety of potential reinforcers, including edibles, toys or objects, entertainment (e.g., music, TV, movies), games, outings, domestic and personal care activities, and various forms of social attention and sensory stimulation (Green, Reid, Canipe, & Gardner, 1991; Pace, Ivancic, Edwards, Iwata, & Page, 1985). (See ch. 3 for preference assessment.) Knowledge about preferred items, events, activities, and other reinforcers is essential in designing positive and rewarding environments that make problem behaviors irrelevant and insure that appropriate adaptive behaviors are efficient and effective in producing preferred outcomes.

8. *What is known about the history of the undesirable behaviors, the programs that have been attempted to decrease or eliminate them, and the effects of those programs*? Learning about the types of supports that have been attempted and their effects can provide clues about the things that influence problem behaviors. For example, if you learn that a time-out program was tried and had the effect of *increasing* the frequency of a behavior, this might indicate that the behavior is motivated by escaping or avoiding situations or demands. In many cases, it may be difficult to obtain clear and reliable information about what has been tried and how well it worked or did not work; however, the attempt should be made.

Summary Hypothesis Statements

Interviews are useful only if they can be summarized into functional assessment hypothesis statements. As noted previously, hypothesis statements take into account all the information gathered from the interview and define the setting events, immediate antecedents, and maintaining consequences for problem behaviors. O'Neill et al. (1997) present a format for writing summary hypothesis statements at the conclusion of interviews using the Functional Assessment Interview (FAI) form. Table 6–3 presents examples of summary hypothesis statements, written in the O'Neill format, derived from an interview completed with teachers working with an elementary school student named Curtis. Note that each statement has the four components described above (i.e., setting events, immediate antecedents, problem behavior, maintaining consequence).

TABLE 6–3
Examples of Summary Hypothesis Statements Derived from a Functional Assessment Interview

Distant Setting Event	Immediate Antecedent (Predictor)	Problem Behavior	Maintaining Consequences
More likely if no breakfast	When Curtis is asked to complete difficult or nonpreferred math and reading tasks	He will yell obscenities and/or throw objects	In order to escape from the tasks
No identified distant setting event	When a peer has a toy or item that Curtis wants	He will pinch and/or scratch the peer	To try to get the person to give him the toy or item
More likely if he got little attention earlier in the day	During group work or other situations in which he is receiving little attention	Curtis will call out a teacher's name and/or pound and slap his desk	To attempt to obtain attention
No identified distant setting event	In a large variety of situations, when Curtis is experiencing "itchiness"	He will scratch his arms repeatedly	To relieve the discomfort
No identified distant setting event	When Curtis is scratching his arms and he is prompted to stop	He will yell obscenities	In order to continue scratching

Curtis is 11 years old and carries the diagnoses of moderate to severe intellectual disabilities and attention-deficit hyperactivity disorder. Curtis has a history of seizures. He is in a regular fourth grade class with 27 other students. His problem behaviors were identified as yelling, throwing objects, pinching or scratching peers, pounding or slapping the desk, calling out the teacher's name, and scratching his own arm (sometimes to the point of bleeding). The hypothesis statements presented summarize results of a Functional Assessment Interview conducted with Curtis' teacher, a classroom assistant, and a behavior consultant working with Curtis' school and family.

Recent Developments in Functional Assessment

Two recent trends in the design of functional assessment interviews have been (a) the design of more efficient interviews for use in schools, and (b) development of interviews that can be done with the student (Kern, Childs, Dunlap, Clarke, & Falk, 1994). The Functional Assessment Checklist for Teachers and Staff (FACTS) is an example of the first trend, and the Student-Directed Functional Assessment Interview (SDFAI) is an example of the second.

Functional Assessment Checklist for Teachers and Staff (FACTS)

March and Horner (1998) have developed a brief functional assessment interview for teachers called FACTS to address the information demands of relatively less complex behavioral problems in schools. This interview collects information similar to the Functional Assessment Interview form (O'Neill et al., 1997) but is designed to be used with teachers in short meetings, lasting 15 to 20 minutes. We have used the FACTS to assess the behavior of "at-risk" students in elementary and middle schools who are presenting minor problem behaviors. The form leads to the development of a hypothesis statement, but without the level of precision and detail of other interviews. The reliability of FACTS was recently confirmed by Lewis-Palmer (1998). A sample of FACTS is included as Figure 6–3.

Student Guided Functional Assessment

To date, functional assessment procedures have been used most often to design support for persons with moderate to severe intellectual disabilities. Recently, however, demonstrations of successful interventions based on functional assessment have been provided for children with emotional and behavioral disorders,

conduct disorders, mild intellectual disabilities, brain injury, and developmentally typical children (e.g., Dunlap et al., 1993; Kern et al., 1994; Todd, Horner, Vanater, & Schneider, 1997).

The success of linking functional assessment and intervention for more intellectually able individuals raises the possibility of collecting information from the person performing problem behavior. Our clinical observations, and those of others, suggest that some students can clearly (a) state preferences for activities or items; (b) describe complaints about assigned work; (c) request alternative activities; (d) point out personal distractions; and (e) describe difficulties with peers. To the extent that these statements are accurate and consistent, personally provided information can supplement, validate, or replace information obtained from teachers, parents, or others.

As one approach to include individuals directly in the functional assessment process, O'Neill et al. (1997) provided the SDFAI for use in school settings. Using this interview form, any student who can provide reliable information can contribute functional assessment information and participate in his or her own support process. In some cases, the student may need assistance from a family member or staff person with whom they are comfortable. These people can provide clarification of questions or provide suggestions or reminders about certain situations. However, some students may have a strong preference for an interview without additional persons present. In either case, the quality or accuracy of such interview information should be confirmed in the same manner as information gathered with any informant interview form or rating scale; that is, through direct observation or systematic functional analysis manipulations.

Research on the SDFAI with typically developing students as well as students with emotional and behavioral disabilities has shown it to be highly reliable in comparison to teacher reports and direct observation (Hagan, 1998; Lewis-Palmer, 1998; Nippe et al., 1998; Reed et al., 1997).

Validate the Hypothesis

While interviews and checklists are perhaps the simplest and most efficient methods for collecting functional assessment information, we believe it is necessary to confirm the information gathered from indirect methods with direct observation data, or, in

FIGURE 6–3

Functional Assessment Checklist for Teachers & Staff (FACTS)

Student _____   Date _____

Grade _____   Staff Reporting _____

Student Profile: *Please use the space below to identify the student's strengths. Some possible strengths include academic interests, social skills, hobbies, sports, etc.*

_____

_____

Directions: *To gain a better understanding of the nature and scope of the problem behavior(s) please check the most relevant item(s). Then use the CONSIDERATION space at the bottom of each section to provide a brief description of the problem behavior(s), predictors, and consequences.*

Problem Behavior(s): Behaviors of concern that have been occurring.

___ Tardy	___ Inappropriate language	___ Disrupts class activities	___ Theft
___ Inattentive	___ Fighting/physical aggression	___ Insubordination/disrespectful	___ Vandalism
___ Sleeping	___ Verbally harasses others	___ Work completion	___ Other _____

CONSIDERATIONS: *What behavior typically occurs first and how does it escalate? What does behavior look like?* _____
_____

Predictor(s) & Setting Event(s): Person(s), place(s), or time(s) where behavior of concern is most likely to occur.

Location	*Person(s)*	*Time*	*Academic Concerns*	*Setting Event(s)*
___ In class	___ Peer(s)	___ Before school	___ All classes	___ Use of medication
___ Hall	___ Teacher(s)	___ Morning	___ Reading	___ Physical health
___ Cafeteria	___ Staff	___ Lunch	___ Math	___ Illegal drug use
___ Bus		___ Home room	___ Spec. ed. eligible	___ Conflict at home
___ Other _____		___ Afternoon	___ Other _____	___ Other _____

CONSIDERATIONS: *A specific activity that is difficult for student? Does behavior occur alone or with peer group?* _____
_____

Consequence(s): What typically happens after behavior of concern occurs?

Obtain Attention	*Escape/Avoid Demand or Situation*	*Current Strategies*
___ Peer attention	___ Escape difficult activity	___ Change seating
___ Adult attention	___ Adult attention	___ Contact parent
___ Activity	___ Negative peer attention	___ Send to office
___ Other _____	___ Other _____	___ Other _____

CONSIDERATIONS: What strategies have been effective? After an incident what does the student obtain (e.g., attention) or avoid (e.g., difficult task)? _____
_____

Summary of Behavior(s)

Directions: Please use the items selected above and information you've written in the CONSIDERATIONS to complete section below.

Predictor(s) & Setting Event(s)	*Behavior(s) of Concern*	*Consequences*

some cases, with direct functional analysis. In this section, we describe the major methods of hypothesis testing, direct observation, and functional analysis.

Direct Observation

Direct observation of behavior is a cornerstone of behavior analysis (Baer et al., 1968). The antecedent, behavior, consequence (ABC) chart (Bijou, Peterson, & Ault, 1968) was an early method to collect systematic direct observation data. ABC charts require recording the behavior when it occurs, a notation regarding the event preceding the behavior (antecedent), and a comment regarding the event(s) that followed the behavior (consequence). ABC charts are limited in that observers typically must write out each event, which can adversely affect reliability. ABC charts also can be difficult to use when tracking high-frequency behaviors. Finally, ABC charts often are used to record only the occurrence of problem behaviors and tell us little about events that may be associated with the *absence* of problem behavior.

An extension of the ABC chart, called *scatterplot analysis*, was developed by Touchette, McDonald, and Langer (1985) and elaborated by Doss and Reichle (1991). The scatterplot is a grid specifying time intervals (e.g., 1 hour or 30-minute periods) on a two-sided matrix with space for behavior codes to be recorded across multiple days. The scatterplot adds the advantage of documenting both when behaviors occur and when they do not. Touchette et al. (1985) found that, by focusing on the features of those periods where problem behavior was observed, interventions that altered those periods resulted in reductions of problem behavior. A more recent adaptation of the scatterplot observation form, incorporating ABC charting as well, provided by O'Neill et al. (1997), is the Functional Assessment Observation Form (Figure 6–4). In each case, the observation system allows identification of events that reliably occur just prior to problem behaviors, and events that occur just after problem behaviors. By identifying these relationships we infer that the antecedent events trigger problem behaviors and the consequence events maintain the problem behaviors. Note that direct observation systems seldom focus on distant setting events.

While direct observation methods tend to be more objective and precise than interviews, the results must also be viewed with caution. Because the observation involves no manipulation or control of tar-

geted variables, the results document correlations between events and behavior, not causal relationships. An example illustrates the potential risk of relying solely on observational data to design an intervention. Consider a case of a young child who engages in severe head banging. A direct observation analysis showed that when the child hit her head, which occurred across a broad range of conditions, the teacher generally went to her, provided a reprimand, and attempted to redirect her to engage in an appropriate behavior. Multiple observations of this interaction would suggest that her head banging is maintained by teacher attention. A more extensive analysis indicated that the child had chronic sinus infections, and head hits lessened the pain from sinus infections. Attempts to replace head banging with requests for attention would have been ineffective. Medication to relieve sinus pain was effective. The message from this example is that multiple factors can affect problem behavior, and care is needed when developing and confirming functional assessment hypotheses.

Some studies have documented that carefully conducted direct observation assessments can be used as the basis for intervention design (Lewis-Palmer, 1998; Mace & Lalli, 1991; March & Horner, 1998; Repp, Felce, & Barton, 1988; Sasso et al., 1992), while others have demonstrated less accurate findings (Lerman & Iwata, 1993). The full range of appropriate applications of direct observation methods have not been documented across settings, subjects, and qualifications of personnel. Future investigations should delineate appropriate applications of direct observation versus experimental analysis methods.

At this time, it appears that direct observation paired with interviews can lead to appropriate hypotheses regarding behavioral antecedents and consequences for many behaviors. The relatively low cost, effort, and skill required to implement these two methods present a practical alternative for practitioners.

Direct observation procedures must be structured to provide clear and useful information, while at the same time not overburdening the people responsible for collecting the data. A strategy for accomplishing this is to use the results of functional assessment interview(s) to guide the direct observation process. Observations, and an observation data form, should focus on the behaviors, relevant situations and antecedent events (i.e., predictors), and functions identified during the interview process (O'Neill et al., 1997).

FIGURE 6-4
Functional Assessment Observation Form

Name: *Darin*

Starting Date: *10/15*   Ending Date: *10/17*

Time	Behaviors: Scream	Self-Hit	Hit Others	Rip/Tear	Demand/Request	Difficult Task	Predictors: Transitions	Interruption	Alone (No Attention)	Waiting Task	Speak to Child	Get/Obtain: Attention	Desired Item/Activity	Self-Stimulation	Demand/Request	Escape/Avoid: Activity/(Transition)	Person	Other/Don't Know	Sent to child	Actual Consequences: Redirect	Comments
8:20 AM / 8:30 / Greeting	8	1	1		1	8, 13							1, 8, 13				8	1		
8:30 / 9:05 / Language	2, 3, 9, 14	2	2, 3, 9, 14		2, 3				2, 3, 14	9	9		2, 3, 14				3	2, 9, 14		MO
9:05 / 9:40 / Math		5				4, 5, 10, 15							4, 5, 10, 15					5		
9:40 / 9:45 / Transition	15																			
9:45 / 10:15 / Health/PE						6										6				
10:15 / 10:30 / Recess																				
10:30 / 11:15 / Reading	7, 11, 12, 16	7, 12, 16	7, 11, 12, 16						7, 12	11, 16			7, 11, 12, 16					7, 12, 16		RJ
Totals	12	8	9		2	6			5	4			10		5					

Events:	1	2	3	4	5	6	7	8	9	10	11	12	13	14	15	16	17	18	19	20	21	22	23	24	25
Date:	10/15							10/16					10/17												

Comments: (if nothing happened in period, write initials)

225

Direct Observation of Darin

Information from earlier functional assessment interviews had indicated that Darin engaged in (a) screams, (b) slaps to his face, (c) hitting others (teachers), and (d) ripping and tearing papers and materials. The interviews led to a hypothesis indicating that these behaviors were most likely to occur when Darin was (a) transitioning from one place to another (e.g., home to school, classroom to gym), (b) asked to speak before the class, or (c) asked to do writing tasks. All of the problem behaviors were identified as being maintained by escape from the aversive features of the three predictor, or trigger, situations.

The hypothesis generated through the interviews guided the direct observation data collection process, beginning with setting up the observation form. Identified target behaviors were listed in the "behaviors" columns, two specific predictors were added to the "predictors" columns on the form, and an "escape activities" column was "personalized" for Darin (i.e., "transitions" were listed). In addition, information about Darin's morning schedule and current classroom consequences for his problem behaviors were used to complete the "time" and "actual consequences" columns of the observation form.

Data were collected across the school day, but only the results from 8:20 AM to 11:15 AM are shown in Figure 6–4. Each time a problem behavior event occurred, the teacher or assistant would record the number of the event (first event, second event, third event) in the appropriate time period row and problem behavior cells. For Darin, the first problem behavior event occurred on October 15 between 8:20 AM and 8:30 AM. Darin screamed and hit his teacher when his teacher asked him to speak in front of the class during the morning greeting time. The teacher's perception was that Darin's behavior was associated with escape from the aversive situation of having to speak in front of the class, and the actual consequence was that Darin was redirected when he hit. The number "1" (first event) was placed in the 8:20 AM to 8:30 AM row for (a) the problem behaviors that

occurred, (b) the predictor events that were in place when the problem behaviors began, (c) the teacher's perception of the function maintaining the behaviors, and (d) the actual consequences applied. The number "1" was then crossed off in the "events" row at the bottom of the form.

Looking at the form after three school days (October 15 to 17) elucidates some interesting patterns. Darin engaged in screaming, self-slaps, and hitting others, but not ripping and tearing. Problem behaviors were most likely (a) during transitions (8:20 AM to 8:30 AM and 9:40 AM to 9:45 AM), (b) when he was asked to speak before the class (during greeting, language, and reading), and (c) when he was asked to do writing tasks (during language and reading). Math, health/PE, and recess were the times when he was least likely to engage in problem behaviors. Darin's problem behaviors were perceived by his teacher and assistant as being maintained by escape from aversive demands or activities, and as such, the current consequences (i.e., sent to hall, redirect) may inadvertently have rewarded his problem behaviors (e.g., produced escape).

In general, the direct observation data in Figure 6–4 provide strong support for the functional assessment hypothesis statements generated from Darin's functional assessment interviews, with the exception that "rip and tear" did not appear to be a major problem. Note that the observation data were collected throughout the school day by those in the setting who knew Darin best. The data do not record a frequency count of each hit or slap as might be done in research-level data collection. However, the data do provide a record of the number of different events (incidents) that included problem behaviors (a total of 16 problem behavior events across the 3-day observation period). By focusing on all the behaviors in a problem event, the form makes data collection easier, yet still allows for a level of accuracy that is useful for decision making. (See chapter 5 for further description of measurement and graphing strategies.)

Consider one direct observation form example based on information gathered on Darin (Fig. 6–4) by his teacher and teaching assistant over three school days. The Functional Assessment Observation Form developed by O'Neill et al. (1997) was used.

There are many forms for collecting direct observation data. A key point is that direct observation systems can be used both to help identify and to

test functional assessment hypotheses. However, for very complex problems, even the additional accuracy of direct observation may be insufficient. In such cases, you may choose to implement functional analysis procedures. These methods can be highly accurate but also require high levels of skill to carry out. We have briefly outlined the major methods here.

Functional Analysis

The final, and most studied functional assessment method, involves experimental manipulation of antecedent and/or consequence events that are believed to control problem behavior (Carr, 1977, 1994; Repp et al., 1988). The conceptual foundation for functional analysis procedures was provided by Skinner (1953), Bijou et al. (1968), and Carr (1977). A landmark study by Iwata, Dorsey, Slifer, Bauman, and Richman (1982) demonstrated an "analogue" functional analysis process for severe self-injury. Children with self-injurious behaviors were presented with conditions where self-injury resulted in (a) escape from task demand, (b) no response because the child was alone, (c) no response while the child played with an adult and preferred toys or objects, or (d) social attention from an adult who was otherwise ignoring the child. The study provided an early demonstration that a type of behavior described with a singular label (i.e., self-injury) occurred at strikingly different rates in different conditions across individual children. Some individuals engaged in high rates of self-injury only when self-injury resulted in escape from difficult tasks. Other individuals engaged in self-injury only when the behavior resulted in adult attention. Still others engaged in self-injury in all conditions. The point was that the same basic behavior, self-injury, occurred for different functions in different individuals,

thereby necessitating different intervention strategies. The authors emphasized how the functional analysis information was of tremendous value in the design of effective interventions, and spurred extensive research and clinical application of functional analysis procedures.

Variations of the basic analogue protocol have been demonstrated in school and community settings (Durand & Carr, 1991; Sprague & Horner, 1992), clinical outpatient settings (Wacker, Steege, Northup, Reimers, et al., 1990), and home settings (Arndorfer et al., 1994; Lucyshyn, Albin, & Nixon, 1997). Some studies have tested the full range of possible functions while others have provided more detailed analysis of the controlling factors of specific functional response classes (e.g., escape-maintained behavior) or demonstrations of teaching replacement behaviors (e.g., communication).

Wacker and his colleagues (Northup et al., 1991; Wacker, Steege, Northup, Reimers, et al., 1990; Wacker, Steege, Northup, Sasso, et al., 1990) have developed a "brief" functional analysis protocol that involves very short (5-minute) sessions in which different functional analysis conditions (e.g., attention, escape) are presented in rapid sequences, and the condition(s) with the highest rates are repeated. The data in Figure 6–5 provide the results from a brief functional analysis that was completed in 90 minutes.

FIGURE 6–5
Brief Functional Analysis

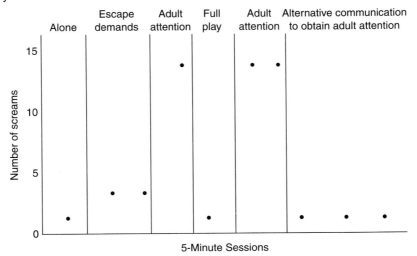

The results provide strong documentation that screaming was maintained by adult attention. These data, combined with interview information, were of direct value in building an effective plan of support, and they document that attention from adults (not escape from demands, or self-induced consequences) maintained problem behavior. The results further indicate that when an alternative communication response was taught, screaming was reduced.

The benefit of precision offered by functional analysis also presents its greatest limitation in applied settings. Functional analysis requires relatively high levels of skill to be carried out effectively and often may require that informed consent and human subjects' approvals be obtained before implementation. In addition, the fact that functional analysis procedures involve creating conditions where problem behaviors are evoked makes the procedure more dangerous and less appropriate than less precise alternatives in some applied contexts and with some behaviors that may be more extreme.

Brief and full functional analyses are the "gold standard" for defining the maintaining function(s) of problem behaviors. The technology can be adapted and applied with success in typical home and community contexts (Berg & Sasso, 1993; Cooper, Wacker, Sasso, Reimers, & Donn, 1990), but our experience is that a functional analysis (a) should only be attempted with the support of a trained behavior analyst and (b) is only needed when other sources of functional assessment information do not provide a clear set of validated hypothesis statements.

This section has defined functional assessment, provided a discussion of the major options for conducting functional assessment, and presented the strengths and weaknesses of each. The next section outlines procedures for using functional assessment hypothesis statements to design effective and efficient behavior supports.

The Design of Comprehensive Behavior Support

Once an initial functional assessment is conducted and the five outcomes for a functional assessment are completed, the process of designing and implementing a comprehensive behavior support plan can truly begin.[1] A behavior support plan provides a guide for the behavior of those people providing support and serves as a blueprint for designing and maintaining effective environments that render problem behaviors irrelevant, inefficient, and ineffective. We often think of a behavior support plan as the plan for changing the behavior of a student. In fact the behavior support plan is designed to describe changes that we as teachers, administrators, family members, friends, and peers will perform. The changes we make in the physical setting, the daily schedule, what we teach, the way we teach, and the way we respond to appropriate and problem behaviors are what will produce changes in the behavior of the student. Behavior plans are for those of us who implement behavior support; change in our behavior changes the behavior of students with problem behaviors. As such, behavior plans should be clear in describing the exact changes expected in the behavior of those who will implement the plan.

Behavior Support Should Be Technically Sound and Contextually Appropriate

In designing a comprehensive behavior support plan, two essential standards exist. First, the plan should be *technically sound* (Horner et al., 1993; O'Neill et al., 1997). This means that the procedures in the support plan are logically linked to the functional assessment hypotheses and grounded in the basic principles of applied behavior analysis (Alberto & Troutman, 1999; Miltenberger, 1997). Research should support the effectiveness and logic behind each procedure used in a plan (e.g., Carr & Carlson, 1993). Second, the plan should be a good *contextual fit* (Albin, Lucyshyn, Horner, & Flannery, 1996; Horner, in press; Lucyshyn & Albin, 1993). How well a support plan "fits" its implementors and settings is likely to influence whether the plan is put in place at all, whether it is implemented with precision, and whether its implementa-

---

[1]In many cases, behavior supports, interventions, or crisis procedures are needed, and are implemented, as functional assessment procedures are in progress and not yet completed. Procedures from a current or past support plan may continue to be used, or new short-term or emergency procedures may be developed and implemented, based on existing information and preliminary hypotheses regarding the functions of problem behaviors. People with severe problem behaviors must receive the support needed to be safe and healthy at all times.

tion will be sustained for a long time. The contextual fit is as important as the technical soundness of the plan. The specific elements of good contextual fit are defined later.

To ensure both the technical soundness and contextual fit of a comprehensive support plan, the design, implementation, evaluation, and modification of the plan should be conducted as a collaborative team process involving all key stakeholders: the people who will implement the plan, family and friends, the person with disabilities, and administrators who must support the process (Anderson, Albin, Mesaros, Dunlap, & Morelli-Robbins, 1993). A collaborative team process also provides the framework for a support approach that is person-focused, longitudinal, and dynamic. Behavior support needs of persons with severe problem behaviors are likely to be long-term. Therefore, support should be designed with longevity in mind and with the expectation that the nature of the support will change as the person's skills, needs, and preferences change. Sustained plan implementation, ongoing monitoring of effects, and timely adaptation and modification of plan procedures and features are essential elements of effective comprehensive behavior support. A collaborative team process involving all key stakeholders facilitates high quality performance of these elements.

Behavior Support Should Be Comprehensive

The objective of comprehensive behavior support is to have a broad positive impact on the life of a person with disabilities and challenging problem behaviors. Successful behavior support should result in real differences in a person's life. Research to date demonstrates the effectiveness of specific procedures to change behavior. The technology of positive behavior support is now focused on integrating this knowledge to create comprehensive support systems. Five features characterize a comprehensive approach to building behavior support.

1. *All problem behaviors performed by the focus person are addressed in a comprehensive support plan.* The need for behavior support is often prompted by the occurrence of a few intense problem behaviors. Teachers and families have noted, however, that multiple occurrences of small intensity behaviors (e.g., whin-

ing, refusal) may be as disruptive and damaging as higher intensity aggression, self-injury, and property destruction (Horner et al., 1992; Turnbull & Ruef, 1996). Research also indicates the value of organizing support around all the problem behaviors that are maintained by the same function (e.g., all behaviors that produce attention, all behaviors that are maintained by escape from tasks) (Sprague & Horner, 1992; Sprague & Horner, in press). Both our current understanding of behavioral theory and the goal of producing change that has a broad impact argue for focusing behavior support on the full range of problem behaviors a person performs, rather than on just one or two high-intensity behaviors.

2. *A comprehensive support plan is implemented across all relevant settings and times of day.* Just as addressing all problem behaviors is important, so too is implementation of behavior support procedures across the relevant scope of a person's entire day. In the past, it was not unusual for individual behavioral interventions to be implemented for limited periods of time, across limited settings or situations (e.g., for 1-hour sessions in a clinic treatment room, during one activity or class period at school). The research literature shows clearly that single intervention procedures can have a dramatic effect in reducing severe problem behavior across brief periods in specific contexts. However, to achieve true lifestyle impact, behavior support must produce broad and lasting effects across the relevant range of contexts, conditions, activities, and routines that a person with severe problem behaviors experiences in the course of the day. Developing comprehensive support strategies that can be implemented and sustained across the entire day and the full range of conditions encountered is a major challenge for positive behavior support (Horner, in press).

3. *A comprehensive support plan blends multiple procedures.* It would be unusual for a single intervention procedure (e.g., a Differential Reinforcement of Other Behavior [DRO] or Differential Reinforcement of Incompatible Behavior [DRI] reinforcement schedule, a good token economy) to address the full spectrum of problem behaviors performed by an individual with severe problem behaviors and cover the full range of settings where problems occur. Comprehensive support will more likely

involve the creative blending of multiple procedures. Strategies for curricular revision and schedule modification will be used to minimize contact with highly aversive events, instructional procedures will build new skills, and consequences throughout the day will be modified to increase the rewards associated with communication and learning and decrease the rewards that follow problem behaviors. Collectively, these multiple changes result in an environment that minimizes and redirects access to problem events, builds new skills, and provides constructive feedback that both promotes appropriate behavior and minimizes the rewards for problem behavior.

4. *Comprehensive support plan procedures are driven by a functional assessment.* One of the most important developments in the area of behavior support is the shift from focus on the topographies and forms of problem behaviors (e.g., self-injurious, head hitting, hand biting) to focus on the functions of problem behaviors (e.g., escape from aversive activities, obtain social attention). Rather than having separate interventions for each behavior, we recognize that all behaviors maintained by the same function (e.g., all behaviors that are associated with escape) can and should be addressed in a support plan with a common set of procedures that relate to the function (Carr et al., 1994; Horner et al., 1993; Lucyshyn & Albin, 1993). We also now recognize that the same behavior may serve multiple functions for a person, being maintained by different consequences in different contexts or situations. For example, inspection of the hypothesis statements for Curtis (Figure 6–3) reveals that, when asked to complete difficult or nonpreferred math and reading tasks, Curtis will yell obscenities in order to escape from the tasks. In a different situation, Curtis will yell obscenities when he is prompted to stop scratching his arms in order to continue scratching. In such cases, separate support procedures must be implemented in the different contexts to address the separate functions of a behavior (Day, Horner, & O'Neill, 1994). Not only does functional assessment guide and integrate our behavior support efforts, but there is growing evidence that the effectiveness of behavior support interventions increases when the procedures implemented are consistent with functional assessment information (Carr et al., in press; Didden, Duker, & Korzilius, 1997).

5. *A comprehensive support plan must "fit" the context and conditions in which it is implemented.* Positive behavior support has moved the delivery of behavioral intervention for persons with severe problem behaviors from specialized and restrictive settings into regular, integrated community settings. The challenge facing families, schools, and community support providers today is to deliver effective behavior support in typical homes, schools, and community settings for as long as such support is needed. The support procedures, in most cases, must be implemented by the typical people (i.e., family members, friends, teachers, classroom assistants, paid caregivers) who live and work in those settings. Simply put, behavior support must be "doable" for typical people in typical settings. A comprehensive support plan that is technically sound is necessary but not sufficient. If the plan does not "work" for all of the stakeholders involved, if it does not "fit" the contexts in which it is implemented, then the procedures specified may not be implemented at all, may be implemented in a haphazard and inconsistent manner, or may be implemented initially but abandoned once any immediate behavioral crisis is past (Albin et al., 1996; Horner, in press).

The concept of contextual fit is defined by five key variables (a) the extent to which the procedures in a plan of support are consistent with the *values* of the people who will implement the plan (e.g., are the implementors comfortable doing what the plan requires?), (b) the extent to which the people who will implement the plan have the *skills* to perform the required procedures (e.g., do they know how to teach new communication skills?), (c) the extent to which the physical, fiscal, and person *resources* are available to carry out the procedures (e.g., is time set aside for instruction, are communication tools purchased?), (d) the extent to which *administrative support* is provided to ensure that a behavior support plan is implemented, monitored, and managed (e.g., are outcome measures collected and reviewed, and are policies in place to support behavior support plan implementation?), and (e) the degree to which plan procedures can be *embedded within the typical routines and activities of daily life* (e.g., can plan procedures be built into regular classroom or home routines, and do plan procedures not disrupt ongoing activities within a setting). In our experience, if support plan procedures require families or teachers (or other direct support providers) to make substantial changes in their regular routines and activities as part of plan implementation, then plan procedures are much less likely to be used across all contexts and times of day, and implementation is much less likely to be sustained over time.

The notion of "contextual fit" is a major development in the technology of positive behavior support. No longer are there assumptions that only one perfect intervention exists and that an effective intervention is defined only by technical features. The assumption now is that there are many different ways to engineer or redesign an environment to gain behavioral goals. Among the many different intervention options, it is essential that selected procedures meet both the technical standards defined by the functional assessment and the requirements for good contextual fit (e.g., the values, skills, resources, and supports available to those who will implement the plan). This emphasis on contextual fit is a direct result of recognizing that positive behavior support is a process of engineering (or redesigning) environments rather than a process of "fixing" children.

Competing Behaviors Model

The competing behaviors model (CBM) provides a conceptual bridge for moving from functional assessment information to the design of a comprehensive behavior support plan (Horner & Billingsley, 1988; Horner et al., 1993; O'Neill et al., 1997). A competing behaviors analysis provides a framework to logically link the plan's multiple intervention procedures and support strategies.

The process for conducting a competing behaviors analysis involves four basic steps: (a) summarize the functional assessment information to write a summary hypothesis statement for each group (i.e., response class) of problem behaviors; (b) identify appropriate desired and alternative behaviors and the contingencies associated with them; (c) identify potential intervention procedures, across four support strategy categories, that promote the occurrence of appropriate behaviors and make problem behaviors irrelevant, ineffective, and inefficient; and (d) select the set of strategies from the options proposed that are technically likely to result in behavior change, and a good contextual fit (O'Neill et al., 1997). Figure 6–6 presents a form that guides the completion of these

four steps and illustrates an example of a completed competing behaviors analysis for Darin.

The *first step* of summarizing functional assessment information to construct a summary hypothesis statement for a response class involves listing, from left to right, the setting event(s), immediate antecedents (predictors), problem behavior(s) in the response class, and maintaining consequence(s) that have been identified in the functional assessment.

The functional assessment for Darin indicates that he slaps himself, screams, and hits others (problem behaviors) when he is presented with difficult tasks (e.g., tasks involving writing or presenting in front of class) or confusing transitions (predictors). These behaviors are maintained by escape from the difficult tasks or transition (e.g., teaching or the transition ends immediately and Darin is removed from the task or situation whenever he hits, screams, or slaps himself) (maintaining consequence). Screaming, hitting, and self-slaps also become more likely when Darin is tired (i.e., mom notes little sleep [less than 6 hrs] the previous night) (setting event). This information would be diagrammed as follows:

Setting Event	Predictors	Problem Behavior	Maintaining Consequence
Less than 6 hours sleep	Presentation of difficult tasks or confusing transitions	Screams, hits others, and/ or slaps self	Escapes task (sent to "quiet" room)

The *second step* in completing a competing behaviors analysis is to identify desired alternative behaviors that will compete with the problem behavior. Two questions can be asked: (a) Given that the setting events and predictors have occurred, what is an appropriate behavior that would be the *desired* behavior for the person to perform in that situation? and (b) Given that the setting events and predictors have occurred, what would be an *alternative* behavior that could produce *exactly the same consequence* as the problem behaviors (i.e., a functionally equivalent behavior) (O'Neill et al., 1997). The answer to the first question leads to what is called the "desired behavior" in Figure 6–6, and the answer to the second produces an "alternative behavior."

For Darin, the desired behavior would be doing or completing the tasks, and the current maintaining consequence for task completion would be teacher praise and a rousing "high five" handshake. A functionally equivalent alternative behavior for

FIGURE 6–6

Diagram of the Competing Behavior Model for Darin

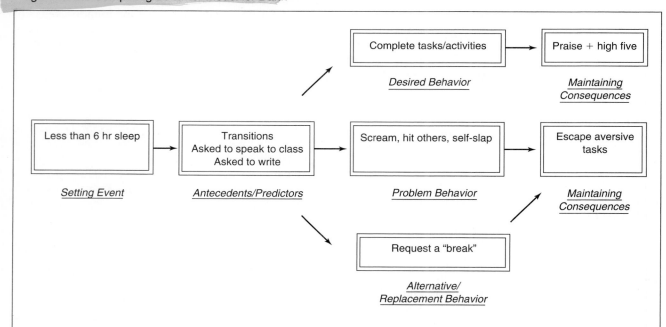

Strategies that Make the Problem Behavior Irrelevant, Ineffective, and Inefficient

Setting Event Strategies	Predictor Strategies	Teaching Strategies	Consequence Strategies
* • Mom contacts teacher to alert after "bad sleep" night and teacher adjusts schedule to reduce difficult tasks • Implement soothing bedtime routine at home • Provide opportunity for nap in nurse's office after "bad sleep" night • Classroom assistant increases one-to-one attention after "bad sleep" night	* • Modify task from speaking in front of class to small group * • Use picture sequence to prompt transitions • Use interspersion strategy for difficult tasks (intersperse difficult with easier tasks) • Offer choices for writing tasks • Use precorrection routine for transitions * • Precorrect or prompt use of "break" requests	* • Teach Darin to request a break • Teach Darin to ask for help * • Teach use of picture sequence system for transitions * • Implement sequenced curriculum to teach & improve writing skills • Teach Darin to speak in front of class using gradually increasing time periods and less familiar topics	* • Increase reinforcers for appropriate task completion (use stickers and other tangibles) * • If problem behaviors occur, prompt use of appropriate communication alternatives (use pictures, request break) * • If problem behaviors occur, block and redirect as needed; do not allow escape (keep working through task)

* Team - selected strategies.

Darin would be requesting a break, at which point he gets to take a break from the task. Requesting a break may not be what Darin's support team members actually desire (i.e., they want the task to be done), but it is an appropriate behavior that serves the same function (i.e., escaping the task) as screaming and hitting the teacher. Requesting a break is an appropriate functionally equivalent response that can compete with hitting (Carr, 1988). Figure 6–6 shows how the desired and alternative behaviors would be entered on the competing behaviors diagram.

A depiction of the competing behaviors analysis provides support team members with a picture of the current contingencies in Darin's life and helps guide the team to constructively change the environment (e.g., contingencies, antecedents, Darin's skills) to make the problem behaviors irrelevant, inefficient, and ineffective.

The *third step* in the competing behaviors analysis process is to build a list of possible behavior support procedures. The goal here is not simply to look for a single intervention that would eliminate the problem behaviors, but to identify a range of strategies and procedures that would reduce the likelihood of problem behaviors and increase the likelihood that either, or both, of the competing behaviors (i.e., desired or alternative) would occur. Such a multicomponent support plan might address setting events (e.g., a soothing bedtime routine to promote sleep, a changed schedule to reduce or eliminate difficult tasks on "bad sleep days"), predictors (e.g., redesign the tasks to make them easier; embed the tasks in a more preferred routine), behaviors (e.g., teach or prompt requesting a break), and consequences (e.g., increase reinforcers for completing the tasks, ensure that hitting does not result in escaping the task but requesting a break verbally does). A comprehensive behavior support plan is likely to include several components or procedures to address the full range of variables that will influence which behaviors occur from among the alternatives available. This third step involves a brainstorming process to create a menu of potential strategies, from which support team members can then select the best options and strategies for their situation. Identify and list as many potential strategies as you can. In this way, the resulting plan is more likely to be both technically sound (i.e., based on the functional assessment) and have good contextual fit (i.e., strategies are identified that work best for the team members and context) (Albin et al., 1996).

The *fourth step* in building a plan of behavior support involves review of the proposed list of strategies, and selection of specific procedures that the team identifies as effective, doable, and an appropriate fit with their skills, values, schedules, resources, and administrative support system. This fourth step is extremely important. The people who will be implementing the intervention (and in many cases, the individual with disabilities) define the final features of the intervention. The first three steps have ensured that technically sound information is being considered. The features of effective behavior support are defined. The final step adds form to those features, and ensures that this form reflects a good fit with the people and context where the intervention will be implemented. This fourth step is of particular importance when a behavioral consultant is involved in the design of support. The behavioral consultant can be of tremendous assistance in the process of functional assessment and coordination of the competing behavior model. The final selection and operationalization of the specific strategies that make up a behavior plan, however, must be done with active participation of people who know the student best and who will be implementing the final plan. Examine the list of the different support strategies identified for Darin's behavior support plan in Figure 6–6. The strategies with an asterisk (*) next to them were selected by his team for inclusion in his plan of support.

Constructing a Written Behavior Support Plan

Elements of an Effective Plan of Support

A written comprehensive behavior support plan should include three major elements: (a) a support plan describing the multiple procedures to be implemented, (b) an implementation plan describing steps and activities for putting the support plan in place, and (c) an evaluation plan for monitoring effects of the support plan and making necessary modifications. The actual format, length, and style of these components may vary. Rather than focusing on a particular form or format, it is useful to focus on the information presented in a written plan and on the processes described. Following are recommendations for the content of a written plan (Horner et al., 1993; Lucyshyn & Albin, 1993; O'Neill et al., 1997).

The First Element: A Written Comprehensive, Multicomponent Behavior Support Plan that is logically linked to functional assessment and that has acceptable contextual fit should include the following information.

1. A *brief rationale for the comprehensive support plan.* Whenever a behavior support plan is proposed and developed, there must be reasons and objectives for the plan that are directly related to the health, safety, and lifestyle of the focus person (Horner et al., 1990; Meyer & Evans, 1989). Every written support plan should begin with a brief rationale explaining the reasons why the plan is being implemented and the overall expectations for the plan's beneficial impact on the person's life. This rationale sets the behavior support plan within the broader context of the person's life.

2. *Operational definitions of problem behaviors.* Comprehensive behavior support plans are developed in response to patterns of behavior that are a problem. Clear definitions of behaviors, stated in observable and measurable terms, are an important initial step in designing a plan. They help a collaborative support team reach consensus on the nature and magnitude of the problems faced and on a vision for the future.

Two important considerations in defining problem behaviors are (a) to define behaviors within the contexts in which they occur, and (b) to focus on response classes and not just individual behaviors (Horner et al., 1993). Too often, problem behaviors are described or defined as if they were characteristics or traits of the person (e.g., he's aggressive, he's a biter, she's noncompliant). Defining problem behaviors within the contexts in which they occur emphasizes that a person's behavior must be understood in relation to the contexts and situations in which it occurs (e.g., when faced with place-to-place or activity-to-activity transitions where he does not know what is happening next, Darin slaps his face with open palm, screams, or hits the adult requesting the transition). In planning support for Darin, it is important to note that slapping his face, screaming, and his "attacking" behaviors are members of the same response class (i.e., are maintained by the same consequence).

3. *Summary (hypothesis) statements from the functional assessment.* For each response class of problem behaviors identified in the functional assessment, a summary (hypothesis) statement should be presented that identifies setting events, antecedents

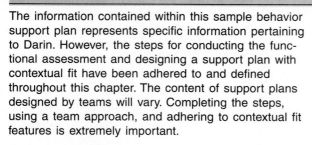

SAMPLE BEHAVIOR SUPPORT PLAN FOR DARIN
Rationale for Support

The information contained within this sample behavior support plan represents specific information pertaining to Darin. However, the steps for conducting the functional assessment and designing a support plan with contextual fit have been adhered to and defined throughout this chapter. The content of support plans designed by teams will vary. Completing the steps, using a team approach, and adhering to contextual fit features is extremely important.

Student: Darin Williams   Adoption Date: 10/24/97
DOB: 4/4/88   Teacher: Ms. Ortiz
Contacts: Dolores Williams   Assistant: Mr. Sears
(555-1234)   Behavioral Specialist:
Jared Williams   Ms. Greig
(555-5678)

Darin communicates with one and two word phrases, plays for long periods of time by himself with a Slinky, and has a history of slapping his face, screaming, and physically attacking adults who work with him. Darin's

outbursts average five times daily at school. In particular, Darin engages in problem behaviors during transitions, during nonpreferred activities, and during activities requiring writing. Darin's life at school and home will be greatly improved by learning new skills to replace his problem behaviors.

Team Agreements
- Darin will receive his education in a regular third grade classroom.
- Darin's behavior support plan will be based on functional assessment outcomes.
- Darin's support plan will be implemented and evaluated on a consistent and regular basis for a specified period of time (not just a week or two).
- Behavioral support for Darin is a high priority since, with age, Darin's aggressive behaviors and face slapping may become more frequent, intense, and problematic and may put him and those around him at even more risk.

Description of Darin's Problem Behavior:

1. *Self-slap.* Darin slaps himself in the face (cheeks and forehead) with an open-palmed hand, using enough force to produce an audible "slap" sound. Touching, rubbing, or tapping his face with no sharp, audible contact are *not* examples of self-slaps.
2. *Scream.* Screaming is defined as loud verbalizations from moderate to high intensity (i.e., clearly above conversation level). Darin's screaming has a high-pitched, piercing quality that is readily identifiable. Multiple screams are coded as a single incident when they occur in the context of continued performance of other problem behaviors (e.g., attacking staff or self-slaps) or when less than 2 minutes with no problem behaviors passes between screams. Low-intensity or conversation level verbalizations (e.g., typical or "excited voice" talking, mumbling, humming, or singing) and loud appropriate verbal communication attempts (e.g., yelling to a peer, calling out teacher name) are *not* examples of Darin's screams.
3. *Hit Others.* Hitting (and kicking) others is defined as Darin striking (i.e., making contact with any degree of force), or attempting to strike (e.g., swinging, punching, or slapping at someone with no contact), other people with an open hand, fist, or foot. This response may involve swinging or flailing arms and feet, punching, or slapping motions with his hands. Contact in the course of appropriate activities or play, such as tapping a shoulder to get someone's attention, should *not* be scored as hitting others.

and predictors, the behaviors in the response class, and the maintaining consequences. These summary statements provide the basis for a competing behaviors analysis, and the subsequent generation of potential intervention procedures. For response classes that have multiple functions, a separate summary statement must be produced for each function, identifying the different setting events and predictors for each different maintaining consequence (i.e., function).

4. An *overview of the general approaches selected to make problem behaviors irrelevant, inefficient, and ineffective.* The competing behaviors analysis form, when completed, provides a listing of potential intervention and support procedures within four types of support strategies: setting event, predictor (immediate antecedent), teaching, and consequence strategies. From these options, the collaborative team selects those strategies for the multicomponent plan that seem most likely to be effective for the focus person and to best fit the contexts in which they will be implemented. An overview of the general approaches selected and the considerations leading to these general approaches should be included in the written plan. This overview is not only useful in reaching consensus on procedures within the original collaborative support team, but it also plays an important role in orienting and training new support team members who must learn and implement the comprehensive plan at later points in time.

 Summary Hypothesis Statement from Darin's Functional Assessment

The functional assessment included completion of the Functional Assessment Interview Form by Darin's teacher, teaching assistant, and mother. In addition, 3 days of direct observation data were collected using the Functional Assessment Observation Form (O'Neill et al., 1997). From this process we believe that when Darin is faced with situations that he finds unpleasant or aversive (i.e., transitions in which expectations are unclear, requests that he speak in front of the class, or tasks that require writing), he is likely to begin slapping his own face, screaming, or physically attacking (hitting) the adult (e.g., teacher, class assistant, parent) making the request. These behaviors are maintained by escape from the situations. Darin is even more likely to engage in these problem behaviors if he is tired (i.e., has had less than 6 hours sleep). A diagram of the hypothesis indicates:

Less than 6 hours sleep	Transitions, requests to speak to class, requests to write	Scream, hit others, self-slap	Escape task, demand or transition
Setting Event	Antecedent or Predictor	Problem Behaviors	Maintaining Consequence

General Intervention Plan for Darin

Overview. Darin's problem behaviors are maintained by escaping three types of situations that he finds aversive.

We believe that during transitions, Darin often is confused about what is happening, and what is expected. He finds this aversive. When he screams and hits, people either help him through the transition or remove him to a more predictable situation.

We also believe that speaking in front of the class is aversive for Darin. Finally, when Darin tries to write, his current skill level makes writing difficult, and he is not as neat as he wants it to be, so he finds the result aversive. Problem behaviors often result in escaping these aversive situations. It also appears that if Darin has a poor night's sleep, the likelihood of problem behaviors increases.

The goals of the intervention will be to (a) reduce the aversive features of the three routines that often lead to problem behaviors, (b) teach Darin an alternative (appropriate) way to escape aversive situations, and (c) no longer allow problem behaviors to be an effective way of escaping aversive situations.

---

5. *Descriptions of each intervention and support procedure to be implemented, including specific procedures, protocols, or scripts for implementation during typical routines, activities, and problem situations.* The core of a written comprehensive behavior support plan is the descriptions of each of the procedures contained in the plan. These descriptions will vary in length and format depending on the specific procedure being described. The written plan must present the procedures in sufficient detail to ensure consistent, high-fidelity implementation. It also must serve as a primary tool for informing new support people about the content of behavior support. Because written support plans often serve more than one function (e.g., clinical implementation guide, administrative accountability, training), a "final" written comprehensive plan may employ multiple formats, including narrative descriptions, summaries, and scripts for specific responses to identified behaviors.

6. *Specification of emergency or crisis procedures, if needed.* An emergency or crisis intervention plan should be included in the comprehensive support plan for any person with severe problem behaviors who engages in (or has some likelihood of engaging in) high-intensity self-injurious, aggressive, or destructive behaviors that threaten his or her safety and health or the safety and health of others. An emergency plan should (a) precisely define what constitutes an emergency, (b) describe in detail the specific intervention procedures to be implemented, (c) define specific criteria for ending implementation of any intrusive or restrictive emergency procedures (e.g., criteria for ending a manual restraint procedure), (d) describe in detail specific procedures for data collection related to the emergency, (e) detail reporting procedures to be followed and identify who should be informed, (f) describe training and caregiver support procedures designed to maintain capacity to respond effectively to emergency behaviors, and (g) describe debriefing, feedback, and other follow-up procedures to be implemented after implementation of crisis intervention.

Emergency or Crisis Procedures

No unique crisis procedures are needed for Darin because he does not present a health or safety risk to himself or to others. Regular classroom and schoolwide safety and support policies will apply.

The Second Element: An Implementation Plan. This element provides a guide for getting the procedures and features of a comprehensive support plan into place and operational. The implementation plan is an often overlooked element of effective behavior support. Unfortunately, we have experienced many cases in which excellent behavior support plans have been developed but never fully implemented. Developing an implementation plan as part of the overall process of providing comprehensive support facilitates both initial and sustained implementation of planned procedures. The implementation plan identifies responsibilities and time lines for activities required to make planned procedures happen. For example, it would identify who will obtain or develop the necessary materials and forms, and when. The implementation plan may also (a) describe procedures for implementing each of the various plan components, (b) identify the sequence in which plan procedures will be implemented, and (c) set target dates and time lines for

Specific Procedures for Darin

Seven specific elements will be implemented throughout the school day. These are:

1. *Picture Sequence for Transitions.* There are four major transitions during the day that are most likely to lead to problem behaviors. For each transition, a picture sequence card will be used. The picture sequence card will identify each step of the transition (e.g., line up, walk down hall, sit in gym, physical education activities). Darin will be shown the picture card just before the transition begins, and each step of the transition will be reviewed. He will carry the card and will be prompted (by teacher or assistant) to identify which step of the card he is on, and which step is next. When he reaches the transition destination, he will place the card in a sleeve on the wall and enter into the new activity.

    Four 20-minute training sessions will be scheduled during the first week of the program to teach Darin how to use the picture cards and to fade the training into the regular daily routine. His prior history with picture sequences should make this amount of training sufficient.

2. *Shift from speaking to whole class to speaking to small group.* It is not necessary for Darin to speak before the whole class to accomplish his current academic objectives. As such, he will not be asked to report to the whole group. He will, however, continue to be asked to report on his work within his smaller reading and language groups.

3. *Teaching writing with precision.* During the next 4 weeks, Darin will have a modified writing assignment that uses tracing skills to help him build competence at forming letters. He will receive daily 20-minute one-to-one instruction with his preferred teaching assistant and substantive praise for his writing. He will be taught to deliver self-praise for his writing and, across the 4 weeks, the size, form and complexity of the writing will be gradually adjusted to approximate typical assignments. Materials recommended by Gleason and colleagues will be adapted for use in the training (Archer & Gleason, 1991).

4. *Teach Darin to request "breaks."* Darin may take a 2-minute break at any time of the day by saying "break please." When he takes a break, he physically moves to the blue desk on the South side of the class and sits with his timer. When the timer sounds, he returns to his desk. The first training Darin will receive in his new program will be 15-minute sessions twice a day on how to signal for a break, how to set the timer, and return when the timer sounds. After he has demonstrated the skill sequence five out of five times with a verbal direction from his teacher (e.g., "ask for a break"), training will be expanded to natural situations where Darin is given assignments or requests that typically evoke problem behaviors (e.g., writing). Training should continue until Darin asks for a break and correctly takes a break (i.e., sets timer and returns when it sounds) with no prompts or assistance for 10 consecutive breaks.

    Before routines that are associated with problem behavior (i.e., greeting, language, transitions, reading), Darin will be reminded to signal if he needs a break.

5. *Minimize the rewards for problem behaviors.* If Darin engages in screaming, hits others, or self-slaps, he will be instructed that his behavior is not an acceptable way to get out of difficult events and that if he needs a break he should ask for a break the right way. Blocking problem behaviors (e.g., protecting Darin, yourself, and others) if they continue to occur and directing or prompting Darin to work on the task should be continued, while also prompting him to ask for a break the right way (e.g., "Darin, say 'break please' if you want a break"). Allow him to take a break as soon as he asks the right way. Do not allow him to escape a situation simply by using his problem behaviors.

6. *Increase rewards for task completion.* The new program will place many new expectations on Darin. To make regular parts of the day maximally rewarding, a 4-week period will occur in which "extra" rewards will be delivered (e.g., stickers, privileges) for work completion.

7. *Modify schedule after nights with little sleep.* Ms. Williams will telephone Ms. Greig on mornings following a night when Darin got less than 6 hours of sleep. Ms. Greig will adjust her schedule to be available to work with Darin during the first 2 hours of the day, using the modified work package developed for days when a substitute teacher is on duty. The goals here are a high level of success on Darin's part, minimal exposure to aversive tasks, and allowing him to get through the portion of the day that typically is most difficult for him.

FIGURE 6–7
Implementation Plan

Date: _Oct. 13, 1997_   Student: _Darin Williams_

Team Members: _Ms. Ortiz, Mr. Sears, Ms. Greig, Mrs. Williams_

Action Team Coordinator: _Ms. Greig_

At the initial action team meeting, use this plan to organize activities and dates.

Activity	People Responsible	Date	Team Meeting
Functional Assessment			
1. Interview	_S. Greig_	_10/13-15_	
2. Observations	_S. Greig_	_10/15-17_	
3. Summarize	_Team_	_10/20_	_10/20 2:30-4:00_
Support Plan Development			
1. Develop considerations for support plan	_Team_	_10/20_	_10/20 2:30-4:00_
2. Firm up support plan	_S. Greig_	_10/24_	_10/24 2:30-4:00_
Support Plan Implementation			
1. Material development	_S. Greig_	_10/24_	
2. Teaching	_S. Greig_	_10/27-10/31_	
3. Coaching and feedback	_All_	_10/27-10/31_	
4. Staff training	_S. Greig_	_10/26 2:30-3:15_	
Monitoring and Evaluation			
1. Managing student information	_Ms Ortiz_	_Daily_	
2. Team meeting times	_All_	_Alternate Fridays 2:30-3:15_ _(11/14, 12/5, 12/19, 1/9, 1/23 . . .)_	

implementation. The implementation plan can be used to identify any necessary resources, training, and strategies for meeting training needs. Just as the comprehensive support plan itself is the product of a collaborative team process, an implementation plan also should reflect consensus from the support team.

The implementation plan also can provide aids (e.g., checklists, one-page summaries) to promote implementation fidelity and long-term maintenance (Lucyshyn & Albin, 1993). Team and caregiver support strategies and procedures for sustaining long-term implementation of a support plan can be incorporated into the implementation plan. Procedures for sustaining a collaborative team process over time and for maintaining the team's focus on their vision and goals for a focus person's lifestyle are essential for the long-term delivery of effective comprehensive behavior support.

Implementation Plan for Darin

Darin's team has agreed to use the Implementation Plan form to identify responsibilities and time lines for the implementation of Darin's support plan. This form (presented in Figure 6–7) lists the major activities to be performed by the implementors, who will do each activity, and when it will be completed.

The Third Element: An Evaluation Plan. The final element should include descriptions of data collection procedures, including forms and directions for using them, and procedures for ongoing monitoring and evaluation of plan effects. The evaluation plan will specify the behaviors to be tracked, the forms to be used, procedures for summarizing and sharing the information collected, and the persons responsible for each of the evaluation activities. A process for regular review and analysis of evaluation information should be identified so that timely decisions can be made regarding ongoing implementation and modification of plan procedures. An effective strategy is to set a regular meeting schedule for the support team to review plan effects and any issues arising from plan implementation.

Darin's Evaluation Plan

Darin's behavior will be monitored daily by using the Functional Assessment Observation Form (O'Neill et al., 1997). A 15-minute meeting will occur at the beginning of each school day for the first week of the plan, and every other Friday thereafter to review the status of Darin's (a) acquisition of new skills (e.g., break training, picture schedule use, writing) and (b) his pattern of problem behaviors.

In addition, Mrs. Williams has asked to use the Functional Assessment Observation Form to monitor problem behavior patterns at home. She will bring this information to the Friday meetings, and the data may be used to extend the program to the home, once success is established at school.

Summary

Positive behavior support is among the most exciting developments in the support technology available to children and adults with severe disabilities. Problem behaviors have long been a major obstacle to important living, educational, and employment opportunities. For too long we have assumed that to be part of typical environments a person first needed to acquire appropriate behaviors. We now have learned that appropriate behaviors are best learned when appropriate supports are delivered *in* typical contexts. The procedures associated with positive behavior support provide the means for assessing and designing support that will both reduce problem behaviors and develop the constellation of skills needed to have a real effect on how a person lives.

This chapter provides (a) a structure for understanding problem behaviors; (b) a set of procedures for conducting assessment that can transform chaotic, painful, confusing situations into understandable, logical patterns that can be addressed; and (c) a process for building support plans that will be both effective and doable.

However, this chapter has not provided a list of intervention techniques. We have not reviewed the critical issues related to identification and use of reinforcement. We have not reviewed the key skills related to curriculum design, delivery of instructional cues, response shaping, fading, prompting, and correcting. We have not reviewed the essential skills of good teaching that are needed for implementation of many positive behavior support plans. We have not reviewed new intervention procedures associated with manipulation of setting events (Carr, et al., 1996; Horner, et al., 1996; Horner, Day, & Day, 1997), use of choice procedures (Dunlap, et al., 1994; Lerman, et al., 1997; Vaughn & Horner, 1997), application of interspersed requests

(Mace & Belfiori, 1990; Horner, et al., 1991), antecedent manipulations (Smith & Iwata, 1997), incorporation of noncontingent reinforcement (Vollmer, Iwata, Zarcone, Smith, & Mazaleski, 1993; Fischer, Iwata, & Mazaleski, 1997), or application of augmentative communication systems (Mirenda, 1997). Part of what makes positive behavior support exciting is that there is a large list of intervention procedures from which to choose. We encourage readers to pursue further information regarding procedures identified in this chapter, as well as other positive behavioral support procedures not mentioned, in the many valuable texts related to positive behavioral support that are available (e.g., Carr et al., 1994; Koegel et al., 1996; Meyer & Evans, 1989; Meyer et al., 1991). Positive behavior support is a structure for using these procedures effectively.

The science of behavior analysis has defined an important set of mechanisms that describe how human beings learn from their environment. This science has been transformed into teaching and support procedures that have the potential to produce important changes in the behavior of children and adults with disabilities. Positive behavior support is the marriage of this science with fundamental values about the way people with disabilities should be part of our society. The challenge is to use the science with precision and the values with distinction. Those implementing positive behavior support need the self-discipline to learn the science before they venture to change someone else's behavior, the wisdom to learn the values so they apply the technology with discretion, and the humility to work collaboratively and to continually assess the impact of interventions on the lives of those who receive support.

Suggested Activities

Take a behavior support plan that you have written or that has been written to support a person you know well. Ask the following questions as you reread the support plan and make modifications where appropriate.

1. Does the plan operationally define the problem behaviors?
2. Does the plan identify all of the behaviors that are of concern?
3. Was the plan developed after a functional assessment was conducted?

4. Does the plan define the hypotheses about the predictor and maintaining events that were identified in the functional assessment?
5. Does the plan identify the critical features that should shape all of the elements of the intervention approach?
6. Does the plan identify specific changes that must occur in the behavior of staff (or family)?
7. Does the plan involve manipulating anything other than consequences for problem behaviors? Are changes in the physical setting defined? Changes in schedule? Changes in training objectives? Changes in staff prompting?
8. Does the plan involve changes that are logically consistent with the assessment assumptions?
9. Does the plan involve procedures that are socially acceptable, likely to be effective, and possible within the local context?
10. Does the plan include monitoring procedures that will assess both the problem behaviors and the larger life-style patterns of the student?
11. Does the plan include an evaluation component that ensures regular (at least weekly) assessment of the effects of the plan?
12. Construct a competing behaviors analysis for the major problem behaviors targeted in the plan. Is the approach defined in the plan logically consistent with your competing behaviors analysis?

Acknowledgments

Preparation of this chapter was supported in part by the U. S. Department of Health and Human Services Grant No. 90DD0439. However, the opinions expressed herein do not necessarily reflect the position or policy of the Department, and no official endorsement should be inferred. The authors gratefully acknowledge the efforts and contributions of Priscilla Phillips and Terri Surratt in preparation of this chapter.

References

Alberto, P. A., & Troutman, A. C. (1999). *Applied behavior analysis for teachers* (5th ed.). Upper Saddle River, NJ: Merrill/Prentice-Hall.
Albin, R. W., Lucyshyn, J. M., Horner, R. H., & Flannery, K. B. (1996). Contextual fit for behavior support plans: A model for "goodness-of-fit". In L. K. Koegel, R. L. Koegel, & G. Dunlap (Eds.), *Positive behavioral support: Including people with difficult behavior in the community* (pp. 81–98). Baltimore: Paul H. Brookes.

Albin, R. W., & Sandler, L. (1998, May). *Contextual fit as a variable affecting the fidelity with which behavior interventions are implemented.* Presentation at the Association for Behavior Analysis Annual Convention, Orlando, FL.

Anderson, J. L., Albin, R. W., Mesaros, R. A., Dunlap, G., & Morelli-Robbins, M. (1993). Issues in providing training to achieve comprehensive behavioral support. In J. Reichle & D. P. Wacker (Eds.), *Communicative approaches to the management of challenging behavior* (pp. 363–406). Baltimore: Paul H. Brookes.

Archer, A., & Gleason, M. (1991). *Skills for school success.* North Billerica, MA: Curriculum Associates.

Arndorfer, R. E., Miltenberger, R. G., Woster, S. H., Rortvedt, A. K., & Gaffaney, T. (1994). Home-based descriptive and experimental analysis of problem behaviors in children. *Topics in Early Childhood Special Education, 14*(1), 64–87.

Baer, D. M., Wolf, M. M., & Risley, T. G. (1968). Some current dimensions of applied behavior analysis. *Journal of Applied Behavior Analysis, 1,* 91–97.

Berg, W. K., & Sasso, G. M. (1993). Transferring implementation of functional assessment procedures from the clinic to natural settings. In J. Reichle & D. P. Wacker (Eds.), *Communicative alternatives to challenging behavior* (pp. 343–362). Baltimore: Paul H. Brookes.

Bijou, S. W., Peterson, R. F., & Ault, M. H. (1968). A method to integrate descriptive and experimental field studies at the level of data and empirical concepts. *Journal of Applied Behavior Analysis, 1,* 175–191.

Brown, F. (1991). Creative daily scheduling: A nonintrusive approach to challenging behaviors in community residences. *Journal of the Association for Persons with Severe Handicaps, 16,* 75–84.

Carr, E. G. (1977). The motivation of self-injurious behavior: A review of some hypotheses. *Psychological Bulletin, 84,* 800–816.

Carr, E. G. (1988). Functional equivalence as a mechanism of response generalization. In R. H. Horner, R. L. Koegel, & G. Dunlap (Eds.), *Generalization and maintenance: Life-style changes in applied settings* (pp. 221–242). Baltimore: Paul H. Brookes.

Carr, E. G. (1994). Emerging themes in the functional analysis of problem behavior. *Journal of Applied Behavior Analysis, 27,* 393–399.

Carr, E. G., & Carlson, J. I. (1993). Reduction of severe behavior problems in the community using a multicomponent treatment approach. *Journal of Applied Behavior Analysis, 26,* 157–172.

Carr, E. G., Horner, R. H., Turnbull, A., Marquis, J., Magito-McLaughlin, D., McAtee, M., Smith, C. E., Anderson-Ryan, K. A., Ruef, M. B., & Doolabh, A. (in press). *Positive behavior support as an approach for dealing with problem behavior in people with developmental disabilities: A research synthesis.* American Association on Mental Retardation Monograph.

Carr, E. G., Levin, L., McConnachie, G., Carlson, J. I., Kemp, D. C., & Smith, C. E. (1994). *Communication based intervention for problem behavior: A user's guide for producing positive change.* Baltimore: Paul H. Brookes.

Carr, E. G., Reeve, C. E., & Magito-McLaughlin, D. (1996). Contextual influences on problem behavior in people with developmental disabilities. In L. K. Koegel, R. L. Koegel, & G. Dunlap (Eds.), *Positive behavior support: Including people with difficult behavior in the community* (pp. 403–423). Baltimore: Paul H. Brookes.

Cooper, L. J., Wacker, D. P., Sasso, G. M., Reimers, T. M., & Donn, L. K. (1990). Using parents as therapists to evaluate appropriate behavior of their children: Application to a tertiary diagnostic clinic. *Journal of Applied Behavior Analysis, 23*(3), 285–296.

Crawford, J., Brockel, B., Schauss, S., & Miltenberger, R. G. (1992). A comparison of methods for the functional assessment of stereotypic behavior. *Journal of the Association for Persons with Severe Handicaps, 17,* 77–86.

Day, H. M., Horner, R. H., & O'Neill, R. E. (1994). Multiple functions of problem behaviors: Assessment and intervention. *Journal of Applied Behavior Analysis, 27,* 279–289.

Didden, R., Duker, P. C., & Korzilius, H. (1997). Meta-analytic study on treatment effectiveness for problem behaviors with individuals who have mental retardation. *American Journal on Mental Retardation, 101*(4), 387–399.

Donnellan, A. M., Mirenda, P. L., Mesaros, R. A., & Fassbender, L. L. (1984). Analyzing the communicative functions of aberrant behavior. *Journal of the Association for Persons with Severe Handicaps, 9,* 201–212.

Doss, S., & Reichle, J. (1991). Replacing excess behavior with an initial communicative repertoire. In J. Reichle, J. York, & J. Sigafoos (Eds.), *Implementing augmentative and alternative communication* (pp. 215–237). Baltimore: Paul H. Brookes.

Dunlap, G., dePerczel, M., Clarke, S., Wilson, D., Wright, S., White, R., & Gomez, A. (1994). Choice making and proactive behavioral support for students with emotional and behavioral challenges. *Journal of Applied Behavior Analysis, 27*(3), 505–518.

Dunlap, G., Kern-Dunlap, L., Clarke, S., & Robbins, F. R. (1991). Functional assessment, curricular revision, and severe problem behaviors. *Journal of Applied Behavior Analysis, 24,* 387–397.

Dunlap, G., Kern, L., dePerczel, M., Clarke, S., Wilson, D., Childs, K. E., White, R., & Falk, G. D. (1993). Functional analysis of classroom variables for students with emotional and behavioral challenges. *Behavioral Disorders, 18,* 275–291.

Durand, V. M. (1998). *Sleep better!: A guide to improving sleep for children with special needs.* Baltimore: Paul H. Brookes.

Durand, V. M., Berotti, D., & Weiner, J. (1993). Functional communication training: Factors affecting effectiveness, generalization, and maintenance. In J. Reichle & D. P. Wacker (Eds.), *Communicative alternatives to challenging behavior: Integrating functional assessment and intervention strategies* (pp. 317–340). Baltimore: Paul H. Brookes.

Durand, V. M., & Carr, E. G. (1991). Functional communication training to reduce challenging behavior: Maintenance and application in new settings. *Journal of Applied Behavior Analysis, 24*(2), 251–264.

Durand, V. M., & Crimmins, D. B. (1988). *The motivation assessment scale: An administration manual.* Unpublished manuscript, State University of New York, Albany.

Fischer, S. M., Iwata, B. A., & Mazaleski, J. L. (1997). Noncontingent delivery of arbitrary reinforcers as treatment for self-injurious behavior. *Journal of Applied Behavior, 30*(2), 239–249.

Giangreco, M. F., & Putnam, J. W. (1991). Supporting the education of students with severe disabilities in regular education. In L. H. Meyer, C. A. Peck, & L. Brown (Eds.), *Critical issues in the lives of people with severe disabilities* (pp. 245–270). Baltimore: Paul H. Brookes.

Green, C. W., Reid, D. H., Canipe, V. S., & Gardner, S. M. (1991). A comprehensive evaluation of reinforcer identification processes for persons with profound multiple handicaps. *Journal of Applied Behavior Analysis*, 24, 537–552.

Guess, D., & Carr, E. G. (1991). Emergence and maintenance of stereotype and self-injury. *American Journal on Mental Retardation*, 96, 299–319.

Hagan, S. (1998). *An examination of classroom management procedures that support middle school students with severe and chronic problem behaviors.* Unpublished doctoral dissertation, University of Oregon, Eugene.

Horner, R. H. (1994). Functional assessment: Contributions and future directions. *Journal of Applied Behavioral Analysis*, 27, 401–414.

Horner, R. H. (in press). Positive behavior supports. In M. Wehmeyer & J. Patton (Eds.), *Mental retardation in the 21st Century.* Austin, TX: Pro-Ed.

Horner, R. H., & Billingsley, F. F. (1988). The effect of competing behavior on the generalization of adaptive behavior in applied settings. In R. H. Horner, G. Dunlap, & R. L. Koegel (Eds.), *Generalization and maintenance: Life-style changes in applied settings* (pp. 197–220). Baltimore: Paul H. Brookes.

Horner, R. H., Day, H. M., & Day, J. (1997). Using neutralizing routines to reduce problem behaviors. *Journal of Applied Behavior Analysis*, 39, 601–614.

Horner, R. H., Day, H. M., Sprague, J. R., O'Brien, M., & Heathfield, L. T. (1991). Interspersed requests: A nonaversive procedure for decreasing aggression and self-injury during instruction. *Journal of Applied Behavior Analysis*, 24(2), 265–278.

Horner, R. H., Diemer, S. M., & Brazeau, K. C. (1992). Educational support for students with severe problem behaviors in Oregon: A descriptive analysis from the 1987–88 school year. *Journal of the Association for Persons with Severe Handicaps*, 17(3), 154–169.

Horner, R. H., Dunlap, G., Koegel, R. L., Carr, E. G., Sailor, W., Anderson, J., Albin, R. W., & O'Neill, R. E. (1990). Toward a technology of "nonaversive" behavioral support. *Journal of the Association for Persons with Severe Handicaps*, 15(3), 125–132.

Horner, R. H., O'Neill, R. E., & Flannery, K. B. (1993). Building effective behavior support plans from functional assessment information. In M. Snell (Ed.), *Instruction of students with severe disabilities* (4th ed.) (pp. 184–214). New York: Merrill/Macmillan.

Horner, R. H., Vaughn, B., Day, H. M., & Ard, B. (1996). The relationship between setting events and problem behavior. In L. K. Koegel, R. L. Koegel, & G. Dunlap (Eds.), *Positive behavioral support: Including people with difficult behavior in the community* (pp. 381–402). Baltimore: Paul H. Brookes.

Hunt, P., Farron-Davis, F., Wrenn, M., Hirose-Hatae, A., & Goetz, L. (1997). Promoting interactive partnerships in inclusive educational settings. *Journal of the Association for Persons with Severe Handicaps*, 22(5), 127–137.

Iwata, B. A., Dorsey, M. F., Slifer, K. J., Bauman, K. E., & Richman, G. S. (1982). Toward a functional analysis of self-injury. *Analysis and Intervention in Developmental Disabilities*, 2, 3–20.

Iwata, B. A., & Fisher, W. W. (1997, May). *Current research on the assessment and treatment of severe behavior disorders.* Symposium presented at the Association for Behavior Analysis Annual Convention, Chicago, IL.

Janney, R. E., & Snell, M. E. (1997). How teachers include students with moderate and severe disabilities in elementary classes: The means and meaning of inclusion. *Journal of the Association for Persons with Severe Handicaps*, 22(3), 159–169.

Kern, L., Childs, K. E., Dunlap, G., Clarke, S., & Falk, G. D. (1994). Using assessment-based curricular intervention to improve the classroom behavior of a student with emotional and behavioral challenges. *Journal of Applied Behavioral Analysis*, 27, 7–19.

Kern, L., Dunlap, G., Clarke, S., & Childs, K. E. (1994). Student-assisted functional assessment interview. *Diagnostique*, 19, 29–39.

Kincaid, D. (1996). Person-centered planning. In L. K. Koegel, R. L. Koegel, & R. Dunlap (Eds.), *Positive behavioral support: Including people with difficult behavior in the community* (pp. 439–465). Baltimore: Paul H. Brookes.

Koegel, L. K., Koegel, R. L., & Dunlap, G. (1996). *Positive behavioral support: Including people with difficult behavior in the community.* Baltimore: Paul H. Brookes.

LaVigna, G. W., & Donnellan, A. M. (1986). *Alternatives to punishment: Solving behavior problems with nonaversive strategies.* New York, NY: Irvington Publishers.

Lerman, D. C., & Iwata, B. A. (1993). Descriptive and experimental analysis of variables maintaining self-injurious behavior. *Journal of Applied Behavior Analysis*, 26, 293–319.

Lerman, D. C., & Iwata, B. A., Rainville, B., Adelinis, J. D., Brosland, K., & Kogan, J. (1997). Effects of reinforcement choice on task responding in individuals with developmental disabilities. *Journal of Applied Behavior Analysis*, 30(2), 411–422.

Lewis-Palmer, T. (1998). *Using functional assessment strategies in regular school classroom settings with students at-risk for school failure.* Unpublished doctoral dissertation, University of Oregon, Eugene.

Lucyshyn, J. M., & Albin, R. W. (1993). Comprehensive support to families of children with disabilities and behavior problems: Keeping it "friendly." In G. H. S. Singer & L. E. Powers (Eds.), *Families, disability, and empowerment: Active coping skills and strategies for family interventions* (pp. 365–407). Baltimore: Paul H. Brookes.

Lucyshyn, J. M., Albin, R. W., & Nixon, C. D. (1997). Embedding comprehensive behavioral support in family ecology: An experimental, single-case analysis. *Journal of Counseling and Clinical Psychology*, 65(2), 241–251.

Mace, F. C., & Belfiori, P. (1990). Behavioral momentum in the treatment of escape-motivated stereotypy. *Journal of Applied Behavior*, 23(4), 507–514.

Mace, F. C., & Lalli, J. S. (1991). Linking descriptive and experimental analysis in the treatment of bizarre speech. *Journal of Applied Behavior Analysis*, 24, 553–562.

March, R., & Horner, R. (1998, May). *School-wide behavioral support: Extending the impact of ABA by expanding the unit of analysis.* Presentation at the Association for Behavior Analysis Annual Convention. Orlando, FL.

Meyer, L. H., & Evans, I. M. (1989). *Nonaversive interventions for behavior problems: A manual for home and community.* Baltimore: Paul H. Brookes.

Meyer, L. H., Peck, C. A., & Brown, L. (1991). *Critical issues in the lives of people with severe disabilities.* Baltimore: Paul H. Brookes.

Michael, J. (1993). Establishing operations. *The Behavior Analyst*, 16, 191–206.

Miltenberger, R. (1997). *Behavior modification: Principles and procedures.* Pacific Grove, CA: Brookes/Cole.

Mirenda, P. (1997). Supporting individuals with challenging behavior through functional communication training and AAC: Research review. *Journal of the International Society for Augmentative and Alternative Communication*, 13(4), 207–225.

Mount, B. (1994). Benefits and limitations of personal futures planning. In V. J. Bradley, J. W. Ashbaugh, & B. C. Blaney (Eds.),

Creating individual supports for people with developmental disabilities (pp. 97–108). Baltimore: Paul H. Brookes.

Neef, N. A., & Iwata, B. A. (1994). Current research on functional analysis methodologies: An introduction. *Journal of Applied Behavior Analysis, 27,* 211–214.

Nippe, G., Lewis-Palmer, T. & Sprague, J. (1998). *Student-guided functional assessment: An analysis of agreement between teachers, students and direct observation.* Manuscript submitted for publication. University of Oregon, Eugene.

Northup, J., Wacker, D., Sasso, G., Steege, M., Cigrand, K., Cook, J., & DeRaad, A. (1991). A brief functional analysis of aggressive and alternative behavior in an out clinic setting. *Journal of Applied Behavior Analysis, 24,* 509–522.

O'Neill, R. E., Horner, R. H., Albin, R. W., Sprague, J. R., Storey, K., & Newton, J. S. (1997). *Functional assessment and program development for problem behavior: A practical handbook* (2nd ed.). Pacific Grove, CA: Brookes/Cole.

Pace, G. M., Ivancic, M. R., Edwards, G. L., Iwata, B. A., & Page, T. J. (1985). Assessment of stimulus preference and reinforcer values with profoundly retarded individuals. *Journal of Applied Behavior Analysis, 18*(3), 249–256.

Reed, H., Thomas, E., Sprague, J. R., & Horner, R. H. (1997). Student guided functional assessment interview: An analysis of student and teacher agreement. *Journal of Behavioral Education, 7*(1), 33–49.

Repp, A. C., Felce, D., & Barton, L. E. (1988). Basing the treatment of stereotypic and self-injurious behaviors on hypotheses of their causes. *Journal of Applied Behavior Analysis, 21,* 281–289.

Salisbury, C. L., Mangino, M., Rainforth, B., Syryca, S., & Palombaro, M. M. (1994). Promoting the inclusion of young children with disabilities in the primary grades: A curriculum adaptation process. *Journal of Early Intervention, 18,* 311–322.

Sasso, G. M., Reimers, R. M., Cooper, L. J., Wacker, D., Berg, W., Steege, M., Kelly, L., & Allaire, A. (1992). Use of descriptive and experimental analyses to identify the functional properties of aberrant behavior in school settings. *Journal of Applied Behavior Analysis, 25*(4), 809–821.

Schmidt, M. W., & Harriman, N. E. (1998). *Teaching strategies for inclusive classrooms: Schools, students, strategies, and success.* Orlando, FL: Harcourt Brace.

Skinner, B. F. (1953). *Science and human behavior.* New York: Macmillan.

Smith, R. G., & Iwata, B. A. (1997). Antecedent influences on behavior disorders. *Journal of Applied Behavior Analysis, 30*(2), 343–376.

Snell, M. E. (1993). *Instruction of students with severe disabilities* (4th ed.). New York: Merrill/Macmillan.

Sprague, J. R., & Horner, R. H. (1992). Covariation within functional response classes: Implications for treatment of severe problem behavior. *Journal of Applied Behavior Analysis, 25,* 735–745.

Sprague, J. R., & Horner, R. H. (1999). Low frequency, high intensity problem behavior: Toward an applied technology of functional assessment and intervention. In A. C. Repp & R. H. Horner (Eds.), *Functional analysis of problem behavior: From effective assessment to effective support.* (pp. 98–116), Belmont, CA: Wadsworth.

Sturmey, P. (1994). Assessing the functions of aberrant behaviors: A review of psychometric instruments. *Journal of Autism and Developmental Disorders, 24,* 293–304.

Sugai, G., & Horner, R. H. (1994). Including students with severe behavior problems in general education settings: Assumptions, challenges, and solutions. In J. Marr, G. Sugai, & G. Tindal (Eds.), *The Oregon conference monograph* (pp. 102–120).

Sugai, G., Horner, R. H., & Sprague, J. R. (in press). Functional assessment-based behavior support planning. *Education and Treatment of Children.*

Todd, A. W., Horner, R. H., Vanater, S. M., & Schneider, C. F. (1997). Working together to make change: An example of positive behavioral support for a student with traumatic brain injury. *Education and Treatment of Children, 20,* 425–440.

Touchette, P. E., MacDonald, R. F., & Langer, S. N. (1985). A scatter plot for identifying stimulus control of problem behavior. *Journal of Applied Behavior Analysis, 18,* 343–351.

Turnbull, A. P. (1997, September). *Getting a life.* Presentation at the Research and Training Center Conference, Santa Barbara, CA.

Turnbull, A. P., & Ruef, M. (1996). Family perspectives on problem behavior. *Mental Retardation, 34*(5), 280–293.

Turnbull, A. P., & Ruef, M. B. (1997). Family perspectives on inclusive lifestyle issues for individuals with problem behavior. *Exceptional Children, 63*(2), 211–227.

Turnbull, H. R., Rainbolt, K., & Buchele-Ash, A. (1997). *Individuals with Disabilities Education Act: Digest and significance of 1997 amendments.* Beach Center on Families and Disability, University of Kansas, Lawrence. Unpublished manuscript.

Van Houten, R., & Rolider, A. (1991). Applied behavior analysis. In J. L. Matson & J. A. Mulick (Eds.), *Handbook of mental retardation* (pp. 569–585). New York: Pergamon Press.

Vaughn, B., & Horner, R. H. (1997). Identifying instructional tasks that occasion problem behaviors and assessing the effects of students versus teacher choice among these tasks. *Journal of Applied Behavior Analysis, 30* (2), 299–312.

Vollmer, T. R., Iwata, B. A., Zarcone, J. R., Smith, R. G., & Mazaleski, J. L. (1993). The role of attention in the treatment of attention-maintained self-injurious behavior: Noncontingent reinforcement and differential reinforcement of other behavior. *Journal of Applied Behavior Analysis, 26*(1), 9–22.

Wacker, D. P., Berg, W. K., Cooper, L. J., Derby, M., Steege, M. W., Northup, J., & Sasso, G. (1994). The impact of functional analysis methodology on outpatient clinic services. *Journal of Applied Behavior Analysis, 27*(2), 405–407.

Wacker, D. P., Steege, M., Northup, J., Reimers, T., Berg, W., & Sasso, G. (1990). Use of functional analysis and acceptability measures to assess and treat severe behavior problems: An outpatient clinic model. In A. C. Repp & N. Singh (Eds.), *Perspectives on the use of aversive and nonaversive interventions for persons with developmental disabilities* (pp. 349–359). Sycamore, IL: Sycamore.

Wacker, D. P., Steege, M. W., Northup, J., Sasso, G., Berg, W., Reimers, T., Cooper, L., Cigrand, K., & Donn, L. (1990). A component analysis of functional communication training across three topographies of severe behavior problems. *Journal of Applied Behavior Analysis, 23,* 417–429.

Walker, H., Colvin, G., & Ramsey, E. (1995). *Antisocial behavior in public schools: Strategies and best practices.* Pacific Grove, CA: Brooks/Cole.

Willis, T. J., LaVigna, G. W., & Donnellan, A. M. (1987). *Behavior assessment guide.* Los Angeles, CA: Institute for Applied Behavior Analysis.

Zarcone, J. R., Rodgers, T. A., Iwata, B. A., Rourke, D. A., & Dorsey, M. F. (1991). Reliability analysis of the motivation assessment scale: A failure to replicate. *Research in Developmental Disabilities, 12,* 349–360.

7

Special Health Care Procedures

Marilyn M. Ault
Jane P. Rues
J. Carolyn Graff
Jennifer F. Holvoet

Students with special health care needs are similar to all other students in terms of their right to an appropriate education in the least restrictive environment, with full family participation. The presence of special health care needs, however, requires additional accommodations in the educational setting. This is best accomplished by training educational staff in the knowledge and skills needed to manage these procedures at school.

 LIZ

Mark was not surprised when he learned that a student enrolling in his class next year would have special health care needs. He had become accustomed to "looking out" for a variety of his students' needs over his 8 years of teaching fifth and sixth grade math and science. In the past he had encountered several medical situations, even emergencies, which had taken him to the emergency room with some students. The episodes that most clearly taught him the necessity of proper training and support resulted from the near death of two students during his fourth and fifth year of teaching. During a spring field trip to gather water quality samples a student was stung by a bee. While Mark was removing the stinger, the student moved rapidly through the stages of anaphylactic shock. Mark was able to call an emergency medical technician (EMT) on his cell phone and arrange to meet an ambulance on the way to the hospital.

The second emergency didn't even occur off campus. During the hot days at the beginning of school, a student returned to his class from playing soccer during gym. It soon became evident that the child was in respiratory crisis. Mark was able to retrieve the student's inhaler from his gym bag and call for EMT assistance. It became very clear to Mark that the outcomes of these situations would not have been so positive had he not been

245

knowledgeable about first aid, known about the medical status of his students, and had a good relationship with the EMT at the local hospital. More typical issues surrounding health care occurred throughout the years including medication administration, burns and wounds, and allergies. Mark felt quite confident that he was prepared to handle any health-related condition.

During the past 3 years of teaching, Mark's school had actively moved towards the practice of full inclusion for all children. Children with a range of disabilities had been enrolled in his classroom and he enjoyed the challenge of including them in science and math activities with their more typical peers. Mark felt he was a contributing part of a team trying to determine how the math and science content could be taught in a way that would be meaningful for their lives. With the support from the consultant teacher, he felt positive about his efforts and their results. Now he was presented with the challenge of including a student with severe cognitive disabilities

who also used a wheelchair to navigate around the building and his classroom. He had dealt with children having both these conditions before. This child, Liz, also used a colostomy bag. Mark knew that the female aide would assist the child in actually changing the bag. He did, however, have a significant role on the team planning for her full inclusion. He, and all her other teachers, had to understand her nonverbal communication indicating discomfort, have knowledge of when typical elimination might occur and how to respond, and perhaps how to integrate the needs of the health care procedure into her educational activities.

In addition to teaching Liz to count and keep track of her own supplies, Mark hoped to use the information he learned from his experience with Liz to expand some of the content addressed in his science class. Mark planned to include typical as well as atypical functioning of many of the systems of the body and how accommodations are made.

Teachers across all grade levels deal with issues surrounding the health care needs of children and youth. This chapter focuses on special health care procedures that are common across a number of health conditions or diagnoses. For example, medication administration, a very common special health care procedure, may be required for students with asthma, allergies, seizures, or constipation. Children with these conditions may also present teachers with additional procedures to be conducted in the classroom, such as oxygen supplementation, resuscitation, and monitoring of nutrition and fluid intake. Although there are also many health conditions that do not require any special health care procedures during the school day, teachers should be aware of the presence of these conditions and their potential effect on learning. Any heath-related condition may have a significant effect on a student's readiness to fully participate in educational activities.

Many students with severe or profound disabilities require the application of one, or many, special health care procedures in order to promote and maintain health (Ault, Guess, Struth, & Thompson, 1989; Graff, Ault, Guess, Taylor, & Thompson, 1990). These health care procedures tend to include seizure monitoring, medication administration, nutrition monitoring and supplementation, teeth and gum care, skin care, and bowel care. A second group of health-related procedures are present less often but may require imple-

mentation during the school day. These include non-oral feeding, atypical elimination, and respiratory management. There is also a third and relatively rare group of procedures that, while effecting student overall health and readiness, generally are not implemented in the school. These may include glucose monitoring and shunt care. This chapter introduces the basic aspects of these procedures within the context of the school day.

Each section addressing a health care issue ends with directions for where to go for further information and training. The Internet is one of the most valuable options available to educators to quickly access current and exhaustive information regarding almost any health condition or procedure. The following advice about the Internet is presented as encouragement and a general guide. We encourage use of the links listed below as well as those following each section.

Where to Go for Further Information or Training on the Internet

The Internet offers many sources of information that were not available even 3 years ago for the educator or parent wishing to address the needs of a student with disabilities. This information can be quite useful, if selected and used with discretion. When in doubt about the reliability of a site, or the veracity of the information found at a site, make sure to check with the student's primary health care provider and the health care coordinator at your school or district. You will easily be able to find, for example, information about:

1. Specific syndromes and the typical symptoms associated with these syndromes
2. Typical medical treatments used to treat certain aspects of specific disabilities
3. Alternative medical treatments that have been successful for some individuals
4. Opportunities to learn from, and confer with, other individuals who either have a specific disability, who are parents of children with that disability, or who are teaching others with the disability.

Information about Disabilities

Much information about specific disabilities (even very rare syndromes) and health care conditions can be used to ascertain the extent of the disability and associated conditions that may also need educational support. Such information can generally be regarded as accurate if published on the Internet by medical practitioners or parental support groups. The best use of the information found in this chapter, or through the Internet sites, is to allow you to ask relevant and informed questions of a parent when a student with a disability is enrolled in a class for the first time. This information can also be quite helpful in ascertaining when certain behaviors may be part of a syndrome. For example, a student receiving a certain medication may experience dryness of the mouth or lethargy. Knowing this and using the tips that other parents and educators have provided to address this problem can certainly make the education of a child more effective. Often these tips are found in discussion groups or chat rooms on Internet sites.

Most of the disability information on the Internet is written from a medical perspective and may use words unfamiliar to an educator. A good medical dictionary or talking with the parents may help clarify most of these terms. Learning the terms is a worthwhile investment for an educator. It allows clearer and more professional communication with many support staff, such as occupational and physical therapists, and also allows better communication when you wish to ask questions of parents or experts either personally or via E-mail.

Some examples of this type of material are:

1. Awesome Library (has links to different types of disabilities and health-related needs): http://www.neat-schoolhouse.org/special-ed.html
2. Blindness Resource Center: http://www.nyise.org/eye.htm
3. LD Online: http://www.ldonline.org/
4. Charcot-Marie Tooth Disorder: http://www.charcotmarie-tooth.org/
5. Prader-Willi Association (take Basic Information link): http://www.pwsausa.org/
6. Cerebral Palsy: http://www.ucpa.org/html/resources/index.html
7. Kids with Cancer: http://www.kidswithcancer.com/
8. AsthmaNet: http://www.njc.org/asthmanet/asthmnet.htm

Since the Internet is a very fluid and dynamic electronic space, it is possible that some of the web addresses provided throughout this chapter will have been moved or changed. Therefore, you should know how to search for material. Use a search engine such as ProFusion (www.profusion.com), Yahoo (http://www.yahoo.com/), Metacrawler (http://www.metacrawler.com), or Inference Find (http://infind.inference.com/infind/), and type in the keyword area or field the name of the syndrome or condition for which you want more information (e.g., asthma, shunt, nasal cannula, cancer). Use capital letters at the beginning of the words, if this is how the syndrome is typically written. Click on the search button. The search engine will work for a minute or so and then will return a list of links. Look for links that have descriptions or an address in the "location" heading of your browser that indicate the site is published by a medical establishment or a national or state association.

Medical Treatments

An educator may be interested in what medical treatments are typically encountered by those individuals with a specific disability. For example, knowing what types of medications are typically prescribed and the intended effect and possible side effects of the medication may help the educator report classroom observations that will be useful to the parents and the physician as they attempt to manage the child's medications. If surgeries are scheduled for a student, knowing more about those surgeries and what type of care the student may need when he or she returns to school may make the experience less traumatic for both. For example, if you have a student return to school in a spica cast, a specially constructed cast to restrict movement, after some hip surgery you will need assistance in determining how to both manage the student's needs and determine the student's ability. You will need to know how to manage this student's toileting without contaminating the cast and how to move or position the child safely. The parent and hospital will provide specific information about your student; general information can be found at, for example, http://www.ccmckids.org/hipspic.htm and other similar sites.

The sites that describe disabilities noted in the previous section often have sections on typical treatments, especially those that are sponsored by medical organizations or hospitals. For example, the Charlotte Institute of Rehabilitation at http://www.charweb.org/health/rehab/scin/urology.html has a whole section on bladder management that includes how the urinary system works, different types of tests the student might encounter, and the procedures and purpose of catheterization. In addition, an educator can search for specific information by using a search engine and typing in the name of the treatment (e.g., spica cast) or medication (e.g., phenytoin [Dilantin]). As a general rule, look for sites such as glossaries or patient information rather than choosing sites that are clearly geared to physicians (e.g., *The Use of Dilantin in Febrile Seizure Management*) or that are clearly personal (*Patty's Dilantin Page*) to find general information. Hospitals or pharmacies often sponsor such sites. Some good sites to start your investigation are:

1. The Virtual Hospital: http://www.vh.org/Patients/ PatientsAnnotatedList.html
2. Connecticut Children's Center Patient Education Guides: http://www.ccmckids.org/ccmc2-1.htm
3. MedWeb: http://www.gen.emory.edu/MEDWEB/ keyword/patient_education/neoplasms.html
4. Implant Dentistry: http://implantdentistry.com/
5. Smart Drugs Glossary: http://www.smartbasic.com/ glos.drugs.dir.html
6. Internet Mental Health Medications (medical text for health professionals): http://www.mental-health. com/p30.html

There are also many Internet sites focusing on disabilities that are developed and operated by parents.

Often these sites have information about alternative treatments for a condition. These treatments, however, are often not endorsed by the medical community and generally are promulgated by word of mouth. They typically seem to work with small subsets rather than all students with a particular disability. When looking at alternative treatment literature, be sure to read both the pros and the cons, so you are an informed reader. You should not make recommendations about alternative treatments, but you could provide information from both sides of the controversy to a family or team searching for ideas, which, of course, should be reviewed by appropriate health care professionals.

Opportunities to Confer with Others

One of the most useful options available on the Internet is the ability to easily correspond with experts about specific problems or areas where more information is needed. This can be a comfort both for the educator and the family. Most pages related to a health condition and those that are sponsored by Departments of Education or Special Education also provide links to the web site manager. By clicking on that link, filling in the E-mail form that results, and clicking on send, you can be put in touch with people who are in a position to help you maximize the positive effect of your interactions with a student who has special health needs or disabilities.

Quality Health Care and Teaching

The process of establishing quality health care in the educational setting means a commitment to (a) incorporating the special health care needs into the ongoing educational program and (b) actively preventing the development of health-related problems or conditions. This commitment must be made by the educational staff as well as the administrative personnel. Teachers, additional staff members, and related service personnel must be willing to attend to special health care procedures throughout the educational day. The building principal, general and special education teachers, director of special education, and other administrative staff members must be willing to support this commitment through the provision of necessary training, location of the classroom or in-structural setting within the school building, and availability of backup support personnel. Collaboration among each of these key groups, including the student's family, is essential to the provision of health care that is safe, consistent, and involves the student in the implementation of the procedure. This respect and collaboration is often exemplified in a transdisciplinary team in which the unifying philosophy is a commitment to sharing information and skills among the various disciplines represented on the team. The richness of these interactions across time encourages the development of a common language and system of communication that facilitates a comprehensive understanding of a student's goals and the educational program to achieve these goals. This team model can be effective, efficient, accountable, and proactive because each team member is responsible for the goals and the opportunities throughout the school day for incidental teaching, embedded teaching, and partial participation.

Integrating Health Care Needs

The first commitment, addressing both the present education and the health requirements of students in the educational setting, confirms the willingness of teachers not to divide students' needs into separate parts and to accept the responsibility to address the educational needs of the total student. The fact that a student has a gastrostomy (i.e., has a tube inserted through the wall of the abdomen in order to receive food and fluids) or a tracheostomy (i.e., has an opening at the base of the throat in order to facilitate breathing) adds to, rather than subtracts from, situations that may provide the content or occasion for instruction. For example, a teacher must include a student's visual or hearing needs when developing an educational plan or instructional strategies. Similarly, a teacher must consider a student's need for bladder catheterization in the identification of functional skills and the development of methods to practice those skills.

At least three instructional procedures facilitate the incorporation of health-related procedures into the educational day. These include incidental teaching, embedded skill teaching (see chapter 4), and partial participation (see chapters 4 and 9). Briefly, incidental teaching is a procedure during which a teacher follows a student's initiation in identifying an interest

or a need. Once the teacher has responded to the signal or initiation presented by the student, the teacher offers an opportunity to practice specific skills. Incidental teaching, usually described in the context of language instruction, can also be applied when responding to a student's need for special health care procedures. Based on an initiation from a student, the teacher can provide, for example, humidified oxygen or a tube feeding, or empty a colostomy bag.

Embedded teaching suggests that multiple skills, addressing many different goals, can be taught simultaneously. Skills involving language, reach and grasp, relaxation, and head control, often taught in small, distributed trial settings (see ch. 4), can be practiced in conjunction with the procedures used for providing oxygen, resting after a seizure, or emptying a colostomy bag.

The third educational procedure, partial participation, provides a framework for the teacher to support the student's participation in a health-related activity as an educational objective. With this approach, the student is not required to independently perform a procedure in order for participation in the procedure to be considered relevant. The student may practice many skills that are part of a special health care procedure and are contributing to greater independence. These may include grasping a toothbrush and spitting after teeth and gum care, visual fixation and swallowing during medication administration, communicating the need for position changes, or grasping the syringe and visual tracking during tube feedings.

Mark planned to implement a sequence in his math class that would allow Liz to keep an inventory of her medical supplies. This included sorting and counting the bags, gauze, and shields. As part of a group activity with her peers related to sets, fractions, and projections, she would also keep a weekly count of use and orders given to the school nurse. Mark would also make sure he and her teammates in the class understood her sign for the need to have her bag changed. Once she signaled her need, a peer would call the health care aide.

Preventing Additional Health Care Problems

In addition to being committed to meeting the present needs of students, teachers must participate in efforts designed to prevent the development of further health-related problems. Problems may result from complications from an already identified condition or from conditions not related to any presently identified problem. The instructional day must routinely include procedures designed to promote the overall health of students. Implementation of special health care procedures must be a high priority in order to maintain student health as well as to contribute to the ability of students to optimally interact with the environment. Health-related procedures include adequate nutrition and hydration, cardiovascular exercise and physical fitness, frequent movement, frequent positioning or repositioning in the upright position, changes in instructional environments and materials, and access to the outdoors and sunshine.

Throughout their careers, teachers encounter students who need a variety of special health care procedures. The need for these procedures in schools occurs with varying frequencies and intensities. This chapter identifies a general body of knowledge and group of skills as "general health care procedures." It also identifies a group of procedures that are present less frequently, identified as "specialized health care procedures." Finally, some procedures seem to occur infrequently and teachers may or may not be expected to participate in their implementation. These procedures are identified as "low-incidence health care procedures." The chapter includes information concerning what is involved in the implementation of the procedures, reasons why this particular knowledge and skill are necessary in the classroom, and directions for further information or training.

What Does a School Nurse Know?

As school systems grew, it became apparent that districts needed to establish a health service system to protect all of the students attending school. Originally, the major function of a school nurse was to protect the entire student population from the spread of common disease. This involved screening for contagious diseases, immunizing students, and implementing basic health instruction in the schools (Walker & Jacobs, 1984). The role of screening for hearing and vision problems was added later.

When dealing with the needs of students who have severe disabilities, a school nurse should function as a member of a group of professionals who bring their expertise together to meet the needs of students. A

teacher should not assume, however, that the school nurse would have the knowledge or skill to address all of the special health care procedures that may be required in the schools. It is not common for a school nurse to have specific knowledge or skill in the implementation of procedures such as catheterization, tracheostomy suctioning, or gastrostomy tube feedings. But given background and training, the school nurse is the most qualified member of the team to take a major role in identifying resources, training, and monitoring special health care procedures for individual students.

General Health Care Procedures

General health care procedures contribute significantly to the overall health and safety of any student in any classroom, but particularly young children and youth with severe or profound disabilities. These procedures, *commonly needed for all students*, include infection control, cardiopulmonary resuscitation, and first aid. The procedures (a) have a broad range of application across many different settings and (b) require that all staff members having direct contact with students be skilled in their application.

Infection Control

The purpose of infection control is to prevent the transmission of disease to children and youth and, secondarily, to prevent the infection of school personnel. Infections occur when organisms enter the body and find an environment that allows them to grow and spread. Some infections, such as chicken pox and colds are an almost expected part of childhood. Other infections, such as AIDS or tuberculosis, which occur in the general public, present minimal risk in the schools if proper control procedures are followed. Infections can be caused by bacteria, viruses, fungi, protozoa, and helminths (parasitic worms). Once an infection is established, there is always a potential for transmission to others.

What Is Involved

Infection control primarily refers to the efforts of public health and school officials to prevent the initial occurrence of infection. Secondarily, it refers to efforts to prevent the spread of an already established infection. Proper immunization, before school enrollment, is the major method of infection control. Children should have begun their immunizations before entry into schools (kindergarten or preschool) and should have received the following: DPT (diphtheria, pertussis, tetanus), OPV (oral polio vaccine), MMR (measles, mumps, and rubella, or German measles), and, possibly, varicella (chickenpox). The schedules for these immunizations have been established by the Centers for Disease Control (CDC) (www.cdc.gov). Additionally, a tuberculin test is given to determine whether a child has been exposed to tuberculosis. A vaccine for *Haemophilus influenzae*, which may be present in influenza type B, is recommended for infants between 2 and 6 months of age (AAFP Recommendation, 1991). *Haemophilus influenzae* is known to cause serious infections, such as meningitis. Immunization for influenza type B is especially recommended for children attending day care centers (Andersen, Bale, Blackman, & Murph, 1986). Immunizations are given because immunity to a disease does not occur unless the child receives an immunization to stimulate production of antibodies to the disease, which is the body's defense against infection.

Infection control also involves using proper procedures to prevent the spread of infection to other children and youth, as well as educators. When a student is identified as having an infection, consultation with the school nurse and the primary health care provider is necessary to determine whether the child should remain in the classroom. If the student remains, then specific procedures designed to prevent the spread of infection without unnecessarily stigmatizing the student must be utilized. Because certain students are more susceptible to infections than others, efforts must be made to maintain or promote the health of the student with the infection as well as those students potentially exposed.

There are some viruses that may be present for varying lengths of time with no symptoms. These include, but are not limited to, cytomegalovirus (CMV), herpes virus, hepatitis A and B viruses, and human immunodeficiency virus (HIV). Preventing the spread of these infections, therefore, requires a clear understanding of how infections are transmitted. For example a child may have acquired CMV infection early in life. The virus will leave the body through saliva or urine only at certain times, with no sign that this is

occurring. School policy may require, therefore, that disposable gloves be used whenever feeding or changing the child's diaper, if such a level of support is required. Because there is a risk to pregnant women, many health authorities also recommend that a pregnant staff person not work directly with a child who has CMV infection. Procedures required to prevent the spread of HIV infection and hepititis should be followed when individuals are exposed to blood, certain other body fluids (i.e., amniotic fluid, pericardial fluid, peritoneal fluid, pleural fluid, spinal fluid, cerebrospinal fluid, semen, and vaginal secretions), or any body fluid visibly contaminated with blood. Since HIV and hepatitis B virus (HBV) transmission have not been documented from exposure to other body fluids, such as feces, nasal secretions, sputum, sweat, tears, urine, and vomitus, extraordinary precautions do not apply. Extreme care procedures should be applied in dental or oral care settings in which saliva might be contaminated with blood (CDC, 1998).

Use in the Classroom

Infections can be spread through various ways, including contact with droplets that are sneezed into the air; contact with secretions from the body, such as saliva, mucus, cerebral spinal fluid, urine, feces, or blood; and ingestion of organisms in food. One can generally assume, however, that most typical contacts with a student bring minimal risk of infection if proper clean procedures are utilized.

The best way to prevent the spread of infection in the classroom is for all students and staff to use clean procedures. The simple and most effective procedure is to engage in proper hand washing, lathering hands with running water and soap. Proper hand washing should always occur after contact with diapers. This is critical between toileting episodes for each child and before handling any food or liquid. Figure 7–1 presents one description of proper hand-washing techniques. Clean procedures also involve the proper washing of school items, such as toys and teaching materials, with disinfectants before the items are shared. This is particularly true if items are mouthed, if saliva is present outside the mouth (e.g., on the hands or clothing), or if sneezing or coughing onto materials is common. For the most effective implementation of clean procedures, classrooms should be equipped with or have access to toileting and hand

FIGURE 7–1
Description of Proper Hand Washing Techniques

How to Wash Your Hands

- Remove jewelry

- Rub foaming soap all over hands especially around and underneath nails and between fingers

- Rub hands under running water and rinse

- Use paper towel to dry, to turn off faucet (if necessary), and to open door to exit (if necessary)

Note: Adapted from Centers for Disease Control [1985]. *What you can do to stop disease in child day care centers.* Atlanta: Department of Health and Human Services.) (Obtain through your local or state department of health or write to: Public Health Advisor, Center for Professional Health and Training, Centers for Disease Control, 1600 Clifton Road, Atlanta, GA 30333.

washing areas that are separate and distinct from food preparation areas.

Where to Go for Further Information or Training
Local health departments and local hospitals with departments or designated individuals responsible for infection control can be contacted for additional information. Many local hospitals are establishing web pages for reference to immunization schedules and infection control procedures. The Centers for Disease Control and Prevention (*www.cdc.gov*) and the American Academy of Pediatrics (*www.aap.org*) provide information and guidelines about infectious diseases, symptoms, modes of transmission, and strategies for prevention.

Cardiopulmonary Resuscitation

Cardiopulmonary resuscitation (CPR) is an emergency procedure used when breathing, or breathing and pulse, have ceased. CPR is not considered a routine procedure for classroom implementation; rather, it is an emergency response. A presentation of CPR is included within the context of this chapter only to provide general information about the procedures. All teachers should receive yearly certification in CPR and should not attempt intervention without current endorsement. CPR, while potentially life sustaining,

may easily result in serious injury and death if not performed correctly (American Academy of Pediatrics, 1993; ParasolEMT, 1998; Sommers, 1992).

What Is Involved
The three basic rescue skills of CPR include opening the airway, restoring breathing, and restoring circulation. The rescuer provides oxygen and, if the heart has stopped, simulates the heart's pumping action through external compression of the chest. It is rare, however, that CPR alone will save a life. CPR applied immediately upon discovery of a casualty and sustained until more advanced life support arrives is the key to saving lives (American Heart Association, 1987). Teachers should be trained in all CPR procedures associated with the ages of the students they teach. Separate procedures have been developed for infants, children, and adults. The procedures briefly described here are for students from 1 to 8 years of age. The procedures for students over 8 years of age of typical size are the same procedures as for adults (see American Heart Association, 1987, for the procedures for adults).

Opening the Airway. Indications that intervention may be necessary are unconsciousness, pupils fixed and dilated, and absent pulse and respiration. When a student is suspected of having respiratory or cardiac arrest, the recommended procedure is to first make an attempt to rouse the student by gently shaking his or her shoulders and shouting "[name], are you okay?" After the attempt to arouse the student is unsuccessful, first call for help. Second, position the student on his or her back, carefully supporting the head and neck in case of injury. Third, open the airway by tilting the student's head backward and lifting the chin.

Restoring Breathing. Determine if the student is still breathing by looking for the rise and fall of the chest and listening and feeling for a breath while holding the airway open. If there is no breath, give the student two breaths using mouth-to-mouth contact, while holding the student's nostrils closed.

Restoring Circulation. Determine whether a pulse is present by feeling for the carotid pulse (on either side of the student's throat, near the Adam's apple), while tilting the head to open the airway.

If the pulse is absent, position your hands in relation to the heart and begin repeated compressions of the chest in a specific rhythm. It is critical that your hands are positioned correctly in relation to the child's heart. If not, the chest compression will seriously damage other vital organs (ParasolEMT 1998). The hands should be located on the lower half of the sternum and compressions are performed at a depth of 2 to 3 centimeters, using the heel of one hand only. Continuously repeat the routine cycle of five chest compressions to one breath, periodically checking for the pulse as long as the pulse is absent and until an emergency medical services (EMS) team arrives. If the pulse returns, check for spontaneous breathing. Give one breath every 4 seconds as long as there is no spontaneous breathing. If the student begins breathing spontaneously, remain beside the student to monitor the breathing and pulse (American Heart Association, 1987). If other persons arrive to assist, they should first contact the EMS team before taking turns in the CPR process, in order to insure that medical assistance arrives as quickly as possible.

Managing an Obstructed Airway. If the student appears to be choking, identify if the airway is completely obstructed by determining if the student can speak or cough. If the student can do either, do not interfere with the student's attempts to force out the object blocking the airway. If the student is unable to speak or cough, assume the airway is blocked and perform the Heimlich maneuver until the object is expelled. This maneuver can be conducted with the student in a standing, sitting, or supine position. To perform the Heimlich maneuver, place the unconscious student on his or her back (a conscious student can be sitting or standing with the rescuer positioned behind the student), supporting the head and neck, and look down into the mouth and airway for an object blocking the airway. Use only your fingers to remove any visible object. If no object is seen or removed, open the airway and attempt to breathe into the student. Then, make a fist with one hand positioned over the fist of the other hand and give 6 to 10 upward thrusts over the abdomen. This describes the Heimlich maneuver for an unconscious student lying on the floor. The procedure is different for a student conscious and sitting or standing. Continue the cycle of looking for the object blocking the airway, opening the airway,

breathing into the student, and performing abdominal thrusts until the student revives or an EMS team arrives (American Heart Association, 1987).

Use in the Classroom

Difficulty breathing is the most frequent medical emergency for children (American Academy of Pediatrics, 1993; Buzz-Kelly & Gordin, 1993; Campbell & Thomas, 1991; CPR-ECC National Convention, 1992a; Harris, Baker, Smith, & Harris, 1984; Sommers, 1992; Soud, 1992). The need for resuscitation may result from injuries; suffocation caused by toys, foods, or plastic covers; smoke inhalation; sudden infant death syndrome; and infections, especially of the respiratory tract, among other conditions (Statistical Resources Branch, 1981). It is unfortunate that the majority of situations resulting in CPR for children are preventable; therefore, instructional settings and routines must be established to ensure environments that are safe (Standards for CPR and ECC, 1986) and foster independence.

Although any individual may need CPR, students with severe disabilities tend to have characteristics that increase the likelihood. Heart defects, seizure disorders, aspiration of fluids or objects, tracheostomies, or excess fluids in the mouth are examples of these characteristics. Feeding characteristics that may result in the need for an emergency response are immature chewing and swallowing and abnormalities of the structure and sensation of the mouth and throat. Children, when compared with older students, are at a higher risk for choking because their airways are smaller and their coughs are weaker (Harris, Baker, Smith, & Harris, 1984).

By starting CPR quickly after a student has stopped breathing or the airway has been blocked, cessation of the pulse, or cardiac arrest, can be prevented (Standards for CPR and ECC, 1986). CPR begun within 4 minutes (or less) after the pulse and breathing have stopped, can be lifesaving. When CPR is begun within 4 minutes, the chances of leaving the hospital alive are four times greater than for the student who does not receive CPR until after 4 minutes. After 4 minutes and without CPR, brain damage begins. After 10 minutes have passed without CPR, brain death is certain because of the lack of oxygen (American Heart Association, 1987).

All teachers and staff at Mark's school routinely update their CPR and first aid certification. Students who use wheelchairs require a slightly more involved response from staff, should resuscitation be needed. Mark's principal made sure that the local hospital provided one-on-one training in a response protocol for a student in a wheelchair, particularly for resuscitation and CPR. Most first aid situations did not require a different response for students who were, or were not, using a wheelchair.

Teachers and other professionals who interact continuously with students having disabilities should be routinely certified in CPR. If a person who is trained in CPR does injure the victim, the state's Good Samaritan laws usually protect that person. These laws prevent a victim (or the victim's family) from suing someone who attempted to perform lifesaving techniques (Batshaw & Perret, 1986). These laws do not cover persons who implement CPR without a current certification.

Where to Go for Further Information or Training

The American Heart Association, local hospitals, the Red Cross, school districts, and other local agencies routinely conduct CPR and management of airway obstruction classes. There are also a number of web sites that deal with the implementation of CPR (e.g., www.yahoo.com/health). Many of these sites, however, do not outline the specific procedures because of the need to have "hands on" training in order to be considered certified to implement the procedure.

First Aid

First aid refers to the administration of emergency assistance to persons who have been injured or are in some physical distress before the arrival of or transportation to a health care professional (Thomas, 1985). The "first aid" procedures administered in most schools are not lifesaving situations, yet unmanaged or improperly managed situations can become life-threatening with serious consequences.

Although a great deal of effort is expended to assure a safe school environment, accidents and injuries will occur. These typically minor events require first aid procedures that can be carried out in the school by the first person on the scene and that can be supported by the school nurse or qualified school staff. Because these events often occur when the teacher is the first available source of assistance, first

aid training should be required of all school staff, taught by competent and certified health care professionals.

Also, it is often the teacher who first recognizes, interprets, and acts on a student's signs and cues that indicate a need for aid. Typically developing children often have conditions that require first aid, such as asthma, allergies, and reactions to medications. Students with special health care needs also present challenges to school staff, because their symptoms may be subtle and difficult to recognize. A student may experience symptoms, such as headache, nausea, or fever, but be unable to describe these symptoms to others. An aware teacher can recognize these signs in all of his or her students.

What Is Involved

Planning. Since situations requiring first aid generally arise unexpectedly, it is critical to have properly trained staff and emergency procedures in place. Careful planning for and anticipation of situations requiring first aid and identification of methods for prevention are essential. An emergency plan and procedures for school staff to follow should include not only the school setting and available resources in that setting, but also settings away from the school campus (e.g., traveling to and from school by bus, a field trip). Plans and procedures for a school should be consistent with the policies established by the school district and with state laws and regulations for school staff.

Procedures could include, for example, assignment of persons responsible for telephoning emergency assistance to transport the student to a source of emergency care when needed; for calling the student's parents; for accompanying the student to the emergency room, physician's office, or other location to receive emergency care; and for attending to the needs of the other students who witnessed the event requiring first aid.

School staff should have telephone numbers for contacting the student's parents during the school day, along with the names and telephone numbers of persons to contact when parents are not available. Additionally, the name and telephone number of the student's health professional should be easily available for school staff responsible for using this information. Telephone numbers for the school nurse, school administrator, ambulance, police department, fire department, paramedics, poison control center, and hospital emergency room should be posted at telephones in the school.

The amount of responsibility individual school staff members have in administering first aid varies in each school district. The number of health care professionals available in school districts also varies. In one school district, a school nurse may be assigned to an individual school and provide services to several hundred students in that school, while in another district, there may be only one nurse for the entire school district. In that instance, a school staff member who is properly trained in first aid or the school administrator may be the person who is contacted in emergency situations. A clearly outlined procedure of the steps to be followed in an emergency should be posted near all telephones.

Students who are at risk for health-related emergencies should be identified, with student and parental permission, and specific plans about what to do in the event of an emergency should be developed and in place (Schwab, 1991). At a minimum the emergency plan should include: the parents' names and telephone numbers, telephone numbers of alternate persons to contact in the event of parental absence or difficulty reaching the student's parents, and the names and telephone numbers of the student's physician or health care professionals (e.g., nurse practitioner, clinical nurse specialist, or physician assistant). In addition to specific information about the steps to be followed for a specific procedure, written parental permission and medical authorization to carry out the interventions at school must included. Information such as the student's allergies, status of immunizations, major medical problems, medications a student is receiving, and other pertinent information in the school records should be available to school staff responsible for using this information. An emergency care plan should also be a part of the student's Individualized Health Care Plan and the student's Individualized Education Plan (IEP). Porter, Haynie, Bierle, Caldwell, and Palfrey (1997) present a collection of very useful documents for use when developing and implementing a plan for the inclusion of children and youth requiring specialized health care procedures in an edu-

cational setting. Figure 7–2 represents a portion of these documents adapted for Liz.

An emergency identification bracelet or necklace should be worn or an emergency information card carried to identify any serious condition or allergies the student has. Such conditions may include diabetes, epilepsy, hemophilia, and potentially serious allergic reactions to medications or insect stings. Along with the condition or allergy, the student's name and blood type should be included. Use of personal emergency identification is especially important as students become older, more independent, and less supervised by persons aware of their potential need for immediate intervention.

Certain supplies are necessary when administering first aid and are usually available in the office of the school nurse. Disposable gloves should be used when staff may have contact with body secretions. These secretions may include urine, blood, mucus drainage, or saliva. The special health care needs of an individual student may dictate additional items that can be kept in a designated location for the student or with the student at all times. Supplies should be checked periodically and replaced as needed.

Although medications are frequently part of a first aid supply, it must be remembered that medication cannot be given without permission from the student's physician. Written parental and medical permission is required for school staff to administer medication. The exact procedure depends on the policies of the local school district and state laws and regulations. Exceptions to this are life-threatening emergencies in which EMT paramedics administer medications as recommended by a physician from the emergency room or hospital where a student is being transported. In this instance, administration of medications may take place on the school campus by staff from the emergency medical service.

Deciding if Emergency Attention Is Needed. School staff should not call paramedics for minor injuries such as minor cuts, bumps, or sprains. Guidelines on when to contact medical professionals may be in place for an individual student, but unexpected emergencies can occur and must be handled immediately. During an emergency situation, such as severe bleeding, shock, or sudden unconsciousness, the paramedics or an ambulance service should be called to take the

FIGURE 7–2
Sample Individualized Health Care Plan for Liz

In Emergency, Notify:

Name: Kathy Clark   Phone: 235-5483   Relationship: aunt

Name: Mike Harmon   Phone 864-4954   Relationship: father

Jane Roaland _____   ____1998-2000____ School Year
School Health Care Coordinator

Mike Slvoski _____
Education Coordinator

Individualized Health Care Plan

Student Information:

Liz Harmon _____   ____2-14-1986_____
Name   Birthdate

Mike and Beth Harmon _____   3316 SW 80 Street Terrace _____
Parent/Guardian   Address

Mother/Guardian: 295-2434 _____   271-1800 _____
                         Home Phone   Work Phone

Father/Guardian: 295-2434 _____   864-4954 _____
                         Home Phone   Work Phone

Primary Care Physician: N. Crouch _____   Phone: 545-2726 _____

Specialty Physicians/Health Care Workers:

_____Wagner, speech/language _____   Phone 235-8476 _____

_____Hoag, wheelchair care _____   Phone 235-8555 _____

_____Martinez, R.N., skin care _____   Phone 675-7983 _____

_____Berle, M.D., internist _____   Phone 295-3434 _____

student to a hospital. When contacting emergency room staff or paramedics for assistance in determining the seriousness of the student's condition, school staff should minimally provide the following information: (a) student's specific complaints or symptoms; (b) when symptoms began; (c) what makes the pain or condition better or worse; (d) what the student was doing when the injury or illness occurred; (e) what changes have occurred since the onset of the injury or illness; (f) what, if anything, the student has swallowed; (g) what medication the student has been taking. When a student is known to have a health problem that can potentially result in a life-threatening situation, inform the emergency room staff and paramedics as allowed by the student's parents. Permission forms previously signed by the student's

FIGURE 7–1
continued

Student-Specific Staff Training:

Subject	Date	By	Attending
Colostomy bag changing at school	8/25/97	Hospital staff	Fifth grade staff
		Burgess	Secretary
Seizure monitoring at school	8/25/97	Hospital staff	Fifth grade staff
		Nelson	Secretary

General Staff Training:

Subject	Date	By	Attending
CPR	8/28-29/97	Red Cross	All staff

Peer Awareness Training:

Subject	Date	By	Attending
Wheelchairs on the playground	9/25/97	Smith	Fifth grade 3rd hr playground
Nonsymbolic communication	11/6/97	Wagner	Turgeon's math class

Note: Adapted from Porter, S., Haynie, M., Bierle, T., Caldwell, T. H., & Palfrey, J. S. (1997). *Children and youth assisted by medical technology in educational settings: Guidelines for care*, Baltimore: Paul H. Brookes.

parents and filed in the student's school record allow this pertinent information to be shared.

First Aid in the Classroom

First aid procedures must be conducted with due regard for the danger of cross-infection. Simple rules of personal hygiene are sufficient to guard both the first aid provider and the student from additional contam-ination (ParasolEMT, 1998). Before providing the aid, wash hands with soap and water, or rinse with antiseptic. If possible, wear gloves, use a protective cloth over clothing, swab the area to be treated with approved antiseptic, and cover any adjacent areas likely to produce infection. During treatment avoid coughing, breathing, or speaking over the wound, avoid contact with body fluids, and use only clean bandages and dressings. After treatment wash your hands with soap and water.

Tissue Injuries

Insect bites or stings. Insect bites or stings can occur at almost any time. The reaction to the bite depends not only on the individual student but also the particular insect. Students may have a reaction of pain, redness, and swelling at the site of the sting. A life-threatening consequence of a sting may be a systemic reaction resulting in anaphylaxis (i.e., a condition that may be mild and include slight fever, redness of skin, and itching or may be severe and include difficulty breathing, violent coughing, cyanosis, fever, changes in pulse, seizures, and collapse). Awareness of the possibility of a severe reaction to a bite or sting allows school staff to help avoid insect bites or prepare to manage the reactions. An anaphylaxis kit containing epinephrine should be available for all students having severe reactions to foods or stinging insects.

Symptoms of a bee sting include evidence of the stinger, pain, swelling, and itching at the site. An allergic reaction also includes breathing difficulties, facial hives and swelling, rapid pulse, and collapse. Remove the stinger by scraping with fingernail or similar object, but *do not* squeeze. Use a cold compress to reduce swelling and pain.

Insects such as mosquitoes, flies, gnats, fleas, and hornets tend to bite exposed parts of the body, while body lice, scabies, and chiggers (mites) tend to establish themselves on areas of the body that are covered by clothing. These bites may manifest as single welts or rashes. Tick bites may be of particular danger because of the possibility of Lyme disease. For all bites, after immediate necessary first aid is applied, the school health care professional should be informed.

Human bites. Human bites may occur accidentally or intentionally. A student may bite himself or herself during chewing or it may be a behavioral problem. Teachers and staff may also be bitten as a result of interacting with a student. Infection can develop rapidly and be extensive because of the variety of organisms present in the mouth and in saliva. Both human and animal bites require careful cleaning with soap and water and irrigation, and they are left open to permit drainage. Keeping the wound open prevents the growth of certain harmful organisms (i.e., anaerobic

organisms) that can survive in tissue and do not require oxygen to live.

Burns. Burns can occur as a result of scalds, electricity, or flames. Although this is unlikely in a school setting because of the efforts to make the school environment safe for children, minor or major burns can occur. Holding the burned area under cool water lessens the pain and cleanses the wound. Do not place ice on the burn; ice will further damage tissue. Sterile gauze bandages may be used to cover the burned areas if necessary. If sterile bandages are unavailable, clean cloth is used to cover the wound until the student is transported for medical attention.

Soft-tissue injuries. There are injuries, excluding bone fractures, that affect the joints and muscles of limbs. Sprains, strains and dislocations are considered soft-tissue injuries; some authorities also include bruising. The treatment of soft-tissue injuries is based on resting the injured part, applying ice packs to limit swelling and reduce pain, applying a firm compression bandage as support, and elevating the limb. The acronym for this treatment is RICE: rest, ice, compression, and elevation (ParasolEMT, 1998).

Abrasions. Abrasions or scrapes occur when there is loss of skin surface, resulting in pinhead-sized openings with fluid or blood oozing. The area should be held under cool running water and washed with soap or a mild nonirritating antiseptic solution. If dirt is in the area, it can be flushed out with normal saline solution (Foster, Hunsberger, & Anderson, 1989).

Laceration. A laceration refers to a wound that has a smooth or irregular tear of the skin and blood vessels. The area should be washed with soap and running water or a mild antiseptic. If suturing is required, it should occur within 6 hours of the injury to prevent scarring.

Puncture wound. A puncture wound refers to the penetration of the skin with a sharp object, such as a nail, pencil, or tooth, causing a small hole in the skin. There is usually little bleeding. The area should be washed with soap and running water or a mild antiseptic solution. A puncture wound should be monitored carefully for signs of infection, and a tetanus booster injection is recommended if the student has not received one within 5 years.

Bleeding injuries. For bleeding injuries that result from a burn, laceration, or puncture wound, many school districts recommend that school staff wear gloves when in contact with blood or body secretions that may contain blood. Concerns about transmission of HIV, HBV, and other organisms that may be present in the blood have resulted in changes in policies in school districts. Authorities have emphasized that any transmission of HIV and HBV most likely involves exposure of skin lesions or mucous membranes to blood and possibly to other body fluids of an infected person (Education and foster care, 1985).

Bone fracture. Signs that a bone fracture may have occurred include crookedness, shortening, or rotation of an extremity; pain or tenderness at the site of the fracture; or swelling and discoloration of the overlying skin because of bleeding around the fracture site. Keep the area immobilized until assistance arrives, and apply cool packs to the area because they may help reduce swelling (Chow, Durand, Feldman, & Mills, 1984). Students who are immobile and do not place weight on their bones are more inclined to experience a fracture when being lifted from a lying position to a sitting position. Since weight bearing contributes to bone density, the bones of such students are frail and tend to fracture more easily (Batshaw & Perret, 1986).

Where to Go for Help

The nearest poison control center is an excellent resource for the school nurse in determining what step should be taken to manage the ingestion of a substance. Emergency care resources in the community may include the local hospital and emergency room staff, health department, and trained EMT paramedics. In some communities, ambulance service, fire department, or police department staff may be properly trained to provide first aid in an emergency. Web sites are also available with general information regarding first aid training (*www.redcross.com*) or procedures (ParasolEMT, 1998).

Specialized Health Care Procedures

A number of special health care procedures, identified in this chapter as "specialized health care procedures," tend to be required frequently, particularly for students with severe or profound disabilities (Ault et al., 1989). These procedures are divided into two distinct groups, reflecting the actions required. The first group of common procedures are those that *require monitoring during the school day* (monitoring procedures). Teachers or designated staff members may be required to record occurrences of an event and monitor the student; no other intervention is required. These procedures can include seizure monitoring, medication administration, and nutrition monitoring and supplementation. The second group of common procedures *requires actual and routine implementation of a specific procedure* to maintain health or prevent the development of additional health-related problems (routine implementation procedures). These include teeth and gum care, skin care, and bowel care.

Monitoring Procedures

Seizure Monitoring

The purpose of seizure monitoring is to keep a record of atypical brain activity in order to provide feedback to the family and health care professionals regarding the effect of seizure treatment. Monitoring, using a form as shown in Figure 7–3, allows us to carefully observe and summarize information about a student's seizures. Systematic observations over time help us distinguish behaviors that are and are not related to the seizure and communicate these observations to the family and physician (Neville, 1997; Williams, et al., 1996). Careful observation of the child's seizure helps us physically protect the child during a seizure.

A seizure is sudden, abnormal bursts of electrical activity in the brain, resulting in a temporary change in behavior. This change in electrical activity may be limited to one area of the brain or may begin in one area and spread to other areas of the brain. If the electrical disturbance is limited to only part of the brain, then the result is a *partial seizure*. For example, the child may experience stiffening or jerking of one arm or leg. If the electrical disturbance affects the entire brain, the result is a *generalized seizure*, which includes grand mal or tonic-clonic seizures.

Epileptic seizures, including febrile seizures, occur in 3% to 5% of children; of the 125,000 new cases that develop each year, up to 50% occur in children and adolescents (Neville, 1997; Murray & Haynes,1996).

FIGURE 7–3

Sample Seizure Documentation Recording Form

Seizure Monitoring Form

Name of Student: _____   Date: _____

Seizure medication: _____   Time of last
administration: _____

Careful observation and documentation will allow you to describe three possible components of the seizure: 1) antecedent events: activities preceding the seizure; 2) seizure activity: motor behavior during the seizure; and 3) postictal state: behavior after the seizure. For each of the following descriptors, note the occurrence or nonoccurrence and indicate by numbering if there was a sequence evident.

Antecedent Events

Classroom activity preceding seizure: _____

Change in student's behavior: _____

Time of onset: _____

Seizure Activity

Areas and sequence of body involved:

      face _____ R arm _____ L arm _____

      trunk _____ R leg _____ L leg _____

Muscle tone: limp _____, rigid _____, alternating limb movements _____

Position of eyes: rolled back _____, turned to R _____, turned L _____

Breathing: beginning of seizure: normal _____, interrupted _____

            middle of seizure: normal _____, interrupted _____

            end of seizure: normal _____, interrupted _____

Skin color: pale _____; blue _____; red _____; other _____

Incontinence: bladder _____; bowel _____

Postictal Activity

Time seizure ended: _____

Duration of seizure: _____

Behavior immediately following seizure:

awake, inactive _____ awake, active _____

crying, agitated _____ drowsy, asleep _____

_____

Person observing seizure/completing form: _____

Studies have indicated that children with other health and developmental problems are less likely to "grow out of their seizures" and less likely to achieve optimal control with anticonvulsants (Kurtz, Tookey, & Ross, 1998; Neville, 1997). Thus, the monitoring of students' seizures has been identified as one of the major health-related procedures performed by the classroom teacher (Ault, et al., 1989.)

What to Do During a Seizure

1. Remain calm. Remember that no one can stop a seizure once it has started.
2. Stay with the student to monitor the student's activity during the seizure.
3. Mentally sequence the events that occurred before the seizure so you can record them later on an appropriate form (see Figure 7–3).
   a. Did the student recognize or signal the onset of the seizure?
   b. Did the student cry out or yell?
   c. What was the student's activity immediately before the seizure?
   d. Who noticed a change in the student's behavior?
4. Loosen tight clothing, especially around the neck.
5. Ease the student to the floor (to avoid a fall), if the student is standing or sitting when the seizure begins. This should be done even if the student is secured in adaptive equipment (i.e., wheelchair, standing frame, prone board).
6. Place a cushion or blanket under the student's head to prevent injury to the head.
7. If possible, position the student on his or her side so that the tongue does not block the airway and the student does not choke on secretions.
8. Place *nothing* (e.g., fingers, objects) in the student's mouth. This could injure the student or result in vomiting.
9. Do not give the student medications or anything to drink during the seizure.
10. Mentally sequence the student's activity during the seizure so that behaviors related to the seizure can be recorded later on an appropriate form (see Figure 7–3).
    a. What time did the seizure begin?
    b. Where on the body did the seizure begin and did it move to another body part?
    c. What were the movements of the head, face, eyes, arms, and legs?
    d. Was the student's body limp or rigid?
    e. Were the student's eyes rolled back, to the right, or to the left? Did they appear glassy?
    f. Did the student stop breathing?
    g. Did the student bite or chew the tongue?
    h. Was the student's skin pale, blue, or reddened?
    i. What time did the seizure end?

What to Do After a Seizure

1. Monitor the student's breathing. If breathing is absent, the emergency medical system must be notified immediately and resuscitation efforts begun.
2. Roll the student onto the left side and clear secretions from the mouth with a suction machine, bulb syringe, or hand wrapped in a handkerchief.
3. Talk or interact with the student to determine level of awareness (i.e., alert, drowsy, confused, unable to respond) and record this information.
4. Determine whether the student is able to move his or her arms and legs or if there is any change in the student's ability to move.
5. Check for loss of control of urine and stool (this can be embarrassing for the student), and determine if the student sustained any injuries (e.g., bleeding from the mouth).
6. Make the student comfortable and quiet, allowing an opportunity to sleep, if necessary (a student may sleep for several hours after a seizure).
7. Record the length of the seizure (in seconds or minutes) and what happened before and during the seizure as described above.

A series of consecutive seizures with no recovery of consciousness lasting longer than 10 to 15 minutes is called *status epilepticus*; this condition is life-threatening and requires immediate medical care (Low, 1982; Dreifuss, Gallagher, Leppik, & Rothner, 1983; Batshaw & Perret, 1986).

Classroom Application. Timely and comprehensive seizure monitoring requires a systematic approach to collecting behavioral data. Adequate preparation for meeting the needs of students with epilepsy requires that the family be consulted regarding the type of seizure as well as typical behaviors seen before, during, and after a seizure.

Communication among school, family, and health care providers will increase the usefulness of seizure monitoring; for example, school staff aware of medication changes can provide feedback to the family and physician on changes in the frequency and intensity of seizures. This information is critical, particularly if the physician is in the process of evaluating the student's prescription and dosage. An increase in the number of seizures per day or per week may indicate that the student is not receiving medication as prescribed, or that the student is in need of a change in medication as a result of a change in the student's metabolism or altered utilization of the medication (Low, 1982). Careful, accurate reporting of seizure activity to parents and health care providers should result in improved seizure management.

Understanding the behaviors that occur before, during, and after a seizure will help the staff prepare the school areas accordingly. For example, a student may become somewhat drowsy approximately 2 hours after administration of a seizure medication, which is generally around 9:30 A.M. In this instance, the teacher needs to plan for activities requiring less interaction and response from the student at this time of day. A student who produces large amounts of secretions during a seizure will need a suction machine or bulb syringe available in the classroom to remove secretions from the mouth.

The potential for injury to the student during a seizure is a concern for all school staff. Students whose seizures are not well controlled can experience a head injury as a result of a seizure-related fall. Often, these students wear a lightweight helmet to protect the head. The student must *never* be restrained during a seizure because of the possibility of physical harm (to the child or the school staff) while the student is held or restrained.

Additionally, the school environment must be as safe as possible for students with seizures. Objects (e.g., furniture, equipment or toys) that could cause an injury should be portable and easy to remove during a student's seizure. Pathways and instructional environments should be wide and free of unnecessary objects (i.e., unused wheelchairs, storage boxes) to minimize the chance of injury during a fall.

Additional Resources. The Epilepsy Foundation of America sponsors a wide variety of programs and activities for persons with epilepsy, as well as workshops and training for staff and educational materials developed for school personnel working with students with epilepsy. Local affiliates can be located in local telephone directories. Information from the national organization is available from:

Epilepsy Foundation of America
4351 Garden City Drive
Suite 406
Landover, Maryland 20785
(301)459-3700 or toll-free 1-800-332-1000

(310)577-0100 for publications
postmaster@efa.org
http://www.efa.org

Medication Administration and Monitoring

The general purpose of administration of medication is to relieve symptoms, to treat an existing disease, or to promote health and prevent disease. Since most medications require administration across the day, many students would be unable to attend school unless medication administration was provided.

Preparation for Administering Medication. Before administering any medication, the policies of the school district related to approval or consent for medication administration must be reviewed. These should include: parent request or authorization to give medication, physician's written approval or request for administration of medication (the prescription on the medication container may be an example), and secure storage for the medication (Gadow & Kane, 1983; Sheets & Blum, 1998). The requirement of a physician's written approval may also apply for over-the-counter (OTC) medications. Any administration of a medication should be recorded, using a log similar to that presented in Figure 7–4.

Administering Medications. The method of administration depends on the developmental age of the student and the student's ability to chew and swallow. For students whose level of physical development is that of an infant or for those who have difficulty retaining food or fluid in the mouth, the student is usually supported in a sitting position. The smaller student may be held; the larger student may remain in a wheelchair or chair (Whaley & Wong, 1987). When holding or supporting a student, maintain a relaxed position to decrease the chances of choking. This may be achieved by insuring the student's neck is flexed, the shoulders are rounded, and the student is in a slightly forward position.

The medication is carefully measured and placed in the student's mouth from a spoon, plastic dropper, or plastic syringe (of course, a syringe without a needle). The dropper or syringe is placed along the side of the student's tongue. The medication is given slowly to ease swallowing and avoid choking. For the student with tongue thrust, it may be necessary to rescue medications from the student's lips or chin

FIGURE 7–4
Medication Information Form

Medication Information Form

Name _____ Age _____

Route _____

Administration Analysis:

Date	Medication	Dosage Indicated	Time Received	Full dosage Received at Time Prescribed		Initials
_____	/_____	_____	_____	Y	N	_____
_____	/_____	_____	_____	Y	N	_____
_____	/_____	_____	_____	Y	N	_____
_____	/_____	_____	_____	Y	N	_____
_____	/_____	_____	_____	Y	N	_____
_____	/_____	_____	_____	Y	N	_____
_____	/_____	_____	_____	Y	N	_____
_____	/_____	_____	_____	Y	N	_____
_____	/_____	_____	_____	Y	N	_____
_____	/_____	_____	_____	Y	N	_____
_____	/_____	_____	_____	Y	N	_____
_____	/_____	_____	_____	Y	N	_____

Maintenance/Episodic Meds and Side Effects	Possible Interactions of Medications
M/E 1. _____	1. _____ & _____ = _____
M/E 2. _____	2. _____ & _____ = _____
M/E 3. _____	3. _____ & _____ = _____
M/E 4. _____	4. _____ & _____ = _____
M/E 5. _____	5. _____ & _____ = _____
M/E 6. _____	6. _____ & _____ = _____

---

and readminister it. If the student uses a suck to take in liquid, the medication can also be slowly pushed into a nipple while the student is sucking (Whaley & Wong, 1987).

If the student is able to swallow a tablet, the medication may be placed on the middle of the tongue. The student can then swallow it with juice or water (Wagner, 1983). Because of the possibility of aspiration (pulling the tablet or secretions into the lungs), a whole tablet should not be given until the student is about 5 years old or demonstrates the necessary oral-motor control to safely swallow the tablet.

Use in the Classroom. Medication given during the school day must generally be made available at the school. The medication container must be labeled with the student's name, dosage, frequency of administration, and the prescribing physician's name. A system for recording and documenting when the medication was administered to a student must be established. Finally, the school district's policy should be reviewed to determine who can administer the medication in the school setting.

The "Five Rights" of Medication Administration. The person administering the medication makes certain that the *right dose* of the *right medication* is given to the *right patient* at the *right time* by the *right route* (Wagner, 1983). These guidelines are used every time a medication is given. A few minutes of double-checking a medication or writing down routine procedure can prevent a serious error that may result in unfortunate experiences for the school staff, the student, and the family.

Where To Go for Further Information or Training. School staff can find more information on administration of medication in the references listed at the end of this section (King, Wieck & Dyer, 1983; Scipien, Barnard, Chard, Howe & Phillips, 1986; Whaley & Wong, 1987; Wong, 1997). Nurses in the school, the physician's office, public health department, or local hospital can provide assistance on methods of administration, side effects and toxic effects of medications, and setting up a medication log for the student. The occupational and physical therapists can provide guidance on proper positioning for medication administration and suggestions on oral or motor problems hindering medication administration. A pharmacist and the student's physician can provide information about the student's medication (i.e., side effects, toxic effects, and interaction among medications).

Growth Monitoring, Nutrition Supplementation, and Feeding Management

Eating is one of the primary experiences in life. It is a universal event for children of all ages, from all cultures and from all socioeconomic classes. The well-nourished child grows at an expected rate, is resistant to illness, and has the energy to take advantage of social and educational opportunities. Adequate nutrition is critical to achieving potential for brain and physical development. An estimated 35% to 40% of children with a chronic disease or chronic disabling condition have a feeding disorder that results in inadequate nutrition and growth retardation. To initiate appropriate intervention, the school team must be aware of children at risk for nutrition problems and

the simple screening methods used to identify these children.

Growth Monitoring Procedures. Growth is a sensitive measure of health, nutritional status, and development. We can monitor the nutritional status of a student by measuring his or her growth. Trends revealed through repeated height and weight measurements can be used to detect growth abnormalities, monitor nutritional status, or evaluate the effects of nutritional or medical interventions. (See Figure 7–5.)

Measuring Weight. Growth measurements must be made accurately and recorded correctly at least three times a year. In order to obtain an accurate weight, a beam scale with nondetachable weights is recommended. This type of scale is commonly found in physician's offices and in the school health office.

The student is weighed in light clothing with shoes removed, wearing as little clothing as possible with consideration given to privacy needs. If the child is unable to bear weight in standing, an adult may hold the student and obtain a combined weight. The adult then subtracts his weight obtained on the same scale at that time from the combined weight.

Measuring Height. A measure of weight does not provide maximum information without corresponding measures of height. Both are needed for an accurate analysis of growth.

In measuring height, a metallic tape or yardstick attached to a flat wall should be used. Any measuring rods attached to a platform or scale, or plastic or cloth tapes are considered inaccurate and should not be used. Ideally, the student must be able to cooperate and stand upright. If not, measures of length may be taken with the student lying down.

Measuring Length. If a student is less than 2 years of age, or is unable to stand unassisted and straight, then he or she may be measured lying down on a measuring board. One person (possibly a parent) holds the student's head so the eyes are looking vertically upward with the crown of the head firmly against the fixed headboard. The second person holds the student's feet with knees and hips extended, and toes pointed directly upward. A movable foot board is brought firmly against the student's heels. Individualized methods of assessing length are necessary when a student is unable to lie with shoulders, hips, and heels aligned. This type of measuring device may be available in the primary health care provider's clinic or in a public health clinic, or the school nurse should be able to locate a measuring board.

Measuring Weight-for-Height. In addition to weight and height measurements, weight-for-height data provide information about a student's growth. The weight for height measurement compares a student to others of his same size, not age. It is of particular importance in monitoring many students with profound disabilities, because these students frequently do not grow at the same rate as other individuals of the same age. A graph for weight-to-height measurement is found on growth charts (see Figure 7–6).

Monitoring Procedures During Eating. Many children with profound disabilities experience difficulty in eating. This may be the result of chronic health problems, early negative oral experience (e.g., tube feedings, intubation, suctioning), neurological problems, fatigue during meals, or a combination of these factors. The special education teacher, trained as an observer of behavior, can play an important role in monitoring the child's feeding abilities, eating behaviors, food intake, and preferences.

Monitoring Intake. Because the process of mealtime or eating extends well beyond the school day, it is critical that the school and family exchange information about changes in eating behavior or volumes of food consumed. Specific behaviors to monitor include: (a) whether a meal lasts less than 10 minutes or longer than 40 minutes; (b) student's behaviors, such as excessive whining, crying, or signs of discomfort, including frequent gagging, coughing or choking; and (c) whether the meal consistently contains items from only two of the four food groups or contains less than suggested amounts for height.

Recording the foods eaten at each meal and the child's responses to the various textures, tastes, and consistencies can provide the family and school with important information about preferences and differential oral-motor responses to the various foods. Some students with profound disabilities are tube-fed or receive a combination of tube and oral meals. For these youngsters monitor over time the amount and types of food ingested both orally and through the tube.

The effect of body position, particularly the head and trunk, on the student's ability to eat are additional observations. These monitoring functions can provide information important to the identification of simple positional interventions or lead to appropriate referrals.

Increasing Caloric Intake. It is a myth that failure to thrive is a necessary part of having a disability. The reason for a child's weight being in less than the 5th percentile for height is often because the child does not get enough calories. Simply increasing the amount of food to facilitate weight gain is often unsatisfactory because of impaired oral-motor function or effects of fatigue. Frequent illness or infection may decrease a child's appetite, as do certain medications.

There are several techniques to increase the number of calories a student consumes when not enough food is consumed to maintain an appropriate rate of growth. The addition of fats (a particularly concentrated source of calories), evaporated milk, wheat germ, or eggs in the preparation of foods increases the caloric and nutrient intake without requiring the students to eat more food. A regular meal pattern with two or three high-calorie snacks per day is also recommended to promote weight gain.

Increasing Fluid Intake. Adequate fluid intake is essential for maintaining health. Children with oral or motor problems often have difficulty with consuming sufficient liquids. This may be caused by an inability to communicate thirst, problems with hand-to-mouth coordination, or problems with sucking, swallowing, or heavy drooling. Many students with oral-motor difficulties are able to consume thickened liquids more successfully than thin liquids. Products commonly used to thicken thin liquids include pureed fruit, baby cereal, yogurt, dehydrated fruits and vegetables, mashed potato flakes, gelatin (added to warm liquids), or commercially available products designed specifically for thickening foods. Fruits and vegetables such as canned fruit, watermelon, cucumbers, and squash are also excellent sources of water.

FIGURE 7–5
Growth Monitoring Form

Growth Monitoring Form

Name _____ Age _____

Special Considerations _____

I. AT RISK FOR GROWTH PROBLEMS
Refer if weight for height is <5% or >95% **OR** if there is no weight gain over 9 month period

FALL _____   WINTER _____   SPRING _____
          (date)   (date)   (date)

Height: Height: Height:

Weight: Weight: Weight:

Ht/Wt%:   Ht/Wt%:   Ht/Wt%

(Plot growth on chart)

II. AT RISK DUE TO MEALTIME CHARACTERISTICS
Refer if 2 or more of these characteristics apply.

_____ Meal lasts longer than 40 minutes.

_____ Student displays discomfort during or after meal, such as

          _____ excessive crying, whining, or signs of discomfort or

          _____ frequent gagging, coughing, choking.

_____ Meal consistently contains items from only two of the four food groups (meat, dairy, vegetables, fruits) or contains less than suggested amounts of food for height.

_____ Drinks less than 4-6 glasses of fluid per day.

III. CHECK MEDICATION INFORMATION FORM FOR MEDICATION THAT COMPROMISES NUTRIENTS AND/OR SUPPRESSES APPETITE

Classroom Adaptations and Applications. Growth is a sensitive measure of health and development. Recording and plotting a child's height and weight, using forms such as those in Figures 7–5 and 7–6, at the beginning, middle, and end of the school year will help monitor the student's growth. Trends revealed through repeated height and weight measurements can be used to detect growth abnormalities, monitor nutritional status, or evaluate the effects of nutritional or medical interventions. A variety of growth charts are available for assessing the growth of children. The growth charts adapted from the National Center for Health Statistics (NCHS) (Hammill, et al., 1979) can be used to assess the growth of most children and should be a permanent part of a child's record. Recognizing that children with disabilities may have different growth expectations than children without disabilities has prompted the recent development of separate growth charts for children with Down syndrome, Prader-Willi syndrome, Turner's syndrome and achondroplasia (dwarfism). Generally these data are recorded and plotted by the school nurse or dietitian, but any member of the team can be trained to measure and record a child's growth.

To determine whether a child is underweight, overweight, or short in stature, the data gathered for a particular student is compared with standard data. Those youngsters who fall at either end of the continuum present a problem. Possible reasons for an underweight condition include improper nutrition resulting from poor caloric intake, chronic disease, dehydration, iron deficiency, infectious disease, or measurement error.

FIGURE 7–6
A Graph for Weight to Height Measurement

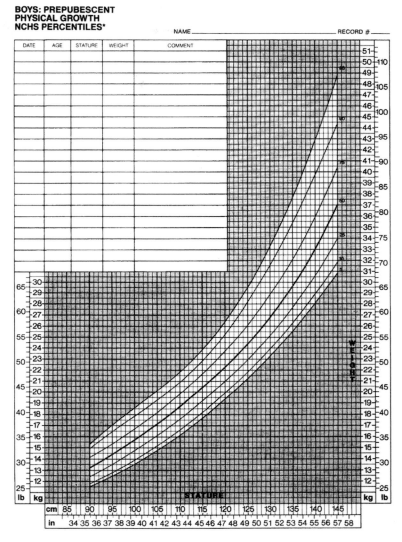

Possible reasons for an overweight condition include higher caloric intake than the child's energy expenditure (common in Prader-Willi syndrome and Down syndrome), edema, and measurement error.

A referral to a nutritionist should be made when:

1. Weight for age is at or below the 5th percentile or at or above the 95th percentile
2. Length for age is at or below the 5th percentile
3. Weight for length is at or below the 5th percentile or at or above the 95th percentile
4. No weight gain in 1 month (for infants from birth to 12 months of age)

5. No weight gain in 3 months (for children from 1 to 2 years of age).

Additional Resources. A registered dietitian can be contacted through a local medical center, hospital clinic, county or state extension service, or state or local chapter of the American Dietetic Association. The request should be for dietitians who work with children who have special health care needs or profound disabilities. In addition, the state's services for children with special health care needs and university-affiliated programs can offer consultation and technical assistance for the development of nutrition services in schools. These agencies may also provide an interdisciplinary feeding clinic or assist you in locating a clinic for evaluation and follow-up of children with complex, chronic feeding disorders.

An additional resource is the University of Iowa Virtual Children's Hospital at http://indy.radiology.uiowa.edu/VCH/>. Look further in the site to find Patient Information by Department: Pediatric Nutrition at http://indy.radiology.uiowa.edu/Patients/IHB/Peds/Diet/PedsDiet.html.

Routine Implementation Procedures

Teeth and Gum Care
The major components of teeth and gum care include oral hygiene, preventive dental care, and good nutrition and eating habits. Some of these components may be addressed instructionally during the school day, and some require cooperation between the school and home. The purpose of including teeth and gum care in the curriculum is to promote the overall health and well-being of the student.

Oral Hygiene and Preventive Dental Care. Regular visits to the dentist may begin as early as 12 months of age. Many factors, such as an improperly formed jaw or teeth, prolonged dependence on the bottle, lack of stimulation from chewing, inadequate cleaning of the teeth and gums, infrequent dental care, and the side effects of medications, can result in unhealthy and malformed teeth and gums. For the child with a disability, it is recommended that dental care begin early, during the first year of life, to establish a preventive program with the parents. Establishing a schedule of routine dental care provides parents with guidance on tooth brushing, dental development, fluoride, oral habits, proper diet, and other issues unique to the child. Routine oral hygiene should begin as early as possible. Starting at birth, clean the baby's gums with a clean damp cloth and progress to tooth brushing as teeth appear.

Infant Dental Care. The following procedure for oral hygiene has been recommended by the American Academy of Pediatric Dentistry (1997):

1. After a bottle, cleanse the baby's mouth with a soft toothbrush dipped in water. Use clean gauze dipped in water if the infant does not like a toothbrush.
2. Do not let the baby fall asleep with a bottle of formula or juice, rather give the baby a bottle of water at naptime.
3. Regular attention to oral hygiene at an early age will establish a routine associated with eating for the child; establish the feeling of having a clean mouth; and desensitize the oral-motor area for the child with increased sensitivity to touch in and around the mouth.

Toothbrushing. The American Academy of Pediatric Dentistry (1997) has suggested the following procedure for toothbrushing:

1. Place the head of a soft toothbrush beside the teeth, with the bristle tips at a 45° angle against the gumline.
2. Move the brush back and forth in short strokes (half a tooth wide) several times, using a gentle "scrubbing" motion.
3. Brush the outer surfaces of each tooth, upper and lower, keeping the bristles angled against the gumline.
4. Use the same method on the inside surfaces of all the teeth, still using short back-and-forth strokes.
5. Scrub the chewing surfaces of the teeth.
6. To clean the inside surfaces of the front teeth, tilt the brush vertically and make several gentle up-and-down strokes with the "toe" (the front part) of the brush.
7. Brushing the tongue will help freshen the breath and clean the mouth by removing bacteria.

Flossing. The American Academy of Pediatric Dentistry (1997) has recommended the following procedure for flossing the student's teeth:

1. Break off about 18 inches of floss, and wind most of it around one of your middle fingers.
2. Wind the remaining floss around the same finger of the opposite hand. This finger will "take up" the floss as it becomes soiled.
3. Hold the floss tightly between the thumbs and forefingers, with about an inch of floss between them. There should be no slack. Using a gentle sawing motion, guide the floss between the teeth. Never "snap" the floss into the gums.

4. When the floss reaches the gumline, curve it into a C-shape against one tooth. Gently slide it into the space between the gum and the tooth until resistance is felt.
5. Hold the floss tightly against the tooth. Gently scrape the side of the tooth, moving the floss away from the gum.
6. Repeat this method on the rest of the teeth. Do not forget the back of the last tooth.

Nutrition. In addition to careful brushing and flossing, a healthy, balanced diet is necessary for teeth to develop properly and for healthy gum tissue to form around the teeth. A healthy diet includes the following major food groups each day: fruit and vegetables, breads and cereals, milk and dairy products, meat, fish and eggs. A diet high in certain types of carbohydrates, such as sugar and starches, may place a child at risk for tooth decay.

"Baby bottle" tooth decay can occur when an infant or toddler is given a bottle filled with milk, formula, fruit juice, or sugared liquids at bedtime, naptime, or for long periods during the day. Excessive exposure to sugar in these liquids can cause teeth to discolor and decay. In a 1-year study of nontraumatic dental emergencies from a pediatric emergency department, 73% of visits were the result of dental caries and 18% resulted from baby bottle tooth decay (Wilson, Smith, Preisch, & Casamassimo, 1997). Children with oral motor problems are at increased risk for this problem because the bottle is often the primary source of nutrition long beyond 12 to 18 months of life. Rigorous attention to oral hygiene is required to maintain healthy teeth and gums.

Classroom Adaptations

Current data on child health suggest that few children receive early periodic screening, diagnosis, or preventive dental treatment. Anticipatory guidance provided through the school can facilitate an interchange on the provision of developmentally appropriate, preventive oral health information and care (Perlman, 1997). The development of a routine of oral hygiene, independent or assisted, that is ongoing and consistent between home and school will help (a) prevent peridontal (or gum) disease by maintaining healthy teeth and gums, (b) promote a healthy diet and good eating habits, and (c) promote correct speech habits and a positive body image (Mott, Fazekas, & James, 1985).

The time required to complete teeth and gum care must be included when planning for the student's individual program. Toothbrushing is performed after meals and snacks; flossing is performed at least once a day. The location (home or school) where flossing is conducted can be designated during the IEP process. Gloves should be used when completing any oral hygiene procedure. Initially the student with a disability may require complete assistance with toothbrushing and flossing. The goal of instruction is for the student to be able to brush his or her teeth independently or with minimal assistance from staff and meaningful participation in the process.

To promote adequate oral hygiene, the student must be positioned to facilitate tooth brushing and flossing. If unable to sit up, the student can be turned onto the side with the face along the edge of a pillow, and a towel and basin placed under the chin. If the student can sit, several positions are suggested. The student can sit on the floor while the adult sits behind him or her on a chair, with the student's head straddled by the adult's thighs. The adult can reach around with one hand supporting the student's chin and brush the teeth with the other hand. A second position may be with the student sitting in a wheelchair, the adult can stand or sit behind the student and reach around with one hand supporting the student's chin and opening the student's mouth. The teeth can then be brushed using the other hand.

Occasionally a child with a severe physical disability and poor oral motor skills has a bite reflex. This involuntary reflex or response often occurs when a spoon, toothbrush, or other object is placed in the child's mouth. If this is a problem when cleaning the teeth, a padded tongue blade or a new, clean rubber door stopper can be placed between the biting surfaces of the upper and lower jaw (Woelk, 1986). This will protect the child's teeth and the individual who is assisting the child with oral hygiene. Toothbrushing can then be carried out with this device holding the mouth slightly open. Brushing should be accomplished in the bathroom in front of a sink with both the student and teacher looking in the mirror.

Additional Resources

The American Dental Association provides information on care of teeth and gums. Information can be obtained from local dentists, the local health department, or:

American Academy of Pediatric Dentistry
211 East Chicago Avenue, Suite 700
Chicago, Illinois 60611-2616
http://aapd.org

Academy of Dentistry for Persons with Disabilities
211 East Chicago Avenue, Suite 700
Chicago, Illinois 60611-2616
(312) 440-2660

Skin Care

The most appropriate skin care treatment in the schools focuses on the prevention of skin breakdown and the development of pressure sores. Because many students spend the majority of their day in a wheelchair, braces, or splints and are dependent on others for position change, it is critical that skin care and skin monitoring be systematically addressed in the classroom.

Skin Monitoring

Maintaining healthy skin. Four objectives must be considered when promoting healthy skin: (a) keeping the skin clean and dry; (b) maintaining proper nutrition; (c) maintaining adequate activity; and (d) reducing periods of continuous pressure on parts of the body across the day.

Clean, dry skin is a necessary requirement for healthy skin. This is particularly important for skin that comes in contact with feces or urine. A primary skin care program should include efforts to reduce or eliminate incontinence; establish toilet training; establish catheterization; or establish frequent routines of checking and changing diapers and cleansing the skin to reduce prolonged exposure of the skin to feces or urine. Moisture, stool, and frequent and excessive washings cause a decrease in the skin's tolerance to friction, leaving it more vulnerable to chafing by diapers and clothing (Jeter & Lutz, 1996). This exposure can also result in the softening or maceration of the skin. Softened skin is at an increased risk for the development of sores. Moisture, from any source, accumulated in folds of the skin around the genitals, thighs, or any place where the skin can rub together will result in redness, irritation, and the

eventual development of sores (Jeter & Lutz, 1996; Walker, 1971). Maceration of the skin by urine and feces adds the excoriating (skin cutting) effects of the decomposing substances in the urine and the infective organisms present in the feces to already damaged tissue, increasing the likelihood that sores will develop.

Sacco (1995) recommends the maintenance of adequate nutrition and hydration as an important strategy in the prevention of pressure sores. Adequate nutrition and hydration allows the body to develop healthy skin and more resistance to bacteria and to pressure sores. Proper nutrition is also critical to support healing when a sore has developed.

Optimal levels of activity also must be encouraged as part of a proactive skin care program. Inactivity can result in increased opportunities for the student to experience pressure on the skin surfaces. Pressure occurs when the skin and subcutaneous tissue is squeezed between an underlying bony prominence and a hard surface, such as a bed or a chair. Unrelieved pressure on the skin squeezes tiny blood vessels, which supply the skin with nutrients and oxygen. Sliding down in a chair or bed (friction or shear force) can stretch or bend blood vessels. When skin is starved of nutrients and oxygen for too long, the tissue dies and a pressure ulcer forms. Certain parts of the body sustain more weight when sitting and lying and are considered pressure-sensitive areas (e.g., the heels, bony prominences along the spinal column, the buttocks). A change in position should occur *about every* 1 *to* 2 *hours* for those students with severe physical disabilities to relieve continuous pressure as well as to increase blood circulation (Sacco, 1995).

The student, whether active or inactive, may also experience pressure from braces, shoes, or sitting in a wheelchair. The same concerns about pressure resulting from inactivity applies to pressure resulting from ill-fitting equipment. The skin underneath braces and splints, or wheelchair seats, should be checked daily to identify persistent red spots. If the spots do not fade within 20 minutes after the pressure is relieved, the health care worker should be notified of (a) ill-fitting equipment and (b) the potential for the development of a pressure sore.

A final aspect of prevention is the need to identify methods the student uses to communicate the presence of discomfort. Often uncomfortable pressure causes a student to move to relieve the discomfort. If the student cannot move to relieve the discomfort, school staff need to be sensitive to changes in mood or posturing as indicators of pain.

Because Liz has reduced sensation and spends the majority of her time sitting in a wheelchair, her skin care program includes diet and fluid monitoring as well as twice daily skin checks. These checks are implemented by the school health professional in the late morning and in the afternoon before she goes home. Liz's therapists have also worked to strengthen her elbow extensors so she can raise herself out of the chair to relieve pressure on her bony prominences (buttocks). Liz does this routinely between classes, providing a minimum of six hourly position changes across the day. Finally, Liz carries a water bottle with her so she has access to fluid whenever needed.

Treating unhealthy skin. When providing care to unhealthy skin, the focus is on treating the skin to promote a return to a healthy condition. The actual care of the unhealthy skin is prescribed by the student's physician or other health care provider or endorsed by the health care worker in the school.

Classroom Adaptation

The student's skin should be examined daily, emphasizing portions of the body susceptible to the development of pressure sores. A rating scale for determining the potential for pressure sore formation has been developed by Gosnell (1973), see Figure 7–7 for an adaptation of the scale. A low score indicates greater susceptibility to developing pressure sores and a high score indicates reduced risk. This scale should be completed annually as part of the overall assessment and program development process.

The school health care worker or the primary care physician should write a general health plan for the student at risk for skin problems. The plan should address the need for routine position changes, cleansing, maintenance of nutrition, and use of lotions or oils on the skin.

Additional Resources

Parents are a valuable resource for school staff when there is question about the condition of the student's skin. The student's physician or health care provider working with the physician can provide assistance and direction on prevention or treatment of skin problems.

The enterostomal therapist from a local hospital can provide assistance in care of the student's skin and the physical and occupational therapist in the school system can help identify positions that will be suitable for the student during certain activities, yet prevent prolonged pressure on a few skin areas.

Also see *http://www.healthfinder.org*, a general health information locator provided by the U.S. government.

Bowel Care

The purpose of attending to bowel care is to be aware of factors that may effect performance and to promote the overall health of a student. Constipation occurs in 5% to 10% of all children (Leung, Chang, & Cho, 1996) but is often more prevalent in children with differences in muscle tone (e.g., children with cerebral palsy and spina bifida). Increased or decreased muscle tone affects coordination of the anal muscles or muscles of the pelvic floor, making it more difficult for the student to have regular bowel movements. These muscle tone differences are compounded by insufficient fiber and water consumption and immobility and may be a side effect of certain medications. Symptoms of constipation can include unexplained fussiness, apparent abdominal pain, decreased appetite, and a swollen abdomen (Hirsch, 1997).

Factors that contribute to optimal bowel functioning include: a diet high in fiber, adequate fluid intake, a regular daily schedule for elimination, an established plan for toilet training (if applicable), an environment conducive to elimination, proper positioning for elimination, and daily physical activity or exercise (Hirsch, 1997; Leung, Chang, & Cho, 1996).

Fiber and Fluid Intake

Diet, particularly fluid and fiber content, is often the first line of intervention to manage the toileting process (Sullivan-Bolyani, Swanson, & Shurtleff, 1984). Fiber is found in raw fruits and vegetables, whole grain breads, and cereals. When the student has difficulty chewing and swallowing, an increase in fiber content may be difficult to achieve. Shaddix (1986) has recommended that the student progress from blended, pureed, or baby foods as rapidly as possible. Commercial baby foods contain very little fiber. To retain some of their fiber content, table foods can be placed in a baby food grinder or food processor to obtain the best texture for the student with

FIGURE 7–7
Screening Tool to Identify Students at Risk for Pressure Sores

Risk of Developing Pressure Sores
Screening Form

Awareness Levels Score

4	Alert/active
3	Alert/inactive
2	Dazed/drowsy
1	Asleep

Communication Ability Score

3	Symbolic
2	Gestures
1	Nonsymbolic

Continence Score

4	Fully controlled
3	Usually controlled
2	Minimally controlled
1	Absence of control

Mobility Score

5	Fully ambulatory
4	Minimally ambulatory
3	Fully mobile with a device
2	Minimally mobile with a device
1	Immobile

Activity/Movement Score

3	Moves self frequently in and out of positions
2	Adjusts self within position
1	Little to no independent movement

Nutrition Score

3	good
2	Fair
1	poor

Name of student _____ Completed by _____

Date									
Score									
Awareness Level									
Communication Ability									
Continence									
Mobility									
Activity/Movement									
Nutrition									
Total									

Note: Adapted from Gosnell, D. [1972]. An assessment tool to identify pressure sores. *Nursing Research, 22,* 55–59.

oral-motor impairment. Shaddix (1986) also recommends serving bran cereal for breakfast or mixing unprocessed bran in food each day to supply additional fiber.

A dietitian is the best person to make changes in the fiber content of the student's diet. Studies have demonstrated that when families are instructed to increase fiber intake, on follow-up their children are consuming less than the recommended fiber intake (McClung & Boyne, 1995). Dietary management requires intensive and ongoing counseling to be effective. The student's physician or other health care professional may recommend a dietitian for this purpose. Most children need between 1 and 2 quarts of fluid a day. Shaddix (1986) recommends using unsweetened juice and water. Prune juice has a natural laxative effect and can be combined with another fruit juice to be more readily accepted by the student. Thickening liquids with items such as infant cereals, blended fruit, or unflavored gelatin may change the consistency of the fluid to be more easily accepted by the student with oral-motor problems. Frequent opportunities to drink small amounts of fluid are often scheduled throughout the day to better meet the fluid needs of the student with difficulty swallowing.

Use in the Classroom
Normal bowel functioning means that the student has a normal schedule of elimination. This developing or existing pattern may be incorporated into an ongoing, or new, toilet training program. Strategies for promoting a normal schedule of elimination include placing the student on the toilet for approximately 10 minutes after meals and snacks to take advantage of the gastrocolic reflex that usually occurs 15 to 30 minutes after meals.

A student's defecation can be facilitated by environmental considerations, positioning of the student, and an increase in the student's overall muscle tone. Stimuli or activities that aid in or detract from the process of defecation should be identified through discussion with the family and school personnel.

A squatting position best facilitates defecation. When a student cannot sit up alone or assume a position similar to squatting, adapted toilet chairs or special positioning may be of assistance. Physical activity and exercise are an active approach to the implementation of a bowel care program. Physical activity can help the fecal material move through the large intestine toward the rectum, facilitating normal bowel patterns. Exercise as a component of bowel care should be conducted daily, in a routine manner (see chapters 8 and 9).

Where to Go for Further Information or Training
Each individual has unique patterns of bowel functioning and the student with a disability brings additional complications to the issue of bowel control. These complications can include oral-motor impairment resulting in inadequate intake of fiber and fluids; medications that alter the consistency, color, and

frequency of bowel movements; decreased levels of activity resulting in improper emptying of the intestines; inadequate innervation of the rectal sphincters; and inability to recognize the urge to defecate.

These problems, if not addressed, affect the student's participation in the curriculum. The physical therapist or occupational therapist can provide a plan for positioning the student during meals and elimination. The dietitian is an important source of information on incorporating fiber in the meals and should work with the occupational therapist on developing an eating plan that addresses both dietary needs and the oral-motor skills of the student.

The student's physician can be helpful in solving problems with diarrhea, constipation, and skin irritation. When diet and adequate fluids are not enough, the physician may recommend supplemental fiber, laxatives, medications, or occasional suppositories and enemas. The communication between school and home regarding the student's status with the bowel management program is critical for success. Atypical bowel elimination procedures (ileostomy and colostomy) are discussed later in this chapter.

Low-Incidence Health Care Procedures

Procedures occurring with low frequency, in less than 25% of students with disabilities, are identified in this chapter as "low-incidence health care procedures." These procedures may be characterized by additional equipment and specialized training and include various nonoral methods for providing nutrients, atypical methods of elimination of feces and urine, respiratory management procedures, and very specific procedures, such as glucose monitoring and shunt care.

Nonoral Feeding Procedures

Gastrostomy and *nasogastric tube feedings* are two methods of providing nourishment other than by mouth. Either of these may be necessary because students cannot eat enough food orally to get needed nutrients and fluid. A *gastrostomy tube* (*G-tube*) is a tube extending through the abdomen into the stomach. The purpose of this tube is to allow liquid nutrients to move into the stomach when a student is unable to take feedings by mouth or is unable to take adequate amounts of food by mouth. Gastrostomy tubes are used for long periods of time or even on a permanent basis. Some students may have a gastrostomy tube and not require feedings through the tube during school hours. Their tubes may be used to supplement oral intake or used when the student is ill or oral intake is not adequate. A *jejunostomy tube* (J-tube) extends through the abdomen into the jejunum, or the second part of the small intestine.

A *nasogastric tube* (NG-tube) extends through the nose, down the throat and esophagus or food pipe, and into the stomach. Some students have nasogastric tubes placed for each feeding, while others have tubes in for several weeks at a time. A *nasogastric tube* is typically a short-term solution to assist a student unable to meet his or her nutritional needs by mouth. Since this may be related to an illness or hospitalization, school staff are less likely to have contact with students having nasogastric tubes and therefore may avoid the issue of accidental placement of a nasogastric tube into the respiratory tract or lungs (Orr, 1997).

What Is Involved
Liquid nutrients can be given as formula or regular food carefully blended to be administered through the tube. Feedings are continuous (liquid nutrients slowly drip through the feeding tube over the entire day or night) or intermittent (larger amounts of liquid nutrients are given during five to eight feedings in a day). The amount of liquid nutrients given through the tube varies for each student and must be determined by the student's health care professional. In addition to formula or blended food, the student's health care professional will recommend a specific amount of water to be given each day.

Students may be fed by *gravity-drip*, *pump*, or *syringe*. A student fed by gravity-drip has a feeding bag hanging on a hanger (or pole) at a height ranging from 8 to 24 inches above the level of the stomach. A clamp is used to regulate the flow of the feeding. Students may receive feedings by gravity-drip continuously or intermittently. However, most students receive feedings by a pump that automatically regulates the flow of liquid nutrients into the gastrostomy tube. The pump may be electric or battery-operated. The student may receive feedings by syringe, a third method. A large syringe is attached to the end of the feeding tube, and liquid nutrients are poured into the syringe. When the

remaining liquid nutrients have flowed into the bottom of the syringe tip, the appropriate amount of water is poured into the syringe and flows into the feeding tube. Liquid is never forced through the feeding tubing.

Instead of a gastrostomy tube that extends out of the student's stomach through the abdomen and is secured beneath the clothing, the student may have a *button gastrostomy*. This is a short tube that fits against the skin on the abdomen and has a small plug that can be removed for feeding. The button gastrostomy tube fits snugly against the student's skin and is not as noticeable to others or to the student. Tubing from the feeding bag can be placed into the button opening, allowing liquid nutrients to flow into the stomach or jejunum (i.e., the first 10 inches of small intestine). When the feeding is completed, the tubing is disconnected, and the opening is closed by the small plug attached to the gastrostomy tube.

Use in the Classroom
Tube feedings should occur during the mealtime or snack time of peers. Students should be fed in as typical a manner as possible to promote the development of mealtime skills. Students are generally in a sitting or upright position for feeding. If neither of these is possible, lying on the right side in an elevated position is acceptable for the feeding. Students should not be fed while lying flat and should remain in a sitting, upright, or elevated position for 1 hour after the feeding.

Students may be offered meals by mouth before, during, or after the tube feeding, depending on the plan established for each student. If oral meals are not allowed, oral stimulation activities should be carried out. These include, at a minimum, oral hygiene procedures described earlier in this chapter; mouth care is essential when a student receives only nonoral feedings. Some students may receive tube feedings as a temporary means of improving their nutritional status and promoting growth until they can receive food by mouth. Because this transition from tube to oral feedings may be challenging to some students, various strategies may be used to promote the transition (Bernbaum, Pereira, Watkins, & Peckham, 1983; Blackman & Nelson, 1985; Glass & Lucas, 1990; Luiselli, 1994; Satter, 1990; Schauster & Dwyer, 1996; Wolff & Lierman, 1994), such as introducing the oral portion of the meal before the tube feeding so that hunger works as a stimulus for eating and using preferred foods for the oral meal, since all necessary nutrients can be fed through the tube.

Feedings are given over the recommended period of time and usually followed by water to flush the tubing. Syringe feedings or intermittent feedings are given over a minimum of 20 minutes (Orr, 1997). Occasionally, medications are given through the tubing before, after, or at some point during the feeding. Make certain that the efficacy of the medication is not changed by the formula. Liquid medications are recommended whenever possible to avoid plugging the tube (Orr, 1997).

Equipment used during tube feedings should be washed thoroughly with warm, soapy water and rinsed well in a sink that is used for food preparation and cleanup. Equipment is allowed to air dry and then stored in a clean, covered container.

Problems that can occur with the feeding include blockage of the tube, the tube slipping out, skin problems, abdominal distention, diarrhea, and constipation. The flow of the liquid nutrients may stop during feeding because of a kink in tubing, viscosity of the liquid, plugging of the tube with medications, or movements of the student. Gentle flushing of the tubing with water can remove plugs and allow feedings to continue (Graff et al., 1990; Orr, 1997). The gastrostomy tube can be squeezed or rolled with the fingers moving slowly down toward the child's stomach (Cusson, 1994). If the tube comes out, a clean gauze pad (or clean cloth) should be placed over the opening. Parents and the school nurse may be trained to replace a gastrostomy tube, so a replacement may be kept at school. The tube must be replaced within 2 hours or before the next feeding (Cusson, 1994). The student's physician must carry out replacement of a J-tube immediately. The tube site is checked daily at school. Redness, swelling, pain or soreness, or drainage around the tube must be reported to the school nurse and parents.

Swelling or distention of the abdomen after feedings, resulting from excessive swallowing of air or gas build-up, may require venting of the tube. This venting may be done in a private area, because of the odor, away from other students (Haynie, Porter & Palfrey, 1989). Diarrhea can occur as a result of using unclean feeding equipment (i.e., equipment contaminated with bacteria), antibiotic therapy, or intolerance to formula. Constipation may occur from lack of fiber

in the liquid nutrients being given to the student. Both of these issues should be discussed with the student's parents and health care professional (Orr, 1997).

If a change in skin color, difficulty with breathing, choking, vomiting, or aspiration of the liquid occurs, the feeding should be stopped immediately and the school nurse contacted. Some students may require suctioning by the nurse or a trained person to remove secretions from the mouth and throat. If suctioning is not successful and the student stops breathing, resuscitation must be initiated.

The student should be able to participate in school activities, including physical education, as determined by the physician on an individual basis.

Where to Go for Further Information or Training

Nurses in the local hospital, pediatrician's office, public health office, or home health agency can provide information on tube feeding. Dietitians in the local hospital or health department can provide information about many formulas used with tube feedings. Medical supply companies may provide information and training in use of the equipment (gastrostomy tube, feeding equipment, and feeding pump).

Summarized information titled "Tube Feeding at Home: Gastrostomy or Jejunostomy" can be accessed through *http://housecall.orbisnews.com*. "Gastrostomy Feedings" can be accessed through *http://wellness.ucdavis.edu*.
Videotapes include:

"Home Gastrostomy Care for Infants and Young Children"
Learner Managed Designs, Inc.
P.O. Box 747
Lawrence, Kansas 66044
Telephone (785) 842-9088
Fax (785) 842-6881

"Making That Important Decision: Parents Perspectives on a G-Tube"
"Life After Your Child's G-Tube Placement"
University of Nebraska Medical Center
Meyer Rehabilitation Institution
Media Resource Center
600 South 42nd Street
Omaha, Nebraska 68198-5450
Telephone (402) 559-7467
Fax (402) 559-5737

Atypical Elimination Procedures: Bowel or Intestinal Ostomy Care

Atypical elimination procedures address methods of eliminating feces and urine that require some type of assistive device or special procedure. While the goal is independent performance of these procedures, students with severe and multiple disabilities generally require assistance with appropriate partial participation goals.

What Is Involved

An *ostomy* is a surgically created opening in the body for the discharge of body wastes (Ostomy Association of Boston, 1995); there are two main types, a *colostomy* and *ileostomy*. When the opening is created from the bowel or intestine and leads to the abdominal surface, a student is able to eliminate feces from the bowel without using the rectum. *Colostomy* refers to an opening created when a portion of the colon or large intestine is removed and the remaining colon is brought to the surface of the abdomen. An *ileostomy* refers to an opening of some portion of the ileum (lower part of the small intestine) onto the abdomen. Feces are eliminated through this opening and collected in a small pouch or bag. The pouch is tightly adhered to the skin around this opening on the abdomen, called a stoma. Since there is no control over when feces move into the pouch, feces collect in the pouch during the school day. This is especially true when a student has an ileostomy. The fecal material passing through the stoma is liquid or a pasty consistency and contains digestive enzymes that can be irritating to the skin. Ostomy care involves procedures to collect feces in an odor-free manner and to keep the skin and stoma healthy and free of irritation.

Ostomy care should be conducted in an area that is private and allows a student to be in the best position for emptying or replacing the pouch. This may be a sitting or reclining position. Extra supplies for changing the pouch should remain at school at all times, along with an extra change of clothes (Haynie, Porter, & Palfrey, 1989). Supplies include a clean pouch, a skin sealant or skin preparation wipe, a skin barrier, a washcloth, and warm water. Skin sealants are used to protect the skin and are used under adhesive materials. Skin barriers are used to protect the skin from fecal material eliminated through the stoma (Hagelgans & Janusz, 1994). Pouches may or may not have adhesive that allows them to adhere to the skin barrier. Pouches can be drainable, with an opening that allows for frequent emptying, or they can have a closed end, to be discarded after one use (Broadwell, 1984).

When the pouch is removed, apply soapy water or solvent to the edge of stoma or opening. The skin is cleaned with warm water or mild soapy water and then thoroughly rinsed and dried. If a skin sealant is used, it is applied to the skin around the stoma and allowed to dry. The skin barrier is applied with the adhesive side toward the skin. The pouch is placed around the stoma and held in place for 1 minute or so (Adams & Selekof, 1986).

A drainable pouch should be emptied when it is one third full to prevent the weight of the feces from loosening it (Dudas, 1982). If possible, the student should be positioned over the toilet seat and the pouch opened and drained into the toilet. After the inside of the pouch is rinsed and dried, the pouch is closed and secured with an ostomy clamp or a rubber band.

Occasionally, a pouch will need to be emptied of accumulated gas. Excessive gas can be caused by certain foods or by swallowing air. A drainable pouch can be opened, and a closed-end pouch can be punctured with a pin, releasing the gas using compression. Tape is placed over the pinholes to avoid leakage (Adams & Selekof, 1986). Either method may result in odor that permeates the pouch and student's clothing. Most pouches contain odor barriers. Charcoal filters or pouch deodorizers may be available from ostomy suppliers to control odor (Bradley & Pupiales, 1997).

Contents of the old pouch are emptied into the toilet, and the old pouch is sealed in a plastic bag and disposed of in a container used for body fluid waste. The stoma and skin around the stoma should be examined during each change of the bag for signs of irritation or redness. The skin should have its natural color, with no flaking or sweating. The stoma should appear pink and moist like the inside of the mouth. Any discoloration should be reported to the school nurse. Since feces are a primary source of infection (see section on infection control), proper hand washing should be carried out after this procedure and at any time there is contact with feces. Gloves are worn during this procedure. Students may not need to wear gloves if they carry out ostomy care without assistance (Haynie, et al., 1989), although hand washing before and after is always required.

Use in the Classroom

A colostomy or ileostomy pouch is usually changed at home. A student, however, may require a change at school for a variety of reasons. A bag may become loose or leak as a result of activity or unintentional pulling on the pouch. A student may also develop diarrhea or excessive gas. Changing of the pouch is recommended between meals, not before meals, because the signs and smells of the ostomy may reduce the student's appetite (Ayello, 1997).

Ostomy care may be done by the student, school nurse, or other school staff person who is properly trained. Some students may require distraction during ostomy care to keep their hands from exploring the pouch and stoma. However, some students may participate in ostomy care by holding supplies and helping clean the stoma area, or they may carry out the procedures themselves (Wong, 1997).

School staff who have regular contact with the student should receive general education about the colostomy or ileostomy and potential problems. Understanding how to manage problems can allow students to continue classroom activities with little interruption. The goal is to promote as much independence and participation as possible.

Where to Go for Further Information or Training

Information and literature on colostomy or ileostomy care can be obtained from:

> The United Ostomy Association
> 36 Executive Park, Suite 120
> Irvine, California 92714
> Toll-free 1-800-826-0826

> The International Association for Enterostomal Therapy (IAET)
> 5000 Birch Street, Suite 400
> Newport Beach, CA 92660

> The American Cancer Society at http://www.cancer.org/

> The United Ostomy Association Inc. at http://www.uoa.org

Atypical Elimination Procedures: Clean Intermittent Catheterization

Students having defects of the spinal cord, such as spina bifida or myelomeningocele, may also have neurologic impairment of the bladder (*neurogenic bladder*) resulting in little or no control over bladder emptying. Typically, the bladder stretches as it fills with urine until full, when nerve signals cause the bladder to contract and empty. Usually, a person can delay bladder emptying and control the occurrences of urination. A neurogenic bladder may overstretch or contract frequently or irregularly, resulting in constant dribbling or incomplete evacuation. *Clean intermittent catheterization* (CIC) is a procedure to empty the bladder and is most frequently used in students with neurogenic bladder (Vigneux & Hunsberger, 1994).

Clean intermittent catheterization involves the insertion of a catheter through the urethra (passageway between the bladder and the opening to the outside of the body) into the bladder. This usually is done every 2 to 4 hours during the day (McLone & Ito, 1998), taking into consideration other activities in the student's day, such as meals and snacks. The area chosen to carry out the procedure should provide privacy and have a sink to allow proper cleansing before and after the procedure.

During the catheterization, a student may sit on the toilet, stand, or lie down. The urine, if not emptied directly into the toilet, should be collected in a container. After thorough hand washing, the area around the opening to the urethra is cleansed with a towelette, or soap and water. Nonlatex gloves are worn, unless the student completes this procedure independently (Haynie, Porter, & Palfrey, 1989). The penis is cleansed using a circular motion, moving outward from the tip. A female student's labia are separated and cleansed, using one down motion. The motion is repeated two or three times, each with a clean towelette. If the student is prone to urinary infections, a wipe containing an antiseptic, such as betadine, may be used for cleansing (Clean intermittent catheterization, 1998).

First, the catheter is lubricated with a water-soluble gel. The catheter is inserted 2 to 3 inches into the urethra of the female student or until urine flows. For a male student, the catheter is inserted an additional 1 to 3 inches, so that it goes into the bladder. Once urine begins to flow, the catheter is held in place (Chapman, Hill, & Shurtleleff, 1979). The catheter is never forced. If unusual resistance is felt, the student's parent must be notified (Haynie et al., 1989). The open end is held over a container or over the toilet to catch the urine. The catheter is gently removed after the urine flow has stopped. If urine begins to flow as the catheter is removed, removal is stopped until the urine flow ceases. Then removal of the catheter is continued. The skin is washed again to remove any urine and prevent odors. The catheter is washed with soapy water, rinsed, air dried, and returned to its carrying case. A self-contained intermittent catheter system allows the catheter to be inserted while remaining sterile. It includes a urine collection bag that eliminates the need for separate containers and extra supplies (The MMG/O'Neil closed intermittent catheterization system, 1998).

Use in the Classroom

A student with a neurogenic bladder has little or no control over the process of emptying the bladder and needs assistance in controlling the release of urine during the school day. The teacher involved in this process should encourage the student to participate in his or her own urinary catheterization as much as possible. To be independent in catheterization, the student should have adequate fine-motor control to manipulate the catheter and clothing, be motivated to learn catheterization, and have the support of the family. Students should be encouraged to participate as much as possible by washing their hands, holding equipment, or participating in whatever activities are appropriate (Taylor, 1990).

> Liz actively participates in her clean intermittent catheterization. She sequences the activities, handing the equipment to the health care professional in order, and signals when done. Liz's assistant talks with her during the ongoing activity to increase her level of participation and understanding of the process.

When students are unable to control the bladder, they may not achieve complete dryness, so protective clothing may be used. Students may also experience leakage when laughing, coughing, or sneezing. An extra set of clothing may be kept at school in case of an accident.

Where to Go for Further Information or Training

Nurse specialists in clinics, urological specialists, and hospitals serving children with myelmeningocele can provide information and assistance in this area. Videotapes on catheterizations, such as "Clean Intermittent Catheterization" can be useful in training others to perform this procedure (available from Learner Managed Designs, Inc., P.O. Box 747, Lawrence,

Kansas 66044; telephone (785) 842-9088; fax (785) 842-6881). A handbook on intermittent catheterization from the Children's Health Care System in Seattle, Washington, is available at http://www.chmc.org/departmt/surgery/cic.htm.

Respiratory Management: Tracheostomy Care

Respiratory management involves procedures to maintain an adequate oxygen level in the bloodstream, it is the process of helping students maintain respiration or breathing. Typically, respiratory management procedures in school involve tracheostomy care, suctioning, oxygen supplementation, and assisted ventilation.

What Is Involved

A *tracheostomy* is a surgically created opening into the trachea. It is created when there is an obstruction in the respiratory tract to prevent movement of oxygen through the trachea, to allow for long-term assisted ventilation and to allow a way to remove aspirated oral secretions by suctioning (Hunsberger & Feenan, 1994). A hollow plastic or Silastic tube, called a *tracheostomy* tube, is placed in this opening and secured by cotton ties or other ties around the neck. The student can then breathe through the trachea rather than through the mouth or nose.

Care of the tracheostomy so that air can move freely includes removal of secretions from the student's trachea, cleaning the tracheostomy tube, care of the skin around the tube, changing the tracheostomy ties, and changing the tracheostomy tube. To remove secretions from the trachea, a suction catheter and tubing are attached to a suction machine. While wearing gloves, a trained individual removes secretions from the trachea. A suction catheter is inserted no more than 0.5 centimeter beyond the tip of the tube to avoid trauma and irritation to the trachea (Wong, 1997). If the student coughs secretions to the outer edge of the tracheostomy tube, the secretions may be removed with a bulb syringe or wiped away from the opening with a clean tissue. Care should be taken to assure that secretions do not come in contact with the skin of the caregiver or the student.

On rare occasions, a tracheostomy tube may come out and require replacement by a properly trained person. The staff person remains with the student and calls for assistance (Haynie, Porter, & Palfrey, 1989). An extra, sterile tracheostomy tube should always be kept in the classroom. If a new, sterile tube is not available, the old tube can be reinserted. Keeping the tracheostomy ties secure helps to ensure that the tube remains in place. Tracheostomy ties are usually changed at home, but if they become soiled, they require changing at school. If soiled ties remain on the student's skin, they can cause irritation.

Changing a tracheostomy tube and cleaning the old tube should be done at home. The skin around the tube is cleaned at least once daily and more often as needed. The student may wear a bib or dressing around the tube to collect secretions coming out of the tube. When the bib is soiled, it is changed during the school day. School staff members should carefully examine the skin around the tube for any signs of redness or irritation. Caregivers should wear gloves or wash their hands carefully before and after tracheostomy care at a sink that is not used for food preparation.

Use in the Classroom

Although the overall number of tracheostomies being performed for children is decreasing, the length of time tracheostomies remain in place is increasing (Carter & Benjamin, 1983; Line, Hawkins, Kahlstrom, MacLaughlin, & Ensley, 1986; Wetmore, Handler, & Potsic, 1982). Parents are routinely trained to care for a child with a tracheostomy at home. When school staff members know that a student will have a tracheostomy tube placed, one or more staff individuals should also be trained with the parents before the student's discharge from the hospital. Even though a teacher may not be designated as the person routinely responsible for changing the tube, all classroom personnel should be able to respond in the event of an emergency. This preparation can help alleviate concern on the part of parents and the school staff and minimize potentially negative responses from the student. Supplies should always be available at school. In addition to learning tracheostomy care, school staff members should be trained in cardiopulmonary resuscitation of a student with a tracheostomy.

Students may use a Passy-Muir speaking valve that allows the student to speak as a result of a positive-pressure closure valve that opens only when the student breathes in to allow air to enter the tracheostomy tube. After the student has breathed in, the positive closure mechanism shuts, forcing air out through the vocal cords, nose, and mouth, thus creating speech (Passy, 1986). The Passy-Muir speaking valve is being used with infants and children to promote speech and language development (Engleman & Turnage-Carrier, 1997).

Other students in the classroom may be curious about the tracheostomy. They should be informed about the purpose of the tracheostomy tube and its importance to the child. They may need reminders not to touch, pull on, or put objects into the tube. When the student is exposed to cold or windy weather, the tracheostomy tube should be covered. The student may wear light clothing to cover the tube or a small pouch known as an "artificial nose" over the opening of the tracheostomy tube. As the student breathes in and out through the "artificial nose," the air is warmed and humidified. This nose can prevent tracheal spasm caused by cold air or irritation of the trachea by dust particles (Hunsberger & Feenan, 1994). Although the student may play outdoors, play near water, such as a swimming pool or stream, is restricted to avoid accidentally getting water in the opening of the tracheostomy tube. Care should also be taken to avoid any talc product, such as baby powder, and fumes, such as paint, varnish, or hair spray (Wong, 1997).

Where to Go for Further Information or Training

Qualified persons, such as nurses and respiratory therapists who have taught the student's parents, can teach tracheostomy care. Cardiopulmonary resuscitation for a person with a tracheostomy requires specialized devices and training.

Resources include:

"Home Tracheostomy Care for Infants and Young Children"
Available from Learner Managed Designs, Inc.
P.O. Box 747
Lawrence, Kansas 66044
Telephone: (785) 842-9088; Fax: (785) 842-6881
Internet address: *http://www.lmdusa.com*

"Suctioning a Tracheostomy" from Children's Hospital Medical Center (Cincinnati), Patient Education Program.
Online address is at
http://www.chmcc.org/pep/pep2076.htm

"Suctioning" from Children's Health, University of California, Davis.

Online address is at *http://wellness.ucdavis.edu/ child_health/...ds/pediatric_tracheostomy/suctioning.html*

Respiratory Management: Suctioning

Suctioning is the removal of secretions from the respiratory tract to allow for breathing. Suctioning may be done through the nose (nasopharyngeal), mouth (oropharyngeal), or trachea. Suctioning in the school setting is most likely to be done through the mouth. A suction catheter (attached to a suction machine by connecting tubing), a bulb syringe, or a DeLee suction catheter may be used to remove secretions from the mouth. These machines produce a suctioning sound when in operation. Because of the unusual characteristic of this sound, it is important to introduce both the machine and its operation to the student's peer group.

What Is Involved

Suctioning is carried out when a student is unable to remove secretions effectively and requires assistance in moving the secretions from a certain area of the body. Signs that a student may need suctioning include audible secretions, symptoms of obstruction, and signs of oxygen deficiency. Large amounts of secretion in the mouth may be visible or partially visible and can be removed by suctioning (Dickey, 1987). Positioning the student on one side allows secretions to move out of the mouth to be suctioned more easily.

Secretions removed with a bulb syringe should be expelled onto a disposal tissue before a second attempt is made to remove additional secretions. Care must be taken to avoid skin contact with the secretions removed from the student's mouth or nose. Thorough hand washing before and after suctioning is essential.

Where to Go for Further Information or Training

Home health nurses, nurses in local hospitals, and respiratory therapists can provide information about and assistance with suctioning. Also look for assistance in your area through the American Lung Association at http://www.lungusa.org.

Respiratory Management: Oxygen Supplementation

Oxygen supplementation is necessary if the current level of oxygen in the body is inadequate because of respiratory or cardiac conditions. Oxygen is given through a nasal catheter (a small catheter is placed into one nostril), nasal prongs (two small plastic prongs fit into the student's nostrils), a face mask (a plastic mask fits over the student's mouth and nose), or a trachea mask (a plastic mask fits loosely over the student's tracheostomy tube). Nasal prongs are the most frequently used method of administering oxygen to children in the home and the community. Because these prongs are sometimes irritating, adaptations may have to be made to the tubing. For example, the prongs may be cut off, leaving holes that can be positioned toward the nostrils so that oxygen can then enter the nostrils through these openings.

What Is Involved

Oxygen should not be given over a prolonged period of time without humidification, since it can dry up secretions and mucous membranes. The flow rate of oxygen is not changed unless ordered by the student's primary care provider. Occasionally, a student needs to have more oxygen during mealtime or certain activities. The student's primary care provider must prescribe this change in flow rate. Indications that the student has an inadequate supply of oxygen include difficult breathing, irritability, increase in respirations, fatigue, pale color, cyanosis (i.e., bluish lips and nail-beds), or increase in the heart rate.

Use in the Classroom

Most likely, a student will receive oxygen from a portable oxygen tank that is attached to a wheeled device or wheelchair and is carried by or with the student. Because oxygen is highly combustible, caution should be taken to avoid using highly flammable substances while oxygen is administered. Open flames from cigarettes or candles, Bunsen burners in chemistry class, electrical equipment that can produce sparks, and items that can produce static electricity must be avoided. Areas where oxygen is being used should be marked with large, easily read warning signs. Administration of oxygen may be a necessary part of a student's health care plan. Oxygen supplementation may be required at all times, or may be given at certain times, such as during meals, snacks, naps, or other activities.

Where to Go for Further Information or Training

Respiratory therapists and pediatric nurses in a local hospital and home health care staff members may provide information about administration of oxygen to children. Medical equipment supply companies can provide useful information about the oxygen tank, humidifier, and the tubing used to administer oxygen. The student's physician is a resource for school staff members when questions arise about the student's responses to oxygen supplementation.

Also look for information with the Children's Hospital Medical Center (Cincinnati) Patient Education Program: Education and Assistance for Parents and Patients. See particularly "Care of Your Child While Receiving Oxygen by Nasal Cannula" at http://www.chmcc.org/pep/pep2048.htm.

Respiratory Management: Mechanical Ventilation

Mechanical ventilation is required when the student is unable to breathe in or breathe out adequately; oxygen supplementation is accomplished using the student's current breathing pattern. Students may be dependent on a ventilator as a result of conditions such as neurological damage, muscle weakness, or severe pulmonary disease (Haynie, Porter, & Palfrey, 1989). Respiratory management in the schools involves monitoring the necessary equipment to allow breathing and to intervene in emergency situations.

What Is Involved

Although there are many different types of ventilators, the most common is a *positive pressure ventilator*. This ventilator breathes for the student by forcing air into the lungs, usually through a tracheostomy tube. A *negative pressure ventilator* creates a negative pressure that pulls the student's chest wall out and air moves into the lungs as a result of this negative pressure. An example of a negative pressure ventilator is the iron lung. These ventilators are used less often than the positive pressure ventilators and do not require a tracheostomy tube.

Use in the Classroom

Students require assisted ventilation for a variety of reasons: fatigue from the increased work of breathing; periods when breathing does not occur spontaneously; or when conditions restrict or prevent adequate ventilation. Students who require ventilatory assistance, as well as their parents, are often anxious when others become responsible for managing this aspect of their daily routine. Anxiety can increase the student's respirations and possibly lead to hyperventilation. Short training periods with the student in the classroom can allow school staff members to acquire understanding of the ventilator and allow the student and parents to begin feeling comfortable.

Carefully planned training sessions with the school staff members who will carry out procedures with the student are crucial. Staff members must feel confident and secure in the procedures they are using, have a clear understanding of all aspects of the procedures, and have plans to follow if problems arise. According to Haynie et al. (1989), a nurse or respiratory therapist who has received specialized training to manage mechanical ventilation should perform care. A trained caregiver should be available to the student in the classroom and in transit to and from school. In addition to knowing how to care for the student and ventilator, these trained persons must know how to provide CPR for the student with a tracheostomy. Back-up electrical power should be available for mechanical ventilator at all times. A resuscitation bag, spare tracheostomy tube, and suction supplies should always be with the student.

Where to Go for Further Information or Training

Respiratory therapists, home health care staff members, nursing specialists working with the student in the hospital setting, and the student's physician can provide information to develop and implement an overall plan for a student's respiratory management.

Also see *http://www.healthfinder.org*, a general health information locator provided by the U.S. government. Also available is "Allergies and Asthmatics Network" at http://www.aanma.org/, a nonprofit membership organization founded in 1985 to help families in their quest to overcome and maintain control of asthma, allergies, and related conditions. Several children's hospitals also provide web-based information: University of Minnesota Department of Pediatrics (*http://www.peds.umn.edu/*) and Gillette Children's Hospital (*http://www.gillettechildrens.org/newwelcomepage.html*).

Glucose Monitoring

Glucose monitoring is a procedure used to identify the amount of glucose (sugar) present in the blood. This is often carried out for students who have diabetes, a disorder in which carbohydrates are unable to be used because of inadequate production or use of insulin. Excessive amounts of glucose are then found in the student's blood and urine.

Type I diabetes or insulin-dependent diabetes, may occur at any age but is more common in youth. Type II, or non–insulin-dependent diabetes, is more common in adults but may occur at any age (American Diabetic Association, 1997a). The four aspects of therapy for type I diabetes are: (a) blood glucose monitoring, (b) insulin injections, (c) dietary modifications, and (d) exercise (Maffeo, 1997). Persons with type I diabetes usually require testing of blood glucose levels three to four times a day; this will likely affect the classroom routine. The optimal number of times a person with type II diabetes should test their blood glucose levels is not known, but it should be done often enough to assist reaching optimal glucose levels (American Diabetes Association, 1997c). Another test used to measure blood glucose levels is glycosylated hemoglobin. The result of this test reveals the overall glucose control over several months and can serve as a "report card" (Bayne, 1997) on dietary and insulin management.

What Is Involved

Glucose monitoring is taught to students and their parents as a method of achieving optimal control of glucose levels and can be carried out relatively easily during the school day. The student's fingertip is pricked with a lancet or spring-activated lancet. When a drop of blood forms, the blood is allowed to drop from the student's finger onto a special reagent strip. The strip is placed into a special meter. A reading of the student's glucose level appears on the meter's screen. If this device is not used, the color of the reagent strip can be compared with the color blocks on the reagent container; this method results in a probable range of glucose levels (Graff et al., 1990). It is important to follow the directions that come with the child's device.

Use in the Classroom

A team approach to therapy or management includes informing teachers, school staff, the peer group, bus drivers, and others who interact with the student about diabetes. The student may wear a Medic Alert bracelet or necklace to provide identification that could be life-saving (Wong, 1997). The teacher and peer group can play a role in helping the student manage his or her disease by providing sugar-free treats or other appropriate foods during holiday and birthday celebrations. Careful monitoring provides accurate, current information on the student's glucose level and allows treatment of levels that are too high or too low. Foods can be given to provide extra glucose, foods can be limited, or insulin can be given. Glucose levels that are too high or too low can affect a student's ability to perform in the classroom. In a position statement on medical care for persons with diabetes, the American Diabetes Association (1997b) noted that it is desirable to test blood glucose levels at school before lunch and when signs or symptoms of abnormal levels are present.

When glucose levels are too high, insulin may need to be given (Graff et al., 1990). Since students with disabilities may not communicate symptoms of low or high glucose levels, parents can be extremely helpful in identifying behaviors that indicate glucose levels are not within the desired range.

Where to Go for Further Information or Training

Information about diabetes can be obtained through diabetes educators, nurse specialists working with children who have diabetes, and dietitians in local hospitals. The American Diabetes Association may have local affiliates that can be contacted for more information.

American Diabetes Association
1660 Duke Street
Alexandria, VA 22314
1-800-ADA-DISC
http://www.diabetes.org

Juvenile Diabetes Foundation
120 Wall Street
New York, NY 10005
1-800-JDF-CURE
http://www.jdfcure.com

Medic Alert
2323 Colorado Avenue
Turlock, CA 95382
(209) 668-3333

Internet resources linking to diabetes-related resources include: *http://casteweb.com/diabetes/d_07_000.htm* and *http://casteweb.com/diabetes/index.html*

Shunt Care

Hydrocephalus is a condition in which the accumulation of excess amounts of fluid in the cerebral ventricles result in enlargement of the ventricles. This enlargement may eventually result in enlargement of the head and subsequent brain damage. A student with hydrocephalus may have a shunt that drains excess fluid from the ventricles of the brain into another part of the body. This fluid is called cerebrospinal fluid and is formed primarily in the ventricles. Shunt care almost exclusively involves procedures to identify when the shunt has malfunctioned.

What Is Involved

Surgical placement of a shunt allows fluid to leave the cerebral ventricles and to move to one of several possible locations for elimination by the body: (a) the peritoneal cavity (ventriculoperitoneal, or V-P shunt); (b) the right upper chamber (atrium) of the heart (ventriculoatrial, or V-A shunt); or (c) the chest cavity (ventriculopleural, or V-P shunt). Valves in the shunt system assure that the fluid flows in one direction, from the brain to the other part of the body. If a shunt becomes obstructed or malfunctions, fluid begins to build up, creating increased pressure in the brain. Signs of shunt malfunction in students include headache, vomiting or change in appetite, lethargy or irritability, swelling along the shunt tract, seizures, deterioration in school performance, neck pain, or personality change (McLone & Ito, 1998). Double vision or blurred vision may also occur.

Use in the Classroom

To assure proper functioning of the shunt, there must be careful observations and reporting of complications to parents or the student's physician. School staff must be aware of the student's usual behavior, level of activities, and responses (Graff et al., 1990). This knowledge will help the school team note changes in level of activity, behavior, and response to and awareness of the environment which may indicate that the shunt is not working. Lethargy, nausea, and vomiting are common signs of shunt malfunc-

tion, but idiosyncratic behaviors are best identified through discussion with the student's parents. There are generally no restrictions on a student's activities, with the exception of exclusion from contact sports when there is a high risk of head injury (Jackson, 1980). Carpeted floors in the classroom can help protect a student who falls in school.

Where to Go for Further Information or Training

Health care professionals working with the student, such as the student's physician (pediatrician or family physician, neurologist, neurosurgeon) and a nurse specialist working with children who have neurologic disorders, can provide additional information. The student's parents can be exceptional resources by providing information about usual behaviors and about behaviors that can be expected when the shunt is not functioning properly.

The Hydrocephalus Association and the Spina Bifida Association of America (SBAA) provide families and professionals with resources on hydrocephalus and its management. The Hydrocephalus Association offers support, education, and advocacy to families and individuals (Tatter, Owen, & Kenyon, 1998).

The Hydrocephalus Association
870 Market Street, Suite 995
San Francisco, CA 94102
415/732-7040

The Spina Bifida Association of America publishes brochures, reports, newsletters, and videotape programs for families and professionals (Spina Bifida Association of America, 1998).
The Spina Bifida Association of America
4590 MacArthur Boulevard, NW, Suite 250,
Washington, DC 20007-4226
202/944-3285

Also see "Children with Spina Bifida: A Resource Page for Parents," produced by the Waisman Center, at http://www.waisman.wisc.edu/~rowley/sb-kids/.

Issues in Providing Special Health Care

Occurrence in Integrated Settings

In the past, the rationale for placement of students requiring complex special health care procedures in restricted settings was that these resources (personnel and equipment) were more efficiently, economically, and reliably provided if all students requiring special health care procedures at school were in close proximity. Separation from peers, however, is in opposition to current efforts toward local school placement, integrated settings, and community-based instruction (Meyer, Peck, & Brown, 1991). It is our position that if a person has been discharged to the home and nonnursing personnel can accomplish the necessary special health care procedures in the home, it is possible to provide these same procedures in the school setting (Porter, et al., 1997). There does not appear to be a medical reason for segregation.

> When Liz was born and the degree of her disabilities became clearer, her parents were very much afraid that Liz would not have the same opportunities and experiences growing up that her sisters had. They liked their neighborhood, their school, and their community. They felt Liz should be a part of all of this, just as her sisters were. Since her birth, Liz had been receiving services through the school district, with home visits from infant and early childhood teachers. When Liz turned 6 she started in a segregated school, but soon the district moved her to an inclusive placement in Liz's neighborhood school. Though not an easy task, the process of including Liz with her peers was and is being accomplished. Her parents, again, were faced with the familiar fears and concerns when Liz had a colostomy. The school personnel, though initially hesitant, were willing to "give it a try." Liz's mom and dad worked closely with the district's health care coordinator to develop a plan for her health management at school. They additionally devised a strategy to both discuss how Liz's presence would affect school personnel and a training program so that everyone would be prepared. Aside from a few days missed because of colds and one case of diarrhea, Liz's attendance has been very good.

Children in Pain

Pain is a sensation in which an individual experiences discomfort, distress, or suffering resulting from irritation or stimulation of sensory nerves (Thomas, 1985). The interpretation of pain usually leads that individual to communicate, either verbally or nonverbally, the onset, intensity and occurrence of pain. Therefore, subjective information and an interpretation of another's communication (see chapter 11 for a discussion of nonsymbolic communica-

tion) is often the basis for treatment or management of pain.

Pain in children has been challenging to assess, particularly when children are preverbal or nonverbal (Foster et al., 1989). The presence of language and cognitive disabilities makes it difficult to rely on reports of pain, and teachers must be very aware of each student's strategy for communicating discomfort or pain. The student's behaviors, expressions, fears, and sources of comfort provide objective information about the student's experience of pain. The different ways a child or youth may express pain is very individual. If possible a student may gesture towards or favor specific areas of the body if the pain is localized. For example, if experiencing a fracture a student may guard an arm or try not to bear weight on a leg. The student may hold his head or stomach, a common response for all persons with stomachaches or headaches, or wince when swallowing or breathing. Often, however, the pain is not localized, or the child is not able to localize the pain or protect an area of the body. In these instances, the only indication that a person is in pain is that the individual is behaving differently than usual. Is the child, for example, more quiet, more irritable, or more lethargic than usual?

It may be the case that some students overreact to episodes of pain. Others, however, may not be aware of pain as an indicator that an injury has occurred. Students with spina bifida have decreased sensation in the lower extremities and may not feel pain, even with a severe injury, such as a burn or fracture (Holvoet & Helmstetter, 1989). Instruments have been developed to assess behavior changes associated with pain, but no useful instruments exist for assessing pain in students with disabilities, who often express themselves nonverbally (Foster et al., 1989). School staff members must rely on their own observations and knowledge about the student along with the information provided by the student's family to make an objective interpretation about a student's experiences with pain.

Children Who Are Dying

When a student's health begins to deteriorate because of an underlying condition or disease, plans for the student's educational program may need to be adjusted to the physical changes that are occurring. The course of the decline as communicated by the parents and physician may allow school staff members to adjust the school program. It is important to plan strategies to assist the student and his or her peers for the deterioration of the child's abilities; and to prepare the peers to handle their feelings before and after the child dies. If a progressive disorder is suspected but a diagnosis has not been made, close monitoring at school can provide information that can help the student's physician diagnose a condition (Holvoet & Helmstetter, 1989).

When a student's condition is expected to worsen or when death is expected within months or years, four options are available. These include (a) focusing on skill training that will maintain the present functioning level as long as possible; (b) teaching skills that are needed in order to compensate for lost ability; (c) aiding the student, family, school, and other students in dealing with increasing deterioration; and (d) lessening the likelihood of secondary complications, such as pain or additional impairment. These options are based on the assumptions that it is important for the student's life to be normal and that part of a child's normal life includes school (Holvoet & Helmstetter, 1989). Some or all of these options may be selected, depending on the student's condition.

School staff members can gain understanding of the degenerative disease and feel comfortable with the student by meeting with the parents and medical staff to learn about the student's condition and what the student can and cannot do and to clarify how to recognize and respond to emergencies (Holvoet & Helmstetter, 1989). When a student dies, school staff members are dealing not only with their own feelings but also with the feelings of other students, parents, and other staff members. It is important to discuss a student's death openly and allow others to express their feelings (Kleinberg, 1982).

Withholding Treatment

The following section discussing the special case of withholding CPR was written by a physician with a long history of educating health care providers in the process of ethical decision making, particularly at the end of life. These are issues that we are facing with increasing frequency; thoughtful discussion will assist us in understanding and evaluating the values involved, our respective roles and responsibilities, and the process through which decisions are made or changed. The intent of this section is not to tell you "what to think" but rather "how to think" about these difficult issues.

Withholding CPR

William G. Bartholome, M.D., M.T.S.

Withholding of a specific health care intervention—cardiopulmonary resuscitation, or CPR—is an example of the challenges facing teachers and schools when a student may have a life-limiting or even terminal illness. Another section of this chapter suggests that teachers and other appropriate school personnel must be trained to provide CPR. The underlying assumption is that any student who would suddenly stop breathing or whose heart would suddenly stop beating would be provided this emergency medical intervention in an effort to rescue them, to resuscitate them.

For some children, parents and health care providers may decide that CPR is either (a) "futile" in the sense that it is unlikely to be effective or (b) inappropriate given the nature of the child's medical condition and prospects for living (Landwirth, 1993). Studies of patient outcomes after CPR have demonstrated that it is often the case that CPR is a brutal and fruitless procedure (Blackhall,1987). It is now known that, in certain populations of seriously ill children, CPR is so rarely successful in saving lives that decisions to withhold it are not only reasonable but ethically required in order to protect the child from the burdens of this highly invasive and often futile procedure (Nelson & Nelson, 1992). In most cases, the decision to withhold CPR will be made initially during the course of the child's hospitalization. Since cardiopulmonary resuscitation is a "routine" procedure in most hospital settings, the decision to withhold CPR is implemented through the mechanism of a "Do Not Resuscitate," or DNR, order. When a patient with a DNR order experiences a "respiratory or cardiac arrest" (the patient stops breathing or the patient's heart stops beating), attempts to restore breathing or heart function (CPR) are not undertaken and the patient is allowed to die.

While it is clearly the case that health care professionals and the facilities in which they work have become increasingly comfortable with decisions to limit certain kinds of life-sustaining treatments (Bartholome, 1991), this is often not the case when these same patients leave the hospital to go back out into the community or back to school. In the past few years, health care professionals, institutions, organizations, and families have worked diligently with emergency medical services (EMS) and agencies to develop methods of implementing the decision to limit treatment, especially decisions to withhold CPR from patients after discharge from hospital (Sachs, Miles & Levin, 1991). Some communities have developed computer registries of DNR patients; some use special out-of-hospital DNR forms, or even special DNR medical alert bracelets. While these procedures may well result in protecting people from inappropriate CPR in their homes, it is unclear how these developments would serve these same individuals outside of the home, in the school.

When children with DNR orders are discharged to home or to another facility, such as a long-term care facility, steps are taken to insure that the order is honored after the child has been discharged. The result is that teachers and school districts are now being asked to develop procedures for including children with DNR orders in the classroom. If teachers and school personnel are to be provided training that would allow them to provide CPR in a school setting, is it also the case that they should be provided training in how to respond to children with DNR orders? If school officials are willing to develop procedures to respond to the special needs of children who may experience a respiratory or cardiac arrest while at school, should they also be willing to develop policies and procedures for honoring DNR orders while these special students are at school? If hospitals and other health care facilities are willing to develop policies and procedures for protecting their patients from inappropriate resuscitative efforts, should not schools, which have adopted policies of always attempting CPR, be willing to do the same to protect students from inappropriate CPR?

Should Schools Honor DNR Orders? Some have argued that it is one thing for health care professionals or even family members to accept the responsibility of honoring DNR orders, but another to expect this kind of responsibility to be undertaken by teachers or school personnel. Younger argues that since school personnel ". . . have neither first-hand knowledge of the patient's clinical status nor the training necessary to make clinical judgments. . .", they should *not be expected to honor* DNR *orders* in the classroom (Younger, 1992). Younger also points out that school personnel, unlike families, have not been provided with training in dealing with and responding to a child who is experiencing a sudden cardiac or respiratory arrest. It may well be the case that a child from whom CPR is withheld may experience seizures or gasping respirations or another kind of "terminal crisis" before death. Is it reasonable to expect that a teacher in a classroom with other students would be capable of providing effective "comfort" to the dying student? Younger proposes that individual schools work out agreements with local emergency medical service agencies to both respond to the 911 call for help, but to provide only comfort to the child. This proposal implies that school districts would "honor DNR orders" by transferring this responsibility on a case-by-case basis to local EMS agencies. Although I feel that there is considerable merit in Younger's proposal, it may not be the case that such arrangements can be made in advance for all children.

Many children who are appropriate candidates for DNR orders have conditions for which a wide range of other life-sustaining treatments (e.g., antibiotics, treatment for status epilepticus) are appropriate and utilized. A DNR order is nothing more than a decision to withhold a specific, burdensome, and often unsuccessful intervention, namely CPR (Council on Ethical and Judicial Affairs, 1990). It has also been argued that a parent's request that a school district honor a student's DNR order might be a very reasonable request, but that it conflicts with the school's obligation to protect other students from the harm that might come from having to witness the child's death in the classroom. No one who has ever witnessed a full-blown CPR attempt, particularly a prolonged and unsuccessful one, would ever make this claim. It could clearly be argued that witnessing the brutality to the child involved in an attempt at CPR is likely to be much more difficult for the child's fellow students than witnessing the loving and caring response of school personnel to a classmate while she or he experiences something that the class had been previously told might happen and had been prepared to deal with if it did.

Summary

To establish quality health care in the educational setting, teachers must (a) incorporate special health care procedures into the educational day and (b) actively prevent the development of related health problems and conditions. This chapter offers guidelines for establishing programs responsive to all of the needs of students. These guidelines address assessing needs, scheduling, gathering student information, monitoring routine procedures, and including special health care procedures as part of the instructional day.

Procedures that should be a part of training for all classroom personnel include infection control, first aid, and CPR. Teachers also should have readily available information concerning the special health care needs of students. This information should minimally include (a) seizure information, with the type, frequency, and response; (b) medication information, with the type, purpose, schedule of administration (even at times other than school hours), and possible side effects or interactions; (c) emergency numbers for family members, the medical facility of choice, and the primary care provider; and (d) specific protocols, or descriptions, of the implementation of special health care procedures for individual students, the person primarily responsible for implementing the procedures, designated backups, and the dates of training of school staff members for the implementation of the procedures.

Teachers should consider the nutrition and hydration needs of their students. Weight-for-height measures, taken regularly over time, provide information on the overall growth and nutritional status of students. Following meals and snacks, some students may need teeth and gum care. Routine monitoring also may include the color of the skin under a brace or at the hips and tailbone. The risk status for pressure sores provides information for considering routine positioning, repositioning a minimum of every 20 minutes, and frequent rotations into the upright position. The frequency of bowel movements and the frequency and qualities of urination are other considerations.

Suggested Activities

1. Complete training for CPR with an emphasis on children and a basic Red Cross first aid course.
2. Monitor the weight for height of a student for whom you feel normal growth is at risk. Plot growth over several months and determine if the student's weight for height places the student below the 5th percentile. Determine whether growth is occurring at an acceptable rate. Discuss your findings with the school nurse or nutritionist.
3. Spend approximately 2 hours participating in a specialty medical clinic focusing on pediatrics, such as a cerebral palsy clinic, a feeding clinic, or a home health nurse clinic. Learn to implement a special health care procedure for a student with whom you are familiar. Develop at least two or three instructional skills that are appropriate for the student to practice during the implementation of the special health care procedure. If possible, implement a plan for the student to practice the skills during the procedure.
4. Find a web site that addresses issues of right to treatment and disability. Make sure the web site is produced either by a medical center, pediatric hospital, state or federal agency, or university.

References

Adams, D. A., & Selekof, L. (1986). Children with ostomies: Comprehensive care planning. *Pediatric Nursing*, 12, 429–433.

American Academy of Pediatrics. (1993). Basic life support training in school. *Pediatrics*, 91(1), 158–159.

American Academy of Pediatric Dentistry. (1997). *Cleaning your teeth and gums*. Chicago: Bureau of Health Education and Audio Visual Services.

American Association of Family Physicians. AAFP recommendation: new Haemophilus influenza type B immunization schedule (1991). *American Family Physician*, 43, 1437–1440.

American Diabetes Association. (1997a). Guide to diagnosis and classification of diabetes mellitus and other categories of glucose intolerance. *Diabetes Care*, 20(1), S21.

American Diabetes Association. (1997b). Standards of medical care for patients with diabetes mellitus. *Diabetes Care*, 20(1), S5–S13.

American Diabetes Association. (1997c). Tests of glycemia in diabetes. *Diabetes Care*, 20(1), S18–S20.

American Heart Association. (1987). *Heartsaver manual: A student handbook for cardiopulmonary resuscitation and first aid for choking.* Dallas, TX: Author.

Andersen, R. D., Bale, B. F., Blackman, J. A., & Murph, J. R. (1986). *Infections in children: A sourcebook for educators and child care providers.* Rockville, MD: Aspen Systems.

Ault, M. M., Guess, D., Struth, L., & Thompson, B. (1989). The implementation of health related procedures in classrooms for students with severe multiple impairments. *Journal of the Association of Persons with Severe Disabilities*, 13, 100–109.

Ayello, E. A. (1997). Bowel Elimination. In P. A. Potter & A. G. Perry (Eds.), *Fundamentals of nursing: Concepts, process, and practice* (4th ed.) (pp. 1348–1352). St. Louis: Mosby.

Bartholome, W. G. (1991) Withholding/withdrawing life-sustaining treatment. In B. Woodrow & M. D. Burgess. (Eds.) *Contemporary Issues in Pediatric Ethics*, pp. 17–40. Waterloo, Ontario: Edwin Mellen Press.

Batshaw, M. L., & Perret, Y. M. (1986). *Children with disabilities* (2nd ed.). Baltimore: Paul H. Brookes.

Bayne, C. G. (1997). How sweet it is: Glucose monitoring equipment and interpretation. *Nursing Management*, 28(9), 52, 54.

Bernbaum, J. C., Pereira, G. R., Watkins, J. B., & Peckham, G. J. (1983). Nonnutritive sucking during gavage feedings enhances growth and maturation in premature infants. *Pediatrics*, 71, 41–45.

Blackhall, L. J. (1987) Must we always use CPR? *New England Journal of Medicine*, 317, 1281–1285.

Blackman, J. A., & Nelson, C. L. A. (1985). Reinstituting oral feedings in children fed by gastrostomy tube. *Clinical Pediatrics*, 24, 434–438.

Bradley, M., & Pupiales, M. (1997). Essential elements of ostomy care. *American Journal of Nursing*, 97(7), 38–45.

Broadwell, D. C. (1984). Study guide for ostomy products. *Journal of Enterostomal Therapy*, 11(2), 74–76.

Buzz-Kelly, L., & Gordin, P. (1993). Teaching CPR to parents of children with tracheostomies. *MCN*, 18(3), 158–163.

Campbell, L. S., & Thomas, D. D. (1991). Pediatric trauma: When kids get hurt. *RN*, 54(8), 32–38.

Carter, P., & Benjamin, B. (1983). Ten-year review of pediatric tracheostomy. *Annals of Otology, Rhinology, & Laryngology*, 92(4), 398–400.

Centers for Disease Control and Prevention. (1998) Update: Universal precautions for prevention of transmission of human immunodeficiency virus, hepatitis B virus, and other bloodborne pathogens in health-care settings. *MMWR*, 37, 377–382, 387–88.

Chapman, W., Hill, M., & Shurtleff, D. B. (1979). *Management of the neurogenic bowel and bladder.* Oak Brook, IL: Eterna Press.

Chow, M. P., Durand, B. A., Feldman, M. N., & Mills, M. A. (1984). *Handbook of pediatric primary care.* New York: Wiley.

Clean intermittent catheterization. (1998, May 31). Seattle, WA: Children's Hospital and Regional Medical Center (online). Available: http://www.chmc.org/departm/surgery/cic.htm

Council on Ethical and Judicial Affairs, American Medical Association. (1990) Guidelines for the appropriate use of do-not-resuscitate orders. *Journal of the American Medical Association*, 265, 1868–1871.

CPR-ECC National Convention (1992a). Pediatric basic life support. *Journal of the American Medical Association*, 268, 2172–2197.

Cusson, R. M. (1994). Altered digestive function. In C. L. Betz, M. M. Hunsberger, & S. Wright (Eds.), *Family-centered nursing care of children* (2nd ed.) (pp. 1413–1505). Philadelphia: W.B. Saunders.

Dickey, S. B. (1987). *A guide to the nursing of children.* Baltimore: Williams & Wilkins.

Dreifuss, F. E., Gallagher, B. B., Leppik, I. E., & Rothner, D. (1983). Keeping epilepsy under control. *Patient Care*, 17, 107–149.

Dudas, S. (1982). Postoperative considerations. In D. C. Broadwell & B. S. Jackson (Eds.), *Principles of ostomy care* (pp. 340–368). St. Louis: Mosby.

Education and foster care of children infected with human T-lymphotropic virus type lymphadenopathy-associated virus. (1985). *MMWR*, 34, 517–520.

Engleman, S. G., & Turnage-Carrier, C. (1997). Tolerance of the Passy-Muir speaking valve in infants and children less than 2 years of age. *Pediatric Nursing*, 23(6), 571–573.

Foster, R. L. R., Hunsberger, M. M., & Anderson, R. D. (1989). *Family-centered nursing care of children.* Philadelphia: W. B. Saunders.

Gadow, K. D., & Kane, K. M. (1983). Administration of medication by school personnel. *The Journal of School Health*, 53, 178–183.

Gastrostomy feedings. (1998, March 2). *Children's Health* (online). Available: http://wellness.ucdavis.edu/child_health/special needs/gastrostomy_feedings/

Glass, R. P., & Lucas, B. (1990). Making the transition from tube feeding to oral feeding. *Nutritional Focus*, 5(6), 1–8.

Gosnell, D. (1973). An assessment tool to identify pressure sores. *Nursing Research*, 22, 55–59.

Graff, J. C., Ault, M. M., Guess, D., Taylor, M., & Thompson, B. (1990). *Health care for students with disabilities: An illustrated medical guide for the classroom.* Baltimore: Paul H. Brookes.

Hagelgans, N. A., & Janusz, H. B. (1994). Pediatric skin care issues for the home care nurse (part 2). *Pediatric Nursing*, 20(1), 69–76.

Hammil, P. V. V., Drizad, T. A., Johnson, C. L., Reed, R. B., Roche, A. F., & Moore, W. M. (1979). Physical growth: National Center for Health Statistics percentiles. *American Journal of Clinical Nutrition* 32, 607–629.

Harris, C. S., Baker, S. P., Smith, G. A., & Harris, R. M. (1984). Childhood asphyxiation by food. *Journal of the American Medical Association*, 251 (17), 2231–2235.

Haynie, M., Porter, S. M., & Palfrey, J. S. (1989). *Children assisted by medical technology in educational settings: Guidelines for care.* Boston: Project School Care, The Children's Hospital.

Hirsch, D. (1997). Constipation. *Exceptional Parent*, 27 (8), 60–63.

Holvoet, J. F., & Helmstetter, E. (1989). *Medical problems of students with special needs: A guide for educators.* Boston: College-Hill.

Hunsberger, M., & Feenan, L. (1994). Altered respiratory function. In C. L. Betz, M. M. Hunsberger, & S. Wright (Eds.). *Family-centered nursing care of children* (2nd ed.), (pp. 1167–1275). Philadelphia: W.B. Saunders.

Jackson, P. L. (1980). Ventriculo-peritoneal shunts. *American Journal of Nursing*, 80, 1104–1109.

Jeter, K. F. & Lutz, J. B. (1996) Skin care in elderly, dependent, incontinent patients. *Advances in Wound Care: Journal for Prevention and Healing*, 9(1), 29–35.

King, E. M., Wieck, L., and Dyer, M. (1983). *Pediatric nursing procedures.* Philadelphia: Lippincott.

Kleinberg, F. (1982). *Educating the chronically ill child*. Rockville, MD: Aspen.

Kurtz, Z., Tookey, P., & Ross, E. (1998). Epilepsy in young people: 23-year follow-up of the British national child development study. *British Medical Journal*, 316, 339–343.

Landwirth, J. (1993). Ethical issues in pediatric and neonatal resuscitation. *Annals of Emergency Medicine*, 22(2 pt 2), 502–507.

Leung, A., Chang, D., Cho, H. (1996). Constipation in children. *American Family Physician*, 54(2), 611–620.

Line, W. S., Hawkins, D. B., Kahlstrom, E. J., MacLaughlin, E. F., & Ensley, J. L. (1986). Tracheostomy in infants and young children: The changing perspective 1970–1985. *Laryngoscope*, 96(5), 510–515.

Low, N. L. (1982). Seizure disorders in children. In J. A. Downey & N. L. Low (Eds.). *The child with disabling illness: Principles of rehabilitation* (pp. 121–144). New York: Raven Press.

Luiselli, J. K. (1994). Oral feeding treatment of children with chronic food refusal and multiple developmental disabilities. *American Journal on Mental Retardation*, 98, 646–655.

Maffeo, R. (1997). Helping families cope. *American Journal of Nursing*, 97(6), 36–39.

McClung, H. J., & Boyne, L. (1995). Constipation and dietary fiber intake in children. *Pediatrics*, 96 997–1000.

McLone, D. G., & Ito, J. (1998). *An introduction to spina bifida*. Chicago, IL: Children's Memorial Hospital Spina Bifida Team.

Meyer, L. H., Peck, C. A., & Brown, L. (1991). *Critical issues in the lives of people with severe disabilities*. Baltimore: Paul H. Brookes.

Mott, S. R., Fazekas, N. F., & James, S. R. (1985). *Nursing care of children and families*. Menlo Park, CA: Addison-Wesley.

Murray, J. A., & Haynes, M. P. (1996). The benevolent overreaction: Nursing assessment and interaction in families coping with seizure disorders. *Journal of Neuroscience Nursing*, 28(4), 252–259.

Nelson, L. J., and Nelson, R. M. (1992). Ethics and the provision of futile, harmful, or burdensome treatment to children. *Critical Care Medicine*, 20, 427–33.

Neville, B. G. R. (1997). Epilepsy in children. *British Medical Journal*, 315, 924–931.

Orr, M. E. (1997). Nutrition. In P. A. Potter & A. G. Perry (Eds.), *Fundamentals of nursing: Concepts, process, and practice* (pp.1089–1127). St. Louis: Mosby.

Ostomy Association of Boston. (1995). Definition of key terms. In *Ostomy resource guide for the Greater Boston Area* (online). Available: http://www.uoa.org/chapc1.html

ParasolEMT. (1998). *http://www.parasolemt.com.au*.

Passy, V. (1986). Passy-Muir tracheostomy speaking valve. *Otolaryngology and Head and Neck Surgery*, 95, 247–248.

Perlman, S. P. (1997). Putting teeth into oral health care: Good care of oral hygiene begins at home. *Exceptional Parent*, 27(8), 32–35.

Porter, S., Haynie, M., Bierle, T., Caldwell, T. H., & Palfrey, J. S. (1997). *Children and youth assisted by medical technology in educational settings: Guidelines for care*. Baltimore: Paul H. Brookes.

American Red Cross. (1998). http://www.redcross.com.

Sacco, M. (1995). Four-step multidisciplinary approach to wound management pays off. *The Brown University Long-Term Quality Letter*, 7(5), 1–2.

Sachs, G. A., Miles, S. H., and Levin, R. A. (1991). Limiting resuscitation: Emerging policy in the emergency medical system. *Annals of Internal Medicine*, 114, 151–154.

Satter, E. (1990). The feeding relationship: Problems and interventions. *Journal of Pediatrics*, 117(suppl), S181–S189.

Schauster, H., & Dwyer, J. (1996). Transition from tube feedings to feedings by mouth in children: Preventing eating dysfunction. *Journal of the American Dietetic Association*, 96(3), 277–281.

Schwab, N. (1991). Guidelines for school nursing documentation: Standards, issues, and models. Scarborough, Maine: National Association of School Nurses.

Scipien, G. M., Barnard, M. U., Chard, M. A., Howe, J., and Phillips, P. J. (Eds.). (1986). *Comprehensive pediatric nursing*. New York: McGraw-Hill.

Sheets, A. H., & Blum, M. S. (1998). Medication administration in schools: The Massachusetts experience. *Journal of School Health*, 68(3), 94–8.

Shaddix, T. (1986). *Meal planning for the childhood years: Nutritional care for the child with developmental disabilities*. Birmingham, NY: United Cerebral Palsy of Greater Birmingham.

Sommers, M. S. (1992). The shattering consequences of CPR: How to assess and prevent complications. *Nursing*, 22(7), 34–41.

Soud, T. (1992). Airway, breathing, circulation, & disability: What is different about kids? *Journal of Emergency Nursing*, 18(2), 107–119.

Spina Bifida Association of America. (1998, June 2). Washington, DC. (online). Available: http://www.healthy.net/pan/cso/cioi/SBAA.HTM

Standards and guidelines for cardiopulmonary (CPR) and emergency cardiac care (ECC). (1986). *Journal of the American Medical Association*, 255, 2905–2989.

Statistical Resources Branch, Division of Vital Statistics. (1981). *Final mortality statistics*. Hyattsville, MD: Author.

Sullivan-Bolyai, S., Swanson, M., & Shurtleff, D. B. (1984). Toilet training the child with neurogenic impairment of bowel and bladder function. *Issues in Comprehensive Pediatric Nursing*, 7(1), 33–43.

Tatter, S. B., Owen, C., & Kenyon, L. (1998, June 2). Hydrocephalus Association Homepage. (online). Available: http://neurosurgery.mgh.harvard.edu

Taylor, M. (1990). Clean intermittent catheterization. In J. C. Graff, M. M. Ault, D. Guess, M. Taylor, & B. Thompson. *Health care for students with disabilities: An illustrated medical guide for the classroom*. Baltimore: Paul H. Brookes.

The MMG/O'Neil closed intermittent catheterization system. (1998, May 31). (online). Available: http://www.mmghealthcare.com.

Thomas, C. L. (1985). *Taber's encyclopedic medical dictionary*. Philadelphia: F. A. Davis.

U.S. Department of Health and Human Services. (1995). *Child health USA '95*. Washington DC: Author.

Vigneux, A., & Hunsberger, M. (1994). Altered genitourinary/renal function. In C. L. Betz, M. M. Hunsberger, & S. Wright (Eds.). *Family-centered nursing care of children* (2nd ed.) (pp. 1516–1517). Philadelphia: W.B. Saunders.

Wagner, M. (Ed.). (1983). *Nurse's reference library (drugs)*. Springhouse, PA: Intermed.

Walker, D. K., & Jacobs, F. H. (1984, Winter). Chronically ill children in school. *Peabody Journal of Education*, 61(2), 28–76.

Walker, K. A. (1971). *Pressure sores: Prevention and treatment*. London: Butterworth & Company.

Wetmore, R. F., Handler, S. D., & Potsic, W. P. (1982). Pediatric tracheostomy experience during the past decade. *Annals of Otology, Rhinology, & Laryngology*, 91, 628–632.

Whaley, L. F., & Wong, D. L. (1987). *Nursing care of infants and children*. St. Louis: Mosby.

Williams, J., Grant, M., Jackson, M., Shema, S., Sharp, G., Griebel, M., Lange, B., Mancias, P., & Bates, S. (1996). Behavior descriptors that differentiate between seizure and nonseizure events in a pediatric population, *Clinical Pediatrics, 35*(5), 243–250.

Wilson, S., Smith, G., Preisch, J., & Casamassimo, P. (1997). Nontraumatic dental emergencies in a pediatric emergency department. *Clinical Pediatrics, 36*(6), 333–338.

Woelk, C. G. (1986). The mentally retarded child and his family. In G. M. Scipien, M. U. Barnard, M. A. Chard, & P. J. Phillips (Eds.). *Comprehensive pediatric nursing* (pp. 639–666). New York: McGraw-Hill.

Wolff, R. P., & Lierman, C. J. (1994). Management of behavioral feeding problems in young children. *Infants and Young Children, 7*(1), 14–23.

Wong, D. L. (1997). *Whaley & Wong's essentials of pediatric nursing* (5th ed.). St. Louis: Mosby.

Younger, S. J. (1992) A physician/ethicist responds: A student's rights are not so simple. (Case presentation and three commentaries in response to the question: Should a school honor a student's DNR order?) *Kennedy Institute of Ethics Journal, 2*(1), 13–19.

8

Promoting Participation in Natural Environments by Accommodating Motor Disabilities

Philippa H. Campbell

Quality programs for individuals with motor disabilities include both *instructional programs* and *physical management routines*. Instructional and therapeutic programs work to develop specific movements for use in performing functional outcomes in communication, mobility, socialization, work, and learning. For example, specifically teaching an individual to perform an assisted standing transfer from a chair to a toilet, a sofa, or the floor requires an instructional program. However, individuals with motor disabilities also require conscientious management of their physical needs while in their home, school, work, and community environments. Lifting, carrying, positioning, feeding, toileting, dressing, and other similar routines must be managed when a person is not able to do the routine independently or may not be independent in all settings. Physical management routines allow adults (or peers) to use procedures that are therapeutic for the muscles, bones, joints, and overall motor limitations that may be present. Lifting a child from an adaptive chair can be done in ways that promote

relaxation or in ways that make a child stiff, uncomfortable, or fearful. A child may be comfortably sitting in an adaptive chair or may be uncomfortably and poorly positioned in an ill-fitting chair.

Occupational and physical therapists, together with family members, teachers, and others, can ensure that the easiest and most efficient ways are used to manage physical care needs in all settings. Ways in which these needs are addressed depend on the age and size of the person with a disability, the degree and type of motor disability, the setting, and the person who will be carrying out the routine. This chapter provides an overview of the guidelines used to accommodate the care needs of individuals with motor disabilities so that they will be able to participate as fully as possible in activities in a variety of environments. Two children, Tommy, a 4-year-old preschooler, and Mackenzie, a high school freshman, are described below and are used as examples to illustrate the ways in which general handling and care routines are individualized for specific children and circumstances.

Tommy

At age 4, Tommy, who has been diagnosed as having cerebral palsy and spastic quadriplegia, remains dependent on his mother and other caregivers for all of his care. Tommy likes a lot of activities that other 4-year-olds enjoy, such as being read stories, making art projects, and playing with toys. Tommy might like to be as independent as other children, but severe stiffness in his arms and legs prevents such independence. Tommy needs to be fed, dressed, and bathed, as well as lifted and carried from place to place. When Tommy's mother is working, Tommy is cared for in a community day care center where he is enrolled in the 4-year-olds' room. At the center and at home, Tommy also receives early intervention services (e.g., special education and therapy services) through his local school district. These specialists help Tommy, the child care program staff, and his family so that Tommy's

care is well managed and that his development in all areas is maximized.

Many of the physical management routines that are provided by adults when children are infants and toddlers will be necessary for Tommy throughout his life. However, over time and with the assistance of his family, caregivers, teachers, and therapists, Tommy may learn to physically do parts of many of his care routines and to perform other routines independently. For example, Tommy participates in dressing and bathing, and his mother and the child care workers are helping Tommy learn to feed himself without assistance. All of Tommy's caregivers work with professionals to learn information, resources, and techniques to manage Tommy's physical care routines, help him participate fully in activities and routines, and promote his ability to become as independent as possible.

 Mackenzie

Mackenzie has been receiving special education and a variety of related services for the past 14 years. She was diagnosed with cerebral palsy at 6 months and began receiving early intervention services shortly thereafter. Now 15 years old, she is a veteran of numerous orthopedic surgeries and, just last year, a selective dorsal rhizotomy surgery was done to help lower the tone in her legs. The surgery improved the ease with which Mackenzie's care needs can be addressed and allowed her to stand with considerable support and assistance.

Mackenzie attends her local high school, where she participates in many classes with her peers. She also participates in other classes where she is learning to do things in the community, such as order food in a restaurant and ride public transportation. The students at the high school have grown up with Mackenzie, who has attended regular schools since kindergarten, and many of them are sensitive to her needs. One of her friends feeds her each day in the cafeteria. Another

spends time with her during swimming. A paraeducator has been assigned to the school to work with Mackenzie and other students with special needs. The paraeducator assists "Mac" in the bathroom and in moving her from one piece of equipment to another. The paraeducator follows team recommendations and helps by making special adaptations and modifying materials so that Mackenzie can do her schoolwork with the other students. Mackenzie is able to get around the school independently using a power chair. She communicates with a communication device and uses a computer with a switch to participate in her classes. Mac receives occupational, physical, and speech language therapy. Her team, which includes her teacher, parents, therapists, and many friends, recognizes her many strengths and has established Individualized Educational Program (IEP) goals that will enable her to be as independent as possible when she finishes high school.

Key Issues in Motor Disability

Most types of pediatric physical disability are identified during infancy or early childhood years. Children with the most severe physical disabilities are likely to be diagnosed early, often at or shortly after birth,

while those with mild physical disabilities or those with some forms of genetically based physical limitations may not be identified until their toddler, preschool, or sometimes even later school years. Physical disability also may be the result of accident or injury that may occur at any time during childhood;

it may be the only disability the child has or may be accompanied by other disorders, such as vision or hearing impairment, intellectual disability, or other types of learning disorders (see Batshaw, 1997, for further discussion of physical disabilities). As a result of the physical or combined disability, children may have difficulties with physical development, learning, or performance.

Tommy has a physical disability that is resulting in difficulties with learning and development in all areas (e.g., gross motor, communication) and with performance of self-care skills, such as self-feeding.

Movement Competence, Adaptation, and Participation

Motor disability may range from severe to mild and may involve the whole body (i.e., arms, legs, head, trunk) or only parts of the body (e.g., one side or both legs). When the motor disability is severe, the whole body is more likely to be involved than when the disability is mild or moderate (Palisano et al., 1997). When motor disability is mild to moderate, there is a greater chance that children will learn to perform the same motor skills that typically developing children master during their early years. Children with mild to moderate disability will learn basic gross motor skills, such as sitting, crawling, and walking, although they may look different or be less coordinated than children without motor disability or may achieve skills at a later time than typical children. Children with severe motor disability may never be able to perform these basic skills because the degree of motor impairment may prevent them from doing so. Severe motor disability may not just affect gross motor skills like mobility but may also influence whether a child is able to learn to eat independently, play with toys, hold a pencil, manage clothing, or even use the bathroom independently. Severe motor disability may impact on performance in many different areas.

Throughout the childhood years, whether at home, in school, or in community settings, participation in typical activities and routines must be promoted, no matter how severe the motor disability. When a motor disability limits performance of skills, participation in typical settings is assured through accommodations, adaptations, assistive technology, or other strategies. The terms *accommodation* and *adaptation* are often used interchangably, but both terms relate to physical ac-

cessibility, or program modifications made to accommodate access and participation. Accessibility results from environmental adaptations (or modifications) that allow an individual with a disability to gain access to a particular setting. Adapting a bathroom with wider doors, grab bars, a higher toilet, special water spigots, or other adaptations makes it possible for people with physical disabilities to access and use the bathroom facilities. *Program adaptations* allow an individual with a disability to participate in the activities and routines of a particular environment or setting. A teacher who tapes a paper to the desk of a student with a physical disability so that the student may still write, draw, or paint on the paper has adapted the activity for the student. *Assistive technology* is generally associated with a particular individual and helps that individual perform specific skills in a different way than typical people do. A communication device enables a student who cannot speak to do so using another means. The communication device may be as simple as pictures or symbols pasted onto cardboard (an example of a low-tech assistive device) or as complicated as a computerized communication device that both speaks and writes. Accommodations, adaptations, and assistive technology all enable children with disabilities to fully participate in typical home, school, and community activities. A child with a physical disability who is unable to run may still be able to participate in a community baseball program (such as Little League) by being the equipment manager or by using an adaptation to hit the ball or by "running" bases by moving a wheelchair.

Mackenzie may participate in ninth grade by achieving all the goals specified on the IEP but might not be able to complete the algebra curriculum.

When motor disability is severe and limits performance of self-care skills, the basic needs of an individual must be managed in the environments or settings where the person spends time (Campbell, 1995). For a child to participate in baseball, ways of managing eating, toileting, and other care needs during the baseball game and in the settings where baseball takes place must be identified. More often than not, these care needs fall to parents, other family members, or hired personal care assistants; a child may be permitted to participate *only* with parents, family members, or a personal care assistant present. There are many reasons why children may be required to participate only if adults are present, and these include perceived safety, liability and risk management, and views that the child needs more assistance than may actually be the case. A better alternative involves good planning and instruction of people who spend time with an individual in a particular setting. For example, the places where baseball takes place may be assessed to determine the accommodations and adaptations necessary for an individual's eating, drinking, and toileting needs to be met. People who are at the community games, such as the coaches or perhaps an older high school student who wishes to volunteer or, depending on age and the situation, the friends and peers of the child, may be taught the best ways of addressing individual needs during baseball games and practice. Assisting in determining strategies for managing care needs is generally the role of occupational therapists (or sometimes physical therapists), but family members and others who are familiar with the child may also be knowledgeable about easy and effective strategies.

Motor Form Versus Function

Most motor disabilities start with an impairment in the brain, nerves, the muscles, or joints of the body. When these impairments are present before or in the early period immediately after a child's birth, they may affect the development of the motor (or other) skills that occur so naturally during most children's early years, resulting in motor disabilities.

> Tommy's motor disability affects not just whether he learns motor skills, such as walking, but also other developmental areas, such as speaking, independent eating, or toileting.

Most motor disabilities are not static; that is, they do not remain the same throughout an individual's lifetime. Some children may acquire motor skills later than would be expected for most children. A child, for example, may learn to walk at age 5 rather than at age 1, which would be more typical. By the time that student has reached adulthood, walking may no longer be possible or preferred. The individual may have learned other more efficient and less taxing ways of getting around, of being mobile without walking. Every motor skill has both a *form* (the pattern used to perform the movement) and a *function* (the purpose of the movement). The purpose of walking, its function, is to enable a person to go from place to place. The form of walking differs based on individual circumstances. People may walk with their legs held far

apart or close together, on their toes, with their knees held together, or using many other patterns. Children with motor disabilities may learn a different form, or way, to accomplish the purpose, or function, of walking. They may get around by propelling a wheelchair or by using a motorized chair. They may move from place to place on their hands and knees or by using a walker. They may use a walker in their homes or classrooms but may use a wheelchair at the shopping center or when outside on the playground. The more severe the motor disability, the more likely a child is to use different rather than typical ways, or forms, of accomplishing motor functions. If a child's hands are fisted and difficult to open for grasp and release, an adapted holder may help the child to write, paint, or draw. Creative expression, a function of writing, drawing, and painting, may be accomplished using a computer with a mouse and appropriate software. Children do not necessarily naturally develop different forms for motor skills. Most often, these different ways of accomplishing basic motor functions must be taught by occupational and physical therapists, speech and language pathologists, teachers, family members, and others who are involved with the child.

Barriers to Motor Competence

Infants and young children may be born with or may acquire physical impairments that affect development, learning of motor skills, or the ways in which particular functions are performed. The severity of the resultant motor disability is dependent not just on the physical impairment but on the ways in which the impairment interacts with environmental challenges, circumstances, and expectations across the life span of the individual (S. K. Campbell, 1997; Lollar, 1994). The expectations of people interact in a number of ways with the circumstances of settings in which a person with motor disabilities spends time. For example, when the people in the settings where a person spends time do not expect the person to participate in activities and routines, opportunities for participation are limited. The person may learn that nothing is expected; it is better to be "helpless" (Seligman, 1975). On the other hand, when expectations and circumstances provide significant challenges for an individual, the person may not be able to be successful and may have low self-esteem or an attitude of never being able to be "right" (Kunc, 1996).

Sometimes parents, educators, or others have goals that emphasize full participation in activities and routines using whatever means are available. These expectations may be achieved through use of whatever motor abilities a student may have as well as with the assistance of adaptations, special materials, assistive devices, or other types of equipment. The goal is for the student to participate as fully as possible irrespective of any negative impact on the motor system.

The degree of muscle tone and secondary disabilities are two factors that affect the ability of individuals with motor disabilities to perform as expected. Opportunities for practice are another factor. Each of these factors can function as barriers to motor competence.

Muscle Tone

Many individuals have motor disabilities that are related to atypical muscle tone. *Muscle tone* is a measure of the tension in individual muscles (or muscle groups). The term *postural tone* is used, also, to describe the degree of tension in muscles throughout the body. Normal postural tone provides sufficient tension in the muscles to hold the body against gravity and to support coordinated movements into and away from gravity. Sufficient postural tone allows a variety of movements, such as reaching, which requires that the arm be held up against the influences of gravity, or rolling from the side onto the back, which requires controlled movement into gravity. Many functional movements are combinations of antigravity (away from gravity) and with-gravity (or into gravity) movement. Standing up from a chair requires movement into gravity to lean forward and away from gravity to put weight on the feet and stand up.

Some individuals with motor disabilities have *hypotonia*, or too little postural tone. This means that they may have difficulty with antigravity postures, such as sitting, or with antigravity (into gravity) movements, such as are required to get from sitting to standing. Other motor disabilities involve too much tone, either in particular muscle groups (such as those in the legs) or throughout the body. The terms *hypertonia* and *spasticity* are used to describe the stiffness that results when the muscles have too much tension. Often, the body or an extremity (e.g., the arms, legs, or head) are pulled by the spasticity into the opposite direction of where the movement should occur. A student who is sitting and who has significant spasticity in the arms,

for example, may have the arms pulled backward behind the trunk by the spasticity, rather than having the arms forward in front of the trunk, a position from which it would be possible to reach.

Combinations of atypical muscle tone are possible, also. Muscle tone in the head and trunk may be low (or hypotonic) and in the arms and legs may be high (hypertonic or spastic). Muscle tone, particularly hypertonia, is influenced not just by the original brain impairment but also by environmental conditions, which may change tone to sudden stiffness throughout the body or in one or more extremities. An unexpected loud noise, for example, may cause a student to become even more spastic. Picking a student up from the floor without preparation and using inappropriate techniques may activate spasticity (and make the motor disability even more difficult to manage). Appropriate physical management routines may maintain the student's muscle tone within more appropriate ranges, making the student more able to assist in the process and making the procedures safer and easier for the people using physical management routines.

Secondary Motor Disabilities

A cycle illustrating the ways in which posture and movement may become more abnormal over time is illustrated in Figure 8–1 (Campbell & Forsyth, 1993). The cycle shows the process that occurs when infants are born with abnormal tone or when atypical muscle tone is acquired through brain damage from accident or injury. Muscle tone, particularly in the head and trunk, is hypotonic for a majority of infants who are born very prematurely or whose brains are damaged by medical conditions associated with prematurity, such as periventricular leukomalacia (PVL) or severe interventricular hemorrhage (IVH). Other infants with motor conditions may also have low tone in the head and trunk during the early stages of their development. Over time, many of these infants begin showing hypertonia in the extremities and, to a lesser extent, in the head and trunk, so that by school age, many of these children demonstrate muscle tone that is largely described as hypertonic or spastic.

The hypotonia in the head and trunk makes it difficult for infants to move against gravity; thus, they may have difficulties (a) in lifting their heads or controlling head movement, (b) with lifting themselves against gravity when lying on their stomachs, or (c) with

FIGURE 8–1
Cycle of the Development of Abnormal Movement. This diagram illustrates the ways in which posture and movement develop abnormally over time. Deviations in postural tone result in postural adjustments that compensate for the inability of tone to hold the body upright against gravity. These adjustments, in turn, influence the kinds of movements that are possible.

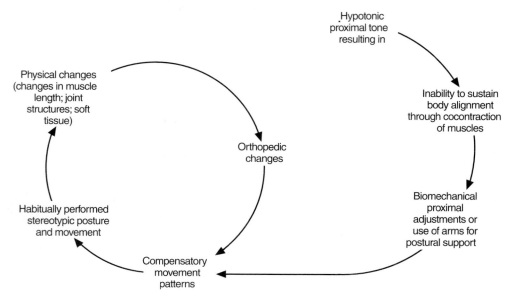

holding themselves upright in sitting. All of these maneuvers require postural tone and movement against gravity. Instead, their heads may fall into gravity or their whole bodies may fall into gravity when they are positioned on their stomachs or seated. The low muscle tone makes it difficult to sustain body alignment through muscle control (or *cocontraction*, a process in which muscles contract together to hold the body or a body part against gravity.) Most young children are intrinsically motivated to move; therefore, children with disabilities figure out different ways of moving and holding themselves in positions that are used by children with normal muscle tone. Our bodies automatically adjust for gravity and other factors associated with movement so that *biomechanical advantage* is achieved. A common example among adults is that we bend our knees when sitting on the floor (rather than sitting with the legs straight out). This compensates for shortness or tightness in the hamstring muscles. These automatic adjustments of the body also may compensate for atypical muscle tone. Another way of compensating for muscle tone is to use the arms to accomplish what the body muscles are unable to do. For example, when we get tired of holding

our trunks up against gravity, we use our arms to support ourselves.

Figure 8–2 illustrates young children sitting using biomechanical adjustments and arm movements to compensate for low tone in the head and trunk. The biomechanical adjustments and arm movements are used to hold the child upright because the muscles in the head and trunk are unable to sustain the necessary cocontraction against gravity. Without these compensations, each of the children would fall over into gravity and would be unable to sit on the floor independently. While each of these children are achieving some degree of independent floor sitting, they are doing so at high physical cost. The negative outcomes of each child achieving sitting may be forgotten when an immediate focus is on gross motor development or skill performance. The fact that a child has accomplished something independently should not outweigh concern about the ways in which this independence has been achieved. The child in Figure 8–2a shows increased tone (or spasticity) in the head and arms. This high tone is stiffening the top of the body so that the child is able to stay upright against gravity with the support of the adult. The child is not in alignment

FIGURE 8–2
Patterns of Muscle Tone and
Biomechanical Adjustments of
Body Parts

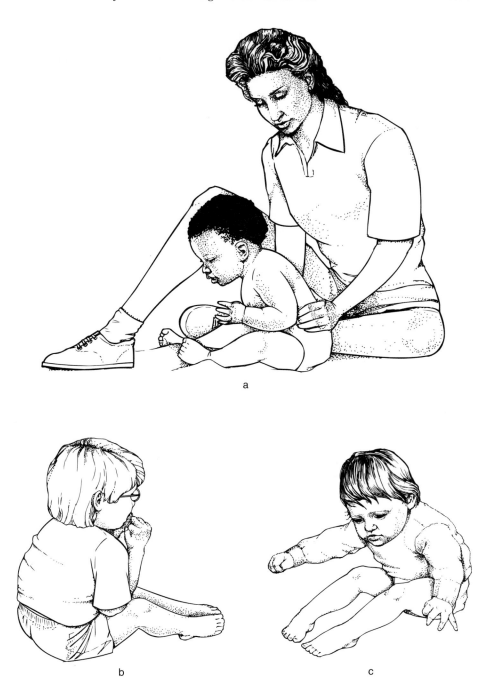

a

b

c

(or truly upright) against gravity but is tilted forward because of lack of sufficient extensor tone in the trunk. This extensor tone would straighten the trunk so that she was sitting on her hips (rather than forward of her hips as is the case in the illustration).

The preschooler in Figure 8–2b is able to floor sit without adult assistance but does so with the upper back rounded forward and the head turtled into the shoulders (a biomechanical compensation) and the arms pulled forward to his chest.

Tommy sits on the floor in this same way although he is only able to maintain the position for a few seconds (and may never be able to maintain the position for longer periods of time because of the spasticity).

The child in Figure 8–2c compensates with arms that are held out and away from the body for balance and stability. The sitting patterns of each of these children, while different from each other, all rely on biomechanical adjustments of the body as well as use of the arms to compensate for low tone in the head and trunk. None of the children are upright and in alignment against gravity, although all of them are sitting. While these compensations make sitting possible, they also (a) increase muscle tone, so that the children are using spasticity to attain sitting; (b) establish posture that is not aligned against gravity; and (c) rely on use of the arms to hold the body upright (making the arms unavailable for functional activity, such as playing with toys or doing other things that would typically be done in a sitting position). Most children do not sit as an end in itself. Rather, they sit so that they can play with objects, watch what is going on around them, or move from sitting into another position, such as crawling, standing, or walking. These children with motor disabilities are able to sit but are not able to sit *functionally*.

Over time, reliance on biomechanical body adjustments or of the arms to support antigravity postures (see Figure 8–1) leads to the development of compensatory movement patterns, which, in turn, lead to practice of poorly coordinated movement patterns, which, in turn, create secondary physical changes in the muscles and joint structures, which, in turn, may result in orthopedic deformities, which induce further development of compensatory patterns, secondary physical changes, and perhaps, more orthopedic deformities. By the time many children with motor disabilities reach school age, secondary motor disabilities and orthopedic deformities have been added to the original motor disability that was present during their infant and early childhood years. Typical secondary disabilities include changes in muscle length, in which muscles may have become overstretched (or elongated) or may have become permanently shortened; muscle weakness; changes in the joints or soft tissues in the joint structures; or deformities, such as subluxation or dislocation of the hips or shoulders.

As students age into adulthood, arthritis or other secondary conditions may also develop (Campbell, 1997).

Hypothetically, each of these secondary changes are preventable through appropriate physical management and coordinated expectations for children's development and learning. More important, however, is that when these secondary conditions develop, they further limit and inhibit a child's ability to perform functional motor skills. A student with severe shortening in the elbow muscles (so that the elbow is bent much of the time) may not be able to reach very far or may be unable to grasp an object because the hand is not well positioned for grasping. A student who acquires tightness and shortening in the muscles of the hips and knees so that they are in a bent position most of the time (as happens when children are positioned too often in sitting) may be unable to stand as an adolescent or adult, making it necessary for two people to move the student from his or her chair to the toilet, onto a school bus, into a car, or into any other position. A student who still has straight knees and hips may be able to assist in transfer by maintaining supported standing balance long enough for another person to do a standing pivot transfer with the student, thereby making the student's physical needs much easier to manage.

Even though Mackenzie has received services since she was an infant, secondary disabilities were acquired. The amount of spasticity in her legs prevented her from being transferred easily, and so a recent surgical procedure has decreased the spasticity in her legs and is allowing her the possibility of learning to stand supported for a long enough period of time (in seconds) to be transferred from one position to another. Even though the surgery has reduced the spasticity, Mackenzie needs to use her legs for supported standing so that she can develop muscle strength for endurance and so that she can learn and practice the skill of standing within the context of transferring from one position to another.

Opportunities for Learning and Practice

For competence in any motor skill to be acquired, sufficient opportunities must be present to perform skills within the contexts in which they are functionally used. This means that a particular motor skill must be practiced often enough to be firmly established as "automatic." When a child is first learning how to go up and down steps, for example, the required movements are thought out and made carefully and slowly. As the child goes up and down steps again and again, greater skill and precision result from the practice of repeating these movements. After much practice, going up and down steps becomes automatic: a motor skill that is performed without even thinking. There are many functional motor skills that become automatic, or are performed without conscious thought. Walking, drinking from a glass, feeding oneself, riding a bike, playing volleyball, reaching for objects, washing dishes, or signing your name are examples of motor skills that become automatic through practice.

Individuals with motor disabilities can best learn new skills through practice. Opportunities for practice can be provided by creating opportunities for a person to perform specific motor skills throughout the day. These motor skills may be incorporated into physical management routines to increase opportunities for practice. A child may be required, for example, to lift the arms up toward the adult before being picked up from the floor, before the tray on the wheelchair is put on or taken off, or before being moved out of a chair. By incorporating movement of the arms into many physical routines, an individual not only partially participates in the care routine but also uses the same motor skill (in this case, lifting the arms up) across routines, thereby practicing this movement numerous times throughout the day. This practice helps to improve the performance of a particular movement pattern and to make performance of the pattern automatic over time.

Tommy's caregivers, teachers, and therapists all incorporate this arm movement into everything they do with Tommy. This means that Tommy gets many more than 100 opportunities a day to practice lifting his arms. Under these conditions, he will learn to lift his arms up more quickly than if only his therapist practices this with him during weekly therapy sessions, and he is less likely to develop muscle tightness and secondary disabilities in his shoulders and arms.

Weight Shifting and Movement Competence

Posture describes the position of the body—sitting, standing, on hands and knees, lying down. *Alignment* is a feature of posture that relates the position of the body to physical planes of space. For example, a per-

son who is sitting in a chair and leaning backward against the back of the chair is in a sitting posture but is out of alignment. An aligned sitting posture in a chair occurs when the person sits straight, with the feet on the floor and the hips and knees bent at right (or 90°) angles. Alignment is important to observe when motor disability is present because the way in which the body is out of alignment is defined by the muscle tone differences, the acquired secondary motor disabilities, and the compensations that are being used to remain upright against gravity or comfortable in a position. Movement results when (a) the body is moved within the same posture, such as when a person reaches down to the floor but remains in sitting or leans forward in sitting to reach an object that is past arm's length or (b) when the body is moved through space, such as in rolling, crawling, walking, running, ice skating, or climbing steps.

All gross motor movements are made up of combinations of *weight shifts* of the body in different planes of space. To lean forward in sitting, the weight of the body must be shifted forward. To walk, body weight must be shifted from side to side and frontwards. When weight is shifted, the weight of the body comes off of one part, resulting in an unweighting that allows isolated movement of an extremity or body part. When a person is standing, for example, the weight of the body is on both feet. Weight bearing surfaces cannot move. Therefore, the weight has to be shifted off of one leg to allow the unweighted leg to move. The leg moves forward in front of the body and now the weight has to be shifted forward onto that leg so that the back leg may be unweighted and can move forward, resulting in walking.

Functional motor skills, such as walking, reaching, or getting into and out of positions, are made up of weight shifts. Particular weight shifts may be difficult for individuals with motor disabilities. A student with spasticity in the legs may have her pelvis and hips pulled backward from the spasticity and tightness in the hip or leg muscles and, therefore, may have difficulty shifting weight forward over the legs, a weight shift that is needed to stand up or be assisted into a standing position easily.

Spasticity in the hip and leg muscles was one of the problems that Mackenzie had before her surgery, and spasticity is also an emerging issue with Tommy, even though he is still young. Tommy's therapists work to prevent the development of secondary disabilities in Tommy's hips and promote opportunities for him to practice shifting his weight forward.

Weight shifts that are important for a child to learn and use should be incorporated into all routines and activities, including physical management routines.

> *For Tommy, the desired motor skill of an anterior to posterior weight shift (i.e., moving the body forward and backward at the hips, such as in leaning forward or backward when sitting), was incorporated into as many physical management routines as possible for Tommy so that, for example, when Tommy was being lifted from any position, the person lifting him created an opportunity for him to practice the anterior/posterior weight shift.*

Coordination of Services and Supports

Professionals of many different disciplines may be involved in working with and assisting individuals with physical disabilities. Physical and occupational therapists, speech language pathologists, assistive technology specialists, vision or hearing specialists or teachers, adaptive physical educators, or recreation therapists are some of the specialists who may be involved with children with disabilities, in addition to regular or special education teachers, paraeducators, child care providers, or other paid caregivers. One of the primary issues for families and people with disabilities is coordination of these services and supports, especially since the constellation of services and supports needed by individuals with motor disabilities of all ages are likely to be provided by a variety of separate agencies, including schools, child care programs, or human service and home health agencies. Various team structures have served as a traditional way for coordinating services (Campbell, 1987; Giangrecco, 1994; Rainforth & York-Barr, 1997), particularly in school settings. *Service coordination* is required in publicly funded statewide systems of early intervention (but not for students in school settings). Service coordinators help families access and use a variety of services and supports and coordinate these services so that they are provided in ways that assist families to promote the development of their infants and toddlers with delayed development. In education, the teacher, special educator, a school social worker, or the child's family may coordinate services. Plans such as the Individual Family Service Plan (IFSP),

used in early intervention; the Individualized Education Program (IEP), required in education; or other plans, such as the Individual Habilitation Plan (IHP), which is for individuals beyond school age or those residing in various types of out-of-home living arrangements, help to outline desired goals and the ways in which services may contribute to the attainment of those goals.

At times, conflicts arise because each professional discipline may view children's disability and development from different perspectives; sometimes these underlying perspectives result in different priorities or goals for children (Campbell & Forsyth, 1993). For example, an occupational therapist who is approaching a child from a particular perspective, such as *sensory integration* (a focus on ways in which the child is processing sensory information), may identify sensory integration dysfunction and view a child's skill limitations in terms of processing of sensory information. The therapist in such a situation would likely establish goals of improving integration of sensory stimuli to enhance a child's fine motor abilities. However, this same child's teacher may have a priority of teaching the child to write and may be more interested in adaptations, such as computer word processing programs that allow a child to write in spite of deficient fine motor abilities. The occupational therapist in this example is focused on improving performance, but the teacher is interested in improving participation. Both professionals recognize the limitation in fine motor skills and the effect of this limitation on a performance area such as writing, but the occupational therapist is using a remedial approach to prepare the child to learn to write using a pencil, and the teacher is addressing the issue from the standpoint of compensation for the fine motor and writing limitation (Campbell, 1987; Dunn, Brown, & McGuigan, 1994; Wilcox, 1989).

> *As Mackenzie entered high school, the limitations that she had in writing became pronounced. Her writing was not easily intelligible and was very laborious, making it difficult for her to write as clearly and as quickly as was needed in her high school program. The occupational therapist wished to have her use a computer for writing but wanted, also, to spend individual therapy time working on fine motor coordination so that Mackenzie's writing would ultimately be improved. Her teacher wanted everything to be adapted so that Mackenzie would not need to write at all and could partici-*

pate via assistive technology. Each of these team members viewed the issues with Mackenzie's writing from a different underlying perspective.

Sometimes different perspectives and approaches can co-exist if professionals are working together. In this example of Mackenzie's writing, the occupational therapist can work on improvements in fine motor coordination as long as adaptations are in place that allow the child to write or do other fine motor skills while acquiring the fine motor competence necessary to perform these skills without adaptations.

Because Tommy's occupational therapist is teaching him to feed himself using an adapted spoon and particular procedures, the child care staff and Tommy's parents and other caregivers each should know how to use both the spoon and the self-feeding teaching procedures and should use them each time Tommy is feeding himself. Because many people will be implementing these teaching procedures with Tommy, consistency is important and can be achieved when the occupational therapist, teacher, parent, and other caregivers discuss the procedures and make sure that they are "doable" by all people and across all settings in which Tommy is fed. Otherwise, Tommy may not learn to feed himself as easily or quickly as when all people who interact with him during eating are teaching him in the same way.

The different viewpoints that may occur when children and students receive multiple services need to be coordinated and integrated if children are to be maximally successful. Participation in typical activities and routines is critical, but participation is not enough to ensure improvements in current motor skills and abilities—or the acquisition of new motor abilities. Motor competence provides a base for future development, learning, and participation and prevents the development of other disabilities that are secondary to the original disability and that occur as a child ages (Campbell, 1997).

Many of the professionals who come into contact with individuals with motor disabilities do so for only short periods of time in that individual's life. One set of therapists and teachers may shift to a new set of professionals as a child moves from early intervention to preschool. Professionals may shift again each time a student moves within the educational system from elementary to middle to high school and then to postschool education or work. Families are the constant in their children's lives and

are often the "historians" of what has occurred earlier in their child's life (Salisbury & Dunst, 1997). Families usually know what has worked or not worked, what has been tried with what result, and what may be easiest for their children. Professionals who develop positive and respectful relationships with parents and family members can learn a great deal about what has happened with the student before that professional entered the student's and family's life. Making sure that parents see themselves as "experts" about their children is an important role for all professionals to play. Most motor disabilities are lifelong; they do not go away or decrease with age or programming. In many instances, motor disabilities become more limiting because of secondary changes that result from poor physical management, insufficient use of adaptive equipment or assistive devices, or overemphasis on independent performance of gross motor skills.

Goals of Proper Physical Management

A primary goal of proper management is *maintaining normal body alignment*. Atypical muscle tone may allow the body to fall out of alignment with less than normal tone (hypotonia) or may pull the body out of alignment with greater than normal tone (hypertonus). The child previously illustrated in Figure 8–2b is being pulled out of alignment by spasticity in the shoulders and arms as well as by spasticity in the hips. The hips have been pulled backward, causing the shoulders and arms to pull forward to allow the child to remain upright. The result is that his back is rounded and not straight (or aligned) over his hips. In contrast, the child in Figure 8–2c is out of alignment because she is falling into gravity. Holding her arms out to the side provides balance and stability so that she does not fall all the way forward. The result is that her spine is not in alignment over her hips and her back is rounded rather than straight (or upright) against gravity. Postural alignment can be achieved with proper positioning and with handling that minimizes the effects of atypical muscle tone and maintains body alignment. In contrast, improper positioning and handling may result in malalignment of the body and development of secondary physical disabilities.

A second goal of proper management is to *encourage as much participation as possible* by the individual and to *prevent the development of secondary muscular and structural disorders*. Individuals who are being moved, fed, dressed, lifted, or positioned may become passive during physical management routines. The routines, also, may become automatic for the individuals implementing them so that the person who is lifting, for example, is no longer thinking about how to do the lift but is just lifting, picking up, or carrying. Opportunities for an individual to physically participate in the physical management routine may become lost when the routines become automatic. Sometimes a major part of a routine may be difficult for an individual to perform and may take too long, given the setting or situation in which the routine is being used. For example, a student may be able to walk to the bathroom with supervision, but it may require 30 minutes for the student to get to the bathroom. Students may participate within routines through communication, such as vocalizing that they are ready to be moved or using eye movement to look at the plate or glass to indicate what they might want next, or through small motor movements, such as opening their hands to have the spoon put in their hands before a hand-over-hand feeding routine or opening their mouths for the spoon or cup. There are many creative ways in which some participation can be incorporated into every physical management routine for every student (see chapters 3 and 4 for further discussion of participation in activities and routines). Many individuals remain dependent on others to physically move them because of the degree of their physical impairment. However, all individuals can learn the motor movement necessary to participate partially in one or more steps of a physical management routine.

The third goal of proper physical management is to move and position individuals in ways that *incorporate practice of desired motor component skills* into as many situations as possible. Often there are one or more motor component skills that are important for an individual to practice. These skills may be incorporated into several physical management routines so that many opportunities to practice are provided throughout the day. Incorporating motor component skills into as many routines as possible is especially important for individuals with severe motor disabilities and for younger children who are just beginning to learn and practice these abilities. Students with severe disabilities are at great risk for developing secondary motor disabilities. Motor abilities can be maintained when they are performed numerous times throughout the day. For younger children who may be just learning a particular motor ability, opportunities for practice enable the skill to become fully integrated across various routines as well as to become automatic.

Physical Management Routines

Most adults lift, carry, or feed infants and young children without thinking about the procedures that they use to accomplish this caregiving. When individuals have severe physical disabilities, however, caregivers must use specific procedures to prevent deformities and secondary physical changes and to provide opportunities for participation. Thus, simple care activities become physical management routines that, ideally, are used by all people involved in caregiving, including parents, teachers, paraprofessionals, therapists, baby-sitters, or respite care workers, nurses, siblings, friends, and peers.

Physical management routines should reflect both the environments in which the routines will be used and the physical needs of the individual. In developing these routines, the team of parents, friends, and professionals who are involved with the individual should also consider the efficiency with which the routines can be carried out (Campbell, 1995). In classroom or group settings, individual caregiving routines should not prevent students from participating in group activities or isolate students from their peers. Eating routines provide a good example. When a student's eating routine takes 1 hour at school, and therefore, the student is fed in a classroom rather than a cafeteria, the social interactions that normally occur in conjunction with eating are lost and the physical management routine isolates the student from his or her classmates. When even 15 minutes are required to reposition a child in adaptive equipment to allow participation in a kindergarten group activity, such as art or reading, the other children are likely to be completing the activity just as the student who has been repositioned is ready to join.

Ecological assessment strategies (described in chapter 3) can help the team establish the steps of a routine and the opportunities for participation at home, school, and in the community (Baumgart et al., 1982; Campbell, 1997; Rainforth & York-Barr, 1997). Management routines are not isolated activities. They have beginning and ending points that link them with events occurring before and after.

Tommy's team completed an ecological inventory (Table 8–1) to help determine the ways in which Tommy could participate in the eating routines in his child care setting. The assessment process helped the team determine the ways in which Tommy, who had been viewed as "needing to be fed," might be able to participate as fully as possible during snack.

Caregiver routines should be individualized according to the needs of each individual, but they also should include a series of activities that are implemented across all routines for all individuals (Stremel et al., 1990). These activities include:

1. Making contact with the individual
2. Communicating what is going to happen in a way the individual can understand
3. Preparing the individual physically for the routine
4. Performing the steps of the routine in ways that require the individual to participate as much as possible

Making contact is important because many individuals with severe disabilities have disorders in vision and hearing as well as posture and movement. Contact to prepare for a care routine may include touching, speaking, gesturing, signing, attracting the individual's attention visually, or a combination of these approaches. When individuals use specific communication systems, such as object cueing, an object may be used in conjunction with speaking to prepare the individual for the caregiving activity (Rowland & Stremel-Campbell, 1987). It is equally important to communicate what is going to happen next (e.g., "I am moving you into your wheelchair because it is time to get on the bus to go home") in ways that the individual can understand. This may mean using speech and gestures, simple language, object cueing, or nonverbal systems, such as tactile or regular signing. A speech and language pathologist or others who know the best ways for a student to receive and understand language and receive communication can help design the best ways for communicating what is going to happen next.

Each caregiving routine should be individualized to both the needs of the individual and the requirements of the environment. Some children with motor disabilities with excessive amounts of spasticity may startle or become stiffer if they are not prepared physically before being moved. Or other students with secondary physical disabilities may be easier to manage if their arms or legs are positioned before attempts are made to move them. There are many strategies that can be used to physically prepare an individual for a physical management routine. The therapists who work with the student are able to demonstrate the best ways of physically preparing individual students. Table 8–2 is an example of a lifting and carrying routine written for Tommy. This routine is implemented in the classroom at Tommy's child care center each time he is lifted and carried to another location. Basic guidelines for each type of caregiving routine (e.g., lifting, carrying, dressing) that apply to all individuals with physical disabilities are discussed in this chapter. These guidelines must be individualized to address the age, size, and motor abilities of an individual; ways of communicating; and environments in which the routines are used. For example, what works best for Tommy's parents at home may not be as easily implemented by other caregivers in his child care center (and vice versa, because of the unique requirements of environments and people). Physical or occupational therapists are a resource for individualized caregiving routines. Together with teachers and family members, written or picture instructions can be developed for how each individualized caregiving routine is to be implemented each time the routine is needed.

As children get older and gain some degree of independence, physical care routines may require less detailed instruction.

Mackenzie's needs are addressed by a number of people including her family and friends, people with whom she spends time in community activities (i.e., her swimming teacher), the paraeducator, and a number of teachers with whom she interacts during a typical high school day. Mackenzie carries her physical care routine plan (Table 8–3) with her in the backpack attached to her wheelchair.

TABLE 8–1
Ecological Inventory of Snack Time

Name: Tommy_____ Environment: 4-Year-Old Classroom_____ Activity: Snack Time_____

		Plan			Observation
Preschooler Inventory	Inventory of Tommy	Skills Tommy May Acquire	Skills Tommy May NOT Acquire	Adaptation Possibilities	Assessment and Plan
Children are at various learning centers and are cleaning up to prepare for snack; children move to snack table and seat themselves (time = 8 min.)	Tommy is standing in stander at art easel being cleaned up by TA, who removes Tommy from stander, carries him to snack table, and positions him in snack chair (time = 10 min.).	Use a motorized chair to go to the snack table.	Transfer from stander to chair or walking device; walking; moving chair with his arms	Motorized chair	Equipment dealer has been contacted to obtain loaner chair to try; Tommy will be placed in a regular wheelchair and will vocalize to indicate that he would like to be pushed or moved and will point with arm movement to show where he wants to go. TA will push Tommy when he indicates and to where he points. Motorized chairs will be tried when available from dealer.
Children wait while designated helper children pass out juice boxes, snack food, and napkins.	Tommy is not yet to the snack table; his food is placed in front of the spot where he will sit.	Tommy can get to the snack table on time if started out from the preceding activity earlier than other children; he is already able to sit and wait.		Adapted chair is needed (and is already available); chair sits on wheeled platform.	TA will start transition from learning centers to snack earlier so that time is available for clean up, transfer, and movement to the snack table and Tommy is with other kids.
Children insert straws in juice boxes, drink independently, and eat snack foods independently, requesting more if they would like additional liquid or food.	Tommy is unable to insert juice straw, drink from straw, or eat finger foods.	Eating spoon foods; drinking from cup with long straw (?) or if held for sipping; can vocalize to request more and can use large arm movement to indicate choice	Finger feeding, especially small foods; drinking from juice box straw	Try different cups; may be able to use Rubbermaid juice box, which has large straw; needs shallow spoon with built up handle; Big Mac switch for requesting more	Embed strategies to teach spoon feeding within snack; work with teacher to have spoon-fed snacks rather than finger snacks. Tommy will use Big Mac switch to request more and large arm movement to indicate choice
Children clean up after snack by throwing juice boxes and napkins away; one helper child passes the basket.	Tommy throws away his napkin (once he is able to grasp it) and can make large arm movements to wipe table.				
Children who need to use the restroom do so after snack; others begin next activity.	Tommy's diapers are changed but he is transferred to the potty for toilet training after snack; this makes him miss the next activity.	He may become toilet trained; learn to transfer from chair to toilet independently; communicate his bathroom needs.		Toilet chair	Wheel (or carry) to the potty chair and place on the chair; do Tommy's clothes for him; sit him on potty for a maximum of 10 minutes, making sure that his tone is relaxed. Encourage Tommy to participate as much as possible. Reward for successes! Take Tommy to next activity.

TA, teaching assistant.

TABLE 8–2
A Routine for Lifting and Carrying

Name: <u>Tommy</u>   Date: <u>5/11/99</u>

Lifting and Carrying Routine
Follow these steps each time you pick Tommy up from the floor or move him from one piece of equipment to another, or move him in the classroom from one location to another.

Step	Activity	Desired Response
Contacting	Touch Tommy on his arm or shoulder & tell him you are going to move him from _____ to _____.	Wait for Tommy to relax.
Communicating	Tell Tommy where you are going and show him a picture or object that represents where he is going. For example, show him his coat and say, "we are going outside now to play."	Wait for Tommy to respond with facial expressions and vocalizations. (Try not to get him so hyped that he becomes more spastic.)
Preparing	Make sure Tommy's muscle tone is not stiff before you move him. Use deep pressure touch with a flat hand on his chest area to help relax him.	Wait to make sure that Tommy's body is relaxed and in alignment (as much as possible).
Lifting	Place Tommy in a sitting position and lift him from sitting unless he is in the stander, where he will need to be lifted from standing. Tell him that you are going to lift him. Put your arms around Tommy's back and under his knees and bend his knees to his chest so that you maintain him in a flexed position.	Wait for Tommy to reach his arms forward toward you and facilitate at his shoulders if he does not initiate reach within 10 sec.
Carrying	Turn Tommy away from you so that he is facing away and can see where you are moving. Lean his back against your body to provide support, and hold him with one arm under his hips with his legs in front. If his legs become stiff, use your other arm to hold his legs apart by coming under one leg and between the two legs to hold them gently apart.	Tommy will be able to see where he is going and can use his arms to indicate location (grossly).
Repositioning	Put Tommy in the next position he is to use for the activity. Tell him what is happening: "Music is next and you are going to sit on the floor so you can play the instruments with Jilly and Susan."	Tommy is ready to participate in the next activity.

Methods of Changing Position

Many different times during a day, individuals who are unable to move themselves independently may need to be lifted and moved from one position to another. Every attempt should be made to design routines that allow participation in whatever ways possible, however limited. A student who is unable to stand independently may still be able to perform an assisted standing transfer, where the feet become a point for pivoting the body from a wheelchair to a classroom chair or onto the toilet. A child who is unable to get to a sitting position independently, may be able to bend her neck and head forward to make it easier for the adult to move her into sitting and then pick her up from the floor.

Lifting

Several standard procedures are incorporated into any method of lifting to make the task physically easier for caregivers. All individually designed lifting programs, even those for infants and small children, should incorporate these procedures. In general, the rule is for adults to *lift with the legs* rather than with the back by squatting down next to a person who is on the floor, holding the person, and then standing up. Lifting improperly may result in physical problems for

TABLE 8–3
Generic Instruction Plan for Mackenzie

When Mackenzie's Peers are Participating In:	Mackenzie Can:
Lessons at their desks	Be called upon to participate Have a peer assist her in writing Use her computer Be involved in community-based instruction
Lunch	Eat with her peers in the lunchroom Be assisted by a peer to go through the lunch line (Mac needs help with reaching and grasping food items.) Balance her cafeteria tray on her lap Use her eyes (eye-pointing skills) or vocalization to answer "yes" or "no" so that she can make choices Be assisted in eating and drinking by her friends Carol or Shawn
Changing classes	Use her motorized chair to get through the halls, especially if she leaves class a few minutes early Be accompanied by another classmate so that someone is available if she needs assistance
Using the bathroom	Use the bathroom on the first floor that has been specially adapted for her Be taken to the bathroom by a female student (Joanie and Susan are often available) Be taken to the bathroom by an aide Help when being transferred from her chair to the toilet (She needs a lot of physical assistance from an adult or another high school student.) Use the toilet independently Assist in managing her clothing Wash her hands independently

Plan modified from Rainforth & York-Barr (1997), *Collaborative teams for students with severe disabilities: Integrating therapy and educational services (second edition)*. Baltimore, MD: Paul H. Brookes.

parents, teachers, or other adults who perform this activity frequently. Back pain and more serious complications are frequent results of using incorrect lifting methods. Younger children are lifted easily by one person. Older children or adults who are severely dependent may require two people to lift them safely.

A number of factors must be considered when determining methods for moving an individual. These include:

1. The specific movements that the individual is able to perform either independently or with assistance
2. The degree of discrepancy in postural (i.e., higher or lower than normal) tone
3. The positions (postures) to be used for instructional activities
4. The adaptive equipment being used for positioning the individual
5. The number, size, and strength of the adults (or peers) who will be moving the individual
6. The size and weight of the individual

Individuals with severe discrepancies in postural tone (either very low tone or very stiff [hypertonic]) are lifted more easily from the floor if they are placed in a sitting position before being lifted. Many children and adults are able to participate partially in a transition from stomach or back lying to a sitting position and may be able to hold on to the caregiver, maintain head position, or assist in other ways during lifting.

Many children are lifted from adaptive equipment, such as wheelchairs or specialized classroom chairs. Figure 8–3 illustrates the routine used to lift a preschooler with stiffness (hypertonus) throughout the body. The adult in this picture is kneeling beside the child who is being lifted out of her adaptive chair. By kneeling next to the child, the adult does not need to bend over and place stress on the back. Instead, the adult will be able to easily pick the child up out of her chair and then stand up from the kneeling position. Physical and occupational therapists can work with teachers and parents to design individualized pro-

FIGURE 8–3
Proper Lifting of a Small Child. Lifting a small child from a chair is easier when the adult kneels down next to the child, so that the adult can pick up the child and then stand up using her legs rather than her back.

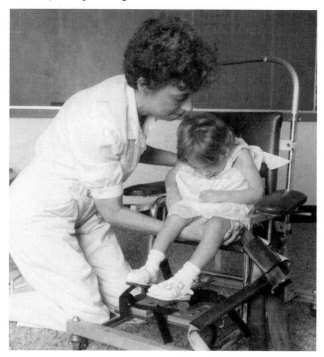

cedures for specific children. Also, many references illustrate appropriate procedures (Fraser, Hensinger, & Phelps, 1990; Hanson & Harris, 1987; Jaeger, 1989).

Transfers

Many individuals with motor disabilities may not need to be lifted or may not require lifting in all situations. Standard methods are typically used to teach children and adults to move independently from one situation into another (e.g., from a chair to the floor, from a chair to the toilet, from one chair to another). The specific methods of transfer directly depend on two factors: (a) the transfer situation (the points between which the individual will be moving), and (b) the parts (or steps) of the routine that an individual can perform independently (Jaeger, 1989). For example, transfer is different from a bed to a chair than from a chair to the floor, and the best ways of accomplishing the transfer depend on factors such as

whether or not the individual can use the arms to partially participate in the transfer.

Physical therapists or occupational therapists should analyze home, school, and typical community environments to determine the most appropriate procedures for each environment and to help individuals achieve transfer as independently as possible. To be motorically efficient, transfer routines for each environment should achieve biomechanical advantage for both the person with a disability and the person helping, if help is needed. Two frequently used basic approaches are standing transfers and sliding transfers, both of which may be accomplished either independently or assisted by another person, depending on the extent of the motor disability. Standing transfers require a minimum of assisted weight bearing on the legs. Sliding transfers require use of the arms for balance and support.

Carrying

Many younger children must be carried within home, early intervention, school, or community environments. Infants are likely to be carried by parents and teachers more often than are school-aged children or adults. Children with severe dysfunction in posture and movement can be difficult to carry for long distances, even when small in size. Instructional programs that focus on independent mobility are important to reduce the need for carrying as children get older and bigger in size. Infant backpacks or "frontpacks" assist the carrying of infants. Equipment, such as strollers, can be selected or specifically designed for infants, toddlers, and preschoolers. Wheelchairs and other types of adaptive seating can be designed for children who are older or extensively dependent.

There are several important guidelines for carrying:

1. The distance any individual is carried should be as short as possible.
2. Routines should be designed to allow maximum individual participation, provide therapeutic management, and capitalize on biomechanical efficiency.
3. Children should be carried in ways that control muscle tone, achieve body alignment, and allow independent performance of selected movements.
4. Methods should be used that are appropriate for the size and strength of the adult as well as for the situation(s) in which carrying is being used.

5. Carrying routines that require adults to use both arms for carrying do not work as well as those requiring one arm or use of the second arm intermittently, because caregivers often need the second arm to open car doors or house doors, carry items (such as a diaper bag), or hold on to another child.

Examples of carrying routines can be found in reference texts (Finnie, 1975; Jaeger, 1989; Scherzer & Tscharnuter, 1990). These reference guides provide illustrated examples of ways to carry children of various sizes and differences in muscle tone. For example, a younger child with hypertonus (increased tone) in the legs may be carried over one of the caregiver's hips to spread the legs and allow the legs to relax or become less stiff. A student with low tone and difficulty with head control may be easier to carry facing frontward, with the legs held together and supported underneath by the caregiver's arm. When muscle tone is not controlled in some way, carrying children, especially for long distances, requires a great deal of strength and endurance on the part of the caregiver. Ideally, carrying routines capitalize on each child's individual abilities to distribute his or her weight evenly and make carrying easier and more efficient.

Positioning

Well-aligned posture results from muscle contractions that maintain the body in positions against varying influences of gravity. Increased muscle tone frequently occurs in response to gravitational effects on the body. An individual who is able to lie on the floor with reasonable postural tone may become hypertonic when placed in a sitting position or may slump. Such changes occur when the motor system is unable to coordinate tone and muscle contractions against the influences of gravity.

Proper positioning can help maintain body alignment and reasonable levels of postural tone by accounting for gravitational influences. Many individuals can be positioned to receive adequate postural support and alignment without the use of extensive adaptive equipment. However, most individuals with severe physical disabilities require at least some adaptive equipment to provide postural support (Bergen, Presperin, & Tallman, 1990; Breath, DeMauro, & Snyder, 1997; Rainforth & York, 1996;

Trefler et al., 1996). Several cautions are critical to remember when using adaptive equipment:

1. Equipment does not *produce* either normalized tone or proper body alignment, since well-selected and well-fitted equipment can only *maintain* postural tone levels and body alignment.
2. Adaptive equipment maintains body alignment only when well fitted and when the individual has been placed properly in the equipment.
3. Adaptive equipment may not produce the specific results desired for each individual, so teachers, parents, and therapists must carefully observe the individual using the equipment over time and in a variety of situations to determine whether or not the desired function is achieved.
4. The length of time the individual is placed in equipment varies on an individual basis, because many individuals with motor disabilities may lack the postural tone necessary to remain in static positions for long periods.
5. Restricting people to one position (even in equipment that fits well and is otherwise comfortable) can produce secondary problems, such as poor circulation, skin ulcerations, muscle tightness, and contractures that lead to deformity.

Teachers and parents should ask therapists to specify the length of time each individual can be positioned in equipment. Some individuals can stand or sit comfortably for long periods of time (2 to 3 hours). Other individuals should be repositioned as frequently as every 20 to 30 minutes.

Selecting Adaptive Equipment

Equipment is available from a wide variety of commercial sources. Each piece of equipment varies in purpose, cost, and durability. Some individuals require equipment that is durable enough to last for several years. Others need positioning equipment only temporarily, until their size changes or their skills change. Because infants and young children are growing, their needs may be met most appropriately by equipment that is highly adjustable or low enough in cost to be replaced when they outgrow it. For example, an insert may be fabricated from tri-wall (e.g., appliance carton weight) cardboard to help position an infant in alignment in a high chair. When this baby becomes a preschooler, a more substantial insert may be needed for the child to sit at the table for snack time at Sunday school.

Equipment must also be appropriate to the environment. A normalized appearance of equipment enhances the social integration of an individual. Another consideration is the extent to which a particular piece of equipment may result in isolation of the infant or child from peers. Much of the currently available equipment for infants and young children has been designed for ease of use by adults or for use in classrooms or programs that are attended only by students or adults with motor disabilities. For example, wheelchairs such as Tumbleform Carrie Chairs, Snug Seats, and travel chairs position young children so that the adults pushing them do not have to bend over. When such wheelchairs are not limited to transportation use only, young children with physical disabilities become positioned higher than their peers and are physically isolated. Young children should be at the same level as their peers, so that they can play and be together with children who do not have physical disabilities in child care, preschool, or community settings. The commercial adaptive equipment business is rapidly growing and changing to meet consumer needs. Being familiar with major equipment vendors or with equipment available through catalogs can help keep teachers and therapists current on the features of various types of equipment. Equipment designers and manufacturers are constantly producing new types of adaptive equipment that may be used easily in the community and in programs and schools that include children with motor disabilities along with typical peers.

Most individuals with severe motor disabilities receive equipment through a number of sources. Some physical and occupational therapists who work with the students in school settings suggest particular pieces of equipment and are responsible for securing and fitting equipment. Alternately, seating clinics that are operated by hospitals and agencies in various states prescribe equipment (all equipment or only seating devices) after the individual has been referred by a physician or therapist or the clinic has been contacted by the family. In other instances, equipment is purchased by families, therapists, or teachers who reviewed product literature and catalogs. Equipment that is paid for through insurance, medical health care plans, or federal medical programs (such as Medicaid) for the most part, requires a physician's

prescription. Some manufacturers and distributors help families and professionals secure the right prescription and complete the necessary paperwork correctly. Seldom are individuals with severe physical disabilities able to use commercially available equipment without adaptation. Parents may experiment with adaptations or may return to clinics or distributors to fit and adjust equipment. Physical and occupational therapists may fit and adjust equipment, also. It is important to contact professionals when equipment does not position an individual adequately or when the body seems to be malaligned.

Use of poorly fitting adaptive equipment may result in secondary motor disabilities, such as changes in muscle length or development of physical deformities. When equipment is too big or too small, for example, the person being positioned is likely to be out of alignment. Being out of alignment may be uncomfortable and make it more difficult for the person to function, but malalignment also changes the length of the muscles or the position of the joints, resulting in the development of additional motor disabilities that were not present during infancy or early years. The most common secondary deformities are those involving the spine. Improper positioning may contribute to *scoliosis* (i.e., a "C" curve in the spine), *kyphosis* (i.e., a rounding of the shoulders), or *lordosis* (i.e., positioning of the pelvis in a tipped forward position with a "sway" back). In addition to the actual secondary problems in the muscles and bones, damage to the internal organs may occur when deformities, such as scoliosis, become severe.

Purposes of Adaptive Equipment

Adaptive equipment has two major purposes:

1. Prevention of secondary motor disabilities, including deformities
2. Enhancement or promotion of functional abilities

Sometimes, these purposes may conflict. For example, many individuals with severe motor disabilities are able to perform functional skills best when positioned in sitting, resulting in their being positioned in sitting most of the time. Sitting, also, may be the easiest position in which to manage a person with motor disabilities across many different environments, another factor which may contribute to sitting being selected as a preferred position. Even though sitting may appear to be the ideal position, when an individual spends most of the time in only one position, secondary disabilities will develop (even when equipment is well fitted and used appropriately). Changes in the length of muscles in the hips and legs occur frequently when an individual is positioned in sitting for the majority of the day. Tightness (or contractures) of the flexor muscles may result, causing the hips and knees to remain in a flexed (or bent) position and preventing them from straightening (or extending) in order to stand or lie with the legs straight. This means that a variety of positions and types of equipment are necessary to prevent secondary disabilities by placing an individual in alternate postures in as normal a body alignment as possible.

Alternate positions may require additional types of adaptive equipment. The functional appropriateness of a position in relation to the setting and activity in which it will be used is of primary importance.

> *Positioning Mackenzie, a high school student, in a side lying position during art class is not socially appropriate, even though the position may be appropriate and the equipment available. Side lying is a good position to use for watching TV at home during the evenings, for sleeping, or for just spending time relaxing. Standing is the best alternative to sitting in a majority of settings and is easily used in most school and work settings.*

Children with even the most severe motor disabilities can be positioned in some form of standing when they are young, but the development of muscle tightness, joint limitations, or deformities may prevent or limit standing possibilities as students get older. Side lying is used to position individuals who are no longer able to achieve sufficient extension in the legs or weight bearing on the feet for even supported standing. Many types of adaptive equipment are available for positioning, and new types become regularly available (Figure 8–4).

Physical and occupational therapists who are employed in clinic or hospital settings may not be fully aware of the home, school, or community environments in which adaptive equipment will be used. When equipment is acquired through a clinic or vendor, parents, teachers, and school-based therapists must communicate information about the settings in which the equipment will be used. A number of pieces of equipment may appropriately position an individual; however, only *one* piece may be appropri-

ate for a school environment, be transportable in the family's car or van, and may work best in their home or in the settings where they spend time with their children. To find out after a piece of equipment has been purchased that it won't fit in the bathroom of the school or in the family car is unfortunate. Most pieces of equipment are quite costly and seldom is their purchase fully covered by insurance or other health care programs; therefore, environmental factors must be considered before equipment is ordered, purchased, or fitted.

Improving Functional Performance

Adaptive positioning equipment itself does not enhance functional abilities. Rather, teachers, therapists, and parents must select and use equipment that places individuals with motor disabilities in positions where they can perform functional movement more easily (Breath, DeMauro, & Snyder, 1997). When motor disabilities are severe, functional skills such as mobility, communication, eating, or class participation are most likely to be possible through arm and hand or head movement. Often, these functional skills require the use of assistive devices, which are accessed through head and arm movement.

> *Mackenzie operates her motorized chair by using a switch interface device that is placed in her head rest. Her head movement activates and directs the movement of the chair.*

Other types of switch interface devices, computers, communication aids, writing devices, adapted feeding equipment, or environmental control units are used by people with physical disabilities. Functional assistive devices enable a person to participate in the task or activity in spite of significant motor disabilities. These assistive devices may be no-tech adaptations or low-tech or high-tech assistive devices.

> *Mackenzie uses a communication device and a computer, both of which are high-tech devices, but she removes printed paper from her printer by using a block of wood that she is able to grasp that has a substance to which the paper adheres. Mackenzie is unable to pick up and grasp the paper with her hand but does so independently using this low-tech device. With her communication device, she is able to ask the paraeducator or the teacher to help her in the bathroom and, when she is positioned in her power chair, she can get to the bathroom independently, change classes by herself, and get*

FIGURE 8–4
Types of Adaptive Equipment Available to Position Students with Motor Disabilities

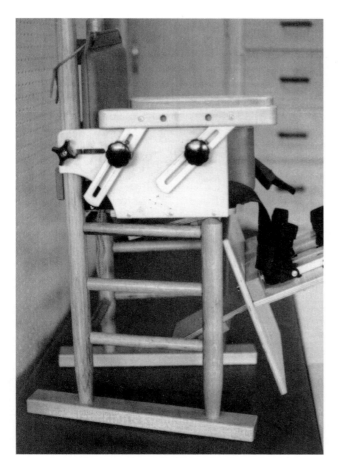

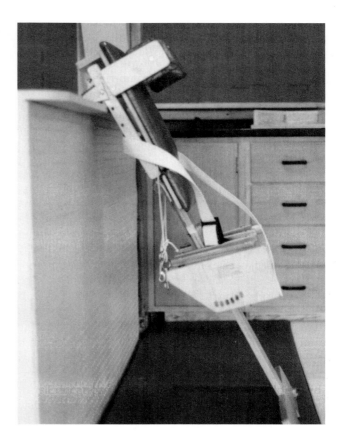

*to the cafeteria, the bus, and her after-school clubs and ac-
tivities. Mackenzie is not able to transfer to the toilet without
assistance or manage her clothing, but managing her toileting routine is far easier because of the independence provided
through her positioning equipment and other devices.*

*Tommy falls forward a lot in sitting, so when he is doing
a painting activity, his day care provider makes sure that he
has an easel in front of him. Sometimes he stands to paint
at the easels in the classroom and sometimes his teacher
places a cardboard easel on the tabletop, which she has made
by taping cardboard into a triangular shape, a no-tech
adaptation.*

Without sufficient trunk control to maintain an upright posture in sitting or standing equipment, many
students may automatically use their arms to help
hold the trunk upright. Using the arms for postural
support inhibits using them for reaching or fine motor
movement. A student may be unable to eat independently, or manipulate learning materials, or even use
a switch. Adaptive positioning equipment that supports the trunk sufficiently enables use of the arms for
more functional purposes than holding the trunk
musculature upright.

Positioning must not only provide body alignment
(to prevent orthopedic problems) and promote use of
the arms and hands but also must relate directly to
the activity.

*When Tommy wants to play in a sand or water table or
paint at an easel, he can do so more easily in some sort of
standing position. The therapists and teachers decide that a
prone stander or supine stander would be most appropriate
for this activity.*

Standing equipment would probably not be best
on the playground or when playing a game like baseball or when working with other children in a group
tabletop activity. Washing dishes may be more easily
facilitated in standing than with sitting equipment
but independent mobility, moving from place to
place, will be easier using adapted seating. A motorized or power chair enables a student to get from
place to place but may not provide the best seating
position when the student is doing classwork with a
computer; another type of adapted seating may promote better seating. Seating that transports a student
safely to and from school may be inappropriate for
classroom use because the student's movement may

be too severely restricted for function in the classroom but restricted sufficiently to ensure safety when
on the bus. Most individuals require a variety of positions and adaptive equipment, not only to prevent
secondary disabilities and deformities and maintain
alignment but also to promote function within the
context of specific activities.

Promoting Community Participation

Many young children and school-aged students receive services in schools and programs that are attended by peers, and participate with their families
and friends in all sorts of community activities. They
may visit the fire house with a Cub Scout troop, attend a birthday party at the home of a friend, swim at
the Y or a community recreation program, attend
church or religious classes, go shopping, visit amusement parks, go to day or overnight camps, see plays
or movies, or participate in any number of other settings. In an ideal world, all environments and settings
would be usable by individuals with motor disabilities. In reality, the necessary adaptations or devices
may not always be available in all settings.

*Mackenzie can get to any bathroom independently in her
power chair but often is unable to get through a standard
doorway, which is likely to be too narrow to accommodate her
chair. Sometimes when visiting a museum or another community building, she is unable to get in the building unassisted because of steps or a ramp that are too narrow for her
chair.*

Because all settings are not fully accessible or
don't accommodate all types of adaptive equipment,
therapists and others need to design secondary
strategies for overcoming these architectural barriers.
Lifting and carrying routines may be needed in some
settings even when individuals are independent in
others. Alternative ways of participating in physical
management routines should be in place for times
when communication aids malfunction, grab bars are
not present in the bathroom, or other environmental
circumstances change.

Well-selected and appropriately-used adaptive
equipment, such as a wheelchair, can promote an individual's ability to use assistive devices (e.g., grab
bars in the toilet area) to enhance participation and
independence. Partial or full independence in self-

care routines such as toileting, eating, bathing, or other care activities may be possible only through both adaptive equipment for positioning (e.g., wheelchairs, toilet chairs, bathing chairs) and accommodations and assistive devices, such as grab bars around the toilet, adapted handles on the sink faucets, special plates and utensils, bars around a person's bed, a washcloth mitt, or other such aids. When needed equipment and devices are not available, an individual may be more dependent in the routine. Procedures for these limited circumstances, as well as those in which all necessary assistance is present, should be designed by teams so that everyone knows what to do and how to do it when circumstances or settings are less than ideal.

> When Mackenzie needs to use a restroom in the community, her toileting routine is more difficult than when she is at home or at school. She is still able to communicate her needs with her communication device and get to the bathroom independently if she is positioned in her power wheelchair. Since her rhizotomy surgery, she is able to bear weight momentarily on her legs and feet, so it is possible to transfer her to a toilet using an assisted standing transfer, which can be managed by one adult. Before the surgery, her legs were so stiff and bent that Mackenzie was unable to physically help in the transfer and two people were needed to lift her onto or off of a toilet. Once on the toilet, someone has to hold her in place, which is not necessary at home or in school, where an adapted toilet chair is used.

Eating and Drinking

Some individuals have severe problems with eating and drinking and must be fed by caregivers to ensure sufficient nutritional intake or to eat safely. Gastrostomies or nasogastric tubes (described in chapter 7), which replace eating and drinking by mouth, are being used for an increasing number of problems, such as gastrointestinal reflux and compromised nutrition, in infants and other individuals (Campbell & Bailey, 1991). Tube feedings can be administered in a school or community setting without too much difficulty if gastrostomies or nasogastric tubes do not have to be inserted daily. Gravity feeding is less cumbersome than continuous pumped feeding, which requires a machine to pump specific amounts of nutritional substance over a preset period of time. Gravity feeding,

which allows the nutritional substance to fill the stomach by gravity, occurs periodically throughout the day.

Teachers, other professionals, or paraprofessionals should be trained to administer feedings and know precautions on a child-by-child basis (Campbell, 1995; Lehr & Noonan, 1989). In addition, a system to communicate between school and home should provide daily exchange of information about the feedings. Finally, attempts should be made to enable children to eat and drink orally, if oral feedings are possible. Parents, speech pathologists, occupational therapists, nutritionists, and physicians should be consulted to develop and monitor feeding programs (Campbell & Bailey, 1991). Many regional specialty medical centers operate feeding clinics to address the needs of the growing number of individuals who require specialized assistance with eating and nutrition.

Many procedures may help an individual eat and drink by using coordinated patterns of movement in the oral motor musculature (Morris & Klein, 1987; Orelove & Sobsey, 1996; Sobsey & Orelove, 1984). Some procedures help a child acquire better patterns of eating and drinking, while others simply make the individual easier to feed. Poorly coordinated movements during eating and drinking may result in gagging on food, choking or aspiration, or poor nutritional intake. Infants, children, and adults may push food out of their mouths with their tongues, have difficulties swallowing, or be unable to chew all foods. Any of these difficulties may increase the time it takes to eat a snack or meal and may make mealtimes unpleasant for both the individual being fed and the caregiver. Some children exert control over mealtimes in many of the same ways used by typically developing children. They may refuse particular types or textures of foods. They may spit food out, try to get out of their chairs, or push food off of the table or tray. Physical management techniques are useful when the issues seem to relate to the motor disabilities. Other approaches, such as behavior assessment, may be required in addition to physical management so that feeding can be a pleasurable experience and accomplished in a reasonable length of time (see chapter 6). Although specialized feeding techniques do not necessarily teach a child to chew or swallow, their use may make mealtimes easier and prevent choking, aspiration, or poor nutritional intake (and poor growth).

Positioning For Proper Feeding

Well-coordinated contractions of the oral motor muscles result in appropriate use of the lips, teeth, tongue, and jaw for eating and drinking (Morris & Klein, 1987). Since the muscles in the oral motor area are not able to contract in coordinated ways if posture is malaligned severely, particularly in the head and shoulders, alignment is the first step for implementing appropriate eating and drinking. Most individuals are fed in a seated position; therefore, alignment should start with the position of the pelvis and hips, which are the primary weight-bearing surfaces in sitting. The spine should align from the supporting base of the pelvis and hips to allow alignment of the head on an erect spine. Tommy is pictured in Figure 8–5. The adaptive seating equipment used with Tommy resulted in proper alignment of the head and neck.

Good alignment is achieved through proper positioning using specialized adaptive equipment where necessary (as illustrated in Figure 8–5). Many individuals have low postural tone in the head, neck, and

FIGURE 8–5
Positioning for Self-Feeding. Tommy is positioned for eating so that his head and neck are reasonably aligned with his trunk. This allows him to be able to move his arm more easily and for his mouth to remain in the same position while he is learning hand to mouth movement patterns required for spoon feeding.

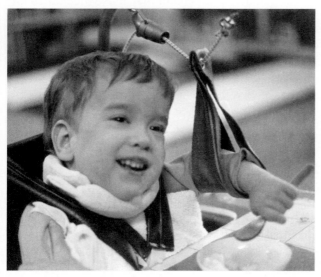

trunk and are unable to maintain the head in alignment on the spine. One method for helping an individual maintain head alignment is to tip the chair backward approximately 10° to 20°. This positioning prevents neck hyperextension (where the head falls backward onto the surface) and keeps the head in an upright position. Another method is to provide additional head and trunk supports. Towel rolls or pieces of foam rubber can be used to provide sufficient temporary supports for the head and trunk. In some instances, a soft cervical collar or an inflatable neck cushion assists in head positioning. Positioning of the head is important (and is dependent on positioning of the hips in a sitting position) because the oral-motor musculature is influenced by head position. When the head is held backward (or hyperextended), the mouth has a tendency to fall open, which makes chewing and swallowing difficult as well as allowing food or liquid to fall out of the mouth easily. If the head is too far forward or drops forward onto the chest, food and liquid may fall out of the mouth easily, as well. Proper alignment of the head makes it easier for food to stay in the mouth and for chewing and swallowing to be successful.

Positioning that also facilitates support for the arms may enable the individual to retain a stable trunk and head during feeding. Ideally, arm support is provided by seating the individual at a table, but wheelchair trays may also be used. Some infants or very young children are more easily fed when not sitting in a highchair or adaptive seating equipment but held by the person feeding them or positioned on the floor. Positions in which an older child is held or seated on the floor should be avoided unless no other position is possible, because these positions are stigmatizing in most school and community settings.

Approaches to Eating and Drinking

Many individuals have difficulty with jaw, lip, tongue, and other movements necessary to take food or liquids into the body. Other individuals have poor eating habits in general or use mealtimes to manipulate behavior of their caretakers. Eating problems are often the result of a combination of both oral-motor incoordination (attributable to motor disabilities) and behavior. Many of the oral-motor coordination difficulties that occur during eating and drinking are the result of the general motor disability. These coordination difficulties often are correctable through attaining proper body alignment. Proper head alignment (see Figure 8–5) changes the position of the jaw and lips, thereby allowing easier mouth closure, swallowing, and chewing. Speech pathologists and occupational therapists can help teachers and parents identify the primary problems that an individual demonstrates when trying to eat. After postural alignment has been addressed, the most appropriate approach for addressing eating difficulties may be selected or individually designed. Differentiating between eating problems that are behaviorally based and those that originate from neuromotor problems is not always easy. A movement such as a tongue thrust, which may be neurologically based, may be used by children (and even infants) functionally, for example, to communicate that the child does not want the food. Observational assessment procedures can help distinguish between neuromotor-based eating problems and behavior based problems and help parents, therapists, and teachers select the most appropriate intervention procedures.

A behavioral approach structures *antecedents* (the events that precede the desired behavior) and *consequences* (the events after the behavior) to enable the individual to manage food more appropriately. This approach works effectively with individuals who have poor eating habits, are exerting control over caregivers during mealtimes, or are using motor patterns for a function other than eating (e.g., communication). Generally, this approach views feeding behaviors, such as pushing food out of the mouth with the tongue and refusing to eat solid foods, as potentially having a function for the child, such as gaining attention, communicating about eating, or stopping the eating activity. Intervention procedures are designed with respect for the function the behavior is achieving (e.g., stopping the feeding activity) and focus on replacing the behavior (e.g., tongue thrusting) with a more appropriate form of behavior (e.g., another way of communicating that the child is all done now or wants a break). Chapter 6 includes information on functional assessment and positive behavior support procedures that can be used to design intervention approaches when children's eating disorders appear to be behavior-based.

A second approach incorporates neuromotor principles into methods used to develop oral-motor coordination (Morris & Klein, 1987). In this approach, problems with eating are viewed as resulting from dysfunction in the motor system. Movement patterns are carefully observed and classified in a detailed assessment completed by a therapist or trained teacher. Intervention methods are selected to normalize muscle tone in the jaw and mouth, if necessary, and to facilitate coordinated patterns of movement in the jaw, lips, and tongue for chewing and swallowing. Behavioral and neuromotor approaches can be combined when professionals work together with parents (and others) to design interventions that are appropriate for the unique characteristics of each child's eating disorder.

Neuromotor Methods to Promote Coordinated Eating and Drinking Patterns

A number of sequenced steps are used when designing interventions to establish the coordinated patterns of movement necessary for efficient eating and drinking.

Positioning

The first step in improving patterns of eating and drinking is to be sure that positioning results in as much body alignment as possible and that the head is in alignment with the shoulders. Only after these things have been accomplished will techniques specific to the oral motor area be maximally effective. However, muscle tone may vary during feeding, especially with students who have increased tone (hypertonus). A student who seems to be in alignment and have reasonable muscle tone may push back and become stiffer each time the spoon is brought to the mouth or may do so when the food on the spoon is something that the child does not want to eat. In some instances, these tone changes are communicating a message (e.g., child does not like food, does not want more, is being fed too quickly) and, in other instances, the tone changes are "involuntary" and are occurring beyond the child's control. When tone changes are associated with a functional purpose for the child (e.g., the tone changes are communicative), the strategies described further in chapters 6, 11, and 12 are used so that a more appropriate way is found to express the function. When tone changes are not communicative (i.e., the child is not expressing a message through tonal changes) a number of strategies may be used to maintain postural tone during feeding. In sitting, for example, a hand placed below the sternum allows a caregiver to use small (subtle) weight shifts across the body midline to reduce excessive muscle tone. Slight downward pressure of the hand on the chest area can facilitate better alignment of the head throughout the meal. Therapists can show teachers and parents the best ways of maintaining tone and alignment throughout the meal when the tone changes are not communicative.

Tommy (see Figure 8–5) has been very difficult to feed since he was an infant. He is now beginning to learn to feed himself part of a meal using a spoon. His positioning during eating supports and assists him to bring the food to his mouth independently. The supports from the chair hold him upright and the assistive device of an arm sling supports his arm against gravity so that he is able to move the spoon to his mouth. When Tommy was younger, his mother described him as "very fussy" during eating and as very difficult to feed. The therapist worked with Tommy and his mother (and other caregivers) so that Tommy learned to vocalize before each spoonful of food that the adult was feeding him. This allowed Tommy to express his "readiness" for the next mouthful and also to select or reject foods that were being fed to him. Tommy's teacher in his day care center uses these same strategies when she is feeding Tommy. Even though Tommy

can bring the spoon to his mouth, he is unable to scoop the food. His caregivers now ask him simple questions, such as "More applesauce?," before assisting him to scoop.

Identify Utensils

The second step is to experiment with eating utensils, bottles, or cups and with various types and textures of foods. Some examples of the different types of spoons and cups that are commonly available are illustrated in Figure 8–6. Some bottles or cups, for example, force the head backward to take in the liquid. Other adaptations, such as bottle straws, allow the bottle to remain upright even when an infant is sucking liquid from the bottom of the bottle. Some nipples work better than others when infants have difficulty sucking. Nipples vary a lot in shape and size, changing the intensity of sucking required to get the liquid. Similarly, cups frequently require the head to be positioned backward because of the shape of the cup. Making a cut out in the cup for the nose (or purchasing one with a cut out) allows the head to remain in an upright (not tilted back) position throughout drinking.

Selecting the most appropriate spoon is very important. Spoons vary a lot in terms of what they are made of, the size and depth of the bowl of the spoon, and the length of the handle. Simply changing from one spoon to another that is better suited to the

FIGURE 8–6
Types of Eating Utensils for Mealtimes

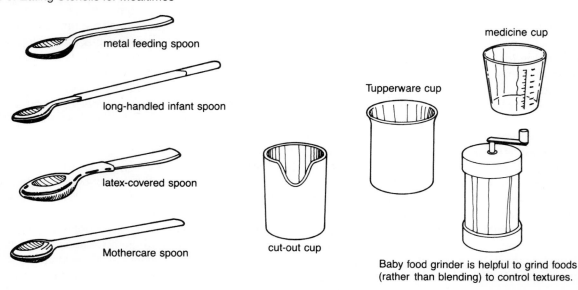

metal feeding spoon

long-handled infant spoon

latex-covered spoon

Mothercare spoon

cut-out cup

Tupperware cup

medicine cup

Baby food grinder is helpful to grind foods (rather than blending) to control textures.

child's needs may make feeding much easier. The mouth area is one of the most sensitive areas in the body. Metal spoons retain heat or cold and may not be ideal for children who do not tolerate temperature variations in the mouth. Spoons that are latex-covered or made of soft plastic may work much better. Other children do better with small amounts of food and are fed more easily from a spoon with a small bowl. When lip movement is a problem, a student may be able to take food off the spoon with the upper lip much more easily when the spoon has a shallow bowl. Occupational therapists, speech language pathologists, or others who specialize in feeding can help parents and teachers explore the range of options that are available. Many of these items are easily purchased in infant stores or departments. Others are available through specialized catalogs.

Determine the Easiest Consistency of Foods or Liquids

Foods or liquids of particular consistencies may be more difficult or more easy for a person to eat. Thickened liquids, for example, are easier for many children to drink from a cup than are thin liquids, such as water or juice. Thickening milk by making a milkshake or apple juice by adding applesauce may make it possible for a child to drink more easily. A blender may be helpful in experimenting with the thickness of liquids as well as for varying the consistency of foods. Grinders also allow food consistency to be changed easily by grinding table foods to different consistencies. The most difficult food consistencies for many students to manage are foods of mixed consistencies, such as vegetable soup or other similar types of soup or macaroni and cheese.

> Tommy (see Figure 8–5) has been learning to feed himself part of a meal using a spoon. Caregivers hold the cup to his lips so that he can drink and still assist with part of the meal. Tommy's muscle tone fluctuates from low tone in the head and trunk to high tone in the arms and legs. Although he is learning to bring the spoon to his mouth and is able to do so assisted by a special spoon and an arm support, he eats foods that have been ground to an even consistency so that complex chewing is not required. These foods stick to the spoon as he is bringing it to his mouth and are easier for him to take off the spoon with his lips. He uses a soft plastic spoon (not a picnic-type hard plastic spoon, which is easily broken) with a built-up handle that has a shallow bowl. The soft plastic protects his teeth and gums if he locks onto the spoon caused by spasticity in the jaw. The built-up handle makes the spoon easier for him to hold.

Techniques to Facilitate Muscle Coordination

The fourth step involves using techniques and procedures designed to improve or facilitate coordination in the jaw, lips, tongue, face, and throat muscles. The muscles in the face and throat, used for eating, drinking, and intelligible speech, produce finely coordinated and highly complex patterns of movement. Therefore, it is important not to start with these techniques but to use them after positioning has been achieved and appropriate utensils are available. Many procedures have been used to teach individuals to accept foods of varying textures, take food from a spoon or fork, or use appropriate tongue movements for chewing or swallowing foods or liquids (French, Gonzalez, & Tronson-Simpson, 1991; Morris and Klein, 1987; Wolf & Glass, 1992). The procedures are individualized to a student's unique pattern of eating or drinking. Specific procedures to normalize tone in the muscles in the face, head, and neck and to promote coordinated use of the oral musculature may be helpful. Speech language pathologists, occupational therapists, or others who have completed training for working with feeding disorders can design and demonstrate eating and drinking routines to improve feeding of individuals in school, at home, or in other settings.

Nutrition

Most people have specific likes and dislikes in food. Others resist specific foods because of sensory characteristics (e.g., temperature, taste, texture). Many individuals with severe neuromotor problems lack sufficient intake of proper foods and liquid because eating and drinking are difficult and time-consuming. These restricted food preferences may lead to poor nutrition, which can result in diminished growth, weight problems, and poor health (Farber, Yanni, & Batshaw, 1997).

Nutrition should be a component of all eating routines but is of critical importance for infants and for individuals who are highly medicated, difficult to feed, or showing poor rates of growth (i.e., height, weight, head growth). Many individuals with complex feeding issues are likely to receive services through a special multidisciplinary feeding clinic team. Early intervention and public school personnel should co-ordinate their efforts with the family and with other professionals. When the amount of food or the nutritional content of what a student is able to eat are in question, nutritional consultations can be obtained, through local hospitals, and visiting nurse agencies, and other home health providers. These consultations can provide information about ways to expand the nutritional content of what a student is eating, maximize caloric intake (if this is necessary), and generally ensure good nutrition.

Independent Eating and Drinking

Instruction leading to independent eating and drinking skills should be initiated as soon as possible (i.e., at 7 to 9 months of age) and when sufficient arm movement is present to bring a spoon to the mouth. Some children may learn to feed themselves independently, but when motor disabilities are severe, self-feeding may allow at least partial participation in eating and drinking. Arm slings (as illustrated in Figure 8–5) and other adaptations may be fabricated to make the movement of the hand to the mouth easier for some individuals. Special feeding devices, such as a bowl or plate that automatically turns to provide the movement necessary to scoop food, are available commercially for individuals who lack sufficient arm movement. The use of devices does not automatically result in independence during mealtimes. Many individuals, especially those with cognitive disabilities, need to be taught to use the devices to feed themselves. Systematic procedures, illustrated next with Tommy (and further described in chapter 9), must be used to teach individuals with movement disorders to eat and drink.

Tommy's child care provider and his mother work on self-feeding when Tommy is having a snack. Snack time has been selected because only a small quantity of food is eaten. Tommy might be able to eat all of the snack by himself eventually, thereby becoming independent at snack time even though he will continue to need assistance during meals. Tommy's self-feeding program requires considerable adaptations, which may not be available in all locations where he may be eating. He needs a special chair to control his posture and head as well as the arm sling to assist him in getting the spoon to his mouth. Both his day care teacher and his mother select foods for snack that Tommy will be able to manage

both on the spoon and in his mouth. Because it motivates Tommy to have peer models and because his teacher does not want him to be "different" from other children, all children in his day care class eat spoon foods during snack. Pudding and applesauce and other similarly prepared fruits have been very popular. Right now, Tommy needs assistance with scooping. An adult guides him through the scooping, using a special bowl that makes scooping easier. Tommy has learned to put the spoon in his mouth and seldom requires any specific direction to do so. Rather, he watches the other children and follows their lead.

Oral-motor competence is not a prerequisite to learning self-feeding skills. Coordination of certain oral movement patterns, however, enhances instruction in self-feeding. For example, a student who is unable to use the lips and teeth to get food from a utensil when being fed by another person will have this same difficulty getting food into the mouth even when the student may be able to bring the utensil to her mouth without assistance. Problems with tongue movement make it difficult to move food from the front of the mouth to the side for chewing and to the back for swallowing. Some individuals compensate for poorly coordinated tongue movement by pushing the food around in the mouth with the fingers or using the spoon to push foods.

Bringing food to the mouth may increase muscle tone for some individuals with severe physical disabilities. This situation has been labeled as "anticipation" (Mueller, 1975), and it results in poorly coordinated oral movement patterns. For instance, with anticipation, increased tone may cause an individual's body to move away from the food and spoon, the jaw to open widely, and the tongue to pull back in the mouth. Each of these patterns make removal of food from the spoon, chewing, and swallowing almost impossible to accomplish without choking. In these instances, children should be "desensitized" to stimuli approaching their faces. During feeding, the caregiver can prepare the child by talking about the food coming or may construct a signal that a child can use to say that they are ready for a next bite or more food. Giving an individual control over when the stimuli (food) will be presented prepares the child for what is going to happen next.

In each individual, tone changes, postural stability, coordinated movement of the oral musculature, and hand-to-mouth movement patterns should be assessed by a professional such as an occupational therapist or speech language pathologist before a decision to teach self-feeding skills is made. Food is a reinforcer for many (but not all) individuals. Teaching an individual to self-feed but to eat with poorly coordinated movements strengthens the behavior of poor oral-motor coordination. However, preventing acquisition of self-feeding skills may result in learned helplessness. Parents and professionals should weigh all factors carefully so that they can design effective overall programming strategies for each situation.

Toileting

Individuals with movement dysfunction can be toilet trained using standard procedures (such as those described in chapter 9) with consideration of several additional factors (Finnie, 1975). Proper positioning is an essential component in effective toileting. Of particular importance are muscle tone, alignment, and postural control in the muscles of the pelvis, hips, and trunk. Reasonably normal degrees of tone must be attained for elimination. For example, individuals with hypertonus, particularly in the pelvis, hips, and legs, may have even greater increases of tone during toileting, thereby preventing elimination. An individual with low tone may lack the muscle contractions necessary for effective bowel and bladder elimination. Proper positioning can promote alignment while providing postural support. Therefore, as with other self-care routines, a first step is to make sure that the individual is properly positioned for the routine.

Adaptive equipment can assist a student to sit appropriately for toileting. Many types of toileting equipment are commercially available (see Figure 8–7 for one example). Additional modifications (e.g., towel roll supports or pads) may be necessary to ensure proper support and alignment when using commercial equipment.

Most toileting areas of community buildings have been modified for use by people in wheelchairs by installing grab bars and high toilets to make independent transfer from a wheelchair easier (or in some cases, possible). These bathroom facilities, however, may not be easily used with children with severe motor disabilities who may need supports for sitting in addition to facilitated transfer.

FIGURE 8–7
Adapted Toilet Chairs Position Comfortably for Toileting

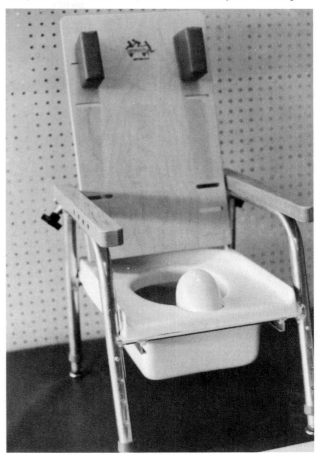

Mackenzie is learning assisted transfer from her power chair (and her regular wheelchair) at school. One bathroom in her high school has been equipped with grab bars and with the special toilet adaptation that Mackenzie needs in order to sit. Although she is able to lean forward and grasp the grab bars, she needs assistance to get out of the chair, turn, manage her clothing, and seat herself on the adapted toilet insert. Mackenzie will probably never be fully independent in toileting because many of the places where she will need to use the bathroom will not have the special adaptations and equipment that are required for her to become independent. However, as Mackenzie learns to assist with the transfer, managing her toileting routine is easier for the caregiver. When Mackenzie was much younger, her mother and her preschool teachers worked to teach her to communicate when

she needed to use the bathroom. They used a Big Mac switch, programming it to say "I need to pee" and making it available to Mackenzie throughout the day. They also made sure that she drank a lot of liquid and that they knew approximately what times during the day she was likely to need to use the toilet. Then, they asked her if she needed to go to the bathroom and prompted her arm movement onto the switch. As soon as Mackenzie activated the switch, the adults lifted her from wherever she was positioned and carried her to a special potty chair. They left her on the chair for a few minutes, using rewards and attention when she was successful.

Another factor that must be considered in toileting is nutritional intake. The amount of liquid that is taken in during the day is of critical importance. Many individuals, particularly those with severe eating problems, consume little liquid during a day. Elimination may be so infrequent as to make training difficult. Specific elimination patterns can be identified by taking baseline data to determine the approximate times during the day, the frequency, and the type of elimination (see chapter 9). Providing liquids approximately every half hour during the day (and particularly in the morning) may be helpful to increase the number of opportunities per day for training.

Many individuals with severe movement dysfunction have particular difficulty with bowel elimination. These difficulties may be associated with poor nutritional intake, medication side effects, physical immobility, poor muscle tone, or other factors (Batshaw, 1997; Orelove & Sobsey, 1996). A person with chronic constipation has great difficulty in acquiring bowel continence. Problems with constipation can be managed through increased liquid intake, adding high fiber foods to the diet, and using mild natural laxatives, such as prune juice. A stool softener can be used as a laxative, or a stronger laxative may be suggested by a physician.

Teachers and parents often do not begin toilet training with a child because of the difficulties that they encounter in positioning or because they do not see the child as "ready" or they generally underestimate the training potential. Fully independent toileting involves not only elimination on the toilet but also communication of toileting needs, mobility to the bathroom, independent transfer onto the toilet, and management of clothing. Although many individuals with motor disabilities are not able to achieve total independence in the toileting sequence, most can at least partially participate in the routine and become regulated to a toileting schedule or be able to communicate the need to use the bathroom. Studies of specific toilet training procedures indicate that most individuals can be trained to some extent, regardless of the cognitive level (see chapter 9 for more information on these procedures).

Dressing

Dressing and undressing without assistance are extremely complex movement tasks. Many of the required motor patterns involve movements of the extremities away from the trunk of the body. Managing fastenings, in contrast, requires finely coordinated manipulation of the fingers. In addition, these gross- and fine-motor movements must be performed while moving from one posture to another. An individual may put on or remove shirts or jackets while in a sitting position; however, to pull pants up or down, the individual must be able to roll or stand. Many individuals with severe movement disorders will always require assistance to dress or undress, but caregivers can use a number of procedures to normalize muscle tone and to facilitate participation.

Positioning for Dressing and Undressing

Typically, children above the chronological age of 12 to 18 months should be dressed and undressed in a sitting position. Sitting is a chronologically age-appropriate position from which to learn necessary arm movements in a less passive position than back lying. Supported sitting, achieved either with equipment or adult support, is necessary for individuals who are unable to sit independently or balance in a sitting position using the trunk muscles. Individuals who need to use their arms to hold themselves upright in sitting are unable to use their arms for movements in and out of clothing and should be supported by equipment or caregivers to allow arm movements.

A variety of types of adaptive equipment may be used to support students who are able to balance in a sitting position and move their arms and legs. Individuals who lack sitting balance or who require

FIGURE 8–8
Promoting Participation in Dressing. During dressing, an adult can hold a small child on the floor to provide postural support for the child and facilitate participation in dressing and undressing.

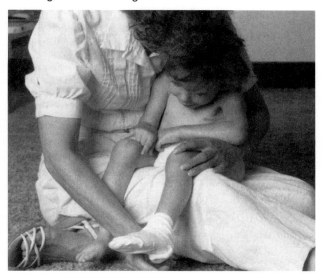

considerable guidance of arm and leg movements can be provided with postural support as is illustrated with the 2-year-old in Figure 8–8. By positioning the child in a sitting position on the adult's legs, the adult is able to provide postural support and maintain this child's muscle tone so that she does not become more stiff during dressing. Alternate positions that can be used for dressing and undressing can be found in Conner, Williamson, and Siepp (1978) and Finnie (1975).

Some activities, such as changing diapers and dressing or undressing infants, cannot be accomplished well with an individual in a sitting position. Changing diapers when infants or young children are lying on their backs is easiest. However, some children with spasticity may become stiffer when placed on their backs. Placing a small pillow under the head or applying pressure with the hands on the chest while bending the individual's hips and legs toward the chest may help reduce stiffness in the legs and make managing the diaper easier. Many children will be easier to lift and carry after diaper changing if moved first from a back lying to a sitting position and then lifted and carried.

Selecting Clothing

As with other self-care activities, careful selection or adaptation of clothing can be very helpful in maximizing participation in dressing or undressing. Some types of clothing are hard to get on or off of any child who is being dressed or undressed. Looser fitting clothing (such as sweat suits), elastic-waisted pants or skirts, or tops with large-sized necks or button fronts or backs are easier to manage for the child or caregiver than more tightly fitted clothing. Most parents of children with motor disabilities learn early on and through experience to purchase easy-to-manage clothing. As children get older, these types of clothing may be more difficult to find or may not match what typical peers are wearing. Adaptations are very helpful in these circumstances. For example, the back of a turtleneck top may be split and hemmed and Velcro fasteners may be sewed to the edges to make dressing and undressing easier. There are also several mail order companies that make fashionable clothing for children and adults with disabilities.

Facilitating Dressing and Undressing

Physical or graduated guidance procedures are used to teach performance of necessary movement patterns for dressing and undressing (see chapter 9 for additional descriptions). Guidance is provided to inhibit stiffness and poorly coordinated patterns of movement and promote coordinated movement patterns. This type of guidance, referred to as *facilitation*, may result in three positive outcomes: (a) the individual being dressed or undressed is partially participating in the activity; (b) individuals whose movements are guided using facilitation methods may be prevented from developing further problems, such as limitations in range of motion of the joints, and (c) repetitive practice of the proper movement patterns may enable individuals to learn to perform the necessary movements as a component of partial or total independence in dressing.

Physical and occupational therapists can design individualized facilitation procedures so that the particular needs of an individual are best addressed. The following general principles, however, can be incorporated during dressing or undressing.

1. Most individuals are best guided by movement from the shoulder or hips (e.g., caregivers can

guide an individual's arm through a sleeve, by moving the arm from the shoulder rather than by pulling the hand through the sleeve).

2. Slow guidance maintains tone better than fast movement, which may produce spasticity; therefore, caregivers should guide the extremities slowly through the clothing rather than quickly.

3. Tone may increase in some individuals when they attempt to initiate movement, so that the effort of producing a required movement may increase arm and leg stiffness and prevent movement from occurring; caregivers can assist individuals who experience this difficulty by guiding the initiation but

letting the individual finish the movement pattern without further assistance.

These procedures will assist in dressing or undressing routines but are not sufficient by themselves as ways of teaching the skills required to be independent. Positioning and facilitation must be combined with specific dressing training procedures (see chapter 9).

Managing Fastenings

Shoelaces, buttons, zippers, belts, and other fastenings require degrees of movement coordination that many individuals with severe motor disabilities are not able to perform. Typical fastenings can be easily avoided by either selecting appropriate clothing or modifying existing clothing. Velcro fasteners in place of shoestrings, buttons, or metal waistband fasteners, for example, may allow independence in dressing without performance of fine manipulations. Additional modifications to make dressing easier are suggested in Table 8–4.

Getting Help from Therapists and Other Specialists: Working as a Team

Occupational and physical therapists, as well as speech and language pathologists and assistive device specialists, and professionals from other disciplines, such as rehabilitation engineers, nurses, or respiratory therapists, may all have specialized information and resources to contribute to developing physical management routines for particular individuals. Therapists and others whose training has been primarily individual-based may approach students with motor disabilities from a standpoint of improving or developing particular motor skills that will, when learned, eventually enable participation in the same activities and in the same ways that typical people participate. Such an approach does not work well when individuals have severe motor disabilities and may never learn the skills used by people without motor problems nor participate in activities in the same ways that typical people do.

Tommy's older brother Steven plays soccer in a community league. Tommy has attended these games since he was an infant and may want to participate when he is old enough for

TABLE 8–4
Clothing Modifications

Problem	Modification
Individual has trouble getting arms through sleeves	Select short-sleeved shirts Select shirts without tight sleeves (short or long), raglan sleeves are good
Individual has trouble buttoning shirt	Select shirts that zip partway down the front Replace buttonholes with Velcro closings Select shirts with large buttons
Individual has trouble getting legs into pants	Select short-legged pants Select pants with wide legs
Individual has trouble getting pants over braces	Slit the pants up the inside of the legs and insert snap tapes, Velcro fasteners, or zipper closings
Individual has trouble with elastic waists	Select pants with waistbands (loose, not tight)
Individual has trouble with fastening pants	Replace the button or hook fastening with Velcro
Individual has trouble with belt	Select a belt with a cinch fastening or with pull-through fastening
Individual has trouble with zippers	Select clothing that zips in the *front* only Use a ring attached to the zipper for easier grasping and pulling
Individual has trouble with buttons (on pants, shirts, jackets, and sweaters)	Replace buttonholes with Velcro fasteners Select clothing without buttons

the league. Though Tommy will never run or kick a ball, there may be ways that he can participate in sports through the community league. Another sport may be easier to adapt for Tommy's physical participation. For example, in baseball, he may be able to attempt hitting the baseball by using a T-ball support. He may be able to be on the swim team, where adaptations will allow him to stay afloat and move his arms and legs. At the least, if sufficient adaptations cannot be made to support his physical participation, he may be able to be the scorekeeper, equipment manager, or time keeper or participate in the team in some way other than by playing the actual sport, but this will only occur if specialists work toward facilitating his participation in whatever ways are possible for him.

The activities that a particular person participates in are linked directly to settings (or environments) in neighborhoods and communities where the individual spends time. When children are young, those activities are influenced by decisions and preferences of their families as well as by opportunity. Children who attend typical child care, preschool, or regular education programs or adults who work in typical work settings have more opportunities for a wider range of experiences and social contacts than do children whose education is based in special settings or individuals who are employed in sheltered workshops. Promoting participation in activities that take place in home, child care, school, community, or work settings results from a collaboration among the individual, the family, specialists, and the people associated with the particular activity or setting.

Tommy wants to swim in the preschool swimming program in his neighborhood recreation center. For this to happen easily, collaboration must occur among the swimming instructor, Tommy's family, and the specialists. The outcome of the collaboration is not to increase Tommy's motor skills, necessarily, but to allow him to benefit from participation in the swimming program. Tommy's participation will be facilitated through management routines for dressing and undressing, toileting, lifting, carrying, and positioning and potentially may require modification of the swimming setting or of the typical activities done during swimming.

Teams need a framework to guide decision making about children's participation and programming within the context of activities and routines that are typical of a particular setting. Special education and related services personnel may use typical home, school, and community settings for special instruction and therapy methods that will enable students to attain their IFSP or IEP goals and objectives. A "best fit" with the activities, routines, and people in typical settings may not occur when specialists try to use these methods, many of which are dependent on one-on-one interactions between adults and students, in typical environments. Many of these methods have been designed and used within clinical or specialized educational settings and do not necessarily adapt well to typical contexts where adult-child ratios may be larger and where there is a focus for the activity as a whole rather than a focus on individual goals. A first goal for all specialists is to ensure that a child is fully included in the activities and routines that typify a particular setting such as a child care center, home, community recreation program, amusement park, library, or neighborhood school (York-Barr, Rainforth, & Locke, 1996). A second goal is to create opportunities for individualized learning.

Specialists, families, and community program personnel can use the diagram in Figure 8–9 to aid in making decisions about the best ways to ensure full inclusion of a person with a disability as well as to determine opportunities for addressing the individual's special learning and therapeutic needs. The diagram starts with identification of desired outcomes. Outcomes may be identified by the student, family members, child care providers, peers and friends, teachers, or other people who spend time with the person. Person-centered planning processes such as the McGill Action Planning System, commonly known as MAPS (Vandercook, York, & Forest, 1989), or discussion with students, their family members (when students are young), or a team that includes both the student and family members can be used to identify desired outcomes. Outcomes are not necessarily written as goals but often represent a broader context or framework for specific goals. For example, when parents and children identify desired outcomes, they are likely to use the context of their family's values, roles, priorities, and concerns as a framework. Outcomes are likely to be expressions of things they would like to change (e.g., "I wish I understood better what John is trying to tell me" or "I'd like be able to bathe Shawn more easily") or things they would like to do (e.g., "We go skiing a lot and we want Susie to be able to do this with us"). Outcomes may be classified as activities (e.g., go skiing), routines (e.g., bathe more easily), or

FIGURE 8–9
This diagram provides a framework for making decisions about whether and when to embed motor learning into activities and routines. A first step is to find out about activities and routines that may not be going well, so that the routine or activity itself can be improved through adaptations or other means. Routines and activities that are going well provide opportunities for learning and a context in which to embed motor learning strategies.

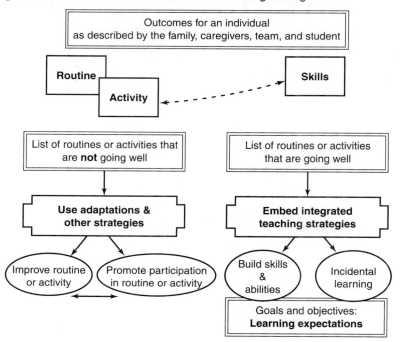

skills (e.g., communicate more clearly). When professionals identify goals for students, they, too, use their experiences with a child as a contextual framework. This perspective typically emphasizes skills that come from the developmental or other types of evaluations they have used as a basis for understanding a child's needs. Professionals are more likely to identify outcomes and goals that are descriptive of skill learning (e.g., walk without support, eat with a spoon, activate a toy with a switch device, communicate with peers).

One outcome is for Tommy to participate in a community preschool swimming program. Tommy's family enjoys and values sports. Each member of the family is involved in some sort of community sports activity, so it is logical that Tommy's family would want to create opportunities for Tommy to participate in sporting activities. Tommy is interested in sports because he has been involved in attending sporting activities with other family members, and he wants to go swimming. However, it is not necessarily a goal for Tommy to learn to swim or to be able to participate in swim-

ming fully independently nor is this an activity that is going to be provided by his child care program or by the team of professionals who provide services to Tommy through his local school district. Rather, the school district team will provide the consultation and assistance necessary to enable Tommy to participate in the community preschool swim program.

The school team working with Tommy started by using the framework outlined in Figure 8–9 to solve problems regarding Tommy's participation in swimming and to identify opportunities within swimming for him to learn and practice goals and objectives included on his IEP. They viewed the swimming program as (a) a setting that included activities and routines in which Tommy could participate and (b) a setting that included opportunities for Tommy to learn and practice IEP goals and objectives. The first step in their problem-solving analysis was to talk with the swim program personnel *to identify any activities and routines that were not going well. The second step was to use adaptations and other strategies to improve routines and ac-*

tivities that were not going well so that Tommy could participate in these activities and routines. The third step was *to identify activities and routines that were going well* so that these activities and routines could provide a context in which Tommy could learn specific skills. The fourth step was *to decide which skills would be taught using specific intervention techniques* within the context of activities and routines that were going well.

In many settings, particular aspects of routines and activities may not be going well for any child, including the child with a disability (Figure 8–10). For example, in child care and preschool settings, transition from one activity (e.g., art) to another (e.g., snack) is often difficult, even without children with disabilities.

In Tommy's swim program, the routine of getting the children undressed and in their suits and into the pool area and into the pool was confusing and somewhat chaotic for everyone. The specialists who were working with Tommy talked to the swim teacher and asked her to identify what was going well and not so well. In the process of this discussion, the teacher described the swimming activities as going well and the routine of getting into the pool as needing to go better. Tommy's team used the framework in Figure 8–10 to identify adaptations and other strategies that would improve the routine generally and that would promote Tommy's participation specifically. The special education teacher visited the swim class and observed that all of the children and their caregivers did not necessarily get undressed and into their suits at the same time, so that some children were ready and in the pool area before other children. The swim teacher tried to have these children line up but they became fidgety while waiting for the other children (who were not yet ready). The special education teacher talked with the swim teacher and they decided to try placing rubber mats next to the pool (environmental modification) so that each child would have his or her own mat and would sit down next to the pool when they were ready. In this way, children were not milling around, they were using a familiar routine (e.g., sit on a mat), and they could still splash their feet in the water while they were waiting. The teachers also decided to have Tommy come early to the program so that there would be plenty of time for him to get his swimsuit on and he would be ready at the same time as the other children (adapting the schedule). His mother agreed to dress him at home in his swimsuit with other loose-fitting clothes on top so that the time required to change his clothes would be lessened. By improving the routine of getting into the pool for all children and for Tommy, opportunities were created for Tommy to practice skills (e.g.,

reaching, forward and backward weight shifts), which were embedded within the routine of preparing for the swim program.

Individuals with motor disabilities may be prevented from participating in a variety of community programs when physical management needs are not easily met (Figure 8–10). For example, any difficulty in getting Tommy undressed or dressed; managing his toileting needs; or lifting, carrying, and positioning

FIGURE 8–10

Hierarchy of Strategies for Accommodations and Adaptations. Adaptations and other types of strategies may be used to improve activities or routines that are not going well in classroom, school, home, or community settings. The outcome of these strategies is to: (a) improve the overall activity or routine for all students in a particular setting and (b) promote participation of the person with a physical disability in the routine or activity. The least intrusive strategies, such as environmental accommodations, are used first, so that students with physical disabilities are not removed from an activity or setting to do something different until all other strategies have failed.

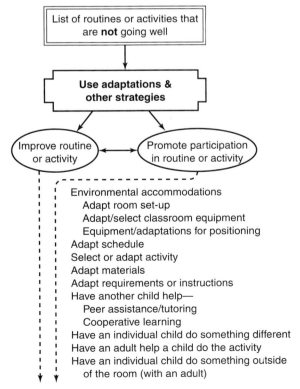

him in the pool area or in the water may become obstacles to his participation in the swimming activity.

*Tommy's mother or babysitter dresses and undresses him in
the locker room for the pool. The adult straddles the bench and
sits Tommy on the end of the bench between the adult's legs.
By leaning forward, the adult is able to control the position of
Tommy's hips and pelvis, keeping them forward to prevent his
legs from stiffening. (If his legs became too spastic, he would
be difficult to control and might slip off the bench). In this position, the adult's hands are free to move Tommy's arms and
legs, using facilitation techniques taught by the physical therapist and making the activity of dressing or undressing one
in which specific therapeutic intervention methods were used
to promote practice of specific skills (e.g., reach forward, forward and backward weight shifts). After Tommy's clothes
have been removed and he is in his swimming trunks, the
adult places her arm under his thighs and stands up, lifting
Tommy at the same time. He is now in a good position in
which to be carried to the swimming pool. Tommy's undressing is going so well that the therapist has suggested that
Tommy may be able to move his own arms out of the shirt
sleeves when taking his shirt off or to stand up, assisted, from
sitting on the bench so that he can walk a few steps assisted
before being carried the rest of the way into the pool. Tommy
will be learning to move his arms and to get to a standing position and move his legs by himself, skills that are identified
as important goals on his IEP. It would be very difficult to use
the undressing routine as an opportunity for new skill learning if getting ready for swimming were not going well, not
just for Tommy but for all the children in the swimming class.*

The same process (Figure 8-10) is applied to resolve
Mackenzie's physical management needs during a Girl
Scout troop outing.

*When Mackenzie was in fifth grade, her Girl Scout troop was
going to visit a farm house, a hands-on museum about living on a farm. The two-story farm house had been built in
the early 1900s, presenting innumerable architectural barriers to her participation. Many routines, such as positioning,
lifting, and toileting, were going to be difficult in this situation. The obvious "solutions" were: (a) having Mac miss the
trip or (b) having her mother go along, so that someone
would be available to lift, carry, and give assistance. Instead,
Mackenzie's mom and the scout leader used the process outlined in Figure 8–10 to create better solutions. First, they
considered adapting the environment. Environmental modifications were not possible in the farmhouse setting, but it
was possible to position Mac in her regular wheelchair, one*

*that was lighter and smaller, instead of her power chair so
that she could remain seated and be moved easily around the
first floor of the museum by another member of her troop
(equipment/adaptations for positioning). The troop leader
called ahead to tell the museum about Mac's abilities and
ask about the activities that would take place at the museum,
so that materials and modifications could be brainstormed
ahead of the visit. The troop made cookies in the farmhouse
kitchen. Mac was able to slip her hand through the large
handles of the old-fashioned cookie cutters and cut out cookies using a large breadboard that was placed across her knees
(adapt materials). A partner used a spatula to move the
cookies onto the cookie sheet. Fortunately, the farmhouse had
a large bathroom on the first floor. Mac could be pushed into
the bathroom and lifted onto the toilet. While she was not
wonderfully positioned, her friend Susan sat on the toilet behind Mac and the troop leader supported Mackenzie from the
front and then lifted her back into her chair (adult assistance). Mackenzie is usually transported in her power chair
in her family's van, which is equipped with a lift. For the
farmhouse trip, she used a special adult-sized support seat
(i.e., car seat) borrowed from a local equipment exchange
program that her therapist knew about and rode in a regular car (equipment/adaptations for positioning).*

*For this visit, Mackenzie's needs were managed without
her mother being required to attend the field trip and without
total adult assistance. More lifting and carrying than normal were needed, because all the special equipment and
adaptations that Mackenzie uses were not available or not
possible at the farmhouse. Mac's therapist spent time one afternoon after school with the Girl Scout troop and showed the
troop leaders how to lift and carry Mac easily and how to
make sure that she was positioned well in her regular chair.
This information was helpful to her troop leaders, who previously had not needed to lift or carry her, because Mac attended the troop meetings in her power chair.*

Specialists have information about ways to adapt
environments or settings as well as ideas about the positions that may work best for an individual with motor
disabilities in a particular circumstance. They know,
also, how to adapt materials or change the sequence
of steps in a routine or alter its requirements.
Teachers, family members, and other adults who interact with children with motor disabilities can see specialists as sources of information and ideas that may
help another adult manage physical needs easily and
with limited effort. Managing care routines easily and
efficiently requires adaptations and skill. Knowing how

to lift a student, for example, is only one part of the process; the second part is carrying it out correctly. The implementation phase requires motor skill and practice on the part of the adults. Many therapists have so many years of experience in using these techniques that they are able to do them automatically. Practice of any motor skill is important because it leads to competence, making the skill easier to use over time.

Many therapists are only now learning how to change their roles and function as consultants (not just direct providers of one-on-one interventions) and are collaborating with teachers and family members to make sure that students' physical needs are managed easily and efficiently. When specialists do not ask how routines are working or what activities in a classroom, home, or community setting are going well or not so well, teachers and parents must communicate this information and ask for assistance. The resources, information, and expertise that specialists may provide make caring for children much easier and expand their opportunities for participating in a wide array of activities. Many families alter their activities because they can't figure out how to do them and include their child with a disability. When specialists help families figure out how their children can participate on the playground or in the local park, or ways to go camping or what to do so a child can ride in an amusement park, children's social and environmental experiences are broadened as are their opportunities for learning. Similarly, when regular education teachers can share with specialists what is difficult within the context of their classrooms, specialists may contribute strategies that will make the situation successful rather than stressful. Problem solving by individuals with various backgrounds and expertise is important. Many of the issues that teams need to address do not have "known" solutions. Rather, the team may have to generate what seems to be an optimal solution (Rainforth & York-Barr, 1997).

When routines and activities are not going well, a first strategy that many adults use is to view the situation as "unworkable" or "not possible," essentially

 Integrated Therapy

Box 8–1

Until recently, most therapy services have been provided to students *directly;* that is, most therapists work one-on-one with students either in their classrooms or in other environments of the school. In many instances, therapists establish their own goals (e.g., physical therapy goals), which may or may not be related to those established by a student's teacher or other therapists, and then work with students individually or in small groups to provide the types of interventions that will assist the student to achieve therapy goals. More recently, therapists have begun to provide *consultation* in addition to direct therapy. When providing consultation, therapists collaborate with teachers, family members, and others to: (a) promote a student's participation in home, school, and community settings and (b) show others how to work on a student's goals within the context of home, school, or community environments.

Integrated therapy is a term that has gained increasing popularity as a way of describing an approach to providing therapy services for infants, toddlers, and students of all ages. Integrated therapy does not describe a particular model for providing therapy services but is a general term used to describe a variety of approaches, most of which share the following features:

- One set of functional goals are outlined on the IFSP or IEP and various services or disciplines contribute their unique expertise and perspective to teaching and learning.
- Services are provided within the context of activities and routines that occur in various home, school, or community settings; that is, students are not removed from typical activities to receive therapy services.
- All the professionals in disciplines associated with a child's or student's needs collaborate together and with the family to determine priorities, plan and implement interventions, and monitor progress.

Other terms besides integrated therapy may be used to describe approaches with similar components, including *transdisciplinary, consultative,* and *collaborative teaming.* Research data show that students whose therapy services are provided in an integrated manner make greater gains in skill learning than do students whose therapy is provided totally through more traditional direct, one-on-one therapy in which services are provided outside of natural contexts. The important point is not what an approach is labeled but that people collaborate and solve problems together so that individuals with motor disabilities may participate fully in life.

excluding a child from participation. The next most commonly used strategy is to ask for adult assistance in the form of a personal assistant for the student. In essence, adults have a natural tendency to start at the bottom of Figure 8–10 and work upwards rather than starting at the top and working down. Teams of educators, family members, and specialists working with a particular student can focus on ways of making participation in typical environments possible. By sharing information and resources, collaborating, and using a problem-solving focus, the physical management routines of students with even the most severe motor disabilities may be managed easily and efficiently in practically all settings and environments.

Summary

Managing the physical care needs of individuals with severe motor disabilities requires creativity, planning, and skill. Physical management routines include lifting, transferring, carrying, positioning, eating and drinking, toileting, and dressing. When these care routines accommodate the needs of each individual, they provide opportunities for partial participation and have a positive impact on physical characteristics, such as muscle tone and the development of secondary motor disabilities. Allowing individuals to participate in their own caregiving to the greatest extent possible may prevent learned helplessness as well as make them less dependent on assistance from others.

Physical management routines need not yield full independence in a particular care activity; many individuals with severe motor disabilities require assistance in these activities throughout their lives. The purposes of these routines are to address care needs with dignity and in ways that promote participation, to manage routines efficiently, and to reduce the likelihood of secondary physical limitations and deformities.

Suggested Activities

1. At the beginning of each school year, work with therapists to assess whether each student's adaptive equipment is suitable for the student and is used properly. Answer the following questions:
   - Does the equipment fit the student?
   - Do the staff members place the student properly in the equipment?
   - Does the equipment produce the desired function over time and across activities?
   - How long should the student remain in the piece of equipment before being repositioned?
   - Is the equipment suited to the student's chronological age and does it allow for a normalized appearance?
   - Does the equipment isolate the student from an activity because of its size, height, or purpose?

2. Observe the typical routines that your students follow during their school day (e.g., arrival and departure on a bus, movement to and from scheduled school locations, use of the restroom, change of diapers, change of clothing for physical education class, or use of the library). For students who are not independent in their movements or ability to communicate, check to see if the following four activities occur during these routines:
   - The adult or peer makes physical contact with the student.
   - The adult or peer communicates what is going to happen in a manner that the student can understand.
   - The adult or peer prepares the student physically for the routine.
   - The adult or peer performs the steps of the routine in ways that allow the student to have choices and require as much participation as possible.

References

Batshaw, M. L. (1997). *Children with disabilities* (4th ed.). Baltimore: Paul H. Brookes.

Baumgart, D., Brown, L., Pumpian, I., Nisbet, J., Ford, A., Sweet, M., Messina, R., & Schroeder, J. (1982). Principle of partial participation and individualized adaptations in educational programs for severely handicapped students. *Journal of the Association for the Severely Handicapped, 7*(2), 17–27.

Bergen, A. F., Presperin, J., & Tallman, T. (1990). *Positioning for function: Wheelchairs and other assistive technologies.* Vallhalla, NY: Vallhalla Rehabilitation.

Breath, D., DeMauro, G., & Snyder, P. (1997). Adaptive sitting for young children. *Young Exceptional Children, 1*(1), 10–16.

Campbell, P. H. (1997). *Therapy in homes and communities.* Unpublished manuscript. Child and Family Studies, Allegheny University of the Health Sciences.

Campbell, P. H. (1995). Supporting the medical and physical needs of students in inclusive settings. In N. Haring & L. Romer (Eds.) *Welcoming students who are deaf-blind into typical classrooms* (pp. 277–305). Baltimore: Paul H. Brookes.

Campbell, P. H. (1987). The integrated programming team: An approach for coordinating professionals of various disciplines for students with severe and multiple handicaps. *Journal of the Association for Persons with Severe Handicaps, 12*(2), 107–116.

Campbell, P. H., & Bailey, K. (1991). Issues in health care in the education of students with the most severe disabilities. In M. C. Wang, M. Reynolds, & H. Walberg (Eds.), *Handbook of special education* (Vol. 4) (pp. 143–160). Oxford: Pergamon.

Campbell, P. H., & Forsyth, S. (1993). Integrated programming and movement disabilities. In M. E. Snell (Ed.), *Instruction of students with severe disabilities* (4th ed.) (pp. 264–289). New York: Merrill.

Campbell, S. K. (1997). Therapy programs for children that last a lifetime. *Physical and Occupational Therapy in Pediatrics, 17*(1), 1–15.

Conner, F. P., Williamson, G. C., & Siepp, J. M. (1978). *Program guide for infants and toddlers with neuromotor and other developmental disabilities.* New York: Teachers College.

Dunn, W., Brown, C., & McGuigan, A. (1994). The ecology of human performance: A framework for considering the effect of context. *American Journal of Occupational Therapy, 48*, 595–607.

Farber, A. F., Yanni, C. C., & Batshaw, M. (1997). Nutrition: Good and bad. In M. Batshaw (Ed.), *Children with disabilities* (4th ed.) (pp. 183–210). Baltimore: Paul H. Brookes.

Finnie, N. (Ed.). (1975). *Handling your young cerebral palsied child at home.* New York: E. P. Dutton.

Fraser, B. A., Hensinger, R. N., & Phelps, J. A. (1990). *Physical management of multiple handicaps: A professional's guide.* (2nd ed.). Baltimore: Paul H. Brookes.

French, C., Gonzalez, R. T., & Tronson-Simpson, J. (1991). *Caring for people with multiple disabilities: An interdisciplinary guide for caregivers.* Tucson, AZ: Therapy Skill Builders.

Giangrecco, M. F. (1994). Effects of a consensus-building process on team decision-making: Preliminary data. *Physical disabilities: Education and related services, 13*(1), 41–56.

Hanson, M., & Harris, S. (1986). *Teaching the young child with motor delays: A guide for parents and professionals.* Austin, TX: Pro-Ed.

Jaeger, D. L. (1989). *Transferring and lifting children and adolescents: Home instruction sheets.* Tucson, AZ: Therapy Skill Builders.

Kunc, N. (1996, April/May). The right to be disabled. *Pennsylvania Early Intervention, 7*(7), 1, 4.

Lehr, D. H., & Noonan, M. J. (1989). Issues in the education of students with complex health care needs. In F. Brown & D. H. Lehr (Eds.), *Persons with profound disabilities issues and practices* (pp. 139–160). Baltimore: Paul H. Brookes.

Lollar, D. J. (Ed.). (1994). *Preventing secondary conditions associated with spina bifida or cerebral palsy.* Washington, DC: Spina Bifida Association of America.

Meyer, L., Peck, C., & Brown, L. (Eds.). (1991). *Critical issues in the lives of people with severe disabilities.* Baltimore: Paul H. Brookes.

Morris, S. E., & Klein, M. D. (1987). *Pre-feeding skills: A comprehensive resource for feeding development.* Tucson, AZ: Communication Skill Builders.

Mueller, H. (1975). Feeding. In N. Finnie (Ed.), *Handling your young cerebral palsied child at home.* New York: E. P. Dutton.

Orelove, F., & Sobsey, D. (1996). *Educating children with multiple disabilities: A transdisciplinary approach.* Baltimore: Paul H. Brookes.

Palisano, R., Rosenbaum, P., Walter, S., Russell, D., Wood, E., & Galuppi, B. (1997). Development and reliability of a system to classify gross motor function in children with cerebral palsy. *Developmental Medicine and Child Neurology, 39*, 214–223.

Rainforth, B., & York-Barr, J. (1996). Handling and positioning. In F. Orelove & R. Sobsey (Eds.), *Educating children with multiple disabilities* (3rd ed.). (pp. 79–118). Baltimore: Paul H. Brookes.

Rainforth, B., & York-Barr, J. (1997). *Collaborative teams for students with severe disabilities: Integrating therapy and educational services* (2nd ed.). Baltimore: Paul H. Brookes.

Rowland, C., & Stremel-Campbell, K. (1987). Share and share alike: Conventional gestures to emergent language for learners with sensory impairments. In L. Goetz, D. Guess, & K. Stremel-Campbell (Eds.), *Innovative program design for individuals with dual sensory impairments* (pp. 49–75). Baltimore: Paul H. Brookes.

Salisbury, C. L., & Dunst, C. J. (1997). Home, school, and community partnerships: Building inclusive teams. In B. Rainforth & J. York-Barr, *Collaborative teams for students with severe disabilities: Integrating therapy and educational services* (2nd ed.). (pp. 57–87). Baltimore: Paul H. Brookes.

Scherzer, A., & Tscharnuter, I. (1990). *Early diagnosis and therapy in cerebral palsy* (2nd ed.). New York: Marcel Decker.

Seligman, M. (1975). *Helplessness: On death, depression, and development.* San Francisco: W. H. Freeman.

Sobsey, R. J., & Orelove, F. (1984). Neurophysiological facilitation of eating skills in severely handicapped children. *Journal of the Association for Persons with Severe Handicaps, 9*, 111–122.

Stremel, K., Molden, V., Leister, C., Matthews, J., Wilson, R., Goodall, D. V., & Holston, J. (1990). *Communication systems and routines: A decision making process.* Washington, DC: U.S. Office of Special Education.

Trefler, E., Hobson, D., Taylor, S., Monaham, L., & Shaw, C. (1996). *Seating and mobility for persons with physical disabilities.* San Antonio, TX: Psychological Corporation/Therapy Skill Builders.

Vandercook, T., York, J., & Forest, M. (1989). The McGill Action Planning System (MAPS): A strategy for building the vision. *Journal of the Association for Persons with Severe Handicaps, 14*(3), 205–215.

York-Barr, J., Rainforth, B., & Locke, P. (1996). Developing instructional adaptations. In F. P. Orelove & D. Sobsey, *Educating children with multiple disabilities: A transdisciplinary approach* (3rd ed.) (pp. 119–159). Baltimore: Paul H. Brookes.

Wilcox, M. J. (1989). Delivering communication-based services to infants, toddlers, and their families: Approaches and models. *Topics in Language Disorders, 10*(1), 68–79.

Wolf, L. S., & Glass, R. P. (1992). *Feeding and swallowing disorders in infancy: Assessment and management.* Tucson, AZ: Therapy Skill Builders.

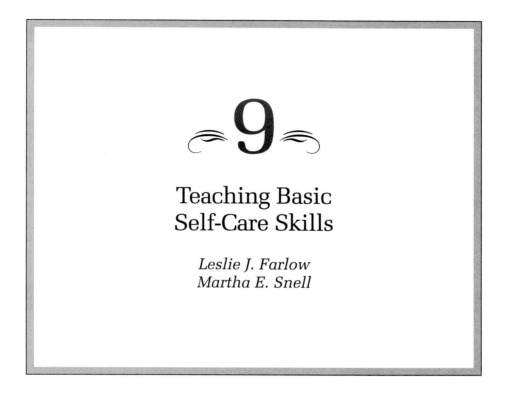

9

Teaching Basic
Self-Care Skills

Leslie J. Farlow
Martha E. Snell

The development of the ability to care for oneself represents the beginning of independence from one's parents. The first time children complete self-care routines (e.g., using the toilet or getting dressed) "by themselves" is considered a major event in most families to be celebrated and recorded. We define this domain to include the basic and routine tasks of maintaining personal hygiene: toileting, eating, dressing, and grooming. For children and young adults with severe disabilities, the ability to manage personal care is of paramount significance, even if management relies somewhat on others. A range of obstacles (e.g., mental, physical, or behavioral disabilities, along with lowered environmental expec-

tations or poor instruction) may slow, limit, or indefinitely postpone development of such basic adaptive skills. This chapter describes proven and socially acceptable methods for assessing and teaching these skills.

Before we begin, we'd like to introduce three students: John, a kindergarten student; Jamal, a teenager in middle school; and Alycin, a young woman well into her transition to adulthood. Within the chapter sections on toileting, mealtime, and dressing, and grooming, we share the related issues faced by these three students and their educational teams. Their instructional programs should help you apply chapter information to your own practices with students.

 John

This is John's first year in an inclusive educational program, and he is assigned to a typical kindergarten classroom. He is very social and appears to like everything about school, especially music and reading. John also

has a great sense of humor, he enjoys "tricking" his teachers into believing that he can't do something. John is identified as having multiple disabilities: cerebral palsy and severe mental retardation.

There are 20 students in his class. Ms. Johnson, the kindergarten teacher, has the services of a part-time teaching assistant and a consulting special education teacher, Ms. Perez. Ms. Perez typically spends about a half hour daily in the kindergarten class teaching small groups of children, working one-on-one with John, or observing to plan adaptations. John's mother participates actively on his team along with an occupational therapist (OT), a physical therapist (PT), and a speech and language pathologist (SLP), all of whom provide services to him several times a week in the context of kindergarten activities.

John uses a wheelchair to travel distances of more than a few feet, but he can walk 3 feet, using two canes, and up to 10 feet when an adult holds him from behind and facilitates hip rotation. In the self-care domain, John is not toilet trained and still wears diapers. He eats finger foods and uses a spoon, but he is messy and does not appear to chew his food thoroughly. John participates in most grooming skills with verbal and physical assistance.

 Jamal

Jamal is an eighth grader with autism. At age 13, he is fairly social with staff and peers and well-liked. Since entering middle school, Jamal has been involved in a Lunch Bunch Club, which means he interacts daily with many other eighth graders, even though he spends about half of his school time learning apart from them (e.g., in the special education room, at the high school where he will be next year, and in many community locations). Jamal uses signing, conventional gestures, and a pocket communication book of symbols and printed words to communicate. He is learning to indicate his dislike of activities in more appropriate ways than shaking his head and humming loudly, jumping up and down, tearing around the room, and yelling, which has been his practice for many years. Now he is learning to communicate his dissatisfaction and make a choice about a change. Jamal likes being around peers but dislikes excessive noise and often reacts by covering his ears.

Unlike many of his peers, Jamal is somewhat oblivious to his appearance, though, at his mother's insistence, he always looks neat and fashionable. His grooming goals include generalization of independent toothbrushing, initiation of hand washing before handling food, and checking his face in the mirror after eating and brushing his teeth. In the dressing area, Jamal is aiming for independence in the school bathroom (i.e., unfastening and fastening his pants, exiting the bathroom with clothes properly arranged and underpants not showing), handling all fasteners on clothing and jackets, and tying his shoes. At lunch time, Jamal's focus is on attaining fluency in cleaning his own place after lunch, setting his own place in the classroom, and asking for what he needs spontaneously.

 Alycin

Alycin, who is 17, will complete her high school program next year and start a post-high program, located in the community, when she is 18. Because of her extensive cerebral palsy, she uses a wheelchair and a computerized communication device with voice output and regularly uses other pieces of adaptive equipment, such as toileting and shower chairs, adapted desk and chair arrangement, and wedges for positioning. Alycin's vision is limited, which means her parents, teachers, and peers rely a lot on telling her where things are and "talking her through" what is happening around her. For her transition years, Alycin and her team have identified skill targets that emphasize less dependence on others and have problem-solved common challenges to her self-care routines. Her self-care skills include indicating when she needs to use the bathroom, partial participation in toileting and many grooming tasks, and active participation in eating, including the use of a mechanized self-feeder for some meals at home and school.

A Rationale for Attaining Proficiency in Self-Care Routines

It is our position that attaining proficiency in self-care must continue to be a priority for instruction for most students with severe disabilities. The most basic and functional skills of human beings are those involved in daily self-care routines. These routines are performed every day, they have strong, lifelong influences upon health, social acceptability, and positive self-image. If not performed by the student, these routines must be completed by someone else or medically managed if the person is to remain healthy and socially acceptable.

While today's prevalence of early intervention should have a positive effect on our students' attainment of these basic skills, there is no guarantee that self-care routines will be taught or will be mastered by elementary-school age. The accommodations allowed and available during the school years often disappear after age 21; young adults who have not achieved the highest degree of independence possible in their daily hygiene may be excluded from many community opportunities as a result. The clock is always ticking for students with severe disabilities.

Additionally, the self-care curricular domain continues to be a priority for parents and contributes greatly to quality of life and to self-determination for individuals with severe disabilities. Parents of students with severe disabilities are often the most vocal supporters of targeting and teaching self-care skills (Hamre-Nietupski, 1993). For instance, when these parents responded to a questionnaire about school curriculum, they agreed that about half of every school day should be devoted to functional skills instruction, which included learning to care for oneself; community skills, such as shopping and street crossing; and work and leisure skills. Parents recommended that the remaining portion of the day's instruction be divided between academics and developing friendships and social relationships with nondisabled peers.

The attainment of proficiency in basic self-care skills (even if proficiency involves some necessary accommodation) makes it possible for our students to meet their own personal needs while it contributes meaningfully to the development of self-

determination and to one's quality of life. There is increasing consensus that the four core dimensions of quality of life are: (a) personal well-being, (b) emotional well-being, (c) personal development, and (d) self-determination (Hatton, 1998; Hughes, Hwang, Kim, Eisenman, & Killian, 1995; Schalock, 1996). Clearly, toileting, eating, and grooming are critical to the first dimension: personal well-being and health. Independent performance of self-care activities are considered milestones in child development. When these milestones are accomplished, they are "celebrated" in families, whether the child is typical or has a disability. This is strong evidence that independent performance of self-care tasks contributes to emotional well-being and personal development.

If the components of self-determination are examined, it becomes clear how aptitude to perform self-care tasks is closely related to this fourth dimension of quality of life. Initiation, persistence, choice making, self-regulation, and self-efficacy are components of self-determination (Brown & Cohen, 1996). Think about it:

- People have many natural opportunities to initiate and persist while completing necessary self-care routines.
- Eating, grooming, and dressing require many choices.
- Independent performance of self-care tasks is a milestone in the development of self-regulation and self-efficacy for typically developing young children.
- Progress in self-care skills provides a sense of self-control and accomplishment for students with disabilities.

Finally, starting in the adolescent years, appropriate dressing and grooming skills are necessary for acceptance in a peer group and also may improve students' access to integrated community environments. With instruction, students with disabilities should be expected to make progress in self-care skills and to demonstrate at least some level of independence from parents and other support providers. This can lead to improved quality of life, increased ability for self-determination, and increased opportunities to develop interactions with peer groups that may lead to positive social relationships.

Problems with Current Research

Even though self-care skills contribute to health, reduce dependence, and add to quality of life, the research basis for instruction of these skills is surprisingly limited. Most of the self-care research since the 1960s exhibits one or more difficulties:

1. It was conducted in segregated school or living settings.
2. It included aversive procedures in the intervention.
3. It is dated.

Today, segregated placements and aversive procedures are not acceptable practices for students with disabilities because (a) we know the power that ordinary peers and life experiences can have for students with disabilities (Meyer, Park, Grenot-Scheyer, Schwartz, & Harry, 1998), and (b) we have seen that more problems than solutions result from the use of aversive methods (Horner & Carr, 1997).

Despite a need for more studies using positive strategies in inclusive educational settings, research in the functional skill domains, including self-care, appears to be declining (Nietupski, Hamre-Nietupski, Curtain, & Shrikanth, 1997). Furthermore, with a reduction in self-care research in general, the areas of dressing and grooming instruction have been significantly less studied than have toileting and eating instruction (Snell, 1997).

General Principles for Developing Self-Care Instruction

Our general principles for developing self-care instruction are summarized in Table 9–1. Teachers, in collaboration with family members, related service personnel, general educators, and the student, choose which skills to address but pay close attention to social, age, and cultural characteristics of teaching procedures and the perspective of peers. Partial (versus full, or nonadapted) participation of skills is judiciously used. Next, team members conduct meaningful assessment, including an inventory of the

TABLE 9–1
Principles for Developing and Implementing Self-Care Teaching Programs

- **Collaborate with team members.** Work collaboratively with the entire team (student, family members, educators, related service personnel, paraprofessionals) to select skills for instruction, set instructional targets, develop instructional programs, and monitor performance.
- **Use procedures that are socially valid, age- and culture appropriate.** Skills selected for instruction and instructional procedures should: (a) be acceptable to those close to the student, the student's peers, and the larger community; (b) be performed by others of the same age in similar ways; and (c) reflect the heritage, religion, and beliefs of the family and student.
- **Involve peers.** Because peers are good judges of "what is appropriate" and "what is socially acceptable," involving them can help teams choose targets, screen teaching approaches (e.g., methods, locations), and decide if the outcomes are acceptable.
- **Use partial participation carefully.** Modify tasks to empower students and enhance learning when mastery of unmodified routines is an unrealistic goal for current instruction. Continuously reevaluate modifications to ensure they are effective, nonstigmatizing, and necessary.
- **Conduct meaningful assessment and use the results.** Meaningful assessment to select skills for instruction should result in knowledge of: (a) what the student is able to do; (b) what skills the student does not perform or does not perform completely; (c) whether unlearned skills are a priority in current or future environments; (d) the way the student participates in performance of tasks and routines; (e) whether skills are performed fluently; and (f) whether skills are performed across settings. Meaningful assessment during instruction provides information about student progress and the need for changes in instruction.
- **Select appropriate settings and schedules for instruction.** Schedule instruction in settings and at times where the skills are most functional. While creating additional opportunities for instruction or providing instruction in isolated settings may sometimes be justified, such decisions must be implemented with caution.
- **Select uncomplicated and effective instructional methods.** Instructional strategies should be easy to use, practical, and result in student progress. Instructional strategies should be matched to the student's stage of learning, specific learning characteristics, and the instructional environment.
- **Consider related skills for instruction.** When teaching core skills within self-care routines, instruction should address related skills, including social and communication skills, initiation, problem solving, and monitoring quality and tempo.

environment to determine which self-care routines and specific skills are the most important for the student to master and what the best schedule and settings are for instruction. Uncomplicated and effective instructional methods should be selected on the basis of the student's specific learning characteristics, the stage of learning, and the instructional environment. Finally, the team should identify related skills (e.g., social, communicative) that should be included in instruction. These eight principles are repeatedly applied by teams as a decision cycle to select skills, evaluate student progress, and adjust teaching strategies.

Collaborate with Team Members

The collaborative team is an ongoing process in which many decisions are made about what to teach, how to teach, and how to improve teaching (for more detail, see chapter 4 and Snell & Janney, 2000). If teams are to be student-centered, the *student* must be a team member. When students are present at their own Individualized Educational Plan (IEP) meetings and team members seek to understand their feelings, ideas, and choices about self-care skills, team decisions are more likely to reflect the student's wishes. We know of several teams who routinely put the student's picture on the meeting table when he or she (or a family member) cannot be present. Likewise, *family members* can provide the team with perspectives that no professional members have, especially in the self-care domain. Involvement of the family in instructional plans can facilitate generalization of the skills from schools or community-based sites to the home environment. If teachers are limited to the traditional school day and settings for instruction and observation, then family members or other support providers must facilitate students' use of the self-care routines where they are especially needed—in the home and the community.

In addition to the student and family, other core team members include teachers. The student's *special education teacher* facilitates the planning of meeting times and location, the agenda, and implementation of actions the team recommends. *General education teachers* must be involved as core members, too, because (a) their classroom activities and teaching schedule are the context for assessment and instruction, and (b) classmates may be included, even if only as informal models for self-care.

When self-care skills are a priority, related services staff make essential contributions for many students. *Occupational therapists* have expertise in the activities of daily living, including self-care skills, and the fine motor development needed for many self-care tasks. For example, Reese and Snell (1991) consulted with an occupational therapist to determine the most appropriate steps for putting on and removing coats and jackets. *Physical therapists* are sources of knowledge on adaptive equipment and overall positioning considerations, which influence skill performance. *Speech and language therapists* have expertise in oral musculature that may be useful in the evaluation of eating and oral hygiene activities. For example, Snell, Lewis, and Houghton (1989) consulted with a speech therapist to determine the most appropriate steps for brushing teeth. *School nurses* may directly assess nutrition, bowel and bladder characteristics, and other health concerns (e.g., seizure disorders, urinary tract infections, vision and hearing concerns) or consult with the student's physician. Sometimes additional school staff are included because they fill important team roles: *paraprofessional staff*, *adaptive physical educators*, and *vision specialists*.

> John's teacher and occupational therapist visited his home to meet with John's parents to complete assessments and observations in the self-care domain. Ms. Perez asked his preschool team members, including his last teacher and mother, about what had been targeted, taught, and successful for John in self-care areas. Ms. Perez also consulted with John's current physical and occupational therapist and his speech therapist. They observed John as he performed self-care tasks. The speech and occupational therapists worked together in the initial development of an eating program and shared their ideas with the team. Since many of John's self-care skills ultimately will be completed in the home environment, Ms. Perez, Ms. Johnson, and the therapists worked closely with John's parents to plan his self-care program.

Use Socially Valid Procedures that Are Appropriate for Age and Culture

Throughout the assessment, instruction, and evaluation process, the team should consider family or support-provider priorities for instruction, peer standards (the skills that the students' peers perform and the ways they perform them), and community norms (the acceptability of the task and the way it is performed). These considerations are often referred to as *social validity* criteria. When targeting skills for instruction, the student teacher should heed family or support-providers' priorities for instruction, the skills that the students' peers perform, the ways peers perform skills, and the acceptability of the task and its performance as viewed by the community. The acceptability of teaching strategies cannot be ignored. Social validity criteria apply to decisions regarding how skills are performed, the materials used for instruction, the prompting procedures, the consequence procedures, and the overall intrusiveness of the procedures. Teams should compare their teaching plans with methods used to teach students without disabilities in similar settings and judge the appropriateness of the techniques. Family team members should also evaluate the fitness of the technique for their son or daughter. Because of the personal and private nature of many self-care skills, it is even more critical that team members evaluate their comfort level with teaching plans. In one study addressing how menstrual care might be taught, nondisabled women in the community were surveyed to determine if instruction should be conducted using a doll rather than on the students (Epps, Stern, & Horner, 1990). Women in the community indicated a preference for instruction using a doll, citing the intrusiveness of instruction on the student and the potential for some students to negatively react to such an approach.

Self-care routines targeted for instruction, as well as the procedures for instruction and monitoring progress, should be age- and culture-appropriate. Skills are *chronologically age-appropriate* for a student when they are performed by others of the same age. The specific ways skills are accomplished as well as the materials and setting used can be influenced by a student's age. A student's chronological age has great influence on whether or not a skill becomes a priority. For example, completely independent toileting may not be an appropriate goal for a preschool or primary school–aged child, since typical children in this age group receive assistance from their parents or siblings in public toilets, with soap and towel dispensers, and even with getting on and off the toilet and manipulating doors, because of the height, size, and novelty of the equipment. When students in elementary school, or older students, are still dependent on teachers and support providers for toileting, eating, and grooming assistance, however, their differences may isolate them from their peers. Age-appropriateness may also affect the selection of crite-

ria. For example, Young, West, Howard, and Whitney (1986) recorded the dressing rate of skilled peers with and without disabilities to calculate an average of these rates, which became the goal rate for instruction.

> *Like some of his peers Jamal wears button-fly designer jeans, but the buttons are very difficult for him to fasten and unfasten. Many peers also wear snap-and-zip jeans, which would be easier for him to handle. At 17, Alycin has her legs and armpits shaved by her mom; in the summer, because Alycin likes to swim, she also has a bikini shave! Alycin likes the process and helps pick out the shaving cream.*

Culturally-appropriate criteria, or practices that family members value that relate to heritage, religious practices, and beliefs, may influence the performance of some self-care skills, particularly diet. Not enough attention has been given to the impact of family values and culture on teaching content. Listening to families as valued team members gives others on the team opportunities to learn about cultural preferences the family may have.

Involve Peers

The ways in which peers perform tasks are important in selecting skills for instruction and determining how they will be performed. Research shows that the attitudes of typical peers toward students with disabilities are better when students who have disabilities are viewed by their peers as being similar to them (Bak & Siperstein, 1987). For example, in the grooming curriculum, this can mean several things: (a) looking similar to their peers in dress, hairstyle, and grooming habits and (b) performing grooming skills at the same time and place. Especially in dressing and grooming, peers may be better models than professional teachers.

> *Now that Alycin spends more time in community-based instruction, she and her team feel she must "dress the part." This means no skirts, because they ride up in the wheelchair, and no shorts, because they are not suitable for a job; instead, she wears long, lightweight pants, which she and several high school friends picked out.*

Nondisabled peers can be involved as task companions, partners, models, or assistants with students who have severe disabilities, though caution must be applied so that one-way helping is not the only outcome (see partial participation in this chapter and chapter 10). Mike's peers in Figure 9–1 assist him

FIGURE 9–1

Mike's Lunch Routine

Mike's routine illustrates partial participation, interaction with peers, and embedded skills: (a) Mike cannot reach into the cafeteria line refrigerator where milk is kept, so a classmate lends a hand; (b) Mike has learned to grasp his lunch money and reach and extend it to the cashier to pay and (c) get his lunch; (d) Mike can eat independently with an adapted spoon and bowl; (e) when Mike needs assistance, he gets it from classmates.

a

b

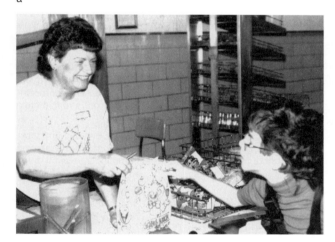

c

d

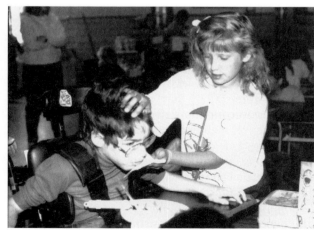

e

by handing him a milk carton and providing assistance with his lunch when he needs it. Those who have used this approach often comment on how students' motivation for learning is high when peers replace adults as learning partners.

> John likes to trick adults by pretending that he cannot do things, but he is very responsive to peer praise and being like his peers. Ms. Perez and Ms. Johnson acknowledge John's accomplishments to his class and encourage students to praise John when he is successful in a task "all by himself."

Staub, Spaulding, Peck, Gallucci, and Schwartz (1996) taught adolescents in junior high to be student aides, which involved ability awareness training, adult modeling, and an accountability system for participation in the student aide program, and scheduled student aides to lend a range of support to students with disabilities in general education classes. Support was given in social, academic, communication, and daily living skills and for appropriate behavior and resulted in many positive outcomes. Here are a few examples in the self-care area:

> Another change is that he can tie his shoes by himself. I taught him how to do that. (student aide) (Staub et al., 1996, p. 201).

> Kelly initially relied on her aide to help her with the locker routine. But now she's doing a great job at it and she's even helping another student in the class with disabilities with her locker routine. (physical education teacher) (Staub et al., 1996, p. 201).

Use Partial Participation Carefully

Partial participation (Baumgart et al., 1982) and adaptations can allow students to participate to some degree in any activity, to attain dignity, and to profit from self-care, rather than remaining totally dependent. However, teachers should not eliminate skills for instruction merely on the basis of perceived difficulty or student characteristics. When the team decides to use partial participation, any adaptations should be designed to be age-appropriate, nonstigmatizing, and practical (Ferguson & Baumgart, 1991). Continuous evaluation of partial participation is critical to determine when assistance can be faded or eliminated, to ensure that modifications result in satisfactory outcomes, and to empower students rather

than humiliate them. Modifications for partial participation include:

1. Modified or adapted materials (e.g., toothbrushes, combs, forks, and cups that are designed for easier gripping; velcro fasteners in place of buttons, hooks, or snaps)
2. Adaptive switches or automated appliances (e.g., hair dryers activated by a pressure switch, battery-powered toothbrushes that provide scrubbing action automatically)
3. Changed sequences within an activity (e.g., allowing a student to put her bathing suit on under her clothes before going to a public pool; sitting on the toilet for balance while scooting underwear down)
4. Personal assistance (e.g., fastening pants for a child in the bathroom, guiding a student's hand to scoop food).

> At home, Myra (Alycin's mom) and Alycin have a long history of using partial participation strategies in self-care tasks; they share the successful ideas with the team. Additional improvements and new ideas evolve from there. For example, Alycin can grasp a wet wash cloth and has the wiping motion, but because of her cerebral palsy, she does not apply enough pressure to get her mouth or arms clean. Still, when showering, Myra gives Alycin a soap mitt and lets her spread the soap on her body, while Myra does any scrubbing that is needed. During the morning routine, Alycin helps by putting her arms up in air as her mom applies deodorant. When it is time to brush teeth, Myra asks Alycin which of several flavors she wants, gives her a "filled" brush, and Alycin does the lateral motion up front, then Myra gets the back teeth as Alycin holds her mouth open. Myra adds: "I do the floss, she holds her mouth open, and the job is done!"

Conduct Meaningful Assessment and Use the Results

Assessment is necessary, for many reasons, to determine:

- What skills the student is able to perform;
- What skills the student does not perform or does not perform completely;
- Whether unlearned skills are a priority now or in future environments;
- How the student participates in performance of tasks or routines;

- Whether the skills are performed fluently;
- Whether skills are performed across settings;
- Whether the student is making progress in instruction;
- Whether or not changes are needed in instruction.

Typically, self-care assessments include the use of interviews and checklists with family members, such as the eating subtest of the Checklist of Adaptive Living Skills (Morreau & Bruininks, 1991) shown in Figure 9–2; environmental assessments; and direct observation (see chapters 3 and 5 for more information on assessment). As noted earlier in this chapter, the assessment process should encompass collaboration with the educational team; social validity; age- and culture-appropriateness; and peer standards.

Informal Assessment

Informal assessments include environmental assessments and interviews. Information may be collected from team members through interview or self-report using a checklist of self-care skills. Interviews may begin with general questions, such as: "Describe Jamal's typical morning routine getting ready for school." Then, as you begin to target priority skills, you may focus on questions about the typical components of self-care routines (Brown, Evans, Weed, & Owen, 1987), such as:

- Can Jamal *brush his teeth*? What kinds of assistance does he need (e.g., complete, more than half, less than half, little, or none)?
- In the *toothbrushing* routine, does Jamal initiate the task, problem-solve, monitor quality, monitor speed, or terminate the task?
- In the *toothbrushing* routine, does Jamal make choices, use communication or social skills, or have interfering behavior?
- Is the *toothbrushing* routine a priority? Are there any specific concerns?

Sometimes individuals or agencies outside the team are also asked about what self-care skills are required in settings that the student uses or may use in the near future. For example:

As John's teachers were preparing for him to enter an inclusive kindergarten, they learned from visiting the kindergarten he would attend that children went to the toilet in groups. They also knew that John could probably learn to respond to peer models for washing hands after toileting. Thus,

a preschool objective was to teach John to attend to several peer models who were students in a Head Start classroom near his room.

Alycin's team called six potential post-school adult agencies to see what kinds of self-care skills were required to participate. Unfortunately, only two provided assistance in toileting transfers and at mealtime; all others required independence or attendant services. This news made the team place more emphasis on improving Alycin's ease with assisted transfers and fluency in feeding herself (finger foods or the self-feeder).

The settings students use influence the selection of skills for instruction. For example, if a student eats most meals in the school cafeteria, then the related skills of cafeteria use may be a priority. As a student becomes older and receives more instruction in the community, then the associated skills of restaurant use and eating at work are appropriate teaching targets. Family-style dining may become a priority if it is preferred by the family or if the student's future placement indicates that it will be needed.

Direct Observation

Some self-care behaviors such as taking a bite, taking a drink or eliminating in the toilet, can be separated from the chain as isolated, discrete skills, but these behaviors usually are taught as part of a routine. For example, the target skill of bladder elimination may be taught in the context of the toileting routine, which is task-analyzed into its component behaviors: walking to the toilet, unfastening clothing, pulling down pants, positioning self on toilet, pulling up pants and underwear, fastening clothing, flushing, washing and drying hands, and returning to previous activity. For some students, asking permission to go to the bathroom or requesting needed assistance will be taught concurrently or added after progress is made on these core steps.

Published task analyses such as those by Baker and Brightman (1997) can be used to guide assessment observations and instruction, but teachers often conclude that it is more practical to develop their own task analyses. Task analyses may be developed by taking several steps: performing the task, observing capable peers perform the task, observing focus students performing the task, and getting team input. Task analyses should reflect the ways others around the student do the task (family members or peers at school) and materials used at home or school or other

FIGURE 9–2

Eating Subtest of the Checklist of Adaptive Living Skills (CALS)

1.2 EATING

Assessment			Skills	Assessment			Skills
DATE	DATE	DATE		DATE	DATE	DATE	
☐	☐	☐	1.2.1 Sucks from a nipple.	☐	☐	☐	1.2.24 Chews food with the mouth closed.
☐	☐	☐	1.2.2 Holds and drinks from a baby bottle.	☐	☐	☐	1.2.25 Swallows food before taking another bite.
☐	☐	☐	1.2.3 Swallows a spoonful of soft food.	☐	☐	☐	1.2.26 Tastes food he or she has not tried before.
☐	☐	☐	1.2.4 Sits in a chair with support, such as a belt or tray.	☐	☐	☐	1.2.27 Sucks on a hard piece of candy.
☐	☐	☐	1.2.5 Holds head up while eating.	☐	☐	☐	1.2.28 Scoops pieces of small solid food, such as peas, with a fork.
☐	☐	☐	1.2.6 Picks up and eats crisp food, such as crackers or cereal, with the fingers.	☐	☐	☐	1.2.29 Wipes own hands and face with a napkin.
☐	☐	☐	1.2.7 Swallows liquids from a cup held by someone else.	☐	☐	☐	1.2.30 Cuts soft food, such as cooked carrots, with the side of a fork.
☐	☐	☐	1.2.8 Scoops soft food, such as cooked cereal, with a spoon.	☐	☐	☐	1.2.31 Pours liquid into a glass from a pitcher or bottle.
☐	☐	☐	1.2.9 Scoops small pieces of solid food, such as stew, with a spoon.	☐	☐	☐	1.2.32 Chooses the fork, knife, or spoon when they are needed to eat different foods.
☐	☐	☐	1.2.10 Drinks from a cup with a handle.	☐	☐	☐	1.2.33 Asks for food to be passed.
☐	☐	☐	1.2.11 Chews and swallows a bite of solid food that is not soft, such as a piece of meat.	☐	☐	☐	1.2.34 Spreads a sandwich spread, such as peanut butter, on bread with a knife.
☐	☐	☐	1.2.12 Takes food into mouth with the tongue (for example, licks ice cream from a cone).	☐	☐	☐	1.2.35 Puts a small amount of seasoning, such as salt or pepper, on food.
☐	☐	☐	1.2.13 Drinks from a glass.	☐	☐	☐	1.2.36 Opens a carton of liquid, such as milk.
☐	☐	☐	1.2.14 Picks up and eats hand-held foods, such as a sandwich.	☐	☐	☐	1.2.37 Places a serving of food from a serving bowl onto his or her plate.
☐	☐	☐	1.2.15 Scoops soft food, such as mashed potatoes, with a fork.	☐	☐	☐	1.2.38 Opens a tab-top can, such as a soda pop can.
☐	☐	☐	1.2.16 Drinks a beverage directly from a drinking fountain.	☐	☐	☐	1.2.39 Takes the cap off a bottle.
☐	☐	☐	1.2.17 Drinks water from a drinking fountain.	☐	☐	☐	1.2.40 Sets the spoon, fork, and knife on the plate when they are not being used.
☐	☐	☐	1.2.18 Sucks liquid through a straw.	☐	☐	☐	1.2.41 Slices soft, solid food, such as a baked potato, into bite-sized pieces with a knife.
☐	☐	☐	1.2.19 Takes paper off of wrapped foods.				
☐	☐	☐	1.2.20 Fills a glass with water from a faucet.	☐	☐	☐	1.2.42 Peels the skin or shell from food, such as an orange or an egg, with fingers.
☐	☐	☐	1.2.21 Drinks a beverage directly from a bottle.				
☐	☐	☐	1.2.22 Tests cooked food or liquids that are hot before eating or drinking them.	☐	☐	☐	1.2.43 Cuts meat into bite-sized pieces with a fork and a knife.
☐	☐	☐	1.2.23 Pierces a piece of solid food, such as meat, with a fork.				

Note: From *Checklist of Adaptive Living Skills (CALS)* (p. 7) by L. E. Morreau and R. H. Bruininks, 1991, Allen, TX: Developmental Learning Materials. Copyright 1991 by DLM. Reprinted by permission.

relevant environments. For many students and self-care targets, consultation with family members, the occupational and physical therapist, or the speech and language therapist greatly improves the task analysis.

Observing the focus student is particularly important when the student has had some experience with the skill. For example, the first author learned from a student with motor involvement that soaping a washcloth for face washing can be accomplished by wadding the washcloth into a ball and then rubbing the cloth across the soap in a stable soap dish. Unfortunately, this lesson was learned only after struggling to teach the student to place the washcloth over an extended palm, to pick up the soap in the other hand, and then to rub the soap on the cloth. Had the student been observed first, the task analysis would have been written to reflect this adapted method.

Select Appropriate Settings and Schedules for Instruction

Once priority skills are selected, teams have several issues to address that concern scheduling and learning setting:

- Where to teach the skill (natural location or elsewhere);
- Whether privacy is appropriate (alongside peers or isolated training);
- When to teach the skill (natural times or nonnatural times, or both);
- How often to teach the skill (natural frequency or increased intensity).

Instruction of activities in the places and at times when the activity is functional is a characteristic of quality programs for students with severe disabilities, because this practice uses normalized routines, allows peer modeling, and promotes skill generalization (Losardo & Bricker, 1994; Sewell, Collins, Hemmeter, & Schuster, 1998). Unfortunately, much of the self-care research has not addressed these issues in the school environment because, beyond preschool, many self-care skills are not used during the school day or are used in private.

Often activity-based self-care instruction, which occurs during natural times for dressing, toileting, and eating, is sufficient for instruction. However, if students are not making progress in a carefully implemented program, then the team needs to consider

---

 An Example of Meaningful Self-Care Assessment

Ms. Perez, John's special education teacher, and Mr. Lee, the occupational therapist, visited John's family at home about a month before his IEP meeting was scheduled. Ms. Perez chose to use the Vineland Scale of Adaptive Behavior to interview John's mother on his adaptive behaviors, in addition to an informal interview and environmental assessment. She took advantage of being in John's home to assess the environments where John completed self-care tasks: his bedroom, the bathroom, the kitchen, and the dining room. Ms. Perez discussed the family's routines in the morning getting ready for school, in the evening getting ready for bed, and mealtimes at home and in the community. What follows are the assessment findings:

John's scores range from 1 year to 3 years on the Vineland. While not toilet trained and still using diapers, his physician says John is physiologically capable of toileting independence. John does eat finger foods without assistance and uses a spoon, but he is

messy and does not appear to chew his food thoroughly. John participates in most grooming skills but still requires some verbal and physical assistance. He can dress independently in clothing with no fasteners, such as elastic-waist pants and T-shirts, but he needs full physical assistance with zippers, buttons, and snaps.

Based on these findings, the team decided a number of things: (a) John's priorities for self-care instruction are toileting independently, chewing food, using a fork, and washing his hands and face; (b) John will receive instruction in mealtime behaviors and fastening clothing only as natural opportunities present themselves; (c) task analyses will be used to guide teaching and to measure John's progress; and (d) the members of the team will keep a time chart to record toileting successes and accidents and a frequency count of correct and incorrect bites for chewing.

increasing instructional intensity or the number of teaching trials. For example, if a student is not successful in learning to toilet with an improved traditional method (explained later in this chapter), teachers may increase fluids to increase opportunities for learning. Because intensive instruction is intrusive to the typical daily routine, it should be considered only when skills are a high priority and after more normalized techniques have been implemented unsuccessfully. Sometimes, instructional intensity can be increased without major schedule adjustments or concern. For example:

> John can work on his eating skills extra times each day because the class has two snacks and lunch. The speech therapist is scheduled for the morning snack, the class aide for lunchtime, and variable staff for the afternoon snack.

Some students with special dietary needs or who are at risk nutritionally require an extra meal or snack during school hours, providing potential instructional opportunities.

The decision to teach in isolation away from peers must be made cautiously. Segregation eliminates social interaction, reduces the probability of skill generalization, and may mean less efficient use of staff time. Certainly, the ultimate goal of instruction is to enable students to use self-care skills appropriately, with as much independence as possible alongside others at home, at friends' homes, at school, and in the community. Given this goal and the fact that students with severe disabilities have difficulty generalizing learned skills from one setting to another, there is clear support for instruction in natural settings. Even when students require specialized equipment to eat or when staff must use therapeutic methods, they can participate with their peers in the lunchroom environment, as illustrated in Figure 9–1 with fourth-grader Mike. Notice that Mike actively participates in the whole routine, even though he has not reached independence on all steps; his team worked out simple adaptations on some steps with cafeteria staff (e.g., taking his milk carton from another student rather than reaching into a cooler), which led to his independence.

Typical reasons teachers cite to justify *initial mealtime isolation* of students with severe movement involvement are: (a) poor motor control, which results in excessive errors even when the student is given a high level of physical support, and (b) increased muscle tone, which may result from noise and distractions, interfere with controlled movement, increase primitive reflexes, and reduce the level of performance. Some students may not want to eat in front of peers; and, while this preference needs to be considered, it may have life long implications for being isolated at mealtime. In contrast, isolation for instruction in many personal care tasks (e.g., toileting and some dressing and grooming tasks that peers do not perform at school), particularly beyond early childhood, is justifiable. Teams may follow two guidelines to determine when to choose isolated self-care instruction over activity-based instruction:

- If the self-care activity is one that other class members perform openly at school (e.g., hand washing, using a utensil at lunch, taking shoes and outer garments off and putting them on for recess), then activity-based, nonisolated teaching may be appropriate. For example, most students do not brush their teeth at school, so if toothbrushing is a priority and school time is devoted to its teaching, then isolated teaching may be best.
- If privacy is natural and appropriate to the task (e.g., toileting, menstrual hygiene, changing clothes before and after swimming), then any instruction should take place in private, although during expected times so that task completion leads to natural outcomes (e.g., swimming follows changing into a swimsuit).

Teams need to carefully explore the reasons for and against increasing opportunities for instruction or for isolated instruction, while giving priority to the viewpoints of family members and the student.

Select Uncomplicated and Effective Instructional Methods

Teachers often recommend that common sense be a primary guideline for designing teaching programs: Programs must be easy to use and practical, but they must also work! This same message has been designated as the *principle of parsimony* by Etzel and LeBlanc (1979), which suggests that when several approaches work, select the simplest. We have found that the most "doable" program that works with an individual student is team-developed—it reflects input from all team members—and is built on consideration of assessment results, involves peers when appropriate, respects student preferences, and is sensitive to age- and culture-appropriateness.

Stages of Learning

The stages of learning (e.g., acquisition, fluency, maintenance, and generalization), which were described in chapter 4, influence the selection of teaching strategies. The existing literature, which can be analyzed according to the stage of learning addressed by the research, has some helpful implications for designing teaching programs.

Acquisition Stage. In this stage of learning, the student does not know how to perform the task without assistance (scoring 0% to 60% correct on assessments. (Students who resist performing self-care tasks, but can, are not in acquisition, but are unmotivated and perform in later stages of learning.) The goal of instruction during this stage of learning is to provide maximal information to the student about how to perform the core steps and related behavior in the routine. Most self-care research has dealt with this stage of learning and has used some sort of physical prompting system in a whole-task presentation. The acquisition strategies with research support are listed in Table 9–2.

While there are no rigid rules for which instructional procedure is most effective at a given stage, there are "rules of thumb": for students who are completely new to a skill (and thus in the acquisition stage of learning), more *intrusive prompts involving physical prompts or physical guidance* may be best. This might mean using graduated guidance, time delay with physical prompts, or a decreasing assistance prompt hierarchy. During the acquisition stage of learning, many students cannot respond to minimal verbal or gesture cues. Teaching time can be lost moving through two or more prompt levels in an increasing hierarchy, such as least prompts if the least intrusive prompts are not yet meaningful (e.g., during initial instruction for brushing hair, the verbal prompt to "make a part" may not be meaningful). Students with motor disabilities also may need the physical guidance initially to learn the physical movements necessary to perform skills. The exception is students who are less able to tolerate physical prompts.

A *whole-task approach* has several advantages at this stage of learning: The task gets done and students have the opportunity to see the functional outcome of the task, which may not be apparent from only one or two steps. The disadvantage is that lengthy tasks may make early learning too complex. Thus, for some students, backward chaining, forward chaining, repeated practice on problem steps, or instruction in smaller skill clusters (core steps only) is more appropriate. After students begin to master the core part of the task, teachers shift the teaching focus to performing fluently, completing entire routines, and transferring use to a range of natural environments.

We next provide examples of application of the instructional strategies to self-care skills. *Graduated guidance*, one of the most intrusive and intensive approaches we describe, has been used to teach self-care skills more often than any other method. Prompts are intensive initially and then faded. Reese and Snell (1991) used graduated guidance to teach three children with severe disabilities, including motor and sensory impairments, to put on and take off jackets and coats. Instruction began with oversized clothes and involved individualized task analyses. They used three levels of prompts, which progressively faded guidance from full to none:

- Full assist (teacher assists by placing a hand over the student's hand);
- Partial assist (teacher uses an index finger and thumb only to assist);
- Touch assist (teacher assists with only one finger).

Full assistance was provided initially and was continued on each task step until the student indicated that less help was needed. This was communicated by: (a) pressure cues from the student, (b) correct responses made during the latency period, or (c) evidence from instructional data that the student had been successful with less help in the previous teaching trials.

Graduated guidance also may be faded by *hand-to-shoulder fading* (Azrin & Armstrong, 1973; Simbert, Minor & McCoy, 1977). In this approach, guidance is faded from hand-over-hand assistance first to a gentle touch on the hand, then to the forearm, to the elbow, to the upper arm, and finally to the shoulder and upper back. A third way to fade guidance is through *backward chaining*, in which guidance is provided from the beginning of the task though all but the last step, when guidance is reduced or delayed. Guidance is gradually faded by reducing assistance on more and more steps from the end to the beginning of the task. In addition to the use of probes and pressure cues from the student, the level of guidance is sometimes

TABLE 9–2
Effective Strategies for Teaching Self-Care Skills

Strategy	Research On Self-Care Skills	Considerations
Graduated Guidance and Decreasing Assistance Provide physical assistance to the student to complete the task, gradually decreasing the amount as the student begins to perform the task either by reducing pressure or by moving your hand from the student's hand to the wrist, to the elbow, to the shoulder, and away. The decreasing assistance variation provides the student with the highest level of assistance the student requires, decreasing assistance based on probe performance.	**Eating** (Albin, 1977; Azrin & Armstrong, 1973; Miller, Patton, & Henton, 1978; Simbert, Minor & McCoy, 1977) **Dressing** (Reese & Snell, 1991; Sisson et al., 1988) **Other daily living skills** (Matson et al., 1990)	• Provides maximal information about how to perform the task, especially for students new to the task, for students with physical disabilities or visual impairments, and for other students who respond positively to physical assistance • Eliminates time going through prompts to which the student will not respond • May limit opportunity for students to perform some steps independently or with less assistance; some risk for providing "too much help" • Not for students who find physical assistance aversive
Shaping Reinforce successful approximations of the desired behavior.	**Eating** (Luiselli, 1991; O'Brien et al., 1972) **Toileting** (Luiselli, 1996) **Toileting and related skills** (Levine & Elliot, 1970; Marshall, 1966; Richmond, 1983)	• Allows student to experience success by rewarding successive approximations • May require extra materials or time (e.g., having a variety of sizes of clothing so student gradually progresses from oversized to natural-sized clothing)
Simultaneous Prompting Cueing the student to look at task materials, give a task request, and prompt and praise through each step of the task. Use probe trials to determine mastery.	**Dressing** (Sewell, Collins, Hemmeter & Schuster, 1998)	• Provides maximal information about how to perform the task, especially for students new to the task, ensuring success • May limit opportunity for students to perform some steps independently or with less assistance; some risk for providing "too much help"
Forward Chaining Providing instruction on the first step(s) of a task until mastery on initial steps is achieved; then providing instruction on the next step(s) until mastery, and so on.	**Toileting and related skills** (Bettison, 1982) **Dressing** (Alberto et al., 1980) **Menstrual care** (Epps et al., 1990; Richman, et al., 1984)	• Breaks tasks into small teachable units for students who are frustrated by prompting through the entire task • May be more difficult for student to understand function or outcome of performance which may affect student's motivation.

reduced after each set number of trials. For students with multiple disabilities who were learning to dress, Sisson, Kilwein, and Van Hasselt, (1988) reduced the level of assistance after every 10 teaching trials.

Decreasing assistance is a variation of graduated guidance. Look at Table 9–3, which describes how assistance was gradually diminished to shape a 3-year-old boy's self-feeding skill (Luiselli, 1991). In this example decreasing assistance was combined with *shaping* and backward chaining; the teacher began in-

struction on the last step (step A) by presenting one bite of food in a spoon at eye level (but no plate). The student was expected to grasp the spoon, bring it to his mouth, consume the food, and withdraw the spoon. When the student got four of the six steps correct, he received a preferred activity (20 seconds of looking at a light box and listening to music). Reinforcers were needed because the student indicated dislike of food by pushing the plate of food away and saying "No." Over training opportunities, the

TABLE 9–2
Effective Strategies for Teaching Self-Care Skills

Strategy	Research On Self-Care Skills	Considerations
Time Delay Over successive trials, small amounts of time are inserted between natural cues and instructional prompts. Prompts selected must be effective for the student.	**Eating** (Collins, et al., 1991). **Brushing teeth** (Snell et al., 1989) **Other daily living skills** (Wolery, et al., 1991)	• Provides maximal assistance for student success • Prompts are easily matched to individual student characteristics. • Delay allows student opportunity to perform independently before receiving assistance • Not for students who have difficulty waiting for assistance
System of Least Prompts Select a hierarchy of 3 to 4 prompts (e.g., verbal, model, physical), present the cue to the student and pause for student response. If student is incorrect or does not respond, present the next least intrusive prompt and again pause. Repeat the procedure until the student is successful.	**Eating** (Banerdt & Bricker, 1978) **Brushing teeth** (Horner & Keilitz, 1975) **Dressing skills** (Young et al., 1986)	• Provides opportunities for the student to perform each step independently or with the least amount of assistance required • Strategy is easily implemented with multiple-step tasks • May be time inefficient for students who require most prompts at the most intrusive end of the hierarchy to perform the task correctly
Modeling or Observational Learning Students watch peers being taught and then are provided direct instruction to complete the task. Students are taught in groups of 2 to 3. Each student is prompted to watch the whole task while the others are instructed.	**Dressing** (Biederman, et al., 1998; Wolery, et al., 1980) **Other daily living skills** (Wolery, et al., 1991) **Handwashing** (Biederman et al., 1998)	• May assist students in learning to "learn through observation" • Allows for efficient instruction by grouping students • Does not provide for privacy • Requires focused visual attention, memory, and ability to imitate • Not appropriate for instructor to perform some self-care tasks for observation (e.g., toileting, complete undressing)
Provide Opportunities and Reinforce Appropriate Behavior Provide opportunities for students to perform appropriate skills or behaviors; provide reinforcement or appropriate consequence contingent on instructional target.	**Toileting** (Hobbs & Peck, 1985) **Eating** (Nelson et al., 1975; Riordan et al., 1980; Riordan et al., 1984; Smith et al., 1983)	• Simple strategy, appropriate in most settings • Many students need more information via prompts or other instruction to perform the behavior

teacher gradually increased both the distance between the spoon and the mouth (conditions A to C in Table 9–3) and the performance criteria for obtaining reinforcement—the teacher expected better and better spoon use. Once the boy brought the spoon from the table to his mouth with 100% accuracy, shaping was also used teach the student to accept the plate of food. First the spoon was placed on a plate-sized circular marker. Then, a plate was placed on the marker, but food was still presented one bite at a time. The fi-

nal step involved presenting the full plate of food and the spoon. This shaping method resulted in independent self-feeding and was retained when checked 12 months after training ended.

Matson, Taras, Sevin, Love, and Fridley (1990) used a decreasing assistance approach to teach brushing teeth, combing hair, dressing, and eating with physical assistance and modeling to three students with autism and mental retardation. During each instructional session, the teacher followed three steps,

TABLE 9–3
Using Decreasing Assistance Plus Shaping and Backward Chaining to Teach Spoon Use

Condition	Criterion	Teacher's Response	Alan's Required Response*
A	C-1	Present one spoonful of food to Alan, at his eye-level.	Grasp spoon, transport to mouth, insert spoon, consume food, withdraw spoon, hand spoon to teacher.
B	C-1	Present one spoonful of food to Alan, one-half way between his eye-level and table top.	Grasp spoon, transport to mouth, insert spoon, consume food, withdraw spoon, hand spoon to teacher.
C	C-1	Present one spoonful of food to Alan while spoon rests on table top.	Grasp spoon, transport to mouth, insert spoon, consume food, withdraw spoon, place spoon on table top.
D	C-1	Present one spoonful of food to Alan while spoon rests on a circular marker [plate size] that is on table top.	Grasp spoon, transport to mouth, insert spoon, consume food, withdraw spoon, place spoon on marker.
E	C-2	Present one spoonful of food in an empty plate positioned on the circular marker.	Grasp spoon, transport to mouth, insert spoon, consume food, withdraw spoon, place spoon in plate.
F	C-3	Place spoon in plate that contains lunch meal [at start of meal].	Grasp spoon, scoop food, transport to mouth, insert spoon, consume food, withdraw spoon, place spoon in plate.

*Underlined responses represent those comprising the six-step feeding trial. Reinforcement was contingent upon 66.6% (4/6) of steps completed at C-1, 83.3% (5/6) of steps completed at C-2, and 100% (6/6) of steps completed at C-3.

Note: Reprinted from "Acquisition of Self-Feeding in a Child with Lowe's Syndrome" by J. K. Luiselli, 1991, *Journal of Developmental Disabilities, 3*, p. 186. Copyright 1991 by Plenum Publishing Corporation. Reprinted by permission.

working with one student at a time. For example, the teacher:

1. Modeled the whole task of tying a shoe, using the student's shoe while giving verbal instructions (e.g., "First, I grab the laces, then I pull them tight. Next I cross this lace over to this side of the shoe. Then I cross the other lace to the other side of the shoe," p. 369).
2. Physically guided the student through the whole sequence (using as little assistance as necessary) with verbal instructions.
3. Asked the student to complete the task with no help and noted which steps the student completed independently.

Thus, a probe of the student's performance was made at the end of each teaching session. The three children improved in their independent ability to perform the tasks, and gains for two of the three participants were maintained over 7 to 12 months.

Time delay (described in more detail in chapter 4) is another effective teaching method. Constant time delay, which involves initial zero-second latencies fol-

lowed by four-second latencies, has been successfully applied to teach basic eating skills (Collins, Gast, Wolery, Holcomb, & Letherby 1991). Table 9–4 shows the task analyses Collins et al. used to teach a group of young students to eat with a spoon, drink from a cup, and use a napkin at meals. Teachers may either increase the delay period gradually in small increments of 1 to 2 seconds (*progressive delay*) or increase delay quickly by moving from no-delay trials to trials delayed by 4 seconds (*constant delay*). Applying the principle of parsimony (Etzel & LeBlanc, 1979), we recommend using constant delay, which is easier to use and which Collins found to be effective.

The *system of least prompts* has been applied to teach dressing skills (Young et al., 1986). During acquisition, the students were prompted first with verbal and gestural prompts when they did not respond or when they made an error. If the verbal or gestural prompt did not result in correct performance, graduated physical guidance was given. Students were given intermittent praise for success during teaching, and praise, hugs, pats, and stickers at the end of the task whenever performance was improved over the previ-

TABLE 9–4
Task Analyses for Teaching Mealtime Skills with Constant Time Delay

Behavior	Discriminative Stimuli	Response
Spoon	"Eat"	Grasp spoon
	Spoon in hand	Scoop food
	Food in spoon	Raise spoon to lips
	Spoon touching lips	Open mouth
	Mouth open	Put spoon in mouth
	Food in mouth	Remove spoon
	Spoon out of mouth	Lower spoon
	Spoon on table	Release grasp
Cup	"Drink"	Grasp cup
	Cup in hand	Raise cup to lips
	Cup touches lips	Tilt cup to mouth
	Liquid in mouth	Close mouth and drink
	Liquid swallowed	Lower cup to table
	Cup on table	Release grasp
Napkin	"Wipe"	Grasp napkin
	Napkin in hand	Raise hand to face
	Napkin touching face	Wipe face
	Face wiped	Lower napkin
	Napkin on table	Release grasp

ous session. Finally, inappropriate behavior, like not attending, was interrupted during training with a stern "No" and a 30-second time-out, which involved the teacher's merely turning away from the student. Once the student could perform a task correctly in a consistent manner without prompts, the training procedure Young and his colleagues used was changed to improve the students' fluency or rate of responding. Difficult steps, which were characterized by hesitation, more frequent errors, or self-correcting, were identified and given repeated practice. Thus, if a student usually hesitated and sometimes erred only when pulling the shirt off his head, he was given ten consecutive trials on this step alone.

Fluency. During fluency learning, students understand the task requirements, but need more practice to perform the skill consistently and at an appropriate pace. Students need to be motivated to improve fluency. When students are near mastery of acquisition learn-

ing (more than 60% of steps correct), it is often time to revise a program, reduce prompts, and address motivation (e.g., shift from antecedent prompting tactics to consequences, making reinforcement contingent on faster or more perfect performance). Targeting more fluent self-care routine performance often means placing an emphasis on *timed performance*: Teachers or students may time their own performance or students can learn to "beat the clock" to be ready for a preferred activity that follows the task. Other strategies to increase student motivation for practicing and perfecting skill routines include:

- Giving the students choices about the order of completing self-care tasks or what tasks to complete;
- Introducing a buddy system so peers can support students;
- Examining teaching methods: Are methods disliked by the student? Overly intrusive? Stigmatizing? Does instruction pull student away from preferred activities?
- Examining task difficulty: Is the student ready for a more challenging extension of the task and a reduction in teacher control? Is the task too difficult?

When difficult steps are simplified or eliminated or students are given extra practice on them, errors can be reduced and fluency enhanced. Fluency in self-care routines may be necessary for students to have the opportunity to use the skill. Consider the child who takes too much time to dress by herself; her parent often will dress her in the interest of a busy family routine. Jamal, the teenager we described earlier, experienced difficulty on one dressing step, which not only kept him from being fluent but also led to problem behavior.

When Jamal finds something intolerable he jumps up and down, screams, and runs. Intolerable events may be unfamiliar situations, changes in familiar routines, or a task he finds too difficult. One example of a difficult task for Jamal was doing up his button-fly jeans. In the toileting routine, Jamal was independent except on "button his jeans by himself." This meant he would leave the bathroom with his pants open, which constituted a social disaster at school! His teacher described one of two things that would happen at these times: (a) He'd wait until someone buttoned his pants or gave him hand-over-hand prompting, which he hated, or (b) his teacher would "back off," give minimal cues but repeat her requests to hurry him (because others wanted to use the bathroom), and he'd get very upset, yell, and jump up and down. After meeting to solve the problem, the team changed the program with good outcomes. His mom agreed to replace button-fly jeans with zipper jeans as he outgrew them, which would simplify the task. The OT cut the button-holes a little bigger, making them easier to button and unbutton (simplify task). Staff let him pick an activity photo, which he engaged in right after buttoning his pants (motivation). He worked by himself but could request "help" by signing (communication in place of problem behavior). Staff helped out little by little and praised him for the buttons he had done alone. Currently, Jamal buttons three and sometimes four of the five buttons.

Maintenance. When students begin to demonstrate some mastery of a task, teachers should select less intrusive strategies, provide more opportunities for students to perform independently (Table 9–2), build skill performance into the schedule as a routine, and fade artificial reinforcement that may have been used. The less intrusive strategies allow instructors to fade their presence altogether. Teachers can fade instruction and build routine performance in a number of ways, including:

- Stepping behind, then away from the student; engaging in other tasks nearby;
- Leaving the task area at gradually increasing but unpredictable times (Dunlap & Johnson, 1985);
- Introducing other students or typical peers into the instructional area, so that teacher time and attention are divided among students and less focused on the target student;
- Eliminating intrusive and special prompts, such as physical guidance and modeling, and including nonspecific prompts, such as simple pointing gestures or nonspecific verbal prompts (e.g., "What's next?");
- Using picture task schedules as "permanent prompts" for students to self-manage their daily self-care and chore routines; involving students in selecting and arranging task photos in a schedule book each morning (Bambara & Cole, 1997; Irvine, Erickson, Singer, & Stahlberg, 1992) (chapter 14 expands on ideas for self-prompting).

Teaching students to self-manage their dressing or grooming performances is a maintenance strategy gaining more attention. Several types of stimuli (e.g., pictures, picture checklists, tape-recorded messages,

and videotapes) can be used to teach students to prompt and monitor their own performance of a series of self-care tasks that they already know how to accomplish in part. For example, Garff and Storey (1998) taught young adults to use a checklist to self-manage hygiene during work, while Lasater and Brady (1995) used video self-modeling to teach shaving. When material prompting stimuli are used, they may or may not be faded, depending on the student, but such prompts are designed by the team to be non-stigmatizing, easily carried, and independently used. For example, students can select and arrange pictures of morning routine tasks in a pocket-sized booklet to be used like a schedule. For other students, a booklet of task pictures (used initially during acquisition training) may be shortened to single task photos and continue to remind students of task steps after teachers have faded their ongoing supervision (Figure 9–3). For students able to operate a small cassette tape recorder, the Pocket Coach (Attainment Company, Inc.) can facilitate self-management; teachers let students or peers record ahead a series of up to fifteen 12-second self-prompting messages (e.g., brush teeth, shave, shower and *shut curtain all the way*; dress, comb hair, straighten bed, *take medication*, and eat; pack lunch and get bus money). When a person presses the *play* button the message plays or repeats, but when the *done* button is pressed, the tape progresses to the next message.

FIGURE 9–3
Task Step Photos for Teaching Jamal Hand Washing

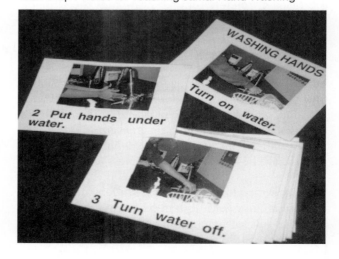

Thinesen and Bryan's (1981) study is a good example of self-management through pictures. They taught three men living in a group home to complete their morning grooming routine using a picture book. The men were given a book holding pictures of the tasks that they needed to complete each morning: (a) making a bed, (b) dressing, (c) washing face with soap, (d) shaving, (e) brushing teeth, (f) cleaning glasses (if needed), (g) combing hair, and (h) returning towel and washcloth to personal hanger. During instruction, a picture of a reinforcer was paired with each task, and each man received the reinforcer when he completed the task. The reinforcement was faded by gradually removing the pictures of reinforcement. The men's independence in completing the grooming routine increased and was still maintained when checked 16 weeks after training. During the follow-up phase, the men had access to a book of task pictures, but did not need them: Two men stopped using the book after the first week, and the third man would open the book to any page and then complete the sequence of tasks.

Generalization. During all the advanced stages of learning (fluency, maintenance, and generalization), it is important to reduce prompting and to fade from artificial to natural consequences. To make school and community environments supportive of skills, teachers may involve peers and show them how to give more natural forms of reinforcement (e.g., high 5, "All right!") and error correction (e.g., "Try it again," point to mistake). Environments should be arranged so that students can use their acquired skills regularly and obtain approval (or learn to give self-approval) for task completion at the end of a time period or after a cluster of related routines are completed (e.g., the three interrelated tasks of using the bathroom, washing hands, and returning independently to work). When students use self-scheduling photo books to plan their daily school schedule, self-reinforcement can be an added component of instruction. For example, students can learn to reinforce themselves: (a) by placing checks in a daily schedule book next to the task photos (plastic-covered photos of themselves), which they have completed; or (b) by removing completed schedule photos from one section of a scheduling book and placing them in another section. If particular steps are hard, the photo might portray the difficult part(s) of

the task, rather than the final step. (Refer to chapter 14 for more ideas on self-directed learning.)

Using multiple instructors (i.e., teachers, peers, therapists, parents) also enhances generalization because students learn (a) that "who's present" is less relevant than are task stimuli and (b) that they can complete the task despite differences between instructors and supervisors. Generalization is facilitated when students are expected to use the target skill during all opportunities across multiple environments (e.g., eating in the school cafeteria, home economics room, and restaurants; using the toilet and washing hands in the classroom toilet, the school restroom, the restaurant restroom, and the locker room). Teaching across multiple settings means the student learns to adjust the skill on the basis of (a) small or even large differences in materials, (b) changing background stimuli (e.g., noise, commotion, temperature), and (c) varying problems that arise. For example, differences from one bathroom to another include the door into the toilet, the presence or absence of a stall, the type of lock on a stall, the height of the toilet, the presence or absence of supports, the location of supports if present, the location and type of the toilet paper dispenser, the height of the sink and faucets, the type of soap dispenser, the type of paper towel dispenser, and the location and accessibility to the trash container. Even in one bathroom, it is not unusual to have several different soap and towel dispensers! Sailor et al. (1986) suggest recruiting speech and occupational therapists to provide therapy during instructional times, a strategy that not only increases the number of instructors but also facilitates the realism and thus the generalization of therapy gains. Teaching across multiple task opportunities facilitates generalization, although learning may be slow initially.

Reinforcement

Reinforcers should also be individually planned. What is socially reinforcing varies from student to student. Some students may need more concrete reinforcers (e.g., associated object present, not a photo), others may need more frequent reinforcement (e.g., praise during the task, preferred activity at the end). What to use, how much, and how to use it must be individualized by the team. The team aims to teach students to attend to natural reinforcers so their criterion performance is not stigmatized by or dependent on artificial reinforcers. For example:

- John's independent toileting is reinforced by having dry pants, increased independence, and privacy and by being like his peers. Feeding himself without spilling is reinforced by reducing his hunger more quickly and being neat like others.
- Jamal's ability to fasten and unfasten his pants by himself means that he finishes faster and he can go alone to the boy's bathroom.
- If Alycin can learn to change her feminine pad by herself, she can enjoy the privacy that goes with performing a very personal task on her own.

Still, during early instruction, especially if students have limited experience with natural reinforcers, completion of self-care activities alone may not be very reinforcing. Teachers should be prepared to use and systematically fade artificial reinforcers during these later phases of instruction.

Consider Related Skills for Instruction

As with many tasks, self-care tasks often have several components (Brown et al., 1987):

- *Core steps*: The essential behaviors that are involved in task completion.
- *Extension skills*: Task-related skills that provide options to expand meaningful participation but without extensive physical requirements (e.g., initiation, preparation, monitoring the quality, monitoring the tempo, problem solving, and termination).
- *Enrichment skills*: Task-related skills that, while not critical to the independent performance of a routine, add to the quality of its performance (e.g., expressive communication, social behavior, and preference or choice).

Understandably, many teachers focus on the core skills first, since these behaviors are what "gets the job done." But self-care routines provide opportunities to teach beyond the core, extending the task to a more useful level of performance and enriching the routine in ways that make it more pleasant and that integrate it with social and communication skills. For example, evening mealtimes for many of us signal a time to relax and connect with friends and family; thus, we socialize and talk to each other and make choices (all enrichment skills). (Annie and Frank in

Figure 9–4 show how they have extended and enriched their eating routines in the school cafeteria and during community-based instruction.)

While eating (i.e., consuming food and beverages by using utensils) means performing the core steps, there are also many ways to extend the core task and make it more complete.

Jamal has learned that the lunch bell signals that his "lunch bunch" peers will arrive and they'll head to the cafeteria, get and pay for their lunches, eat together, and when finished, will clean up by taking their trays and trash to the recycling bins and leaving utensils at the dish station. When Jamal learned to respond to the lunch bell and his lunch partners' arrival, he learned to initiate on his own. Mastering the lunch line (waiting, getting each item, paying) allowed Jamal to carry out preparation steps on his own. Jamal learned to watch his peers' cues to monitor his eating tempo (eat until the group is also done) and to monitor quality and solve problems by watching others as they cleared their places and recycled their trash into the right receptacles. After this is done, he knew that lunch was over (termination) and headed back to his home room.

Reflect on the school-aged self-care routines that lend themselves to socialization, communication, and choice: the extension skills. It is not unusual to see high school girls conversing while doing hair and putting on makeup between classes. Joyce's fingernail-painting routine (see Figure 9–5) is one routine that embeds many social, choice-making, and communication skills. We recommend that teachers enhance task analyses by adding extension and enrichment components to the core task and that they plan to teach during natural opportunities for these routines to occur, particularly when peers are involved. Students can be taught to communicate the desire to begin and end grooming tasks. For example, a student without independent mobility skills could request to be taken to the school bathroom to brush her hair after recess and request to be taken to class before she is late. Choice and approval of finished products are also communication skills that can be embedded into self-care routines. For example, a student who does not have the motor skills to style her hair may be able to initiate a need for grooming, make choices about style and accessories, and approve the final style.

With many self-care tasks, students can have a voice in the task outcome (i.e., making choices

FIGURE 9–4
Middle School Students Extend and Enrich Lunch Time
(a) Annie has the opportunity to communicate with the cafeteria cashier; and (b) interacts with a peer who helps her balance a cup for drinking. (c) Frank at a community-based eating activity where he communicates his need for assistance in getting more food by pointing to his picture board on his lap; and (d) Frank chooses what he wants, and his teacher gives physical guidance with serving.

a

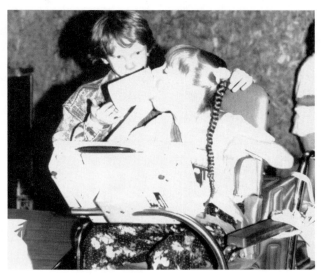

b

c

d

about clothes and hair) and should have an awareness of the personal nature of some tasks. Some students may be put at risk because instructors have accidentally taught them that it is acceptable to undress and toilet in front of a variety of adults. Students need to learn to discriminate and respond differently to trusted adults and mere acquaintances or strangers.

FIGURE 9–5
Painting Fingernails
Student partially participates in nail care activity by (a) requesting application of nail polish and giving directions on color preference with an eye gaze communication board, (b) holding still as nails are done, and (c) showing manicure to a classmate.

a

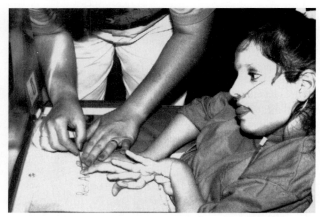

b

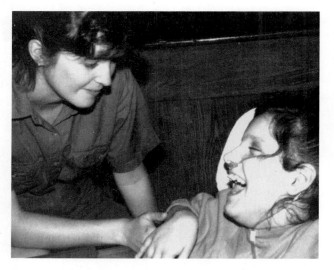

c

In the remainder of the chapter, we direct the focus first to toileting skills, then to feeding, and finally to dressing and grooming skills.

Special Considerations for Toileting

Assessment and Instruction

Toileting behavior is one of the most difficult self-care skills to teach because it requires an awareness of in-ternal stimuli (e.g., bladder fullness, bowel tension) and a lengthy sequence of related skills, which must be learned in part or full for the skills to be useful. In this section, we discuss the process for teaching these skills: (a) the prerequisites for toilet training, (b) assessment of daytime performance, (c) approaches for teaching daytime toileting, and (d) approaches for teaching nighttime toileting. (See Chapter 7 for bowel and bladder management for students who require atypical elimination procedures and Chapter 8 for specific toileting considerations for students with motor disabilities; see also Orelove and Sobsey, 1996, and Shephard, Procter, and Coley, 1996.)

Prerequisites for Toilet Training

Three characteristics are essential for readiness for toilet training. These characteristics are interdependent and relate to physiological development—specifically, the maturity of the central nervous system and the muscle sphincters involved in elimination.

- Stability in pattern of elimination
- Daily 1- to 2-hour periods of dryness
- A chronological age of 2 years or older

Generally, students who are ready for training have one bowel movement daily and three to five urinations, but many differ from this pattern. Urination and bowel responses should occur within predictable daily time periods, not randomly.

Assessment of Toileting Performance

In addition to the environmental assessments and task-analytic assessments of related behavior, a toileting or elimination record should be used to record periods of dryness, urinations, and bowel movements (see Figure 9–6 as an example.) The toileting record is a weekly grid with dates and time intervals of 15, 30, or 60 minutes on which school staff, parents, or care providers record type and location of elimination. At least during baseline (the period before a teaching program starts), it is essential to change the student into dry clothing immediately after each accident, accompanied by neutral teacher-student interaction (neither punishing or reinforcing), so that each accident is not confused with earlier accidents.

The purposes of baseline charting vary, depending on the method of toilet training and whether training will initially extend across home and school environments. Traditional toileting approaches rely on knowing the student's natural elimination schedule. To discover whether reliable toileting patterns exist and what these patterns are, most recommend that baseline charting continue for a minimum of at least 2 weeks, with a possible extension to 30 days if necessary (Baker & Brightman, 1997; Fredericks, Baldwin, Grove, & Moore, 1975; Giles & Wolf, 1966). It is wise

to continue charting throughout a toilet training program (a) so progress can be assessed by comparing successful eliminations to accidents, and (b) so training can be extended to additional "typical times" as the student demonstrates success for the initial target times.

Students' peers may be aware that a classmate is being toilet trained because of the frequency of removing the child to a nearby bathroom. As such issues arise, teachers should handle them with care and perhaps as part of peer planning groups (chapter 4). The team must be sensitive to the student's right to privacy when selecting the location for baseline assessment and training. We suggest that records be easily accessible by team members who will be recording information, but still secure and private— never taped to the bathroom wall.

The data collection form in Figure 9–6 illustrates one method for monitoring student toileting behavior during the school day; it can be extended to cover all waking hours. In classrooms, we suggest using 15- or 30-minute intervals. While shorter recording intervals (15 or 30 minutes) are more demanding on staff, they give a more accurate picture of the student's elimination pattern.

For one week Ms. Perez and her assistant, Ms. Anderson collected baseline data somewhat sporadically on a 30-minute interval elimination record, but no steady pattern emerged. Because this was a priority skill for John, the team decided to take two more weeks of data but increase pants checks to 15-minute intervals, as illustrated in Figure 9–6, and to assign staff to time intervals to improve their record keeping. At each interval, the assigned adult removed John to a private area and checked his diapers. If he had urinated, a U was recorded in the pants column; if he was dry, a D was recorded in the same column. Whenever he used the toilet, his performance was recorded in the toilet column as student initiated (+) or adult initiated (−). John did not have a bowel movement at school during baseline, which is why BM was not recorded. Ms. Johnson offered her students an opportunity to go to the bathroom upon arrival, on the way to and from physical education and lunch, and before leaving school. During these times, John was taken to the bathroom and these opportunities are recorded in the toilet column. On only one adult-initiated opportunity did John eliminate on the toilet (day 7 at 1:00). On day 6, staff found they were not as regular in their checks as they wanted to be and decided to record the exact time John was checked or eliminated (if known).

FIGURE 9–6

Data Recorded During the Last 7 Days of Baseline and the First 2 Days of Instruction from John's Toileting Program

Elimination Record

Student's Name: John Recorder(s): Perez, McLean, Lee, Anderson

	Baseline Data: Week 2											Instruction			
	Day 1		Day 2		Day 3		Day 4		Day 5		Day 6		Day 7	
	Mon		Tues		Wed		Thurs		Fri		Mon		Tues	
Time	Pants	Toilet	Pants	Toilet	Pants	Toilet	Pants	Toilet	Pants	Toilet	Pants	Toilet	Pants	Toilet
8:30 arrival		D−		D−		D−		D−	U			D−		D−
8:45 ind	D				D		D		D					
9:00 group	D		D		D		D		D		D		D	
9:15 group	D		D		D		D		D					
9:30 center	D		U		D		D		D		U (9:30)		D	
9:45 center	D		D		U		D		D				U (9:47)	
10:00 center	U		D		D		U		U			D−		D−
10:15 PE		D−		D−	U			D−		D−		D−		
10:30 PE														
10:45 language		D−	U					D−		D−		D−		
11:00 language	D		D		D		D		D		U (11:05)		D	
11:15 prep		D−		D−		D−		D−		D−		D−		D−
11:30 lunch	D		U		D		D		D		U (11:30)		U (11:35)	
11:45 lunch														
12:00 story		D−		D−		D−		D−		D−		D−		D−
12:15 rest	D		D		D		D		D					
12:30 rest	D				D				D		D		D	
12:45 art	U		D		U		U		U (12:45)				U (12:50)	
1:00 recess	D		U		D		D		D			D−		U− (1:05)
1:15 group	D		D		D		D		U			D−		
1:30 dismissal	D		D		D		D		D			D−	D	

Key: D = dry; U = urination; BM = bowel movement; toilet codes: + = student initiated, − = adult initiated; blank = unable to check; L = lunch.

Other: _____

Note: If it is possible to record the exact time of the elimination, use the second line for that time period.

After reviewing all 10 days of baseline data (7 of which are shown in Figure 9–6), four time periods were selected during the day for instruction: 9:45—before the 9:45 to 10:00 time when John usually urinated; 11:30—before lunch; 12:45—after lunch (because John used the bathroom then to clean his face and hands) before the 1:00 time John usually urinated; and right before dismissal, because John's mother reported he was usually wet when he arrived home. In addition, as John was usually wet on arrival at school, he was always changed at 8:15. John's bladder training plans involved taking him 5 to 10 minutes before his usual urination times.

In addition to elimination, assessment should address the skills involved in the toileting routine. Table 9–5 sets forth 12 basic toileting components and lists potential teacher cues and student behaviors that relate to each component. Some components, such as pants down and up and hand washing, have multiple steps. Teachers should develop a task analysis that suits the individual but that is also generic enough to be used with the variety of toilets a particular student uses during the training period.

Whenever team members took John to the toilet, they taught John to use his canes to walk from his wheelchair to the toilet and provided related skills instruction. On the days when he wore clothing with fasteners, they taught fastening and unfastening, but he was taught to flush and wash his hands after toileting every time.

The specific student behaviors and their order in a task analysis also must be considered by the team. For example, with younger children, a better method of teaching wiping requires the child to stand up and then wipe rather than to remain seated. If skirts or dresses are worn, the "pants up and down" sequence changes. Some students with physical disabilities may be more independent if they sit or lean on the toilet to remove their pants. The most "typical" urination position for boys is to stand and face the toilet, and for girls, it is to sit. However, initially, boys as well as girls are taught to use the toilet while sitting; later, boys who have adequate motor control will be taught to stand.

For Alycin, partial participation is necessary for the task steps of pulling pants down and sitting on the toilet. Partial participatory steps are incorporated into her task analysis:

At home, Alycin's mom uses a one-person supported transfer, which involves Alycin being pulled to standing (Alycin can bear weight), pivoted in place, and having her pants lowered (by mom); lowering Alycin onto the adapted toilet seat; and fastening the seat belt. School staff will work with the OT, PT, and mom to modify their two-person transfer so it can be safely executed by one person, making toileting at job settings more feasible. The three will also problem-solve ways for Alycin to be actively involved.

As Alycin's case illustrates, the toileting components, teachers' teaching cues, and student behaviors listed in the task analysis must be individualized.

Approaches for Teaching Daytime Toileting

In this section, we describe several broad approaches to teaching daytime toileting: traditional, improved traditional, and rapid. The primary difference between traditional and rapid methods is the toileting schedule:

- Traditional methods (day and night) rely on toileting students when they are likely to experience bowel or bladder tension (when the bowel or bladder is naturally full).
- Rapid methods (day and night) require students to consume extra fluids, creating more frequent bladder tension and thus additional opportunities for toileting.

Most children learn to control their bowel movement without accidents before they acquire bladder control, and they master daytime before nighttime control. This general pattern also is true for individuals with disabilities, though there are exceptions.

Traditional Toilet Training Methods

Training Considerations. Before beginning instruction, the instructional team must consider clothing, toileting position, and task order. Clothing students in training pants or ordinary underwear rather than diapers is recommended, as it can facilitate detection of accidents during baseline and training (Dunlap, Koegel, & Koegel, 1986). Removing diapers allows learners to experience the naturally unpleasant feedback from wet or soiled clothing that modern diapers have virtually eliminated; these naturally occurring, uncomfortable consequences of accidents can contribute to faster learning. However, without diapers,

TABLE 9–5

Basic Behavior Components in Toilet Training with Teaching Cues and Initial Student Behaviors

Behavior Component	Teacher's Training Cue (Individualized to Suit Student)	Initial Forms of Student's Behavior[3]
Recognizing the need	Do you have to go?[1]	Senses internal stimuli May show outward behavior (grabs genitals, grimaces)
Waiting	Do you have to go?[1]	Senses internal stimuli May show outward behavior (grabs genitals, grimaces)
Entering the rest room.	Go to the toilet.	Walks directly to rest room.
Pulling pants down	Pull your pants down	(Unfastens belt, buttons, zippers) Hooks thumbs into tops of underpants Pushes underwear and outerwear to at least mid-thigh
Sitting on the toilet	Sit on the toilet.	Sits on the toilet seat.
Eliminating	"Pee"[2]	Eliminates.
Using toilet paper	Wipe yourself.	Stands. Reaches and grasps toilet paper. Pulls out and tears off an appropriate amount. Bends and wipes self. Drops paper into toilet.
Pulling pants up	Pull up your pants.	Grasps top band of underpants. Pulls up and into place. Grasps outer pants at waist. Pulls up and into place. (Fastens buttons and zippers.)
Flushing	Flush the toilet.	Places hand on top of flusher. Pushes down on flusher.
Washing hands	Wash your hands.	Approaches sink. Turns water on. Wets hands. Picks up soap and rubs hands. Replaces soap. Soaps hands. Holds hands under water and rinses hands.
Drying Hands	Dry your hands.	Reaches for and grasps paper towel dispenser crank. Turns crank several turns to release appropriate amount. Grabs paper and tears off. Holds paper between hands while turning hands. Drops paper into trash.
Exiting the rest room.	Time for _____.	Leaves rest room. Goes to next activity.

[1]The internal cue of bladder or bowel tension becomes the controlling stimulus after training is complete.

[2]Use language suited to the student's chronological age, the setting (school or home), and family practice.

[3]Behavior form may change in later learning (e.g., boys may stand to urinate); task steps will vary to suit conditions and student.

students' toileting accidents can be noticed by peers and be stigmatizing, especially beyond the preschool years. Teams (including family members) must decide the appropriateness of having students wear diapers or not and may make exceptions to this guideline to avoid noticeable accidents. Training pants with plastic pants over them may allow the student both privacy and feedback. For some students, it may be best to remove diapers only with intensive or isolated instruction or if training occurs at home during summer vacation. Teams may decide that wearing diapers in school even when training is under way may be the appropriate choice.

Stages of Toileting Training

Usually as students learn toileting they move through stages, somewhat parallel to the stages of learning, discussed earlier. Some students attain all three stages, others may attain only the first or the first and second stages.

Stage 1: Regulated Toileting. The first stage of toileting is learning to become regulated to a toileting schedule (also called habit-trained or conditioned). Students who acquire reliable patterns of bowel movements and urination can stay dry if someone else reminds or assists them to go to the toilet at scheduled times. School staff can observe the signals that elimination is imminent and then prompt students to use the toilet; alternately staff can take students to the toilet at certain times (e.g., after lunch, before the students' bedtime, at the parents' bedtime). Keeping a fairly stable eating and drinking pattern paired with reinforcement for correct toileting behavior helps students achieve toileting regulation.

John's data in Figure 9–6 indicates that he is at this stage of toilet training: regular periods of dryness and elimination, but only rare eliminations on the toilet and no self-initiations.

Stage 2: Self-initiated Toileting. The second toileting stage toward independence is self-initiation and involves learning to discriminate the natural cues of bladder fullness (for bladder control) and pressure in the lower bowel (for bowel control). During this stage of learning, we want students to make a connection between these internal stimuli and the response of eliminating on the toilet. Giving positive feedback as soon as students eliminate on the toilet helps them

make this connection. Once a student is sitting on the toilet, teachers may make regular checks and (depending on its appropriateness) listen or look for urination or defecation so they can provide reinforcing feedback with little delay. Students may tell someone or signal a need to use the bathroom or they may seek permission or simply initiate toileting on their own; these are signals both for enthusiastic praise and getting them to a bathroom quickly with as little help as necessary.

Generally, Alycin can initiate the need for a toilet, and her pattern of elimination is very regular. Several initiation challenges remain for her and school staff: (a) Alycin being able to reliably signal others with her electronic communication board, (b) staff learning to attend to Alycin's requests and act upon them, (c) staff more efficiently providing assistance to get her to a toilet and make the transfers from wheelchair to toilet, and (d) Alycin learning to participate in the toileting components more quickly.

Stage 3: Toileting Independence. The final stage in the toileting process is gaining independence. Independent students not only are aware of the need to toilet but also manage clothing and related cleanup skills (e.g., wiping, flushing, washing hands). At this stage, trainers fade themselves out of the bathroom during routine toileting and the focus shifts to skill generalization, fluency and proficiency issues (e.g., speed, elimination of all accidents, social awareness), and routine performance. For many students, nighttime training may also be initiated at home.

Jamal is working on independence: he self-initiates, has not had an accident at school for over a year, and can perform most of the related skills. Once Jamal learns to unfasten and fasten his pants, he will have achieved independence.

Several authors recommend training steps and related practices that may make traditional bowel or bladder training more successful (Baker & Brightman, 1996; Fredericks et al., 1975; Linford, Hipsher, & Silikovitz, 1972; Schaefer & DiGeronimo, 1997):

1. Continue diapers when students are neither bladder or bowel trained; the training focus typically will be bowel training first because it is easier to learn; also accident cleanup is easier and involves giving less attention. Any accidents are changed in the bathroom without a fuss. If bladder training is the focus, training pants are better than diapers,

but the team needs to decide depending on the circumstances.

2. Learn how the student signals the need to eliminate. Signals for a bowel movement are more obvious (e.g., gets quiet, squats, strains, red in face). Whenever these signals occur, take the student to the bathroom even if it is not a scheduled time, and then record these times on the record.

3. Follow the toileting schedule consistently, changing times only after the team analyzes new elimination patterns and elects to make adjustments.

4. Use the regular toilet, with adaptations added only as necessary: (a) to keep the student's feet flat on the floor or on a nonslip support and (b) to keep the student sitting securely (e.g., toilet seat inset). Sometimes (as in Alycin's case) specialized toilet chairs are needed, support bars (as in John's case), or perhaps even potty seats (if the child is younger than age 5 and very small). If students are unstable while sitting, they will have trouble relaxing the sphincters that control elimination. When needed, team members should pool their talents to generate appropriate adaptations that are nonstigmatizing and practical.

5. Keep the toileting time positive but not distracting. Any rewarding activities (e.g., toy play, books) should take place after toileting and out of the bathroom. Unneeded conversation (e.g., social talk, singing, rhymes) is kept to a minimum, though talking about the toileting task in ways suited to the student *is* appropriate.

6. Take the student to the toilet according to schedule or when a need is signaled. Approximately:
   - 15 minutes before the scheduled time for *bowel* training
   - 5 to 10 minutes before the scheduled time for *bladder* training

   The specific length of time for sitting on the toilet should be determined on the basis of individual student characteristics. The student should be placed on the toilet long enough to have the opportunity to eliminate but not for so long that toileting becomes aversive.

7. Reinforce the student when elimination occurs. If elimination does not occur, return the student to the classroom for a 5- to 10-minute interval and then return to the toilet. Continue the alternating intervals until elimination occurs. Record any extra toileting times and the outcomes.

8. Continue elimination records so the team can evaluate progress and adjust toileting times as needed.

9. Consider extending goals as the student is successful (e.g., add more times, add bladder training, move from regulation to a focus on self-initiation and then independence).

Table 9–6 illustrates some of the basic rules of a traditional toilet training approach (Hobbs & Peck, 1986).

TABLE 9–6
The Rules of Toilet Training

Do	Do Not
• Reinforce students for using the toilet (e.g., praise, physical contract, tangibles, as appropriate for age, student, setting).	• Do not reinforce students when wet. Do not talk, scold, or give eye contact or unneeded touch.
• When there is an accident, clean the student without delay.	• Avoid letting students get social reinforcement while wet or soiled.
• Until students are clean, remove them from class activities, without reprimand.	• Do not let students get used to being wet or soiled.
• In private, clean students impersonally with damp towel after accidents (should be neutral, not reinforcing); dress in dry clothing.	• Do not give showers or baths to wet or soiled students.
	• Do not let students eat or continue eating when an accident occurs before or during a meal. Clean the student first.
• Give students regular opportunities to use the toilet (e.g., once every 2 hours or more often).	• Do not skip or delay a scheduled toileting.
• Stay with or nearby students while they are on the toilet, listen and watch for their elimination, and reinforce eliminations immediately.	• Do not leave students during toiletings because you may miss an opportunity to reinforce eliminations. Do not delay reinforcement.

Note: Adapted from Hobbs, T., & Peck, C. A. (1986). Toilet training people with profound mental retardation: A cost effective procedure for large residential settings. *Behavioral Engineering, 9,* p. 53.

Improved Traditional Methods

When traditional toilet training is insufficient, teachers may consider one or more of the following procedures: (a) pants inspections, (b) consequences for accidents, (c) increased fluids, or (d) the use of moisture-signaling devices.

Pants Inspections and Reinforcement. Pants checks consist of assessing whether or not a student is wet or dry and providing appropriate feedback (reinforcement for continence or signaling a need to change if wet). During the first two phases of toileting (regulation and self-initiation), pants checks serve to increase student awareness of being wet or dry. When learning to become independent, pants checks can help students maintain continence. These checks were introduced as a component of rapid training programs (Azrin & Foxx, 1971; Foxx & Azrin, 1973). The technique consists of three steps:

1. Question the student about dryness, using simple phrases and gestures (e.g., "Are you dry?").
2. Prompt the student (in a manner that respects his or her privacy) to look at and feel the crotch area of the pants.
3. If the pants are dry, reinforce with praise for dryness ("Good, you have dry pants! Pick a music tape."). If the pants are wet, indicate their wetness with disappointment and withhold reinforcement ("Oh, you have wet pants. No music.").

Specific length of intervals between pants checks, their timing, the feedback given for wetness and dryness, and reinforcement for continence should be individualized by the team to suit the student. Feedback should always be directed toward increasing student awareness of being dry and wet; when wet, pants should be changed.

> John's first instructional program consisted of the traditional methods described above, half hourly pants inspections, and enthusiastic verbal praise for dry pants. When this was not successful, pants checks were increased to 15-minute intervals whenever sufficient staff were present in the room.

Consequences for Accidents. When students are learning toilet control and are purposefully taken out of diapers, some accidents must be expected. Thus, a regular procedure for responding to accidents should be planned by the team. In most cases, extinction

(planned ignoring) will be the consequence of choice, however, the team may consider several options:

1. *Extinction.* Following an accident, change the student's pants and clean the student in a neutral manner, with little socialization. Be careful not to provide any reinforcing activity too soon after an accident (Hobbs & Peck, 1985).
2. *Disapproval.* As soon as an accident is discovered, approach the learner *in a manner that respects his or her privacy*, have the student feel and look at the pants, and express some disapproval in your words and facial expressions ("Oh, you wet your pants." or "No music. You have wet pants."). Leave the student wet for up to a few minutes to experience the discomfort. Then change the student, using the extinction procedure.
3. *Cleanup.* Require the student to participate in washing themselves and changing their clothing. Student cleanup should be implemented as a natural consequence with little socialization. Requiring the student to repeatedly practice going to the toilet or to do more than required (e.g., mop the entire floor where the accident occurred instead of just cleaning the soiled area of the floor; changing all clothing when only training pants were soiled) is aversive and should not be used. Use the cleanup participation strategy cautiously, as students who require prompting to clean themselves up may be reinforced by attention for the accident or may become upset emotionally. Also, some students who clean themselves independently may find it reinforcing to leave classroom demands.

The approaches for handling accidents must be carefully matched to a given student. Note that if extinction is selected, neither disapproval nor student cleaning up of accidents should be used. However, disapproval and cleanup consequences may be used together, or disapproval may be used alone. Cleanup typically includes mild disapproval.

Regulating or Increasing Fluids. Another strategy to improve instruction when students are not making progress is to control or increase the frequency of instruction by loosely regulating or by increasing the student's fluid intake. Loosely regulating fluids simply involves scheduling the times of day that a student has fluids (not necessarily an increased amount) so it is coordinated with toileting instruction. For example, if, during baseline, a teacher notes that a student tends to urinate approximately 2 hours after drinking, the teacher could schedule a fluid break 2 hours before a convenient time to implement toileting instruction in an appropriately private setting. We do not know of any research on this method of informally redistributing the fluids that would be drunk or offering an extra drink to coincide with scheduled toilet training. If used, several practical guidelines should be followed, which are addressed after a discussion on increasing fluids.

Alternately, having the student drink one to three small glasses of juice, milk, or water during the school day can provide more opportunities for the student to eliminate and therefore to receive instruction. The use of increased fluids, or hydration, as a means of promoting urination and, thus, extending the opportunities for bladder training must be ac-

companied by certain precautions. When the intake of water or other liquids is forced or encouraged over an extended period, the balance of electrolytes in the body may be seriously endangered. *Hyponatremia*, or a low serum sodium level, may result. Hyponatremia is associated with nausea, vomiting, muscular twitching, grand mal seizures, and coma (Thompson & Hanson, 1983). This condition "constitutes a serious medical emergency requiring prompt sodium replacement therapy and other medical support" (p. 140).

If the team decides to increase fluids, we recommend that fluids not be increased by more than three small servings. This will allow regulation of toileting opportunities without putting the student's health at risk. Fluid regulation also must be used cautiously and teams must be flexible in their plans: If students want fluids when not scheduled to have them or do not want them when scheduled to have them, the plans for fluid

 John's Toilet Training

When John's team looked at his instructional data, they decided that his pattern of elimination was too variable to predict full bladder times accurately. They decided to attempt to stabilize the morning urination pattern by giving John a 6-oz beverage of his choice as soon as he arrived at school, and again at lunch. With the fluid increase, John consistently urinated around 9:30 and 12:30, so his teachers selected 9:20 and 12:20 for toileting times. On John's first occurrence of urinating in the toilet (2 days after the program revision), Ms. Perez cheered for him. John praised himself, saying that he had gone to the bathroom "like big boys do." Within 2 weeks, John was no longer having accidents at school. His mother reported that John was still arriving home wet. When giving John an additional opportunity to use the toilet before leaving was unsuccessful, the team decided to eliminate the extra fluid at lunchtime. This solved the problem on the bus, but John continued to have toileting accidents at home.

The next phase of the program planning concerned the home: (a) the use of diapers was stopped, (b) John's mom took him to the toilet every 2 hours, and (c) John was praised for having dry pants. These procedures were successful in getting John to maintain dry pants for 1 month both at home and school.

Then, John's team began self-initiation training at school. Instead of automatically taking John to the bathroom at designated times, they asked (as is typical to do in Kindergarten), "Does anyone need to use the bath-

room?" If John did not respond, they prompted him to raise his hand and took him to the bathroom. When he responded in the affirmative to the question without prompts for 1 week, they no longer prompted him to use the toilet. If he raised his hand, they took him to the toilet; if he did not, they allowed him to continue his classwork. John remained dry and spontaneously requested to go to the bathroom. At this point, the teachers withdrew the increased fluids.

John successfully maintained dry pants for 2 months with self-initiated requests only. Then, his mother reported that he began having accidents at home and on the bus again. Within a few days, the accidents began at school also. John's mother reported that his father had received a temporary transfer and was living in another town for 3 months. John's accidents seemed to occur only when his father was away, not when the father was home with the family. The team decided that John's mom and his two teachers would re-institute verbal reminders for using the toilet. Every hour, John was taken to the bathroom if he needed to go. His response was honored; if he said yes, he'd go to the toilet, but if he said no, he continued his activity. Finally, his dad agreed to call daily and praise John for his successes at school and home in toileting and other areas. This procedure reduced accidents to one or two a month. When John's father returned home, the hourly prompts were faded and John continued his success in toileting.

regulation must changed to reflect students' requests. Increased fluids should not be forced on students when they indicate they do not want them.

Moisture Signaling Devices. One possible reason students may not learn toileting is delayed feedback. Students who wear modern disposable diapers often feel little discomfort when they are wet, and teachers may be unable to identify exactly when elimination occurs. Learning to associate bowel or bladder tension with elimination (e.g., sphincter relaxation) is facilitated when students are quickly taken to the toilet during urination or bowel movement and receive approval. Moisture-signaling devices are used to signal the moment of elimination.

Two types of moisture-detection or urine-signaling devices have been used along with other teaching methods:

1. Toilet alert: A special potty chair or a small toilet bowl that fits under the regular toilet seat which catches eliminations and triggers an auditory signal through the detection of moisture (Foxx & Azrin, 1973; Herreshoff, 1973), and
2. Pants alert: Training underpants that detect moisture when students eliminate in their clothing (Mahoney, Van Wagenen, & Meyerson, 1971; Van Wagenen & Murdock, 1966; Smith, 1979). These special underpants involve a circuit and switch plan somewhat similar to the toilet signal; the signaling device is attached to the pants, shirt, or vest pocket.

Both devices involve a low-voltage circuit being completed when moisture activates the switch for the auditory signal. The signal allows staff to provide students with appropriate feedback the moment an elimination occurs. Moisture-detecting switches connected to a potty chair or toilet inset signals the moment for positive reinforcement; moisture-detecting underpants signal the moment an accident occurs. Thus, reinforcement and accident procedures can be implemented without delay. (Refer to Azrin, Bugle, and O'Brien, 1971; Herreshoff, 1973. These devices are available through the Sears & Roebuck Co. and the J.C. Penney catalogs and are carried by many local pharmacies; pediatricians also can direct parents or teachers to suppliers.)

Despite the efficiency of signaling the moment of elimination, the disadvantages of moisture-signaling equipment in a toileting program are multiple. The equipment, which is noisy and fairly obvious (especially when it signals), can be quite stigmatizing to students who use it. If students spend time in regular education classes and activities in the school and community, such equipment use may not be appropriate. Other problems with the device include expense, breakdown, or failure (Mahoney, et al., 1971; Smith, 1979). However, for some students, moisture-signaling equipment may be appropriate during, for example, an at-home summer program. Teams should view moisture-signaling devices as optional and for use in unusual situations in which toileting progress has been minimal and toileting control is relatively important for the individual.

Rapid Training Programs

Current Views of "Rapid" Approaches. "Rapid" toilet-training methods actually are rather complex training packages based primarily on the research of Azrin and Foxx (Azrin & Foxx, 1971; Foxx & Azrin, 1973, 1974) or of Van Wagenen, Mahoney, and colleagues (Mahoney, Van Wagenen, & Meyerson, 1971; Van Wagenen, Meyerson, Kerr, & Mahoney, 1969; Van Wagenen & Murdock, 1966). Some components of the packages (e.g., pants inspections, moisture-detection devices) have already been discussed. The packages are described as "rapid" because the program usually is delivered with high intensity, and researchers often have reported rapid changes in student performance. However, the intensity of the delivery conflicts with some of the accepted best practices in the field today, and the speedy results have not been consistently replicated by others.

Most applications of rapid approaches to toilet training have employed one or more of the following questionable practices: (a) fluid increases that may be dangerous; (b) removal of the student from all or most instruction other than toileting; (c) removal of the student from opportunities to participate in interactions with nondisabled peers; and (d) the likelihood of excessive punishment. Two rapid approaches (Mahoney, Van Wagenen, and Meyerson, 1971; Richmond, 1983) are less intrusive and nonaversive in their application; we describe only Richmond's procedure because, unlike Mahoney's approach, it does not require expensive, specialized signaling equipment.

Richmond's Rapid Procedure. Four preschool children with profound retardation were successfully toilet trained with increased opportunities to use the toilet.

Intervention consisted of four training phases (i.e., toileting every 15 minutes, every 30 minutes, every hour, every 2 hours), each lasting 1 week, and followed by a posttraining, or maintenance, phase. Each toileting trip was proceeded by a pants check. If no accident was detected, the child was praised for having dry and clean pants ("Good for you, Danny, your pants are dry and clean."). The teacher then asked the child, "Do you need to use the toilet?" The child was prompted to respond and go to the rest room. In the rest room, the child was praised for engaging in the related toileting behaviors (e.g., pulling pants down and up). If necessary, graduated guidance was used for these behaviors. Social praise and liquids were given for successful toileting, and no comments were made when accidents occurred. Extra fluids served both as reinforcers and to increase the frequency of urination. When an accident was detected, the teacher gave a brief reprimand and simple correction (i.e., the child was responsible for getting a clean set of clothes, removing the dirty clothes, washing soiled body areas, disposing of dirty clothes, and dressing). Their schedule for morning preschool continued even with the frequent toileting interruptions. Richmond's results offer encouraging news to teachers in that simple toileting methods applied in a consistent manner can be effective over a 9- to 15-week period without extreme techniques or schedule changes.

Eliminating Toileting Accidents

There is less research that deals with the problems of partial toileting control during waking hours. Two somewhat different approaches have been used to eliminate toileting accidents once bladder control is attained. The first approach is to ensure continuity of treatment across the settings a person uses daily. Dunlap, Koegel, and Koegel (1984) employed the combination of training methods (i.e., pants checks, urine-sensitive pants, reinforcement for success, and graduated guidance for related behaviors) on a schedule of once or twice an hour. They found that when similar approaches were employed at either the school or the homes of three young students with autism, students made no clear progress toward mastery. Only when training methods were consistently and simultaneously implemented across these and the other community settings that the students visited daily were steady gains made in successful toileting. One adult per child was designated as the pro-

gram coordinator, whose job it was to (a) initiate contact with a designated support provider in each setting, (b) ensure that this person understood the teaching and data collection methods, (c) ensure that the child carried written instructions to facilitate consistent use of procedures by staff, (d) ensure full-day coverage, (e) contact trainers immediately after the first day to check the procedure and answer questions, and (f) continue regular phone contacts with trainers to promote coordination and consistent implementation of treatment. For two of the four students, however, infrequent bowel accidents continued for several months after bladder control was attained, making the effects of the continuity-of-treatment approach on bowel accidents less clear.

In the second approach to reducing bladder accidents, Barmann, Katz, O'Brien, and Beauchamp, (1981) combined hourly pants checks with a somewhat normalized version of positive practice or cleaning up after accidents (i.e., a punishment technique in which a student is required to restore a situation after an accident to an extreme level of cleanliness). For example, when the three boys with moderate to severe mental retardation were dry they were praised verbally, but when wet they were required to: (a) get a towel, (b) clean up all traces of urine or feces, (c) go to their bedroom and get clean pants, and (d) place the wet pants in a diaper pail. The pants check and praise for dry pants were used in both the home and the school, while positive practice was required only at home to test whether its effects generalized into the classroom. For all three students, the procedures led to substantial improvements over their baseline accident levels of 3 to 4 accidents daily. Once overcorrection was instituted in the home, there was an immediate decline in accidents there and at school, followed by complete elimination of accidents.

Encopresis, or partial bowel control, can take two forms: (a) retentive (extreme constipation) and (b) nonretentive (soiling). Treatment programs must match the type of encopresis and the actual and likely reasons for its presence. Boon and Singh (1991) and Doleys (1985) recommend individually designed teaching programs that emphasize reinforcement for appropriate bowel movements, periodic pants checks, and possible use of laxatives or enemas in the early stages of training, but no punishment.

Approaches for Teaching Nighttime Toileting

Fredericks et al. (1975) and Linford et al. (1972) describe variations in traditional nighttime training procedures that they found successful in individuals having severe disabilities, but they unfortunately do not report any objective outcome data. Support providers using a traditional approach should follow the general steps listed below.

Traditional Procedures

1. Decrease the liquids a student has during the evening; 1 1/2 to 2 hours before bedtime, no more fluids are given.
2. Ask the student to go to the toilet just before a fixed bedtime.
3. Before training starts (during baseline), check the student every hour, if possible, to obtain a night elimination schedule.
4. Analyze 2 weeks of records and identify the time that is typical for accidents. About 30 minutes before this typical accident time constitutes a time for training; target a second earlier training time about 1 to 2 hours after going to bed. Once these two target times are identified begin training.
5. Before bedtime, instruct the student in simple language and gestures (and perhaps showing a reinforcer) that a dry bed will be rewarded in the morning (e.g., a special breakfast food, toy, an activity). In the morning, check the bed and enthusiastically reinforce the student if it is dry. Ignore wet beds.
6. Check the student for accidents or dryness about 1 to 2 hours after going to bed, and record results on a nighttime chart.
   a. If dry, wake and reinforce the student (this step may be omitted).
   b. If wet, wake and neutrally change the pants, pajamas, and sheets. Involving the student neutrally in some cleanup is an option the team may consider.
7. Also awaken the student 30 minutes before the usual accident time and, if not wet, direct him or her to go to the toilet. Require that the student sit on the toilet without sleeping for 5 minutes, or less if the student urinates. Praise and chart successes but neutrally return an unsuccessful student to bed, charting a failure to eliminate.
8. If the student is wet when awakened, neutrally clean the student and return him or her to bed, chart the accident, and awaken the student earlier the following night.
9. Once the wake-up time that allows the person to be toileted once and remain dry has been identified, strengthen the student's ability to withhold urine for longer periods each night by gradually moving the wake-up time in intervals of 10-15 minutes forward or backward depending on whether the time was closer to bedtime (add time) or wake up time (subtract time). Continue charting accidents.
10. Continue to provide powerful reinforcers in the morning for dry beds while giving social praise during the night for correct elimination or dry bed checks.

Signaling devices have been developed to assist in nighttime toilet training and have been used successfully with students having multiple disabilities (Coote, 1965; Lovibond, 1963; 1964; Mowrer & Mowrer, 1938; Seiger, 1952). Moisture-signaling devices tend to take several weeks or months to establish initial control, but do so in about 80% to 90% of people who have nocturnal enuresis. Unfortunately, relapse is common (Lovibond, 1964; Sloop & Kennedy, 1973; Smith, 1981). When a team elects to use moisture-signaling devices, they must understand the equipment, familiarize the student with it, and ensure that the student will not be injured from potential misuse.

Special Considerations for Eating and Mealtime

Assessment and Instruction

Eating is perhaps the most functional and frequently used of all self-care skills. When developing individualized plans for teaching eating and mealtime behavior, teams focus on the general goals of healthy eating (e.g., meeting nutritional needs, eating without choking) and eating as independently as possible. This section of the chapter addresses elements of assessing and teaching basic mealtime skills in learners whose objectives aim or will aim for self-feeding. Two other chapters address issues we do not cover but which are relevant for many students: nutrition monitoring and supplementation and nonoral feeding procedures (chapter 7) and specific feeding and eating considerations for students with motor disabilities (chapter 8). Current references supplement the coverage of these topics (Case-Smith & Humphry, 1996; Christensen, in press; Orelove & Sobsey, 1996).

Eating is unique in the self-care domain because, in addition to filling our primary needs for nutrition, mealtimes are often a time for socializing. Mealtimes mean conversation, getting together with friends and family, sharing, and enjoying food. This should be true for students with disabilities, too. Pleasant and gratifying mealtimes can enhance the maintenance and generalization of eating skills and the social and communication skills embedded in eating routines. Teams should structure mealtime and eating instruction so social opportunities are not lost but used for learning and enjoyment.

Eating is also unique in the self-care domain because the need for instruction must be considered in light of nutritional needs. Individual student characteristics influence the amount of teaching time. Ideally, some instruction can be provided on core and related skills throughout each entire meal and snack. However, some students (i.e., those with physical disabilities, just beginning to learn self-feeding or exhibiting interfering behaviors) require unusually long mealtimes and may become fatigued and discontinue eating. If a student is not eating enough to maintain nutrition or the mealtime instruction is interfering with time to teach other priority goals, teachers may schedule instruction initially for the first one third to one half of the meal, and more fully assist the student during the remainder.

The Sequence for Teaching Mealtime Skills

The core eating skills typically are taught in a general developmental sequence beginning with various aspects of dependent feeding (e.g., anticipates spoon, uses lips to remove food with utensils), eating finger foods, eating with a spoon, drinking from a cup, using a fork, spreading and cutting with a knife, serving food, using condiments, and displaying good table manners. In general, targets should be both realistic in relation to the current performance of students and also immediately or subsequently relevant (prioritized by the family or teacher as being needed on a regular basis). Additionally, students must learn to eat a variety of foods, since food refusal and food overselectivity can put students at risk nutritionally, for growth, and for other health problems.

Not all eating skills, however, should be taught in a developmental sequence. Incorporating into mealtime routines the related skills a student can do or can learn will facilitate improvements in independence later. For example:

> When Alycin was very young and highly dependent on others for feeding, parents and teachers taught her to initiate eating by making the sign for eat and vocalizing the "Eee" sound. Then, they put her bib on her tray and she learned to feel for and grasp it.

Likewise, teaching skills in a functional order, even if not the developmental order, may be the best option. For example, Mary, who is age 8, knows how to use a spoon without spilling, but does not use a fork or cut with a knife. Developmentally, she "should" master these first, but her team has decided that using a napkin and going through the lunch line are more functional, even if she bypasses fork and knife use for now.

Prerequisites for Instruction in Self-Feeding

For students to be successful in learning self-feeding, they need an active gag reflex and the skills of sucking, maintaining closed lips, swallowing, biting, and chewing. Mastery of these basic skills greatly reduces the risk of choking. Before beginning assessment or instruction, students should be in the proper position for eating, even when they do not have extensive or obvious motor disabilities or high or low tone in their muscles. Proper position has a big impact, not only on learning and success with eating, but also on the prevention of choking and the aspiration of food. The student's head must be stable, in midline, and with the chin and jaw as near to parallel with the floor as possible.

Monitoring Student Performance at Mealtimes

Monitoring at mealtimes can be challenging during phases when the student still requires physical assistance. Eating skills and related mealtime behaviors may be measured in several ways: (a) frequency or percent of correct responses, (b) duration or rate of correct responses, (c) frequency or percent of errors, (d) duration or rate of errors, and (e) task-analytic assessment. (Chapter 5 describes these measurement methods in more detail.) Team members can observe and assess throughout an entire meal routine, for part of a meal, for several trials (e.g., eating with a spoon, drinking from a cup), or can observe the after-effects of eating (e.g., assess the mess on the table and floor). One decision that affects these choices is whether the behavior is viewed as being a discrete or isolated behavior or as a task composed of component skills. For example, spoon use has been defined as a discrete behavior: "Moving appropriate food from the container (e.g., pudding, soup) with the spoon held in one hand, by the handle, right side up and without spilling (except back into the container from which the food was taken)" (O'Brien & Azrin, 1972, p. 391). The same skill has also been defined as a task made up of component steps: "Grasp spoon, scoop food, raise spoon to lips, open mouth, put spoon in mouth, remove spoon, lower spoon, release grasp" (Collins, et al. 1991, p. 163) (see Table 9–4).

Related and embedded skills may also be a focus for monitoring instruction. Figure 9–7 shows how a teacher collected data on the component skills for eating lunch in a school cafeteria by using a task analysis while counting the number of correct fork use responses in the first 10 opportunities.

Mike (introduced in Figure 9–1) has just gotten an electric wheelchair and needs to learn how to control it. In addition, he is beginning to use an augmentative communication device (i.e., a folder with pages for specific activities during the day). Mike has some verbal language, so his teacher is monitoring greeting skills, too. Skills in these three areas (i.e., mobility, communication, social skills) are embedded in the task of getting lunch in the cafeteria. The targeted eating skill for Mike is stabbing bites of food with his fork. The teacher collects data on the number of correct stabs (e.g., stabs a bite of food on the first attempt and moves the food into his mouth with no spilling). In the cafeteria line, peers help Mike reach for food items and put them on his tray and also provide guidance on operating the wheelchair. Task steps for peers and cafeteria workers are noted in parentheses in the task analysis.

For Mike's instructional program, data are summarized by percentage of steps correct in the total task; the frequency of bites with appropriate fork use (i.e., no assistance and no spills off the plate); and the frequency of embedded skills (e.g., communication, mobility, and social steps).

During the first 2 weeks of the program, the teacher monitors student and peer tutor performance and models appropriate prompts for the peers; she collects data daily during this ini-

tial period. As peers begin to provide appropriate levels of assistance, the teacher withdraws and lets the peers implement the program independently, observing and collecting data less often, while Mike, the peer assistants, and the cafeteria workers informally report on Mike's progress.

The combination of embedding related priority skills into the lunch routine with using peer models constitutes a powerful approach for building mealtime skills.

Team members should expect students to be messy while they are learning to eat. Spilling and other errors of untidyness go along with learning to eat with one's fingers and with utensils, using adapted utensils or eating equipment, and drinking from a glass. If spilling and messiness errors continue as students acquire the basic steps, teachers should conduct observations and task analytic assessments to determine where the errors occur in the response chain (e.g., locating food, grasping utensils, scooping out of the bowl, bringing food to the mouth, putting food into the open mouth, leaving food in the mouth, chewing food, swallowing food) and why (e.g., poor lip closure around the spoon). Messiness is not only influenced by the student's level of skill but also by the student's muscle tone and control, the sitting position, the type and consistency of food, and the utensils, cups, or adapted equipment.

Alycin has been making progress using her electric self-feeder independently. Once set up and positioned, the self-feeder requires that someone monitor the food on the rotating plate, but Alycin can operate the switch to activate the spoon that dips automatically into the food as the plate turns. Alycin's mom has learned a lot about the required casserole food consistency that keeps spilling to a minimum. She makes lasagna 16 different ways and freezes it so the family can eat most meals together, while Alycin uses her self-feeder. The new self-feeder they hope to purchase will help Alycin eat soups, cereal, and ice cream.

At an early planning meeting, the OT initially suggests that adapted equipment will help John with his messiness. Therefore, Ms. Perez gives him a bowl with a built-up side and utensils with built-up handles. Although John is neater with the built-up materials, he complains about not having a cafeteria tray like others. Later, because John prefers the natural materials, the team decides to eliminate the special bowl and utensils and use reinforcement for neatness. At school, neatness is rewarded with preferred activities. At home, John's mother agrees to serve ice cream contingent on having a

FIGURE 9–7

Data Sheet for Component Skills of Eating in the School Cafeteria

Student: Mike

Program manager: Carla

Setting and time: Lunchroom, 11:35

Peers: Bill, Jane, Karen

Stimulus: Teacher tells students that it is time for lunch

Procedure: System of least prompts (SLP) for all steps except wheelchair

Graduated guidance (GG) for wheelchair steps

Date	10/5	10/6	10/7		
1. Initiates driving wheelchair to area where lunch folder is kept (mobility)	H	H	H		
2. Picks up folder and places on tray	P	P	G		
3. Navigates hallway to get to cafeteria (mobility)	H	H	H		
4. Enters line and positions chair in front of milk cooler (mobility)	H	H	H		
5. Opens folder and points to picture indicating milk choice (communication) (Peer: Gets milk and puts on tray)	P	G	V		
6. Moves to food area (mobility)	H	H	H		
7. Greets cafeteria worker (social) Cafeteria worker asks Mike what he wants to eat	V	+	+		
8. Points to picture indicating choice (communication) (Peer: Puts plate on wheelchair tray)	G	V	+		
9. Moves to salad/dessert area (mobility)	H	H	L		
10. Points to salad/dessert choices in communication folder (communication) (Peer: Puts items on tray)	V	V	V		
11. Moves chair to cashier (mobility)	H	H	L		
12. Greets cashier (social)	V	V	+		
13. Hands lunch money to cashier	G	G	G		
14. Waits for change to say "thank you" (social)	+	+	+		
15. Goes to lunch table (mobility)	H	H	H		
Percent steps correct (out of 15)	6%	13%	33%		
• Correct fork use responses during first ten opportunities (10)	III	IIII	IIII		
Embedded skills (13) • Communication (3)	0	0	2		
• Mobility (7)	0	0	0		
• Social (3)	1	2	3		

Key: + = Independent
SLP: *V*erbal, *G*esture, *P*hysical
GG: *H*and-over-hand, *L*ight touch, *S*hadow

clean table and floor area after eating. This is effective on most days. However, some foods, like lasagna, prove particularly difficult to eat. For difficult foods, John is given the adapted materials. With these procedures in effect, John is able to eat in the cafeteria with his kindergarten class and to eat more neatly at home.

Instructional Strategies for Eating and Mealtimes

A variety of methods have been successful in teaching mealtime skills (Table 9–2). Specifically, shaping and physical prompting procedures (including physical prompts on time delay and graduated guidance) have been shown to promote the acquisition of eating skills. Sometimes, these strategies have been combined with error correction, but positive procedures alone have been successful in other cases. Generally, graduated guidance and shaping are the recommended procedures for building basic eating and self-feeding skills during the acquisition stage.

Once students have learned the basic core eating skills (e.g., pick up spoon, scoop food), other teaching methods have been demonstrated to be more effective to promote learning in more advanced stages. For example, skills can be maintained and made more fluent with simple reinforcement (e.g., praise and confirmation: "That's right!") and error correction. The procedures used to correct errors in these later stages of learning may include teachers' or peers' verbal statements and models (observation learning; see Table 9–2).

Next we discuss special considerations in the teaching of eating finger foods, drinking from a cup or glass, and using utensils and provide examples of graduated guidance and shaping.

Eating Finger Foods

The first sign of independence in self-feeding is the predictably messy stage of eating finger foods. If the team's initial observations emphasize needs in utensil use as well as coordination of grasp, lift, and placement of finger foods in the mouth, finger food instruction should have priority. At this early stage, students use pincer grasps and hand-to-mouth movements to pick up food in combination with the sucking, gumming, chewing, and swallowing of many soft foods, such as bananas and saliva-softened toast. Eating finger foods provides essential opportunities

to improve the movements necessary for later utensil use. Finger feeding also allows opportunities for continued instruction in chewing. Teachers can use meal and snack times to introduce students to a variety of textures and tastes.

For Alycin, an adapted sandwich holder does not really work; it tends to smash her sandwich and she cannot eat the end; instead Alycin eats a lot of finger foods, which someone holds out for her to grasp. Her favorites are rolled up cheese and sandwich meat.

Drinking from a Cup or Glass

Initially, students help parents or teachers hold the cup or glass and lift it to the mouth. At this early stage, and when individuals first drink from a cup independently, they use both hands. When students have the potential to master drinking from a cup without assistance, straw use also may be taught, but typically, this is not taught until after drinking from a cup is learned. For students like Alycin, who cannot acquire independence in cup drinking, drinking liquids from stabilized cups through straws is a good alternative means to achieve complete independence.

Alycin has been drinking on her own for years. She uses her Dynovox (or indicates by yes or no responses) to tell what beverage she wants and, once poured into her sports cup (covered with a straw), it is placed into a stabilized cup holder within reach on her tray or in a holder on her self-feeder tray.

Use of a straw also may be a functional skill for students in restaurants and cafeterias, where most peers or customers drink from straws. As with finger feeding, the learning process is messy.

The type of cup chosen for training may influence the initial success of students. Stainback and Healy (1982) suggest that short, squat cups that do not turn over easily and can be held without difficulty are best to begin with. With preschool-aged students, a weighted cup may be appropriate, although most cups of this style have a clear association with infants and are not age-appropriate. Similarly, whereas double-handled cups are easier to hold, they also may not be age-appropriate in design. However, plastic-handled coffee mugs (with or without the top) may be a good substitute. Durable plastic cups are obviously safer to use than are containers made of glass, brittle plastic, or paper. Spouted or nipple cups should never be used, because they stimulate abnormal sucking and do not allow students to master the correct drinking response, but sports cups with built-in straws are easily available and often used by teens and adults (Mueller, 1975).

The amount of liquid in a cup should not be excessive (to reduce spilling) but also should not be so insufficient that students need to tip their heads too much to drink, increasing the difficulty of the task. Adapted cups that are cut out on the upper side (for the nose) can allow students with physical disabilities to drink all of the fluid without tilting their heads at all (see Figure 8–6).

After students learn to drink holding handled cups or small glasses with both hands, teachers can begin to emphasize a reduction in spilling. Spilling can occur while drinking but may also happen as a cup or glass is grasped, lifted, or replaced on the table. Eventually, as drinking and other self-feeding skills improve, students should be reminded to lift glasses with only the dominant hand.

Using Utensils

Once students have the skills of grasping finger foods, moving food from a table to the mouth with their fingers, along with the basics (i.e., lip closure, chewing, and successful swallowing), teams can plan instruction on using utensils. At this time, observations should be made to assess the student's ability to pick up and eat with a spoon. Using utensils can be taught simultaneously with instruction on drinking from a cup.

Typically, utensil use is taught sequentially, from the simplest skill to the most difficult. Spoon use is the simplest of the utensil skills, followed in order of difficulty by eating with a fork, transferring spreads with a knife, spreading with a knife, cutting finger-grasped bread with a knife, and cutting meat with a fork and knife. The typical sequence is: (a) spoon, (b) fork for spearing, (c) knife for spreading, and (d) knife and fork for cutting. Children may be able to eat using utensils in a palm-down finger or fist position. Teachers may use this grasp for initial instruction and teach the more mature, palm-up position after students have made gains in their ability to eat independently.

At age 6, John needs to learn to cut bites of food with a fork. At a team meeting, the occupational therapist (OT) shares her concerns that John will not acquire cutting with a fork

FIGURE 9–8
Everyone benefits when students learn to eat independently.

until his fine-motor abilities improve. The team still decides to teach fork use, but it is not a priority for John. Ms. Perez and an assistant teach cutting with a fork, using graduated guidance at the beginning of lunch whenever foods require cutting with a fork. The prompt levels that they use are full assistance on the hand, light assistance on the hand, assistance on the wrist, assistance at the elbow, assistance at the shoulder, and independence. Ms. Perez and the assistant fade the prompts as they notice improvement in John's independent movements. Although John does not master cutting with a fork before the end of the year, he learns to cut soft foods like cooked vegetables, fish, and cake by himself.

Addressing Problem Behaviors at Mealtimes

A large portion of research on eating has addressed related problem behaviors, such as eating too rapidly (Favell, McGimsey, & Jones, 1980; Luiselli, 1988; Knapczyk, 1983) and eating too slowly (Luiselli, 1988). In this section, we describe teaching approaches found useful in shaping skills, promoting neatness, and reducing problem eating behavior (e.g., eating too fast or too slowly, food refusal, food selectivity, stealing others' food). These methods include: pacing prompts, changing the eating environment, and shaping appropriate behavior through various consequence approaches (i.e., contingent reinforcement and error correction, contingent reinforcement alone, and altering reinforcement schedules). More serious eating problems, such as pica (i.e., eating nonedible substances), excessive weight gain, and extreme food refusal are not addressed here. Teams facing these problems may need to broaden the team membership to include medical input and to use additional assessment tools (e.g., functional assessment to study the conditions that seem to be maintaining the behavior; medical assessments and health monitoring). (Chapter 6 addresses functional assessment; chapter 7 discusses health monitoring).

Pacing Prompts to Slow Eating Rate. Instruction aimed at pacing may be needed for some students in the fluency stage of learning: for example, students who have the ability to use utensils or to drink from cups or eat finger foods but do so too quickly or too slowly. Prompts to slow down or speed up a student's pace of eating, referred to as *pacing prompts*, have been an effective way to establish an appropriate rate for eating. Excessively rapid eating can be a serious problem because of social acceptability and potential health problems (e.g., vomiting, aspiration, poor digestion). A survey of persons with severe and profound retardation living in institutions (Favell et al., 1980, p. 482) defined "normal" eating rates as about eight bites per minute with the total meal consumed in 15 to 20 minutes. "Rapid" eaters, however, "consumed food at rates sometimes exceeding 20 bites per minute, and finished their entire meal within 1 to 3 minutes" (p. 482).

In one pacing prompt approach, Luiselli (1988) taught a girl with deafness and mental retardation to pause for 5 seconds between bites and thereby decrease her rate of eating. The teacher was positioned to block the left hand from leaving the student's lap and to physically guide the girl's right hand. The girl was allowed to take one bite. Then, the teacher guided the girl's hand to the table, and she was prompted to keep her hand on the table until the food had been swallowed and to wait an additional 5 seconds. After a reasonable rate of eating was achieved, the physical prompt was faded and used only after errors.

Knapczyk (1983) used another variation of pacing prompts to reduce rapid and sloppy eating in a student with cognitive and motor disabilities (i.e., mod-

erate cerebral palsy with poor arm and hand coordination). The student used a spoon, but only ate pureed foods and did not pause between bites. Frequently, he performed the eating cycle without putting any food on his spoon, and excessive spilling occurred during every meal. During the first phase of instruction, the teacher placed one spoonful of food into an empty bowl and gave verbal instructions with manual guidance to eat the spoonful and lay down the spoon. This procedure was repeated until the student followed the request without help. The amount of food was increased gradually over 9 days, until the student was able to consume his entire meal and still pause between bites. During follow-up, pureed food was changed to solid food without any disruption of pausing between bites.

Pacing Prompts to Speed Up Eating Rate. Pacing prompts have also been used to increase the rate of eating. Luiselli (1988) increased the rate of eating in two girls with dual sensory impairments: one girl took approximately 1 hour to complete meals and the other initiated self-feeding only for hamburgers. The teacher provided pacing prompts for the slow eater after every 40-second pause, guiding the girl's hand to grasp the food and bring it to her mouth. The girl's rate of eating increased and her need for prompts decreased during the treatment phase.

Pacing prompts to promote self-initiation of eating in the second girl consisted of the following steps:

- Physical guidance to get food to within 2 inches of her mouth and a 5-second pause to allow her to place food in her mouth.
- If the student consumed the food, she received specific verbal praise and a sip of cold water (a preferred reinforcer).
- If the food was not consumed, the teacher returned the girl's hand to the table and waited 15 seconds for the next prompted trial.

Although the student's level of self-feeding was extremely variable, the treatment resulted in marked gains in food consumption.

Consequence Procedures. Several studies have applied primarily consequence methods to address utensil use and improvements in eating a variety of foods. Riordan and colleagues (Riordan, Iwata, Wohl, & Finney, 1980; Riordan, Iwata, Finney, Wohl, & Stanley,

1984) reduced food refusal and selectivity in younger students with severe disabilities by using reinforcement alone. In the first study, the number of correct bites and foods across food groups was increased by presenting two children with bites of a more preferred food after every bite or sip of a less preferred item (Riordan et al., 1980). When some students began to hold food in their mouths, the program was adapted, and reinforcement was presented only after they swallowed. Reinforcement was faded by gradually increasing the number of bites and the variety of food items that students had to consume to earn the preferred food.

Riordan et al. (1984) employed similar procedures to decrease food refusal and increase the variety of foods eaten by four children who were "at risk" as a result of malnutrition. During the baseline, a variety of foods were presented for the students. Foods accepted during baseline were used during intervention as reinforcers for the other foods. During the teaching phase, when a student accepted a target food, the behavior was reinforced with a bite of a preferred food. One child was reinforced with toy play because she did not regularly accept any food item. All students showed improvement in the number and variety of foods accepted when reinforcement was made contingent on the acceptance of a nonpreferred food. Their improvements were maintained with an intermittent schedule of reinforcement, and parents were able to apply the same methods at home. Follow-up results indicated that all children ate more food, more varied foods, and gained weight. One student's improvement even allowed the removal of a gastrostomy tube for feeding, and another student's improvement led to development of self-feeding skills.

Altered reinforcement schedules were also used by Riordan et al. (1984) to increase a student's ability to accept and eat a range of foods. Rather than moving reinforcement to the end of the meal, intermittent reinforcement (i.e., bits of preferred foods) was used throughout the meal. Because most of us rotate across different food items during a meal, the practice of alternating bites of preferred foods (intermittent reinforcement) with bits of less preferred food is a normalized way to fade reinforcement contingencies.

The problem behaviors of *food stealing* and *scavenging*, often observed in older research done in institutions, may possibly be identified in some students in school settings. Smith, Piersel, Filbeck, and Gross

(1983) used a change in the eating environment plus shaping of appropriate behavior to reduce food stealing in a young woman with severe retardation. The program started by seating the student at a table away from others and giving her frequent reinforcement with favorite foods for longer and longer periods of no stealing. Over successive treatment phases, peers were seated by the woman and reinforcement was gradually reduced. If she did steal food, the stolen food was removed. Then the young woman was moved back to her peers' table to eat, and researchers randomly chose one of three meals a day as the "training meal," when reinforcement was contingent on no stealing. When the treatment was delivered at one random meal daily, the behavior was reduced in all meals. Then, because she could sit with others and not steal or scavenge, reinforcement was faded so it was available only at the end of the meal; her behavior reduction was maintained under these conditions.

Other researchers have attempted to increase appropriate mealtime behaviors and decrease problem behaviors with potentially aversive strategies. These approaches have been based on the rationale that students allowed to steal food or eat with their hands have little reason to learn to use utensils. The mildest aversive technique used for these mealtime-related problems has been a brief nonexclusionary time-out from eating (also referred to as interruption-extinction). Nonexclusionary time-out has been effective in improving mealtime behavior in individuals with severe disabilities (Barton, Guess, Garcia, & Baer, 1970; Christian, Holloman & Lanier, 1973; O'Brien & Azrin, 1972; Song & Gandhi, 1974). For some students, a 30-second removal of the plate or tray has been an aversive consequence strong enough to eliminate food stealing, food throwing, mouth stuffing, eating with hands, and inappropriately using utensils. Note, however, that while Barton et al. (1970) found that these briefly applied punishment procedures quickly eliminated stealing, treatment guidelines may prevent the elimination of students' meals as a violation of their basic rights. Teams will need to rigorously apply a range of positive methods before even considering approaches that involve punishment.

Informal assessment revealed that John is able to chew his food, that he is able to keep his mouth closed while chewing (although he doesn't usually do so), and that he responds to verbal cues. The team decided that Ms. Perez and the assis-

tant should use verbal prompts and reinforcement to teach John to consistently and thoroughly chew his food with his mouth closed. Once the program was under way, they noted that he sometimes responded to verbal prompts by opening his mouth wider, thrusting his tongue, shaking his head from side to side, and laughing. To counter these "silly" behaviors, the team agreed that Ms. Perez and the assistant should use a brief interruption-extinction consequence along with the prompting program. When John opens his mouth while chewing, they remove his tray until he closes his mouth, completes chewing, and swallows. This time-out is never more than 30 seconds. Separately, Ms. Perez talks to John's peers and problem-solves how they might help reduce John's silliness. Classmates decide they will not laugh or smile when John engages in silly behaviors but will try hard to notice his neat eating (with his mouth closed). Two boys admit to having a hard time remembering to eat with their mouths closed, so they suggest sitting nearby and "working" with John on this same skill of neat eating. Several classmates who are extra-good models will sit among them. These procedures prove effective, and after 10 days of the extinction procedure, John consistently keeps his mouth closed to chew and swallow.

Special Considerations for Dressing and Grooming

Assessment and Instruction

Having some ability to participate, fully or partially, in grooming and dressing activities and the responsibility for doing so not only lightens the load on care providers but also opens numerous opportunities for choice and control in one's life. Individuals who dress and groom themselves to suit peer and community standards make better impressions on others. For these reasons, instructional goals in grooming and dressing typically receive priority ratings by families and support providers. In response to a questionnaire, parents ranked skills in the domestic domain as significantly the most important among the curricular areas (Epps & Myers, 1989).

In this last section, we talk about the teaching of dressing and grooming skills. Our discussion covers: (a) the range of skills, (b) instructional considerations, (c) materials, (d) embedded behaviors, and (e) recent research. Our focus is primarily on learners who will become actively involved or independent in their daily routines of dressing and grooming.

Chapter 7 addresses issues related to dressing: positioning considerations and teaching tactics for students with motor disabilities and atypical muscle tone. These current references provide more information: Christensen, in press; Orelove and Sobsey, 1996; Shephard, Procter, and Coley, 1996; Snell and Vogtle, in XX.

Range of Skills

The dressing and grooming curriculum for students with severe disabilities encompasses routines that almost everyone engages in at least daily: (a) brushing teeth, (b) combing and brushing hair, (c) washing face and hands, (d) showering or bathing, (e) using deodorant, (f) dressing, (g) undressing, (h) selecting appropriate clothing, and (i) evaluating one's appearance and making adjustments if necessary. The more difficult tasks in dressing and undressing include shoe tying and fastening and unfastening buttons, snaps, hooks, zippers, ties, and belts. Grooming routines performed less frequently include: clipping, filing, or painting fingernails; menstrual hygiene; shaving face, underarms, or legs; and applying makeup. Routines such as shaving and makeup are specific to the student's gender and personal preference. Other skills, such as bathing or showering, washing hands, brushing teeth, and menstrual care are critical for maintaining good hygiene. Finally, skills that are nonessential, such as painting fingernails (see Figure 9–4), wearing makeup, or grooming a beard, can be very important to certain individuals.

Instructional Considerations

When students with disabilities have friends of the same age and gender who are able to perform the skills they are trying to master, learning by observing them and by getting their assistance offers a viable supplement to teacher-directed trials. Supporting this practice are several areas of research. First, it appears that scheduling increased opportunities to practice a task being taught facilitates learning (Lehr, 1985), although teachers must clearly balance any need for intensive instruction on a skill with the student's learning needs in other areas and with the learning needs of classmates. Second, work by Wolery and his colleagues (Table 9–2) emphasizes the effectiveness of learning by observing others perform. Third, research indicates that spacing the learning opportunities, or trials, on a given skill across the day is more conducive to learning than is massing trials in a concentrated shorter period of time (Mulligan, Lacy, & Guess, 1982). Fourth, learning grooming tasks under natural conditions (e.g., time of day, location) is more likely to speed learning (Freagon & Rotatori, 1982) and to promote skill transfer and retention (Reese & Snell, 1991; Snell et al., 1989). Finally, making the teacher's presence and supervision less predictable to learners (i.e., the teacher comes and goes at random times during the students' performance of grooming tasks, providing teaching and reinforcement when present) has been shown to result in increased attending to tabletop tasks and better performance with children who have autism (Dunlap & Johnson, 1985). Taken together, these studies lend some support to the use of typical peers as models and informal task assistants during some natural grooming opportunities.

> *Jamal will need a lot of instruction before he can tie his shoes by himself, but his teacher is optimistic. She lets him get extra practice on tying simple knots by tying plastic grocery bags when he gathers and packages things for recycling with other eighth graders. Since they have started recycling three times a week, Jamal has learned to make the half knot. Peers also are good models: They are willing to slow down their tying and verbalize the steps while he watches.*

Dressing and Grooming Materials

When selecting materials for instruction, teachers should use real materials (e.g., clothing, toothbrushes, deodorant) as much as possible. However, the use of larger clothing for initial instruction, faded over time to appropriate clothing sizes has been demonstrated as a potent strategy (Azrin, Schaeffer, & Wesolowski, 1976; Diorio & Konarski, 1984; Reese & Snell, 1991). The use of larger buttons to introduce buttoning was also effective (Kramer & Whitehurst, 1981). Surprisingly, Kramer and Whitehurst (1981) also found it easier for children to button the top buttons that were out of view rather than beginning with lower buttons.

To promote generalization of dressing and grooming skills to new materials and settings, students must be taught using a variety of materials and settings. Teams should decide what materials and what settings are most appropriate (e.g., nonstigmatizing, preferred, privacy) and most feasible (e.g., close, fit daily schedule). Sometimes in grooming instruction, teachers are not able to use real materials and may supplement with artificial or simulated materials. Two such times concern teaching simple wound care and the instruction of women on menstrual hygiene. In the latter instance, instruction needs to be regular and to last longer than a single menstrual cycle. Epps et al. (1990) compared two instructional approaches, both of which involved simulation: (a) changing artificially stained underwear or a pad on oneself and (b) using a doll and materials to practice these same maneuvers. Women taught using the dolls did not demonstrate generalization of their skills to themselves, but once they were given instruction on themselves, they were able to perform these same skills during their menses. When using task simulations to teach, match the simulation to the actual task as much as possible. The authors in this study agreed with this general practice. They noted that changing pads on dolls differs greatly from performing the same task on oneself. In addition, they found that when the simulated menstrual amount and stain was dissimilar from the woman's actual menses onset, generalization was worse than when the similarity was close. Their materials included examples of different colors and styles of underwear; underwear with stains in different locations; and underwear with no stains. As we mentioned earlier in this chapter, Epps and her colleagues also learned that ordinary women in the community expressed a preference for teaching initially on dolls rather than on the individual herself; thus, instructional methods need to be designed to effectively promote efficient learning and generalization for individual learners, while also being socially acceptable to those who do the teaching.

Embedded Behaviors in Dressing and Grooming Routines

Dressing and grooming routines provide numerous opportunities to develop self-determination through enrichment skills, such as making choices, communicating preferences, and interacting socially. For some, dressing and grooming are opportunities to express creativity in choosing clothing, hair styles, and other fashions. The extension skills of initiating tasks, persisting through completion, solving problems, and monitoring speed and quality are a big part of independence in the grooming and dressing domain. Extension skills can be performed on a partial or full participation basis. (Figure 9–9 illustrates how extension and enrichment skills can be embedded in the grooming task of brushing or combing hair.)

Recent Studies in Dressing and Grooming Research

Observation Learning or Modeling

Several recent studies lend support to the practice of learning by watching others perform competently or by watching others being taught. This ordinary teaching approach has been called by different names: observation learning (Shoen & Sivil, 1989; Wolery, Ault, & Doyle, 1992), passive observation (Biederman, Fairhall, Raven, & Davey, 1998), and self-modeling (Dowrick & Raeburn, 1995). Wolery et al. (1992) have demonstrated several important features of *observation learning*:

- Students are taught in small groups of 2 or 3 and focus on similar skills.
- Students are asked or prompted to watch the student who is being taught as he or she performs the skill.

FIGURE 9–9
Task Analysis for Grooming Hair

Domain: Personal Management					
Interval/Form: Daily/Fixed					
Routine: Grooming Hair	Yes	No	NA	With Adaptation	Comments
1. Grooms or indicates need to groom at such times as when hair is messy, before going out, after gym (initiate)					
2. Finds and selects needed items such as comb, brush, or pick (prepare)					
3. Combs, brushes, or picks hair (core)					
4. Checks hair for neatness (monitor quality)					
5. Grooms hair within acceptable time (monitor tempo)					
6. If a problem arises, such as a tangle or can't find brush, will take action to remove problem (problem solve)					
7. Puts comb or brush away, cleans up loose hairs if necessary (terminate)					
8. Expresses or communicates about any aspect of hair grooming, such as need for haircut or style (communication)					
9. Makes choices concerning hair grooming, such as choosing between comb or brush, type of barrette, hairstyle (choice)					
10. Grooms hair according to social standards, in acceptable settings, responds appropriately to comments of others (social behavior)					

Note: Adapted from "Delineating functional competencies: A component model" by F. Brown, I. M. Evans, K. Weed, and V. Owen, 1987, *Journal of the Association for Persons with Severe Handicaps.* Adapted with permission.

- Students in the group take turns performing the target skill while others observe.
- One student can be taught half a task while others watch; instruction then moves to another in the group for the other half. Students can learn some or all of the task steps that they have only observed.

Passive modeling, also used with chained tasks, involves instructors as models who demonstrate the whole dressing or handwashing task. Observing students are then given turns to perform but receive little or no verbal or gestural prompts or even social praise. Passive modeling was more effective than both interactive modeling (i.e., hand-over-hand instruction with ongoing verbal prompts and praise) and less rigorous verbal prompting (Biederman et al., 1998).

Video self-modeling is a little different from the other observation approaches in that students review videos of their mastery performances, edited to omit errors and produce recording of "advanced" skills. Dowrick and Raeburn (1995) made videos of students ranging in age from 5 to 13 performing skills (with the needed supports) that were priorities for them: dressing upper garments, dressing outer clothes, and other non–self-care skills. Students all had motoric disabilities (e.g., cerebral palsy, spina bidifa). Camera shots showed closeups of key component behaviors. The edited tape showed students as much more competent performers than they actually were because the tapes omitted errors and views of therapists providing assistance. To test the effects of self-modeling, some priority tasks were randomly chosen for each student for the video treatment, while no videos were made of other tasks. Over a 2-week period students could watch their videotape without discussion and all did. Consistently children were judged to have made significantly more progress on tasks involving self-modeling, and those gains did not lapse but continued over time. These findings on the positive effects of video replay suggest the potential that self-observation may have as a teaching strategy for dressing, alone or in combination with other methods.

Simultaneous Prompting

Simultaneous prompting involves intermittent probe trials and teaching trials. During *probe trials*, students are asked to perform the entire task without assistance, errors are ignored, and these steps completed for the student without comment. *Training trials* involve cueing the student to look at task materials, giving a task request, and prompting and praising the student on each step of the task, with an activity choice reinforcer at the end. Sewell et al. (1998) used simultaneous prompting during activity-based routines to teach two preschoolers with developmental delays to take off shoes, socks, and pants and to put on shirts, shoes, and jacket. Skills were taught in the context of routine activities that required the skill (e.g., taking off socks before dress-up play, sensory play, ball-bin play, and rest time; putting shirt on for dress-up play, water play, and "messy" art activities). The teacher assessed student performance in a probe trial each morning and completed one-on-one instruction throughout various times of the day. The teacher first provided an attentional cue (e.g., "Look, [student's name]" or "Look at [article of clothing]") and then gave full physical assistance and verbal directions and explanations throughout the task. The student received continuous verbal reinforcement as long as she allowed physical assistance. The students also got to perform a preferred task after the dressing skill was performed. The teacher used a variety of clothing to encourage generalization.

While it may seem strange that prompts are not faded during training trials, it is the contrast between training trials (all prompted) and probe trials (no prompts) that gives (a) students an opportunity to perform without assistance and (b) teachers an opportunity to view student learning. Probe trials must be given daily. When learning occurs, training trials end and team members aim for skill maintenance.

Other Teaching Techniques

Another method used with grooming skills is forward chaining, which involves teaching in a forward direction through task steps and "building" a student's performance as each additional step is learned (Figure 9–10). Forward chaining has been used to teach menstrual care (Epps, Stern, & Horner, 1990; Richman, Reiss, Bauman, & Bailey, 1984). Epps et al. faded prompts by requiring students to return to the beginning of the task after errors, until they performed without a prompt. Thus, whenever students made an error, they practiced the appropriate response with the prompt until performing correctly. Then, the student was instructed to begin the task again and no prompt was given. This procedure was

Grooming Application to John

John's team views dressing and grooming as priority areas. Because he is 6 years old and has many other needs and motor limitations, most objectives in the dressing and grooming areas reflected partial participation. The skills his team selects for instruction are those John uses most often: washing hands, washing face (needed after all meals), and unfastening and fastening clothing for toileting.

The team examined John's schedule and identified natural opportunities for teaching these skills. Washing hands and manipulating fasteners are taught whenever John goes to the bathroom. Washing his face is taught after lunch. At school, Ms. Perez or her assistant teach all skills in the boy's bathroom. At home, John's mother teaches in the family bathroom. Later in the school year, when a male teaching assistant, Mr. McLean, is hired to work with the primary grades, the team decides to ask him to teach John when other boys are present in the bathroom. John has some experience with washing his face and hands, and he is able to complete some steps with minimal guidance. These skills are task-analyzed and taught to John, using a system of least prompts.

Manipulating fasteners is a more difficult skill for John because of the fine-motor requirements. The OT helps team members design a simple version of graduated guidance to teach the skills, so John will get the feel of the motions required. Prompting begins with full physical assistance but changes based on the pressure cues of John's improved performance of the skill steps; as he initiates successfully, guidance is reduced to shadowing.

At the end of the year, John sometimes demonstrates the ability to wash his face and hands independently, but he also requires verbal reminders at times. The team's plan is to fade verbal reminders by having Mr. McLean stand just outside the bathroom door to observe and praise successful efforts. He notes that John sometimes throws away a paper towel without washing his hands. Although John is not at 100% accuracy, he is correctly imitating the behaviors of his typical peers, who do not always wash their hands either. By the end of the school year, John needs only reminders to check how his face looks after washing but still requires some physical assistance with fasteners.

repeated until the student could perform the entire task without any errors.

Richman et al. (1984) used an alternate approach to teach feminine hygiene. On the first trial, the women were prompted through the entire task. Then they were allowed to perform independently on the

FIGURE 9–10
Physical Therapist Uses a Forward Chaining Total Task Approach to Teach Natalie to Wash Her Hands

task until their first error. Errors were followed by having the women practice the missed step with verbal assistance until they could complete the step independently. Next, they were asked to begin the task again from the beginning. Five women mastered three variations of the feminine hygiene task when confronted with (a) a stain on their underwear, (b) a stain on their pad, or (c) a stain on both pad and underwear. The women were able to generalize the skills to their own menses.

Summary

The self-care domain consists of basic tasks for maintaining personal hygiene: toileting, eating, dressing, and grooming. For students who do not master self-care skills in the early childhood years, these skills continue to be a priority area for instruction for individuals and families. Justly or not, independence in self-care continues to make more postschool options available to individuals with disabilities. Independence and participation in one's own self-care contributes to personal and emotional well-being and self-determination. Despite the importance of self-care skills, current research in the area is lacking, particularly in teaching methods that involve positive strategies and inclusive environments.

Assessment, program development and implementation, and evaluation require collaboration, consideration of social validity, age- and culture-appropriate practices, involvement of peers, and consideration of partial participation. In addition to the student, the family, and the teachers involved with the student, occupational therapists, speech and language therapists, and physical therapists have expertise related to the self-care domain. Social validity requires consideration of family and support providers' perceptions, peer standards, accepted practice in the settings where instruction is implemented, and community standards in planning assessment and instructional procedures. Strategies and materials should be appropriate to the chronological age of the student and the practices and values of family members related to heritage, religion, and custom. Peers may play a critical role in setting standards for performance, providing models and reinforcement, being learning coaches, and supporting students' growth in independence in self-care domains. Finally, teachers should not eliminate students from instruction because the student may not become fully independent in self-care skills. Rather the judicial and cautious use of partial participation should be considered and continually evaluated.

Meaningful assessment is used to determine skills the student performs and what skills may require instruction. Assessment should address the environments where students use self-care skills. Informal and formal interviews are useful, as well as careful observation in environments the students currently use and will use in the future and observation of the student performing self-care tasks targeted for instruction.

Before instruction, the educational team must decide on the appropriate settings and schedule for instruction. Especially in the self-care areas of toileting, eating, and, to some extent, grooming, privacy is a critical consideration. The student's need for meaningful interactions with peers and need for privacy in instruction in self-care skills must be carefully balanced.

Teachers should select the simplest effective strategy that meets the individual student's needs for instruction. Effective strategies in the self-care domain include: observational learning, shaping, time delay, graduated guidance, and the system of least prompts during the acquisition stage. Fluency may be improved with a focus on motivation for increasing time and accuracy of performance. Sometimes motivation may be enhanced by providing choice or peer supports. Other strategies for fluency include extra progress on problem steps and pacing prompts. Careful and systematic fading of instructional procedures and reinforcement should be planned for the student's maintenance phase. Maintenance of skills should be monitored until the team is convinced that the student will continue to perform needed self-care routines independently. Generalization of performance across settings and materials should be evaluated, facilitated, or instructed as necessary. Reinforcement for tasks should also be individualized to student characteristics.

Instruction in self-care provides many natural opportunities to incorporate related social, communication, and mobility instruction. Additionally, educational teams should plan for instruction in the extended skills related to initiation, quality, tempo, problem-solving and termination. For some students, instruction in related skills may be the purpose of instruction during self-care activities and routines.

Special considerations in toileting include examination of students' physiological readiness and assessment of natural toileting patterns. Instruction in toileting may be successful using traditional methods or improved traditional methods, including reinforcement for dry pants, consequences for accidents, regulating toileting times, or moisture-signaling devices. Some students may require rapid training programs.

Eating and mealtime instruction also requires the assessment of physiological readiness. Additionally, consideration of appropriate foods and materials for instruction is required. Eating finger foods is typically the first self-feeding skill to develop, followed by drinking from a cup and using utensils. Much of the eating research has focused on problem behaviors such as food over-selectivity and rapid eating. Pacing prompts and consequence procedures have been successfully used to reduce problem behaviors.

Individual preference is a critical consideration in many grooming and dressing skills (e.g., whether or not to shave, choice of style in clothing). Careful communication with student, family, and peers is necessary to determine appropriate choices in this area. There are fewer natural opportunities for dressing and grooming during school than for the other self-care areas of eating and toileting. The educational team must evaluate the priority of instruction, the need to create artificial times and places, and the use of groups for instruction. As with eating, special materials (e.g. larger sizes, Velcro fasteners) may be needed for teaching dressing to some individuals. Recent research in this area has shown that various forms of observational learning (i.e., modeling, passive modeling, and video self-modeling), as well as simultaneous prompting, are successful in teaching grooming and dressing.

Suggested Activities

1. Are your instructional programs in self-care consistent with current best practices? Find out by completing the following program evaluation and improvement checklist for each self-care objective for a particular student you know well.

Skill Objective: _____

The Skill or Routine

- Is it functional for this student (i.e., needed now and in the future, essential to health or social acceptability, valued by family and peers)? YES NO
- Is it appropriate for the student's age? YES NO
- Do the conditions and criteria reflect the functional needs of the student? YES NO

Teaching Methods

- Does instruction include related skills (i.e., extension beyond the core task steps) and opportunities for enriching the task with student communication, choice, and socialization? YES NO
- Do methods emphasize natural cues and task materials? YES NO
- Do methods include a range of routine times and locations for teaching? YES NO
- Can natural reinforcers or incentives be used to promote motivation? YES NO

- Do methods reflect those that have worked with this student in the past? YES NO
- Do methods reflect socially and culturally valid approaches? YES NO
- If adaptations are used (e.g., modified materials, partial participation) do they reflect the rule: as little as necessary? YES NO
- Are teaching methods team-generated? YES NO

Evaluation

- Were starting points for teaching determined from baseline assessments? YES NO
- Has the team developed simple but effective methods to monitor student performance and learning across settings? YES NO
- Are these evaluation data used to make improvements in the program? YES NO

2. Are you using partial participation with students to complete self-care routines? If so, answer the following questions to check the appropriateness of your application.

- Did planning include input from therapists, the student, and family members? YES NO
- If adaptations are used to simplify the cognitive aspects of a task (e.g., photos to prompt morning grooming sequence), does the student know how to use the adaptations or will instruction address this learning? YES NO
- Does the student have some control with or over the task or routine? YES NO
- Will you monitor the student's performance regularly so participation can be increased or made more natural if progress seems to indicate these changes are suitable? YES NO
- Is the form of partial participation used suited to the student's age and personal preferences (e.g., adapted clothing, physical assistance)? YES NO
- If protheses or adaptive equipment are used, are they durable and suited for use in all or most environments where the skill is needed (e.g., a battery-operated toothbrush, adapted eating utensils)? YES NO
- Does partial participation appear to improve the student's enjoyment of the task, inclusion with peers, and the ease with which the student completes the task? YES NO

- Does partial participation result in good outcomes in this routine (e.g., clean teeth)? YES NO
- Is the partial participation approach practical for the student and for care providers or peers who might assist (e.g., not too slow, effective, flexible in lots of situations, does not require excessive materials)? YES NO

References

Alberto, P., Jobes, N. Sizemore, A. & Doran, D. (1980). A comparison of individual and group instruction across response tasks. *Journal of the Association for Persons with Severe Handicaps*, 5, 285–293.

Albin, J. B. (1977). Some variables influencing the maintenance of acquired self-feeding behavior in profoundly retarded children. *Mental Retardation*, 15(5), 49–52.

Azrin, N. H., & Armstrong, P. M. (1973). The "mini-meal": A method for teaching eating skills to the profoundly retarded. *Mental Retardation*, 11(1), 9–11.

Azrin, N. H., Bugle, C., & O'Brien, F. (1971). Behavioral engineering: Two apparatuses for toilet training retarded children. *Journal of Applied Behavioral Analysis*, 4, 249–253.

Azrin, N. H., & Foxx, R. M. (1971). A rapid method of toilet training the institutionalized retarded. *Journal of Applied Behavior Analysis*, 4, 89–99.

Azrin, N. H., Schaeffer, R. M., & Wesolowski, M. D. (1976). A rapid method of teaching profoundly retarded persons to dress by a reinforcement-guidance method. *Mental Retardation*, 14(6), 29–33.

Bak, J. J., & Siperstein, G. N. (1987). Similarity as a factor effecting change in children's attitudes toward mentally retarded peers. *American Journal of Mental Deficiency*, 91, 524–531.

Baker, B. L., & Brightman, A. J. (1997). *Steps to independence: Teaching everyday skills to children with special needs* (3rd ed.). Baltimore: Paul H. Brookes.

Bambara, L., & Cole, C. L. (1997). Permanent antecedent prompts. In M. Agran (Ed.) *Self-directed learning: Teaching self-determination skills* (pp. 111–143). Pacific Grove, CA: Brookes/Cole.

Banerdt, B., & Bricker, D. (1978). A training program for selected self-feeding skills for the motorically impaired. AAESPH *Review*, 3, 222–229.

Barmann, B. C., Katz, R. C., O'Brien, F., & Beauchamp, K. L. (1981). Treating irregular enuresis in developmentally disabled persons. *Behavior Modification*, 5, 336–346.

Barton, E. S., Guess, D., Garcia, E., & Baer, D. (1970). Improvement of retardates' mealtime behaviors by timeout procedures using multiple baseline techniques. *Journal of Applied Behavior Analysis*, 3, 77–84.

Baumgart, D., Brown, L., Pumpian, I., Nisbet, J., Ford, A., Sweet, M., Messina, R., & Schroeder, J. (1982). Principle of participation and individualized adaptations in educational programs for severely handicapped students. *Journal of the Association for Persons with Severe Handicaps*, 7, 17–27.

Bettison, S. (1982). *Toilet training to independence for the handicapped: A manual for trainers*. Springfield, IL: Charles C. Thomas.

Biederman, G. B., Fairhall, J. L., Raven, K. A., & Davey, V. A. (1998). Verbal prompting, hand-over-hand instruction, and passive observation in teaching children with developmental disabilities. *Exceptional Children*, 64, 503–511.

Boon, F. F. I., & Singh, N. (1991). A model for the treatment of encopresis. *Behavior Modification*, 15, 335–371.

Brown, F., & Cohen, S. (1996). Self-determination and young children. *Journal of the Association for Persons with Severe Handicaps*, 21, 22–30.

Brown, F., Evans, I., Weed, K., & Owen, V. (1987). Delineating functional competencies: A component model. *Journal of the Association for Persons with Severe Handicaps*, 12, 117–124.

Case-Smith, J., & Humphry, R. (1996). Feeding and oral motor skills. In J. Case-Smith, A. S. Allen, & P. N. Pratt (Eds.), *Occupational therapy for children* (3rd ed.) (pp.430–460). St. Louis: Mosby.

Christian, W. P., Hollomon, S. W., & Lanier, C. L. (1973). An attendant operated feeding program for severely and profoundly retarded females. *Mental Retardation*, 11(5), 35–37.

Christensen, C. H. (in press). *Ways of living* (2nd ed.). Bethesda, MD: American Occupational Therapy Association.

Collins, B. C., Gast, D. L., Wolery, M., Halcombe, A., & Leatherby, J. G. (1991). Using constant time delay to teach self-feeding to young students with severe/profound handicaps: Evidence of limited effectiveness. *Journal of Developmental and Physical Disabilities*, 3, 157–179.

Coote, M. A. (1965). Apparatus for conditioning treatment of enuresis. *Behaviour Research and Therapy*, 2, 233–238.

Diorio, M. A., & Konarski, E. A., Jr. (1984). Evaluation of a method for teaching dressing skills to profoundly mentally retarded persons. *American Journal of Mental Deficiency*, 89, 307–309.

Doleys, D. M. (1985). Enuresis and encopresis. In P. H. Bornstein & A. E. Kazdin (Eds.), *Handbook of clinical behavior therapy with children* (pp. 412–440). Homewood, IL: Dorsey Press.

Dowrick, P. W., & Raeburn, J. M. (1995). Self-modeling: Rapid skill training for children with physical disabilities. *Journal of Developmental and Physical Disabilities*, 7, 25–37.

Dunlap, G., & Johnson, G. (1985). Increasing the independent responding of autistic children with unpredictable supervision. *Journal of Applied Behavior Analysis*, 18, 227–236.

Dunlap, G., Koegel, R. L., & Koegel, R. K. (1984). Continuity of treatment: Toilet training in multiple community settings. *Journal of the Association for Persons with Severe Handicaps*, 9, 134–141.

Dunlap, G., Koegel, R. L., & Koegel, L. K. (1986). *Toilet training for children with severe handicaps: A field manual for coordinating procedures across multiple community settings*. Huntington, WV: Autism Training Center, Marshall University.

Epps, S., & Myers, C. I. (1989). Priority domains for instruction, satisfaction with school teaching, and postschool living and employment: An analysis of perceptions of parents of students with severe and profound disabilities. *Education and Training in Mental Retardation*, 24, 157–167.

Epps, S., Stern, R. J., & Horner, R. H. (1990). Comparison of simulation training on self and using a doll for teaching generalized menstrual care to women with severe mental retardation. *Research in Developmental Disabilities*, 11, 37–66.

Etzel, B. C., & LeBlanc, J. M. (1979). The simplest treatment alternative: The law of parsimony applied to choosing appropriate instructional control and errorless learning procedures for the difficult-to-teach child. *Journal of Autism and Developmental Disorders*, 9, 361–382.

Favell, J. E., McGimsey, J. F., & Jones, M. J. (1980). Rapid eating in the retarded: Reduction by nonaversive procedures. *Behavior Modification*, 4, 481–492.

Ferguson, D. L., & Baumgart, D. (1991). Partial participation revisited. *Journal of the Association for Persons with Severe Handicaps*, 16, 218–227.

Foxx, R. M., & Azrin, N. H. (1973). *Toilet training the retarded: A rapid program for day and nighttime independent toileting.* Champaign, IL: Research Press.

Foxx, R. M., & Azrin, N. H. (1974). *Toilet training in less than a day.* New York: Simon & Schuster.

Freagon, S., & Rotatori, A. F. (1982). Comparing natural and artificial environments in training self-care skills to group home residents. *Journal of the Association for Persons with Severe Handicaps*, 7(3), 73–86.

Fredericks, H. D. B., Baldwin, V. L., Grove, D. N., & Moore, W. G. (1975). *Toilet training the handicapped child.* Monmouth, OR: Instructional Development Corporation.

Garff, J. T., & Storey, K. (1998). The use of self-management strategies for increasing the appropriate hygiene of persons with disabilities in supported employment settings. *Education and Training in Mental Retardation and Developmental Disabilities*, 33, 179–188.

Giles, D. K., & Wolf, M. M. (1966). Toilet training institutionalized severe retardates: An application of operant behavior modification techniques. *American Journal of Mental Deficiency*, 70, 766–780.

Hamre-Nietupski, S. (1993). How much time should be spent on skill instruction and friendship development? Preferences of parents of students with moderate and severe/profound disabilities. *Education and Training in Mental Retardation*, 28(3), 20–231.

Hatton, C. (1998). Whose quality of life is it anyway? Some problems with the emerging quality of life consensus. *Mental Retardation*, 26, 104–115.

Herreshoff, J. K. (1973). Two electronic devices for toilet training. *Mental Retardation*, 11(6), 54–55.

Hobbs, T., & Peck, C. A. (1985). Toilet training people with profound mental retardation: A cost effective procedure for large residential settings. *Behavioral Engineering*, 9, 50–57.

Horner, R. H., & Carr, E. G. (1997). Behavioral support for students with severe disabilities: Functional assessment and comprehensive intervention. *Journal of Special Education*, 31, 84–104.

Horner, R. D., & Keilitz, I. (1975). Training mentally retarded adolescents to brush their teeth. *Journal of Applied Behavior Analysis*, 8, 301–309.

Hughes, C., Hwang, B., Kim, J. H., Eisenman, L. T., & Killian, D. J. (1995). Quality of life in applied research: A review and analysis of empirical measures. *American Journal on Mental Retardation*, 99, 623–641.

Irvine, A. B., Erickson, A. M., Singer, G. H., & Stahlberg, D. (1992). A coordinated program to transfer self-management skills from school to home. *Education and Training in Mental Retardation*, 27, 241–254.

Knapczyk, D. R. (1983). Use of teacher-paced instruction in developing and maintaining independent self-feeding. *Journal of the Association for Persons with Severe Handicaps*, 8(3), 10–16.

Kramer, L., & Whitehurst, C. (1981). Effects of button features on self-dressing in young retarded children. *Education and Training of the Mentally Retarded*, 16, 277–283.

Lasater, M. W., & Brady, M. P. (1995). Effects of video self-modeling and feedback on task fluency: A home-based intervention. *Education and Treatment of Children*, 18, 389–407.

Lehr, D. (1985). Effects of opportunities to practice on learning among students with severe handicaps. *Education and Training of the Mentally Retarded*, 20, 268–74.

Levine, M. N., & Elliot, C. B. (1970). Toilet training for profoundly retarded with a limited staff. *Mental Retardation*, 8(3), 48–50.

Linford, M. D., Hipsher, L. W., & Silikovitz, R. G. (1972). *Systematic instruction for retarded children: The illness program.* Part 3. Self-help instruction. Danville, IL: Interstate.

Losardo, A., & Bricker, D. (1994). Activity-based intervention and direct instruction: A comparison study. *American Journal on Mental Retardation*, 98, 744–765.

Lovibond, S. H. (1963). The mechanism of conditioning treatment of enuresis. *Behaviour Research and Therapy*, 1, 17–21.

Lovibond, S. H. (1964). *Conditioning and enuresis.* New York: Macmillan.

Luiselli, J. K. (1988). Improvement of feeding skills in multi-handicapped students through paced-prompting interventions. *Journal of the Multi-Handicapped Person*, 1, 17–30.

Luiselli, J. K. (1991). Acquisition of self-feeding in a child with Lowe's syndrome. *Journal of Developmental and Physical Disabilities*, 3, 181–189.

Mahoney, K., Van Wagenen, R. K., & Meyerson, L. (1971). Toilet training of normal and retarded children. *Journal of Applied Behavior Analysis*, 4, 173–181.

Marshall, G. R. (1966). Toilet training of an autistic eight-year-old through conditioning therapy: A case report. *Behaviour Research and Therapy*, 4, 242–245.

Matson, J. L., Taras, M. E., Sevin, J. A., Love, S. R., & Fridley, D. (1990). Teaching self-help skills to autistic and mentally retarded children. *Research in Developmental Disabilities*, 11, 361–378.

Meyer, L. H., Park, H., Grenot-Scheyer, M., Schwartz, I. S., & Harry, B. (1998). *Making friends.* Baltimore: Paul H. Brookes.

Miller, H. R., Patton, M. E., & Henton, K. R. (1971). Behavior modification in a profoundly retarded child: A case report. *Behavior Therapy*, 2, 375–384.

Morreau, L. E., & Bruininks, R. H. (1991). *Checklist of adaptive living skills* (CALS). Allen TX: Developmental Learning Materials.

Mowrer, O. H., & Mowrer, W. M. (1938). Enuresis: A method for its study and treatment. *American Journal of Orthopsychiatry*, 8, 435–459.

Mueller, H. (1975). Feeding. In N. R. Finnie (Ed.), *Handling the young cerebral palsied child at home* (pp. 113–132). New York: E. P. Dutton.

Mulligan, M., Lacy, L., & Guess, D. (1982). Effects of massed, distributed, and spaced trial sequencing on severely handicapped student's performance. *Journal of the Association for the Severely Handicapped*, 7(2), 48–61.

Nelson, G. L., Cone, J. D., & Hanson, C. R. (1975). Training correct utensil use in retarded children. *American Journal of Mental Deficiency*, 80, 114–122.

Nietupski, J., Hamre-Nietupski, S., Curtain, S., & Shrikanth, K. (1997). A review of curricular research in severe disabilities from 1976 to 1995 in six selected journals. *Journal of Special Education*, 31, 36–55.

O'Brien, F., & Azrin, N. H. (1972). Developing proper mealtime behaviors of the institutionalized retarded. *Journal of Applied Behavior Analysis*, 5, 389–399.

O'Brien, F., & Azrin, N. H. (1972). Developing proper mealtime behaviors of the institutionalized retarded. *Journal of Applied Behavior Analysis, 5,* 389–399.

O'Brien, F., Bugle, C., & Azrin, N. H. (1972). Training and maintaining a retarded child's proper eating. *Journal of Applied Behavior Analysis, 5,* 67–73.

Orelove, F. P., & Sobsey, D. (1996). *Educating children with multiple disabilities* (3rd ed.). Baltimore: Paul H. Brookes.

Reese, G. M., & Snell, M. E. (1991). Putting on and removing coats and jackets: The acquisition and maintenance of skills by children with severe multiple disabilities. *Education and Training in Mental Retardation, 26,* 398–410.

Richman, G. S., Reiss, M. L., Bauman, K. E., & Bailey, J. S. (1984). Teaching menstrual care to mentally retarded women: Acquisition, generalization, and maintenance. *Journal of Applied Behavior Analysis, 17,* 441–451.

Richmond, G. (1983). Shaping bladder and bowel continence in developmentally retarded preschool children. *Journal of Autism and Developmental Disorders, 13,* 197–205.

Riordan, M. M., Iwata, B. A., Finney, J. W., Wohl, M. D., & Stanley, A. E. (1984). Behavioral assessment and treatment of chronic food refusal in handicapped children. *Journal of Applied Behavior Analysis, 17,* 327–341.

Riordan, M. M., Iwata, B. A., Wohl, M. K., & Finney, J. W. (1980). Behavioral treatment of food refusal and selectivity in developmentally disabled children. *Applied Research in Mental Retardation, 1,* 95–112.

Sailor, W., Halvorsen, A., Anderson, J., Goetz, L., Gee, K., Doering, K., & Hunt, P. (1986). Community intensive instruction. In R. Horner, L. Voeltz, & B. Fredricks (Eds.), *Education of learners with severe handicaps: Exemplary service strategies* (pp. 251–288). Baltimore: Paul H. Brookes.

Schaefer, C. E., & DiGeronimo, T. F. (1997). *Toilet training without tears* (rev. ed.). New York: Signet Books.

Schalock, R. L. (Ed.). (1996). *Quality of life.* Washington, DC: American Association on Mental Retardation.

Seiger, H. W. (1952). Treatment of essential nocturnal enuresis. *Journal of Pediatrics, 40,* 735–749.

Sewell, T. J., Collins, B. C., Hemmeter, M. L., & Schuster, J. W. (1998). Using simultaneous prompting within an activity-based format to teach dressing skills to preschoolers with developmental delays. *Journal of Early Intervention, 21,* 132–142.

Shephard, J., Procter, S. A., & Coley, I. L. (1996). Self-care and adaptations for independent living. In J. Case-Smith, A. S. Allen, & P. N. Pratt (Eds.), *Occupational therapy for children* (3rd ed.) (pp. 526–580). St. Louis: Mosby.

Shoen, S. F., & Sivil, E. O. (1989). A comparison of procedures in teaching self-help skills: Increasing assistance, time delay, and observational learning. *Journal of Autism and Developmental Disorders, 19,* 57–72.

Simbert, V. F., Minor, J. W., & McCoy, J. F. (1977). Intensive feeding training with retarded children. *Behavior Modification, 1,* 512–529.

Sisson, L. A., Kilwein, M. L., & Van Hasselt, V. B. (1988). A graduated guidance procedure for teaching self-dressing skills to multihandicapped children. *Research in Developmental Disabilities, 9,* 419–432.

Sloop, W. E., & Kennedy, W. A. (1973). Institutionalized retarded nocturnal enuretics treated by a conditioned technique. *American Journal of Mental Deficiency, 77,* 712–717.

Smith, L. J. (1981). Training severely and profoundly mentally handicapped nocturnal enuretics. *Behaviour Research and Therapy, 19,* 67–74.

Smith, Jr., A. L., Piersel, W. C., Filbeck, R. W., & Gross, E. J. (1983). The elimination of mealtime food stealing and scavenging behavior in an institutionalized severely mentally retarded adult. *Mental Retardation, 21,* 255–259.

Smith, P. S. (1979). A comparison of different methods of toilet training the mentally handicapped. *Behaviour Research and Therapy, 17,* 33–34.

Snell, M. E. (1997). Teaching children and young adults with mental retardation in school programs: Current research. *Behaviour Change, 12,* 73–105.

Snell, M. E., Lewis, A. P., & Houghton, A. (1989). Acquisition and maintenance of toothbrushing skills by students with cerebral palsy and mental retardation. *Journal of the Association for Persons with Severe Handicaps, 14,* 216–226.

Snell, M. E., & Vogtle, L. (2000). Methods for teaching self-care skills. In C. Christensen (Ed.), *Ways of living: Self care strategies for special needs* (2nd ed.) (pp. 57–81). Rockville, MD: The American Occupational Therapy Association.

Song, A. Y., & Gandhi, R. (1974). An analysis of behavior during the acquisition and maintenance phases of self–spoon feeding skills of profound retardates. *Mental Retardation, 12*(1), 25–28.

Stainback, S. S., & Healy, H. A. (1982). *Teaching eating skills: A handbook for teachers.* Springfield, IL: Charles C Thomas.

Staub, D., Spaulding, M., Peck, C. A., Gallucci, C., & Schwartz, I. S. (1996). Using nondisabled peers to support the inclusion of students with disabilities at the junior high school level. *Journal of the Association for Persons with Severe Handicaps, 21,* 194–205.

Thinesen, P. J., & Bryan, A. J. (1981). The use of sequential pictorial cues in the initiation and maintenance of grooming behaviors in mentally retarded adults. *Mental Retardation, 19,* 247–250.

Thompson, T., & Hanson, R. (1983). Overhydration: Precautions when treating urinary incontinence. *Mental Retardation, 21,* 139–143.

Van Wagenen, R. K. Meyerson, L., Kerr, N. J., Mahoney, K. (1969). Rapid toilet training: Learning principles and prothesis. *Proceedings of the 77th Annual Convention of the American Psychological Association, 4,* 781–782.

Van Wagenen, R. K., & Murdock, E. E. (1966). A transistorized signal-package for toilet training of infants. *Journal of Experimental Child Psychology, 3,* 312–314.

Wolery, M., Ault, M. J., & Doyle, P. M. (1992). Teaching students with moderate to severe disabilities. White Plains, NY: Longman.

Wolery, M., Ault, M. J., Gast, D., Doyle, P. M., & Griffen, A. K. (1991). Teaching Chained Tasks in Dyads: Acquisition of Target and Observational Behaviors. *Journal-of-Special-Education, 25,* 198–220.

Young, K. R., West, R. P., Howard, V. F., & Whitney, R. (1986). Acquisition, fluency training, generalization, and maintenance of dressing skills of two developmentally disabled children. *Education and Treatment of Children, 9,* 16–29.

10

Peer Relationships

Debbie Staub
Charles A. Peck
Chrysan Gallucci
Ilene Schwartz

 Karly

For the last 45 minutes of the school day the children in the K-2, multi-age class at Jane Austen Elementary have choice time. Choice time begins with the children gathered as a large group. As the children seat themselves on the rug, one of the teachers describes the array of activity choices available for that day. Some of the chcices are consistent from day to day, such as spending time in the "reading loft." Most choices, however, are prepared to reflect the theme being addressed through a variety of curriculum units in the class. This year, teachers have chosen to focus on cultural diversity around the world. They have been learning recently about Great Britain and the royal family. Consequently, many choices around the room reflect something about British culture. What better than to have a "tea time" in the dress-up area? Karly, a child with Down syndrome, and Deanne, her typically developing friend, quickly raise their hands for this activity. They "dress" for tea, then sit down to have a proper tea party, complete with sophisticated manners and conversation. They take turns playing the "Queen":

"First, I'll be the Queen, then you can, OK?" says Deanne. "You have to call me Your Majesty, you know" (giggling). Karly watches as Deanne raises her tea cup with exaggerated formality. She carefully copies Deanne's movements. "My turn," she says. "Now you call me majesty." Karly and Deanne take sips of "tea," and invite another child to join their party. The three groan audibly when the teacher announces cleanup and school dismissal time. At home later that evening, each of the girls shares the experience with her parents. Deanne asks her mother, "Can I have Karly over to play tomorrow? Can we make our own tea party?"

Human beings are the most profoundly social of all creatures. Our development, well-being, and happiness are utterly dependent on the quality of our relationships with others. From the earliest establishment of regularity and predictability of social exchanges between infants and caregivers (Kaye, 1982) to our uniquely human construction of "webs of significance" and meaning as adults (Geertz, 1973), the social relationships of our lives form the crucible within which we come to know the world, each other, and ourselves (Bruner, 1990). With this viewpoint in mind, we attempt in this chapter to highlight the role that social relationships play in the development of children and youth with disabilities and to describe some of the strategies teachers and other caregivers can use to support this process.

Neither cognitive (e.g., Piaget, 1972) nor behavioral (e.g., Bijou & Baer, 1961) theorists have denied the importance of social relationships to child development. However, the analysis of social relationships has not been central to these traditions nor to the teaching strategies that have emerged from them. In contrast, contemporary perspectives on development, based on the work of Vygotsky (1978) and other sociocultural theorists, place issues of relationship at the fulcrum of their claims about how children become competent members of human communities (e.g., Bruner, 1996; Cole, 1996; Lave & Wanger, 1991). Of course, children participate regularly in a wide variety of social relationships with family members, teachers, and many other adults. The specific focus of our discussion and recommendations here are on some of the important issues that arise from considering the function of relationships between children and youth with disabilities and their peers. Figure 10–1 shows children enjoying each other's company at lunch, an important social time of the day.

The vignette with which we began our chapter illustrates a number of possible ways in which the social dimensions of Karly's life are likely to affect her development. First, Karly's interactions with her friend Deanne are an important context in which she learns new skills. Deanne models language and behavior that are appropriate and useful to Karly as a means of participating in the "tea party" and similar social situations. Karly attends carefully to these cues, as she is excited and motivated by the tea party as a drama, and her roles as both "queen" and "subject." This social experience with dramatic play is likely to both be in-

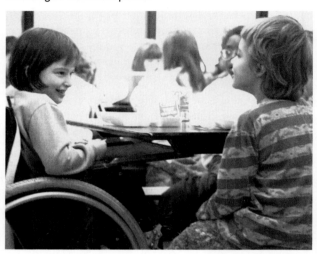

FIGURE 10–1
Lunchtime is often hurried but filled with social exchanges between peers.

formed by her understanding of the curriculum unit on Great Britain and to contribute to that understanding. At a deeper level, Karly's participation in the large group meeting, in which the teacher describes possible choices children may make, constitutes a social context in which she may learn to attend to instructions given in a group, to observe what the group is doing as a cue for what is expected of her ("mass modeling"), and to make choices and regulate her behavior independent of one-to-one adult intervention. All of these may be recognized as critical skills for competent participation in a tremendous variety of highly valued activities, roles, and settings within our culture.

Second, the special friendship Karly enjoys with Deanne functions as both a source of personal support and as a meaningful context for her participation in this activity. For example, Deanne provides needed and appropriate support for Karly in learning what behavior is required for appropriate participation in the tea party: she shows her how to be the "queen," gives useful feedback about the performance, and guides her through the chaotic transition from the large group to small-group activities. In addition, Karly's motivation to participate in the tea party appears to be closely related to her relationship with Deanne as "best friends." They gleefully raise and wave their hands to indicate they want to be partners; they look at each other and moan when the teacher says its time to stop. They seem to enjoy, as adults might say, their "connection."

From Karly's point of view, the new cognitive, language, and social skills demanded by this social situation constitute, in part, the means by which she can participate in a relationship she values greatly (Halliday, 1975). Thus, the tea party, the behaviors required to participate, and the social relationships which underlie all of it, form a web of connections that make the activity meaningful to Karly, Deanne, and others in the class. The significance of this web of connection between context, behavior, and social relationships is of enormous importance for teachers who struggle daily with the problem of making learning meaningful for their students. We believe teachers' difficulties in constructing meaningful learning experiences for their students are caused in large part by a curriculum in which "skills" are viewed as behaviors rather than as complex context-behavior relationships (Haring, 1992).

A third way in which social relationships in Karly's life affect her development has to do with the effect these relationships have on her peers. For example, Deanne's mother and teachers comment often about how much she has learned and benefited through her friendship with Karly, in which she plays a role as a leader and nurturer (which is new for her). These things make Deanne feel good about herself (Peck, Donaldson, & Pezzoli, 1990), but they also increase her positive impact on Karly's development. As Deanne learns more about the ways in which Karly communicates, the situations she struggles with, the things she enjoys, and the things they enjoy in common (like dress up games), Deanne becomes better able to support Karly's participation in a variety of activities, including many they particularly enjoy with each other. Deanne and her mother begin to invite Karly over after school regularly, and the two girls begin to enjoy outings to the park, and to other children's homes together. All of these constitute opportunities for Karly to participate in new activities, roles and settings—and all demand that she learn new skills. Viewed in this way, we may recognize that Karly's development is intertwined with Deanne's in many important ways. In fact, we may see development in general as a process of co-evolution or transactional change between individuals and their social environments (Brofenbrenner, 1979; Sameroff & Chandler, 1975).

The other issues raised above clarify how important it is for teachers and other professionals concerned with the development of children, youth, and adults with moderate and severe disabilities to undertake a careful analysis of the kinds of social experiences and relationships in which these individuals participate in their daily lives. Of course, this is not a simple undertaking. In the following section, we describe a conceptual framework we and our colleagues have developed which helps make sense of the complex connections between social experiences, skill acquisition, and participation in valued roles, activities and settings (Billingsley, Gallucci, Peck, Schwartz, & Staub, 1996; Peck, et al., 1994). We then offer a set of recommendations for intervention based on this framework. We conclude our chapter with some suggestions regarding assessment and evaluation strategies that we believe are useful in documenting outcomes related to peer relationships and with comments related to the effect of experiences with the inclusion of students with severe disabilities on the lives of nondisabled children. But first we introduce three children with moderate and severe disabilities whose experiences and outcomes in inclusive settings will be used to illustrate critical functions that social relationships play in providing opportunities to learn new skills, to achieve a sense of membership or "belonging" to valued social groups, and as a means of supporting participation in valued roles, activities, and settings.

Three Case Examples

Ray

Ray is a 12-year-old boy who experiences severe developmental delays caused by a rare genetic disorder, tuberous sclerosis. Ray has attended inclusive classrooms since second grade with his age-appropriate peers and presently attends a general education sixth grade class. He has shown very uneven progress over the years, partially due to his severe seizure disorder and the medications that are administered to control it. Ray exhibits many of the characteristics associated with the tuberous sclerosis syndrome, such as, frequent seizure activity and self-stimulatory and ritualistic behaviors. He is nonverbal and walks with an awkward gait. His communication skills are limited, though he often communicates protests or desires through vocalization. Despite these, and other significant disabilities, Ray has experienced a variety of positive outcomes in the context of his inclusion in regular classes over the past 4 years.

Carrie

We began following Carrie, who has Down syndrome, when she was in fourth grade. Her teachers and peers characterized her as a playful, occasionally stubborn or shy, and always interesting child. Carrie has always been small for her age, and her carrot-top hair, perhaps a symbol of her fiery personality, hangs close to her shoulders. Currently in ninth grade at her neighborhood junior high school, Carrie has attended inclusive classrooms since second grade. She is quite verbal but has some speech difficulties. She works with a communication specialist on her articulation and voice volume regularly. Many times her peers understand her communication better than the adults in her life. Her reading level is close to that of a typical first grader's. Carrie takes great pride in being a member of her school. In the past couple of years, she has shown significant growth in her ability to do things independently.

Cole

Cole is a 17-year-old young man with severe disabilities who attends high school as a junior. We started collecting data on Cole's inclusive experiences in his fifth and sixth, multi-age classroom during his sixth-grade year. We followed Cole throughout his 3-year junior high school experience (grades seven through nine).

Cole contracted spinal meningitis at age 1, resulting in early paralysis and severe seizures. Cole's serious health problems and challenging behaviors (e.g., tantrums, aggression toward adults and objects) have often been frustrating for both his family and teachers. However, his parents and teachers are convinced that Cole has benefited greatly from, and contributed to, the inclusive classrooms in which he has participated over the past several years.

Described by his neurologist as having one of the most severe cases of seizure disorders in the state, Cole's "good" days and "bad" days are often determined by his rate of seizure activity and the effects of the medication he must take to control them. Cole has strong social initiation skills, and his expressive vocabulary has increased greatly in the past few years. Because of an increase in violent behaviors the summer of his seventh-grade year, Cole's parents enrolled him in a behavioral treatment group home for 18 months. During that time, Cole was able to continue his education at the junior high school he had been attending. Currently Cole lives with a foster family in close proximity to his parents, whom he sees regularly.

Peer Relationships and Developmental Outcomes

In this chapter, and elsewhere (Billingsley, et al., 1996; Peck, et al., 1994), we make the claim that participation in socially valued roles, activities, and settings is both the most fundamental outcome of the developmental process and the primary means by which development is achieved. This view is at odds with views of development as acquisition of skills, which has dominated the field of special education, including special education for individuals with severe disabilities, for many years. We do not consider skills to be unimportant. Rather we broaden our analysis of how students with severe disabilities come to be more competent members of human communities to include more detailed consideration of the relationships between skill acquisition and a variety of social context factors.

Our changing views of development have emerged in part from a 4-year program of research in which we have followed 43 children with moderate or severe disabilities who have been enrolled full-time in regular classrooms. From the fall of 1992 to the summer of 1996, colleagues from the Inclusive Education Research Project (Peck, White, Billingsley, & Schwartz, 1992) and the Consortium of Collaborative Research on Social Relationships on Children and Youth with Diverse Abilities (Meyer, Harry, Schwartz, Grenot-Scheyer, & Park, 1992) collected and analyzed data from multiple sources, including classroom observations; interviews with teachers, parents, nondisabled peers, and paraeducators; video recordings and documents such as IEPs; and examples of children's work, in an effort to describe outcomes that occur for students in inclusive school programs. An important feature of this work has been our efforts to construct an understanding of outcomes for students with disabilities in active dialogue with parents, teachers, and students. In these conversations, and in the more "objective" data we collected, we were confronted again and again by compelling evidence of change in children's lives that was not adequately described in terms of the simple acquisition of skills. Using hundreds of excerpts from our observational and interview data, we implemented inductive category formation techniques, as described by Lincoln and Guba (1985), and cross case analysis techniques, explained by Miles and Huberman (1984), to develop a conceptual framework that describes the types of outcomes we observed for students with severe disabilities in inclusive school settings. This framework clarifies the ways in which skill development is embedded in the social contexts and relationships of a student's life. Because the framework was developed out of our observations of fairly typical school settings, including regular classrooms, playgrounds, cafeterias, and other activity contexts, it offers considerable guidance for teachers and specialists who wish to use these settings as a context for supporting the development of learners with severe disabilities.

The Outcome Framework

The outcome patterns that have emerged in our follow-along data set are conceptualized in terms of three broad domains. First, our findings suggest that many of the children we studied in inclusive classrooms were in fact learning many of the same types of skills that have been the traditional focus of special education outcome assessment. These include social and communication skills, academics, and functional skills. A second domain of outcomes we observed was the extent to which children with severe disabilities achieve membership or a sense of belonging in the formal and informal groups that make up the social fabric of the classroom and school (Schnorr, 1990). Finally, we observed that children in inclusive classrooms may develop a wide variety of personal relationships with other children. Each of these broad outcome domains (i.e., membership, relationships, and skills) have strong effects on each other. Moreover, each of the domains may be viewed in terms of its relationship with a higher order outcome, which we conceptualized as increased participation in valued roles, activities, and settings of the community and culture (Bronfenbrenner, 1979; Lave & Wenger, 1991). Figure 10–2 depicts the relationship between each of the three outcome domains and the higher order goal of increased participation.

FIGURE 10–2
Inclusive Education Research Group Outcome Framework

Ultimately, peer relationships are both an end in themselves (and an important one) and an important means of support that enable a child to participate in a variety of valued roles, activities, and settings. Relationships between children with severe disabilities and their nondisabled peers are strongly related to other types of outcomes, including the child's individual skills (e.g., social and communication skills) and status as a "member" of the class or social group. We describe each of these outcome domains in more detail.

Membership

We have used the term "membership" to refer to the phenomenological sense of belonging to a social group, such as a classroom, cooperative work group, or friendship clique. Membership is not something we can observe directly. However, we can (and routinely do) make inferences about the extent to which a child is treated as a member of a group by observing things such as accommodations group members make to include a child, shared symbols used by the group (e.g., special T-shirts, team names, uniforms), and rituals that occur in the group context (e.g., special greetings, activities or roles performed only by group members).

Membership is an important outcome in and of itself in the lives of children, including those with severe disabilities. In fact, membership outcomes have received very high "importance" ratings from parents and teachers in social validation studies of the outcome framework (Peck et al., 1994). However, the extent to which students with severe disabilities are viewed as "members" of the classroom also affects the kinds of opportunities they are likely to have for participating in social relationships, as well as other classroom activities (Schnorr, 1990). These opportunities for participation, in turn have an effect on skill development.

Relationships

This domain of outcomes refers to the characteristics and extent of personal (dyadic) relationships between children with disabilities and their peers. We characterized relationships between students with disabilities and other individuals (both with and without disabilities) on the basis of consistencies in their social interactions over time, interviews with teachers and parents, and (when possible) informal interviews with children themselves. As in most relationships, the qualitative features of the social relationships we observed between individual children are not static, but often vary in specific contexts (Fiske, 1992).

Clearly, a high-priority outcome for children with severe disabilities, as for any child, is the development of friendships. Friendships have, in fact, been the focus of most analyses of social relationships in the professional literature to date (Haring, 1991; Meyer, Park, Grenot-Scheyer, Schwartz, & Harry, 1998a). However, other types of relationships also play an important role as sources of learning and support for students with severe disabilities. Our observations of the variety of relationships that emerge between children with disabilities and their nondisabled peers led us to identify four "types" of relationships: play/companion, helper (giver), helpee (receiver), and conflictual, each of which offers important learning opportunities for children.

Skills

The third domain of outcomes we observed in inclusive classrooms is comprised of the behavioral competencies children develop over time; these have been the predominant focus of traditional outcomes assessment in special education. Skills, particularly social and communicative skills, strongly affect (but do not exclusively determine) the extent to which students with severe disabilities are able to participate in a variety of social roles, activities, and settings. Our

analysis of what children learn in inclusive settings, and how they learn, suggests that many critical skills are acquired in the contexts of social activities in which personal relationships and membership play an important part. For example, in the vignette that begins this chapter, it is easy to envision how Karly is taught to take a variety of roles within the tea party, how she may learn about the meaning of concepts like "queen" and "England," and perhaps most important, how she may learn how to observe her friend Deanne as a source of guidance about how to behave in this activity (Apolloni & Cooke, 1975). In other classrooms, we have observed children learning new skills in the context of counting out materials for distribution to classmates, checking off the names of children for a lunch count, reading a simplified script for a role in a class play, and many other social activities.

Linkages Among Outcome Domains

The relationships among the outcomes described above are transactional. The quality of a child's social relationships with peers is affected by (and affects) the child's status as a member of the group and is also affected by (and affects) the skills the child develops. All of these factors contribute to the student's access and participation in valued roles, activities, and settings in the school and community. The richest examples of inclusive educational practice we have observed suggest that multiple outcomes were likely to accrue to the students involved. The vignette provided at the beginning of this chapter illustrates this: when engaged in the "tea party" with her friend Deanne, Karly was learning skills, experiencing a sense of membership in her class, and engaging in a playful and companionable interaction with a classmate.

The framework we have described above carries some important implications for understanding issues of curriculum and instruction for learners with severe disabilities and others. First, the framework rejects the separation of social and academic outcomes that has been so prevalent in the field of special education. In fact, our observations suggest that the social aspects of a child's life in school (which we have defined in terms of membership and relationships) constitute the motivational contexts in which many fundamental life skills are learned. The false dichotomization of social and academic or other skill outcomes may in fact lead teachers away from creating functional and meaningful instructional contexts for learners with severe disabilities. Teachers who are falsely led by this dichotomization may focus solely on teaching skills or working on relationships.

Recognizing the important linkages among membership, relationships, and the development of critical skills carries the important implication that removing students from rich social contexts to emphasize one type of outcome (e.g., pulling a student out of the regular classroom for one-to-one skill instruction) is likely to affect the student's opportunities related to other outcome domains (Schnorr, 1990). For example, if Karly had been pulled away from her general education classroom during "choice time" to work one-on-one with a speech therapist on communication skills, valuable opportunities for both her social, functional, and academic development would have been lost. For teachers and others concerned with planning activities that enhance the development of students with severe disabilities, our model suggests many ways in which interventions can be designed that take advantage of the natural learning processes that are embedded in typical classroom life and other rich social contexts.

In the following section, we illustrate how the outcome framework can be used to describe and evaluate the peer relationships in the lives of Ray, Carrie, and Cole, the three children introduced earlier in this chapter. In particular, we draw the reader's attention to the critical functions that each child's social relationships play in providing opportunities to learn new skills, to achieve a sense of membership or "belonging" to valued social groups, and to support participation in valued roles, activities, and settings.

Three Case Illustrations

Ray

Relationships. "Ray and I are friends because we liked most of the things that the other one liked to do—like, I like to kick a ball and he likes to kick a ball. I like to be with him and he likes to be with me. I like to see him and he likes to see me. He likes to go on the slide and so do I. He likes to walk and I like to walk. He likes to look at pictures and I like to look at pictures. He likes to think and I like to think." (Typically developing fourth-grade classmate of Ray's)

Two significant findings emerged from our data with regard to Ray's relationships with other children. First, Ray's typically developing peers became accustomed to Ray's unique behaviors (i.e., self-stimulating, humming, wandering around the classroom in circles). His peers became comfortable in his presence. Second, by his third-, fourth-, and fifth-grade years, Ray was more attentive and responsive to his typically developing classmates and their social initiations. These peer interactions were often the contexts in which Ray demonstrated his clearest communicative behaviors, and his peers were often able to interpret his attempts at communication more effectively than adults. Ray had a system of buddies who helped him and spent time with him during arrival, recess, lunch, and some academic periods. There were also three typically developing girls who became particularly connected to Ray, taking a nurturing, helping role with him. While many of these peer supports were initially nurtured by Ray's teachers, Ray's peers soon took responsibility and initiative for these interactions with Ray.

> *Membership. The teaching assistant, Ray and three typically developing girls from Ray's class chat in the cafeteria while they eat. At one point they discuss how many years they have been in class with certain people. Susan says, "I've been with Ray for 3 years." Ray smiles, and Susan continues, "And next year it will be 4 years, at least I hope you'll still go here next year, Ray." Allison adds, "Yeah, because you have lots of people who like you and who care about you here." (Observation from Ray's fourth-grade class)*

We found many indications of Ray's membership in his classes and school. During fourth grade, Ray was recognized in the school newsletter for his contribution to the recycling effort. Ray was often included in small groups where his participation was supported by his peers. Ray's teachers, teaching assistants, and classmates considered Ray as a member of their class and school, and they missed him when he was absent or too sleepy to participate because of seizures. While his peers worried about Ray's health and seizures, they also encouraged Ray to do well and they took pride in his accomplishments.

Skills. Ray's growth in skills was variable and often related to his rate of seizure activity. Over the course of our observations, he learned to sit quietly and participate in a variety of large group activities. He learned to enjoy being read to, and nondisabled peers would often initiate this activity with him. While Ray relied on adult support for many of his self-help skills, he learned how to make his way through the routine and schedule of the school day. He also learned several school jobs such as recycling, sweeping, loading the pop machine and delivering school mail. He usually completed these tasks with the support of a typically developing classmate.

Carrie

Relationships. "*I think one of the things I see right now is Carrie's ability to have true friends. I'm talking about kids who call her on the phone and invite her to their house. That has happened more and more this year.*" (*Carrie's sixth-grade teacher*).

For Carrie, interactions with her typically developing classmates have been her greatest source of support and joy. We observed her peers helping her with academic work, making accommodations to include her in activities, and giving her feedback about her social behaviors. Carrie also developed several lasting friendships over the 4 years of our research. In fourth grade, she was a peer tutor ("helper") for a first-grade class, and in seventh grade, she helped another child with disabilities at the junior high school on an informal basis.

Conflictual interactions with peers have been an ongoing issue for Carrie (i.e., grabbing at others, trashing other's personal property), but in this area, Carrie made perhaps her greatest improvement. Her peers learned to communicate with her about their feelings regarding these behaviors and Carrie, who very much wants to be liked by her peers, has responded to their feedback.

Membership. "*Yeah, she's a member of our class, I mean she does everything that everyone else does. She helps in the class garden, even though she might not do it as well as other kids can. I mean it's fine. It turns out in the end. She can say that she helped in the garden and she helped do stuff in our class, because she does a lot of things.*" (*Carrie's sixth-grade classmate*)

The extent to which Carrie was viewed as a full member of her class varied over the course of the 4 years we followed her. Several factors contributed to this variation, but most notable was the type of class-

room context that Carrie participated in. For example, in fourth grade with a general education teacher who strongly supported cooperative learning in the class, Carrie was included in all of the class activities and assignments. However, with a more traditional general education teacher during her fifth-grade year, Carrie spent a considerable amount of her school day being pulled out of her classroom for specialized instruction. During her sixth-grade year, she was perceived by both the general education teacher and her peers as an important, contributing member of the class. She participated in small academic groups who were studying literature, social studies, and math. She was assigned roles in these groups, and accommodations were made so she could actively participate and contribute in a meaningful way. In junior high, Carrie has become a participant in some of her general education classes but is on the periphery of becoming a fully accepted member.

Skills. "*I think that so much of her actual academic and functional development is because she has had lots of peers to model from, lots of peers to support her, to reinforce her. She sees meaning for what she is doing rather than being in some isolated situation.*" (*Carrie's mother during Carrie's sixth-grade year*)

Carrie showed growth and improvement in all skill outcome areas during her participation in our research. In fourth grade, Carrie's teacher reported that she exhibited more appropriate social skills with her peers and that she was making verbal requests to adults more frequently. In fifth and sixth grades, Carrie showed academic improvement in math, reading, writing, and computer use. In functional skills, Carrie became more responsible and independent, both at home and at school. Carrie's mother and sixth-grade teacher also reported that Carrie made remarkable growth in her communication skills. Her articulation was greatly improved and she was talking louder and more frequently to peers and adults.

Cole

Relationships. Cole saw Chris (one of his student aides) walk in the room. As Chris walked toward Cole, Cole got very excited and said in a real distinct voice, "There's Chris! Look, he's back!" Chris smiled and said, "Hi, Cole." Cole said, "He's back, he's back!" (Observation notes during Cole's ninth-grade year)

Many of the interactions that Cole had with his peers in sixth grade were typical of "helpee" relationships. His peers helped Cole behave appropriately in class, and they found ways to insure his participation. Outside of class, other boys often met him at the bus, and invited him to play basketball during recess time. His teacher commented: "You just get so much more out of Cole when he's with his peers." When Cole moved on to junior high he was observed engaging in many more friendly interactions with peers. He became particularly fond of older, typically developing male students at the junior high school and was often found "hanging out" with them. He continued to receive help from several student aides who accompanied him to his classes throughout the school day (Staub, Spaulding, Peck, Gallucci & Schwartz, 1996). While Cole has not had friendships with typically developing peers that have extended beyond the school campus, his peers seem very genuine in their affection for Cole.

> *Membership. "Cole sat down between Paul and another of his classmates and started eating his lunch. He talked to Paul, and sat listening to peers as they talked. He occasionally repeated things they said, and they all laughed."* (*Observation notes, sixth grade*)

As a sixth grader, Cole was very much a member of his class. He attended sixth-grade graduation, as well as an overnight camping trip with the entire sixth grade at his elementary school. During his first year at junior high, Cole followed a class schedule similar to that of his typically developing classmates. However, during the last 2 years, Cole began to spend more time helping with school jobs and engaging in schoolwide recreation activities. A favorite activity during his sophomore year was to attend the varsity football games.

> *Skills. "Cole used to be real shy. He'd duck his head and not say a word and close his eyes if someone came close. Now he can talk about anything!"* (*Typically developing friend in eighth grade*)

Cole's most significant growth has been in social communication. For example, he learned how to interact much more appropriately with his peers, how to share, and how to wait for his turn patiently. He also displayed better receptive communication skills, which were reflected in his increased ability to follow directions. We observed Cole initiating many more

social interactions with his typically developing peers, and we noticed an increased use of complete sentences to express his feelings or describe his day. He has learned a limited number of traditional academic skills, such as number and word recognition and counting, as well as independently moving through functional routines in his school and community, such as packing his lunch, taking the bus, and moving between classes at the junior high.

Relationships and Learning

These vignettes about Ray, Carrie, and Cole show how central the social relationships of each of these students' lives are to their learning. Their opportunity to interact with their nondisabled classmates is one of the strongest motivations to participate in classroom activities. Teachers for each of these students comment on how other children understand their communicative attempts, make accommodations to enable their participation in activities, and give them helpful prompts and feedback about their behavior. One day we observed an interaction between Cole and two of his friends that brings many of these issues into focus:

> *Cole, Chris, and Justin are sitting together as one of several small groups in the class. Cole whispers to Chris and laughs. Chris laughs and then asks Cole to pay attention to the teacher. Cole watches the teacher for a few minutes, then turns to Justin and burps. Justin laughs. Chris tells Cole to knock it off. Chris then scratches the top of Cole's head. Cole does the same thing back to Chris. When their group is called up to perform their report, Chris tells Cole: "Just watch me and do what I do."*

While some might see this interaction as a bit unruly, and perhaps even counterproductive to the lesson being presented, we see it as a rich example of how typical classroom life is planted with opportunities for learning for students like Cole. First, it is clear that Cole is highly motivated to interact with his buddies. His communication attempts are, in fact, richly rewarded with their attention and laughter. In addition, one student takes an active role in teaching Cole to pay attention to what the teacher is saying and to what is happening in the group activity. Chris's final admonition to Cole, "Just watch me and do what I do", is focused on perhaps one of the most important social skills Cole must learn if he is to get along without the direct assistance of others in complex social settings: learning to observe the behavior of people around him as a source of guidance about how to "fit in" to a social situation.

In the following section, we use our conceptual framework to suggest a variety of curriculum goals related to social relationships, as well as intervention strategies for addressing them. In making these recommendations, we depart intentionally from the traditional curriculum emphasis on acquisition and generalization of specific skills in favor of a more holistic view of student learning and development in which outcomes are conceptualized in terms of increased student participation in valued roles, activities, and settings. This approach recalls early insights about the value of "partial participation" proposed by Diane Baumgart and her colleagues (Baumgart et al., 1982; Ferguson & Baumgart, 1991). We further develop the notion of participation here by placing it in the context of contemporary theories of situated learning (e.g., Lave & Wenger, 1991), as well as our own observations of student development in the context of inclusive schools. Our assumption, supported by the theories of situated learning, is that students acquire specific skills (including important cognitive, communicative, and academic skills) in the context of engaging in meaningful activities in which their participation is supported by other children, teachers, and other adults.

Strategies for Intervention

Our suggestions for intervention strategies related to social relationships are based on three sources. First, recommendations are based on what we have observed in studying students with severe disabilities in inclusive classrooms over the past 4 years (Meyer, et. al., 1992; Peck, et. al., 1992). Second, our observations are based on sociocultural theories of human development that we found of enormous value in making sense of what we observed (Cole, 1996; Lave & Wenger, 1991; Vygotsky, 1978). These views place the process of joint activity, or participation, at the center of the developmental process. Development is thus seen as a process of mutual change and adaptation, rather than as a process that takes place exclusively within the learner (Lave & Wenger, 1991). The third source of influence consists of feedback from teach-

ers, special educators, and parents about what is really workable in the context of typical practice (Meyer, Park, Grenot-Scheyer, Schwartz & Harry, 1998b; Salisbury, Gallucci, Palombaro, & Peck, 1995).

Designing "Usable" Interventions

After a series of meetings with constituent groups, school-based teacher teams, and groups of adolescents attending inclusive schools, Meyer et al. (1998b) developed a list of guidelines for intervening in the social lives of children with disabilities. They suggest that interventions should be:

1. Doable in context. Interventions must be based on an understanding of the "average" classroom and what are practical and reasonable expectations.
2. Feasible with available resources. A careful analysis of long-term available resources should precede the implementation of an intervention.
3. Sustainable over time. Time for sharing ideas and expertise is essential for sustaining the life and quality of an intervention.
4. Constituency owned and operated. For interventions to be created, facilitated, and supported by the ones carrying them out makes a large difference in how and for how long they are carried out.
5. Culturally inclusive. Interventions must be consistent with and respectful of the values, behaviors, and beliefs of the ones implementing and receiving them.
6. Intuitively appealing. Does the intervention make good, common sense? Is it appealing to the recipients and the ones carrying it out?

One approach to developing intervention strategies that reflects many of these guidelines is to identify practices that teachers, specialists, and others have found successful within inclusive classrooms (Salisbury et al., 1995). In the context of our follow-along research, we have had the opportunity to observe and record a variety of classroom practices that were associated with positive outcomes for children with and without disabilities. Although these practices have not been subjected to rigorous experimental analysis, they are perhaps best considered as a source of "ideas" that classroom teachers, special educators, and others may find of value in developing their own solutions to the ongoing and dynamic issues and problems of planning effective interventions. Although we organize our observations about classroom practice below in terms of specific themes and subthemes within our conceptual framework, many of the most promising things we have observed teachers doing are likely to have an effect on all three of the outcome domains (social relationships, membership, and skills).

Recognizing and Supporting a Range of Relationships

Social relationships between students with severe disabilities and their peers take a wide variety of forms. In analyzing our follow-along data, we identified four major types of peer relationships that were evident in the lives of the students we studied: 1) play/companionship, 2) helpee, 3) helper, and 4) conflictual. Each of these types of relationships offer somewhat different developmental opportunities; participation in such a "range of relationships" is an important advantage to students (Gaylord-Ross & Peck, 1985). In the next section, we present examples of each of these types of relationships and describe some strategies we have observed teachers use to support students' learning in each.

Play/Companion Relationships

The play/companionship theme refers to relationships that revolve around the mutual enjoyment of an activity or interaction. The importance of play/companionship relationships and friendship as a dimension of a satisfying human life is widely acknowledged (Forest, 1991; Haring; 1991; Strully & Strully, 1985). We also believe these kinds of relationships are extremely important for children as contexts for the development of social and communication skills and as avenues for achieving membership in larger social groups. When children repeatedly choose to spend time playing together or "hanging out", showing a preference for each other's company, they begin to achieve some of the richer outcomes of "friendship" (Epstein & Karweit, 1983). The following excerpt from our observations illustrates the kind of play/companion relationship we often saw in inclusive classrooms:

It is free time. Marcy, a second grade student with Down syndrome and moderate developmental delays, goes to the house area in the loft. Mellanie, a typically developing classmate, is there. Marcy smiles happily on seeing Mellanie, and the girls begin to chase each other up and down the loft. Both girls are laughing and smiling. Mellanie stays in the loft, and Marcy runs up the loft. Mellanie then chases Marcy to the stairs. Marcy runs back up the stairs. They do this over and over—maybe 20 times before the teacher calls an end to free time.

In spite of the technology that has been made available to educators today, teachers cannot "program" their student's friendships. But they can build connections that foster and support friendships between and among their students. Teachers can use practices that encourage student participation, they can provide situations like the free-time activity described above that allow and encourage playful interactions to occur, and they can model caring, respectful, and interested attitudes toward each of their students. The following are some strategies for supporting play/companion relationships.

Time and Opportunity. Students with moderate and severe disabilities and their classmates need varied, frequent, and regular opportunities to interact with each other. No matter how supportive the classroom may be for building and sustaining friendly relationships, if the student with disabilities is seldom present, it will be difficult for them to develop relationships in that setting (Schnorr, 1990). Furthermore, students with disabilities who do spend the majority of their school day in their general education classroom need to be engaged in activities that encourage frequent peer interaction and general social skills development. Our observations suggest that classrooms in which positive social relationships are more likely to develop are those in which children are given lots of opportunities to work together in a variety of small and large groups, to talk with each other about the work they are engaged in, and to assist one another with academic and other classroom activities (Salisbury, et. al., 1995; Salisbury & Palombaro, 1998). The richness of Carrie's relationships with her peers during her sixth-grade year was directly related to her teacher's design of a classroom environment with these very characteristics. In contrast, classrooms that are dominated by teacher talk, individual seatwork, and activities in which helping one another is viewed negatively (and sometimes even defined as "cheating") are less suited for peer interactions of any kind, much less those we advocate here. Likewise, Carrie's placement in a general education fifth-grade class that reflected some of these characteristics provided her with very few opportunities to interact socially with her classmates.

Classroom Climate. The impact of the general emotional tone or climate of a classroom environment on children's feelings and performance has been well-documented (Moos, 1979). While many benefits for children with and without disabilities derive from establishment of a warm and caring classroom environment (Noddings, 1992), the emergence of play/companion relationships between children with severe disabilities and their typically developing classmates is likely to be particularly affected. In a climate in which children feel themselves vulnerable to judgment, rejection, and exclusion, they are not likely to take social risks inherent in affiliating themselves with peers who are obviously "different" in ways that are devalued in our culture. In order to make the classroom a safe and supportive place for typically developing children to develop positive personal relationships with their most vulnerable peers, it must be made a safe place for all kinds of differences to be acknowledged and accepted. The establishment of such a climate may not be an easy task in schools and communities in which some students experience judgment and exclusion related to race, social class, gender, or ethnicity. Thus, the task of making the climate of classrooms and other social settings safe and supportive for children with disabilities is fundamentally and inextricably linked with making these settings safe and supportive for all children (Meyer et al., 1998a).

Paradoxically, the obvious vulnerability of students with severe disabilities may function as an opportunity for teachers to create a more caring and accepting classroom climate by demonstrating that even its most vulnerable members are respected and included (Peck, Gallucci, Staub & Schwartz, 1998). For example, in Ray's fourth-grade class, the "talking stick" activity honored a different student each day for their unique contributions to the class:

> The "talking stick," a short totem pole such as a piece of wood, is passed around the circle of students. Each day the talking stick is given to a selected "honored student," and the other classmates go around the circle and make compliments to him or her. (Observer comment about the "talking stick" activity).

Ray was never short-changed on compliments by his classmates on the day he was the "honored" student for the talking stick activity. Ray's classmates were able to identify his unique strengths and thus celebrate his differences. Moreover, the participation of Ray and others we observed in regular classrooms served as a context for students to clarify and affirm important values and practices related to individual rights, inclusion, and participation in the classroom.

Cooperative Goal Structures. Bryant (1998), Sapon-Shevin (1992), Putnam (1993), and others have noted that classrooms using cooperative goal structures may help generate friendships and foster the development of a variety of social and communicative skills that are important for all students. However, setting up cooperative group activities does not in itself assure that positive interactions, relationships, and academic outcomes will occur. The success of such arrangements is dependent on thoughtful planning, guidance and support from the teacher (Cohen, 1986). In cooperative activities that include students with severe disabilities, considerable creativity is often required to insure their meaningful participation. While teachers must be careful not to delegate too much responsibility to their typically developing students for creating accommodations for students with disabilities, peers can be a valuable source of creative ideas (Salisbury et al., 1995), as the following excerpt reveals:

> A group of students are planning a skit as part of their Winter Holiday pageant. One member of the group is Cathy, a student with moderate developmental disabilities and limited verbal skills. Her classmates are anxious that she not be left out of the dialogue of the skit and decide to record her parts on a tape player, which she activates when cued. (Observation notes)

The planning and preparation of Cathy's role in the skit turned out to be one of the real highlights of the work the students did on the skit, and one of the most meaningful aspects of the pageant.

Classroom Structures: Physical Considerations. The physical arrangements of a classroom may set the occasion for student interactions, and the development of social relationships. Flexibility of seating arrangements, the amount of space available to carry out activities, and the placement of the teacher's desk are all factors that influence interactions in the classroom setting (Epstein & Karweit, 1983):

In Carrie's sixth-grade general education classroom, her teacher had salvaged an old couch, which he covered with an attractive blanket and placed by the only window in the classroom. This spot has became an important setting for Carrie to engage in many playful interactions with her nondisabled classmates. (Observer comment)

Teachers as Models. Studies suggest that children are more likely to acquire positive attitudes and behaviors when they experience warm and affectionate relationships with their teachers (Solomon, Watson, Delucchii, Schapps & Battistich, 1988). Many of the teachers we observed successfully serving children with disabilities in their regular classrooms were also notable for the respect, warmth, and compassion they demonstrated for every one of their students. They designed their classroom environment to promote student interaction, but they also showed students the kinds of behavior they expected by taking time to listen to students, by treating their feelings with respect, and by avoiding critical and judgmental behavior toward students. We believe nondisabled students are extremely sensitive to the ways in which the classroom teacher, and other adults, respond to children with disabilities. The extent to which they see acceptance and caring modeled by the teacher has a great impact on their own interpretation of being "different" in the classroom, not only for their peer with disabilities, but for themselves.

Mr. Jones, Ray's fifth-grade teacher, set aside the last 10 minutes of each day to have class discussion. On one occasion, students wanted to discuss ways that they thought they were being treated unfairly by Mr. Jones. Even though the students were critical of Mr. Jones during this discussion, he told his students how much he appreciated their honesty and feedback. He also thanked them for helping him become a better teacher. This positive handling of criticism was often modeled by the students when they too were faced with dealing with criticism. (Observer comment)

Helpee Relationships

We observed numerous social relationships in which the student with disabilities was consistently the recipient of assistance or support from another child. We termed these "helpee" relationships. Clearly, these kinds of relationships evolve naturally in the context of many social settings in which students often need special support for participation.

In eighth-grade home economics class, the teacher asks the students to go to their cooking stations and complete the steps of making lasagna. Jackie, a "student aide" for Gina, a 13-year-old girl with cerebral palsy who uses a wheelchair, pushes Gina to an adapted kitchen counter. The teacher hands Gina an egg. Jackie physically guides Gina, cracking open the egg and putting it in a bowl. While Jackie guides Gina through this process, she quietly encourages her and tells Gina, "You're doing a good job."

We found many examples in our data of students with moderate and severe disabilities being helped by their typically developing peers in a variety of ways (see also Janney & Snell, 1996). We observed typically developing students naturally helping out by picking up dropped items, cueing a student with disabilities to participate, or showing them where they should be. We observed peers helping classmates with disabilities with their school work, making transitions, and prompting appropriate behavior. In these instances, it was often seatmates, buddies, or small group members who offered the most help. While we observed help being provided in natural ways, we also found many examples of help being provided that was purposefully planned by teachers. At Gina's junior high school, for example, typically developing students were trained as student aides to provide assistance to students with moderate and severe disabilities in each of their inclusive general education classes. We also noticed adults requesting help or support from nondisabled peers in the context of recess buddies, transition partners, or academic tutors.

There is a large body of literature on typically developing peers providing support to students with disabilities. Increases in social skills (e.g., Haring & Breen, 1992; Staub & Hunt, 1993), conversational turn-taking (Hunt, Alwell, & Goetz, 1988), and improvements in academic skill development (Delquadri, Greenwood, Whorton, Carta, & Hall, 1986) for students with moderate and severe disabilities at the elementary and secondary levels have all been associated with peer support programs. While we are in agreement with these authors in recognizing the value of relationships in which students with severe disabilities are receivers of help from others, we also have observed a number of issues with these relationships that raise concern.

Helping and Friendship. For many years, Meyer et al. (1988) have noted the potential for relationships in which students were consistently receiving help from others (what we have termed "helpee" relationships) to have adverse affects on the emergence of other kinds of peer relationships, including friendships (Voeltz, 1982). In our own research, Theresa's and Cathy's story provides an illustration of how too much "help" may sometimes interfere with friendship.

> *Theresa's and Cathy's friendship began in the third grade when they first made a connection on the school playground. Theresa, a very shy typically developing child, saw that Cathy, who has severe disabilities, was in need of a friend. Perhaps identifying with this need, Theresa initiated an interaction with Cathy that led to a two-year friendship between the girls. However, by the time the two girls were attending their inclusive fifth-grade class together, Theresa's friendship with Cathy had changed and its primary function had become helping. Theresa's ability to understand Cathy's communication attempts may have been one important reason as to why their relationship had shifted, as teachers began to routinely assign Theresa to help Cathy in a variety of classroom activities. Before the end of their fifth-grade year, Theresa had become Cathy's designated caretaker. Their classroom teacher and the special education assistant, challenged by supporting a classroom of 30 students, two of whom had moderate or severe developmental delays, began to rely on students who were most "connected" to the child with disabilities as a primary source of support. Sadly, Theresa became more and more overwhelmed as this responsibility grew, finally expressing relief when she and Cathy were not assigned to the same classroom the following year. What had begun as a real expression of interest, caring, and support had become an overwhelming responsibility for this fifth-grade girl, leading her to withdraw from the relationship* (Staub, Schwartz, Gallucci & Peck, 1994).

Cathy's and Theresa's relationship raises some important issues for consideration when assigning typically developing students to help classmates or peers with disabilities. First, if typically developing students are asked to take on the role of tutor or caretaker for a classmate with disabilities, are they given the opportunity to communicate their dissatisfaction, discomfort, or unpreparedness for this role? Second, how does the role of helper affect the relationships among teacher, students without disabilities, and the student with disabilities? Third, considering respect

and value for individual diversity and ability levels, how much "help" should adults be expecting typically developing students to provide their peers with disabilities and how should this help be structured so that there is a balance between giving and taking (Staub et al., 1994)? Finally, how can students with severe disabilities be provided with the opportunity to "choose" the student they would like to receive help from (Janney & Snell, 1996)?

Strategies for Supporting Helpee Relationships. Relationships in which students with severe disabilities receive help from peers are perhaps the most frequent and naturally occurring of those we observed. However, we have noted a tremendous difference between classrooms in which these relationships are planfully supported by adults and those in which students are left to themselves to figure out when and how to help. Following are some strategies for structuring and supporting helpee relationships:

1. Classwide helping procedures. Teachers can support students to have a voice in how the classroom is conducted, addressing issues of providing "help" to each other in ways that do not take over the activity. Teachers can also discuss with their students the kinds of help peers with disabilities may require. If these discussions take place within the context of issues about all students helping each other, more naturalized systems of support may develop. We observed several classrooms where students and teachers had incorporated "helping" rules (Janney & Snell, 1996). For example, in Karly's and Deanne's multi-grade, K-2 classroom, the "ask three before me" rule required students to ask at least three other classmates before they went to the teacher for assistance. The "elbow partner" rule was used when students were in need of help. For this rule, they were to first ask a classmate to their right elbow for help and, if that didn't work, ask a classmate to their left elbow for help.

2. Peer tutoring programs. Teachers can also set up structured systems, such as peer tutoring or peer buddy programs. We have described one such program, operated at the junior high school level, in some detail (Staub et al., 1996). Several components of the program were believed to contribute to its success. First, the open and frank ability

awareness discussions that took place during the first week of the school year gave students an opportunity to learn about differences among people, and in the discussions, they could express any fears and misconceptions they may have regarding disability issues. Second, the student aide role at Kennedy Junior High was highly valued by teachers, staff, and fellow classmates. Students who participated in the program received a good deal of recognition for their work. Finally, the special education teacher who carried out the student aide program was planful about balancing "helping" with opportunities for friendly interactions to occur. The student aides and the students with moderate and severe disabilities went on outings in the community, played games during "down" time, and occasionally attended plays or sporting events after school hours.

Unhelpful Help. Giangreco and his colleagues (Giangreco, Edelman, Luiselli, & MacFarland, 1997) have recently described some of the problems that may develop when adult aides are in one-to-one tutoring roles with students with disabilities in inclusive classrooms. We have noticed some of the same problems in some peer-helping relationships. Peers are sometimes unaware of the needs of students with disabilities to do things for themselves, and may rush in to help in ways that interfere with learning. Students who are in helping relationships with peers who have disabilities should receive direct guidance and support from teachers in making judgments about when help is needed and when it is not. Furthermore, students need to learn to ask students with disabilities if they want or need help before assuming they do and providing the help anyway (Janney & Snell, 1996).

Helper Relationships

This outcome theme refers to relationships and interactions in which the student with disabilities provides support or assistance to another child. This type of relationship is relatively unusual for children with disabilities—an observation we find distressing. Examples we observed of children with disabilities participating in relationships as helpers, rather than as "helpees," were rich with opportunities for learning and self-concept enhancement. These relationships may also serve an important function in educating others about the many ways in which individuals with disabilities can make meaningful contributions to the welfare of others:

> *The students in Mr. Hathaway's sixth-grade class are working on their journals. Jonathan, a student with autism, is typing his journal onto the computer. As he slowly types the words into the computer, he is interrupted as Amy sits down beside him, her notebook in hand: "Hey, Jon, how do you spell 'conscience'?" asks Amy. A few minutes later, as Jonathan returns to his seat, another student stops him as he walks by, "Jon, how do you spell 'mechanical'?" (Jonathan is acknowledged to be the best speller in Mr. Hathaway's class.)*

In another situation we observed, Carrie served as a "peer tutor" for a first-grade class during the year she was in fourth grade. Once a week, Carrie would visit the first grade class to listen to the typically developing students read. This relationship gave Carrie a chance to experience herself in a role in which she was giving, rather than receiving, help and she consistently responded with some of her most independent and mature behavior. Likewise, she was providing an "ear" to the first graders who were in need of practicing their reading skills. The effects of such an experience on Carrie's self-esteem were certainly important. The first graders benefited from having an eager listener attend to their reading and, perhaps more important, they had the opportunity to see an older child with Down syndrome as a competent and mature role model.

Strategies for Supporting Helper Relationships. Teachers and other adults must usually plan opportunities for students with disabilities to help others. These opportunities may be focused on helping individuals, such as Carrie's work with first graders, or they may be group focused, such as having a student regularly pass out materials to their classmates. When students have special skills, such as Jon's, teachers may create a role for the student in which those skills can be used to assist others.

With support from teachers, many older students with moderate or severe disabilities may be able to develop meaningful helper relationships with younger children. In schools with preschool programs, child care programs for younger children, and (in high schools) teen parent programs, there may be many useful contexts in which students with disabilities can develop relationships in which they are the "helper." In our experience, the possibility and value of such relationships is seldom recognized by adults.

Conflictual Relationships

Students with severe disabilities, like other students, have occasional conflict with peers. In a few instances, we observed relationships in which there was repeated verbal or physical conflict between the same two students. We termed such relationships conflictual or adversarial. The following vignette is an example of two students, one with a disability and one without, who experienced conflict with one another for almost an entire school year over the attention of a girl in their fifth-grade class:

> Jake, a child with moderate developmental delays, walks over to Connor, a typically developing student, who is standing alone watching the other kids play at recess. Jake starts pushing Connor against the wall. He does this for several minutes. Connor walks away from Jake, but Jake follows him, still pushing at him. In between pushes, Jake gets right in Connor's face and looks at him with an angry expression. (Observer comment: Earlier in the day, Connor pushed Jake out of the way so he could stand next to Erika in line [the girl they both like].)

Other instances of conflict we observed included students who were fighting, teasing, or arguing with each other. In younger children, we found conflict over toys or games, especially within unstructured situations such as free time or recess. In the intermediate grades and into junior high school, we sometimes observed instances of students with disabilities exhibiting aggressive or inappropriate behaviors toward other students, particularly on the playground.

Strategies for Supporting Learning in Conflictual Relationships. Conflictual relationships between students with and without disabilities, although unpleasant, can serve as important learning opportunities, just as they do when conflict arises between students without disabilities. Teachers can be planful in problem solving and conflict resolution skills in the hope that students will learn from their conflicts with their peers. In some cases, students may learn to use structured strategies, such as the "conflict wheel" (Jones & Jones, 1990), to solve problems with each other. In other cases, group discussion and collective brainstorming and planning in class meetings may be used to ad-

dress problems with individuals, small groups, or the entire classroom community (Nelson, Lott, & Glenn, 1993).

A particularly problematic issue we have observed repeatedly has to do with the reluctance of many typically developing students to provide direct and honest feedback to peers with disabilities about undesirable or inappropriate behavior:

> Carrie is sitting with her friends Terry and Yolanda at lunch. The girls are chatting and eating. Carrie has gotten some mayonnaise from her sandwich on her hands. Suddenly she leans over and wipes her hand on Terry's sleeve. "Oh . . . gross," exclaims Yolanda quietly to Terry. Neither of the girls say anything directly to Carrie. They move down the table so Carrie cannot reach them. (Observation notes, Carrie's fourth-grade year)

This vignette illustrates what we came to term the problem of "double standards," which both children and adults often use in responding to the behavior of students with moderate or severe disabilities. While there are many situations in which tolerance, understanding, and accommodation are called for in supporting students with disabilities, there are also many in which tolerance may be viewed as disabling. In this situation, Carrie needed clear and direct feedback from her peers about her inappropriate behavior. Equally important, her peers needed to know how to set boundaries for what they would tolerate, in ways that allowed them to remain comfortable in their relationship with Carrie. Simply moving away from Carrie was not a productive solution to this conflict for any of the students involved. Teachers have an important role to play in teaching nondisabled children how to be honest and direct with their peers with disabilities. In many cases, this involves helping nondisabled students appreciate the importance of their feedback to the learning of their peers with severe disabilities.

Recognizing and Supporting Membership

Outcomes related to the domain we have termed "membership" are essentially phenomenological in nature, referring to the sense of "belonging," which students with disabilities may experience in a variety of formal and informal group contexts in inclusive schools. An important issue to consider in planning supports for students with disabilities in the membership domain is that the perceptions of adults regarding who is and is not a member of the group may not be consistent with those of students (Schnorr, 1990). In this context, teachers should develop the ability to listen carefully to what students have to say about their social experiences in the classroom and school (Grenot-Scheyer, Staub, Peck, & Schwartz, 1998).

We observed five contexts in which teachers, parents, and students viewed membership as an important outcome for students with disabilities. These include: 1) small groups that were developed by teachers or peers, 2) the class, 3) the school, 4) friendship cliques and 5) outside groups.

Small Group Membership (Teacher-Developed)

Carrie participates in a discussion with four typically developing classmates about the "Faithful Elephants," an award-winning short story. Carrie looks at sketches Anna has made from the story and points out different things she sees. Anna asks her, "Carrie, who do you think the person with the stick is?" Carrie smiles and says, "He feeds the elephant." Children around the group smile with appreciation at her response. Sharon, another group member, shares her "sketch to stretch" with the other students and they respond to what they see in her sketch.

Description. In our observations, we found students with disabilities were often members of small groups at stations or centers, of reading or literature groups, in theme-related project groups, in art project groups, or in teacher-led games. We also found that the students with disabilities took a variety of roles in these groups, including listening, reading, sharing turn-taking, and contributing to group work.

Strategies for Supporting Membership in Small Groups. Perhaps the most critical strategy for supporting the membership of students with severe disabilities in small groups has to do with the general quality of the groupwork itself. There is a well-developed literature describing design and implementation of groupwork within regular classrooms that include a diverse array of student backgrounds and abilities (Cohen, 1986; Putnam, 1993). An important feature of cooperative learning methods within these small group contexts is provision for each student to make a substantial contribution to the group, without having to make the *same* contribution (Cohen, 1986).

Carrie's teacher often used reader's theater (Routman, 1994) as a means of demonstrating student's knowledge and comprehension at the completion of a novel or chapter of a book. As each reading group finished a novel, they wrote a script that represented the novel. All group members were expected to participate in the skit about the book, including Carrie, who was a beginning reader. However, the lines of the script that Carrie was expected to read, while they gave her a meaningful and sometimes central role in the skit, were tailored to her reading abilities. Carrie's general education teacher wrote about these experiences: "The students with disabilities have shined during these skits. They take pride in their performance and become totally engaged in the learning experience. At times they need prompts or reminders, but their group members take ownership and help each other as needed." (Pernat, 1995, p. 17).

In order for some students with disabilities to participate as members of small groups, teachers may need to make accommodations in the activities. The special education consulting teacher can assist the classroom teacher to plan roles and accommodations for individual student participation in groups. However, we have observed some of the best accommodations to be those invented by other students. Theresa found various ways to communicate with her classmate Cathy, who is nonverbal. Based on her experiences, Theresa played an active role in developing a communication book for Cathy, and showing others how to use it. Nondisabled students are able to invent these and other accommodations for peers with disabilities only when they are in classrooms in which teachers respect their ideas and actively solicit their input.

Small Group Membership (Peer-Developed)

Description. This outcome theme refers to formal and informal groups organized by students themselves, such as teams for basketball at recess or groups of children playing a game during free time in the classroom. The following vignette illustrates how Cole, a student with severe developmental delays, participated in a daily basketball game at recess:

Cole is waiting his turn to shoot the ball during the basketball game. He takes two steps forward and shoots underhand, his preferred method of shooting. He misses the first shot, but makes the second. (You're only allowed one shot, but nobody says anything about him making a second shot.)

After he makes it, he looks around and all four of the kids in line say "Good job," or "All right Cole!" (Observation notes from Cole's sixth-grade year)

Many of the same qualities of the small groups that are developed by teachers were evident in small groups that are peer-developed. For instance, students with disabilities in these small groups were given a role, specific accommodations were made by typically developing students to support their participation, and rituals (such as "high fives" and exclamations of "nice shot") were performed by group members.

Strategies for Supporting Small Group Membership (Peer-developed). Teachers can support membership in small groups developed by students by creating unstructured situations for play and exploration (i.e., setting up free choice centers, not excluding students with disabilities from important "breaks," such as recess, and providing games and other interactive materials for use during free time). Teachers can also plan ahead for peer support by doing ability awareness training, setting up buddy systems, and having class discussions about ways in which peers with disabilities can be included in peer-directed activities (Gallucci, Staub, Peck, Schwartz, & Billingsley, 1996).

Class Membership

Description. This outcome theme refers to the student's belonging to the class as a social group. We observed many examples of students with disabilities receiving the same roles, symbols, and rituals of the class as their typically developing peers, suggesting that they were "members" of these communities:

Ninth-grade band: Cole walks to the band room with his "student aide" for that period. About 30 kids are hanging out in front of the classroom. Cole is greeted by several students as they wait for the teacher. "Are you going to the game this afternoon?" one student asks. Cole nods. The teacher arrives and the kids file into the room and start to take their instruments out and practice. The band teacher hands Cole a couple of percussion sticks and reminds him what to do. Cole hits his sticks together in time with the rest of the band members. (Observation notes, Cole's ninth-grade year)

The examples of class membership we found included students having roles in special events such as class plays, assembly presentations, parades, games,

or celebrations. Students with disabilities were also often assigned roles within the class, such as taking attendance or passing out materials. Symbols of class membership we observed included certificates, portfolios, class hats worn for special occasions, being the "kid of the week," or being included on a classroom reading chart. Students with disabilities followed class schedules similar to that of their classmates and were included in the activities of the class or classes with adult and peer support.

Strategies for Supporting Class Membership. The overall social climate and sense of community that prevails in a classroom has a great impact on the likelihood that students with disabilities will be included as full members. One of the processes through we which we observed classroom teachers develop a stronger sense of community is the class meeting (Nelson, et al., 1993). Class meetings are conducted in the general tradition of the "town meeting"; they may take a variety of forms but have as a common goal the creation of opportunities for children to have a voice in decisions about how the class is conducted and in setting norms and expectations for behavior in the classroom community. Schneider (1996), suggests that the first meeting begin with the inquiry: "What kind of classroom community do we want to have?" The meetings, once established, become a regular event.

In one fifth-sixth, multi-grade class we observed, the topic of class membership came up during a class meeting. The group of students were concerned that one of their classmates, a student with autism, was being excluded from literature groups to work individually with a special education assistant. The group of students felt this was an important time for their classmate to be included "in the work we do." The students talked about the issues and agreed that everyone should participate in literature groups in whatever way they could. Adjustments were made in the schedule of the student with disabilities, and accommodations were made to the curriculum. The student with autism soon became an active and valued member of a literature group. Equally important, all of the students in this class experienced themselves as having some influence over how their class was run. Indeed, it actually became more of "their" class through this process of figuring out how to include their classmate with autism.

School Membership

Description. Membership outcomes at the level of the school as a group were indicated by (a) the student's participation in school rituals and activities, (b) by accommodations made by adults and other students to support such participation, (c) by the display of symbols of membership (such as school sweatshirts, logos, or other artifacts), and (d) by their presence in special settings, such as schoolwide assemblies and sporting events. Many times, the participation of students with disabilities in these events took on a personal and social significance that reflected the importance of membership to the student and others:

> It is Friday morning assembly time. The principal of Austen Elementary School reads a list of names of students who have completed school service projects. The principal calls out Karly's name. Karly stands up with the rest of the students whose names the principal has called. She has a big smile on her face. Everyone clearly knows her, and the students clap for her and others as she beams with pride.

Strategies for Supporting School Membership. Opportunities for students to participate in school events that both reflect and contribute to a sense of membership are plentiful in most schools. In many schools we have observed, the importance of these opportunities is not recognized.

Teachers, administrators, and parents who appreciate the value of children's experience of belonging at school can plan to include students with disabilities in active roles at school assemblies, in taking turns announcing the daily bulletin over the school public address systems, and in playing a "typical" role at the schoolwide level, such as taking tickets at a school basketball game. In addition, membership can be promoted by planning necessary supports and accommodations to insure that students participate in schoolwide rituals and celebrations, including, of course, graduation (see chapter 16). We found symbols of membership more evident at the upper elementary and middle school years, when these issues become more salient for all students. For example, symbols of membership at the middle school level included students with disabilities having a class schedule, receiving a report card, carrying a school bag, or wearing a school sweatshirt. While many of these symbols of membership are taken for granted

by many students, the absence of such symbols for students with severe disabilities may serve as subtle indicators to other students and adults of the marginalized social position of students with disabilities.

Friendship Cliques

Description. Membership within a friendship clique refers to a student belonging to a group of mutual friends, whether or not there is a close relationship with any individual in the group. As described in the vignette below, Carrie played each day with the same group of girls from her fourth-grade class during recess for more than 2 months:

> Carrie leaves the cafeteria with Lindsay, Chelsea, and Jackie, heading to the playground, all holding hands. They run to the tire swing. Carrie, Lindsay, and Chelsea climb on the tire and Jackie pushes them. Chelsea climbs off and sits on a log watching. Carrie and Lindsay swing for awhile. Both are laughing really hard and trying to make the swing go faster.

Strategies for Supporting Membership in Friendship Cliques. As any parent knows, a child's membership in a friendship clique is one of the most valued experiences in a child's life, and if it doesn't occur naturally, it is one of the most difficult outcomes for adults to create. In our observations, this outcome was a relatively rare occurrence. The heart of friendship is voluntary association. Adults can create environments in which it is relatively safe for children to befriend vulnerable peers (Forest, 1991; Haring & Breen, 1992) and they can create social contexts in which it is attractive for nondisabled students to "hang out" (Gaylord-Ross, Haring, Breen, & Pitts-Conway, 1984), but friendship is ultimately a matter of choice among peers. The few examples of this outcome theme we found included children playing with the same group of peers every day at recess or walking home regularly with the same group of friends.

While it may be difficult for teachers to "program" membership in friendship cliques for their students with severe disabilities, they may facilitate the development of groups from which these cliques may spring. For example, in several schools we worked with teachers to create a regular meeting time for peers to discuss issues of inclusion, which encompassed development of support systems for peers with disabilities. We did not include the students with disabilities in these discussions because the typically developing students expressed that they would be uncomfortable talking about their classmates in their presence. One of the effects of these groups was that some typically developing students began to feel more skillful at including students with disabilities in a variety of regular peer activities, some of which extended beyond school contexts (Gallucci et al., 1996).

Outside Groups

This final membership theme reflected a student's membership in community-based groups such as church choir, soccer team, Cub Scout troop, and an after-school folk dancing club. These groups may not be formally affiliated with the school, but nevertheless may be composed of children who meet each other at school, or who develop relationships that extend across both settings. In our follow-along research, parents reported a variety of these kinds of experiences. Karly was a member of her Brownie troop, which met once a week for an hour. Jonathan, a nonverbal student with autism, participated in his Sunday school classes at his community church. Carrie received her first communion with her typically developing peers from school. Interventions to support a students' membership in groups outside of school need not be highly technical. Parents and teachers may advocate for the student's participation in these groups and provide an array of peer supports and accommodations, in much the same way as in classroom settings. Intervention begins, of course, with recognition of the value of membership in these groups as both an experience in itself and as a context for the development of skills and the enhancement of personal relationships.

The intervention strategies that have been presented here, although focused on supporting outcomes in membership and relationships, do not preclude the importance of traditional skill development for individuals with severe disabilities. Indeed, the very skills educators work so hard on "teaching" students with severe disabilities (e.g., social communication skills, functional routines) were often acquired as an embedded outcome, along with the outcomes of membership and relationships. The reader is referred to chapters 8–15 in this text for more information on skill development for students with severe disabilities.

Assessment and Evaluation of Peer Relationships

The systematic assessment of social behavior of individuals with disabilities is a relatively recent endeavor within the field of special education and related disciplines. Since the publication of Strain, Cooke, and Apolloni's (1976) seminal book on the measurement and analysis of social behavior of students with developmental, learning, and behavioral disabilities, assessment approaches have relied primarily on the methodological strategies of applied behavior analysis. These approaches to measurement have been extremely valuable in identifying functional relationships between a variety of instructional variables and student social behavior. Recently, behavior-analytic methods have been extended conceptually and methodologically to the analysis of contextual factors affecting the quality and quantity of social relationships between students with disabilities and their peers (Breen & Haring, 1991; Haring, 1992; Haring & Kennedy, 1990). In addition, Kennedy and his colleagues (e.g., Kennedy, Horner, & Newton, 1989; Kennedy & Itkonen, 1994) have demonstrated the value of methods drawn from social and community psychology in analyzing the networks of social relationships in which individuals with disabilities participate (see chapters 3 and 6 for further description of quantitative assessments). These measurement approaches share a common focus on dimensions of social behavior that may be reliably quantified, such as the number of interactions a student with disabilities has with her peers or the duration of engaged time spent participating in an activity. With adaptation, such techniques can be highly useful to classroom teachers. However, our own work has been inspired in good part by our experience that social relationships between children with disabilities and their nondisabled peers, as well as other outcomes of their participation in regular class settings, are often not described adequately by quantitative measures.

There are several issues that constrain the effectiveness of quantitative measures as a means of documenting and evaluating change in social relationships, particularly when they are used in isolation. These include: (a) the relative inflexibility of such measures in capturing unanticipated dimensions of change, (b) their relative insensitivity to issues of meaning embedded in social situations, and (c) the fact that teachers often find these data of limited value in their daily work (Ferguson, 1987; Grigg, Snell, & Lloyd, 1989; Meyer & Evans, 1993). We do *not* suggest that quantitative measures be abandoned. However, in our own efforts to document outcomes for students with severe disabilities that their parents and teachers affirm as meaningful and important, we have found narrative data to be extremely valuable (see Schwartz, Staub, Gallucci, & Peck, 1995, for an elaboration on these arguments). We have used a variety of simple data collection techniques drawn from the qualitative research tradition to enrich our description, analysis, and understanding of what is happening in students' social lives at school and elsewhere. Next, we briefly describe some of these techniques, including narrative observational records and interviews, and how we have used them. More complete accounts of how qualitative research strategies may be used to describe and evaluate change in educational settings are offered by Bogdan and Biklen (1992), Hubbard and Powers (1991), and others.

Narrative Observational Records

Observational data recorded as narrative offer a highly flexible means of documenting the rich and dynamic flow of classroom events, which can be useful to any classroom teacher. Rich narrative descriptions of behavior in situational contexts may be a valuable source of insight about what is going on in a social setting. Figure 10–3 presents an example of the kinds of data (i.e., field notes) we have found of value in evaluating social relationships between children. Collected regularly (e.g., daily, weekly, monthly), these descriptive accounts may be valuable in assessing qualitative changes in relationships over time and in evaluating differences in behavior across context. For example, narrative descriptions of interactions might help identify issues related to the quality of "helping" relationships emerging for children across the school year. Five examples of issues that we have observed to be of concern in some classrooms, and that might be evaluated using narrative data, include:

1. To what extent is assistance from peers and adults really helpful (or unneeded, intrusive, stigmatizing)?
2. Are nondisabled children becoming de facto aides to children with disabilities?

3. What are the attitudes, interpretations, and responses of nondisabled children who are not directly involved in inclusive classrooms (e.g., children on the playground or in the cafeteria)?
4. How do nondisabled peers respond to "inappropriate" behaviors of peers with disabilities? (e.g., Are they direct in giving feedback to the child? Do they respond pejoratively?)
5. In what ways are issues of inclusiveness part of regular class meetings and discussions, and to what extent are these issues considered to be about all children in the classroom and not just those with identified disabilities?

Interviews

Interviews are another source of data teachers may find useful in evaluating social relationships among students. In fact, interviews provide a source of insight about how students perceive their relationships, which may be uniquely valuable to teachers and other adults, who often have only partial understanding of the students' point of view. For example, we recently interviewed nondisabled fifth- and sixth-grade children about their experiences in inclusive classrooms (Peck et al., 1998). We were interested in how these students perceived the process of full inclusion of peers with moderate and severe disabilities in their classrooms. From the interviews, we learned much of value about how nondisabled students perceive membership in the class, including the ways in which membership was negotiated as a complex interplay of conflicting values related to the "fairness" of being treated "the same as us" (i.e., not receiving "special" treatment) and the "fairness" of receiving needed supports. From these interviews, we also discovered some ways in which adults were sometimes perceived as using a "double standard" to evaluate the behavior of students with disabilities. Nondisabled students were adamant that this kind of adult behavior detracted greatly from their peers with disabilities being viewed by other children as class members.

Figure 10–4 depicts a general interview protocol we have used with nondisabled peers and adults, such as teachers, parents, and classroom aides, to gather descriptions of social exchanges, friendship, and other relationships between students with disabilities and their nondisabled peers.

FIGURE 10–3
Field Notes Example

Classroom: Century Elementary, Grade 4, Room 23
Focus Student: Steven
Date: 9/29/98
Start time: 1:40   End time: 2:40
Observer: Cap

Context: The entire class is in the room. The desks are arranged in groups of 3 or 4, except for Randy and Steven, who are sitting together in an area to the side of the classroom. Students are sitting and working quietly, and the noise level in the class is low. Steven (S.) is working with a teaching assistant (TA) on a math assignment.

1:40
The teacher calls students up to the front of the room to read what they have written about the math problem. S. continues to work quietly on his assignment, as the TA leaves the room. The teacher comments briefly on each student's presentation, and then asks questions of the class. Students raise their hands to answer the questions. S. looks up to watch one girl as she discusses her assignment.

1:50
The class is dismissed for a break. Students are shuffling about, and the noise level is higher. S. is pushing a chair around the classroom, and then he sits down in it. The class is lined up in two lines (by gender), waiting to go outside. S. has gotten up and is playing with a paper airplane, trying to keep it away from one of his peers. S. is the last one to get in line. [Observer comment: How often does this happen? How do peers feel about this?]

1:55
S. walks out with Tara. She wanders off, and S. walks over to Kenny. They walk out to the soccer field. S. follows Kenny and stands by him on the field. They are both on the field, but are not actually playing, just watching. S. follows K. off the field, then walks back over to Tara. He stands very close to her and then says something. A game of tag starts between S., T., and a group of four girls. S. stops to talk with his classroom teacher, Linda, and then returns to the game. The kids are laughing and smiling. S. is "it" now, and Linda tells him "Run! Run!" He gets tagged, and runs after the person who tagged him [Observer comment: S. seems very much a part of this informal group. They seem to really enjoy his participation].

2:10
The tag group has broken up, the kids going off in different directions. S. stays and talks with Linda. She leads S. over to the tetherball court, and asks the kids playing if S. can join them. She roots for him, "Go, Steven!" They play for a few minutes, but the other student is then called in from his recess. S. runs off with another girl (Carrie), and together they look into a classroom window. Linda calls the class back in from recess.

A feature of this and other interview protocols we have used is that it begins with an open-ended question, asking for description rather than evaluation of "what's going on" in relation to the student with disabilities or others in the classroom. We also attempt to establish trust with the interviewee by assuring them that they do not have to answer every question and that they can stop whenever they want. Using an open-ended interview strategy allows the adult or student being interviewed an opportunity to bring up issues of concern that the interviewer may not know to ask about. This information may be of great value to specialists, teachers, and others who are trying to develop a richer understanding of the social experiences

and relationships of students with severe disabilities for the purpose of designing interventions, as well as monitoring and evaluating change.

Analyzing and Evaluating Narrative Data

The value of narrative (qualitative) data as a source of information about what is going on in the social lives of students with disabilities is enhanced to the extent that these data are read and analyzed regularly. Simply jotting down observational notes or excerpts from conversations with children and others will not in itself necessarily lead to greater understanding of what is going on in the classroom. But the reflection

FIGURE 10–4

Nondisabled Peer Interview

The purpose of this interview is to gather information about how the student perceives the social relationships of a classmate with significant disabilities. We have found it useful to begin the interview process by conducting informal observations of contexts in which the informant student is interacting with the student with disabilities. These concrete activity contexts are then used as a referent for discussion of the social relationships between the informant student, other members of the classroom, and the peer with disabilities.

Begin the interview by explaining that you are interested in helping the student with disabilities participate as fully as possible in the activities of the classroom, and that the informant student can help you understand how things are going in many classroom situations that are hard for the teacher to get around to observe directly (e.g., group work, paired reading, peer tutoring, recess).

Activity Contexts (list at least 3 areas, e.g., recess, lunch, P.E.)

1) _____

2) _____

3) _____

Questions

(Adapt these as needed, but ask for general descriptions, examples, and illustrations of what's going on before asking for evaluative comments).

1) Tell me about some of your experiences in [activity context 1].
   How do you feel about this activity?
   How do you think other kids feel about it?
   How do you think [student with disabilities] experiences this activity?

2) What about [activity context 2]? (same probe questions as for activity context 1)

3) Tell me about [activity context 3] (same probe questions as above)

4) What kinds of changes have you seen in the ways in which [student with disabilities] relates to you, and to other kids, over the past [weeks, months]?

5) How do you think we can help [student with disabilities] be a member of our class? Have fun with other kids? Get help when it's needed?

---

involved in regular and systematic analysis of the data does. This analytic process need not be highly formal, but it should be ongoing. Furthermore, it should involve all the members of the team, including the special educator, general educator, parent(s), and any other individuals providing services to the student (e.g., paraeducator, physical therapist). The use of a reflective journal may add considerably to the depth of this process of "re-searching" the data for patterns of behavior, context events, or other factors affecting social relationships. Hubbard and Powers (1991) describe a variety of specific techniques teachers have used for analysis of narrative data, such as looking for common themes across journal entries or identifying information that doesn't seem to fit to bring up possible issues of concern.

Nondisabled Students and Severely Disabled Peers: All True Benefits Are Mutual

Research and development work related to social relationships between children with severe disabilities and their nondisabled peers has been focused almost exclusively on the functions of these relationships in the lives of children with disabilities (Haring, 1991; Meyer, et al., 1998a; Strully & Strully, 1985). At one level, this focus is understandable in view of the many ways in which individuals with disabilities have been routinely excluded from participation in valued roles, activities, and settings within American society. However, we also believe that our cultural interpretations of disability as deficiency, with our attendant focus on programs of "treatment" and "remediation," have functioned to obscure questions about the potential contributions that individuals with disabilities may make to our lives and to our society (Wolfensberger, 1983). One of the most robust phenomena we have observed in our inclusive schools research is the positive value many nondisabled students place on their relationships with peers who have severe disabilities. Indeed, the relatively few studies that have been carried out to evaluate the impact of these relationships on nondisabled students are quite consistent in their findings (Staub & Peck, 1994, 1995). Specifically, it is clear that nondisabled students are perceived by themselves, their parents, and their teachers as benefiting in a variety of ways from their relationships with peers who have severe disabilities. These include:

1. Increased understanding of how other people feel;
2. Increased acceptance of differences in appearance and behavior;
3. Increased sense of self-worth in contributing to the lives of others;
4. Increased sense of commitment to personal principles of social justice (Biklen, Corrigan, & Quick, 1989; Helmstetter, Peck, & Giangreco, 1994; Murray-Seegert, 1989; Peck et al., 1990; Peck, Carlson, & Helmstetter, 1992; Staub, 1998; Staub et al., 1994).

In addition, the academic progress of nondisabled students is not harmed by the inclusion of students with severe disabilities in regular classes (Peck et al., 1992; Hollowood, Salisbury, Rainforth, & Palombaro, 1995; Sharpe, York, & Knight, 1994).

Perhaps most exciting is the reciprocity of outcomes between students with and without moderate and severe disabilities that emerged from many of the relationships we observed over the course of our follow-along research. Three outcomes that we perceived to be mutually beneficial included: (a) warm and caring companionships, (b) increased growth in social cognition and self-concept, and (c) the development of personal principles and an increased sense of belonging (Staub, 1998).

Companionship

One of the most important functions of relationships is to enable us to feel safe, loved, and cared for. When

Karly and Deanne first became acquainted in their K-2, multi-age class, they each needed a friend. Both were shy, hesitant, and often intimidated by the activity that surrounded them. By becoming companions, they found comfort in each other's presence in an overwhelming situation:

> Deanne is truly a friend for Karly. They hang out, they comfort each other, and they are always hugging and holding hands. Karly and Deanne truly have a "bud" friendship. You don't want to be friends with everyone in the classroom necessarily, but everyone has a need for at least one buddy. That's what they provide to each other. (Karly's and Deanne's teacher).

Growth in Social Cognition and Self-Concept

We found that several of the nondisabled children who participated in our research identified as "connected" to their peers with disabilities and became more aware of the needs of their disabled peers. These nondisabled children became skilled at understanding and reacting to the behaviors of their classmate with disabilities. Stacy, a nondisabled peer of Carrie's who attended class with Carrie for many years, was perceived to have benefited from her longstanding relationship with Carrie:

> I think Stacy is at a point where she looks at Carrie as a friend, and I think inclusion, overall, has benefited Stacy in the sense that Stacy will never judge someone by their mental ability, whether they have Down syndrome or are developmentally delayed. I think she's come to a point where later on in life, if she has a chance to hire someone that could do the job with a disability, she would be the first one to say "yeah." (Carrie's and Stacy's sixth-grade teacher)

Likewise, having a relationship with Stacy was very important to Carrie's own sense of self-worth. Stacy not only provided Carrie with a model for how to socialize appropriately, but she also helped Carrie feel better about herself:

> Stacy has had an enormous impact on Carrie's behavior. Carrie wants to do the 'right thing' in front of Stacy and you can really tell that she feels reinforced when Stacy compliments her on her behavior or actions. (Carrie's mother)

Development of Personal Principles

Children are extremely vigilant about the way vulnerable peers are treated by other children and by adults (Bukowski, Newcomb, & Hartup, 1996). While the risks of vulnerability, including social rejection and exclusion, are commonly recognized for children with disabilities, the meanings that nondisabled students may construct about the experiences they observe in relation to their peers with disabilities have received little empirical attention from researchers and little practical attention from educators. We believe that there may be considerable risks for nondisabled students that are constituted by their belief that it is not safe to be weaker than others in our society. Significantly, the likelihood of children drawing this conclusion appears to be compounded, not reduced, when vulnerable peers are sent away (to other classes, to other schools).

Viewed from this perspective, the inclusion of children with severe disabilities in regular classes creates both risk and opportunity for all children. The creation of classroom and school communities in which developmental differences are accepted, and vulnerability is not observed to produce exclusion, may represent one of our most powerful opportunities to make schools psychologically safer and more humane places for all children. The social relationships that develop between children with disabilities and their nondisabled peers thus constitute a wonderful opportunity for all educators. For the benefits of these relationships to be realized, it is essential that educators, parents, and other adults concerned with the well-being and development of children recognize the deep ways in which our relationships with people with disabilities offer us possibilities to see, and to redefine, who we are.

Brittany [Ray's nondisabled classmate] definitely keeps us on our toes. One day last week, Ray was really having a hard time—lots of screaming and fussing. I asked his teaching assistant to take him for a walk. I was stressed that the kids were getting stressed. Brittany came up to me and said, "I think we should ignore Ray's screaming and find something that he wants to do in class. Think how bad he feels being sent out of the room." Well, how do you respond to that? What it did was force me to push for a better communication system on his part, and the special education staff have really responded positively. But really, it caused me to look at Ray differently. Not as a child with disabilities, but as a classmate, a peer. (Ray's fourth-grade teacher).

Summary

This chapter highlights the importance of social relationships in the lives of all children. The level of importance and value that teachers place on supporting and facilitating their student's relationships will influence greatly their successful development. It is our hope that this chapter has provided ideas and tools for teachers to use in this important capacity.

Suggested Activities

1. Plan to spend at least 40 minutes in an inclusive classroom to observe a target student's interactions with his or her peers. Write down your observations in an objective fashion (e.g., provide a running account of what you observe without comment or judgment). After your observation, read over your notes and write your responses to the following:
   a. What looked "right" about the interactions I observed? (For example, nondisabled students were treating student with severe disabilities respectfully, student with severe disabilities was included in conversations)
   b. What looked "uncomfortable" about the interactions I observed? (For example, nondisabled students were treating the student with severe disabilities as a nonmember of their class, student with disabilities was isolated from all conversations and activities taking place in the classroom).
   c. What was working well in the classroom environment for promoting peer interactions? (For example, the arrangement of desks allowed for easy conversation among students, the teacher used cooperative learning activities to promote interactions)
   d. What barriers were evident in the classroom environment that interfered with students' interactions? (For example, a class rule was that students were not to talk with one another during activities, teacher spent too much time "lecturing" to students).
2. Looking back over your responses to the items in question 1, develop an action plan that specifies how the classroom environment could be arranged to facilitate more appropriate peer interactions.

What are things the teacher(s) could do? What environmental changes would you recommend? What types of activities would facilitate more peer interactions? Name at least five things that could be done to promote more appropriate peer interactions in the classroom.

3. Think about a student who has severe disabilities. Using the style of the case illustrations presented in this chapter (e.g., Ray, Carrie, Cole), write a brief case summary for your student, which reflects his or her outcomes in the areas of membership, relationships, and skills. Conclude your case summary by writing one to two paragraphs on the types of supports and contexts that you believe have facilitated these outcomes. Use your case summary to present at the student's next IEP meeting or planning meeting as a vehicle for selecting appropriate goals and objectives for the student.

References

Apolloni, T., & Cooke, T. P. (1975). Peer behavior conceptualized as a variable influencing infant and toddler development. *American Journal of Orthopsychiatry, 45*, 4–17.

Baumgart, D., Brown, L., Pumpian, I., Nisbet, J., Ford, A., Sweet, M., Messina, R., & Schroeder, J. (1982). The principle of partial participation and individualized adaptations in educational programs for severely handicapped students. *Journal of the Association for Persons with Severe Handicaps, 1*, 17–27.

Bijou, S., & Baer, D. (1961). *Child development I: A systematic and empirical theory.* Englewood Cliffs, NJ: Prentice-Hall.

Biklen, D., Corrigan, C., & Quick, D. (1989). Beyond obligation: Student's relations with each other in integrated classes. In D. Lipsky & A. Garnter (Eds.), *Beyond separate education: Quality education for all* (pp. 207–222). Baltimore: Paul H. Brookes.

Billingsley, F., Gallucci, C., Peck, C., Schwartz, I., & Staub, D. (1996). "But those kids can't even do math": An alternative conceptualization of outcomes for inclusive education. *Special Education Leadership Review, 3*, 43–56.

Bogdan, R., & Biklen, S. (1992). *Qualitative research for education: An introduction to theory and methods.* Boston: Allyn & Bacon.

Breen, C., & Haring, T. G. (1991). Effects of contextual competence on social initiations. *Journal of Applied Behavioral Analysis, 24*, 337–347.

Brofenbrenner, U. (1979). *The ecology of human development.* Cambridge, MA: Harvard University Press.

Bruner, J. (1990). *Acts of meaning.* Cambridge, MA: Harvard University Press.

Bruner, J. (1996). *The culture of education.* Cambridge, MA: Harvard University Press.

Bryant, B. K. (1998). Children's coping at school: The relevance of failure and cooperative learning for enduring peer and academic success. In L. H. Meyer, H. S. Park, M. Grenot-Scheyer, I. S. Schwartz, & B. Harry (Eds.), *Making friends: The influences of culture and development* (pp. 353–368). Baltimore: Paul H. Brookes.

Bukowski, W. M., Newcomb, A. F., & Hartup, W. W. (1996). *The company they keep: Friendship in childhood and adolescence.* New York: Cambridge University Press.

Cohen, E. (1986). *Designing groupwork: Strategies for the use of heterogeneous classrooms.* New York: Teachers College Press.

Cole, M. (1996). *Cultural psychology: The once and future discipline.* Cambridge, MA: Harvard University Press.

Delquadri, J., Greenwood, C. R., Whorton, D., Carta, J. J., & Hall, V. R. (1986). Classwide peer tutoring. *Exceptional Children, 52*, 535–542.

Epstein, J. L., & Karweit, N. (1983). *Friends in school: Patterns of selection and influence in secondary schools.* New York: Academic Press.

Ferguson, D. L. (1987). *Curriculum decision making for students with severe handicaps: Policy and practice.* New York: Teachers College Press.

Ferguson, D. L., & Baumgart, D. (1991). Partial participation revisited. *Journal for the Association for Persons with Severe Handicaps, 16*, 218–227.

Fiske, A. P. (1992). The four elementary forms of sociality: Framework for a unified theory of social relations. *Psychological Review, 99*, 689–723.

Forest, M. (1991). It's about relationships. In L. Meyer, C. Peck, & L. Brown (Eds.) *Critical issues in the lives of people with severe disabilities* (pp. 399–407). Baltimore: Paul H. Brookes.

Gallucci, C., Staub, D., Peck, C., Schwartz, I. & Billingsley, F. (1996). *But we wouldn't have a good class without him: Effects of a peer-mediated approach on membership outcomes for students with moderate and severe disabilities.* Unpublished manuscript. Seattle: University of Washington.

Gaylord-Ross, R., Haring, T., Breen, C., & Pitts-Conway, V. (1984). Training and generalization of social integration skills with autistic youth. *Journal of Applied Behavior Analysis, 17*, 229–247.

Gaylord-Ross, R., & Peck, C. A. (1985). Integration efforts for students with severe mental retardation. In D. Bricker & J. Filler (Eds.), *Serving students with severe mental retardation: From research to practice* (pp. 185–207). Reston, VA: Council for Exceptional Children.

Geertz, C. (1973). *Interpretation of cultures.* New York: Basic Books.

Giangreco, M., Edelman, S., Luiselli, T., & MacFarland, S. (1997). Helping or hovering? Effects of instructional proximity on students with disabilities. *Exceptional Children, 64*, 7–18.

Grenot-Scheyer, M., Staub, D., Peck, C. A., & Schwartz, I. S. (1998). Reciprocity and friendships: Listening to the voices of children and youth with and without disabilities. In L. H. Meyer, H. S. Park, M. Grenot-Scheyer, I. S. Schwartz, & B. Harry (Eds.), *Making friends: The influences of culture and development* (pp. 149–168). Baltimore: Paul H. Brookes.

Grigg, N. C., Snell, M., & Lloyd, B. (1989). Visual analysis of student evaluation data: A qualitative analysis of teacher decision making. *Journal of the Association for Persons with Severe Handicaps, 14*, 23–32.

Halliday, M. (1975). *Learning how to mean: Explorations in the development of language.* London: Edward Arnold.

Haring, T. G. (1991). Social relationships. In L. Meyer, C. Peck, & L. Brown, (Eds.), *Critical issues in the lives of people with severe handicaps* (pp. 195–217). Baltimore: Paul H. Brookes.

Haring, T. G. (1992). The context of social competence: Relations, relationships and generalization. In S. Odom, S. McConnel, & M. McEvoy, (Eds.), *Social competence of young children with disabilities: Issues and strategies for intervention* (pp. 307–320). Baltimore: Paul H. Brookes.

Haring, T. G., & Breen, C. G. (1992). A peer-mediated social network intervention to enhance the social integration of persons with moderate and severe disabilities. *Journal of the Association for Persons with Severe Handicaps, 13,* 20–27.

Haring, T., & Kennedy, C. (1990). Contextual control of problem behavior in students with severe handicaps. *Journal of Applied Behavior Analysis, 23,* 235–243.

Helmstetter, E., Peck, C. A., & Giangreco, M. F. (1994). Outcomes of interactions with peers with moderate or severe disabilities: A statewide survey of high school students. *Journal of the Association for Persons with Severe Handicaps, 19,* 263–276.

Hollowood, T. M., Salisbury, C. L., Rainforth, B., & Palombaro, M. M. (1995). Use of instructional time in classrooms serving students with and without severe disabilities. *Exceptional Children, 61,* 242–253.

Hubbard, R., & Powers, B. (1991). *The art of classroom inquiry.* Portsmouth, NH: Heineman.

Hunt, P., Alwell, M., & Goetz, L. (1988). Acquisition of conversation skills and the reduction of inappropriate social interaction behaviors. *Journal of the Association for Persons with Severe Handicaps, 13,* 20–27.

Janney, R., & Snell, M. (1996). How teachers use peer interactions to include students with moderate and severe disabilities in elementary general education classes. *Journal of the Association for Persons with Severe Handicaps, 21,* 72–80.

Jones, V., & Jones, L. (1990). *Comprehensive classroom management.* Boston: Allyn & Bacon.

Kaye, K. (1982). *The mental and social life of babies: How parents create persons.* Chicago: University of Chicago Press.

Kennedy, C. H., Horner, R., & Newton, S. (1989). Social contacts of adults with severe disabilities living in the community: A descriptive analysis of relationship patterns. *Journal of the Association for Persons with Severe Handicaps, 14,* 190–196.

Kennedy, C. H., & Itkonen, T. (1994). Some effects of regular class participation on the social contacts and social networks of high school students with severe disabilities. *Journal of the Association for Persons with Severe Handicaps, 19,* 1–10.

Lave, J., & Wenger, E. (1991). *Situated learning: Legitimate peripheral participation.* New York: Cambridge University Press.

Lincoln, Y., & Guba, E. (1985). *Naturalistic inquiry.* Beverly Hills: Sage.

Meyer, L., & Evans, I. (1993). Science and practice in behavioral intervention: Meaningful outcomes, research validity and usable knowledge. *Journal of the Association for Persons with Severe Handicaps, 18,* 224–234.

Meyer, L., Harry, B., Schwartz, I., Grenot-Scheyer, M., & Park, H. S. (1992). *The consortium for collaborative study of social relationships.* Proposal submitted to the U.S. Department of Education. Syracuse, NY: Syracuse University.

Meyer, L. H., Park, H., Grenot-Scheyer, M., Schwartz, I., & Harry, B. (Eds.) (1998a). *Making friends: The influences of culture and development.* Baltimore: Paul H. Brookes.

Meyer, L. H., Park, H. S., Grenot-Scheyer, M., Schwartz, I. S., & Harry, B. (1998b). Participatory research approaches for the study of

the social relationships of children and youth. In L. H. Meyer, H. S. Park, M. Grenot-Scheyer, I. S. Schwartz, & B. Harry (Eds.), *Making friends: The influences of culture and development* (pp. 3–30). Baltimore: Paul H. Brookes.

Miles, M., & Huberman, A. (1984). *Qualitative data analysis: A sourcebook of new methods.* Beverly Hills: Sage.

Moos, R. (1979). *Evaluating educational environments.* San Francisco: Jossey-Bass.

Murray-Seegert, C. (1989). *Nasty girls, thugs, and humans like us: Social relations between severely disabled and nondisabled students in high school.* Baltimore, MD: Paul H. Brookes Publishing.

Nelson, J., Lott, L., & Glenn, H. (1993). *Positive discipline in the classroom.* Rocklin: Prima Publishing.

Noddings, N. (1992). *The challenge to care in schools.* New York: Teachers College Press.

Peck, C. A., Carlson, D., & Helmstetter, E. (1992). Parent and teacher perceptions of outcomes for typically developing children enrolled in integrated early childhood programs: A statewide survey. *Journal of Early Intervention, 16,* 53–63.

Peck, C. A., Donaldson, J., & Pezzoli, M. (1990). Some benefits nonhandicapped adolescents perceive for themselves from their social relationships with peers who have severe handicaps. *Journal of The Association for Persons with Severe Handicaps, 15,* 241–249.

Peck, C., Gallucci, C., Staub, D., & Schwartz, I. (1998). *The function of vulnerability in the creation of inclusive classroom communities: Risk and opportunity.* Paper presented at the annual meeting of the American Educational Research Association. San Diego, CA, April.

Peck, C. A., Schwartz, I., Staub, D., Gallucci, C., White, O., & Billingsley, F. (1994). *Analysis of outcomes of inclusive education: A follow-along study.* Paper presented at the annual meeting of the Association for Persons with Severe Handicaps. Atlanta, GA, December.

Peck, C. A., White, O., Billingsley, F., & Schwartz, I. (1992b). *The inclusive education research project.* Proposal submitted to the U.S. Department of Education. Vancouver, WA: Washington State University.

Pernat, D. (1995). Inclusive education and literacy: Engaging a student with disabilities into Language Arts activities in a sixth grade classroom. *Network, 4,* (4), 12–19.

Piaget, J. (1972). *Origins of intelligence in children.* New York: International University.

Putnam, J. (1993). (Ed.) *Cooperative learning and strategies for inclusion.* Baltimore: Paul H. Brookes.

Routman, R. (1994). *Invitations: Changing as teachers and learners in K–12.* Portsmouth, NH: Heineman.

Salisbury, C., Gallucci, C., Palombaro, M., & Peck, C. (1995). Strategies that promote social relationships among elementary students with and without severe disabilities in inclusive schools. *Exceptional Children, 62,* 125–137.

Salisbury, C., & Palombaro, M. M. (1998). Friends and acquaintances: Evolving relationships in an inclusive elementary school. In L. H. Meyer, H. S. Park, M. Grenot-Scheyer, I. S. Schwartz, & B. Harry (Eds.), *Making friends: The influences of culture and development* (pp. 81–104). Baltimore: Paul H. Brookes.

Sameroff, A., & Chandler, M. (1975). Reproductive risk and the continuum of caretaking casuality. In F. Horowitz, M. Hetherington,

S. Scarr-Scalapatek, & G. Siegel (Eds.), *Review of research in child development, (vol 4)*. Chicago: University of Chicago Press.

Sapon-Shevin, M. (1992). Student support through cooperative learning. In W. Stainback & S. Stainback (Eds.), *Support networks for inclusive schooling* (pp. 65–80). Baltimore: Paul H. Brookes.

Schneider, E. (1996, Sept.). Giving students a voice in the classroom. *Educational Leadership*, 22–26.

Schnorr, R. (1990). Peter? He comes and he goes . . . First graders' perspectives on a part-time mainstreamed student. *Journal of the Association for Persons with Severe Handicaps*, 15, 231–240.

Schwartz, I. S., Staub, D., Gallucci, C., & Peck, C. A. (1995). Blending qualitative and behavior analytic research methods to evaluate outcomes in inclusive schools. *Journal of Behavioral Education*, 5, 93–106.

Sharpe, M. N., York, J. L., & Knight, J. (1994). Effects of inclusion on the academic performance of classmates without disabilities. *Remedial and Special Education*, 15, 281–287.

Slavin, R., & Hansell, S. (1983). Cooperative learning and intergroup relationships: Contact theory in the classroom. In J. L. Epstein & N. Karweit (Eds.), *Friends in school: Patterns of selection and influence in secondary schools* (pp. 93–114). New York: Academic Press.

Solomon, D., Watson, M. S., Delucchi, K. L., Schapps, E., & Battistich, V. (1988). Enhancing children's prosocial behavior in the classroom. *American Educational Research Journal*, 25, 527–554.

Staub, D. (1998). *Delicate threads: Friendships between children with and without special needs in inclusive settings*. Bethesda, MD: Woodbine House.

Staub, D., & Hunt, P. (1993). The effects of a social interaction training on high school peer tutors of schoolmates with severe disabilities. *Exceptional Children*, 60, 41–57.

Staub, D., & Peck, C. A. (1994/1995). What are the outcomes for nondisabled kids? *Educational Leadership*, 52, 36–40.

Staub, D., Schwartz, I. S., Gallucci, C., & Peck, C. A. (1994). Four portraits of friendship at an inclusive school. *Journal of the Association for Persons with Severe Handicaps*, 19, 314–325.

Staub, D., Spaulding, M., Peck, C. A., Gallucci, C., & Schwartz, I. S. (1996). Using nondisabled peers to support the inclusion of students with disabilities at the junior high school level. *Journal of the Association for Persons with Severe Handicaps*, 21, 194–205.

Strain, P., Cooke, T., & Apolloni, T. (1976). *Teaching exceptional children: Assessing and modifying social behavior*. New York: Academic Press.

Strully, J., & Strully, C. (1985). Friendship and our children. *Journal of the Association for Persons with Severe Handicaps*, 10, 224–227.

Voeltz, L. M. (1982). Effects of structured interactions with severely handicapped peers on children's attitudes. *American Journal of Mental Deficiency*, 86, 380–390.

Vygotsky, L. (1978). *Mind in society*. Cambridge, MA: Harvard University Press.

Wolfensberger, W. (1983). Social role valorization: A proposed new term for the principle of normalization. *Mental Retardation*, 21, 234–239.

≈11≈

Nonsymbolic Communication

Ellin Siegel
Amy Wetherby

Symbolic modes of communication rely on forms that represent, or stand for, something else, such as the word *shoe*, spoken or signed, referring to the shoe that you put on this morning. Combining the words *my* and *new* with the spoken or signed word *shoe* requires understanding of the formal rules of language. However, many individuals with severe disabilities have limited ways of expressing themselves or understanding those around them. These individuals communicate without using symbols, such as talking, signing, or pictures.

 Marina

Marina is 3 years old and began attending an early intervention center last year. At age 1½, she was not walking or talking but laughed frequently and always wanted to be near the "action" of her two older siblings and her parents. Marina's parents became very skilled at noticing and interpreting her subtle movements and facial expressions. She smiled often as her head bobbed up and down. Her parents helped her learn to make choices by directing her gaze toward desired items. Her family learned to understand how Marina's body movements meant that she wanted a favorite game or event to occur.

For example, Marina would rock back and forth in a wagon to get her brother to pull it and attempt to climb on her mother's back to get a ride. Figure 11–1 is another example of how Marina's family learned to understand her nonsymbolic expressions.

By age 2½, Marina began having seizures, and her parents sought further medical testing, which led to the diagnosis of Angelman syndrome. This syndrome was first identified by Dr. Harry Angelman in 1965. Major clinical characteristics include microbrachycephaly (small

FIGURE 11–1
Marina enjoys interactions with her mother. They have learned how to read each other's expressions, and their enjoyment in this familiar peek-a-boo game is obvious.

head with a flattened occiput), abnormal results on electroencephalogram (EEG), an awkward gait, severe language impairment (usually without speech), excessive laughter, a protruding tongue, the mouthing of objects, and intense curiosity (Dooley, Berg, Pakula, & MacGregor, 1981; Williams & Frais, 1982.)

A great deal of familiarity with Marina and her behavior was needed before the intervention staff could readily interpret her behaviors. The onset of her seizures led Marina to regress. Now, medication controls Marina's seizures but makes her fatigue easily. Her abilities fluctuate. The staff members are trying to not only interpret

Marina's behaviors but also encourage her to use the behaviors that she used intentionally before the Angelman syndrome progressed and to solidify Marina's communication by developing her awareness of the effects that her communicative behaviors have on her family and her intervention staff. In addition, the staff is trying to get Marina to use more conventional gestures and to expand her use of eye gaze to be more understandable and readable to people who are less familiar with her. The conventional gestures of giving an object, raising her arms to be picked up, holding an object up to show it, and reaching are being targeted.

                                                    Ryan

When Ryan sees you approach him, he usually smiles, reaches toward you to shake hands, and vocalizes. He is a 16-year-old teenager who has limited peripheral vision and a mild hearing loss. He enjoys attention and expresses his interest by smiling at familiar people, extending his fisted hands toward objects or people, and making eye contact. Because of severe motor impairments, Ryan relies on others to move him. He has a variety of supported positions, including side lying, sitting in three different chairs that can be easily adapted for him, and sitting in a motorized wheelchair. It is difficult for Ryan to maintain his head erect for very long when seated, and adaptations are needed to aid him. Ryan needs to be moved to new positions every hour.

Ryan is in the local high school in his community, where he rotates through many different subjects and spends part of the day in the community. He has developed some friendships with his peers, especially since he began assisting the football team. Paired with other assistants assigned to the football team, Ryan takes care of the towels in the locker room and on the field (i.e., laundering, folding, handing them out using specialized equipment designed for these tasks). He also helps with getting drinks to the players. Ryan tends to wait for others to interact with him but will indicate his interest in maintaining interactions by increasing his vocalizations or body movements. He turns his head away or is quiet when he wants to terminate or deter an interaction.

Nonsymbolic Skills

This chapter focuses on individuals who do not use or understand symbols and the rules of language. Instead, these individuals rely on their own bodies and current contexts to communicate. Their communication may include facial expressions, body movements, gazing, gesturing, and touching. This communication has been referred to by many different terms, such as prelinguistic, prelanguage, and nonverbal. The authors of this chapter prefer to use the word nonsymbolic, in order to focus on what individuals are doing. Nonsymbolic behavior is viewed as a legitimate form of communication and not just a transition to another stage. Because some individuals with severe disabilities rely primarily on nonsymbolic skills, it is crucial to recognize each individual's current communication repertoire and to strive to expand it.

The Impact of the Disability

No single disability or combination of impairments distinguishes which individuals communicate primarily in a nonsymbolic manner. An individual who communicates in this way may have dual sensory impairments, severe motor impairments, or profound mental retardation combined with a health impairment. Individuals who use nonsymbolic communication from a heterogeneous group. All young children communicate without symbols during the first year of life, and for some, this mode continues for many years beyond the early developmental period. Communication partners (school staff members such as teachers and speech language therapists) must recognize nonsymbolic communication skills and have strategies to enhance these skills for young children as well as older children who use this communication mode.

The Tri-Focus of Intervention

Most school staff and other communication partners expect to observe and respond to language. Because they typically use spoken language to communicate, they have difficulty adjusting their expressive messages to individuals with severe disabilities. Yet, all of us use nonsymbolic expressions. When Mary asks you where Sam has gone, you tip your head in the direc-

tion Sam went. When a waitress is at the table next to you, you lift your coffee cup in the air, hoping that she will come to give you a refill. You may not be fully aware, however, of the many forms of nonsymbolic communication and may not systematically use nonsymbolic communication to enhance communication skills (Beukelman & Mirenda, 1998; Stillman & Siegel-Causey, 1989).

Many successful interactions occur between communication partners and individuals who communicate nonsymbolically. When a child cries, a staff member tries to relieve discomfort. A reach toward the juice pitcher conveys the message to pass the pitcher. These are examples of nonsymbolic communication, which plays a key role in most interactions, especially with individuals who do not use symbols or whose understanding of symbols is limited (Stillman & Siegel-Causey, 1989).

The tri-focus framework (Siegel-Causey & Bashinski, 1997) incorporates concepts from various fields into three primary components: the learner, the partner, and the environmental context. Figure 11–2 displays the interactive nature of the components. The tri-focus framework recognizes that communication interactions are experienced mutually by communication partners and learners and that both parties are reciprocally affected. Because communication is a dynamic process involving at least two people, the willingness of individuals without disabilities to interact may be influenced by the limited behavioral repertoires of individuals with severe disabilities. Therefore, the focus of intervention is on enhancing the communication skills of learners with nonsymbolic abilities and of their communication partners.

FIGURE 11–2
The Tri-Focus Framework

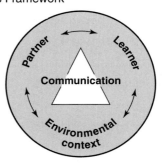

Copyright 1996 by E. Siegel-Causey and S. Bashinski. Reprinted with permission.

An additional aspect of this intervention approach is recognizing the influence of the environmental context on communication interactions and in particular the learner. In the tri-focus framework, the context encompasses all aspects of the setting; specifically, physical and social aspects of the environment. Addressing the physical and social aspects of the environment is another dimension that should be considered as communication partners attempt to enhance nonsymbolic communication and responsiveness of learners with severe disabilities. Physical refers to the broad settings (e.g., home, school, community) and the specific contexts that an intervention occurs within, such as snack, physical education, or free play. In addition, physical attributes, such as lighting, noise level, and materials, present in the specific context are considered (Ault, Guy, Guess, Bashinski, & Roberts, 1995). Social environment includes aspects such as the peers and adults within close proximity of the learner, overall activity level of the setting, and the amount and type of social interaction or contact being provided to the learner by partners (Ault et al., 1995).

Figure 11–3 provides an overview of the tri-focus framework. The triple focus on learner, partner, and environment has considerations that should help the partner plan areas to assess and the related interventions to implement. We focus this chapter using these three components: understand the learner (assessment), broaden the partner's role (use nonsymbolic strategies and guidelines as part of intervention), and improve environmental contexts (modify the environment, use physical and social supports as part of intervention). The next section provides information related to early communication development and recognition of what nonsymbolic communication encompasses.

Early Communication Development

It is sometimes difficult to interpret messages of individuals who use nonsymbolic expressions, especially since most of us function in a world of symbols. Individuals with severe disabilities need to be systematically taught to interact, are likely to learn to communicate first about their own wants and needs, and are most likely to communicate in their familiar environments (Coots & Falvey, 1989; Falvey, 1986; Gaylord-Ross & Holvoet, 1985). Next, this chapter explores issues raised in the developmental literature to help individuals who communicate nonsymbolically. It presents the critical aspects of communication, including the emergence of communication and the parameters of nonsymbolic communication acquisition.

Critical Aspects of Communication

To develop or enhance strategies for individuals who communicate nonsymbolically, communication partners must be aware of the variables that influence early communication development. The development of communication occurs during a critical period of acquisition of linguistic and nonlinguistic skills (Bates, O'Connell & Shore, 1987; Duchan, 1995; Dunst, Lowe, & Bartholomew, 1990; Wetherby, Reichle, & Pierce, 1998). Communication is a developmental process involving reciprocal interactions between individuals. Understanding and enhancing communication requires building on existing nonsymbolic behaviors that are communicative signals or that have the potential to be communicative.

When Marina was young her parents built on her subtle movements, facial expressions, and laughter. When she

FIGURE 11–3
Overview of Tri-Focus Framework

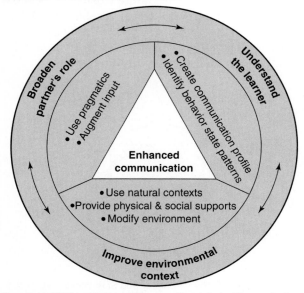

smiled, her parents smiled in reaction. They interpreted her smile as a signal of "I want" or "like" within the specific activity and repeated the event. At this early level of communication, Marina did not realize that her facial expression (i.e., smile) could signal a message to her family.

Developmental research shows that infants communicate before they talk, and that this communicative ability evolves during the first few years of life (Bates, 1979; Bloom, 1993; Bruner, 1981; Dore, 1986; McLean & Snyder-McLean, 1978; Siegel-Causey & Downing, 1987; Wetherby, Reichle, & Pierce, 1998). The information compiled from research on the nonsymbolic stage in typical development is particularly relevant to individuals with severe disabilities who communicate in a similar manner. The developmental literature, then, can provide relevant and solid bases for forming assessment and intervention strategies for any individual who is communicating at these early stages of communication development. Information on how typically developing children acquire and use communication can provide a framework for understanding how individuals with nonsymbolic skills develop communication, guiding the strategies used to assess communication and prioritizing the educational goals. Extensive reviews of the developmental research in relation to the nonsymbolic stage of development and the communicative abilities of children with severe disabilities include Siegel-Causey, Ernst, and Guess (1987, 1989), Siegel-Causey and Guess (1989), Wetherby and Prizant (1992), and Wetherby, Warren, and Reichle (1998).

The study of language development has shifted the emphasis from the *structure* of language (e.g., grammatical rules, size of vocabulary) to the use of language as a social tool to communicate. The aspect of language that deals with the social rules governing the use of language is called *pragmatics*. Pragmatics has its roots in speech act theory, which describes the basic unit of communication as the "speech act" and underscores the notion of speech as action. According to speech act theory (Austin, 1962; Muma, 1986; Searle, 1969), each speech act consists of three components: (a) the "perlocution," which is the effect of the message on the listener; (b) the "illocution," which is the purpose of the message as planned or intended by the speaker, and (c) the "locution," which is the referential meaning of the message and includes the proposition (new information or explicit content)

and the presupposition (assumed information or implicit content) of the message.

The concept of a speech act may be extended to apply to nonsymbolic communicative acts. Thus, a "communicative act" may include two components, the intention (illocution) and the function (perlocution). At a nonsymbolic level, a child uses a sound, movement, or gesture to indicate wants and needs. When a child progresses to a symbolic level, he or she uses symbols (e.g., words, signs, pictures) to express intent. At this level, the communicative act includes propositional content (i.e., words that refer to things) and is considered a speech act.

The constructs of intention and function are critical to a discussion of nonsymbolic communication. Since communication involves a dyadic interaction between a sender and a receiver, communicative intent must be considered in relation to the function of communication. *Intention* refers to the plan of the sender of a message, and *function* refers to the purpose of the act as interpreted by the receiver of the message. Look at Figure 11–4, and read about this nonsymbolic communication act:

> *Marina looks at and reaches toward her ball, looks at her mother, looks back at the ball, and looks up at her mother. As a result, her mother tips the basket so that Marina can reach the ball. Marina's plan was to get the ball and play with Mom. The function of Marina's signal was to request an action, and her mother interpreted the signal as intended by Marina. The success of a communicative act depends upon whether or not the sender's intention is appropriately interpreted by the receiver of the message. Marina's interaction with her mother was a successful communicative interaction.*

A Three-Stage Communication Progression

The emergence of communication is a developmental process involving reciprocal interactions between a caregiver and child. Bates and associates (Bates, 1979; Bates, Camaioni & Volterra, 1975) have provided a theoretical framework to describe the emergence of communication and language. Borrowing terminology from the speech act theory of Austin (1962), they identified three stages in the development of communication. From birth, the infant is in the "perlocutionary stage." The infant's behavior systematically affects the caregiver, and thus, serves a

FIGURE 11–4

In the photo at left, Marina reaches toward the toy basket to request her ball (intention). In the photo (right), Marina's mother interprets the action to mean that Marina wants a toy (function) and tips the basket so that Marina can reach inside.

communicative function, although the infant is not yet producing signals with the intention of accomplishing specific goals. At about 9 months of age, most children move to the "illocutionary stage" and begin to use preverbal gestures and sounds to communicate intentionally; that is, the child deliberately uses particular signals to communicate for preplanned effects on others. At about 13 months of age, the child progresses to the "locutionary stage" and begins to construct linguistic propositions while communicating intentionally with referential words. Thus, communication and language development can be conceptualized as a three-stage process, involving movement from perlocutionary (preintentional) communication to illocutionary (intentional preverbal) communication to locutionary messages (verbal language) used intentionally to communicate. This model has been adapted for application to the emergence of communication in individuals with severe disabilities (e.g., Beukelman & Mirenda, 1998; McLean & Snyder-McLean, 1988; Musselwhite & St. Louis, 1988; Stremel-Campbell & Rowland, 1987).

An important assumption of this model is that all individuals communicate in some way. In applying this model to individuals with severe disabilities, communicative partners play a critical role in interpreting behaviors that are communicative. The model also highlights the broad range of communicative abilities spanning the perlocutionary and illocutionary stages. Understanding the developmental progression from perlocutionary to illocutionary communi-

nication can help partners detect and enhance progress in subtle but critical aspects of communicative development.

> For example, when Ryan was a toddler, he did not intentionally communicate (perlocutionary stage). Tom, a peer, and Ryan are seated across from each other at a table in their preschool. On the table is a large switch connected to a toy that has sound and movement linked to many small, colorful toy birds. Ryan squeals in delight each time Tom uses the switch to make the toy movements occur. Ryan's vocal expressions became a humming sound when the toy's noises and movements stopped. Tom, with help from staff, learns to react to the humming as if Ryan expressed "I want more." Later Ryan was taught to hum and look at Tom to signal "more," and he also was taught to use the switch.

It is important for communication partners to understand how communication emerges, because nonsymbolic communication may be the primary or only means used by individuals with severe disabilities. Communicative interactions are rooted in early social and affective development in infants. Gaze, the expression of emotion, body movement, and orientation are signals (or forms) that guide the responses to infants and regulate social interactions. Interpretations of and contingent responsiveness to the preintentional communicative signals of infants play important roles in the development of intentional communication (Dore, 1986; Dunst, Lowe, & Bartholomew, 1990; Yoder, Warren, McCathren, & Leew, 1998). Early social interactions involving shared affective experi-

TABLE 11–1
Speech Act Theory and Nonsymbolic Behaviors

Definition	Nonsymbolic Messages	Interpretation or Meaning	Speech Act Messages	Interpretation or Meaning
Perlocution: the effect or function of the message on the listener; interpretation of behaviors as if they were intentional	Ryan's first moves toward his book bag.	His friend interprets this to mean that Ryan wants the book bag and says, "Hey, you want some help buddy?"	Says "mm" after he swallows a bite of his sandwich.	His teacher assumes that he wants another bite and says, "Here's your sandwich."
Illocution: the meaning of the message as planned by the speaker; using behaviors and conventional gestures with the intent of affecting the behavior of others	Ryan looks at his friends when the bell rings before gym class.	Ryan wants his friend to push him to gym class.	Andy says "nn" and turns his head away when the teacher puts the sandwich toward his mouth.	Andy is full.
Locution: using words with the intent of affecting the behaviors of others	—	—	Andy smiles and says "yes" when his teacher extends his cup of juice toward him.	Andy uses words to convey wanting a drink.

Note: Based on *How to Do Things with Words* by J. Austin, 1962, Cambridge, MA: Harvard University Press, and *The Emergence of Symbols: Cognition and Communication in Infancy* by E. Bates, 1979, New York: Academic Press.

ences lead to awareness of the effects that their behaviors have on others (Bruner, 1981; Corsaro, 1981; Dore, 1986). Thus, the responsiveness of communicative partners to preintentional communicative behaviors plays a critical role in developing communication skills.

The speech act theory and its relationship to nonsymbolic behavior is described with example in Table 11–1.

Intentional Behavior

Intentionality may be defined as the deliberate pursuit of a goal (Flavell, 1963). Behavior is intentional if an individual has an awareness or mental representation of the desired goal as well as the means to obtain the goal (Piaget, 1952). Parallels in the development of intentionality are seen in cognitive and social domains. For example, if a child wants a toy on a shelf out of reach, the child may pull a chair over to the shelf, climb on the chair, and get the toy. This exam-

ple does not involve social interaction to obtain the goal. This same goal may also be obtained through social communicative behavior. For instance, rather than using a chair, the child may pull on the caregiver's pant leg, point to the toy on the shelf, and vocalize until the caregiver gives him or her the toy.

Wetherby and Prizant (1989) conceptualize intentional communication along a developmental continuum beginning with automatic, reflexive reactions. Children then develop awareness of goals but do not have plans to achieve the goals. With advancing knowledge of communicative partners, children coordinate their behaviors to pursue their goals. Further development in intentionality is evident in the use of repair strategies when communicative attempts are not met with success. Rudimentary efforts to repair involve repeating a signal to persist in achieving a goal. More sophisticated efforts involve modifying the form of the signal. Simple, coordinated, and alternative plans to achieve goals develop from 9 to 18 months of age, during sensorimotor stages V and VI (Bates et al., 1975; Harding, 1984; Wetherby, Alexander, & Prizant, 1998).

> *Ryan has developed repair strategies. For example, his friend Matt is helping him get to their next class, art. As he enters the room, his teacher points to Matt's project and says, "Ryan, where is your <u>project</u>?" Ryan looks at her and vocalizes, "EHH". "Don't worry, Matt can take you back to your <u>locker</u>." Ryan looks at the art teacher, vocalizes louder, and pulls his head to the right side of his wheelchair. "Oh, is it in your <u>backpack</u>?" she says, as she points to his backpack. Ryan smiles.*

Conversational Roles

Communication involves taking turns between being a sender of a message (expressive role) and being a receiver (receptive role). Communicative partners interacting with nonsymbolic learners must be aware of these dual roles. Individuals with disabilities, too, must function as both senders and receivers of messages. Figure 11–5 shows Marina and her mother in these dual communication roles.

Nonsymbolic communicators are individuals who use primarily nonsymbolic communication as senders. The receptive abilities of nonsymbolic communicators may be comparable to or better than their

FIGURE 11–5
Marina and her mother both act as senders and receivers of messages.

expressive abilities. Before children comprehend the meaning of words, they use a variety of contextual cues to determine a response strategy and thus they may appear as if they comprehend specific linguistic information (Chapman, 1978; McLean & Snyder-McLean, 1978; Miller & Paul, 1995). For example, when a child is standing in front of a sink and an adult points to the faucet while saying "wash hands," the child can figure out how to respond without comprehending the word wash or hands. As children move to the illocutionary stage of communication expression, they begin to comprehend nonverbal cues provided by their caregivers, including gestures, facial expression, and directed eye gaze (e.g., an adult pointing to or looking at an object "means" the child should give or attend to that object). Children may also respond to paralinguistic cues by using intonation to determine how to respond (e.g., loud voice and volume "means" angry). At this stage, children also may respond to situational cues by using the immediate environment and knowledge of what to do with objects to respond (e.g., observe what others do, drink from a cup, put objects in a container). As children progress to the locutionary stage of expression, they begin to comprehend the meanings of familiar words, but continue to be guided by the context. It is easy to overestimate a child's comprehension of language if one is not aware of the nonverbal, paralinguistic, or situational cues that the child may be using to determine how to respond. The development of comprehension response strategies serves as a bridge to the comprehension of word meanings. That is, contextual cues provide children with strategies for responding and guide them to the meanings of words.

Recognizing Nonsymbolic Communication

Nonsymbolic communication is a reciprocal interaction involving reception (i.e., understanding others' behavior) and expression (i.e., using behavior to signal others). Figure 11–6 depicts the reciprocal nature of communication between a learner and a partner. The overlapping circles depict the communication partner's abilities to use both nonsymbolic and symbolic behaviors.

In considering nonsymbolic communication, it is necessary to identify the observable behaviors that may serve a communicative function. The first para-

meter is to consider how the learner communicates, or the *form* of communication. Nonsymbolic communication may be conventional in form if the meaning of the behavior is shared by a community and is generally recognizable. Examples of conventional gestures are giving, showing, reaching, pointing, and open-palm requesting. However, nonsymbolic communication may be unconventional or idiosyncratic and understood only by someone who is very familiar with the individual and the context. Table 11–2 presents examples of forms that nonsymbolic communication may take, including unconventional forms, such as standing by a sink to request a drink or scratching oneself to protest an action.

A second parameter to consider is the function, or purpose, served by the communicative behavior. Children use presymbolic gestures and vocalizations to communicate for a variety of purposes before the emergence of words (Bates, 1979; Coggins & Carpenter, 1981; Harding & Golinkoff, 1979; Wetherby, Cain, Yonclas, & Walker, 1988; Wetherby & Prizant, 1993). Bruner (1981) suggests that children use communication to serve three functions during the first year of life: (a) *behavior regulation*, which is communicating to get others to do something or to stop doing something (i.e., request an object or action or protest an object or action); (b) *social interaction*, which is communicating to get others to look at or notice oneself (e.g., request a social game, greet, call, showoff); and (c) *joint attention*, which is communicating to get others to look at an object or event (e.g., comment on an object or action, request information). Studies of the communicative functions of individuals with severe disabilities also demonstrate a pattern of relatively strong use of behavior regulation functions and limited use of social interaction and joint attention functions (Cirrin & Rowland, 1985; Ogletree, Wetherby, & Westling, 1992; Wetherby, Cain, Yonclas, & Bryan, 1988; Wetherby, Prizant, & Hutchinson, 1998). Table 11–3 presents examples of nonsymbolic forms of communication for the three major functions of behavior regulation, social interaction, and joint attention.

The forms of communication used by individuals with severe to profound mental retardation has been distinguished on the basis of *contact gestures* versus *distal gestures* (McLean, McLean, Brady, & Etter, 1991). This distinction is consistent with developmental

FIGURE 11–6
Reciprocal nature of communication interactions

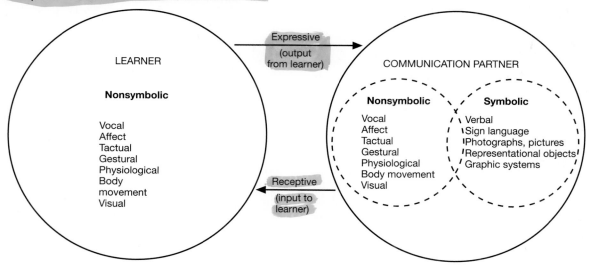

NONSYMBOLIC

Vocal—Using sounds and utterances produced
    by voice
Affect—Displaying a feeling or emotion
Tactual—Using touch (stimulation of passive
    skin receptors and active manipulation
    and exploration)
Body movement—General motion of body
    such as leaning, pulling away, or swaying
Gestural—Using movement of the limbs or
    parts of body
Physiological—Displaying functions of body
    such as alertness or muscle tone
Visual—Using sense of sight

SYMBOLIC

Verbal—Using words
Sign language—Using system of hand and
    arm gestures
Photographs and pictures—Using visual
    representation or image
Representational objects—Using miniature
    objects to depict real objects or activity;
    using portions of a real object to depict
    a real object or activity
Graphic system—Using a method of symbols
    (Blissymbolics, Rhebus pictures)

Note: Adapted from "Introduction to Nonsymbolic Communication" by R. Stillman and E. Siegel-Causey. In *Enhancing Nonsymbolic Communication Interactions Among Learners with Severe Handicaps* (p. 4) by E. Siegel-Causey and D. Guess (Eds.), 1989, Baltimore: Paul H. Brookes. Reprinted by permission of Paul H. Brookes Publishing Company, P.O. Box 10624, Baltimore, MD 21285-0624.

patterns. At about 9 months of age, children first use contact gestures, in which their hands come in contact with an object or person (e.g., giving an object, showing an object, pushing an adult's hand). By about 11 months, children use distal gestures, in which their hands do not touch a person or object (e.g., open-hand reaching, distant pointing, waving) (Bates et al., 1987). McLean et al. (1991) found that the adolescent and adult participants who used only contact gestures used communication for behavior regulation functions only, while the participants who used distal gestures used communication for behavior regulation and joint attention functions. That is, the adolescents or adults who used contact gestures communicated by leading others' hands to request actions, while those who used distal gestures drew the attention of others to an object by pointing. Additionally, those using distal gestures attempted to clarify their messages when there was a breakdown in communication and communicated at a higher rate than did those using contact gestures. Figure 11–7 shows Marina using contact gestures.

TABLE 11–2
Forms of Learner Nonsymbolic Communication

Generalized movements and changes in muscle tone

- Excitement in response to stimulation or in anticipation of an event
- Squirms and resists physical contact
- Changes in muscle tone in response to soothing touch or voice, in reaction to sudden stimuli, or in preparation to act

Vocalizations

- Calls to attract or direct another's attention
- Laughs or coos in response to pleasurable stimulation
- Cries in reaction to discomfort

Facial expressions

- Smiles in response to familiar person, object, or event
- Grimaces in reaction to unpleasant or unexpected sensation

Orientation

- Looks toward or points to person or object to seek or direct attention
- Looks away from person or object to indicate disinterest or refusal
- Looks toward a suddenly appearing familiar or novel person, object, or event

Pause

- Ceases moving in anticipation of coming event
- Pauses to await service provider's instruction or to allow service provider to take turn

Touching, manipulating, or moving with another person

- Holds or grabs another for comfort
- Takes or directs another's hand to something
- Manipulates service provider into position to start an activity or interactive "game"
- Touches or pulls service provider to gain attention
- Pushes away or lets go to terminate an interaction
- Moves with or follows the movements of another person

Acting on objects and using objects to interact with others

- Reaches toward, leans toward, touches, gets, picks up, activates, drops, or pushes away object to indicate interest or disinterest
- Extends, touches, or places object to show to another or to request another's action
- Holds out hands to prepare to receive object

Assuming positions and going to places

- Holds up arms to be picked up, holds out hands to initiate "game," leans back on swing to be pushed
- Stands by sink to request drink, goes to cabinet to request material stored there

Conventional gestures

- Waves to greet
- Nods to indicate assent or refusal

Depictive actions

- Mimes throwing to indicate "throw ball"
- Sniffs to indicate smelling flowers
- Makes sounds similar to those made by animals and objects to make reference to them
- Draws picture to describe or request activity

TABLE 11–2
continued

Withdrawal

- Pulls away or moves away to avoid interaction or activity
- Curls up, lies on floor to avoid interaction or activity

Aggressive and self-injurious behavior

- Hits, scratches, bites, spits at service provider to protest action or in response to frustration
- Throws or destroys objects to protest action or in response to frustration
- Hits, bites, or otherwise harms self or threatens to harm self to protest action, in response to frustration, or in reaction to pain or discomfort

Note: From "Introduction to Nonsymbolic Communication" by R. Stillman and E. Siegel-Causey. In *Enhancing Nonsymbolic Communication Interactions Among Learners with Severe Handicaps* (p. 7) by E. Siegel-Causey and D. Guess (Eds.), 1989, Baltimore: Paul H. Brookes. Reprinted by permission of Paul H. Brookes Publishing Company.

TABLE 11–3
Examples of Nonsymbolic Communicative Functions

Communicative Function	Communicative Form (Nonsymbolic Examples)
Behavior regulation: to get others to do something or stop doing something	
Request object or action	• Learner *looks* at or *reaches* toward an object that is out of reach • Learner in need of assistance *gives* an object to open or activate it • Learner *holds* up an empty cup to get a refill
Protest object or action	• Learner *pushes* other's hand away to stop being tickled • Learner *cries* in response to a toy's being put away • Learner *throws* undesired object
Social interaction: to draw attention to oneself	
Request social routine	• Learner *taps* other's hand to request continuation of tickling • Learner *looks* at other and laughs to keep a peek-a-boo game going
Request comfort	• When distressed, learner *reaches* toward caregiver to get comforted • Learner *raises* arms to get picked up and comforted • Learner *wiggles* in chair to get other to adjust his or her position
Greet	• Learner *waves* hi or bye • Learner *extends* arm in anticipation of other's shaking to say good-bye
Call	• Learner *tugs* on other's pant leg to get other to notice him or her • Learner *vocalizes* to get other to come to him or her
Show off	• Learner *vocalizes* a raspberry sound, *looks* at other, and *laughs* to get a reaction
Request permission	• Learner *holds* up a cookie to seek permission to eat it
Joint attention: to draw attention to an object or event	
Comment on object or action	• Learner *shows* a toy to get other to look at it • Learner *points* to a picture on the wall to get other to look at it
Request information	• Learner *holds* up a box and *shakes* it with a questioning expression to ask what's inside • Learner *points* to a picture in a book and *vocalizes* with rising intonation to ask what it is

FIGURE 11–7
Marina is using contact gestures successfully with her mother.

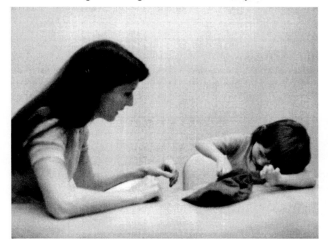

The Capacity for Symbols

Along with the social bases of communication and language development, the cognitive bases of language acquisition has received continuing attention in the literature. Piaget (1952) suggested that sensorimotor cognitive knowledge (i.e., knowledge about how things in the world work) provides the basis for the emergence of symbol use. Language is one manifestation of the capacity to use symbols (other symbolic functions are deferred imitation, play, drawing, and visual imagery). Piagetian theory has influenced the current view that language is derived from a broad cognitive knowledge base and has stimulated the search for cognitive prerequisites to language acquisition. There is accumulating evidence of parallels between cognition and the emergence of preverbal communication and first words (Bates & Snyder, 1987; Rice, 1983; Wetherby et al., 1998). In a cross-sectional study of 25 typically developing children, Bates found that the following sensorimotor skills were correlated with the emergence of language: imitation, tool use, communicative intent, and object use. Thus, the potential for movement toward a symbolic communication system in learners with severe disabilities may be better understood by considering skills that enhance the capacity for symbol use and using a framework of assessment that includes the continuum from non-symbolic to symbolic skills.

Assessment

This section presents a structure for the assessment of nonsymbolic communication of individuals with severe disabilities. Given the interrelated nature of the learner, partner, and environment, it is suggested that assessment include each of these three aspects. Table 11–4 displays the tri-focus on learner, partner, and environment. In the second column is a listing of considerations that can serve as assessment questions to guide the staff. These questions can help partners consider the important aspects to assess about the learner, partner and environmental variables. The last column provides an overview of the interventions that are linked to each focus on learner, partner, and environment. The assessment content in

TABLE 11–4
Considerations and Interventions Using the Tri-Focus Framework

Focus	Considerations	Interventions
#1: Understanding the learner who has severe disabilities	*What is the learner's communication profile?*	
	Consider the progression of communicative development	Identify learner's level of symbolization
		Identify learner's level of intentionality
	View challenging behavior as communication	Relate learner's expressions to partners' actions
	Attend to behavior state patterns	Facilitate alert, responsive state behavior
#2: Broadening the communication partner's role	*How can I help the learner communicate better?* *How can I communicate better with the learner?*	
	Consider the pragmatic perspective	Use pragmatics: Enhance sensitivity Increase opportunities Sequence experiences
	Attend to elements of choice making	Implement continuum of choice formats
	Consider augmented input	Augment vocal input: Enhance meaning Facilitate retention
#3: Improving the environmental context	*What combination of influences can improve the context of the interaction?*	
	Attend to natural contexts	Provide both physical and social natural supports
		Use relevant, natural contexts
	Consider external influences on state behavior	Modify environment: Adjust sensory qualities Alter movement and orientation of the learner's body Change learning atmosphere
		Consider environmental influences in combination

Note: Adapted from Siegel-Causey, E., & Bashinski, S. M. (1997). Enhancing initial communication and responsiveness of learners with multiple disabilities: A tri-focus framework for partners. *Focus on Autism and Other Developmental Disabilities, 12* (2), 105–120.

Table 11–4 provides the structure for the rest of this chapter.

Quality communication assessment procedures measure typical and spontaneous behaviors, are conducted by familiar persons, employ real-life materials and naturalistic activities, and translate information into relevant functional skills. In addition to pinpointing a learner's current repertoire, a partner must address the communication skills required in the current and future environments. Multiple strategies and sources of information should be used to assess current and future communication repertoires adequately to meet the needs of individuals with severe disabilities. Available strategies include commercially available instruments, communication and language samples, behavioral assessment, ABC analysis, and oral-motor assessment. Further details about assessment are discussed in chapters 3, 5, and 6; oral-motor assessment is discussed in chapter 8.

In the next section, we address assessment of the learner's behaviors, the partner's role, and the environment. We begin assessment with the first focus: *understanding the learner by using a communication profile*. Next, we address the second focus: *the broadening of partner roles* by assessing current patterns of partners' communication style. Finally we address the third focus: *environment* in terms of what may be influencing communication.

Assessment: Understanding the Nonsymbolic Communicator Using a Learner Profile

Assessment of nonsymbolic communication should identify not only what individuals cannot do but also what they *can* do. Thus, the assessment should profile the limitations and abilities across cognitive, social, communicative, and motor domains. Communication partners should begin with the assumption that individuals with nonsymbolic skills *are* communicating and that the purpose of communication assessment is to identify *how and why* the individual uses communication. The use of a communicative profile of the learner will assess important behaviors.

Learner Communicative Profile

1. Communicative forms
   a. Behavior state patterns
   b. Vocalizations, gestures, etc.
   c. Challenging behavior

2. Communicative functions
3. Intentionality
4. Readability of signals
5. Repair strategies
6. Capacity for symbols

Communicative Forms

In the assessment of nonsymbolic communication, a related primary goal is identifying the repertoire of communicative forms used by an individual (concept introduced in section on recognizing nonsymbolic communication). The forms of communication used by the learner provides important information for intervention planning. A comparison of vocal and gestural forms should be made. Consideration should be given to both conventional forms and idiosyncratic forms. For gestural communication, contact gestures should be differentiated from distal gestures. One key to distinguishing communicative forms from general behaviors is that forms are linked to specific behaviors used to convey messages.

> *Marina's communicative forms include generalized movements (e.g., increased hand shaking, moving torso), vocalizations (e.g., undifferentiated vowels, laughs, cries), facial expressions (e.g., smiles, grimaces), orientation with her head and eyes to objects or actions of interest, pauses, reaches toward desired objects, body moves to request action, and withdrawal to avoid activity.*

However, many of Marina's forms may be exhibited by learners with more motor impairments than she has.

> *For Ryan and other learners with severe motor impairments, partners must be attuned to more subtle movements and a smaller range of movements as the communicative forms (e.g., increased tone, stop or start of a vocalization).*

One assessment strategy as you build the learner's communication profile is to formally identify the learner's current communicative forms. A gestural dictionary (Beukelman & Mirenda, 1998) or, as we refer to it, a communication dictionary, is one strategy that provides a way to document what the learner communicates, what the family and staff are interpreting each form of communication to mean, and how a partner should react when the form is expressed by the learner. Two considerations need to be addressed in setting up a communication dictionary; how it is organized and how it is displayed. The dictionary should be available for partners to access easily and can be organized in a variety of ways, such as listing each form categorized by body parts starting with head (e.g., head: shaking, movement to side; face: wide open mouth, neutral) or in alphabetical order (e.g., aah sound, arching of back, body movement forward). The selected format should be easy for partners to use. Secondly, some practitioners have found it helpful to have the dictionary displayed in more than one way (poster board in classroom, listed on cards in a wallet-photo holder the learner carries, in a notebook) so that all partners have access to the current list during their interaction with the learner. Collecting and revising the communication dictionary is part of assessing the learner's communication and of building a communication profile. Updating the communication dictionary, on a periodic basis, documents the changes in forms used by the learner and provides an assessment record of the changes accomplished across the school year, as more forms are developed or as forms become more conventional. An example of a communication dictionary is provided in Table 11–5.

TABLE 11–5
Communication Dictionary

Student: <u>Ryan</u>   Date: <u>October 1998</u>

Settings: classes, one-to-one intervention

What the Learner Does (Form)	What it Means (Function)	How We React (Consequence)
Turns head away from activity or person	I don't want to do this or I am done	Respond as if expressed "no" and stop the activity. Tell Ryan what you responded to. ("I see that your head turned.")
Increases vocalizations	I like this	Continue activity. Tell him what made you continue. ("I can hear that you like this.")
Eye gaze*	This is the item or person I want	Respond as if he selected what he gazed at. Tell him what made you respond. ("You are looking at Tom. Do you want to go with him?")

*Emerging

Behavior state is a physiologic condition that reflects the maturity and organization of an individual's central nervous system. The term "behavior state" is also used to refer to an individual's ability to internally and externally mediate interactions with the environment (Rainforth, 1982). Behavior state observations generally include assessment of sleep, drowsiness, awake behavior (e.g., orienting, interacting), agitation (e.g., crying, aggression, self-abuse), and stereotypic behavior. Research findings (Guess et al., 1990; Guess, Roberts, et al., 1991, 1993; Guess, Roberts, Siegel-Causey, & Rues, 1995; Guess, Siegel-Causey, et al., 1993; Guy, Guess, & Ault, 1993; Richards & Sternberg, 1992, 1993) suggest that state behavior has a significant influence on alertness and responsiveness of learners who have multiple disabilities and, indirectly, on their learning, development, and overall quality of life. These learners' state profiles frequently reveal high occurrences of behaviors that impede progress in educational programs, and particularly affect communication intervention (e.g., drowsiness, sleep, stereotypy). Low occurrences of overt responses or little action, another characteristic of state organizational patterns in learners with severe disabilities, further results in an extremely limited response repertoire. These limitations set the stage for little diversity and fluency in the learner's use of their small repertoire in the complex environments of school and community.

To better understand the overall state behavior of individuals with severe disabilities, Guess et al. (1990) studied occurrences of each of eight behavior states in 50 learners with severe disabilities in educational settings. Aggregate results showed that these learners exhibited alert, responsive behavior states only 58% of the time; they spent the remaining 42% in states not optimal for learning (i.e., sleep, drowse, daze, stereotypy, or agitation). These results were replicated in a second study (Guess et al., 1995) that yielded highly similar results. Such a state profile is highly discrepant from the profiles of youngsters who do not have disabilities; the amount of time nondisabled infants and children spend in alert, responsive states averaged at 75% or greater. The fact that learners with multiple disabilities display low rates of overt responses, have externally limited response repertoires, and spend significantly less time in alert states than typical children unquestionably affects their development of effective communication skills.

It is important to consider the learner's typical levels of alertness within the contexts of educational environments. Several authors have extended the research in behavior state and have developed and researched assessment strategies to be used by educational personnel. The ABLE (Analyzing Behavior State and Learning Environments) model (Ault et al., 1995) provides systematic assessment competencies via a CD-ROM format. Richards and Richards (1997) recently described techniques for classroom observation. The educational partners would observe the student's level of alertness across the school day to determine if irregular patterns are present (e.g., excessive sleepiness or drowsiness, high rates of self-stimulation). If patterns are noticed, using the assessment protocols from ABLE (Ault) or Richards and Richards (1997) can help document these patterns and link to interventions aimed at increasing or decreasing alertness levels. (Intervention is addressed later in regard to environmental considerations.)

High Levels of Alertness and Challenging Behavior. An additional consideration is whether any of the forms of communication may interfere with social acceptance or not (e.g., self-injury, aggression). Behavior state research (e.g., Guess, Siegel-Causey et al., 1993) has identified patterns of stereotypy, agitation, aggression, or self-injurious behavior that appear to represent high levels of alertness. These same behaviors have been identified as "challenging," or "problem," behaviors. Whether the behaviors are deemed as part of the behavioral state schema or as challenging behaviors, we believe they should be viewed as a form of communication and need to be understood in relation to an individual's entire repertoire of communicative forms. The first step in assessing these forms is to review the communication dictionary that was done as part of the communication profile and note if any of these behaviors might indicate challenging behaviors (see Table 11–5). If a behavioral state assessment was conducted as part of the communication profile, review this to see if high level of arousal (e.g., agitation, self injury, stereotypy) states were present. If challenging behavior or high levels of arousal were present, these would be assessed further in terms of communicative functions.

Siegel-Causey and Bashinski (1997) have suggested that challenging behaviors be assessed as indicators of behavior state and applied as a communicative form. Thus, the assessment techniques for addressing challenging behavior as communicative (e.g., Durand & Crimmins, 1992; O'Neill et al., 1997) provide relevant strategies to supplement those listed here (chapter 6). A clear description of the form of the challenging behavior is essential to understanding the contextual variables that influence the behavior (see Carr et al., 1994; O'Neill, Vaughn, & Dunlap, 1998; Reichle & Wacker, 1993).

Communicative Functions

A third goal of assessment is identifying the reasons that an individual uses communication. That is, what range of communicative functions does the individual display? The three communicative functions common to individuals who communicate nonsymbolically (i.e., using communication to regulate behavior, to engage in social interaction, and to reference joint attention) provide a useful framework. Partners should determine whether an individual uses any of the functions to convey messages. For example, Marina displays the communicative functions of regulating behavior (e.g., requesting objects or actions, protesting objects or actions) and engaging in social interaction (e.g., requesting social games, calling).

Educational partner(s) should be aware of the variety of nonsymbolic forms the learner may use. The Checklist of Communicative Functions and Nonsymbolic Forms (Figure 11–8) can help the educational partner link the learner's forms and functions. A first step would be to circle the nonsymbolic forms (across the top of the checklist) that are known to be in the learner's repertoire; the partner may want to add in other forms that are unique to the learner that may not be listed in Figure 11–8. The staff person would then conduct observations in a natural context in which the learner is involved in activities where partner(s) are present. As the observation unfolds, the observer identifies (or hypothesizes) for each nonsymbolic form observed the possible function. Then the observer checks which area applies: behavior regulation, social interaction, joint attention, or other functions. The checklist provides an overview of the current nonsymbolic forms used and the various functions for which the forms are used. It is suggested that the checklist be completed across a variety of activities and be repeated periodically across the school year. The information from the checklist provides a measure of the current level of communication and an

FIGURE 11–8
Checklist of communicative functions and nonsymbolic forms

Student: ____________

Date: ________ Setting: ________

Context: ____________

____

Observer: ____________

Communicative Functions	Nonsymbolic Forms: Generalized Movements or Tone Changes	Vocalizations	Facial Expressions	Orientation	Touching or Manipulating Objects	Acting on Objects or Using objects	Pause	Assuming Positions or Mobility	Conventional Gestures	Depictive Actions	Aggressive or Self-Injurious Behavior	Withdrawal	Other: ____	Other: ____	Other: ____	Other: ____
Behavioral Regulation																
Request Object/Action																
Protest Object/Action																
Social Interaction																
Request Social Routine																
Request Comfort																
Greet																
Call																
Showing Off																
Request Permission																
Joint Attention																
Comment on Object/Action																
Request Information																
Other Functions																

overview of the possible intervention emphasis in terms of (a) altering or expanding forms, (b) expanding number of forms used, (c) expanding frequency of use of forms, (d) expanding number of functions, and (e) expanding frequency of use of functions. Over time, these checklists could be used to show rate of progress and success of intervention efforts or to point out that little progress has been made and that intervention efforts warrant revision.

To provide comprehensive assessment, if forms of challenging behavior were identified with the learner's *communication profile*, (see p. 423), further assessing the functions of challenging behaviors may be helpful. A number of researchers (e.g., Horner, O'Neill, & Albin, 1991; O'Neil et. al., 1997; Wacker et al., 1990) have considered the impacts of challenging behavior in terms of their communicative functions. It has been suggested that much of the challenging behavior exhibited by those with more severe disabilities may be communicative (Carr & Durand, 1985; Carr et al., 1994). Using a communicative approach guides the assessor to identify whether a particular communicative form functions as a request, a rejection, a comment, or a means to escape or avoid a situation, to gain access to desired items, or to obtain attention (Brady & Halle, 1997; Carr et al., 1994; Durand & Crimmins, 1992; O'Neill et al., 1997). (Refer to chapter 6 for more information).

Intentionality

A fourth goal of assessment is identifying the degree of intentionality for each communicative function.

Recall that communication may range on a continuum from preintentional to intentional. Intentionality cannot be measured directly; it must be inferred from observable behaviors displayed during interactions. One approach to inferring intentionality at the preverbal level is to define intentional communication operationally, based on a set of behavioral criteria (Bates, 1979; Bruner, 1978; Harding & Golinkoff, 1979). Such behavioral evidence includes:

1. Alternating gaze between the goal and the listener
2. Persistent signaling until the goal is accomplished or failure is indicated
3. Changing the signal quality until the goal has been met
4. Ritualizing or conventionalizing the form of the signal within specific communicative contexts
5. Awaiting a response from the listener
6. Terminating the signal when the goal is met
7. Displaying satisfaction when the goal is attained or dissatisfaction when it is not

An individual may not display all of these behaviors, but the more behaviors displayed, the more likely that the behavior is intentional communication. For Chris, intentionality is just emerging. In the photo sequence (Figure 11–9), one can see that he gazes directly at the listener. It would be important to teach him to alternate this gaze between the listener and the object or event he desires. He will be able to display more intentionality if this skill is present. He also awaits the response of Samantha to activate the toy. The staff would need to assess the learner across a variety of activities and observe as to whether any of the seven intentional behavior indicators (just listed) are present. The more behaviors present, the more intentional the communicator.

It is important to view intentionality as a developmental process and to evaluate the degree of intentionality in reference to changes in behaviors that imply anticipation and expectation. It is also important to detect increased intentionality and to view it as progress.

Marina is just beginning to show intentionality by her alternating gaze and persisting until a goal is met.

Readability of Signals

A fifth goal of assessment is determining the degree of readability of nonsymbolic communicative behaviors. Readability refers to the clarity of a commu-

FIGURE 11–9

Chris is positioned in the side-lyer next to his peer, Samantha, who holds the toy cow. As an educator assists him in finding the switch, Chris looks toward Samantha (function = engage in social interaction). Samantha smiles to indicate she wants Chris to activate the toy (function = behavior regulation).

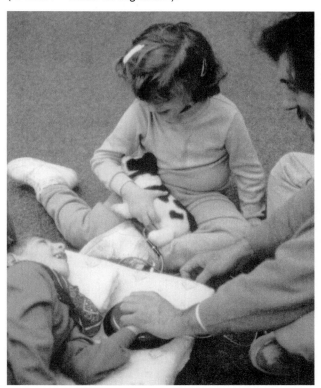

nicative signal and to the ease with which the signal can be interpreted. Readability is influenced by the degree of familiarity of the communication partner with the learner as well as the conventionality of the signal. Ability to use social-affective signals enhances readability by clarifying the learner's emotional state (Prizant & Wetherby, 1990; Kublin et al., 1998). Motor ability is a major factor influencing the clarity of gestural and vocal communications and the support of social-affective signals.

Marina's family members find Marina to be very readable, but less familiar people find Marina difficult to understand.

Repair Strategies

A sixth goal of assessment is identifying repair strategies. Communication breakdowns are frequent when there is limited readability of signals. Therefore, ability to repair communicative breakdowns contributes to communicative competence (Prizant & Wetherby, 1990; Kublin et al., 1998). An opportunity for repair occurs when a learner initiates a communicative behavior and the interactant fails to respond or responds in a manner that violates the learner's intention.

> Marina wiggles in her stroller to request out; if the interactant fails to respond, this is an opportunity for Marina to repair in order to clarify what she wants.

Opportunities for repair should be systematically provided and the ability to repair should be evaluated. It should be determined whether the learner persists by repeating the same signal or by modifying the behavior. An absence of repair strategies is reflected in abandoning a communicative goal if it is not immediately achieved. The ability to modify a signal to repair communicative breakdowns allows greater reciprocity and promotes more successful social exchanges.

> Marina generally abandons a goal if it is not met immediately, but she is beginning to repeat her signals for behavior regulation. Still, she does not modify her signals if her goals are not met.

Individuals with severe disabilities are likely to display repair strategies. Brady, McLean, McLean, and Johnston (1995) studied repairs of 28 individuals with severe to profound mental retardation who resided in an institution. Each participant was provided with five opportunities to repair when their requests for help were not responded to or misunderstood in a variety of ways and five opportunities to repair when their requests for attention to an object or event were similarly not responded to or misunderstood. They found that 25 of the 28 participants initiated at least one repair. Significantly more participants repaired when requests for help were misunderstood. The participants who did repair tended to either repeat the same signal or change to a different signal. Adding information (additions) were used rarely by these participants. For individuals who used serious challenging behavior as a form of communication, the problem behavior may be a repair strategy used when more conventional forms are not successful. Furthermore, the ability to repair with appropriate behaviors may lead to reductions in challenging behaviors (Wetherby, Alexander et al., 1998).

Capacity for Symbols

A seventh goal of assessment is consideration of the learner's capacity for symbol use across activities. By definition, learners who communicate nonsymbolically do not use symbols expressively. However, there may be variation from individual to individual in terms of their understanding (reception) of symbolic input. Their understanding may range from no or little comprehension of speech or graphics (e.g., line drawings, photos) to some comprehension of speech and graphics to understanding of speech or graphics. Thus, receptive language and comprehension response strategies should be evaluated as you build the learner's assessment profile. Capacity for symbols focuses first on the individual's readiness to attach symbolic expressions to their known nonsymbolic forms and to further teach them to use symbols for expression.

Knowledge of skill level on cognitive tasks that are correlates of language (i.e., tool use, causality, imitation, object use) can help partners understand the capacity of learners for communication skills in reference to other domains of knowledge. In other words, learners' communicative strategies should be considered in reference to their problem-solving and learning strategies. In determining the learner's communication profile, it is particularly important to consider how learners use objects to obtain a goal, understand the source of actions, observe and attempt to imitate the behaviors of others, and explore the functional uses of objects. For example, a child who attempts to obtain a toy that is on a shelf out of reach by moving a chair to the shelf, climbing on the chair, and getting the toy is demonstrating mental representation skills in tool use. A child who attempts to obtain a cracker that is out of reach by rolling to the low cupboard that the cracker box sits on, reaching for the box and scooting it off the shelf, and vocalizing so someone will help open it is demonstrating similar representational skills.

An understanding of the cognitive skills of learners can provide information about strengths and interests that can be used to develop communication abilities. The transition from presymbolic to symbolic activities is a critical milestone that is evident in the use of objects and play. As children are able to symbolize, they show increasing capacity to use objects for specific functions, in pretend actions toward others, and for building (Lifter & Bloom, 1998). There is a strong relationship between object knowledge or use in play and the emergence of words. Wetherby and Prutting

(1984) describe specific procedures adapted from developmental literature for setting up assessment probes for tool use, causality, imitation, and object use. For individuals with limited motor abilities, microswitches or other adaptive devices are needed to assess cognitive knowledge.

We have now provided suggestions about how to gather assessment information to develop a learner's communicative profile, including assessment of (a) the forms of communication, (b) the communicative functions, (c) the degree of intentionality, (d) the readability of communicative signals, (e) repair strategies, and (f) the capacity for symbolic communication.

The Communicative Environment

A learner's communicative profile provides information about only part of the communicative interaction. It is also necessary to assess the quality of the physical and social aspects of the communicative environment. Use of the environmental context within the tri-focus framework incorporates both the communicative context and setting variables of the social and physical environment. It is important that assessment procedures expand upon the information gained from the "learner communicative profile" and create a "partner communicative profile (social environment) and environmental profile (physical)."

Assessment: Understanding the Social Environment Using a Partner Profile

Partner Communicative Profile

Social Environment

1. Opportunities to initiate and respond to communication
2. Social supports present
   a. What is there to communicate about?
   b. Who is available to interact with?
3. Interaction styles of communication partners

The first step would be to understand (a) who is available to communicate with during the natural routines and (b) the relationship the learner has with these partners. Major dimensions of the communicative social environment include (a) opportunities for learners to initiate and respond to communication, (b) social supports present, and (c) the interaction styles of communicative partners.

Opportunities

The educational settings and activities vary a great deal in regard to the quality and quantity of opportunities for communication. School staff partners must ask whether situations and persons in the environment provide ample opportunities to initiate and respond to communication for the three major communicative functions. That is, do learners have opportunities to use communication in order to get others to do things (behavior regulation), to draw attention to themselves (social interaction), and to direct others' attention to objects or events (joint attention)?

Opportunities to use communication for behavior regulation generally involve situations in which an individual needs to request assistance or objects that are out of reach, to make choices about desired objects or activities (e.g., food items, toys, games, or play partners), and to indicate undesired objects or activities. Opportunities to regulate behavior should occur throughout activities, not just when materials are first presented or activities are first initiated. Evaluation of behavior regulation opportunities provides information about whether or not there is a need to make environmental arrangements to increase opportunities for communication (Peck, 1989).

Opportunities to use communication for social interaction and joint attention are more likely to occur within repetitive, turn-taking interactions. Bruner (1978, 1981) suggests that joint-action routines provide optimal opportunities for communication development and provide foundations for learning to exchange roles in conversation. A joint-action routine is a repetitive turn-taking game or activity in which there are attention and participation by both the learner and the caregiver, exchangeable roles, and predictable sequences (Snyder-McLean, Solomonson, McLean, & Sack, 1984). A prototypical example of a joint-action routine for infants and toddlers is the game of peekaboo (Bruner & Sherwood, 1976), which caregivers may play hundreds or thousands of times during the first year of a child's life. A joint-action routine may include activities involving preparation of a specific product (e.g., food), organization around a central plot (e.g., pretending), or cooperative turn-taking games (e.g., smiling in response to one's name during a song) (Snyder-McLean et al., 1984).

For example, in the set-up for Ryan's role with helping the football team, there are many aspects that are prepared in a repetitive manner. His joint action routine begins as he and Andy (his friend) approach the clothes dryers and Andy assists with set-up of the jig that helps Ryan remove the clothes. Ryan smiles at Andy when the jig is set comfortably and he can reach into the dryer and the empty basket. They interact back and forth as Andy sets the jig each time and Ryan pulls the towels into the basket in front of his wheelchair. The routine continues until each dryer is emptied.

In assessment, it is important to consider how the structure of activities influences communication. Snyder-McLean et al. (1984) delineate eight critical elements of successful joint-action routines for the assessment of the communicative environments (Table 11–6). Both the quantity and quality of joint-action routines should be evaluated. Activities that learners and partners routinely engage in at home, in the classroom, or in the community are potential joint-action routines that should be evaluated for these eight elements.

It is imperative to link the eight critical elements with the learner's chronological age when selecting materials, settings, and people for the routines. Possible home activities include eating meals, dressing, bathing, and playing. Possible school activities include eating snacks and meals, domestic activities

(e.g., doing laundry and preparing meals), and leisure activities. Possible community activities include riding the bus, going shopping, and eating in a restaurant. These elements provide a structure to activities that allows the nonsymbolic learner to anticipate the nature and sequence of the activity and participate maximally, and thus, enhance communication (Duchan, 1995; Kublin et al., 1998; Snyder-McLean et al., 1984).

Using the elements from Table 11–6, here is an example of a joint action routine.

1. *An obvious unifying theme*: *Ryan and Andy preparing for football practice.*
2. *Requirement for joint focus and interaction*: *They both have been assigned to get the locker room set up before practice begins.*
3. *A limited number of clearly defined roles*: *Andy assists with some of Ryan's setup. Ryan completes some tasks alone and some with assistance from Andy. Andy does some tasks on his own.*
4. *Exchangeable roles*: *For some jobs, it doesn't matter who does what task. For instance, shutting the dryer and washer doors and pushing the baskets to the sorting area.*
5. *A logical, nonarbitrary sequence*: *The young men proceed logically to wash, dry, fold, and store the locker room towels.*

TABLE 11–6
Critical Elements of Effective Joint-Action Routines

---

1. *An obvious unifying theme or purpose* to relate the actions of different individuals engaged in the routine and provide a theme that is meaningful and recognizable to all participants. There are three general types of routines:

   - Preparation or fabrication of a specific product (e.g., food preparation, product assembly)
   - Routines organized around a plot or theme (e.g., daily living routines, pretend play scenarios)
   - Cooperative turn-taking games or routines (e.g., songs with spaces to fill in, peekaboo)

2. *A requirement for joint focus and interaction* to establish need for interaction and negotiation.
3. *A limited number of clearly delineated roles,* but at least two different roles that are definable and predictable (e.g., speaker and listener, giver and receiver).
4. *Exchangeable roles* so that the individual is assigned to more than one role in the same routine.
5. *A logical, nonarbitrary sequence* that is determined by the nature of the activity and can be predicted by the outcome or product.
6. *A structure for turn taking in a predictable sequence* that allows the individual to anticipate when to wait and when to initiate a turn.
7. *Planned repetition* over time to establish role expectancy and sequence predictability, used within a daily time block to offer several turns to each individual.
8. *A plan for controlled variation* that introduces novel elements against a background of familiarity and expectancy to evoke spontaneous comments in the following ways:

   - Interrupt the routine or violate expectations
   - Omit necessary materials
   - Initiate a routine and "play possum"
   - Initiate old routines with new contents
   - Introduce new routines with old contents

Note: Adapted from "Structuring Joint-Action Routines for Facilitating Communication and Language Development in the Classroom" by L. K. Snyder-McLean, B. Solomonson, J. E. McLean, and S. Sack, 1984, *Seminars in Speech and Language, 5*(3), pp. 216–218.

6. *A plan for controlled variation: Natural interruptions or violations occur in their routine, such as finding personal clothes items with the towels or running out of soap. These events allow for Ryan and Andy to communicate with each other and, of course, goof around, such as when Ryan used his jig to fling a pair of underwear into Andy's pile of towels.*

Social Supports

What activities are like and the presence of other people (peers, adults) are social aspects that affect learners' communication interactions. A nurturant atmosphere fosters warmth and security. The learner needs to have a relationship with partners that develops over time, so that in a natural way, a sense of trust and sharing develops between them. Communication interventions should facilitate interactions and relationships with others, particularly peers without disabilities, staff members, and community members. The need for positive relationships and friendships is universal. Falvey and Rosenberg (1995) provide a practical overview of strategies for promoting peer relationships and building a sense of belonging, which need to be considered in addition to nonsymbolic assessment strategies. (Chapter 10 also contains information on social relationships.)

In addition to promoting the natural development of relationships and friendships, it is important to determine if, from *the learner's perspective*, the social environment and specific contexts are positive and conducive to interactions? This may be viewed from the learner's perspective in terms of: "What is there to communicate about?" and "Who is available to interact with?" Taking time to reflect on these questions may help staff assess these social supports. The partner is trying to determine what aspects are used or available to provide contexts that the learner finds interesting and responsive. The assessment information gleaned helps to develop a "picture" of the current social environment.

Some strategies of assessment best apply to learners in the perlocutionary stage.

When Marina first entered the preschool, the staff members and peers provided many opportunities for her to express whether or not she wanted an activity to continue and to choose what would happen next. A staff member would be assessing the number and kind of opportunities Marina had to impact the activity within familiar routines.

The assessment profile would help determine how many routines appear repetitive, familiar, and fun to Marina. If some routines met this criteria, the as-sessment profile for the social environment would then expand to examine the opportunities for communication.

As Marina's friend pushed her in the swing, he stopped the swing periodically and asked: "Fun, Marina?" "Do you want to swing more?" "Do you want to go on the merry-go-round?"

As individuals move toward the illocutionary stage, they should have social supports that provide opportunities to initiate interactions, maintain interactions, and terminate interactions, while realizing that their behaviors affect others.

As Marina learned that the staff members and peers understood her expressions, she signaled her needs more readily. As she was swinging, she smiled and vocalized to her friend. When she wanted to stop, she put her head down and stopped vocalizing.

When partners maintain a nurturant environment and increase opportunities, individuals who communicate with nonsymbolic behaviors are more likely to discover that their behaviors can control others and that they can initiate these behaviors to communicate.

Interaction Style

Communicative behavior is influenced not only by the opportunities for communication but also by the interaction styles communicative partners use and the social supports available. Therefore, it is important to evaluate the partners' interaction styles to determine if the partners are using styles that foster communication or that inhibit it. The caregivers' contingent social responsiveness to a child's behavior is a major influence in the child's developing communicative competence (Dunst et al., 1990; Yoder, et al., 1998).

School staff partners should think about the unique ways that they talk, gesture, and share "who they are" as they interact with others.

Sam, Ryan's teacher, tends to speak quietly, look directly at his communication partners, and use touch only to emphasize important points. He always wears blue jeans and short-sleeved T-shirts, uses musk cologne, and has glasses. Martha, a speech-language therapist, speaks loudly, uses her tone of voice to convey emotion, and is affectionate and demonstrative with touch and gestures. She usually wears long dresses, wears her hair in a braid, and does not use perfume. Sam and Martha work with the same learners, and their interaction styles and personal behaviors influence each learner differently.

Understanding may be influenced by how a communication partner expresses himself or herself. A student may receive the most salient information through nonsymbolic means.

Carol attends to Sam when he touches her or is close enough for her to smell his cologne, although for most of their interactions, she tends not to notice Sam until he redirects her attention by raising his voice and being more animated. She becomes very attentive and animated the moment she hears Martha's voice and strives to encourage Martha to interact with her. Ryan, however, prefers Sam's quiet voice and limited touch and tries to avoid Martha's demonstrative nature and loud voice.

Developmental literature provides guidelines for assessing interaction styles of caregivers (Girolametto, Greenberg, & Manolson, 1986; MacDonald, 1989; MacDonald & Carroll, 1992; Yoder et al., 1998). Based on developmental guidelines for children at nonsymbolic stages of communication, interaction styles should be evaluated to determine if the following features are present:

1. Waiting for the learner to initiate communication by pausing and looking expectantly.
2. Recognizing the learner's behavior as communication by interpreting the communicative function that it serves.
3. Responding to the learner's communicative behavior in a manner that is consistent with the communicative intention of the learner and that matches the communicative level of the learner.

Table 10–7 provides a format that can be used to assess these features.

Thus, if a learner is requesting an object, does the communicative partner give the desired object immediately? If the learner is requesting comfort, does the communicative partner provide social or physical attention to the learner? If the learner is directing attention, does the communicative partner attend to the object or event that the learner is drawing attention to?

Marina and her friend Jody, a peer without disabilities, are serving a snack. Jody has the juice pitcher and Marina has the cups. Jody looks at Marina as they approach Arturo's place at the table (waiting for communication). Marina smiles and places the cup in front of Arturo. Jody looks at Marina and then at the cup (recognizing and interpreting the communication function). "OK, I pour juice, huh?" and Jody pours the juice (responding contingently and matching the communicative level).

An interaction that does not contain the features of interaction style (see previous list) that promote nonsymbolic communication may occur inadvertently.

Marina and Lois, the paraeducator, are serving a snack. Lois smiles and says, "Give Arturo a cup next." This request will help Marina know how to proceed and will speed up the serving process. However, it does not provide Marina an opportunity to communicate and does not allow her to "direct" Lois to pour juice. Thus, Marina's partner did not wait for her to communicate.

Partners must adjust their behaviors to match the communication level of each learner. MacDonald (1989) provides the analogy of being on a staircase with a child so that the partner has one foot on the child's step and the other foot on the next step. In the

TABLE 10–7
Assessing Nonsymbolic States of Interaction Styles

Features observed in partners were: _____

Feature	*Yes.* What was observed?	*No.* What alternatives to use?	*Unclear.* What might we try next time?
1. Does partner wait for communication?			
2. Does partner interpret behavior (form) and assign a function?			
3. Does partner respond consistently and matched to learner's level?			

assessment of a communication partner's interaction style, it is important to consider the balance between the individual and the partner. That is, communicative partners should ask whether or not the interaction is reciprocal (i.e., each individual should influence and respond meaningfully to the other individual).

Assessment: Understanding the Physical Environment Using an Environmental Profile

In addition to social aspects, the second primary dimension of the environment to consider is the effect of physical variables on the communication contexts and interactions.

Environmental Profile

Physical

1. Learner's interest in activity
2. Learner's access to materials
3. Changes in learner's position
4. Activity level of immediate environment

Physical Aspects of the Environment

During instruction or interactions, the physical environment is part of the context that influences how well communication is exchanged between the learner and the educational partner. The materials available, type of activity, and body position of the learner are areas that need to be assessed. These variables have been shown to influence the alertness of learners with severe disabilities.

External Influences on State Behavior

Behavioral state is a manifestation of a learner's physiological condition. State behavior itself and changes in state behavior do *not* represent learned responses (Ault et al., 1995; Rainforth, 1982). It has been suggested that changes in behavior state can be facilitated through systematic arrangements of instructional environments and influenced by external variables (Ault et al.; Guess et al., 1990). Behavior state research has documented five primary variables that are associated with the occurrence of either alert or sleepy states: (a) failure to attend to the variables of social contact provided to a learner, (b) a learner's static body position, (c) the type of activity, (d) availability of materials, and (e) activity level in the immediate environment.

In addition to these primary variables, field evaluation using the ABLE model (Ault et al., 1995) yielded data that suggested a more direct relationship between

TABLE 10–7
Assessing the Physical Environment

Primary features observed in physical setting were: _____

Feature	*Yes.* What was observed?	*No.* What alternatives to use?	*Unclear.* What might we try next time?
1. Is the learner supported in a static position that allows interaction?			
2. Is the activity of interest?			
3. Are the materials easy to access given the learner's sensory and motor skills?			
4. Is the activity level in the immediate environment conducive to attention to the interaction?			

changing environmental characteristics and influencing behavior state. A well-engineered environment was associated with learners' display of alert, responsive state behavior. Conversely, this study also demonstrated that when educational staff did not systematically manage environmental characteristics, the learners displayed more behavior states that were nonoptimal for learning (i.e., sleep, drowse, daze, agitation). Systematic instructional application of the ABLE model techniques yielded significant decreases in nonoptimal behavior states. The reader is encouraged to review the ABLE techniques for more detail on how to enhance the environment to influence behavior state. There are some simple ways of assessing some of these variables. While building the profile to observe what partners' interaction styles are, the physical environment can also be assessed using the form shown in Table 10–8 on the previous page.

Strategies for Assessing Nonsymbolic Communication

Three strategies may be used in assessing nonsymbolic communicative behaviors:

1. Interviewing familiar people
2. Observing in natural contexts
3. Gathering communication samples

Interviews

The first strategy is to interview people who are very familiar with the learner to document the repertoire of communicative behaviors and purposes for communicating across a variety of environments. Teachers, parents and other relatives, and service providers who interact with a learner on a regular basis are good candidates. Peck and Schuler (1987) describe a communication interview that provides a format for identifying the variety of forms of communication used for different communicative functions and also addresses the use of repair strategies. O'Neill et al. (1997) provides a Functional Assessment Interview (FAI) to collect information about events that influence challenging behavior. The FAI incorporates both functional assessment of the challenging behaviors and the primary communication repertoire of the person across communication functions such as requesting or showing. These aspects of the FAI may be another valuable interview format to use. Communication interviews are effective in assessment because they provide a great deal of information

in a relatively short period of time and this information may be used to plan further assessment.

Observations in Context

A second strategy for assessment is to observe communicative behaviors occurring in natural contexts (Wetherby & Prizant, 1997). Observations provide opportunities to gather information about learners as well as about interactants. Observational checklists may be used to organize recordings from naturalistic observations. Figure 11–8 is an example of an observation checklist that incorporates communicative functions with nonsymbolic forms.

Checklists use categorical systems determined on an a priori basis. Therefore, clinicians and educators should be open to the possibility of communicative behaviors that are not included on a particular checklist after gathering information from an interview with familiar individuals. One way to circumvent this problem is using a checklist only after gathering information from an interview with familiar individuals. Checklists are used most typically while observing children and while observing videotaped naturalistic communicative interactions in several environments.

Communication Sampling

A third strategy used in assessment is that of communication sampling. The purpose of communication sampling is to gather a representative sample of communicative behaviors in a relatively short period of time. Although checklists may be scored while a school staff person is observing, videotaping a communication sample is optimal. Videotaping provides the most objective and the richest data collection procedure for analyzing communicative behaviors. Videotaping also allows repeated observations of behaviors, providing opportunities to note subtle and fleeting behaviors or responses that may be missed during ongoing dyadic interactions.

In contrast to the use of checklists, communication sampling involves designing situations to entice learners to initiate and participate in communicative interactions. Free play within joint-action routines may be used (Snyder-McLean et al., 1984), but learners must have ample opportunities to initiate a variety of communicative acts. If a learner does not initiate readily, communicative temptations are useful (Wetherby & Prizant, 1989; 1993; Wetherby & Prutting, 1984).

Communicative temptations involve opportunities that entice specific attempts at communication. One example is activating a windup toy, letting it deactivate, and then waiting and looking expectantly at the learner. This provides opportunities for the learner to request assistance at getting the toy to activate, to protest about the ceasing of action, or to respond in other ways. Another example is giving the learner a block to put away in a box, repeating this several times so that the learner expects a block, and then giving a different object, such as a toy animal or a book. The novel object may tempt the learner to communicate about the unexpected object or to protest over the change in objects. In Figure 11–5, it appears that Marina is tempted by the bubbles that her Mother has deliberately placed out of reach.

Because temptations may be presented nonverbally, they circumvent the problem of a learner's limited comprehension of language. Although each temptation should be designed with at least one particular function in mind, any one temptation may potentially elicit a variety of communicative functions (Wetherby & Rodriguez, 1992). Communicative temptations should not be the only interactive technique used in the communication sample, but they may be useful as warm-ups or supplements to unstructured interactions.

An accurate assessment of nonsymbolic communication depends on observation of a learner over a period of time in a variety of communicative situations with different communicative partners. Thus, assessment should be viewed as an ongoing process rather than episodic. Furthermore, since communication is a dyadic process, assessment must consider the learner's communicative behavior in relation to the characteristics and interaction styles of communicative partners (Kublin et al., 1998; Mirenda & Donnellan, 1986; Peck & Schuler, 1987) and the characteristics of the environment (Siegel-Causey & Bashinski, 1997).

Intervention Methods

Traditionally, intervention has focused on promoting speech and language development. Speaking and communicating have been viewed synonymously (Calculator, 1988). Efforts were focused on remediation, including drilling in discrimination and teaching speech as a behavior within one-to-one isolated ther-

apy sessions (Bedrosian, 1988; Coots & Falvey, 1989; Musselwhite & St. Louis, 1988). This focus on speech excluded many students with severe disabilities, who were described as "not ready" for communication development or enhancement. Previously, the belief was held that before a child could benefit from augmentative and alternative communication interventions, a criterion level of cognitive ability was necessary (Rice & Kemper, 1984). Such beliefs are no longer supported (Musselwhite & St. Louis, 1988; Norris & Hoffman, 1990). The current trend is to provide communication intervention that matches the learner's skills, regardless of the mode of expression.

There has been a gradual expansion related to the communication needs of learners with severe handicaps (Baumgart, Johnson, & Helmstetter, 1990; Beukelman & Mirenda, 1998); Beukelman & Yorkston, 1989; Calculator & Jorgensen, 1994; Goetz & Sailor, 1988; Halle, 1985; Musselwhite & St. Louis, 1988; Reichle, York, & Sigafoos, 1991) and in facilitating prespeech development (Johnson, Baumgart, Helmstetter, & Curry, 1996; Langley & Lombardino, 1991; Noonan & Siegel-Causey, 1997; Rowland & Stremel-Campbell, 1987; Schuler & Prizant, 1987; Siegel-Causey & Bashinski, 1997; Siegel-Causey & Downing, 1987; Siegel-Causey & Guess, 1989; Stillman & Battle, 1984).

Current research and theory suggest that:

1. Interventions should focus on interactions that are learner-centered within the natural environments of the school, home, and community.
2. Systematic instruction should be responsive and nondidactic.
3. A number of intervention strategies may enhance early communication, such as naturalistic teaching procedures including time delay (Halle, Marshall, & Spradlin, 1979), mand-model (Warren, McQuarter & Rogers-Warren, 1984), and incidental teaching (Hart & Risley, 1975). (See chapter 12.)
4. A gestural dictionary or communication dictionary should be used so partners respond to idiosyncratic gestures consistently (Mirenda, 1988; Beukelman & Mirenda, 1998);
5. Use scripted routines (Beukelman & Mirenda, 1998),
6. Use joint-action routines (Snyder-McLean et al., 1984),
7. Provide choice-making opportunities (Guess, Benson, & Siegel-Causey, 1985; Peck, 1989; Brown, Belz, Corsi, & Wenig, 1993),

8. Use augmented input (Romski & Sevcik, 1993; Rowland, Schweigert, & Prickett, 1995; Wood, Lasker, Siegel-Causey, Beukelman & Ball, 1998).
9. Use interrupted behavior chains (Allwell, Hunt, Goetz, & Sailor, 1989; Goetz, Gee, & Sailor, 1985; Hunt, Goetz, Alwell, & Sailor, 1986).

Next, this chapter provides interventions that facilitate communication for both a learner and his or her partners in interactions and are a synthesis of many intervention methods. An overview of the intervention methods covered in this Chapter is shown in Table 11–7.

A Reciprocal Assessment Focus

Numbers 1 through 3 in Table 11–7 have already been described and are provided as a review here. First, school staff partners should conduct an assessment of the learner's communication (learner communicative profile) and the communicative environment (partner communicative profile and environmental profile). This will provide an overview of the (a) current status of communication patterns of learner and partner, and (b) the current environmental contexts. This process is likely to help educational partners to recognize the effect of communication interactions on both the learner and his/her partner(s). Communication inter-

---

TABLE 11–7

Methods to Enhance a Partner's Communication with Learners Who Have Nonsymbolic Skills

1. Conduct assessment of the learner's communication (learner communicative profile) and the communicative environment (social and physical environmental profile) to recognize the effects of communication interactions on both you and the learner and the influence of the environment.
2. Design instructional interventions that are functional, systematic, and useful within naturally occurring routines.
3. Determine potential communication content from activities that occur in present and future environments.
4. Use the following intervention guidelines to enhance your nonsymbolic and symbolic expressions: (a) increase opportunities, (b) sequence experiences, and (c) augment input.
5. Use the following intervention guideline to enhance your nonsymbolic understanding (reception): enhance sensitivity.
6. Use the following intervention guidelines to enhance the communication contexts and to attend to external influences on state behavior: (a) provide physical supports, (b) provide social supports, (c) adjust sensory qualities, (d) alter movement and orientation of learner, and (e) change learning atmosphere.

---

vention is best viewed as a reciprocal process between a partner and a learner. The learner may be the responder and thus influenced by how clearly he or she understands (responder receptive understanding). Then, the partner's expressions are the focus. Alternately, the learner may be the initiator. Then, the partner's understanding is influenced by how clearly the learner expresses himself or herself (initiator expressive competence). The strategies to enhance the learner's expressive communication should include augmenting the educational partner's instruction and strengthening the learner's communication repertoire. Interactions are influenced by what both the initiator and responder do, rather than assuming that either partner has deficits to remediate.

Functional, Systematic Methods in Natural Routines

As educational partners deliver communication instruction, they must incorporate sound instructional methods, regardless of the intervention approach. All communication instruction should occur within the routines of the day and natural environments (within the home, school, or community) so that learners not only communicate better or more but also recognize that communication always serves a purpose. This approach uses a collaborative model of service delivery, with all staff members collaboratively establishing goals and facilitating cross-disciplinary training. (Refer to chapter 4 for more information.)

Potential Communication Content

In addition to being aware of the influence that interactional style has on receptive understanding, school staff partners should consider the activities that occur in the educational setting. What activities are conducive to joint-action or turn-taking segments? Are staff members and peers conducting activities that use these attributes? From the learner's perspective, what is there to communicate about in each familiar activity? Such questions may help partners discover potential communication content. For example:

Using an adaptation that facilitates handling and transferring, Ryan hands out towels to the team at the football games. This activity has the available content of Ryan's indicating to the peer that he is ready with a towel, that he recognizes individual friends and favorite players, that he wants to move his wheelchair or change his position, that he has finished the job, that he wants to start a conversation, and so on.

Thus, school staff partners may recognize a wide range of targets for instruction and develop additional targets to generalize to other activities that typically occur. Then, the educational team, including the family, can prioritize the communicative targets that are most functional and generalize across people, events, and environments.

Intervention Guidelines to Enhance Partner's Symbolic Expression

The following guidelines are based on previous work (Siegel-Causey & Guess, 1989) of Siegel-Causey, the senior author, and more recent work (Siegel-Causey & Bashinski, 1997): (a) increase opportunities, (b) sequence experiences, (c) enhance sensitivity, (d) augment input, (e) attend to natural contexts, and (f) modify the environment. These guidelines evolved as part of an overall intervention for interacting with learners who have severe handicaps (Siegel-Causey & Guess, 1989). They are not arranged in a sequential manner. Rather, educational partners should incorporate the relevant components of the six guidelines during any individual communicative interaction.

Figure 11–10 displays the intervention guidelines that will be explained in the next pages. The outer, shaded circle contains the four communication

FIGURE 11–10
Intervention Guidelines in Relation to the Context of the Environment

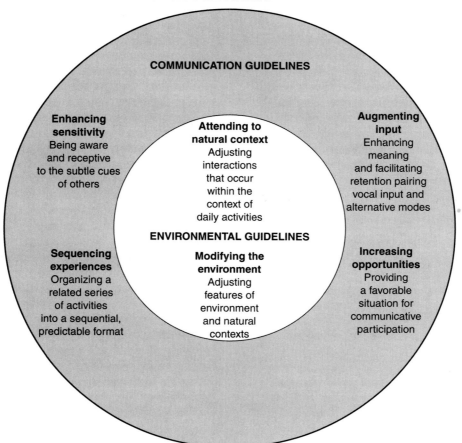

Note: Adapted from "Procedures for Enhancing Nonsymbolic Communication" by E. Siegel-Causey, C. Battle, and B. Ernst. In *Enhancing Nonsymbolic Communication Interactions Among Learners with Severe Handicaps* (p. 25) by E. Siegel-Causey and D. Guess (Eds.), 1989, Baltimore: Paul H. Brookes.

guidelines of enhancing sensitivity, augmenting input, sequencing experiences, and increasing opportunities. The inner, white circle contains the two environmental guidelines of attending to natural contexts and modifying the environment. These six guidelines form the philosophical basis of the intervention methods that are focused on the educational partner.

1. Partners should enhance their use of nonsymbolic and symbolic expressions.
2. Partners should enhance their nonsymbolic understanding.
3. Partners should enhance communication contexts and attend to influences on state behavior.

The four guidelines in Figure 11–10 and their corresponding strategies form a philosophy of intervention that promotes the premise that partners should expect learners to communicate. Expecting communication can create an atmosphere that is positive and promotes reciprocal exchanges. For example:

> Jack, Ryan's friend, expects that Ryan will communicate as they take off their coats upon entering the room. This allows Jack to be ready to respond to Ryan's initiations and expressions. Since Jack has had a variety of interactions with Ryan, he is familiar with Ryan's nonsymbolic ways of communicating, he can predict what this activity will be like, and he is alert to opportunities that occur naturally in their routine. (Jack uses the guideline of increasing opportunities and enhancing sensitivity.)

An initial focus of some communication interventions is to encourage learners to convey messages. Some learners are discouraged from communicating because of the great physical or cognitive effort required, while others have had infrequent opportunities to communicate (MacDonald, 1985; Musselwhite & St. Louis, 1988). Still others are at the perlocutionary stage and do not understand that their behaviors can affect others. Thus, the focus may be to teach learners that they can affect people and events. We believe that all of the guidelines and strategies in this section can help learners progress on a continuum of development from perlocutionary to locutionary to illocutionary expressions. In addition, the strategies allow learners to control interactions as they initiate, maintain, and terminate communication exchanges. Partners can implement the six intervention guidelines in Figure 11–10 by using

the corresponding strategies in Figure 11–11. A detailed description of the procedures necessary to implement the strategies does not fit within the scope of this chapter. Instead, the chapter presents the purpose of the guidelines, the potential effects of the guidelines on partners and learners, and brief descriptions of the strategies. Examples highlight the roles of partners and learners.

When using the intervention guidelines, remember to:

1. Use relevant and functional tasks, age-appropriate methods and materials, and natural contexts.
2. Expect communication.
3. Establish a desire to communicate.

Increasing Opportunities

Creating situations that empower learners to communicate can promote their participation in interactions. The strategies to increase opportunities include (a) using time delay, (b) providing choices, (c) creating need for requests, (d) providing opportunities to interact, and (e) facilitating alert, responsive behavior (Halle, 1984; Siegel-Causey & Bashinski, 1997; Siegel-Causey & Guess, 1989).

School staff partners can insert pauses (time delay) in interactions so that learners can initiate a change in the interchange, maintain the interchange, or terminate it. Increasing opportunities can be beneficial to learners at both the perlocutionary and illocutionary stages, providing clear opportunities for "my turn" or emitting an expression.

At the perlocutionary stage, partners can help learners recognize that they have signals. Thus, partners convey information with the behaviors expressed by the individual. For example:

> At a snack with Marina, when the juice pitcher is passed around the table, the partner used Marina's own behavior, fluttering his hands and saying, "Ahga," as the juice pitcher gets closer to him. To expand the communication opportunities, the partner increased his vocalizations and looked at Marina (rather than pouring the juice). Marina then had an opportunity to jointly attend to the juice pitcher, request juice herself, or terminate the interaction.

As learners move to a more illocutionary level, they begin to seek social interaction (initiate) and to obtain changes in actions or objects (e.g., initiate, main-

FIGURE 11–11
Intervention Guidelines and Corresponding Strategies

Enhancing the partners' nonsymbolic and symbolic expressions to the learner

Increase opportunities	**Sequence experiences**	**Augment input**
• Create need for requests	• Encourage participation	• Enhance meaning
• Facilitate alert, responsive state behavior	• Establish routines	• Facilitate retention
• Provide choices	• Provide turn-taking opportunities	
• Provide opportunities to interact		
• Use time-delay		

Enhancing the partners' understanding of the learner's nonsymbolic communication

Enhance sensitivity
• Recognize individual's readiness for interaction
• Recognize nonsymbolic behaviors
• Respond contingently
• Respond to expressions and challenging behavior as communicative behavior
• Respond to individual's level of communication

Enhancing the learner's communication contexts and attending to external influences on the learner's state behavior

Attend to natural contexts	**Modify environment**
• Provide physical supports	• Adjust sensory qualities
• Provide social supports	• Alter movement and orientation of learner
	• Change learning atmosphere

Note: Based on Siegel-Causey, E., Battle, C., & Ernst, B. (1989). Procedures for enhancing nonsymbolic communication. In *Enhancing Nonsymbolic Communication Interactions Among Learners with Severe Handicaps* (p. 25) by E. Siegel-Causey and D. Guess (Eds.), Baltimore: Paul H. Brookes; and Siegel-Causey, E., & Bashinski, S. M. (1997). Enhancing initial communication and responsiveness of learners with multiple disabilities: A tri-focus framework for partners. *Focus on Autism and Other Developmental Disabilities, 12* (2), 105–120.

tain, and terminate the movement of a windup toy). Also, they can direct attention to an object or event (e.g., get peers' attention on the waves in a pool). In the same snack situation, a need for requests could be incorporated.

> *Her teacher is "busy" when Marina finishes her juice. Thus, if Marina wants more to drink, she will need to get the partner's attention so that he would pour the juice.*

The right to choice and self determination are highly valued, and many sources for understanding the issues about choice-making and providing interventions are now available (e.g., Bambara & Koger, 1996; Bannerman, Sheldon, Sherman, & Harchik, 1990; Brown et al., 1993). Siegel-Causey and Bashinski (1997) suggested that choice making involves two aspects: (a) displaying preferences, and (b) making decisions. To display a preference, the learner recognizes that options exist, has a propensity (liking) toward something, and makes a communicative expression (choice) about that item or occurrence.

> *Ryan is given the opportunity to choose which peer he wants to work with during football practice tasks. Ryan needs to be able to recognize that there are peers present today to choose from, that he feels like being with one of them (propensity), and can convey this preference by gazing at the peer he prefers.*

It is important to consider the learner's level of receptive understanding and symbolization, and it may be necessary to implement choice-making instruction on a continuum from simple to complex. One level most applicable to learners who communicate nonsymbolically is a simple active or passive choice system with two options (Beukelman & Mirenda,

1998). The learner gets choice "X" when passive (for doing nothing) and choice "Y" when active (for doing something). Another applicable level is two-item active choices using real objects (Beukelman & Mirenda, 1998). The types of items in the two-choice array can be (a) two preferred options (Writer, 1987), (b) one preferred and one nonpreferred option, or (c) one preferred option and a "blank" or "distracter" option (Reichle et al., 1991; Rowland & Schweigert, 1990). The educational partner should select the option that will promote the learner's understanding that their behavior influenced the interaction. Learning to make choices should be a positive experience, thus starting with two preferred options is usually favored.

Choice Diversity. Brown et al. (1993) presented a model of choice diversity that expands traditional choice-making options by analyzing opportunities for choices within specific routines. Daily routines and activities in the school setting have many opportunities for choice making. According to Brown et al., there are seven categories of choice that are available within the context of most daily routines: within activities, between activities, refusal, where, when, who, and terminate. Each routine could be analyzed by partners, and the aspects of choice making to provide (e.g., within, who, terminate) would be selected for an individual time frame or day (for more information, refer to Brown et al., 1993). For example:

> During a leisure activity routine, Marina can be given the opportunity to choose listening to music or to have a book read to her (between activity). If Marina chooses to listen to music, she can be given the opportunity to choose either listening to rock or country music (within activity). Marina can also be given the opportunity to choose where (either lying on the mat or sitting in a rocking chair), and with whom to listen to music (either with Paul, or her friend Jody). Marina can also choose not to listen to music and not to be read a book (refusal) and choose to end the activity when she wants (terminate). The educational team decides which aspects of these options would be implemented in the leisure routine with Marina.

Facilitating alert, responsive state behavior is highly interrelated with knowledge of the learner. The learner's level of symbol understanding and intentionality is assessed via the communication profile. The outcome of the profile also includes identifying all expressions, including challenging behaviors, and

linking these to identification of their form and function. Intervention to facilitate state behavior, at the perlocutionary level, will focus on establishing the relationship between what the learner expresses and the actions of other people and environmental events. Perlocutionary nonsymbolic behaviors generally include relaxing or stiffening of the body; total body movement; arm, leg, or hand gestures or movements; and vocalizations (e.g. crying, cooing, noise making). For example:

> The peer stops the country music CD that he and Tom are listening to and starts to play another. Tom's legs stiffen and he begins to vocalize. His peer looks over, attending to the change in Tom's expression. "Hey buddy, you want to hear it still?" He reactivates the music and Tom relaxes and quiets down. Tom's level of alertness (agitation expressed via vocalizations and stiffening of his body) was noticed by his peer and affected the activity.

The learner who is building intentional behavior will use nonsymbolic behavior to affect actions of people and the environment. Nonsymbolic behaviors used purposefully in the early stages of intentionality generally include actions such as approaching or avoiding people, materials, or activities; contacting or pushing or pulling people, materials, or activities; smiling; and pointing.

The learner who communicates at a nonsymbolic level is limited to expressions focused on his or her current behavior state or on something that can be touched, looked at, or directly perceived through a sensory system. The preintentional and intentional behaviors may appear very similar in form and may affect the partner similarly whether the expressions were reactions (perlocutionary) or actions displayed for the purpose of achieving desired effects from the partner (illocutionary).

Sequencing Experiences
Routines help organize experiences for learners. Establishing routines can provide familiar interaction patterns for learners and allow them active roles in exchanges. (The strategies to sequence experiences are derived from the eight critical elements of effective joint-action routines in Table 11–6.) It is important to (a) establish routines, (b) provide turn-taking opportunities, and (c) encourage participation. Sequenced experiences are appropriate for helping learners move from the perlocutionary stage to the illocutionary

stage. Games and familiar routines often have a component of "your turn, my turn," which helps learners realize that they can express themselves. For example:

> Marina helps pour juice with her friend Jody. Each time that Jody moves the pitcher forward, Marina moves a cup toward the pitcher. This interchange occurs repeatedly as they pour juice for their classmates.

Routines such as self-care, leisure, and transition between activities and places provide redundancy and these recurring events across environments can be structured to encourage the learner to anticipate what may occur next (refer to next section for use of object schedules and calendar boxes for helping learners anticipate or recall events).

Routines can be established by educational partners to help ensure consistency and opportunities for communication across the activities of the day. The use of planned "dialogues" (Siegel-Causey & Guess, 1989) structures routines for the multiple partners so that communication is expected and consistent reciprocal roles between the learner and partners is promoted. An example dialogue was provided earlier in the chapter (Table 11–6). Similarly, "scripted routines" delineate the specific verbal and touch cues the partner should provide and the pauses and the precise actions of the partner within natural events (Beukelman & Mirenda, 1998).

Building on the Brown, et al. (1987) component model, Rainforth and York-Barr (1997) suggest that routines be examined in terms of sequential components (i.e., initiation, preparation, core, and termination) and interwoven components, such as preferences, communication, and social intervention. Partners can analyze routines that are already familiar and provide the learner with a role within the sequential components. The educational partners may select dialogues, scripted routines, or routine components to help sequence the experiences for the learner and thus encourage more participation and communication.

Initially, learners at the perlocutionary level do not realize that they can control their own behaviors or that their behaviors affect a game or routine. However, sequenced experiences allow learners to experience maintaining and terminating interactions. As learners develop more illocutionary skills, they can anticipate steps in a sequence and initiate parts of a routine or game.

Augmenting Input

The use of verbal input paired or "augmented" with another mode of communication may enhance the learner's understanding (comprehension of messages received). The strategy of enhancing meaning, commonly used by interventionists, may help the learner receive information more clearly because verbal input is elaborated upon with another mode. The alternative mode may include concrete gestures, touch cues, real objects, photographs, or pictures. The strategy of facilitating retention aids the learner's recall of a message or event through an object, gesture, or photograph. The use of an object schedule or calendar box may facilitate a learner's recall and anticipation of familiar activities (Rowland & Schweigert, 1990; Stillman & Battle, 1984).

Intervention to Enhance Partner's Understanding of Nonsymbolic Communication

The following guideline and strategies enhance the understanding of partners and the nonsymbolic expressions of learners. An example also illustrates the strategies for interaction.

Perceiving, interpreting, and responding to nonsymbolic behaviors helps partners concentrate on what learners do. In addition, such responsiveness can help make learners aware of other people as partners in interactions. The strategies to enhance sensitivity include (a) recognizing nonsymbolic behaviors, (b) responding contingently, (c) recognizing readiness for interactions, (d) responding to the level of communication and (e) responding to expressions and challenging behavior as communicative.

At the perlocutionary stage, learners do not realize that their behaviors can affect others, but the intervention focus is on always noticing and responding to the expressions of learners. At the perlocutionary level, partners continue to notice the expressions of learners and respond to those expressions as if they were communicative. As learners express in a more illocutionary manner (with intentionality), partners can note nonsymbolic behaviors that display a readiness for interaction and respond with expressions that are at the same level.

Regardless of the level of intentionality, partners can enhance their sensitivity to learner expressions and capitalize on opportunities for communication in two ways. First, the partner and all team members can become familiar with the learner's nonsymbolic behavior. This familiarity will be a primary outcome of creating the learner profile. Assessment outcomes about forms and functions of the learner's communication should be reviewed to help the team identify patterns and relationships of behavior. A second aspect of being sensitive is for partners to recognize the nonsymbolic behavior and respond contingently to these behaviors using a communicative level matched to the learner's understanding. The use of a gestural dictionary (Beukelman & Mirenda, 1998) or communication dictionary (Table 11–5) provides a means to list and describe the learner's nonsymbolic (and symbolic) behavior so that familiar and unfamiliar partners will have a source that provides current, accurate information. The dictionary describes the learner's current forms of expression, along with their meanings, and suggestions for how to respond appropriately (what partners should consistently do). The learner profile and gestural dictionary are not strategies per se, but sets of information about the learner that are likely to provide partners with concrete ways to understand what the learner expresses and those alert, responsive behaviors that can be responded to in a consistent manner. Thus, sensitivity is enhanced by being familiar with the breadth of the learner's forms of communication and by assigning meaning to those expressions contingently.

In Figure 11–12, Paul, a school staff partner, waits for Chris to indicate interest in activating the switch (increasing opportunities to create a need for requests). When Chris smiles and vocalizes at Paul (his signals that communicate behavior regulation and social interaction), Paul helps position Chris's arm so that he can more easily engage the switch (enhancing sensitivity by responding contingently).

Intervention to Enhance Communication Contexts

As the learner and partner communicate, the environment influences the interaction. Interactions that occur in natural contexts provide a dynamic environment for communication and take advantage of the influences of the physical and social aspects. The partner uses the learner's communication interests and participation needs within interactions that occur naturally or as part of daily activities and routines.

FIGURE 11–12
Paul is following the intervention guidelines and strategies to enhance Chris's communicative expressions.

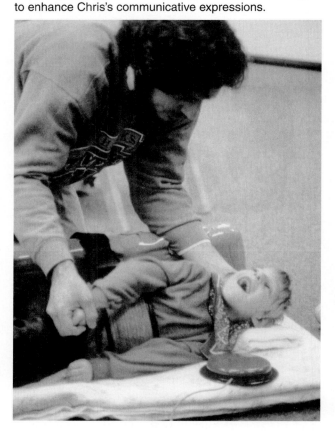

Direct teaching and instructional techniques that provide the learner with consistent stimulus-response-consequence arrangements is crucial. The intent of direct, systematic instruction is to enhance or highlight for the learner the relationship of stimulus, response, and consequences (Noonan & Siegel-Causey, 1997) (see also chapter 4) and will be most effective when implemented in naturally occurring activities. Using incidental teaching embraces this approach by teaching skills at times that they are needed and relevant (see Kaiser, Chapter 12).

Enhance Communication Contexts and Attend to External Influences on State Behavior

In addition to using structure in natural routines and embedding instruction within them, learners with severe disabilities may require additional physical and social supports to promote learning. The educational team should first consider how the learner participates by using participation analysis or ecological assessment to determine what factors may contribute to the difference between the learner's participation and that of his or her peers (Beukelman & Mirenda, 1998; McCormick, 1997; Noonan & Siegel-Causey, 1997). (Chapter 3 contains information about these processes).

One factor in decreased participation may be environmental. The partner may need to change the physical supports to increase the learner's performance. Some physical supports that may enhance participation might include using interesting and manipulable materials that can be part of an activity, adapting the materials that are part of the activity, or increasing personal assistance. The social supports, such as involving peers as facilitators, using group project activities, and teaching social communication strategies to students in the activity may also enhance instruction.

Team members modify the environment, including the sensory qualities, in order to assist the learner to interact with others in a functional manner, while displaying more alert, responsive state behavior. The ABLE field study (Ault et al., 1995) validated techniques for facilitating alert, responsive behaviors. They found three environmental characteristics: (1) sensory qualities, (2) movement and orientation of the learner's body, and (3) learning atmosphere that most influenced responsive behaviors. This research yielded data that suggested a direct relationship between changing the environmental characteristics and influencing behavior state.

Sensory qualities that can be modified encompass visual, auditory, tactile, gustatory, and olfactory stimuli. The partner determines whether certain features of sensory stimuli in the activity (or that could be added to the activity) would have an activating or soothing effect on the learner. For example, direct versus indirect light, materials highlighted with bright or neutral backgrounds, or a change from light to deep pressure may produce responsive behavior in the learner.

Similarly, the partner can evaluate the effects of movement and orientation of the learner's body. Team members may consider tempo or movement of the learner's body parts, or the learner's body tilt and po-

sition when on various adaptive equipment. The final consideration involves assessing the learning atmosphere. For example, what effects do secondary noise, location changes, and activity level nearby have on an individual learner? The minor changes or manipulations of these environmental characteristics could easily be implemented within the context of natural environments in conjunction with partner strategies from this chapter (refer to Ault et al., 1995, for more about environmental features).

An Example

It is important to incorporate the intervention guidelines into natural routines, as displayed in the photo sequence in Figure 11–13. Jona, an interventionist, tells Chris that it is time for music. She waits for his vocal and hand movements that signal that he agrees; then she picks him up.

Once he is face to face she asks who he wants for a music buddy, lists two peers, and then repeats their names, pausing after each name for his response. He vocalizes to choose one peer, and she places him in his chair. She pauses before strapping his feet and looks at him; this is Chris's cue to move his foot into place and Jona thanks him.

The dialogue in Table 11–8 presents ways to incorporate intervention into the daily context of interactions (Siegel-Causey & Guess, 1989). This table is set up in three columns. The left-hand column identifies partner behaviors and the intervention guideline or strategy being used. The bold type denotes the partner's use of a specific intervention within the dialogue. Italics in the learner and peer column designate their communications.

The methods in this chapter can help school staff members become partners with the learners who use nonsymbolic communication. These methods should be embedded in an instructional system for communication that fits within the overall education program of each learner. The methods lend themselves best to instruction that uses all relevant skill areas covered in this textbook, because although learners may have expressive communication skills that are primarily nonsymbolic, they may also have receptive communication skills that are symbolic. Therefore, the interventions for nonsymbolic communication should be supplemented with the information in this text on functional communication.

FIGURE 11–13
Jona, an interventionist, uses intervention strategies within the naturally occurring event of moving Chris to a new position.

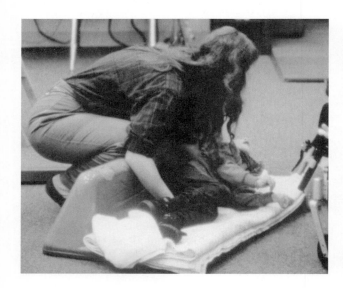

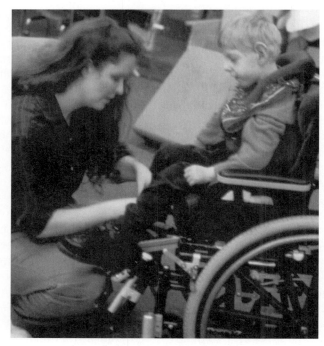

TABLE 11–8
Dialogue Before Snack in Marina's Classroom

This classroom has students with disabilities and typical peers who are 3 to 5 years of age. It is time for snack, and each student has a role. The teacher, Rachel, has paired Marina and Jody together for many classroom activities. Marina has missed school for the last month because of hospitalizations for extensive seizures. Jody is a typical peer, who is extremely quiet and reluctant to interact with other children. Rachel feels that Jody can benefit from helping Marina get back into the school routine and from having structured interactions to communicate about.

Intervention Guidelines and Strategies	Interventionist	Learner and Peer
	Rachel says to the group, "Class, it is time to prepare for snack. You will find a job and a partner on the snack picture board here." Rachel points to the bulletin board that displays photographs of student pairs and a photograph of the job each pair is to complete.	
Opportunity: Provide opportunities to interact	"Who wants to find a job?" Rachel *pauses* and *looks* around the circle. A few students raise their hand, and Rachel calls them up to find their picture. "What job did Andy and Josh find?" Rachel extends the photo that Andy and Josh found under their pictures and shows it to the children. She pauses in front of Jody. "What job is in this picture?"	
		Jody whispers, "Tablecloth."
	"Great, Jody. That's right, it is a tablecloth. Pass the photo to Marina. Marina, get ready." Rachel knows that Jody will barely extend the photo to Marina. Thus, Marina will have to reach out to get it. Rachel wants Marina to practice reaching out for items so that she can learn that this is a good way to request things she wants.	
Sequencing: Encourage participation	"Where is the photo, Marina?" Rachel says as she *looks quizzically and extends her palms upwards.*	
		Marina looks at Rachel's hands and laughs.
Sensitivity: Respond to the individual's level of communication	"You're happy! Let's find the photo." Rachel *guides Jody to extend the photo toward Marina.*	
		Marina laughs again and reaches toward the photo that Jody has extended in front of her.
Sensitivity: Recognize nonsymbolic behavior	*"Marina, you want the photo!"* Rachel exclaims.	
		Marina takes the photo.
Augmenting: Enhance meaning	Rachel points out the tablecloth in the photo that Marina now holds and *gestures, as if laying it out as she says,* "Put out tablecloth?"	
		Marina touches the photo. Jody looks over at the snack area, where the tablecloths are stacked on a shelf.
Sensitivity: Recognize nonsymbolic behaviors	*"Yes, Jody, I see you looking at the snack area.* Andy and Josh are going to put the tablecloth out." Rachel continues to call students up to find their snack jobs on the photo board. Soon, it is Marina and Jody's turn.	
Sequencing: Encourage participation	*"Who wants a job?"*	
		Jody looks at the photos of her and Marina.

(continued)

TABLE 11–8
(continued)

Intervention Guidelines and Strategies	Interventionist	Learner and Peer
Sensitivity: Respond contingently	*"Right, Jody, your picture is still here,"* Rachel *says as she points* to the photos of Jody and Marina.	
Sequencing: Encourage participation	"Who is in the picture with you?" Rachel *asks.*	
		Jody looks at Marina. Marina laughs.
Sequencing: Provide turn taking	Rachel *extends the photo* toward the girls.	
		Marina turns toward the photo.
Sensitivity: Recognize nonsymbolic behaviors	*"Yes, Marina, this is your job,"* says Rachel.	
		Jody moves toward Rachel, and Marina crawls to follow her. Jody takes the photo from Rachel.
	Rachel encourages Jody to show the photo to Marina in the same manner as they did with the photo of the tablecloth.	
Sequencing: Encourage participation	Rachel asks, *"What job is in the picture?"*	
		Jody whispers, "Napkins."
Sensitivity: Respond to the individual's level of communication.	"Napkins!" Rachel *says as she gestures toward Jody and Marina and pretends to hand out napkins.*	
Augmenting: Enhance meaning		
		Jody watches. Marina laughs and touches Rachel's hands.
Opportunity: Provide opportunities to interact	"Marina, where are the napkins?" Rachel *asks as she shrugs her shoulders and looks around the room.*	
		Marina turns toward the shelves and begins to crawl to them.
Sensitivity: Respond contingently	*"Marina sees the napkins,"* Rachel says with a loud and happy tone in her voice. "Are you going to help with your job, Jody?" Jody slowly follows Marina to the shelf.	
		Marina giggles and watches Jody follow her.
	Rachel continues to guide the girls as needed to complete their job of putting out the napkins and encourages them to interact as opportunities arise.	

Summary

This chapter focuses on learners who use nonsymbolic communication and partners working with these learners. Researchers and practitioners in the field of severe disabilities and speech language pathology have only begun to recognize the broad spectrum of communication intervention needs of individuals who have disabilities. A new emphasis on and inclusion of instructional methods and procedures for enhancing the primary repertoire of communication form a foundation for the development of symbolic and augmentative communication.

School staff members have an array of sources that can help them provide instruction that matches the learner's communication level. School staff partners should provide instruction with a sound understanding of the broad continuum of communication, beginning with nonsymbolic communication and continuing to symbolic communication. Marina, Ryan, and all of the other learners who communicate primarily using nonsymbolic skills have a quality instructional program when partners enhance the skills that the learners already have. The goal is to use methods that incorporate nonsymbolic skills and build upon the present repertoire of communication skills to move learners to the most sophisticated system of communication possible for them.

Suggested Activities

1. Select a learner who uses primarily nonsymbolic communication. Write down the activities that occur with partners (peers or adults). Select one activity that you participate in and analyze the interaction: What intervention strategies will you apply based on your analysis?
2. Think about your personal style of interacting with learners who have severe disabilities.
   a. Pick one of these learners.
   b. Who are his or her favorite peers?
   c. Who are his or her favorite adults?
   d. What information can you gather that will help determine what this learner prefers in terms of interactional style?
   e. How does your style match the learner's preferences?
3. Select a learner and an activity that you engage in with that learner. Analyze the activity in terms of the naturally occurring opportunities for the learner to communicate. Which opportunities do you respond to? Are there any opportunities that you inadvertently preempt? Try writing a dialogue to enhance the activity.

Learner Behavior	What I Think It Means	How I Respond	Effectiveness of Interaction	Possible Changes

References

Alwell, M., Hunt, P., Goetz, L., & Sailor, W. (1989). Teaching generalized communicative behaviors within interrupted behavior chain contexts. *Journal of the Association for Persons with Severe Handicaps, 14*, 91–100.

Ault, M. M., Guy, B., Guess, D., Bashinski, S., & Roberts, S. (1995). Analyzing behavior state and learning environments: Application in instructional settings. *Mental Retardation, 33*, 304–316.

Austin, J. (1962). *How to do things with words.* Cambridge, MA: Harvard University Press.

Bambara, L. M., & Koger, F. (1996). *Opportunities for daily choice making.* Washington, DC: American Association on Mental Retardation.

Bannerman, D. J., Sheldon, J. B., Sherman, J. A. & Harchik, A. E. (1990). Balancing the right to habilitation with the right to personal liberties: the rights of people with developmental disabilities to eat too many doughnuts and take a nap. *Journal of Applied Behavior Analysis, 23*, 78–89.

Bates, E. (1979). *The emergence of symbols: Cognition and communication in infancy.* New York: Academic Press.

Bates, E., Camaioni, L., & Volterra, V. (1975). The acquisition of performatives prior to speech. *Merrill-Palmer Quarterly, 21*, 205–226.

Bates, E., O'Connell, B., & Shore, C. (1987). Language and communication in infancy. In J. Osofsky (Ed.), *Handbook of infant development* (pp. 149–203). New York: Wiley.

Bates, E., & Snyder, L. (1987). The cognitive hypothesis in language development. In I. Uzgiris & J. Hunt (Eds.), *Infant performance and experience* (pp. 168–204). Chicago: University of Illinois Press.

Baumgart, D., Johnson, J., & Helmstetter, E. (1990). *Augmentative and alternative communication systems for persons with moderate and severe disabilities.* Baltimore: Paul H. Brookes.

Bedrosian, J. L. (1988). Adults with mildly to moderately severe mental retardation: Communicative performance, assessment and intervention. In S. N. Calculator & J. L. Bedrosian (Eds.), *Communication assessment and intervention strategies* (pp. 265–307). Boston: College-Hill.

Beukelman, D. R., & Mirenda, P. (1998). *Augmentative and alternative communication: Management of severe communication disorders in children and adults* (2nd ed.) Baltimore: Paul H. Brookes.

Beukelman, D. R., & Yorkston, K. M. (1989). Augmentative and alternative communication application for persons with severe acquired communication disorders: An introduction. *Augmentative and Alternative Communication, 5,* 42–48.

Bloom, L. (1993). *The transition from infancy to language.* New York: Cambridge University Press.

Brady, N. C., & Halle, J. W. (1997). Functional analysis of communicative behaviors. *Focus on Autism and Other Developmental Disabilities, 12* (2), 95–104.

Brady, N. C., McLean, J. E., McLean, L. K., & Johnston, S. (1995). Initiation and repair of intentional communication acts by adults with severe to profound cognitive disabilities. *Journal of Speech and Hearing Research, 38,* 1334–1348.

Brown, F., Belz, P., Corsi, L., & Wenig, B. (1993). Choice diversity for people with severe disabilities. *Education and Training in Mental Retardation, 28,* 318–326.

Brown, F., Evans, I., Weed, K., & Owen, V. (1987). Delineating functional competencies: A component model. *Journal of the Association for Persons with Severe Handicaps, 12*(2), 117–124.

Bruner, J. (1978). From communication to language: A psychological perspective. In I. Markova (Ed.), *The social context of language* (pp. 17–48). New York: Wiley.

Bruner, J. (1981). The social context of language acquisition. *Language and Communication, 1,* 155–178.

Bruner, J., & Sherwood, V. (1976). Early rule structure: The case of peekaboo. In J. Bruner, A. Jolly, & K. Sylva (Eds.), *Play: Its role in evolution and development* (pp. 277–285). London: Penguin.

Calculator, S. N., & Jorgensen, C. M. (1994). *Including students with severe disabilities in schools: fostering communication, interaction, and participation.* San Diego: Singular.

Calculator, S. N. (1988). Exploring the language of adults with mental retardation. In S. N. Calculator & J. L. Bedrosian (Eds.), *Communication assessment and intervention strategies* (pp. 523–547). Baltimore: University Park Press.

Carr, E. G., Levin, L., McConnachie, G., Carlson, J., Kemp, D., & Smith, C. (1994). *Communication-based intervention for problem behavior: A user's guide for producing positive change.* Baltimore: Paul H. Brookes.

Carr, E. G., & Durand, V. M. (1985). Reducing behavior problems through functional communication training. *Journal of Applied Behavior Analysis, 18,* 111–126.

Chapman, R. (1978). Comprehension strategies in children. In J. Kavanagh & W. Stragne (Eds.), *Speech and language in the laboratory, school and clinic* (pp. 308–330). Cambridge, MA: MIT Press.

Cirrin, F., & Rowland, C. (1985). Communicative assessment of nonverbal youths with severe/profound mental retardation. *Mental Retardation, 23,* 52–62.

Coggins, T., & Carpenter, R. (1981). The communicative intention inventory: A system for observing and coding children's early intentional communication. *Applied Psycholinguistics, 2,* 235–251.

Coots, J., & Falvey, M. A. (1989). Communication skills. In M. A. Falvey (Ed.), *Community based curriculum* (2nd ed.) (pp. 255–284). Baltimore: Paul H. Brookes.

Corsaro, W. (1981). The development of social cognition in preschool children: Implications for language learning. *Topics in Language Disorders, 2,* 77–95.

Dooley, J., Berg, J., Pakula, Z., & MacGregor, D. (1981). The puppet-like syndrome of Angelman. *American Journal of Disordered Children, 135,* 621–624.

Dore, J. (1986). The development of conversation competence. In R. Scheifelbusch (Ed.), *Language competence: Assessment and intervention* (pp. 3–60). San Diego: College-Hill Press.

Duchan, J. (1995). *Supporting language learning in everyday life.* San Diego: Singular Press.

Dunst, C., Lowe, L. W., & Bartholomew, P. C. (1990). Contingent social responsiveness, family ecology, and infant communicative competence. *National Student Speech Language Hearing Association Journal, 17,* 39–49.

Durand, V. M., & Crimmins, D. B. (1992). *The motivation assessment scale (MAS) administration guide.* Topeka, KS: Monaco.

Falvey, M. A. (1986). *Community-based curriculum: Instructional strategies for students with severe handicaps.* Baltimore: Paul H. Brookes.

Falvey, M. A., & Rosenberg, R. L. (1995). Developing and fostering friendships. In M. A. Falvey (Ed.), *Inclusive and heterogeneous schooling: Assessment, curriculum, and instruction* (pp. 267–283). Baltimore: Paul H. Brookes.

Flavell, J. (1963). *The developmental psychology of Jean Piaget.* New York: Van Nostrand.

Gaylord-Ross, R. J., & Holvoet, J. F. (1985). *Strategies for educating students with severe handicaps.* Boston: Little, Brown.

Girolametto, L. E., Greenberg, J., & Manolson, H. A. (1986). Developing dialogue skills: The Hanen early language parent program. *Seminars in Speech and Language, 7,* 367–382.

Goetz, L., Gee, K., & Sailor, W. (1985). Using a behavior chain interruption strategy to teach communication skills to students with severe disabilities. *Journal of the Association for Persons with Severe Handicaps, 10,* 21–30.

Goetz, L., & Sailor, W. (1988). New directions: Communication development in persons with severe disabilities. *Topics in Language Disorders, 8*(4), 41–54.

Guess, D., Ault, M. M., Roberts, S., Struth, J., Siegel-Causey, E., Thompson, B., & Bronicki, G. J. (1988). Implications of biobehavioral states for the education and treatment of students with the most profoundly handicapping conditions. *Journal of the Association for Persons with Severe Handicaps, 13,* 163–174.

Guess, D., Benson, H. A., & Siegel-Causey, E. (1985). Concepts and issues related to choice making and autonomy among persons with severe disabilities. *Journal of the Association for Persons with Severe Handicaps, 10,* 79–86.

Guess, D., Roberts, S., Siegel-Causey, E., & Rues, J. (1995). Replication and extended analysis of behavior state, environmental events, and related variables in profound disabilities. *American Journal on Mental Retardation, 100,* 36–51.

Guess, D., Roberts, S., Siegel-Causey, E., Ault, M. M., Guy, B., Thompson, B., & Rues, J. (1991). *Investigations into the state behaviors of students with severe and profound handicapping conditions.* (Monograph No. 1) Lawrence, KS: University of Kansas Department of Special Education.

Guess, D., Roberts, S., Siegel-Causey, E., Ault, M. M., Guy, B., Thompson, B., & Rues, J. (1993). An analysis of behavior state conditions and associated environmental variables among students with profound handicaps. *American Journal on Mental Retardation, 97,* 634–653.

Guess, D., Siegel-Causey, E., Roberts, S., Guy, B., Ault, M. M., & Rues, J. (1993). Analysis of state organizational patterns among students with profound disabilities. *Journal of the Association for Persons with Severe Handicaps, 18,* 93–108.

Guess, D., Siegel-Causey, E., Roberts, S., Rues, J., Thompson, B., & Siegel-Causey, D. (1990). Assessment and analysis of behavior state and related variables among students with profoundly handicapping conditions. *Journal of the Association for Persons with Severe Handicaps, 15,* 211–230.

Guy, B., Guess, D., & Ault, M. M. (1993). Classroom procedures for the measurement of behavior state among students with profound disabilities. *Journal of the Association for Persons with Severe Handicaps, 18,* 52–60.

Halle, J. (1984). Arranging the natural environment to occasion language: Giving severely language-delayed children reason to communicate. *Seminars in Speech and Language, 5*(3), 185–197.

Halle, J. (1985). Enhancing social competence through language: An experimental analysis of a practical procedure for teachers. *Topics in Early Childhood Special Education, 4*(4), 77–92.

Halle, J. W., Marshall, A. M., & Spradlin, J. E. (1979). Time delay: A technique to increase language use and facilitate generalization in retarded children. *Journal of Applied Behavior Analysis, 12,* 431–439.

Harding, C. (1984). Acting with intention: A framework for examining the development of the intention to communicate. In L. Feagans, C. Garvey, & R. Golinkoff (Eds.), *The origins and growth of communication* (pp. 123–135). Norwood, NJ: Ablex.

Harding, C., & Golinkoff, R. (1979). The origins of intentional vocalizations in prelinguistic infants. *Child Development, 50,* 33–40.

Hart, B., & Risley, T. R. (1975). Incidental teaching of language in the preschool. *Journal of Applied Behavioral Analysis, 8,* 411–420.

Horner, R. H., O'Neill, R. E., & Albin, R. W. (1991). *Supporting students with high intensity problem behavior.* Unpublished manuscript, University of Oregon, Eugene.

Hunt, P., Goetz, L., Alwell, M., & Sailor, W. (1986). Using an interrupted behavior chain strategy to teach generalized communication responses. *Journal of the Association for Persons with Severe Handicaps, 11,* 196–204.

Johnson, J. M., Baumgart, D., Helmstetter, E., & Curry, C. A. (1996). *Augmenting basic communication in natural contexts.* Baltimore: Paul H. Brookes.

Kublin, K. S., Wetherby, A. M., Crais, E. R., and Prizant, B. M. (1998). Using dynamic assessment within collaborative contexts: The transition from intentional to symbolic communication. In A. Wetherby, S. Warren, & J. Reichle (Eds.), *Transitions in prelinguistic communication* (pp. 285–312). Baltimore: Paul H. Brookes.

Langley, M. B., & Lombardino, L. J. (Eds.). (1991). *Neurodevelopmental strategies for managing communication disorders in children with severe motor dysfunction.* Austin, TX: Pro-Ed.

Lifter, K. & Bloom, L. (1998). Intentionality and the role of play in the transition to language. In A. Wetherby, S. Warren, & J. Reichle (Eds.), *Transitions in prelinguistic communication* (pp. 161–195). Baltimore: Paul H. Brookes.

MacDonald, J. D. (1985). Language through conversation. In S. Warren & A. Rogers-Warren (Eds.), *Teaching functional language* (pp. 89–122). Baltimore: University Park Press.

MacDonald, J. D. (1989). *Becoming partners with children: From play to conversations.* Chicago: Riverside.

MacDonald, J., & Carroll, J. (1992). Communicating with young children: An ecological model for clinicians, parents, and collaborative professionals. *American Journal of Speech-Language Pathology, 1,* 39–48.

McCormick, L. (1997). Ecological assessment and planning. In L. McCormick, D. Loeb, & R. Schiefelbusch (Eds.), *Supporting children with communication difficulties in inclusive settings: school-based language intervention* (pp. 223–256). Boston: Allyn & Bacon.

McLean, J., McLean, L., Brady, N., & Etter, R. (1991). Communication profiles of two types of gesture using nonverbal persons with severe to profound mental retardation. *Journal of Speech and Hearing Research, 34,* 294–308.

McLean, J., & Snyder-McLean, L. (1978). *A transactional approach to early language training.* New York: Merrill/Macmillan.

McLean, J., & Snyder-McLean, L. (1988). Applications of pragmatics to severely mentally retarded children and youth. In R. L. Schiefelbusch & L. L. Lloyd (Eds.), *Language perspectives: Acquisition, retardation and intervention* (pp. 255–288). Austin, TX: Pro-Ed.

Miller, J., & Paul, R. (1995). *The clinical assessment of language comprehension.* Baltimore: Paul H. Brookes.

Mirenda, P. (1988, August). *Instructional techniques for communication.* Paper presented at the Annual Augmentative and Alternative Communication for Students with Severe Disabilities Special Education Innovative Institute, Fremont, CA.

Mirenda, P. L., & Donnellan, A. M. (1986). Effects of adult interaction style on conversational behavior in students with severe communication problems. *Language, Speech and Hearing Services in the Schools, 17,* 126–141.

Muma, J. (1986). *Language acquisition: A functionalistic perspective.* Austin, TX: Pro-Ed.

Musselwhite, C. R., & St. Louis, K. W. (1988). *Communication programming for persons with severe handicaps: Vocal and augmentative strategies* (2nd ed.). San Diego: College-Hill Press.

Noonan, M. J., & Siegel-Causey, E. (1997). Special needs of young children with severe handicaps. In L. McCormick, D. Loeb, & R. Schiefelbusch (Eds.), *Supporting children with communication difficulties in inclusive settings: school-based language intervention* (pp. 405–432). Boston: Allyn & Bacon.

Norris, J., & Hoffman, P. (1990). Language intervention in naturalistic environments. *Language, Speech, and Hearing Services in the Schools, 21*(2), 72–84.

Ogletree, B., Wetherby, A. & Westling, D. (1992). A profile of the prelinguistic intentional communicative behaviors of children with profound mental retardation. *American Journal on Mental Retardation, 97,* 186–196.

O'Neill, R. E., Horner, R. H., Albin, R. W., Sprague, J. R., Storey, K., & Newton, J. S. (1997). *Functional assessment and program development for problem behavior: A practical handbook.* Pacific Grove, CA: Brookes/Cole.

O'Neill, R., Vaughn, B., & Dunlap, G. (1998). Comprehensive behavioral support: Assessment issues and strategies. In A. Wetherby, S. Warren, & J. Reichle (Eds.), *Transitions in prelinguistic communication* (pp. 313–341). Baltimore: Paul H. Brookes.

Peck, C. A. (1989). Assessment of social communicative competence: Evaluating environments. *Seminars in Speech and Language, 10,* 1–15.

Peck, C. A., & Schuler, A. L. (1987). Assessment of social/communicative behavior for students with autism and severe handicaps. The importance of asking the right question. In T. L. Layton (Ed.), *Language and treatment of autistic and developmentally disordered children* (pp. 35–62). Springfield, IL: Charles C. Thomas.

Piaget, J. (1952). *The origins of intelligence in children*. New York: Basic Books.

Prizant, B., & Wetherby, A. (1990). Assessing the communication of infants and toddlers: Integrating a socioemotional perspective. *Zero to Three*, 11, 1–12.

Rainforth, B. (1982). Biobehavioral state and orienting: Implications for educating profoundly retarded students. *Journal of the Association for the Severely Handicapped*, 6, 33–37.

Rainforth, B., & York-Barr, J. (1997). *Collaborative teams for students with severe disabilities: integrating therapy and educational services*. Baltimore: Paul H. Brookes.

Reichle, J., York, J., & Sigafoos, J. (1991). *Implementing augmentative and alternative communication*. Baltimore: Paul H. Brookes.

Reichle, J., & Wacker, D. (Eds.) (1993). Communication and language intervention series: vol. 3. *Communicative alternatives to challenging behavior: Integrating functional assessment and intervention strategies*. Baltimore: Paul H. Brookes.

Rice, M. (1983). Contemporary account of the cognition/language relationship: Implications for speech-language clinicians. *Journal of Speech and Hearing Disorders*, 48, 347–359.

Rice, M. L., & Kemper, S. (1984). *Child language and cognition: Contemporary issues*. Baltimore: University Park Press.

Richards, S., & Richards, R. (1997). Implications for assessing biobehavioral states in individuals with profound disabilities. *Focus on Autism and Other Developmental Disabilities*, 12 (2), 79–86.

Richards, S. B., & Sternberg, L. (1992). A preliminary analysis of environmental variables affecting the observed biobehavioral states of individuals with profound handicaps. *Journal of Intellectual Disability Research*, 36, 403–414.

Richards, S. B., & Sternberg, L. (1993). Corroborating previous findings: Laying stepping stones in the analysis of biobehavioral states in students with profound disabilities. *Education and Training in Mental Retardation*, 28, 262–268.

Romski, M. A., & Sevcik, R. A. (1993). Language learning through augmented means: The process and its products. In A. Kaiser & D. Gray (Eds.), *Enhancing children's communication: Research foundations for intervention* (pp. 85–104). Baltimore: Paul H. Brookes.

Rowland, C. & Schweigert, P. (1990). *Tangible symbol systems: Symbolic communication for individuals with multisensory impairments*. Tucson, AZ: Communication Skill Builders.

Rowland, C., Schweigert, P. D., & Prickett, J. G. (1995). Cummunication systems, devices, and modes. In K. M. Huebner, J. G. Prichett, T. R. Welsch, & E. Joffee (Eds.), *Hand in hand: essentials of communication and orientation and mobility for your students who are deaf-blind* (pp. 219–259). New York: American Foundation for the Blind.

Rowland, C., & Stremel-Campbell, K. (1987). Share and share alike: Conventional gestures to emergent language for learners with sensory impairments. In L. Goetz, D. Guess, & K. Stremel-Campbell (Eds.), *Innovative program design for individuals with dual sensory impairments* (pp. 49–75). Baltimore: Paul H. Brookes.

Schuler, A. L., & Prizant, B. M. (1987). Facilitating communication: Prelanguage approaches. In D. J. Cohen & A. M. Donnellon (Eds.), *Handbook of autism and atypical developmental disorders* (pp. 301–315). New York: Wiley.

Searle, J. (1969). *Speech acts: An essay in the philosophy of language*. Cambridge, England: Cambridge University Press.

Siegel-Causey, E. & Bashinski, S. (1997). Enhancing initial communication and responsiveness of learners with multiple disabilities: A tri-focus framework for partners. *Focus on Autism and Other Developmental Disabilities*, 12 (2), 105–120.

Siegel-Causey, E., & Downing, J. (1987). Nonsymbolic communication development: Theoretical concepts and educational strategies. In L. Goetz, D. Guess, & K. Stremel-Campbell (Eds.), *Innovative program design for individuals with dual sensory impairments* (pp. 15–48). Baltimore: Paul H. Brookes.

Siegel-Causey, E., Ernst, B., & Guess, D. (1987). Elements of nonsymbolic communication and early interactional processes. In M. Bullis (Ed.), *Communication development in young children with deaf-blindness: Literature review III* (pp. 57–102). Monmouth, OR: Communication Skills Center for Young Children with Deaf-Blindness.

Siegel-Causey, E., Ernst, B., & Guess, D. (1989). Nonsymbolic communication in early interactional processes. In M. Bullis (Ed.), *Communication development in young children with deaf-blindness: Literature review IV* (pp. 69–122). Monmouth, OR: Communication Skills Center for Young Children with Deaf-Blindness.

Siegel-Causey, E., & Guess, D. (Eds.). (1989). *Enhancing nonsymbolic communication interactions among learners with severe handicaps*. Baltimore: Paul H. Brookes.

Snyder-McLean, L. K., Solomonson, B., McLean, J. E., & Sack S. (1984). Structuring joint-action routines for facilitating communication and language development in the classroom. *Seminars in Speech and Language*, 5(3), 213–228.

Stillman, R. D., & Battle, C. W. (1984). Developing prelanguage communication in the severely handicapped: An interpretation of the van Dijk method. *Seminars in Speech and Language*, 5(3), 159–170.

Stillman, R., & Siegel-Causey, E. (1989). Introduction to nonsymbolic communication. In E. Siegel-Causey & D. Guess (Eds.), *Enhancing nonsymbolic communication interaction among learners with severe disabilities* (pp. 1–13). Baltimore: Paul H. Brookes.

Stremel-Campbell, K., & Rowland, C. (1987). Prelinguistic communication intervention: Birth-to-2. *Topics in Early Childhood Special Education*, 7(2), 49–58.

Wacker, D. P., Steege, M. W., Northup, J., Sasso, G., Berg, W., Reimers, T., Cooper, L., Cigrand, K., & Donn, L. (1990). A component analysis of functional communication training across three topographies of severe behavior problems. *Journal of Applied Behavior Analysis*, 23, 417–429.

Warren, S. F., McQuarter, R. J., & Rogers-Warren, A. K. (1984). The effects of mands and models on the speech of unresponsive socially isolated children. *Journal of Speech and Hearing Disorders*, 47, 42–52.

Wetherby, A., Alexander, D., & Prizant, B. (1998). The ontogeny and role of repair strategies. In A. Wetherby, S. Warren, and J. Reichle (Eds.), *Transitions in prelinguistic communication* (pp. 135–160). Baltimore, MD: Paul H. Brookes.

Wetherby, A., Cain, D., Yonclas, D., & Walker, V. (1988). Analysis of intentional communication of normal children from the prelinguistic to the multi-word stage. *Journal of Speech and Hearing Research*, 31, 240–252.

Wetherby, A., & Prizant, B. (1989). The expression of communicative intent: Assessment issues. *Seminars in Speech and Language, 10,* 77–91.

Wetherby, A., & Prizant, B. (1992). Profiling young children's communicative competence. In S. Warren & J. Reichle (Eds.), *Causes and effects in language assessment and intervention* (pp. 217–253). Baltimore: Paul H. Brookes.

Wetherby, A., & Prizant, B. (1993). *Communication and Symbolic Behavior Scales-Normed Edition.* Chicago, IL: Applied Symbolix.

Wetherby, A., & Prizant, B. (1997). Communication, language, and speech disorders in young children. In S. Greenspan, J. Osofsky, & S. Wieder (Eds.), *Handbook of Child and Adolescent Psychiatry* (pp. 473–491). NY: Wiley.

Wetherby, A., Prizant, B. & Hutchinson, T. (1998). Communicative, social-affective, and symbolic profiles of young children with autism and pervasive developmental disorder, *American Journal of Speech-Language Pathology,* 7, 79–91.

Wetherby, A., & Prutting, C. (1984). Profiles of communicative and cognitive-social abilities in autistic children. *Journal of Speech and Hearing Research,* 27, 364–377.

Wetherby, A., Reichle, J., & Pierce, P. (1998). The transition to symbolic communication. In A. M. Wetherby, S. F. Warren, & J. Reichle (Eds.), *Transitions in Prelinguistic Communication* (pp. 197–230). Baltimore: Paul H. Brookes.

Wetherby, A., & Rodriguez, G. (1992). Measurement of communicative intentions during structured and unstructured contexts. *Journal of Speech and Hearing Research,* 35, 130–138.

Wetherby, A., Warren, S., & Reichle, J. (Eds.) (1998). *Communication and language intervention series: vol. 7. Transitions in prelinguistic communication.* Baltimore: Paul H. Brookes.

Wetherby, A., Yonclas, D., & Bryan, A. (1989). Communicative profiles of handicapped preschool children: Implications for early identification. *Journal of Speech and Hearing Disorders,* 54, 148–158.

Williams, C., & Frais, J. (1982). The Angelman ("happy puppet") syndrome. *American Journal of Medical Genetics,* 11, 453–460.

Wood, L., Lasker, J., Siegel-Causey, E., Beukelman, D., & Ball, L. (1998). Input framework for augmentative and alternative communication. *Augmentative and Alternative Communication,* 14, 261–267.

Writer, J. (1987). A movement-based approach to the education of students who are sensory impaired/multihandicapped. In L. Goetz, D. Guess, and K. Stremel-Campbell (Eds.) *Innovative program design for individuals with dual sensory impairments* (pp. 191–223). Baltimore: Paul H. Brookes.

Yoder, P., Warren, S., McCathren, R. & Leew, S. (1998). Does adult responsivity to child behavior facilitate communication development? In A. M. Wetherby, S. F. Warren, & J. Reichle (Eds.), *Transitions in prelinguistic communication* (pp. 39–58). Baltimore: Paul H. Brookes.

12

Teaching Functional Communication Skills

Ann P. Kaiser

Communication is an essential skill for students with severe disabilities. Many students with severe disabilities acquire communication skills only when they have systematic instruction and support for using new skills. A critical issue in teaching communication to these learners is insuring that the forms of communication which are taught are used meaningfully in social interactions. Functional communication skills are communication forms that work to inform listeners of students' needs, wants, interests, and feelings. Functional skills allow students to achieve their desired ends. These skills are the means for social interaction and sharing of intentions with others. They are a keystone for learning to express choices and build-

ing independence. Such skills may take many different forms, including verbalizations, signs, gestures and the use of augmentative devices; what is critical is that meaning or function of the form is shared by students and their conversational partners. For most learners with severe disabilities, functional communication skills are most easily acquired when they are taught in everyday contexts, to achieve specific social goals in interactions with conversational partners who are familiar and preferred.

During the last 15 years, naturalistic strategies for teaching functional communication have been demonstrated to be effective for increasing everyday communication by students with severe disabilities. These strategies begin with the learner's intention to communicate and systematically provide models of appropriate communication forms and meaningful social consequences for communication attempts.

The author wishes to thank Susan Copeland for her assistance in the literature review for this chapter.

Lizabeth

Lizabeth is a 4-year-old who has autism. At this time, Lizabeth has no spoken words, but she is learning to use a communication book to signal her basic wants and needs. She has learned to use pictures for requesting more of any object, food, or event; to ask for help; to indicate she needs to use the potty; to say no; and to ask for her favorite stuffed toy. She will soon be learning to use the labels for other preferred items and activities.

Lizabeth has attended a preschool sponsored by her family's church since age 3. She is the only child with a

disability in her class of 12 children. An itinerant special education teacher visits the classroom 2 days a week and works with Lizabeth in the classroom. The special education teacher consults with the two classroom teachers. The two most challenging issues for her teachers are understanding Lizabeth's needs and wants and engaging her in the activities of the classroom. Lizabeth often prefers to watch activities while standing away from the rest of the children. When verbally requested or physically directed toward an activity, she typically protests by crying and physically resisting.

Social communication is the meaningful exchange of information by two persons. Social communication can be verbal and linguistic; it may also be nonverbal, symbolic, or gestural. The broadening of our understanding of the range of forms social communication may take has opened the door to new approaches to teaching functional communication skills to persons with severe disabilities. The premise that the communicative function of an event is of primary importance has refocused our teaching efforts to ensure that newly learned communication forms are immediately functional for the individual. As we teach, we now ask: Does the student's use of this new form result in sharing of information between conversational partners? At the same time, there has been an increased appreciation for the variety of communication forms (i.e., spoken language, signed language, pictures, natural gestures) that may be used to communicate functionally.

Behavioral technology that was developed to teach specific skills to individuals with limited language has not been discarded. Rather, the application of this technology has been extended to teaching functional skills in more natural settings. Working with persons who have severe disabilities has drawn attention to the critical needs of this population and to the limits of existing language intervention technology. It is increasingly clear that teaching functional communication skills may require an approach to intervention that is different from that for teaching the rudiments of a formal linguistic repertoire. An emphasis on functional communication has important implications for both teaching strategy and curriculum content.

Research provides data supporting this shift in emphasis. Generalization and maintenance of newly learned communication skills have been shown to require specific planning (Kaiser, Yoder, & Keetz, 1992;

Kristi

Kristi is a bright-eyed 9-year-old with a charming smile and lots of energy. She is a full participant in the third-grade classroom she attends in her neighborhood school. Along with 20 other children, she receives academic instruction that is designed to fit her developmental needs in the context of cooperative learning groups, individualized tutoring, and traditional classroom activities. Kristi's special education teacher collaborates with her classroom teacher in planning and implementing instruction. In addition, Kristi works with a speech therapist and a physical therapist 3 days each week.

Kristi has multiple disabilities: a vision impairment corrected with glasses, a moderate level of motor con-

trol that limits her mobility, and moderate to severe cognitive limitations. Although she is socially engaging and frequently interacts with adults and peers, her formal communication skills are limited. Only when prompted does Kristi currently use the six signs that she learned in one-to-one training with her speech therapist. Kristi does not yet sign with peers or spontaneously initiate communication. Kristi's parents are very interested in learning ways to facilitate Kristi's communication at home, and Kristi's teachers are motivated to enhance Kristi's participation in classroom social and academic interactions.

Carter

Carter is a 10-year-old boy with autism. His spoken language is limited to one- and two-word utterances, but he understands longer sentences if the referent is fairly concrete. Carter's favorite activities include visiting his grandparents and looking at family picture albums. Carter is a fan of all kinds of sports, which he watches on television. He also likes to throw a football with his older brother. Carter is sometimes echoic and will repeat the last word or two of utterances directed to him.

Carter's mother, Catherine, has been taught to use responsive interaction and milieu teaching during everyday interactions with Carter at home. She is careful to respond to Carter's verbal and nonverbal initiations, expand his one- and two-word utterances into short sentences, and prompt Carter to make verbal choices whenever it is appropriate.

Warren & Rogers-Warren [Kaiser], 1985). Both longitudinal analysis (Warren & Rogers-Warren [Kaiser], 1983) and specific experimental analysis (Anderson & Spradlin, 1980) have demonstrated that limited generalization of newly learned language skills by individuals with severe disabilities is a typical training outcome when training occurs outside the settings where the newly learned skills are required. Clearly, limited generalization is a major barrier to acquisition of a functional communication repertoire, and teaching strategies must include plans to surmount this barrier.

Along with the shift toward teaching functional skills in the natural environment has come greater attention to the immediate success of students in affecting communication partners and in achieving their specific social intentions. While teaching new skills continues to be important, facilitating communicative interactions during training has become an issue for interventionists. The emphasis in communication intervention for students with severe disabilities has shifted from "training for tomorrow" to "training for today."

For students like Kristi and Lizabeth, the difference in emphasis translates into selecting an alternative mode of communication (e.g., signing or communication book) that is easier for them to acquire than the verbal mode, teaching responses that have an immediate function in indicating needs and wants, and providing specific training to promote generalized use of new skills in everyday conversational contexts. To ensure that skills are functional and generalized, training occurs in the settings where communication is ongoing. Dinner at home, recess on the playground with peers, lunch in the cafeteria, and bus rides to school are settings for training in addition to the classroom or speech therapy room. Before teaching new skills, teachers must assess the individual's needs for communication and the environmental demands for communication as well as the individual's existing skills. The new emphasis on generalized functional skills requires the use of instructional strategies that take advantage of naturally occurring opportunities to teach language and to promote generalization.

 Michael

Michael is a 15-year-old student with mental retardation and a moderate hearing loss. He uses a wheelchair. His communication skills include single words and two-word phrases. He struggles to articulate sounds clearly because of his hearing loss. It is important to maintain face-to-face visual contact with Michael when speaking to him so that he can see as well as hear what is being said. Michael uses a picture book to support his verbal communication, especially with peers who have difficulty understanding him. Michael is socially responsive to peers and enjoys participating in a variety of activities.

Michael is enrolled in a multiability, prevocational high school program. Much of the instruction in this program takes place in community settings. Like other high school students, Michael has several different teachers across a typical school day. His special education teacher and his speech therapist work with his other teachers to individualize his vocational training and academic instruction to fit his communication abilities.

The new goals for communication training and the methods for accomplishing that training challenge teachers and therapists to change their behaviors as well. These changes are of two types.

1. Teachers must be both communicators and facilitators of communication.
2. Teachers must have an expanded repertoire of technical skills to ensure effective training.

The first change requires teachers to effectively communicate with students and to respond to the existing communication styles and modes of the students. The second change requires teachers to have skills in conversational interaction style, arranging the environment, behavior management, assessment, and specific techniques of language intervention. When teachers leave the one-to-one therapy setting and move into the classroom, the playground, and the community, they must adapt their teaching to fit the context.

Throughout this chapter, the term "teachers" is used to include any adult who teaches new communication skills—teachers, classroom assistants, speech and language clinicians, parents, and all other adults who interact with students to promote their communication development. Peers can also facilitate and support the use of new communication skills; however, their role will most often be as conversational partners or as a collaborator with an adult, rather than as an instructor.

Overview of Milieu Teaching

This chapter focuses on the use of Enhanced Milieu Teaching (EMT) strategies for communication intervention with individuals who have severe disabilities. Milieu Teaching is a naturalistic approach to teaching communication skills in everyday communication contexts, which uses environmental arrangement, specific natural prompts for language, and functional consequences to increase the frequency and complexity of students' communication. In discussing the principles of Milieu Teaching, we assume that most readers already have knowledge of basic direct instructional techniques. Figure 12–1 provides an overview of the components of effective Milieu Teaching. Thus, those techniques are not described in detail when they are referred to in the text. Our perspective in this chapter is largely behavioral, with a strong functional and social interactionist orientation. Core principles of effective communication and naturalistic teaching are derived from an eclectic theoretical base.

Many individuals with severe disabilities do not use the verbal modality as their primary means of communication. The principles outlined in this chapter can be applied to teaching alternative communication modes. In general, the same instructional procedures will be used. Several important points about alternative and augmentative communication in general should be noted.

FIGURE 12–1
Components of Effective Milieu
Teaching

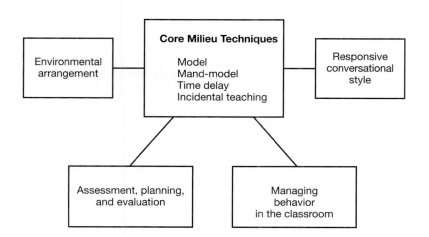

1. The selection of communication mode should be based on current student and environmental assessments (Romski & Sevcik, 1992; Wacker & Reichle, 1993). Choosing an appropriate mode of communication requires knowledge of the student's physical, cognitive, and intentional communication abilities and knowledge of the opportunities for and barriers to communication for the student. Expert assistance in evaluating students for use of alternative or augmentative communication modes should be sought.

2. In some cases, students may need exposure to or practice using a new mode of communication in addition to naturalistic teaching. For example, students may require initial practice in operating a computer-based communication system or in learning sufficient motor imitation skills to allow efficient imitation of a simple sign. These practice opportunities can occur concurrent with naturalistic teaching; there is no advantage to waiting until the student is "ready" for teaching in functional contexts.

3. In order for a communication system to be functional, the adults (and, ideally, peers) who will be the student's communication partners must have knowledge of the system sufficient for teaching and responding to the student's communicative attempts. Communication partners who are teaching new forms must have a repertoire of those forms so that they can model and expand in natural contexts.

4. There is no evidence to suggest that using an alternative communication mode reduces a student's chances of learning to speak; in contrast, pairing nonverbal and verbal communicative forms may facilitate learning both forms (Romski & Sevcik, 1992). Thus, introducing an augmentative or alternative system as soon as the student demonstrates the minimal cognitive and intentional communication abilities to support the use of the system is highly recommended. Spoken language can always be modeled concurrently to provide opportunities to learn both verbal and alternative forms of communication.

With these caveats in mind, examples of applications with learners who use alternative or augmentative systems have been included throughout the chapter.

The Goals of Language Intervention

The overriding goal of language intervention is to increase students' functional communication. As obvious as this goal is, functional communication can be forgotten in a classroom where several students have significant communication needs and teaching new skills requires many trials before acquisition of even a simple response is assured. Faced with the many needs and modest skill repertoires of individuals with severe disabilities, it is easy for teachers to lose sight of the goal of language intervention, which is increasing the students' ability to share information, feelings, and intentions with communication partners.

Communication as a Short-Term Target

There is a particular need to consider functional communication as a short-term training objective as well as a long-term goal. Target forms (words, signs, gestures) should be usable immediately. Although some potential targets may be logical in terms of existing skills, they may not be particularly functional in terms of immediate usefulness (e.g., naming colors is an early skill acquired by typical children, but this skill may not be immediately functional for students with severe disabilities and limited communication repertoires.) The specific form does not render a target dysfunctional. Instead, its usefulness in the student's communicative environment determines the function.

For example, emerging phonemes such as /ba/ and /ma/ are highly functional communication forms for very young children who are developing normally (see chapter 11). The caregivers for such young children attend to new phonetic forms as if those forms had communicative intent. In contrast, teaching Kristi to articulate early phonemes such as /ba/ and /ma/ will do little to increase her current functional communication skills unless persons in the environment respond to them in functional and systematic ways. Signs and picture selection are forms that Kristi can use immediately to indicate desired objects or activities are more functional choices for her.

Making Training Functional

Three steps can be taken to increase the functionality of short-term training targets: (a) select forms known to be functional in a particular setting frequented by the student; (b) teach the student to use new forms in a functional manner; and (c) prepare conversational partners in the environment to respond to new forms in ways that make these forms functional. Functional forms for training can be determined by observing the settings in which students spend time and noting the interactions in which they engage and the communication required to participate in those interactions.

By observing Kristi throughout her day, a list of communication opportunities can be compiled. Certainly, Kristi needs greeting skills as she gets on the bus and as she enters the classroom. She needs simple requests to obtain classroom materials and to ask for assistance. She needs to be able to indicate her food preferences at lunch. It would be enjoyable for her to be able to indicate to a peer that she would like to play and to comment on her favorite activities. From the list of opportunities, a set of potential target forms can take into account Kristi's preferences. It makes sense to teach generic forms (such as "help"); however, specific forms that allow students to acquire things she prefers (i.e., a hug, a favorite book, access to a computer game) also should be taught.

Forms become functional only when the environment responds to their use in particular ways. Teaching a form in its functional communicative context gives meaning to an otherwise arbitrary sign or word. That is, meaning derives from the consequences of attempted communication.

When Kristi signs "Julie come" and her friend joins her at the lunch table, she has demonstrated that she can express her communicative intent. Her signs have meaning and function for her.

Ensuring functional use may require intervention to help conversational partners become responsive to the emerging communication skills of students. This is particularly true when students are using an alternative communication mode, have unclear articulation, or have a history of limited language use. Often the greatest barrier that students must overcome is the effectiveness of less desirable strategies such as hitting or grabbing materials. If conversational partners respond more quickly and more consistently to these behaviors than to emerging forms of "standard" communication, it will be difficult to learn and use these new forms.

Functional Communication

Communication shares feelings, needs, or information. Functional communication begins with a con-

nection between people. It does not depend on the specific form of the communicative act or utterance.

In Kristi's case, signing her request for a friend to come is not functional unless her friend responds to the request. Her friend may need support from a teacher (such as a prompt to respond or a verbal interpretation of Kristi's sign) to understand and respond to Kristi's attempt to communicate. Training parents, classroom aides, community service providers (i.e., bus driver), and peers to pay attention and respond to such communication attempts is often critical for functional language intervention.

Effective social communication interventions, such as Milieu Teaching, require increasing the interaction skills of the target students and the conversational partners (Hunt, Alwell, & Goetz, 1988; Ostrosky, Kaiser, & Odom, 1993). Coaching peers to initiate communication and to respond to students' communication attempts may be nearly as important as teaching new forms. Similarly, supporting conversational interaction by providing a common topic (i.e., a photo album containing pictures of a student's family and favorite activities [Hunt et al., 1988]) or providing toys or activities enjoyed by both students with disabilities and their peers (Ostrosky et al., 1993) may be a necessary environmental change.

Lizabeth's 4-year-old classmates easily learned words for the five pictures in her communication book when their teacher used a large-group time to talk about ways to communicate. The teacher first asked the children to name some ways they let people know what they want. They talked about using words, about pointing, nodding heads, and taking things they wanted. The teacher showed them Lizabeth's book and asked them to name each picture. Some pictures were easy to name (i.e., potty, toy); others were a little harder (i.e., more, no, help). They practiced pointing to and naming the pictures. The teacher told them that Lizabeth was just learning to use these pictures to communicate. She suggested that they watch very carefully when Lizabeth pointed to a picture and that they say the name of the picture so Lizabeth could hear the word. Every day for 2 weeks after the initial large-group activity, the teacher asked the children to name a time when they had helped Lizabeth use her book. During play and snack, the teacher set up opportunities for Lizabeth to communicate with peers and used the Milieu Teaching strategies to prompt peer-directed communication.

When functional communication is the primary goal of language intervention, the intervention must occur in natural settings, address students' immediate communication needs, and enhance students' interactions with communication partners.

Milieu Teaching Strategies

Milieu Teaching refers to language and communication training procedures that are (a) brief and positive in nature, (b) carried out in the natural environment as opportunities for teaching functional communication occur, and (c) occasioned by student interest in the topic. Milieu Teaching (or incidental teaching, as it has sometimes been called) provides specific instruction about the form, the function, and the social use of language and is most effective when it is embedded in a responsive conversational style. Teaching opportunities that develop in the context of meaningful social interaction between partners with shared interests are most likely to result in learning new and functional forms of communication.

Guidelines for Milieu Teachers

- Teach when the student is interested.
- Teach what is functional for the student at the moment.
- Stop while both the student and the teacher are still enjoying the interaction.

There are important differences between traditional language instruction and Milieu Teaching. In traditional models of language instruction, the basic structure of the teaching interchanges is predetermined by the teacher's agenda for training. Specific trials are constructed to provide practice with particular linguistic forms, and standard consequences are selected to reinforce or correct the responses of students. For example, during a 20-minute session, a student might be presented with 30 opportunities to name common objects. Each time, the teacher holds up the object and says, "What is this?" When the student responds, the teacher praises her; if the student gives an incorrect answer or does not answer at all, the teacher models the correct response. Although Milieu Teaching shares some of these features, it differs in important ways. Teaching occurs in the natural environment in response to the interests of students and incorporates functional consequences. Successful Milieu Teaching more closely resembles a conversation than

a rote instructional episode. During Milieu Teaching, teachers or peers and the student communicate in a meaningful, responsive way.

In order to effectively use Milieu Teaching, teachers must:

1. Arrange the environment as a context for conversation.
2. Communicate with students using a responsive, interactive style.
3. Be able to fluently use the four core Milieu Teaching techniques (i.e., model, mand-model, time delay, and incidental teaching).
4. Be skilled in assessment and planning for Milieu Teaching.
5. Be sufficiently skilled in managing behavior to insure time, space, and opportunities for communication in the classroom.

Why Milieu Teaching Is Effective for Learners with Severe Disabilities

Milieu Teaching procedures are well-suited for teaching functional language skills to students with severe disabilities.

Michael is a 15-year-old student with mental retardation and a moderate hearing loss. When teaching Michael new language skills, Michael's teachers match his intentions (e.g., greeting, answering, requesting, commenting) and the complexity of his language (e.g., single words with some simple two-word requests). They model appropriate new vocabulary and two- and three-word phrases when his attention is focused on something of interest to him in the environment (e.g., a favorite material, an activity, a peer), when he has a specific need or desire, or when he can make a choice. Michael uses both verbalizations and pictures to communicate; teachers model using language and pictures.

Teachers attempt to fit their requests for language and their models as closely as possible to Michael's emerging skills. They teach forms that are just slightly more advanced than his current spontaneous language. Since Michael uses a few two-word utterances, such as "want" plus a noun (e.g., "want Coke") to make requests, the teachers work to expand Michael's requesting repertoire by modeling a variety of new nouns in combination with the verb "want" and by adding a pronoun (e.g., "I want chips"). Modeling a new form occurs as Michael attends to the specific aspect of the environment that a new label describes. Teachers update Michael's communication book by pointing to the pictures representing new labels while verbally modeling the complete utterance.

Successful Milieu Teaching occurs only when a student's language works to control the immediate environment. Teaching new requesting forms is most effective when Michael has indicated his desire for a specific object (e.g., his favorite record, his new baseball cap, another sandwich) or a specific activity (e.g., getting a soft drink, getting assistance in putting on his sweater). Initiations and requests signal that Michael has specific communicative intentions and that he already has made discriminations among many aspects of the communication context (e.g., what he wants, the presence of a cooperative partner, that language is needed to communicate his request). Prompting or modeling language that matches Michael's intentions helps him learn how language functions to control the environment. Furthermore, requiring elaborated language also teaches Michael that specific forms work more effectively than general or incomplete ones.

Modeling a New Form in a Functional Context

Michael: (*Reaching for a videotape that has fallen on the floor next to the teacher*)

Teacher: *Want tape* [*model plus point to the picture of tape*]

Michael: *Want it.*

Teacher: *Say "Want <u>tape</u>"* [*corrective modeling plus point to the picture*]

Michael: *Want tape.* (*Pointing to picture*)

Teacher: *Oh, you want the tape* (*points to the picture*). *Here, let me get it for you.* (*Picks up tape from the floor and hands it to him.*)

Milieu Teaching also may help students develop strategies that increase their naturally occurring language learning. Michael is being taught to attend to both the presence of a conversational partner and his own needs as opportunities to talk. When he initiates, his verbal behavior results in specific consequences. Thus, Milieu Teaching is likely to increase Michael's initiations and positive interactions with adults.

Milieu Teaching promotes establishment of response classes, composed of functionally equivalent communication forms. In Milieu Teaching episodes, Michael hears at least two utterances that serve the same purpose: the original form he produces and the elaborated form that is modeled by the teacher.

When Michael requests more milk at lunch by saying "milk" and pointing to the picture of milk, his teacher models a

slightly more elaborate request, "milk, please." Michael has an opportunity to equate his existing single-word request with a more polite form of requesting. When teachers and his parents provide Michael with another container of milk accompanied by additional descriptive talk (e.g., "it's chocolate milk" or "yes, you can have more milk"), several forms are paired with the same function during a very brief interaction.

Finally, teaching in communicative contexts facilitates generalization to other conversational interactions. Teaching incorporates a variety of stimuli that occur in naturalistic contexts. Thus, students are not likely to become "stimulus-bound" to the same extent observed after traditional one-to-one training. Teaching in response to Michael's attention to a specific object or event increases the likelihood that Michael will learn new labels and simple request forms without the use of massed trials and intensive practice or teacher-selected reinforcers that may mitigate against generalization.

Milieu Teaching Procedures

This section describes four Milieu Teaching procedures: (a) modeling, (b) the mand-model procedure, (c) the time delay procedure, and (d) the incidental teaching procedure. Table 12–1 summarizes the teaching techniques used in each of these procedures.

Modeling

Modeling is used during the initial stages of teaching a new form, when a student has not acquired independent production of the form. Modeling may be considered the most fundamental Milieu Teaching process. The four primary goals of child-directed modeling are (a) building turn-taking skills, (b) training generalized imitation skills, (c) establishing a basic vocabulary, and (d) participating in conversations that occur outside the training context. Modeling can be used in environments that are arranged to facilitate communication by students. The teacher first establishes joint attention[1] by focusing attention on the

---

[1]Joint attention refers to an occasion when two communication partners (e.g., teacher and student; two peers) are simultaneously attending to each other, the same material, or activity. Joint attention increases the level of engagement between partners and the likelihood of shared communication.

TABLE 12–1
A Summary of Milieu Language Teaching Techniques

Model Procedure	Mand-Model Procedure
• Use the model procedure to teach new forms. • Note student interest. • Establish joint attention. • Present a verbal model related to the student's interest. • A correct student response receives immediate praise, verbal expansion, and (when material is being withheld) access to material. • An incorrect or absent student response is followed by a corrective model. • A correct student response receives immediate praise, verbal expansion, and access to material. • An incorrect or absent response to the corrective model is followed by corrective feedback plus access to material.	• Use the mand-model procedure to prompt functional use of emerging forms. • Note student interest. • Establish joint attention. • Present a verbal mand related to student interest. • A correct student response receives immediate praise, verbal expansion, and (when material is being withheld) access to material. • An incorrect or absent student response is followed by a second mand (when student attention is high and when the student is likely to know the answer) or a model (when student interest is waning and the student is unlikely to know the answer). • A correct response to a mand or model is followed by immediate praise, verbal expansion, and access to material. • Steps involved in the model procedure follow an incorrect student response to a corrective mand or model.
Time Delay Procedure	**Incidental Teaching Procedure**

• Use time delay to teach more spontaneous use of emerging forms.
 	
• Identify occasions when a student is likely to need materials or assistance.
 	
• Establish joint attention.
 	
• Introduce time delay.
 	
• A correct student response (i.e., student communicates what he or she needs) receives immediate praise, verbal expansion, and materials or assistance.
 	
• An incorrect or absent student response is followed by application of the mand-model procedure (if student interest is high and the student is likely to know the answer) or application of the model procedure (if student interest is waning and the student is unlikely to know the answer).
	• Use incidental teaching whenever the student requests.
	
	• Identify occasions when a student is verbally or nonverbally requesting materials or assistance.
	
	• Establish joint attention.
	
	• Use the occasion to teach more intelligible, complex, or elaborated language/communication skills by applying steps of the:
	  a. Model procedure (use to train new or difficult forms or structures or to improve intelligibility).
	  b. Mand-model procedure (use to train complexity and conversational skills).
	  c. Time delay procedure (use to train a student to initiate verbal or nonverbal communicative behavior about environmental stimuli).

student and on what the student is interested in. Next, the teacher presents a verbal model that is related to the student's immediate interest. If the student imitates the model correctly, immediate positive feedback (which includes an expansion of the student's response) and the material of interest are offered to the student. Then, the student's response is expanded to present another model of more complex language for future responses.

If the student does not respond to the initial model or responds with an unintelligible, partial, incorrect, or unrelated response, the teacher estab-

lishes joint attention again and presents the model a second time (a corrective model). Figure 12–2 is a picture of Scotty pointing in his yearbook and his mother providing a corrective model for Scotty to try again. A correct student response again results in immediate positive feedback and expansion of the student's utterance and access to the material. If an incorrect response follows the corrective model, the teacher provides corrective feedback by stating the desired response and then gives the topic material to the student. All milieu procedures have a modeling component that includes the steps described here.

FIGURE 12–2

Scotty points out his friend in his year book. In response to his pointing, his mother prompts him to say his friend's name by modeling "Karen." When Scotty approximates ("Aren") the modeled name, his mother provides a corrective model ("Karen") and waits for Scotty to try again.

Figure 12–3 is a flowchart showing the steps of the modeling procedure.

Modeling Language that Matches the Student's Intention

Michael: (*Touching the front of his jacket and looking at the teacher.*)

Teacher: Say, "New jacket." (*Model is followed by a teacher pause to give the student time to respond.*)

Michael: . . . *jacket.*

Teacher: <u>New</u> *jacket.*

Michael: *New jacket.*

Teacher: *Oh, I like your new jacket! Let me see the back.*

Modeling may be used to increase the complexity of Michael's requesting. Michael and two peers are taking videotapes from the shelf to play on the VCR. Michael looks at his friend, who is holding a favorite videotape, and gestures to request the friend to give the tape to him.

Teacher: *Tell Jamie, "Play tape"* [model]

Michael: *Play.* [partial student response]

Teacher: *Play* <u>tape</u>. [corrective model]

Michael: *Play tape.* [correct student response]

Teacher: *Right, you want Jamie to play the tape for you. Let's help him put it in the VCR.* [acknowledgment + expansion + natural consequence]

Mand-Model Procedure

The mand-model procedure was developed by Rogers-Warren [Kaiser] and Warren (1980) to actively program for the generalization of language skills from one-to-one sessions to the classroom. Generalization was programmed by training classroom teachers to increase the number of opportunities for students to display newly learned language in the classroom.

FIGURE 12–3
The Model Procedure Flowchart

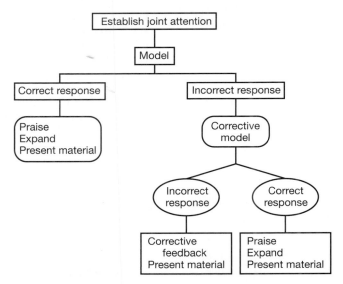

During the mand-model procedure, a variety of interesting materials are provided. When a student approaches a material (toy truck), the teacher mands (verbally instructs) the student to request what he wants (e.g., "Tell me what you want"). If the student gives an appropriate response, the teacher responds positively and descriptively (e.g., "Okay, you want the red truck") and provides the requested material. If the student does not respond or gives an incorrect response, the teacher provides a model for the student to imitate. By presenting two choices, the teacher allows the student to make language immediately functional in indicating his choice.

Use of the mand-model procedure is arranged and initiated by teachers. Teachers are responsive to what students are interested in and only present mands when there is a meaningful opportunity for the student to control the environment through communication. The particular goals toward which the mand-model process is directed are (a) establishing joint attention (topic selection) as a cue for verbalization, (b) teaching turn-taking skills, (c) teaching students to provide information on verbal request or instruction, and (d) teaching students to respond to a variety of adult verbal cues. The mand-model procedure differs from modeling by including a nonimitative verbal prompt in the form of a question (e.g., "What do you need?") or a choice (e.g., "We have crayons or paints; which one would you like?") or a mand (e.g., "Tell Jamie what you want"). The presentation of corrective models of appropriate responses when a student responds incorrectly or fails to respond to the mand (i.e., question, choice, or request) is identical to the sequence in the model procedure. Figure 12–4 is a picture of Jeremy and his mother Karen, illustrating the mand-model procedure.

Michael and two peers are taking tapes from the shelf to play on the VCR. Michael looks at his friend, who is holding a favorite tape and gestures to request the friend to give the tape to him.

Teacher: *Tell Jamie what you want. [mand]*

Michael: *(No response.)*

Teacher: *Say, "Play tape please." [model]*

Michael: *Play tape. [partial student response]*

Teacher: *Play tape, please. [corrective model]*

Michael: *Play tape, please. [correct student response]*

FIGURE 12–4

Jeremy and Karen are waiting for the picnic lunch to be served. Karen asks Jeremy what he wants for lunch (a mand). Jeremy presses the symbol for sandwich. Karen expands his response and acknowledges his choice ("Oh, you want a sandwich. That's a great choice. I hope we have sandwiches for lunch.")

Teacher: *You asked Jamie to play the tape please. Jamie can you play the tape for Michael? [acknowledgment + natural consequences; Note that the teacher facilitates the peer providing the natural consequence for Michael's verbal request.]*

Choice-making mands are particularly effective variants of the mand-model procedure. Choice-making mands begin with a statement to students about the available choices (e.g., "There are cheese sandwiches and peanut butter sandwiches for lunch"). They are followed by asking students to indicate a preference (e.g., "What would you like?"). The subsequent steps are identical to those just described. Asking students to indicate a preference using a question or request form that the students are likely to hear in everyday conversations promotes generalization in similar but unprogrammed choice situations.

Real questions or real choices form the basis of the mand-model procedure. Real questions and choices allow the student to truly communicate preferences and gain control over the environment. In contrast, questions that test the student's knowledge or seek only to get the student to perform a response are not truly functional communication exchanges because the adult already knows the answer. Use of the mand-model procedure should support students in becoming more independent and teachers in learning to ask for and respond to student preferences.

Time Delay Procedure

Conversation should involve not only responding to another person's models and mands for verbalization but also initiating communication about various aspects of the environment. The time delay procedure was developed to establish environmental stimuli instead of simply presenting models and mands as cues for verbalization. The effects of the time delay procedure alone were experimentally demonstrated in studies by Halle and his colleagues (Halle, Baer, & Spradlin, 1981; Halle, Marshall, & Spradlin, 1979). Adults in these studies (e.g., care-giving staff members and teachers) were instructed to attend to individual students by introducing a time delay in situations where the students were likely to need assistance or materials. Time delay has also been used in combination with interrupting a chain of behaviors (Gee, Graham, Goetz, Oshima, & Yoshioka, 1991) and with a systematic reduction in prompting (Gee, Graham, Sailor, & Goetz, 1995). For example, when a student is assembling a pizza box as part of his vocational training, he learns sequential steps: (a) Place cardboard, (b) fold along lines, (c) tuck end tabs, (d) secure with tape, and (e) fold down top). A time delay just before step d might be used to prompt the student to request help from his job coach to "hold please."

Steps of the time delay procedure include:

1. The teacher is in proximity to and looking at the student.
2. The teacher pauses when student attends to the material (e.g., looks at job coach and then at box) or nonverbally signals his communicative intent (e.g., points to the object).
3. Positive feedback and immediately offering the desired material or assistance follow student verbalizations.
4. Verbal prompts follow incorrect student responses.

The time delay procedure may be used effectively in prompting Michael's language interactions with persons in the community. The teacher casually may block the door while talking to another student until Michael verbalizes and points to a picture ("Open, please"). A cafeteria worker may hold on to Michael's tray until he requests it ("Tray, please").

Any regular routine, (e.g., entering and exiting a classroom, cleaning up after an activity, transitioning into a new task) may be interrupted by pausing between routine steps, focusing attention on the student as a prompt for communication, waiting for a communicative request, and finally, providing the requested action when the student communicates.

Michael is assembling a bicycle gear by taking parts from each of six containers and fitting them together.

Teacher: (*Placing her hand over the second container in a natural way, she looks up at Michael and waits for him to verbalize.*) [*delay or pause 2 to 5 seconds*]

Michael: Washer. [*partial student response*]

Teacher: Say, "Want washer." [*corrective model*]

Michael: Want washer. [*correct student response*]

Teacher: Yes, Michael, you want a washer. Help yourself. [*acknowledgment + expansion + natural consequence*]

Time delay alone or in combination with other fading and chaining procedures may be especially useful with students who are echolalic (e.g., frequently imitate or repeat the exact words spoken to them). Often students with autistic characteristics repeat the last words of a prompt. The use of nonverbal prompting helps avoid the automatic echoing of a response and transfers stimulus control to the social and contextual cues. For students like Carter, time delays may prompt language without inadvertently eliciting echoic responses.

Teacher walks up to Carter as he comes down the hall toward his homeroom and locker.

Teacher: "Hi, Carter."

Carter: "Hi, Carter." (*echoic response*)

Teacher: (*Casually stands in front of Carter's locker then looks up at him*) (*time delay*)

Carter: "Move!"

Teacher: "I will move. Now you can get in your locker." Moves aside to give Carter access. [*acknowledgment + expansion + natural consequence*]

Incidental Teaching Procedure

A fourth strategy has been developed for teaching more elaborate language and for improving conversational skills about particular topics. Incidental teaching is used when the student makes a request. The first step in the incidental teaching procedure is arranging the environment in ways that encourage the student to request materials and assistance. This can be achieved by attractively displaying potential reinforcers within the student's view but out of reach. A student who verbally or nonverbally requests materials or assistance is identifying what is a reinforcer at that moment. The teacher responds by modeling, manding, or delaying for a more elaborated response or for additional information. When the student responds appropriately, the teacher gives the item of interest while affirming and repeating the answer in an expanded fashion (thereby presenting a model of more complex language for future student responses).

If the student does not respond appropriately to the mand or time delay prompts, the teacher instructs the student to imitate a model of an appropriate elaboration. The adult then confirms the accuracy of the student's imitation, repeats and expands what the student said, and gives the student whatever he or she requested. Because teaching to a reinforcer is possible only as long as the item or event is really of interest to the student, episodes are brief and positive in nature. Ability to request verbally or nonverbally and ability to imitate target forms are the only prerequisite student skills for incidental teaching.

> *Carter and a peer have been taken to a variety store to purchase a birthday present for a classmate. They are looking at a rack of baseball caps.*
>
> *Carter*: (*Pointing to a blue cap.*) *Cap.* [*initiation*]
>
> *Teacher*: *Tell me which one you like.* [*mand*]
>
> *Carter*: (*Continuing to point.*)
>
> *Teacher*: *Say, "Blue cap."* [*corrective model*]
>
> *Carter*: *Blue cap.* [*correct student response*]
>
> *Teacher*: *Here you go. You like the blue cap. Do you think Jimmy will like this one?* [*natural consequence + acknowledgment + expansion*]
>
> *Carter*: (*Nodding his head yes.*)

Figure 12–5 is a flowchart showing the incidental teaching procedure. Note that student requests may be followed by the model, mand-model, or time delay procedure.

When to Use Each of the Four Procedures

Two general guidelines apply when selecting one of the four Milieu Teaching procedures. First, select the procedure that is the most natural to the ongoing interaction. For example, asking a question (using the mand-model procedure) is natural when a student's intentions or desires are not clear or when asking for

FIGURE 12–5
The Incidental Teaching Procedure Flowchart

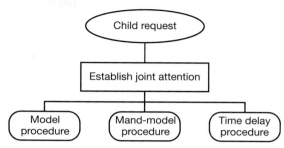

specification would be usual (e.g., "Would you like milk or iced tea?"). The model procedure is used whenever the student does not know the appropriate response. For example, if the student does not know the name of an object, it is appropriate to begin by modeling the label for the student to imitate (e.g., "These are Lego blocks").

Second, use the procedure that provides the level of support the student needs to make an appropriate communicative response. Modeling provides maximum support for a student's response; time delay provides no initial verbal support. The mand-model procedure provides a middle level of support and can be tailored to fit a student's skills by either asking a question only or providing two named choices followed by a question (e.g., "I have cheese sandwiches and peanut butter sandwiches. What do you want?").

Incidental teaching differs from the other three procedures because it always follows a student request. Thus, incidental teaching should be used only when the student has made a request. Requests can be verbal, vocal, or gestural. How the teacher responds to the student's request in order to prompt elaborated language depends on the level of support the student requires to respond appropriately. In all uses of the Milieu Teaching procedures, incomplete or incorrect student responses are followed by support for a correct response (i.e., if a student cannot respond to a mand, a model of the correct response is offered.) Every episode includes a positive consequence, continuing communication, and modeling of an expanded form of the prompted response. The goals in all applications of the procedures are to ensure that the interaction is as communicative, natural, and positive as possible and that interactions end with the students' gaining the specified reinforcers.

Learning to notice individual students' varied forms of requesting is a challenging task for teachers who want to use incidental teaching. Echoes, utterances, repeated gestures, and problem behavior that are not prototypical forms of communication (e.g., banging a hand on the table) and vocalizations with and without gestures may be requests. For students with limited physical mobility, eye gaze and head turns may function as requests. Students with autism and limited verbal skills may have very few obvious requests, but systematic observation can help in identifying their unique forms and reinforcers.

Environmental Arrangement Strategies

Children learn what language is by learning what language can do (Bates, 1976; Hart, 1985). The function of language depends upon its effect on the environment, and a critical aspect of Milieu Teaching is environmental arrangement. An environment that contains few reinforcers, few objects of interest, or meets students' needs without requiring language is not a functional environment for promoting language. Settings where peers have limited communication skills can also limit students' opportunities for learning and using communication skills. Environments in which language teaching takes place should be designed to recruit and capture students' interests in materials and events. Such environments increase opportunities for Milieu Teaching and facilitate communicative initiations, such as requesting and commenting by students.

Using the environment to prompt language involves (a) a focus on making language part of students' routines, (b) including interesting materials and activities in the environment, (c) providing adults and peers who encourage students to use language and who respond to their attempts to communicate, and (d) establishing a contingent relationship between access to materials or assistance and language use during at least some routines and activities. Research suggests that environmental arrangement is an important strategy for teachers who want to promote communication in classrooms (Alpert, Kaiser, Hemmeter, & Ostrosky, 1987; Haring, Neetz, Lovinger, Peck, & Semmel, 1987). To encourage the use of language, classrooms and other communication settings should be arranged so that interesting materials and activities are available. Teachers should

mediate the environment by presenting desired materials and activities in response to students' requests and other uses of language (Hart & Rogers-Warren [Kaiser], 1978). Contingent provision of desired materials serves the important function of reinforcing language use.

Six environmental strategies have been shown to increase the likelihood that students will show interest in the environment and make communicative attempts and that teachers will prompt language about things of interest to the students. These strategies include (a) providing interesting materials, (b) placing some materials in sight but out of reach, (c) providing small portions of needed or desired materials, (d) providing choice-making opportunities, (e) setting up situations in which students need assistance, and (f) creating unexpected situations. The goal is to provide clear and obvious prompts. Attractive materials and activities function as both discriminative stimuli and reinforcers for language use. Table 12–2 summarizes and gives examples of these six environmental strategies.

Interesting Materials

Materials and activities that students enjoy should be available in the environment. Students are most likely to initiate communication about the things that interest them. Thus, increasing interest in the environment increases the likelihood of language use as well as opportunities for language teaching. It may be helpful to assess students' preferences and to arrange settings so that preferred materials and activities are included. Age appropriateness and context appropriateness should be considered along with the students' preferences.

Environmental arrangement can be used to promote peer interactions. Peers can provide assistance, additional materials, present choice-making opportunities, and interact in the context of interesting materials. With peers present, the teacher can mediate the interaction (i.e., provide prompts to the student to address the peer: "Tell Janie, I want another turn shooting the basket"). Alternatively, peers can be taught simplified milieu strategies to use directly with the student. (See Hancock & Kaiser, 1996, for an example.)

Guidelines for Milieu Teaching by Peers

- Environmental arrangement supports both the peer and the student.

TABLE 12–2
Arranging the Environment to Encourage Communication

1. **Interesting materials.** Students are likely to communicate when things or activities in the environment interest them.

   Example: James lay quietly on the rug, with his head resting on his arms. Ms. Davis sat at one end of the rug and rolled a big yellow ball right past James. James lifted his head and looked around for the ball.

2. **Out of reach.** Students are likely to communicate when they want something that they cannot reach.

   Example: Mr. Norris lifted a drum off the shelf and placed it on the floor between Judy and Annette, who were both in wheelchairs. Mr. Norris hit the drum three times and then waited, looking at his two students. Judy watched and clapped her hands together. Then, she reached for the drum with both arms outstretched.

3. **Inadequate portions.** Students are likely to communicate when they do not have the necessary materials to carry out an instruction.

   Example: Mr. Robinson gave every student except Mary a ticket to get into the auditorium for the high school play. He told his students to give their tickets to the attendant. Mr. Robinson walked beside Mary toward the entrance. When Mary reached the attendant, Mr. Robinson paused and looked at Mary. She pointed to the tickets in his hand and signed, "Give me." Mr. Robinson gave her a ticket and she handed it to the attendant who said, "Thank you. Enjoy the play."

4. **Choice-making.** Students are likely to communicate when they are given a choice.

   Example: Peggy's favorite pastime is listening to tapes on her tape recorder. On Saturday morning, Peggy's father said to her, "We could listen to your tapes" (pointing to the picture of the tape recorder on Peggy's communication board) "or we could go for a ride in the car" (pointing to the picture of the car). "What would you like to do?" Peggy pointed to the picture of the tape recorder. "OK, let's listen to this new tape you like," her father said as he put the tape in and turned on the machine.

5. **Assistance.** Students are likely to communicate when they need assistance in operating or manipulating materials.

   Example: Tammy's mother always places three clear plastic containers with snacks (cookies, crackers, popcorn) on the kitchen table before Tammy returns from school. When Tammy arrives home and is ready for a snack, she goes to the table and chooses what she wants. The containers are hard to open, so Tammy usually brings the container with her chosen snack to her mother. Her mother responds to this nonverbal request by modeling a request form that specifies Tammy's choice (e.g., "Open popcorn.")

6. **Unexpected situations.** Students are likely to communicate when something happens that they do not expect.

   Example: Ms. Esser was helping Kathy put on her socks and shoes after rest time. After assisting with the socks, Ms. Esser put one of the shoes on her own foot. Kathy stared at the shoe for a moment and then looked up at her teacher, who was smiling. "No," laughed Kathy, "my shoe."

- Simple prompt sequences are used: only one prompt; correction, if needed; positive natural consequences.
- Emphasize functional use.
- Keep interactions positive and teaching brief.

Out of Reach

Placing some desirable materials within view but out of the students' reach prompts students to make requests to gain access to the materials. Materials may be placed on shelves, in clear plastic bins, or simply across a table during a group activity. Students' requests create opportunities for language teaching. When students request a specific material, they are specifying their reinforcer at that moment (Hart & Rogers-Warren [Kaiser], 1978). Thus, a teacher who prompts language and provides the requested mater-

ial after a communicative response effectively reinforces that response. For students who have limited motor skills, materials should be within their visual field, slightly out of reach, and far enough apart from other materials to allow a teacher or peer to interpret the nonverbal or verbal requests.

At home, Carter's mother keeps three of his favorite objects (i.e., a pack of baseball cards, a small trophy from his softball team, and a yo-yo) on the window sill above the sink. At supper time, Carter likes to be in the kitchen with her while she cooks dinner and later cleans up. Carter cannot reach over the sink to the window. He initiates by pointing and naming the object he wants. Carter's mother uses this opportunity to prompt a short sentence (e.g., "I want yo-yo") in an incidental teaching episode. Responding to Carter's initiations also reminds his mom to take a few minutes to talk to

Carter during this busy time of day. Her attention to his initiations also supports his positive behavior at a time of day when he presents challenging behavior.

Inadequate Portions

Providing small or inadequate portions of preferred materials (e.g., blocks, crackers, or turns on a computer game) is another way to arrange the environment to promote communication. During an activity that the students enjoy, the teacher can control the materials so that the students have only a limited amount. When the students have used the materials initially provided, they are likely to request more. When they initiate with requests for more, the adult has the opportunity to model and prompt more elaborate language as well as to provide functional consequences for the communicative attempts. Teachers may also set up the environment so that students request materials from each other.

Choice Making

On many occasions, two or more options of activities or materials can be presented so that students can make a choice. To encourage students to initiate language, the choice may be presented nonverbally (e.g., by holding up two tools for opening a carton in either hand or by presenting three snack options on a tray). Students may be most encouraged to make a choice when one of the items is much more preferred and the other is much less preferred or disliked. Figure 12–6 is a picture of Scotty shooting baskets with his mother.

> *Lizabeth's teacher sets up a tray with two options at snack time: apples and crackers with peanut butter. She asks a peer to offer each child in the class a choice of snacks. Lizabeth prefers apples and does not like peanut butter. When the peer holds out the tray with choices and Lizabeth reaches for the apples, the teacher points to the picture of apples in Lizabeth's communication book and says "Oh Lizzie, you want apples. Good choice!" After the snack routine is established, the teacher will prompt Lizabeth to indicate to the peer what she wants using her book (e.g., the teacher will say, "Show Peter what you want," as she places the communication book where Lizabeth can respond.)*

Assistance

Creating a situation where students are likely to need assistance increases the likelihood of communication

FIGURE 12–6
Scotty loves to shoot baskets. His mother uses the opportunity to prompt Scotty to indicate that he wishes to continue the game. She use a choice mand; "Should we stop or play more?" Scotty says and signs "More." His mom replies, "Great, we'll shoot some more baskets."

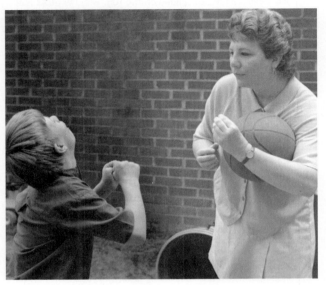

about that need. Attractive materials that require assistance may encourage students to request help. For example, a difficult-to-open container of a preferred food (e.g., chocolate milk) may provide an excellent opportunity to prompt "open" or "help."

Unexpected Situations

The final environmental strategy is to create a need for communication by setting up situations that violate the expectations of students. Children learn routines and expect that things will happen in a particular order. When something unexpected happens, they may be prompted to communicate. Of course, use of this strategy must be tailored to the individual skills of the students and to their familiar routines. Sometimes, students need support in recognizing an unexpected situation. The teacher may need to indicate to the student that something is funny or unusual.

Ideally, use of the environmental strategies results in attracting students' interest and evoking communicative responses. Teachers should either reinforce an acceptable response or use a Milieu Teaching procedure to prompt a corrected response or a more complex verbal response. If the environmental strategy captures students' attention but does not evoke communication, teachers should use a Milieu Teaching procedure to prompt a contextually relevant and appropriate response.

Nonverbal cues accompanying the environmental arrangement strategies should be faded out over time so that students are responding more to things of interest in the environment and less to arranged cues (Halle et al., 1979). For example, it may be necessary at first for teachers to shrug their shoulders, raise their eyebrows, and tilt their head while extending their hands containing two different materials, in order to direct students' attention to the materials and to the opportunity for choice making. As students become more skilled at initiating requests, teachers should give fewer and less obvious nonverbal prompts.

Environmental strategies must be tailored to each student's cognitive level and responsiveness to the environment. For example, unexpected situations depend on students noticing unusual or unexpected happenings. If a student does not notice, there is no opportunity to practice a communicative response. Environmental strategies are most effective when they cue communicative responses that are emergent in students' repertoires. Environmental arrangements provide nonverbal cues for communication. Thus, they may help students progress toward a more spontaneous use of their newly acquired skills.

> *Inadequate portions of Kristi's favorite food at lunch serves as a cue for her to spontaneously attempt to sign "more."*

> *When a peer who is handing out passes for the Friday night football game gives Michael only one pass (a planned implementation of inadequate portions), Michael says, "Want more."*

How teachers and others respond to students' communication attempts when these attempts are elicited by environmental arrangement is extremely important. Immediate attention, feedback, and access to the desired material or requested assistance, as well as a positive response, are essential for reinforcing communication attempts. As in all applications of Milieu Teaching, episodes that begin with environmental arrangement should be brief, positive, successful for students, and reinforcing for the use of language and social engagement with adults.

The best uses of environmental arrangement are truly natural, thereby creating opportunities for functional communication. Providing choices is a strategy that can be used naturally in many different contexts. Other strategies, such as inadequate portions and out of reach, should be used carefully and not overused. Environmental arrangement can also support peer communication. Peers can present materials and activities when the student requests. It is important to help peers understand the basic principles of Milieu Teaching if they are going to be prompting specific forms of communication (e.g., teach to the students' interests, be positive, keep episodes short, and always follow through with natural consequences), but increasing responding to student communication may require only brief instructions and feedback to peers.

Responsive Conversational Style

One of the important evolutions in Milieu Teaching and other forms of naturalistic communication intervention during the last few years is the greater emphasis on responsive conversational style (Kaiser, Hancock & Hester, 1998).

Responsive conversational style is a general interaction approach that supports students' communication and greatly enhances the naturalistic qualities of Milieu Teaching. Responsive conversational style sets a social context for language in the same way that environmental arrangement sets a physical context. Together, responsive conversational style and environmental arrangement create a supportive interactional context for conversation-based teaching. When a responsive interaction is established between teachers and students, communication is ongoing and offers many opportunities for specific but highly natural teaching. Responsive conversational style has four components:

1. Establishment of joint and mutual attention
2. Turn-taking
3. Contingent responsiveness
4. Positive affect

Joint attention occurs when teachers and students are focused on the same activity or material. For example, when a teacher watches closely while a student moves a toy truck back and forth on the floor in front of him, the teacher and student are jointly attending to the student's activity. Mutual attention occurs when students and teachers look at each other as they talk. In an ideal conversation, there is both joint attention to the student's ongoing activity and mutual attention between the student and the teacher. Joint attention allows teachers to focus their comments and requests for language on the objects and activities that are of immediate interest to the students. Mutual attention helps maintain communicative engagement between the conversational partners and increases the likelihood that students' requests and comments will be understood and responded to appropriately.

Turn-taking refers to the exchange of communication turns by students and teachers in a conversation. Ideally, conversational turns are balanced so that each communicator's turns are of similar length and complexity. Turns can be taken nonverbally or verbally. Many students with severe disabilities initiate infrequently. Thus, developing a more even balance of turns may require teachers to talk less, to take shorter turns, and to attend carefully to the students' attempts to communicate and various ways of taking turns. Pausing to allow time for students to respond is an easy way to increase opportunities for students to take their turns. Ending an adult turn with a question (i.e., a turnabout) can also promote student turn-taking; but the adult must ask a question the student understands and then wait for a response.

The following examples illustrate balanced and unbalanced turn-taking.

Unbalanced Turn-Taking

Mr. G.: *Hi there, Markus! What are you doing? Do you like that puzzle? It's a baseball player.*

Markus: *Me ball, too.*

Mr. G.: *Oh, you like baseball? Do you watch baseball on TV? I never miss a game. I watched three games this weekend. Well, it's time to clean up. Do you need some help? Ok, you do it. I'll be back.*

Balanced Turn-Taking

Mr. G.: *Hi there, Markus! (Pause.)*

Markus: *Hi!*

Mr. G.: *Hey, you've got the baseball player. (Pause.)*

Markus: *Me ball, too.*

Mr. G.: *You like baseball?*

Markus: *(Nods yes.)*

Mr. G.: *You like baseball. I bet you watch it on TV.*

Markus: *Me. (Nods yes.)*

Mr. G.: *You watch baseball on TV.*

Contingent responsiveness means that teachers respond to students' communication attempts quickly and meaningfully. Noticing and responding to student communication attempts are essential in establishing a conversation. Such responsiveness reinforces attempts to communicate and indicates to students that teachers are available as communication partners. Although some attempts will be missed in the context of a busy classroom, teachers should seek to be as responsive to student communication attempts as possible. When students communicate at low rates and there are relatively few potential communication partners in a setting, teacher responsiveness is especially important.

Meaningful adult responses are related to the communicative intention, or functional content, of the students' utterances. These utterances continue the students' topics. To respond in a meaningful way, teachers must try to understand what it is that students wish to communicate and tailor their responses accordingly. The communicative attempts of students with severe language disabilities are not always easily understood. However, when teachers have established joint and mutual attention and have arranged the environment to promote communication, understanding students' messages is easier. The following examples contrast a conversation in which a teacher is contingently responsive with one in which she is not.

Contingently Responsive Conversation

Marci is emptying her backpack (a book, her glasses, a note from her mother, a package of tissues). Her teacher, Mrs. B., is standing by Marci's locker, waiting for Marci to finish.

Marci: *(Takes out her glasses and looks at them.)*

Mrs. B.: *Oh, Marci, there are your glasses. (Pause.) Shall I help you put them on?*

Marci: *(Hands Mrs. B. the glasses and looks at her.)*

Mrs. B.: *(Takes the glasses, looks back at Marci, smiles, and then helps Marci put the glasses on.)*

Marci: *(Takes out the note from her mother and plays with it.)*

Mrs. B.: *You brought a note from your mom. (Watches Marci and pauses.) Marci, is that note for me?*

Marci: *Note. Yes.*

Mrs. B.: *(Looks at Marci and extends her hand. Waits.)*

Marci: *Here. (Gives note.)*

Mrs. B.: *Why, thank you, Marci. Let's see what your mom has to say. (Holds note where she and Marci can look at it while she reads it.)*

Noncontingent Conversation

Mrs. B.: *Good morning, Marci. Put your things away and come sit down.*

Marci: *(Takes out her glasses.)*

Mrs. B.: *Hurry, Marci. We're running late.*

Marci: *(Takes out a note from her mother.)*

Mrs. B.: *(Reaches for note and takes it.) Thank you. I'll read this later.*

Marci: *Note?*

Mrs. B.: *Hurry. It's late.*

Positive affect includes smiling, gentle touching, use of the student's name, a warm tone of voice, and an affirming style of interaction. Students who have limited verbal communication may be particularly sensitive to the nonverbal messages that communication partners send. Teachers who indicate their interest in a student by making themselves physically available and affirming students' attempts to communicate invite conversation. In contrast, adults or peers who speak loudly, do not match their pace and style to that of the students and who are not gentle in their physical contact with students discourage communication, even if they do not intend to do so. Positive affect indicates interest, liking, respect, and availability for conversations with students. Positive affect should be an ongoing aspect of interactions with students who have severe disabilities as well as creating a social context for Milieu Teaching.

Michael's job coach is careful to establish physical contact with him at the beginning of a work period. He greets Michael face to face and shakes his hand or touches his shoulder. He expresses his positive regard for Michael with smiles, nods, and gestures as well as words. Because Michael has a hearing loss, his job coach makes sure peers also communicate with Michael with their facial expressions, physical proximity, gentle touching, and gestures.

Peers may need special instructions about the importance of these aspects of communication for students with disabilities. Talking with a warm tone, conveying positive affect, and being relatively gentle in physical exchanges does not come naturally to most children and teens. Teacher modeling of a responsive conversational style with all students and some open discussion of ways in which students can communicate with each other, especially their peers with disabilities, can support modest changes in interactional style.

Research on Milieu Teaching

More than 30 empirical studies have examined the effects of Milieu Teaching. Four variants of Hart and Risley's (1968) original model of incidental teaching have been analyzed experimentally: (a) *modeling* (Alpert & Rogers-Warren [Kaiser], 1985); (b) *manding and modeling* (Cavallero & Bambara, 1982; Hemmeter, Ault, Collins & Meyers, 1996; Warren et al., 1984); (c) *time delay* (Charlop & Walsh, 1986; Halle et al., 1981; Halle et al., 1979; Oliver & Halle, 1982; Schwartz, Anderson, & Halle, 1988); and (d) *incidental teaching* (Alpert & Kaiser, 1992; Hart & Risley, 1968, 1974, 1975, 1980; Hemmeter & Kaiser, 1994). In general, the modeling, mand-modeling, and time delay are variants of the original incidental teaching model. In these procedures, there is increased adult support for children who are low-frequency initiators and whose language skills are relatively limited. Incidental teaching is simply the use of models, mands, and time delays in response to student requests.

Milieu Teaching involves the application of behavioral teaching procedures in naturalistic, conversational settings (Hart & Rogers-Warren [Kaiser], 1978). While Milieu Teaching is firmly rooted in the behavioral principles of stimulus control and reinforcement, the interactional aspects of this method are consistent with those described in naturally occurring facilitative language learning contexts (Hart, 1985). Emphasis on the development of responsiveness, turn taking, mutual engagement, joint attention, and topic elaboration is consistent with developmental analyses of mother-child interactions (Bruner, Roy, & Ratner, 1980; Hart & Risley, 1988; Moerk, 1983; Schacter, 1979).

Research has demonstrated that Milieu Teaching is effective in teaching a range of productive language skills to individuals with mental retardation and other language-related disabilities. (A comprehensive review of this literature may be found in Kaiser et al., 1992.) A range of language responses (e.g., single words, adjectives, simple utterances [one to four words], compound sentences, specific requests, general requests) in both verbal and nonvocal modes have been taught. Milieu Teaching positively affects general language skills as measured by changes in complexity of utterances and vocabulary diversity (Hart & Risley, 1975, 1980; Rogers-Warren [Kaiser] & Warren, 1980; Warren et al., 1984). Generalization across settings has been reported for some subjects in each study in which it has been assessed (Alpert & Kaiser, 1992; Alpert & Rogers-Warren [Kaiser], Cavallero & Bambara, 1982; Halle et al., 1979; Halle et al., 1981; Hancock & Kaiser, 1996; Hart & Risley, 1974, 1975; McGee, Krantz, & McClannahan, 1985; Warren et al., 1984). Finally, for children with initially low levels of responsiveness and initiations, Milieu Teaching has resulted in increased levels of these specific social communicative behaviors (Halle et al., 1981; Hancock & Kaiser, 1996; Hart & Risley, 1980; Warren et al., 1984).

There is considerable evidence that children's initiations, responses, participation in conversation, and requesting using trained utterances can be systematically increased using milieu procedures (Charlop & Walsh, 1986; Haring et al., 1987; Haring, Roger, Lee, Breen, & Gaylord-Ross, 1986; Schwartz et al., 1988). Studies that have measured broader effects on language development (Alpert & Rogers-Warren [Kaiser], 1985; Hart & Risley, 1975, 1980; Hemmeter & Kaiser, 1994; Warren & Bambara, 1989; Yoder, Kaiser, & Alpert, 1991) report modest changes in more global measures of language development. A recent study comparing applications of Milieu Teaching by parents and therapists of preschool children with significant language disabilities found that children in both the parent- and teacher-implemented conditions made significant gains in most measures of language development compared to a nontreatment control group (Kaiser, Lambert, Hancock, & Hester, 1998). Follow-up data collected 6 months after the end of the primary intervention indicated that children in both groups maintained their gains and continued to show growth on standardized measures; however, children whose parents were taught to use the milieu strategies made significantly greater gains during the follow-up period than children who were taught by therapists. These findings suggest the particular value of involving family members in the implementation of Milieu Teaching.

Sixteen children with autism were included in this study (Kaiser et al., 1998). The children with autism increased their verbal communication during the Milieu Teaching interventions when implemented by either parents or therapists, and the results for children with autism did not differ from those of other children (Kaiser et al., 1998; Kaiser, Hancock, Nietfeld, & Delaney, 1996). These results, along with those of Hamilton and Snell (1993), suggest that Milieu Teaching may be successful in improving the communication skills of students with autism. There has been much discussion on the outcomes of intensive didactic intervention on the functioning of children with autism (McEachin, Smith, & Lovaas, 1993); however, findings to date do not establish that didactic training is better than more naturalistic approaches to language intervention (Gresham & MacMillan, 1997). To date, there is evidence that Milieu Teaching procedures can increase the language and communication skills of students with autism.

Implementing Milieu Teaching

Implementing Milieu Teaching requires more than skill in using each of its three components. Assessment of child skills, selection of targets, structuring the setting to promote naturalistic teaching, and evaluating both the implementation and the student's progress must be addressed to ensure that this instructional strategy is effective.

Data Collection and Evaluation

Effective Milieu Language Teaching is data-based. Many aspects of the process may be monitored. At a minimum, it is recommended that data be kept on the following dimensions:

1. The number of Milieu Teaching episodes per day and the targets taught in these episodes: A total of 10 to 15 episodes per day is a reasonable teaching base. Typically, students will have a small number of targets (two to five) and there should be at least two or three opportunities to teach each target.
2. The number of student initiations across the day or during selected activities: an increase in the number of student initiations is often one of the primary effects of Milieu Teaching. *Initiations* typi-

cally are defined as directed speech that occurs in the absence of an adult verbal stimulus (e.g., a request). Noting the content of student initiations is useful in assessing progress; selecting activities, materials, and consequences, and establishing new language targets.

3. The responsiveness of the student to Milieu Teaching procedures: Responsiveness can be measured by counting the number of appropriate student responses to questions, mands, models, and delays. For example, a teacher could determine the number of times a student responded to 10 different questions across the day. Responsiveness to 65% to 70% of the Milieu Teaching procedures should be considered adequate if each episode ends positively and contains appropriate models of the target behavior.

4. Use of the target skills by students outside of teaching episodes: This indicates a level of unprompted generalizations of the target skill across forms, as well as across people and settings.

Each of these dimensions can be monitored using a simple tally sheet. Data sheets can be index cards or Post-it notes attached to a lesson plan. An activity-specific data sheet cues the teacher when and how to prompt, as well as providing space for data collection. Post-it notes on the student's communication book, wheelchair, or desk can be used for simple data collection. Daily monitoring is ideal; however, systematic sampling of different activities across several days provides a more balanced evaluation than does casual monitoring across an entire day. Non–data-based Milieu Teaching is likely to be highly erratic and, like any such approach, may prolong the use of ineffective strategies, depriving students of critical learning time. Monitoring is especially important when several students are being targeted for Milieu Teaching. Table 12–3 is a sample data sheet used to collect data for three students across the varied activities of a school day.

How to Use Milieu Language Teaching

Milieu Teaching can be used either as a primary language intervention approach or in combination with direct teaching one-on-one to facilitate generalization and promote further acquisition. When used as a primary intervention approach, Milieu Teaching should be applied systematically in routine interactions with the student, in small groups, and at any other time a need for language use can be specified. Skilled teachers can provide Milieu Teaching within the context of classroom and daily living activities without disrupting those activities.

Planning classroom activities and routines around Milieu Teaching opportunities ensures that it will occur. Routines provide extra support to students who are learning language because the context is familiar and the expectations for communication are clear. Table 12–4 is a completed planning sheet used to organize the activities of a preschool classroom around opportunities for Milieu Teaching.

Activity-based instruction (Bricker & Cripe, 1989) is similar to Milieu Teaching, except that it includes a range of social, motor, communicative, and cognitive skills. In activity-based instruction, materials are selected and settings are arranged to facilitate active child engagement, provide opportunities for learning language and other skills, and promote natural opportunities for incidental teaching.

Another highly effective strategy is to embed Milieu Teaching into instruction on academic, work, or independent living tasks. Communication integrated with teaching of other skills further ensures that the natural functions of communication are being learned.

> *Michael is learning to ride the bus from his home to his job training site. His job coach prompts him to greet the driver, to respond when other passengers ask him questions (e.g., "How are you? Where are you going?"), and to thank the driver as he gets off the bus. These verbal skills are functional and well-integrated with other daily living skills: waiting for the bus, getting on, putting money in the coin receptacle, watching for his stop, and checking for his belongings before departing the bus.*

Figure 12–7 shows a cluster of skills being taught. Communication goals have been embedded in a task that teaches several skills simultaneously. The asterisks mark the communication teaching opportunities that have been included in the sequence. In this example, a student, Kelly, is being taught to sign. In the grooming sequence, Kelly practices washing her face and combing her hair. The teacher uses time delays to prompt Kelly to sign for soap, towel, comb, and, if needed, help from the teacher. Initially, the teacher modeled by pointing to the photos, providing the verbal label, and prompting Kelly to imitate, but now she focuses her attention on Kelly and waits for Kelly to request the needed objects. The teaching of labels

TABLE 12–3

Data Collection Across the Day for Three Students

	Student: Mina			Student: Kristi			Student: Caryn	
Setting	Times	Prompts/ Consequences	Setting	Times	Prompts/ Consequences	Setting	Times	Prompts/ Consequences
Target 1: want + noun			**Target 1:** photo + label			**Target 1:** two words		
breakfast	//	S, TD	breakfast	///	MQ, MQ, MQ	group	/	S +
group	/	MQ	small group	/	M +	math	/	TD
Target 2: new noun labels			**Target 2:** request assistance			**Target 2:** action verbs		
math	/	M	arrival	/	S +	group	/	M +
hall/transition	/	M	departure	/	S +	self-help	/	M +
bus	/	M +(peer)				transition	/	M +
Target 3: _____			**Target 3:** _____			**Target 3:** request assistance, "help, please"		
						breakfast	/	MQ +
						self-help	/	TD +

Setting: Specify activity when response occurred.

Times: Use slash (/) for each occurrence.

Prompts: (Record one symbol for each occurrence) M = model; S = spontaneous; + = acknowledged by adult or peer; MQ = mand or question; TD = time delay.

TABLE 12–4
Environmental Arrangement and Milieu Teaching Planning and Data Collection Form

Activity PlayDoh

Date 8-1-91

Materials of Interest
1. 2 cans PlayDoh
2. 4 cookie cutters
3. 2 rolling pins
4. _____

Basic Arrangement
1. Cookie cutters on tray
2. Lids on PlayDoh
3. Rolling pin on shelf
4. _____

Child	Environmental Arrangement	Target	Milieu Procedure	Child Response	Comments
Bill	1. Opening PlayDoh (assistance)	Sign "help"	Model	Signed	Only one model!
	2. Present two cookie cutters (choice-making)	Point to preference	Model with physical assistance	Initiated point	Did not need prompt
	3.				
Margaret	1. Small portion of PlayDoh (small portions)	Sign "want more"	Model "want more"	Want more	Needed two models
	2. Present two cookie cutters (choice-making)	Sign shape of cookie cutter	Time delay and model "want star"	Want	Time delay, two models then physical guidance for "star"
	3.				
Mary	1. Opening PlayDoh (assistance)	"Help, please"	Incidental teaching	"Help please"	Mary is requesting
	2. Present two colors of PlayDoh (choice-making)	"Want ___"	Incidental teaching	No response	Consistently nonverbal
	3. Roll PlayDoh without pin (assistance)	"Need pin"	Incidental teaching	"Need pin"	Models are effective, mands are not
Ginny	1. Small portion of PlayDoh (small portions)	Point to PlayDoh	Time delay	Pointed	Exaggerated time delay to elicit response
	2. Present three cookie cutters on tray (choice-making)	Point to cookie cutter	Time delay	Pointed	Exaggerated time delay to elicit response

Milieu procedures: Model   Mand-model   Time Delay   Incidental Teaching

475

FIGURE 12–7
Skill Sequence Including Opportunities to Train
Communication Skills

Skill Sequence for Kelly

1. Knee walks to sink (gross motor)
2. Turns water on (fine motor)
3. Signs *soap* (communication)*
4. Signs *towel* (communication)*
5. Washes and dries hands (self-help)
6. Turns water off (fine motor)
7. Signs *comb* (communication)*
8. Combs hair (self-help)

---

*Communication training opportunities

and requesting fits well with the grooming task and helps the student acquire appropriate and situation-specific language.

Table 12–5 shows communication targets and Milieu Teaching procedures for three students during lunch. These students routinely enter the lunch room, ask for specific foods, make a choice of drinks, move to a table, and ask to sit next to a peer. Each student has three communication targets, appropriate for aspects of their established routine. Note that for Kristi, who is just learning signs, pointing to communicate

is taught along with the sign "eat" to specify her food choices, because she does not have specific food labels yet. Similarly, Jamie, who uses a picture book to communicate, is encouraged to point, vocalize, and attempt "please" as part of her functional communication training. Data can be collected on the lesson plan sheet using the columns immediately adjacent to where the target is listed. Social goals, such as looking at peers, getting peers' attention before communicating, and using "please" are taught concurrently with the target communicative form.

Assessment

The general purposes of assessment are:

1. To describe the student's existing communication skills
2. To gather a database for prescribing treatment goals and strategies for intervention

When Milieu Teaching is proposed as an intervention strategy, both student skills and environmental demands for language must be assessed to formulate a functional intervention plan.

Performing an Environmental Inventory

The purpose of an environmental inventory is to identify the environments in which students need com-

TABLE 12–5
Milieu Prompts and Communication Targets During Lunch

Students		Contexts							Total Correct
		Order food		Order drinks		Ask to sit with peer			
Kristi	Prompt	Model		Mand-model		Model			
	Target	Point + "eat" (sign)	+	"Juice" or "milk" (sign)	−	"Sit" (sign) + look at peer	+		3/3
Martin	Prompt	Time delay		Time delay		Mand-model			
	Target	"I want + _____." (3-word request)	+	"I want + _____." (3-word request)	+	"(Name), sit here."	−		2/3
Jamie	Prompt	Mand-model		Mand-model		Model			
	Target	Show picture + "please"	+	Show picture + "please"	+	Show picture + vocalize to get attention	+		3/3

+, correct response; −, incorrect response or no response.

munication skills. Since almost every setting requires such skills, the first step of an environmental inventory is to list the settings where a student spends the majority of his or her time. First, settings are identified (e.g., home, school, church, transportation vehicles); then specific activities (e.g., eating, helping with chores at home, ordering and paying in a restaurant) within each setting are listed and particular communication demands are identified.

Table 12–6 is an environmental inventory that describes communication opportunities during a ride to school each morning. The setting (bus to school) is identified and five discrete activities during the ride are indicated. For each activity, general communication opportunities are listed and a potential trainer is identified. To plan an intervention, specific forms and functions of language must be delineated and a teaching plan must be specified along with a potential teacher.

An environmental inventory should be based on direct observation of the student in the potential teaching settings plus informal interviews with significant others. Informal interviews are especially helpful in selecting settings for teaching and in clarifying whether information gained during direct observation is representative of both the student and the environment. Table 12–7 summarizes a plan for intervening

to teach a student to greet the driver and peers during the student's ride to school.

Assessing Student Skills

Two general classes of assessment information are related to student skills. The first is a comprehensive overview that describes cognitive functioning, social skills, motor skills, and communication abilities. This chapter does not describe ways to obtain this type of information. The second type of assessment examines students' actual performance of communicative behaviors in the settings identified through environmental inventory. This section focuses on the second type of assessment information. (More information is available in chapters 3 and 5).

Individual students are often assessed many times in the course of a few years. Thus, existing information should be reviewed to determine where new information is needed and to glean information about intervention strategies that have been used successfully in the past. While some test results are useful, past training data may yield even more useful information about the interventions that have been effective, the duration of training to expect for new skills, and the specific skills that have been taught. Information about the ability of students to generalize new information is especially valuable. Additional

TABLE 12–6
Environmental Inventory for Community Setting: Taking the Bus to School

Activities	Communication Demands/Functions	Possible Training Site	Trainer	Comments	Target Forms
Getting on bus	Greet driver	Yes	Mom or sibling	Mom willing; sibling may be	"Good morning"
Greeting driver	Ask social questions	No	No trainer, driver too busy	Check for generalization from other social talk training	
Greeting riders	Friends greet, ask social questions	Yes	Normal peer or sibling	Two classmates are willing and ride the same bus	"Hello" + *name* "I'm fine" "I'm _____"
Ride to school	Varied questions, can comment on environment	Yes	Normal peer or sibling	Two classmates	3 words, context appropriate; also yes or no
Getting off the bus	Say goodbye to driver and passengers, greet teacher or aide who meets	Maybe	Teacher or aide who greets students at school	Could coordinate with Mom on greeting	"Goodbye" "Hello" + *name*

TABLE 12–7
Milieu Intervention Plan with Sibling: Bus to School

| Student | Tommy | Date | January 10–30, 1998 | Trainer Responsible | Teacher aide with sibling |
| New Training | | Generalization Training | XX | | |

Activity	Trainer	Language Targets	Procedure	Data/Monitoring
Greeting driver	Sibling	"Good morning" + eye contact, smile	Sibling *models,* verbal praise for success, one corrective model, driver responds positively	Sibling records on note card for teacher, teacher summarizes and gives sibling feedback
Responding to driver	Sibling	"Fine" in response to "How are you?"	Sibling *models,* prompts if needed, acknowledges	
Greeting friends	Sibling	"Hello" + *name*	Sibling *mands* (say "hello" to your friend), models if needed, expands, and acknowledges	
Responding to friends	Sibling	Varies: Reply "hello" Answer "fine" Answer "yes" or "no"	Sibling *models* appropriate reply, uses delayed modeling, expands, and praises	
Getting off bus	Teacher's aide	"Goodbye" "See you"	Aide *models,* prompts if needed, acknowledges	

assessments should provide new or more specific information about the students' skills. Unless there is a reason for repeating an entire assessment, teachers should repeat only the portions where new learning is likely to have occurred. Discrepancies between skills acquired in training and the use of these skills in conversational settings should be identified. Previously taught forms are ideal beginning points for Milieu Teaching, because most students benefit from support to generalize and maintain those forms. Initial Milieu Teaching attempts are likely to be successful with forms previously learned in other settings.

Assessing functional communication skills involves observing students in the activities identified in their environmental inventory and answering the following five questions.

Functional Communication Skill Assessment
1) What do the students find interesting in this setting? To answer this question, observe the students and note the people, objects, and events to which they attend. Determine if and how the students initiate socially to the people in the setting and if they are responsive to particular people. Note the subjects or aspects of the environment that engage the attention of the students.

2) What communication functions do the students exhibit in this setting? Seven basic communication functions should be considered: greetings, protests, requests for objects, requests for attention, requests for assistance, commenting, and answering (Table 12–8). Settings in which adult-initiated interactions are infrequent may offer few opportunities for answering and commenting. Thus, it is important to notice whether opportunities occur and how the students respond to those opportunities.

3) What forms do the students use to express these functions? Communication functions can be expressed verbally and nonverbally. Students with severe disabilities often have idiosyncratic ways of expressing functions. For example, a student may throw objects in protest rather than nod or say, "No." A student such as Kristi, who has a limited sign repertoire, may use a single gesture to indicate requests for help, for objects, or to invite joint play. Understanding a student's idiosyncratic communication forms is sometimes difficult but always worth the time invested in observation and analysis, because current communication forms are the beginning point for teaching more elaborated language.

4) What communication skills in the student's repertoires can be the base for building new language

TABLE 12–8
Basic Communication Functions

Functions	Possible Forms
Greetings	Waves Eye contact "Hello" "Name"
Requests for assistance	Gesture to come Giving object for which assistance is needed Taking the adult's hand and directing the adult to the task Crying "Help" Use of the adult's name
Requests for object	Pointing Attempting to grab the object Taking the adult's hand and directing it to the object Verbal requests: "Give me," "Want that" Naming object
Requests for information	Echoic imitation "What?" Eye contact plus quizzical look Showing object (requesting name or function of object)
Protests	"No" Pushing the adult away Crying Turning away from the adult or peer Throwing objects
Comments	Echoic imitation Pointing to the object Showing the object to the adult

skills? General information about students' skills gleaned from the review of existing language assessments could be used to determine the beginning skills to be taught with the milieu method. For example, the outcomes of criterion-referenced assessment of Kristi's signs or of Michael's single-word vocabulary and two-word phrases should be integrated with the assessment of communication performance in natural settings. Kristi's teacher might review her records and prepare a list of signs she has been taught in the past. Using this list, the teacher could construct a probe or test in which Kristi is given two opportunities to make each sign in response to planned presentations of objects or events. Any signs that Kristi has mastered in the probe or test setting should then be assessed in everyday settings. Information collected in natural settings should indicate whether Kristi spontaneously uses the sign to request or initiate interactions or whether she uses the sign in response

to questions (e.g., "What do you want?") or mands (e.g., "Tell me what you want to do next.")

Discrepancies between tested performance and naturalistic performance are ideal beginning points for Milieu Teaching interventions to promote generalization. The milieu method teaches skills slightly in advance of the students' current functional repertoires. Often, this requires generalization training to transfer already-learned forms into their functional contexts. Language goals may include enlarging the student's vocabulary, extending the number of different forms used to express an already-mastered communicative function (e.g., greetings), and teaching new ways to use and combine existing skills. Language skills that already have been acquired receptively but are not yet in the productive repertoire are also potentially excellent targets.

Michael understands many more labels than he uses spontaneously; these labels would be good targets in simple two-word phrases with already mastered verbs (e.g., go library, go gym, go homeroom).

5) What social communication strategies are used by the students? To answer this question, students must be observed interacting in the setting. The purpose of this observation is to determine when students are socially responsive and what basic in-teractional skills they already have. Milieu Teaching procedures strengthen and train interactional skills as well as communication skills. Table 12–9 is a checklist of basic communication strategies. Basic strategies include attention to persons and objects in the environment, responsiveness to adult and peer verbalizations, and initiating communicative interactions.

TABLE 12–9
Communication Strategies Checklist

Attention

_____ Student visually attends to adults when they talk
_____ Student visually attends to peers when they talk
_____ Student visually attends to a referent (object or person) named by an adult or a peer
_____ Student visually attends to novel or changing aspects of the environment
_____ Student attends when instructed to do so
What objects or activities have you seen the student attending to?

Responsiveness

_____ Student is socially responsive to adults (smiles, greets, acknowledges, approaches them)
_____ Student is socially responsive to peers
_____ Student complies with instructions
_____ Student responds verbally (any mode) to simple greetings, questions
_____ Student responds verbally (any mode) to comments
_____ Student accepts invitations to join activities (play together, share material, sit next to peer)
_____ Student can take turns nonverbally (in games or routines)
_____ Student imitates motor behavior spontaneously
_____ Student imitates verbal behavior spontaneously
_____ Student imitates motor behavior when prompted
_____ Student imitates verbal behavior when prompted

Initiative

_____ Student greets others spontaneously
_____ Student nonverbally initiates play or activity
_____ Student verbally (any mode) initiates (other than greetings)
_____ Student shares materials without prompting from an adult or a peer
Are there any other situations in which the student initiates?

What are the strengths in this student's communication?

When is this student most likely to communicate?

What are the barriers to communication for this student? (What aspects of the environment make communication difficult?)

When is this student least likely to communicate?

Other Observations

*Combining Environmental Information
and Student Assessments*

The final step in assessment is to combine information gathered about the environment and students' skills (see Functional Communication Skill Assessment Checklist) in order to make a plan for training. The training plan should specify:

1. The mode(s) for student communicative responses (e.g., verbal, sign, symbol system, or a combination of these);
2. Specific communication targets described in terms of both linguistic form and communicative function;
3. Where teaching will occur;
4. How the teaching environment should be restructured to include Milieu Teaching interactions;
5. Who will do the teaching;
6. What assistance the teacher may need to apply Milieu Teaching strategies;
7. Whether supplemental instruction is needed in addition to Milieu Teaching, and when this instruction will be provided.

The student communication mode(s) and specific training targets should be derived primarily from student assessments with the planning team's consensus, but targets and mode(s) should also be determined by the characteristics of the settings. If no one in a student's most frequented settings has knowledge of signs and if the student's significant others are unwilling to learn a signing symbol system, a communication board with pictures may be a more useful mode of communication.

The first training setting should be one in which the target skills will be most functional, but it should also be one in which milieu intervention is relatively easy to apply. Identification of teachers who can apply the milieu techniques effectively is essential. Often, new instructors need support to begin intervention. Assistance in identifying interactions for teaching and training specific language targets and instruction in modeling, manding, time delay, and feedback should be part of the trainers' preparation. Continued feedback to teachers is also needed if the intervention is to be effective.

Finally, some skills may need supplemental didactic instruction (e.g., intensive practice in an instructional setting). For example, when teaching a student an initial set of signs or to associate pictures with objects,

places, and activities, massed trial practice may be useful for training the basic motor skills involved in producing the sign. Didactic instruction and Milieu Teaching can proceed concurrently. Trainers can determine if more intensive teaching is needed by monitoring student performance and noting the actual number of Milieu Teaching trials that students are receiving and their progress toward criterion performance. If the number of trials is low or students are not acquiring the target form after a reasonable length of time (e.g., 3 weeks of six trials each day), then massed trial instruction may be added to facilitate acquisition, and Milieu Teaching may be continued to ensure generalization to functional use. Other considerations include the symbol system taught, the functionality of the specific student's targets, and the adequacy of implementation of the milieu procedures.

To meet the goal of functional language, the effectiveness of intervention must be assessed at frequent intervals in natural settings. If students' functional communication repertoires are not expanding during intervention, adjustments in teaching tactics and target skills should be made. A sort of bottom-line question should be posed at 3-month intervals: What does this student communicate effectively now that he or she was unable to communicate 3 months ago? Assuming regular teaching sessions, even students with severe disabilities should show progress toward more functional skills after 3 months of training.

Generalized Skills Teaching

One of the strengths of a Milieu Teaching approach is that it is designed to facilitate generalization. Multiple exemplars (e.g., several linguistically similar forms which serve the same function) in functional communication contexts and naturally occurring reinforcers make the generalization of newly-trained forms likely. When students have several appropriate forms that communicate their needs and wants effectively, they are likely to use them. However, when planning a milieu intervention, it is still important to consider the issues surrounding the generalization of language training.

Language generalization occurs at several levels. Using a specific communication function (e.g., requests) or form (e.g., adjective-noun combinations, such as "red ball") across individuals and settings is an important but relatively simple type of generalization. Formation of a generalized concept, such as "ball," "cup," or "go," without either over-generalizing or undergeneralizing the word representing the concept is a more difficult type of generalization. Generative language use (i.e., spontaneously initiating novel, meaningful word combinations in varied communication situations) is the most complex type of generalization.

Generalization is an aspect of the learning process. Learning may be characterized as consisting of three overlapping levels or stages. First is the acquisition level, where students learn the basic response or skill (e.g., the word "ball" is associated with a spherical object). Language teaching typically is concentrated on this level. Simple form-object and form-event relationships are taught and new skills are introduced as soon as students evidence associative learning. Next is the generalization level, when students begin to use the new response under a variety of conditions. They may overgeneralize or undergeneralize use of the response as they explore its potential functions and discover its essential attributes and delimiters. This level of language learning frequently has been ignored in language teaching, although many students with severe disabilities need help "fine-tuning" their use of forms. Finally, the third level of learning is characterized by competence, or fluency in using the learned response. At this level, students approximate adult competence in use of the response. The students know when to use the response and when not to use it. The response is used generatively. That is, it is integrated with other communicative responses in the students' repertoires. This level of language learning, which is the desired outcome of intervention, typically has been overlooked completely in training.

For example, Carter is beginning to learn some three-word phrases (e.g., "give me some," "play new game") He typically uses his newly learned phrases in one of two ways. He either uses the phrase only in the exact circumstance it was learned (i.e., he uses it too specifically or undergeneralizes) or he uses the phrase across many settings and contexts, some of which are not appropriate (i.e., he overgeneralizes it). Carter may only say "give me some" when requesting popcorn from his mother but not use it when requesting other foods or comic books from his friends. Milieu Teaching may be used to prompt Carter to apply his newly learned phrases to a variety of contexts in which they are appropriate.

The three levels of learning are interrelated. If teaching at the basic acquisition level produces well-discriminated responses (i.e., students learn to associate the word "ball" with only one or two particular balls), then generalization is unlikely unless it is programmed subsequently. If generalization is restricted or fails to occur, students have no basis for attaining competence. An effective language teaching approach must ensure that learning occurs across all three levels.

Initial acquisition, generalization, and maintenance use are influenced by a number of variables that relate to the nature of the training, environmental support for trained language, and the criteria for mastery of the trained responses. Variables that relate specifically to training outcomes include (a) what is taught; (b) who teaches; (c) how functional, reinforcing, and consistent the consequences for communication are; (d) where teaching occurs; (e) how the content is organized; (f) what criteria for learning are applied; and (g) how responsive students' environments are to new learning.

What Is Taught?

Both the forms of communication (e.g., words, sentences, signs, and gestures) and their functions (e.g., greetings, commenting, questioning, requesting) must be learned if new skills are to be used. Simply put, the content of training must be functional for students, and they must have experience using the content in a functional manner during training.

New forms should map communicative functions that students have already acquired. For example, since Michael already requests objects (e.g., milk, video tape), a new form of requesting (e.g., "give me" + noun label) can be taught easily. New forms for training should be only slightly more complex than the forms that students currently use to express a particular function. Conversely, when teaching a new function, such as requesting information, it is easiest to begin with an already known form, or to teach the function with a single, simple form.

Who Teaches?

The simple answer to this question is everyone. As many people as possible who come in contact with students regularly and are willing to be either spontaneous teachers or trained teachers should be involved. Specific Milieu Teaching techniques can enhance the natural abilities of teachers, therapists, and parents. Milieu Teaching is a particularly feasible approach, because training can be incorporated easily into routine activities throughout the day. Parents and significant others can be effective in facilitating generalization through their Milieu Teaching.

When family members are willing, they can also teach new skills appropriate to settings outside of schools (Kaiser, et al. 1998). Family members are especially important as collaborators for ensuring that students maintain newly learned skills. These people may use Milieu Teaching procedures across the range of daily interactions to prompt functional use of forms that students have already learned. Milieu Teaching procedures implemented in a naturalistic and conversational style should promote the functional use of students' skills without changing conversations into formal teaching interactions. Research comparing parent-implemented and therapist-implemented Milieu Teaching found that young children with disabilities, including children with autism, showed greater language growth over a 6-month period after intensive intervention when their parents implemented Milieu Teaching than when it was implemented only by a therapist (Kaiser et al., 1998b). Parent-implemented training may be especially important for students who require intensive intervention over long periods of time, and practice in specific social contexts, especially students with autism.

> Carter is a 10-year-old boy with autism, whose spoken language is primarily one- and two-word utterances. Carter's mother, Catherine, has been taught to use responsive interaction and Milieu Teaching during everyday interactions with Carter at home. She is careful to respond to Carter's initiations, expand his one- and two-word utterances, and to prompt Carter to make verbal choices whenever it is appropriate.
>
> Carter (looking at a picture of his grandparent's house in a family album): "House."
>
> Catherine (coming over to look at the picture): "Yes, it's Granddad's house."
>
> Carter: "Go house."
>
> Catherine: "You like to go to Granddad's house, don't you?"
>
> Carter: "Go Granddad?"
>
> Catherine: "We can't go to Granddad's house today. We could call him or write him a note."
>
> Catherine: (goes to desk and points to first the phone and then to a notepad) "Would you like to call Granddad or write Granddad a note?"

> Carter: (points to phone)
>
> Catherine: "Call Granddad."
>
> Carter: "Call Granddad."
>
> Catherine: "OK, we'll call Granddad. I'll call and you can talk." (Dials number and waits; when phone is answered, she says) "Hi Dad, Carter wants to say hello to you." (Hands phone to Carter)
>
> Carter: (Takes phone and places it next to his ear but does not say anything)
>
> Catherine: Say "Hi, Granddad!"
>
> Carter: "Hi, Granddad."
>
> Granddad: "Hi there, Carter!"

How Are Students Reinforced?

To be generalized, language must come under the control of a breadth and range of naturally occurring consequences. To the greatest extent possible, only student-selected naturally occurring reinforcers should be used in training (e.g., preferred activities, toys or materials). If this is not possible initially with some training targets, then systematic introduction of naturally occurring consequences must be a central part of the training process. Consequences should always include continued positive interaction with teachers, meaningful comments related to students' responses, and expansions of student's utterances. These interactional and linguistic consequences are the typical natural results of everyday language use.

In the previous example with Carter and his mother, Catherine, several natural consequences occurred: (a) Catherine responded to Carter's initiation with continued attention and talk about his topic (his granddad's house); (b) Carter chose a means to contact his granddad and Catherine followed through with his choice, so that the natural consequence of his choice was placing the call; (c) finally, Catherine prompted Carter to say hello to his granddad and his granddad responded in a conversational and natural way.

Where Does Teaching Occur?

Language should be taught in settings where communication naturally occurs. Milieu Teaching can occur at home, on the playground, in the lunchroom, in the community, during academic activities, in the hallway, on the bus, during family outings, and in all the daily routines in which language is functional. With normally developing children, parents and teachers rarely set aside a particular time for specifically teaching language or other skills. There are too many other things to be done. Language is taught informally in the course of typical activities, such as eating, dressing, toileting, bathing, and transitions between activities. In general, the same model should apply for students who have severe disabilities. In the classroom and in community instruction, it is important to integrate language into teaching other skills within which the use of language normally occurs.

Responsive Environments Are Essential to New Learning and Generalization

One way to program for generalization is to introduce a new skill into its natural community of reinforcement (Stokes & Baer, 1977). That is, to allow the student to experience the naturally occurring positive outcomes of communication. As students acquire new skills and their behaviors change, natural environments must respond in ways that support those changes. During normal development, adaptation naturally occurs in mother-child interactions. Mothers are aware of their children's improved skills because they are in close contact with the children and expect them to change (Newport, 1976). When students have severe disabilities, adults sometimes lose the expectation that the students will change. In busy classrooms, teachers may not have much time to notice a student's attempts to comment using newly learned signs, pictures, or words. Thus, potential conversational partners may fail to respond differentially when change and growth do occur. Peers, teachers, and parents can become more responsive to the communication of students with severe disabilities' skill repertoires, when they have information about changes in the students' communication. When these people respond to new forms and provide consequences for their use, they help students generalize and maintain new skills. Again, providing opportunities for students to use new forms is an important step toward ensuring maintenance.

> For example, in Michael's and Kristi's cases, their parents should be provided with regular updates on newly learned words and signs. In classrooms, demonstrations of new skills can help peers and teaching staff members recognize new communication forms.
>
> Kristi is given the opportunity to show the new signs she has learned in a large-group activity.
>
> Michael is invited to show his friends pictures or objects and to label these pictures or objects with his newly learned words.

Designing an Optimal Teaching Approach

Each of the preceding variables (what to teach, who teaches, where teaching occurs) should be directly addressed in designing an individualized communication training program for a student. Generalization should be assessed on a weekly basis. Parents should be asked to note the use of new forms, and their help in promoting generalization should be sought. A simple report form, such as the one shown in Table 12–10, can be used to both assess generalization and prompt adults to facilitate language use.

Table 12–11 is a generalization planning worksheet developed to monitor and plan for generalization. The basic strategy is to plan training to include multiple, functional exemplars; to probe for simple generalization across persons, settings, and objects; to monitor generalization observed in functional contexts; and to remediate any observed problems in generalization. The worksheet should be updated on a weekly basis and shared with everyone involved in the students' training. Sharing data and brainstorming innovative approaches to support generalization and maintenance should be a collaborative team activity.

Jordon's special education teacher, his regular kindergarten teacher, his speech and language pathologist, and his mother form a planning team that focuses on Jordon's communication needs. This team follows a series of steps in developing a functional language training program for Jordon that uses Milieu Teaching strategies.

Gathering New Information

First, functional communication skills that will give Jordon more control over his physical and social environment are identified by conducting an environmental inventory in the settings in which Jordon spends the majority of his time. For these environments (his kindergarten class, playground, and home), the following information is determined:

1. The major activities that occur within the environment, for example:
   - Kindergarten class—large group, small group, snack or lunch, and gym or recess.
   - Playground—swings, riding push toys, and slide.
   - Home—meals, bedtime or story time, trips in the car, and play with favorite toys.
2. Basic communication skills that will help Jordon function more independently and that will facilitate increased participation in activities.

TABLE 12–10
Report Form for Assessing Generalization

Student Kristi			**Date** March 3, 1998	
Person Reporting Sharon (Mom)			**Mode** Sign	

Target	Status	When Was Target Used? How Often?	New Context
1. ___Help___	Kristi has this one really well at school	Opening jar, 1 time; trying to get toys from sibling, 3 times	Trying to get arm in coat
2. ___Candy___	Kristi's favorite	Lots of times! She really likes to try this request	None
3. ___Potty___	Maintaining use of this word as a request	About 5 times (always appropriate)	No, she uses it by herself appropriately
4. ___Hug___	Just started training this word	Not seen	Build a routine with Mom and Dad
5. _____			

Comments and Suggestions

I think "hug" will need prompting. Kristi doesn't know how to ask for hugs yet. I may be missing some things she signs because her signing is not precise and I sometimes don't recognize her gestures as specific signs.

3. The individuals in each environment or activity who are the logical candidates to be Milieu Teachers and the current skills of each individual.

4. Whether the materials available and the arrangement of the environment are optimal for promoting initiations and choice making by Jordon and facilitating the application of Milieu Teaching procedures.

Information needed to complete the environmental inventories for activities occurring in Jordon's classroom is readily available. Jordon's mother describes his home activities. Jordon's special education teacher and his speech and language clinician divide the responsibility of observing Jordon at school and at home after school. For each environment, they also obtain information about strategies currently being

 An Application of Milieu Teaching

Jordon is 5 years and 3 months old. At 4 months, Jordon contracted cerebrospinal meningitis and was hospitalized for 5 weeks. As a result of the meningitis, Jordon experienced significant brain damage, which resulted in hemiplegia of the left side and severe mental retardation.

Jordon lives at home with his mother, his 12-year-old sister, and his maternal grandmother. He attends a regular kindergarten class from 9:00 AM to 3:00 PM, Monday through Friday. Jordon is seen by the school's speech and language clinician twice each week for small-group language instruction. Both the speech clinician and the

special education teacher consult with Jordan's kindergarten teacher. Late afternoons are spent at home with his grandmother and his sister, when she arrives home from school. Jordon's mother comes home from work around 6:00 PM Weekends are generally less structured. On Saturday mornings, Jordon usually attends a young children's story hour at the local library. Jordon also spends time in other activities, such as going to the grocery with his mother, going to the playground with his sister, and accompanying his grandmother as she does chores around the house.

TABLE 12–11
Generalization Planning Worksheet

Student Michael   Trainer Martha (teacher)   Date 1/30/99

| Form | Training Criterion Met (Date and %) | Generalization Probed | | | Spontaneous Use Observed | | Further Training Needed? (Date, Plan, Person Responsible) |
		Setting (%)	Trainer (%)	Stimuli (%)	Prompted (No. and Occasion)	Unprompted (No. and Occasion)	
Photo + label (help, book, finished)	10/14/98 100%	100	100	85	One time (book) in response to time delay by teacher	Three times (help): 1. When he couldn't reach his jacket 2. When he wanted teacher assistance with his backpack 3. When a peer took his paper	"Finished" will be trained at home beginning 2/12/99. Mom and Dad will build into mealtime routine in morning and evening

used to teach language, the responsiveness of teachers to Jordon when he shows interest in something or attempts to communicate, and opportunities for Jordon to control his physical and social environment.

Second, interviews are conducted to get information from significant others as a basis for planning a functional communication program. The five questions discussed earlier are posed:

1. What does Jordan find interesting in this setting?
2. What communication functions does he exhibit in this setting?
3. What forms does he use to express these functions?
4. What existing communication skills can be the basis for building new skills?
5. What social communication strategies does Jordan use in this setting?

The special education teacher interviews the teacher and teaching assistant in the kindergarten class, the physical therapist, and the peer tutor who works with Jordon. Jordon's mother interviews his grandmother, his sister, and the story-time coordinator at the Saturday morning library program. The interviews are designed to obtain specific information about the existing environmental demands for Jordon to communicate, the social and communicative behaviors exhibited by Jordon in each setting, and the minimal skills that Jordon needs to improve his ability to interact and communicate with others in the environment. The planning team uses the interview data to verify, clarify, and augment their observational data and to gain insight into the ability of significant others to identify and foster Jordon's communicative behavior.

Third, in addition to taking into account environmental characteristics and demands, Jordon's planning team specifies child characteristics essential to consider in developing an individualized, functional communication training program for Jordon. Test results (including the results of diagnostic testing) and informal observation provide relevant information about Jordon's receptive language and expressive communication skills, motor development, and sensory abilities. Reports from teachers and significant others provide information about his social interaction strategies, preferred activities, and engagement with the physical environment.

1. What does Jordan find interesting? Jordan's interests vary by setting. At home, he likes to look at books alone or with an adult or his sister, to be pushed in a swing, and to ride the merry-go-round on the nearby playground. He likes to ride in the car. He also likes to look at mechanical things, such as the vacuum cleaner, the coffee maker, and the blender when they are operating. He enjoys meals and especially likes having a snack with his sister when she arrives home after school. He seems to enjoy story time at the library as long as he can see the pictures. At school, Jordan does not seem interested in many of the classroom activities (e.g., large group, going to most centers, working independently on preacademic tasks). He does like to look at books, watch and manipulate the Playskool television, and to be pushed on the swing during outdoor time. The physical therapist reports that Jordan seems very interested in mechanical toys (e.g., a wind up top, a toy truck with a turning cement mixer, race cars that move on a track).

2. What communication functions does Jordon exhibit? At home, Jordon dependably greets his family, he protests when he does not get his way or he does not want to do something. He sometimes requests objects and assistance. At school, Jordon demonstrates these same functions (i.e., greetings, protests, requests) but seems to be less consistent. For example, he greets his physical therapists and speech clinician, but does not always greet his classroom teacher and never greets peers. He does protest when peers take toys or interfere with his activities.

3. What forms does Jordon use to express these functions? In all settings, Jordon vocalizes, to greet others (except peers). He reaches for objects, looks at adults, vocalizes, to request, and vocalizes cries and sometimes tantrums to protest. Jordon spontaneously produces a variety of one-syllable sounds but does not yet use them to signal specific functions. His mother reports that he can wave goodbye with his right hand with minimal prompting. He waves goodbye at story time and with familiar adults if his mother prompts him.

4. What existing skills can be the basis for building new skills? Jordon can take turns nonverbally (e.g., alternating putting objects in a basket, pushing a car back and forth) and vocally (e.g., making sounds when an adult imitates him). He is able to

do picture-to-object and object-to-picture matching and he is working on a program that teaches him to point to an object after presentation of its verbal label. He can also imitate motor gestures with his right hand (e.g., wave "hi," touch his head, tap his leg). He responds to the word "no" by stopping whatever he is doing. Testing has shown that Jordon has good visual and auditory functioning. His motor development limits both his mobility and, to an extent, his engagement with objects, toys, and peers. Jordon basically does not use the left side of his body. He keeps his left hand tightly clenched and his arm drawn upward. He can sit independently for long periods and is able to pivot around in a circle. He is able to roll from one place to another but typically relies on prompting to do so.

5. What social communication strategies does Jordon use? Jordon gets attention from his mother, his sister, his grandmother, his teachers, and his physical therapist by visually following the person until he can establish eye contact. Upon making eye contact, Jordon smiles and sometimes produces a string of sounds. He can also vocalize and reach for objects and coordinate his attention by looking at an adult, reaching for the object and vocalizing, then looking back at the adult. He smiles and turns toward adults when they speak to him. He responds to his name and to familiar words and simple phrases (e.g., his sister's name, car, eat, potty, time to go) with appropriate anticipatory responses (e.g., looking around for his sister, vocalizing and smiling when it is time to go in the car or eat). He will occasionally respond to a peer by taking a toy the peer offers. He will protest to peers but does not initiate eye contact, vocalizations or smiling toward peers.

Planning the Functional Communication Program

Fourth, Jordon's team plans his functional communication program by considering the data on child performance and learning characteristics in light of the data obtained from the environmental inventories. They begin by determining target responses that are slightly above Jordon's current level of functioning and that are functional across environments and activities. Selected training targets include "more," "help," and pointing to one of two pictures to choose

one of the two represented objects (i.e., choice making). The team feels that many natural opportunities to teach each of these targets will occur across the primary activities and environments.

His team next considers the communication mode to be used in teaching each response. A review of Jordon's expressive modalities indicates that he spontaneously produces a variety of sounds but he does not imitate sounds. He uses his right hand to point to things that he wants and also for picture-object and object-picture matching. He has virtually no use of his left hand. Because this disability places limitations on the repertoire of signs he can ultimately produce and because he already shows some degree of skill using pictures, Jordon's teachers decide that his primary communication system should involve a picture communication board. However, they will always include models of verbal responses.

In summary, three beginning goals are selected for Jordon:

1. Sign "help" (modified).
2. Sign "more" (modified).
3. Indicate choices by pointing on a communication board.

The next step in planning Jordon's communication program is determining how and when to teach these goals. Appropriate vocal stimuli (words) will be paired with pictorial stimuli (pictures representing concepts). Vocal imitation training will be concomitant with the nonvocal communication training. Initially, concrete pictoral stimuli should be used. This poses a problem for training the more abstract concepts of "help" and "more." The teachers decide to teach Jordon to express these responses by producing signs that are modified to accommodate his physical disability. Verbal imitation training of "help" and "more" will accompany the respective sign training.

The third goal, indicating choice, uses the communication board. Initially, two pictures are presented. Beginning with two pictures is appropriate because Jordon already understands that pictures stand for aspects and actions. As Jordon becomes more proficient in using the communication board, additional pictures will be added gradually. The pictures on the communication board vary and are functionally related to the activity at hand. Once Jordon indicates his choice, he is given access to that material.

Fifth, the planning team next discusses the techniques they will use to train the target responses. Milieu Language Teaching procedures are selected.

Model Procedure. Initially, the model procedure would be used to train "help" and "more" at times when Jordon appears to need help or want more of something. The team agrees that they will attempt to give Jordon the opportunity to express each function himself before modeling the appropriate (modified) sign. For example, when Jordon correctly imitates each sign 80% of the time, the teachers will interchange use of the mand-model and time delay procedures to elicit responses. (Attempts by Jordon to indicate "help" or "more" that are followed by the model, mand-model, or time delay procedure technically represent applications of the incidental teaching procedure, i.e., a child's request followed by the model, mand-model, or time delay procedure). In addition to collecting performance data on sign production, the team collects data on vocal imitation training that accompanies each nonverbal training trial. Three Milieu Teaching techniques, the mand-model, time delay, and incidental teaching procedures, are used to teach Jordon to make choices using the communication board. An example of how each of these techniques is applied for this purpose follows.

Mand-Model Procedure. The mand-model procedure is used when Jordon indicates a choice in response to his teacher's presenting two alternatives.

After Jordon has learned to respond by imitating his targets during the model procedure, the mand-model procedure is introduced. When it is Jordon's turn during music group, the teacher shows him the bells and the tambourine. She then places his communication board showing a picture of each of these objects and asks, "Which musical instrument do you want?" If Jordon does not respond or if he makes an incomplete or unclear response, the teacher prompts by presenting a model of the correct response (i.e., demonstrates a clear pointing response to the picture that Jordon appears to favor), or she physically prompts Jordon to make a clear response. The teacher then verbally expands Jordon's nonvocal response (e.g., "You want the bells") and provides an appropriate (i.e., appropriate for the situation and Jordon's level of

functioning) verbal model (e.g., "bells"). After use of the model procedure to train "bells," Jordon is given the bells to shake.

Delay Procedure. The delay procedure is to support Jordon in learning to initiate using his targets. It will be introduced after Jordon has some success using targets in the model and mand-model procedures.

In free play, when Jordon visually expresses interest in a toy, the teacher presents his communication board displaying pictures of the toy of interest and another toy. The teacher looks at Jordon for about 5 seconds but says nothing (delay). If Jordon points to either picture, he receives the corresponding object. A point to the "wrong" picture (i.e., Jordon shows displeasure upon receiving the object) or an incomplete or unclear response results in a mand or model prompt with or without a physical prompt, as necessary. An appropriate verbal model is presented before delivering the chosen toy.

Incidental Teaching Procedure. The incidental teaching procedure is used on occasions when Jordon requests a material or activity. It can be introduced at any point in training because it embeds the model, the mand-model, or time delay procedures as needed to support Jordon's use of his targets.

For example, if Jordon points to the record player, the teacher presents his communication board, displaying pictures of the record player and something else. She then uses the mand-model or delay procedure to elicit a pointing response. Verbal and physical prompts are presented as necessary. Before giving Jordon access to the record player, the model procedure is applied to elicit an appropriate vocal or pointing response.

As a sixth step, several additional tasks are completed in developing Jordon's communication training programs. The team writes task-analyzed instructional programs, including levels of prompts, vocal imitation training procedures, and criterion performance levels for each communication objective. Procedures for data collection and data sheets also are developed. The members of the team agree to do Milieu Language Teaching whenever naturalistic opportunities occur, and especially in the context of other kinds of skill training. Data are collected daily on a minimum of 10 trials for each objective. However, training occurs during other naturalistic teaching opportunities throughout the day. The teachers decide to use certain situations as training settings and other situations as generalization settings. In school, Jordon's communication goals are trained formally during small-group sessions in both his early intervention class and his kindergarten class, during snack, and at recess. Probes for generalization are conducted during large-group sessions, lunch, and gym. Information obtained during the environmental inventories indicates that training to use environmental arrangement strategies and the Milieu Teaching techniques is appropriate for Jordon's mother and his grandmother. Jordon's early intervention teacher, who has had previous Milieu Teaching experience, plans to provide this training by visiting Jordon's home once each week for 2 months. Periodic posttraining visits are made to Jordon's home to assess the Milieu Teaching and to provide feedback and additional training as necessary.

Seventh and finally, the team considers whether didactic communication training should be conducted in conjunction with the naturalistic communication training. The consensus is to implement only the naturalistic training procedures initially. Jordon's vocal imitation skills are monitored carefully and, if the anticipated rate of acquisition is not achieved within 4 months, the issue of concomitant didactic training on vocal imitation skills will again be considered.

Summary

This chapter focuses on applying Milieu Teaching strategies in teaching functional language skills to students with severe disabilities. Choosing milieu strategies requires consideration of the larger system in which language instruction occurs. Thus, the concluding section of this chapter focused on changes that the choice to teach functional language may require in the environments of a student, if the goal of usable skills that are generalized across appropriate settings and events is to be realized.

Teaching functional language is a curriculum goal that requires support from a variety of persons in the larger ecosystem in which instruction occurs. Teaching functional language may require a larger number of persons sharing the responsibility for training than does direct instruction, which occurs only in the classroom. A functional approach to language increases the number of settings in which teaching occurs to include all settings in which communication skills are needed. Functional teaching cannot be limited to classrooms, lunchrooms, playgrounds, vocational settings, homes, transportation vehicles, or the community. All may be necessary training sites. Functional language teaching is integrated into other activities. It is not separate from social interaction or from the learning and application of cognitive skills. The choice to teach functional language implies that training will be more frequent and more dispersed than can easily be managed by speech clinicians who see individual children for two or three sessions each week. Significant others in the life of students must be involved in training new language. The first significant trainer for students with severe disabilities is likely to be a teacher; the second significant trainer is usually a parent or a primary caregiver. Classroom aids, siblings, other therapists, and possibly classmates may also serve as trainers.

Planning begins by gaining consensus that teaching functional language is a priority. Speech clinicians, teachers, parents, and program administrators must agree that language teaching will be a shared responsibility and that language cannot be taught separately from other skills, if it is to be functional. Also, plans for teaching functional language must be embedded in the other aspects of the curriculum for each student. A truly critical step in planning is allocation of resources for training. Assigning responsibility, providing necessary training, facilitating access to appropriate training settings, and sharing information are essential aspects of allocating resources for functional language training. Finally, part of the planning effort must be the development of problem-solving strategies through team collaboration, because problems undoubtedly arise when such broad-based instruction is undertaken.

Not surprisingly, teachers who choose the goal of teaching functional language often must advocate building a system in which meeting this goal is possible. Functional language teachers must enlist the cooperation and support of colleagues who work with their students. Functional language teachers may find it necessary to provide training for willing colleagues and to negotiate compromises with less willing ones. Student progress data may be used for a new purpose—demonstrating that a functional approach produces the desired changes in communication. Choosing to implement a functional teaching approach may require improving one's own skills, learning new ways to teach, and learning ways to promote environmental support for language.

Suggested Activities

1. Observe a young child with disabilities for a period of 1 to 2 hours. Note the ways in which the child attempts to communicate and the ways in which the adults in the environments respond. From these observations and your notes, identify at least five opportunities to teach a functional language skill. Describe the context, the skill, and the procedure you would use to teach the skill.

2. One of the most important skills that a teacher must master is clear communication about communication. Review Michael's case study at the beginning of this chapter. Then role-play, explaining his skills, his needs, and the basics of Milieu Teaching to Michael's home room general education teacher. This exercise works best in teams of three: (a) one person explains, (b) one person plays the general education teacher, and (c) one person evaluates the interaction and gives feedback. Switch roles and use what you learn from one another. Summarize what you have learned after all three people have role-played.

3. Consider how to create a classroom that is a "context for conversation." Choose a type of classroom that reflects the age and most appropriate options for students of interest to you. Include the following: (a) how teachers will interact with students, (b) the classroom schedules, (c) the physical design of the classroom, and (d) training for teaching assistants and peers. List five simple things that you might do to promote communication in the classroom.

References

Alpert, C. L., & Kaiser, A. (1992). Training parents as milieu language teachers. *Journal of Early Intervention*, 16(1), 31–52.

Alpert, C. L., Kaiser, A., Hemmeter, M. L., & Ostrosky, M. (1987, November). Training adults to use environmental arrangement strategies to prompt language. Paper presented at the annual meeting of the Division of Early Childhood, Council on Exceptional Children, Denver, CO.

Alpert, C. L., & Rogers-Warren, A. K. (1985). Communication of autistic persons, characteristics and intervention. In S. F. Warren & A. K. Rogers-Warren (Eds.), *Teaching functional language* (pp. 123–155). Baltimore: University Park Press.

Anderson, S. R., & Spradlin, J. E. (1980). The generalized effects of productive labeling training involving comment object classes. *Journal of the Association for the Severely Handicapped*, 5, 143–157.

Bates, E. (1976). Pragmatics and sociolinguistics in child language. In D. Morehead & A. Morehead (Eds.), *Normal and deficient child language*. Baltimore: University Park Press.

Bricker, D., & Cripe, J. (1989). Activity-based intervention. In D. Bricker (Ed.), *Early intervention for at-risk and handicapped infants, toddlers and preschool children* (pp. 251–274). Palo Alto, CA: VORT Corp.

Bruner, J., Roy, C., & Ratner, N. (1980). The beginnings of requests. In K. E. Neelson (Ed.), *Children's language* (vol. 3, pp. 91–138). New York: Gardner.

Cavallero, C. C., & Bambara, L. (1982). Two strategies for teaching language during free play. *Journal of the Association for the Severely Handicapped*, 7(2), 80–93.

Charlop, M. H., & Walsh, M. E. (1986). Increasing autistic children's spontaneous verbalizations of affection: An assessment of time delay and peer modeling procedures. *Journal of Applied Behavior Analysis*, 19, 307–314.

Gee, K., Graham, N., Goetz, L., Oshima, G., & Yoshioka, K. (1991). Teaching students to request the continuation of routine activities by using time delay and decreasing physical assistance in the context of chain interruption. *Journal of the Association for Persons with Severe Handicaps*, 16, 154–167.

Gee, K., Graham, N., Sailor, W., & Goetz, L. (1995). Use of integrated general education and community settings as primary contexts for skill instruction for students with severe, multiple disabilities. *Behavior Modification*, 19, 33–58.

Gresham, F. M., & MacMillan, D. L. (1997). Autistic recovery? An analysis and critique of the empirical evidence on the early intervention project. *Behavioral Disorders*, 22(4), 185–201.

Halle, J. W., Baer, D. M., & Spradlin, J. E. (1981). Teachers' generalized use of delay as a stimulus control procedure to increase language use in handicapped children. *Journal of Applied Behavior Analysis*, 14, 387–400.

Halle, J. W., Marshall, A. M., & Spradlin, J. E. (1979). Time delay: A technique to increase language use and facilitate generalization in retarded children. *Journal of Applied Behavior Analysis*, 12, 431–440.

Hamilton, B., & Snell, M. E. (1993). Using the milieu approach to increase spontaneous communication book use across environments by an adolescent with autism. *Augmentative and Alternative Communication*, 9, 259–272.

Hancock, T. B., & Kaiser, A. P. (1996). Siblings' use of milieu teaching at home. *Topics in Early Childhood Special Education*, 16(2), 168–190.

Haring, T. G., Neetz, J. A., Lovinger, L., Peck, C., & Semmel, M. I. (1987). Effects of four modified incidental teaching procedures to create opportunities for communication. *Journal of the Association for Persons with Severe Handicaps*, 12, 218–226.

Haring, T. G., Roger, B., Lee, M., Breen, C., & Gaylord-Ross, R. (1986). Teaching social language to moderately handicapped students. *Journal of Applied Behavior Analysis, 19*, 159–171.

Hart, B. (1985). Naturalistic language training strategies. In S. F. Warren & A. Rogers-Warren (Eds.), *Teaching functional language* (pp. 63–88). Baltimore: University Park Press.

Hart, B. M., & Risley, T. R. (1968). Establishing the use of descriptive adjectives in the spontaneous speech of disadvantaged preschool children. *Journal of Applied Behavior Analysis, 1*, 109–120.

Hart, B. M., & Risley, T. R. (1974). Using preschool materials to modify the language of disadvantaged children. *Journal of Applied Behavior Analysis, 7*, 243–256.

Hart, B. M., & Risley, T. R. (1975). Incidental teaching of language in the preschool. *Journal of Applied Behavior Analysis, 8*, 411–420.

Hart, B. M., & Risley, T. R. (1980). In vivo language intervention: Unanticipated general effects. *Journal of Applied Behavior Analysis, 12*, 407–432.

Hart, B. M., & Risley, T. R. (1988). Incidental strategies. In R. L. Schiefelbusch (Ed.), *Language competence: Assessment and intervention* (pp. 213–225). San Diego: College Hill.

Hart, B. M., & Rogers-Warren, A. K. (1978). Milieu teaching approaches. In R. L. Schiefelbusch (Ed.), *Bases of language intervention* (vol. 2, pp. 193–235). Baltimore: University Park Press.

Hemmeter, M. L., Ault, M. J., Collins, B. C., & Meyers, S. (1996). The effects of teacher-implemented feedback within free time activities. *Education and Training in Mental Retardation and Developmental Disabilities, 31*, 203–212.

Hemmeter, M. L., & Kaiser, A. P. (1994). Enhanced milieu teaching: Effects of parent-implemented language intervention. *Journal of Early Intervention, 18*, 269–289.

Hunt, P., Alwell, M., & Goetz, L. (1988). Acquisition of conversation skills and the reduction of inappropriate social interaction behaviors. *Journal of the Association for Persons with Severe Handicaps, 13*, 20–27.

Kaiser, A. P., Hancock T. B., & Hester, P. P. (1998a). Parents as co-interventionists: Research on applications of naturalistic language teaching procedures. *Infants and Young Children, 10*(4), 1–11.

Kaiser, A. P., Hancock, T. B., Nietfeld, J. P., & Delaney, E. (1996). Adapting enhanced milieu teaching for children with autism. Paper presented at the meeting of DEC International Early Childhood Conference on Children with Special Needs, Phoenix, AZ.

Kaiser, A. P., Lambert, W., Hancock, T., & Hester, P. P. (1998b). *Differential outcomes of naturalistic language intervention.* Paper presented at the 31st Annual Gatlinburg Conference on Research and Theory in Mental Retardation and Development Disabilities, Charleston, SC.

Kaiser, A. P., Yoder, P. J., & Keetz, A. (1992). Evaluating milieu teaching. In S. F. Warren & J. Reichle (Eds.), *Causes and effects in communication and language intervention* (pp. 9–47). Baltimore: Paul H. Brookes.

McEachin, J. J., Smith, T., & Lovaas, O. I. (1993). Long-term outcome for children with autism who received early intensive behavioral treatment. *American Journal on Mental Retardation, 97*, 359–372.

McGee, G. G., Krantz, P. J., & McClannahan, L. E. (1985). The facilitative effects of incidental teaching on preposition use by autistic children. *Journal of Applied Behavior Analysis, 18*, 17–31.

Moerk, E. L. (1983). *The mother of Eve as a first language teacher.* Norwood, NJ: Ablex.

Newport, E. L. (1976). Motherese: The speech of mothers to young children. In N. J. Castellan, D. B. Pisoni, & G. R. Potts (Eds.), *Cognitive theory* (vol. 2, pp. 177–218). Hillsdale, NJ: Lawrence Erlbaum Associates.

Oliver, C. B., & Halle, J. W. (1982). Language training in the everyday environment: Teaching functional sign use to a retarded child. *Journal of the Association for the Severely Handicapped, 7*(3), 50–62.

Ostrosky, M. M., Kaiser, A. P., & Odom, S. L. (1993). Facilitating children's social communicative interactions through the use of peer-mediated interventions. In A. P. Kaiser & D. B. Gray (Eds.), *Enhancing children's communication: Research foundations for intervention* (vol. 8, pp. 7–43). Baltimore: Paul H. Brookes.

Rogers-Warren, A. K., & Warren, S. F. (1980). Mand for verbalization: Facilitating the display of newly-taught language. *Behavior Modification, 4*, 361–382.

Romski, M. A., & Sevcik, R. A. (1992). Developing augmented language in children with severe mental retardation. In S. F. Warren & J. Reichle (Eds.) *Causes and effects in communication and language intervention* (pp. 113–130). Baltimore: Paul H. Brookes.

Schacter, F. F. (1979). Everyday mother talk to toddlers: Early intervention. New York: Academic Press.

Schwartz, I. S., Anderson, S. R., & Halle, J. W. (1988). Training teachers to use naturalistic time delay: Effects on teacher behavior and on the language use of students. *Journal of the Association for Persons with Severe Handicaps, 14*, 48–57.

Stokes, T. F., & Baer, D. M. (1977). An implicit technology of generalization. *Journal of Applied Behavior Analysis, 10*, 349–367.

Wacker, D. P., & Reichle, J. (1993). Functional communication training as an intervention for problem behavior: An overview and introduction to our edited volume. In J. Reichle & D. P. Wacker (Eds.) *Communicative alternatives to challenging behavior: Integrating functional assessment and intervention strategies* (vol. 3)(pp. 1–8). Baltimore: Paul H. Brookes.

Warren, S. F., & Bambara, L. M. (1989). An experimental analysis of milieu language intervention: Teaching and action-object form. *Journal of Speech and Hearing Disorders, 54*, 448–461.

Warren, S. F., McQuarter, R. J., & Rogers-Warren, A. K. (1984). The effects of teacher mands and models on the speech of unresponsive language-delayed children. *Journal of Speech and Hearing Research, 51*, 43–52.

Warren, S. F., & Rogers-Warren, A. K. (1983). Setting variables affecting the display of trained noun referents by retarded children. In K. Kernan, M. Begab, & R. Edgerton (Eds.), *Environments and behavior: The adaptation of mentally retarded persons* (pp. 257–282). Baltimore: University Park Press.

Warren, S. F., & Rogers-Warren, A. K. (1985). Teaching functional language: An introduction. In S. F. Warren & A. K. Rogers-Warren (Eds.), *Teaching functional language* (pp. 3–23). Baltimore: University Park Press.

Yoder, P. J., Kaiser, A. P., & Alpert, C. L. (1991). An exploratory study of the interaction between language teaching methods and child characteristics. *Journal of Speech and Hearing Research, 34*, 155–167.

13

Teaching Functional Academics

Diane Browder
Martha E. Snell

With increased opportunities to be part of general education and to use the community, students with severe disabilities have more need for academic skills than ever before. While some students may learn a broad range of useful academic skills, others will need a functional approach that focuses on acquiring a few, precisely defined academic skills for use in everyday activities, both in and out of school. These functional academic skills typically include sight word reading and skills to read numbers, count, use money, and tell time. Some students may also learn some writing, spelling, and computation skills. This chapter describes considerations for targeting and teaching these skills.

Three students with rather different needs and abilities are described in the following vignettes to illustrate how these teaching considerations are applied. These students are 7-year-old Sharon, who spends much of her day in her second-grade classroom; sixth-grader Simon, who is 11 years old and attends middle school; and Jerome, an 18-year-old young man who is well into realizing his transition plan. All students participate in general education, although each with different objectives and intensities. Both Simon and Jerome take part in community-based instruction, although Simon spends more time using his functional academics in the context of middle school activities.

Sharon is 7 years old and has Down syndrome. She has been classified as having moderate mental retardation. She is nonverbal and uses some signs and pictures to communicate. Sharon is a student in Ms. Farmer's second-grade class. Sharon's parents want her to learn to read, write, and perform basic math so that she will have a foundation of skills for participation in general education throughout her school career. During most of the day, she participates in the second-grade lessons in ways that Ms. Farmer and her special education teacher, Mr. Albert, have planned for her. For example, when Ms. Farmer gives seat work in language arts, Sharon practices reading Dolch sight words and other key sight words (e.g., her name, her hometown, "girls") with a fourth-grade peer tutor. Because she does not use speech to communicate, Sharon responds to her tutor's questions (e.g., "Find the word 'the'") by pointing or locating a word card or by using her communication device, an Introtalker (©Prentke Romich Co.), a digitized speech output communication device that is controlled by pressing preprogrammed keys with pictures or symbols to activate a voice.

Sharon practices writing her name on her own by using a template (a cardboard cutout of her name that she moves her pencil through). Sometimes she works on the Edmark reading computer program with Ms. Forest, the special education aid. Although Sharon does not read at the second-grade level, she participates in small-group reading lessons by listening to her peers read and attending to the pictures. She answers questions by pointing to the pictures in the stories or signing.

Ms. Farmer uses cooperative learning groups frequently, especially for science and social studies. For example, when groups were assigned the task of developing a poster to describe weather conditions, each student was given information resources. Sharon was given a National Geographic with pictures of heavy rainstorms. She contributed to her group's poster by cutting out and adding a picture to help them describe rain.

With the speech therapist, Sharon gets intensive instruction to learn to read and use new pictures and words for communication. Mr. Albert gives Sharon addi-

tional tutoring in sight words and using money with a group of students. This small group instruction focuses on the upcoming "weekly special." For example, the group learns the sight words for making cupcakes using a box mix or practices the next dollar strategy to go to Burger King (Box 13–1). Once a week, Mr. Albert helps Sharon use her new academic skills by either making a purchase at the school store or in the community or through cooking or another activity.

The following are the academic objectives on Sharon's Individualized Educational Plan (IEP):

When given an array of Dolch functional sight words on flash cards or her Introtalker and asked, "Find the word _____", Sharon will point to the correct word within 3 seconds on 3 out of 3 days.

With the aid of a template, Sharon will write her full name with all letters formed correctly on 3 out of 3 days.

When given short passages or sentences of known words, with newly mastered words added weekly (e.g., Dolch words, Edmark words), Sharon will read brief passages and point to pictures to indicate comprehension, maintaining 90% correct on this weekly test.

When given known functional sight words in the context of a daily living activity (e.g., cooking), Sharon will demonstrate comprehension of the words in performing the activity. Criterion: applies 90% of words independently.

When participating in a second-grade reading group, Sharon will demonstrate listening comprehension by pointing to a picture in the story for 4 out of 5 days each week.

Given a personal schedule, Sharon will follow it to begin each day's activity by reading the word and time and then selecting appropriate materials for all activities of the day. Criterion: independent for 2 weeks (schedule changes daily).

When she has the opportunity to make a purchase at school or in the community, Sharon will use the "next dollar strategy" to select the correct money amount for 5 out of 5 purchases.

Simon

Simon, an 11-year-old, has autism. Most of his elementary years were spent in a self-contained classroom for children with autism. Recently, his parents and teachers have developed ways for him to spend more of his time in general education. During his elementary years, Simon acquired some useful academic skills: counting to 50, adding and subtracting single digit numbers, and reading words and simple phrases. He reads about 50 sight words including a mix of high-frequency words (Dolch words) and words from daily living (e.g., food words, directions from cassette player, school schedule words). Simon can distinguish between denominations of money and count dollar bills by one. Simon's challenge is using his skills in context. For example, he has not yet mastered using the next dollar method because he has difficulty counting if he does not begin with "one." Although he can read the words on a food package, he does not initiate the steps to prepare the food. He can read the words on his schedule, but does not seem to know to go to the math room when the schedule says "math."

Simon likes school, textbooks, notebooks, bookbags, and other school supplies. While he had some difficulty being with five new teachers and almost 100 new students his first weeks of middle school, he shows a strong preference for having his own desk, books, and supplies in each class. His teachers plan to use the school's supply "store" twice a week to provide easy opportunities to make small purchases and give him practice with reading (purchase list) and money skills.

Simon uses Ms. Jones' tutoring and study hall area as his home base between classes. There he learns to read his schedule and identify where to go next. Ms. Jones is recruiting eighth graders from the student tutoring program to assist in his schedule use by prompting him to read the schedule word and find his class. In most of his classes, Simon will look at the textbook pictures as the teacher lectures, but he also has specific related tasks for each class to keep him actively involved. For example, Simon might select and use in some way the relevant labeled pictures from his "photo notebook" of pictures related to the class topics; each picture in the notebook has brief labels he has added as an ongoing homework project. During seat work, he works through a folder that Ms. Jones gives him for each period. Depending on the class, this folder includes match-to-sample practice with sight words, computation of prices with a calculator, and practice writing his name in cursive as a signature. When possible, Ms. Jones adapts the general education teacher's own worksheets to incorporate these skills in some way:

- Finding the words "men" and "women" on a social studies page
- Signing his name in cursive on each page of a science handout
- Locating pictures from his photo notebook to illustrate circled words

In his language arts class, Ms. Jones joins the class to teach vocabulary words to Simon in a small group of classmates. She uses a constant time delay procedure (see chapter 4). Each student is learning a different word set depending on their reading level. Interestingly, Simon is incidentally learning some of his peers' words that far exceed his "reading level."

In home economics and shop, Simon and two other students receive support from Mr. Sanchez, the paraprofessional who works with Ms. Jones. Mr. Sanchez keeps a list of sight words, measurement skills, and other tasks used in these classes that can also be practiced during other times of the day. Mr. Sanchez' goal is to create opportunities daily for Simon to use some of his academic skills in the shop or home economics activity and to "connect" Simon to a classmate who works alongside him for these applied activities. Sometimes such applications occur naturally (e.g., the home economics lesson is on preparing box mixes using sight words Simon knows). Other times, Mr. Sanchez creates opportunities (having Simon subtract a measurement in shop class to determine how long his board will be after he saws it.)

One period a day, Simon leaves school for a community setting, where he is taught by Ms. Jones or a job coach. Two days a week, he has an exploratory "job," which changes every month; these early work experiences are part of his first transition plan, written into his recent IEP. Currently, he is working in a plant nursery and is learning to use a sight word/picture schedule to follow in doing his jobs. The job coach uses a feedback procedure to help him read and follow the schedule each day. During the other days of the week, Simon receives instruction in making purchases, using a restaurant, and using other community resources. Ms. Jones sets up each activity to incorporate a variety of academic skills, such as using a word/symbol list or using numbers. Just before the community outing, Ms. Jones tutors Simon in the academic skill to be used that day. For example, they might do a sight word drill using a grocery list or practice

continued

counting money. The following are a sample of academic objectives from Simon's IEP:

> Across a variety of general education contexts, Simon will sign his name in cursive on each class handout on 5 out of 6 opportunities for 2 out of 2 days.
>
> During general education class time involving independent seat work, Simon will initiate getting out his folder to practice known academic skills, remaining on task with no more than one prompt from the general education teacher in 20 minutes.

> When given opportunities to purchase at school or in the community, Simon will apply his academic skills to read a shopping list and select the correct money amount. Criterion: makes purchases independently on 4 out of 5 days.
>
> Given a written schedule of classes, Simon will read the name of each class and find it by the time the bell rings for 5 out of 5 days.
>
> Given sight words presented in a variety of materials and activities, Simon will generalize his skills to read and apply the words with at least 5 demonstrations of generalization weekly.

 Jerome

Jerome is 18 years old and is a senior in his high school. He will go through graduation and then advance to a full-time job and community-based life skills training program during the last 3 years of special education services. In addition to a severe intellectual disability, Jerome has physical limitations and uses a wheelchair, which he is unable to operate by himself. He communicates in several ways: facial expressions, vocalizations, and by using a Dynavox, a dynamic voice output electronic communication board with pictographic symbols for each word/phrase, which he operates with a hand switch attached to his tray (©Prentke Romich Co.).

Although Jerome likes school, he finds academics to be a challenge. Jerome has learned to read six sight words: "Jerome," "Central" (his high school), "men," "Coke" (a favorite beverage), "X-Files" (a favorite TV show), and "basketball" (his favorite sport). These words are on his communication board along with numerous picture symbols he uses to communicate (e.g., picture symbols for "I want," "Let's stop now," "Let's talk"). Jerome has participated in a Best Buddies program at his high school for the past 2 years; his buddy, Max, is a senior and on the varsity basketball team. Being a Buddy means that Jerome and Max spend time together each week hanging out; once a week Jerome eats with Max and his friends. During basketball season, Jerome attends many practice sessions with another pair of buddies to watch Max and the team play.

In math Jerome can now recognize the numbers 1 through 59 and uses this knowledge to read digital clock times and prices. When prompted where to look, he can distinguish between types of dollar bills (e.g., fives versus ones). Jerome loses track when counting items, but can count more accurately by pushing things across his tray into a counting jig. Given Jerome's age and academic level, he and his team have decided to make all of his academic training as "real world" as possible (a specific, embedded approach).

Through his friendship with Max, Jerome has a lot of high school friends who help him get to his classes. Jerome and his teachers have selected classes that use creative approaches to instruction (e.g., media, student presentations, cooperative learning, Internet) and give him the opportunity for social interactions and exposure to a variety of curricula in interesting ways. This year he is taking drama, business math, and world geography because these classes meet these criteria; he has a study hall, where he gets tutoring from his special education teacher. The rest of his blocked schedule is divided between three periods of community-based instruction and peer tutoring at school.

Ms. Johnson, Jerome's special education teacher, creates ways during each new academic unit for Jerome to learn and use a new sight word or math skill that is applicable within the class. For example, in drama he is learning to use the words "applause," "actors," "play," and "lines;" the stage crew is exploring a way to connect Jerome's switch so he have an active part in the productions by operating the curtains. With Max, his buddy, he is learning to read the school names for each competing basketball team (coded with their school colors) and keeps a record of the wins and losses in his basketball Dynovox file. In business math, he does at least one problem on the calculator or computer with a peer's assistance.

Like many other students in his high school, Jerome has chosen a work/study curricular track in which he leaves school 2 to 3 hours early for a job. During this time he receives both community-based instruction and job training from Ms. Johnson or a job coach. On the way to the job, Jerome is learning to read familiar signs and to discriminate between the "walk" and "don't walk" sign. Jerome now works in a K-Mart as a greeter. Jerome is learning to read the aisle marker words at the store where he works. He also is learning to order from the menu in the store's restaurant and to pay for his food.

Here are some of the academic objectives from Jerome's IEP:

During each new academic unit in his general education classes, Jerome will learn at least one new sight word or one new math response and will apply this response in the class on at least 3 out of 5 days (e.g., pressing the word for "applause" in drama; selecting the word "United States" when shown a map in geography).

Using his Dynovox file, Jerome will keep score during sports events by finding the correct team name and tallying points with score correct for 3 out of 3 games.

In Business Math class, or when planning a community purchase, Jerome will use a calculator to add prices with all steps of the task analysis correct for 3 out of 3 days.

On the way to work, Jerome will identify when the street sign says "Walk" versus "Don't Walk" and will nod to indicate he is ready to cross the street safely for 10 out of 10 days.

When working as a store greeter, Jerome will select the correct aisle marker description on his Dynovox when asked, "Where is _____?" with 8 out of 8 aisle markers correct for 5 out of 5 days.

Overview of Functional Academics

The Importance of Functional Academics

Functional academics are simply the most useful parts of the "three R's"—reading, writing, and arithmetic. However, what is "useful" must be defined individually by studying each student's current daily routines, predicting future needs, and establishing a set of priorities in basic math and reading, as well as money, time, counting, and writing skills. Functional academics are skills, often learned early in general education, that have lifelong application in performing activities of daily living.

For some students, the mastery of several key functional reading or math responses can increase a student's independence and self-direction at home, work, school, or in the community. These functional responses can be pivotal in enabling a person to access services, to actively participate, to indicate a choice, or to be independent. For example, by learning some specific sight words, students may be able to recognize warnings on product labels (Collins & Stinson, 1995), prepare menus (Collins, Branson, & Hall, 1995), do chores or follow a schedule of chores (Browder, Hines, McCarthy & Fees, 1984; Lalli & Browder, 1993), select television shows or movies, or shop for groceries (Schuster, Griffen, & Wolery, 1992). Other students might learn sight words related to their general education grade level curriculum: for example, words from a seventh-grade social studies unit on South American countries or a science lesson on fossils that their classmates are learning in more depth (Johnson,

Schuster, & Bell, 1996). While these words may not be frequently used, they allow meaningful participation in adapted class activities alongside peers. Sometimes students with severe disabilities may master targeted sight words in small, heterogeneous groups with classmates who are nondisabled but also need word practice (Schoen & Ogden, 1995).

In math, pivotal skills for a student might involve counting dollars or discriminating between classes of money allowing him or her to make store purchases independently (Westling, Floyd, & Carr, 1990) or buy lunch or snacks (Gardill & Browder, 1995; McDonnell, 1987). By learning number comparisons, students can do comparison shopping (Sandknap, Schuster, Wolery & Cross, 1992). Like reading, math facts might also be learned in a heterogeneous group of students with and without disabilities who need some direct instruction (Whalen, Schuster, & Hemmeter, 1996). Some students with severe disabilities may progress beyond these basic academic responses and benefit from the direct and remedial instruction in academics described in methods textbooks for students with milder disabilities. Most students, however, will acquire some high-priority sight words, counting or classification skills, and number recognition. These pivotal academic skills can be applied to a broad range of life activities and are the focus of this chapter.

Selecting Functional Academic Skills for Instruction

To determine the functional academic priorities for an individual student, two instructional decisions need to be made. The first decision involves selecting the approach and outcomes for academic instruction and the second involves curriculum planning

Select a Teaching Approach

There are four basic options for approaching the instruction of academic skills (Table 13–1). These include:

- General education curriculum (with or without adaptations)
- Functional, generalized skills usable across life routines
- Embedded academic skills for specific life routines
- Adaptations to bypass academic skills

In the first approach, general education curriculum (with or without adaptations), the expectation is for the student to master grade level material with outcomes similar to students who are nondisabled, though perhaps at a much slower pace. This approach most often suits students without disabilities or students who have minimal learning difficulties in acad-

emics. For example, students with autism may be able to master grade level material. In the second approach, functional, generalized skills usable across life routines, the expectation is that the student will master some pivotal skills, such reading a sight vocabulary, counting, and recognizing numbers, and use these skills in a variety of school, home, and community activities. In the third approach, embedded academic skills usable in specific life routines, the goal is for the student to learn some academic skills as part of a daily living routine (e.g., grocery shopping, as shown in Figure 13–1). Unlike a functional generalized skills approach, in an embedded academic approach, the student may not be able to generalize these academic responses to activities beyond the ones in which they are taught. The last approach, adaptations to bypass academic skills, involves using adaptations, such as money envelopes, counting boards, preset alarm signals on a watch, or color coding, to avoid the required academic skill altogether (e.g., reading, counting, or time-telling), while still participating in the ac-

TABLE 13–1

Approaches for Teaching Functional Academics

Academic Approach	Learning Outcomes	Example
General education curriculum with or without adaptations	Student will master grade level material with outcomes similar to most classmates.	Simon completes the unit on the solar system with sixth-grade science class. For his group project, Simon helps to make the styrofoam model of Saturn.
Functional, generalized skills usable across life routines	Student will learn some pivotal skills (i.e., useful word and number recognition and counting) and use them in home, school, and community activities.	Sharon is mastering generalized counting skills. She can count dollars to make a purchase, objects to do simple addition in math class, and ingredients when cooking with her mother. She not only learns sight words related to daily activities, such as following her schedule, but also learns high-frequency words that she uses in reading and other academic subjects.
Embedded academic skills usable in specific life routines	Student will acquire an academic response as part of a daily life routine (e.g., use money to buy school lunch; use time and word schedule to organize day).	Jerome has a sight word vocabulary of five words. He uses each of these words in a specific way. For example, he finds his name on a set of job cards at his work site. He can select a sweatshirt that has the name of his school to wear on school spirit day.
Adaptations to bypass academic skills	Student will learn to use adaptations that avoid the need for an academic skill (e.g., money envelopes, bus passes).	Because it is difficult for Jerome to count money, his teacher helps him use a predetermined amount of money to make purchases (e.g., a dollar for a soda.)

tivity. The last two approaches require that instruction occurs in realistic settings so that students learn to transfer their skill to life routines. While a functional, generalized skills approach involves some instruction under realistic conditions, it may also include some academic drills (e.g., massed trial instruction of a list of functional sight words). This chapter focuses on the second and third approaches: functional, generalized skills usable across life routines and embedded academic skills usable for specific life routines.

FIGURE 13–1

(a) Dave uses a price record when he goes grocery shopping to write down his grocery list. (b) He enters the rounded-up price in the far right column. (c) He totals up the rounded-up prices to calculate how many one dollar bills he will need. (d) Dave counts out the number of dollars and pays for his groceries.

a

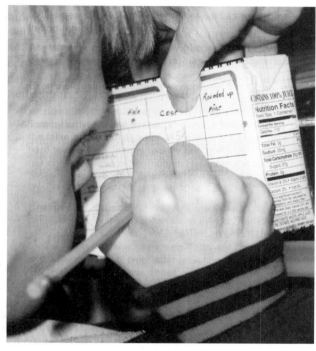

b

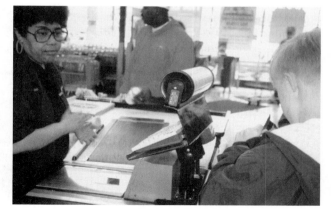

c

d

Chapter 14 provides examples of permanent prompts that can be used to bypass academic instruction.

To determine which approach to use, the planning team will consider six factors:

- The student's preferences
- The parents' preferences
- The students' chronological age or how many years left in school
- The student's current and future settings
- The student's rate of learning academic skills
- The student's other skill needs

Sharon, the second grader who was described earlier, is just beginning academic instruction and her parents place a priority on learning academic skills. Sharon might have several academic goals in functional generalized skills (e.g., counting money) combined with numerous opportunities to keep pace with the general education curriculum, with materials adapted as needed.

The sixth grader named Simon, who likes academic instruction, has mastered about 50 sight words and can count accurately by ones to 30; his team might target a combination of some functional, generalized academic skills (e.g.,

sight words usable in school and community settings, comparing prices or times) and some more specific skills. In the specific, embedded approach, Simon might be taught precise ways to use his existing counting and reading abilities (e.g., counting when starting at any number, using the next dollar strategy to buy items at the school store as illustrated in Box 13–1, reading a word schedule to get to classes).

In contrast, think of Jerome, the high school student we described earlier who had years of instruction on counting money and reading sight words, but made minimal progress, and dislikes this instruction. This teenager might be more motivated if all his instruction is focused on real life routines and targeted either specific, embedded academics (e.g., recognizing classroom numbers; using sight words to follow a job list) or strategies to bypass academics that require too much time to teach (e.g., learn to show a bus pass rather than count out needed change). Table 13–2 gives some suggested guidelines for determining what academic approach to choose for a student.

Carry Out Curriculum Planning

Once an academic approach (or combination of approaches) is determined, curriculum planning is

---

"One More Than" Technique, or "Next Dollar Strategy"

Box 13–1

"One More Than" Technique

Stimulus: Teacher/cashier requests the amount needed: "That will be thirteen dollars and eight cents."
Target Response: Using $1 bills, the student counts out one more than the number of dollars named (e.g., 13).
Teaching tips: Teacher role playing the cashier states prices as _____ dollars and _____ cents. Begin with practice prices from the whole dollar price group (0 to $5.00), then move to progressively more difficult price groups ($5.01 to $10.00, $10.01 to $20.00). As part of feedback for correct responses, restate the correct amount and the rule: "Fourteen dollars. That's right, fourteen dollars is one more than thirteen dollars." Incorrect responses are followed by a model of the technique and an opportunity to try again. If still wrong, go to a different price.

"One More Than" Plus the Cents Pile Modification

Stimulus: Cashier gives price requests that include the shortened form, omitting the word "dollar" (e.g., "Four fifty-two").
Response: Using $1 bills, the student puts one dollar aside in the "cents pile," counts out the requested dollar amount, and then combines the two piles and gives the total to the trainer/cashier.
Teaching tips: This modification might only be taught if the simpler method is not learned.

"Say-Back" Method

Stimulus: Cashier states prices in the shortened form, omitting the word "dollar" (e.g., "Two sixty").
Response: Student is taught to say back to the trainer/cashier the amount in terms of dollars and cents (i.e., "Two dollars and sixty cents") before counting out the correct number of dollar bills.
Teaching tips: This approach may not be needed for all students.

Reference: Test, Howell, Burkhart, & Beroth (1993)

TABLE 13–2
Guidelines for Choosing an Academic Approach

Student: _____ Grade/Age: _____ Date: _____

Individuals completing form: _____

Directions to complete form: Team members should independently complete the form for a particular student.

1. How well does the student like academics?
   A. Lots   B. Some   C. Not at all

2. How important are academics to the parents?
   A. High   B. Medium   C. Low

3. How old is the student?
   A. Elementary   B. Middle school   C. High school

4. How many life skills does this student lack for his or her age?
   A. A few   B. Some   C. Lots

5. How well has the student learned academic skills in the past?
   A. Well or no opportunity yet
   B. Some sight words and math skills acquired
   C. Minimal progress after years of instruction

6. To what extent do the other activities in the student's daily schedule require academic skills?
   A. Lots—most of day has an academic focus
   B. Some
   C. Minimal (e.g., student is mostly in community job that does not require academic skills)

Directions for using the results: Team members should discuss their ratings and reach consensus on each item. The number of A, B and C ratings for the group are totalled below. If primarily "A" responses are indicated, the student is a candidate for functional, generalized academics and may also be a candidate for general education (with or without adaptations). A mix of "A" and "B" ratings may suggest functional, generalized academics and some embedded academics. Mostly "C" ratings may suggest an embedded academic approach in which skills are only introduced as part of life routines or may support modifications to by-pass academics.

"A" ratings: _____/6   "B" ratings: _____/6   "C" ratings: _____/6

---

needed. Ryndak and Alper (1996) suggest a twofold approach to this planning:

First, determine general education outcomes.

Second, identify functional priorities.

For general education outcomes, the team first reviews the scope and sequence of the curriculum in the general education classes a student will take and selects specific outcomes that may be relevant to this student. Then by reviewing the student's life domains (i.e., school, vocational, home, recreational, community), the team selects life skill priorities for each domain. To determine which priority skills (IEP objectives) are addressed in each general education class, team members examine the general education out-

comes for every class and select life skills that overlap with the outcomes and can be applied in that class. Some life skills need to be addressed in contexts outside the general education classroom; these are identified and placed into the student's school and community-based schedule. For example,

Sharon will work on writing her name with a template in her second-grade class during: a) handwriting, b) social studies (putting her name on handouts), and c) art (putting her name on her projects).

Jerome will work on gaining new academic sight words during his drama, business math, and world geography classes. In contrast, he will learn to apply new functional sight words during his job training and community-based instruction. He will learn to use a calculator during his business

math class, but will apply this skill to make purchases at the school store and in the community.

Many times functional academic skill priorities will emerge when the team completes an ecological inventory of a student's life domains. Other functional academic skills may emerge from reviewing the general education curriculum apart from a specific student and determining functional life applications for some objectives (e.g., science labs and home economics lend themselves to following sequenced, written or pictured directions, reading numbers, and measuring things). Giangreco, Cloninger, and Iverson (1993) describe this cross prioritization process in *Choosing Options and Accommodations for Children* (COACH) by identifying three basic ways to teach students with severe disabilities in general education activities.

1. Students have the same learning outcomes in the same learning activities as their general education classmates.
2. Students focus on the same curriculum area, doing the same activity, but have different goals and objectives (multilevel curriculum and instruction), which works well for teaching functional, generalized academics.
3. All students participate in the same lesson but learn skills from different curricular areas (curricular overlapping).

Let's examine several examples.

Multilevel:

In a math class where students are working on number comparisons (less than and greater than), Sharon participates in math (same curriculum) doing the same class activity (comparing sets of numbers), but with a different, less complex objective (she compares two-digit prices by sorting price tags while others complete problems comparing three- or four-digit numbers).

Curriculum Overlapping:

Simon participates in a science lesson and performs the lab work with a partner (same activity), but Simon has two reading goals—to follow picture/word sequenced directions and to read the functional sight words related to safety, such as "hot" and "caution" (different curricular area: reading).

Both Giangreco et al. (1993) and Ryndak and Alper (1996) note that sometimes a fourth alternative is needed in curriculum planning. Sometimes a

student needs an alternative activity outside of the general education class in order to learn adequately or because a class activity cannot be easily adapted. For example, when the class takes tests, Simon and Jerome leave to practice purchasing at the school store or to participate in community-based instruction using newly acquired functional academic skills.

Teaching Strategies for Functional Academics

Once a teacher has determined what to teach and when to teach it in the daily schedule, planning is needed on the specific instructional methods to use. From the research on functional academics, some highly effective teaching strategies have emerged. Some are applicable to general education contexts, others are more suitable for private tutoring or teaching in the context of a life routine. This section discusses: (a) where to teach functional academics, (b) formats for instruction, (c) peer tutors, (d) prompting and feedback procedures, (e) designing and selecting materials, (f) planning for generalization, and (g) skill maintenance.

Where to Teach Functional Academics

One of the biggest challenges teachers of students with severe disabilities face is their students' difficulty with skill generalization. Will students be able to transfer their learning from the classroom to the school, home, and community? Or will they be unable to use a skill they learned in school once outside the classroom? A failure to transfer skills can happen for many reasons, but might best be viewed as incomplete learning.

For example, Simon recognizes many sight words, but can not apply these in the context of daily living activities.

There are many reasons why students may fail to generalize. Some students may not recognize the stimuli that signal a need for a skill, because these signals are different from those in the classroom. Other students may be confused by the many differences between the classroom and real life use (e.g., extra people, environmental distractions, many noises) or because a student does not know how to adjust a known response to suit the particular situation. There are a number of ways teachers can facilitate skill generalization. One important way is to choose locations and materials that encourage generalization.

The three primary locations for teaching functional academics involve "tabletop" instruction, simulations, and in vivo instruction.

- Tabletop instruction simply means that teachers or tutors use the traditional approach of sitting at a table, desk, or other surface to teach the skills. Tabletop instruction typically takes place in the classroom.
- Simulations involve teaching in adapted locations or with set-ups that are intended to reproduce in part the real activity or situation. Simulations usually are arranged in classrooms or schools to avoid traveling to an actual community location.
- In vivo ("in life") instruction means that teaching takes place in an actual location where the activity can occur. In vivo instruction takes place away from the classroom: in the school building (making purchases in the cafeteria or at the school vending machine), on the school grounds (reading signs), or some place in the community.

While teaching materials used in each type of instruction may vary, simulated and in vivo instruction typically involve real materials. In tabletop instruction, teachers can use teaching materials that range from the regular instructional articles that others in the class are using (e.g., texts, worksheets, objects to manipulate, word/number cards) to real objects that relate to the life skill and the in vivo setting (food containers for reading, coins and bills for making change). If the materials and task structure can be made more like its application for some or most of the learning opportunities, this helps the student make the connection between the skill learned in school and the same skill used elsewhere. Teachers should match the location and teaching materials to the academic approach (Table 13–1). For example, functional, generalized academics often are taught in a tabletop lesson with occasional probes of the student's generalization to a real or in vivo location. In contrast, teaching embedded academic skills necessitates an opportunity to perform the activity in the natural context or in a simulation of it. Students with severe disabilities have learned many different academic skills using a tabletop instruction format:

- Reading sight words (Gast, Wolery, Morris, Doyle, & Meyer, 1990; Schoen & Ogden, 1995)
- Using a calculator to plan purchases (Frederick-Dugan, Test, & Varn, 1991)
- Learning to count "one-more-than" a stated price (Denny & Test, 1995)

Researchers and practitioners caution teachers to check students' use of the skills learned at a table in real situations that are suitable for them. Thus, 6-year-old Sharon might be asked to read her target words learned in the classroom when she is at home reading a library book with her father or sister; and middle-schooler Simon will spend time using the next dollar method, once mastered at school, in the grocery store and at a fast food restaurant during community-based instruction.

Teaching in an in vivo location has also been successful for:

- Reading sight words as they are encountered in a community outing (Cuvo & Klatt, 1992; Schloss et al., 1995)
- Selecting coins and reading prices while using vending machines (Browder, Snell, & Wildonger, 1988)
- Using the next dollar strategy (counting "one-more-than") while purchasing food in a restaurant (McDonnell & Ferguson, 1988)

The caution that goes along with in vivo instruction is having enough opportunities to learn the skill. For example, although Simon will have a chance for instruction on many different tasks on the trip to McDonald's, there is only one natural chance to use the next dollar strategy: when the cashier tells him the price of his purchase. This may be the most difficult skill of all the tasks at the fast food restaurant, thus Simon's teachers will want to create more opportunities to teach this skill so he learns it. They could have him apply the strategy to other students' purchases (who don't need to learn the skill); staff might order coffee and have Simon tell them the number of dollars needed. Alternately, they could give him some practice totals, role-playing the cashier once they are seated, then go back and buy a dessert. Although shopping in a grocery store allows repeated opportunities to use the same skill (e.g., by subtotaling items in the basket to keep within a budget), this changes the nature of the task.

There are also examples in the research whereby students with disabilities learned through school or home simulations to perform activities without ever being taught in the in vivo location:

- Using a bank lobby simulated in the classroom, students learned to cash checks and later demonstrated generalization (Bourbeau, Sowers, & Close, 1986).
- An adult learned to make withdrawals of money using a simulated automatic teller (Shafer, Inge, & Hill, 1986). When generalization probes showed incomplete transfer, Shafer et al. (1986) adapted the simulation to address the problems (e.g., performing responses faster so the real machine did not end a transaction).
- Children with autism who were taught to shop for groceries using a simulated store demonstrated some transfer of skills to actual stores, but some in vivo remediation was also needed (Alcantra, 1994).

Thus the caution for teachers using simulations is that probes are needed because transfer may not be successful or may be incomplete. Generalization from tabletop instruction to in vivo applications have had similar mixed results. For example, Colyer and Collins (1996) taught students a next dollar strategy for store purchases and got both acquisition and generalization to varied community stores. In contrast, Collins and Stinson (1995) taught reading product labels but were disappointed with the minimal transfer to reading actual product labels in grocery stores. Cuvo and Klatt (1992) compared different ways to teach sight words: using flash cards, a video simulation, and in vivo training. They found excellent generalization to community sight word reading for students with moderate and mild mental retardation regardless of whether words were taught by flash cards or video.

From this research, several recommendations can be made regarding the teaching context for functional academics. First, the best practice is that teachers supplement more frequent tabletop instruction (using realistic materials and requests) with some in vivo instruction. Usually students have the most time available for learning functional academic skills when they are in school settings, and most students will benefit from some tabletop instruction in functional academics (e.g., flash card drills of sight words, practice counting out money or reading clock times). But, as the research indicates, teachers must not assume that skills learned in a classroom will be used appropriately outside the classroom. Students need instructional opportunities to use skills in real life contexts. Some skills can be practiced in other school contexts, such as purchasing in the cafeteria, buying something from a vending machine, reading a daily schedule, or reading menus in home economics class (see Figure 13–2). Still, scheduling community instruction allows students the opportunity to apply these skills more broadly. For example, students can practice functional reading and math skills by purchasing items in department stores, shopping for groceries, eating in restaurants, and working in their jobs (e.g., job schedule; time management). How much community exposure is needed will depend on the individual student's needs and learning characteristics.

Second, generalization to community settings may be encouraged by designing instruction to closely match the materials and responses used in the community. A "close match" need not require expensive or even real materials, but it does require teachers to study the response sequences needed in vivo and the range of stimuli students must learn to respond to. For example, Colyer and Collins (1996) credited their

FIGURE 13–2

Before a trip to the community store, students use a number line to count out the number of dollars they will need.

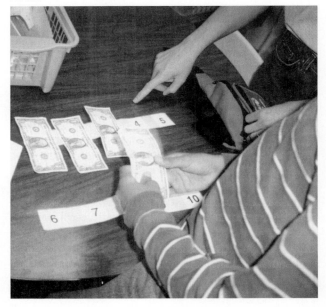

students' successful generalization of the next dollar strategy from the classroom to community stores to their verbal prompting strategy, which matched the natural cues observed in their area stores (e.g., cashiers always stated the price and prices usually were not visible on cash registers). Thus, while careful design of classroom and simulated instruction need not mean increased expense or time investment, teachers should identify both the relevant and typical conditions involved in using a skill and incorporate those characteristics into instruction (see chapter 14 for more suggestions for designing effective simulations).

Format for Instruction: Group Instruction and Observational Learning

Small-Group Instruction
A strong body of research has emerged demonstrating that students do not require one-on-one teaching arrangements to learn functional academic skills but can learn well in small groups (e.g., Doyle, Gast, Wolery, & Ault, 1990; Farmer, Gast, Wolery, & Winterling, 1991; Gast et al., 1990; Kamps, Leonard, Dugan, Boland, & Greenwood, 1991; Kamps, Walker, Locke, Delquadri, & Hall, 1990; Schoen & Ogden, 1995). By teaching in small groups, teachers can maximize the amount of instruction students receive and minimize "down time" when little learning takes place.

Several principles should guide teachers who use small groups:

- Select a group of about 3 to 5 students.
- Students need not be matched in ability; students will have individualized learning objectives in the same or different academic skill areas. When observational learning is used, all students should be taught the same skill area (e.g., spelling, math facts).
- The attention of some students will be more focused if they make an attending response to the target stimuli before making the academic response (e.g., look at a coin before counting it, take a word card before reading it, trace a word before matching it to a picture, read a math problem before giving the sum).
- Several methods may be used to enhance group instruction: individual and choral responding, multi-

ple rather than single target responses (point to and say word, match word to sample, match word to picture, say and write word), individualized sets of media materials for each student, rotation of materials and concepts to keep interest high, frequent student-to-student responding where students give peers requests, prompts, or feedback, and fast-paced random opportunities to respond.
- Systematic prompting and feedback is used as each student responds to the teaching materials (e.g., constant time delay and specific praise).
- To keep students attending, call on them randomly (versus round robin) and praise students for watching their peers' trials.

Sometimes it is feasible to use larger classroom-based group instruction (15 students) for daily, 30-minute, simulated practice sessions on purchasing skills just before their actual community use. For example, Westling et al. (1990) used large group simulation practice and found that students with severe disabilities were able to generalize their skills to a broad range of stores. The keys to successful group instruction appear to lie in several characteristics: the individualization of instruction, the active involvement of each group member, and the match between the natural environment and the teaching cues, stimulus materials, and target responses.

Observational Learning
Teachers and researchers have known for many years that students can benefit from each other's instruction. But work by Gast and his colleagues clarifies how to structure small groups so these benefits are realized. For example, Gast et al. (1990) taught sight words to five students in a small group. Each student was taught a different list of sight words. Probes of all words taught indicated that students had learned some of each other's words through observation: Brent was able to read some of the words Andrea had been taught and Andrea could read some of Jaime's words. Similarly, when Whalen et al. (1996) taught math facts in a small group, they found that students learned not only their own math facts, but some of their peers' facts too. These examples of observational learning were not random; they occurred when teachers were using precise prompting and feedback with individual students taught as a small group. Additionally, teachers encouraged group members

to attend to each student's trial by using a cue: "Everybody look".

When observational learning techniques were applied to teach reading to preschoolers with developmental disabilities, Alig-Cybriwsky, Wolery, and Gast (1990) found that observational learning was enhanced even more by an attentional cue that also prompted the target response (spelling the letters of the word presented), rather than using a general cue ("All look"). For example, when the instructor used a general attentional cue in teaching the word "boys" to the group, the teacher told the children "All look" before asking one student (e.g., Pete) to read the word. In using the specific attentional cue, the teacher held up the flash card of "boys" and said, "Let's say the letters." The teacher then said each letter ("b") and waited one second for the children to repeat the letter ("b") and continued until the whole word was spelled ("b-o-y-s"). If any child did not participate in the group spelling of each letter, he or she was asked to spell the word again with the teacher. Then, the teacher asked one student (e.g., Pete) to read the word aloud.

Observational learning has been successful in small groups of students (some with disabilities and some without) in general education classes with either the teacher or a teaching assistant in charge (Kamps et al., 1990; Schoen & Ogden, 1995; Whalen et al., 1996). Group members in Schoen and Odgen's work learned their words and some of those taught to other members. The findings of this study also supported teachers' use of specific attentional cues (the student traced the letters of the stimulus word presented with a marker before reading the word) instead of requesting students' eye contact at the beginning of each trial.

In summary, students who are learning material in the same content area can be grouped for instruction, and observational learning may be encouraged (Box 13–2). This is done by teaching each student a set of academic responses (which may be different or the same across students) but prompting all students to

---

Using Observational Learning to Teach Students

Box 13–2   When you teach students in groups of 2 or 3 and incorporate observational learning methods, each student will learn their own information as well as some of their group members' information (from 30% to 50% of the untaught task) by watching the other students being taught. You can use either chained tasks (multiple step) or discrete response tasks (single response) taught in a tabletop format:

1. Chained tasks (e.g., operating a coin washer/dryer; using a recipe to make lunch) (Wolery et al., 1991)
   - Ask both "Are you ready?"
   - Get an affirmative from students ("yes").
   - Teach half the task to the first student and the second half to the second student, *or* teach related but non-identical chains to each (e.g., student reads aloud the directions on washer and loads washer, adds soap and coins, and starts, other students operate dryer).
   - Before starting the task, the first student asks the second student to "Watch me".
   - The second student agrees to watch by saying "OK" (promoting more active observation).
   - Use constant time delay (0 seconds on first trial, 5 seconds delayed prompt on rest of trials) to teach each step in order.
   - When finished with first half of chained task, prompt the second student to give check mark or praise to the first student, then repeat with second half of chain, teaching the second student.
   - Test students weekly to see how much they have learned through observation and how much needs to be directly taught.
2. Tabletop instruction (e.g., reading words, identifying pictures of places in community) (Collins & Stinson, 1995)
   - Each student is given a different, small set of functional words, clock times, money amounts, or other information they need to learn.
   - Use the attention requests in the previous example.
   - Arrange seating so students see each others' task stimuli.
   - Keep turns short, avoid "round-robin," and use random turns.
   - Use direct instruction: clear requests, prompts that allow time to respond, and corrective or praise feedback.
   - Test students on their own targeted information and the information they observe.

watch each trial. One of the most encouraging aspects of this research on group instruction and observational learning is that groups can be formed with students of mixed ability in general education with excellent outcomes.

Incidental Learning in the Context of Systematic Instruction

One of the challenges of using systematic prompting and feedback, even in small group settings, is finding enough time to teach all students all of their IEP objectives. In general education contexts where students need the opportunity to participate in typical class activities, as well as receive specialized instruction, this problem can be even more frustrating to teachers. An interesting way to maximize the use of available structured teaching time is to teach two responses at once: targeted functional responses and incidental functional responses. The typical way this is achieved is to give students instructive feedback that provides information beyond the target information. To illustrate, when teaching students with moderate mental retardation to read product warning labels, Collins and Stinson (1995) gave information on the words meanings as part of their feedback to students. For example, after the student read the word "irritant," the teacher said, "Good, 'irritant.' An eye irritant means a product that can hurt your eyes." Although the students never were asked to state these meanings in the training trials, they were able to reproduce some of them on probes. Similarly, Singleton, Schuster, and Ault (1995) taught community signs, but added the descriptive incidental information to the feedback statement. For example, with the sign and word "barber," the teacher said, "Good, 'barber'. Barber means a haircut." Thus, if incidental information is embedded into the task, some of it can be learned, while students also learn the targeted information.

The incidental information can be added into one of three positions: request, prompt, or feedback and can be used to teach future objectives (Box 13–3).

The incidental information provided in instruction does not have to be from the same curricular area. For example, the Whalen et al. (1996) study, which focused on teaching math facts to a heterogeneous group in general education, also included exposing the students to flash cards of sight words as instruc-

tive feedback. For example, after the student looked at the math flash card and answered that 2 + 2 = 4, the teacher said, "Good, '4'. This word is 'cheese,'" while showing a target sight word on a second flash card. (The word 'cheese' came from the student's sight word list.) The purpose of this approach was to maximize learning when systematic instruction could be arranged in the general education class. Students learned all their math facts, (some of their peers' math facts through observational learning,) and some of the incidental sight words even though they never were asked to repeat the sight words or their peers' math facts during instruction.

The incidental information added to the task also may be the material that comes from an upcoming, future objective. For example, Wolery, et al., (1991) introduced sight words as incidental information that were embedded in the feedback statements while the teacher taught students to name photos of pertinent community people. After showing a picture of a veterinarian, and the student saying "vet," the teacher praised the student and then showed the flash card for the word "vet" while repeating the word. Introducing the sight words did not decrease the efficiency of the photo instruction. That is, presenting more information did not make it more difficult for the students to learn the photo names. An encouraging outcome was that showing the sight words decreased the time needed to learn these words later on; that is, words that had been previewed as incidental information during photo instruction were learned more quickly than nonpreviewed words.

Peer Tutors

Another way to maximize instructional opportunities for teaching functional academics is to use peer tutors. Collins, Branson, and Hall (1995) recruited high school students in an advanced English class to tutor their peers with moderate mental retardation in reading. Tutoring provided the English students with an experience to reflect on during their writing assignments, while the students with moderate mental retardation learned to read cooking words and generalized them to a cooking activity in the home economics room. These high school tutors were taught specific teaching approaches including time delay prompting.

In other examples of peer tutoring, tutors have relied on using scripts of teaching procedures (Wolery,

Box 13–3

Embed Incidental Information and Teach More

When you use a tabletop format to teach small groups of two to four students, you can embed incidental, but functional, information into the task request, the prompt, or the consequences. Many students will acquire some of the incidental information in addition to their target information.

Target Information: the primary set of responses the student is to learn (e.g., sight words, shape names, math facts)

Incidental Information: a second set of reponses that the teacher models during instruction, but does not ask the student to repeat (e.g., word definitions, colors, spelling words, associated facts [location of a community service, type of food: breakfast, dairy product])

1. Embed incidental but relevant information into the target task in one of three positions (consequence, prompt, or request):
   Target Task: Read product warning words on cards (flush, harmful, caution)
   Incidental Information: Definition or spelling of target word (e.g., "flush means to rinse with water")
   A. Place incidental information in *consequence* position:
      Cue: Product warning label with the word "Flush."
      Student: "Flush."
      Teacher: **"Yes, that is right: FLUSH,** *and it means to rinse with water."*
   B. Place incidental information in the *prompt* position:
      Cue: Sight word "Eggs."
      Student: (No response: waits for teacher's prompt.)
      Teacher: **"The word is 'eggs.'** *We eat them for breakfast."*
   C. Place incidental information into the *request:*
      Cue: Flash card "Milk."
      Teacher: "What *dairy food* is this?"
2. Select incidental information from functional academic objectives targeted for the near future
   Target Task: Identifying photos of restaurants and stores in the community
   Future Information: Reading the names of these places (K-Mart, McDonald's, CVS Drug Store, Kroger's)

Show a group of photos, and ask the student to touch one ("Find K-Mart"). After a student touches the named photo, praise the student while also showing or giving the student the word card for that photo and reading it aloud: "Right, that's K-Mart; this says 'K-Mart'." Later, their ability to identify photos and to read words is assessed. Reading instruction will focus on the words not learned incidentally, while learned words will simply be reviewed.

Werts, Snyder, & Caldwell, 1994). For example, a group of 13 tutors learned to use scripts of a systematic method to teach sight words and then rotated teaching responsibility across tutees but were still consistent in their methods. Students with disabilities can also serve as tutors for each other or for younger students (Snell & Janney, in press). For example, Koury and Browder (1986) found that students with moderate mental retardation could use constant time delay accurately to teach sight words to other students in their class.

In business math class, a peer named Michael works with Jerome to learn to use a calculator. The special education teacher taught Michael how to follow the task analysis for calculator use and to prompt Jerome (using least intrusive

prompts) to enter each numeral and symbol in adding two prices. Michael, who finishes his own work quickly, initiates these lessons daily. They often use a calculator program on the classroom computer. When finished, he and Jerome look up sports stories together on the internet.

Prompting and Feedback Procedures

Much of the instruction in functional academics involves teaching students to recognize words, pictures, numbers, or symbols on sight and associate them with meaning connected to their routine lives (e.g., to select the correct restroom, to count out a specific value in coins). The most basic type of academic skill needed by students is recognizing visual, printed stimuli; teaching these skills requires teachers to use appropriate stimulus control procedures. The second type of academic skill needed involves making a meaningful association between the visual stimuli and routine activities or applied tasks; teaching these associations requires that teachers use generalization procedures. Many procedures exist for both stimulus control and generalization. Some of these methods involve designing and remembering complex teaching steps or developing multiple materials. Others are simple to design and implement.

When teaching, Etzel and LeBlanc (1979) recommend the principle of parsimony: Use the simplest, but still effective method. More complex procedures to teach skills like sight words are not always more ef-fective (Browder & Lalli, 1991). More complex methods also might not be the most efficient, in that they take more teaching or preparation time than simpler methods (Schuster, et al., 1992). Described next are six methods for prompting and feedback, presented in an approximate order of difficulty (Table 13–3). (Some teachers may find these procedures to be simpler or more difficult than the order given here.)

Practice with Feedback

The simplest method to teach a skill is to give the student multiple opportunities to practice the target responses, while providing feedback on their responses. Feedback usually involves correcting errors

TABLE 13–3
Prompt and Feedback Procedures

Prompting and Feedback Procedures	Description (Simplest to More Complex Procedures)
Practice with Feedback	Give student repeated opportunities to use skill and provide information on their performance (e.g., praise for correct answers and correction for errors).
Simultaneous Prompting	Give the student a request to make the target response and prompt the correct response at the same time (often using a model prompt). Give daily probes or opportunities to respond without any prompts and record performance.
Constant Time Delay	During initial requests to make the target response, prompt the correct response at the same time (without any delay: at zero delay). These initial trials look like simultaneous prompting. After a trial or several trials (or a session or sessions), insert a short latency (e.g., 4 seconds) between the request for the response and the prompt. Continue this constant delay of the prompt until learning occurs (i.e., when student responds repeatedly before the prompt). If errors occur, reintroduce zero delay for several trials.
Progressive Time Delay	During initial requests to make the target response, prompt the correct response at the same time (without any delay: at zero delay). These initial trials look like simultaneous prompting. After a trial or several trials (or a session or sessions), gradually over successive trials and learning sessions increase the latency from zero to a ceiling of 4 to 8 seconds (depending on the student and task). These increases may be made in 1- or 2-second increments. Continue with the longest delayed prompt until learning occurs (i.e., when student responds repeatedly before the prompt). If errors occur, reintroduce a prompt at a briefer delay (or even at zero delay) for several trials.
Least Intrusive Prompts	Following each task request, students are given a latency to respond with no assistance; then, as needed, are given progressively more assistance with time to respond, until the student makes the correct response. Errors are interrupted with additional assistance and time to respond. The typical prompt hierarchy is: verbal instructions, model or demonstration, followed by physical assistance
Stimulus Fading and Stimulus Shaping (Task Demonstration Model)	Both methods rely on "within stimulus prompts" being built into the teaching materials, rather than prompts that model the correct response. When within stimulus prompts use stimulus fading to teach a discrimination, the prompts (color coding or a superimposed picture) are gradually eliminated over successive exposures. When within stimulus prompts use stimulus shaping to teach, the difficulty of the discrimination becomes harder over successive exposures to a word or number (e.g., choose from more distracting word cards; the incorrect word options are closer to the correct option). The Task Demonstration Model makes use of both approaches plus general case procedures and simple-to-difficult responses.

and providing praise for correct responses, and sometimes is referred to as "postresponse prompting" because assistance is given after the student tries the response. After a correct response, the teacher gives some type of praise statement and repeats the response (e.g., "Good, the word is 'women'"). Additional reinforcement strategies may be used with some students, such as getting tokens, stars or stickers, or keeping track of correct answers (self-monitoring by stacking the correct stimulus cards or punching a counter).

After an error, the student is corrected in some way that is informative but not aversive. Error correction lets students know that their answer was not correct and provides the correct answer. For example, if the word 'exit' is presented and the student says "keep out", the teacher would correct the student by saying "No, the word is 'exit'." Sometimes the student is asked to repeat the correct response. For example, Van Houten and Rolider (1989) found that more math facts were learned when students who missed a fact were told "No" in a neutral tone of voice, then given the whole problem plus the answer (e.g., "9 + 7 = 16"), and finally given a repeat of the trial ("What does 9 + 7 equal?"). Error correction can be more elaborate, for example, by having the student repeat the word several times or spelling or tracing the word (Browder & Shear, 1996; Singh & Singh, 1988). Generally, error correction should be direct and immediate and should actively involved the learner. (See Box 13–4)

Lalli and Browder (1993) compared three of the more complex teaching procedures (i.e., stimulus shaping, stimulus fading, and progressive time delay) with a feedback procedure in teaching adults with moderate mental retardation to read words from a grocery list and chores schedule. When Lalli and Browder found that the adults learned the sight words equally well across procedures, they replicated the simplest procedure, practice with feedback, to teach the adults a new set of words for shopping and completing chores. The participants learned the words and were able to use them to complete these tasks. These findings reinforce the advice to use the simplest but still effective methods; for many situations the procedures of "practice with feedback" may be the best choice.

Feedback procedures can work well in a peer tutoring format. For example, Barbetta, Miller, Peters, Heron, and Cochran (1991) taught tutors to draw a happy face on the back of a word card when the student read a word correctly. If a word was read wrong, the tutor gave the correct answer. Cards with three happy faces went into a "stop" pocket in their tutoring folders for occasional review. Unlearned words went into a "go" pocket in the tutoring folder. The tutor also helped the student complete a bar graph for the number of words read correctly. Although implemented by peer tutors with students who had learning disabilities, other research that has used similar feedback procedures successfully with students having moderate and severe disabilities, suggesting that this peer tutoring folder might have value with more students.

Computer assisted instruction lends itself to practice with feedback procedures. Baumgart and VanWalleghem (1987) used a computer format to

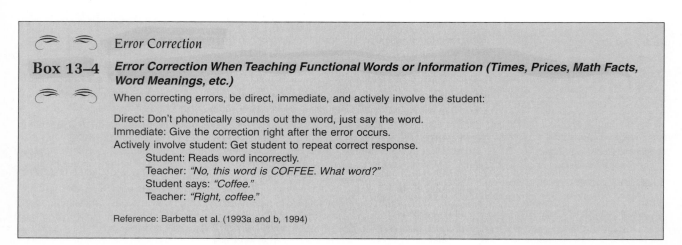

Error Correction

Box 13–4 ***Error Correction When Teaching Functional Words or Information (Times, Prices, Math Facts, Word Meanings, etc.)***

When correcting errors, be direct, immediate, and actively involve the student:

Direct: Don't phonetically sounds out the word, just say the word.
Immediate: Give the correction right after the error occurs.
Actively involve student: Get student to repeat correct response.
    Student: Reads word incorrectly.
    Teacher: *"No, this word is COFFEE. What word?"*
    Student says: *"Coffee."*
    Teacher: *"Right, coffee."*

Reference: Barbetta et al. (1993a and b, 1994)

teach grocery words to three adults with moderate mental retardation. When incorrect, the adults received feedback with a chance to try the response again. When correct, the computer program provided them with a praise statement. Teachers will benefit from keeping in close touch with the instructional software that is available. Reviews of available software will let teachers evaluate new programs for their strengths and weaknesses as drill and practice tools, their cost, and their appeal to students (Closing the Gap, 1998). Another option is for teachers to use an "authoring tool," such as IntelliPics or HyperStudio, to create their own functional academic computer activities. The advantage of using an authoring program is that teachers can customize the computer tasks specifically to individual student needs.

During computer lab two to three times a week, Sharon and some of her second-grade classmates use computer programs to practice reading and math. These programs give repeated opportunities to associate quantities with numbers and words with pictures, actions, or sounds. Sharon gets immediate feedback from the computer and another opportunity to respond with assistance when she makes an error. The only difference between Sharon's use of the computer and that of her classmates is the choice of software, which is more applicable to her reading level. Some of her favorite programs are Words Around Me (©Edmark) and Simon Sounds It (©Don Johnson) (refer to listing in Table 13–4).

A variation of a feedback procedure is the interspersal method for teaching skills like sight words, math facts, coin values, and time reading (Browder & Shear, 1996). In the interspersal method, new stimuli on flashcards are intermixed with old stimuli on flashcards using a high ratio of known to unknown and a rapid drill format. For example, two new words may be introduced with 10 known words, which means the

---

TABLE 13–4
Commercial Academic Materials

Language Arts

- Developing Alphabet Skills
  Edmark Corporation
  P.O. Box 3903
  Bellevue, WA 98009-3903

- Developmental 1 Reading Laboratory
  Science Research Associates, Inc.
  155 N. Wacker Drive
  Chicago, IL 60606

- Edmark Reading Program, Level 1
  EBSCO Curriculum Materials
  Division of EBSCO Industries Inc.
  Box 11542
  Birmingham, AL 35202

- Edmark Reading Program, Level 1 Software
  EBSCO Curriculum Materials
  Division of EBSCO Industries Inc.
  Box 11542
  Birmingham, AL 35202

- Functional Reading Series
  Edmark Corporation
  P.O. Box 3903
  Bellevue, WA 98009-3903

- High Hat Early Reading Program
  American Guidance Service
  Publishers' Building
  P.O. Box 99
  Circle Pines, MN 55014-1796

- I Can Print
  ASIEP Education Company
  P.O. Box 12147
  Portland, OR 97212

- ITL
  American Guidance Service
  Publishers' Building
  P.O. Box 99
  Circle Pines, MN 55014-1796

- Level 1, Mini Set
  Edmark Corporation
  P.O. Box 3903
  Bellevue, WA 98009-3903

- Level 1 Software, Classroom Version
  Edmark Corporation
  P.O. Box 3903
  Bellevue, WA 98009-3903

- Name Writing
  Pro-Ed
  8700 Shoal Creek Boulevard
  Austin, TX 78758

- Reach for Reading
  Modern Curriculum Press
  13900 Prospect Road
  Cleveland, OH 44136

- Reading for Independence
  Science Research Associates, Inc.
  155 N. Wacker Drive
  Chicago, IL 60606

TABLE 13–4

continued

- Reading for Understanding 1, 2, 3
  Science Research Associates, Inc.
  155 N. Wacker Drive
  Chicago, IL 60606

- Real Reading
  Edmark Corporation
  P.O. Box 3903
  Bellevue, WA 98009-3903

- The Sensible Pencil
  Edmark Corporation
  P.O. Box 3903
  Bellevue, WA 98009-3903

- SRA Skills Series
  Science Research Associates, Inc.
  155 N. Wacker Drive
  Chicago, IL 60606

- WRITE-Right Now!
  Edmark Corporation
  P.O. Box 3903
  Bellevue, WA 98009-3903

Math

- I can + and − Arithmetic Program
  ASIEP Education Company
  P.O. Box 12147
  Portland, OR 97212

- Real-Life Math
  Pro-Ed
  8700 Shoal Creek Boulevard
  Austin, TX 78758

Other Curricula and Software

- Community Places
  Attainment Company Inc.
  504 Commerce Parkway
  Vernona, WI 53593

- Cues
  Attainment Company Inc.
  504 Commerce Parkway
  Vernona, WI 53593

- Employment Signs
  Attainment Company Inc.
  504 Commerce Parkway
  Vernona, WI 53593

- Home Cooking
  Attainment Company Inc.
  504 Commerce Parkway
  Vernona, WI 53593

- Information Signs
  Attainment Company Inc.
  504 Commerce Parkway
  Vernona, WI 53593

- Looking Good
  Attainment Company Inc.
  504 Commerce Parkway
  Vernona, WI 53593

- Plan Your Day
  Attainment Company Inc.
  504 Commerce Parkway
  Vernona, WI 53593

- Resource Directory (of Available Software)
  Closing the Gap
  P.O. Box 68
  Henderson, MN 56044
  www.closingthegap.com

- Safety Sign
  Attainment Company Inc.
  504 Commerce Parkway
  Vernona, WI 53593

- Select-a-Meal
  Attainment Company Inc.
  504 Commerce Parkway
  Vernona, WI 53593

- Sentence Master
  Laureate
  110 E. Spring St.
  Winooski, VT 05404-1898
  (800) 562-6801
  www.laureatelearning.com

- Shopping Smart
  Attainment Company Inc.
  504 Commerce Parkway
  Vernona, WI 53593

- Simon Spells
  Simon Sounds It (for students working on phonics)
  Don Johnston, Inc.
  1000 N. Rand Rd.
  Wauconda, IL 60084-0639
  (800) 999-4660
  www.donjohnston.com

- Stepping Out
  Attainment Company Inc.
  504 Commerce Parkway
  Vernona, WI 53593

- Words Around Me
  TouchMoney
  Dollars & Cents Series
  Edmark
  P.O. Box 97021
  Redmond, WA 98073-9721
  (800) 362-2890
  www.edmark.com

possibility for error is reduced and many trials are devoted to review. The cards are exposed, responded to, and placed in another pile if correct. Unless the student makes an error, the drill continues uninterrupted, with the student controlling the cards. The advantages of this rapid drill format are that students make a large number of responses in a short time frame and can minimize "teacher talk" by continuing to respond correctly.

In the drill, one new word is introduced at a time in this sequence: first new word/one known word/first new word/two known words (one at a time)/first new word/three known words/first new word/four known words/first new word/five known words/second new word/first new word/one known word/second new word/first new word/two known words. . . . (ending after five new words have been interspersed) with first new word/second new word/third new word/five known words. This procedure can be simplified by having a stack of known words and a stack of new words. After each new word presentation, the necessary number of known words are drawn from the "known stack" and read by the student. The new word continues to be "sandwiched" between these sets of known words until it has been introduced at least 10 times. This is repeated for each new word. In the study by Browder & Shear (1996) the students with moderate mental retardation and behavior disorders learned to independently control the flash cards, interspersing known words as they read aloud. The interspersal sequence created 101 trials to read words: 71 trials of known words and 30 trials (10 each) for the unknown words. These 101 trials were presented in less than 20 minutes because there was no teacher talk unless an error was made. When an error was made, an elaborated correction procedure is used (e.g., word was spelled or traced and repeated several times). Intermixing known material with new material can also be an effective strategy to encourage maintenance of known material (Doyle, Wolery, Ault, Gast, & Wiley, 1989).

In general, the practice with feedback procedure is a simple beginning point for teaching systematically and can be highly effective for students. Descriptive praise ("Good, the word is milk"), opportunities to practice a correct response after an error is made, instructive feedback, and interspersal of known items all may enhance a feedback approach. The more complex teaching methods that we describe next all incorporate the basic elements of the practice with feedback approach and this, in part, explains their effectiveness.

Simultaneous Prompting with Modeled Response

An alternative to feedback procedures that rely on postresponse prompting (prompting correct response after an error) is to use an antecedent prompting strategy (prompting before an error can be made). One of the least complex methods of antecedent prompting is to model the correct response (e.g., Teacher shows a flash card with the word hamburger and says "Read the word 'hamburger'"). Presenting a prompt before the response on each teaching trial, without fading it, is called "simultaneous prompting" (Schuster et al., 1992). In using this method, the teacher always tells the student the correct response (e.g., models reading the word; states the price) and has the student repeat this model. To determine which responses no longer need prompting, the teacher gives a test before the next lesson. In simultaneous prompting, testing simply involves withholding the prompt, but giving feedback. For any responses known on the test, the teacher no longer uses a prompt in teaching.

Simon, the sixth grader who can read many words but does not associate meaning with them, accompanies Pete, his eighth-grade peer tutor, to various locations in the school to have his lesson. Each day his tutor uses simultaneous prompting to teach each word 2 to 3 times but also tests each word once. Pete takes Simon to a location and points to the word on the flash card and on the door, saying "Read the words 'Boy's Restroom.'" Simon holds the flash card and repeats the word. Then Pete says "That's our bathroom," and Simon, says "Our bathroom." This same routine is repeated in front of the Girl's bathroom ("Read the words 'Girl's Restroom'") and Pete models, "This is NOT our bathroom." Pete teaches the associated meaning through gestures and/or simple phrases for each target word: e.g., math (the room he has a class), exit (the way outside), office (the principal), cafeteria (eat lunch). On Friday, Simon is tested. Pete gives the test by walking to the various locations in a random order, handing Simon the word cards, and waiting for Simon to locate the word, read it aloud, and tell its associated meaning. Simon gets to hold onto the cards he gets right, and Pete makes a record of them upon their return to the tutor office.

The advantage of simultaneous prompting is that it can produce errorless learning without the teacher designing and using a fading method like time delay. The disadvantage is that some students may become dependent on prompts. An essential feature of simultaneous prompting is the use of daily or frequent probes of the student's learning; this gives students an opportunity to make the target response without prompting or feedback. If learning does not seem to progress, teachers may want to use a different prompting procedure.

It is important to comment on the use of picture cues, which are sometimes used to prompt sight word reading. While not all functional words can be depicted with pictures, many community words are associated with logos, colors, or symbols. Unfortunately pictures may also create a "blocking effect" in which the student responds to the picture rather than looking at the word stimulus and thus may slow down word acquisition (Singh & Solman, 1990) (Box 13–5). In general, pictures of words are not recommended as good prompts for teaching reading. The exceptions are words typically portrayed with the natural cues of pictures, shapes, or color coding (e.g., K-Mart, McDonalds and their arches, stop signs). It seems more efficient to teach these words as community signs rather than as words in isolation. For example, Singleton, Schuster, and Ault (1995) successfully taught students to read words of this type (e.g., KOA, Food Mart, and Denny's) and did not isolate the word from its associated logo.

Constant Time Delay

There will be some times when teachers prefer using a procedure in which prompts are systematically faded. This decision is most appropriate if a learner's progress is slowed down by errors or if a learner becomes prompt-dependent in a simultaneous prompting procedure (i.e., only states the response when given a teacher model). Time delay is a procedure involving very brief periods of teacher silence and inactivity, during which students have the opportunity to respond without prompts; this approach can produce near errorless learning in many students with disabilities.

Initially, in a time delay procedure, the teacher immediately gives the prompt while simultaneously presenting the target stimuli (e.g., says the word while showing the flash card). The prompt, which often involves saying the answer or pointing to the correct

---

      Rules for Using Pictures to Teach Words

Box 13–5   When teaching students to read functional words, don't use pictures to teach words because the picture tends to block their attention to the word unless there is a picture or logo that serves as a natural cue for the word.

When a Picture or Logo Serves as a Natural Cue for a Sight Word

- Test first to see if a student knows the meaning of the logo or picture apart from the word (e.g., red and white soda can with word "Coke" hidden).
- Divide the words into two groups: those whose picture or representation can be named correctly (teach reading of these words first) and those whose meaning is not clear or known (teach reading of these words after the student learns to connect meaning with their picture or logo).
- Some associated logos, pictures, or symbols for words in the first group will always be associated with the word and should not be taught apart from the word (e.g., McDonalds and the golden arches). Others may be taught both with and without the logo (e.g., "Coke" as it appears on soda can is with logo; "Coke" as it appears on a menu may be without logo.)

When the Word Does Not Typically Appear with a Picture or in Logo Form

- When teaching words that do not typically appear with a picture or logo, just use the printed word as the stimulus.
- *Warning:* if pictures are used as a prompt, students may focus on the picture because it is a known stimulus and tend not to look at the word; this tendency acts to block learning the printed word.

Reference: Singh & Solman (1990)

choice, is provided at zero seconds delay, that is, simultaneous with the request to respond. Over successive teaching opportunities, the teacher adds a latency (a few seconds) between the target stimuli and the prompt, thus giving the learner an opportunity to respond without assistance. The simplest way to delay assistance is to use a constant time delay. After an initial trial, session, or some number of sessions at zero delay, the teacher waits a defined latency (e.g., 4 seconds) before giving the prompt. This prompt delay or latency remains constant for the remainder of instruction until the student has learned to make the correct response ahead of the 4-second delayed prompt. Typically, students will learn the correct responses with few or no errors. Thus, time delay is called an errorless procedure. If errors occur, however, the teacher may reintroduce simultaneous prompting or may teach the student to wait for the prompt, if he or she seems unsure of the answer.

Mr. Sanchez identified some measurement skills (using a ruler to tell the length of boards, using graduated measuring cups—1, ½, ⅓, ¼) and sight words (measure, length, cook, mix, stir) for Simon to learn for shop and home economics classes. To make the task more interesting, Simon's special education teacher, Ms. Jones, created a short, daily small-group session involving two nondisabled peers who also would benefit from instruction in measurement and reading. She planned to alternate between two reading tasks (e.g., "What does this say?," shows word card and student reads; "Show me what it means," student picks up utensil and gestures how to use it) and one measuring task ("How many inches is this?," places an even length board by a ruler, and student reads the length from the rules). She taught using constant time delay (4 seconds) in combination with the guidelines for observational learning so that each student would learn some through the observation of the other's targeted tasks. Ms. Jones taught the first few days using simultaneous prompting on the first trial (zero delay) followed by a 4-second delay on the next trials. Mr. Sanchez observed, then they rotated and she provided him with feedback. On the third day, all the task requests were followed by a 4-second delayed model prompt (no more use of zero delay "warm up" trial). Some students in the small group had already mastered a few of the tasks by getting three consecutive, unprompted, correct responses. When this happened, since all target tasks are represented on cards, the teacher added in a new item (a word or measurement card) to that student's task pile and placed the known item in that student's periodic review pile.

Constant time delay lends itself well to group instruction. For example, Gast et al. (1990) used constant time delay to teach sight words to students with moderate mental retardation. Constant time delay also has been applied by peer tutors who are nondisabled (Collins et al., 1995; Wolery et al., 1994) or who have disabilities (Koury & Browder, 1986). Constant time delay has been implemented during community-based instruction of sight words (Cuvo & Klatt, 1992) and has worked well in teaching money skills (Gardill & Browder, 1995; Whalen et al., 1996). Because of the potential efficiency of errorless teaching procedures (i.e., fewer teaching sessions to criterion) and its applicability to a wide range of teaching contexts (i.e., group instruction, peer tutoring, community-based instruction), teachers might elect to teach most skills like sight words and money selection with constant time delay. Others might prefer simultaneous prompting (remaining at zero delay and using probes to determine mastery), which may be easier to implement and more efficient for some students (Schuster, et al., 1992).

Progressive Time Delay

An alternative method of fading prompts is progressive time delay. In this approach, the teacher also begins with simultaneous prompting (zero delay), but the latency of the delay of the prompt is increased gradually (e.g., from 0 seconds to 2 seconds to 4 seconds and up to 6 or 8 seconds or higher) until the student "anticipates" the correct response (answers correctly before the teacher's prompt). Progressive time delay also has been demonstrated as effective in teaching sight words, either individually (Browder & D'Huyvetters, 1988) or in group instruction (Browder et al., 1984; Collins & Stinson, 1995), and in teaching money skills (Browder et al., 1988; Frederick-Dugan et al., 1991). For some students, progressive delay may be a powerful and efficient teaching technique for learning responses with few to no errors. The disadvantage of progressive time delay is that it may be difficult to implement because teachers must keep track of the delay level and student responses from trial to trial or session to session. This can become especially complex if the delay level varies across the target stimuli (e.g., across words) or across students within a group.

Jerome and his teachers decided that he would benefit from learning to recognize several key times during the school day (time to leave for work, to start and end work, and times for each of his classes and therapy). They chose progressive time delay because he was used to the method, was not being taught in a group (less difficult to use with one student), and was easily discouraged by errors. To teach Jerome to read the specific digital clock times in his schedule, the teacher had him look at the time displayed digitally on the clock (or on his watch) and then touch the matching photo (from an array of three photos). In this first teaching phase, the photo also had the digital time written below the picture of the activity. When he could locate each schedule card that matched the digital clock time, he then was taught to find the correct picture card at the beginning of each class. The goal was to have him learn to initiate the next activity at the correct time by following a picture schedule.

In the first phase, the teacher began with zero delayed prompts. That is, she read the digital time on Jerome's watch and then pointed to the correct activity photo. Jerome then imitated looking at his watch and pointing to the correct picture. She then reset his watch for the next time and repeated this procedure for all the schedule times. She repeated these zero delayed prompts for 2 days of instruction and advanced by 2-second increments after each 2 days of instruction. If an error occurred (e.g., at 6-second delays), the teacher dropped back to zero delay for 1 day, then to 2 seconds less than the previous delay level for another day (e.g., 4 seconds), then back to the former delay level for 2 days of no errors (e.g., 6 seconds). Once a delay of 8 seconds was reached, training remained there until Jerome could "beat the delay" by responding correctly beforehand. This tabletop instruction was followed, in the second phase, by training in vivo use of his schedule. Just before changing classes, Jerome's peer or teacher escort prompted him to look at his digital watch and point to the picture of his next class on his schedule display. Jerome received assistance to wheel his chair to the next class when he told his escort where to take him by pointing to this picture (see Table 13–5).

In addition to its complexity as a disadvantage, some researchers have reported that progressive delay may teach some students to wait for the teacher's cue and thus encourage prompt dependence (Glat, Gould, & Stoddard, 1994). For example, Glat et al. found that participants learned merely to wait for the cue to point to the correct sight word and became dependent on the prompts. This was corrected in the following way: After the teacher's request ("Find the word, "exit,"), but before the delay trial was intro-

duced, students repeated the word ("Exit"); this was followed by the delay period, the prompt (as needed), and the student's pointing response. This adaptation of having the student say the word (an attentional cue) before pointing to the correct word card "broke" the prompt dependence and led to the students' mastery of the words. Interestingly, in teaching children with autism to point to the correct Chinese letter, Leung and Wu (1997) also found it beneficial to have the participants repeat the name of the target letter before pointing to the correct choice in an array, a response which focused student attention on the controlling stimulus. If oral reading, rather than pointing, is the target response, some other attentional cue, such as tracing the letters on the flash card, might be used. For example, the teacher might say, "Trace the word. . . . Now read the word (waits delay interval). . . . The word is 'soda.'" Tracing the word might encourage the student to anticipate the teacher's prompt and read the word independently. Because of complexities, such as keeping track of the delay level and discouraging prompt dependence, progressive delay is not usually selected for group instruction and peer tutoring. Constant time delay is the simpler and still effective choice.

Least Intrusive Prompts

The system of least intrusive prompts involves following a hierarchy of prompts that are organized by the amount of assistance the student requires to make the correct response. The usual hierarchy used involves:

1. A latency where no prompt is given (often 3 to 5 seconds) and the student can respond independently
2. A verbal prompt (e.g., "Touch the word 'math'")
3. A model prompt (e.g. "Touch the word 'math' like this"; models touching correct word card)
4. A physical prompt (e.g., "Let me help you touch the word 'math'"; guides student's hand to touch the word card "math")

Each prompt is followed by a latency period, giving the student time to respond. Any errors are interrupted by giving the next prompt in the hierarchy. This procedure typically is not used when teaching functional academics, because it may be less efficient than other procedures, such as time delay (Gast, Ault, Wolery, & Doyle, 1988). It also can be difficult and

TABLE 13–5

A Sequence of Time-Telling Objectives for Jerome Taught by Using an Embedded Approach and Progressive Time Delay

Discriminative Stimulus	Prompt	Student Response	Consequence
Phase 1: Match to Sample Instruction			
The teacher shows each of the times from Jerome's daily schedule (e.g., 10:26) on a flash card and an array of 3 cards with similar times (10:15, 9:26) and says, "Find the matching schedule card." This is repeated for 20 different flash card times.	If Jerome waits for help, the teacher points to the correct choice. • On first 2 days, give prompt at no delay. • On next 2 days, give prompts at 2 seconds delay. • On next 2 days, give prompt at 4 seconds delay. • Continue adding 2-second delays per day up to 8 seconds. If more than 2 errors occur during one session, begin fading schedule again at zero delay.	To respond correctly (before or after the prompt), Jerome points to the card in the array that matches the flash card.	Confirm correct "Yes, that's 10:26." And give incidental information, "That's when you have math." Or, corrects error, "No, this 10:26."
Phase 2: Receptive Reading of Digital Time			
The teacher puts out an array of 3 cards showing digital times and says, "Point to ___" (e.g., "Point to 11:15")	If Jerome waits for help, the teacher models pointing to the correct card. This prompting is also given on a progressive time delay schedule, beginning at zero delay the first day and adding 2 seconds each day	Jerome points to the correct time card.	Same as above—praise or error correction.
Phase 3: Using Watch or Clock to Initiate Next Activity			
Jerome's digital clock is his discriminative stimulus	If Jerome does not begin the next activity, the teacher prompts Jerome by pointing to the time and the schedule picture on his communication board. For the first two sessions, the teacher prompts checking the clock and schedule as soon as the time appears on Jerome's clock. For each of the next two sessions, the teacher delays this prompt by 5 seconds; adding 5 seconds every 2 days up to a 30-second delay.	Jerome looks at his clock and asks for help to move to the next activity by pressing the picture on his communication board.	Teacher praises correct response; corrects errors by saying, "No, you have—[e.g., math] now."

awkward to design a hierarchy of prompting for a verbal response like reading sight word or stating a word's definition.

However, when it is desirable to focus the student's attention on the natural cues in the environment before making the target response, least intrusive prompting may be an appropriate approach. For example, Colyer and Collins (1996) taught students in vivo to use the next dollar strategy and wanted them to attend to the natural cue of the cashier stating the price out loud. The printed price was inconsistently visible on cash registers, so teachers wanted their students to listen for the price instead. Colyer and Collins began each teaching trial by stating the price in the same manner as a cashier would (consistent natural cue). This verbal statement used the shorthand way that cashiers state prices ("Five ninety-seven"). The first prompt in the hierarchy was to show the price on a flash card to simulate the cash register (cash registers that showed the price were inconsistently present as a natural cue). The second level of prompt was to show the flash card again and use an expanded price statement that cashiers sometimes used ("Five dollars and ninety-seven cents"). If this was ineffective, the teacher used a third level of prompt: she told the student what money to get out ("Give me five dollars and one more for cents"). If ineffective, a fourth prompt was used (she modeled counting out the amount). Students mastered the next dollar strategy and generalized it to community stores with some additional tutoring on special problems (e.g., prices under a dollar). The in vivo training, such as Coyler and Collins conducted, also could be combined with table top or simulated instruction at school to increase the number of learning opportunities, while still giving students exposure to the generalization setting.

Stimulus Fading and Stimulus Shaping

Sometimes students do not respond well to teacher-delivered prompts or become overly dependent on these. Other times, students need to use self-instruction (e.g., remind themselves, keep track of their performance, self-assess) or perform seat work without teacher assistance. In these instances, materials may be used that actually prompt the student to respond in the absence of a teacher. When prompts are built into the materials, they are called "within stimulus prompts" because they use some type of visual or au-

ditory cue within the material to enhance the stimulus to which the student is to respond. For example, the correct word in an array might be color-coded.

"Within stimulus prompts" may involve one of two procedures to teach the student: stimulus fading or stimulus shaping. In stimulus fading, a within stimulus prompt (e.g., color coding or a superimposed picture on a word) is gradually eliminated by reducing the salience (or obviousness) of the prompt. For example, progressive photocopying of a picture (or adding layers of tissue paper) results in less distinct copies with successively dimmer images, thereby shifting the learner's focus from the picture of the word to the word itself. (Copy the picture or glue tissue paper on the picture separate from the word and then glue the word on so that the word does not become lighter.) Similarly, color coding, which might highlight all the prices costing more than one dollar, can be reduced to smaller and smaller dots or to faded color highlights, again forcing attention to shift to the number of digits. An illustration of stimulus fading from a picture prompt to the word stimulus is shown in Figure 13–3.

FIGURE 13–3
Stimulus Fading from a Picture Prompt
to the Word Stimulus

Some years ago, stimulus fading was the primary method used in research on teaching sight words to individuals with mental retardation (e.g., Dorry & Zeaman, 1975). Although effective, this method requires many hours of preparing specialized materials. Although there still are applications of stimulus fading to teach such skills as letter discriminations (Hoogeven, Smeets, & Lancioni, 1989) and sight words (Lalli & Browder, 1993), time delay has come to replace stimulus fading. Time delay requires no special material adaptations, and thus is simpler to use, but still is highly effective. However, as teachers explore more options for inclusive settings, stimulus fading may gain increased recognition, because materials can be prepared in advance for students to use with minimal supervision in general education classrooms. Within stimulus prompts also can help some students use the general education materials (e.g., by color-coding answers in a spelling or math workbook).

Stimulus shaping involves the use of a series of increasingly more difficult discriminations to teach words or symbols. The following number identification task of locating specific numbers from an array of flash cards shows how the difficulty increases as the symbols on the flash cards look more and more like each other:

Objective: To discriminate the numerals 1 through 9

Instructional Arrangement: An array of four flash cards lies on the table in front of the student. (These arrays can also be prearranged as a student worksheet.)

Request: "Find number 2"

Early teaching trial: ☐ 2 ☐ ☐

Middle teaching trial: 2 ✳ ▲ ➡

Later teaching trial: ◯ 5 2 1

The illustration in Figure 13–4 shows how materials are prepared for teaching sight word reading through stimulus shaping in the *Edmark Reading Program* (1972). The target word is presented in an array of cards with distracter symbols. Over several teaching sessions (each row is one teaching trial), these distracters become more similar to the target word and the difficulty of the discrimination increases. In the newer versions of the Edmark program such as the *Edmark Functional Word Series* (1990),

FIGURE 13–4
An Example of Stimulus Shaping

horse	—	—
ft	horse	un
ros	fuvx	horse
sho	horse	rwao
	horse	

Note. From "Errorless Discrimination and Picture Fading as Techniques for Teaching Sight Words to TMR Students" by B. F. Walsh and F. Lamberts, 1979, American Journal of Mental Deficiency, 83(5), p. 474, Copyright (1979) by American Association on Mental Retardation. Reprinted by permission.

computer graphics are used to develop this easy-to-difficult discrimination.

McGee, Krantz, and McClannahan (1986) used stimulus shaping to teach students with autism to point to the words for play materials in an incidental teaching format. As students showed an interest in a play material, the target word and up to four distracters were presented to the child. The words were from labels on storage boxes for the play materials. Other labeled boxes were used as distractors. Over time, the distracters were made more like each other and students worked harder to make the discrimination (i.e., read the word to find the correct box). Stimulus shaping can also be used more independently by students; for example, the *Edmark Functional Word Series* (1990) has student worksheets that can be completed independently and computer programs that use stimulus shaping that require students to "click on" the correct answer.

An innovation in the use of stimulus fading and shaping procedures is the task demonstration model, which has been applied both to reading (Karsh & Repp, 1992; Karsh, Repp, & Lenz, 1990) and to math skills (Repp, Karsh, & Lenz, 1990). The task demonstration model is an instructional method that incorporates principles of generalization from general case instruction (explained later in this chapter) and teaches a hierarchy of simple to more difficult skills: match-to-sample, identification, and naming. In the task demonstration model, teachers instruct students to discriminate relevant stimulus dimensions (or S+) from irrelevant stimulus dimensions (or S−). Relevant stimulus dimensions are those symbol characteristics (e.g., curvature of a line, shape, number of lines, presence of a dot) that are critical for making that symbol what it represents and not something else. Irrelevant stimulus dimensions are the features of a symbol that have no meaningful bearing on the symbol's meaning. Consider the examples of the numeral "1" illustrated next:

$$1 = 1 = 1 = 1 = 1 = 1$$

What are the relevant dimensions of the numeral "1"?

The relevant dimension (S+) is the single vertical line. Notice how every example has this vertical line.

What are the irrelevant dimensions of the numeral "1"?

The use of a horizontal base, a slanted "flag" at the top of the numeral, and the size of the numeral are examples of irrelevant dimensions (S−).

The goal for students taught through the task demonstration model is that they be able to read target stimuli (words or numbers) however they may be encountered in the natural context.

Several steps are involved in using the task demonstration model:

1. Prepare a wide variety of flash card materials that vary all the irrelevant dimensions (e.g., color, size, and typeface of letters, numbers, and shapes; size, color, and shape of flash card). This variation over successive trials will allow students to differentiate the relevant stimulus dimensions (i.e., S+ or correct choices) (e.g., the letters "m-e-n") from the irrelevant dimensions, such as the color of the flash card or type or size of the letters in a word.

2. Plan the order of teaching so that the distracter symbols and words (the S− flash cards or the incorrect choices) are:
   (a) initially, very different from the correct choice, or S+ (e.g., use dashed lines as distractors:--- men ---)
   (b) later, moderately different from the correct choice (e.g., use contrasting words: toy men box)
   (c) finally, only slightly different from the correct choice. (e.g., use similar words: met men ten)

3. Expect students to start by learning simpler responses and progress to more difficult responses:
   (a) initially, "read" by matching the word shown to them to one from an array of words using a match-to-sample response
   (b) later, "read" by pointing to the word (spoken by the teacher: "Find cat") in an array of words
   (c) finally, read by stating the word shown on a flash card ("What is this?")

4. Before teaching starts, students are probed for their ability on each skill (e.g., match-to-sample, identification (point to word), and naming (reading) words). During training, students' ability to read (name) words or numbers by stating the word or number shown on a flash card is assessed regularly as the primary evaluation.

While the task demonstration model requires the preparation of some materials, it has been found to be more efficient than a system of least prompts in teaching adolescents with moderate mental retardation sight words (Karsh et al., 1990) and naming numbers (Repp et al., 1990). Students acquired basic academic skills more quickly with a task demonstration model than with a system of least prompts. This may be because the within stimulus prompts better focused the students' attention to the word configuration. Thus for some teachers and students, the task demonstration model may be more useful for teaching academics.

Summary on Prompting and Feedback Procedures

The last decade has provided a strong body of research on effective methods for teaching functional academic skills, such as sight words, math symbols, time discriminations, and money computation. The challenge for teachers is to determine which methods work best for them, for their teaching assistants and students, and for the settings where they teach. Teachers are recommended to begin with the principle of parsimony by choosing the simplest, but still effective procedure. To "overdo" procedures for one teaching plan may cost the time needed to address another skill that requires extra effort.

Teachers also should consider which methods will blend best into the teaching context. Simpler procedures like feedback, simultaneous prompting and probes, or constant time delay can work well in a general education context with group instruction or with peer tutoring. In contrast, teachers may select some more complex procedures, such as stimulus shaping, to design materials that can be student-directed during class seat work times; in other cases, pre-programmed workbook or computer programs may already encompass effective stimulus shaping or stimulus fading procedures.

Another consideration when selecting instructional procedures is the student's preferences or reaction to different teaching methods. For example, some students may prefer an interspersal method in which they control the flash card presentations in drill format, while others may like to be given rapid response trials within small groups (thus involving one of the first three methods in Table 13–2). Other students may prefer workbooks, worksheets, or computer programs that make use of stimulus shaping or fading methods. A student who has a history of learning academic skills with a certain approach may prefer this approach. Other students may prefer the variety of a new teaching method. Students who slow their work rate or get disruptive when they make errors will do best with an errorless or low-error method (e.g., time delay, system of least prompts) (Wolery, Ault, & Doyle, 1992).

Finally, teachers should take into account the research findings on the efficiency of these teaching procedures with academic skills. These findings show that least intrusive prompting tends to be less efficient with academic skills than other procedures, such as time delay or the task demonstration model. However, least prompts may still be used in teaching functional academics when the method can help focus attention on natural cues in either a classroom simulation or a community setting. More appropriate teaching methods like time delay also can be used for the one or two difficult academic steps that might appear in a lengthy chain of responses in activities like using a commercial washing machine or ordering (and paying) at a fast food restaurant, while least prompts is used to teach all the remaining activity steps.

Also, a note of caution is needed about the instructional efficiency findings: The difference in time to mastery in this comparative research is often small (less than an hour across many days of training to reach criterion). If a procedure like least prompts is preferred by a student, easier for a teacher to use, or more applicable to a given setting, then teachers are encouraged to use it.

Designing and Selecting Materials to Encourage Learning

In general, teachers will want to use as many real materials as possible in teaching functional academics. For example, personal calendars, real clocks, money, store coupons and flyers, food packages, and slides, videos or photos of aisle markers, community signs, and fast food ordering areas all make excellent teaching materials for functional academics instruction. Some students may also benefit from commercial materials that provide opportunities to learn basic academic skills. Some commercial materials that may be applicable are given in Table 13–4.

Community-based instruction can be economically supplemented with videotape simulations taken in a variety of community settings. Work by Haring, Breen, Weiner, Kennedy, and Bednersh (1995) demonstrated the value of videotape simulations for promoting generalization when used in conjunction with small group instruction at school and intermittent in vivo training. Teachers may find that "homemade" videotapes of volunteer peers following the target task steps can offer a time-saving way to supplement small-group learning and increase the saliency of the simulated materials. The videotape is used to teach students to focus on relevant setting stimuli, to learn the task sequence visually and possibly verbally, to anticipate upcoming steps, to solve problems in a more concrete manner, and to encourage self-instruction (e.g., "I need to look at my list . . . OK, now I need to find the diary products . ."; "That's the express line, do I have 10 or less things in my basket?").

Teachers can systematically combine videotapes with small-group instruction in the following way. Students sit at a table in a small group facing the video equipped with any shopping materials they are learning to use (e.g., shopping word or picture lists, single dollar bills, paper and pencil for recording rounded up amounts, calculators). The tape is shown and then paused just after each sequenced step. Using the small-group instructional techniques described earlier, teachers (or tutors) pose questions that are pertinent to the behavior coming up. For example:

- Pause tape after the individual is shown entering store. Ask: "Where is she going?" (e.g., to get a cart; to find the right aisle; to walk down the first aisle).

- Pause tape after shopper finds the correct item or aisle. Ask "What should she do now?" (e.g., look at her list and check the products).
- Pause tape after shopper selects needed item. Ask "What did she select?" "What should she do now?" (e.g., she got bananas; check them off and look on her list again; she got soup, round up the price, write it on her paper, then look at her list again).

Videos (or slides) can be made of many community situations where academic skills are required including fast food or "sit-down" restaurants (entering; ordering, paying, sitting, eating, and exiting), bank lobbies, movie theaters, public libraries, laundromats, drug stores, and clothing stores. Most community locations will agree to having an informal video made when they understand its training purpose ahead of time. Sometimes a student film club or even a tutoring group may be interested in making the videotape. However, planning is essential if the videos or slides are to be useful for teaching!

1. Teachers must identify the specific steps to be taped or photographed and their order.
2. The detail or close-up shots required should be carefully thought through beforehand so the tape illustrates an accurate sequence, shows the relevant stimuli clearly, and can be used as an instructional tape.
3. It is good to have a diversity of taped sequences that illustrate a range of shopping situations and a variety of stores. (The general case methods described later in this chapter may be used to select the best variety of locations that will produce greater skill generalization).

Videos and slides from the nearby community are an excellent way to make in-school instruction of academic skills more meaningful and increase the likelihood of generalization. In addition, most students tend to like videos, especially when peers they know are pictured.

Planning for Generalization

How or if students manage to achieve generalization depends in part on the ways their teachers plan instruction. There are several approaches teachers can build into their plans to promote skill generalization; the four approaches listed next (and described in more detail later) are arranged from simple to more difficult to use: (a) functional skills, realistic simulations, and in vivo probes; (b) multiple exemplars, (c) general case instruction, and (d) stimulus equivalence.

Functional Skills, Realistic Simulations, and in Vivo Probes
Without the transfer of reading and number use from the classroom tabletop to the real world, academic skills may not indeed be "functional" for students with disabilities. Most of the sight word research has demonstrated that students learn to read words presented on flash cards, but it has not demonstrated functional use of these words in the context of some activity (Browder & Xin, 1998; Snell, 1997). Teachers can encourage functional use of academic skills by following several steps:

1. Develop school instruction plans based on ecological inventories of activities that may require functional academics and are suited to the person's age, interests, and potential adult needs. The best way to make academic instruction functional is to begin with the activity, not the skill. The teacher asks, "In what activities will the student need to read sight words?," and then selects activities and teaches sight word reading in that context, using any natural cues available, such as commercial logos. The teacher also asks, "In what activities will the student need to use money or count or know numbers for time-telling or measurement?" Then the teacher selects the most appropriate activities and uses them (simulated and real) to provide a context for teaching the related money and counting skills, while using materials that increase the connection between classroom setting and the activity setting.
2. Use real materials and examples in school-based instruction and teach the response that is required in the target activity. During instruction, have students practice the response in the way it will be used in community contexts. For example, the teacher may have students "show how much money is needed for lunch" rather than asking students to learn the names for money (e.g., nickel, dime, ten-dollar bill). Students who can move about, like Simon, also need to learn to select money amounts while standing and without a counting surface.
3. Schedule opportunities for using target activities and skills outside the classroom and check on gen-

eralization. Some school environments can provide excellent practice opportunities (e.g., reading a school schedule, purchasing at the school store). Additionally, older students, such as Simon and Jerome, need some time to try out their skills in community or job contexts.

The Multiple Exemplar Approach

One easily implemented strategy to enhance generalization is to teach numerous examples from a stimulus or response class. Solnick and Baer (1984) used this classic approach to teach number-numeral correspondence to preschool children. The five worksheet formats that they selected for instruction required both stimulus generalization (counting different objects) and response generalization (e.g., drawing a line from the numeral 3 to three buttons; circling two apples in a row when given the number 2). The experimenters tested the youngsters on each of the five worksheet formats and then chose one format for instruction. When the students mastered this format, the children were tested on all formats again. If test results revealed that they did not generalize their counting to the other worksheets, a second worksheet format was selected and taught. This process of teaching and testing for generalization continued until testing revealed that the children could count using any of the worksheets; generalization to all five formats occurred after children received training on up to three formats. The children also generalized from the number group taught (numbers 1 through 3) to new number groups that they had not been taught (numbers 4 through 6 or 7 through 9). This study illustrates the benefits of teaching multiple exemplars of the target skill that require students to learn several variations of the response needed and to use those responses in the presence of a variety of stimulus materials.

The steps that teachers might take to use the multiple exemplar strategy can be illustrated as follows:

The teacher's objective was for Simon to be able to recognize his name across a variety of materials (e.g., class materials, his lunchbox, mail, a job time card). He would also be making a variety of responses when viewing his name (e.g., selecting his own folder, punching his time card, carrying his lunch). Thus, Simon would be learning both stimulus generalization (across materials) and response generalization (what to do when he saw his name). The teacher then selected

a set of materials with Simon's name (i.e., lunchbox, timecard, class folder, toolbox). She probed his response to all of these materials. When Simon did not respond to his name, she began by teaching the first material (to read his name on his lunchbox and carry it to the cafeteria). She then checked for generalization across the other materials. When Simon did not respond to his name for other materials, she taught the second exemplar (to punch in using his own time card). She then probed again and found Simon could now generalize. That is, he could find his own folder and carry it to his desk and locate his own toolbox in shop and place his tools there.

General Case

The term "general case instruction" refers to the practice of defining the range of responses and stimuli that need to be mastered, and then using this information to select the most logical items to teach first—items that will enable students to transfer their learning to other items not directly taught (Horner & McDonald, 1982; Sprague & Horner, 1984). The general case approach is a more sophisticated version of the multiple exemplar method in that the "best exemplar(s)" is identified. Becker, Engelmann, and Thomas (1975) said, "The general case has been taught when, after instruction on some tasks in a particular class, any task in that class can be performed correctly" (p. 325). Although teaching the general case may require more planning time, it ultimately may save teaching time.

Gardill and Browder (1995) used time delay and a general case approach to teach students to associate an adequate amount of money with specific pictured food or snack purchases. Students learned to discriminate food or snack items by whether they cost one of three amounts of money: three quarters for any vending machine purchase, a one-dollar bill for a variety of convenience store snacks, or a five-dollar bill for lunch (a range of stimuli). Pictures of a wide variety of potential purchases were selected that sampled the range of variation in the three cost classes. One set of pictures was used for teaching and a second set was used to probe generalization of the target response (e.g., pointing to the correct money amount: quarters, one-dollar bill, or five-dollar bill). The practice of teaching individuals to associate a cash amount with various types of purchases was an adequate and simpler response to learn than counting out exact change. Similarly, the task demonstration model described earlier in this chapter uses a general case approach by teaching from a wide variety of materials. The steps to use a general case approach are:

1. Define the instructional universe.
   The goal is for Sharon to tell time using any analog clock with the numerals 1 through 12 and an hour and minute hand.
2. Define the stimulus and response variation.
   The teacher will use a variety of clocks with different colors, numeral shapes, and hand sizes.
3. Select exemplars that sample the range of variation.
   The teacher chose three clocks and a watch that had these contrasts.
4. Vary the irrelevant features.
   The teacher was careful to vary which clock she used with each clock time (e.g., not always use watch for 3:00 P.M.)
5. Teach one set of exemplars and probe the others. Teach a second exemplar and so forth until mastery occurs.
   The teacher alternated which clock or watch she used each day in teaching. One day a week, she probed how well Sharon generalized to a novel (untaught) clock or watch.

Stimulus Equivalence

A third approach to generalization is to develop and sequence instruction to encourage stimulus equivalence. Stimulus equivalence is based on the mathematical principle of transitivity. This principle states that if a = b and b = c, then a = c. That is, if you teach two of three inter-related skills, the third skill may be learned through generalization by means of stimulus equivalence. For example, a student who knows that four quarters equals a one-dollar bill and that the printed price $1.00 equals a one-dollar bill could probably use either four quarters or a one-dollar bill in a vending machine item with a price of $1.00.

Stimulus equivalence may have particular applicability to teaching reading comprehension. In early studies, Sidman (1971) and Sidman and Cresson (1973) noted equivalence transfer in teaching sight words to learners with severe mental retardation. They found that once students could match the spoken word ("car") to a picture and point to the word c-a-r when told "car" (steps 3 and 5 in Table 13–6), they could then match a picture and printed word or read aloud the printed word (steps 6, 7, and 8 in Table 13–6).

Similarly, Skinner (1957) proposed several decades ago that comprehension problems are, in fact, language deficiencies. Thus, following the stimulus equivalence approach, teachers tackle reading comprehen-

sion by teaching language equivalencies. The assumption is that when students (a) learn to associate pictures with spoken words and (b) learn to associate printed words with spoken words, they would likely transfer their learning and (c) know how to pair printed words with their pictures. Browder and D'Huyvetters (1985) illustrated just such a transfer in teaching children with moderate mental retardation and emotional disturbance to reach sight words. Once the children could name objects (e.g., figures of man, woman, boy, girl) and read these as sight words, they were able to match the sight words and figures to demonstrate comprehension with no further training. (see Table 13–7.)

Equivalence can be used with math skills too. Stoddard, Hurlbert, Manoli, and McIlvane (1989) used stimulus equivalence to teach coin combinations to individuals with mental retardation. For example, they taught facts (a) and (b), and found that students readily transferred their learning to fact (c); for example, (a) a quarter = 25 cents; (b) 2 dimes and 1 nickel = 25 cents; (c) a quarter = 2 dimes and 1 nickel. Similarly, Kennedy, Itkonen, and Lingquist (1994) demonstrated how to use transitivity in teaching students to classify food sight words by their food groups.

Summary

Regardless of the methods teachers use to promote generalization of skills in their students, instruction and learning should be regarded as incomplete until meaningful generalization and routine skill use are observed. Most teachers will find the first two approaches discussed in this section (i.e., functional skills, realistic simulations, and in vivo probes and multiple exemplars) to be the easiest ways to teach skill generalization.

Skill Maintenance

Maintaining one's academic skills once learned is another important stage of learning. The best preventative to forgetting is regular use. When the academics skill taught can be readily used in daily activities and routines, then regular use is easily achieved and skill maintenance is more likely. Maintenance, in contrast to generalization, is simpler because it means retention over time in the same situations rather than transfer to new situations. Math and reading skills learned during activities like buying a school lunch,

TABLE 13–6

Stimulus Equivalence and Reading

Skill	Definition	Stimulus (visual or auditory)	Response (name or match)
1. Identity picture matching	Match sample picture to picture	🚗	👧 🥛 🐕 🚗 🛒 👦 🍎 🐈
2. Identity word matching	Match sample printed word to printed word	car	girl drink dog car bus boy apple cat
3. Auditory comprehension *	Match sample spoken word to picture	"car"	👦 👧 🐕 🐈 🛒 🚗 🥛 🍎
4. Picture naming	Name a sample picture	🚗	"car"
5. Auditory comprehension **	Match sample spoken word to printed word	"car"	boy girl dog cat bus car drink apple
6. Reading comprehension ***	Match sample picture to printed word	🚗	apple car boy dog bus girl drink cat
7. Reading comprehension ***	Match sample printed word to picture	car	🍎 🚗 👦 🐕 🛒 👧 🥛 🐈
8. Oral reading ***	Name (read) sample printed word	car	"car"

*When skills 3 and 5 were mastered, students demonstrated a transfer of their learning to skills 6, 7, and 8 without additional learning.

TABLE 13–7

An Example of Stimulus Equivalence and Reading

Reading skill	Equivalence	Example
1. Teach auditory comprehension of pictures	a = c stated word = picture	"Mop" = 🧹
2. Teach auditory receptive reading	a = b stated word = word card	"Mop" = MOP
3. Probe for transfer of learning to reading comprehension tasks	b = c word card = picture	MOP = 🧹

opening a locker, finding one's papers by name recognition, and getting to a therapy appointment on time are naturally repeated each time the activity occurs; but staff and peers must let the student be independent and use the skill. The best way to promote skill maintenance is through regular use:

1. Target skills that will be needed by a particular individual currently and are likely to be useful later in life.
2. Choose skills that contribute to active participation in age-appropriate activities, preferred by the student and valued by peers and family members.
3. Keep track of what is learned and design students' schedules so learned skills are either built on or used as is; IEP objectives should not only pertain to teaching new skills (acquisition) but also should address maintenance and generalization.
4. Successful skill generalization to settings the student regularly uses in and outside the school increases the probability that skills will be maintained through regular use.

Functional Reading and Language Arts Instruction

To plan a functional reading and language arts program, the teacher begins by considering the outcomes desired for the student (refer back to Table 13–1). Will the goal for Sharon be to use her sight vocabulary across a variety of school and community activities (i.e., a generalized approach to reading)? Or, is the desired reading outcome to read a limited set of words while participating in shopping, leisure, cooking, or other activities (i.e., reading skills embedded into highly specific routines)? What other language arts outcomes are relevant for Sharon: comprehension, handwriting, spelling? Because she is young and has some reading skills already, her teachers will probably aim for broader reading and language arts outcomes (i.e., general education curriculum with adaptations or functional generalized skills). The approaches for reaching for these differing outcomes and goals are described next.

Generalized Functional Reading

In a generalized, functional reading approach, the goal is for students to have enough of a sight word vocabulary to be able to scan printed materials and glean the key information needed in a given activity. For example:

> Erin can scan a TV program listing, locate the name of a favorite show, and identify the time it begins. In the morning, she can scan the weather report in the newspaper, picking out key words to learn how to dress appropriately. At work, she can check the bulletin board for simple messages like "Friday—casual dress" or "Pick up paycheck by 4:00 PM."

The best way for teachers to plan reading instruction is through the use of key activities in the student's current and future environments. Table 13–8 lists categories of printed materials and examples of related reading activities, many of which could serve as a context for teaching generalized reading From these activities, a sight word vocabulary can be identified that students learn to read and apply across a variety of activities. For example, a student may learn sight words to read the weather report in the newspaper (see Figure 13–5).

If students make good progress in learning functional words, or if students are young, it may be valuable to introduce a vocabulary of often-used words found in most printed literature. For example Fry's list of 300 "instant words" (Fry 1957, 1972), the Dolch list of 200 words (Dolch, 1950), and the revised Dale list of 769 words (Stone, 1956) are lists of words that appear frequently in beginning reading programs. The school's reading specialist may be a good resource for these word lists. The Dolch word list can be found in many commercial beginning reading materials. Many of these high-frequency words do not have an immediate functional application as isolated words (e.g., "red", "in"), but they can be combined into functional phrases with the targeted activity-related words. For example, the teacher might use recipe phrases (e.g., "Put in" with picture of oven). These words may also help students participate in general education class activities where class work directions, word experience stories, charts, class newspapers, and bulletin board labels often make use of high-frequency words.

Another important category of functional words are the names of key people and labels in the student's environment and in their daily routine. Many elementary general education classes repeatedly use words like "math" and "reading" to help students know their schedule and assignments. Similarly, the names of

TABLE 13–8
Common Printed Materials

Printed Materials	Examples
Signs and Labels	Road signs, room labels, clothing tags, medicine labels, billboards, street signs, store signs
Schedules and Tables	TV guide, bus and train schedules, game schedules, movie listings, school and work schedule, library and swim schedule
Maps	City, street, road, global, weather
Categorized Listings and Indices	Yellow pages, indices in books, want ads, dictionary
High-Interest, Factual Materials	Sports events, news reports, stories
Illustrated Advertisements	Department stores, yellow pages, grocery stores, magazines
Technical Documents	Sales contracts, insurance policies, guarantees, apartment lease
Sets of Directions	Prescription and over-the-counter medicines, recipes, opening packages, use of tools or equipment, crafts, games, assembly of materials
Fill-In Blank Forms	Banking forms, job applications, car registration, credit card application, tax forms, bank account application, hospital entry form

some staff and classmates might be taught to help students know who will be working with them.

Sight Word Instruction

To plan instruction of key sight words, the teacher can select from the prompting and fading methods described earlier in this chapter. The most prevalent method found in the research to teach sight words is constant time delay. This method can easily be used

FIGURE 13–5
A Teacher Works with Charles on Interpreting the Day's Weather Report in the Paper.

in a group instruction format. Time delay also can be combined with observational learning and the instruction of incidental information (Gast et al., 1990; Schoen & Ogden, 1995).

Word Analysis

One limitation of whole-word methods of teaching reading is that students may not generalize their skills to new words; words are learned as separate units rather than teaching phonetic rules. Some research with individuals having moderate mental retardation has demonstrated that students with moderate disabilities can learn several methods of word analysis (e.g., Entrikin, York, & Brown, 1977; Hoogeven, et al., 1989):

1. Phonetic analysis, or sounding out words
2. Structural analysis, or recognizing meaning units such as parts of compound words, prefixes, suffixes, and contractions
3. Contextual analysis, or using the meaning of the sentence and preceding sentence to determine an unknown word

Many commercial materials exist that provide skill sequences for teaching phonics and other word analysis skills (e.g., Science Research Associates' Developmental 1 Reading Laboratory). The general education teacher or reading specialist often can recommend materials for students who can benefit from further instruction in word analysis. Because word analysis training is difficult to apply to immediate functional use (e.g., identifying the short "a" sound), it should augment, not replace, sight word instruction. Learning sight words only without any word analysis goals may be the main focus for some students because of their age, rate of learning, or need for all instruction to be applicable in daily routines.

Comprehension Skills
The first step in sight word learning is to identify a word that is named (e.g., "Find coffee") by pointing to it in an array (receptive reading) or by saying it aloud when presented with a single flash card (expressive reading). Comprehension requires making a second response to the sight word. This second response shows that the student understands the meaning of the printed word. Comprehension can be demonstrated in several ways by asking the student: (a) to pair the word with a picture, (b) to demonstrate the activity, (c) to point to an associated object or location, or (d) to make some other type of academic comprehension response (e.g., circle a word or a picture). Functionality is increased when comprehension involves using the word in the context of a daily routine.

> Simon reads the word on his schedule and selects the correct materials for that activity (e.g., gym bag for "gym"). Or, he reads the word in a recipe and begins the cooking response (e.g., "stir"). Or, Sharon finds her name on a paper and takes it to her table.

Some students with severe disabilities are excellent decoders and can read a wide variety of words—they have generalized word analysis skills—but they do not understand the meaning, that is, they lack comprehension of the words. As described earlier in the section on stimulus equivalence, a lack of reading comprehension usually indicates that the student lacks language comprehension. To help students begin making links between the printed words and their meanings, the teacher can probe the students' listening (auditory) comprehension. That is, the teacher says the word and notes whether a student understands its meaning (e.g., find the gym bag when the teacher says "gym"). If not, the teacher will want to focus sight word instruction on using the word in context rather than in tabletop drill. For example, the teacher might show a student word cards of their key schedule words (e.g., physical education, chorus, home room, math) and ask him or her to read the

word and locate the associated photo of the classroom and teacher. Even though the student may be able to read entire sentences, instruction would begin at the level of the student's listening comprehension (e.g., single sight words or short phrases).

Comprehension can be encouraged by using a language experience approach (LEA), which involves composing simple stories (Nessel & Jones, 1981). This approach has the advantages of providing vocabulary that is familiar to the student and relates to a recently experienced activity. In the LEA process, the student dictates a story to a teacher or tutor who then records it, adding words, if needed. Once written, reading instruction focuses on the dictated story or passages. Topics for the story can be school events, community-based instruction, activities with friends, family events, or other areas of interest to the student. To use this passage for reading instruction, the teacher or peer tutor may (a) put new words on flash cards for sight word instruction, (b) ask comprehension questions, (c) ask the student to select a picture or photograph for the story, or (d) have the student photocopy, type, or recopy the story for a permanent storybook. Word cards can be arranged to make new sentences. Some students like to have a storage box for their words, and, depending on their skills, word cards can be arranged behind alphabet cards, making them easier to find and allowing additional learning opportunities involving alphabetization and initial letter recognition whenever getting out or replacing word cards. Figure 13–6 shows an example of a language experience approach story. In this student-dictated story, the underlined words were those supplied by the teacher.

Spelling and Writing
A generalized approach to functional reading may also involve teaching students some spelling and writing skills. It is important to note that students can learn to read sight words without first learning to name the letters of the alphabet; knowing the names of letters is a skill that can consume a lot time without necessarily having great benefit for learners with more extensive disabilities. However, if spelling becomes a goal, letter naming would be important.

One way to introduce spelling skills is through incidental learning by spelling sight words as they are taught. For example, Wolery, Ault, Gast, Doyle, and Mills (1990) spelled each sight word in a group lesson with students who had mild disabilities. Spelling the

FIGURE 13–6

Example of a Language Experience Story Composed by a Student and Used to Teach Passage Reading.

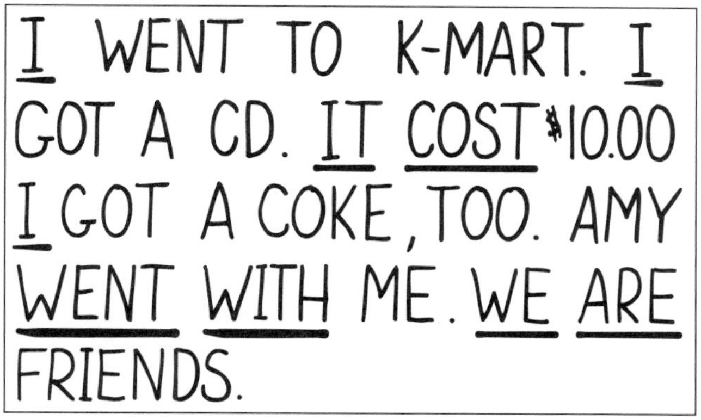

```
I WENT TO K-MART. I
GOT A CD. IT COST $10.00
I GOT A COKE, TOO. AMY
WENT WITH ME. WE ARE
FRIENDS.
```

words helped focus the students' attention, and some students also learned to spell the words.

If writing is a goal, a good starting point is the student's own name. The movement involved in making each letter can be task analyzed. The teacher may use prompting that facilitates learning the motor response (e.g., graduated guidance) to help the student learn to make each stroke. (Graduated guidance is described in chapter 9.) Or the student may use a template to practice his or her name without teacher assistance.

Specific, Embedded Reading

Some students may only learn to read a small sight vocabulary (less than 20 words) or only a couple of key words. By carefully choosing these key words, this sight word vocabulary can be an asset to performing daily routines. Because these words will always be read while performing the activity, the teacher chooses an activity from student's current daily priorities. When possible, these words are also chosen for long-term utility (e.g., name recognition, work-related words). The following discussion addresses some of the ways to teach reading using a specific, embedded approach.

Picture-Word Instruction Booklets

Picture-word instructions can help individuals self-manage their activities. Picture-word booklets have been designed to teach cooking by recipes, multiple

step housekeeping chores, and other daily living skills (Browder et al., 1984; Johnson & Cuvo, 1981) and to increase independence in vocational settings (Agran, Fodor-Davis, Moore, & Deer, 1989). Teaching younger students the skills of following picture-word instruction booklets also can have longitudinal benefit as students learn to use books for self-instruction on new skills. Some students may be able, or may prefer, to use books that only have words. For example, Browder and Minarovic (in press) taught three adults with moderate mental retardation to read sight words that helped them remember a sequence of job tasks in their paid community jobs. In this study, a cook's assistant in a restaurant learned to read the words: garlic bread, dishwasher, pots, and trays. The individuals first learned to read the sight words during massed trial practice prompted by progressive time delay; instruction took place just before work at nearby library or home. Then, while on the job, they learned to self-manage their sequence of job tasks using these words and a "did-next-now" self-management strategy (Agran & Moore, 1994). After completing one job, the employee would check off the word "trays" and say, "Did 'trays'"; read the next word on the list, "garlic," and say, "Next, 'garlic bread'"; and restate the word as she moved to the materials needed: "Now garlic bread". The employees became independent in moving from task to task with this self-instructional approach.

Reading to Make Choices

One of the most important ways sight words can be used is to make choices in daily life. As much as possible, these choices should relate to the individual's preferences. For example, knowing some sight words can provide students a means of selecting options from a menu, finding a favorite Internet site, identifying the time for a TV show, selecting a type of ice cream in the grocery store, or obtaining a preferred soda at a vending machine. Some choices will have "correct answers" that are needed to participate appropriately or safely in community settings, such as students who can read sight words and symbols to select the correct restroom, avoid doors that say "Use other door", pick the theater in a multiplex cinema that corresponds with the purchased ticket, and so on. Teachers can also introduce "menus" of options like free time activities in the classroom that the student can read and choose.

Reading for Orientation and Mobility

Sight words can enhance students' mobility at school and in the community, enabling them to find their way around school buildings, and in stores, libraries, restaurants, medical office buildings, and other places. For example, aisle marker words from the grocery store may be taught to improve the ability to locate products (Karsh et al., 1990); signs of familiar landmarks like "barber", "KOA", and "Denny's" can be taught to help students identify community landmarks (Singleton et al., 1995). Familiar street signs and bus names are other options for this instruction.

Container and Product Discrimination

Shopping for groceries, preparing food, doing laundry and other daily living activities often require discrimination between different containers. Sometimes students benefit from learning to select their family's cereal or detergent brands; parents might send money and a short shopping list to school thereby providing a meaningful task for the community-based training context. Other students will benefit from learning to discriminate edible products from nonedible products. Store coupons provide an easily accessible material for teaching product reading and they also contain the natural cues for product discrimination (e.g., the color of the box, product logo). Grocery shopping may also be taught using videotaped instruction of a grocery store's aisles and pictures of products to be located (Alcantara, 1994). Aeschleman and Schladenhauffen (1984) had students develop their own symbols for a class of grocery items (e.g., a pretzel to symbolize salty snacks). The students then used their own grocery lists in shopping.

Reading to Gain Information or to Function in Social Settings

Even with limited reading skills, students can use their reading to gain information or to function in social settings. For example, students who recognize their own names can use this information to find their own belongings or an assigned area (e.g., names on desks or work lockers). Knowledge of a few weather sight words and symbols and practice with the newspaper will allow an individual to determine the upcoming weather from the paper's daily report. Communication skills can sometimes be enhanced by teaching students to read and use symbols or words. For example, Osguthorpe and Chang (1988) taught students who had no reading or symbolic

communication skills to use a computerized Rebus symbol processor to communicate. The students learned to associate a Rebus picture with spoken labels of things and events in their environment (e.g., ride, bus, want, goodbye, eat). Because the computer printed out communication as Rebus word combinations, others could read their communication as well.

Another category of sight words that provide information includes product warning labels. For example, in Collins and Stinson's (1995) work described earlier, students learned to read words like "precaution," "harmful," "induce vomiting," and "caution." The teacher used instructive feedback to teach students the definitions of these words. For example, "'harmful if swallowed' means 'don't drink it'." Students were probed on their ability to read these words on actual product labels. Linking reading instruction to actual products and contexts is key to their functional use. Teaching a word like "danger" or "caution" in isolation may not help a student avoid a dangerous situation. By contrast, the teacher can teach students to read the safety word ("caution") and to verbalize its meaning ("don't walk there"), and then purposefully expose students to the safety words during community-based instruction (e.g., reading the word "caution" on yellow warning tape at a construction site, indicating an area closed to pedestrians).

Writing

Students who are only learning to read a few sight words may be able to learn to write their name for lifelong use as a signature. If not, the student may learn to use a rubber stamp signature or a distinctive mark. Similar to Aeschleman and Schladenhauffen (1984), teachers may help students find their own distinctive mark that will be enhanced through instruction to use as a "signature".

Students Who Are Linguistically Diverse

Some students with severe disabilities are from linguistically diverse homes. For example, in Rafael's home Spanish is the primary language, but English is the primary language at school. When teaching sight words to students like Rafael, it is important to conduct ecological inventories and determine if the words students will encounter at home are English, Spanish, or some other language. Teachers should not assume that the printed language encountered most often outside of school is English. For example, some neighborhoods may have nearly all signs in Spanish (e.g., food words on grocery store, street signs), while others neighborhoods will be predominantly English. In a study evaluating bilingual instruction with students having moderate mental retardation who came from Spanish speaking homes, Rohena-Diaz (1998) found that most community signs were in English in the favorite stores used by the families. Thus, English aisle marker words were taught, but the language of instruction was varied to be either English or Spanish. Using constant time delay and massed trial classroom instruction, Rohena-Diaz (1998) found comparable word acquisition and generalization to store settings with both English and Spanish instruction compared to a control condition of word exposure only. Rohena-Diaz noted that teaching functional sight words using constant time delay was compatible with recommendations for teaching English as a second language. Results may also have been influenced by the teacher's skill in talking informally with the students and their families in Spanish when not conducting the reading lessons. Overall, these results demonstrate that students with moderate mental retardation who are linguistically diverse can learn English sight words with constant time delay instruction.

Functional Math

Generalized Functional Math

In a generalized approach to functional math, students will learn a variety of money combinations and price reading, to tell time with a digital clock (and perhaps an analog clock as well), and to compute small sums with or without a calculator (e.g., to balance a checkbook). Students who have generalized outcomes will be able to transfer these skills to novel contexts, such as being able to read a broad range of prices on a variety of price tags or telling time from a variety of clocks. Each of these skills is now described.

Counting and Numerals
Counting objects to obtain the total number or to get a specific number is a useful skill often included in the math objectives for students learning by the gen-

eralized approach. Even being able to count up to five can be applied in numerous situations: table setting, helping adults pass things out in class, playing board games, craft or art projects, money skills and number line use, and work and volunteer settings. The sequenced steps for teaching counting and one-to-one correspondence and using numerals can be found in Table 13–9 (Resnick, Wang, & Kaplan, 1973). These two sequences are valuable for planning assessments and instructional steps for counting and number use skills. Both sequences get more difficult with each added skill; unit one is taught with quantities to 5 and then repeated as unit two with quantities to 10, followed by units three and four on numerals, first from 1 to 5 and then from 1 to 10.

For example, to teach counting, this approach suggests teaching rote counting (first to 5 and later to 10) first. Once counting by rote to 5 is mastered, the student learns to use that skill to count moveable objects (unit one, skill two), then to count fixed, but ordered objects (skill three):

☆ ☆ ☆ ☆   and   ✿ ✿

and then fixed, but unordered objects:

☆   ☆

☆   ☆   ☆

With these math sequences, it is best to use materials from daily classroom, school, and home routines, and then find ways to use the skills once learned. One important "generalizable" math skill is identifying and entering numbers. Wacker et al. (1988) taught students with moderate mental retardation to enter numbers into a computer file, a checkbook, or a calculator. They found that this skill was enhanced by having students say the number aloud before entering it, using what they called a "say, then do" approach. Being able to read and enter numbers can help students in planning purchases, performing some simple data entry jobs, and computing on a calculator.

The listing of ordered skills for numeral use in Table 13–9 can help organize number instruction from easy to more difficult. Note that the first three skills would be:

- Given two sets of numbers, the student matches them in pairs (match to sample).

TABLE 13–9
Sequenced Objectives for Counting, One-to-One Correspondence, and Numerals

Units 1 and 2: Counting and One-to-One Correspondence

1. The student can count (rote counting).
   "Count" or "Count to _____"
2. Given a set of moveable objects, the student can count by moving them out of the set while counting (touch-move-counting)
   "Count how many pencils" (group of moveable objects)
3. Given a fixed ordered set of objects, the student can count the objects.
   "Count the cups" (objects in a row)
4. Given a fixed unordered set of objects, the student can count the objects.
   "Count the quarters" (an unordered array of objects)
5. Given a stated number and a set of objects, the student can count out a set of the stated size.
   "Count out three plates" (a stack of objects that can be moved)
6. Given a stated number and several sets of fixed objects, the student can identify a set that matches the stated number.
   "Find the group with four animals" (three sets of objects varying in number)
7. Given two sets of objects, the student can pair objects and state whether the sets are the same in number.
   "Are these groups the same?" (two sets of objects the same or different in number)
8. Given two unequal sets of objects, the student can pair objects and state which set has more.
   "Which group has more pennies?" (two sets of objects with differing amounts)
9. Given two unequal sets of objects, the student can pair objects and state which set has less.
   "Which group has less pennies?" (two sets of objects with differing amounts)

Units 3 and 4: Numerals

1. Given two sets of numerals, the student can match the numerals.
   "Match the same numbers"
2. Given a numeral stated and a set of printed numerals, the student can select the stated numeral.
   "Find the 7" (numerals 2, 6, 8, and 7 are missing)
3. Given a numeral (written), the student can read the numeral.
   "What this number?" (show numeral)
4. Given several sets of objects and several numerals, the student can match numerals with appropriate sets.
   "Put the numbers with the piles" (two numeral cards and two piles of coins)
5. Given two numerals (written), the student can state which shows more (or less).
   "Look at these numbers . . . get the one that is more." (two different number cards)
6. Given a set of numerals, the student can place them in order.
   "Put these numbers in order" (2 to 5 number cards)
7. Given numerals stated, the student can write the numeral.
   "Write the number two."

Units 1 and 3 involve sets of up to five objects; Units 2 and 4 involve sets of up to 10 objects.

Note: From "Task analysis in curriculum design: A hierarchially sequenced introductory mathematics curriculum," by L. B. Resnick, M. C. Wang, & J. Kaplan, 1973, *Journal of Applied Behavior Analysis, 6,* p. 699. Copyright 1973 by *Journal of Applied Behavior Analysis.* Adapted with permission.

- Given a stated number and an array of number cards, the student locates the stated number (identification).
- Given a number card (written number), the student reads the number (naming).

Some students may be able to learn to name numbers with flash card drills using either using simple feedback or time delay procedures. Others may bene-

fit from the task demonstration model that uses stimulus shaping and general case instruction to teach generalized number naming (Repp et al., 1990).

Generalized Money Use

Two approaches can be taken for learning to count money. In the first, students learn to use dollars before other currency, and then to use coins if and when dollars are mastered. Dollars are taught first because they have the greatest applicability in purchasing. Change that accumulates is taken to a bank to be converted to dollars. A sequence for teaching students to use dollar bills is shown in Table 13–10.

Students can also be taught to read the prices of anticipated purchases. The prompting and fading methods described earlier (e.g., feedback procedures or constant time delay) have been effective in teaching price reading. Some students may not be able to master reading the full price in dollars and cents, but may be able to learn what has been called the "next dollar strategy" or the "one-more-than strategy" (Box 13–1). In this approach, the student focuses on the first number the cashier states in the price and gives one dollar more (Test, Howell, Burkhart, & Beroth, 1993). Investigators using this strategy have found that two modifications might help some students perform better if the shortened "one-more-than" strategy proves too difficult. For some students, this strategy is easier if they are taught the cents pile modification: to put a single dollar aside in the "cents pile" before counting out the number of dollars named by the cashier (e.g., cashier asks for 4 dollars and 20 cents; student puts one dollar aside for the 20 cents, then counts out four dollars in another pile, and combines the two piles and hands them to the cashier). Other students will make fewer errors when they learn the "say-back" method of restating the price before counting out the number of dollars needed—from the cashier's shortened version of "two forty," to the longer version of "two dollars and forty cents" (Colyer & Collins, 1996; Test et al., 1993). Some students may need extra practice on exact dollar amounts or amounts under one dollar (Colyer & Collins, 1996; Denny & Test, 1995). Students may be able to learn to use higher denominations of bills (fives and tens) after learning the one-more-than technique (Denny & Test).

Students need to determine if they have enough money to buy desired items. One way students can learn this is to select items in advance and use a calculator to determine if they will have enough money to cover these purchases (Frederick-Dugan, et al., 1991). For example, Simon has $10.00, he may use the store flyer from K-Mart or another store to select possible items to buy. First, Simon will list the items in order of preference or need. Then, following a task analysis for calculator use like that shown in Table 13–11, he determines what can be bought that does not result in the calculator showing a minus (overspending). If the items are taxable, it is sometimes simplest to teach students to bring "tax quarters" (change to give to cover the tax) to go with the ten dollar bill, rather than teaching computation of tax.

TABLE 13–10

A Dollar-First Sequence for Teaching Money Skills

The following sequence is more appropriate than teaching coins first to older students:

1. One-Dollar Bill. Use of $1 for small purchases. (Change can be saved in a personal bank at home and converted to dollars by caregivers or at a commercial bank.)
2. Ones to Tens. Use of $1 bills needed for purchases up to $10.00 by using the "one-more-than" strategy (e.g., for $5.49, give 5 ones and "one more").
3. Ten-Dollar Bill. Use of $10 bills for large purchases. Use a number line or "one-more-ten-than" strategy (e.g., for $36.59, give 3 tens and "one more ten").
4. Mixed Tens and Ones. Student learns to count up "one more than" using first tens; then ones (e.g., $36.59, give 3 tens, 6 ones, and "one more" one-dollar bill).
5. Equivalence. Student learns to use equivalent bills (e.g., five-dollar bill=five ones; two fives=ten-dollar bill or ten ones).
6. Coins. Teach counting coins once use of bills is mastered. Teach counting by fives, beginning with nickels following the sequence by Lowe and Cuvo (1976), described in this chapter.

TABLE 13–11

Task Analysis for the Use of a Calculator for Planning Purchases

1. Turn calculator "on."
2. Enter allowance ($10.00). Enter first digit, "1".
3. Enter second digit of allowance, "0".
4. Enter third digit of allowance, "0".
5. Enter fourth digit of allowance, "0".
6. Enter subtraction sign, "−".
7. Enter first digit of item selected from store flyer ($5.98). Enter "5".
8. Enter second digit of selected item. Enter "9".
9. Enter third digit of selected item. Enter "8".
10. Enter equals, "=".
11. State if negative number ("minus" or "no minus").
12. State if can buy (e.g., "No minus. I can buy it," or "Minus, I can not buy it.").

After students have mastered using dollars, or if students are in elementary school, the teacher may teach coin counting and combinations. In *The Syracuse Community-Referenced Curriculum Guide*, Ford, Davern, Schnorr, Black, and Kaiser (1989) provide a skill sequence that can be combined with math instruction for young students. Students learn to count and to use a number line and a calculator to plan and make purchases. A critical feature of this money program is that students apply whatever level of money and number line skills they have to make purchases. For example, students with skills to count pennies would count how many pennies they have (e.g., seven) and then consult the number line to see if this is enough to purchase five cents' worth of gum. This also might be done by matching the pennies to five circles on a picture of gum to see if there are enough pennies. Table 13–12 provides an abbreviated version of the Ford et al. sequence (1989).

For older students, dollar bills may still be used for most purchases, but activities like vending machines might be used to teach coin counting (Trace, Cuvo, & Criswell, 1977). Lowe and Cuvo (1976) designed a skill sequence for teaching coins that simplifies the process by teaching students to count all coins in varying units of fives (e.g., count two dimes by tapping each twice and counting: "five-ten" then "fifteen-twenty"). This simplified approach may be especially beneficial for the older student learning to count coins. Each coin was also associated with a finger(s) prompt. To count nickels, students used their index finger counting by five for each nickel. After mastering nickels to a dollar, students learned to count dimes. Dimes were counted by giving two taps per coin with the paired index and middle finger ("five-ten" . . . "fifteen-twenty" . . . for two dimes). Next, students learned to count combinations of nickels and dimes, continuing to count by fives. After learning to count nickel and dime combinations, quarters were learned by tapping each coin five times with all fingers of the hand and counting by fives to 25. Pennies were learned last and require counting up by one (may be omitted). Additional research revealed that moving the coins a short ways from the group of uncounted coins while counting (a touch-move-count approach) facilitated this learning (Borakove & Cuvo, 1976). In this coin counting sequence (Lowe & Cuvo, 1976), students learn to arrange coins by decreasing value and then count the more valuable coins first, with pennies counted last.

For example, if Simon learned to use this approach, he would count a combination of five coins totaling 55 cents (one quarter, two dimes, and two nickels), by first arranging them as follows: quarter, dime, dime, nickel, nickel. Next he would use the counting sequence and finger-tapping outlined as:

TABLE 13–12
A Sequence to Teach Counting and Money Skills Simultaneously

The following sequence is especially appropriate for young children:

1. Count pennies to 10 cents (count by ones to 10).
2. Equate 10 pennies to 1 dime (both are 10).
3. Count dimes to 1 dollar (count by tens).
4. Count quarters to 1 dollar (25, 50, 75, 1 dollar).
5. Equate 2 quarters plus dimes to 1 dollar (count by tens beginning with 50).
6. Count nickels to 1 dollar (count by fives).
7. Count quarters plus nickels (count by fives beginning with 25, 50, or 75).
8. Count dimes plus nickels (count by tens and then switch to counting by fives).
9. Count quarters plus dimes (count by fives beginning with 25 or 50).
10. Count quarters, dimes, and nickels (count 25 or 50, then by tens, and then by fives).
11. Count 1-dollar bills to $10.00 (use a number line to round up from dollars and cents to compute affordability).
12. Count 1-dollar and 5-dollar bills to $20.00.
13. Count 10-dollar and 1-dollar bills to $20.00.
14. Count 10-dollar, 5-dollar, and 1-dollar bills to $20.00.
15. Use a calculator to compute affordability of multiple purchases.

Note. Based on "Money Handling" by A. Ford, L. Davern, R. Schnorr, J. Black, and K. Kaiser. In *The Syracuse Community-Referenced Curriculum Guide for Students with Moderate and Severe Disabilities* (pp. 117–148) by A. Ford, R. Schnorr, L. Meyer, L. Davern, J. Black, and P. Dempsey (Eds.), 1989, Baltimore: Paul H. Brookes. Copyright (1989) by Paul H. Brookes. Used with permission.

Coin	Finger Prompt	Student Taps Coin and Says
Quarter	5 fingers	"5, 10, 15, 20, 25
Dime	2 fingers	30, 35
Dime	2 fingers	40, 45
Nickel	index finger	50
Nickel	index finger	55 . . . it's 55 cents."

One of the most complex money skills is change computation. This skill probably should be taught last in a money sequence. Cuvo, Veitch, Trace, and Konke (1978) taught change computation to students with moderate mental retardation who knew how to count coins. Students learned to count correct change given back after a purchase. Since most adults who are nondisabled do not take the time to count their change, it seems reasonable that this complex skill may be one that is not taught, unless there is specific vocational reason to target it (a job as a cashier).

Time Management

Because of the proliferation of digital watches and clocks and the comparative ease of digital displays over analog clocks, the most efficient method to teach time telling is with digital numbers. This can be achieved using the same options of prompting and fading methods recommended for teaching sight words. A good beginning point may be to teach the students to read key times in their daily schedules and to identify when they appear on a watch. A skill sequence to teach students digital time might shape students' discrimination across numbers. For example, the sequence of instruction might be:

1. Recognize one number of time for next activity up to 9.
   (e.g., After the clock shows 7, student watches for the 8 to turn on television show.)
2. Recognize two numbers for time of next activity up to 12
   (e.g., Student waits for watch to show a 12 to go to lunch room (12:00) or for watch to show 10 in last two numbers to go home (3:10).)
3. Recognize two numbers up to 59 to know exact time
   (e.g., Student learns to punch in at job training site at exactly 8:47).

One disadvantage of digital time telling is that it is more complex to determine how close a given time is to the target time (e.g., 2:27 is very close to 2:30, as is 1:57 to 2:00). With analog clocks, the student can watch the minute hand to see it getting closer to the target time. A skill sequence to teach analog time telling that requires few prerequisites is the O'Brien (1974) program, which is shown in Figure 13–7. Note that in this skill sequence, students learn

to tell time to the nearest quarter hour, not to the minute.

For time management, students also need to be able to follow schedules and use a calendar. Martin, Elias-Burger, and Mithaug (1987) taught students in a vocational training program to change work tasks based on a printed schedule of words or pictures paired with times. If students did not change work stations within 5 minutes of a scheduled time, they received a verbal prompt to do so and were given feedback to look at the schedule (time and activity). Younger students might be taught to use classroom clocks and self-initiate changes from one classroom activity to the next according to schedules with times. Older students might use personal time schedule cards and their own watch to monitor when to change classes, attend therapy, or meet the bus for community-based instruction.

Calendar time is also key to planning daily, weekly, and monthly activities. This task might be taught by using individual appointment books of small month-by-month calendars (week and daily planners may be less functional as they correspond less to the monthly calendars used in most environments). Students learn to locate the current month and day to note any special events. Then notices of future events can be recorded by finding that month and day.

Computation and Measurement

Some students benefit from learning addition and subtraction skills, which can be taught as a sequenced curriculum (Resnick, et al., 1973). Many commercial programs exist that can be used to teach computation. Some students may learn to add by using their counting skills. For example, Irvin (1991) taught children with moderate mental retardation rote counting to 20 and to count up from any number (e.g., from 5 to 10). Using this rote counting skill, students learned to add by counting sets of dots. For example, to add 3 + 5, the student would be given sets of three dots and five dots. The student would count the three dots, and then shift to the next set counting up from three (i.e., 4, 5, 6, 7, 8) to get the sum of eight.

Often flash card drills of basic addition and subtraction facts are a useful way to build these skills to a more automatic level. Whalen et al. (1996) used group instruction of flash card drills with constant time delay. Students learned their own math facts and

FIGURE 13–7

Steps in the O'Brien Program for Telling Time

I. Reading the Hour Hand
   Step 1: Match number to clock face number
       Phase   1: 1,   (numbers on the clock)
                2: 1, 8
                3: 1, 8, 5
                4: 1, 8, 5, 4
                5: 1, 8, 5, 4, 10
                6: 1, 8, 5, 4, 10, 9
                7: 1, 8, 5, 4, 10, 9, 2
                8: 1, 8, 5, 4, 10, 9, 2, 6
                9: 1, 8, 5, 4, 10, 9, 2, 6, 11
              10: 1, 8, 5, 4, 10, 9, 2, 6, 11, 7
              11: 1, 8, 5, 4, 10, 9, 2, 6, 11, 7, 3
              12: 1, 8, 5, 4, 10, 9, 2, 6, 11, 7, 3, 12
              13: 1, 8, 5, 4, 10, 9, 2, 6, 11, 7, 3, 12
   Step 2: "Point to the number _____ on the clock face."
       Shown the number, point to its match on the clock.
       In 13 phases (see above), number held farther and farther away from clock.
   Step 3: "Point to number _____ on the clock face."
       (Not shown the number.)
   Step 4: Imitation of number name. "This is number _____.
       What number is this? Say "_____.' (Point to number on clock face.)
   Step 5: Number naming. "What number is this?' (Point to number on clock face.)
   Step 6: Reading the hour hand. "What number does the hour hand Point to?"

II. Reading the Minute Hand
   Step 7: Discrimination of hour and minute hand. "Point to the hour hand.' "Point to the minute hand."
   Step 8: Read minute hand—imitation. "What does the minute hand say? Say 'o'clock'.' ("o'clock,' "30,' "15,' "45")
   Step 9: Read the minute hand (no verbal prompt).

III. Read the Nearest Quarter Hour Setting
   Step 10: Read hour hand when not exactly on a number.
       Phase 1: Move hour hand clockwise.
              2: Only 2 numbers on clock. Hour hand between them. "Which number did the hour hand Point to last?"
              3: All numbers showing.
              4: Hour hand between and minute hand on 9.
              5: Hour hand between and minute hand on 3.
              6: Hour hand between and minute hand on 6.
              7: Hour hand between or on and minute hand 12, 9, 3, 6.
                 "What number does the hour hand point to?"
                 "What number does the minute hand read?"
                 "What time is it? Say _____."
   Step 11: Read time to quarter hour. "What time is it?"
   Step 12: Read time between quarter hour as "It's about _____."
       "What time is it? Say about _____."
   Step 13: Read time between quarter hours. No prompt. "What time is it?"
       Phase   Distance from nearest quarter hour
         1   1 minute
         2   1, 3
         3   1, 3, 5
         4   1, 3, 5, 7
         5   0, 1, 3, 5, 7

Note: From "Instruction in Reading a Clock for the Institutionalized Retarded" by F. O'Brien, 1974, Unpublished manuscript. Southern Illinois University. Reprinted by permission.

those of their peers. Whalen et al. also introduced some sight words for incidental learning during these math drills. Students also can learn to perform computation by using calculators and to discriminate between whether to add or subtract (Lancioni, Smeets, and Oliva, 1987). Some students with disabilities may be able to keep pace with the general education math class assignments by using calculators (Horton, 1985). If such skills are taught, teachers are urged to find many ways for addition and subtraction skills to be used by students in their daily routines, using functional materials and situations.

Students may also benefit from learning basic measurement skills of length (ruler), volume (cups and tablespoons measures), and weight. Smeenge, Page, Iwata, and Ivancic (1980) developed a skill sequence to teach measurement to an adolescent and two adults who had multiple disabilities. Students learned to compare lengths to determine if they were the same or different; then to determine if one was shorter or longer; and finally to use a ruler to measure feet and inches.

Specific, Embedded Math Skills

In a specific, embedded approach to math, responses are only taught in the context of the activities in which they are used. That is, the teacher would not use tabletop instruction in counting, money use, or telling time, but instead would only teach the math responses as they are embedded in task analyses of daily living. For example, to teach money use, the student is taught to make purchases. Some students for whom a specific, embedded approach is targeted, may learn to use the next dollar strategy to make purchases (McDonnell & Ferguson, 1988), but others who cannot count by ones might simply learn to associate specific types of money with specific types of purchases. For example,

Gardill and Browder (1995) taught students to use: (a) quarters for vending machines, (b) one-dollar bills for single items from a convenience store, and (c) five-dollar bills to purchase lunch. Other students may learn to use a predesignated amount of money for a specific setting. McDonnell (1987) taught students with severe disabilities to take out a single one-dollar bill from a group of five ones to purchase an item in a fast food restaurant or convenience store.

For time management, in an embedded approach, the student may be taught to follow specific digital times in a daily schedule and to attend to natural cues that tell when to begin and end tasks. For example, students may learn the specific times classes begin but also know to follow peers as they prepare to change classes. In a work setting, a student may determine break time by matching a pictured clock time on their schedule with the wall clock or their watch (Connis, 1979). Some students may not be able to follow a digital clock but may be able to set a timer to signal a break time. Others may simply prefer to have their watches set to beep at designated times and learn both how to turn off the beeper and what the signal means. Sometimes students benefit from learning to follow a picture or object schedule, using natural cues like finishing one task to signal when to check the schedule for what to do next.

In an embedded approach, students probably will not learn computation skills. Students may learn to identify specific numbers within activities. For example, students may learn to dial a telephone number using a match-to-sample strategy (Lalli, Mace, Browder, & Brown, 1989), while others may learn to read vending machine prices that are common to the community: 55 cents, 60 cents, 70 cents, 75 cents (Browder et al., 1988). What is taught to students taking the embedded approach must be linked to the skill needs identified in their ecological inventories and taught within a meaningful activity-based context.

Summary

Academic instruction is gaining in popularity for students with severe disabilities, in part because of inclusion and participation in the general education curriculum. Functional academics, in contrast to the curriculum in general education, are skills that have immediate utility in daily living. The best reasons for including functional academics in a student's curriculum are: (a) it will enhance the student's participation in daily routines and (b) it may open valuable opportunities for jobs, volunteer activities, and leisure enjoyment later in life.

Decisions must be made about what approach to take for teaching academics. Additionally, teachers will want to plan how to address the academic skills that overlap between the student's ecological inventory and those taught or used in the general education classes in which they are enrolled. Although some students with severe disabilities may be able to learn some of the general education curriculum with accommodations, this chapter has focused more on students who will not likely be able to do so. Instead, functional academic skills are chosen that can be coordinated with the general education curriculum but can also be used in daily routines.

The two primary approaches teachers use to teach functional academics are: a) functional, generalized academic skills that are usable in life routines and b) embedded academic skills for specific life routines. Which approach is taken and whether to teach functional academics at all depends on the student and parental preferences and individual student characteristics. Once an approach is identified, ecological inventories of both the general education curriculum and the student's life domains are needed to select specific skills (see chapter 3). Further planning is needed to determine whether curriculum overlapping or a multilevel curriculum approach will be used to adapt instruction in the general education classroom.

Once specific skills have been chosen, the teacher develops the instructional plan. Functional academics can be taught in tabletop lessons, through simulations, or in community settings. Because students typically spend more time in school than in the community for most of their school career, some tabletop academic instruction is warranted. At the same time, it is essential that students have the opportunity to practice these skills in real settings. Students with severe disabilities can learn well through group instruction and may learn peers' material as well as their own (i.e., observational learning). Instructional time can also be maximized by teaching a second response using instructive feedback, requests, or prompts (i.e., embed incidental information).

Several options exist for designing prompting and feedback. In general, teachers should consider simplicity and student preference in selecting from the many procedures demonstrated as effective in the research literature. These procedures include feedback, simultaneous prompting, constant time delay, progressive time delay, least intrusive prompts, and stimulus fading and stimulus shaping (including the task demonstration model). Consideration also needs to be given to planning for generalization by using real materials, well-designed simulations, and providing opportunities to use functional academic skills in ac-

tual settings. Teachers may also teach students to generalize by using one of four methods: (a) functional skills, realistic simulations, and in vivo probes, (b) multiple exemplars, (c) general case instruction, and (d) stimulus equivalence procedures.

To teach functional reading, real life materials and activities provide the best resource for selecting sight words. In a generalized academic approach to functional reading, students may learn high frequency sight words (e.g., Dolch) as well as words from daily living activities. Word analysis may also be targeted. Comprehension is best addressed by teaching the language concepts associated with the sight words. Student-composed stories can provide an excellent resource to teach comprehension. In a specific, embedded approach to reading, teaching may focus on instruction booklets, reading to make choices, reading to communicate, reading for mobility, and health and safety.

In teaching functional math, a generalized approach would focus on student mastery of using dollars, and perhaps coins, to make a wide range of purchases. Students might also learn some computation, or to use a calculator. Being able to tell time with a digital or analog clock might also be a priority. In a specific, embedded approach to math instruction, students will learn simplified ways to use money to make purchases, such as counting out the next dollar or picking a type of money for a purchase (e.g., five-dollar bill for lunch). Time management may involve learning specific clock times or setting a timer. Some number recognition or matching might also be used in the context of activities such as using a telephone or money access machine.

Overall, functional academic skills need to be selected that maximize students' participation in their daily routines. When applying this guideline to individual students, the educational team should balance targeted academic responses that can increase a student's participation in general education with those that will have long-term application in that student's life and immediate use at school or in the home and community.

Suggested Activities

1. Outline a talk for parents about the different academic approaches; their expected outcomes; and examples of each. Share the guidelines for deter-

mining an academic approach with parents and solicit their feedback on the academic outcomes they hope to see their children attain.

2. Develop an instructional plan to teach Sharon (see introductory vignette) sight words in a group format with peers who are learning different words than Sharon. Brainstorm a list of functional sight words for Sharon that would be related to finding her way around her elementary school. Check with a second-grade teacher to identify words for second graders who might benefit from this small-group instruction. Consider how Sharon might also learn some of these second-grade words through observational learning of the peer's instruction in the small group. How might the lesson be further enhanced by using incidental information about the word's meaning? How could you test for Sharon's observational and incidental learning?

3. Obtain a copy of your school district's standard course of study (general education curriculum) for one age level or subject. Brainstorm how students could use some of their functional academics skills to participate more fully in these subjects.

References

Aeschleman, S. R., & Schladenhauffen, J. (1984). Acquisition, generalization, and maintenance of grocery shopping skills by severely mentally retarded adolescents. *Applied Research in Mental Retardation, 5,* 245–258.

Agran, M., Fodor-Davis, J., Moore, S., & Deer, M. (1989). The application of a self-management program on instruction-following skills. *Journal of the Association for Persons with Severe Handicaps, 14,* 147–154.

Agran, M., & Moore, S.C. (1994). How to teach self instruction of job skills. *Innovations.* Washington, DC: American Association on Mental Retardation.

Alcantara, P. R. (1994). Effects of videotape instructional package on purchasing skills of children with autism. *Exceptional Children, 61,* 40–55.

Alig-Cybriwsky, C., Wolery, J., & Gast, D. L. (1990). Use of a constant time delay procedure in teaching preschoolers in a group format. *Journal of Early Intervention, 14,* 99–116.

Barbetta, P. M., Miller, A. D., Peters, M. T., Heron, T. E., & Cochran, L. L. (1991). Tugmate: A cross-age tutoring program to teach sight vocabulary. *Education and Treatment of Children, 14,* 19–37.

Barbetta, P. M., Heron, T. E., & Heward, W. L. (1993a). Effects of active student response during error correction on the acquisition, maintenance, and generalization of sight words by students with developmental disabilities. *Journal of Applied Behavior Analysis, 26,* 111–119.

Barbetta, P. M., Heward, W. L., Bradley, D. M., & Miller, A. D. (1994). Effects of immediate and delayed error correction on the acqui-sition and maintenance of sight words by students with developmental disabilities. *Journal of Applied Behavior Analysis, 27,* 177–178.

Barbetta, P. M., Heward, W. L., & Bradley, D. M. C. (1993b). Relative effects of whole-word and phonetic-prompt error correction on the acquisition and maintenance of sight words by students with developmental disabilities. *Journal of Applied Behavior Analysis, 26,* 99–110.

Baumgart, D., & Van Walleghem, J. (1987). Teaching sight words: A comparison between computer-assisted and teacher-taught methods. *Education and Training in Mental Retardation, 22,* 56–65.

Becker, W., Engelmann, S., & Thomas, D. (1975). *Teaching 2: Cognitive learning and instruction.* Chicago: Science Research Associates.

Borakove, L. S., & Cuvo, A. J. (1976). Facilitative effects of coin displacement on teaching coin summation to mentally retarded adolescents. *American Journal of Mental Deficiency, 81,* 350–356.

Bourbeau, P. E., Sowers, J. A., & Close, D. W. (1986) An experimental analysis of generalization of banking skills from classroom to bank settings in the community. *Education and Training in Mental Retardation, 21,* 98–107.

Browder, D., & D'Huyvetters, K. (1988). An evaluation of transfer of stimulus control and of comprehension and sight word reading for children with mental retardation and emotional disturbance. *School Psychology Review, 17,* 331–342.

Browder, D., Hines, C., McCarthy, L. J., & Fees, J. (1984). Sight word instruction to facilitate acquisition and generalization of daily living skills for the moderately and severely retarded. *Education and Training in Mental Retardation, 19,* 191–200.

Browder, D., & Lalli, J. (1991). Review of research on sight word instruction. *Research in Developmental Disabilities, 12,* 203–228.

Browder, D., & Minarovic, T. (in press). The use of sight words by adults with mental retardation to self-manage job tasks in competitive job settings. *Education and Training in Mental Retardation.*

Browder, D., Snell, M., & Wildonger, B. (1988). Simulation and community-based instruction of vending machines with time delay. *Education and Training in Mental Retardation, 23,* 175–185.

Browder, D., & Shear, E. (1996). Interspersal of known items in a treatment package to teach sight words to students with behavior disorders. *Journal of Special Education, 29,* 400–413.

Browder, D., & Xin, Y. (1998). A meta-analysis and review of sight word research and its implications for teaching functional reading to individuals with moderate and severe disabilities. *Journal of Special Education, 32,* 130–153.

Closing the gap (1998). *Resource directory.* Henderson, MN: Closing the Gap.

Collins, B. C., Branson, T. A., & Hall, M. (1995). Teaching a generalized reading of cooking product labels to adolescents with mental disabilities through the use of key words taught by peer tutors. *Education and Training in Mental Retardation and Developmental Disabilities, 30,* 65–76.

Collins, B. C., & Griffen, A. K. (1996). Teaching students with moderate disabilities to make safe responses to product warning labels. *Education and Treatment of Children, 19,* 30–45.

Collins, B. C., & Stinson, D. M. (1995). Teaching generalized reading of product warning labels to adolescents with mental disabilities through the use of key words. *Exceptionality, 5,* 163–181.

Colyer, S. P., & Collins, B. C. (1996). Using natural cues within prompt levels to teach the next dollar strategy to students with disabilities. *Journal of Special Education, 30,* 305–318.

Connis, R. (1979). The effects of sequential picture cue, self-recording, and praise on the job task sequencing of retarded adults. *Journal of Applied Behavior Analysis*, 12, 355–361.

Cuvo, A. J., & Klatt, K. P. (1992). Effects of community-based videotape, and flash card instruction of community-referenced sight words on students with mental retardation. *Journal of Applied Behavior Analysis*, 25, 499–512.

Cuvo, A., Veitch, V., Trace, M., & Konke, J. (1978). Teaching change computation to the mentally retarded. *Behavior Modification*, 2, 531–548.

Denny, P. J., & Test, D. W. (1995). Using the one-more-than technique to teach money counting to individuals with moderate mental retardation: A systematic replication. *Education and Treatment of Children*, 18, 422–432.

Dolch, E. W. (1950). *Teaching primary reading* (2nd ed.). Champaign, IL: Garrard Press.

Dorry, G. W., & Zeaman, D. (1975) Teaching a simple reading vocabulary to retarded children: Effectiveness of fading and nonfading procedures. *American Journal of Mental Deficiency*, 79, 711–716.

Doyle, P. H., Gast, D. L., Wolery, M., & Ault, M. J. (1990). Use of constant time delay in small group instruction: A study of observational and incidental learning. *Journal of Special Education*, 23, 369–385.

Doyle, P. H., Wolery, M., Ault, M. J., Gast, D. L., & Wiley, K. (1989). Establishing conditional discriminations: Concurrent versus isolation-intermix instruction. *Research in Developmental Disabilities*, 10, 349–362.

Edmark Reading Program (1972). Redmon, WA: Edmark.

Edmark Functional Word Series (1990). Redmon, WA: Edmark.

Entrikin, D., York, R., & Brown, L. (1977). Teaching trainable level multiply handicapped students to use picture cues, context cues, and initial consonant sounds to determine the labels of unknown words. AAESPH *Review*, 2, 169–190.

Etzel, B. C., & LeBlanc, J. (1979). The simplest treatment alternative: The law of parsimony applied to choosing appropriate instructional control and errorless instructional control and errorless learning procedures for the difficult-to-teach child. *Journal of Autism and Developmental Disorders*, 9, 361–382.

Farmer, J. A., Gast, D. L., Wolery, M., & Winterling, V. (1991). Small group instruction for students with severe handicaps: A study of observational learning. *Education and Training in Mental Retardation*, 26, 190–201.

Ferguson, B., & McDonnell, J. (1991). A comparison of serial and concurrent sequencing strategies in teaching generalized grocery item location to students with moderate handicaps. *Education and Training in Mental Retardation*, 26, 292–304.

Ford, A., Davern, L., Schnorr, R., Black, J., & Kaiser, K. (1989). Money handling. In A. Ford, R. Schnorr, L. Meyer, L. Davern, J. Black, & P. Dempsey (Eds.), *The Syracuse community-referenced curriculum guide* (pp. 93–116). Baltimore: Paul H. Brookes.

Frederick-Dugan, A., Test, D. W., & Varn, L. (1991). Acquisition and generalization of purchasing skills using a calculator by students who are mentally retarded. *Education and Training in Mental Retardation*, 26, 381–387.

Fry, E. (1957). Developing a word list for remedial reading. *Elementary English*, 33, 456–458.

Fry, E. (1972). *Reading instruction for classroom and clinic*. New York: McGraw-Hill.

Gardill, M. C., & Browder, D. M. (1995). Teaching stimulus classes to encourage independent purchasing by students with severe behavior disorders. *Education and Training in Mental Retardation and Developmental Disabilities*, 30, 254–264.

Gast, D. L., Ault, J. A., Wolery, M., & Doyle, P. M. (1988). Comparison of constant time delay and the system of least prompts in teaching sight word reading to students with moderate mental retardation. *Education and Training in Mental Retardation*, 23, 117–128.

Gast, D. L., Wolery, M., Morris, L. L., Doyle, P. M., & Meyer, S. (1990). Teaching sight word reading in a group instructional arrangement using constant time delay. *Exceptionality*, 1, 81–96.

Giangreco, M. F., Cloninger, C. J., & Iverson, V. S. (1993). *Choosing options and accommodations for children*. Baltimore: Paul H. Brookes.

Glat, R., Gould, K., & Stoddard, L. T. (1994). A note on transfer of stimulus control in the delayed-cue procedure: facilitation by an overt differential response. *Journal of Applied Behavior Analysis*, 27, 699–704.

Haring, T. G., Breen, C. G., Weiner, J., Kennedy, C. H., & Bednersh, F. (1995). Using videotape modeling to facilitate generalized purchasing skills. *Journal of Behavioral Education*, 5, 29–53.

Hoogeven, F. R., Smeets, P. M., & Lancioni, G. E. (1989). Teaching moderately mentally retarded children basic reading skills. *Research in Developmental Disabilities*, 10, 1–18.

Horner, R. H., & McDonald, R. S. (1982). A comparison of single instance and general case instruction in teaching a generalized vocational skill. *Journal of the Association for the Severely Handicapped*, 7, 7–20.

Horton, S. (1985). Computational rates of educable mentally retarded adolescents with and without calculators in comparison to normals. *Education and Training of the Mentally Retarded*, 20, 14–24.

Irvin, K. (1991). Teaching children with Down syndrome to add by counting-on. *Education and Treatment of Children*, 14, 128–141.

Johnson, B. F., & Cuvo, A. J. (1981). Teaching cooking skills to mentally retarded persons. *Behavior Modification*, 5, 187–202.

Johnson, P., Schuster, J., & Bell, J. K. (1996). Comparison of simultaneous prompting with and without error correction in teaching science vocabulary words to high school students with mild disabilities. *Journal of Behavioral Education*, 6, 437–458.

Kamps, D. M., Dugan, E. P., Leonard, B. R., & Daoust, P. M. (1994). Enhanced small group instruction using choral responding and student interaction for children with autism and developmental disabilities. *American Journal of Mental Retardation*, 99, 60–73.

Kamps, D. M., Leonard, B. R., Dugan, E. P., Boland, B., & Greenwood, C. R. (1991). The use of ecobehavioral assessment to identify naturally occurring effective procedures in classrooms serving students with autism and other developmental disabilities. *Journal of Behavioral Education*, 1, 367–397.

Kamps, D., Walker, D., Locke, P., Delquadri, J., & Hall, R. V. (1990). A comparison of instructional arrangements for children with autism served in a public school setting. *Education and Treatment of Children*, 13, 197–215.

Karsh, K. G., & Repp, A. C. (1992). The task demonstration model: A concurrent model for teaching groups of students with severe disabilities. *Exceptional Children*, 59, 54–67.

Karsh, K. G., Repp, A. C., & Lenz, M. W. (1990). A comparison of the task demonstration model and the standard prompting hierarchy in teaching word identification to persons with moderate retardation. *Research in Developmental Disabilities*, 11, 395–410.

Kennedy, C. H., Itkonen, T. L., & Lindquist, K. (1994). Nodality effects during equivalence class formations: an extension of sight word reading and concept development. *Journal of Applied Behavior Analysis*, 27, 673–684.

Koury, M., & Browder, D. (1986). The use of delay to teach sight words by mentally retarded peer tutors. *Education and Training of the Mentally Retarded*, 221, 251–258.

Lalli, J. S., & Browder, D. M. (1993). Comparison of sight word training procedures with validation of the most practical procedure in teaching reading for daily living. *Research in Developmental Disabilities*, 14, 107–127.

Lalli, J. S., Mace, F. C., Browder, D., & Brown, K. (1989). Comparison of treatments to teach number matching skills to adults with moderate mental retardation. *Mental Retardation*, 27, 75–83.

Lancioni, G. E., Smeets, P. M., & Oliva, D. (1987). Introducing EMR children to arithmetical operations: A program involving pictorial problems and distinctive-feature prompts. *Research in Developmental Disabilities*, 8, 467–485.

Leung, J., & Wu, K. (1997). Teaching receptive naming of Chinese characters to children with autism incorporating echolalia. *Journal of Applied Behavior Analysis*, 30, 59–68.

Lowe, M. L., & Cuvo, A. J. (1976). Teaching coin summation to the mentally retarded. *Journal of Applied Behavior Analysis*, 9, 483–489.

Martin, J. E., Elias-Burger, S., & Mithaug, D. E. (1987). Acquisition and maintenance of time-based task change sequence. *Education and Training in Mental Retardation*, 22, 105–119.

McDonnell, J. (1987). The effects of time delay and increasing prompt hierarchy strategies on the acquisition of purchasing skills by students with severe handicaps. *Journal of the Association for Persons with Severe Handicaps*, 12, 227–236.

McDonnell, J., & Ferguson, B. (1988). A comparison of general case in vivo and general case simulation plus in vivo training. *Journal of the Association for Persons with Severe Handicaps*, 13, 116–124.

McGee, G. G., Krantz, P. J., & McClannahan, L. E. (1986). An extension of incidental teaching procedures to reading instruction for autistic children. *Journal of Applied Behavior Analysis*, 19, 147–157.

Nessel, D. D., & Jones, M. B. (1981). *The language experience approach to reading*. New York: Teachers College.

O'Brien, F. (1974). *Instruction in reading a clock for the institutionalized retarded*. Unpublished manuscript. Anna State Hospital and Southern Illinois University.

Osguthorpe, R. T., & Chang, L. L. (1988). The effects of computerized symbol processor instruction on the communication skills of nonspeaking students. *Augmentative and Alternative Communication*, 4, 23–34.

Repp, A. C., Karsh, K. G., & Lenz, M. W. (1990). Discrimination training for persons with developmental disabilities: A training for persons with developmental disabilities. A comparison of the task demonstration model and the standard prompting hierarchy. *Journal of Applied Behavior Analysis*, 23, 43–52.

Resnick, L. B., Wang, M. C., & Kaplan, J. (1973). Task analysis in curriculum design: A hierarchically sequenced introductory mathematics curriculum. *Journal of Applied Behavior Analysis*, 6, 697–710.

Rohena-Diaz, E. (1998). *A comparison of English and Spanish instruction in teaching sight words to students with moderate mental retardation who*

are linguistically diverse. Unpublished doctoral dissertation. Lehigh University, Bethlehem, PA.

Ryndak, D. L., & Alper, S. (1996). *Curricular content for students with moderate and severe disabilities in inclusive settings*. Needham Heights, MA: Allyn & Bacon.

Sandknap, P. A., Schuster, J. W., Wolery, M., & Cross, D. P. (1992). The use of an adaptive device to teach students with moderate mental retardation to select lower priced grocery items. *Education and Training in Mental Retardation*, 27, 219–229.

Schloss, P. J., Alper, S., Young, H., Arnold-Reid, G., Aylward, M., & Dudenhoeffer, S. (1995). Acquisition of functional sight words in community-based recreational settings. *Journal of Special Education*, 29, 84–96.

Schoen, S. & Ogden, S. (1995). Impact of time delay, observational learning, and attentional cueing upon word recognition during integrated small group instruction. *Journal of Autism and Developmental Disorders*, 25, 503–519.

Schuster, J. W., Griffen, A. K., & Wolery, M. (1992). Comparison of simultaneous prompting and constant time delay procedures in teaching sight words to elementary students with moderate mental retardation. *Journal of Behavioral Education*, 2, 305–325.

Shafer, M. S., Inge, K. J., & Hill, J. (1986). Acquisition, generalization, and maintenance of automated banking skills. *Education and Training of the Mentally Retarded*, 21, 265–272.

Singleton, K. E., Schuster, J. W., & Ault, M. J. (1995). Simultaneous prompting in a small group instructional arrangement. *Education and Training in Mental Retardation and Developmental Disabilities*, 30, 218–230.

Sidman, M. (1971). Reading and auditory-visual equivalence. *Journal of Speech and Hearing Research*, 14, 5–13.

Sidman, M., & Cresson, O., Jr. (1973). Reading and cross modal transfer of stimulus equivalences in severe retardation. *Journal of the Experimental Analysis of Behavior*, 37, 5–22.

Singh, N. N., & Singh, J. (1988). Increasing oral reading proficiency through overcorrection and phonic analysis. *American Journal on Mental Retardation*, 93, 312–319.

Singh, N. N., & Solman, R. T. (1990). A stimulus control analysis of the picture-word problem in children who are mentally retarded: The blocking effect. *Journal of Applied Behavior Analysis*, 23, 525–532.

Singleton, K. C., Schuster, J. W., & Ault, M. J. (1995). Simultaneous prompting in a small group instruction arrangement. *Education and Training in Mental Retardation and Developmental Disabilities*, 30, 218–230.

Skinner, B. F. (1957). *Verbal behavior*. New York: Appleton-Century Crofts.

Smeenge, M. E., Page, T. J., Iwata, B. A., & Ivancic, M. T. (1980). Teaching measurement skills to mentally retarded students: Training, generalization, and follow-up. *Education and Training in Mental Retardation*, 15, 224–229.

Snell, M. E. (1997). Teaching children and young adults with mental retardation in school programs: Current research. *Behaviour Change*, 14, 73–105.

Snell, M. E., & Janney, R. E. (2000). *Social relationships and peer support*. Baltimore: Paul H. Brookes.

Solnick, J. V., & Baer, D. M. (1984). Using multiple exemplars for teaching number-numeral correspondence: Some structural aspects. *Analysis and Intervention in Developmental Disabilities*, 4, 47–53.

Sprague, J. R., & Horner, R. H. (1984). The effects of single instance, multiple instance, and general case training on generalized vending machine use by moderately and severely handicapped students. *Journal of Applied Behavior Analysis, 17,* 273–278.

Stoddard, L. T., Hurlbert, B. B., Manoli, C., & McIlvane, W. J. (1989). Teaching money skills through stimulus class formation, exclusion, and component matching methods: Three case studies. *Research in Developmental Disabilities, 10,* 413–439.

Stone, C. B. (1956). Measuring difficulty of primary reading material: A constructive criticism of Spache's measure. *Elementary School Journal, 6,* 36–41.

Test, D. W., Howell, A., Burkhart, K., & Beroth, T. (1993). The one-more-than technique as a strategy for counting money for individuals with moderate mental retardation. *Education and Training in Mental Retardation, 28,* 232–241.

Trace, M. W., Cuvo, A. J., & Criswell, J. L. (1977). Teaching coin equivalence to the mentally retarded. *Journal of Applied Behavior Analysis, 10,* 85–92.

Van Houten, R., & Rolider, A. (1989). An analysis of several variables influencing the efficacy of flashcard instruction. *Journal of Applied Behavior Analysis, 22,* 111–120.

Wacker, D. P., Berg, W. K., McMahon, C., Templeman, M., McKinnery, J., Swarts, V., Visser, M., & Marquardt, P. (1988). Evaluation of labeling-then-doing with moderately handicapped persons: Acquisition and generalization with complex tasks. *Journal of Applied Behavior Analysis, 21,* 369–380.

Westling, D. L., Floyd, J., & Carr, D. (1990). Effects of single setting versus multiple setting training on learning to shop in a department store. *American Journal on Mental Retardation, 94,* 616–624.

Whalen, C., Schuster, J. W., & Hemmeter, M. L. (1996). The use of unrelated instructive feedback when teaching in a small group instructional arrangement. *Education and Training in Mental Retardation and Developmental Disabilities, 31,* 188–202.

Wolery, M., Ault, M. J., & Doyle, P. M. (1992). *Teaching students with moderate to severe disabilities.* New York: Longman.

Wolery, M., Ault, M. J., Gast, D. L., Doyle, P. M., & Mills, B. M. (1990). Use of choral and individual attentional responses with constant time delay when teaching sight word reading. *Remedial and Special Education, 11,* 47–58.

Wolery, M., Doyle, P. M., Ault, P. M., Gast, D. L., Meyer, S. L., & Stinson, D. (1991). Effects of presenting incidental information in consequent events on future learning. *Journal of Behavioral Education, 1,* 79–104.

Wolery, M., Werts, M. G., Snyder, E. D., & Caldwell, N. K. (1994). Efficacy of constant time delay implemented by peer tutors in general education classrooms. *Journal of Behavioral Education 4,* 415–436.

Home and Community

Diane M. Browder
Linda M. Bambara

In the current era, approaches to supporting individuals with severe disabilities within their homes and communities are undergoing important transformations as self-determination is more fully understood. To understand this transformation, consider the focus of the past three decades. In the 1970s, many professionals believed that individuals with severe disabilities needed to earn the right to live in the community by learning skills that qualified them for deinstitutionalization. With rulings such as *Haldermann v. Pennhust State School and Hospital* (1979), the legal right of community living was established. Individuals no longer needed a certain level of daily living skills for community access. In the 1980s, a large body of research emerged on teaching skills to individuals with severe disabilities for managing their homes and gaining access to their communities. Teachers focused on teaching skills in home and community settings, and students often spent large portions of their day away from the school building. In the 1990s, students with severe disabilities gained increased access to full-time membership in general education. With the advent of full inclusion, special education teachers often struggled with the trade-off between offering life skills instruction in "real" nonschool environments and encouraging students with severe disabilities to have a typical full-time school day in general education classes. In the current era, this tension between full-time participation in general education classes and community-based instruction is not fully resolved.

This chapter adheres to several values in describing how teachers can encourage students to gain skills for their homes and community. First, decisions on what and where to teach must be made in partnership with individuals with severe disabilities and their families. Second, instruction needs to be planned to encourage the student's self-determination by teaching choice, honoring preferences, and encouraging self-directed learning. Third, instructional strategies that can be blended with typical general education environments and also encourage interaction with peers at school, home, or in the community

Julia Romano

Julia, a petite 14-year-old with moderate mental retarda-tion, is an active, happy eighth-grader in her middle school. Since Julia's earliest school days, her parents have insisted that she be included in general education classrooms and have full opportunity to participate in the school activities of her choice. Although Julia's eighth-grade schedule was difficult to design, she now attends an array of academic and nonacademic classes with her schoolmates. Julia is also a member of the middle school chorus and an after-school art club. As an active teen with tremendous school spirit, Julia loves to attend school games and dances with her friends.

One day early in the school year, Julia's parents re-ceived an invitation to attend a transition planning meet-ing with the school's transition coordinator. This invitation took Julia's parents by surprise. Like many parents of young teens, they were more focused on Julia's current needs as a teenager than on her adult life. Julia had not thought much about her life as an adult either and her goals were uncertain. As they began to talk, both Julia and her parents expressed their dream for Julia to live in

her own home someday, work in a job she enjoys, and be active in her community as she has been at school. They recognized the importance of beginning to plan now.

Although the Romanos believed it would be beneficial for Julia to begin learning the daily living and community skills needed for postschool life, they had one unsettling concern. They worried that training for adult living would take Julia away from what she loved most—her school classes, activities, and classmates. Julia's parents had worked hard for Julia to be fully included. They were not willing to sacrifice Julia's current needs as a middle school student in planning for her future needs, at least not at age 14. They feared that during the transition plan-ning meeting, they would have to make a choice.

Questions for Planning and Instruction
1. How can Julia's instructional needs in home and com-munity skills be addressed without detracting from typical school experiences?
2. What skills should be addressed that could best ad-dress her current and future needs?

---

need to be identified. Fourth, home and community skills gain importance as students become older. Children typically rely mostly on their caregivers for daily living (e.g., meal preparation) and community access (e.g., going to restaurants). In contrast, an im-portant part of adolescents' transition to adulthood is their increased autonomy in their home (e.g., fixing their own breakfast) and community (e.g., meeting friends at a restaurant). We illustrate these four val-ues by sharing glimpses from the lives of three stu-dents: Julia (age 14), Rico (age 9), and Aaron (age 21). We will begin with Julia.

Planning Instruction to Enhance Skills for Home and the Community

Providing support for individuals to have enhanced quality of life in their homes and communities in-volves much more than instruction. For some individ-uals, the primary support need may be getting help rather than learning to perform specific routines. For example, assistance in budgeting may make it possi-ble to buy prepared meals or to get help for house-cleaning. Some individuals manage some parts of their home and community routines through reliance on a roommate or significant other who is especially

adept in home management. For example, one room-mate may do all of the cooking and another does the laundry. In contrast, some people pursue home and community skills as a special interest or hobby. When activities such as home management and shopping are highly preferred, the individual may pursue exten-sive training in these areas. For example, a high school student may take 3 years of home economics classes or do an internship to learn more about bank-ing. Planning instruction to enhance home and com-munity skills should be framed in the broader context of this overall support planning. When taking this per-son-centered approach to planning instruction for home and community, it is important to focus on self-determination as a context and goal of instruction.

Self-Determination: A New Era for Home and Community Instruction

During the 90s, we entered a new pedagogical era of self-determination, one that emphasizes the value of individuals with disabilities directing their own lives. As described by Martin and Marshall (1995), self-determined individuals "know what they want and how to get it" (p. 147). This simple definition has strong implications for daily living and community instruction.

Knowing what one wants requires a self-awareness of likes and dislikes, needs and abilities, capacities and limitations, and goals and dreams. The implication for students with severe disabilities is that the development of self-awareness requires continuous experience in option-rich community settings so that individuals can learn about themselves and what the community has to offer (Bambara, Cole, & Koger, in press; Wall & Datillo, 1995).

Knowing how to get what one wants involves the skills or competence needed to control or direct one's life. Self-determination would advance very little if the individual did not have the skills needed to pursue goals and participate in daily activities that are both necessary and preferred. Thus, instruction for daily and community living plays an important role in the enhancement of self-determination.

However, personal control or autonomy need not be considered absolute. Having control over one's life may involve directing others to act on one's behalf or using resources or noninstructional supports to get what one needs (Kennedy, 1996). Skill instruction is only one form, albeit an important one, of support for helping people achieve what they want. Community inclusion and a "good life," for example, may be achieved through a variety of means, including the supports and accommodations provided by friends and family, personal care assistants, self-advocacy groups, assistive technology, and environmental adaptations. The main point is that whether acting independently or with the assistance of others, self-determined people set the direction and course for their lives.

The concept of self-determination has strongly influenced instruction for the home and the community in at least two important ways. It provides the overall context or value base for determining what to teach, and just as importantly, how to teach in a way that emphasizes student control over learning.

Self-determination influences the format of instruction by emphasizing student direction and empowerment. The learner is viewed as a partner in the instructional process. Once meaningful instructional goals are targeted, the instructor gives students control during instruction by offering multiple and diverse opportunities for choice making (Bambara & Koger, 1996; Brown, Belz, Corsi, & Wenig, 1993). For example, the instructor might offer the student a choice of when or where to conduct the lesson, a choice of materials, a choice of activity sequence or instructional formats, and the opportunity to change,

take a break from, or terminate an activity if the student is experiencing difficulty. The instructor also follows the student's lead and interests. This includes honoring the student's spontaneous choices or suggestions for instruction, and modifying instruction according to the student's preferred learning style.

Self-determination is also enhanced during instruction via the principle of partial participation (Ferguson & Baumgart, 1991) and the use of adaptive aids to maximize self-sufficiency. Under the principle of partial participation, students are never denied access to preferred or meaningful activities because they do not have the skills (or potential) for complete independent participation. Rather, the instructor asks:

- What noninstructional supports are needed to make participation in targeted activities meaningful for the student?
- To what extent can and does the student wish to actively participate?
- How can instruction be used to enhance the student's independence, albeit partial independence?

Once these questions are answered, the instructor carefully blends instructional support with other forms of personal assistance (e.g., supports provided by peers, job coach, or personal aid) to provide immediate access to daily routines and preferred activities.

After swimming lessons at her school, Julia turns the hair dryer on and off and blows the dampness from her hair, while her buddy Susan directs the tip of the dryer for final styling.

The use of adaptive aids or permanent prompts during instruction (e.g., use of picture cues, color-coded oven and range dials, templates for telephone dialing) can further enhance empowerment by lessening the demands of the task and expediting self-sufficiency and student control.

In addition to influencing how to teach, the concept of self-determination has direct influence on what to teach. Skills for daily and community living should be directly related to the student's and family's preferences and visions for the future. More than being "functional" in the eyes of professionals, instructional goals are personalized according to the individual's unique interests and needs. Almost any daily living or community skill could potentially enhance learner control; however, those that facilitate self-determination are those that are useful from the learner's perspective. That is, they provide the skills needed to participate in preferred activities (e.g., school chorus, Little League baseball) and necessary activities (e.g., taking medications, food shopping) and to achieve long range or future goals (e.g., learning how to use public transportation to access a preferred job). Broadly classified, skills for self-determination related to this chapter include: (a) task-, activity-, or routine-specific skills, such as matching clothing, preparing dinner, or getting ready for work in the morning, and (b) generic empowerment skills that are applicable across tasks, activities, and routines. Generic empowerment skills enable learners to initiate, take action, and direct the course of their lives. These may include skills in choice making, decision making, problem solving, self-regulation or self-management, goal setting, self-advocacy, and leadership.

Guidelines to Plan Instruction

At the beginning of this chapter, several values were stated to guide planning instruction for home and the community. These values are now translated into specific guidelines for instructional planning.

Value One: Plan in Partnership with Students and Their Families

Guideline One: Use Person-Centered Planning Strategies

If instruction is viewed as a form of support, then the question is: What form of instruction is needed or wanted? To enhance self-determination, instruction for daily and community living must be person-centered. What to teach and how to teach must fit within the context of the student's and family's preferences, priorities, and visions or goals for the future.

Person-centered planning is a collaborative process involving the student, family members, teachers, specialists, and, as needed, support personnel from non-school services (e.g., mental health, Office of Vocational Rehabilitation, residential supports). Through collaborative problem solving and discussions among team members, person-centered planning aims to (a) describe a desirable future for the student, (b) delineate the activities and supports necessary to achieve the desired vision, and (c) mobilize existing resources to make the vision become a reality (Vandercook, York, & Forest, 1989). From an instructional perspective, person-centered planning can help ensure

that teaching is coordinated with other forms of support and that the goals of instruction are unified toward achieving a desired life for the student. Person-centered planning may be achieved by structured action planning or more informally, through collaborative meetings with families (Gage & Falvey, 1995).

Structured Action Planning

A variety of structured person-centered planning processes have emerged over the past 10 years. These structured approaches guide educational teams through a comprehensive information gathering and planning process to address the student's wants and needs. Some of these include: Personal Futures Planning (Mount & Zwernick, 1988); Life Style Planning (O'Brien, 1987); The McGill Action Planning System, or MAPS (Vandercook, et al., 1989); and Planning Alternative Tomorrows with Hope, or PATH (Pearpoint, O'Brien, & Forest, 1992). Although each differs somewhat in format and focus, (e.g., Life Style Planning focuses on adults, while MAPS emphasizes the inclusion of students in school communities), all of the structured processes guide teams to consider at least five essential questions.

First, what is the student's history and current life situation? Here teams contribute information that will paint a life history for the student. Both positive and negative events are noted. Additionally, teams describe both positive and negative aspects of the student's current life. For example, in O'Brien's Life Style Planning (1987), teams are asked to describe the student's current life along five dimensions: choice, relationships, competence, community presence, and respect.

Second, what are the strengths and gifts of the student? The purpose of this question is to focus the team on building a vision based on the student's strengths and preferences, rather than the student's deficits.

Third, what is the vision or dream for the student? After considering the first two questions, the team members paint a picture of an ideal life for the student for the next several years of childhood or as an adult. Team members are encouraged to think about what they want for the student and what the student would want for himself or herself.

Fourth, what are the team's fears, obstacles, or challenges to building a better life for the student? This question guides teams to consider fears about change and obstacles that may thwart the student's dreams with the aim of eliminating each one.

Fifth, what are the priorities and goals for the future, and what will it take to make the vision happen? Once the team has a vision for the future, team members then focus on how to get there. They set priorities for achieving both short- and long-range goals, consider how to eliminate obstacles, and in a very specific way, identify how to use and direct supports toward achieving desirable outcomes.

Due to their comprehensiveness, structured action planning approaches are useful when it is important to set new directions for the student, such as planning for transition to postschool life or greater inclusion in school. This structured action planning is now described for Julia, a 14-year-old who is in the eighth grade in a middle school.

Mr. and Mrs. Romano were concerned about the transition planning process for their daughter, Julia. They feared that transition planning would result in a heavy vocational emphasis that would take Julia away from the current school activities that she loved. Julia's parents were later relieved to discover that the transition coordinator selected MAPS (Vandercook et al., 1989) to help them clarify what was important to Julia and to begin to think about her future as an adult.

By answering the questions (Table 14–1), Julia and her parents set priorities for the next 3 years. Julia will continue to be enrolled in general education classes, but her curriculum will be modified to reflect a stronger focus in daily and community living instruction. Instructional targets will include skills that will be useful to Julia now and in the future and that can be taught within general education classes. Community-based instruction will be achieved through Julia working with the community training specialist for one period, 4 days per week. As an additional priority, and in preparation for Julia's postschool life, Julia's family will begin to explore options for residential, community, and employment supports. The transition coordinator will help Julia and her family connect with adult services for this initial planning.

Table 14–1 illustrates the outcomes of the MAPS process for Julia (Vandercook et al., 1989).

TABLE 14–1
McGill Action Planning System (MAPS) Planning Process Outcomes for Julia

---

What is Julia's History?

Julia is a 14-year-old teen with Down syndrome.
Julia's parents have always felt strongly about inclusion.
Julia attended segregated preschool and school programs until age 8.
At her parents' insistence, Julia was fully included in a second-grade class.
Continued full inclusion through the eighth grade (current grade).
Julia has had a happy childhood, doing activities typical for her age.
Grade 6 was bad for Julia—first year at middle school. "New" kids from other elementary schools ridiculed her, called her "retard."
Problem solved after a schoolwide intervention emphasizing friendships for all.

Who is Julia?

Julia is a friendly, social girl who enjoys typical "teen" stuff.
She is very persistent.
She likes to be independent.
She likes to complete what she has started.
She is very methodical in her approach to things.
She laughs and giggles easily.
She's a "girl's girl": likes to primp, wear new clothes, have her nails done, wear makeup.
She likes to stay busy and go places.
She loves to sing and draw.
She is somewhat gullible—easily led by peers she considers to be her friend.

What is Your Dream for Julia? What Are Your Dreams for Her As An Adult?

In General

For Julia to continue to be a part of her school.
For Julia to be happy, healthy, and safe.
To be able to pursue activities that she enjoys.
To have friends and people that care about her.

TABLE 14–1
continued

___

As an Adult:

To live in an apartment with friends, family, or people who care about her.
To live close to family.
To have her independence but also the supports she needs to do what she wants.
To be involved in her community doing things she wants to do.
To have a competitive job that she likes.
To live in a community that will offer many opportunities and that will accept her for her gifts and talents.

What is Your Nightmare?

That Julia will be denied typical middle school and high school experiences.
That the focus on her "adult" needs will take her away from typical school activities.
That she will be lonely.
That she will be unhappy.
That once she graduates she will not be given the support she needs to achieve her goals.
That she will be put on a waiting list for adult services.
Once living on her own, she will be completely dependent on the "good" graces of others: lack independence.
Once she graduates, the good life that she has built so far will stop: no more friends, no more activities, waiting for a job.

What Are Julia's Strengths, Gifts, and Abilities?

Julia is very persistent and will work hard at the things she enjoys or wants.
Julia has wonderful social skills, people are drawn to her.
She's easy going.
Julia loves to sing, draw, and swim.
Julia loves to be around people.

What Are Julia's Needs?

Julia enjoys and therefore needs to attend school with her same-age peers, doing typical school activities.
Julia needs to continue with the school activities that she enjoys: swimming, chorus, art.
Julia and her family need to begin exploring options for Julia's adult life.
Julia needs to develop daily living and community living skills that will enhance her independence now and in the future. Some areas include:

- Basic cooking skills
- Community travel and safety skills
- Consumer skills (e.g., purchasing clothing, food shopping, ordering at restaurants)
- Use of communication tools (e.g., using the telephone, using newspapers and Internet to access information)

Julia needs to develop personal care skills appropriate for her age (to help Julia to feel good about herself). Some areas include:

- Skin care for a teen
- Teen grooming (e.g., styling hair, applying makeup and nail polish)
- Clothing selection and care
- Sex education

What Would Julia's Ideal Day Look Like and What Must Be Done to Make It Happen?

For At Least the Next 3 Years:

Julia will maintain her current level of participation in regular education classes and after-school activities.
Daily living and community living skills will be integrated within her regularly scheduled classes. For community-based instruction, Julia will meet with a community training specialist one period a day, four times per week.
Julia's weekly schedule will reflect her interests as well as her academic, social, and daily and community living needs (e.g., school chorus, swimming/gym, home economics, social studies, science, art, computers, community-based instruction).

To Prepare for the Future:

Julia and family will explore adult services options.

Rico Hernandez

Rico Hernandez, 9 years old, attends a third-grade class in his neighborhood school with the assistance of a full-time one-to-one paraprofessional. He has autism and is performing close to grade level academically in most subject areas, but he requires intensive wraparound support through mental health services because of severe behavioral challenges and life skill needs.

Mrs. Hernandez, Rico's mother, thought she would never see the day when her son would be in a general education classroom. She and her husband are extremely proud of their son's accomplishments, yet at the same time, they were becoming increasingly concerned about Rico's display of challenging behaviors at home and his lack of participation in household routines. They asked for a team meeting, consisting of Rico's teachers, support staff, and behavior specialists from the mental health services, to address their concerns.

After conducting a functional assessment and through many team discussions, it appeared that Rico's challenging behaviors, consisting of screaming, tantruming, and self-injury (face slapping), were most often associated with transitions or changes in routines or activities. The team speculated that from Rico's perspective almost any activity not anticipated by him (e.g., being asked to put his toys away while watching TV, going to a different grocery store, having an unexpected visitor in the home) constituted a change of activity. As Rico's tantrums increased in frequency and intensity as a result of his physical growth, Mrs. Hernandez placed less demands on him to participate in the household routines. With the family's hectic schedule, it was often easier to complete Rico's chores for him.

Mrs. Hernandez also feared bringing Rico with her in the community. She worried not only about the potential for challenging behavior but also for Rico's safety. Rico would become preoccupied with other thoughts and frequently wander away from his mother. Mrs. Hernandez reported that one day, while grocery shopping, she turned her back for a minute, only to find Rico walking aimlessly in a busy parking lot. With the growing concerns about Rico's safety and behavior, he spent most of his free time at home doing little but watching television.

The team noted that Rico had had important success at school. With the assistance of the paraprofessional, he was completing adapted class assignments and participating in activities. In contrast, Rico rarely interacted with his peers. Mrs. Hernandez expressed her concern to the team that her son was socially isolated at school and had no friends. Rico often sat alone at recess while his classmates played kickball and volleyball. Mrs. Hernandez said she was worried that Rico was becoming increasingly dependent on the paraprofessional and could not function without her. She also wondered if the other children hesitated to play with Rico because he always had an adult nearby.

Questions for Planning and Instruction

1. How can Rico's participation in family routines and activities be enhanced, while decreasing instances of challenging behaviors?
2. How can Rico be encouraged to have more involvement with his peers during leisure at school and home?
3. How can Rico's community access be encouraged? What supports will be needed for his behavior and safety?
4. In what ways can Rico's teachers and home support work together to meet Rico's needs at home?

Collaborative Meetings

Not all person-centered planning requires a comprehensive approach or the development of a new vision for the future. Sometimes, teams need to come together to solve problems around specific issues, focusing on the goals and preferences of the student and family. This can be accomplished through informal, collaborative meetings, as in Rico's case.

In Rico's case, Mrs. Hernandez, Rico's teachers, the behavior specialist from mental health services, and the therapeutic support staff (TSS) met to address the questions posed in the case study. The team members collaborated to coordinate their support for Rico and his family. The teacher agreed to design instructional strategies to meet priority objectives, teach as many as were relevant in school, and teach the TSS how to implement instruction in the home. Instructional targets selected were to teach Rico (a) to follow a picture schedule to enhance predictability of activities at home and increase independence at school, (b) to complete daily routines at home, (c) to learn community travel skills (e.g., following his parents or classmates when traveling independently around the school), and (d) to master the basics of organized ball games, such as kickball and T-ball.

Instructional targets were integrated with other forms of support including behavioral support, respite care, enrolling Rico in Junior League sports, and getting him involved in school recess activities.

Value Two: Encourage Student's Self-Determination

Guideline Two: Enhance Choice, Self-Prompting, and Self-Management

Self-determination is an ongoing, developmental process. The more opportunities for self-determination, the greater its growth. More than just an outcome of instruction, self-determination should be viewed as a source of empowerment during instruction. Self-determination is enhanced when students are involved in their own learning. Here we discuss three approaches for student empowerment: (a) choice, (b) self-prompting, and (c) self-management.

Choice

When teachers select instructional goals that reflect preferences, they are honoring student choice. This is the first level of choice in instruction. The second level involves embedding multiple choice opportunities into instruction so that students can self-direct their own learning.

Choice, or the act of selecting among presented alternatives, is an expression of preference. All people have preferences. The role of the instructor is to ensure that student preferences for learning are recognized and honored. This communicates respect for each student's individuality and enhances motivation for learning. Not surprisingly, many studies have shown that when preferences are incorporated during instruction, student participation is enhanced (e.g., Bambara, Ager, Koger, 1994; Dunlap et al., 1994). Furthermore, choice can lead to the reduction of problem behaviors, especially when student protests or disruptions during instruction are related to low opportunities for student control (e.g., Bambara, Koger, Katzer, & Davenport, 1995; Dunlap et al., 1994; Dyer, Dunlap, & Winterling, 1990).

The choice diversity model (Brown, Belz, Corsi, & Wenig, 1993) provides one strategy for embedding choice into the instruction of daily home and community routines. In this approach, teachers first analyze steps or component parts of a routine, and then identify the types of options that can be made available during each step. Many different options can be embedded within instructional routines. Teachers might first consider offering between-activities options to start an activity.

In a kitchen clean-up routine, Rico is offered the choice of clearing the table or stacking the dishes in the dishwasher.

Then, once an activity is selected, additional within-activity options are presented.

Rico's teacher offers him a choice of materials (e.g., sponges, dish soap), choice of sequence (e.g., cups or plates first), choice of when to complete the activity (e.g., now or later), and a choice of partners (e.g., with or without help from Mom).

Two additional options, the choice to refuse participation and to terminate an activity, are opportunities that must always be made available to students during instruction. If refusals are high, it may suggest that the activity is not meaningful or preferred by the student.

Within activity choices can be powerful motivators for participation and are especially helpful for enhancing learner control when between-activity options are limited. For example, Bambara and colleagues (1995) task analyzed three home routines: vacuuming, dusting, and snack preparation, for one man with severe disabilities who required the assistance of staff, but refused to participate in activities when prompted. In this study, prompts for step completion (e.g., "get the vacuum cleaner," "plug in the vacuum," "get the carpet deodorizer") were translated into choice opportunities (e.g., "Would you like to start by vacuuming the living room or the dining room?" "Would you like to plug the vacuum cleaner in that outlet or this one?" "Would you like to use the country air or herbal scent spray?"). When choices were embedded in the routines, the man completed each activity willingly; however, when choices were absent, he refused participation and protested by engaging in challenging behaviors. In this case, participation was enhanced when the man was given more control.

In addition to identifying choice opportunities, instructors should consider how to best present options to match the learner's communication mode and choice-making skills (Bambara & Koger, 1996). Some learners benefit when choice options are presented with actual objects and some respond better to pictures rather than words. Other individuals indicate their choice by pointing, labeling, or grimacing. Also, consideration should be given to the type of choice-related questions or prompts. Closed questions that delineate alternatives (e.g., "Do you want to iron in the living room or in the kitchen?") are useful when the student is unfamiliar with potential choice. Later, once options are known by the student, teachers may prompt choice by using open-ended questions (e.g., "What do you want to do now?"). To enhance self-initiations (e.g., unprompted choice responses), instructors are encouraged to honor students' spontaneous choices whenever practical (e.g., "Thanks for telling me you want to wear your blue sweater!") and should expect that, as students learn the power of their choice making, spontaneous choices will increase.

Not all students know how to make choices, however, and in such cases, choice making can be taught during home and community routines by (a) prompting the student to make a choice response (e.g., guiding the student to touch a preferred item) and (b) providing the selected item upon each choice selection (Bambara & Koger, 1996). Through repeated opportunities across daily routines, the student will learn eventually how to make meaningful selections. In the meantime, instructors should carefully attend to learners' subtle, nonverbal cues of preference (e.g., smiles, active participation) and rejection (e.g., facial grimace, pushing objects away) to assure that the learners' preferences are being honored.

Self-prompting

Teaching students to learn from themselves or their environment can also facilitate self-determination. Learners with severe disabilities can become overly dependent on instructor cues and fail to self-initiate home and community skills or self-correct when problems arise. Self-learning may be enhanced by teaching students to respond to natural cues or permanent prompts, a procedure called self-prompting.

Ford and Mirenda (1984) describe ways to build natural cues into instruction by pointing out salient features of natural cues (e.g., wrinkles in a bed) and using nonspecific prompts (e.g., "What's next?"). Other examples of teaching students to use cues contained within home and community environments include: (a) color-coding or labeling possessions with name tags; (b) using placement as a cue, such as hanging

matching outfits together; (c) color-coding temperature levels on stove or oven dials; (d) amplifying natural auditory cues, such as traffic sounds for pedestrian training; and (e) using unrelated, naturally occurring events to signal the onset of an activity (e.g., begin dinner when the television news comes on).

To enhance maintenance and generalization, cues in the criterion environment (the home or the community) should be included in training simulations. For example, Livi and Ford (1985) found that the transfer of a daily living skill (food preparation) from a training site to the student's own home was best when the teacher replicated cues found in the home. One student who had been taught to toast bread failed to locate the bread at home, but, when the training site replicated the family's practice of keeping the bread in the refrigerator instead of in a breadbox, the student transferred the skill to his home without any home-based instruction.

In many cases, when errors do not pose dangers, teachers should encourage students to self-correct using the cues provided by the error. This means that teachers modify their teaching approach so that increased response prompts are withheld for a longer latency after a student error has been made or replaced by gestures or questions that emphasize error cues.

When Julia forgets to get all the items from the refrigerator to make a meal, the teacher may hesitate when Julia reaches the step requiring mixing in the eggs and let her discover the eggs are missing. If Julia somehow skips the step, the teacher might ask, "What's missing?" or "What did you forget?"

Such approaches probably work best once students have learned some of the task rather than in the early acquisition stage.

Some students may have difficulty learning from and responding to natural cues in their environment. Even after natural cue instruction, they may continue to have trouble knowing when to initiate activities, remembering what comes next in a lengthy activity sequence, or just seem to need instructional prompts to complete an activity. As an alternative to natural cues, students may be taught how to use permanent prompts to guide their learning. Permanent prompts are "extra" stimuli or cues, such as pictures, written words, or tape recordings, that students learn to control to enhance their independence. Permanent prompts act like memory aids, similar to how recipe books, appointment books, and things-to-do lists assist adults in their daily routines.

Pictures can provide an excellent form of graphic assistance for students with severe disabilities because of their versatility with nonreaders. Typically, pictures representing an activity or a step in a routine or task are placed in a photo booklet or on a wall chart for easy accessibility. Students are then taught to "look and do," which means referring to the pictures as they complete each activity or step in a sequence. Again, as much as possible, these activities should incorporate student preference.

Pictures of Rico's after-school home routine (e.g., put backpack away, make a snack, put out the trash, watch TV, set the table for dinner) may be placed on a wall chart in the kitchen. Rico would be guided to look at the chart, initiate the first activity, and return to the chart for the next activity once the previous one was completed.

Students with disabilities have been taught to follow pictures as a guide to preparing meals (e.g., Martin, Rusch, James, Decker, & Trytol, 1982), to setting up and performing complex job tasks (e.g., Wacker & Berg, 1984; Wacker, Berg, Berrie, & Swatta, 1985), to using a microcomputer (Frank, Wacker, Berg, & McMahon, 1985), and to managing daily or weekly schedules for leisure activities, work, housekeeping, or grooming (e.g., Bambara & Ager, 1992; Irvine, Erickson, Singer, & Stahlberg, 1992; Krantz, MacDuff, & McClannahan, 1993; Sowers, Verdi, Bourbeau, & Sheehan, 1985). Pictures also may be used to assist learners to shop for groceries (e.g., Matson, 1981) and order foods at restaurants.

In addition to promoting independence, picture prompts may also aid the generalization of a learned task or routine to new settings. Once a student learns how to "read" pictures in one situation, the pictures may then be used in different settings to guide student performance on the same or similar tasks (Irvine et al., 1992; Wacker et al., 1985). For example, Irvine et al. (1992) taught four high school students with moderate to severe disabilities to follow picture cues to complete school and home routines. Training began at school. Once the students followed pictures at school, one student initiated home activities without further instruction. The three other students needed additional instruction on how to use the pictures at home, but this was completed in far less time than the original training.

Rico's teachers think picture prompts have important implications for him. The more intensive training in using picture prompts for home routines will be completed in school by Rico's teacher. Rico's parents or the therapeutic support aide will then assist Rico to generalize picture reading to home as needed.

When pictures are not suitable to learner needs, other forms of self-prompting can be tried. For example, Alberto, Sharpton, Briggs, and Stright (1986) taught four adolescents with moderate and severe disabilities to use self-operated audio prompts played through a Walkman-type cassette player to guide them through operating a washing machine, preparing a meal, and performing a vocational assembly task. For readers with mild disabilities, McAdam and Cuvo (1994) used written directions to assist learners to complete housecleaning tasks. Like pictures, both audio prompts and written directions have enhanced learners' generalization to different settings (Briggs, Alberto, Sharpton, Berlin, McKinley, & Ritts, 1990; McAdam & Cuvo, 1994).

Self-management

Another way to promote self-direction in home and community routines is to incorporate self-management in instruction. Self-management can be defined as a "personal and systematic application of behavior change strategies that result in the desired modification of one's own behavior" (Heward, 1997, p. 517). Technically speaking, choice making and self-prompting are aspects of self-management; however, to truly self-manage behavior, a combination of multiple components are needed, such as goal setting (setting personal performance goals), self-monitoring (recording progress toward goals), self-evaluation (evaluating the acceptability of performance outcomes), and self-reinforcement (rewarding oneself for a job well done).

Although there are many methods of self-management, self-instruction and self-scheduling are two that have direct applicability for home and community use. In self-instruction, students are taught to self-talk through the steps of a home, community, or leisure activity, self-evaluating their performance as they go along. Agran, Fodor-Davis, and Moore (1986) taught job sequencing skills to four adolescents with mental retardation enrolled in a hospital work program. The students were taught to verbalize a "did-next-now" strategy to complete a lengthy cleaning sequence (e.g., "I just brought the bucket into the room. I need to fill the bucket. I'm going to fill the bucket now"). Hughes (1992) taught four individuals with severe disabilities to use self-instruction to solve task-related problems at home by identifying the problem (e.g., "lamp not plugged in"), stating the correct response (e.g., "got to plug in"), evaluating the response (e.g., "fixed it"), and self-reinforcing (e.g., "good"). More recently, Gomez and Bambara (1996) used self-instruction to teach complex problem solving to adults with severe disabilities in their home. In this study, the adults were guided to consider more than one solution to a problem (e.g., "My toothbrush is missing. Look on the counter. Look in the cabinet. Ask for help.").

Self-scheduling, a self-management strategy that can facilitate daily and weekly planning, can give people with severe disabilities a way to self-direct and control the multiple tasks needed for daily living. Through self-scheduling, learners are guided to select activities that are both enjoyable and necessary, plan when to do them that day or several days in advance, and use their schedule to initiate the planned activities (Bambara & Ager, 1992; Bambara & Koger, 1996).

To summarize this guideline, self-determination can be enhanced when students are involved in their own learning. Choice-making, self-prompting, and self-management are several ways that students can begin to take direction while learning the tasks needed for home and community life.

Self-determination skills are important for Aaron to learn as he prepares to transition into his new apartment. Aaron Williams is a young man in his last year of public school services. Aaron is working hard with his parents and the transition team to plan his next steps as an adult.

When Aaron and his team met, they discussed ways to enhance Aaron's skills to "be on his own." They compared living in an apartment to his current life at home. The team quickly realized that Aaron would have a lot more choices to make when he was on his own! For example, he would be deciding what to have for dinner, when to go to bed, what to wear, and who to invite for a visit. He might decide to go out for the evening and would need skills to request support from his personal attendant. Aaron and his parents made a list of decisions that he could begin making right away in his family home. His teacher helped him make a list of decisions he could start making during his

---

 Aaron Williams

Aaron is a young man with severe cognitive delays and physical disabilities. Owing to a stroke at age 8, he is paralyzed from the waist down and has limited use of his right arm and hand. He moves about freely in his automated wheelchair and communicates with gestures, pictures, and a touch talker.

At age 21, Aaron is in his last year of public school services. This last year is devoted to helping Aaron transition to his own apartment and find a job. Aaron has completed several years of person-centered planning with his transition team, and his goals are clear. He wants to live in his own apartment with a roommate who shares his interest in music and sports. He also wants a job that pays well, but gives him flexible or part-time hours because he tires easily. Because of his love of school and desire to improve his career options, Aaron has been taking classes at the community college since he was 18 with support from the public school transition coordinator. Aaron wants to continue taking courses and maybe explore a new college environment. Because of his physical challenges, Aaron will need 24-hour support from a personal care attendant to address his basic daily living, health, and safety needs. He also needs specialized transportation. Another challenge Aaron faces is that he has not had many experiences of being "on his own."

Partially resulting from his physical challenges, Aaron has spent most of his time at school or home. His family has worked hard to make their home accessible for Aaron but have found it difficult to find the resources (e.g., finances, physical assistance, transportation) to help Aaron spend time in the community. Aaron has had training in community activities through his school program.

Aaron's transition into a job and a home of his own will require the coordinated efforts of his planning team, which includes his parents, the transition coordinator, the county case manager from developmental disabilities services, and representatives from supported employment and supported living providers. The team has begun to brainstorm ways to help Aaron meet his goals. For example, the case manager will help the family explore affordable housing options, and his teacher will help him place an ad for a roommate at the college housing office.

Questions for Planning and Instruction
1. What skills does Aaron need and want that will enhance his competence and help him maintain control over the direction of his life?
2. How can instructional support be coordinated with the other forms of support that Aaron needs and wants?

school day. The team also targeted self-scheduling as a way for Aaron to take more control of his day.

Value Three: Choose Instruction that Blends with General Education Contexts and Encourages Peer Interaction

Guideline Three: Use Efficient Strategies, Peer Instruction, and Observational Learning

With the increasing emphasis on school inclusion, planning teams may need to give new thought to how skills for home and community settings can be taught. Questions that can be asked to guide this planning are:

- What setting will be used for instruction? Can the skills be embedded in typical school activities and routines? If not, will a simulated activity be feasible and effective? Or, is it best to schedule instruction in the settings where the skills are typically used (e.g., the community)?
- How can generalization be encouraged? How many different settings will be needed for this generalization to be demonstrated?
- How can instruction be made more effective and efficient? Can peers be involved?

Choosing the Instructional Setting

The challenge in teaching school-aged students skills for the home and community is that these settings differ greatly from typical school settings. Students may not generalize skills taught in school to community contexts (Snell & Browder, 1986). To meet this challenge, teachers can take one of three approaches: (a) embedding home and community skills in typical school routines and settings, (b) using school-based simulations of home and community settings, and (c) conducting in vivo instruction. If one of the first two school-based options is selected, it is important to plan some probes in community settings and collaboration with caregivers to determine that skills are generalizing to these other settings.

To embed skills in typical school routines, the teacher considers how each priority home or community skill can be incorporated in existing school activ-

ities. For example, Gardill and Browder (1995) taught purchasing skills using the school store, cafeteria, and vending machines, as well as community settings. Similarly, food preparation might be incorporated with a general education unit in social studies or science or as part of a special activity offered to all students in a club or study hall format. Some housekeeping skills can be taught as classroom chores that all students share (e.g., emptying trash, cleaning a classroom sink after art projects).

The second alternative is to use school-based simulations of community and home activities. For example, Sowers and Powers (1995) implemented a community training program that included: (a) strategy planning for community participation, (b) training in a school-based simulation, and (c) collaboration with caregivers for in vivo instruction. In the strategy planning, Sowers and Powers (1995) observed the students' purchasing food at a fast food restaurant and reviewed each step of the task analysis to determine if the student could learn the step without an adaptation and, if not, what adaptation could be made. For example, some of the strategies targeted for a participant named Paul were:

- Paul will drive his scooter up to the clerk at the counter. He will always take his scooter so he can move on his own.
- Paul will get a five-dollar bill out of a fanny pack positioned in the front.
- Paul will use a cupholder. (A cupholder was purchased for Paul and was placed on his chair before he left home. He took the drink from the clerk and placed it in the cupholder.)
- Paul will position his scooter next to the bench in the dining area and transfer.

The instructor taught the adapted task analysis in a simulation of the fast food restaurant in a school conference room. The instructor had available the food items from the community restaurant (i.e., a take-out order) for instruction that the student had ordered earlier in the day. The instructor then role played with the student how to order the food and clean up. Two practice trials were conducted by rewrapping the food after the first trial. The student could eat the food after the second practice. Once the student had mastered the steps of the task analysis, the instructor invited the students' caregiver (e.g., parent or group home staff) to come to school to participate in the simulation. The caregivers were given the strategy planning along with six rules for encouraging the student to perform these steps for him or herself.

1. *Before leaving home, review with the student how she/he will perform each step.*
2. *Don't jump in to help too quickly, even if the student seems to be struggling a little in trying to do a step; allow a few minutes to try before helping.*
3. *If you do help, don't do the whole step; assist just a little to get him or her going.*
4. *If the student makes an error, allow the opportunity to correct it before stepping in to help.*
5. *If the clerk tries to deal with you, direct him or her to the student.*
6. *On the way home, communicate your pride in accomplishment; discuss any steps he or she has difficulty with and what she or he needs to do next time to perform the step more independently or easily.* (Sowers & Powers, 1995, p. 213)

The caregiver watched the instructor give the student any needed assistance in the role play of purchasing the food and then provided assistance on the second trial. This caregiver training took a total of 1 hour. Observations of the student on four weekly visits to fast food restaurants demonstrated that they did generalize their skills. They also maintained their skills on visits with their caregivers, when observed 6 weeks later.

Community-based instruction, or even the simulations, might be taught with peer instruction. Peers could be taught to use strategies that encourage independence in a community setting. In some high schools, seniors have the privilege of eating lunch out. The teacher might facilitate having the student join peers for lunch in a local fast food restaurant.

Why do students sometimes demonstrate generalization from simulations to in vivo settings and other times do not? Some of the literature on using simulations offers guidelines for increasing the likelihood that skills will transfer. First, the simulation should carefully replicate the stimuli and responses found in the community or home setting (Horner, McDonnell, & Bellamy, 1986; Nietupski, Hamre-Nietupski, Clancy, & Veerhusen, 1986). For example, in using classroom-based simulations of vending instruction, Browder, Snell, and Wildonger (1988) used photographs of vending machines. Each photograph was enlarged and glued to a stationary box to form a miniature machine. To use the simulated machine, students inserted coins in an actual slot cut on the picture. The dropping coins

made a "clinking" sound similar to a vending machine as they dropped into the box. When the student pushed one of the buttons on the picture, the teacher slid the food or drink under the box and the student had to reach under to retrieve it. Similarly, Shafer, Inge, and Hill (1986) simulated an automatic teller (ATM) with a box that had a slot with flipcards to show the written messages, painted numbers, and slots for the bank card, money, and receipt. Neef, Lensbower, Hockersmith, DePalma, and Gray (1990) adapted a cardboard furniture box to make a life-sized simulated washing machine.

A second consideration in planning the simulation is to use multiple exemplars and stimulus variation. For example, Neef et al. (1990) compared training a single example of laundry use to multiple exemplars in simulated and in vivo instruction. The single example training focused on one community laundromat or cardboard box simulation. In multiple exemplar training, the participant either went to multiple laundromats or trained with multiple sets (several simulated box models) of washers and dryers. Participants used coins and actual laundry detergent in these simulations. Interestingly, Neef et al. (1990) found that students generalized their laundry skills when introduced to multiple exemplars. That is, generalization was limited when only one community or school simulation was used, but multiple school simulations were as effective as multiple community simulations.

The third consideration in using school-based simulations is to include some opportunities to apply skills in actual community or home settings. All of the research using simulated instruction has included community probes of skills. These probes provide students with the exposure to the natural variation of community contexts that cannot be fully simulated at school. The advantage of using simulations is that these community probes may be scheduled much less frequently than would be needed if relying on community-based instruction alone. For home skills, rather than community probes, collaboration with caregivers can help determine if skills performed at school are being used at home. A parent conference similar to that in Sowers and Powers (1995) in which the caregiver sees and participates in the simulation may be especially beneficial in encouraging this generalization.

A third option is to conduct in vivo instruction in the community or home. When students are past typical school age but still receiving educational services (i.e., ages 19 to 21), the focus of instruction will probably shift from school inclusion to job training and community access. Some students who are over age 18 may receive instruction in higher education contexts (e.g., community college), but most will also have community-based instruction. During the transition years (age 14 and older), students may also have direct community-based instruction for part of their school day, especially when: (a) this is a student and parental priority, (b) this instruction can be scheduled as one or more periods of the student's class schedule and does not require the student to be "pulled" in the middle of a general education class, and (c) other students leave school on a regular basis (e.g., to travel with school teams to sports events, to work at a half-day job program, to participate in honors activities, to

attend a vocational-technical center). At the elementary level, direct community-based instruction may be less of a priority and more disruptive to the classroom routine in some schools. In other situations, direct community-based instruction may be a strong student and parent priority (e.g., to teach safe street crossing) and may be less disruptive (e.g., in elementary schools that use a lot of individualized pull-out programs for music, sports, the arts, and other special interests). For example, in one elementary school known to the authors, students flow in and out of their classes all day for one-to-one instrument lessons, to participate in student council, for individualized reading instruction, and for small group instruction with computers. Even when using in vivo instruction, teachers need to remember that it is important to encourage generalization by using a variety of sites.

  Balancing Community-Based Instruction and General Education Inclusion

Box 14–1

Maintaining inclusion in general education contexts is an important priority. Community-based instruction can often compete with this goal unless careful consideration is given to the student's chronological age, individual priorities, and the culture of the school. Here is how this issue was addressed for each of the case studies.

Elementary School

For some students, community-based instruction may not receive much emphasis during the elementary years beyond capitalizing on school field trips. In contrast, for Rico, community skills were a high priority because of issues of safety and behavioral support. His mother, Mrs. Hernandez sought ways that she could take Rico into the community safely. In Rico's schools, students often left the class for a variety of activities (e.g., student council, music lessons, and enrichment activities). Rico's departures for community-based instruction were made part of the school's enrichment activities and students took turns going with him to stores and restaurants. Most students were eager to have their turn for this special event. Rico received weekly community-based instruction from the special education teacher with a different peer serving as a role model each week.

Middle School and High School

Community-based instruction is a part of many student's transition plans. Julia was just at the beginning of transition planning and continued to have strong priorities within the general education context. Julia's middle school had a food court in the cafeteria, which provided an excellent location for learning fast food purchasing. She also could learn to purchase items at the school store. Her home economics class provided a context for learning skills for home settings. The special education teacher also collaborated with the home economics teacher to plan biweekly shopping trips for Julia and some of her classmates to buy supplies for the class. These shopping trips gave her the opportunity to learn grocery shopping and pedestrian skills while still having contact with her peers.

Postsecondary Years

Students who are 19 to 21 years of age need educational opportunities outside of high school. General education inclusion in a high school is no longer an age-appropriate match. At this age, the entire school day will probably be spent in community and job settings. Some students may also receive instruction at a community college and in apartment settings. Aaron had not actually attended the local high school since he was 18, although he still was receiving public school special education services. Instead, he attended classes at the community college, tried part-time jobs, and learned new community skills with instructional support from a team that included the special education teacher, a paraprofessional, and a job coach.

> *General Case Instruction*
>
> **Box 14–2**   General case instruction emphasizes selecting and teaching examples so that students learn to perform skills across the full range of settings and materials that they confront. The five steps to set up general case instruction are:
>
> **1.** Define the instructional universe.
> **2.** Write a generic task analysis
> **3.** Select teaching and testing examples that sample the range of stimulus and response variation
> **4.** Teach
> **5.** Test

General Case Instruction

Teachers can also maximize what time is available for home and community instruction by making it as effective and efficient as possible. General case instruction is one of the ways to maximize instructional effectiveness (see Box 14–2). General case instruction has been effective in teaching students skills such as using vending machines (Sprague & Horner, 1984),

telephones (Horner, Williams, & Steveley, 1987), and restaurant use (McDonnell & Ferguson, 1989) and to teach requesting help in community contexts (Chadsey-Rusch, Drasgow, Reinoehl, Hallet, Collet-Klingenberg, 1993).

General case instruction can be illustrated through the example of how to teach Rico to use convenience stores with a companion. First, an

FIGURE 14–1

Robert, at age 20, receives most of his educational support in community settings. One of the benefits of his part-time job in a martial arts center is free classes.

instructional universe is defined. Generalization becomes unwieldy unless these parameters are defined.

Rico's teachers must answer several questions: Is the goal for Rico to be able to use all convenience stores in his neighborhood? In his city? In the world? The teacher decides to focus on teaching Rico to use convenience stores in his region (the Lehigh Valley of Pennsylvania).

As shown in Table 14–2, four convenience stores are identified for the general case analysis.

Second, the teacher writes a generic task analysis for purchasing a snack at the store. Next, the teacher analyzes the stimulus and response variation in each store (Table 14–2). Third, the teacher selects which stores will be used for training. The teacher chooses a 7-Eleven, a Penn Supreme, and the school cafeteria snack line (which offers snack foods like ice cream to supplement school lunch) because these three stores sample the range of variation in Rico's home community as shown in the table. The teacher will also test Rico at other stores, including

the Nick's Market and Kate's One-Stop Shopping. Rico will receive daily instruction in the school cafeteria and weekly instruction at a convenience store on Fridays. Every fourth Friday, the teacher will use a novel convenience store to check for generalization. This will continue until Rico demonstrates both mastery and generalization.

Efficient Teaching Strategies

Two other ways the teacher can maximize instructional time for teaching home and community skills is to use observational learning and instructive feedback. For example, Griffin, Wolery, and Schuster (1992) taught students with moderate mental retardation to make a milkshake, scrambled eggs, and pudding in a small-group format involving three students. To maximize instructional efficiency, one student received direct instruction using prompting for each step of the task analysis with constant time delay. At the same time

TABLE 14–2
General Case Analysis

Generic Responses: Task Analysis (TA)	Instructional Universe: Convenience stores in Lehigh Valley, PA Assessment Data: Sites to sample stimulus/response (S/R) variation (parentheses show S/R variation for that TA step in that site)				Assessment Summary: Generalization
	Penn Supreme	**Nick's**	**7-Eleven**	**Kate's**	
1. Enter store	+ (electric door)	− (push)	− (pull)	− (push)	Push/pull door
2. Locate item	− (multiple aisles)	− (display case)	− (aisles)	+ (behind clerk)	Scan aisles and cases
3. Pick out item	+ (bottom shelf)	− (open case)	− (top shelf)	+ (clerk selects)	Shelf location and opening case
4. Take item to counter	+ (large counter)	− (small counter)	− (small counter)	N/A	Size/location of counter
5. Wait in line	+	+	+	N/A	Mastered
6. Pay cashier	− (clerk states price)	+ (clerk extends hand)	− (clerk states price)	− (clerk states price)	Verbal cue states
7. Take change/ item	− (change with no bag)	− (no bag)	− (change and bag)	+ (bag)	Unbagged item Change cups
8. Leave store Number Correct/ Total	+ (electric door)	− (pull)	− (push)	− (pull)	Push/pull door
Responses:	5/8	2/8	1/8	3/6	
Date of Probe:	Nov. 3	Nov. 10	Nov. 12	Nov. 15	

Key: + = Independent correct; − = incorrect or needed prompting, N/A = not applicable to that site.
Note: Reprinted from "Functional Assessment" by R. Gaylord-Ross and D. M. Browder, in *Critical Issues in the Lives of People with Severe Disabilities* (p. 58) by L. H. Meyer, C. A. Peck, and L. Brown (Eds.), 1991, Baltimore: Paul H. Brookes. Reprinted by permission.

the instructor prompted and reinforced the other two students to observe and follow instructions by turning the pages of a picture recipe. Even though each student only received direct instruction on one of the three recipes, they learned most of the steps of all three. Similarly, Schoen and Sivil (1989) taught pairs of students to get a drink and make a snack using observational learning. Hall, Schuster, Wolery, Gast, and Doyle (1992) also taught food preparation in pairs, but they selected direct instruction for half of the task analysis with one student, then switched to the second student to teach the rest of the recipe. Each day, the students alternated who started first. To encourage generalization for materials, the instructor also selected multiple brands of the food products, varying the brand used across sessions.

Instructional time may also be enhanced by giving extra information either by adding it to the prompts or to supplement feedback. Jones and Collins (1997) employed a system of least intrusive prompts to teach three microwave recipes to adults with moderate mental retardation. During each prompt, they added extra information on nutrition and safety. For example, while prompting the participant to get the mix, the teacher would say "Get the mix [verbal prompt] . . . . it is healthy because it contains milk." [extra information]. While prompting using a hot mitt, the teacher said, "Use a mitt . . . the food may be hot and could burn you." Extra information was also given as feedback. For example, after completing the task analysis to microwave a baked potato, the teacher said, "A baked potato is a good food because it is lowfat and won't make you gain weight." Participants learned not only to prepare the microwave recipes, but also learned some nutrition and safety facts.

General case instruction, observational learning, and adding extra information can encourage general education inclusion by making community and home instruction more efficient, but peer instruction can facilitate social inclusion. For example, Collins, Branson, and Hall (1995) taught high school students from an advanced English class to teach recipe sight words to students with moderate mental retardation. Students read each word and then found it in the recipe on the product's box or container. The advanced English students wrote about their teaching experiences as part of their English assignments. The

students with moderate mental retardation learned to read the recipe words and were able to prepare the recipes in probes conducted in the home economics room and a nearby home.

In another program that involved typical peers as tutors, which was developed by Collins, Hall, and Branson (1997), students with moderate mental retardation learned leisure skills by playing cards or a video game or watching a sports video. The special education teacher conducted daily systematic instruction using a system of least prompts to teach each step of a task analysis for each leisure skill. Once a week, the peers who were nondisabled joined the class to probe the students' use of the leisure skill.

Besides using direct prompting or probing skills, peer tutors can also model skills for students with disabilities to learn through observation. For example, Werts, Caldwell, and Wolery (1996) had peers model school-related tasks such as sharpening a pencil, using a tape recorder, and using a computer. The peer model would demonstrate each step of the task analysis while saying it aloud. The students with disabilities were then probed on their ability to perform the task. This modeling continued until the students had mastered the tasks through observational learning.

To summarize this guideline, teachers can enhance students' participation in general education and inclusion with peers by making the time devoted to teaching community and home skills as efficient as possible, by recruiting peers as instructors, and by using school settings and school-based simulations as adjuncts to community-based instruction. Teachers may also enhance generalization by collaborating with caregivers for carryover of newly learned community and home skills.

Rico's team thinks he'll benefit from peer instruction on several new leisure skills (e.g., playing computer games and putting sports cards in collection books). His teacher decides to simulate some home training by teaching chores and safety at school. Rico's mother is invited for a school conference to observe Rico and participate in giving him the assistance he needs to perform these skills. The teacher also uses some intensive instruction in street crossing safety with a general case approach so Rico can learn skills that will work in a variety of street crossing situations.

Value Four: Home and Community Skills Gain Importance as Students Become Older

Guideline Four: Use Transition Planning to Focus Community-Based Instruction

Wehman (1997) noted that the seven most common transitions youth with disabilities face as they approach adulthood concern employment, living arrangements, getting around in the community, increased financial independence, making friends, sexuality and self-esteem, and having fun. To help adolescents meet these challenges, community, home, employment, and social skills will gain increasing priority as students progress through their last years of school. Many of the skills described in this chapter are more suitably age-appropriate for adolescents and young adults. For example, adolescents may vacuum, do laundry, and prepare meals, but young children typically do not. Adolescents may open their first bank account and start going to the movies and restaurants without their parents. By contrast, children may do chores, pick up their laundry, and prepare snacks but typically go to the movies or restaurants with an adult.

With this increasing priority, teachers may focus more time and planning on skills for the home and community during the transition years (age 14 and older).

Julia, who is 14, will probably have more objectives related to domestic and community skills than Rico, who is 9 years old. Aaron's greatest instructional needs at age 21 are using community resources, establishing his own home, and obtaining a job. Many of his IEP objectives will be related to home, community, and employment skills.

Although the transition years may be a time for increased community-based and home instruction, this instruction may not look like that typical of past eras because of the awareness gained through person-centered planning. Conducting community-based instruction from a person-centered planning perspective means that preferences should be honored about what to learn and where to learn it (Browder, Bambara, & Belfiore, 1997). Skills and instruction should be selected that enhance the person's dignity in community contexts and do not create stigma. For example, in public, prompting should be given discreetly so that others are not aware that the person is receiving assistance. In some situations, simulations and private tutoring may be used to allow intensive instruction initially (e.g., use of an automated teller machine).

Aaron's case can illustrate how current community-based instruction has changed from the 1980s.

In the 1980s, Aaron's teacher probably would have based skill selection almost entirely on an ecological inventory of Aaron's community sites. For example, the teacher would have noted that Aaron lived near a grocery store that his family used. After identifying this site, the teacher would define its activities and teach Aaron to select groceries using a picture list and to pay for them at the checkout counter. Similarly, community-based instruction in a fast food restaurant and bank would have been planned. Although all of these are important and "functional" skills, they may not reflect Aaron's unique preferences and goals.

In the first decade of the next century, things are done differently:

Aaron's IEP looks quite different because of the increased emphasis on his right to self-determine his future in the community. Aaron's teacher identifies skills not only through an inventory of the student's community, but more importantly, by brainstorming with students and their planning team about their preferences and future goals. From such a discussion with Aaron, the team notes that he does not like grocery shopping and often has shown distress during outings to the store. He likes going to restaurants and banks during off hours when they are quiet but strongly dislikes crowds and waiting in line. From this perspective, plans are made to teach Aaron to select groceries to be purchased by an assistant or roommate as an alternative to going to the store himself. Instruction is also targeted to increase Aaron's independence in a restaurant and to gain new skills, such as communicating with a friend during lunch. The teacher works with Aaron on developing prompting that is effective and efficient but does not stigmatize him in public. Aaron also learns to schedule restaurant outings using a calendar so that he knows how to select quieter days and times (e.g., weeknights versus Friday). The team also decides to tutor Aaron in using a money access machine and to cash checks with a cashier by private simulation conducted daily in a conference room. Once a week, his job coach provides community support for Aaron to go to his home bank, where he will choose whether to use the automated teller or to seek the assistance of the cashier. Aaron's IEP reflects his own unique preferences and needs related to home and community skills.

To summarize the guideline on transition planning, home and community skills become increasingly important as students progress through the high school years. Older students' IEPs may reflect more objectives related to these areas than younger students. By contrast, these IEP objectives should also stem from the student's own preferences and transition goals. Rather than simply asking if the objective is "functional," teachers need to consider whether the objective enhances the student's self-determination of his or her future plans.

Resources for Planning Instructional Support

Skills for the Home

This section describes specific ideas for teaching skills that are necessary in home settings. Before focusing on specific teaching ideas, it is important to consider where and when these skills will be taught. While students may learn simple skills such as preparing snacks or dusting in their classroom, if this instruction is atypical in that setting, it may stigmatize the student. The student may also not understand when and why to perform the skill when instruction in home activities is inserted in a classroom routine and setting. In contrast, home skills may be simulated successfully with a specially designed space. Most middle and high schools have home economics suites that offer a context for all students to learn daily living skills during their school day. This space may be well suited as a context for teaching the skills described next. This instruction may be incorporated with the general education classes in home economics by planning for inclusion, or students may receive private tutoring from their teacher or peers during periods when the room is free. Sometimes it may be necessary to create additional space for teaching daily living skills if the current facilities are over-scheduled or lack necessary equipment. Some teachers schedule instruction in daily living skills in community homes. This community-based option may be especially appropriate for older students (ages 19 to 21).

Food Preparation

Students are often highly motivated to participate in food preparation instruction because of the benefit of being able to consume the results (Figure 14–2)! In contrast, food preparation can be difficult to plan and teach because of the specialized setting and equipment needed and cost of supplies. Schuster (1988) suggested several ways that a program may offset the expense of teaching food preparation, including: (a) obtaining donations from civil organizations, (b) using lunch money (with the parents' permission) to prepare the student's lunch, (c) collecting lab fees from parents, (d) operating a school vending machine and using the profits to cover the costs of food, and (e) operating a schoolwide food service program on a cost basis (e.g., selling bagels or donuts in the morning). Students also may be able to practice with real preparation materials several times before preparing the food for consumption. For example, Schleien, Ash, Kiernan, and Wehman (1981) had students practice boiling an egg, broiling a muffin, and baking a frozen dinner. The same egg was reboiled for practice and the frozen dinner was an empty tray with foil. Although students need to experience the natural consequences of consuming the food they prepare, they may be able to understand the importance of practicing a few times before using the real materials.

Food preparation instruction has several components: planning meals or snacks, preparing the food items, safe food storage, and cleaning up. When teaching students to plan what foods to prepare, honor any dietary restrictions, respect both cultural and familial preferences (e.g., meatless or no pork), honor personal preferences, and encourage nutrition. Some students may benefit from learning recipe planning as described by Sarber and Cuvo (1983). In their study, adults with mental retardation learned to plan meals using a board that had color cues for each food group. For example, peaches were cued for the fruits and vegetable group. Beef stew was cued as both meat and vegetables. After planning the menus, the participants learned to develop a grocery list to purchase necessary items. Sarber, Halasz, Messmer, Bickett, and Lutzker (1983) applied a similar approach to teach a mother with mental retardation to plan nutritious meals for her family. Arnold-Reid, Schloss, and Alper (1997) implemented the system of least prompts to teach participants to plan meals according to the four food

FIGURE 14–2

Jamal uses pictures to help guide him through the task of making toast. In (a) he touches the picture and then follows the actions involved by placing bread in the toaster and pushing the handle down to start the toaster (b). Later he follows step 6 (c) and spreads butter on each slice of toast (d).

a

b

c

d

Thanks to Vicky Block of Charlottesville High School and Deb Morris of Walker School and their students for sharing their work with us.

groups. The meal chart used is shown in Figure 14–3. Because one participant had to limit sweets owing to health concerns, these were listed in a column called the "Dreaded Other." The participant, Joseph, learned to only have an item in the "Dreaded Other" column as an occasional treat. Since participants had difficulty filling out the chart, instruction was adapted by teaching either sight words or picture identification related to commonly eaten foods and enlarging the chart. After completing the chart, the participants planned a grocery list. Similarly, Reitz (1984) taught adults with mental retardation to self-monitor their food intake

FIGURE 14–3
Meal Chart Used to Self-Monitor Healthy Eating

The Food Groups					
Cross out items not eaten and fill in substitutions. Check item if eaten.					
Meals	**Vegetables and Fruit**	**Meat**	**Dairy**	**Bread and Cereal**	**Dreaded Other**
Breakfast	✔ Juice		✔ Milk	✔ Cereal	
Lunch	✔ Tomato and lettuce	✔ Hamburger	✔ Cheese	✔ Bun	✔ Brownie
Snack	✔ Grapes				(Candy Bar)
Dinner	✔ Carrot	✔ Chicken		✔ Rice	

Note: Adapted from Arnold-Reid, P. J., Schloss, S., & Alper, S. Teaching meal planning to youth with mental retardation in natural settings. *Remedial and Special Education, 18,* 166–173. Copyright (1997) held by Pro-Ed. Adapted with permission.

using the basic food groups. Through self-monitoring and cash reinforcement, the participants learned to have a healthier diet. Participants who do not have the academic skills to read or write food names in planning menus or self-monitoring their diet may benefit from a picture system. The *Select-A-Meal Curriculum* from the Attainment Company provides commercial materials that can be helpful for menu planning or restaurant use (see Table 14–3).

Besides teaching healthy menu planning, food preferences should be honored. Some students may be able to describe the foods they want to learn to prepare. For students with more severe disabilities, preference assessment can be applied to determine which foods to select (Lohrmann-O'Rourke & Browder, in press). To conduct this preference assessment, the teacher might show the student an array of pictures or packages of food and wait for the student to select one by touching it, gazing at it, or making some other response. Or, the teacher may offer samples of foods and then have students choose from among the samples. The teacher would repeat the choices, rotating some different food options to see if a preference emerges.

Once the specific foods have been selected, consideration can be given to how to teach the recipe. One option is to use a special picture recipe book, such as the *Home Cooking Curriculum* listed in Table

14–3. Singh, Oswald, Ellis, and Singh (1995) taught individuals with profound mental retardation to prepare a dessert (pineapple mousse) using a picture cookbook with line drawings that was developed by Hopman & Singh (1986). First the instructor pretrained the recipe by demonstrating each step and having the participant practice it five times (guided rehearsal) per session. The instructor continued to use this demonstration method for five additional instructional days. Then, to teach the student to prepare the menus by following the picture, the instructor used a most to least intrusive prompting system beginning with gestural and verbal prompts and fading to verbal prompts and then, no prompting.

For students who have some sight word reading, it may be beneficial to teach the reading of recipes written on food packages. For example, in the study by Collins et al., (1995) in which peers from an advanced English class taught students with moderate mental retardation to read food package words, the words were taught using constant time delay. The tutor also gave feedback on the meaning of the word by pointing to the utensil or product needed to make the cooking response. Students practiced reading the recipe words in daily sessions and then applied them to prepare the actual recipes during generalization probes with the teacher.

TABLE 14–3

Commercial Materials Used in Teaching Daily Living and Community Skills

From: THE ATTAINMENT COMPANY (1-800-327-4269)
PO Box 930160
Verona, WI 53593-0160

Keeping House Curriculum

Task analysis and suggested activities for teaching housekeeping (vacuuming, bathrooms, laundry). Picture cards and booklet to self-schedule chores. Video illustrating many of the activities.

Home Cooking Curriculum

Picture recipes for 37 foods in a laminated format that can be used while cooking. Also has an instructor's guide and videos teaching the basics of cooking.

Plan Your Day Curriculum

Appointment book and picture cards that can be used for daily, weekly, and 6-month plans. Examples of picture cards include sports events, movies, party, and renting videos.

Select-A-Meal Curriculum

Contains 144 pictures of foods, color-coded, which can be used in a booklet to plan and place an order in a restaurant. Instructor's guide focuses on teaching restaurant skills. Cards may also be useful for menu planning and assessing food preferences.

From: THE JAMES STANFIELD PUBLISHING COMPANY (1-800-421-6534)
PO Box 41058
Santa Barbara, CA 93140

First Impressions Video Series

Videotapes that use humor and clear examples to teach the basics of grooming, dress, hygiene, and attitude. Appropriate for use with adolescents and adults with developmental disabilities.

Circles I, II, and III

Videotape series and color-coded chart of worksheets to teach students about intimacy and relationships. For example, teaches participants to discriminate between who to trust with a hug and who not to hug. Circles II focuses on avoiding sexual abuse and Circles III on avoiding sexually transmitted diseases.

Sexuality Education for Persons with Severe Developmental Disabilities

Slides teach parts of male and female body, appropriate social behavior (e.g., private versus public behavior), and physical examination. Slides are of real people and are sexually explicit.

Janet's Got Her Period

In this video with live actresses, a young girl learns to manage her period from her mother and sister.

Community Man

In an entertaining format, this videotape series teaches safety, when to call 911, how to interact appropriately with police, how to get medical care, and how to use the pharmacy.

TABLE 14–4

Instructions for Audiovisual
Self-Prompting System

Task:	Making Microwave Popcorn
Self-Prompting System:	Digivox Communication Board with picture overlay and speech output

Sample Step	Visual Cue (Picture)	Auditory Cue
1. Put bag in, right side up	Bag inside, right side up	"Put bag in, like this"

Teacher's Use of System of Least Prompts to Encourage Use of Audiovisual System

1. Verbal:	"Touch the picture again." (Referring to picture overlay on device.)
2. Verbal:	"Touch the picture again to hear how to put the bag in." (Referring to audio)
3. Gesture:	"Touch the picture like this." Touches picture and points to bag.
4. Model:	Repeats verbal prompt above and then models placing bag in microwave.
5. Physical:	Repeats verbal prompt above and guides hand to place bag in microwave.

Note: From L. C. Mechling & D. L. Gast, 1997. Combination audio/visual self-prompting system for teaching chained tasks to students with intellectual disabilities. *Education and Training in Mental Retardation and Developmental Disabilities, 32,* 138–153. Copyright (1997) by Division of Mental Retardation and Developmental Disabilities, Council for Exceptional Children. Used with permission.

Students who cannot read sight words or use line drawings may benefit from audiotaped recipes. Trask-Tyler, Grossi, and Heward (1994) taught adolescents with developmental disabilities to prepare recipes using audiotaped directions. The participants carried a tape recorder in the pocket of a cooking apron. At the end of each step, the tape beeped so that the student would know to turn it off and perform the step. The instructor selected a system of least to most intrusive prompts to teach the students to use the taped messages to perform the recipes. The students were able to master the trained recipes and generalize to similar recipes using the audiotape.

The advantage of employing picture, word, or audiotaped recipes is that they encourage self-directed learning as described earlier in this chapter. Often students will need teacher prompting to learn to use the materials for self direction. Teachers have several alternatives for this prompting. One alternative is the system of least intrusive prompting (Mechling & Gast, 1997; Trask-Tyler et al., 1994). For example, Mechling and Gast (1997) taught students to use a combination picture and audiotape recipe book that was made with a communication board with picture overlays and speech output (Digivox). If students were unsure of the step, they could re-press the button to hear the instructions again. The instructor gave progressive assistance, which is described in Table 14–4.

The teacher may also select the system of least prompts to teach additional information about food preparation. Jones and Collins (1997) taught three microwave recipes: hot chocolate, popcorn, and baked potato preparation. In their system of prompting, shown in Table 14–5, additional information was given as part of the prompting and feedback.

Time delay, an alternative to the system of least prompts, can be used to teach participants to read sight words contained in recipe or instruction booklets (Browder, Hines, McCarthy, & Fees, 1984; Gast, Doyle, Wolery, Ault, & Farmer, 1991). Constant time delay is also effective for teaching food preparation in a group instruction format (Griffin, Wolery, & Schuster, 1992; Hall, Schuster, Wolery, Gast, & Doyle, 1992; Schoen & Sivil, 1989). The challenge of teaching food preparation to a group is having enough supplies for everyone to make the recipe. Rarely is it feasible or practical for each person in the group to perform all the steps of the task analysis. For example, if four students in a group each prepare a box of instant pudding, there will be 16 servings to consume! An alternative is to have each student prepare part of the recipe while the others watch.

Sometimes teacher prompting is selected to teach the student to prepare simple items for which no recipe is needed. Schuster and Griffin (1991) used constant time delay to teach students to prepare a drink mix (Kool-Aid). The participants with moderate

TABLE 14–5
Embedding Extra Information in System of Least Prompts

Target Skill: Making hot chocolate

Step of Task Analysis	Prompt Hierarchy	Extra Information Given
Gather materials	Wait for independent	
	Indirect verbal: "What do you need?"	"The mix is healthy. It contains milk."
	Direct verbal: "Get the mix and cup."	
	Gesture/verbal: "Get the mix and cup." (Point to mix & cup)	
	Model/verbal: "Get the mix and cup like this . . ." (model)	

Examples of Other Nutrition and Safety Information Given for Hot Chocolate

Fill the cup with water.	"Drink 6 glasses of water each day."	
Push start.	"Don't cook too long. The water could boil and burn you."	
Put on hot mitts.	"The mitts keep your hands from getting burned."	

Note: From G. Y. Jones & B. C. Collins, 1997. Teaching microwave skills to adults with disabilities: Acquisition of nutrition and safety facts presented as nontarget information. *Journal of Developmental and Physical Disabilities, 9,* 59–78. Copyright (1997) by Plenum Publishing Corp. Adapted with permission.

mental retardation all learned to make this drink independently. In contrast, many food items are more complex; individuals who are nondisabled often rely on recipes in preparing these items. Teacher prompting can be crucial in assisting students with severe disabilities to learn to use picture, packaged, or audiotaped recipes. The outcome of this instruction is student-directed learning: that is, by learning to follow these recipe aids, the student will be able to teach themselves to prepare foods without the teacher's help. Sanders and Parr (1989) taught independent meal preparation to adults with mild and moderate mental retardation and demonstrated that participants could prepare untrained recipes. Similarly, Browder et al. (1984) demonstrated generalization to untrained recipes.

The teaching challenge is to design instructional strategies to be efficient and effective, while also encouraging generalized use of self-prompting guides like picture or audiotaped recipes. The following guidelines are offered for making instruction efficient while encouraging self-directed learning:

1. Teach food preparation in a small group (two or three people), giving each person the opportunity to prepare part of the recipe, while the others watch and follow the recipe using pictures, the package, or an audiotape.

   For example, in preparing a box cake mix, Sam adds the ingredients and prepares the pan using a picture recipe, while Connie follows, using her own recipe. Then, Connie uses the mixer and pours the mix into the pan and places it in the oven, while Sam follows his picture recipe.

2. Use a prompt system like constant time delay or the system of least prompts, being careful to prompt following the recipe.

   The teacher uses a verbal and gesture prompt: "Look at the next step and do it."

3. Consider including additional information about nutrition or safety in the prompting or feedback.

   If applied, make this information the same statement used consistently across teaching trials, (e.g., "Use a hot mitt to keep from being burned").

4. Probe for generalization to untrained recipes that use the same type of picture, package, or audio-tape system.

Probes whether Sam and Connie can make boxed cheesecake by following the picture recipe.

Housekeeping and Laundry

To manage a home, individuals need strategies to keep pace with the ongoing demands of housecleaning and laundry (Figure 14–4). Even when outside help can be procured (e.g., a maid service or cook), ongoing chores still must be performed. As students make the transition from relying on their parents to clean and do their laundry to caring for their own clothes and living space, they need to learn two important sets of skills: (a) how to perform housekeeping and laundry tasks, and (b) how to manage their time to keep pace with the ongoing demands of these tasks.

To teach housekeeping skills, the instructor typically uses a task analysis of the skill and a prompting system, such as least intrusive prompts or time delay. Whether to teach the entire task or some portion of it will depend on the complexity of the task and the students' current skill level. For example, McWilliams, Nietupski, and Hamre-Nietupski (1990) taught students bedmaking using a system of least prompts and forward chaining. The instructor selected the home living center in the school as an instructional setting. In contrast, Snell (1982) used progressive time delay to teach the entire task of bedmaking. Students learned to strip and make their beds.

Similarly, in teaching laundry skills, researchers have used the system of least prompts (Cuvo, Jacobi, & Sipko, 1981), time delay (Miller & Test, 1989), and most to least prompting (Miller & Test, 1989). McDonnell and McFarland (1988) found whole task instruction to be more efficient than chaining in teaching laundry skills. Miller and Test (1989) found time delay to be slightly more efficient than most to least prompting. In applying these strategies to individual students, it is important to consider how the student learns best. One teacher might follow the research on efficiency and begin by teaching the entire task analysis (whole task instruction) using a time delay system. Another teacher might choose least intrusive prompting or chaining after observing the student's prior performance with these methods.

Another alternative is to encourage student-directed learning by using a self-operated audio-prompting system. Briggs et al. (1990) taught students with moderate and severe disabilities to operate a washing machine, clean a toilet, and clean mirrors using a taped script that they played while wearing a Walkman tape player. The script gave both verbal prompts and praise. The following sample from the Briggs et al. (1990) audio tape illustrates how the script contained prompting, self-checking of outcomes, seeking help as needed, and praise. When the bell sounded, the participant turned off the tape and performed the step.

> "Open the box and take out one set (two packets) of blue detergent.
>
> Put them in the washer." (bell)
>
> "Can you see the blue packets on top of the clothes? If you can't see them, call the teacher for help." (bell)
>
> "Good job! Now close the detergent box and put it back in the cabinet. Close the cabinet door." (bell)

Some families use commercial laundromats. This skill requires training to generalize across different types of machines and to community settings. Morrow and Bates (1987) compared using pictures, a cardboard replica of a machine, and a real machine to teach community laundry skills. While all three sets of materials were effective, students still needed some practice in the community laundromat to generalize their skills to that setting. In contrast, Neef, et al. (1990) found that generalization to community settings occurred if the school simulation introduced a range of training examples. That is, instructors adapted multiple cardboard boxes to simulate a variety of machines found in the community. They also found that community-based training did not generalize to new laundromats unless multiple settings were trained. Thus, for most students who will be using community laundromats, training across community sites is recommended. Providing some school-based simulated training combined with practice in varied community laundromats may be more practical than trying to develop several simulated machines and store them at school.

Once students learn the basics of housekeeping, they need to learn self-management skills to keep pace with the demands of these chores. Pierce and Schriebman (1994) used pictures to teach children

FIGURE 14–4

This student is learning to use a community laundromat. Here he is learning the steps of a task analysis for folding clothes. He also has instructional plans for using the coin-operated washer and dryer.

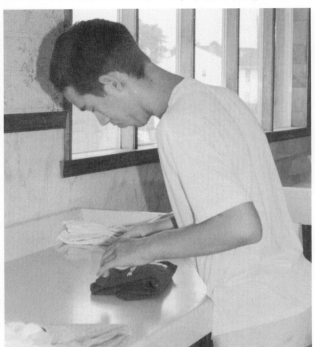

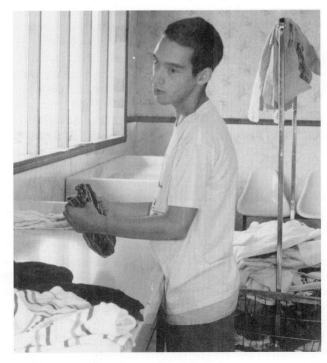

with autism to perform various daily living skills independently. Students were given a photo album with one step on each page and a picture for that step of the task analysis. A felt dot glued to the bottom of the page made the booklet's pages easier to turn. The instructor employed three training phases. In the first, the instructor taught receptive labeling of all the photos. In the second, students learned to choose a reinforcer, turn a page in the book, perform the response, and self-reinforce. In the third phase, the instructor faded her presence by saying, "Good work. I'll be back in a minute," and leaving the area while the student worked alone. By using these photo books, the students learned to set a table, make a bed, make a drink, get dressed, and do laundry without an adult nearby.

Once students learn to perform the skill independently, they can begin to self-schedule these activities. Lovett and Haring (1989) taught adults with mild and moderate mental retardation to self-manage their daily living skills using self-recording, self-evaluation, and self-reinforcement. Tasks were divided into daily, weekly, and occasional schedules. The participants used the planning form to self-select when to perform these tasks. Using instructions, modeling, and feedback, the trainers taught participants to use this form to self-record when each task was completed. If participants did not achieve 100% accuracy for self recording, the trainers introduced self-reinforcement, (e.g., participation in a leisure activity) to improve this accuracy. Upon mastery of self-recording, the participants learned to graph their performance on a simple percentage chart and then determine whether they had made progress. Once successful in self-evaluation, participants learned to self-reinforce (e.g., go to the movies if tasks were completed on time). An adaptation of this self-management training is shown in Table 14–6.

The teacher helped Julia and her mother negotiate Julia's chores. The teacher also negotiated with the mother giving Julia more flexibility in choosing when to complete her chores. Julia chose specific times with her mother's guidance. In a language arts class, the teacher and peers taught Julia to read the names of her chores and the times (e.g., days of the week). The teacher also taught her how to make checks on the form by talking about what Julia had or had not done the night before at home. Once Julia could check the form accurately, the teacher met with Julia and her mother to review

how Julia could "take charge" of her own chores using her charts. The teacher and Julia's mother helped Julia make up her list of "treats" for self-reinforcement. Julia then used her new self-management program at home with support from her mother as needed.

In doing housekeeping and laundry, students can also encounter problems that prevent task completion unless they develop problem-solving skills. Hughes, Hugo, and Blatt (1996) taught students to use self-management strategies to solve problems encountered in performing daily living skills. The problems introduced were: (a) not having the right utensil to make toast, (b) trying to vacuum when the vacuum was unplugged, and (c) cleaning up when there were bread crumbs under the table or game pieces in the area to be vacuumed. In the self-instruction strategy, participants learned to: (a) state the problem, (b) state the response, (c) self-evaluate, and (d) self-reinforce. The instructor taught the strategy by modeling the problem-solving step, having the participant say what to do as the instructor performed it, and then having the participant do the step while saying the problem-solving strategy. For example, to cope with an unplugged vacuum, the participant would say:

1. "The vacuum won't run." (state the problem)
2. "Plug it in." (state the response)
3. "I plugged it in." (self-evaluate)
4. "Great job!" (self-reinforce)

Home Safety and First Aid

One emergency response needed by all individuals is to escape safely from any building when there is a fire or other emergency. Haney and Jones (1982) taught four school-aged children to escape from a simulated fire in a home setting. Props were designed to make the training more realistic. For example, hot and cold pads were used to change the touch temperatures of doors and a tape recording of the home's fire alarm system was played. The instructor used a system of least prompts to teach the steps of the task analysis. Rae and Roll (1985) similarly employed a system of least prompts to teach evacuation. They also measured evacuation time to be sure students could leave the building in the time recommended by the fire department. Sometimes, for students like Rico, school fire drills can be upsetting and confusing (Box 14–3).

TABLE 14–6
Self-Management of Daily Living

Step One: Identify Daily, Weekly, and Occasional Tasks

Student: Julia   **Age:** 14

Tasks	Daily	Weekly	Occasional
	Wash hair	Clean bedroom	Budget allowance
	Blow-dry hair	Help with laundry	Shop for clothes
	Wash face	Vacuum den	
	Select clothes	Change cat box	
	Feed cat	Clean out bookbag	
	Help with dishes	Help buy groceries	

Step Two: Have Student Select When to Perform These Tasks

Julia's Daily Schedule

Time	Task	Yes	No	Notes
6:30 AM	Wash hair, face			
7:00 AM After breakfast	Select clothes			
7:15 AM After dressed	Blow-dry hair			
5:00 PM Before dinner	Feed the cat			
6:00 PM After dinner	Help with dishes			

Julia's Weekly Schedule

Day	Task	Yes	No	Notes
Sunday	Free!!			
Monday	Change cat box.			
Tuesday	Help with laundry (wash towels.)			
Wednesday	Free!! Pep club night.			
Thursday	Help with groceries.			
Friday	Clean out bookbag.			
Saturday	Vacuum den. Clean bedroom.			

Step 3. Teach Student to Self-Record When Task Completed and to Self-Reinforce

Julia's "Treats" for Getting Chores Done

When I finish	I will . . . .
My hair and getting dressed	Treat myself to cherry lip gloss, nail polish, a hair clip, or other item from my treats drawer.
Feeding the cat	Hold the cat as she purrs.
Helping with dishes	Pick out snack cake or other treat.
"Extra" from my weekly list	Eat my snack cake and watch a TV show.
My Saturday chores	Call whichever relative I choose (e.g., Aunt Marie).

How Rico Learned to Participate in Fire Drills

Box 14–3

Whenever the school fire alarm sounded, Rico would begin to scream and slap his face. Feeling pressured to evacuate the students safely, the third-grade teacher and paraprofessional would plead with him to leave. They had even tried carrying him out of the building, but Rico became aggressive. The special education teacher designed a fire evacuation simulation training program for Rico. Each day, at a different time, the special education teacher or the paraprofessional asked Rico to choose two classmates from among those who had finished their work to practice a fire drill. In the first phase, the teacher rang a small buzzer briefly (a second) and used least prompts to teach Rico to follow the two chosen classmates to the school yard. Rico received continuous praise by the teacher and peers as he followed them without screaming or self-injury. When he returned to the classroom, he was given the choice of listening to a musical relaxation tape or looking at a book (activities which he liked and found calming). Over time, the teacher made the buzzer longer and louder until it was more similar to the school fire alarm and faded praise to an intermittent schedule. Some of the peers who had frequently been chosen were then recruited to encourage Rico to follow them during an actual fire drill. When the next fire drill occurred, the peers went to Rico and calmly asked him to follow them. Rico went with them, but wanted to hold their hands. He cried, but was not screaming. At the end of the fire drill, Rico returned and went directly to the relaxation tape just as he had done during simulations. The decision was made to continue the training program, but to fade to a weekly schedule.

Students also may encounter emergencies that require knowing first aid skills. Spooner, Stem, and Test (1989) taught students to communicate an emergency, apply a bandage, take care of minor injuries, and respond to someone else choking. The instructor selected group instruction followed by individual practice sessions with a model and probe. The task analyses used are shown in Table 14–7. These first aid skills can also be taught with constant time delay (Gast, Winterling, Wolery, & Farmer, 1992), by using puppet simulations (Marchand-Martella, Martella, Christensen, Agran, & Young, 1992a), or peers who role play having wounds (Marchand-Martella, Martella, Christensen, Agran, & Young, 1992b).

Students may also need to learn other home safety skills to live more autonomously in their homes. For example, Winterling, Gast, Wolery, and Farmer (1992) taught students with moderate mental retardation to discard broken glass. The instructor taught the skill with constant time delay and simulations of broken glass (paper). Students practiced the skill in both their classroom and the home economics room. Tymchuk, Hamada, Andron, and Anderson (1990) taught mothers with mental retardation to assess and respond to 14 safety categories in their homes. They learned to recognize and correct hazards that could cause fire (e.g., matches left unattended), electric shock (e.g., hairdryer used over sink of water), suffocation (e.g., plastic bags), choking by young children (e.g., small objects on floor), and falls (e.g., clutter on floors and stairs).

Telephone Use

Telephone use can be related to a variety of daily living skills, such as placing orders, calling friends, or coping with an emergency. Risley and Cuvo (1980) taught emergency phone use. Their task analysis was similar to that of Spooner et al. (1989), but they also had pictures of emergency situations to begin each simulated emergency call.

Emergency calls are only one type of telephone use. Horner, Williams, and Steveley (1987) applied general case instruction to teach generalized phone use to four high school students with moderate and severe mental retardation. The instructional universe included frequently made and received calls. Training variations included the type of phone, its location, the person calling or being called, and the topic of conversation (e.g., to leave a message, place an order, make plans). Following instructions across these variations, students were able to make a wide range of phone calls.

Sometimes students lack the academic skills needed to dial the phone. Lalli, Mace, Browder, and Brown (1989) taught an adult with little number recognition to dial the phone by matching numbers to the phone. Current technology makes it possible to bypass this step altogether by using speed dialing or voice activation on a home or office phone. In contrast, teaching number matching may still be important for using public phones.

TABLE 14–7
Task Analysis of First Aid

Communicating an Emergency	Applying a Plastic Bandage
1. Locate phone	1. Look at injury
2. Pick up receiver	2. Find bandages needed
3. Dial 9	3. Select proper size
4. Dial 1	4. Find outside tabs of wrapper
5. Dial 1	5. Pull down tabs to expose bandage
6. Put receiver to ear	6. Find protective covering on bandage
7. Listen for operator	7. Pull off by tabs, exposing gauze portion
8. Give full name	8. Do not touch gauze portion
9. Give full address	9. Apply to clean, dry skin
10. Give phone number	
11. Explain emergency	
12. Hang up after operator does	

Taking Care of Minor Injuries	First Aid for Choking
1. Let it bleed a little to wash out the dirt	1. Let the person cough and try to get object out of throat
2. Wash with soap and water	2. Stand behind victim
3. Dry with clean cloth	3. Wrap your arms around victim
4. Open plastic bandage	4. Make a fist with one hand, placing the thumb side of the clinched fist against the victim's abdomen—slightly above the navel and below the rib cage.
5. Cover with bandage (hold by the edges)	5. Press fist into abdomen with a quick, upward thrust
6. Call 911 if severe and no adult available	6. Repeat step 5 as needed.

Note: From "Teaching First Aid Skills to Adolescents Who Are Moderately Mentally Handicapped" by F. Spooner, B. Stem, and D. W. Test, 1989, *Education and Training in Mental Retardation, 24,* p. 343. Copyright 1989 by the Division on Mental Retardation and Developmental Disabilities, Council on Exceptional Children. Reprinted by permission.

Sex Education

Another daily living skill is self-management of personal sexuality. McCabe and Cummins (1996) compared the attitudes of adults with mild mental retardation to those of young adults in a psychology class towards sexuality and found that adults with mental retardation had less knowledge about all issues except body parts and menstruation and were less experienced in intimacy and sexual intercourse. They also had more negative feelings about sexual issues. Wolfe and Blanchett (1997) note that sex education is an important part of transition planning. Their survey on educators' attitudes towards sex education supported the importance of teacher-parent collaboration in teaching this information.

Research examples provide some guidance on how to teach menstrual care. For example, Epps, Stern, and Horner (1990) taught girls to manage their periods by using simulations and general case instruction. The James Stanfield video "Janet's Got Her Period" listed in Table 14–3 can provide a good resource for introducing the concept of menstrual care. In this video, a sister and mother teach Janet how to use sanitary products to manage her period.

Planning what to teach in the area of sex education can be difficult. Collaboration between the teacher and parents is important to honor the family's values and determine what information is most relevant for an individual student. One area of sex education that can be especially appropriate to teach for school and the community is that of recognizing and respecting personal boundaries. Students sometimes do not discriminate between who can be trusted with a hug and who cannot or lack understanding about their personal versus public body parts or activities. The "Circles" curriculum listed in Table 14–3 provides videotapes and color coding to teach students to discriminate among different types of relationships. For example, the purple private circle is for the student alone. Some "circles" (relationships) welcome hugs, but some hugs should give the people space between bodies (friends versus lovers). People in the red zone (strangers) are not given physical or verbal contact. This program can be used to teach avoidance of sexual harassment and abuse and helps the participant know how to let relationships develop from acquaintances to friendships. By selecting photographs of people the student knows and color coding them, the discrimination can be made more concrete. Students also may need to practice their ability to discriminate when encountering people in the community. For example, the teacher might say "What zone is Mr. Jones? He's an acquaintance. What do we do? Just wave—no hugs." For students who make inappropriate physical contact with the teacher or others, the teacher may use color coding on clothing to help the student know what "zones" are appropriate (e.g., a green patch on the arm to tap her for attention). Aaron's parents had some specific concerns that needed to be considered in planning for his transition to supported living (see Box 14–4).

Skills For the Community

An important part of a student's transition to adult living is to acquire the skills needed for community settings. These skills include public safety, mobility in the community, and use of community resources like stores, banks, and restaurants. As described earlier in this chapter, teachers will often use some combination of school and community instruction to address these skill needs for students who are in the middle and high school years. Students who are beyond high school age need age-appropriate alternatives to a high school building. These alternatives may include a job, college classes, and an apartment with substantial community-based instruction. Younger students (elementary age) may focus more on school-based skills but also may receive some community-based instruction, depending on their individual needs and parental preferences.

Safety Skills

To gain increased autonomy in the community, students need to acquire skills for public safety. Collins, Stinson, and Land (1993) addressed this need by teaching students with moderate mental retardation to cross streets and use public phones. Collins et al. (1993) compared teaching these skills only in the community setting versus using a combination of simulation and community-based instruction. In the classroom simulation, the instructor created the simulation with masking tape to outline streets and by

---

    Aaron's Sex Education Program

Box 14–4

After Aaron's last transition planning meeting, his mother, Ms. Williams, asked to talk with his special education teacher, Mr. Delaney, privately. Ms. Williams said that one of her greatest fears about Aaron's transition to supported living was that someone would sexually abuse him. She shared that she and her husband had not known how to explain sex to Aaron or help him understand his physical maturity. In a follow-up meeting with Aaron's parents, Mr. Delaney shared the *Circles I and II* and *Sexuality Education for Persons with Severe Developmental Disabilities* curricula (see Table 14–3). He recommended teaching Aaron body parts, discrimination of private and public body zones, appropriate social behavior, and abuse prevention. Mr. Delaney suggested teaching these skills in a classroom format with three other young men who needed similar training by using the slides, videos, and pictures available in the commercial curricula. He recommended inviting young adults from an area college, who did date-rape prevention training sessions, to talk about self-esteem and the body. He also proposed including Aaron in some of the residence hall training sessions at this college because the role play situations would help Aaron generalize his "no/go/tell" abuse prevention skills. He encouraged the Williams to talk with Aaron about their values related to human sexuality. Mr. Delaney also invited Aaron and the Williams to a program on "Sexuality and Disability." At this program, a couple with disabilities would be sharing their story about overcoming others' resistance to their dating, privacy, and marriage. Before implementing these plans, Mr. Delaney submitted a written proposal of the sex education program to both his supervisor and the parents for written approval. He also planned to keep detailed written lesson plans for the material covered in each day's lesson that could be shared with the students' parents or his supervisor whenever requested.

using a disconnected phone. The instructor applied progressive time delay to teach the task analysis for each skill. Although results were mixed with the simulation providing no clear advantage over in vivo instruction alone, the simulation may be useful to augment community-based instruction when time, resources, and school-based priorities limit in vivo training time.

Another aspect of public safety is to avoid abduction. Watson, Bain, and Houghton (1992) taught children with moderate mental retardation to discriminate between familiar people and strangers. When approached by a stranger on the street, the children learned a "no-go-tell" response. That is, they learned to tell the stranger no, to leave the area, and to tell another adult what happened. People unfamiliar to the children were employed by the researchers to approach the children in the community to determine if they had mastered the skills. The children did use their "no-go-tell" response sequence. Similarly, Haseltine and Miltenberger (1990) taught adults with mild mental retardation self-protection through role play. Participants also learned a "no-go-tell" response to refuse advances, leave the area, and tell a trusted adult what happened.

Purchasing

Another popular area for instruction is making purchases in the community (shopping). Three important questions teachers need to consider before teaching students to make purchases are:

1. Is the goal to teach the student to make a specific purchase (e.g., school lunch) or a set of purchases (e.g., use of convenience stores)? That is, to what extent will generalization be taught?
2. To what extent will the student be taught to apply academic skills to use money while purchasing (e.g., counting dollars) versus using compensatory strategies (e.g., preselected money amount)?
3. How can the student gain autonomy in purchasing?

If the goal is for the student to learn to purchase a short list of items in the grocery store that is used consistently by the student's family, the teacher might focus on teaching list reading and item selection in a school simulation and then provide community-based instruction in that one store. In contrast, if the goal is for the student to be able to use a wide variety

of stores to make different types of purchases (e.g., clothing, leisure materials, groceries), training should focus on this variation in both school- and community-based instruction.

Generalization in Purchasing

Several researchers have addressed the issue of how many settings are needed for students to master purchasing skills. One outcome of this research is the realization that students perform best when they learn to respond to the variation in community stores. This may be achieved through using simulations that introduce this variation. For example, McDonnell and Horner (1985) created slides to introduce a wide variety of stores and found better generalization of skills than in using community-based training in only one store. Westling, Floyd, and Carr (1990) applied role play to teach community purchasing, trained in one community store, and found generalization across stores. Similarly, Aeschleman and Schladenhauffen (1984) found community generalization from role play training. Haring, Kennedy, Adams, and Pitts-Conway (1987) trained young adults with autism to shop by using their school cafeteria and a convenience store near the school. When this training did not yield generalization across stores, they trained using videotapes of a variety of stores. Students were then able to purchase in a bookstore, drugstore, and grocery store.

While these studies provide important evidence that well-designed training using videotapes, slides, or role play can produce generalization to the community, they must be viewed with caution. McDonnell, Horner, and Williams (1984) found that participants with moderate and severe mental retardation failed to generalize from role play or slides to the community until given community-based instruction. Similarly, Alcantara (1994) found progress with simulated instruction with videotapes, but not mastery for all students until in vivo instruction was introduced. As a general guideline, some community probes are needed to ensure that students are generalizing their skills from school to actual community contexts. In contrast, well-designed simulations can encourage generalization across community settings better than training in only one community context.

Teaching Money Use

A second aspect of teaching purchasing is to help students know how to use their money. Several recommendations for teaching money skills can be found in the chapter on functional academics, including supplying a preselected amount of money (McDonnell & Horner, 1985), teaching students to use certain denominations of money for specific purchases (Gardill and Browder, 1995), and teaching a "one more than" money counting strategy (Test, Howell, Burkhart, and Beroth, 1993).

To gain autonomy in purchasing, students need not only to know how to use money but also how to plan their purchases and perform the steps of a purchasing routine (Figure 14–5). To teach students to plan purchases, Sandknop, Schuster, Wolery, and Cross (1992) taught students to select the lower-priced item from among grocery prices. Using constant time delay, the instructor taught students to look at two prices on a number line that was written vertically to determine which was "lower." Across training phases, students learned to compare not only the first digit of the price, but then the second, third, and fourth. Frederick-Dugan, Test, and Varn (1991) developed a general case analysis of three types of purchases: food, clothing, and hygiene items. The instructor showed the student pictures of items from each category and a price up to $20.00. The students determined if they could buy the items by using a calculator. The instructor used progressive time delay to teach the students to compare the price to the money they had to determine if it could or could not be purchased.

Autonomy in Purchasing

Autonomy can also be encouraged by teaching students to make the purchase with little to no teacher assistance. To be successful, the student may need social skills, as well as knowing the specifics of how to make the purchase at the register. Westling et al. (1990) taught these social skills as part of a purchasing program. These social skills are shown in Table 14–8 in a program designed for Julia to purchase items at discount department stores. By learning skills such as asking for help and being polite, Julia is more likely to have positive experiences when shopping alone or with friends.

One set of social skills that may be needed is asking for help. Chadsey-Rusch, Drasgow, Reinoehl, Hallet, and Collet-Klingenberg (1993) developed a general case approach to teach students to request help in community settings. For example, students might ask for help to negotiate curbs in getting into the store. Or,

like Julia's example in Table 14–8, students may learn to ask for help across a variety of situations encountered in the store (e.g., finding the store section, finding the item on the shelf). With these social and communication skills, students can learn to navigate community routines like purchasing with no more teacher assistance than they need or want.

Dining Out and Buying Snacks

Another popular community activity is dining out and purchasing snacks at convenience stores or vending machines. Many of the instructional procedures that have been described earlier in this chapter have also been used to teach dining out or snack purchases, including general case instruction (McDonnell & Ferguson, 1988; Sprague & Horner, 1984), time delay (Browder et al., 1988; McDonnell, 1987), least intrusive prompts (McDonnell, 1987; Storey, Bates, & Hanson, 1984), and most to least intrusive prompts with chaining (McDonnell & Laughlin, 1989). The school cafeteria provides an important and easy resource for learning to purchase food. Teachers will probably also want to include community-based instruction for dining out to enhance motivation, generalization, and choice. Research supports all three of these benefits for community-based instruction. In evaluating motivation, Belfiore, Browder, and Mace (1993) found that adults with severe disabilities had more adaptive behaviors and fewer maladaptive behaviors when having a beverage in a community setting compared with a day program. Belfiore, Browder, and Mace (1994) observed that these same adults were more likely to show distinctive preferences for beverages when in community restaurants. In studying generalization, researchers found benefits for using a general case approach across community settings (McDonnell & Ferguson, 1988; Sprague & Horner, 1984).

Community settings also may provide more opportunity for students to learn choice-making skills. Cooper and Browder (in press) taught adults with severe disabilities to make four distinctive choices while using fast food restaurants, including the entry/exit doors, the specific food to be purchased, the condiments or paper products desired, and the choice of seating. They found that teaching these choices increased the participants' independent performance of the purchasing routine more than the

FIGURE 14–5

(a) Pete "preps" for his trip to the community with his teacher by making a picture shopping list and then gathering his money and ID. (b) Once at K-Mart, Pete and his teacher practice safe crossing of the street, (c) get a shopping cart, and begin searching for the items on their list. Pete searches the shelf (d) while using his picture shopping list and (e) compares the brand picture to the actual items in order to select an item that matches his list.

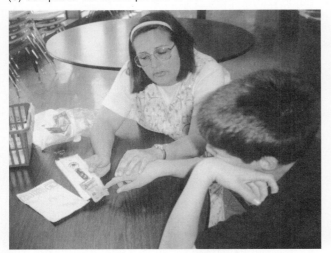

a

b

c

d

FIGURE 14–5 *(continued)*
Finally, (f) Pete finds a short line and pays for the items he has selected.

e   f

Thanks to Vickie Block of Charlottesville High School and Deb Morris of Walker School and their students for sharing their work with us.

TABLE 14–8
Task Analysis of Shopping Skills

Student: Julia	**Skill: Purchasing at discount department stores (e.g., K-Mart, Walmart)**
Purchasing Step	**Related Social Skill**
1. Enter door	Wait turn if needed
2. Go to correct store section	Ask help to find correct section
	Say "thank you" when given help
3. Find correct shelf	Ask help if can't find item on shelf
	Say "thank you" when given help
4. Select correct item(s)	
5. Go to register	Wait turn at checkout counter
	Keep cart from bumping others
6. Put item on counter	Greet cashier
7. Take out money	
8. Use "next dollar strategy"	
9. Give money to cashier	
10. Put change and receipt away	
11. Pick up purchased item	Say "goodbye" or "thanks"
12. Exit store	Wait turn at door to exit

Note: From D. L. Westling, J. Floyd., & D. Carr, 1990. Effects of single setting versus multiple setting training on learning to shop in a department store. *American Journal on Mental Retardation, 94,* 616–624. Copyright (1990) by American Association on Mental Retardation. Adapted with permission.

use of least intrusive prompting alone. The method employed to teach these choice-making skills is shown in Table 14–9.

Given the advantage of teaching students skills for purchasing snacks or meals in the community at least some of the time, it is notable that simulations can provide an important resource for this instruction as well. Earlier in this chapter, the work of Sowers and Powers (1995) was described, in which real food items were brought in to train a simulation in a school setting. The students' parents learned to implement the program for family carryover. Browder, Snell, and Wildonger (1988) employed a simulation of vending machines as an adjunct to community-based instruction, which helped to save both time and money. Similarly, teachers of elementary and high school students may choose to augment community-

based instruction by teaching purchasing in the school cafeteria, at a school vending machine, and with classroom simulations of community settings. In contrast, students who are postsecondary age can receive all of their instruction in community contexts. For example, these older students may learn to purchase food on a break in their job or in a community college setting or while dining at a fast food restaurant with friends.

Community Leisure

Besides dining out, another enjoyable community activity is participating in leisure activities. These activities may include going to concerts or movies, participating in fitness classes, walking in the park, participating in clubs, and going to special commu-

---

TABLE 14–9
Prompting Choice in Restaurants for Individuals with Severe Mental Retardation Who Are Nonverbal

Choice:	Entry door
Options:	Teacher escorts participant to two adjacent entry doors.
Prompting Choice:	1. Teacher waits for participant to select a door 2. Teacher points to the two doors and says, "Which one?"
Feedback:	If participant touches a door, teacher praises, "Great choice!" If participant does not teacher says, "I'm not sure which door you want. Let's use this one" (and points to one).
Prompting Performance:	1. Teacher waits for participant to open selected door. 2. Teacher uses verbal, "Open the door." 3. Teacher uses gesture/verbal, "Open this door." 4. Teacher uses partial physical guidance and verbal, "Let me help you get the door open."
Choice:	Food selection
Options:	Teacher offers two pictures of food or drink.
Prompting Choice:	1. Teacher waits for participant to touch one picture. 2. Teacher points to the pictures and says, "Which one?"
Feedback:	If participant touches a picture, teacher praises, "Fine! You'd like a Coke today." If participant does not touch, teacher says, "I'm not sure what you want today. Let's try french fries."
Prompting Performance:	1. Teacher waits for participant to hand cashier the food picture. 2. Teacher uses verbal, "Hand her/him the picture." 3. Teacher uses gesture/verbal, "Hand her/him the picture" (pointing to cashier). 4. Teacher uses partial physical guidance, "Let me help you give him/her the picture."

Note: From K. J. Cooper & D. M. Browder (1998). Enhancing choice and participation for adults with severe disabilities in community settings. *Journal of the Association for Persons with Severe Handicaps, 33,* 252–260. Copyright (1999) by The Association for Persons with Severe Handicaps. Adapted with permission.

nity events. A challenge in providing leisure instruction is determining where and how to teach so that students learn skills without losing the chance to make friends and have fun. One opportunity to provide intensive leisure instruction in inclusive contexts for school-aged students is a school- or community-sponsored summer program. Hamre-Nietupski et al. (1992) described an approach to extended school year programming that focused on inclusive leisure activities. An extended school year program is a public school service that is offered to students with severe disabilities beyond the typical 180-day school year because it is needed to prevent skill regression. Not all students with severe disabilities qualify for these services, but those who do sometimes end up in segregated summer programs unless creative options like inclusive leisure activities are considered. Hamre-Nietupski et al. (1992) selected local playground programs, the swimming pool, and week-long camps to design an inclusive extended school year program. The special educators planned jointly with the recreational staff to adapt activities for increased participation. In this inclusive leisure program, a T-ball was used during softball and a large dowel was used for roasting hot dogs.

In addition to summer programming, school and community extracurricular activities provide opportunities for leisure instruction. For example, many schools have music groups, pep clubs, special interest (such as computers) clubs, and intramural sports. Through collaboration with the sponsors of these activities and the student's caregivers, arrangements can be developed for the student with severe disabilities to have access to these opportunities. Important considerations in planning these activities include: (a) assessing and honoring individual preferences for activities, (b) teaching individuals to self-initiate leisure activities, and (c) providing instruction or support to participate in inclusive settings. Each of these considerations is now described.

Honoring Choice in Leisure Activities

Most people pursue leisure activities for relaxation, fun, friendship, or fitness. An important aspect of leisure activities that makes them fun and relaxing is that they are optional. People choose what to do with their leisure time, including the choice to do nothing! Similarly, individuals with severe disabilities need the opportunity to choose how to spend leisure time. While some individuals will be able to make these choices by telling others what they want to do or by initiating activities on their own, others need the opportunity to sample new leisure options to decide which to pursue. Sometimes these choices can then be expressed through selecting pictures of the activities or by using some other communication system (e.g., signing, communication board).

A challenge some teachers face is understanding the activity preferences of students who do not have a formal system of communication. Research on preference assessment with students who do not have symbolic communication has focused on selecting objects that can then be used or consumed (Lohrmann-O'Rourke & Browder, 1998). In contrast, selecting an activity requires using some type of symbolic representation of the options. Browder, Cooper, and Lim (1998) demonstrated how to teach using symbols to choose leisure activities. In a three-phase study, they first assessed participants' preferences for activities at community sites and in a day program by timing the duration of their participation in activities at each site. Once clear preferences emerged, they taught the participants to select an object to represent each activity. Using massed trials and a time delay prompting system, the instructor taught the participants to select a golf ball for golf, a library card to go to the library, a nametag for a club, or shoes for an aerobics class. This instruction occurred immediately before beginning the leisure activity. Because the focus of the study was the choice of leisure settings (community versus day program), participants learned to associate different objects with the same activity in different settings. For example, an orange golf ball was chosen for the day program site and a white golf ball for the community golf course. Once the participants mastered associating the object with the activity, the third phase of the intervention was to give the participants a choice between settings (e.g., orange versus white golf ball). The participant was then given assistance (e.g., transportation and an instructor) to go to the chosen setting and engage in the activity. Interestingly, all three participants consistently chose the community-based activities.

Although this study focused on choice of settings, the teacher might want to use objects associated with different leisure activities that are all community-based. For example, an empty popcorn container might be used for the movies (or a ticket), a baseball cap of a favorite team might be selected for attending a sports event, or a program might be used for the theater or a concert. Whatever object is chosen, the student may need direct instruction for several months to master the association between the object and the activity before using the object to make a meaningful choice.

Teaching Self-Initiation of Leisure Activities

The second consideration in planning instruction for leisure activities is to encourage the students' self-direction in activities. The pictorial self-management that Pierce and Schriebman (1994) developed to teach children with autism to self-initiate daily living activities might also be adapted for leisure activities. For example, students could be taught to use a photo book to select and begin an activity. Students who can use picture symbols may also be able to learn to self-schedule leisure activities. Bambara and Ager (1992) taught adults with developmental disabilities to use pictures to self-schedule leisure activities in the up-coming week. The participants also initiated contact with staff to request any necessary support (e.g., transportation or an escort). The pictures used were from the Attainment Company's "Plan Your Day Curriculum" shown in Table 14–3. Devine, Malley, Sheldon, Datillo, and Gast (1997) also evaluated an intervention to teach adults with mild to moderate mental retardation to initiate leisure activities. Similar to Bambara and Ager (1992), they taught participants to use a calendar and pictures for self-scheduling. They also compared having the participants put a reminder on their wall calendar to giving participants a morning phone call prompt about the selected activity. Both prompting methods increased participants' self-initiation of community leisure activities (Box 14–5).

Instruction for Participation in Leisure Activities

In addition to teaching students responses that can be used to choose and self-schedule leisure activities, instruction and other forms of support may also be needed to participate in these activities. Some students will benefit from direct instruction using a task analysis and prompt system, such as time delay or least intrusive prompting. For example, Zhang, Gast, Horvat, and Datillo (1995) taught adolescents with severe disabilities "lifetime sport skills," including bowling, overhand throwing, and short distance putting. The instructor employed a physical prompt and con-

---

  Aaron's Winter Break

Box 14–5

Aaron enrolled in classes at his area community college and found a part-time job in the bookstore. The college and bookstore were closed for a month between the fall and spring semesters. Aaron's teacher, Mr. Delaney, needed to plan ways to provide meaningful instruction related to his IEP during this "downtime." After interviewing some of Aaron's classmates, Mr. Delaney found that many students looked forward to this break as extended leisure time. Mr. Delaney decided to use this time to teach Aaron to self-schedule leisure activities and to make arrangements for support to participate. For example, the paraprofessional who served as Aaron's job coach was available to provide assistance in leisure activities while the college bookstore was closed. Because Aaron lived in an urban area, there were a number of cultural events, museums, sports events, and seasonal activities from which to choose. Mr. Delaney also encouraged Aaron to make specific plans with fellow students during the last week of classes. Aaron invited classmates to join him by handing them an informal note that Mr. Delaney had helped him prepare on the computer. By the time school was out, Aaron had a calendar of both scheduled activities and open days. At the beginning of each day, Mr. Delaney taught Aaron to review his plans for the day. If he had free time, Aaron chose an activity from a picture list of options. He then created a picture schedule for the day by putting the pictures in sequence. Aaron then requested any needed assistance. For example, Mr. Delaney had Aaron use his touch talker to request the van. Mr. Delaney would then call to check the schedule with the public transportation company. If arrangements could not be made on short notice, Aaron put the picture in a stack of items to be considered for the next week and selected another picture. Aaron then scheduled a week ahead for activities that required more planning. For example, on Wednesday, he selected pictures for the next Wednesday's schedule. He then requested assistance that would be needed. For example, he would again press "van" to ask Mr. Delaney to try to schedule transportation for the next week or "time" to ask him to check to see if the special museum exhibit would still be open the next week.

stant time delay to fade teacher assistance. All of the participants mastered the sport skills. Similarly, Bolton, Belfiore, Lalli, and Skinner (1994) taught adults with severe to profound mental retardation to putt in golf. They used stimulus fading by introducing guide boards for the golf ball that were then faded in size until the participant could get the ball in the hole with no guide.

Leisure skills can also be taught using self-directed learning strategies. LeGrice and Blampied (1994) employed videotaped prompting to teach adolescents with moderate mental retardation to operate a video recorder and personal computer. To teach the participants to use the video to self-instruct, the instructor would give a nonspecific verbal prompt, e.g., "What's next?", and show the videotaped step. If the participant did not perform the step, the video was rewound and the step was shown again until the participant performed the step using the video. Self-management strategies can be especially useful for fitness activities. Ellis, Cress, and Spellman (1990) taught individuals with moderate to severe mental retardation to increase their duration of walking in either hallways or on a treadmill with self-monitoring and self-reinforcement. During hall walking, the participant carried batons (like relay racers in the Olympics) and discarded one after each lap. When they had discarded all batons, they gave themselves a sticker in a notebook. Using a changing criterion design, the instructor helped the participants increase the number of batons carried (laps walked) across time. Similarly, in using the treadmill, the participants learned to set the timer for longer periods of time across weeks of training.

Since many leisure skills are performed with family members or at home, it may also be beneficial to get interested family members involved in instruction of leisure skills. For example, Wall and Gast (1997) taught caregivers (i.e., adult sibling, parent, houseparent) to teach leisure skills to adolescents with moderate mental retardation. The caregivers learned to use task analyses and constant time delay to teach activities like horseshoes, checkers, croquet, board games, and turning the radio to a preferred station.

If developed well, leisure instruction need not impede the social benefits of participating in inclusive leisure settings. Vandercook (1991) taught adolescents with severe mental retardation two activities that were popular with youth in their school (bowling

and pinball). After determining the least intrusive effective prompt for each student, the teacher instructed the students in the bowling and pinball skills at the community bowling alley. Once a week participants with severe disabilities bowled with peers who were nondisabled. During this weekly bowling time with peers, the teacher did not interact with the dyad nor prompt performance of bowling and pinball. As participants increased their bowling and pinball skills with the teacher, they generalized these skills to their weekly time with a peer. The peers also indicated a significant increase in their scores on attitude towards individuals with disabilities.

Breen and Haring (1991) evaluated how important it was for the peers with disabilities to have direct training in the leisure activity selected for peer inclusion. They selected eight computer games and provided intensive training in four of the games before setting opportunities for the adolescents with moderate mental retardation to play the games with their peers who were nondisabled. The instructor used a task analysis and least intrusive prompting to teach the four trained games. Using an alternating treatment design, they found that social initiations, game satisfaction, and peer satisfaction were all higher when playing the trained games versus the untrained games. This study and the work of Vandercook (1991) illustrate the potential need to provide intensive teacher training as an adjunct to opportunities to engage in activities with peers.

While both of these studies trained and then simply observed peer interaction, some individuals with more severe disabilities may need ongoing, intensive support to participate in the leisure activity. When this occurs, the teacher may be able to transfer support to peers in the context of the activity. For example, Cooper and Browder (1997) trained adults with severe disabilities to participate in a water exercise class at the YMCA. Once each participant could perform the exercise response with a minimum of prompting, the instructor encouraged peers to exercise beside the participant and offer occasional verbal prompting. Another alternative is to involve peers as tutors from the beginning of leisure instruction.

Another way to promote self-initiated leisure skills is to teach students an entire leisure routine. Sometimes the reason students cannot self-initiate a leisure activity is because they have learned only one component of the activity (e.g., how to bowl) rather than the entire routine. Schleien, Certo, and Muccino (1984) illustrated how to teach an entire routine of using a bowling alley to a student with severe mental retardation. Instruction focused not only on how to bowl, but also on how to purchase a drink, and use the vending machine. The participant was able to generalize these skills to three other bowling alleys without additional instruction. Taylor, McKelvey, and Sisson (1993) also taught the entire routine for two skills (ordering a pizza and renting a video) to individuals with multiple disabilities (visual and physical impairments, mental retardation). For ordering the pizza, the skill cluster included using the phone, interacting with the delivery person, cutting and serving the pizza, and cleaning up. The students were also taught problem solving skills. In renting a video, the students learned to ask the counter person to recommend a video if they could not find one that they liked or to help them find one on the shelf. Both skill clusters were taught in school simulations using a system of least prompts and "props" (e.g., pizza box, video boxes, phone).

Banking

To participate in many of the community activities described, students will need to acquire money management skills. The chapter on functional academics describes how to teach money skills. This section describes approaches to teaching bill paying and banking. LaCampagne and Cipani (1987) describe a method for teaching adults with mild and moderate mental retardation to pay their bills. Instructional materials included a checkbook, check recorder, several real bills with their payment envelope (e.g., electric company, credit card, telephone bill), and a calculator. Through task analytic instruction, the participants learned to write a check, record the amount in their checkbook, and put the payment in the payment envelope. Zencius, Davis, and Cuvo (1990) taught similar skills but used a personalized system of instruction in which students could proceed through learning the materials at their own pace.

Besides paying bills, students also can benefit from knowing how to use the bank. McDonnell and Ferguson (1989) taught high school students with moderate disabilities to use both an automated teller and to cash checks in a bank, while also comparing the use of a decreasing prompt hierarchy with constant time delay. All instruction was community-

based. Both methods of prompting were effective, but the decreasing prompts were slightly more efficient. Using an automatic teller can be taught in school through simulated instruction. Shafer, Inge, and Hill (1986) made a simulated automatic teller from plywood. They found that the simulated instruction was more private and prevented the problem of the machine confiscating the card when too many mistakes were made. Bourbeau, Sowers, and Close (1986) developed a similar simulation in a school workroom. The participants with mild mental retardation mastered using the simulated automated teller and generalized their skills to a real machine in the community. In contrast, Shafer et al. (1986) found that generalization to the community automated teller was incomplete until some in vivo remedial training was conducted.

For either recording checks or using an automatic teller, some students may need to learn a strategy to enter numbers accurately. Wacker et al. (1988) found that teaching individuals with moderate mental retardation self-labeling increased their number entry accuracy. To self-label, students said each number aloud. Students learned to "say then do" the number entry. That is, they said each number aloud before entering it into a calculator or computer.

Community Mobility

Community mobility involves pedestrian safety, being able to use public transportation, and finding locations in the community. The research on street crossing shows that this is one set of community skills for which in vivo instruction has clear advantages over classroom simulations (Marchetti, McCartney, Drain, Hooper, & Dix, 1983; Matson, 1980; Page, Iwata, & Neef, 1976). For some students, the most important street crossing skill to master is crossing streets with an escort (a partial participation goal). The task analysis focuses on walking or propelling a wheelchair near the escort, stopping at curbs, crossing when given a verbal or physical cue, and crossing without stopping in the street. For other students, the outcome is independent street crossing. When independence is the goal, it is important to take a general case approach to teach the variations of streets encountered in a particular community (Horner, Jones, & Williams, 1985). For example, the range of stimulus variation the student may encounter includes the speed of cars, the number of cars, changes in lights, the type of pedestrian signals (e.g., words, pictures), the number of lanes, traffic directions (e.g., one-way or two-way), the angle of crossing (e.g., straight, diagonal), and the type of street (e.g., stop sign, traffic light). Horner et al. (1985) trained on 10 different streets daily and probed with untrained streets until it was clear that participants could cross a variety of streets safely.

Some individuals with severe disabilities need instruction to learn to walk from one location to another without stopping, wandering, or sitting down on the ground. Gruber, Reeser, and Reid (1979) taught four men with profound mental retardation to walk from one building to another in an institution by using backward chaining. The men learned to walk the last fourth of the way to their school, then half the way, and so on until they could walk the entire path alone. Similarly, Spears, Rusch, York, and Lilly (1981) taught a boy to walk from his school bus to his classroom. They used pacing prompts (verbal reminders) to encourage the boy to keep walking without pausing. An alternative to teaching the individual to walk to the destination without pausing is to encourage socialization along the way. For example, Collozi and Pollow (1984) taught elementary-aged students to walk from the school lobby to their classrooms but allowed time for social exchanges along the way.

Individuals who use wheelchairs may also learn to wheel themselves to the desired location or to indicate where they want to go through the use of pictures (Reid & Hurlburt, 1977).

In Aaron's pedestrian program he is taught to indicate by gesture when it is safe to cross; to choose to operate his motorized wheelchair alone or to request assistance, depending on the type of street and his own preference at the time; and to steer his wheelchair safely near other pedestrians using the sidewalk.

Another pedestrian skill is to find the way to a given location. Finding locations in some communities is complex and may require recognition of key landmarks. Singleton, Schuster, and Ault (1995) taught students to recognize community signs (e.g., "barber," "Denny's," "KOA") and their meaning. For example, students learned that a barber gives a haircut. Although not a focus of their instruction, such community sign recognition could be combined with teaching individuals a familiar route, such as walking to work or to the local community recreation center.

In some contexts, getting to these desired locations requires using public transportation, such as the bus or subway. Bus riding can be taught with some simulated practice. For example, slides can be developed to help students learn key landmarks to know when to get off the bus (Neef, Iwata, & Page, 1978; Robinson, Griffith, McComish, & Swasbrook, 1984). Such simulations do not always produce generalization to actual buses (Coon, Vogelsberg, & Williams, 1981); in contrast, individuals with severe disabilities can learn bus riding when all instruction is community-based (Sowers, Rusch, & Hudson, 1979). Table 14–10 provides a response sequence for

TABLE 14–10
Task Analysis for Teaching Bus Riding with Simulation

Students: Julia, Tom, Sarah	Skill: Bus Riding
Step of Task Analysis	**Video, Slide, or Picture Simulation**
1. Walk to bus stop	Pictures of nearby bus stops
2. Wait at bus stop	Show people waiting for bus
3. Identify correct bus	Pictures of buses that come to that stop
4. Signal bus to stop	Show person waving hand
5. Wait in line to enter bus	Show people in line
6. Enter front door of bus	Pictures of both bus doors
7. Give driver bus pass	Show driver and have real passes
8. Sit in empty seat or stand	Show seats that are empty and full
9. Identify destination	Pictures of landmarks
10. Pull cord for stop	Picture of cord
11. Exit rear door	Picture of inside bus doors
12. Move away from bus	Show person correct (moving away) and wrong (walking in front of bus)

teaching bus riding that uses simulations as an adjunct to community-based instruction. To practice bus riding, the teacher shows slides (or video clips) for each response in the task analysis.

> *When teaching Julia and some classmates to take the city bus to the mall, the teacher showed a videoclip or slides of bus stops near the school. When the correct bus stop was shown, students were encouraged to raise their hands. The teacher asked one student to verbalize what they do, "We get on the bus by Jack's Diner." She then showed video clips or slides of the various buses that stop at that destination. When the bus that says "West Mall" was shown, students again raised their hand and someone stated the step. This procedure continued until all steps were rehearsed. Next, the students applied these skills in an actual trip to the mall.*

Summary

In the past, professionals sometimes believed that individuals with severe disabilities gained access to home and community options by mastering skills for these contexts. As awareness increases about self-determination, it becomes clear that there are no prerequisite skills for having a home of one's own and having full access to the community. Increased awareness about inclusion in general education also has raised questions about using the school day for community-based instruction. This chapter describes how daily living and community skills can be taught in ways that honor and encourage self-determination and general education inclusion. Based on the research literature to date, some community-based instruction or probes are needed to ensure that skills learned through school opportunities or simulations generalize to real settings. For students who are beyond the typical school age, most of this instruction will probably take place in the community.

Procedures were given for teaching skills for home and the community that encourage student-directed learning, incorporate peer instruction and interaction when possible, and use powerful teaching strategies, such as constant time delay and least intrusive prompting. Readers are encouraged to select teaching techniques based on individual student characteristics and preferences rather than assuming that one method (e.g., one prompting system) is "best" for all individuals. This chapter included research-based guidelines for teaching food preparation, home management, safety, dining out, purchasing, leisure skills, banking, and community mobility. Person-centered planning is needed to determine which of these skills are relevant for an individual student.

Suggested Activities

1. Plan a school schedule for a student like Aaron, whose case study was described in this chapter. Assume that because Aaron is 21 years old, he will receive instruction in community contexts. If Aaron has a part-time job that lasts 3 hours per day, how and where will he spend the rest of his 6-hour school day? Who will provide his instruction?
2. Given the person-centered planning for Julia shown in Table 14–1, brainstorm a list of leisure activities. Consider her preference for being with her middle school friends. How might some of the community and domestic skills Julia needs be taught in the context of these activities?
3. Identify two community activities for Rico. What method of prompting might be used in teaching these skills to Rico? How can you avoid stigmatizing Rico while teaching in the community? Also make a list of several ways choice making can be incorporated during community-based instruction in these activities with Rico. How will you encourage Rico to make choices while in community activities? What advantages might this choice making have for Rico?

References

Aeschleman, S. R., & Schladenhauffen, J. (1984). Acquisition, generalization, and maintenance of grocery shopping skills by severely mentally retarded adolescents. *Applied Research in Mental Retardation, 5,* 245–258.

Agran, M., Fodor-Davis, J., & Moore, S. (1986). The effects of self-instructional training on job task sequencing: Suggesting a problem-solving strategy. *Education and Training of the Mentally Retarded, 21,* 273–281.

Alberto, P. A., Sharpton, W. R., Briggs, A., & Stright, M. H. (1986). Facilitating task acquisition through the use of a self-operated auditory prompting system. *Journal of The Association for Persons with Severe Handicaps, 11,* 85–91.

Alcantara, P. R. (1994). Effects of a videotape instructional package on the purchasing skills of children with autism. *Exceptional Children, 6,* 40–55.

Arnold-Reid, G. S., Schloss, P. J., & Alper, S. (1997). Teaching meal planning to youth with mental retardation in natural settings. *Remedial and Special Education*, 18,(3) 166–173.

Bambara, L. M., & Ager, C. (1992). Use of self-scheduling to promote self-directed leisure activity in home and community settings. *Journal of the Association for Persons with Severe Handicaps*, 17, 67–76.

Bambara, L. M., Ager, C., & Koger, F. (1994). The effects of choice and task preference on the work performance of adults with severe disabilities. *Journal of Applied Behavior Analysis*, 27, 555–556.

Bambara, L. M., Cole, C., & Koger, F. (in press). Translating self-determination concepts into support for adults with severe disabilities. *Journal of The Association for Persons with Severe Handicaps*.

Bambara, L. M., & Koger, F. (1996). Opportunities for daily choice making. *Innovations*. Washington, DC: American Association on Mental Retardation.

Bambara, L. M., Koger, F., Katzer, T., & Davenport, T. (1995). Embedding choice in daily routines: An experimental case study. *Journal of The Association of Persons with Severe Handicaps*, 20, 185–195.

Belfiore, P. J., Browder, D. M., & Mace, F. C. (1993). The effects of community and center-based settings on the alertness of persons with profound mental retardation. *Journal of Applied Behavior Analysis*, 26, 401–402.

Belfiore, P. J., Browder, D. M., & Mace, F. C. (1994). Assessing choice-making and preference in adults with profound mental retardation across community and center-based settings. *Journal of Behavioral Education*, 4, 217–225.

Bolton, J. L., Belfiore, P. J., Lalli, J. S., & Skinner, C. H. (1994). The effects of stimulus modification on putting accuracy for adults with severe or profound mental retardation. *Education and Training in Mental Retardation and Developmental Disabilities*, 29, 236–242.

Bourbeau, P. E., Sowers, J., & Close, D. W. (1986). An experimental analysis of generalization of banking skills from classroom to bank settings in the community. *Education and Training of the Mentally Retarded*, 21, 98–106.

Breen, C. G., & Haring, T. G. (1991). Effects of contextual competence on social initiations. *Journal of Applied Behavior Analysis*, 24, 337–348.

Briggs, A., Alberto, P., Sharpton, W., Berlin, K., McKinley, C., & Ritts, C. (1990). Generalized use of a self-operated audio prompt system. *Education and Training in Mental Retardation*, 25, 381–389.

Browder, D. M., Bambara, L. M., & Belfiore, P. J. (in press). Using a person centered approach in community-based instruction. *Journal of Behavioral Education*.

Browder, D. M., Cooper, K. J., & Lim, L. (1998). Teaching adults with severe disabilities to express their choice of settings for leisure activities. *Education and Training in Mental Retardation and Developmental Disabilities*, 33, 228–238.

Browder, D. M., Hines, C., McCarthy, L. J., & Fees, J. (1984). A treatment package for increasing sight word recognition for use in daily living skills. *Education and Training of the Mentally Retarded*, 19, 191–200.

Browder, D. M., Snell, M. E., & Wildonger, B. A. (1988). Simulation and community-based instruction of vending machines with time delay. *Education and Training in Mental Retardation*, 23, 175–185.

Brown, F., Belz, P., Corsi, L., & Wenig, B. (1993). Choice diversity for people with severe disabilities. *Education and Training in Mental Retardation*, 28, 318–326.

Chadsey-Rusch, J., Drasgow, E., Reinoehl, B., Hallet, J., & Collet-Klingenberg, L. (1993). Using general-case instruction to teach spontaneous and generalized requests for assistance to learners with severe disabilities. *Journal of the Association for Persons with Severe Handicaps*, 18, 177–187.

Collins, B. C., Branson, T. A., & Hall, M. (1995). Teaching generalized reading of cooking product labels to adolescents with mental disabilities through the use of key words taught by peer tutors. *Education and Training in Mental Retardation and Developmental Disabilities*, 30, 65–75.

Collins, B. C., Stinson, D. M., & Land, L. (1993). A comparison of In Vivo and simulation prior to In Vivo instruction in teaching generalized safety skills. *Education and Training in Mental Retardation*, 28, 128–142.

Collozi, G. A., & Pollow, R. S. (1984). Teaching independent walking to mentally retarded children in public school. *Education and Training of the Mentally Retarded*, 22, 97–101.

Colyer, S. P., & Collins, B. C. (1996). Using natural cues within prompt levels to teach the next dollar strategy to students with disabilities. *Journal of Special Education*, 30, 305–318.

Coon, M. E., Vogelsberg, R. T., & Williams, W. (1981). Effects of classroom public transportation instruction on generalization to the natural environment. *Journal of the Association for the Severely Handicapped*, 6, 46–53.

Cooper, K. J., & Browder, D. M. (1997). The use of a personal trainer to enhance participation of older adults with severe disabilities in community water exercise classes. *Journal of Behavioral Education*, 7, 421–434.

Cooper, K. J., & Browder, D. M. (In press). Enhancing choice and participation for adults with severe disabilities in community-based instruction. *Journal of the Association for Persons with Severe Handicaps*.

Cuvo, A. J., Jacobi, E., & Sipko, R. (1981). Teaching laundry skills to mentally retarded students. *Education and Training of the Mentally Retarded*, 16, 54–64.

Denny, P. J., & Test, D. W. (1995). Using the one-more-than technique to teach money counting to individuals with moderate mental retardation: a systematic replication. *Education and Treatment of Children*, 18, 422–432.

Devine, M. A., Malley, S., Sheldon, K., Datillo, J., & Gast, D. L. (1997). Promoting initiation of community leisure participation for adults with mental retardation. *Education and Training in Mental Retardation and Developmental Disabilities*, 32, 241–254.

Dunlap, G, dePerczel, C. S., Clarke, S., Wilson, D., Wright, S., White, R., & Gomez, A. (1994). Choice making to promote adaptive behavior for students with emotional and behavioral challenges. *Journal of Applied Behavior Analysis*, 27, 505–518.

Dyer, K., Dunlap, G., & Winterling, V. (1990). Effects of choice-making on the serious problem behaviors of students with severe handicaps. *Journal of Applied Behavior Analysis*, 15, 515–524.

Ellis, D. N., Cress, P. J., & Spellman, C. R. (1990). Using timers and lap counters to promote self-management of independent exercise in adolescents with mental retardation. *Education and Training in Mental Retardation*, 27, 51–59.

Epps, S., Stern, R. J., & Horner, R. H. (1990). Comparison of simulation training on self and using a doll for teaching generalized menstrual care to women with severe mental retardation. *Research in Developmental Disabilities*, 11, 37–66.

Ferguson, D. L., & Baumgart, D. (1991). Partial participation revisited. *Journal of The Association for Persons with Severe Handicaps*, 16, 218–227.

Ford, A., & Mirenda, P. (1984). Community instruction: A natural cues and correction model. *Journal of The Association for Persons with Severe Handicaps, 9,* 79–88.

Frank, A. R., Wacker, D. P., Berg, W. K., & McMahon, C. M. (1985). Teaching selected microcomputer skills to retarded students via picture prompts. *Journal of Applied Behavior Analysis, 18,* 179–185.

Frederick-Dugan, A., Test, D. W., & Varn, L. (1991). Acquisition and generalization of purchasing skills using a calculator by students who are mentally retarded. *Education and Training in Mental Retardation, 26,* 381–387.

Gage, S. T., & Falvey, M. A. (1995). Assessment strategies to develop appropriate curricula and educational programs. In Falvey (Ed.), *Inclusive and heterogeneous schooling: Assessment, Curriculum, and Instruction* (pp. 59–86). Baltimore: Paul H. Brookes.

Gardill, M. C., & Browder, D. M. (1995). Teaching stimulus classes to encourage independent purchasing by students with severe behavior disorders. *Education and Training in Mental Retardation and Developmental Disabilities, 30,* 254–264.

Gast, D. L., Doyle, P. M., Wolery, M., Ault, M. J., & Farmer, J. A. (1991). Assessing the acquisition of incidental information by secondary-age students with mental retardation: Comparison of response prompting strategies. *American Journal on Mental Retardation, 96,* 63–80.

Gast, D. L., Winterling, V., Wolery, M., & Farmer, J. A. (1992). Teaching first-aid skills to students with moderate handicaps in small group instruction. *Education and Treatment of Children, 15,* 101–124.

Gomez, O., & Bambara, L. M. (December, 1996). *Complex problem solving.* Paper presented at the 22nd Annual Convention of The Association for Persons with Severe Handicaps, New Orleans, Louisiana.

Griffin, A. K., Wolery, M., & Schuster, J. W. (1992). Triadic instruction of chained food preparation responses: Acquisition and observational learning. *Journal of Applied Behavior Analysis, 25,* 257–279.

Gruber, B., Reeser, R., Reid, D. H. (1979). Providing a less restrictive environment for profoundly retarded persons by teaching independent walking skills. *Journal of Applied Behavior Analysis, 12,* 285–297.

Hall, M. G., Schuster, J. W., Wolery, M., Gast, D. L., & Doyle, P. M. (1992). Teaching chained skills in a non-school setting using a divided half instructional format. *Journal of Behavioral Education, 2,* 257–279.

Hamre-Nietupski, S., Nietupski, J., Krajewski, L., Moravec, J., Riehle, R., McDongal, J., Sensor, K., & Cantine-Stull, P. (1992). Enhancing integration during the summer: Combined educational and community recreation options for students with severe disabilities. *Education and Training in Mental Retardation, 27,* 68–74.

Haney, J. L., & Jones, R. T. (1982). Programming maintenance as a major component of a community-centered preventive effort: Escape from fire. *Behavior Therapy, 13,* 47–62.

Haring, T. G., Breen, C. G., Weimer, J., & Kennedy, C. H. (1995). Using videotape modeling to facilitate generalized purchasing skills. *Journal of Behavioral Education, 5,* 29–53.

Haring, T. G., Kennedy, C. H., Adams, M. J., & Pitts-Conway, V. (1987). Teaching generalization of purchasing skills across community settings to autistic youth using videotape modeling. *Journal of Applied Behavior Analysis, 20,* 86–96.

Haseltine, B., & Miltenberger, R. G. (1990). Teaching self-protection skills to persons with mental retardation. *American Journal on Mental Retardation, 95,* 188–197.

Heward, W. L. (1997). Self-management. In J. O. Cooper, T. E. Heron, W. L. Heward (Eds.), Applied behavior analysis (pp. 515–549). Columbus, OH: Merrill.

Hopman, M. W., & Singh, N. N. (1986). *I can cook: A special cookbook in picture and words.* Christchurch: New Zealand: Flour Power Press.

Horner, R. H., Jones, D. N., & Williams, J. A. (1985). A functional approach to teaching generalized street crossing. *Journal of the Association for Persons with Severe Handicaps, 10,* 71–78.

Horner, R. H., McDonnell, J. J., & Bellamy, G. T. (1986). Teaching generalized skills: General case instruction in simulation and community settings. In R. H. Horner, L. H. Meyer, & H. D. Fredericks, (Eds.), *Education of learners with severe handicaps: Exemplary service strategies* (pp. 289–314). Baltimore: Paul H. Brookes.

Horner, R. H., Williams, J. A., & Steveley, J. D. (1987). Acquisition of generalized telephone use by students with moderate and severe mental retardation. *Research in Developmental Disabilities, 8,* 229–248.

Hughes, C. (1992). Teaching self-instruction utilizing multiple exemplars to produce generalized problem-solving by individuals with severe mental retardation. *American Journal on Mental Retardation, 97,* 302–314.

Hughes, C., Hugo, K., & Blatt, J. (1996). Self-instructional intervention for teaching generalized problem-solving within a functional task sequence. *American Journal on Mental Retardation, 100,* 565–579.

Irvine, B. A., Erickson, A. M., Singer, G., & Stahlberg, D. (1992). A coordinated program to transfer self-management skills from school to home. *Education and Training in Mental Retardation, 27,* 241–254.

Jones, G. Y., & Collins, B. C. (1997). Teaching microwave skills to adults with disabilities: Acquisition of nutrition and safety facts presented as non-targeted information. *Journal of Developmental and Physical Disabilities, 9,* 59–78.

Kennedy, M. J. (1996). Self-determination and trust: My experience and thoughts. In D. J. Sands and M. L. Wehmeyer (Eds.), *Self-determination across the life span: Independence and choice for people with disabilities* (pp. 37–50). Baltimore: Paul H. Brookes.

Krantz, P. J., MacDuff, M. T., & McClannahan, L. E. (1993). Programming participation in family activities for children with autism: Parents' use of photographic activity schedules. *Journal of Applied Behavior Analysis, 26,* 137–138.

LaCampagne, J., & Cipani, E. (1987). Training adults with mental retardation to pay bills. *Mental Retardation, 25,* 293–303.

Lalli, J. S., Mace, F. C., Browder, D. M., & Brown, D. K (1989). Comparison of treatments to teach number matching skills to adults with moderate mental retardation. *Mental Retardation, 27,* 75–83.

Le Grice, B., & Blampied, N. M. (1994). Training pupils with intellectual disability to operate educational technology using video prompting. *Education and Training in Mental Retardation and Developmental Disabilities, 29,* 321–330.

Livi, J., & Ford, A. (1985). Skill transfer from a domestic training site to the actual homes of three moderately handicapped students. *Education and Training of the Mentally Retarded, 20,* 69–82.

Lohrmann-O'Rourke, S., & Browder, D. M. (1998). Empirically based methods of preference assessment for individuals with severe disabilities. *American Journal on Mental Retardation, 103,* 146–161.

Lovett, D. L., & Haring, K. A. (1989). The effects of self-management training on the daily living of adults with mental retardation. *Education and Training in Mental Retardation, 24,* 306–323.

Marchand-Martella, N. E., Martella, R. C., Agran, M., Salzberg, C. L., Young, K. R., & Morgan, D. (1992a). Generalized effects of a peer-delivered first aid program for students with moderate intellectual disabilities. *Journal of Applied Behavior Analysis, 25*, 841–851.

Marchand-Martella, N. E., Martella, R. C., Christensen, A. M., Agran, M., & Young, KR. (1992b). Teaching a first aid skill to students with disabilities using two training programs. *Education and Treatment of Children, 15*, 15–31.

Marchetti, A. G., McCartney, J. R., Drain, S., Hooper, M., & Dix, J. (1983). Pedestrian skills training for mentally retarded adults: Comparison of training in two settings. *Mental Retardation, 21*, 107–110.

Martin, J. E., & Marshall, L. H. (1995). Choice Maker: A comprehensive self-determination transition program. *Intervention in School and Clinic, 30*, 147–156.

Martin, J. E., Rusch, F. R., James, V. L., Decker, P. J., & Trytol, K. A. (1982). The use of picture cues to establish self-control in the preparation of complex meals by mentally retarded adults. *Applied Research in Mental Retardation, 3*, 105–119.

Matson, J. L. (1980). A controlled group study of pedestrian-skill training for the mentally retarded. *Behavior Research and Therapy, 18*, 99–106.

McAdam, D. B., & Cuvo, A. J. (1994). Textual prompts as an antecedent cue self-management strategy for persons with mild disabilities. *Behavior Modification, 18*, 47–65.

McCabe, M. P., & Cummins, R. A. (1996). The sexual knowledge, experience, feelings, and needs of people with mild intellectual disability. *Education and Training in Mental Retardation and Developmental Disabilities, 31*, 13–21.

McDonnell, J. J., & Horner, R. H. (1985). Effects of in vivo versus simulation-plus-in vivo training on the acquisition and generalization of grocery item selection by high school students with severe handicaps. *Analysis and Intervention in Developmental Disabilities, 5*, 85–91.

McDonnell, J. J., & Ferguson, B. (1989). A comparison of time delay and decreasing prompt hierarchy strategies in teaching banking skills to students with moderate handicaps. *Journal of Applied Behavior Analysis, 22*, 85–91.

McDonnell, J. J., Horner, R. H., & Williams, J. A. (1984). Comparison of three strategies for teaching generalized grocery purchasing of high school students with severe handicaps. *Journal of the Association for Persons with Severe Handicaps, 12*, 123–133.

McDonnell, J. J., & Laughlin, B. (1989). A comparison of backward and concurrent chaining strategies in teaching community skills. *Education and Training in Mental Retardation, 24*, 230–238.

McDonnell, J. J., & McFarland, S. (1988). A comparison of forward and concurrent chaining strategies in teaching laundromat skills to students with severe handicaps. *Research and Intervention in Developmental Disabilities, 9*, 177–194.

McWilliams, R., Nietupski, J., & Hamre-Nietupski, S. (1990). Teaching complex activities to students with moderate handicaps through the forward chaining of shorter total cycle response sequences. *Education and Training in Mental Retardation, 25*, 292–298.

Mechling, L. C., & Gast, D. L. (1997). Combination audio/visual self-prompting system for teaching chained tasks to students with intellectual disabilities. *Education and Training in Mental Retardation and Developmental Disabilities, 32*, 138–153.

Miller, U. C., & Test, D. W. (1989). A comparison of constant time delay and most-to-least prompts in teaching laundry skills to students with moderate retardation. *Education and Training of the Mentally Retarded, 24*, 363–370.

Morrow, S. A., & Bates, P. E. (1987). The effectiveness of three sets of school-based instructional materials and community training on the acquisition and generalization of community laundry skills by students with severe handicaps. *Research in Developmental Disabilities, 8*, 113–136.

Mount, B., & Zwernick, K. (1988). *It's never too early, it's never too late.* St. Paul, MN: Metropolitan Council.

Neef, N. A., Iwata, B. A., & Page, T. A. (1978). Public transportation training: In vivo versus classroom instruction. *Journal of Applied Behavior Analysis, 11*, 331–344.

Neef, N. A., Lensbower, S., Hockersmith, I., DePalma, V., & Gray, K. (1990). In vivo versus simulation training: An interactional analysis of range and type of training exemplars. *Journal of Applied Behavior Analysis, 23*, 447–458.

Nietupski, J., Hamre-Nietupski, S., Clancy, P. L. & Veerhusen, K. (1986). Guidelines for making simulation an effective adjunct to in-vivo community instruction. *Journal of the Association for Persons with Severe Handicaps, 11*, 12–18.

O'Brian, J. (1987). A guide to lifestyle planning: Using the Activities Catalog to integrate services and natural support systems. In B. Wilcox and G. T. Bellamy (Eds.), *A comprehensive guide to The Activities Catalog: An alternative curriculum for youth and adults with severe disabilities* (pp. 175–189). Baltimore: Paul H. Brookes.

Page, T. H., Iwata, B. A., & Neef, N. A. (1976). Teaching pedestrian skills to retarded persons: Generalization from the classroom to the natural environment. *Journal of Applied Behavior Analysis, 9*, 433–444.

Pearpoint, J., O'Brien, J., & Forest, M. (1992). PATH: *Planning alternative tomorrows with hope.* Toronto, Ontario, Canada: Inclusion Press.

Pierce, K. L., & Schriebman, L. (1994). Teaching daily living skills to children with autism in unsupervised settings through pictorial self-management. *Journal of Applied Behavior Analysis, 27*, 471–481.

Rae, R., & Roll, D. (1985). Fire safety training with adults who are profoundly mentally retarded. *Mental Retardation, 23*, 26–30.

Reid, D. H., & Hurlburt, B. (1977). Teaching non-vocal communication skills to multi-handicapped retarded adults. *Journal of Applied Behavior Analysis, 10*, 591–603.

Reitz, A. L. (1984). Teaching community skills to formerly institutionalized adults: Eating nutritionally balanced diets. *Analysis and Intervention in Developmental Disabilities, 4*, 299–312.

Risley, R., & Cuvo, A. (1980). Training mentally retarded adults to make emergency telephone calls. *Behavior Modification, 4*, 513–525.

Robinson, D., Griffith, J., McComish, L., & Swasbrook, K. (1984). Bus training for developmentally disabled adults. *American Journal of Mental Deficiency, 89*, 37–43.

Sanders, M. R., & Parr, J. M. (1989). Training developmentally disabled adults in independent meal preparation: Acquisition, generalization, and maintenance. *Behavior Modification, 13*, 168–191.

Sandknop, P. A., Schuster, J. W., Wolery, M., & Cross, D. P. (1992). The use of an adaptive device to teach students with moderate mental retardation to select lower priced grocery items. *Education and Training in Mental Retardation, 27*, 219–229.

Sarber, R. R., & Cuvo, A. J. (1983). Teaching nutritional meal planning to developmentally disabled clients. *Behavior Modification*, 7, 503–530.

Sarber, R. E., Halasz, M. M., Messmer, M. C., Bickett, A. D., & Lutzker, J. R. (1983). Teaching menu planning and grocery shopping skills to a mentally retarded mother. *Mental Retardation*, 21, 101–106.

Schleien, S. J., Ash, T., Kiernan, J., & Wehman, P. (1981). Developing independent cooking skills in a profoundly retarded woman. *Journal of the Association for the Severely Handicapped*, 6, 23–29.

Schleien, S. J., Certo, N. J. & Muccino, A. (1984). Acquisition of leisure skills by a severely handicapped adolescent: A database instructional program. *Education and Training of the Mentally Retarded*, 19, 297–305.

Schleien, S. J., & Larson, A. (1986). Adult leisure education for the independent use of a community recreation center. *Journal of the Association for Persons with Severe Handicaps*, 11, 39–44.

Schoen, S., & Sivil, E. O. (1989). A comparison of procedures in teaching self-help skills: Increasing assistance, time delay, and observational learning. *Journal of Autism and Developmental Disorders*, 19, 57–72.

Schuster, J. W. (1988). Cooking instruction with persons labeled mentally retarded: A review of literature. *Education and Training in Mental Retardation*, 23, 43–50.

Schuster, J. W., & Griffen, A. K. (1993). Teaching a chained task with a simultaneous prompting procedure. *Journal of Behavioral Education*, 2, 299–315.

Shafer, M. S., Inge, K. J., & Hill, J. (1986). Acquisition, generalization, and maintenance of automated banking skills. *Education and Training of the Mentally Retarded*, 21, 265–272.

Siafoos, J. (1997). The empowered life. *International Journal of Disability, Development and Education*, 44, 283–284.

Singh, N. N., Oswald, D. P., Ellis, C. R., & Singh, S. D. (1995). Community-based instruction for independent meal preparation by adults with profound mental retardation. *Journal of Behavioral Education*, 5, 77–92.

Singleton, K. C., Schuster, J., & Ault, M. J. (1995). Simultaneous prompting in a small group instructional arrangement. *Education and Training in Mental Retardation and Developmental Disabilities*, 30, 218–230.

Snell, M. E. (1982). Teaching bed making skills to retarded adults through time delay. *Analysis and Intervention in Developmental Disabilities*, 2, 139–155.

Snell, M. E., & Browder, D. M. (1986). Community-referenced instruction: Research and issues. *Journal of the Association for Persons with Severe Handicaps*, 11, 1–11.

Sowers, J., & Powers, L. (1995). Enhancing the participation and independence of students with severe physical and multiple disabilities in performing community activities. *Mental Retardation*, 33, 209–220.

Sowers, J., Rusch, F. R., L. & Hudson, C. (1979). Training a severely retarded young adult to ride the city bus to and from work. *AAESPH Review*, 4, 15–23.

Sowers, J., Verdi, M., Bourbeau, P., & Sheehan, M. (1985). Teaching job independence and flexibility to mentally retarded students through the use of a self-control package. *Journal of Applied Behavior Analysis*, 18, 81–85.

Spears, D. L., Rusch, F. R., York, R., & Lilly, M. S. (1981). Training independent arrival behaviors to a severely mentally retarded child. *Journal of the Association for the Severely Handicapped*, 6, 40–45.

Spooner, F., Stem, B., & Test, D. W. (1989). Teaching first aid skills to adolescents who are moderately mentally handicapped. *Education and Training in Mental Retardation*, 24, 341–351.

Sprague, J. R., & Horner, R. H. (1984). The effects of single instance, multiple instance, and general case training on a generalized vending machine use by moderately and severely handicapped students. *Journal of Applied Behavior Analysis*, 17, 273–278.

Storey, K., Bates, P., & Hanson, H. B. (1984). Acquisition and generalization of coffee purchase skills by adults with severe disabilities. *Journal of the Association for Persons with Severe Handicaps*, 9, 178–185.

Taylor, J. C., McKelvey, J. L, & Sisson, L. A. (1993). Community-referenced leisure skill clusters for adolescents with multiple disabilities. *Journal of Behavioral Education*, 3, 363–386.

Test, D. W., Howell, A., Burkhart, K., & Beroth, T. (1993). The one-more-than technique as a strategy for counting money for individuals with moderate mental retardation. *Education and Training in Mental Retardation*, 28, 232–241.

Trask-Tyler, S. A., Grossi, T. A., & Heward, W. L. (1994). Teaching young adults with developmental disabilities and visual impairments to use tape-recorded recipes: Acquisition, generalization, and maintenance of cooking skills. *Journal of Behavioral Education*, 4, 283–311.

Tymchuk, A. J., Hamada, D., Andron, L., & Anderson, S. (1990). Home safety training with mothers who are mentally retarded. *Education and Training in Mental Retardation*, 24, 142–149.

Vandercook, T. (1991). Leisure instruction outcomes: Criterion performance, positive interactions, and acceptance by typical high school peers. *Journal of Special Education*, 25, 320–339.

Vandercook, T., York, J., & Forest, M. (1989). The McGill action planning system (MAPS): A strategy for building the vision. *Journal of the Association for Persons with Severe Handicaps*, 14, 205–215.

Wacker, D. P., & Berg, W. K. (1984). Training adolescents with severe handicaps to set up job tasks independently using picture prompts. *Analysis and Intervention in Developmental Disabilities*, 4, 353–365.

Wacker, D. P., Berg, W. K., Berrie, P., & Swatta, P. (1985). Generalization and maintenance of complex skills by severely handicapped adolescents following picture prompt training. *Journal of Applied Behavior Analysis*, 18, 329–226.

Walker, R., & Vogelsberg, R. T. (1985). Increasing independent mobility skills for a woman who was severely handicapped and non-ambulatory. *Applied Research in Mental Retardation*, 6, 173–183.

Wall, M. E., & Datillo, J. (1995). Creating option-rich learning environments: Facilitating self-determination. *Journal of Special Education*, 29, 276–294.

Wall, M. E., & Gast, D. L. (1997). Caregivers' use of constant time delay to teach leisure skills to adolescents or young adults with moderate or severe intellectual disabilities. *Education and Training in Mental Retardation and Developmental Disabilities*, 32, 340–356.

Watson, M., Bain, A., & Houghton, S. (1992). A preliminary study in teaching self-protective skills to children with moderate and severe mental retardation. *Journal of Special Education*, 26, 181–194.

Wehman, P. (1997). *Life beyond the classroom: Transition strategies for young people with disabilities*. Baltimore, Md: Paul H. Brookes. 57–76.

Werts, M. G., Caldwell, N. K., & Wolery, M. (1996). Peer modeling of response chains: Observational learning by students with disabilities. *Journal of Applied Behavior Analysis*, 29, 53–66.

Westling, D. L., Floyd, J., & Carr, D. (1990). Effects of single setting versus multiple setting training on learning to shop in a department store. *American Journal on Mental Retardation*, 94, 616–624.

Winterling, V., Gast, D. L., Wolery, M., & Farmer, J. A. (1992). Teaching safety skills to high school students with moderate disabilities. *Journal of Applied Behavior Analysis*, 25, 217–227.

Wolery, M., Ault, M. J., Gast, D. L., Doyle, P. M., & Griffen, A. K. (1991). Teaching chained tasks in Dyads: Acquisition of target and observational behaviors. *Journal of Special Education*, 25, 198–220.

Wolfe, P. S., & Blancett, W. J. (1997). Infusion of sex education curricula into transition planning: obstacles and solutions. *Journal of Vocational Rehabilitation*, 8, 143–154.

Zencius, A. H., Davis, P. K. & Cuvo, A. J. (1990). A personalized system of instruction for teaching checking account skills to adults with mild disabilities. *Journal of Applied Behavior Analysis*, 23, 245–252.

Zhang, J., Gast, D., Horvat, M., & Datillo, J. (1995). The effectiveness of constant time delay procedure on teaching lifetime sport skills to adolescents with severe to profound intellectual disabilities. *Education and Training in Mental Retardation and Developmental Disabilities*, 30, 51–64.

15

Vocational Preparation and Transition

M. Sherril Moon
Katherine Inge

This chapter provides a framework for preparing students with severe disabilities for meaningful employment. We illustrate (with the examples of two students, Heather and Jane) how to plan and implement transition activities, and we also describe the essential characteristics of secondary vocational programs for students with severe disabilities. Throughout the chapter, we emphasize how vocational preparation must be coordinated along with many other facets of secondary programming as students make the transition from school to adulthood.

 Heather

Heather is a 16-year-old sophomore who has Down syndrome and moderate to severe mental retardation. She has no major physical problems but is 20 pounds overweight. Her nutritional and exercise routines are inconsistent, but her parents are aware that this area is crucial to her future quality of life. She has a functional vocabulary and can read and understand most words and phrases considered essential for community mobility. She can use money to make purchases using a "next dollar" strategy. She is very social and has participated in many school, church, and community extracurricular activities, such as Scouts, church camp, Sunday school, pep club, YMCA

programs, and Special Olympics Partners sports activities. Her 18-year-old sister has included her in many social activities with slightly older teenagers.

Two years ago, Heather entered her neighborhood middle school where she participated in four inclusive class periods (i.e., language arts, physical education, social studies, and science), one resource room period, and 2 hours of community-based and functional academic training. She had several peer buddies and peer tutors and was a member of the science club and pep club. Part of her community-based instruction included career exploration. She indicated a preference for office and clerical work or work in retail clothing stores, though she performed well as a school office messenger in an in-school work internship. Currently, she is working in a 6-week unpaid internship at Kohl's department store as a stocker.

Heather is in her first year of a comprehensive high school where her sister is a senior. She is included in regular academic classes during the morning and two afternoons each week. On Mondays, Wednesdays, and Fridays, she receives vocational training and functional skills instruction in the community. Her next internship will be in the fast food area to provide additional work-place experience to help Heather choose the type of job that she may be interested in pursuing. Specific preference data will be documented during this internship. Heather is slated to participate in the school's summer work program for students with disabilities, where she will be paid as an hourly employee. The goal of her vocational training program during this school year is to identify two job categories in which she shows a preference and to increase skill acquisition so that she can have a paid work experience in one of those areas during the summer.

 Jane

Jane is a 19-year-old student whose abilities are challenged by cerebral palsy and moderate mental retardation. She has limited use of her arms and hands as a result of spasticity, which is evident when she attempts to complete motor activities. Jane's hands usually are fisted, and she has a great deal of difficulty opening them to use functionally. Jane independently uses a power chair by pushing a joystick with her right fist. Her communication skills are also challenged by spasticity. She can communicate verbally with family members and friends; however, unfamiliar persons usually do not understand Jane.

Jane can read on a first- or second-grade level and has a functional vocabulary. She can do simple addition and subtraction and uses a calculator to figure multiple purchases. She has just opened a joint savings and checking account at a local bank and is working on managing a monthly budget. Jane is friendly but very shy and does not have many friends, an area in which she has expressed concern. She is an only child who lives with her mother and her maternal grandmother.

For the first 3 years of high school, Jane has attended a self-contained class in a regular high school, which is not her neighborhood school. For the past school year, she has been included in a community-based program that focuses on field trips rather than Individualized Educational Plan (IEP) goals. For instance, the class goes to a fast food restaurant one week and bowling the next. Jane's involvement has been limited because of her physical disabilities. The teacher or aide typically provides all the support for her to participate, such as translating her requests to "strangers." Jane has also gone to one vocational training site that was established for her class at a local thrift store. Jane's teacher physically assists her in sorting clothes that need to be hung on hangers and those which need to be folded.

Jane has expressed an interest in attending the school's new postsecondary program at a local community college. This new program, for students with severe disabilities between the ages of 19 and 21, includes academic programs at the college, social opportunities with students at the college, and paid work opportunities. Jane's chances of being accepted are good, but there are only 30 positions now open for 110 students who have applied.

Defining Transition

Employment is only one area in which middle and secondary school-aged students with disabilities must receive consistent transition planning and instruction. Other areas for which students must be prepared to live happily as adults include independent living, community mobility, financial and medical security, friendship and sexuality needs, and physical fitness and recreation access, as well as choice making and self-determination, or self-advocacy (Wehman, 1996). To insure that students receive transition service delivery in these areas as part of their special education programs, the Individuals with Disabilities Educational Act (IDEA), PL 101-476, signed into law in October, 1990, defined transition as the following:

coordinated set of activities for a student, designed within an outcome-oriented process, which promotes movement from school to post-school activities, including post-secondary education, vocational training, integrated employment (including supported employment), continuing and adult educa-

tion, adult services, independent living, or community participation. The coordinated set of activities shall be based upon the individual student's needs, taking into account the student's preferences and interests, and shall include instruction, community experiences, the development of employment and other post-school adult living objectives, and when appropriate, acquisition of daily living skills and functional vocational evaluation . . .

(D) A statement of the needed transition services for students beginning no later than age 16 and annually thereafter (and, when determined appropriate for the individual, beginning at age 14 or younger), including, when appropriate, a statement of the interagency responsibilities or linkages (or both) before the student leaves the school setting, and

(F) In the case where a participating agency, other than the educational agency, fails to provide agreed upon services, the educational agency shall reconvene the IEP team to identify alternative strategies to meet the transition objectives. (National Association of the State Directors of Special Education, 1990, p. 2)

The 1997 IDEA Amendments, PL 105-17, broadened the focus of transition by lowering the age at which transition service needs are stated in the IEP. PL 105-17, Section 614, states that:

beginning at age 14, and updated annually, a statement of the transition service needs of the child under the applicable components of the child's IEP that focuses on the child's courses of study (such as participation in advanced-placement courses or a vocational education program) (IDEA, 1997, p. 84)

The 1997 Amendments in Section 602 also state that:

beginning at age 16 (or younger, if determined by the IEP team), a statement of needed transition services for the child, including, when appropriate, a statement of interagency responsibilities or any needed linkages (IDEA, 1997, p. 46)

According to IDEA regulations, assessment, training, and support needs related to the transition outcomes of employment, independent living, or any area of adult functioning should be included in the Individualized Educational Plan (IEP). A statement of needed services is required along with goals and related activities or objectives, timelines for meeting each goal, and persons or agencies responsible for implementing each goal. Goals must be based on student interests and preferences, which must be documented in the IEP. Education personnel responsible for initiating the transition planning process when or before students turn 14 must invite the student, parents, and

other advocates or agency representative outside the school who potentially would facilitate the accomplishment of any current or future transition goals.

Characteristics of Effective Vocational Preparation and Transition Programs

Little empirical evidence exists indicating exactly which secondary and transition practices lead to the achievement of successful adult outcomes such as employment, independent living, or community participation (Everson, 1993). However, over the past 20 years, surveys of professionals, advocates, and parents (Sale, Metzler, Everson, & Moon, 1993); results of model demonstration projects (Wehman, 1996); and follow-up or follow-along research on the outcomes of graduates from special education programs (Blackorby & Wagner, 1996) have contributed to the identification of a set of characteristics of effective transition programs. There is now an abundance of literature outlining entire models and step-by-step strategies for implementing and evaluating secondary programs for students across the entire range of disabilities (McDonnell, Mathot-Buckner, & Ferguson, 1996). Those practices particularly targeted to students with severe disabilities and specifically related to their vocational preparation are described here.

Understanding Which Services Are Available in Your Community

Successful transition depends on local collaboration among educational and community agencies, businesses, and families. Although schools must take the lead in coordinating the planning process and providing initial case management and skills training, the process cannot be completed until other groups or individuals assume the responsibility for follow-up services and continual case management. Meaningful transition cannot occur unless educators use ecological analysis and functional needs assessment to explore and update all possible local employment and volunteer work options while students are still in school (Sitlington, Neubert, Begun, Lombard, & Leconte, 1996). Continual surveying of options facilitates the appropriate variety of vocational experiences and job modifications or job creations needed for students with severe disabilities (Sowers & Powers, 1991). Table 15–1 includes some of the critical questions

TABLE 15–1

Questions for Evaluating Secondary and Adult Employment Training Programs for Individuals with Severe Disabilities

Questions for Secondary School Programs

1. What is the school's philosophy of secondary education for students with moderate and severe disabilities?
2. Does anyone collect data to determine what outcomes former students achieve and what services former students use? Are the students' satisfied with their outcomes? Are school personnel satisfied with the outcomes?
3. To what degree are students included in academic classes and social activities with their peers without disabilities?
4. Does classroom training target functional, age-appropriate activities within the framework of an adapted regular curriculum?
5. Do students receive community-based training (as opposed to intermittent field trips)? If yes, in what curricular domains? How frequently?
6. Is community-based instruction individualized to meet the needs of specific students?
7. How many students receive vocational education services?
8. Are students given the opportunity to participate in a variety of vocational training experiences?
9. Do these vocational training experiences reflect the students' work interests and choices?
10. Do vocational training programs support job placements before or immediately after leaving school? Do students retain paid jobs after graduation with the support of community agencies?
11. Do secondary vocational programs collect situational assessment data as well as formal assessment data?
12. Do students receive formal transition planning beginning at age 14?
13. Are parents and students actively involved in transition planning and implementation? How are student interests and preferences determined? Are person-centered planning tools used?
14. What professionals and agencies are involved in transition planning? Are there transition specialists who coordinate the planning process?
15. Are parents and students provided with information on locally available adult services? Are school personnel knowledgeable about referral procedures and eligibility information?
16. Are release-of-information procedures in place to release student records to adult providers?
17. Are parent and peer support groups available during the transition years?
18. Are transition goals on IEPs and Individual Written Rehabilitation Plan goals coordinated?

Questions for Adult Community Programs

1. What is the name of the program, and what image does the name invoke?
2. Does the program have a mission statement? What is its overall philosophy toward employment for individuals with severe disabilities?
3. What population(s) does the program serve?
4. What are the program's eligibility requirements? Are there any prerequisite skills required? How many candidates are on the waiting list?
5. What range of services are offered: postsecondary vocational training? vocational evaluation? situational/behavioral assessments? job-seeking skills? career counseling? job placement? supported employment? sheltered employment? day activity programs?
6. Are services community-based, facility-based, or both?
7. What types of jobs are being developed by the agency? Do individuals have career choices? Do students who enter agencies get to retain paid jobs that they had while still in school?
8. How many candidates are placed in integrated community employment each year? How many are maintained? What is the program's definition of "successful"?
9. What are the average worker's earnings hourly, weekly, monthly, yearly? Do workers receive fringe benefits?
10. What is the average number of hours worked by individuals daily and weekly? Is the work temporary or seasonal?
11. What long-term supports are provided by the agency? What happens to workers if they lose a job in the community?
12. What is the ratio of workers with disabilities to nondisabled workers? Do workers have opportunities for physical and social integration?
13. What are the agency's primary funding sources?
14. Is the program accessible by public transportation or does the program provide specialized transportation?
15. What is the ratio of staff to workers? (differentiate between direct and administrative)
16. Are the program's services "customer" driven? Are the customers (e.g., individuals with disabilities, employers, parents) satisfied with the services that they receive?

Note: Adapted from Wehman, P., Moon, M. S., Everson, G. M., Wood, W., & Barcus, M. (1988). *Transition from school to work: New challenges for youth with severe disabilities* (pp. 56–57). Baltimore: Paul H. Brookes.

that should be asked when evaluating the appropriateness and effectiveness of secondary and adult employment programs for individuals with severe disabilities.

Few communities have the full range of integrated work options for students with severe disabilities once they exit secondary school programs (Wehman, 1996). Even more undesirable options, such as day activity centers or sheltered workshops, have long waiting lists or a large number of prerequisite entry requirements, such as independent toileting or complete absence of "behavioral differences." Integrated options, such as supported employment, may be restricted to individuals with less severe disabilities or may not exist at all in some communities (Moon, Inge, Wehman, Brooke, & Barcus, 1990). It is critical that educators and families determine before a student reaches the age of 14 what services exist, what services need improvement, and what services must be created. Table 15–2 describes typical adult or community service employment alternatives that school personnel and families should investigate at the local level to determine what is available. Furthermore, the critical questions included in Table 15–1 can be used to specifically determine the quality of the various employment alternatives.

Many educators and family members of students with severe disabilities do not understand that most adult services are *eligibility*-driven rather than *entitled* in the way that special education is. In other words, residential programs, counseling and therapy programs, and even the federal and state vocational rehabilitation system have eligibility, or entrance, prerequisites that may exclude persons with severe disabilities (Szymanski, Turner, & Hershenson, 1992). These programs are governed by different laws and policies, and no umbrella agency, such as the special education system, coordinates the services.

Therefore, it is critical for families and educators to begin to understand the milieu of programs and laws that affect the transition outcomes of students with disabilities. For instance, the Rehabilitation Act Amendments of 1992 (P.L. 102-569) specifically address the fact that many students with the most severe disabilities exit school requiring rehabilitation services (Inge, Dymond & Wehman, 1996). This important law includes a definition of transition services that duplicates that found in IDEA. In addition, these Rehabilitation Act regulations mandate that each state develop a plan requiring that the state rehabilitation agency address the development of policies to

TABLE 15–2
Typical Adult Service and Community Employment Alternatives

1. *Competitive (unsupported) employment*—on company payroll with benefits and without trainer or support from a human services agency.
2. *Job placement, or transitional support into regular employment*—short-term help from an agency, such as the state vocational rehabilitation agency, in finding and getting adjusted to a job.
3. *Supported employment*—job placement, training, and continuing support for as long as necessary in an integrated community business. Supported employment can be in the form of an individual placement or a group model of several workers, such as an enclave or mobile work crew. Workers earn minimum wage or better.
4. *Volunteer work*—unpaid work that is preferred or chosen by an individual for reasons other than "daily support." This is usually done for community service organizations, such as the SPCA, a hospital, or the National Cancer Society. Labor laws define what types of work are considered volunteer. Workers with disabilities cannot volunteer to do work that would pay a wage to employees without disabilities.
5. *Sheltered work*—work done in a sheltered workshop where the majority of workers are disabled and earn subminimum wages. Sheltered workshops can offer a variety of employment and evaluation services, such as work activity, work adjustment training, vocational evaluation, long-term sheltered employment, and work activity programs.
6. *Work activity center–based or nonintegrated day programs*—focus on "prevocational" skills, such as motor tasks or self-care skills.
7. *Day activity or adult day care center–based, nonintegrated programs*—usually have a therapeutic or nonvocational emphasis, depending on the funding source.

ensure coordination between the rehabilitation and state education agencies.

Although access to vocational rehabilitation is eligibility-driven, teachers and parents should be aware that P.L. 102-569 is guided by the "presumption of ability" (Button, 1992). In other words, students with a disability, regardless of the severity of the disability, are presumed to be able to achieve employment with the appropriate services and supports. The burden of proof for accessing needed services and supports shifts from the individual to the rehabilitation system. To deem a student "too severely disabled" for services, the rehabilitation counselor must be able to demonstrate that the student would be unable to achieve any employment outcome.

When a counselor is determining a student's eligibility, he or she must consider existing data first.

This can include information and data provided by the student with a disability, the family, advocates, and education agencies. The use of existing data for determining eligibility for rehabilitation services has major implications for school systems (Inge, Dymond, & Wehman, 1996). Students who exit school with resumes and references from community-based vocational experiences have documentation that demonstrates the feasibility of employment outcomes.

Although Table 15–3 outlines some of the programs and laws that special educators must understand, this list is by no means exhaustive. Ultimately, educators and other agencies must educate each other at the local level, so that fragmented or overlapping services do not result.

TABLE 15–3
Laws and Programs Crucial to Transition Planning for Citizens with Disabilities

Laws Governing Programs for Citizens with Disabilities

- Americans with Disabilities Act (ADA)
- Carl D. Perkins Vocational Education and Applied Technology Act
- Developmental Disabilities Assistance and Bill of Rights Act
- Fair Labor Standards Act (FLSA)
- Goals 2000: Educate America Act
- Individuals with Disabilities Act (IDEA)
- Workforce Investment Act
- Social Security Act
- School to Work Opportunities Act
- Technology-Related Assistance Act for Individuals with Disabilities (Tech Act)

Government Programs

- Supplemental Security Income (SSI)—direct cash payments to eligible persons with disabilities
- Social Security Disability Insurance (SSDI)—direct cash payments to adult disabled children over age 18 who are children of disabled workers eligible for social security
- Plans for Achieving Self Support (PASS)—a work incentive program for SSI beneficiaries who return to work that allows exclusion of certain expenses in calculating SSI benefits
- Impairment-Related Work Expense (IRWE)—a work incentive program for SSI and SSDI beneficiaries that allows exclusion of certain expenses in calculating the benefit level for determining if work is substantial
- Medicare—national health care insurance for the elderly and some persons with disabilities (many SSDI recipients are eligible for Medicare)
- Medicaid—payment for medical services for persons meeting needs test (most SSI recipients are eligible)
- Home- and Community-Based Medicaid Waiver—allows states to apply to use Medicaid funds for noninstitutional settings
- Intermediate Care Facilities for the Mentally Retarded (ICFMR)—funding to states for residential placements for Medicaid recipients requiring certain health care services (typically supports state-operated institutions and some group homes)
- Vocational Education—public school programs providing career education in the form of technical school education, apprenticeships, internships with business, high school-college partnership programs that include students with disabilities
- Vocational Rehabilitation—funds to state vocational rehabilitation agencies from the US Department of Education; provides services related to employment of persons with disabilities (includes supported employment)
- Parent Training Centers—grants to organizations through EHA, Part D, to provide information and training to parents of students with disabilities
- Independent Living Centers—grants to states (usually the vocational rehabilitation agency) to provide independent living services to individuals with severe disabilities
- Child Labor Restrictions—Department of Labor guidelines on vocational education, volunteer work, and unpaid job training for students with disabilities

Supporting Families

As a student with disabilities reaches adolescence and then later reaches adulthood, her family faces two of the most difficult and stressful transitional periods (Turnbull & Turnbull, 1997). Educators must support families in a variety of areas, such as deciding what to include in the school curricula (e.g., sexuality education and self-determination skills) and looking into future supported work and living options. Research has shown that parental participation in the transition process is critical (McNair & Rusch, 1991), but that family priorities are not necessarily valued by professionals involved in the planning process (Steineman, Morningstar, Bishop, & Turnbull, 1993). For example, most transition planning focuses on employment as the major postsecondary outcome, while many parents are likely to view the development of social relationships, personal care, and appropriate adult living opportunities as more crucial (Hanley-Maxwell, Whitney-Thomas, & Pogoloff, 1995). Open and honest communication between families and professionals is essential if the transition process and outcomes are really going to be meaningful. (See chapter 2 for a discussion of parent involvement in the planning process.)

Professionals must continually obtain information from parents by asking them questions and listening and by using written questionnaires and person-centered planning meetings (Miner & Bates, 1997; Wehman, 1995). Parents must assume more responsibility by signing off on the IEP as the responsible party on particular goals; exploring residential, employment, and leisure options; sharing specific paid job leads; promoting independence and self-determination in their son or daughter; and inviting particular agency and advocacy groups to become part of the transition process. Families and professionals should participate together in evaluating existing school and community programs and in the startup of new or improved support or service systems.

Determining Student Preferences and Interests

As Wehman (1996) pointed out, the earliest transition models did not emphasize student choice in the process of moving from school to work and adult living. Fortunately, student or adult customer choice now is recognized as the focus of service delivery. Many agree that students with disabilities who practice self-

determination have better adult outcomes (Wehmeyer & Kelchner, 1995). The implication is that students must participate in a wide variety of employment situations so that they can develop true preferences or dislikes and so that they can have real opportunities to increase skills, which can change preferences over time (Winking, O'Reilly, & Moon, 1993). Realistic, community-based assessment procedures must also be used so that students are not unfairly deemed ineligible for vocational education and vocational rehabilitation programs, as historically has been the case. A variety of ecological assessment procedures (Sitlington, Neubert, Begun, Lombard, & Leconte, 1996) and entire curricula (Field & Hoffman, 1994) now exist that promote student choice and self-determination in the secondary schools and transition process. Legal mandates in IDEA and the Rehabilitation Act Amendments also require the documentation of student preferences for transition goals in the IEP and individual choice in the development of the Individual Written Rehabilitation Plan (IWRP) goals.

One of the best ways to ensure active student involvement in the transition process is to use a student or person-centered planning process to establish transition goals (Miner & Bates, 1997). This approach, which focuses on the desires and needs of the student and her family in helping the student achieve her dreams, has three characteristics (Mount, 1994), which include: (a) focusing on everyday activities as a basis of planning for the future, (b) emphasizing family and community connections rather than particular services, and (c) not relying on a single person or agency to do everything. A variety of person-centered planning approaches exist and have been referred to as personal futures planning, essential lifestyle planning, circles of friends, McGill Action Planning System (MAPS), and Planning Alternative Tomorrows with Hope (PATH) (Falvey, Forest, Pearpoint, & Rosenberg, 1992). More on person-centered planning can be found in chapter 3 and later in this chapter.

Balancing Vocational Preparation with Inclusion and Other Programs

Most secondary programs for students with severe disabilities have emphasized job training and community functioning in natural settings and, in so doing, have also limited the amount of time these older students spend in integrated academic or social settings in their neighborhood schools with peers of the same age (Falvey, Gage, & Eshilian, 1995). With the success of inclusive education now well documented, the lack of access to inclusive school-based activities and classes for older students with severe disabilities raises some concerns (Tashie & Schuh, 1993). This is particularly true when students lack opportunities to learn social and communication skills by interacting frequently with same-aged, nondisabled peers (McDonnell et al., 1996). Inclusion in school-based programs promotes social skill development, the most critical skill in job retention, and it helps students without disabilities develop positive attitudes toward their peers with disabilities (Wehman, 1996). Considering this, one must ask whether work or community-based programs are always more appropriate than an academic setting for teaching these related skills.

As students with severe disabilities reach the age of 18 or 19, a time when most students are graduating from high school, it is age-appropriate for them to spend more time in employment or other postsecondary situations where they can learn to work with and interact socially with other young adults. Many school systems are now starting *postsecondary programs for students with severe disabilities who are ages 18 to 21 that are located on local college campuses*. State-supported community colleges make excellent partners in such programs because of shared funding sources and a similar mission in serving local graduating students during their first 2 years after high school. In these programs, staffed by public school secondary and transition specialists, students can spend 20 or more hours each week in paid employment and still spend significant time during the school day in college and tutorial classes or college-sponsored activities developing functional, academic, and social skills.

Some experts have advocated that students with severe disabilities spend the entire regular school day in school-based inclusive programs, while receiving job and community-based training on weekends, during summer vacation, or after school hours (Tashie & Schuh, 1993). Unfortunately, in most states there are no programs or individuals other than public school personnel who can do this kind of training for school-aged individuals, and it is unrealistic to expect educators to work these extra hours when most are

already overworked and underpaid. Therefore, secondary programs must seek a balance for each student during regular school hours. The amount of job training should depend on a number of factors, including age, student preference, availability and quality of social interaction in each setting, and level of social, work-related, and specific vocational skill development.

Collaborating with a Team for Successful Transition

Effective transition planning depends on formal, functional linkages at the national, state, local, and individual student levels among the student, family, educators, human service agencies, local service providers, advocates, and businesses (Hasazi, 1985). Recent research has shown that collaborative structures at the state, and most importantly, at the local levels are crucial in successful service delivery (Furney, Hasazi, & DeStefano, 1997). The efforts of several states to formalize transition practices across agencies has been thoroughly documented (Bates, Bronkema, Ames, & Hess, 1992). Everson (1993) wrote that states must develop formal *cooperative agreements* between state level agencies, such as education, vocational rehabilitation, and developmental disabilities, in order to shape legislation, to provide a framework for local planning, and to advocate for appropriate budgets. Cooperative agreements can specify functions such as establishing agendas for inservice training, defining responsibilities of various team members, and providing some standard procedures for local teams (Wehman, 1996). Fortunately, IDEA provides some guidelines for working with state and local agencies and families in developing transition goals on the IEP, and almost all states have now developed official guidelines for implementing IDEA transition requirements.

Local teams, comprised of representatives from agencies or individuals typically on an IEP team, collaborate for the purpose of assessing, changing, and monitoring local transition efforts, and a team functions according to the needs of transition-aged students and the quality of secondary and adult service programs. The questions included in Table 15–1 can be used to conduct a community needs assessment. Local teams must also provide avenues for information exchange and training among families, agencies, and businesses. Ultimately, a local team must examine IEPs to make sure that they are functional, promote self-determination, and lead to effective adult outcomes and that they will transfer over into goals on adult service plans, such as IWRPs and individual habilitation plans (IHPs).

Individual Transition Planning and the IEP

The individual transition planning team consists of the student, significant others to the student; educators; adult service providers at the local level; appropriate human service agencies who provide case management, funding to local providers, or direct services; advocates; and local employers. Team members must collaborate to develop and implement transition goals and activities on a student's IEP. These goals must be based on the student's preferences and interests, ideally determined by multiple experiences and a long-running personal futures planning process. IDEA further facilitates the monitoring of transition goals by stating that any agency or individual on the planning team, either from within or outside of the school system, can sign off as the responsible party for seeing that a particular goal is met. To establish priority goals for any student with severe disabilities, an individual transition team should consider developing goals and related activities from the following areas: vocational training, paid employment, postsecondary education, independent living, financial skills, daily living needs, recreation, medical needs, transportation, advocacy or self-advocacy needs, and social and sexual needs.

The number and type of transition goals depends on the needs of each student within and across all areas. For example, Heather needs several goals related to vocational training because, at age 16, her skill level and preferences are not yet established. Also, she is already included in regular education classes and many extracurricular activities, in which other skills can be developed. Jane, aged 19, on the other hand, has paid employment, but she needs skill development and support in other areas, particularly social and friendship development and age-appropriate academic areas. Therefore, her vocational goals may not be a priority until after she is accepted into the postsecondary program. Heather's primary IEP transition goal, related to vocational training and employment, is shown in Figure 15–1.

FIGURE 15–1
Heather's IEP Vocational Training Goal

Goal #1

Heather will participate in unpaid work training in three job types to include stocking, food industry, and hotel janitorial positions so that she can express more accurately her preferences for paid employment positions by the end of the school year.

Level of Current Performance

Heather participated last year in an in-school work internship for 6 weeks as a school office messenger. She has expressed the desire to do this type of work in the future. To date, she has no other training experiences.

Activities Needed to Accomplish Goal

1. Heather will work in all training sites on M, W, F from 9:30 AM to 11:30 AM for a period of 8 to 12 weeks in each site.

2. At 2-week intervals on each site, Heather will verbally answer questions concerning her desire to do future work in this area.

3. Job supervisors will evaluate Heather's performance at midterm and at the end of each training cycle.

4. Heather will review a videotape of her work at the end of each training period and discuss her work performance and preference for future work of this type.

5. Heather will develop a resume at the end of the school year listing her work experiences to date.

Date of Completion

6/1/99

Person(s) Responsible for Implementation

Heather, transition specialist, job trainer (teaching assistant)

School-Based Vocational Preparation

Vocational preparation at the middle and high school levels should lead to meaningful work in the community now that supported employment is a reality backed by legislation, a firm research base, and a rapidly developing technology, which makes paid work possible for citizens with the most severe disabilities (Sowers & Powers, 1995). Effective vocational training actually starts during the elementary years, during which learning to take responsibility, paying attention to natural cues, responding to a schedule, acquiring social skills, appropriate communication skills, self-monitoring and choice-making skills, and understanding the meaning of jobs or careers are emphasized (Hutchins & Renzaglia, 1990; Meers, 1992). As the student becomes older, inclusion in school programs and activities shifts to community programs, in which job-related tasks, community mobility, and functional academic skills are taught in the settings in which they will be used (McDonnell et al., 1996). Actual training in real jobs should begin at the secondary level, where this instruction must be balanced with teaching work-related academic skills, social skills, and age-appropriate curriculum content areas in school settings alongside same-age peers who are not disabled (Putnam, 1994; Stainback & Stainback, 1992). The final years of school for students with severe disabilities between the ages of 19 and 22 should involve paid work and opportunities to continue learning and socializing with young adults. This implies that education moves out of the high school and into community, work, and postsecondary academic settings for the entire school day. Regardless of the age of the student, vocational training must focus on common outcomes and incorporate critical elements. These elements or outcomes are listed in Table 15–4 and are described further in this section.

TABLE 15–4
Critical Elements and Outcomes of School-Based Vocational Preparation

---

- Longitudinal instruction of work-related skills occurs across grades and settings, including inclusive school-based activities and classes, work sites, and community environments.
- Continual assessment of work preferences and interests begin in middle school and is documented in IEP starting at age 14 so that a career path is established.
- Community referenced employment training is based on the local economy.
- Job training occurs across a variety of real jobs in real employment settings.
- Community-based training sites meet labor law requirements.
- Systematic, behavioral procedures and natural supports are used to teach vocational skills.
- Assistive technology is used when needed to facilitate student independence.
- Paid work is sought for students exiting school along with appropriate support services, such as social security benefits or work incentives.

Longitudinal Instruction of Work-Related Skills Across Grades and Settings

Vocational training must be coordinated with all other areas of a student's life, especially for those with the most severe disabilities, for whom life skills in domestic and community environments and appropriate social and communication skills may ultimately be more critical (Wehman, 1996). Therefore, instruction of generalized work behaviors that are also crucial to survival in other environments should comprise much of the vocational curriculum until the student is in the last 3 or 4 years of school (usually ages 18 to 22). This kind of approach allows for some job sampling in real job sites and even some part-time paid employment, while still permitting inclusion in age-appropriate content areas and instruction in nonvocational community skills, such as transportation, and community leisure participation.

> *For example, Heather spends a good portion of her school week in regular school programs, but still has unpaid job experiences in real employment sites, where her preferences are assessed and specific work behaviors are taught. She also spends some time in other community environments learning mobility skills, functional academic, and communication techniques and sampling leisure and social alternatives. Paid work opportunities are part of her summer school program, an age-appropriate option for a 16-year-old. Most of Heather's functional academic, social, and communication needs are taught both in school settings through the modification of curriculum content areas and within the context of community and job site training programs.*

Many work-related behaviors must be taught early on, usually beginning in the elementary grades, and continually assessed and instructed under changing environmental conditions. These work-related behaviors include: caring for personal hygiene needs, using various transportation modes, taking short breaks, appropriately asking for assistance, getting to tasks or areas on time and within a certain time frame, learning to delay reinforcement, paying attention to natural cues and directions, getting along socially with individuals and groups of people, sharing items, adjusting to changes in a schedule, following a schedule in some format, understanding basic access, safety, and danger symbols used in the community, eating a meal or snack in a public area or fast food environment, using a communication system with strangers or coworkers, making purchases such as vending items, and responding to correction or criticism, understanding the concept of pay for work, and budgeting from a paycheck.

Identifying a Career Path

Critical to developing vocational goals and activities for transition is the concept of identifying the *career path* that a student wishes to pursue. The foundation for this career path can be laid by using person-centered planning strategies (O'Brien & Lovett, 1992; Pearpoint, O'Brien, & Forest, 1993). With any needed support, the student identifies a group of people or "circle of support" to assist in exploring what his or her future would be like. The central concept to a person-centered approach is encouraging students to "dream" about their futures and possible careers.

Students' dreams about work should never be limited by existing services and programs. In addition, teachers, parents, related-service professionals, and others involved in the student's life should not make judgments about the student's choices or limit a career path. For instance, many students with the most significant disabilities may be discouraged by professionals who do not believe that they have the abilities for achieving their goals. They are directed to existing vocational training experiences that have been established for other students rather than the more challenging task of identifying training sites specific to their interests. In some cases, the students may even be directed towards the most restrictive choices, such as day activity centers or sheltered workshops, because the transition team lacks the vision to push the service delivery system. However, the transition years must be used to fully explore options and demonstrate that all students can be included in their communities. This is accomplished by recognizing that within each student's dream is a beginning for matching him or her to an environment of choice.

A student with a disability who dreams of being a movie star, for instance, is no different from students without disabilities who have the same dream. Instead of telling the student with a disability that her dream is unrealistic, she should be directed to work experiences in environments that reflect her interests. She may pursue part-time jobs such as the ticket taker or concession stand operator at the local movie

theater. There also may be opportunities in a video store, a costume store, or some other similar environment in which the student is exposed to a component of her dream. Once these environments are identified, the student should have vocational training experiences across several options to see if any of these will meet her interests or preferences.

MAPS *as a Planning Tool*

MAPS is a one person-centered tool that has been used to assist students in planning their futures (Falvey, Forest, Pearpoint, & Rosenberg, 1992). This is an adult- or peer-facilitated process in which a facilitator and sometimes a recorder work with a student and a support team to identify the student's gifts and strengths as well as to plan for the future. There are six key questions that should be addressed during a MAPS meeting. These questions usually are answered in order and all should be discussed. The student selects people to assist in the planning process.

The key to successfully completing a MAPS plan is to have a positive approach to the process. The student's gifts and talents should be highlighted, and she or he should never be described in terms of a disability label or problem. If the student is challenged by a specific issue, the team needs to state the issue in terms of support needs. Jane, for example, dreams of becoming a secretary or teacher. This became clear to her parents when they initiated a MAPS meeting to plan for their daughter's future. Instead of making judgments about this being an unrealistic goal, her circle of support has begun to make plans to determine a career path in one of these areas. A summary of Jane's MAPS plan is located in Figure 15–2.

PATH *as a Planning Tool*

PATH is another process that can be used to identify a student's dreams and goals for employment. PATH evolved from the MAPS process and was designed to put into place a plan of action for the focus person (Pearpoint et al., 1995). Literally, the process can identify an employment "path" for the student to pursue.

Similar to MAPS, the PATH process consists of a series of steps or questions that constitute the meeting, which is led by a group facilitator. The facilitator is preferably neutral and not a member of the student's transition team. The facilitator's responsibility

FIGURE 15–2
Jane's MAPS

1. What is Jane's history or story?
   - She is 19 years old and lives with her mother.
   - Her parents are divorced, and she has two older sisters who are both married with children.
   - Her mother is an elementary school teacher.
   - Her father is a lawyer.
   - She lives with her mother, but she visits with her father and his wife at least one weekend a month.
   - The families are friendly, and Jane loves both her parents.

Medical:

Normal delivery, parents soon noticed that there were problems when Jane did not roll over, sit up, or crawl as her other siblings had. Eventual diagnosis of cerebral palsy. Parents were told to institutionalize Jane, since she would never walk or talk. Parents were told that she would never develop intellectually. Overall, Jane is very healthy.

Educational:

Jane's school years have been spent in special classes for students with severe disabilities. She has little opportunity to interact with nondisabled same-age peers. Out-of-school activities have consisted primarily of field trips rather than community-based instruction experiences.

Communication:

Jane communicates verbally with her entire family. School has attempted to use pictures, since individuals who do not know Jane have a difficult time understanding her.

Social:

Jane enjoys social interactions and relationships. She has friends at church and in her neighborhood; however, most of them are older friends of her mother.

2. What are your dreams for Jane?
   - Will be able to communicate with others.
   - Will have a job working in a daycare, because she really loves children.
   - Have friends her own age and an active social life.
   - Won't have to depend on her parents.
   - Able to live independently in an apartment of her own.
   - Healthy and safe.

3. What are your nightmares for Jane?
   - Will not find the key to making her dreams reality.
   - Will have to live in a nursing home.
   - No friends or supports.
   - Unable to communicate her choices and needs.
   - Will be placed in a sheltered workshop or day activity center.
   - Will be judged by her disabilities and not her abilities!

is to assist the group in addressing each of the eight steps of PATH. These steps include:

1. The dream
2. Sensing the goal, positive and possible
3. Grounding in the now
4. Who do we enroll?
5. Recognizing ways to build strength
6. Charting actions for the next 3 months
7. Planning the next month's work
8. Committing to the next steps

The discussion of the PATH steps can direct the student's transition activities for the coming year. The PATH could focus specifically on one target area, such as a PATH for employment or independent living goals. In any event, the team must be committed to following through with the plan, or the process yields a nice graphic without outcomes.

MAPS, PATH, *and Collaborative* IEPs

MAPS and PATH do not take the place of transition plans or IEPs (Malatchi & Inge, 1997). They are com-

4. Who is Jane and what does she like?
   - Loves children.
   - Likes music and watching comedy shows on TV.
   - Has a great sense of humor!
   - She is very expressive, affectionate, exuberant, curious, expressive, and intuitive.
   - Enjoys going to concerts and plays.
   - She is an aunt, sister, daughter.
   - She is wonderful and much loved!

5. What are Jane's strengths, gifts, and talents?
   - Strong desire to communicate and lots to say.
   - Easy to motivate and knows what she likes and dislikes.
   - Motivated by praise and acceptance.
   - Able to get herself where she wants to go in her power chair.
   - Very outgoing.
   - Likes to read simple books and look at magazines.
   - Enjoys typing notes to her sisters and father using a head pointer and an electric typewriter.

6. What are Jane's needs and challenges?
   - Communication with friends and teachers.
   - Facilitation in developing a circle of friends.
   - Participation in meaningful educational experiences leading to employment.
   - Self-help issues in the workplace and the community.
   - Independent living skills.
   - Support from community agencies to achieve dreams.
   - To feel a sense of acceptance, belonging, and community.

Action Plans for Jane

- Transition team (including parents) will meet within 1 month to begin planning for graduation from high school.
- IEP will be functional, goals stated in proactive language, and include interactions with friends.
- Jane will be evaluated for an augmentative communication device within 2 months.
- After the evaluation, the support team will meet to discuss options and a plan of action.
- Jane will volunteer to work with the nursery group at her church within the next 2 weeks and continue weekly throughout the next year.
- School will identify three different community-based training sites related to Jane's specific interests (e.g., childcare and office work). She will receive one-to-one support and training throughout the coming school year in these two experiences.
- Jane and her teacher will visit the new postsecondary program at the local community college within the next 2 months. They will review the curriculum to determine which courses may be related to her expressed interests.
- Support team will identify needed supports in the community for independent living services.
- Jane will review and select at least one independent living class at the local Center for Independent Living during the next month.

panion tools that can enhance transition planning. They can give direction to the legal documents and provide a starting point in identifying the student's goals for the future.

There are no rules related to whether a team uses a MAPS or PATH approach, and both seem to be excellent tools when beginning a transition planning process. Some teams may choose to use MAPS initially and then use PATH in later years when vocational interests become clearer. These person-centered tools facilitate positive input from all participants, create positive pictures of a student, and actively involve the student in his or her transition plan (Malatchi & Inge, 1997).

Employment Training Related to the Local Economy

In some instances, students may be able to identify a specific career path in their person-centered plans. Others have such limited exposure to the workplace that they need to have a variety of experiences that reflect the local labor market. These training experiences assist in the identification of the student's preferences. Therefore, each school system's vocational curriculum should be specific to the community as well as based on the expressed interests of the students. This requires continual assessment of the local labor market to determine the major employers in the community, the types of employment most commonly available, and the type of employment that has been obtained by individuals with disabilities (Moon et al., 1990).

Teachers may accomplish this task by surveying their local Chamber of Commerce, reading the newspaper want ads, looking in the telephone yellow pages, completing follow-up contacts with school graduates, and contacting adult service agencies and supported employment programs to determine job placements for individuals with severe disabilities. Renzaglia and Hutchins (1988) suggest generating a list of local businesses and categorizing them by job types (e.g. clerical, food service, industrial). After a list of businesses has been generated, the teacher or school representative should initiate contacts with a sampling of employers to identify the types of jobs that would be available to students on graduation. Based on interviews with employers, observation in the business community, and students' interests, teachers are prepared to design a community-referenced vocational curriculum.

Job Training Across a Variety of Real Jobs in Real Employment Settings

Options for vocational training can be considered to include: simulated work in the classroom, school building, and grounds; "real" work in the classroom obtained from community organizations; school-based vocational activities alongside actual school employees; community-based training sites; volunteer work; and supported employment positions in the community. Teachers are cautioned regarding the difficulty of simulating the demands of a real work environment within the school setting, such as interactions with coworkers and customers, productivity issues, and other characteristics of the workplace (e.g. noise, orienting in a large space) (Inge et al., 1996; Moon et al., 1990). Therefore, each student's schedule should reflect a portion of his or her vocational activities in the community as well as within the school building.

Several suggestions and considerations are offered to teachers who are designing a vocational program using a school- or community-based training approach.

1. Community labor analysis: A *community labor analysis* must be completed for selecting vocational objectives, regardless of the training location. Do not fall into the trap of obtaining work from the school office or community agency to complete in the classroom if it does not reflect future job possibilities in the community.
2. School versus real work sites: School-based programs should be reserved for younger students (under age 14) when vocational training in a real work site is not an option because of labor law requirements (Inge, Simon, Halloran, & Moon, 1993). Whenever possible, students should be trained alongside school employees when completing vocational activities in the school building and grounds.
3. Transitions in school programs: As students move from elementary school to high school, they should have the opportunity to complete a variety of jobs in a number of different settings to assist in developing a work history, determining job preferences, identifying future training needs, and determining skill characteristics for supported employment job matching. This information can be shared, as the student moves through the school years, with teachers and adult service agencies to facilitate the transition process from school to work. As previously stated in this chapter, students who have documentation that they are able to achieve an employment outcome have a solid foundation for entering the vocational rehabilitation system.

Figure 15–3 provides a vocational community-based training summary for Heather at the end of a semester or three 6-week grading periods, in which she experienced three different training sites. Since she was uncertain of her job preferences, her transition team determined that she would have the opportunity to experience three different sites during the school year. Her documentation includes work task and environmental preferences, training needs, and recommendations for matching her abilities to a paid work experience.

FIGURE 15–3
Report of Vocational Training Experiences

Community-Based Training Report
Student: Heather
Date of Report: June 1

During the past $4\frac{1}{2}$ months or one semester, Heather has received community-based vocational training at Hechinger's, Howard Johnson's, and Shoney's. She worked at each job site for 2 hours, 4 days a week, over a 6-week period. Each of the training sites involved different job duties and work environments.

Training Site #1

At Hechinger's, Heather had several work stations where she put up stock and "fronted" the shelves. This required her to reposition merchandise from the back of a shelf to the front, organizing the items in neat rows. Heather was required to orient to large areas in the store and had frequent contact with customers. By the end of the training session, she was able to independently match stock in boxes to the correct location on the shelves, lift stock weighing up to 20 pounds, recognize and set aside damaged items and opened packages, maneuver a loaded stock cart throughout the store, and respond appropriately to customer questions; Heather was taught to say "please ask at the service desk" when customers approached her for information.

Training Site #2

At Howard Johnson's, Heather's job was to clean the restroom (e.g., sinks, toilets, sweeping, and mopping the floor) and vacuum the motel lobby. This position involved moving between two different work stations in the front of the motel. Heather reached skill acquisition on the bathroom tasks within 4 weeks of training; however, she could not perform the skill to production standards, and therefore the remainder of her placement focused on increasing her speed. During the last 2 weeks, her time to complete the task decreased from 90 minutes to 50 minutes after a reinforcement program was implemented. Heather did not reach skill acquisition on the vacuuming task.

Training Site #3

Heather's position at Shoney's focused on busing tables and rolling silverware. Rolling silverware was a seated job duty that occurred in a secluded section of the dining room, while busing tables required orienting to the entire restaurant, continuous standing, and frequent interactions with customers and coworkers. Heather reached independence on both tasks by the end of the training period. She was very meticulous and took great care in performing her work. At times, this hampered her ability to achieve the production speed of her coworkers.

Summary:

Heather performed well in both large and small work environments and was able to remain on task in environments where there were unfamiliar people. She seemed to prefer working in public environments with Shoney's being the work site of choice. Heather consistently displayed a positive attitude, arriving at work each day motivated and eager to work. Heather's socialization with customers and coworkers was both appropriate and pleasant. She was able to respond to yes or no questions accurately, initiate "hello" and "goodbye," and carry on short conversations with coworkers. Training sessions were scheduled between 7:30 AM and 3:00 PM, and she maintained the same enthusiasm and speed across all training times. The system of least intrusive prompts was the most effective instructional strategy used with Heather. She consistently worked at a slow, steady pace for up to an hour and a half before needing to take a break. Heather's physical strength is good, and she was able to carry a 30- to 40-pound bus pan full of dishes from the dining room to the dishroom.

Points to consider when seeking employment:

1. The best instructional strategy for Heather is the system of least prompts.
2. Heather likes to self-monitor her work using a picture card and check system. She learned to do this independently during the Shoney's placement.
3. Heather is able to orient in large and small work environments.
4. She prefers to work in settings where she has frequent contact with coworkers and customers. She appeared especially motivated in the food service setting.
5. Heather has a positive attitude. She is motivated by work and is receptive to instruction from a job trainer.
6. Heather's endurance remained consistent for $1\frac{1}{2}$ hours between 7:30 AM and 3:00 PM.
7. Physical strength is good, and Heather can carry a 40-pound bucket for short distances (about 15 feet).

FIGURE 15–3
continued

Future Training Recommendations:

1. Increase opportunities for Heather to purchase items in the community using a "money card." She is currently unable to perform tasks such as using a vending machine independently.

2. Provide opportunities for Heather to perform tasks while standing to increase her endurance for job placement. She also has a tendency to stand and rock from foot to foot rather than maintaining a firm base of support.

3. Establish jobs and errands for Heather to complete that require her to verbally interact with adults. Focus on maintaining eye contact when performing these duties.

4. Provide opportunities for Heather to work toward increasing her speed and production rate on a task.

5. Refer for supported employment placement during next year of school before graduation.

Note: Adapted from Vocational Options Project, Rehabilitation Research and Training Center, Virginia Commonwealth University.

Establishing Community-Based Training Sites

The steps in developing community-based training sites include: (a) identifying appropriate businesses, (b) contacting the personnel director or employer, (c) meeting labor law requirements, (d) identifying and analyzing appropriate jobs, and (e) scheduling community-based instruction.

Identifying Appropriate Businesses

First, teachers should contact adult service agencies within their communities to determine the location of supported employment placements. These sites may not be appropriate for community-based instruction, since the presence of unpaid students may confuse the supervisors and result in inappropriate work expectations and labor law violations. Moon et al. (1990) state that it is helpful to identify businesses that offer several different job types for ease of organizing, scheduling, and transporting students for community-based vocational training. For instance, a local mall may have several businesses that could provide training sites while dispersing students and trainers within a reasonable distance of each other. Other options could include the local hospital, an industrial park or business complex (assuming the businesses targeted are considered nonhazardous), or a community college or university. In any event, the businesses should represent jobs that reflect student choice as well as ones that are available and within a reasonable transportation distance from the school and students' homes. It may not be appropriate to select a job at the local business complex that would

translate into a 45-minute ride to and from the school building or students' homes.

Contacting the Personnel Director or Employer

Pumpian, Shepard, and West (1988) recommend identifying a task force within the school to identify businesses to contact for community-based instruction. This task force may serve as a network in the business community, which can provide invaluable employer contacts and resources (Brooke, Inge, Armstrong, & Wehman, 1997). In addition, the network can include school system contacts as well as contacts provided by parents, family members, and friends.

One individual should be identified to approach employers regarding use of their business for community-based training sites. If it is not possible to identify one person for all initial contacts, the school should maintain a list of businesses that have been approached as community-based training sites to prevent duplication of effort. This transition coordinator or teacher would be responsible for contacting the personnel director or company manager by phone or letter to set up an appointment to discuss the school's program in detail.

Contacts by letter should always be followed with telephone communication. The content of the letter or phone conversation should include a brief description of the school program, identification of potential job types available in the business, and possible times for an appointment to visit. During the initial site visit, the teacher should discuss the responsibilities of the school trainer, student, employer, and coworkers. In addition, the employer should understand the labor law requirements that need to be met regarding unpaid work experiences. The contact person also should be prepared to discuss insurance coverage by the school system and liability issues, as well as the development of a training agreement with the business. If the employer agrees to establish a training site, the teacher should schedule a time to meet with the department supervisors where the students will be working in order to develop task analyses and job duty schedules. A thank you note is always appropriate, regardless of the outcome of the initial contact.

Meeting Labor Law Requirements

Understanding a number of key concepts and issues is critical to successfully implementing the guidelines that were released by the Departments of Education and Labor. First, the primary intent of the *Fair Labor Standards Act* (FLSA) is to ensure that individuals are not exploited in the workplace (Halloran & Johnson, 1992). One way to make certain that students with disabilities are not exploited in nonpaid vocational training is to ascertain that a "nonemployment relationship" exists between the students and the employer. In other words, *the relationship exists for training purposes only, and activities completed by students do not result in an immediate advantage to the business.*

A number of factors are considered when determining whether a business is benefitting from having students in community-based instruction. First, the student(s) and teacher (or other school representative) cannot complete an employee's job duties while the employee is reassigned to other work tasks that are not usually his or her responsibility. The employee must continue to do his or her work while the student is trained on those tasks as well. This has been referred to as "shadowing" the regular employee (Inge et al., 1993). In addition, students cannot perform services that, although not ordinarily performed by employees, clearly benefit the business.

Before placing a student in a community business for instruction, the transition team must identify the goals and objectives that are to be trained and include them in the student's I.E.P. In addition, the teacher must make sure that the employer, student, and parents understand that the placement (a) is intended for training purposes and (b) is a nonpaid experience and that (c) the student is not guaranteed a job after the training is complete. It is important to

develop an agreement between all parties concerned that specifically states the intent of community-based vocational instruction including the Department of Labor and Department of Education guidelines. This agreement will be signed and dated by parents and student, school representative, and business representatives. Teachers need to realize that all of the criteria spelled out in the guidelines released by these two federal departments must be met in order to assert that an employment relationship does not exist. Fines can result, and businesses can be held responsible for back wages if violations are identified. Figure 15–4 contains these guidelines.

Labor Law Guidelines: Cases in Point

The following situations, related to Heather and Jane, show how some training or unpaid work experiences can conflict with labor law guidelines. Each situation must be individually analyzed according to the criteria shown in Figure 15–4.

Heather's Case

Heather's transition team, consisting of her teacher, the transition coordinator, her parents, and Heather, decides that she should participate in a minimum of three vocational training placements during the school year. Heather has not yet expressed a specific career preference so she will have three different training opportunities, including retail sales and food service. (See Figure 15–3 for work duties.) However, the team feels that it is important to determine whether Heather prefers the hardware store to the clothing store environment. All work tasks are specified in Heather's IEP, data will be collected, and a summary of each training experience will be written up for her school records. Heather, her parents, and each employer will sign an agreement before training, stating that these are nonpaid work experiences to benefit Heather and not the companies. A teacher or aide will be with Heather at all times to provide supervision, instruction, and data collection. Each experience will provide 120 hours of training experience within a real work environment.

Response to Heather's Case

One problem area is that the community-based training experiences at the hardware store and clothing store represent the same job type (e.g., Heather will be stocking merchandise). Some teachers may interpret the guidelines to mean that Heather could have 120 hours of training at the hardware and 120 hours at the clothing store during the school year, since

FIGURE 15–4
Labor Law Guidelines

Where *all* of the following criteria are met, the U.S. Department of Labor will *not* assert an employment relationship for purposes of the Fair Labor Standards Act.

- Participants will be youth with physical and/or mental disabilities for whom competitive employment at or above the minimum wage level is not immediately obtainable and who, because of their disability, will need intensive ongoing support to perform in a work setting.
- Participation will be for vocational exploration, assessment, or training in a community-based placement work site under the general supervision of public school personnel.
- Community-based placements will be clearly defined components of individual education programs developed and designed for the benefit of each student. The statement of needed transition services established for the exploration, assessment, training, or cooperative vocational education components will be included in the students' Individualized Education Program (IEP).
- Information contained in a student's IEP will not have to be made available; however, documentation as to the student's enrollment in the community-based placement program will be made available to the Departments of Labor and Education. The student and the parent or guardian of each student must be fully informed of the IEP and the community-based placement component and have indicated voluntary participation with the understanding that participation in such a component does not entitle the student-participant to wages.
- The activities of the students at the community-based placement site do not result in an immediate advantage to the business. The Department of Labor will look at several factors.
  1. There has been no displacement of employees, vacant positions have not been filled, employees have not been relieved of assigned duties, and the students are not performing services that, although not ordinarily performed by employees, clearly are of benefit to the business.
  2. The students are under continued and direct supervision by either representatives of the school or by employees of the business.
  3. Such placements are made according to the requirements of the student's IEP and not to meet the labor needs of the business.
  4. The periods of time spent by the students at any one site or in any clearly distinguishable job classification are specifically limited by the IEP.
- While the existence of an employment relationship will not be determined exclusively on the basis of the number of hours, as a general rule, each component will not exceed the following limitation during any one school year:
  Vocational exploration: 5 hours per job experienced
  Vocational assessment: 90 hours per job experienced
  Vocational training: 120 hours per job experienced
- Students are not entitled to employment at the business at the conclusion of their IEP. However, once a student has become an employee, the student cannot be considered a trainee at that particular community-based placement unless in a clearly distinguishable occupation.

An employment relationship will exist unless *all of the criteria* described in this policy guideline are met. Should an employment relationship be determined to exist, participating businesses can be held responsible for full compliance with FLSA, including the child labor provisions.

Businesses and school systems may at any time consider participants to be employees and may structure the program so that the participants are compensated in accordance with the requirements of the Fair Labor Standards Act. Whenever an employment relationship is established, the business may make use of the special minimum wage provisions provided pursuant to section 14(c) of the Act.

Note: Reprinted from United States Department of Education. (1992). *Guidelines for implementing community-based educational programs for students with disabilities.* Washington, D.C.: United States Department of Labor.

they are two different work sites. This is not the case, because the tasks performed at the stores are not from *clearly different job classifications*. In Heather's example, the teacher should monitor the training experiences to ensure that Heather receives only 120 hours of vocational training in stocking, regardless of the number of sites in any one school year. A second problem exists with the agreement with the various employers; it also should specify that Heather and her teacher are not displacing company employees, filling vacant positions, or otherwise benefiting the business during community-based instruction. For instance, Heather and her teacher would need to "shadow," or work alongside, regular employees while completing the work tasks at the job sites.

Jane's Case

Mrs. Jones is Jane's vocational instructor and is attempting to find all of her students "volunteer" positions within the community for at least 2 hours per week to help them gain work experiences. Mrs. Jones' cousin, Ms. Andrews, runs a day care center and suggests that she would be willing to have one student work for her every Monday afternoon from 3:30 P.M. to 5:30 P.M. Ms. Andrews would be willing to have a student come into the office and type simple memos. This job would be considered a "volunteer position." Mrs. Jones thinks that this might be a great opportunity for Jane, since her cousin will provide all of the supervision, and Jane will have an opportunity to be around small children, which was one of her interest areas. Mrs. Jones doesn't plan on listing these activities as part of Jane's IEP, since Jane is volunteering her time during nonschool hours.

Response to Jane's Case

Students who have disabilities can volunteer their time in the same way as their peers without disabilities (Inge et al., 1993). For instance, Mrs. Jones should try to identify typical volunteer positions with the United Way, SPCA, church, or other local charity organization for Jane. But, in this situation, it is unlikely that any 19-year-old student would volunteer for 2 to 4 hours of nonpaid office work. Jane must be paid at least minimum wage if this is not a training experience. If it is a training experience, it must be in the IEP and meet all labor law guidelines.

Another option to volunteering might be to determine if the students are able to meet the production levels for these particular jobs. If not, the teacher could consider assisting the employer (her cousin) to file for a *Special Handicapped Worker Certificate*. This certificate can be used when production levels for a particular job fall below the norm. The employer is generally responsible for obtaining a certificate of this type, however a rehabilitation counselor or school representative can submit a group application for all students and employers participating in a school work experience program. The important thing to note is that *the certificate must be in effect before employment*. Regional Department of Labor offices, Wage and Hour Division, have the directions and forms. Jane may

qualify for subminimum wage if she cannot work at the established company rate of production; however, if she is meeting the standard set by the company, she should be paid minimum wage for her work.

Analyzing the Work Culture and Identifying Potential Duties

During this step, the teacher needs to determine if there are any special requirements that the students must follow while on the work site. For instance, does the employer or supervisor want the student(s) to wear a uniform or specific clothing? What entrance should be used, and is it important to report to the supervisor upon arrival? Do employees have assigned lockers and can one be available to the student(s)? Is there an identified break area and employee bathroom? Are there any restricted areas or activities that can be identified? All of this information should be recorded and placed in a file that can be accessed by all school personnel. This would be particularly important during teacher absence when another school employee must supervise the site.

Initial information to identify potential jobs within a business can be obtained from the personnel director or employer. Often this individual will be able to provide written job descriptions that can be useful in identifying job types; however, observation at the work sites usually is more beneficial for job identification (Moon et al., 1990). When selecting activities, the teacher must be careful not to replace a worker within the job site as mentioned in the previous section. Therefore, the tasks targeted should provide enough space for the student(s) and teacher to shadow employees.

Scheduling Community-Based Instruction

Creative use of school personnel to schedule and transport students for community-based instruction clearly is the greatest challenge for administrators and teachers of students with severe disabilities (Hutchins & Talarico, 1985). A number of model demonstration programs across the country have identified solutions for scheduling and transportation issues (Baumgart & Van Walleghem, 1986; Hutchins & Talarico, 1985; Nietupski, Hamre-Nietupski, Welch, & Anderson, 1983; Wehman, Moon, Everson, Wood, & Barcus, 1988). Staffing solutions have included team teaching; use of volunteers, paraprofessionals, peer tutors, graduate students, and student teachers; heterogeneous groupings of students; staggered student training schedules; and use of support personnel providing integrated therapy services. Transportation issues have been resolved using volunteers' or parents' cars with mileage reimbursement, coordination of training schedules with regular school bus schedules, use of public transportation, use of school district vehicles, and walking to sites within short distances. Each school system must select procedures that are effective for their specific needs. A rule of thumb for scheduling purposes is to have no more than four students per training site per instructor; however, fewer would be more effective for skill development.

Selecting Systematic Behavioral Procedures to Teach Vocational Skills

Once the sites have been identified and a schedule for student placement determined, the teacher must design instructional programs outlining how each student will be taught job skills and other related activities, such as social skills. This analysis includes identifying the areas in which various job tasks are performed, establishing a work routine, identifying natural supports and natural cues in the workplace, and designing appropriate training and support strategies. Usually, working one shift before introducing students to the training sites is sufficient for completing these activities. *Remember that each skill that a student is learning on a job site must have an objective in the student's* IEP. Training objectives are written to include the observable behaviors that will be taught, the conditions under which they will occur, and the criteria that will be used to evaluate the student's performance. Ensuring that objectives are written for each student will also decrease the chance that community-based instruction turns into field trips.

Identifying Natural Supports

The first step in training is to identify the natural supports that may be available to students in the workplace and assist the student in accessing those supports. The use of the word *natural* implies that the supports are ones that are *typically* available to all workers in the workplace, not artificially contrived by the teacher. As such, natural supports can be referred to as *workplace supports*, which naturally occur on the job site. Workplace supports may include but are not limited to such things as a coworker mentor who assists a student in learning the job; a supervisor who

monitors work performance; a coworker who assists the student in developing social relationships, orientation training, or other company-sponsored training events; and an employee assistance program.

The role of the teacher is to assist the student in identifying and reviewing the variety of supports available and in selecting the ones that facilitate inclusion in the workplace. Companies vary in the number of workplace supports available. For instance, one company may have an intensive orientation and training program, while another has none. In addition, the support must be analyzed to determine if it meets the needs of the student. A one-time, 2-hour lecture on company policies may be of little benefit to the student, while a coworker who explains the "unwritten rules" of the workplace to all new employees may be an extremely valuable resource.

The teacher should not expect that employers and coworkers will automatically provide "natural supports" to a student. Some individuals initially may feel uncomfortable providing instruction and supervision to a worker with a disability. The teacher can model appropriate social interactions and training techniques that will assist coworkers and supervisors to become proficient and comfortable in assisting the student. This can be as subtle as encouraging coworkers to direct questions and conversation to the student rather than to the teacher from the first day of training. Another example may be the teacher who assists the student in learning the names of coworkers as quickly as possible. Trainer support must be analyzed carefully. Something as simple as where the teacher stands during instruction can place a barrier between the student and coworkers.

Inge and Tilson (1997) suggest that four questions be considered when choosing the best supports for the student in the workplace.

1. What are the possible workplace support resources?
2. Which strategies match the learning style or needs of the student?
3. What are the student's, employer's, coworker's choices?
4. Which support option results in or promotes student independence?

Initially, identifying and discussing the various support options with the student, employers, and coworkers is the teacher's role during community-based training. In most instances, a combination of strategies will be selected to promote skill acquisition. This combination of supports may include natural supports from coworkers, natural cues, compensatory strategies, as well as instruction from the teacher or coworkers. In other words, all supports needed may not be natural! Determining which combination promotes learning is the key to gradually increasing the student's independence in the workplace. Table 15–5 provides a summary of a range of supports that may assist a student in becoming independent in the workplace.

Natural Cues

A *natural cue* represents some feature of the work environment, job tasks, or activities that signals to a student what to do next. Typically, a natural cue is one that the student can see, hear, touch or feel, or smell and has not been changed or added to the worksite. Examples may include the color of a cleaning supply, an on/off indicator light, a buzzer on the service door, the telephone ringing, announcements over a loudspeaker, the "body language" of a coworker, and the placement or location of work materials (e.g., mail in an "in" box, dirty dishes on an unoccupied table).

When a natural cue is present or occurs during the student's work routine, he or she either attends to the cue and responds correctly, or does not attend to the cue at all, or responds incorrectly. For instance, a student may respond to the buzzer on the service door by opening it for the delivery person (the correct action); he or she may ignore the buzzer and continue pricing merchandise (no response); or he or she may go ask another worker to open the door (incorrect response). Obviously, if the student attends to and responds to a natural cue, instruction is not required. However, some students must learn to recognize and attend to these cues. The teacher should work with the student, the employer, and coworkers to identify the natural cues in the workplace that can assist the student in completing his or her tasks successfully. Often, the coworkers and supervisor can be the most valuable source for this information.

Some students still may fail to respond or recognize a cue, even after it is pointed out to them. One way to call attention to the cue may be to initially add an extra or artificial cue to the natural one. This *extra cue* can enhance the relevant features of the naturally occurring one.

TABLE 15–5
Examples of Workplace Supports

Strategy	Example
Self-monitoring	*Student has difficulty completing work within a specified time period.* Student uses a timer and a chart to monitor how long it takes to complete a specific job duty. Feedback from the chart assists the worker in meeting the job expectations.
Picture Cue	*Student has difficulty discriminating between work supplies.* Tape a picture of the work task on each container.
Color Cue	*Student has difficulty selecting her time-card to punch in.* Put a colored dot on the time card to assist the student in selecting her card.
Pre-taped instructions	*Student has difficulty reading copy requests to determine work assignments.* Tape record instructions for copy requests.
Visual Cue	*Student has difficulty remembering when to re-stock the condiment bar.* Place a piece of masking tape on the inside of the condiment bar as a visual reminder.
Auditory Cue	*Student has difficulty taking breaks on time.* Student uses a pre-programmed wrist watch.
Coworker Support	*Student has difficulty orienting in more than one to two work areas.* Coworkers bring copy requests to the copy room rather than ask the student to collect the work across multiple offices.
Reinforcement	*Student has difficulty meeting production standard.* Provide feedback hourly and ask student to assist with greeting restaurant patrons if a pre-agreed upon amount of work has been completed.

Adapted from: Inge, K. J., & Tilson, G. (1997). Ensuring support systems that work: Getting beyond the natural supports vs. job coach controversy. *Journal of Vocational Rehabilitation.*

Heather, who is filling a condiment bar on an "as needed" basis at her Shoney's vocational training placement, did not respond to the naturally occurring cue of the empty bins. A piece of tape was placed on the inside of the bins to signal her that a bin needed filling. The tape highlighted the relevant feature of the work task, the empty bin, to which Heather was not responding. Whenever extra cues are added to the work environment or work tasks, the teacher needs to consider fading them as the student begins to notice and correctly respond to the naturally occurring ones.

The supervisor or coworkers can be approached about assisting the student with natural or extra cues. Or, they may volunteer to check that added cues are not removed by other employees who are unfamiliar with the student's training program, and so forth. In fact, coworkers often discover that cues added for the student are beneficial to them in performing their work tasks.

As the coworkers and supervisors assist students with disabilities in identifying natural cues, they may begin to assist with identifying other strategies to assist the students. "Setting the stage" for positive interaction may facilitate the development of natural supports that are not contrived by the teacher. Ultimately, this may lead to the employer realizing that employees with disabilities can be easily supported in the workplace.

Systematic Instruction

Even after the identification of natural supports and natural cues in the workplace, the student most likely will need more intensive instruction. This includes developing a task analysis (TA) of the job tasks that have been identified for community-based instruction. This task analysis of each skill that the student will be learning must be written before bringing the student(s) to the work site. The best way to accomplish this is first to observe the coworkers performing the task and then to complete it yourself. Steps in a task analysis should be stated in terms of observable behaviors with each step representing one work "behavior." Once the step is complete, a visible change in the job task or process occurs. When writing the steps, the teacher may want to word them in the form of a verbal cue (e.g., push the "off" button). This provides a cue for using the steps of the task analysis as verbal prompts during instruction. There are several other tips for developing task analyses for vocational instruction in real work sites that may be critical for a student's skill acquisition and quality performance. These can be found in Table 15–6. See chapters 3 and 4 for additional information on task analyses.

After the initial analysis, the teacher should check with the supervisor to ensure that the task is being

TABLE 15–6
Tips for Writing Task Analyses for Community-Based Instruction

1. State steps in terms of observable behaviors.
2. Write steps in adequate detail with only one behavior per step.
3. Test the task analysis to ensure that each step results in a visible change in the job task or process.
4. Order steps from first completed to last completed.
5. Word steps as verbal cues.
6. Build natural cues and compensatory strategies into the task analysis.
7. Consider efficiency; use both hands with the least amount of movement.
8. Eliminate discrimination by avoiding need for judgment in the task (e.g., vacuuming in a pattern results in a clean rug versus needing to determine where the rug is dirty).

performed correctly. If modifications are made to the task to accommodate a specific student, this too should be approved by the employer. Finally, the teacher should have a schedule that outlines the tasks that will be performed while the students are on the site and the time frame in which activities will be performed. This sequence of job duties is necessary, since it is as important for students to learn to follow a work schedule as it is to complete individual work tasks. A job duty schedule with accompanying information can be found in Figure 15–5 for one of Heather's training sites.

Collecting Baseline and Probe Data

To effectively monitor the success of community-based vocational programs, the teacher must select a data-collection procedure for each skill receiving instruction (Inge et al., 1996; Inge & Wehman, 1993). These data are also needed to ensure that the school system is not violating labor law regulations for non-paid work experience. For instance, a student whose data show that she has reached skill acquisition and is performing at 100% of production standard should not be working in a nonpaid training site.

Teachers should consider the intrusive nature of the data collection when working with students in the community. While at times it may be appropriate to collect data on clipboards in the school, this strategy may call attention to the students' disabilities and isolate them in a community setting. Nonintrusive

FIGURE 15–5
Community-Based Job Duty Schedule

Training Schedule

Community-Based Training Site: Shoney's

Area Supervisor: Mrs. Mary Miller

Teacher Completing Form: Stacy D.

☒ Daily (Training tasks remain the same from day to day)

☐ Varies day to day (If checked here, complete a separate form for each day's schedule)

If above box is checked, indicate
day for which this form is completed:

☐ Mon ☐ Tues ☐ Wed ☐ Thurs ☐ Fri

Approximate Time	Vocational Training Tasks
1:00 PM–1:15 PM	Punch in, set up work area
1:15 PM–1:30 PM	Roll silverware
1:30 PM–2:00 PM	Bus tables
2:00 PM–2:15 PM	Break in employee lounge
2:15 PM–3:00 PM	Roll silverware
3:00 PM–3:30 PM	Greet customers in the front lobby
3:30 PM	Punch out—go to McDonald's

Comments: Heather should wear dark blue pants and a white shirt for this training site. Report to Mrs. Miller upon arrival.

If she is not in the stock room, call ext. 75 and report to Bill. Heather will work with Laura (coworker) on all tasks.

SIGNATURE/TITLE: _____ DATE: _____

strategies are recommended, such as collecting information on index cards or small pieces of paper that can be put into a pocket.

Two alternative strategies have been described in the literature as appropriate for collecting baseline and probe data: single- and multiple-opportunity probe procedures (Brooke et al., 1997). The critical component of both of these strategies is allowing the student to perform the task independently without providing feedback, reinforcement, or prompting. Initial data collection is referred to as a baseline and should be conducted at least once before the initiation of any skill acquisition program. Data collection, thereafter, is referred to as a probe and should be col-

lected at least once a week before the beginning of a training session. Typically, a skill is considered learned when the student performs the task correctly for three or four consecutive probe trials (Inge, et al., 1996; Moon et al., 1990), although it still may be forgotten or fail to generalize to other settings.

Baseline and probe data form a record of whether the student performs the step in the task analysis correctly (+) or incorrectly (−). Use of a *multiple-opportunity probe* requires that the student be assessed on his or her performance on every step of the task analysis. The second procedure, known as a *single-opportunity probe*, calls for the teacher to discontinue the assessment as soon as the student makes an error (Moon et al., 1990; Snell, 1978). Specific guidelines for each type of data collection are described in Table 15–7.

There are several things to consider when deciding whether to use a single- or multiple-opportunity probe in the workplace. First, data collection should not be time-consuming or interrupt the natural flow of the workplace. Use of a multiple opportunity data collection procedure could limit the amount of training time available on the site. For instance, if every

TABLE 15–7
Guidelines for Collecting Probe Data

Multiple Opportunity

1. Have the student move to the appropriate work area unless movement is the first step of the task analysis.
2. Stand beside or behind the student so that data collection does not interrupt the work flow.
3. Tell the student that he or she is going to complete the job without assistance to see how much he or she can do independently.
4. Provide the work cue (e.g., "roll the silverware").
5. Do not provide any further verbal instructions, prompts, or reinforcement.
6. Wait a specified latency period (e.g., 3 seconds) for the student to initiate a response.
7. Record (+) for correct performance or (−) for incorrect performance on the task analysis recording sheet.
8. If a response is incorrect or the student does not initiate a step within the latency period, complete the step yourself (if necessary) or position the student to perform the next step in the task analysis. (Do not take the student's hands and perform the step with him or her. This would be considered a physical prompt.)
9. Continue to move through all steps in the task analysis in this manner from first to last.

Single Opportunity

1. Have the student move to the appropriate work area unless movement is the first step of the task analysis.
2. Stand beside or behind the student so that data collection does not interrupt the work flow.
3. Tell the student that he or she is going to complete the job without assistance to see how much he or she can do independently.
4. Provide the work cue (e.g., "roll the silverware").
5. Do not provide any further verbal instructions, prompts, or reinforcement.
6. Wait a specified latency period (e.g., 3 seconds) for the student to initiate a response.
7. Record a (+) for correct performance.
8. As soon as the student makes an error or fails to respond within the latency period, discontinue the probe and score a (−) for all remaining steps in the task analysis.

step in operating the dish machine were tested, limited time for training would be available. Finally, coworkers may question the use of a multiple-opportunity strategy that appears to be more like testing than work in a real community environment.

A single-opportunity probe, however, allows for testing to stop as soon as the student makes an error, at which time training is initiated. This may be a more natural and efficient way to take data that maximizes training time on the job site. For instance, single-opportunity probes could be used predominately, and a multiple-opportunity probe initiated occasionally to determine exactly which step the student is having difficulty performing. Teachers should assess the work environment and the length of the task to determine the most appropriate strategy for data collection. (See chapter 5 for additional discussion of baseline strategies.)

Selecting an Instructional Strategy

Least Prompts

The majority of the literature on teaching job tasks to individuals with severe disabilities focuses on the use of least prompts as the teaching strategy of choice (Cuvo, Leaf, & Borakove, 1977; Test, Grossi, & Keul, 1988). Least prompts is also referred to as a response prompt hierarchy, since the trainer progresses from the least amount of assistance (usually a verbal prompt) to the most intrusive (usually a physical prompt) until one prompt stimulates correct responding.

A least prompt strategy can be very effective for teaching skills on community job sites. Teachers are encouraged to consider various types of prompts in addition to the traditional verbal, model, and physical sequence. For instance, as a student becomes more proficient on a work site, try using an indirect verbal prompt in the sequence such as, "What do you do next?" before using the verbal prompt specific to the step in the task analysis. This may be effective also for training students who have long been dependent on teachers for verbal instruction. In addition, gestures, such as touching the student's arm, can be used instead of a full model prompt or partial physical assistance.

Regardless of the types of prompts selected, the teacher should establish a latency period or time that he or she will wait for the student to respond before providing the next level of prompt. Usually a student should be given a latency of approximately 3 to 5 seconds. Students with physical disabilities, however, require longer latency periods based on their movement limitations, which should be determined on an individual basis. Finally, the teacher is cautioned to deliver each prompt only once before moving to the next more intrusive prompt. A least prompt training program that was used with Jennifer, a student with spina bifida, at one of her vocational sites can be found in Figure 15–6.

Time Delay

The use of time delay on vocational training sites is another viable option for teachers of students with severe disabilities (Moon et al., 1990). There are several critical components to a time delay procedure (Gast, Ault, Wolery, Doyle, & Belanger, 1988).

1. Prompt: First, the teacher must select a prompt that will consistently assist the student to perform the task correctly.
2. No delay: Initially, the prompt is given simultaneously with the request to perform the job duty. (By pairing the prompt with the request to perform a work task, the student is not allowed to make errors initially.)
3. Delay: Gradually, increasing amounts of time (usually seconds) are waited between giving the request to perform the task and providing the prompt to complete the skill correctly.

4. Number of trials or delay level: The number of trials at each delay level and the length of the delay should be determined before initiation of the program.

The delay procedure allows the teacher to gradually fade assistance until the student performs without prompting. For example, a set number of trials are determined for zero delay, the next set at 2 seconds, the next at 4 seconds, and so on, until the student performs without assistance.

Unlike the system of least prompts, time delay requires that the teacher select one prompt for use during the instructional program. Therefore, the procedure would be particularly useful if a student has consistently demonstrated a preference for one type of prompt. For example, if a student has shown that he or she always responds to a model prompt without making errors, the teacher can use models but fade them through delay (Moon et al., 1990). Monitoring of the training data is essential to ensure that the student is not making errors during the procedure. If this is the case, the teacher should consider selecting another prompt to provide an errorless learning experience. Figure 15–7 provides an example of a time delay program used on Jennifer's community-based training site. (See chapter 4 for further discussion of time delay.)

FIGURE 15–6
Instructional Program Using Least Prompts

Program: Putting Shirts on Hangers

Student: Jennifer

Community-based site: Burlington Coat Factory/Warehouse

Program objective: Given a box of shirts and a rack of hangers, Jennifer will place all of the shirts in the box on hangers with 100% accuracy according to the steps in the task analysis for three consecutive probe trials.

Rationale: Jennifer needs to participate in a vocational training program within the community to prepare her for employment by her last year of school. This job will provide her with a training experience similar to a position that she may obtain when she is older.

Student characteristics: Jennifer is 16 years old with severe mental retardation and paraplegia from spina bifida. She currently uses a manual wheelchair for transportation, which she sometimes refuses to do independently. Upper extremity functioning is within normal limits, however, Jennifer is unable to bear weight or move her lower extremities. She uses a "reacher" available from the Fred Sammons catalog to assist her in completing tasks. This will be incorporated into the task analysis for hanging shirts at Burlington Coat Factory.

FIGURE 15–6
continued

Task analysis: (1) Take shirt out of box; (2) Tear wrapper off of shirt; (3) Remove pins from the collar; (4) Remove the paper; (5) Shake out the shirt; (6) Lay the shirt flat on the table; (7) Pick up a coat hanger; (8) Open the bottom of the shirt; (9) Put hanger into shirt; (10) Pull shirt over hanger; (11) Shake out shirt; (12) Hang shirt on the rack; (13) Take another shirt out of the box.

Data collection: A baseline of performance will be collected the first day Jennifer is on the work site. Thereafter, probe data will be collected before each training session for the first shirt placed on a hanger. Use a single-opportunity probe procedure for both baseline and probe testing with a 5-second latency period between steps. Have Jennifer move to the work station and give the cue, "Place the shirt on a hanger." Record a (+) for all independent correct responses. Do not provide prompts or reinforcement. As soon as Jennifer makes an error, discontinue the probe and begin the training session.

Behavior change procedures: A system of least prompts using verbal, model, and physical assistance will be implemented for this program. Provide the instructional cue; if Jennifer completes the first step in the task analysis correctly, move on to the next step in the chain. If she does not respond within 5 seconds or begins to make an error, provide a verbal prompt specific to the first step in the task (i.e., pick up a shirt). If she responds correctly, move to the next step in the task analysis. If she does not respond within 5 seconds, or does so incorrectly, to the verbal prompt, provide a model prompt. Move on to the next step in the task if Jennifer responds correctly to the model prompt. If no response is made within 5 seconds or she initiates an incorrect response, provide a physical prompt to complete the step in the task analysis. Train all steps in the task analysis in this manner, moving from the first step to the last.

Data collection during training procedures: Use the task analysis data sheet for data collection. Score a (+) for independent correct responses, a (V) for correct responding after a verbal prompt, an (M) after a model prompt, and a (P) for completing a step with a physical prompt. Training data may be collected on a representative sample of trials during the time on the job site. For instance, the teacher could collect five trials during the beginning, middle, and end of the training session. It is not necessary to record every trial that is completed.

Reinforcement: Reinforce Jennifer on a fixed ratio schedule of every two steps in the task analysis with verbal praise specific to work behavior. ("That's good looking at your work." "I like the way you are hanging up the shirts.") Talk to the coworker and supervisor about socially reinforcing Jennifer for work well done. For instance, ask the supervisor to give a "thumbs-up" sign when passing the work area if Jennifer is on task. Provide a break after 1 hour of work in the employee break room. At the end of each training session, give her $1.00 to spend at McDonald's on the way back to school for a job well done.

When Jennifer is performing 30% of the steps in the task analysis independently, fade the verbal reinforcement on a fixed ratio schedule of every three steps. Continue the other components of the reinforcement procedures outlined above.

When Jennifer is performing 50% of the steps in the task analysis independently, provide verbal reinforcement on a variable ratio schedule of every five steps in the task analysis. Continue with the other reinforcement strategies.

When Jennifer is performing 75% of the steps in the task analysis independently, verbal reinforcement should be provided at the end of the task. Continue to encourage the supervisor and coworkers to praise and interact with Jennifer for work well done. Also continue to provide a break daily and trip to McDonald's.

Generalization and maintenance:

1. After Jennifer is performing 50% of the steps in the task analysis for *an entire box of shirts,* begin to step 3 feet away from her on those steps that she has demonstrated skill competence. Verbally praise her on an average of every three shirts placed on hangers. Interrupt errors and provide instruction as needed by moving back to Jennifer's side and using the least prompt strategy.

2. After Jennifer is performing 75% of the steps in the task analysis for *an entire box of shirts,* step 6 feet away from her on those steps that she has demonstrated skill competence. Continue at this distance until she reaches the program objective. Interrupt errors and provide instruction as needed by moving back to Jennifer's side and using the least prompt strategy.

3. Test for generalization to other types of items that can be placed on hangers.

4. When Jennifer has demonstrated 100% correct responding on all steps of the task analysis for an entire box of shirts for three consecutive probe sessions, the task is considered learned.

Note: Data should be reviewed regularly to ensure that Jennifer is not performing the task to company production standards or displacing the regular worker's job. If this occurs, the teacher needs to advocate for employment or remove Jennifer from the training site.

FIGURE 15–7
Instructional Program Using Time Delay

Program: Rolling Silverware

Student: Heather

Community-based site: Shoney's Restaurant/Dining Room

Program objective: Given a stack of napkins, a container of silverware, and the teacher positioned 10 feet from the student, Heather will roll silverware with 100% accuracy according to the steps in the task analysis for one entire training session.

Rationale: Heather needs to have community-based vocational training experiences in order to prepare her for the transition from school to work. Learning to complete a job task such as rolling silverware in a busy dining room setting will begin to help her develop community work skills. Heather will also have the opportunity to work alongside a company employee who is responsible for rolling silverware.

Student characteristics: Heather is a 16-year-old sophomore who has Down syndrome and moderate-to-severe mental retardation. She has no major physical problems and good physical strength. Heather has a positive work attitude, is motivated to do a good job, and is receptive to feedback from others.

Task analysis: (1) Place napkin in front of you; (2) Pick up knife; (3) Place knife in middle of napkin; (4) Pick up fork; (5) Place fork on top of knife; (6) Pick up corner of napkin; (7) Fold napkin over silverware to corner; (8) Hold silverware in the middle; (9) Turn silverware on its side; (10) Pick up corner of napkin; (11) Fold over end of silverware; (12) Hold end over silverware; (13) Pick up other corner of napkin; (14) Fold over other end of silverware; (15) Roll silverware in napkin; (16) Get a plastic bag; (17) Put silverware in bag; (18) Stack bag in silverware container.

Data collection: A baseline level of performance will be collected the first day Heather is on the work site. Thereafter, probe data will be collected before each training session for the first set of silverware rolled. Use a multiple-opportunity probe procedure for both baseline and probe testing with a 3-second latency period between steps. Have Heather move to the work station and give the cue, "roll the silverware." Record a (+) for an independent correct response and a (−) for an incorrect or no response. If Heather makes an error on a step or fails to respond within the latency period of 3 seconds, position her to complete the next step in the task analysis. If necessary, complete the step for her when she does not initiate a response or performs incorrectly. Do not provide any prompts or reinforcement.

Behavior change procedures: Use a time delay procedure with a physical prompt to train the steps in the task analysis. The teacher will position herself slightly to the side and behind Heather for instruction.

1.) A zero delay will be used for the first 25 trials of rolling silverware. Place the materials on the table and provide the instructional cue. Immediately provide the physical prompt through each step in the task until completion.

2.) Beginning on the 26th trial, a backward chaining procedure will be implemented. Continue to implement a zero delay on all steps of the task except the last one (stack bag in silverware container). Train this step by using a 2-second delay before providing the physical prompt. In other words, once step 17 of the task has been prompted using a zero delay, pause for 2 seconds to see if Heather performs the step without prompting. Correct performance should be reinforced. If she does not respond within the 2 seconds, provide the physical prompt. If she begins to make an error at any time during the 2 seconds, interrupt the error and provide the physical prompt. Continue with this procedure for the next 15 trials. Thereafter, increase the delay level for each 15 trials to 3, 4, and 5 seconds with the maximum delay level set at 5 seconds. When Heather has performed the last step in the task for 5 consecutive trials without prompting, begin training on the prior step in the chain. Continue all other steps in the task analysis at zero delay.

3.) Train each prior step in the chain in this manner until Heather is performing the task independently.

4.) Error Correction: Interrupt errors using a physical prompt if Heather begins to make an incorrect response on any step of the task. If three errors occur in a row on any one step, provide 10 trials at zero delay. Return to the previous delay level.

Data collection during training procedures: Use the task analysis data sheet for training data. Score a (*) on the data sheet for *prompted* correct responses on those steps being trained using the backward chaining procedure. Score a (+) for *unprompted* correct responses and a (−) for any incorrect response. Five consecutive (+) scores indicate that Heather has met the criteria for that step and training should begin on the prior step in the chain.

FIGURE 15–7
continued

Reinforcement: Provide a continuous schedule of reinforcement for each step in the task analysis on the first 25 trials (e.g., "That's the way to work." "Good looking at your work." "I like the way you are getting the silverware!"). After each set of silverware is rolled and placed in the container, check off on a reinforcement card that work has been completed. At the end of the training session, show Heather her card and pay her $1.00 for working. She can use this money to buy something on the job site or save it to spend later.

After the first 25 trials have been completed, reduce verbal reinforcement to a variable ratio schedule of three steps for prompted correct responses in the task analysis. Continue the card procedure. Always provide verbal reinforcement for steps completed without prompting. Use specific praise that provides feedback for the response:

1. "Good, picking up the fork."
2. "I like the way you folded the napkin."
3. "That's how you stack the silverware!"

After 50 trials have been completed, reduce verbal reinforcement to a variable ratio schedule of five steps for prompted correct responses. Continue the check card and verbal praise for each unprompted correct response.

Once Heather is performing a step independently for 10 consecutive trials, begin to fade your verbal reinforcement to every other correct response. After 20 consecutive trials on a step have been performed, discontinue verbal reinforcement on that step, fading to the check card system at the end of the entire task. Review data daily to ensure that the schedule of reinforcement is sufficient for skill acquisition. Modify as necessary.

Generalization and maintenance:

1. When Heather performs the task with 100% accuracy for three consecutive probe trials, the teacher will move to a seat across the table and implement a 6-second delay procedure. That is, if Heather does not complete a step in the task analysis within 6 seconds, a physical prompt will be provided. No comment will be made nor should Heather receive reinforcement on that step. At this time, the teacher should discontinue the use of the initial task cue and fade to the natural cue of materials on the table. Place a check on Heather's card after every two napkins rolled with silverware.
2. When Heather performs with 100% accuracy for one training day with the teacher sitting across the table, move 10 feet away from her. Continue with the 6-second delay and reinforcement on the check card every three task completions.
3. When Heather performs with 100% accuracy for one training day with the teacher 10 feet away from her, the program objective will be met.

Note: Data should be reviewed regularly to ensure that Heather is not rolling silverware independently to company production standards or displacing the regular worker's job. When this occurs, the teacher needs to advocate for employment or remove Heather from the training site.

Compensatory Strategies

Adding *compensatory strategies* to the instructional program can enhance a student's ability to learn and perform work tasks correctly. A compensatory strategy is any material or additional instruction, such as audiotaped directions or a jig for counting items, that compensates for the inability to independently perform certain aspects of a job (Inge et al., 1996). In some instances, using a compensatory strategy can eliminate instruction and allow the student to participate in activities that he or she otherwise could not. For instance, a student may use a "money card" to purchase a soda from the break room vending machine.

The money card eliminates the need for the student to learn the differences among coins or the actual amount that is required to access the machine. Remember, the steps in using a compensatory strategy may require instruction and should be included within any task analyses that are developed.

If compensatory strategies are targeted, they must be designed with input from the student, employer, and coworkers. In addition, care should be given to the design and construction of materials to ensure that they do not stigmatize the student. Materials, when possible, should be those that any adult could access within a work environment and would be accepted by the work culture where they are used. For instance, if a picture book is selected to assist a student in remembering his or her work schedule, the employment specialist and student should work together in the design of the booklet. Some of the things they may want to consider include the following. First, pictures should be concise and eliminate unnecessary information. Next, the number of pictures in the booklet should be evaluated. Too many may distract or confuse the student rather than assist in task completion. Third, the size of the booklet must be evaluated. Does it draw attention to the student? Could it be made small enough to fit in a pocket? Fourth, the materials should be simple to use. Is there a less complicated strategy that is just as effective? For instance, evaluate if the student could learn to use a written list of job tasks rather than a bulky picture book.

The same questions applied to designing a schedule reminder can be applied to almost any compensatory strategy used on a job site. Competency strategies should be simple to use and concise and the least intrusive strategy should be selected that will assist the student in performing his or her job duties. A list of common compensatory strategies used in vocational training programs can be found in Table 15–8.

Self-Management Strategies

Self-management has been referred to as self-monitoring, self-observation, self-evaluation, self-reinforcement, self-instruction, and self-assessment, to mention a few terms (Browder & Shapiro, 1985; Kazdin, 1984). Self-management strategies may be applied either before or after the targeted job duty or skill to assist the student in performing a task successfully and independently. For instance:

- The student may use a preset alarm on a watch to determine when it is time to take a break.
- A student may use a compensatory strategy, such as a picture book of tasks that need to be completed during the day.
- Another example is a student who evaluates his or her work performance in order to self-reinforce, such as marking checks on a card for a specific amount of work, which is later exchanged for a reinforcer.

Self-management usually entails instructing the student to independently self-monitor by using nat-

TABLE 15–8
Compensatory Strategy Ideas

The student can't remember his or her sequence of job duties.

- Written list
- Audiocassette
- Picture book
- Assignment board
- Flow chart

The student has difficulty reading copy requests to determine work assignments.

- In/out boxes for each coworker, requesting work with name or picture of coworker on box
- Special form highlighting relevant features of the task, such as thickly outlined box where number of copies is written
- Audiocassette requests for copy work

The student can't count to package work materials.

- Strips of tape on table which correspond to number of items in package
- Picture of number of items in the package
- Box with number of dividers that corresponds to number of items in package
- Sample of package for matching work

The student can't distinguish money to purchase a snack in the snack bar.

- A money card to match amount for standard purchase
- Correct change in a coin purse
- Next dollar amount strategy

ural cues, adding external cues and prompts, compensatory strategies, or assistive technology devices. This instruction can be provided by the teacher, friends, a family member, coworkers, or the supervisor, depending on the student's support needs. For instance, a family member may assist the student in checking off days on a calendar to determine when he or she goes to the community-based training site. A coworker may instruct the same student to use a timer to monitor production, while the teacher assists the student in using a picture book to sequence job tasks. Clearly, combining the use of compensatory strategies, natural cues, natural supports, and systematic instruction is the key to successful skill acquisition for students with significant disabilities in the workplace.

Special Considerations for Students with Physical Disabilities: Assistive Technology

A student with physical challenges has specialized support needs that should be identified before graduation that are related to independent living as well as employment (Inge & Shepherd, 1995; Sowers & Powers, 1991). These challenges can be met with assistive technology devices and services. The 1994 Reauthorization of the Technology-Related Assistance for Individuals Act (Tech Act) defined assistive technology (AT) devices and services:

> The term assistive technology device means any item, piece of equipment, or product system, whether acquired commercially off the shelf, modified, or customized, that is used to increase, maintain, or improve functional capabilities of individuals with disabilities [20 U.S.C. § 140(25)].

> The term assistive technology service means any service that directly assists an individual with a disability in the selection, acquisition, or use of an assistive technology device [20 U.S.C. § 140(26)].

There is a continuum of complexity in technology related to the device as well as the type of materials or manufacturing techniques used to produce the device (Inge & Shepherd, 1995). Low technology usually includes devices that are simple, with few or no moveable parts (Mann & Lane, 1991). These are devices that students use on job sites that may include (a) dycem (a nonskid mat that can stabilize work materials for the student), (b) keyguards, (c) book stands, (d) reachers, (e) laptray, or (f) builtup or enlarged handles on utensils or work tools. Low technology devices can be purchased almost anywhere from hardware stores to catalogs or can be made from materials that are found in a home workshop. Usually, these devices are low-cost and can be obtained quickly. High technology devices are defined by the use of electronics and specialized manufacturing techniques and materials (Anson, 1992). High technology is most often associated with computers, robotics, environmental control units, power wheelchairs, and so forth. High-tech devices are typically available through vendors from companies specializing in adaptive merchandise.

Possible sources for funding assistive technology include IDEA, Section 504 of the Rehabilitation Act, Medicaid, Social Security work incentive programs, and private insurance (Wallace, 1995). School district obligations to provide AT services and devices are defined by federal and state laws requiring school districts to provide special education and related services to students with disabilities and federal and state laws prohibiting discrimination against persons with disabilities. In addition, policy letters have been issued by the Office of Special Education Programs (OSEP), which has clarified the school districts' responsibilities in providing assistive technology (Inge & Shepherd, 1995). In August of 1990, the Office of Special Education Programs (OSEP) stated that assistive technology is a part of establishing the student's IEP (RENSA, 1992, pp. 34–35). This policy letter made it clear that school districts cannot deny AT to a student with a disability if the technology has been deemed necessary for the child to receive a free and appropriate public education.

Selecting the Device

Technology support needs should be identified after the student has selected a career path or potential job. This is very different from identifying devices and services and then trying to fit them into a job site. Once vocational training opportunities or a paid work experience are identified, options for supporting the student using technology should be explored. Some ways to deal with this issue include: (a) renting equipment, (b) borrowing a device from another individual who is using the technology that is being considered, (c) contacting the state assistive technology project (many programs have lending libraries), and (d) using equipment that is owned by the school system. Often, low technology solutions can be purchased or made at minimal cost that can be absorbed by the school system.

All options for assisting the student in completing the job task should be considered. High technology devices are not always the best solution. Alternatives may include adapting the skill sequence, eliminating difficult steps from the task analysis, or asking a coworker to provide assistance. As with all solutions, the least intrusive and most natural one should be identified. A student may be able to use a high technology device, but a quicker and more natural solution may be to seek personal assistance. In addition, the physical characteristics of the device must be acceptable to the student or he or she will simply not use the assistive technology.

After Jane's person-centered planning meeting, Jane and her teacher went to the local community college to review the new postsecondary program for students with severe disabilities. During the visit, the teacher and Jane realized that she would have a great deal of difficulty getting around the campus in her current power chair, which was more than 8 years old and did not navigate the rough terrain, including gravel and dirt paths. Jane's transition team referred her for an evaluation by the school's physical therapist. The therapist visited the campus, evaluated Jane's chair, and made recommendations to her physician. This included a head-activated switch rather than joystick, since the physical therapist felt that the use of her arm increased Jane's spasticity and difficulty in moving. The physician also felt that a new chair was necessary, and he wrote a prescription for the device. Since this was considered durable medical equipment, the funding source of choice was Medicaid. By using this option, the power chair purchased belonged to Jane and would transition with her to future environments.

Jane was accepted to the postsecondary program in the fall of the following school year as planned by her transition team. The community college had a part-time position located within the registrar's office, which matched one of Jane's interests: secretarial or office work. Jane and her transition team decided that this would be a job which would assist her in making some decisions about future employment. The supervisor in the office agreed to hire Jane for 10 hours a week to assist the office manager in maintaining a database on current and past students. The task identified for her was to assist the office manager in entering student data. At first this task seemed too difficult, since Jane was unable to use her hands to manipulate papers. The task was analyzed by the school system's occupational therapist and a number of simple solutions were identified. Jane's technology solutions can be found in Figure 15–8.

In addition, the teacher provided input into systematic instruction procedures that would assist Jane in learning the task. Time delay with a verbal prompt was used to teach her the data entry program. Thus a combination of assistive technology, coworker supports, and teacher training facilitated Jane's independence in this workplace. A table of how these supports combined to facilitate community employment for Jane can be found in Figure 15–9.

Finally, Jane's teacher knew that she must consider the instruction of related issues that are critical to employment success for students with the most severe disabilities. These may include toileting, eating

and drinking, communication, and mobility. These tasks, as well as the actual work duties, must be taught in the natural environment using systematic instruction procedures and may require modification from the manner in which they are performed at home or school. Jane chose to wear an adult protection garment rather than ask a coworker to assist her in the restroom, because it is difficult for one person to transfer Jane, who cannot stand and bear any of her own weight. However, a student worker volunteered to assist Jane with filling her sport bottle as well as eating a snack during break. This provided for important socialization time between Jane and her coworker, which ultimately developed into a nonwork relationship.

Paid Employment

Providing students with a variety of work experiences using the planning and instructional strategies described in this chapter should lead to paid employment for most students with disabilities. Whether it is part-time or full-time will depend on the needs and preferences of each student and her family as she exits the school system. It will also depend on the capacity of businesses, family and friend networks, and community systems to provide continual support to the worker. At any rate, most experts agree that paid employment experience before graduation should be the ultimate vocational goal for most students with significant disabilities. Research has shown that students with paid jobs before graduation are more likely to be employed as adults (Blackorby & Wagner, 1996; Hasazi, Gordon, & Roe, 1985). Of course, a variety of factors must be considered by a transition team before paid jobs are pursued. For example, younger students, between the ages of 16 and 19, may benefit more from inclusion in school-based classes where social and communication skills and work-related academic skills are stressed. For other students, regardless of age, developing work preferences and general skills through participation in short-term training placements may be more crucial. Many students may benefit from inclusion in regular vocational education programs, as long as the content is directly related to the local labor market. Research has shown that participation in such classes is positively related to postschool employment of students with disabilities

FIGURE 15–8
Jane's Assistive Technology Solutions

Jane's Job: Entering names and addresses into a mailing list

Jane's Strengths:

- Types simple letters to friends and family members using a head pointer on a manual typewriter.
- Can copy whatever is written on paper with accuracy even if she can't read the words.
- Is very social and expresses an interest in learning to use a computer for data entry.
- Uses a power chair for mobility.
- Can lift her right arm to shoulder height.
- Is extremely motivated to work.

Jane's Work Challenges:

- Cannot use her fingers to grasp objects.
- Is not able to manipulate paper for data entry.
- Must rely on others for daily care activities.
- Does not have any computer training or previous work experiences.

Issue #1: Jane's headpointer slips when striking the keys.

Solution: *An eraser was put on the end of her headpointer.*

Issue #2: Jane cannot access upper case keys or press more than one key at a time.

Solution: *A DOS-based program called "Sticky Keys" was put on Jane's computer.*

Issue #3: The computer is at a low level; accessing it is awkward.

Solution: *A stand was made to position the computer keyboard at an angle that was easy for Jane to access.*

Issue #4: Jane has difficulty keeping her place on the paper listing the data to enter.

Solution: *A stand, which was available at an office supply store, was adapted with a motorized paper guide. Jane used a switch to move the guide down the page. This assisted her in keeping her place for data entry.*

Issue #5: Jane cannot manipulate paper for data entry.
Requests arrive on telephone message pads, business cards, and scrap pieces of paper.

Solution: *Jane's supervisor suggested taping requests to standard size paper. She offered to do this for her.*

Issue #6: Jane has difficulty reading small print.

Solution: *Type was enlarged on the copy machine.*

Issue #7: How will Jane turn the sheets of paper?

Solution: *Jane pushed the pages off the typing stand using her head pointer.*

Issue #8: Jane couldn't stack finished work.

Solution: *A box, which caught the finished pages, was attached to her stand.*

Issue #9: Jane can't use the telephone to call her supervisor for assistance.

Solution: *The phone receiver was placed on a goose neck holder. Jane uses her headpointer to access the touch tone buttons. She was also given an emergency alarm button. The receiver unit is kept by the supervisor. Whenever she needs immediate assistance, Jane can push her alarm button.*

FIGURE 15–9

Jane's Supports for a Job in the Community

Student is to enter data into community college mailing list.

Challenges:

- Learning how to use the data entry program
- Physically manipulating the work materials
- Meeting production goals

Student needs to enter addresses using a computer.

1. Accommodations (low technology devices)	Teacher works with supervisor and student to modify the work space. Teacher finds a work table that is accessible for student. Work site pays for table. Teacher gets blocks to raise the table to adequate work height. Student brings head pointer to work to use for data entry. Stand is made to tilt computer keyboard for easy access. "Sticky Keys" is loaded onto the computer.
2. Instruction (time delay)	Teacher and coworker develop task analysis for data entry. Student, supervisor, and teacher decide that the teacher will assist the student in learning the data entry program using a time delay strategy with a verbal prompt. Teacher carefully fades assistance, using the time delay strategy.
3. Color cue	Student and teacher discuss mistakes in data entry. Student is having difficulty distinguishing among the number "one," the letter "el" (1), and the letter "eye". The teacher uses a pink and green highlighter pen to add a color cue. This cue is faded as the student begins to distinguish the letters.

Student needs to use the telephone to buzz supervisor for assistance.

1. Accommodations (low technology device)	Teacher brainstorms with the supervisor and employee how the student will contact the supervisor when assistance is needed. Teacher identifies a device to hold the telephone receiver. Supervisor provides money to pay for device. Student uses head pointer to punch buttons on the phone.
2. Coworker assistance	Coworker offers to check to make sure phone is in the device at the beginning of the work day.

Student needs a way to manipulate the paper with names for data entry.

1. Specialized accommodation	A work stand and paper holding device are designed by the therapist with a paper guide that the student moves down the page by pushing a switch.
2. Coworker assistance	Coworker offers to place pages on device at the beginning of the work day. She also offers to enlarge the type on the pages on the copy machine so that it is easier for student to read.
3. Instruction	Student, teacher, and supervisor discuss training on device. Student decides that the teacher will develop a task analysis and train her to use the device.

Student needs to increase data entry speed.

1. Self-monitoring	Supervisor, student, and teacher discuss the need for increased production. Teacher obtains a timer and records student's data entry speed. He presets the timer for a faster time. Student uses the timer to monitor data entry speed.
2. Reinforcement	Coworker offers to check on the student and praise when she notices that student is meeting the time requirement.

Note: Adapted from Inge, K. J., & Tilson, G. (1997). Ensuring support systems that work: Getting beyond the natural supports vs. teacher controversy. *Journal of Vocational Rehabilitation, 9*(2), 133–142. Reprinted with permission.

(Hasazi et al., 1985; McDonnell et al., 1996). Two of the most important considerations for obtaining paid jobs are:

1. How paid work may affect Social Security benefits that a student and his family now receive.
2. Whether or not paid work placement will be supported by some formal or informal system after the student leaves school.

Social Security Benefits and Work Incentives

Parents have a number of concerns regarding the effect of employment on the benefits their sons or daughters receive from Social Security Income (SSI) and Social Security Disability Insurance (SSDI) programs. The concerns include loss of or reduction of SSI payments, which can lead to loss of medical benefits, particularly Medicaid. Teachers must become informed regarding these issues and be able to assist parents in understanding the regulations in order to facilitate employment for students with severe disabilities.

In January of each year, Congress establishes a *Federal Benefit Rate* (FBR) which is the maximum dollar amount that a student or couple can receive in SSI cash benefits on a monthly basis (O'Mara, 1991). The amount a student actually receives is based on his or her resources, living arrangements, unearned income, and earned income. For instance, a student living with her parents and receiving food and shelter is considered to be receiving in-kind support. The SSI check would be reduced by one third of the amount of the FBR. In addition, any earned income from employment should be reported to the Social Security office for consideration in the monthly payment. Parents need to understand that the Social Security office must be notified in writing each time a student starts working, stops working, or when there is a change in monthly work earnings, because these changes affect the amount of SSI a student receives each month. They may also affect a student's eligibility to receive SSDI.

Students who receive SSDI will be affected by an incentive known as the *Trial Work Period*. Unlike SSI, where a student's benefits are decreased based on the amount of money earned, SSDI recipients must be reevaluated for SSDI eligibility following a 9-month Trial

Work Period. At the conclusion of the Trial Work Period, the case is reviewed to determine whether the student has reached "substantial gainful activity." *Substantial gainful activity* (SGA), at the time of this writing, is defined as monthly earnings that exceed $500. Benefits are terminated for all students who earn more than $500 a month (SGA), however those students whose monthly earnings do not reach the SGA level continue to receive their full SSDI benefit. Students who are determined to be ineligible for SSDI after their 9-month Trial Work Period qualify for an *Extended Period of Eligibility*. This work incentive provides SSDI benefits to students during any months that they do not reach substantial gainful activity. The Extended Period of Eligibility is available for 36 months following the 9-month Trial Work Period. In order to receive benefits during the extended period, the student or his or her family must notify the person's Social Security Representative.

Social Security work incentives. The Social Security Administration provides several work incentives for SSI and SSDI recipients, which can help them to keep their benefits while they work. Some of the work incentives apply to both SSI and SSDI, while others are specific to only one of the programs. These work incentives are described here.

All students who receive SSI qualify for an *Earned Income Exclusion*. This incentive allows most recipients to keep a portion of their original monthly SSI benefit even after they start working. The amount of SSI they receive depends on the amount of money they earn and whether they qualify for any other work incentives. Once the Social Security Office is notified of employment, the Earned Income Exclusion is automatically calculated when determining the recipient's new SSI benefit. It is not necessary to submit any additional paperwork to claim an earned income exclusion.

A special work incentive is also available for youth under age 22 who are employed while they are still enrolled in school. The *Student Earned Income Exclusion* allows an SSI recipient to exclude up to $400 of earned income a month, with a maximum of $1,620 a calendar year. This exclusion applies consecutively to months in which there is earned income until the exclusion is exhausted, or the student is no longer considered a child. The Student Earned Income Exclusion is calculated before any other work incentive, such as the Earned Income Exclusion, is taken.

This work incentive helps students retain more of their original SSI check while working and remaining in school.

For a student to claim the exclusion, documentation must be provided that the student was regularly attending school in at least 1 month of the current calendar quarter, or expects to attend school for at least 1 month. In addition, Social Security will need to be notified of the amount of the student's earned income. Regularly attending school means that the student must be enrolled in and taking one or more courses and attends the class regularly. More specifically, the student is (a) in college or university for 8 hours a week; (b) in grades 7 through 12 for 12 hours a week; (c) in a training course to prepare for employment for 12 hours per week; or (d) for less time than indicated above for reasons beyond the student's control, such as illness. This work incentive should also be automatically calculated by the Social Security Office.

SSI recipients who need additional financial resources to help them get or maintain employment may submit a *Plan for Achieving Self-Support* (PASS) (O'Mara, 1991). This work incentive enables students to set aside a portion of their earned income in a special savings account in order to save and pay for services that will allow them to achieve their employment goals. A PASS can be written to cover almost anything that is determined to be work-related. Some examples include specialized transportation, assistive technology devices, tuition, job coach services, and safety equipment. A PASS may be written at any time during a student's employment. Currently, all PASS plans must be submitted to the Social Security office in Baltimore and may take up to 6 months for approval. Therefore, a better and quicker alternative for the student may be an *Impairment-Related Work Expense* (IRWE). Another advantage to the IRWE is that, unlike the PASS, its use is not time-limited.

An IRWE allows students to deduct the cost of work-related expenses from their earnings before calculations are made to determine their SSI or SSDI benefit. An IRWE must include work expenses directly related to a student's disability and paid for by that student. The expenses must be paid within the month the student is working and not reimbursed by another source. An IRWE is not a written plan, but rather a monthly report of expenditures used by the Social Security representative in calculating total countable income and determining continued eligibility or the amount of monthly cash payments. The Social Security Administration must have proof for every IRWE claimed by the worker with a disability. This includes the following: (a) name and address of prescribing source (e.g., doctor, vocational rehabilitation counselor); (b) impairment for which the IRWE is prescribed; and (c) receipts and canceled checks. Some of the expenses that may be reimbursed using an IRWE include the following: attendant care services, assistive technology, drugs and medical services, transportation costs, and guide dogs, to mention a few. The expense must be submitted and approved by the Social Security Administration in order for this work incentive to take effect.

Remember that these regulations require that the Student Earned Income Exclusion is taken away before any other work incentive is used. In many cases, a student will not be making enough money to take both this exclusion and an IRWE or PASS simultaneously. However, once the student exclusion is exhausted for the calendar year, the student may consider using an IRWE or writing a PASS to further facilitate meeting employment goals while maintaining SSI or SSDI benefits.

Employment Support After Graduation

The transition team responsible for providing on-the-job training during a student's final paid job placement before graduation must address a number of issues, including job-specific skill training, changes in Social Security benefits, family satisfaction, transportation details, social and communication skill development, and most importantly, who will assume responsibility for the student's job performance after he or she graduates. This final issue is probably the most pressing one facing families and individuals with disabilities today, *because no particular agency is mandated to serve individuals with disabilities in any capacity once they leave special education!*

Despite the lack of appropriate community services available to young workers with severe disabilities, agencies are slowly changing, and newer, more innovative employment supports are springing up across the country. Also, creative solutions to the problems are being developed as special and vocational educators forge agreements and work cooperatively with businesses, government, and community agencies.

One of the most exciting developments is the use of workplace supports (Inge & Tilson, 1997) as described earlier in this chapter, which allow school or community service agencies to more quickly fade financial and personnel support from workers.

When workers with disabilities need continuing supported employment services, a variety of funding and program options should be sought (Brooke et al., 1997). In most localities employment support services for adults with disabilities are provided by not-for-profit agencies that receive funding on a per customer basis from a variety of sources including vocational rehabilitation, state developmental disabilities agencies, Medicaid, Social Security work incentives, and special state-legislated allocations. Many of these agencies provide supported employment as well as traditional sheltered work, work evaluation, and day activity programs. It is imperative that a transition team specifically inquire about how training and support are provided before a student moves into one of these agency programs. For example, some agencies may have constraints on the type or amount of community or supported employment training they can provide because of funding mandates from particular state or federal sources. Agencies in the past have pulled workers from paid jobs in real work sites back into sheltered employment in order to retain dollars allotted for that person from state developmental disability resourceÛ or other sources. In most states, dollars can be shifted from traditional service delivery modes to supported employment through creative and collaborative agreements at the local, state, and federal levels. For example, Medicaid money can fund supported employment, although some local programs have been slow to use this resource for supports other than traditional day habilitation or residential services.

By using the questions in Table 15–1, a transition team can assess the ability of an adult agency to provide appropriate employment support to a young adult leaving school. Of course, regardless of the quality of services provided by any agency, it can accept or reject a potential consumer of its services despite the needs or desires of that consumer. Most adult services have long waiting lists and entry into any program is typically competitive. The individual who receives support from a community agency is the one whose team worked very early on to understand exactly how to qualify for each particular program. Ultimately, the best way for a school vocational program to ensure that a student gets and keeps paid employment is to help the student get the job and to develop long-term supports that are not agency-specific and firmly in place before graduation.

Summary

IDEA (PL 105-17), according to the 1997 Amendments, broadened the focus of transition and lowered the age at which these services begin to age 14. This law mandates that assessment, training, and supports related to employment, independent living, or any area of adult functioning be included in a student's IEP. Providing transition services is a longitudinal process involving collaboration among a student, her family, school professionals, community support services, and the business community. Although special education is ultimately given the responsibility of implementing transition goals and activities, transition planning affects all curriculum areas. Decisions continually have to be made regarding which instructional areas are most important and when and where training and support should be provided. Student preferences must be assessed throughout the years and this must be matched to the availability of employment, residential options, and social or leisure programs in the community.

Although the availability and quality of community support services for adults with disabilities is improving, there are long waiting lists for all programs, none of which are mandated. Therefore, transition teams must still work to find the critical supports or teach the most important skills related to adult functioning before the young adult reaches age 21 and must leave the school system. They must also work together to understand the strengths and needs of current school and community programs so that families, at an early stage, can begin to untangle the array of laws, agencies, and programs that will affect their son or daughter with a severe disability through the life span.

Suggested Activities

1. Design a transition planning process appropriate to your community. Identify the agencies or organizations and the individuals representing those groups that should meet to establish the transition procedures for students with disabilities.

2. Identify employment opportunities in your community, based on:
   a. conversations with a chamber of commerce representative
   b. conversations with the labor department,
   c. conversations with a vocational rehabilitation agency, and
   d. searches in the local Sunday newspaper "help wanted" section.

References

Anson, D. (1992). *Rehabilitation 492: Technology in rehabilitation and education course syllabus*. Seattle: University of Washington, Department of Rehabilitation Medicine, Division of Occupational Therapy.

Bates, P., Bronkema, J., Ames, T., & Hess, C. (1992). State-level interagency planning models. In F. Rusch, L. DeStefano, J. Chadsey-Rusch, L. Phelps, & E. Szymanski (Eds.), *Transition from school to adult life: Models, linkages, and policy* (pp. 115–129). Sycamore, IL: Sycamore Publishing.

Baumgart, D., & VanWalleghem, J. (1986). Staffing strategies for implementing community-based instruction. *Journal of the Association for Persons with Severe Handicaps*, 11, 92–102.

Blackorby, J., & Wagner, M. (1996). Longitudinal postschool outcomes of youth with disabilities: Findings from the National Longitudinal Transition Study. *Exceptional Children*, 62, 399–413.

Brooke, V., Inge, K., Armstrong, A., & Wehman, P. (Eds.). (1997). *Supported employment handbook: A customer-driven approach for persons with significant disabilities*. Richmond, VA: Virginia Commonwealth University.

Browder, D. M., & Shapiro, E. S. (1985). Applications of self-management to individuals with severe handicaps: A review. *Journal of the Association for Persons with Severe Handicaps*, 10(4), 200–208.

Button, C. (1992, October/November). P.L. 102–569: A new season for the rehabilitation act. *Word from Washington*. Washington, DC: United Cerebral Palsy Association.

Cuvo, A. J., Leaf, R. B., & Borakove, L. S. (1977). Teaching janitorial skills to the mentally retarded: Acquisition, generalization, and maintenance. *Journal of Applied Behavior Analysis*, 11, 345–355.

Everson, J. (1993). *Youth with disabilities: Strategies for interagency transition programs*. Boston: Andover Medical Publishers.

Falvey, M., Gage, S., & Eshilian, L. (1995). Secondary curriculum and instruction. In M. Falvey (Ed.), *Inclusive and heterogeneous schooling: Assessment, curriculum and instruction* (pp. 341–362). Baltimore: Paul H. Brookes.

Falvey, M. A., Forest, M., Pearpoint, J., Rosenberg, R. L. (1992). *All my life's a circle: Using the tools of circles, MAPS and PATH*. Toronto, Canada: Inclusion Press.

Field, S., & Hoffman, A. (1994). Development of a model for self-determination. *Career Development for Handicapped Individuals*, 17(2), 159–169.

Furney, K., Hasazi, S., & DeStefano, L. (1997). Transition policies, practices, and promises: Lessons from three states. *Exceptional Children*, 63, 343–355.

Gast, D. L., Ault, M. F., Wolery, M., Doyle, P. M., & Belanger, J. (1988). Comparison of constant time delay and the system of least prompts in teaching sight word reading to students with moderate retardation. *Education and Training in Mental Retardation*, 23, 177–188.

Halloran, W. D., & Johnson, W. (1992). Education-industry collaboration: Guidelines for complying with the Fair Labor Standards Act. *American Rehabilitation*, 18(4), 21–23.

Hanley-Maxwell, C., Whitney-Thomas, J., & Pogoloff, S. (1995). The second shock: A qualitative study of parents' perspectives and needs during their child's transition from school to adult life. *Journal of the Association for Persons with Severe Handicaps*, 20(1), 3–15.

Hasazi, S. B., Gordon, S., & Roe, R. (1985). Factors associated with the employment status of handicapped youth exiting high school from 1979–1983. *Exceptional Children*, 51(6), 455–469.

Hutchins, M., & Renzaglia, A. M. (1990). Developing a longitudinal training program. In F. R. Rusch (Ed.), *Supported employment* (pp. 365–380). Sycamore, IL: Sycamore Publishing.

Hutchins, M., & Talarico, D. (1985). Administrative considerations in providing community integrated training programs. In P. McCarthy, J. Everson, S. Moon, & M. Barcus (Eds.), *School to work transition for youths with severe disabilities*. Richmond, VA: Virginia Commonwealth University.

Individuals with Disabilities Education Act, 20 U.S.C. 1400 (1997).

Inge, K. J., Dymond, S., & Wehman, P. (1996). Community-based vocational training. In P. J. McLaughlin & P. Wehman (Eds.), *Mental retardation and developmental disabilities* (2nd ed.) (pp. 297–316). Austin, TX: Pro-Ed.

Inge, K. J., & Shepherd, S. (1995). Assistive technology and school system personnel. In K. F. Flippo, K. J. Inge, & J. M. Barcus (Eds.), *Assistive technology: A resource for school, work, and community* (pp. 133–166). Baltimore: Paul H. Brookes.

Inge, K., Simon, M., Halloran, W., & Moon, M. S. (1993). Community-based vocational instruction and labor laws: A 1993 update. In K. Inge, & P. Wehman (Eds.), *Designing community-based vocational programs for students with severe disabilities* (pp. 51–80). Richmond, VA: Virginia Commonwealth University.

Inge, K. J., & Tilson, G. (1997). Ensuring support systems that work: Getting beyond natural supports versus job coach controversy. *Journal of Vocational Rehabilitation*, 9, 133–142.

Inge, K. J., & Wehman, P. (Eds.). (1993). *Designing community-based vocational programs for students with severe disabilities*. Richmond, VA: Virginia Commonwealth University.

Kazdin, A. E. (1984). *Behavior modification in applied settings* (3rd ed.). Homewood, IL: Dorsey Press.

Malatchi, A., & Inge, K. J. (1997). *Whose life is it anyway?: A look at person-centered planning and transition* (on-line). Available: http://www.vcu.edu/rrtcweb/techlink.

Mann, W. C., & Lane, J. P. (1991). *Assistive technology for persons with disabilities: The role of occupational therapy*. Rockville, MD: American Occupational Therapy Association.

McDonnell, J., Mathot-Buckner, C., & Ferguson, B. (Eds.) (1996). *Transition programs for students with moderate/severe disabilities*. Pacific Grove, CA: Brooks/Cole Publishing.

McNair, J., & Rusch, F. R. (1991). Parent involvement in transition programs. *Mental Retardation*, 29(2), 93–101.

Meers, G. D. (1992). Getting ready for the next century. *Teaching Exceptional Children*, 24(2), 36–39.

Miner, C. A., & Bates, P. E. (1997). Person-centered transition planning. *Teaching Exceptional Children*, 66–69.

Moon, M. S., Inge, K. J., Wehman, P., Brooke, V., & Barcus, J. M. (1990). *Helping persons with severe mental retardation get and keep employment: Supported employment issues and strategies.* Baltimore: Paul H. Brookes.

Mount, B. (1994). Benefits and limitations of Persons Futures Planning. In V. J. Bradley, J. W. Ashbaugh, & B. C. Blaney (Eds.). *Creating individual supports for people with developmental disabilities: A mandate for change at many levels* (pp. 97–108). Baltimore: Paul H. Brookes.

National Association of the State Directors of Special Education. (1990). *Education of the handicapped act amendments of 1990 (P.L. 101–476): Summary of major changes in parts A through H of the act.* Washington, DC: Author.

Nietupski, J. A., Hamre-Nietupski, S., Welch, J., & Anderson, R. J. (1983). Establishing and maintaining vocational training sites for moderately and severely handicapped students: Strategies for community/vocational trainers. *Education and Training of the Mentally Retarded*, 18, 169–175.

O'Brien, J., & Lovett, H. (1992). *Finding a way toward everyday lives: The contribution of person centered planning.* Harrisburg, PA: Pennsylvania Office of Mental Retardation.

O'Mara, S. (1991). Current Social Security incentives and disincentives. In S. L. Griffin, & W. R. Grant (Eds.), *Rehabilitation counselor desk top guide to supported employment.* Richmond, VA: Virginia Commonwealth University.

Pearpoint, J., O'Brien, J., & Forest, M. (1993). PATH: *a workbook for planning positive possible futures: Planning alternative tomorrows with hope for schools, organizations, businesses, families.* Toronto, Canada: Inclusion Press.

Pumpian, I., Shepard, H., & West, E. (1988). Negotiating job training stations with employers. In P. Wehman & M. S. Moon (Eds.), *Vocational rehabilitation and supported employment* (pp. 177–192). Baltimore: Paul H. Brookes.

Putnam, J. W. (1994). *Cooperative learning and strategies for inclusion: Celebrating diversity in the classroom.* Baltimore: Paul H. Brookes.

Renzaglia, A. & Hutchins, M. (1988). A community-referenced approach to preparing persons with disabilities for employment. In P. Wehman & M. S. Moon (Eds.), *Vocational rehabilitation and supported employment* (pp. 91–110). Baltimore: Paul H. Brookes.

RENSA Technical Assistance Project (1992). *Assistive technology and the individualized education program.* Washington, DC: RENSA Press.

Rusch, F., Szymanski, E., & Chadsey-Rush, J. (1992). The emerging field of transition services. In F. Rusch, L. DeStefano, J. Chadsey-Rush, A. Phelps, & E. Szymanski (Eds.), *Transition from school to adult life: Models, linkages, and policy* (pp. 5–16). Sycamore, IL: Sycamore Publishing.

Sale, P., Metzler, H., Everson, J., & Moon, S. (1993). Quality indicators of successful vocational transition programs. *Journal of Vocational Rehabilitation*, 1(4), 47–64.

Sitlington, P., Neubert, D. A., Begun, W., Lombard, R. C., & Leconte, P. J. (1996). *Assess for success: Handbook on transition assessment.* Reston, VA: Council for Exceptional Children, Division on Career Development and Transition.

Snell, M. (Ed.). (1978). *Systematic instruction of the moderately and severely handicapped.* Columbus, OH: Charles E. Merrill Publishing.

Sowers, J., & Powers, L. (1991). *Vocational preparation and employment of students with physical and multiple disabilities.* Baltimore: Paul H. Brookes.

Sowers, J., & Powers, L. (1995). Enhancing the participation and independence of students with severe physical and multiple disabilities in performing community activities. *Mental Retardation*, 33(4), 209–220.

Stainback, S., & Stainback, W. (1992). *Curriculum considerations in inclusive classrooms: Facilitating learning for all students.* Baltimore: Paul H. Brookes.

Steineman, R. M., Morningstar, M. E., Bishop, B., & Turnbull, H. R. (1993). Role of families in transition planning for young adults with disabilities. *Journal of Vocational Rehabilitation*, 3(2), 52–61.

Szymanski, E. M., Turner, K. D., & Hershenson, D. (1992). Career development of people with disabilities: Theoretical prospective. In F. R. Rusch, L. DeStephano, J. Chadsey-Rusch, A. Phelps, & E. M. Szymanski (Eds.), *Transition from school to adult life: Models, linkages, and policy* (pp. 391–406). Sycamore, IL: Sycamore Publishing.

Tashie, C., & Schuh, M. (1993, Spring). Why not community-based instruction? High school students belong with their peers. *Equity and Excellence*, p. 15–17.

Technology-related assistance for Individuals with Disabilities Amendments of 1994, PL 103–218. (March 9, 1994). Title 29, U.S.C. 2201 et seq; U.S. *Statutes at Large*, 108, 50–97.

Test, D. W., Grossi, T., & Keul, P. (1988). A functional analysis of the acquisition and maintenance of janitorial skills in a competitive work setting. *Journal of the Association for Persons with Severe Handicaps*, 13, 1–7.

Turnbull, A., & Turnbull, H. R. (1997). *Families, professionals, and exceptionality.* Upper Saddle River, NJ: Prentice-Hall.

Vandercook, T., York, J., & Forest, M. (1989). The McGill Action Planning System (MAPS): A strategy for building the vision. *Journal of the Association for Persons with Severe Handicaps*, 14, 205–215.

Wallace, J. F. (1995). Creative financing of assistive technology. In K. F. Flippo, K. J. Inge, & J. M. Barcus (Eds.), *Assistive technology: A resource for school, work, and community* (pp. 245–268). Baltimore: Paul H. Brookes.

Wehman, P. (1995). *Individual transition plans: The teacher's curriculum guide for helping youth with special needs.* Austin, TX: Pro-Ed.

Wehman, P. (1996). *Life beyond the classroom: Transition strategies for young people with disabilities* (2nd ed.). Baltimore: Paul H. Brookes.

Wehman, P., Moon, M. S., Everson, J. M., Wood, M., & Barcus, M. (1988). *Transition from school to work: New challenges for youth with severe disabilities.* Baltimore: Paul H. Brookes.

Wehmeyer, M. & Kelchner, K. (1995). *Whose future is it anyway? A student directed transition planning process.* Arlington, TX: ARC National Headquarters.

Winking, D., O'Reilly, B., & Moon, M. S. (1993). Preference: The missing link in the job match process for individuals without functional communication skills. *Journal of Vocational Rehabilitation*, 3(3), 27–42.

16

The Promise of Adulthood

Philip M. Ferguson
Dianne L. Ferguson

In his last year of high school, Ian Ferguson learned to fly. This was quite an accomplishment for someone labeled severely mentally retarded and physically disabled. As Ian's parents, we marveled at his achievement and worried about the law of gravity. Let us explain.

As part of Ian's final year as a student, he enrolled in "Beginning Drama." Following his carefully designed transition plan, Ian spent most of the rest of his day out in the community: working at various job sites, shopping at various stores, eating at various restaurants. But he began each day in drama class with a roomful of other would-be thespians. The logic behind Ian's participation in the class at the time was that it might lead somehow to his adult participation in some aspect or other of community theater. You see, while Ian's vision is poor, his hearing is great. In fact he finds odd or unexpected sounds (human or otherwise) to be endlessly amusing. During high school, one of our more insightful friends bought Ian a set of sound tapes of the type used by theater groups (e.g., "Sound A-24, woman screaming, 27 seconds" [screaming ensues]; Sound A-25,

man sneezing, 15 seconds . . .") as called for by various productions. Surely, we reasoned, Ian could learn to control his laughter long enough to help in such offstage activities as the making of sound effects. Furthermore, the drama teacher at Ian's high school just happened to be quite active in community theater in our town. Our objective, then, was really to see if we could figure out how Ian might participate in community theater productions as an adult leisure activity, possibly "networking" with the drama teacher to gain an entree into that group.

To our pleasure, Ian benefited in many more unexpected ways from his introduction to the dramatic arts: memorization, articulation, expressiveness, and social interaction. He also learned to "fly." A major part of the first few weeks of class involved Ian's participation in "trust" exercises. Some students fell off ladders, trusting their classmates to catch them. Others dived off a runway with the same belief that their friends would break their fall. The exercise that Joe, the teacher, picked to challenge Ian was called "flying." Seven or eight of Ian's classmates were to take him out of his wheelchair and raise him up and down in the air, tossing him just a little above their heads.

> *Now, the first time they tried this everyone was very tense. Both Joe and Leah (Ian's support teacher) were nervous; it was an adventure for them as well. The students released Ian's feet from their heel straps, unbuckled his seat belt, and, leaning over en masse, lifted him out of his chair. Joe and Leah positioned themselves at the most crucial locations on either side of Ian, and slowly—together with the students— began to raise Ian's supine body with their hands. Now it was Ian's turn to be nervous. Ian's spasticity makes it impossible for him to break a fall by throwing out his arms. Several painful crashes have left him with a strong fear of falling at the first sensation of being off balance or awkwardly positioned. Like many folks who experience his kind of physical disability, Ian has a hard time trusting strangers to move the body that he has so little control over. As the students lifted him, he clutched nervously at the only wrist within reach of the one hand he can use, trying to find something to hold on to. His voice anxiously wavered "Leah, Leah," seeking reassurance that this was, in fact, a wise course of action. It was pretty scary for Ian, and pretty risky for everyone else. But the exercise went well. Months later, when the drama class repeated some of the same trust exercises, Ian greeted Joe's suggestion that he "fly" with an eager response of "Out of chair! Out of chair!" That is how Ian learned to "fly" in his last year of school. The secret was learning to control the fear of falling, and it's a lesson that has served us well in the ensuing years.*

We tell this story about "flying" in drama class because it metaphorically captures the simultaneous sensations of excitement and anxiety that we experienced as Ian finished high school and launched himself into adulthood. We were fairly certain that Ian had some mixed feelings as his old routines and familiar settings vanished and new activities and settings took their place. The people in Ian's social network of formal and informal supports and friendship also recognized the responsibility that enough hands be there to "catch" Ian if he started to fall. As Ian left the relative stability of public school, grounded as it is in legal mandates and cultural familiarity, we worried about the thin air of adulthood where formal support systems seemed to promise little and accomplish even less.

Eight years later Ian lives in his own home, works at a job that he has enjoyed for nearly 7 years, and en-

joys an active schedule of household tasks, social engagements, weekends away, and occasional vacations. He has even participated as a member of the cast in a local production of *Oklahoma!* directed by his high school drama teacher. He is supported in his adult life by a network of paid and unpaid people, a personal support agent, and our ongoing involvement to ensure that his life is more okay than not okay from his point of view most of the time.

Our journey through these years has been difficult, often confusing and frustrating, but also filled with many exciting achievements. We have all learned a good deal about how one young man can negotiate an adult life and the kinds of supports that requires. Still, we continue to struggle with a variety of thorny issues. How do we make sure that Ian's life is really his life, and not one that merely reflects the regulations, Individual Program Plan (IPP) procedures, agency practices, and other formal service trappings? How do we ensure that Ian's life is not a program? How do we assure ourselves that Ian is somehow contributing to all the choices that get made about what constitutes a good adult life for him?

We have created new options for Ian and others as we have struggled to answer these questions. We have also increased our understanding of what it means for someone who has a variety of significant disabilities to be adult.

Understanding Adulthood

In this chapter we want to explore this status of adulthood and how it applies to people with severe disabilities. Our point is not that people with severe disabilities who are over the age of 18 or 21 are somehow not adults; of course, they are adults. The problem is that our field has not spent enough time thinking through exactly what that means in our culture and era. Adulthood is more than simply a chronological marker that indicates someone is above a certain age. As important as having a meaningful job is, or living as independently as possible, adulthood seems to involve more than this. As one social commentator has framed this distinction, "In many ways, children may always be children and adults may always be adults, but conceptions of 'childhood' and 'adulthood' are infinitely variable" (Meyrowitz, 1984, p. 25). If it is our responsibility as teachers and parents of students with severe disabilities to "launch" them as successfully as possible into adulthood, then it should be worthwhile to reflect on what promises such a role should hold. What is the promise of adulthood for people with severe disabilities?

We are not so bold as to think we can fully answer that question in this chapter. Our effort here will be to begin a discussion of the issue that we think needs to continue within the field of severe disabilities in general. We will organize our effort into three main sections: (1) understanding adulthood; (2) denying adulthood; and (3) achieving adulthood. Finally, throughout our discussion, our perspective will be unavoidably personal as well as professional. We will not pretend to be some anonymous and "objective" scholars writing dispassionately about the abstraction of adulthood for people with severe disabilities. Our son, Ian, is one of those people, and he is far from an abstraction to us. We will mention him throughout this chapter to illustrate some points we make and to explain our perspective better. However, we will also not write only as Ian's parents. We will draw upon our own research and that of other professionals and scholars in disability studies to bolster our discussion as well. Such a mixture of the personal and professional perspective does not only affect us as the writers; it should also affect you as a reader. You should read and respond to this chapter as a discussion of the concept of adulthood in general, but also as it fits (or does not fit) with your own personal experiences of people with severe disabilities.

The Changing Status of Adulthood

The status of adulthood in our society is both simple and complex, obvious and obscure. At one level, it is a seemingly straightforward matter of age. Any one who is over the age of 18 (or certainly 21) is an adult, pure and simple. The process is automatic: one "gains" adulthood through simple endurance. If you live long enough, you cease being a child and become an adult, with all the attendant privileges (often fewer than hoped) and responsibilities (often more than imagined) conferred by that status. In legal terms, one could even be judged incompetent to manage one's affairs but still remain an adult in this chronological sense.

At an equally basic level, adulthood can mean simply a state of biological maturity. In such terms, an adult is someone who has passed through the pubertal stage and is physiologically fully developed. This sense of adulthood most directly reflects the word's etymology. Our word "adult" (as well as "adolescence" for that matter) comes from the Latin "adolescere," which literally means "to grow up." As with the chronological meaning, this biological interpretation also is still common and largely accurate as far as it goes: to be an adult is, at least in a physical sense, to be grown up, mature, fully developed.

However, it seems clear to us that the matter is more complicated than this. Adulthood in our culture is much more than mere biology (Bouwsma, 1976; Dannefer, 1984) or chronology (Kett, 1977; Meyrowitz, 1984). Such factors convey a sense of precision and permanence about the concept that simply ignores the process of social construction by which every culture imbues such terms with meaning.

Historically, we know that the beginning age for adulthood has been a surprisingly flexible concept even within the confines of Western culture (Modell, Furstenberg, & Hershberg, 1978). Philippe Aries (1962) has gone so far as to argue that childhood itself, as an important social distinction, was not "discovered" in Europe until the 16th century. Before then, he argues, children were treated in essence as little more than the "miniature adults" familiar to us through the portrayals of children in medieval art (Aries, 1962). One need not concur with all of Aries' conclusions (Hanawalt, 1993), however, to still find value in his evidence of the dramatic variability of adult-child relationships in history. Adolescence, for example, was reported in a 16th century French compilation of "informed opinion" as being the third stage of life, lasting until 28 or even 35 years of age (Aries, 1962). On the other hand, in colonial New England, legal responsibility for one's personal behavior began at "the age of discretion," which usually meant 14 to 16 years old (Beales, 1985), and many children left home for their vocational apprenticeships as early as age 10 or 12 (Beales, 1985; Kett, 1977).

At the end of the nineteenth century in Europe and America a period of postadolescent "youth" emerged, where children of the upper and middle classes (mainly males at first, but now including females) could choose to postpone their adulthood by extending their professional training into their late 20s. As Wohl (1979) defines this role, the key distinction lay in the extended status of economic dependency for these college students. Taylor (1988) is even more specific: "Physically and psychologically adults, these individuals have not yet committed to those institutions which society defines as adult—namely, work, marriage and family" (p. 649).

In general, most social historians argue that today's transition to adulthood has much less flexibility and is more compressed in time span (Anderson, 1971; Modell et al., 1978) than that accepted by earlier generations. Even this current pattern may be changing, however. Recent census information suggests that many children are continuing (or returning) to live in their parents' home. If this is for something more than economic convenience, the transition period may be extending once more (Pillemer & Suitor, 1991, p. 144).

Given this historical variability, how might we elaborate an understanding of adulthood that goes beyond age? How can we describe the social construction of adulthood? Finally, how do these social and cultural dimensions of adulthood affect the experiences and opportunities of people with severe disabilities? We will address these questions by examining some of the dimensions of adulthood and their symbolic significance.

The Dimensions of Adulthood

As Ian's parents, we naturally thought it was important that Ian graduate from high school. More to the point, however, we felt it was extremely important that he participate as fully as possible in his high school's commencement exercises. The graduation ritual itself seemed crucial to us. It took planning, coordination, cooperation, and compromise by a number of people to make that participation happen, but happen it did, as the picture of Ian in his cap and gown shows (Figure 16–1). Now, while Ian certainly enjoyed his graduation (especially the part where people applauded as he crossed the stage) we doubt that he fully comprehended what the event was all about. And missing the graduation ceremony would not have lessened the skills Ian had learned in high school, threatened the friendships he had forged, or worsened his prospects for a smooth transition from school to work. In other words, the importance of Ian's participation in commencement was largely symbolic. It symbolized for us many of the same things that a son or daughter's graduation from high

FIGURE 16–1
Ian at His High School Graduation Ceremony

school symbolizes for most parents. In addition, we felt there were other symbols of inclusion, accessibility, and social tolerance with significance beyond Ian.

Few events are as loaded with symbolism as a graduation ceremony. It is perhaps the closest our secular society comes to a formal rite of passage from childhood to adulthood. Still, most of our actions as humans have some embedded symbolic meaning beyond their basic behavioral components. Much of what we are trying to capture in an understanding of adulthood occurs at this symbolic level of meaning. There are three important dimensions to this symbolic understanding (Table 16–1).

The Dimension of Autonomy

Perhaps the most familiar and common symbols of adulthood in our society are those that convey a

TABLE 16–1
Dimensions of Adulthood

Autonomy:	Being your own person, expressed through symbols of:	
	Self-Sufficiency:	Especially economic self-sufficiency, or having the resources to take care of oneself. Includes emotional self-sufficiency, or the ability to "make it" on one's own. Marks a shift from economic consumption to consumption and production.
	Self-Determination:	Assertion of individuality and independence. The ability to assure others that one possesses the rational maturity and personal freedom to make specific choices about how to live one's life.
	Completeness:	A sense of having "arrived." A shift from future to present tense. No more waiting.
Membership:	Community connectedness, collaboration, and sacrifice expressed through symbols of:	
	Citizenship:	Activities of collective governance from voting and participation in town meetings to volunteering for political candidates; expressing your position on issues with money, time, or bumper stickers; or recycling to protect the shared environment.
	Affiliation:	Activities of voluntary association, fellowship, celebration and support from greeting the new family in the neighborhood with a plate of cookies to being an active member of the church, participant in the local service or garden club, or being a member of the local art museum.
Change:	Adulthood as an ongoing capacity for growth rather than the static outcome of childhood. Change occurs for adults as they change jobs, move to new apartments or houses, relocate to new communities, or go back to school to learn new jobs or hobbies. Change also occurs as old friends and family members move away and new friendships are formed.	

sense of personal autonomy reserved for those we perceive as fully adult. This dimension emphasizes the status of adulthood as an outcome, a maturational completion. It remains close to biological origins of adulthood as the state of being fully developed. From this perspective, the changes that happen from the first moment of adulthood to the last are either thought of as variations on an established biographical theme or the increasingly unwelcome physical signs of a body on the downhill side of middle age. These dimensions of autonomy can be seen to inhere in several aspects of life commonly associated with adulthood.

Self-Sufficiency. One of the most often cited features of adulthood is an expectation of self-sufficiency. At the most fundamental level, this usually means economic self-sufficiency. Whether by employment, inherited wealth, or social subsidy, adulthood entails the belief that one has the resources to take care of oneself. As the quotation cited earlier mentioned, this sense of self-sufficiency entails a transition from a primary existence of economic consumption to one of rough balance between consumption and production. Theoretically,

even our welfare system works to preserve and enhance the self-sufficiency of individuals by providing temporary support and training.

However, self-sufficiency goes beyond this economic sense to also include elements of emotional adequacy. Adulthood usually has the sense of having the emotional as well as economic resources to "make it on one's own." People who are thought to whine about trivial complaints are often told to "grow up" or "quit acting like a baby." The point is not that all adults are, in fact, emotionally stable and secure (much less self-sufficient). Moreover, there are important differentiations by gender in how our culture portrays emotional maturity. Still, in some sense or other, such emotional competence in the face of life's adversities is presented as a normative goal for adults.

Last year Ian earned about $4,500 in his job at the university. While this job and these earnings are important to his life as an adult, they do not begin to cover his living, to say nothing of his recreational, expenses. Even with the social service support dollars made available to him, the life he is creating for himself exceeds his available economic resources too much of the time. However, Ian has a job and social *service dollars to support his efforts. Many people with significant disabilities have none or what they do have are woefully inadequate. Poverty and disability have a long history, and self-sufficiency and poverty are incompatible.*

Self-Determination. Self-determination and self-sufficiency are often treated as synonymous in terms of adulthood. However, while recognizing that the terms are closely related, we want to use the term self-determination to refer to a more active assertion of individuality and independence. An autonomous adult in this sense is someone who has the rational maturity and personal freedom to make specific choices about how to live his or her life. Autonomous adults make decisions and live with the consequences.

Certainly, from the perspective of childhood this dimension of autonomy must seem the most promising. Self-determination involves all of the accoutrements of freedom and control that seem so oppressively and unreasonably denied as we suffer through the indignities of adolescence. We can live where we want, change jobs if we want, make our own judgments about what debts to incur, what risks to take, and make our own decisions when faced with moral dilemmas. We can even stay up late if we want, or go shopping at 10:00 in the morning. However, these newly available privileges are quickly coupled with newly assumed responsibilities. What seems a distant prize amidst the rules and restraints of life at age 13, becomes a meager consolation amidst the decisions and debates of life at thirtysomething. Sometimes adulthood is not all it is cracked up to be.

For persons with severe disabilities, the concept of self-determination is both challenging and promising and has become a new focus of discussion and research (Brown, Gothelf, Guess, & Lehr, 1998; Ferguson, 1998; Sands & Wehmeyer, 1996; Wehmeyer, 1998). As a concept, self-determination could change not just what happens in the lives of people with significant disabilities, but more fundamentally, how we think about such things as services, supports, interventions, and outcomes.

The latest example of the role of self-determination, and the challenges in understanding and interpreting it for people with severe disabilities, came to us wrapped in a Christmas Eve invitation.

Ian invited us to his house for Christmas Eve. Previously we had always celebrated holidays in our home, even after Ian moved into his own house. Of course, most families eventually face such a time when the location for holidays and other family rituals shifts from the parents' home to the childrens'. What is hard for us to unravel in our relationship with Ian, however, is just how this particular transitional invitation occurred. Did Ian somehow arrive at the determination that it was time to shift our holiday celebrations to his own home? Did his housemates, Robin and Lyn, who had been helping him can fruits and vegetables, make jam and breads, and decorate and arrange baskets for weeks, "support his choice" to invite us over or shape his choice on his behalf? Did they somehow teach him how and why he might wish to request our presence at this holiday celebration?

For individuals whose communication skills are limited and for whom our understanding of their preferences and point of view is incomplete at best, it is difficult to figure out when they are making choices—determining things for themselves—and when it is the interpretations of others that really shape the outcomes. At the same time, it seems better to try to guess at another's perspective and preferences than to ignore them altogether. At still other times, it may well be that no choice is made despite the opportunity.

"Do you want eggs, pancakes or bagels for breakfast tomorrow?" we asked Ian recently during an overnight visit. "Bagels," was his prompt reply. "Do you want bagels, pancakes, or eggs?" Phil tried again, wondering if Ian was really listening and choosing. "Eggs," Ian just as promptly replied.

Over the years we have tried various little tests like this to check whether Ian's answers are choices or just his effort to support the conversational exchange by repeating the last thing he heard. Of course, questioning his apparent choices could seem unsupportive of his efforts to determine things for himself. Perhaps the admission that we question his response is as important as whether or not he is really choosing. These are the essential questions and dilemmas of self-determination for Ian and others with similar disabilities, and one that we will return to throughout this chapter.

Completeness. Perhaps the common element in all the various dimensions of adulthood as autonomy is a sense of completeness. What one gains with the trappings of self-determination and self-sufficiency is obviously more than the imagined pleasures of doing totally as one pleases. Adulthood brings no guarantees of living happily ever after. Rather than the fragile rewards of choosing well and wisely, adulthood seems only to guarantee the opportunity to finally make those choices, from silly to serious, on one's own. Adulthood has to do with feeling like you always know how to act: what to order and how much to tip in any restaurant. Most of us have felt the pain of youthful uncertainty in "grown up" situations. We struggle to manage our youthful discomfort in the fervent belief that each event will eventually bring the longed-for knowledge and confidence to cover all situations. In reality, of course, the completeness really comes with the ability to be comfortable with one's uncertainties.

Adulthood brings a sense of completeness that is never there in the preparatory mode of childhood. The fact that many of us continue to feel a lack of completeness in some situations well past middle age merely attests to the powerfulness of the notion of completeness to our understandings of adulthood. A continuing struggle for us is to make sure that Ian's adulthood is complete in this way. Even though he has continued to learn many things since high school graduation, we have tried to make sure that his learning of new skills or information is not an expectation of his supporters. It is a difficult balance to achieve. ian, and all other adults, need to be afforded opportunities to continue to learn and grow, but without the trappings of preparatory training or schooling. If we think of life as a type of language then adulthood as autonomy would seem to be a move from the future to the present tense as the primary one in which we tell our life stories.

The Dimension of Membership

Sometimes it seems that we allow the dimension and symbols of autonomy to exhaust our understanding of adulthood. Adulthood in this view is essentially a matter of independence. This can create problems when we ask society to respond to all people with severe disabilities as "fully adult," since many of these people are limited by their disability from demonstrating such independence in ways that are similar to the ways typically used. Indeed, for many people, this limited independence is precisely what the label of "disability" means in the first place. However, we would argue that limiting our understanding of adulthood as "being able to do it by yourself" is problematic for all adults whether or not they have a disabil-

ity. There is an equally important dimension in understanding adulthood that serves as a crucial counterbalance to the individualistic emphasis on autonomy. This dimension includes all of those facets of adulthood that involve citizenship affiliation and that must be supported by the collaboration and sacrifice of others. We collectively refer to these facets as the dimension of membership. If adulthood as autonomy is a move to life in the present tense, then adulthood as membership recognizes that life is plural rather than singular, communal as well as individual.

Citizenship. Anthropologists have perhaps contributed most to our understanding of the communal aspects of adulthood in most cultures, including our own. They have described in detail the rituals and responsibilities that societies attach to adult status. In a very real sense, it is only with these rites of passage into adulthood that we become full members of our communities. In part, this involves an element of responsibility for others and the community in general. Voting and other acts of collective governance are the most obvious signs of this theme and perhaps seem the most daunting for some adults with severe disabilities.

> We have not pursued voting as a way for Ian to explore this aspect of membership, mostly because we fear that providing the assistance he would need might really just result in one of us having the advantage of two votes. However, there are other ways Ian can exercise community responsibility. Stuffing envelopes, for example, or passing out campaign information, are ways we think Ian can contribute to the political life of his community. Actively recycling by using his backpack instead of bags when shopping, expressing his political opinions on issues of accessibility with the "Attitudes are the Real Disability" bumper sticker affixed to the back of his wheelchair; or helping clean up trash from a vacant lot in his neighborhood: these are all ways Ian participates as a citizen of our community.

Adults are citizens with duties of civic participation that are neither expected nor allowed for children. Once again, the point is not that all—or even most—of us fulfill these duties of citizenship. Indeed, our country's practice of excessive individualism has been well and recently documented (Bach, 1994; Bellah, Madsen, Sullivan, Swidler, & Tipton, 1985, 1991). Still, the pursuit of our own individual, independent agendas has not removed the ideal of community citizenship as something we endorse in theory. We may not practice what we preach, but we still give the sermon on a regular basis.

Affiliation. The communal dimension of adulthood is not only about some grudging performance of civic duties, or even a cheerful altruism of civic sacrifice. An important aspect of communal adulthood lies in the various examples of voluntary association, fellowship, celebration and support that adults typically discover and create (Figure 16–2). One of the most common signs of adulthood, for example, is the intentional formation of new families and the extension of old ones. Through formal and informal affiliations adults locate themselves socially as well as geographically. You might live on the east side of town, belong to the square dance club, attend the Catholic church, and have a spouse and two kids. We might live in a downtown condo, belong to the library patrons' society, participate in community theater, and volunteer at the local rape crisis center. The particular array of affiliations can differ dramatically. However, in the aggregate those affiliations help define a community; just as the community, in turn, helps define each of us as adults. Through their affiliations adults support and define each other.

The definitional power of our affiliations seems to us very true for Ian and other adults who require similar supports. Ian's

life tends to reflect the people in his life. Right now his two primary support people like to camp, go fishing, and boating. So Ian does, too. Moreover, Ian's community of Eugene, Oregon, is one that prizes such outdoor activities, and so there are many groups and opportunities that encourage these hobbies. A few years ago, when Ian was in his early 20s, dancing and pool were favorite pursuits of his supporters and Ian obligingly enjoyed these activities just as much. At the same time, Ian has his own longstanding hobbies (e.g., casino gambling), and any long-term friends will probably need to enjoy the bells and whistles of Las Vegas and Reno as well. (Figure 16–3).

The Dimension of Change

We said earlier that adulthood as autonomy could be metaphorically described as a move from the future to the present tense. The dimension of adulthood as membership shows that the description requires a

FIGURE 16–3
A Favorite Activity is Hitting the Slot Machines at a Nearby Casino

FIGURE 16–2
Ian often Meets Friends at One of the Local Pubs

plural rather than a singular construction. Let us follow our metaphorical logic in this final dimension of adulthood and argue that a dynamic approach to life demands that adulthood must finally be understood as a verb, not a noun. If adulthood can be seen as an outcome of childhood, it should also be seen as part of the process of life. In the biological sense, adulthood may indeed represent a kind of developmental maturity; in a social and psychological sense, it can also represent phases of continued growth.

Of course, this aspect of adulthood has been the focus of increased attention in developmental psychology since the seminal work of Erik Erikson (1950) on the eight "crises" or stages of the life cycle, four of which occur in adulthood. Subsequent psychologists have variously refined and revised this work (Erikson & Martin, 1984; Levinson, 1978; Vaillant, 1977). Sociologists and historians have added an important sociocultural perspective to these stages within the life span (Dannefer, 1984; Elder, 1987; Hareven, 1978). In general, however, these developmentalist writers share an emphasis that has increased our awareness of adulthood as more than an undifferentiated expanse of life between adolescent impatience and elderly reflection. We now recognize adulthood as a period of both realization and continued transition.

As with most scholarly "discoveries," the understanding of adulthood as full of change and development is neither new nor scholarly. As a theme it runs through some of our richest traditions. One theologian (Bouwsma, 1976) has identified the Judeao-Christian tradition as one in which adulthood "implies a process rather than the possession of a particular status or specific faculty" (p. 77). He goes on to describe the key element for adulthood in this tradition not as the completion of growth, but as the "capacity for growth" (p. 81). However, it is perhaps the Confucian tradition that best captures this understanding of adulthood with its depiction of life as a journey in which one is always "on the way."

Adulthood conceived in this way is not so much a state of attainment as a process of becoming. The emphasis instead is on the process of living itself. The maturation of a human being is viewed as an unfolding of humanity in the world. For without self-cultivation as a continuous effort to realize one's humanity, biological growth becomes meaningless. (Wei-Ming, 1976, p. 109)

On his next birthday Ian will be 30. For most adults the thirtieth birthday is one of a number of milestone adult birthdays, beginning, of course, with the twenty-first. Since Ian was 21, he has become a different person. His tastes in music are still eclectic, but he seems to enjoy the occasional concert with his parents more than he did 7 or 8 years ago. He's gained some weight, has fewer adolescent pimples, and we've been told he has a few early gray hairs (we haven't spotted them yet). More than changes in his appearance, however, he approaches age 30 with a different demeanor. He can be serious or consoling when the occasion demands, although he could not tell you what those words mean. He has experienced the death of grandparents, lost friends and support workers, and learned how to be alone in ways that are different than when he lived with us. We don't know how Ian thinks about these changes, but we can tell that he is aware of them. We wonder what changes his 30s will bring.

For many people with disabilities these three dimensions of adulthood occur only partially, often in terms of approximations of the symbols the rest of us use to identify others and ourselves as adults. Table 16–2 illustrates some examples of these symbols that

TABLE 16–2
Symbols of Adulthood: Some Examples

Symbols of Autonomy

- Having a source of income, a job or wealth.
- Making your own choices, both the big important ones and the little trivial ones.
- No more waiting for the privilege of doing what you want, how you want, when and with whom you want to do it.

Symbols of Membership

- A voter registration card.
- Membership cards for organizations and clubs.
- An appointment calendar and address book.
- Season tickets, bumper stickers, charitable contributions of time and money.

Symbols of Change

- Marriage
- Acquiring new hobbies
- Children
- New jobs and homes
- Learning new skills
- Old friends

---

are present in many adult lives, though not many adult lives of people with disabilities. If we only assess the symbols we each can claim, however, we may make the mistake of denying the status of adulthood to people with disabilities. Symbols are important, but they are not the whole story. One way we evaluate our success at supporting Ian's adulthood is to examine periodically just how each of these dimensions is visible in his life. How does the daily round of Ian's life reflect ways of becoming a unique member of our community? Are his activities, affiliations, and ways of participating varied? Do they change over time? Do they reflect a changing understanding among his circle of family, friends, and supporters of Ian's own preferences and choices? We'll return to these questions later with examples that might help you see how these dimensions of adulthood can apply in the life of a person with severe disabilities. First, however, let us examine more completely why these notions have been so difficult to apply to this group of people.

Denying Adulthood

If the symbolic meaning of adulthood involves the dimensions of autonomy, membership, and change, then how have those dimensions affected our understanding of adults with severe disabilities? The evidence of problems in the quality of life for many of these individuals is apparent even to the casual observer. Almost every state has long waiting lists for residential and employment opportunities of any kind in the community, even grossly inadequate and needlessly segregated ones (Ferguson & Ferguson, 1986; Mank, 1994; O'Brien, 1994). Although the number of people with developmental disabilities residing in private or public institutions has dramatically declined over the last decade, the federal and state Intermediate Care Facilities/Mental Retardation (ICF/MR) program (part of Medicaid) still spends almost $7 billion to keep people in large congregate care facilities (Braddock, Hemp, Parish, & Westrich, 1998; Hemp, Braddock, & Westrich, 1998). For over 15 years, evidence has mounted for the economic and social benefits of supported employment for adults with developmental disabilities. Yet unemployment and segregated day programs still dominate the vocational services offered to such individuals (Blanck, 1998; McGaughey, Kiernan, McNally, Gilmore, & Keith, 1994;

National Organization on Disability, 1998; Wehman, 1997). For individuals with severe disabilities, in particular, this empirical evidence of a poor quality of life must also be understood in a historical context.

If you examine the history of adulthood for people with severe disabilities, you find a story not only of symbolic deprivation but also of economic deprivation. Indeed, at the heart of our discussion is the belief that the two are inextricably related. Symbols of adulthood accompany the practice of being an adult. Or to reverse the logic, the denial of adulthood to people with severe disabilities has been symbolic as well as concrete. Recent movements to recognize the full range of rights and responsibilities of adults with severe disabilities can best be understood in light of this history of denial.

Unending Childhood

Wolfensberger (1972) not only helped popularize the principle of normalization as a basic orientation for human services, he deserves credit for raising our awareness of the symbolic dimensions of discrimination and stigma in the lives of people with severe disabilities. In particular, he helped highlight how society referred to people with mental retardation in terms and images that suggested a status of "eternal childhood." Over 25 years later, it is still frustratingly common to hear adults with severe disabilities described by the construct of "mental age": "Johnny Smith is 34 years old, but has the mind of a 3-year-old." How often, in your experience, have you heard an adult with mental retardation referred to as "Mr. Jones" or "Ms. Smith," instead of Joey or Janie? In an interview we did some years ago (Ferguson, Ferguson, & Jones, 1988), an elderly parent of a 40-year-old son with Down syndrome described him as a sort of disabled Peter Pan: one of the "ever-ever children." "This thing about normalizing will not happen . . . they'll always be childlike" (p. 109).

Such language, of course, symbolically reflects and reinforces infantilizing attitudes and practices that deny adults with disabilities the range of opportunities appropriate for their age. It denies them the "right to grow up" (Summers, 1986) and violates one of the fundamental tenets of the normalization principle as a guide for human services (Nirje, 1970; Wolfensberger, 1972). Specifically, it attacks the symbols of adulthood embedded in the dimensions of autonomy and membership. If you never grow up, the symbols of independence—autonomy, membership, and change—simply do not apply. "Ever, ever children" continue to be tolerated and excluded, cared for and protected, and never consulted, included, or supported to change. Ironically, the status of eternal childhood even attacks the dimension of change. Normally, the dimension of change is important to both childhood and adulthood. However, the permanence of an inescapable assignment of childishness denies people with severe disabilities even that promise of growth and change that real children enjoy.

Fortunately, the myth of eternal childhood as the "inevitable" fate for people with severe disabilities is much less powerful than it was 10 or 20 years ago. We like to think that today's generation of young parents is less likely than our generation to learn from professionals that their sons and daughters are "ever-ever children." Increasingly, it seems that both professionals and the general public are aware of the stigmatizing assumptions built into childish terms of reference. Such now popular terms among professionals as "clients" and "consumers" may still be a bit too depersonalized and bureaucratic, but at least they avoid the eternal child stereotypes of calling 40-year-old men and women "boys and girls." Appearance and activities are also more and more likely to avoid the most obviously childish examples (e.g., adults playing with simple puzzles or toys, carrying school lunch boxes to work). We are gradually moving away from our infantilizing images of the past.

Of course, if symbols only are changed then the true movement to adulthood will still be stalled. We remember working at a large state institution for people with severe disabilities some 20 years ago. This institution closed in June of 1998, but at the time, a number of people who worked there had apparently gotten only part of the message about treating people as adults. As a result, over a period of months all of the adult men on one ward grew beards and smoked pipes. Nothing else changed in their lives to encourage their personal autonomy, much less their membership in the community. The beards and pipes were simply empty symbols of adulthood that had no grounding in the daily lives of indignity and isolation that the men continued to lead. Alternatively, allowing someone the choice to risk his or her health by not wearing a seatbelt in the car or by eating three large pizzas for dinner in the name of autonomy and adult independence also misses the point, resulting instead in a limitation of adulthood, perhaps quite literally if that person's health is threatened by such risky choices.

> Left to his own devices, Ian might always "choose" to watch cartoons or drink chocolate milk or any number of other choices that might be more typical of a young child. Once in awhile, these choices are fine. Recently Dianne bought and drank a quart of chocolate milk, serving some taste nostalgia. But as a steady diet, such choices do not communicate the full range of options most adults enjoy. Part of truly supporting Ian's adulthood is making sure he has enough experience of lots of different options to make adult decisions.

Unfinished Transition

An important part of the move away from the unending childhood view of severe disability has occurred in the greatly increased programmatic attention paid to the transition period from school to adult life (Jorgensen, 1998; Wehman, 1997; Wehmeyer, Agran, & Hughes, 1998). This focus on transition has certainly clarified the right of people with severe disabilities not to remain forever imprisoned by images of childhood. It has led to a heightened awareness on the part of the special education community that what happens after a student leaves school is perhaps the most crucial test of how effective that schooling was. In terms of program evaluation, the emphasis on transition planning in the schools has clearly identified adulthood as the ultimate outcome measure for the process of special education.

However, as a cultural generalization, an escape from unending childhood has not yet meant an entrance into full-fledged adulthood for people with severe disabilities. Instead of eternal childhood, we see their current status as one of stalled or unfinished transition: a "neither-nor" ambiguity in which young people with severe disabilities are no longer seen as children, nor yet as adults. Understood chronologically, of course, the transition process cannot be stalled. As children get older, the transition process automatically occurs and they become adults whether society admits it or not. Bureaucratically, the transition process also seems to take an inexorable course from school to adult services. Transitions might succeed or fail, but cannot be stalled from this perspective. As with adulthood itself, however, transition too, can be viewed symbolically. It is in this symbolic sense that people with severe disabilities can become embedded in a permanent process of incomplete transition.

Several scholars have suggested the anthropological concept of liminality as most descriptive of this situation (Murphy, Scheer, Murphy, & Mack, 1988; Mwaria, 1990). Liminality refers to a state of being when a person is suspended between the demands, and opportunities, of childhood and adulthood. Many societies use various rituals of initiation, purification, or other transitions to both accomplish and commemorate a significant change in status. In many cultures where these rituals retain their original intensity, the actual event can last for days or months. During such rituals, the person undergoing the process is said to occupy a liminal (or "threshold") state. According to one author,

> [P]eople in a liminal condition are without clear status, for their old position has been expunged and they have not yet been given a new one. They are 'betwixt and between', neither fish nor fowl; they are suspended in social space without firm identity or role definition. . . . In a very real sense, they are nonpersons, making all interactions with them unpredictable and problematic. (Murphy, et al., p. 237).

When the rituals end, the liminality ends, and the people assume their new roles within the society.

For too many adults with severe disabilities, one could say the transition to adulthood is a ritual that once never began and now begins but seldom ends. Instead they remain on the threshold of adulthood in a kind of permanent liminality: "suspended in social space."

> In retrospect, it seems the graduation ritual that we fought so hard for Ian to participate in, served more to mark an ending as a child or student, than a clear beginning of a full adult life. It is as though we launched Ian into flight without a location from society where he can land. Much of the intervening years have focused on trying to find the runway that would lead to Ian's adult life.

We see this liminality in the kinds of social responses to adults with severe disabilities that perpetuate social isolation in the name of autonomy. Professionals who tell parents they need to "back off" from involvement in their newly adult son's or daughter's life, so they can begin to build their own separate life apart from the ties of family and home, sometimes end up isolating the new adult by removing the most effective advocates for an expanded membership in the community. Parents and professionals who conspire (usually with purely benevolent intentions) to create a facade of independence for adults with severe disabilities by allowing them trivial, secondary, or coerced choices instead of true self-determination (Knowlton, Turnbull, Backus, & Turnbull, 1988) trap adults in the isolation of liminality in another way.

> For example, some of Ian's high school friends are in residential programs where they might be allowed to choose pizza for dinner, but not when or with whom they will eat it. Similarly, they might choose how the furniture in their room is arranged, but not where or with whom they live. Such incomplete choices merely create the illusion of adulthood.

In still other instances, adults are given a plentiful supply of token affiliations and social activities with no attention to the symbols of self-sufficiency represented by a real job with real income, making the illusion incomplete in yet another way. Such an ambiguous social status will continue to frustrate individuals in their efforts to define themselves as adult. Society in general will continue to feel uncomfortable in the presence of such people, not knowing how to respond.

> Ian's own transition seemed at risk of this liminal status for the first few months after graduation. He continued to live in our home and his only "job" was a volunteer job that he had begun when in high school. His personal agent and personal support staff created a schedule of personal and recreational activities to fill his days. While Ian certainly enjoyed this round of activity, it felt to us, and we think to him as well, like a kind of holding pattern. He was waiting for his chance to enter the routines and responsibilities of adulthood. The meantime schedule of activity was a substitute, and one we all hoped would not last long.

Unhelpful Services

Although the special education system must share part of the blame for this unfinished process of transition, much of the responsibility must fall upon an "adult" service system plagued with problems of poor policy, inadequate funding, and ineffective programs (Ferguson, & Drum, 1990; Ferguson, Hibbard, Leinen & Schaff, 1990; Smull & Bellamy, 1991). From our perspective, the traditional human service system has by now emerged as a major contributor to the continued denial of adulthood for people with severe disabilities and their families. Of course, there are significant exceptions to this generalization across the domains of residential programs (Howe, Horner, & Newton, 1998; Taylor, Bogdan, & Racino, 1991), employment support (Mank, Cioffi, & Yovanoff, 1997), and leisure and recreation (Anderson, Schleien, & Seligmann, 1997; Dattilo & Schleien, 1994; Germ & Schleien, 1997). Nor is this meant to gainsay the good intentions of most of the professionals who participate in the formal system. Nonetheless, there is a growing consensus that examples of successful programs and helpful professionals happen in spite of, not because of, the formal service system.

Many analysts of the social service system continue to point to fundamental inadequacies in adult services (Conley & Noble, 1989; Ferguson, Hibbard, et al., 1990; McKnight, 1985, 1995; Smull & Bellamy, 1991). Although each of these analyses has its own list of problems, they all include some basic complaints. We will briefly mention three of these issues that correspond to the three dimensions of adulthood we have already set forth. These three issues are (1) clienthood, (2) anonymity, and (3) chronicity.

Clienthood

The traditional service system promotes "clienthood" rather than adulthood. This is unavoidably a role of dependency either explicitly or implicitly. The role has many versions but perhaps the most familiar is that which imposes a model of medical or behavioral deficit as the dominant rationale for service decisions. In this rationale, the essential orientation for service delivery is that the individual with the disability has something that needs to be cured or remediated. Just as patients are expected to follow the doctor's orders and take the prescribed medicine, so are people with disabilities expected to follow their "individual habilitation plans," work hard to improve (Bickenbach, 1994; Lane, 1992; McKnight, 1995; Phillips, 1985), and abide by the suggestions of their designated professionals (e.g., case managers, job coaches, residential providers).

This dependency is perhaps most familiar in those aspects of the welfare system (e.g., Supplemental Security Income, Social Security Disability Income, Medicaid) that incorporate economic disincentives to vocational independence. But it is equally powerful at the more personal level through a tendency that

Seymour Sarason (1972) has called "professional preciousness." Professional preciousness refers to the tendency of professionals to define problems in terms that require traditionally trained professionals (like themselves) for a solution. Thus, case managers sometimes define a client's needs according to what the system happens to provide (Taylor, 1988, in press; Williams, 1983). Opportunities for meaningful employment are overlooked or unsought unless they have been developed through the proper channels of certified rehabilitation professionals rather than untrained but willing coworkers (Nisbet & Hagner, 1988). Those who find the penalties too high for participation in such a system can "drop out," but only at the risk of losing all benefits (especially health care) and without official standing as "disabled" at all (Ferguson, Hibbard, et al., 1990). By limiting the avenues for achieving jobs, homes, and active social lives to the "disability-approved" services offered through the formal service system, clienthood undermines autonomy.

> We have strived to create options for Ian that use the social service system, but reject this status of clienthood, at least from Ian's point of view, and perhaps more importantly, from the point of view of his direct supporters. Although Ian's living situation is possible because of the official funding category of "supported living" and his job support dollars are provided through the category of "supported employment," there are no service programs that dominate his day to day choices and routines. Our collective efforts to support Ian's definition of his own life has allowed us to meet the necessary rules and regulations, but protect Ian and his supporters from having to attend to them constantly. It has become the responsibility of Ian's personal support agent to make sure that the penalties of participation in the service system are minimized so that Ian may develop his own adult identity apart from that of social service system client.

Anonymity

The traditional system not only promotes dependency but also creates a kind of bureaucratic isolation in which procedures replace people and standardization overwhelms context. Certainly this is, in part, simply a function of the size of the programs and the numbers of people involved. However, it goes beyond this to a style of entrenched centralization and controls that pursues efficiency above all else. This often leads to situations of sterility and isolation in programs that are ostensibly intended to increase a person's social integration. The need for efficient purchasing and supply often leads to so much similarity in the possessions and activities of clients that the individual becomes swallowed up in a collective personnel that diminishes each member's uniqueness. It seems unlikely that the individuals in a dozen group homes and apartments operated by the same supported living agency all like the same brand of ice cream, prefer the same laundry detergent, and choose the same color paper napkins.

An even more powerful example involves the types of relationships many people with severe disabilities experience. One thing that seems important to the kinds of social relationships and friendships that most of us enjoy is "knowing each others' stories." The very process of a developing friendship usually involves learning about each other through the stories of experiences and history shared in conversation.

> When people enter Ian's life, we support the developing relationship by sharing much of Ian's story for him. If he lived in a community residential program, however, the constant turnover of staff and the demands for confidentiality might so limit what others know about his life that he is rendered virtually anonymous except for what can be readily observed and directly experienced.

One parent expressed this frustration with the impersonal "atmosphere" she had observed in group homes:

> [W]hat I'm seeing is that, while moving away from institutionalization, a group home is still an institution. Those people aren't living there because they're family or because they've chosen to be there. They are living there because it is cost-efficient for the Mental Health Division, Okay! . . . [There is] a lack of privacy, a lack of your own personal belongings. You have the staff, and that's a staff; they don't love you. (Ferguson, Ferguson, & Jeanchild, 1990, pp. 9–10)

Ironically, this social isolation and anonymity stems from the same kind of overemphasis on individualization that we described in the last section as at the root of clienthood. The result of the permanent clienthood is not only dependency, but also a concomitant loss of community and the informal sources of support and affiliation available there. Clienthood undermines autonomy; anonymity undermines membership. Both serve to undermine full adulthood.

Chronicity

The final barrier that seems an unavoidable facet of the traditional support system is something we call "chronicity." Chronicity is the officially delivered, systematic denial of lifelong change and growth. Chronicity is created by professional pronouncements that someone or some group is unsusceptible to further development. Again, this barrier results from the dominance of what might be called a "therapeutic model" in the overall design of services. For those who "respond to treatment" in this model, there is a future of more treatment, more programs, and more clienthood. However, for those whose disability is judged so severe as to be beyond help (i.e., "incorrigible," "incurable," "hopeless," "ineducable"), there is a professionally ordained abandonment. The person becomes "caught in the continuum" (Taylor, S. J., 1988), whereby expansion of adult opportunities is denied as premature while commitment to improvement is abandoned as unrealistic. For example, even service reforms such as supported employment that were initially developed specifically for people with severe disabilities have been denied to people with the most severe disabilities, who are judged to be "incapable of benefiting" from vocationally oriented training (Ferguson & Ferguson, 1986). In this orientation, the system presents full adulthood for people with severe disabilities as something that must be "earned," a reward handed out piecemeal by professionals to people judged capable of continuing to progress. Failure to progress in the past justifies compressed opportunities in the future.

Let us finish our discussion of the denial of adulthood for people with severe disabilities by summarizing the symbols of denial, which we have described in Table 16–3.

The Dilemma of Adulthood

All of this leaves those of us who wish to see the promise of adulthood fulfilled for people with severe disabilities with a frustrating dilemma: How can we help people with severe disabilities gain access to the cultural benefits of community membership and personal autonomy associated with adulthood without neglecting the continued needs for adequate support and protection that did not end with childhood? Let us offer a fairly minor example of this dilemma.

TABLE 16–3
Symbols of Denial of Adulthood: Some Examples

Unending Childhood

- Childish, diminutive names like Bobby and Susie.
- Enforced dependency that permits others to make all important choices.
- Few life changes.

Unfinished Transition

- No more school, but no job, home, or affiliations in the community.
- Rituals for ending, but not for beginning.
- Acquisition of visible but empty symbols like beards and pipes, but no jobs, homes, or community affiliations.

Unhelpful Services

- Clienthood: A focus on remediation and readiness determined through the mechanisms of professional preciousness.
- Anonymity: Service standards and procedures that overwhelm individuality and uniqueness.
- Chronicity: The professional decision to deny lifelong change because the client is insusceptible to further development.

If someone asked Ian if he wanted to watch cartoons or "60 Minutes" on television, he would almost certainly choose the cartoons. The cartoons are lively, have lots of odd noises and music. A Mike Wallace interview just does not match up.

Concerned as we are with Ian's adult status, should we honor his choice as an autonomous adult and turn on the cartoons even though we know it is an activity commonly associated with young children? Or should we override his choice, in the belief that in this case the outcome (i. e., watching more adult entertainment) is more important than the process (i.e., allowing him to independently choose what he watches)? Perhaps we should not offer him the choice in the first place, confident that we will select a much more age-appropriate program? In the long run, we might argue, this will enhance Ian's image and expand his opportunities for affiliation and membership in a community of adults. Finally, we might look at this example of his viewing habits as an area of learning for Ian and emphasize the dimensions of change for him. In so doing, we might honor Ian's choice for now while simultaneously exposing him to more options that might be equally appealing but less childish

(perhaps MTV as a compromise between Mike Wallace and Mickey Mouse).

Our society and its formal support systems have effectively denied full adulthood to people with the most severe disabilities by approaching it in a one-dimensional way that allows no depth or variation to the ways people might achieve such a status. Making shallow and incomplete choices, having activities, but not jobs and homes of their own all approach, but ultimately only imitate and parody, "life in the community" for people with severe disabilities.

In such an approach, excessive emphasis on symbols of autonomy might actually diminish a person's access to membership symbols. Having only a volunteer job is not the same as volunteering your free time after work at a paid job. Making sure a young adult lives apart from previous family and friends in the pursuit of an image of self-sufficiency, for example, may restrict the adult's involvement in activities and groups that those very family and friends might help to access. Just moving to a community residence that creates a "disabled" round of life activity when family and friends might help really support an individual's options for more varied choices limits rather than expands options for expressing adulthood.

Similarly, excessive emphasis on change might perpetuate the liminal position of being permanently stuck on the threshold of full adulthood, spending one's days in endless preparation for life instead of actually living it. This is perhaps most common for those young adults that leave the cultural preparatory experience of schools only to find themselves in a day program or residential service that continues a readiness training focus. Many young adults with significant disabilities still leave high school for the continued preparation of work training programs and sheltered workshops. We wonder how many adults "retire" from such programs when they reach their 60s without ever "graduating" to real jobs.

Indirectly, such one-dimensional service offerings can de-emphasize the importance of societal reform to accommodate a broader range of acceptable adult behavior. Instead, we believe that a full understanding of the multidimensional aspects of adulthood in our tradition and culture allows a more productive and flexible approach to the dilemma of balancing self-sufficiency with support and social accommodation with personal development.

Ron works at the same university we do. He lived in a large institution for people with mental retardation until he was in his 40s. Now he works delivering mail from the dean's office to other parts of the college. Ron doesn't talk and has a history of lashing out at himself and others when he is confused or unclear about what is happening to him. When you encounter him in the mail room and say "hello" he will often respond by retreating, avoiding eye contact, and making his own unique sounds. To many people, these responses seem like he is retreating and uncomfortable with these interactions. Over time, however, those who persistently greet and interact with Ron realize that these responses are an acknowledgement and, perhaps, a recognition of a familiar face.

For us as parents, it seems that the professionals have done a good job of convincing society to recognize the importance of a transition from childhood but have not fully discovered what that process should be a transition to. We are, as it were, in mid-journey on the trail toward adulthood for people with severe disabilities. As professionals it seems to us that our field has not adequately understood the complexity of the journey or the character of its destination. Without such an understanding, the process of achieving adulthood—symbolically or otherwise—for people with severe disabilities will never reach a conclusion.

Having said that, and having explored the dilemma of adulthood for people with severe disabilities in some depth, we must now turn to the good news. Answers are emerging. Perhaps we have moved past the midpoint of our journey, at least for some adults with significant disabilities. Our last section will explore some of these developments after a brief summary review.

Achieving Adulthood

Let us try to summarize our discussion thus far. The promise of adulthood in our society should be more than a job, a place to live, and being on one's own. A full understanding of the meaning of adulthood must look at the structure of symbols and imagery that surround this culturally defined role. In looking, we found that we could organize that symbolic structure around the three dimensions of autonomy, membership, and change. We elaborated the dimension of autonomy into three elements (self-sufficiency, self-

determination, and completeness), and membership into two elements (citizenship and affiliation). Then we discussed the ways in which our current service options tend to deny full participation in these dimensions. Even though some of the symbols of autonomy, membership and change might be attempted, too often the result for persons with severe disabilities is really experience of unfinished transition or unhelpful services.

Despite recent and helpful moves within the field of special education and disability services to focus on the importance of the transition process from school to adult life, we argued that most adults with severe disabilities remain on the threshold of adulthood in this fuller sense of substantive participation in both the symbols and the substance of multidimensional adulthood. An unhelpful service system helps perpetuate this unfinished transition by encouraging professional dependency, social isolation, and personal chronicity. This leaves us with a dilemma of how to surround people such as Ian with resources that recognize their needs without denying their adulthood. The good news is that it really is possible. The bad news is that it is only present for a few so far. There is still much to do.

We believe that the solution to the dilemmas we have raised about adulthood lies in the merger of a reformed support system with a multidimensional understanding of adulthood. In this section, we first outline at least some of the key themes of this new paradigm for support services that respond to the barriers to adulthood that the current system continues to create and maintain despite these new efforts. Next we will look at how these themes are starting to play themselves out in terms of the three dimensions of full adulthood that we have discussed. We think that, taken together, these expanded versions of support and adulthood really do provide an inclusive approach to achieving a high quality of adult life for all people, even those with the most severe disabilities or intensive support needs. Finally, we freely admit that probably nowhere in our country could one find all of the elements of this new approach in place, fully functioning. However, we also believe each of the elements does exist somewhere for some people right now, and for some, we are beginning to achieve several elements. There is increasing reason for optimism that systemic change is starting to occur. The challenge we face is "simply" to fill in the gaps.

The Concept of Support

The significant reforms of the past 20 years in developmental disabilities have occurred mainly under the banners of deinstitutionalization and normalization. We need to recall the massive shift of people from large, segregated settings to much more community-based arrangements that has occurred in less than 3 decades (Lakin, White, Prouty, Bruininks, & Kimm, 1991; Taylor et al., 1991). In the last few years, even some of the money to support these people has made a similar shift from institution to community (Braddock et al., 1998). However, while only partially achieved, normalization and deinstitutionalization now need to be joined (or perhaps even replaced) by a new banner if we are to revitalize the move toward continued restructuring of policy and practice. Many of the critics of the current adult service system have also discussed the message that this new banner needs to convey (Campbell & Oliver, 1996; Ferguson, Ferguson, & Blumberg, 1997; McKnight, 1987, 1995; O'Brien & Murray, 1997; Roeher Institute, 1996). It has become increasingly possible to see the outline of an effort to move beyond the perceived limitations of deinstitutionalization and normalization as policy guidelines to an emphasis on support and self-determination.

The central feature of this new, and admittedly sporadic, effort to radically reorient adult services is an expanded understanding of the concept of "support" and its relationship to self-determination. One way of summarizing the conceptual model that seems to govern this effort is "supported adulthood." The supported adulthood approach is the result of an inductive process. Its unifying vision has emerged out of disparate reform initiatives from across several service domains, including supported employment, supported living, supported education, supported recreation, and supported families.

What Is New About Supported Adulthood?

What is new in all of these types of service reform initiatives within the adult service system? How do they address the criticisms already discussed? There is more going on than a simple commitment of the field to redress past institutional wrongs by eliminating segregated options. There is also more than an attempt to make people "appear" normal. The central theme is in the expanded interpretation of what is and is not supportive of a full adult life in the community. The common purpose is in the effort to recognize a dual sense of independence and belonging as the most basic benefits of social support programs. This enriched notion of "support" has indicated a way out of the conceptual dilemma whereby people with disabilities had either to earn their presence in the community with total independence and self-sufficiency or be inserted there with the type of bureaucratic arrogance so common to social welfare programs. In either case, the result was all too often a kind of clustered isolation associated with the overlapping problems of perpetual clienthood and excessive individualism already described. The image of the 10-bed group home comes to mind, with residents separated from their neighbors simply by the size and regimentation of their house. It became a place of work for direct care staff rather than a home where people lived. To adopt the terminology of the New Testament, adults with severe disabilities were "in" the community but not "of" it; only there was no saving grace to justify their separateness.

What is new in the notion of supported adulthood is a guiding commitment to participation and affiliation rather than control and remediation. "Support" becomes an adjective, modifying and enriching an adult's capacity for participation in and contribution to his or her community. Support cannot be a predefined service available to any who meet eligibility criteria. The real message of initiatives such as supported employment and supported living is, or should be, that all people do not have to be totally independent in terms of skills, or fully competitive (or even close) in terms of productivity, to be active, growing, valued adult members of their communities.

Components of Supported Adulthood

There seem to be at least five features of this expanded approach to support for adults with severe disabilities and their families: (a) natural contexts; (b) informal supports; (c) user definitions; (d) local character; and (e) universal eligibility.

Natural Contexts

The traditional welfare approach to services for people with severe disabilities has been the creation of special settings, with special staff, and separate bureaucracies (e.g., institutions, self-contained schools, and sheltered workshops). Part of the economic irrationality of many of the current approaches is that funding tracks continue to direct financial resources into these settings, even as the field increasingly recognizes their inadequacies (e.g., the continuing institutional bias of ICF/MR payments; see Braddock, et al., 1998). Certainly, the situation is improving, as states have finally tipped the balance in financial support toward community programs. The spread of Home and Community Based Support (HCBS) waivers has allowed the federal government to work more closely with states in removing policy barriers that previously kept Medicaid dollars from flowing into progressive community settings. All of these trends show a growing appreciation for the value of the natural context as the location of choice for people with disabilities, regardless of the domain of life being discussed.

Supported adulthood requires a reliance on natural contexts in the design and location of its supports. To adopt a linguistic metaphor, support must become an adjective or adverb that "modifies" an existing, natural setting, rather than creating a separate one. This shift directly challenges the traditional belief that the more intensive the support needs, the more segregated the setting had to be (Taylor, S. J., 1988; Taylor, in press). Instead, the focus on natural settings allows the intensity of support to be truly individualized from context to context instead of programmatically standardized along an arbitrary service continuum (AAMR, 1992).

The supported adulthood approach brings progressively intensive support to those individuals who need it without abandoning the community setting. The assumption driving the design of services within this approach is that vocational "programs" for people with severe disabilities should occur in those settings within the community where work naturally occurs, not in specially created sites or segregated settings (Mank, 1996). Homes should be in neighborhoods where other people live (Ferguson, Ferguson & Blumberg, 1997; Walker, in press). A preference exists for the generic service instead of the specialized one whenever possible. The appeal of natural contexts, then, is two fold: it returns to a reliance on the community setting, thereby combating the isolating tendencies of "specialized" programs, and it encourages independence by placing people outside the "protected" environment of segregated programs.

A shift to natural contexts occurred for Ian during those last couple of years of high school when our focus had fully shifted to his impending transition. One aspect of his transition plan was an increased focus on exploring employment options in various community locales. One of these—doing laundry at the local YMCA for the next day's fitness enthusiasts—continued as a volunteer job that earned Ian a free membership for a couple of years after he finished school. Another way his transition experience drew upon natural community contexts was the "Out to Lunch Bunch" and "Men About Town" activities that were a regular part of his weekly schedule. Ian's teachers supported these small groups of students to help each other scan community event calendars, plan outings, invite friends or family members, and manage all the necessary logistics to accomplish the plan. We were the beneficiaries of more than one lunch date with Ian at some new restaurant he was learning to patronize.

Informal and Formal Support Resources

A second, and related, element is the recognition that support should be informal as well as formal. This element directly challenges the problems identified with the traditional client-based role for individuals with severe disabilities and their families. In practical terms, informal—or natural—support is what people who are not paid for the "services" provide (e.g., emotional support, practical assistance, moral guidance). As we mentioned earlier, as long as a professional-client model governs the provision of adult developmental disability services, then support, by definition, will be organized and controlled by the formal service system. Efforts that most closely adhere to a supported adulthood approach are always bureaucratically "thin" and not necessarily oriented toward direct service provision. Such efforts recognize that the best support is that which is most natural, and most embedded within the social relationships of the individual with disabilities. As with the element of natural contexts, this has the added benefit of economic prudence.

The most important outcome, however, is improved effectiveness. The critical outcome measure is no longer whether someone receives "services," but rather whether someone's quality of life improves. The emphasis is that the individual finds the support needed regardless of where that support originates. The neighbor who decides at the last minute to invite

Ian to accompany him to a ball game is just as supportive—if not more so—of leisure activity as the official recreational therapist with a scheduled swim time each week, and should be recognized as such. A nondisabled coworker reminding Ian to keep the strange noises to a minimum counts as no less supportive of vocational success than if the reminder had come from a trained vocational rehabilitation specialist. The point—at least from our perspective—is not that all formal support services should be withdrawn or avoided, but that they should be seen as only one source of the support that all of us need at one time or another.

User Defined

An emphasis on informal supports and natural contexts leads logically to a third feature of the supported adulthood approach. The individual receiving the support is the only one who can define what is or is not supportive. Again, this directly challenges the controls of the bureaucratic structures to establish what "services" shall be available to an adult with a severe disability. Instead, the approach endorsed by all of the examples of supported adulthood is to empower the individual to make such determinations. For example, a young man with aggressive behavior might use his behavioral repertoire to indicate a clear preference for spending his residential support dollars to maintain him in a duplex with one other roommate, rather than the eight-person group home originally offered him. In some situations, the "user" might be a family as a whole rather than any one individual.

Local Character

A fourth common feature in examples of supported adulthood is a recognition that support should be community referenced. The emphasis here is that not only should individuals define what is and is not supportive, but that, once defined, that support should then take on the shape and texture of the local culture's traditions, values, and opportunities. The most obvious level of community referencing is at the basic effort to "fit in." For example, using a group home model as the exclusive type of residential service arrangement may foreclose the opportunities provided in many urban communities of apartment settings. Recreational opportunities should support and (if needed) provide training in locally valued activities

(e.g., making a good ski run in Colorado, making a good pastrami on rye in New York City) instead of rigidly adhering to some standardized agenda that seems to imply: "All people with severe disabilities should learn to bowl (or swim, or play cards)." Ian's swimming lessons at the YMCA, for example, helped him overcome a fear of water. As a result he has gone on river rafting excursions; a popular pastime where he lives in Oregon (Figure 16–4). Community referencing should go beyond this level, however, to also draw upon the traditions and values within a local culture.

What we are advocating by "local character" is not a simple nostalgia for some imagined era of small town harmony; tradition can include a recognition of difference, even tension, that support for people with severe disabilities should not ignore in the single-minded pursuit of peaceful conformity. A tradition of resistance can also be supportive when identified as a valuable and important part of a local culture.

> *For example, Ian lives in Oregon in a city with an active tradition of strong minority voices and social activism. Environmental issues alone offer any number of opportunities for citizenship and affiliation, depending on the side you*

FIGURE 16–4
Whitewater Rafting on the McKenzie River in Oregon

choose to support. Ian already contributes his voice to at least some environmental debates in his use of canvas bags or his backpack when shopping. During a public employees' strike a few years ago at the University of Oregon, Ian joined in support of his coworkers on picket lines. We do not know what Ian understood about the reasons for the strike, we expect it was very little, but he was aware that the routines were different and that people he worked alongside were not at their posts. Joining the community expression of resistance, regardless of his level of understanding of the issues, not only allowed Ian to support his coworkers, but increased their willingness to contribute to his support in other ways.

There is also a strong disability rights organization in our community. Although individuals who experience cognitive limitations have not been well-represented in the disability rights movement, and while Ian is not yet a member of the local group, he is assisted to contribute his support for disability issues. In the course of his job, Ian serves the university as an unappointed disability advocate and semiofficial "accessibility tester". During one period he began to consistently run into trouble with one of the automatic doors at the same campus building. The building was first on his morning route to deliver food supplies to cafes around campus. When he pressed the access panel to operate the door, nothing happened. Repeated calls by Ian's coworker to the physical plant resulted in frustration on all sides for awhile. Whenever the repair team tested the panel it worked, but the very next morning it would not work for Ian. Eventually, careful sleuthing by his coworker and others resulted in the discovery that during routine maintenance at night the emergency switch was being turned off. After this incident, Ian was occasionally asked to try out a new door or entry or ramp to test its effectiveness for someone with Ian's type of wheelchair and skills. Our point is that supported adulthood requires attention to not just local traditions of peace, harmony and patriotism, but also to the minority voices and social activism that might afford rich and preferred opportunities for community participation and contribution.

Universal Eligibility

Finally, a fifth feature of most of the emerging examples of supported adulthood, and perhaps the most controversial, is the principle of universal eligibility. Everyone who requires support to experience the full promise of adulthood should receive it. Unfortu-

nately, in our individualistic system of support services, the inevitable scarcity of programs has usually led to either a crisis-oriented or means-tested determination of eligibility. Since there are simply not enough formal resources for all who genuinely require them, only those who meet a more stringent test of poverty or extremity of need, whether temporary or chronic, receive services. In Moroney's now classic analysis (1986), such approaches are described as reactive or residual. That is, such limitations perpetuate the acknowledged problems of the welfare state programs that we summarized earlier. They tend to be stigmatizing, lack cost-effectiveness (because not preventative), and be destructive of personal independence and community membership (because of competition for services).

The customary rationale for this limited eligibility is inevitably tied to the professional-client orientation to support services. If we break away from that constraint, however, then the universalizing of disability policy seems much more feasible (McKnight, 1995; O'Brien & Murray, 1997; Zola, 1989). For example, if formal support services are the only officially recognized, legitimate responses to an identified social need, then competition for scarce resources seems endemic. If informal supports are included and existing natural contexts are preferred, then the available resources for support are dramatically multiplied. The addition of informal support to the equation automatically increases the total of recognized resources. Equally important, formal support dollars become more cost effective when used to encourage this informal sector rather than to pay the salaries of bureaucrats.

There is danger here as well, of course. The emphasis on informal supports can provide "cover" for those politicians and administrators who simply want to avoid the expense and challenge of meeting their responsibilities. The legal protections embedded in such landmark legislation as the Individuals with Disabilities Education Act and the Americans with Disabilities Act remain necessary for neglect of responsibility. Recognizing the value of informal supports should never become code words for ripping up the social safety net for those who need it most.

Dimensions of Adulthood Revisited

Given the elements of this reform toward a reconceptualization of services as part of something called supported adulthood, we now want to return our attention to the three key dimensions of adulthood that we have mentioned throughout this chapter. How might the elements of supported adulthood reveal themselves across these three dimensions of autonomy, membership, and change? We use Ian as an extended example in order to personalize our discussion.

Supported Autonomy

The years since graduation have been exciting and productive for Ian. He now enjoys many of the symbols of autonomy that we outlined earlier. Still, Ian will never be completely self-sufficient in many of the most important aspects of life. He will probably never have the independent judgment to make reliable decisions about some of the more fundamental areas of life: religious beliefs and abstract principles of moral behavior, long-term financial planning, or when it is safe to cross a busy street corner. However, with appropriate support he can attend church if he wants to (assuming it is accessible), reciprocate the kindness of friends and strangers, manage a small bank account, and even negotiate an intersection at rush hour. Self-sufficiency certainly entails a number of discrete skills and resources that Ian will never be able to develop or discover on his own. However, self-sufficiency also conveys a pattern of life that goes beyond individual tasks or skills. In this expanded sense, Ian's autonomy is enhanced by appropriate types and levels of ongoing support.

Work life is perhaps the single area that is most commonly associated with personal autonomy. For Ian, the promises of supported employment have been exciting and rewarding. He has a great job! And one that is uniquely suited to his skills and personality. Ian's a very outgoing kind of guy who likes to be out and about, driving his wheelchair, and meeting people. The food services located in the University's student union decentralized a few years ago by putting small cafés in a number of the classroom buildings around campus. Like most university campuses, however, space is at a premium, and the cafes can only store a small number of supplies. Since the center of campus is closed to cars and trucks, and even bicycle riding is supposed to be banned, Ian offered the only legal vehicle that could convey supplies. With the assistance of Vocational Rehabilitation, a carrier was designed that fits on the back of his wheelchair for carrying these supplies, and he enjoys a regular route that takes him all over campus, meeting and greeting lots of different people. This

past year his job was expanded to include collecting the bank at each café and getting it safely back to the student union.

Getting and maintaining this job has not always been easy. Some of the coworkers hired to support Ian have not been as successful as others. As supervisors and student employees change, Ian's personal support agent—a person hired by Ian as an advocate and intermediary with family, officials, and support providers (Ferguson, Ferguson, & Blumberg, 1997)—has sometimes needed to help the new coworkers understand supported employment and its role in Ian's life. Despite these continuing challenges, however, Ian enjoys his job and misses working when the university is on term break. We have seen his language and communication skills continue to grow and expand in the years since graduation and suspect his daily encounters with new people have contributed. Ian illustrates just how important it is for the developmental disability service system to ensure appropriate levels and types of ongoing support to maintain him in his job. It is a commitment that should be more universally made and kept (Bellamy, Rhodes, Mank, & Albin, 1988; Kiernan & Schalock, 1989; Mank, 1996; Wehman & Kregel, 1995).

Ian also illustrates the contribution that effective high school transition services can make to successful adult experiences after school. Ian did not learn to deliver food in high school. However, what he did learn was what it meant to "have a job." He did learn more about making decisions. He did learn how much he enjoyed "going to work." That is, the dimension of autonomy gained important concrete application for Ian as he sampled a variety of possible employment opportunities in high school and participated in other opportunities for making choices that mattered.

In March 1997, Ian moved into his own home (Figure 16–5). As with most transitions in life, Ian's move included elements of both change and continuation. He ended that phase of living at home with his parents and began the exciting new journey of a more separate life away from home. In this effort, he was supported in a variety of ways and by a variety of sources.

Ian is benefiting from the increasing availability of "supported living" options within the service system. Simply put, supported living means that, within the limits that all of us must recognize, Ian should be able to live where he wants (in his own, fully accessible house in a low-income neighborhood), with whom he wants, for as long as he wants, with the ongoing support needed to make that happen (Howe, Horner, & Newton, 1998; Taylor, Biklen, & Knoll, 1987; Taylor

FIGURE 16–5
Ian's New House and Front Yard

et al., 1991). For Ian, this support comes from Robin and Lyn, his live-in companions, Alina and Andy who support him during some parts of his week, and Susan, his personal support agent.

Supported Membership

For us, as Ian's parents, it seems that the community is the safest place for him to be. The more hands that are there to catch him when he falls the better. We firmly believe that the more deeply embedded Ian· is in the life of his neighborhood, workplace, and the city in general, the more people there will be who will notice if he is not there and who will work to keep him there as a member of his community. Part of this involves some effort to allow Ian to fulfill his duties of citizenship. Ian has volunteered for several agencies or causes that he supports and enjoys. In addition to volunteering at the YMCA that we mentioned earlier, Ian has also delivered mail at a nearby long-term care facility and helped a couple of times to put up posters around town advertising upcoming concerts for a local musical festival. It is important for Ian's membership in his community that he be given the support he needs to support his friends and neighbors.

One creative example of how Ian was supported to help his neighbors occurred soon after he moved into his own house.

We learned that a "lawn party" had been scheduled for an upcoming weekend. Imagining cool drinks, snacks, and lots of get-acquainted conversation among neighbors, we looked forward to the day. There was some cold water, but in this case the lawn party was a group effort to lay the new sod supplied by the building contractor on the group of homes just completed. Ian attended and watched with a supervisory flair until one neighbor struggling to drag the roller used to press the sod into the newly prepared earth declared spiritedly that Ian "wasn't going to get out of doing his fair share." He grabbed some rope and tied the roller to Ian's electric wheelchair and began directing what turned out to be somewhat wavy, but still effective roller tracks in the sod.

Affiliations for pure fun and recreation are also important. The obvious term to capture the spirit of such activities is supported recreation. Instead of separate, specialized, professionally defined recreational opportunities, the emphasis within progressive programs is now on the use of generic programs in the local community. Instead of Ian going to a special bowling night for all of the people labeled mentally retarded in the whole county, the effort might be to let him choose what he wants to do for fun in the community, and then arrange the supports and small groups necessary to allow those choices to be honored (Dattilo & Schleien, 1994; Germ & Schleien, 1997).

Ian's recreational affiliations have changed over the years since graduation, depending on his support people and their friends. Many of Ian's friends and acquaintances have been made through the social networks of his employees: their friends become Ian's friends. Ian still sees a couple of classmates from high school for pizza dinners and occasional picnics or backyard parties with the help of his supporters, who suggest such options and help Ian to proffer the invitation and organize the logistics. For several years after leaving school Ian and his high school teacher, Leah, pursued their interest in theater by attending several productions, including an increasing number of musicals. We supported this new interest by purchasing or borrowing records of the score so Ian could become familiar with all the songs. We inevitably got a little tired of the current selection, but by the time Ian and Leah set out for the play, Ian could practically sing along.

Ian's current housemates enjoy camping, and together they are exploring the accessibility of campgrounds and recreation areas in Oregon and Washington (see Figure 16–6). We support Ian's vacations and weekends away by making sure his van is in good traveling condition and by helping Ian contribute his share of the costs.

FIGURE 16–6
Ian and Lyn Enjoy Camping Trips to a Nearby Lake

Supported Change

Perhaps the central aspect here is to make sure Ian has the information and opportunity to expand the choices he has surrounding his autonomy and membership. Supported change should not involve a lifetime of programs, interventions, training, and habilitation plans. However, it should encourage a lifelong growth and development that will allow Ian to change his preferences as he learns new things. It should allow his relationships with people to evolve and develop without the frenzied impermanence of various paid staff who are here one month and gone the next. Ian should be supported in activities that will create new levels of independence, but even more in activities that will create new breadth of experience. Finally, Ian should be helped to learn how to make his choices known in effective yet appropriate ways. Supported change should help Ian alter or minimize those behaviors that reduce his personal attractiveness to other members of his community (Ferguson, D. L., 1998).

Many of these natural changes are occurring for Ian. His volunteer jobs have changed, as have his duties at his paid job. His first housemate, Faith, moved on to another phase of her own life, making it possible for Robin, who had worked for Ian some years previously, to come back into his life. New support people, Lyn and Alina, are introducing him to new experiences and opportunities. As we mentioned earlier, Ian

continues to learn. He's certainly talking more and about more things. Under Robin's tutelage, his cook's helper skills have greatly expanded, and we hear that he's actually beginning to enjoy sleeping outside during camping trips.

Through all of these changes, we learn more about how to engage Ian as an author in the adult life that is emerging. As we have watched Ian gradually separate his life from ours, our goal has not so much been one of self-determination in the particularly individual sense in which it is often applied to people with severe disabilities (Brown, et al., 1998; Ferguson, 1998; Wehmeyer, 1998). Instead, we have sought with Ian a good life. We can support Ian's autonomy, membership, and change. We can also support a growing self-sufficiency, and completeness, but supporting self-determination has forced us to shift our thinking from Ian's individual agency to our collective negotiations.

Philosophers have long talked about the importance of "agency" to our understanding of what it means to be an individual. What they mean by that term is our personal ability to act on the world around us; to be our own agents of change. The challenge of Ian, and others with even more significant cognitive (and physical, and sensory, and medical) disabilities is how close they seem to come to the absence of agency in key parts of their lives. We really do not know what Ian realizes about himself, though we would dearly love to know. Perhaps we should not assume that Ian finds meaning similar to our own experiences of the characteristics of self-regulation, empowerment, and autonomy so often cited as central to self-determination. Certainly we are all interdependent, but the truth of the matter is that the balance of interdependence in Ian's relationships is disproportionate in most matters as compared with our own. He *is* more dependent. He requires more care. He determines fewer things in the course of a day, week, or year than each of us do. Yet he does contribute in some very important ways to what occurs in his life. Does he choose? Sometimes. But, more often, he sort of indirectly influences people and events to end up being more okay than not okay from his point of view, even when we do not know, and perhaps cannot imagine, what his point of view is at the time. We want Ian to have a life that is more okay than not okay from his point of view most of the time.

One way we have found helpful to think of these issues is to borrow a couple of literary metaphors.

Literary critics try to discover what a particular text means. Part of discovering the meaning of a text, or the "social text" of any person's life, is finding out what the authors of that text intended it to mean—to gather and take into account all the possible constructed meanings. That is never enough, however. The meaning of any text, including the social text of a life, belongs as well to the text itself, and gets determined by each of us who "read" or participate in it. What even casual observers think about Ian's life contributes to his story and influences the next chapters.

To pursue the metaphor a bit further, like many conventional texts, social texts often have multiple authors. Ian, and others with limited communication skills, can contribute as co-authors to the text. Even if they do not noticeably interpret any particular experience for themselves, in any strong sense of human agency, by shaping the collective story in whatever way others can comprehend, the social text is enriched with their contribution for others to interpret and elaborate.

This past Christmas Ian made strawberry jam, marinated mushrooms, canned pears, and applesauce as holiday gifts. In past years, he has made refrigerator magnets and tree ornaments. In other years, he has gone shopping for socks, tea, coffee, really good chocolates, and jewelry. In still other years, it was winter scarves and decorative candles. The results of his holiday efforts are certainly shaped by those that support his participation in the season. This is a part of the complexity of Ian's adulthood that we have come to understand. His taste and choices always reflect the people in his life. Our Christmas gifts come as much from them as from Ian. For our part, we have come to love the variety and choice that go into the content of Ian's gifts. Of course, we also cherish the self-satisfied smile that he always has when he hands us the present as something that is uniquely Ian's.

The most recent Christmas Eve party was at Ian's house. Robin and Lyn might have wanted company at least as much as Ian wanted to open presents in his house around the tree he had helped to decorate. Robin's collection of antique Santa Clauses, and her efforts to display them, deserved a party to appreciate them. It felt a bit odd to us to be out on Christmas Eve, but we were willing to try to help create our adult son's Christmas traditions. It was a text we all wrote together. Ian participated as an author, but how much was "written" by him and how much by others of us must and will vary. The point is that we see him as co-author and can help each other take special notice of what seem to be his par-

ticular contributions. His contributions on this occasion were his ebullient renditions of carols, his energetic opening of gifts, his enthusiastic greeting when we arrived, and his just-controlled crabbiness about the finger-food supper.

If Wehmeyer (1998) is correct and self-determination is a dispositional characteristic, perhaps energy, enthusiasm, ebullience, and crabbiness are expressions of it. We would suggest, however, that it is the balance between Ian's expression of such feelings and our identification of them that, for him, are the keys to whatever self-determination will ever mean for him. It is a jointly authored account.

Multidimensional Adulthood

For us the final key to understanding the full meaning of supported adulthood—indeed, of adulthood itself—is to recognize that it has no one single meaning. Autonomy is a very important dimension of adulthood, but there are others. Unfortunately most attempts to describe the promise of adulthood for people with severe disabilities have tried to accomplish it by making careful discriminations in the meaning of autonomy and independence so as to account for the genuine limits in self-sufficiency that severe disability might actually impose (this seems especially true of severe cognitive disability).

We believe that a multidimensional approach to adulthood allows a clearer way of interpreting the situation. Instead of trying to subsume everything that we want to include under the single rubric of independence, a multidimensional approach allows us to thicken our description of adulthood with the additional—but co-equal—strands of membership and change that lead to the more accurate notion of adult "interdependence."

As we have described earlier, Ian's cognitive limitations and multiple disabilities are significant enough that the strand of autonomy in his version of adulthood may not be as strongly visible as his strand of membership. The strand of personal change and growth may allow the balance between the other two strands to change over his lifetime. It seems to us that a full understanding of adulthood in our society would allow us to avoid dilemmas of linear, one-dimensional thinking where degrees of "adultness" occur on a single line of autonomy and independence. Adding other dimensions is not an excuse for limiting Ian's independence; it is an interpretation that expands his adulthood. Ian's adulthood is an expression of the relationships he has with his parents, his paid supporters, his friends, and his neighbors that contribute to defining what happens to him day to day. To truly support his adulthood, we are striving for relationships that nourish rather than smother, relationships that flourish rather than atrophy, and relationships that author rich stories of lives lived rather than reports of outcomes achieved.

Some Dangers Ahead

A *Cautionary Conclusion About Unkept Promises*

At its broadest application, supported adulthood seems to provide an important summary of how social services in general might accomplish a practical merger of personal independence and community support. However, broad claims of relevance and value for such ideas should always be chastened by the history of social reform efforts in our country. Too often our reform optimism has been followed by decades of unintended consequences that seem all too predictable in retrospect.

There is a definite danger that arguments in favor of the supported adulthood approach could overemphasize the cost-effectiveness of such elements as the use of natural contexts and the encouragement of informal supports. Some economic savings may, indeed, be available through these approaches. However, as experience with the deinstitutionalization movement has shown, effective community support can suffer if justified primarily on the basis of financial savings. The arguments for adopting supported adulthood logic must be careful not to imply any enthusiasm for underfunded social programs. The economic justification for the approach is that it rationalizes spending by tying it directly to valued outcomes, not that it saves money.

A second danger with supported adulthood is to justify unintentionally an even greater reliance upon a charity model of social support. One of the risks in calling for procedures such as increased reliance on community-based responses that encourage informal supports is the creation of a one-sided, libertarian abandonment of legitimate government responsibility to ensure the health and welfare of its citizens with disabilities. Of course, this move to the privatization

of welfare gained popularity during the Reagan administration and seems to be enjoying continuing appeal. The problem is that the charity model almost unavoidably accepts the systemic inequities that occasion the need for charity in the first place. An effective disability policy must challenge inequity and discrimination in our society with distributive and protective systems within the formal structure of social agencies. Supported adulthood should illuminate a comprehensive, egalitarian approach to a national disability policy, not just look for a "thousand points of light" in a darkened age of social divisions resulting from our class structure and continuing racial, gender, cultural, and religious discrimination.

A final danger in the approach is closely related to the potential overemphasis on charity. Just as the rediscovery of informal supports and natural contexts can be exaggerated into a privatized social policy of volunteers and cheerful givers, so can the concomitant de-emphasis on traditional versions of formal supports lead to an overblown antiprofessionalism. Certainly, those within the field of disability services must recognize the value of properly focused expertise and technology in improving the quality of some people's lives. The contention that excessive professionalism has often encouraged a dependency role for disabled people should not entail the abandonment of all the wonderful advances made in the behavioral and life sciences. Professionals have their place—albeit less unilateral and less monopolistic—in supported adulthood.

Despite these very real dangers of misapplication or distortion, the value of moving rapidly toward a vision of supported adulthood is worth the risk. To us it seems to represent the only hope that Ian's "flight" into full adulthood will be a smooth one. There are thousands of Ians "taking off" every year in our society. We have made implicit promises to all of them for as full and rewarding a lifetime as they can achieve. The true risk is the human cost of not doing everything we can to fulfill those promises.

Suggested Activities

1. Think about and discuss with your colleagues the ways in which you do and do not operate as an "adult" in terms of (1) self-sufficiency and (2) autonomy.

2. Think about and discuss with your colleagues all the things, events, and supports you obtain from your own parents or other family members.

3. Inventory all the services available for an individual with significant disabilities in your community. Try to identify the following things about each agency or group providing services:
   - Mission and philosophy of those providing the service
   - Approach to supporting the person with disability
   - Role of the family in program design, monitoring, and improvement
   - Role of the adult in program design, monitoring, and improvement

4. Visit a residential or vocational program in your community that works with individuals with significant intellectual disabilities. Try to listen and notice things that reveal the ways in which the people served and supported by the program or service think of themselves as adults and are thought of by others as adults.

5. Talk with someone who works directly with individuals with significant disabilities (e.g., in a vocational support agency or a residential program). Find out how he or she views adulthood for the people they try to support.

6. Talk with a parent or a sibling of an adult with significant disabilities about his or her perspectives on how best to support the family member with the disability.

References

American Association on Mental Retardation (1992). Adult service applications. *Mental retardation: Definition, classification, and systems of supports* (9th ed.) (pp. 135–146). Washington, DC: Author.

Anderson, L., Schleien, S. J., & Seligmann, D. (1997). Creating positive change through an integrated outdoor adventure program. *Therapeutic Recreation Journal, 31,* 214–229.

Anderson, M. (1971). *Family structure in nineteenth century Lancashire.* Cambridge, England: Cambridge University Press.

Aries, P. (1962). *Centuries of childhood: A social history of family life* (R. Baldick, Trans.). New York: Vintage Books. (Original work published in 1960).

Bach, M. (1994). Quality of life: Questioning the vantage points for research. In M. H. Rioux & M. Bach (Eds.), *Disability is not measles: New research paradigms in disability* (pp. 127–151). North York, Ontario: L'Institut Roeher Institute.

Beales, R. W., Jr. (1985). In search of the historical child: Miniature adulthood and youth in Colonial New England. In N. R. Hiner &

J. M. Hawes (Eds.), *Growing up in America: Children in historical perspective* (pp. 7–24). Chicago: University of Illinois Press.

Bellah, R. N., Madsen, R., Sullivan, W. M., Swidler, A., & Tipton, S. M. (1985). *Habits of the heart: Individualism and commitment in American life.* Berkeley: University of California Press.

Bellah, R. N., Madsen, R., Sullivan, W. M., Swidler, A., & Tipton, S. M. (1991). *The good society.* New York: Alfred A Knopf.

Bellamy, G. T., Rhodes, L. E., Mank, D. M., & Albin, J. M. (1988). *Supported employment: An implementation guide.* Baltimore: Paul H. Brookes.

Bickenbach, J. E. (1994). Voluntary disabilities and everyday illnesses. In M. H. Rioux & M. Bach, (Eds.), *Disability is not measles: New research paradigms in disability* (pp. 109–125). Toronto: L'Institut Roeher Institute.

Blanck, P. D. (1998). *The Americans with Disabilities Act and the emerging workforce: Employment of people with mental retardation.* Washington, DC: American Association on Mental Retardation.

Bouwsma, W. J. (1976). Christian adulthood. *Daedalus: Journal of the American Academy of Arts and Sciences, 105*(2), 77–92.

Braddock, D., Hemp, R., Parish, S., & Westrich, J. (1998). *The state of the states in developmental disabilities.* Washington, DC: American Association on Mental Retardation

Brown, F., Gothelf, C. R., Guess, D., & Lehr, D. (1998). Self-determination for individuals with the most severe disbilities: Moving beyond chimera. *Journal of the Association for Persons with Severe Handicaps, 23,* 17–26.

Campbell, J. & Oliver, M. (1996). *Disability politics: Understanding our past, changing our future.* New York: Routledge.

Conley, R. W., & Noble, J. H., Jr. (1989). Changes in the service system for persons with disabilities. In W. E. Kiernan & R. L. Schalock (Eds.), *Economics, industry, and disability: A look ahead* (pp 37–45). Baltimore: Paul H. Brookes.

Dannefer, D. (1984). Adult development and social theory: A paradigmatic reappraisal. *American Sociological Review, 49,* 100–116.

Dattilo, J. (1991). Recreation and leisure: A review of the literature and recommendations for future directions. In L. H. Meyer, C. A. Peck, & L. Brown (Eds.), *Critical issues in the lives of people with severe disabilities* (pp 171–193). Baltimore: Paul H. Brookes.

Dattilo, J., & Schleien, S. J. (1994). Understanding leisure services for individuals with mental retardation. *Mental Retardation, 32,* 53–59.

Elder, G. H., Jr. (1987). Families and lives: Some developments in life-course studies. *Journal of Family History, 12,* 179–199.

Erikson, V. L., & Martin, J. (1984). The changing adult: An integrated approach. *Social Casework: The Journal of Contemporary Social Work, 65,* 162–171.

Erikson, E. H. (1950). *Childhood and society.* New York: W. W. Norton.

Ferguson, D. L. (1998). Relating to self-determination: One parent's thoughts. *Journal of the Association for Persons with Severe Handicaps, 23,* 44–46.

Ferguson, D. L., & Ferguson, P. M. (1986). The new victors: A progressive policy analysis of work reform for people with very severe handicaps. *Mental Retardation, 24,* 331–338.

Ferguson, P. M., & Drum, C. (1990). *Policy analysis report: 1990 Oregon Assessment Project.* Eugene, OR: University of Oregon, Bureau of Governmental Research and Service, Specialized Training Program.

Ferguson, P. M., Ferguson, D. L., & Blumberg, E. R., with Ferguson, I. (1997). Negotiating adulthood: Kitchen table conversations about supported living. In P. O'Brien & R. Murray (Eds.), *Human services: Toward partnership and support* (pp. 189–200). Palmerston North, New Zealand: The Dunmore Press.

Ferguson, P. M., Ferguson, D. L., & Jeanchild, L. (1990). *Case study report: 1990 Oregon Assessment Project.* Eugene, OR: University of Oregon, Bureau of Governmental Research and Service, Specialized Training Program.

Ferguson, P. M., Ferguson, D. L., & Jones, D. (1988). Generations of hope: Parental perspectives on the transitions of their children with severe retardation from school to adult life. *Journal of the Association for Persons with Severe Handicaps, 13,* 177–187.

Ferguson, P. M., Hibbard, M., Leinen, J., & Schaff, S. (1990). Supported community life: Disability policy and the renewal of mediating structures. *Journal of Disability Policy Studies, 1,* 9–35.

Germ, P. A., & Schleien, S. J. (1997). Inclusive community leisure services: Responsibilities of key players. *Therapeutic Recreation Journal, 31,* 22–37.

Hanawalt, B. (1993). *Growing up in medieval London: The experience of childhood in history.* New York: Oxford University Press.

Hareven, T. (Ed.). (1978). *Transitions: The family and the life course in historical perspective.* New York: Academic Press.

Hemp, R., Braddock, D., & Westrich, J. (1998). Medicaid, managed care, and developmental disabilities. In D. Braddock, R. Hemp, S. Parish, & J. Westrich, *The state of the states in developmental disabilities* (pp. 55–66). Washington, DC: American Association on Mental Retardation.

Howe, J., Horner, R. H., & Newton, J. S. (1998). Comparison of supported living and traditional residential services in the state of Oregon. *Mental Retardation, 36,* 1–11.

Jorgensen, C. M. (1998). *Restructuring high schools for all students: Taking inclusion to the next level.* Baltimore: Paul H. Brookes.

Kett, J. F. (1977). *Rites of passage: Adolescence in America, 1790 to the present.* New York: Basic Books.

Kiernan, R. W., & Schalock, R. L. (Eds.) (1989). *Economics, industry, and disability: A look ahead.* Baltimore: Paul H. Brookes.

Knowlton, H. E., Turnbull, A. P., Backus, L., & Turnbull, H. R., III. (1988). Letting go: Consent and the "Yes, but . . ." problem in transition. In B. L. Ludlow, A. P. Turnbull, & R. Luckasson (Eds.), *Transitions to adult life for people with mental retardation: Principles and practices* (pp. 45–66). Baltimore: Paul H. Brookes.

Lakin, K. C., White, C. C., Prouty, R. W., Bruininks, R. H., & Kimm, C. (1991). *Medicaid institutional (ICF-MR) and home and community-based services for persons with mental retardation and related conditions.* Report No. 35. Minneapolis: University of Minnesota, Institute on Community Integration/UAP.

Lane, H. (1992). *The mask of benevolence: Disabling the deaf community.* New York: Knopf.

Levinson, D. (1978). *Seasons of a man's life.* New York: Knopf.

Mank, D. (1994). The underachievement of supported employment: A call for reinvestment. *Journal of Disability Policy Studies, 5*(2), 1–24.

Mank, D. (1996). Natural support in employment for people with disabilities: What do we know and when did we know it? *Journal of the Association for Persons with Severe Handicaps, 21,* 174–177.

Mank, D., Cioffi, A., & Yovanoff, P. (1997). Analysis of the typicalness of supported employment jobs, natural supports, and wage and integration outcomes. *Mental Retardation, 35,* 185–197.

McGaughey, M. J., Kiernan, W. E., McNally, L. C., Gilmore, D. S., & Keith, G. (1994). *Beyond the workshop: National perspectives on integrated employment.* Boston: Institute for Community Inclusion.

McKnight, J. L. (1985). A reconsideration of the crisis of the welfare state. *Social Policy, 16*(1), 27–30.

McKnight, J. L. (1987). Regenerating community. *Social Policy, 17*(3), 54–58.

McKnight, J. L. (1995). *The careless society: Community and its counterfeits.* New York: Basic Books.

Meyrowitz, J. (1984). The adultlike child and the childlike adult: Socialization in an electronic age. *Daedalus: Journal of the American Academy of Arts and Sciences, 113*(3), 19–48.

Modell, J., Furstenberg, F. F., Jr., & Hershberg, T. (1978). Social change and transitions to adulthood in historical perspective. In M. Gordon (Ed.), *The American family in social-historical perspective* (pp. 192–219). New York: St. Martin's Press.

Moroney, R. M. (1986). *Shared responsibility: Families and social policy.* Chicago: Aldine.

Murphy, R. F., Scheer, J., Murphy, Y., & Mack, R. (1988). Physical disability and social liminality: A study in the rituals of adversity. *Social Science and Medicine, 26,* 235–242.

Mwaria, C. B. (1990). The concept of self in the context of crisis: A study of families of the severely brain-injured. *Social Science and Medicine, 30,* 889–893.

National Organization on Disability/Louis Harris and Associates (1998). *Louis Harris and Associates 1998 survey of Americans with disabilities.* Washington, DC: National Organization on Disability.

Nirje, B. (1970). The normalization principle: Implications and comments. *British Journal of Mental Subnormality, 16,* 62–70.

Nisbet, J., & Hagner, D. (1988). Natural supports in the workplace: A re-examination of supported employment. *Journal of the Association for Persons with Severe Handicaps, 13,* 260–267.

O'Brien, J. (1994). Housing policy for persons with mental retardation: Summary and recommendations. In *The national reform agenda and people with mental retardation: Putting people first* (pp. 123–150). Washington, DC: President's Committee on Mental Retardation.

O'Brien, P., & Murray, R. (Eds.). (1997). *Human services: Towards partnership and support.* Palmerston North, New Zealand: The Dunmore Press.

Phillips, M. J. (1985). "Try harder": The experience of disability and the dilemma of normalization. *Social Science Journal, 22*(4), 45–57.

Pillemer, K., & Suitor, J. J. (1991). Sharing a residence with an adult child: A cause of psychological distress in the elderly. *American Journal of Orthopsychiatry, 61,* 144–148.

Roeher Institute (1996). *Disability, community and society: Exploring the links.* Toronto: L'Insitut Roeher Institute.

Sands, D. J., & Wehmeyer, M. L. (Eds.). (1996). *Self-determination across the life span: Independence and choice for people with disabilities.* Baltimore: Paul H. Brookes.

Sarason, S. B. (1972). *The creation of settings and the future societies.* San Francisco: Jossey-Bass.

Smull, M. W., & Bellamy, G. T. (1991). Community services for adults with disabilities: Policy challenges in the emerging support paradigm. In L. H. Meyer, C. A. Peck, & L. Brown (Eds.), *Critical issues in the lives of people with severe disabilities* (pp. 527–536). Baltimore: Paul H. Brookes.

Summers, J. A. (Ed.) (1986). *The right to grow up: An introduction to adults with developmental disabilities.* Baltimore: Paul H. Brookes.

Taylor, S. J. (1988). Caught in the continuum: A critical analysis of the principle of the least restrictive environment. *Journal of the Association for Persons with Severe Handicaps, 13,* 45–53.

Taylor, S. J. (in press). On the possibility of reaching a common ground: The continuum and current controversies. *Journal on Developmental Disabilities*.

Taylor, S. J., Biklen, D., & Knoll, J. (Eds.). (1987). *Community integration for people with severe disabilities*. New York: Teachers College Press.

Taylor, S. J., Bogdan, R., & Racino, J. (Eds.). (1991). *Life in the community: Case studies of organizations supporting people with disabilities*. Baltimore: Paul H. Brookes.

Taylor, T. (1988). The transition to adulthood in comparative perspective: Professional males in Germany and the United States at the turn of the century. *Journal of Social History, 21,* 635–658.

Vaillant, G. E. (1977). *Adaptation to life*. Boston: Little, Brown & Co.

Walker, P. (in press). From community presence to sense of place: Community experiences of adults with developmental disabilities. *Journal of the Association for Persons with Severe Handicaps*.

Wehman, P. (1997). *Exceptional individuals in school, community, and work*. Austin, TX: Pro-Ed.

Wehman, P., & Kregel, J. (1995). At the crossroads: Supported employment a decade later. *Journal of the Association for Persons with Severe Handicaps, 20,* 286–299.

Wehman, P., Moon, M. S., Everson, J. M., Wood, W., & Barcus, J. M. (1988). *Transition from school to work: New challenges for youth with severe disabilities*. Baltimore: Paul H. Brookes.

Wehmeyer, M. (1998). Self-determination and individuals with significant disabilities: Examining meanings and misinterpretations. *Journal of the Association for Persons with Severe Disabilities, 23,* 5–16.

Wehmeyer, M. L., Agran, M., & Hughes, C. (1998). *Teaching self-determination to youth with disabilities: Basic skills for successful transition*. Baltimore: Paul H. Brookes.

Wei-Ming, T. (1976). The Confucian perception of adulthood. *Daedalus: Journal of the American Academy of Arts and Sciences, 105,* 109–123.

Williams, G. H. (1983). The movement for independent living: An evaluation and critique. *Social Science and Medicine, 17,* 1003–1010.

Wohl, R. (1979). *The generation of 1914*. Cambridge, MA: Harvard University Press.

Wolfensberger, W. (1972). *The principle of normalization in human services*. Toronto: National Institute on Mental Retardation.

Zola, I. K. (1989). Toward the necessary universalizing of a disability policy. *Milbank Quarterly, 67,* (Suppl. 2, Pt. 2), 401–428.

Author Index

Subject Index